New Perspectives on

CREATING WEB PAGES WITH HTML AND XML

Comprehensive

PATRICK CAREY
Carey Associates, Inc.

MARY KEMPER
Contributing Author

THOMSON
COURSE TECHNOLOGY

Australia • Canada • Mexico • Singapore • Spain • United Kingdom • United States • Japan

New Perspectives on Creating Web Pages with HTML and XML—Comprehensive
is published by Course Technology.

Managing Editor:
Rachel Crapser

Associate Product Manager:
Brianna Germain

Composition:
GEX Publishing Services

Senior Editor:
Donna Gridley

Marketing Manager:
Susan Ogar

Text Designer:
Meral Dabcovich

Senior Product Manager:
Kathy Finnegan

Developmental Editor:
Paul Griffin

Cover Designer:
Efrat Reis

Technology Product Manager:
Amanda Young

Production Editor:
Jennifer Goguen

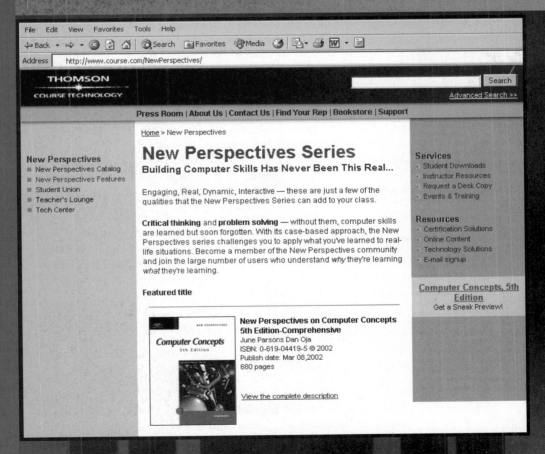

Preface

New Perspectives

Course Technology is the world leader in information technology education. The New Perspectives Series is an integral part of Course Technology's success. Visit our Web site to see a whole new perspective on teaching and learning solutions.

File   Edit   View   Favorites   Tools   Help

← Back ▾ → ▾ ⊗ ⊠ ⌂ | ◎Search ☆Favorites ⊕Media ⊗ | ⬚▾ ⊜ ⊞ ▾ ⊟

Address | http://www.course.com/NewPerspectives/

THOMSON
COURSE TECHNOLOGY

[   ] Search

Advanced Search >>

Press Room | About Us | Contact Us | Find Your Rep | Bookstore | Support

Home > New Perspectives

New Perspectives
- New Perspectives Catalog
- New Perspectives Features
- Student Union
- Teacher's Lounge
- Tech Center

New Perspectives Series
Building Computer Skills Has Never Been This Real...

Engaging, Real, Dynamic, Interactive — these are just a few of the qualities that the New Perspectives Series can add to your class.

Critical thinking and **problem solving** — without them, computer skills are learned but soon forgotten. With its case-based approach, the New Perspectives series challenges you to apply what you've learned to real-life situations. Become a member of the New Perspectives community and join the large number of users who understand *why* they're learning *what* they're learning.

Featured title

New Perspectives on Computer Concepts
5th Edition-Comprehensive
June Parsons Dan Oja
ISBN: 0-619-04419-5 © 2002
Publish date: Mar 08,2002
680 pages

View the complete description

Services
- Student Downloads
- Instructor Resources
- Request a Desk Copy
- Events & Training

Resources
- Certification Solutions
- Online Content
- Technology Solutions
- E-mail signup

Computer Concepts, 5th Edition
Get a Sneak Preview!

Computer Concepts
5th Edition

New Perspectives—Building Computer Skills Has Never Been This Real

Why New Perspectives will work for you.

Critical thinking and **problem solving**—without them, computer skills are learned but soon forgotten. With its **case-based** approach, the New Perspectives Series challenges students to apply what they've learned to real-life situations. Become a member of the New Perspectives community and watch your students not only **master** computer skills, but also **retain** and carry this **knowledge** into the world.

New Perspectives catalog
Our online catalog is never out of date! Go to the Catalog link on our Web site to check out our available titles, request a desk copy, download a book preview, or locate online files.

Complete system of offerings
Whether you're looking for a Brief book, an Advanced book, or something in between, we've got you covered. Go to the Catalog link on our Web site to find the level of coverage that's right for you.

Instructor materials
We have all the tools you need—data files, solution files, figure files, a sample syllabus, and ExamView, our powerful testing software package.

How well do your students know Microsoft Office?
Experience the power, ease, and flexibility of SAM XP and TOM. These innovative software tools provide the first truly integrated technology-based training and assessment solution for your applications course. Click the Tech Center link to learn more.

Get certified
If you want to get certified, we have the titles for you. Find out more by clicking the Teacher's Lounge link.

Interested in online learning?
Enhance your course with rich online content for use through MyCourse 2.0, WebCT, and Blackboard. Go to the Teacher's Lounge to find the platform that's right for you.

Your link to the future is at
www.course.com/NewPerspectives

What you need to know about this book.

- The HTML CD in the back of the book provides extra documentation, a clip art gallery, sound and video library, and a wide selection of Web page authoring software.

- This book includes a 120-day evaluation copy of XML Spy 4.3 – a leading XML editor.

- ExamView testing software gives you the option of generating a printed test, LAN-based test, or test over the Internet.

- The coverage of HTML code has been updated to reflect HTML 4.01 standards, and be compatible with Internet Explorer 6.0 and Netscape Navigator 6.0.

- Students will appreciate the coverage of XHTML in the tutorials and in an XHTML appendix.

- Students will gain confidence as they learn how to bind XML fields with specific elements in an HTML document, and to populate tables with the content of XML documents.

- This book provides extensive coverage of DTDs, namespaces, and schemas. Students learn how to validate a single document, combined from the contents of several XML files. XML documents are validated using the validation commands in XML Spy.

CASE	TROUBLE?	SESSION 1.1	QUICK CHECK	RW
Tutorial Case Each tutorial begins with a problem presented in a case that is meaningful to students. The case sets the scene to help students understand what they will do in the tutorial.	**TROUBLE? Paragraphs** These paragraphs anticipate the mistakes or problems that students may have and help them continue with the tutorial.	**Sessions** Each tutorial is divided into sessions designed to be completed in about 45 minutes each. Students should take as much time as they need and take a break between sessions.	**Quick Check Questions** Each session concludes with conceptual Quick Check questions that test students' understanding of what they learned in the session.	**Reference Windows** Reference Windows are succinct summaries of the most important tasks covered in a tutorial. They preview actions students will perform in the steps to follow.

BRIEF CONTENTS

TABLE OF CONTENTS

Creating Web Pages with HTML

Tutorial 6   HTML 6.03

Creating Web Page Forms

Designing a Product Registration Form

Tutorial 7   HTML 7.01

Working with Cascading Style Sheets

Designing a Style for a Web Site at Maxwell Scientific

Tutorial 8   HTML 8.01

Programming with JavaScript
Creating a Programmable Web Page for North Pole Novelties

Acknowledgments

I would like to thank the people who worked so hard to make this book possible. Special thanks to Mary Kemper for her work in revising HTML Tutorials 1 and 2; Anne Nelson, for her work in updating HTML Appendices D, F, G and H; Paul Griffin, our Developmental Editor, for his excellent ideas and suggestions that improved the manuscript; and to Amanda Young, our Technology Product Manager, who kept the book on task and on target. Other people at Course Technology who deserve credit are Rachel Crapser, Managing Editor; Donna Gridley, Senior Editor; Brianna Germain, Associate Product Manager; Danielle Power, Production Editor; Jennifer Goguen, Production Editor; Aimee Poirier, Production Editor; John Bosco, Quality Assurance Project Leader; and John Freitas, Jeff Schwartz, and Vitaly Davidovich, Quality Assurance Testers.

Feedback is an important part of writing any book, and thanks go to the following reviewers for their ideas and comments: Eric Johnston, Candace Garrods of Red Rocks Community College, Anne Nelson of High Point University, Craig Shaw of Central Community College – Hastings, WJ Patterson of Sullivan University, and John Whitney of Fox Valley Technical College. Special thanks to reviewer Robert Cormia of Foothill College, who was instrumental with advice on the schema and namespace material.

I want to thank my wife Joan for her love and encouragement, and my six children: John Paul, Thomas, Peter, Michael, Stephen, and Catherine, to whom this book is dedicated.

—Patrick Carey

New Perspectives on

CREATING WEB PAGES
WITH HTML

3rd Edition

Read This Before You Begin

To the Student

Data Disks

To complete the Level I tutorials, Review Assignments, and Case Problems, you need one Data Disk. Your instructor will either provide you with this Data Disk or ask you to make your own.

If you are making your own Data Disk, you will need **one** blank, formatted high-density disk. You will need to copy a set of files and/or folders from a file server, standalone computer, or the Web onto your disk. Your instructor will tell you which computer, drive letter, and folders contain the files you need. You could also download the files by going to www.course.com and following the instructions on the screen.

The information below shows you the Data Disk you need so that you will have enough disk space to complete all the tutorials, Review Assignments, and Case Problems:

Data Disk 1

Write this on the disk label:
Data Disk 1: HTML Tutorials 1 and 2

When you begin each tutorial, Review Assignment, or Case Problem, be sure you are using the correct Data Disk. Refer to the "File Finder" chart at the back of this text for more detailed information on which files are used in which tutorials.

See the inside front cover of this book for more information on Data Disk files, or ask your instructor or technical support person for assistance.

Using Your Own Computer

If you are going to work through this book using your own computer, you need:

- **Computer System** A text editor and a Web browser (preferably Netscape Navigator or Internet Explorer, versions 4.0 or higher) must be installed on your computer. If you are using a non-standard browser, it must support frames and HTML 4.0 or higher.

- **Data Disk** You will not be able to complete the tutorials or exercises in this book using your own computer until you have your Data Disk.

Visit Our World Wide Web Site

Additional materials designed especially for you are available on the World Wide Web. Go to http://www.course.com/NewPerspectives.

To the Instructor

The Data Disk Files are available on the Instructor's Resource Kit for this title. Follow the instructions in the Help file on the CD-ROM to install the programs to your network or standalone computer. For information on creating Data Disks, see the "To the Student" section above.

You are granted a license to copy the Data Files to any computer or computer network used by students who have purchased this book.

OBJECTIVES

In this tutorial you will:

- Explore the structure of the World Wide Web

- Learn the basic principles of Web documents

- Create an HTML document

- View an HTML file using a Web browser

- Use HTML tags for text, headings, paragraphs, and lists

- Insert character tags into an HTML document

- Insert an inline graphic image into an HTML document

- Add special characters to an HTML document

- Insert horizontal lines into an HTML document

DEVELOPING A BASIC WEB PAGE

Create a Web Page for Stephen Dubé's Chemistry Classes

CASE

Stephen Dubé's Chemistry Classes

Stephen Dubé teaches chemistry at Robert Service High School in Edmonton, Alberta (Canada). In previous years, he has provided course information to students and parents with handouts. This year, he wants to put that information on the World Wide Web, where it will be easily accessible by everyone. Eventually, he hopes to post homework assignments, practice tests, and even grades on the Web site. Stephen is new to this technology and has never created a Web page. He has asked you to create a Web page for his class.

SESSION 1.1

In this session you will learn the basics of how the World Wide Web is structured and how it operates. You will then begin to explore the HTML language that is used to create Web sites.

Introducing the World Wide Web

Before you start creating a Web page for Stephen, it's a good idea to first look at how and why the World Wide Web was developed in the first place.

In order for computers to share resources efficiently, they can be linked together in a structure called a **network**. If the computers are close together, as they would be in the computer lab at Mr. Dubé's school, the network is called a **local area network** or **LAN**. A network that covers a wider area, perhaps several buildings or cities, is called a **wide area network** or **WAN**. Because networks are so useful, it is not surprising that their use led to a "network of networks" called the **Internet**.

The Internet consists of millions of interconnected computers that enable users to communicate and share information. The physical structure of the Internet uses fiber-optic cables, satellites, phone lines, and other telecommunications media to send data back and forth (see Figure 1-1).

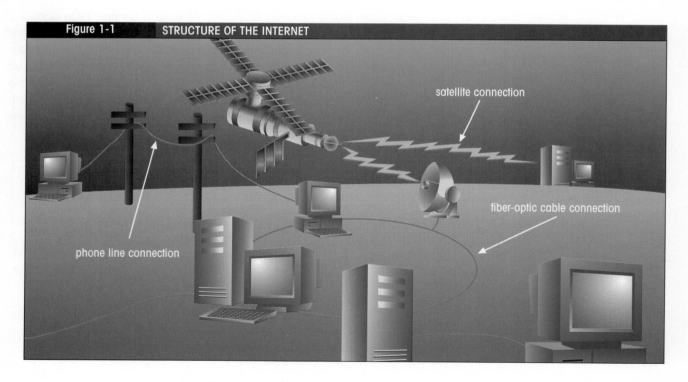

Figure 1-1   **STRUCTURE OF THE INTERNET**

satellite connection

fiber-optic cable connection

phone line connection

Before 1989, using the Internet was not without its problems and challenges. Many Internet tools required users to master a bewildering array of terms, acronyms, and commands before they could navigate the Internet. What users needed was a tool that would be easy to use and would allow quick access to any resource on the Internet, regardless of its location. This tool would prove to be the World Wide Web.

The Development of the World Wide Web

In 1989, Timothy Berners-Lee and other researchers at the CERN nuclear research facility near Geneva, Switzerland, laid the foundation of the World Wide Web, or the Web. They wanted to create an information system that made it easy for researchers to locate and share data and that required minimal training and support. They developed a system of **hypertext documents**, electronic files that contain elements that you can select, usually by clicking a mouse, to open other documents, and so on.

Hypertext offered a better way of locating information. When you read a book, you follow a linear progression, reading one page after another. With hypertext, you progress through pages in whatever way is best suited to you and your objectives. Hypertext lets you skip from one topic to another, following a path of information that interests you. Figure 1-2 shows how topics can be related in a hypertext fashion, as opposed to a linear fashion.

Figure 1-2	LINEAR VERSUS HYPERTEXT DOCUMENTS

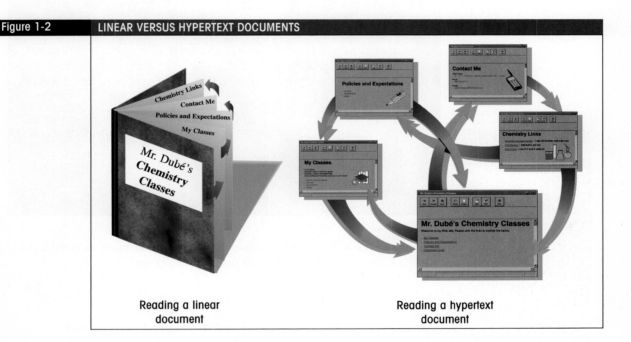

Reading a linear document

Reading a hypertext document

The key to hypertext is the use of **links**, which you activate (usually with a mouse click) to move from one topic to another. Activating a link takes you to another section of the document, or it might take you to another document entirely. A link can open a document on your computer or a document on a computer anywhere in the world.

The hypertext approach proved to be so useful that within a few years it became the dominant method of sharing and retrieving information on the Internet, becoming known as the **World Wide Web**, or more simply the **Web**.

Documents on the Web are known as **Web pages**, but they're not limited to text. Web pages can contain images, video and sound clips, and even programs that run directly from a Web page. The Web designer has a great deal of control over the format of the page. As Figure 1-3 shows, a Web page is not only a source of information, it can also be a work of art.

Figure 1-3   **WEB PAGE WITH INTERESTING FONTS, GRAPHICS, AND LAYOUT**

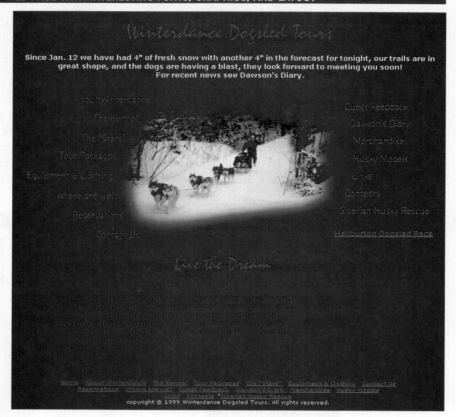

As you will see in this book, another feature that continues to contribute to the Web's popularity is the ease with which Web pages can be created.

Web Servers and Web Browsers

A Web page is stored on a **Web server**, which makes the page available to users of the Web. To view the page, the user runs a **Web browser**, a software program that retrieves the page and displays it (see Figure 1-4).

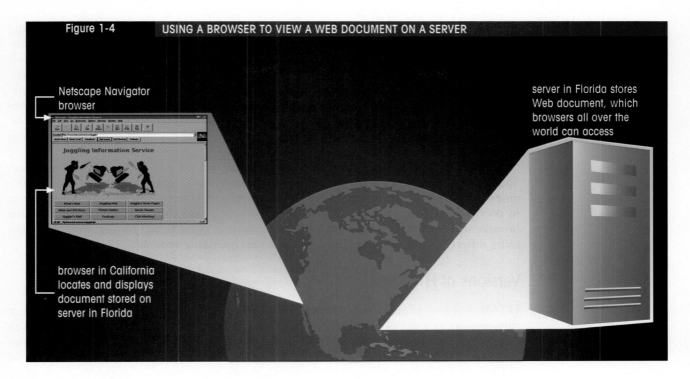

Figure 1-4   **USING A BROWSER TO VIEW A WEB DOCUMENT ON A SERVER**

Netscape Navigator browser

Juggling Information Service

browser in California locates and displays document stored on server in Florida

server in Florida stores Web document, which browsers all over the world can access

Browsers can either be text-based, like the Lynx browser found on UNIX machines, or graphical, like the popular Internet Explorer and Netscape browsers. With a **text-based browser**, you navigate the Web by typing commands; with a **graphical browser**, you use the mouse to move from page to page. Browsers are typically installed on personal computers, but increasingly, devices such as cell phones and PDAs (personal data assistants) are providing Web capability.

HTML: **The Language of the Web**

Web pages are text files, written in a language called **Hypertext Markup Language** or **HTML**. A **markup language** is a language used to describe the content and format of documents. HTML was developed from the **Standard Generalized Markup Language (SGML)**, a language used for large-scale documents. SGML proved to be too cumbersome and difficult for use on the Internet, and thus HTML was created based on the principles of SGML.

The success of the World Wide Web is due in no small part to HTML. HTML allows Web authors to create documents that can be displayed across different operating systems, and the HTML code is easy enough to use that even nonprogrammers can learn to use it. Millions of Web sites are based on HTML, and there is every indication that HTML will continue to be the dominant language of the Web for a long time to come.

HTML describes the format of Web pages through the use of **tags**. Text appearing in the document's heading is marked with a heading tag. Text appearing in a bulleted list is marked with a list tag, and so on. It's the job of the Web browser to interpret these tags and render the text accordingly.

There are a few good reasons to put the formatting in the control of the Web browser rather than the Web server. Web pages must be able to work well with a wide variety of operating systems and browsers. Because different operating systems and browsers differ in how they display information, it would be a daunting task to create a page for all users. Portability frees Web page authors from this concern.

For the most part, Web designers don't have to worry about what devices users are using to display a Web page because HTML works with everything from clunky teletypes to highly sophisticated PDAs. HTML is also supported by nonvisual media such as speech recognition software. Web pages can even be rendered in Braille.

Of course, portability does limit a Web designer's ability to precisely define the appearance of a Web page. For this reason, HTML uses **style sheets**, with which a Web designer can explicitly define the fonts and formatting the Web browser applies to the document. The use of style sheets is an advanced topic that should be mastered only after becoming familiar with basic HTML.

Another reason to put the formatting choices in the browser's control is speed. Specifying the exact appearance of a page can dramatically increase both the size of the document file and the time required to retrieve it. It is more efficient to allow the Web browser to do the work. The disadvantage of this approach is that you cannot be sure how each browser will display your document. For this reason, it's a good idea to view your Web page using different browsers, and if possible, different operating systems.

Versions of HTML

HTML has a set of rules, called **syntax**, that specify how document code is written. These rules appear as a set of **standards** or **specifications** developed by a consortium of Web developers, programmers, and authors called the **World Wide Web Consortium**, more commonly known as the **W3C**. Figure 1-5 presents a history of the various versions of HTML that have been released by the W3C. For more information on the W3C, see their Web site at **http://www.w3c.org**.

Figure 1-5		VERSIONS OF HTML
VERSION	**DATE**	**DESCRIPTION**
HTML 1.0	1989–1994	The first public version of HTML which included browser support for inline images and text controls.
HTML 2.0	1995	The first version supported by all graphical browsers. It introduced interactive form elements such as option buttons and text boxes. A document written to HTML 2.0 should be compatible with all browsers on the World Wide Web.
HTML 3.0	1997	This version included additional support for creating and formatting tables and expanded the options for interactive form elements.
HTML 4.01	1999	This version added support for style sheets to give Web designers greater control over page layout. It added new features to tables and forms and provided support for international features. This version also expanded HTML's scripting capability and added increased support for multimedia elements.
XHTML 1.0	2001	This version is a reformulation of HTML 4.01 in XML and combines the strength of HTML 4.0 with the power of XML. XHTML brings the rigor of XML to Web pages and provides standards for more robust Web content on a wide range of browser platforms.

Extensions, XML, and the Future

The world of Web browsers is a competitive one, and over the years each browser has added **extensions** to HTML that support new features. Netscape and Internet Explorer have added the most extensions to HTML, and often these extensions have been adopted in subsequent sets of standards released by the W3C. These extensions have provided Web page authors with more options, but at the expense of fragmenting Web page development and decreasing compatibility across browsers.

Before using an extension, the Web designer needs to determine which browsers and browser versions support it and, if necessary, create a workaround for browsers that do not support the extension. All of this extra work complicates Web page development and betrays the simplicity of HTML that made it so integral to the success of the Web in the first place.

Primarily for this reason, future Web development is focusing more on XML and XHTML. **XML (Extensible Markup Language)** is used for developing document content. With XML, Web designers can create their own tags and attributes for their documents. XML combined with style sheets provides the same functionality as HTML, but with greater flexibility. **XHTML (Extensible HyperText Markup Language)** is a stricter version of HTML, designed to overcome some of problems that competing HTML standards have introduced, and to better integrate HTML with XML.

Don't worry about HTML becoming obsolete anytime soon. There is a significant amount of overlap between HTML and XML coding. HTML is an excellent stepping stone to the various languages of the future.

Tools for Creating HTML Documents

Because HTML documents are text files, the only software you need to create them is a basic text editor such as Windows Notepad. If you want a software program to do some of the work of creating an HTML document, you can use an HTML converter or an HTML editor.

An **HTML converter** takes text in one format and converts it to HTML code. For example, you can create the source document with a word processor such as Microsoft Word, and then have the converter save the document as an HTML file. Converters have several advantages. They free you from the laborious task of typing HTML code, and, because the conversion is automated, you do not have to worry about typographical errors in your code.

Converters have the disadvantage of creating HTML code that may be longer and more complicated than it needs to be, resulting in larger-than-necessary files. Also, if you need to edit the HTML code directly, it is more difficult to do so with a file created by a converter.

An **HTML editor** helps you create an HTML file by inserting HTML codes for you as you work. HTML editors can save you a lot of time and help you work more efficiently. They have many of the same advantages and limitations as converters. They do let you set up your Web page quickly, but to create the finished document, you often still have to work directly with the HTML code.

Session 1.1 QUICK CHECK

1. What is hypertext?

2. What is a Web server? A Web browser? Describe how they work together.

3. What is HTML?

4. How do HTML documents differ from documents created with a word processor such as Word or WordPerfect?

5. What are the advantages of letting Web browsers determine the appearance of Web pages?

6. What are HTML extensions? What are some advantages and disadvantages of using extensions?

7. What software program do you need to create an HTML document?

In the next session, you'll begin writing your first HTML document, using a text editor.

SESSION 1.2

In this session you begin entering the HTML code for Stephen's Web page. You'll learn how to create and apply HTML tags to format page headings, paragraphs, lists, and individual characters.

Creating an HTML Document

It's always a good idea to plan the appearance of your Web page before you start writing code. Each semester, Stephen distributes a handout listing his classes and describing his class policies. He thinks this handout is a good place to start for his Web site (see Figure 1-6).

Figure 1-6	STEPHEN'S PAPER HANDOUT

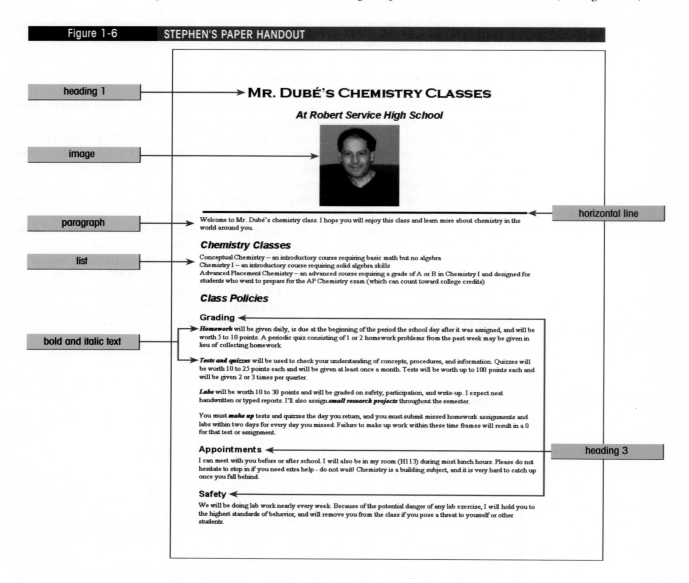

Stephen's handout includes several features that he would like to include on his Web page. A heading prominently displays his name, and beneath the heading is his photo and a horizontal line. The handout has a brief introductory paragraph and is divided into two sections: Chemistry Classes and Class Policies. In the Chemistry Classes section there is a list of the three classes he teaches. In the Class Policies section, three smaller headings list and describe his policies on Grading, Appointments, and Safety.

As you can see, Stephen's handout has three heading levels, a list, formatted characters such as bold and italic text, a horizontal line, and an image. When he creates the Web page with HTML, he wants to include these features. As you help Stephen create this document for the Web, you should periodically refer to Figure 1-6.

HTML Syntax

An HTML file contains both formatting tags and content. **Document content** is what the users see on the page, such as headings and images. **Tags** are the HTML codes that control the appearance of the document content.

The HTML syntax for creating the features that Stephen wants in his page follows a very basic structure. HTML tags are applied to document content using the following syntax:

```
<tag attributes>document content</tag>
```

where *tag* is the name of the HTML tag, *attributes* are properties of the tag, and *document content* is the actual content that appears in the Web page. This type of tag is known as a **two-sided tag** because it contains an **opening tag** that tells the browser to turn on a feature and apply it to the content that follows, and a **closing tag** that turns off the feature. Note that closing tags are identified by the slash (/) that precedes the tag name.

Not every tag is two-sided. Some tags are **one-sided tags** or **empty tags**, because they require only a single tag without content. The syntax for a one-sided tag is simply:

```
<tag attributes>
```

A one-sided tag is used to insert noncharacter data into the Web page, such as a graphic image or a video clip. You'll see examples of one-sided tags later in the tutorial.

Let's look at the first line of the course handout, "Mr. Dubé's Chemistry Classes," from Figure 1-6. You can format this line with the HTML tag as follows:

```
<h1 align="center">Mr. Dube's Chemistry Classes</h1>
```

Here the <h1 align="center"> opening tag instructs the browser to display the text that follows the tag in an h1 (heading level 1) format. ("h1" stands for Heading 1; you'll learn what this means later.) The HTML code also includes the **align attribute**, which instructs the browser how to align the text (in this case, centered). Following the opening tag is the content: "Mr. Dubé's Chemistry Classes". Finally, the </h1> tag signals the browser to turn off the h1 format.

Remember that each browser determines the exact effect of the h1 tag. One browser might apply a 14-point Times Roman bold font to Heading 1 text, whereas another browser might use 18-point italic Arial. In each case, the font is appropriately larger than the lower-level headings such as h2, h3, etc. Figure 1-7 shows how three different browsers might interpret this line of HTML code.

Figure 1-7	INTERPRETATION OF THE <H1> TAG BY DIFFERENT BROWSERS
BROWSER INTERPRETING THE <H1> TAG	**APPEARANCE OF THE DOCUMENT CONTENT**
Browser A	Mr. Dubé's Chemistry Classes
Browser B	**Mr. Dubé's Chemistry Classes**
Browser C	*Mr. Dubé's Chemistry Classes*

Tags are not case sensitive. Both the Internet Explorer and Netscape browser will treat the <h1> tag as they do the <H1> tag. However, in the interest of consistency, the current standard is to display all tags in lowercase letters. We'll follow this lowercase convention throughout this book.

Creating Basic Tags

When you create a Web page, the first step is to identify the markup language being used, identify the document's key sections, and assign a title to the page.

In the steps that follow, type the text exactly as it is displayed. To create an HTML file, you need a text editor such as Notepad or WordPad.

To create an HTML file:

1. Place your Data Disk in drive A.

TROUBLE? If you don't have a Data Disk, you need to get one. Your instructor will either give you one or ask you to make your own. See the Read This Before You Begin page at the beginning of the tutorials for instructions.

2. Create a new document with a text editor.

TROUBLE? If you don't know how to locate, start, or use the text editor on your system, ask your instructor or technical support person for help.

3. Type the following lines of code into your document. Press the **Enter** key after each line. Press the **Enter** key twice for a blank line between lines of code.

```
<html>
<head>
<title>Mr. Dube's Chemistry Classes</title>
</head>

<body>
</body>

</html>
```

Note that the name Dube should contain an accent mark over the "e". You'll learn how to add special characters such as accent marks later in the tutorial.

4. Using your text editor, save the file as **chem.htm** in the tutorial folder of the tutorial.01 folder on your Data Disk, but do not close your text editor. The text you typed should look similar to the text displayed in Figure 1-8.

Figure 1-8	INITIAL HTML TAGS IN NOTEPAD

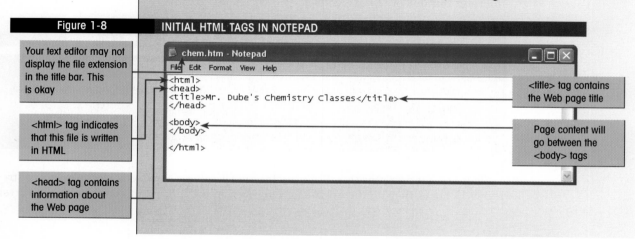

Your text editor may not display the file extension in the title bar. This is okay

<html> tag indicates that this file is written in HTML

<head> tag contains information about the Web page

<title> tag contains the Web page title

Page content will go between the <body> tags

TROUBLE? If you don't know how to save a file on your Data Disk, ask your instructor or technical support person for assistance.

TROUBLE? Don't worry if your screen doesn't look exactly like Figure 1-8. The text editor shown in the figures is the Windows Notepad editor. Your text may look different. Take the time to ensure that you entered the text correctly.

TROUBLE? If you are using the Windows Notepad text editor to create your HTML file, make sure you don't save the file with the extension .txt, which is the default for Notepad. Using an invalid file extension renders the file unreadable to Web browsers, which require .htm or .html as file extensions. So make sure you save the file with an .htm or .html file extension.

TROUBLE? If you are using Microsoft Word for your text editor, be sure to save your files as Web page files and not as Word documents.

The opening and closing <html> tags bracket the remaining code you'll enter in the document. This indicates to a browser that the page is written in the HTML language. While you don't have to include this tag, it is necessary if the file is to be read by another SGML application. Moreover, it is considered good form to include it.

The <head> tag identifies the area where you enter information about the Web page itself. One such piece of information is the title of the page, which is displayed in the title bar of the Web browser. This information is entered using the <title> tag. The title in this example is "Mr. Dube's Chemistry Classes".

Finally, the portion of the document that Web users will see is contained between the <body> tags. At this point, the page is blank, with no text or graphics. You'll add those later. The <head> and <body> tags are not strictly required, but you should include them to better organize your document and make the code more readable to others. The extra space before and after the <body> tags is also not required, but it makes your code easier to understand, especially as you add more code and it becomes more complex.

Displaying Your HTML Files

As you continue adding to Stephen's HTML file, you should occasionally view the formatted page with your Web browser to verify that there are no syntax errors or other problems. You may even want to view the results using different browsers to check for compatibility. In the steps and figures that follow, the Internet Explorer browser is used to display Stephen's page as it is developed. If you are using a different browser, ask your instructor how to view local files (those stored on your own computer rather than on the Web).

To view Stephen's Web page:

1. Start your browser. You do not need to be connected to the Internet to view local files stored on your computer.

TROUBLE? If you try to start your browser and are not connected to the Internet, you might get a warning message. Netscape Navigator, for example, gives a warning message telling you that it was unable to create a network socket connection. Click OK to ignore the message and continue.

2. After your browser loads its home page open the **chem.htm** file that you saved in the tutorial folder of the tutorial.01 folder on your Data Disk.

Your browser displays Stephen's file, as shown in Figure 1-9. Note that the page title, which you typed earlier between the <title> tags, appears in the browser's title bar.

TROUBLE? To open a file in most browsers, click File on the menu bar, click Open, and click the Browse button to locate the file.

TROUBLE? Depending on the browser you're using, you may have to use a different command to open the file from your Data Disk. Talk to your instructor or technical support person to find out how to open the file.

Figure 1-9	THE INITIAL HTML FILE IN INTERNET EXPLORER

the title you entered
between the <title> tags

address box indicates
the name and location
of the HTML file

page content will
appear here

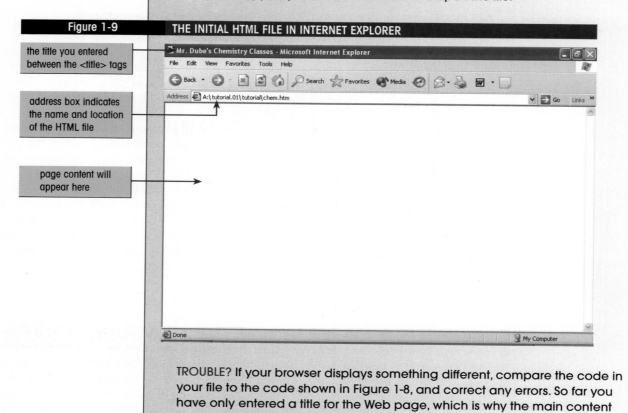

TROUBLE? If your browser displays something different, compare the code in your file to the code shown in Figure 1-8, and correct any errors. So far you have only entered a title for the Web page, which is why the main content area of the Web page is blank.

Creating **Headings, Paragraphs, and Lists**

Now that the basic structure of Stephen's page is set, you can start filling in the page content. A good place to start is with the headings for the various sections of the document. You need a heading for the entire page and headings for each of two sections: Chemistry Classes and Class Policies. The Class Policies section has three additional headings for Grading, Appointments, and Safety. You can create all these headings using HTML heading tags.

Creating Heading Tags

HTML supports six levels of headings, numbered <h1> through <h6>, with <h1> being the largest and most prominent. Headings are always displayed in a bold font. The syntax for a heading tag is:

```
<hy>heading text</hy>
```

where *y* is a heading numbered 1 through 6 and *heading text* is the text that is displayed in the heading.

Figure 1-10 illustrates the general appearance of the six heading styles. Your browser might use slightly different fonts and sizes.

| Figure 1-10 | SIX HEADING LEVELS |

This is an h1 heading
This is an h2 heading
This is an h3 heading
This is an h4 heading
This is an h5 heading
This is an h6 heading

REFERENCE WINDOW   **RW**

Creating a Heading Tag
- Open the HTML file with your text editor.
- Type <h*y*> where *y* is the heading number you want to use.
- If you want to use a special alignment, specify the alignment attribute setting after *y* and before the closing symbol, >.
- Type the text that you want to appear in the heading.
- Type </h*y*> to turn off the heading tag.

As of HTML 3.2, the heading tag can contain additional attributes, one of which is the alignment attribute. Stephen wants some headings to be centered, so you'll be using align attribute tags as shown in the code that follows.

To add headings to the chemistry file:

1. Using your text editor, open **chem.htm** if it is not currently open.

2. Place the insertion point after the <body> tag, press the **Enter** key to move to the next line, and then type the following code. Be sure to press the **Enter** key at the end of each line of code.

```
<h1 align="center">Mr. Dube's Chemistry Classes</h1>
<h2 align="center">at Robert Service High School</h2>
<h2>Chemistry Classes</h2>
<h2>Class Policies</h2>
<h3>Grading</h3>
<h3>Appointments</h3>
<h3>Safety</h3>
```

The revised code is displayed in Figure 1-11. To make it easier for you to follow the changes to the HTML file, new and modified text in the figures is highlighted in red. This will not be the case in your own text files.

| Figure 1-11 | ENTERING HEADING TAGS AND TEXT |

```
<html>
<head>
<title>Mr. Dube's Chemistry Classes</title>
</head>

<body>
<h1 align="center">Mr. Dube's Chemistry Classes</h1>
<h2 align="center">at Robert Service High School</h2>
<h2>Chemistry Classes</h2>
<h2>Class Policies</h2>
<h3>Grading</h3>
<h3>Appointments</h3>
<h3>Safety</h3>
</body>

</html>
```

3. Save chem.htm in the Tutorial folder of the Tutorial.01 folder on your Data Disk. You can leave your text editor open.

The first two headings use the align="center" attribute to center the text on the page. The two <h2> headings Chemistry Classes and Class Policies and the three <h3> headings in the Policies section, however, are aligned left, which is the default setting.

To display the revised version of the chemistry page:

1. Return to your Web browser. Note that the previous version of chem.htm probably appears in the browser window.

2. To view the revised file, click **View** on the menu bar, and then click **Refresh**. If you are using Netscape, you will need to click **View** and then click **Reload**.

TROUBLE? If you closed the browser or the file in the last set of steps, reopen your browser and the chem.htm file.

The updated file looks like Figure 1-12.

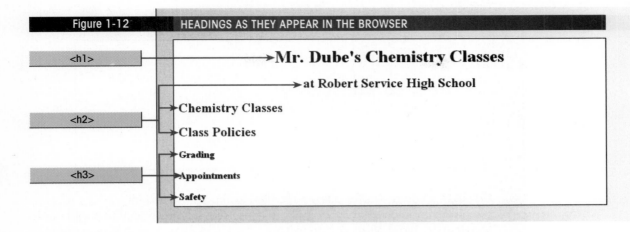

Figure 1-12   HEADINGS AS THEY APPEAR IN THE BROWSER

Entering Paragraph Text

The next step is to enter text information for each section. If your paragraph does not require any formatting, you can enter the text without tags.

REFERENCE WINDOW   RW

Creating a Paragraph
- Using your text editor, open the HTML file.
- Place the insertion point where you want the paragraph to start.
- Type <p> to begin the paragraph.
- Enter the text for the paragraph.
- Type </p> to close the paragraph tag.

Stephen's introductory paragraph, which appears just below the horizontal line in his handout, does not require formatting, so you can enter the text without any HTML formatting tags. He would like to revise the paragraph that appears in Figure 1-6 slightly so that it applies to his Web page.

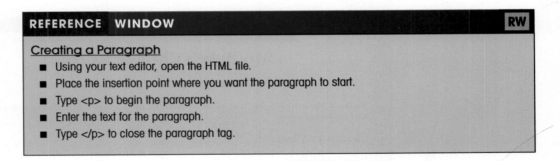

To enter paragraph text:

1. Using your text editor, open **chem.htm** if it is not currently open.

2. Place the insertion point at the end of the line that specifies the <h2> heading "at Robert Service High School", and press the **Enter** key to create a blank line.

3. Type the following text. As you type, let the text wrap to the next line; don't press Enter.

   ```
   Welcome to Mr. Dube's Web site. I hope you will use
   this site to learn more about your class, my
   expectations, and chemistry in the world around you.
   ```

   Your text should be placed after the first <h2> head and before the <h2> Chemistry Classes head, as shown in Figure 1-13. Check your work for mistakes, and edit your file if necessary.

Figure 1-13   ENTERING PARAGRAPH TEXT

```
<html>
<head>
<title>Mr. Dube's Chemistry Classes</title>
</head>

<body>
<h1 align="center">Mr. Dube's Chemistry Classes</h1>
<h2 align="center">at Robert Service High School</h2>
Welcome to Mr. Dube's web site. I hope you will use this site to learn more about your class, my
expectations, and chemistry in the world around you.
<h2>Chemistry Classes</h2>
<h2>Class Policies</h2>
<h3>Grading</h3>
<h3>Appointments</h3>
<h3>Safety</h3>
</body>

</html>
```

TROUBLE? If you are using a text editor like Notepad, the text might not wrap to the next line automatically. Do not press the Enter key. Instead, you might need to select the Word Wrap command from the Format menu, or a similar command, so you can see all the text on your screen.

3. Save your changes to chem.htm.

4. Using your Web browser, refresh or reload chem.htm to view the text you've added. See Figure 1-14.

Figure 1-14   PARAGRAPH TEXT IN THE BROWSER

Mr. Dube's Chemistry Classes

at Robert Service High School

Welcome to Mr. Dube's Web site. I hope you will use this site to learn more about your class, my expectations, and chemistry in the world around you.

Chemistry Classes

Class Policies

Grading

Appointments

Safety

Now you need to add the four paragraphs under the Grading heading and a single paragraph under both Appointments and Safety. Be sure to press the Enter key only where indicated. It is important to allow your text editor to wrap the text to the next line.

To enter remaining paragraphs:

1. Using your text editor, open **chem.htm** if it is not currently open.

2. Place the insertion point at the end of the <h3> Grading heading and then press the **Enter** key to create a blank line.

3. Type the following text:

```
Homework will be given daily, is due at the beginning
of the period the school day after it was assigned, and
will be worth 5 to 10 points. A periodic quiz
consisting of 1 or 2 homework problems from the past
week may be given in lieu of collecting homework.
```

4. Press the **Enter** key two times and then type:

```
Tests and quizzes will be used to check your
understanding of concepts, procedures, and information.
Quizzes will be worth 10 to 25 points and will be
given at least once a month. Tests will be worth up to
100 points and will be given 2 or 3 times a quarter.
```

5. Press the **Enter** key two times and then type:

```
Labs will be worth 10 to 30 points and will be graded
on safety, participation, and write-up. I expect neat
handwritten or typed reports. I'll also assign small
research projects throughout the semester.
```

6. Press the **Enter** key two times and then type:

```
You must make up missed tests and quizzes the day you
return, and you must submit missed homework assignments
and labs within two days for every one day you missed.
Failure to make up work within these time frames will
result in a 0 for that test or assignment.
```

TROUBLE? Note that in Stephen's handout, a keyword or phrase is bold in each paragraph. You'll learn how to format text, such as bold, later in the tutorial.

7. Move to the end of the <h3> Appointments heading, press the **Enter** key once, and then type:

```
I can meet with you before or after school. I will also
be in my room (H113) during most lunch hours. Please do
not hesitate to stop in if you need extra help -- do not
wait! Chemistry is a building subject, and it is very
hard to catch up once you fall behind.
```

8. Move to the end of the <h3> Safety heading, press the **Enter** key once, and then type:

```
We will be doing lab work nearly every week. Because of
the potential danger of any lab exercise, I will hold
you to the highest standards of behavior, and will
remove you from the class if you pose a threat to
yourself or other students.
```

Figure 1-15 shows the new code in Stephen's file.

Figure 1-15	ADDING THE SIX REMAINING PARAGRAPHS

```
<body>
<h1 align="center">Mr. Dube's Chemistry Classes</h1>
<h2 align="center">at Robert Service High School</h2>
Welcome to Mr. Dube's Web site. I hope you will use this site to learn more about your class,
my expectations, and chemistry in the world around you.
<h2>Chemistry Classes</h2>
<h2>Class Policies</h2>
<h3>Grading</h3>
Homework will be given daily, is due at the beginning of the period the school day after it was
assigned, and will be worth 5 to 10 points. A periodic quiz consisting of 1 or 2 homework
problems from the past week may be given in lieu of collecting homework.

Tests and quizzes will be used to check your understanding of concepts, procedures, and
information. Quizzes will be worth 10 to 25 points and will be given at least once a month.
Tests will be worth up to 100 points and will be given 2 or 3 times a quarter.

Labs will be worth 10 to 30 points and will be graded on safety, participation, and write-up. I
expect neat handwritten or typed reports. I'll also assign small research projects throughout
the semester.

You must make up missed tests and quizzes the day you return, and you must submit missed
homework assignments and labs within two days for every one day you missed. Failure to make up
work within these time frames will result in a 0 for that test or assignment.
<h3>Appointments</h3>
I can meet with you before or after school. I will also be in my room (H113) during most lunch
hours. Please do not hesitate to stop in if you need extra help -- do not wait! Chemistry is a
building subject, and it is very hard to catch up once you fall behind.
<h3>Safety</h3>
We will be doing lab work nearly every week. Because of the potential danger of any lab
exercise, I will hold you to the highest standards of behavior, and will remove you from the
class if you pose a threat to yourself or other students.
</body>
```

9. Save your changes to chem.htm.

10. Using your Web browser, refresh or reload chem.htm and view the changes. Figure 1-16 displays the revised version.

Figure 1-16	THE PARAGRAPHS DISPLAYED BY THE BROWSER

Mr. Dube's Chemistry Classes

at Robert Service High School

Welcome to Mr. Dube's Web site. I hope you will use this site to learn more about your class, my expectations, and chemistry in the world around you.

Chemistry Classes

Class Policies

Grading

four grading paragraphs are not separated →

Homework will be given daily, is due at the beginning of the period the school day after it was assigned, and will be worth 5 to 10 points. A periodic quiz consisting of 1 or 2 homework problems from the past week may be given in lieu of collecting homework. Tests and quizzes will be used to check your understanding of concepts, procedures, and information. Quizzes will be worth 10 to 25 points and will be given at least once a month. Tests will be worth up to 100 points and will be given 2 or 3 times a quarter. Labs will be worth 10 to 30 points and will be graded on safety, participation, and write-up. I expect neat handwritten or typed reports. I'll also assign small research projects throughout the semester. You must make up missed tests and quizzes the day you return, and you must submit missed homework assignments and labs within two days for every one day you missed. Failure to make up work within these time frames will result in a 0 for that test or assignment.

As you can see from Figure 1-16, the text you typed into chem.htm looks nothing like what is displayed in the browser. Instead of being separated by blank lines, the four Grading paragraphs are running together. What went wrong?

Remember that HTML formats text only through the use of tags and ignores such things as extra blank spaces, blank lines, or tabs. To demonstrate this, study the following three examples of code that look different:

```
<h1>To be or not to be. That is the question.</h1>
<h1>To be or not to be.    That is the question.</h1>
<h1>To be or not to be.
            That is the question.</h1>
```

Though the spacing in these three examples is different, the three examples would look identical in a browser.

At first glance, the Grading section did not appear to need any formatting other than bolding some words. However, we now know that each new paragraph needs to be set off by a blank line. To add this space between paragraphs, you use the **paragraph tag, <p>**, which adds a blank paragraph (the extra line you need) to separate a block of text from text that precedes it.

To add paragraph tags for blank lines:

1. Using your text editor, open **chem.htm**.

2. Modify the Grading text, bracketing each paragraph between a **<p>** and **</p>** tags, so that the text reads as follows:

```
<p> Homework will be given daily, is due at the
beginning of the period the school day after it was
assigned, and will be worth 5 to 10 points. A periodic
quiz consisting of 1 or 2 homework problems from the
past week may be given in lieu of collecting
homework.</p>
<p>Tests and quizzes will be used to check your
understanding of concepts, procedures, and information.
Quizzes will be worth 10 to 25 points and will be
given at least once a month. Tests will be worth up to
100 pointsand will be given 2 or 3 times a quarter.</p>
<p> Labs will be worth 10 to 30 points and will be
graded on safety, participation, and write-up. I expect
neat handwritten or typed reports. I'll also assign
small research projects throughout the semester.</p>
<p>You must make up missed tests and quizzes the day
you return, and you must submit missed homework
assignments and labs within two days for every one
day you missed. Failure to make up work within these
time frames will result in a 0 for that test or
assignment.</p>
```

TROUBLE? If adding the new tags results in awkward word wrapping, adjust the formatting as necessary to keep your file clear and easy to read.

3. Save your changes to chem.htm.

4. Using your Web browser, refresh or reload chem.htm. The text in the Grading section is now properly separated into distinct paragraphs, as shown in Figure 1-17.

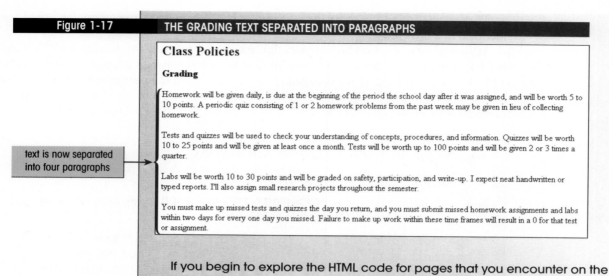

Figure 1-17 — THE GRADING TEXT SEPARATED INTO PARAGRAPHS

Class Policies

Grading

Homework will be given daily, is due at the beginning of the period the school day after it was assigned, and will be worth 5 to 10 points. A periodic quiz consisting of 1 or 2 homework problems from the past week may be given in lieu of collecting homework.

Tests and quizzes will be used to check your understanding of concepts, procedures, and information. Quizzes will be worth 10 to 25 points and will be given at least once a month. Tests will be worth up to 100 points and will be given 2 or 3 times a quarter.

Labs will be worth 10 to 30 points and will be graded on safety, participation, and write-up. I expect neat handwritten or typed reports. I'll also assign small research projects throughout the semester.

You must make up missed tests and quizzes the day you return, and you must submit missed homework assignments and labs within two days for every one day you missed. Failure to make up work within these time frames will result in a 0 for that test or assignment.

text is now separated into four paragraphs

If you begin to explore the HTML code for pages that you encounter on the Web, you may notice that the <p> tag is sometimes used in varying ways. This is because in early versions of HTML, <p> was a one-sided tag. However, both the latest HTML specifications and XHTML require a two-sided tag, so you should follow that convention in your documents.

Creating Lists

You still need to enter the list describing Stephen's three chemistry courses. HTML supports three kinds of lists: ordered, unordered, and definition.

An **ordered list** is used to display information in a numeric order. The syntax for creating an ordered list is:

```
<ol type="option">
     <li>Item1
     <li>Item2
     ...
</ol>
```

where *option* specifies the type of character to number the list and *Item1*, *Item2*, etc, are items in the list. The type attribute must have one of the following values: "1", "a", "A", "i", or "I".

- A value of "1" displays a list with numbers.
- The values "a" and "A" create a list with either lowercase or uppercase letters.
- The values "i" and "I" create a list with Roman numerals.

If you omit the type attribute, browsers assume that you want to create an ordered list using numbers.

For example, Stephen might want to list the three classes from the least difficult to the most difficult. To do so, the following code can be used to list the courses from easiest to hardest in an ordered list:

```
<ol type="1">
     <li>Conceptual Chemistry
     <li>Chemistry
     <li>Advanced Placement Chemistry
</ol>
```

and the browser displays the text as:

1. Conceptual Chemistry

2. Chemistry

3. Advanced Placement Chemistry

If you change the value of the type attribute to "a", the browser displays the text as:

a. Conceptual Chemistry

b. Chemistry

c. Advanced Placement Chemistry

If you remove an item from the list, HTML updates the numbers to accurately reflect the new order.

You can also create an **unordered list**, in which list items are not listed in a particular order. The syntax for an unordered list is:

```
<ul type="option">
     <li>Item1
     <li>Item2
     ...
</ul>
```

where the type attribute can have one of the following values: "disc", "circle", or "square". A value of "disc" inserts a bullet before each list item, "circle" instructs the browser to use an open circle, and "square" creates a filled-in square.

If Stephen wanted to display his classes without regard to their importance, you could create the following unordered list:

```
<ul type="circle">
     <li>Conceptual Chemistry
     <li>Chemistry
     <li>Advanced Placement Chemistry
</ul>
```

and the browser would display the list as:

° Conceptual Chemistry

° Chemistry

° Advanced Placement Chemistry

Ordered and unordered lists can also be nested inside one another. For example, to create the following list of numbered and bulleted items:

1. Homework

   • Given daily

   • Worth 5 to 10 points

2. Quizzes

   • Given at least once a month

   • Worth 10 to 25 points

you would use the following HTML tags:

```
<ol>
    <li>Homework
        <ul type="disc">
            <li>Given daily
            <li>Worth 5 to 10 points
        </ul>
    <li>Quizzes
        <ul type="disc">
            <li>Given at least once a month
            <li>Worth 10 to 25 points
        </ul>
</ol>
```

A third list type you can create with HTML is a definition list. A **definition list** is a list of terms, each followed by a definition line that is typically indented slightly to the right. The syntax for creating a definition list is:

```
<dl>
    <dt>term1 <dd>definition1
    <dt>term2 <dd>definition2
...
</dl>
```

where *term1*, *term2*, etc. are the terms in the list, and *definition1*, *definition2*, etc. are the term definitions.

If Stephen wanted to create a list of his classes and briefly describe each one, he could use a definition list. To create a definition list for his classes, you would enter the following code:

```
<dl>
<dt>Conceptual Chemistry<dd>An introductory course
requiring basic mathematics but no algebra
<dt>Chemistry I<dd>An introductory course requiring solid
algebra skills
<dt>Advanced Placement Chemistry<dd>An advanced course for
students who passed Chemistry I with an A or B and who want
to prepare for the AP Chemistry exam (which can count toward
college credits)
</dl>
```

A Web browser displays this code as:

Conceptual Chemistry

    An introductory course requiring basic mathematics but no algebra

Chemistry I

    An introductory course requiring solid algebra skills

Advanced Placement Chemistry

    An advanced course for students who passed Chemistry I with an A or B and who want to prepare for the AP Chemistry exam (which can count toward college credits)

REFERENCE   WINDOW   RW

Creating Lists

- Using your text editor, open the HTML file.
- Place the insertion point in the document where you want the list to appear.
- Type <ol> to start an ordered list, <ul> to start an unordered list, or <dl> to start a definition list.
- For each item in an ordered or unordered list, type <li> followed by the text for the list item. For each item in a definition list, type <dt> before the term and <dd> before the definition. Note that both <li> and <dt> are one-sided tags, so there is no closing tag.
- To turn off the list, type </ol> for an ordered list, </ul> for an unordered list, and </dl> for a definition list.

In his handout (Figure 1-6), you notice that Stephen's classes are not displayed in a bulleted or numbered list. You decide that the list will look fine as an unordered list, using the default bullet.

To add an unordered list to the chemistry file:

1. Using your text editor, open **chem.htm** if it is not currently open.

2. Place the insertion point at the end of the line specifying the "Chemistry Classes" heading and press the **Enter** key to create a blank line.

3. Type the following code:

```
<ul>
<li>Conceptual Chemistry: An introductory course
requiring basic math but no algebra
<li>Chemistry I: An introductory course requiring solid
algebra skills
<li>Advanced Placement Chemistry: An advanced course
requiring a grade of A or B in Chemistry I and designed
for students who want to prepare for the AP Chemistry
exam (which can count toward college credits)
</ul>
```

The new lines in the file should look like Figure 1-18.

Figure 1-18	ENTERING AN UNORDERED LIST

```
<html>
<head>
<title>Mr. Dube's Chemistry Classes</title>
</head>

<body>
<h1 align="center">Mr. Dube's Chemistry Classes</h1>
<h2 align="center">at Robert Service High School</h2>
Welcome to Mr. Dube's Web site. I hope you will use this site to learn more about your class,
my expectations, and chemistry in the world around you.
<h2>Chemistry Classes</h2>
<ul>
<li>Conceptual Chemistry: An introductory course requiring basic math but no algebra
<li>Chemistry I: An introductory course requiring solid algebra skills
<li>Advanced Placement Chemistry: An advanced course requiring a grade of A or B in Chemistry I
and designed for students who want to prepare for the AP Chemistry exam (which can count toward
college credits)
</ul>
<h2>Class Policies</h2>
<h3>Grading</h3>
<p>Homework will be given daily, is due at the beginning of the period the school day after it
was assigned, and will be worth 5 to 10 points. A periodic quiz consisting of 1 or 2 homework
problems from the past week may be given in lieu of collecting homework.</p>
```

4. Save the file when you are sure that it matches the code in Figure 1-18.

5. Using your Web browser, refresh or reload chem.htm. The latest version of the file is displayed in Figure 1-19.

Figure 1-19	THE UNORDERED LIST IN THE BROWSER

Mr. Dube's Chemistry Classes

at Robert Service High School

Welcome to Mr. Dube's Web site. I hope you will use this site to learn more about your class, my expectations, and chemistry in the world around you.

Chemistry Classes

- Conceptual Chemistry: An introductory course requiring basic math but no algebra
- Chemistry I: An introductory course requiring solid algebra skills
- Advanced Placement Chemistry: An advanced course requiring a grade of A or B in Chemistry I and designed for students who want to prepare for the AP Chemistry exam (which can count toward college credits)

Stephen's page now includes a list formatted to closely resemble his course handout. If your browser does not display a page that looks like Figure 1-19, return to the HTML file and check for errors in the code that you entered.

Creating **Character Tags**

So far in this tutorial, you've worked with HTML tags that format either the entire document or individual lines of text. HTML also lets you format individual characters. A tag that you apply to an individual character is called a **character tag.** There are two types of character tags: logical and physical. **Logical character tags** specify how you want to use text, not necessarily how you want it displayed. Figure 1-20 lists some common logical character tags.

Figure 1-20	COMMON LOGICAL CHARACTER TAGS

TAG	DESCRIPTION
\<em\>	Indicates that characters should be emphasized in some way. Usually displayed with italics.
\<strong\>	Emphasizes characters more strongly than \<em\>. Usually displayed in a bold font.
\<code\>	Indicates a sample of code. Usually displayed in a Courier font or a similar monospace font.
\<kbd\>	Used to offset text that the user should enter. Often displayed in a Courier font or a similar monospace font.
\<var\>	Indicates a variable. Often displayed in italics or underlined.
\<cite\>	Indicates short quotes or citations. Often italicized by browsers.

For example, if you want some text to stand out from the rest of the page, you could use the \<em\> tag; one browser might render the text in bold, while another might use italics.

Figure 1-21 shows examples of how these tags can be displayed in a browser. Note that you can combine tags, allowing you to create bold and italic text by using the \<em\> and \<strong\> tags, for example.

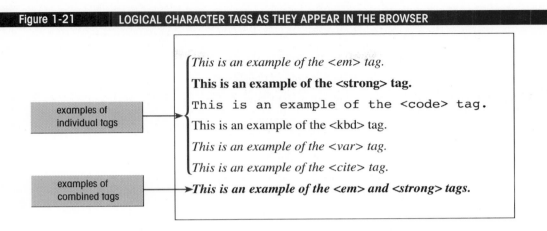

Figure 1-21   LOGICAL CHARACTER TAGS AS THEY APPEAR IN THE BROWSER

examples of individual tags

This is an example of the <em> tag.

This is an example of the <strong> tag.

`This is an example of the <code> tag.`

This is an example of the <kbd> tag.

This is an example of the <var> tag.

This is an example of the <cite> tag.

examples of combined tags

This is an example of the <em> and <strong> tags.

When you combine tags, it is a good idea for one tag to completely contain the other. For example, you can combine the <em> and <strong> tags like this:

```
<em><strong>strong emphasized text</strong></em>
```

But you should *not* overlap the opening and closing tags, as shown in the following code:

```
<em><strong>strong emphasized text</em></strong>
```

Some browsers cannot interpret combined tags. Combining tags also makes code more difficult to follow.

Web designers can also use **physical character tags** to format text. Figure 1-22 shows common examples of physical character tags.

Figure 1-22   COMMON PHYSICAL CHARACTER TAGS

TAG	DESCRIPTION
<b>	Enclosed text is bold.
<i>	Enclosed text is italic.
<u>	Enclosed text is underlined.
<tt>	Enclosed text is typewriter text, which is a monospace font such as Courier.
<big>	Enclosed text is displayed bigger than surrounding text.
<small>	Enclosed text is displayed smaller than surrounding text.
<sub>	Enclosed text is displayed as a subscript, in a smaller font if possible.
<sup>	Enclosed text is displayed as a superscript, in a smaller font if possible.

Figure 1-23 shows examples of how these tags can be displayed in a browser. Note that underlined text can sometimes be confused with hyperlinked text (which is usually underlined), and for that reason, use of the <u> tag is discouraged.

Figure 1-23   **PHYSICAL CHARACTER TAGS AS THEY APPEAR IN THE BROWSER**

This is an example of the <b> tag.

This is an example of the <i> tag.

<u>This is an example of the <u> tag.</u>

`This is an example of the <tt> tag.`

This is an example of the <big> tag.

This is an example of the <small> tag.

This is an example of the $_{<sub> tag.}$

This is an example of the $^{<sup> tag}$.

Given the overlapping functions of logical and physical character tags, which should you use to display text in an italicized font, <em> or <i>? Some older versions of browsers are text-based and cannot display italics, so these browsers ignore the <i> tag. If you suspect that many of your users are using older browsers, you should use a logical tag. Otherwise, use physical tags, which are more common and easier to interpret.

Only the Grading section in Stephen's handout requires the use of character tags, where he wants to highlight certain key words of each grading topic. He decides to use a combination of the <b> and <i> tags to display the key words in bold and italics.

To add character tags to the chemistry file:

1. Using your text editor, open **chem.htm** if it is not currently open.

2. Type the <i> and <b> tags around the keywords in the Grading section of the handout as follows:

   ```
   <i><b>Homework</b></i> will be given daily…
   <i><b>Tests and quizzes</b></i> will be used…
   <i><b>Labs</b></i> will be worth…
   <i><b>small research projects</b></i> throughout the
   semester…
   <i><b>make up</b></i> missed tests and quizzes…
   ```

   See Figure 1-24.

Figure 1-24   **APPLYING CHARACTER TAGS**

```
<h2>Class Policies</h2>
<h3>Grading</h3>
<p><i><b>Homework</b></i> will be given daily, is due at the beginning of the period the school
day after it was assigned, and will be worth 5 to 10 points. A periodic quiz consisting of 1 or
2 homework problems from the past week may be given in lieu of collecting homework.</p>

<p><i><b>Tests and quizzes</b></i> will be used to check your understanding of concepts,
procedures, and information. Quizzes will be worth 10 to 25 points and will be given at least
once a month. Tests will be worth up to 100 points and will be given 2 or 3 times a quarter.
</p>

<p><i><b>Labs</b></i> will be worth 10 to 30 points and will be graded on safety,
participation, and write-up. I expect neat handwritten or typed reports.  I'll also assign
<i><b>small research projects</b></i> throughout the semester.</p>

<p>You must <i><b>make up</b></i> missed tests and quizzes the day you return, and you must
submit missed homework assignments and labs within two days for every one day you missed.
Failure to make up work within these time frames will result in a 0 for that test or
assignment.</p>
```

3. Save your changes to chem.htm.

4. Using your Web browser, refresh or reload chem.htm. The updated Grading section of your page should look like Figure 1-25.

| Figure 1-25 | THE EFFECT OF THE CHARACTER TAGS IN THE BROWSER |

Class Policies

Grading

text formatted with bold and italics

Homework will be given daily, is due at the beginning of the period the school day after it was assigned, and will be worth 5 to 10 points. A periodic quiz consisting of 1 or 2 homework problems from the past week may be given in lieu of collecting homework.

Tests and quizzes will be used to check your understanding of concepts, procedures, and information. Quizzes will be worth 10 to 25 points and will be given at least once a month. Tests will be worth up to 100 points and will be given 2 or 3 times a quarter.

Labs will be worth 10 to 30 points and will be graded on safety, participation, and write-up. I expect neat handwritten or typed reports. I'll also assign *small research projects* throughout the semester.

You must *make up* missed tests and quizzes the day you return, and you must submit missed homework assignments and labs within two days for every one day you missed. Failure to make up work within these time frames will result in a 0 for that test or assignment.

5. If you are continuing to Session 1.3, leave your text editor and browser open. Otherwise you can close them at this time.

You have finished adding text to Stephen's online handout. In Session 1.3, you will add special formatting elements such as horizontal lines and images to the Web page.

Session 1.2 QUICK CHECK

1. Why should you include the <html> tag in your Web document?

2. What is the syntax for creating a centered Heading 1?

3. What is the syntax for creating a paragraph?

4. If you want to create an extra blank line between paragraphs, why can't you simply add a blank line in the HTML file?

5. Show the syntax for creating an ordered list, an unordered list, and a definition list.

6. List two ways of italicizing text in your Web document. What are the advantages and disadvantages of each method?

SESSION 1.3

In this session you'll insert three special elements into Stephen's Web page: an image, a special character for the "e" in his last name, and a horizontal line separating his picture and page title from the rest of the Web page.

Inserting a Graphic

One feature of Web pages that has made the Web so popular is the ease with which images can be displayed. Images can be displayed in two ways: as inline images or as external images.

An **inline image** is displayed directly on the Web page and is displayed when the page is accessed by a user. An inline image can be placed on a separate line in your HTML code, or it can be placed directly within a line of text—hence the term inline. Inline images should be in one of two file formats: GIF (Graphics Interchange Format) or JPEG (Joint Photographic Experts Group). Image editing applications such as Adobe Photoshop can be used to convert images to either the GIF or JPEG file format.

An **external image** is not displayed with the Web page. Instead, the browser must have a file viewer, which is a separate program that the browser launches when it encounters an external image file. Most browsers make it easy to set up viewers for use with the Web. External images have one major disadvantage: you can't actually display them on the Web page. Instead they are represented by an icon that a user clicks to view the image. The advantage is that external images are not limited to the GIF or JPEG formats.

REFERENCE   WINDOW   **RW**

Inserting an Inline Image
- Using your text editor, open the HTML file.
- Place the insertion point where you want the inline image to appear.
- Type <img src="*file*"> where *file* is the name of the GIF or JPEG image file.

Stephen has decided to use an inline image rather than an external image. The syntax for creating an inline image is:

```
<img src="file">
```

where *file* is the name of the image file. If the image file is located in the same folder as the HTML file, you do not need to include any file location path information. However, if the image file is located in another folder or on another computer, you need to include the full location path and use the src attribute. Tutorial 2 discusses directory paths and filenames in more detail. For now, assume that Stephen's image file is located in the folder that contains the HTML file.

The image file that Stephen wants you to use is a photograph of himself that has been saved as a JPEG file. The image is displayed in Figure 1.26. The image file **dube.jpg** is located in the Tutorial folder in the Tutorial.01 folder on your data disk.

Figure 1-26   **IMAGE FOR THE TOP OF STEPHEN'S PAGE**

Because this file includes the title of the page, you no longer need the text "Mr. Dube's Chemistry Classes at Robert Service High School" that you entered earlier.

Stephen wants to center the image on the page. There is no attribute in the <img> tag that allows you to center it on a page, but you can nest the <img> tag within a paragraph tag, <p>, and then center the paragraph on the page using the align="center" attribute for the <p> tag. This has the effect of centering all of the text in the paragraph, including any inline images.

To add Stephen's image to the Web page:

1. Using your text editor, open **chem.htm**.

2. Near the top of the file, select the two lines of code just below the <body> tag (from the <h1> opening tag to the </h2 > closing tag), and then press the **Delete** key.

3. Press the **Enter** key to insert a blank line if necessary, and then type:

   ```
   <p align="center"><img src="dube.jpg"></p>
   ```

4. Save your changes to chem.htm. See Figure 1-27.

Figure 1-27	ADDING THE IMAGE FILE

```
<html>
<head>
<title>Mr. Dube's Chemistry Classes</title>
</head>

<body>
<p align="center"><img src="dube.jpg"></p>
Welcome to Mr. Dube's Web site. I hope you will use this site to learn more about your class,
my expectations, and chemistry in the world around you.
<h2>Chemistry Classes</h2>
```

use the <p> tag so you can center the image

5. Using your browser, refresh or reload chem.htm and compare your Web page to Figure 1-28.

Figure 1-28	THE IMAGE FILE AS IT APPEARS IN THE BROWSER

MR. DUBÉ'S CHEMISTRY CLASSES AT ROBERT SERVICE HIGH SCHOOL

Welcome to Mr. Dube's Web site. I hope you will use this site to learn more about your class, my expectations, and chemistry in the world around you.

Chemistry Classes

Stephen is pleased with the way the image looks. Your next task is to format the e at the end of "Dubé" to include the accent. You do this using special character symbols.

Adding **Special Characters**

Occasionally you will want to include special characters in your Web page that do not appear on your keyboard. For example, a page might require mathematical symbols such as β or μ, or you might need to place the copyright symbol © to show that an image or text is copyrighted.

Stephen needs to use a special symbol, the accented "é," in his last name, which appears twice in his Web page: once in the title at the top of the page, and again in the short introductory paragraph. You've just inserted a graphic that includes the é at the top, so you need to add the symbol only once.

HTML supports the use of character symbols that are identified by a code number or name. To create a special character, type an ampersand (&) followed either by the code name or the code number, and then a semicolon. Code numbers are preceded by a pound symbol (#). Figure 1-29 shows some HTML symbols and the corresponding code numbers or names. A more complete list of special characters is included in Appendix B.

SYMBOL	CODE	CODE NAME	DESCRIPTION
©	&#169;	&copy;	Copyright symbol
®	&#174;	&reg;	Registered trademark
•	&#183;	&middot;	Middle dot
º	&#186;	&ordm;	Masculine ordinal
TM	&#153;	&trade;	Trademark symbol
			Nonbreaking space, useful when you want to insert several blank spaces, one after another
<	&#60;	&lt;	Less than symbol
>	&#62;	&gt;	Greater than symbol
&	&#38;	&amp;	Ampersand

Figure 1-29 — SPECIAL CHARACTERS AND CODES

To add a character code to the chemistry page:

1. Using your text editor, open **chem.htm** if it is not currently open.

2. In the "Welcome to Mr. Dube's Web site" paragraph, select the **e** in "Dube" and then type **&#233** so that the code reads as follows:

```
Welcome to Mr. Dub&#233's Web site
```

3. Save your changes to chem.htm.

4. Using your Web browser, refresh or reload chem.htm. Figure 1-30 shows Stephen's page with the accented é in his last name.

Figure 1-30 — SPECIAL CHARACTER IN THE BROWSER

accented é added to last name

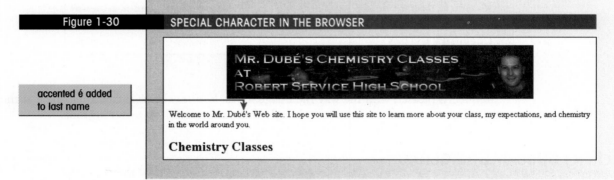

The final thing Stephen wants to include in his page is a horizontal line separating his picture and the large title at the top from the rest of the page.

Inserting Horizontal Lines

The horizontal line after Stephen's photo and title in Figure 1-6 improves the appearance of his paper handout, and he'd like to duplicate that look on the Web page. The syntax for creating a horizontal line is:

```
<hr align="align" size="size" width="width" color="color"
noshade>
```

where *align* specifies the horizontal alignment of the line on the page (center, left, or right), *size* specifies the height of the line, *width* indicates the width of the line, *color* indicates the color of the line, and *noshade* specifies that the browser display a solid line. Note that the color attribute is supported by Internet Explorer but not Netscape.

The size and width attributes are measured in either **pixels** (a square dot on your computer screen about 1/72 inch wide) or as a percentage of the screen width. For example, <hr width="50%"> instructs the browser to place the line so that its length covers half of the width of the page. Figure 1-31 shows how a browser would interpret the following lines of HTML code:

```
<hr align="center" size="12" width="100%">
<hr align="center" size="6" width="50%">
<hr align="center" size="3" width="25%">
<hr align="center" size="1" width="10%">
```

Figure 1-31	DIFFERENT LINE STYLES

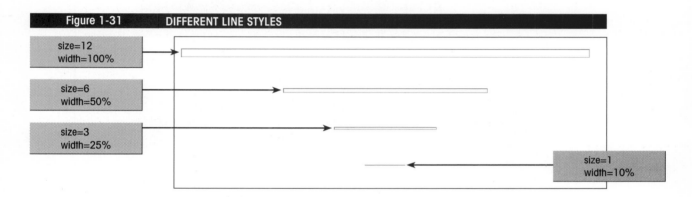

To add a horizontal line to the chemistry file:

1. Using your text editor, open **chem.htm** if it is not currently open.

2. At the end of the line specifying the dube.jpg image (just above the "Welcome" paragraph), press the **Enter** key to insert a new blank line.

3. In the new line, type **<hr>**.

4. Save your changes to chem.htm.

5. Using your Web browser, refresh or reload the chem.htm file. The new horizontal line is displayed in Figure 1-32.

Figure 1-32	HORIZONTAL LINE ADDED TO THE PAGE

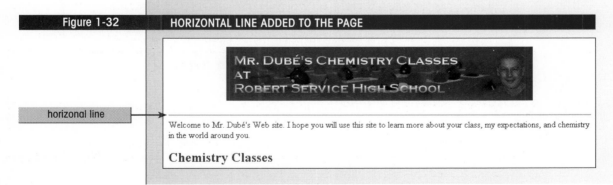

Now that you've completed the Web page for Stephen, you decide to print both the text file and the Web page as it appears in the browser for his review.

To print the text file and Web page:

1. Using your browser, carefully compare your Web page to Figure 1-33, which shows the entire page. If you see any errors, return to your text editor to fix them. When the page is error-free, use your browser to print the page.

Figure 1-33   **STEPHEN'S COMPLETED CHEMISTRY PAGE**

Welcome to Mr. Dubé's Web site. I hope you will use this site to learn more about your class, my expectations, and chemistry in the world around you.

Chemistry Classes

- Conceptual Chemistry: An introductory course requiring basic math but no algebra
- Chemistry I: An introductory course requiring solid algebra skills
- Advanced Placement Chemistry: An advanced course requiring a grade of A or B in Chemistry I and designed for students who want to prepare for the AP Chemistry exam (which can count toward college credits)

Class Policies

Grading

Homework will be given daily, is due at the beginning of the period the school day after it was assigned, and will be worth 5 to 10 points. A periodic quiz consisting of 1 or 2 homework problems from the past week may be given in lieu of collecting homework.

Tests and quizzes will be used to check your understanding of concepts, procedures, and information. Quizzes will be worth 10 to 25 points and will be given at least once a month. Tests will be worth up to 100 points and will be given 2 or 3 times a quarter.

Labs will be worth 10 to 30 points and will be graded on safety, participation, and write-up. I expect neat handwritten or typed reports. I'll also assign *small research projects* throughout the semester.

You must *make up* missed tests and quizzes the day you return, and you must submit missed homework assignments and labs within two days for every one day you missed. Failure to make up work within these time frames will result in a 0 for that test or assignment.

Appointments

I can meet with you before or after school. I will also be in my room (H113) during most lunch hours. Please do not hesitate to stop in if you need extra help -- do not wait! Chemistry is a building subject, and it is very hard to catch up once you fall behind.

Safety

We will be doing lab work nearly every week. Because of the potential danger of any lab exercise, I will hold you to the highest standards of behavior, and will remove you from the class if you pose a threat to yourself or other students.

2. Using your text editor, print chem.htm, and compare it to the following code. When you are finished, you can close your text editor and browser unless you are continuing on to the Review Assignments.

```
<html>
<head>
<title>Mr. Dube's Chemistry Classes</title>
</head>
<body>
<p align="center"><img src="dube.jpg"></p>
<hr>
Welcome to Mr. Dub&#233's Web site. I hope you will
use this site to learn more about your class, my
expectations, and chemistry in the world around you.
<h2>Chemistry Classes</h2>
<ul>
<li>Conceptual Chemistry: An introductory course
requiring basic math but no algebra
<li>Chemistry I: An introductory course requiring solid
algebra skills
<li>Advanced Placement Chemistry: An advanced course
requiring a grade of A or B in Chemistry I and designed
for students who want to prepare for the AP Chemistry
exam (which can count toward college credits)
</ul>
<h2>Class Policies</h2>
<h3>Grading</h3>
<p><i><b>Homework</b></i> will be given daily, is due at
the beginning of the period the school day after it was
assigned, and will be worth 5 to 10 points. A periodic
homework quiz consisting of 1 or 2 homework problems
from the past week may be given in lieu of collecting
homework.</p>
<p><i><b>Tests and quizzes</b></i> will be used to check
your understanding of concepts, procedures, and
information. Quizzes will be worth 10 to 25 points and
will be given at least once a month. Tests will be worth
up to 100 points and will be given 2 or 3 times a
quarter.</p>
<p><i><b>Labs</b></i> will be worth 10 to 30 points and
will be graded on safety, participation, and write-up.
I expect neat handwritten or typed reports. I'll also
assign <i><b>small research projects</b></i> throughout
the semester.</p>
<p>You must <i><b>make up</b></i> missed tests and quizzes
the day you return, and you must submit missed homework
assignments and labs within two days for every one day
you missed.
Failure to make up work within these time frames will
result in a 0 for that test or assignment.</p>
<h3>Appointments</h3>
I can meet with you before or after school. I will also
be in my room (H113) during most lunch hours. Please do
not hesitate to stop in if you need extra help -- do not
wait! Chemistry is a building subject, and it is very
hard to catch up once you fall behind.
<h3>Safety</h3>
We will be doing lab work nearly every week. Because of
```

Note:
Continued on
next page

```
the potential danger of any lab exercise, I will hold you
to the highest standards of behavior, and will remove you
from the class if you pose a threat to yourself or other
students.
</body>
</html>
```

Stephen is pleased with your work on his Web site and feels that it effectively captures the look and feel of the original handout. You explain to him that the next step is adding hypertext links to his Web page so that you can add contact information and create links to the interesting chemistry Web sites you've discovered. You'll do this in Tutorial 2.

Session 1.3 QUICK CHECK

1. How would you insert a copyright symbol, ©, into your Web page?

2. What is the syntax for inserting a horizontal line into a page?

3. What is the syntax for creating a horizontal line that is 70% of the display width of the screen and 4 pixels high?

4. What is an inline image?

5. What is an external image?

6. What is the syntax for inserting a graphic named mouse.jpg into a Web document as an inline image?

7. What are two graphic file formats you can use for inline images?

REVIEW ASSIGNMENTS

After further review, Stephen decides that he wants you to add a few more items to the Web page. In the Chemistry Classes section, he wants you to add a new class that he'll be offering next semester. He would like a numbered list in the Safety section listing his five main safety rules. He would also like to add a whimsical sentence at the bottom of the site to let his students know that though he is serious about learning and safety, he wants his classes to be fun. He'd like the line to read: "Chemistry with Dubé is like medicine with a spoonful of $C_{12}H_{22}O_{11}$!". $C_{12}H_{22}O_{11}$ is the formula for sugar. You'll use the <sub> tag to format the subscript numbers in the formula. You suggest to him that adding a horizontal line to separate this line from the rest of the page would be a nice touch, and he agrees.

The file you'll create is shown in Figure 1-34.

Figure 1-34

MR. DUBÉ'S CHEMISTRY CLASSES AT ROBERT SERVICE HIGH SCHOOL

Welcome to Mr. Dubé's Web site. I hope you will use this site to learn more about your class, my expectations, and chemistry in the world around you.

Chemistry Classes

- Conceptual Chemistry: An introductory course requiring basic math but no algebra
- Chemistry I: An introductory course requiring solid algebra skills
- Applied Chemistry: An introductory course requiring solid algebra skills and an interest in using critical thinking to solve real-world, chemistry-related problems
- Advanced Placement Chemistry: An advanced course requiring a grade of A or B in Chemistry I and designed for students who want to prepare for the AP Chemistry exam (which can count toward college credits)

Class Policies

Grading

Homework will be given daily, is due at the beginning of the period the school day after it was assigned, and will be worth 5 to 10 points. A periodic quiz consisting of 1 or 2 homework problems from the past week may be given in lieu of collecting homework.

Tests and quizzes will be used to check your understanding of concepts, procedures, and information. Quizzes will be worth 10 to 25 points and will be given at least once a month. Tests will be worth up to 100 points and will be given 2 or 3 times a quarter.

Labs will be worth 10 to 30 points and will be graded on safety, participation, and write-up. I expect neat handwritten or typed reports. I'll also assign ***small research projects*** throughout the semester.

You must ***make up*** missed tests and quizzes the day you return, and you must submit missed homework assignments and labs within two days for every one day you missed. Failure to make up work within these time frames will result in a 0 for that test or assignment.

Appointments

I can meet with you before or after school. I will also be in my room (H113) during most lunch hours. Please do not hesitate to stop in if you need extra help -- do not wait! Chemistry is a building subject, and it is very hard to catch up once you fall behind.

Safety

We will be doing lab work nearly every week. Because of the potential danger of any lab exercise, I will hold you to the highest standards of behavior, and will remove you from the class if you pose a threat to yourself or other students.

1. Follow my written and oral directions carefully and immediately.
2. Never perform any procedure not specifically directed by me or assigned in the lab.
3. No playful behavior is permitted in the lab.
4. Safety equipment must be worn as directed at all times, even if you find it uncomfortable or unbecoming.
5. No food, drinks, or loose clothing are permitted in the lab.

Chemistry with Dubé is like medicine with a spoonful of $C_{12}H_{22}O_{11}$!

To complete this task:

1. Using your text editor, open **chem.htm** located in the tutorial folder of the tutorial.01 folder on your Data Disk. This is the file you created over the course of this tutorial.

2. Save the file on your Data Disk in the tutorial.01/review folder with a new name, **chem2.htm**, so that you leave your work from the tutorial intact.

3. In the unordered list section, after the line specifying the Chemistry I class, add a new item to the list using the </i> tag to specify the following:

   "Applied Chemistry: An introductory course requiring solid algebra skills and an interest in using critical thinking to solve real-world, chemistry-related problems"

4. Move to the Safety section of chem2.htm.

5. After the paragraph describing Stephen's safety standards, use the <nl> and <li> tags to create a numbered list with the following five list items:

   1. Follow my written and oral directions carefully and immediately.
   2. Never perform any procedure not specifically directed by me or assigned in the lab.
   3. No playful behavior is permitted in the lab.
   4. Safety equipment must be worn as directed at all times, even if you find it uncomfortable or unbecoming.
   5. No food, drinks, or loose clothing are permitted in the lab.

Explore ▶ 6. Go to the end of the file, and just before the closing </body> tag, insert a blank line and enter the code for the following text:

   "Chemistry with Dube is like medicine with a spoonful of $C_{12}H_{22}O_{11}$!"

   You'll need to enter the symbol **&#233** for the accented é at the end of his name, and the <sub> tag for each of the three numbers that need to be formatted as subscript characters. Your code should look like the following:

   <p>Chemistry with Dub&#233 is like medicine with a spoonful of C₁₂H₂₂O₁₁!</p>

Explore ▶ 7. Insert a blank line before the code you just entered, and then type the code for a horizontal line using the <hr> tag. Set the thickness of the line to 6 pixels.

8. Save your changes to chem2.htm.

9. View the file with your Web browser and compare it with Figure 1-34.

10. Correct any errors that you see, and then print a copy of the page as viewed by your browser and a copy of the code in your text editor.

11. Close your browser and text editor.

CASE PROBLEMS

Case 1. ChildLink, Inc. You are on the board of directors for ChildLink, Inc., a small, nonprofit agency in Las Cruces, New Mexico that provides financial and emotional support for families with children who have newly discovered physical or mental disabilities. The agency received significantly more donations in the last year than expected, and it has decided to offer qualifying clients temporary help with housing and medical costs. The board has asked you to post the eligibility requirements and application process on the Web. The page should appear as displayed in Figure 1-35.

Figure 1-35

ChildLink of Las Cruces

A Loving Connection between Children with Disabilities and the Resources They Need

Temporary Financial Assistance Available

To be eligible for this program, you must meet the following criteria:

- Have a child with a physical or mental disability diagnosed within the last 6 months (the diagnosis can be prenatal or at any age)
- Be at or below the State of New Mexico's poverty line

To apply, please do the following:

1. Pick up an application from ChildLink (address below)
2. Assemble the following papers:
   a. Your completed application
   b. Doctor's record of your child's diagnosis
   c. Tax records or New Mexico Social Services certificate of your income level
   d. Your lease, mortgage, or medical bills, depending on which you need help with
3. Make an appointment with a ChildLink volunteer, available these times:
   a. Ida: MW 10:30 a.m. to 3:30 p.m.
   b. Juan: TR 9:00 a.m. to noon
   c. Chris: F 10:30 a.m. to 3:30 p.m.

ChildLink

1443 Cortnic Drive

Las Cruces, NM 88001

505-555-2371

The page needs an inline image, three headings, a list of eligibility requirements, and application instructions. Two of the items in the list also have nested lists.

To create this page:

1. Start your text editor program.

2. Type the <html>, <head>, and <body> tags to identify different sections of the page.

3. Save the file as **child.htm** in the case1 folder of the tutorial.01 folder on your Data Disk.

4. Within the head section, insert a <title> tag with the text, "ChildLink Temporary Financial Assistance". This text appears in the title bar of the browser.

5. Within the body section, create an <h1> heading with the text "ChildLink of Las Cruces", and center the heading on the page using the align attribute.

6. Below the <h1> heading, create an <h3> heading with the text "A Loving Connection between Children with Disabilities and the Resources They Need", and center the heading on the page.

7. Below the <h3> heading, create an <h2> heading with the text "Temporary Financial Assistance Available", and center the heading.

8. Below the <h2> heading, create an <h4> heading with the text "To be eligible for this program, you must meet the following criteria:". Leave this heading left-aligned.

Explore 9. Below the <h4> heading, create a bulleted list using the <ul> tag and the type attribute to make the bullet a square. Include the two list items shown in Figure 1-35. Make sure you include a closing </ul> tag.

10. Below the closing </ul> tag for the bulleted list, create an <h4> heading with the text "To apply, please do the following:". Leave this heading left-aligned.

11. Below the second <h4> heading, create an ordered list with the three items shown in Figure 1-35. Make sure you include a closing </ol> tag.

Explore 12. Within the "Assemble the following papers:" item, create an ordered list with the four items shown in Figure 1-35. Use the type attribute to have this nested list numbered with a, b, c, and d.

Explore 13. Within the "Make an appointment" list, create another ordered list with the three volunteer names and times as shown in Figure 1-35, again using the type attribute to number the list with a, b, and c.

14. Below the numbered list, type the address shown in Figure 1-35 using the <p> tag to keep each line separate. Remember to right-align the paragraphs and to use the <b> and <i> tags for the ChildLink name.

15. After the <h3> heading ("A Loving Connection...") near the top, insert the inline image **newborn.jpg** (located in the case1 folder of the tutorial.01 folder on your Data Disk), centered on the page.

16. After the image, insert a horizontal line that extends the width of the page and is 1 pixel in height.

17. Save the file, view it in your browser, compare it to Figure 1-35, and then make any corrections necessary in your text editor.

18. Add <p> tags where necessary to insert blank lines to space the text, image, and horizontal lines attractively.

19. Save the file again, view it with your Web browser, print it from the browser and the text editor, and then close your browser and text editor.

Case 2. Mathematics Department, Coastal University Professor Laureen Coe of the Mathematics Department at Coastal University in Beachside, Connecticut is preparing material for her course on the history of mathematics. As part of the course, she has written short profiles of famous mathematicians. Laureen would like you to use content she's already written to create several Web pages to be placed on the Coastal University's Web server. You'll create the first one in this exercise. A preview of one of the pages about the mathematician Leonhard Euler is shown in Figure 1-36.

Figure 1-36

Euler, Leonhard

(1707-1783)

The greatest mathematician of the eighteenth century, **Leonhard Euler** was born in Basel, Switzerland. There, he studied under another giant of mathematics, **Jean Bernoulli**. In 1731 Euler became a professor of physics and mathematics at St. Petersburg Academy of Sciences. Euler was the most prolific mathematician of all time, publishing over *800 different books and papers*. His influence was felt in physics and astronomy as well. Euler's work on mathematical analysis, Introductio in analysin infinitorum (1748) remained a standard textbook for well over a century. For the princess of Anhalt-Dessau he wrote *Lettres à une princesse d'Allemagne* (1768-1772), giving a clear non-technical outline of the main physical theories of the time.

One can hardly write mathematical equations without copying Euler. Notations still in use today, such as e and π, were developed by Euler. He is perhaps best known for his research into mathematical analysis. Euler's formula:

$$cos(x) + isin(x) = e^{(ix)}$$

demonstrates the relationship between analysis, trignometry and imaginary numbers, in one beautiful and elegant equation.

Leonhard Euler died in 1783, leaving behind a legacy perhaps unmatched, and certainly unsurpassed, in the annals of mathematics.

Math 895: The History of Mathematics

To complete this task:

1. Using your text editor, open **eulertxt.htm** located in the case2 folder of the tutorial.01 folder on your Data Disk, and save it as **euler.htm**.

2. Add the opening and closing <html>, <head>, and <body> tags to the file in the appropriate locations.

3. Insert "Leonhard Euler" as a page title in the head section of the document.

4. Insert the inline image **euler.jpg** (located in the case2 folder of the tutorial.01 folder on your Data Disk) at the top of the body of the document.

5. Format the first line of the page's body, "Euler, Leonhard", with the <h1> tag, and format the second line of the page's body, "(1707-1783)", with the <h3> tag.

6. Add the appropriate paragraph tags, <p>, to the document to separate the paragraphs.

7. Within the first paragraph, display the names "Leonhard Euler" and "Jean Bernoulli" in boldface. Italicize the phrase "800 different books and papers", and underline the publication "Introductio in analysin infinitorum".

8. Replace the one-letter word "a" in "Lettres a une princesse d'Allemagne" with an *à*, using the character code &agrave, and then italicize the entire name of the publication.

9. In the second paragraph, italicize the notation "e" and replace the word "pi" with the inline image **pi.jpg**, located in the case2 folder on your Data Disk.

10. Center the equation and italicize the letters "x", "i", and "e" in the equation. Display the term "*(ix)*" as a superscript, using the <sup> tag.

11. Format the name of the course at the bottom of the page using the <cite> tag.

12. Add horizontal lines before and after the biographical information.

13. Save euler.htm, and then print it from your text editor.

14. View the file in your Web browser, and then print a copy of the page as displayed by the browser.

Case 3. Frostbite Freeze You are on the organizing committee for the Frostbite Freeze, Montana's craziest running race. The Frostbite Freeze is a fun but competitive event held each January in Butte, Montana, and you've volunteered to publish the race results on the Web. You'd like to have a snowflake background behind the text, which you can do using a graphic image. Such backgrounds are called tile-image backgrounds because the image is repeated throughout the entire page. To create a tile-image background, you must have an image in either GIF or JPEG file format. You insert the file in the background by adding the background attribute to the <body> tag with the syntax:

```
<body background="filename">
```

You have a JPEG file named **flakes.jpg**, which contains a pattern of repeating snowflakes. You also have a JPEG file named **runner.jpg**, a picture of a Frostbite Freeze racer. A preview of the page you'll create is shown in Figure 1-37.

Figure 1-37

Frostbite Freeze

Montana's Craziest Footrace

The results are in...

257 runners braved the -10° weather on January 19 and ran, in one fashion or another, the icy 5-kilometer course through downtown Butte. About half the runners sported costumes rather than serious running gear, and many runners posted good times (costumed or not). For many, this was the season's first run (not race – *run*), a motivational warm-up for the fun and work that lies ahead.

Awards were given for best time in four age categories for both sexes.

Girls 14-19

Jamie Harrington 19:33 · Sorcia Besay 20:06 · Rachel Stores 25:44

Boys 14-19

Bruce Bevin 18:55 · Endre Witthoeft 19:46 · Joe Wesevich 21:19

Women 20-39

Marie Sillers 17:45 · Denise Wortenhau 18:33 · Lorel Dwiers 18:56

Women 39-49

Jannie Gilbert 17:48 · Mia Saphi 19:23 · Dawn Severson 21:31

Women 50+

Julia Gent 21:09 · Mandy Reming 34:24 · Sung Bon 41:02

Men 20-39

Gary Cruz 17:11 · Lanny Sorla 18:40 · Kip Oestin 18:55

Men 40-49

Steve Jackson 18:50 · Jim Kostenberger 24:33 · Lee Whisten 27:18

Men 50+

Billy Tisa 18:22 · Alois Anderson 28:48 · Lyle Tolbor 35:46

To create this page:

1. Using your text editor, open **frosttxt.htm** from the case3 folder of the tutorial.01 folder on your Data Disk, and then save it as frostrun.htm.

2. Insert the <html>, <head>, and <body> tags in the appropriate locations.

3. Insert a <title> tag in the head section, giving the Web page the title "Frostbite Freeze Results".

4. Insert the **flakes.jpg** file (in the case3 folder) as the background for the page. To do this, modify the <body> tag to read:

   ```
   <body background="flakes.jpg">
   ```

5. Format the text "Frostbite Freeze" with the <h1> tag and center it on the Web page.

6. Format the text "Montana's Craziest Footrace" with the <h2> tag and center it on the page.

Explore 7. Insert a horizontal line below the <h2> heading that is 50% of the width of the screen, is 10 pixels wide, and is purple. (*Hint*: use the color attribute and the word "purple.")

8. Format the text "The results are in" with the <h3> heading tag, leaving the text left aligned.

Explore 9. Add ellipses (…) after the text "The results are in" so it reads, "The results are in…" You'll need to use the character for the ellipses symbol, which you can find in Appendix B of this book.

10. Add a degree symbol after "-10" in the first line of the first paragraph. (The degree symbol is also located in Appendix B.)

11. Insert <p> tags around the two main paragraphs (one starts with "257 runners" and the other starts with "Awards were given").

12. Near the end of the first text paragraph, format the word "run" that appears in parentheses in Figure 1-37 with italics using the <i> tag.

13. Add <p> tags around each of the eight age-sex categories (for example, "Girls 14-19"). (*Hint*: For Steps 13, 14, and 15, use your text editor's copy and paste functions to reduce the amount of typing you have to do.)

14. Format the eight age-sex categories with bold using the <b> tag.

15. Insert a middle dot symbol, with a nonbreaking space on each side of the dot, between each of the three names in each of the eight age-sex categories, as shown in Figure 1-37. To do this, type &#183 after the time for the first two names in each category. Because you are inserting nonbreaking spaces, make sure there is no space after the time or before the next name. For example, in the Girls 14-19 category, the names appear as

   Jamie Harrington 19:33 &#183 Sorcia Besay 20:06 &#183 Rachel Stores 25:44

16. Insert the inline image **runner.jpg** (located in the case3 folder of the tutorial.01 folder on your Data Disk) between the top two headings, as shown in Figure 1-37. Center it on the page.

17. Save frostrun.htm and print it from your text editor.

18. View the file in your Web browser and print it from your browser.

Case 4. Create Your Own Resume Using the techniques from this tutorial, design and create a resume for yourself. Be sure to include these features: section headings, bulleted or numbered lists, bold and/or italic fonts, paragraphs, inline graphic images, and horizontal lines.

1. Start your text editor, and then create a file called **myresume.htm** in the case4 folder of the tutorial.01 folder on your Data Disk. Type the appropriate HTML code and content.

2. Add any other tags you think will improve the appearance of your document.

3. You could take a picture of yourself to your lab or a local office services business and have it scanned. If you do, save it as a GIF or JPEG file. Then place the graphic file in the case4 folder of the tutorial.01 folder on your Data Disk. Add the appropriate code in your myresume.htm file. If you don't have your own image file, use the file **kirk.jpg** located in the case4 folder of the tutorial.01 folder on your Data Disk.

4. Test your code as you develop your resume by viewing myresume.htm in your browser.

5. When you finish entering the code, save and print the myresume.htm file from your text editor.

6. View the final version in your browser, print the Web page, and then close your browser and text editor.

QUICK | CHECK ANSWERS

Session 1.1

1. Hypertext refers to text that contains points called links that allow the user to move to other places within the document, or to open other documents, by activating the link.

2. A Web server stores the files used in creating World Wide Web documents. The Web browser retrieves the files from the Web server and displays them. The files stored on the Web server are described in a very general way; it is the Web browser that determines how the files will eventually appear to the user.

3. HTML, which stands for Hypertext Markup Language, is used to create Web documents.

4. HTML documents do not exactly specify the appearance of a document; rather they describe the purpose of different elements in the document and leave it to the Web browser to determine the final appearance. A word processor like Word exactly specifies the appearance of each document element.

5. Documents are transferred more quickly over the Internet and are available to a wider range of machines.

6. Extensions are special formats supported by a particular browser, but not generally accepted by all browsers. The advantage is that people who use that browser have a wider range of document elements to work with. The disadvantage is that the document will not work for users who do not have that particular browser.

7. All you need is a simple text editor.

Session 1.2

1. The <html> tag identifies the language of the file as HTML to packages that support more than one kind of generalized markup language.

2. <h1 align="center"> Heading text </h1>

3. <p> Paragraph text </p>

4. HTML does not recognize the blank lines as format elements. A Web browser ignores blank lines and runs the paragraphs together on the page.

5. Ordered list:

   ```
   <ol>
       <li> List item
       <li> List item
   </ol>
   ```

   Unordered list:

   ```
   <ul>
       <li> List item
       <li> List item
   </ul>
   ```

   Definition list:

   ```
   <dl>
       <dt> List term <dd> Term definition
       <dt> List term <dd> Term definition
   </dl>
   ```

6. <em> Italicized text </em>

   and

   ```
   <i> Italicized text </i>
   ```

   The advantage of using the <em> tag is that it will be recognized even by older browsers that do not support italics (such as a terminal connected to a UNIX machine), and those browsers will still emphasize the text in some way. The <i> tag, on the other hand, will be ignored by those machines. Using the <i> tag has the advantage of explicitly describing how you want the text to appear.

Session 1.3

1. ©

2. <hr>

3. <hr width="70%" size="4">

4. An inline image is a GIF or JPEG file that appears in a Web document. A browser can display it without a file viewer.

5. An external image is a graphic that requires the use of a software program, called a viewer, to display it.

6. <img align="left" src="**mouse.jpg**">

7. GIF and JPEG

In this tutorial you will:

- Create hypertext links between elements within a Web page

- Create hypertext links between Web pages

- Review basic Web page structures

- Create hypertext links to Web pages on the Internet

- Distinguish between and be able to use absolute and relative pathnames

- Create hypertext links to various Internet resources, including FTP servers and newsgroups

ADDING
HYPERTEXT LINKS TO A WEB PAGE

Developing a Chemistry Web Site with Hypertext Links

CASE

Creating a Chemistry Web Site, continued

In Tutorial 1 you created the basic structure and content of a Web page for Stephen Dubé, a chemistry teacher in Edmonton, Alberta. Stephen has made a few changes to the Web page, and he has ideas for additional content. Stephen notes that although the appearance of the Web page reflects the course handout on which he originally based his Web page, there are some limitations that he would like to see removed. For example, students and their parents must scroll through the document window to find information about his classes. Stephen wants to make it as easy to navigate from topic to topic on his Web page as it is to scan the single-page handout.

Stephen also wants to add more information to his Web site, but he is concerned about making the original page too large and difficult to navigate. He'd like to have a separate page that lists the ways students and parents can contact him (office hours, e-mail, phone numbers, and so forth). He also has found several helpful chemistry Web sites that he'd like to share with his students.

SESSION 2.1

In this session, you'll create anchors on a Web page that let users navigate to specific points within a document. After creating anchors, you'll create and test your first hypertext link.

Creating a Hypertext Document

In Tutorial 1 you learned that a hypertext document contains **hypertext links**, items that you can select, usually by clicking a mouse, to view another topic or document, often called the **destination** of the link. These links can point to another section in the same document, to a different document, to a different Web page, or to a variety of other Web objects, which you'll learn about later in this tutorial.

Stephen's Web page has two main sections: Chemistry Classes and Class Policies. You and Stephen have made some modifications, including removing the <h2> heading "Class Policies" and upgrading the three <h3> headings to <h2> headings. You have also added the new Applied Chemistry course to the Classes list, the numbered list to his Safety section, the spoonful of sugar sentence, and some horizontal lines. However, because of the document window's small size, the opening screen shows only the first heading in the document. The browser in Figure 2-1 displays Stephen's photo, his introductory paragraph, and the beginning of his Classes list, but nothing about Grading, Appointments, or Safety; users must scroll through the document to locate this information.

Figure 2-1	OPENING SCREEN OF STEPHEN'S CHEMISTRY PAGE

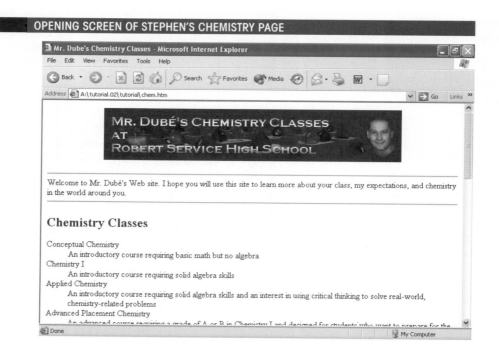

Without hypertext links, you can do little to show more of Stephen's page in the browser except remove the image file or move it to the end of the page, which he doesn't want you to do. One solution is to place text for the four headings (Classes, Grading, Appointments, and Safety) at the top of the document and make these headings hypertext links. When users open Stephen's page, they'll not only see his name and photo, but they will also see links to the main parts of his page. They can then click a link and navigate to that section of the document. The hypertext links that you create here point to sections within the same document. You'll create these hypertext links in Stephen's page using the following steps:

1. Type the headings into the HTML file.

2. Mark each section in the HTML file using an anchor. You'll learn about anchors shortly.

3. Link the text you added in Step 1 to the anchors you added in Step 2.

You can accomplish the first step using techniques you learned in Tutorial 1. You need to open the Chemistry text file in your text editor and then enter the text. You want the text to appear just above his introductory paragraph, as shown in Figure 2-2.

Figure 2-2	TEXT LINKS STEPHEN WANTS TO ADD

Classes · Grading · Appointments · Safety

Welcome to Mr. Dubé's Web site. I hope you will use this site to learn more about your class, my expectations, and chemistry in the world around you.

To achieve this, you place the text within paragraph tags that you'll center, and then you'll add the middle dot symbol (•) with a space on each side. You could type all the text into the HTML file on the same line, but to keep the HTML file as legible as possible, you'll add the text in two lines instead. This way, when you add more tags to the text later, it will still be easy to read. Remember, with HTML, placing text on different lines in the text file does not affect its appearance when viewed with a browser.

To add text that will become links in the Web page:

1. Start your text editor.

2. Open **chemtxt.htm** from the tutorial folder in the tutorial.02 folder on your Data Disk, and then save it as **chem.htm** in the tutorial folder so that the original remains intact.

TROUBLE? If you can't locate **chemtxt.htm** in the Tutorial folder in your text editor's Open dialog box, you may need to set the file type to All Files.

3. Before "Welcome to Mr. ....," type the following, pressing the **Enter** key at the end of each line:

```
<p align="center">
Classes &#183; 
Grading &#183; 
Appointments &#183; 
Safety</p>
```

See Figure 2-3. The new code uses the <p> tag with the center attribute to center the text. It includes the special character codes   and ·, which insert a middle dot surrounded by nonbreaking spaces, to separate the section headings.

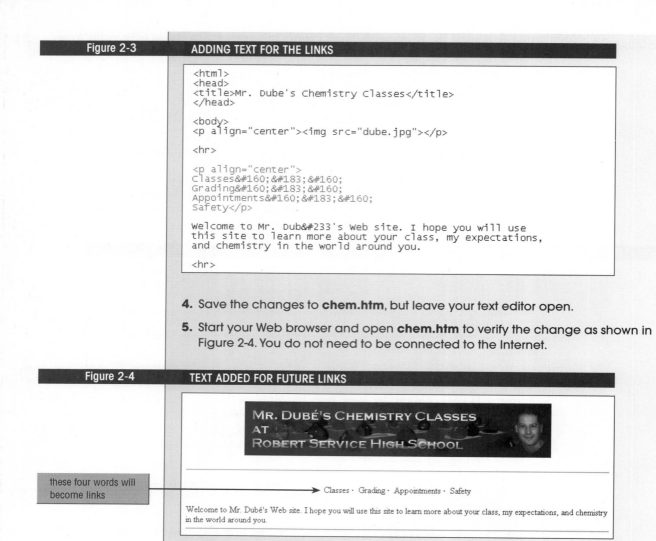

Figure 2-3   ADDING TEXT FOR THE LINKS

```
<html>
<head>
<title>Mr. Dube's Chemistry Classes</title>
</head>

<body>
<p align="center"><img src="dube.jpg"></p>

<hr>

<p align="center">
Classes &#183; 
Grading &#183; 
Appointments &#183; 
Safety</p>

Welcome to Mr. Dub&#233;'s web site. I hope you will use
this site to learn more about your class, my expectations,
and chemistry in the world around you.

<hr>
```

4. Save the changes to **chem.htm**, but leave your text editor open.

5. Start your Web browser and open **chem.htm** to verify the change as shown in Figure 2-4. You do not need to be connected to the Internet.

Figure 2-4   TEXT ADDED FOR FUTURE LINKS

MR. DUBÉ'S CHEMISTRY CLASSES
AT
ROBERT SERVICE HIGH SCHOOL

these four words will become links → Classes · Grading · Appointments · Safety

Welcome to Mr. Dubé's Web site. I hope you will use this site to learn more about your class, my expectations, and chemistry in the world around you.

Creating Anchors

Now that you've created the text describing the different sections of the Web page, you need to locate each heading in the document and mark it using the <a> tag. The <a> tag creates an **anchor**, text that is specially marked so that you can link to it from other points in the document. Text that is anchored is the destination of a link; it is not the text you click on. You assign each anchor its own anchor name, using the "name" attribute. For example, if you want the text "Chemistry Classes" to be an anchor, you could assign it the anchor name "cc":

```
<a name="cc">Classes</a>
```

Later, when you create a link to this anchor from the headings you just inserted at the beginning of Stephen's page, the link will point to this place in the document, identified by the anchor name, cc. Figure 2-5 illustrates how the anchor you create works as a reference point to a link.

Figure 2-5 | **HOW AN ANCHOR WORKS**

Classes · Grading · Appointments · Safety

Welcome to Mr. Dubé's Web site. I hope you will use this site to _____ out your class, my expectations, and chemistry in the world around you.

Chemistry Classes

Conceptual Chemistry
> An introductory course requiring basic math but no algebra

Chemistry I
> An introductory course requiring solid algebra skills

Applied Chemistry
> An introductory course requiring solid algebra skills and a_____ using critical thinking to solve real-world, chemistry-related problems

Advanced Placement Chemistry
> An advanced course requiring a grade of A or B in Che_____ nd designed for students who want to prepare for the AP Chemistry exam (which can count toward college __

Grading

Homework will be given daily, is due at the beginning o____ iod the school day after it was assigned, and will be worth 5 to 10 points. A periodic quiz consisting of 1 or 2 homew___ blems from the past week may be given in lieu of collecting homework.

Tests and quizzes will be used to check your und_____ing of concepts, procedures, and information. Quizzes will be worth 10 to 25 points and will be given at least once a m____ ests will be worth up to 100 points and will be given 2 or 3 times a quarter.

Labs will be worth 10 to 30 points and will be ____ed on safety, participation, and write-up. I expect neat handwritten or typed reports. I'll also assign *small research* ___*cts* throughout the semester.

You must *make up* missed tests and quizz____ e day you return, and you must submit missed homework assignments and labs within two days for every one day you m____ t. Failure to make up work within these time frames will result in a 0 for that test or assignment.

Appointments

I can meet with you before or after school. I will also be in my room (H113) during most lunch hours. Please do not hesitate to stop in if you need extra help -- do not wait! Chemistry is a building subject, and it is very hard to catch up once you fall behind.

Safety

We will be doing lab work nearly every week. Because of the potential danger of any lab exercise, I will hold you to the highest standards of behavior, and will remove you from the class if you pose a threat to yourself or other students.

1. Follow my written and oral directions carefully and immediately.
2. Never perform any procedure not specifically directed by me or assigned in the lab.
3. No playful behavior is permitted in the lab.
4. Safety equipment must be worn as directed at all times, even if you find it uncomfortable or unbecoming.
5. No food, drinks, or loose clothing are permitted in the lab.

Chemistry with Dubé is like medicine with a spoonful of $C_{12}H_{22}O_{11}$!

An anchor doesn't have to be text. You can also mark an inline image as an anchor using the same syntax:

```
<a name="photo"><img src="dube.jpg"></a>
```

In the above example, you anchor an image. You can create a link to this photo from other points in the document by using the anchor name "photo." As you'll see, adding an anchor does not change your document's appearance in any way. It merely creates locations in your Web page that become destinations of links.

REFERENCE WINDOW   **RW**

Creating Anchors

- Using your text editor, locate the text or graphic you want to anchor.
- Before the text or graphic, place the tag
  <a name="anchor_name"> where anchor_name is the name you assign to your anchor.
- Immediately after the text or image, place a closing </a> tag to turn off the anchor.

For Stephen's Chemistry file, you decide to create four anchors named cc, gra, app, and safe that correspond to Chemistry Classes, Grading, Appointments, and Safety sections.

To add anchors to the section headings:

1. Using your text editor, open **chem.htm** if it is not currently open.

2. Locate the <h2> heading for the Chemistry Classes section. This line currently reads:

   ```
   <h2>Chemistry Classes</h2>
   ```

3. Add an anchor tag around the Chemistry Classes heading so that it reads:

   ```
   <h2><a name="cc">Chemistry Classes</a></h2>
   ```

4. Locate the <h2> heading for the Grading section. This line currently reads:

   ```
   <h2>Grading</h2>
   ```

5. Add an anchor tag around the Grading heading so that it reads:

   ```
   <h2><a name="gra">Grading</a></h2>
   ```

6. Locate the <h2> heading for the Appointments section, which reads:

   ```
   <h2>Appointments</h2>
   ```

   and add an anchor tag so that it reads:

   ```
   <h2><a name="app">Appointments</a></h2>
   ```

7. Locate the <h2> heading for the Safety section, which reads:

   ```
   <h2>Safety</h2>
   ```

   and add an anchor tag so that it reads:

   ```
   <h2><a name="safe">Safety</a></h2>
   ```

8. Save your changes to **chem.htm**.

9. Using your Web browser, refresh or reload chem.htm, and scroll through the file to confirm that it appears unchanged. Remember that the anchors you placed in the document are reference points and do not change the appearance of the Web page.

   TROUBLE? If you see a change in the document, check to make sure that you correctly typed the code for adding anchors.

You created four anchors in the Web page. The next step is to create links to those anchors.

Creating **Links**

After you create the anchors that serve as destinations for your links, you need to create the links themselves. For Stephen's page, you want to link the headings that you centered above the introductory paragraph to the four sections in the document. Figure 2-6 shows the four links you want to create.

Figure 2-6   **LINKS YOU'LL CREATE**

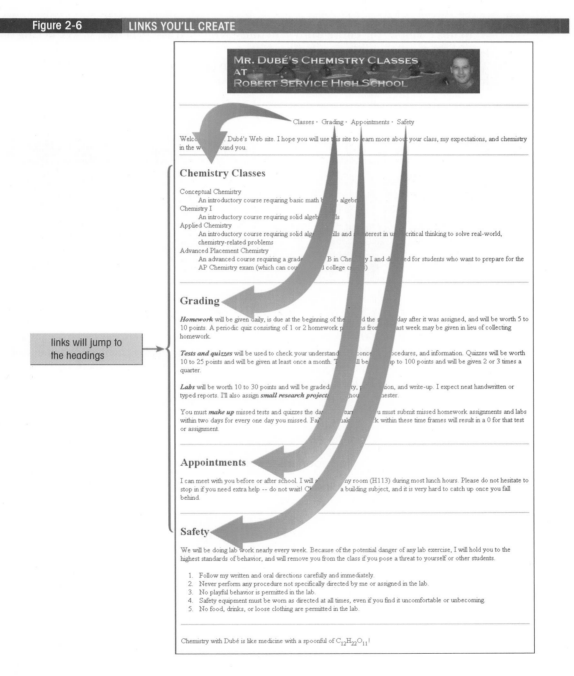

To create a link to an anchor, you use the same <a> tag you used to create the anchor. The difference is that instead of using the name attribute to define the anchor, you use the **href**

attribute, which is short for **Hypertext Reference**, to indicate the location to jump to. "href" can refer to an anchor that you place in the document or, as you'll see later, to a different Web page or a resource anywhere on the Internet. The <a> tags used to create links are sometimes called **link tags**.

You link to an anchor using the anchor name preceded by a pound (#) symbol. For example, to create a link to Stephen's Grading heading, you use the anchor name "gra" and the following HTML code:

```
<a href="#gra">Grading</a>
```

In this example, the entire word "Grading" is defined as a hypertext link. Clicking on any part of the word Grading (in a browser) navigates you to the location of the gra anchor.

You can also designate an inline image as a hypertext link. To turn an inline image into a hypertext link, place it within link tags, as follows:

```
<a href="#app"><img src="dube.jpg"></a>
```

REFERENCE WINDOW   RW

Linking to Text Within a Document

- Using your text editor, mark the destination text with an anchor, if you haven't already done so.
- Locate the text or image you want to designate as the link.
- Before the text or graphic, place the tag
  <a href="#anchor_name"> where anchor_name is the name of the anchor.
- Close the link tag with the </a> closing tag after the text or graphic you designated as the link.

It is important to note that the href attribute is case sensitive. Because of this, the anchor name "EMP" is not the same as "emp". Therefore, you should be careful to make each anchor name unique within a document. Using the same anchor name more than once creates confusion, and your links won't go where you expect them to.

In the current HTML document, you've created four anchors to which you can create links. You're ready to place the link tags around the appropriate text in the HTML file.

To add link tags to the Chemistry file:

1. Using your text editor, open **chem.htm** if it is not already open.

2. Locate the following lines of code:

```
<p align="center">
Classes &#183; 
Grading &#183; 
Appointments &#183; 
Safety</p>
```

and add the <a href> tags so the code reads:

```
<p align="center">
<a href="#cc">Classes</a> &#183; 
<a href="#gra">Grading</a> &#183; 
<a href="#app">Appointments</a> &#183; 
<a href="#safe">Safety</a></p>
```

3. Compare your **chem.htm** file to Figure 2-7.

Figure 2-7 ADDING LINK TAGS

```
<body>
<p align="center"><img src="dube.jpg"></p>

<hr>

<p align="center">
<a href="#cc">Classes</a> &#183; 
<a href="#gra">Grading</a> &#183; 
<a href="#app">Appointments</a> &#183; 
<a href="#safe">Safety</a></p>

Welcome to Mr. Dub&#233;'s web site. I hope you will use
this site to learn more about your class, my expectations,
and chemistry in the world around you.
```

4. Save your changes to **chem.htm**.

5. Using your Web browser, refresh or reload **chem.htm**. The headings should now be a different color and be underlined. This is the standard formatting for links. See Figure 2-8.

Figure 2-8 TEXT LINKS IN THE BROWSER

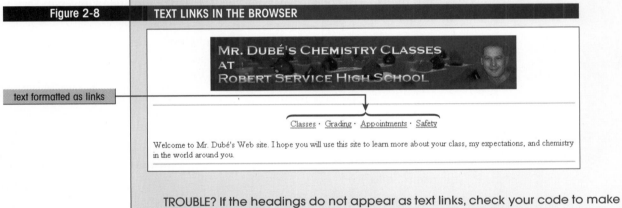

text formatted as links

TROUBLE? If the headings do not appear as text links, check your code to make sure that you are using the <a> and </a> tags around the appropriate text, the href attribute within the tag, and the quotes and # symbols, as shown previously.

Before continuing, you should verify that the links work as you expect them to. To test a link, simply click it and see where it takes you.

To test your links:

1. Click one of the links. Your browser should display the section of the document indicated by the link. If it does not, check your code for errors by comparing it to Figure 2-7.

2. Click each of the other links, scrolling back to the top of the page after each test.

3. If you are continuing to Session 2.2, leave your browser and text editor open. If you are not, you can close them at this time.

TROUBLE? If your links still don't work, make sure you used the correct case and that you coded the anchor and link tags correctly.

When you add an anchor to a large section of text, such as a section heading, make sure to place the anchor within the heading tags. For example, write your tag as:

```
<h2><a name="gra">Grading</a></h2>
```

not as:

```
<a name="gra"><h2>Grading</h2></a>
```

The latter example can confuse some browsers. The general rule is to always place anchors within other tag elements. Do not insert any tag elements within an anchor, except for tags that create document objects such as inline graphics.

You show the new links to Stephen and he's confident that they will help his students and their parents to quickly find the information they want. In the next session, you'll learn how to create links that allow users to navigate to other HTML documents.

Session 2.1 QUICK CHECK

1. What is the HTML code for marking the text "Colorado State University" with the anchor name "csu"?

2. What is the HTML code for linking the text "Universities" to an anchor that is named "csu"?

3. What is wrong with the following statement?

   <a name="info"><h3>For more information</h3></a>

4. What is the HTML code for marking an inline image, **photo.jpg**, with the anchor name "photo"?

5. What is the HTML code for linking the inline image **button.jpg** to an anchor with the name "links"?

6. True or False: Anchor names are case-sensitive.

SESSION 2.2

In Session 2.1 you created hypertext links to locations within the same Web page. In this session you'll create links to other Web pages.

Stephen wants to add two more pages to his Chemistry site: a page showing his contact information and a page listing his favorite chemistry links. Both of these pages, in turn, require links of their own, making it easy to go from each of the three pages to the others. Figure 2-9 shows what he has in mind.

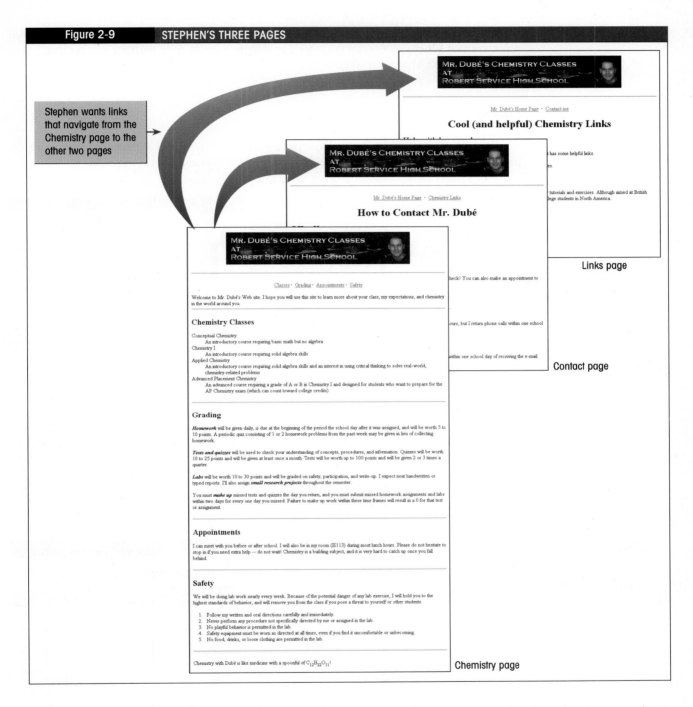

Figure 2-9   STEPHEN'S THREE PAGES

Before you start linking documents together as Stephen has instructed you to do, it would be a good idea to take a look at the basics of Web page structures.

Web **Page Structures**

The three pages that will make up Stephen's chemistry site, Chemistry, Contacts, and Links, are part of a system of Web pages. Before you set up links for navigating a group of Web pages, it's worthwhile to map out exactly how you want the pages to relate, using a technique known as storyboarding. **Storyboarding** your Web pages before you create links helps you determine which structure works best for the type of information you're presenting. You want to ensure that readers can navigate easily from page to page without getting lost.

You'll encounter several Web structures as you navigate the Web. Examining some of these structures can help you decide how to design your own system of Web pages.

Linear Structures

Figure 2-10 shows one common Web page structure, the **linear structure**, in which each page is linked to the next and to previous pages, in an ordered chain of pages.

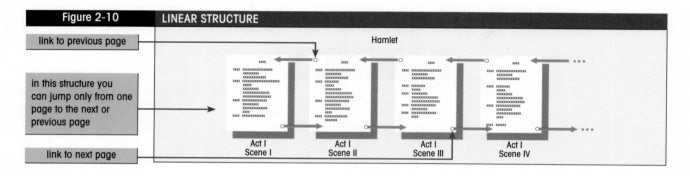

Figure 2-10   LINEAR STRUCTURE

You could use this type of structure in Web pages that have a defined order. Suppose that a Web site of Shakespeare's *Hamlet* has a single page for each scene. If you use a linear structure for these pages, you assume that users want to progress through the scenes in a particular order.

You might, however, want to make it easier for users to return immediately to the opening scene, rather than backtrack through several scenes to get to their destination. Figure 2-11 shows an **augmented linear structure**, in which you include a link in each page that jumps directly back to the first page, while keeping the links that allow you to move to the next and previous pages. This kind of storyboarding can reveal approaches to organizing a Web site that otherwise you may have overlooked.

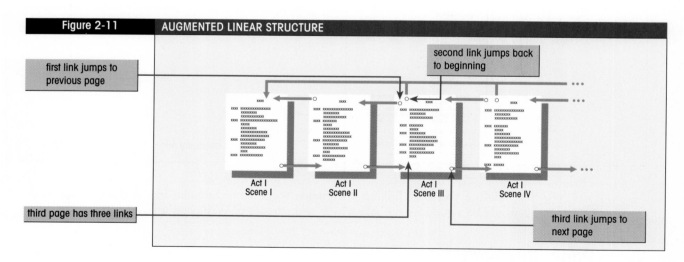

Figure 2-11   AUGMENTED LINEAR STRUCTURE

Hierarchical Structures

Another popular structure is the hierarchical structure of Web pages, shown in Figure 2-12. A **hierarchical structure** starts with a general topic that includes links to more specific topics. Each specific topic includes links to yet more specialized topics, and so on. In a hierarchical structure, users can move easily from general to specific and back, but not from specific to specific.

Figure 2-12	HIERARCHICAL STRUCTURE

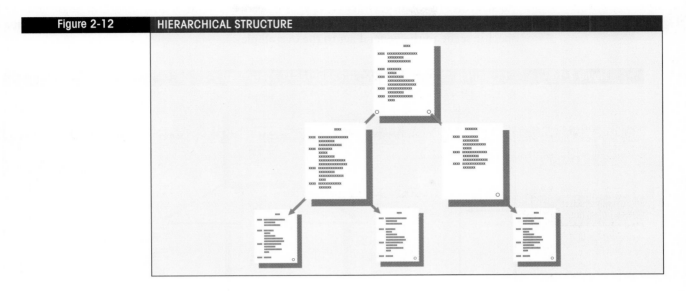

As with the linear structure, including a link to the top of the structure on each page gives users an easy path back to the beginning. Subject catalogs such as the AltaVista directory of Web pages often use this structure. Figure 2-13 shows this site, located at *http://www.altavista.com.*

Figure 2-13	HIERARCHICAL STRUCTURE ON ALTAVISTA WEB PAGE

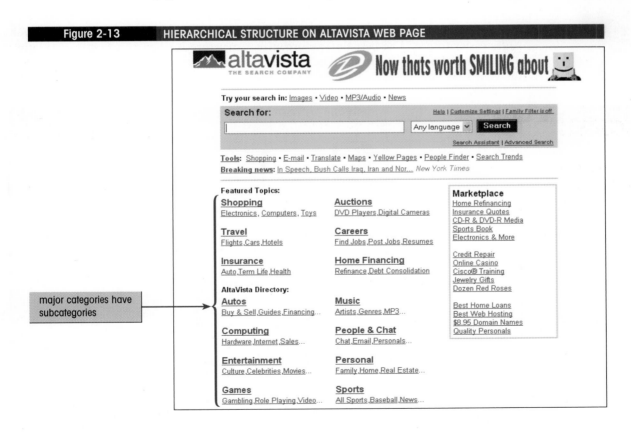

Mixed Structures

As you may have guessed, you can also combine structures. Figure 2-14 shows a hierarchical structure in which each level of pages is related in a linear structure. You might use this system for the *Hamlet* Web site to let the user move from scene to scene linearly, or from a specific scene to the general act to the overall play.

Figure 2-14	COMBINATION OF LINEAR AND HIERARCHICAL STRUCTURES

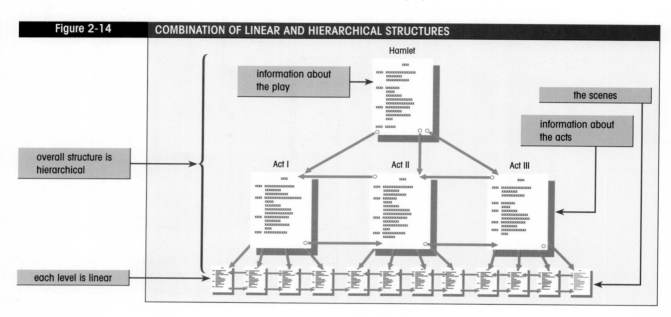

As these examples show, a little foresight can go a long way toward making your Web pages easier to use. The best time to organize a structure is when you first start creating pages, when those pages are small in number and more easily managed. If you're not careful, your structure might look like Figure 2-15.

Figure 2-15	MULTIPAGE DOCUMENT WITH NO COHERENT STRUCTURE

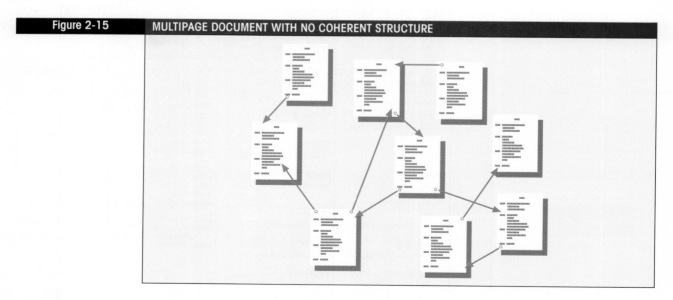

This structure is confusing, and it makes it difficult for readers to grasp the contents of the overall Web site. Moreover, a user who enters this structure at a certain page might not be aware of the presence of the other pages.

Creating **Links Among Documents**

You and Stephen discuss the type of structure that will work best for his chemistry pages. He wants students to be able to move effortlessly between the three documents. Because there are only three Web pages in this site and all focus on the same topic, you decide to include links within each document to the other two. For this relatively simple, three-page Web site, the structure shown in Figure 2-16 works just fine.

Figure 2-16   **STRUCTURE OF MARY'S WEB PAGES**

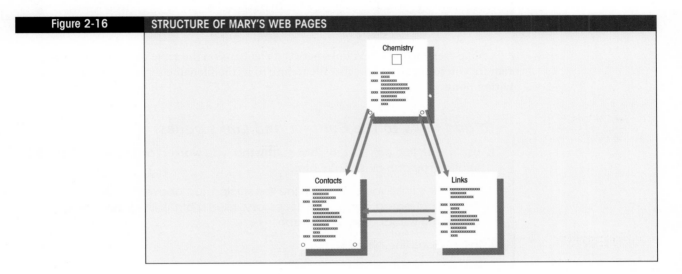

Stephen has given you the information to create two additional HTML files: **conttxt.htm**, a page containing his contact information; and **linktxt.htm**, a page containing links to various chemistry Web sites that he has found particularly helpful to his students. These files are located in the tutorial folder in the tutorial.02 folder on your Data Disk. You should save the text files with new names, **contact.htm** and **links.htm**, to keep the originals intact.

To rename the conttxt.htm and linktxt.htm files:

1. Using your text editor, open **conttxt.htm** from the tutorial folder in the tutorial.02 folder on your Data Disk, and save it as **contact.htm**.

2. Using your text editor, open **linktxt.htm** from the tutorial folder in the tutorial.02 folder, and save it as **links.htm**.

Linking to a Document

You begin by linking Stephen's Chemistry page to the Contact and Links pages. Use the same <a> tag with the href attribute that you used earlier. For example, if you want a user to be able to click the phrase "Contact me" to navigate to the contact.htm file, you enter the following HTML code in your current document:

```
<a href="contact.htm">Contact me</a>
```

In this example, the phrase "Contact me" is linked to the HTML file contact.htm. In order for the browser to be able to locate and open contact.htm, it must be in the same folder as the chem.htm file, the document containing the link.

REFERENCE WINDOW RW

Linking to a Document on Your Computer

- Using your text editor, locate the text or image you want to act as a link.
- Before the text or image, insert the following code:

  `<a href="filename">`

  where filename is the name of the destination document.
- After the text or image link, place the tag `</a>`.

Unlike creating hypertext links between elements on the same page, this process does not require you to set an anchor in a file to link to it; the filename serves as the anchor or destination point.

To add links to the Contact and Links pages:

1. Using your text editor, open **chem.htm** that you worked on in Session 2.1 of this tutorial. You can close **links.htm**.

2. Locate the links you created in the last session, just above the introductory "Welcome" paragraph, and if necessary, insert a blank line below the links and above the introductory paragraph.

3. In the blank line, type:

   ```
   <p align="center">
   <a href="contact.htm">Contact me</a>
   ```

   Do not include a closing `</p>` tag; you'll do that in a moment.

4. Press the **Enter** key to move to the next line, and then type:

   ```
    &#183; 
   <a href="links.htm">Chemistry Links</a></p>
   ```

   See Figure 2-17.

Figure 2-17 | **LINKING TO OTHER FILES**

```
<body>
<p align="center"><img src="dube.jpg"></p>

<hr>

<p align="center">
<a href="#cc">Classes</a> &#183; 
<a href="#gra">Grading</a> &#183; 
<a href="#app">Appointments</a> &#183; 
<a href="#safe">Safety</a></p>

<p align="center">
<a href="contact.htm">Contact me</a>
 &#183; 
<a href="links.htm">Chemistry Links</a></p>

Welcome to Mr. Dub&#233;'s web site. I hope you will use
this site to learn more about your class, my expectations,
and chemistry in the world around you.
```

`<a>` tags to point to other files

5. Save your changes to **chem.htm**.

6. Using your Web browser, view **chem.htm**. The two new, external text links are displayed below the four internal links, as shown in Figure 2-18.

| Figure 2-18 | BROWSER DISPLAYING LINKS TO OTHER DOCUMENTS |

links to the Contact and Links pages

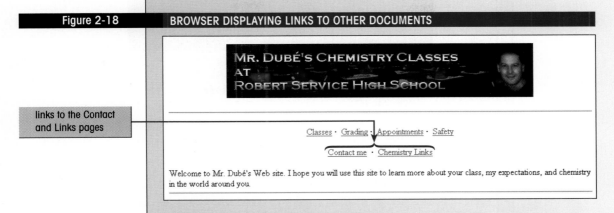

7. Click the **Contact me** link to verify that you navigate to the Contact page as shown in Figure 2-19.

| Figure 2-19 | CONTACT PAGE IN THE BROWSER |

How to Contact Mr. Dubé

Office Hours

I'm in my room, H113, during the following times each day:

- 6:45 a.m. until Period 1 begins at 7:30 a.m.
- lunch hour (11:10 a.m. to 11:50 a.m.)
- 2:30 p.m. until at least 3:00 p.m.

I am often there earlier in the morning and later in the afternoon, so stop by to check! You can also make an appointment to see me if those times don't work for you.

Address and Phone

You can write me at 5587 Abbot Road, Edmonton, Alberta T5H 4G9.

My phone number is 780-555-0955, ext. 230. I am unreachable during class hours, but I return phone calls within one school day of receiving a message.

E-mail

E-mail is a great way to reach me. I answer e-mails from students and parents within one school day of receiving the e-mail. My address is sdube@eps.edmonton.ab.ca.

TROUBLE? If the link doesn't work, check to see that **chem.htm** and **contact.htm** are in the same folder on your Data Disk.

8. Go back to the Chemistry page (usually by clicking a Back button on the toolbar of your browser), and then click **Chemistry Links** to verify that you navigate to the Links page as shown in Figure 2-20.

Figure 2-20	LINKS PAGE IN THE BROWSER

Cool (and helpful) Chemistry Links

Help with homework

<u>Homework Central</u> No, this site won't do your homework for you, but it has some helpful links.

<u>Academic Assistance</u> A free service offering help in a variety of disciplines.

Practice tests and quizzes

<u>Aufbaul</u> An extensive and somewhat unconventional on-line resource for tutorials and exercises. Although aimed at British middle-school students, this will likely be suitable for high school and college students in North America.

<u>ChemTutor</u> Basic help for high school and college chemistry students.

Research resources

<u>ChemTeam</u> A solid chemistry course with plenty of links.

<u>Chemistry Coach</u> A collection of great links for high school chemistry.

The next step is to add similar links in the contact.htm and links.htm files that point to the other two pages. Specifically, in contact.htm, you need to add one link to chem.htm and another to links.htm; in links.htm you need one link to chem.htm and another to contact.htm. This way, each page will have links that point to the other two pages.

To add links in the Contact page to the Chemistry and Links pages:

1. Using your text editor, open **contact.htm** from the tutorial folder in the tutorial.02 folder on your Data Disk.

2. Locate the <hr> tag near the top of the page, and then in the blank line below it, type the following:

```
<p align="center">
<a href="chem.htm">Mr. Dub&#233;'s Home page</a>
 &#183; 
<a href="links.htm">Chemistry Links</a></p>
```

3. Compare your code to Figure 2-21.

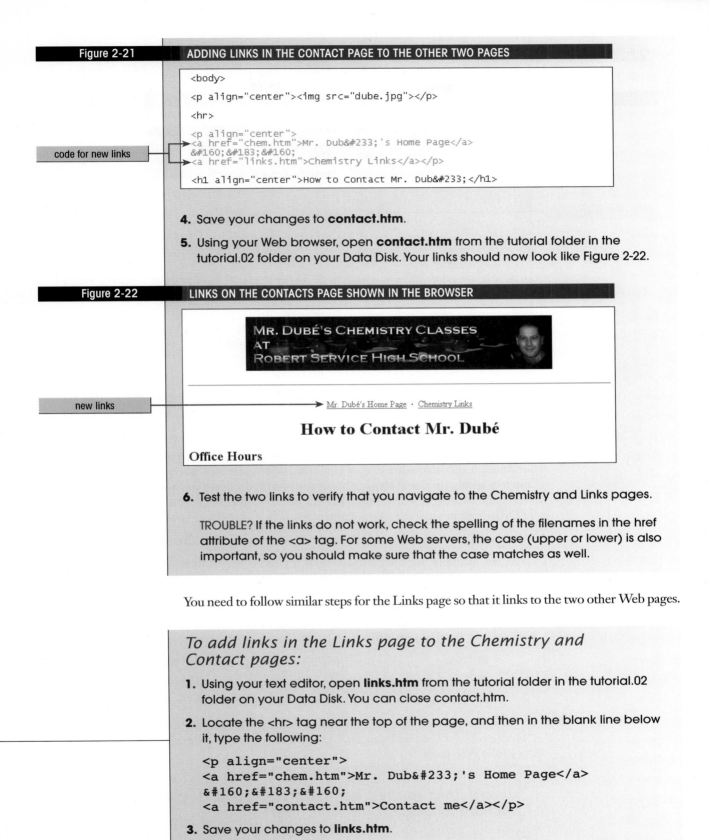

| Figure 2-21 | ADDING LINKS IN THE CONTACT PAGE TO THE OTHER TWO PAGES |

```
<body>

<p align="center"><img src="dube.jpg"></p>

<hr>

<p align="center">
<a href="chem.htm">Mr. Dub&#233;'s Home Page</a>
 &#183; 
<a href="links.htm">Chemistry Links</a></p>

<h1 align="center">How to Contact Mr. Dub&#233;</h1>
```

code for new links

4. Save your changes to **contact.htm**.

5. Using your Web browser, open **contact.htm** from the tutorial folder in the tutorial.02 folder on your Data Disk. Your links should now look like Figure 2-22.

| Figure 2-22 | LINKS ON THE CONTACTS PAGE SHOWN IN THE BROWSER |

MR. DUBÉ'S CHEMISTRY CLASSES
AT
ROBERT SERVICE HIGH SCHOOL

new links

Mr. Dubé's Home Page · Chemistry Links

How to Contact Mr. Dubé

Office Hours

6. Test the two links to verify that you navigate to the Chemistry and Links pages.

TROUBLE? If the links do not work, check the spelling of the filenames in the href attribute of the <a> tag. For some Web servers, the case (upper or lower) is also important, so you should make sure that the case matches as well.

You need to follow similar steps for the Links page so that it links to the two other Web pages.

To add links in the Links page to the Chemistry and Contact pages:

1. Using your text editor, open **links.htm** from the tutorial folder in the tutorial.02 folder on your Data Disk. You can close contact.htm.

2. Locate the <hr> tag near the top of the page, and then in the blank line below it, type the following:

```
<p align="center">
<a href="chem.htm">Mr. Dub&#233;'s Home Page</a>
 &#183; 
<a href="contact.htm">Contact me</a></p>
```

3. Save your changes to **links.htm**.

4. Using your Web browser, open **links.htm** from the tutorial folder in the tutorial.02 folder on your Data Disk. You should see the links shown in Figure 2-23.

Figure 2-23	NEW LINKS ON THE LINKS PAGE

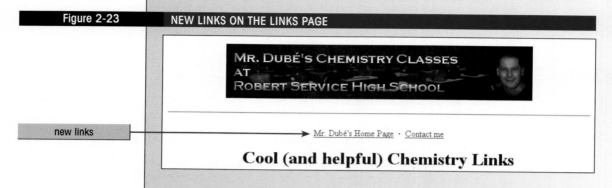

new links

Mr. Dubé's Home Page · Contact me

Cool (and helpful) Chemistry Links

5. Click the two links to verify that you navigate to the Chemistry and Contact Web pages.

Now that you have established links among the three Web pages, users can easily navigate to and from each of the three pages.

Linking to a Section of a Document

When testing your links, you may have noticed that you always navigate to the top of the destination page. What if you'd like to navigate to a specific location elsewhere in a document, rather than to the top of the page? To do this, you can set anchors as you did in Session 2.1 and link to an anchor you create within the document. For example, to create a link to a section in the Web page home.htm marked with an anchor name of "interests," you create an anchor in home.htm in the section on Interests, and then enter the following HTML code in your current document:

```
<a href="home.htm#interests">View my interests</a>
```

In this example, the entire text, "View my interests," is linked to the Interests section in the home.htm file, via the anchor name "interests." Note that the pound symbol (#) in this tag distinguishes the filename from the anchor name (that is why you included the # symbol earlier when linking to anchors within the same document).

Stephen wants to link three of the topics in his Grading section to specific sections in the Links page. The links.htm file already has these anchors in place:

- "home," for the chemistry links related to help with homework
- "test," for the chemistry links on practice tests and quizzes
- "search," for the chemistry links that are helpful in preparing research projects

Now you need to link the phrases listed in the Grading section of the Chemistry file ("Homework," "Tests and quizzes," and "small research projects") to these three anchors in the Links Web page.

To add links to the Chemistry Web page that navigate to anchors located in the Links Web page:

1. Using your text editor, open **chem.htm**. You can close the Links file at this time.

2. Locate the Grading section near the middle of the chemistry file.

As you enter the following code, be sure not to alter any other code, such as the \<p>, \<i>, and \<b> tags.

3. Locate the word "Homework" and replace it with the following code:

```
<p><i><b><a href="links.htm#home">Homework</a></b></i>
```

4. Locate the phrase "Tests and quizzes" and replace it with the following code:

```
<p><i><b><a href="links.htm#test">Tests and quizzes</a>
</b></i>
```

5. Locate the phrase "small research projects" and replace it with the following code:

```
<i><b><a href="links.htm#search">small research
projects</a></b></i>
```

See Figure 2-24.

Figure 2-24   **ADDING LINKS TO SPECIFIC LOCATIONS IN A PAGE**

```
<h2><a name="gra">Grading</a></h2>
<p><i><b><a href="links.htm#home">Homework</a></b></i> will be given
daily, is due at the beginning of the period the school day
after it was assigned, and will be worth 5 to 10 points.
A periodic quiz consisting of 1 or 2 homework problems from the past
week may be given in lieu of collecting homework.</p>

<p><i><b><a href="links.htm#test">Tests and quizzes</a></b></i> will
be used to check your understanding of concepts, procedures, and
information. Quizzes will be worth 10 to 25 points and will be given
at least once a month. Tests will be worth up to 100 points
and will be given 2 or 3 times a quarter.</p>

<p><i><b>Labs</b></i> will be worth 10 to 30 points
and will be graded on safety, participation, and write-up.
I expect neat handwritten or typed reports. I'll also assign
<i><b><a href="links.htm#search">small research projects</a></b></i>
throughout the semester.</p>

<p>You must <i><b>make up</b></i> missed tests and quizzes
the day you return, and you must submit missed homework assignments
and labs within two days for every one day you missed.
Failure to make up work within these time frames will result
in a 0 for that test or assignment.</p>

<hr>
```

6. Save your changes to **chem.htm**.

7. Using your Web browser, refresh or reload **chem.htm**. The phrases in the Grading section are now displayed as text links, as shown in Figure 2-25.

Figure 2-25   **LINKS IN THE CHEMISTRY PAGE THAT POINT TO ANCHORS IN THE LINKS PAGE**

Grading

Homework will be given daily, is due at the beginning of the period the school day after it was assigned, and will be worth 5 to 10 points. A periodic quiz consisting of 1 or 2 homework problems from the past week may be given in lieu of collecting homework.

links

Tests and quizzes will be used to check your understanding of concepts, procedures, and information. Quizzes will be worth 10 to 25 points and will be given at least once a month. Tests will be worth up to 100 points and will be given 2 or 3 times a quarter.

**Labs** will be worth 10 to 30 points and will be graded on safety, participation, and write-up. I expect neat handwritten or typed reports. I'll also assign _small research projects_ throughout the semester.

You must _**make up**_ missed tests and quizzes the day you return, and you must submit missed homework assignments and labs within two days for every one day you missed. Failure to make up work within these time frames will result in a 0 for that test or assignment.

8. Click the three links you created to verify that you navigate to the appropriate places in the Links page.

TROUBLE? If you are having problems with your links, remember that anchors are case sensitive. Be sure you typed "home", "test", and "search" in all lower-case letters.

9. If you are continuing to Session 2.3, you can leave your browser and text editor open. Otherwise, close them.

With these last hypertext links in place, you have given users of Stephen's Web page easy access to additional information. In the next session, you'll learn how to create hypertext links that navigate to documents and resources located throughout the Internet.

Session 2.2 QUICK CHECK

1. What is storyboarding? Why is it important in creating a Web page system?

2. What is a linear structure?

3. What is a hierarchical structure?

4. What is the purpose of the pound symbol (#) when creating a link to an anchor in a separate Web page?

5. What code would you enter to link the text "Sports info" to the HTML file sports.htm?

6. What code would you enter to link the text "Basketball news" to the HTML file sports.htm at a place in the file with the anchor name "bball"?

SESSION 2.3

In Session 2.2 you created links to other documents located within the same folder as chem.htm. In this session you'll learn to create hypertext links to documents located in other folders as well as to other locations on the Internet. You'll also see how to display linked documents in separate browser windows.

Stephen wants to add a new link in the Chemistry page that points to the College Board's Web page on Advanced Placement tests. This Web page provides an overview of the Advanced Placement program and provides help for preparing for the AP tests. Before you can create this link for Stephen, you need to review the way HTML links to files located in different folders and computers.

Linking to Documents in Other Folders

Until now you've worked with documents located in the same folder. When you created links to other files in that folder, you specified the filename in the link tag but not its location. Browsers assume that if no folder information is given, the file is in the same folder as the current document. In some situations, such as when working with large multidocument systems that span several topics, you might want to place different files in different folders to help you stay organized.

When referencing a file located in a different folder than the link tag, you must include the location, or **path**, for the file. HTML supports two kinds of paths: absolute paths and relative paths.

Absolute Pathnames

An **absolute path** provides a precise location for a file. With HTML, absolute pathnames begin with a slash (/) and are followed by a sequence of folders beginning with the highest-level folder and proceeding to the folder that contains the file. Each folder is separated by a slash. Finally, after you type the name of the folder that contains the file, you type a final slash and then the filename itself.

For example, consider the folder structure shown in Figure 2-26.

Figure 2-26	FOLDER TREE

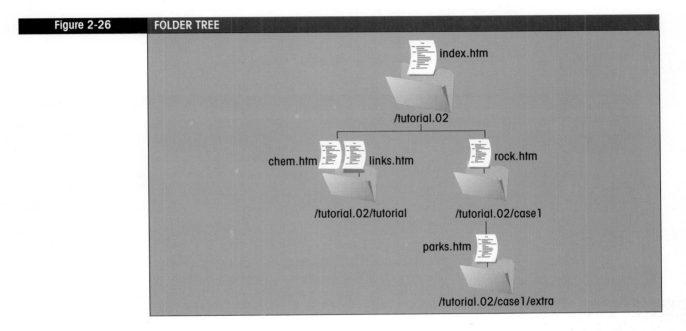

Figure 2-26 shows five HTML files that are located in four different folders. The top-most folder is the tutorial.02 folder. Within the tutorial.02 folder are the tutorial and case1 folders, and within the case1 folder is the extra folder. Figure 2-27 shows absolute path-names for the five files.

Figure 2-27	ABSOLUTE PATHNAMES

ABSOLUTE PATHNAME	INTERPRETATION
/tutorial.02/index.htm	The index.htm file in the tutorial.02 folder
/tutorial.02/tutorial/chem.htm	The chem.htm file in the tutorial folder, a subfolder of the tutorial.02 folder
/tutorial.02/tutorial/links.htm	The links.htm file in the same folder as the chem.htm file
/tutorial.02/case1/rock.htm	The rock.htm file in the case1 folder, another subfolder of the tutorial.02 folder
/tutorial.02/case1/extra/parks.htm	The parks.htm file in the extra folder, a subfolder of the /tutorial.02/case1 folder

Even the absolute pathnames for files located on different computers begin with a slash. To differentiate these files, HTML requires you to include the drive letter followed by a vertical bar (|). For example, a file named "chem.htm" in the tutorial.02 folder on drive C of your computer has the absolute pathname "/C|/tutorial.02.chem.htm".

Relative Pathnames

When there are many folders and subfolders involved, absolute pathnames can be cumbersome and confusing. For that reason, most Web designers use **relative pathnames** in their hypertext links. A relative path specifies the location for a file in relation to the folder containing the current Web document. As with absolute pathnames, folder names are separated by slashes. Unlike absolute pathnames, however, a relative pathname does not begin with a slash. To reference a file in a folder directly above the current folder in the folder hierarchy, relative pathnames use two periods (..).

For example, if the current file is chem.htm, located in the /tutorial.02/tutorial folder shown in Figure 2-26, the relative pathnames and their interpretations for the other four files in the folder tree are displayed in Figure 2-28.

Figure 2-28	RELATIVE PATHNAMES
RELATIVE PATHNAME	**INTERPRETATION**
../index.htm	The index.htm file in the folder one level up in the folder tree from the current file
../tutorial/chem.htm	The chem.htm file in the tutorial subfolder one level up in the folder tree from the current file
rock.htm	The rock.htm file in the same folder as the current file
extra/parks.htm	The parks.htm file in the extra subfolder, one level down from the current folder

A second reason to use relative pathnames is that they make your hypertext links portable. If you have to move your files to a different computer or server, you can move the entire folder structure and still use the relative pathnames you've specified for the hypertext links. If absolute pathnames are used, each link has to be revised. This can be a very tedious process.

Linking to Documents on the Internet

Now you can turn your attention to creating a link on Stephen's chemistry page to the Advanced Placement page. To create a hypertext link to a document on the Internet, you need to know its URL. A **URL**, or **Uniform Resource Locator**, specifies a precise location on the Web for a file. The URL for the College Board Web page, for example, is *http://www.collegeboard.com/ap/students/*. You can find the URL of a Web page in the Location or Address box of your browser's document window.

Once you know a document's URL, you can create a link to it by adding the URL to the <a> tag along with the href attribute in your text file. For example, to create a link to a document on the Internet with the URL *http://www.mwu.edu/course/info.html*, you use this HTML code:

```
<a href="http://www.mwu.edu/course/info.html">Course
Information</a>
```

This example links the text "Course Information" to the Internet document located at *http://www.mwu.edu/course/info.html*. As long as your computer is connected to the Internet, clicking the text within the tag navigates you to the document located at the specified URL. Note that this link is for illustrative purposes only.

<u>Linking to a Document on the Internet</u>
- Using your text editor, locate the text or image you want to designate as the link.
- Before the text or image, place the tag <a href="url"> where url is the URL of the Web page you are linking to.
- Following the text or image, insert the </a> closing tag.

Displaying Linked Documents in a New Window

By default, each Web page you open is displayed in the main browser window, replacing the one you were viewing last. This means that when users click Stephen's AP Chemistry link, they will leave his Web site; to get back, they would have to click their browser's Back button. He would prefer that his Web site stay open, and that when a link navigates to a page outside of his chemistry site, a second browser window opens. This will allow students and parents to "stay" with his chemistry Web site, even as they're browsing other sites.

To force a document to appear in a new window, you use the target attribute in the href tag. The general syntax is:

```
<a href="url" target="window">Hypertext</a>
```

where *url* is the URL of the page, and *window* is a name assigned to the new browser window. The value you use for the target attribute doesn't affect the appearance or content of the window; it's simply used by the browser to identify the different open windows in the current browser session.

You can set up your external hyperlinks to open in the same browser window by using the same value for the target attribute.

If you do, the first hyperlink clicked opens the new window and displays the contents of the external file. As subsequent external hyperlinks are clicked, they replace the contents of the already opened window, and the contents of the main browser window remain unaffected.

If you want your external documents to be displayed in their own browser window, you can assign a unique target value for each hyperlink, or you can assign the _blank keyword to the target attribute as follows:

```
<a href="url" target=_blank>Hypertext</a>
```

Note that you do *not* enclose the _blank keyword in quotation marks.

In the links at the top of the page, Stephen wants to add the link text "College Board AP" to navigate to the College Board Advanced Placement page. Because this is a page outside of his chemistry site, he wants it to appear in a new browser window. He'll give the new browser window the target name "new_window".

To add a link to the College Board AP page from Stephen's Chemistry page:

1. Using your text editor, open **chem.htm**, the file you worked on in Session 2.2 of this tutorial.

2. Locate the links section near the top of the page.

3. In the code containing "Contact me" and "Chemistry Links", place the insertion point just before the closing </p> tag, press the **Enter** key to create a blank line, and then type the following code:

```
 &#183;&160;
<a href="http://www.collegeboard.org/ap/students/"
target="new_window">
AP Information</a>
```

Be sure to leave the closing </p> tag intact.

4. Save your changes to **chem.htm**.

5. Using your Web browser while connected to the Internet, open **chem.htm**. The College Board entry should look like the text link shown in Figure 2-29.

Figure 2-29   LINK TO ANOTHER PAGE ON THE WEB

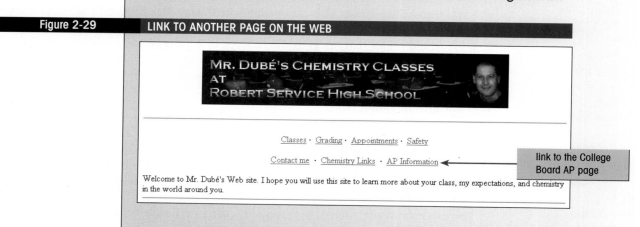

link to the College Board AP page

6. Click the **AP Information** link to navigate to the College Board Web site. The page is displayed in a new window as shown in Figure 2-30.

Figure 2-30   COLLEGE BOARD AP PAGE

Stephen's Chemistry page remains open in the original browser window

AP page in a separate browser window

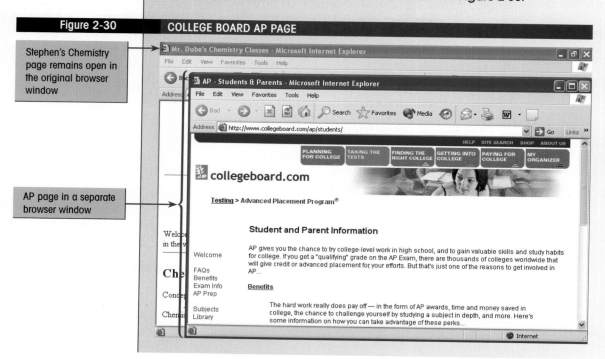

TROUBLE? If the College Board AP page doesn't display right away, it might just be loading slowly on your system. If the page fails to display, verify that your computer is connected to the Internet. Also, since Web pages are updated regularly, the page may look quite different from the one shown in Figure 2-30.

7. Close the second browser window and return to Stephen's Web page in the main browser window.

Linking to Other Internet Objects

Occasionally you see a URL for an Internet object other than a Web page. Remember that one reason for the World Wide Web's success is that it allows users to access several types of Internet resources with a browser. The method you used to create a link to the College Board Advanced Placement page is the same method you use to create links to other Internet resources, such as FTP servers or Usenet newsgroups (you'll learn what these are in the sections that follow). Only the URL for each object is required.

Each URL follows the same format. The first portion of the URL identifies the **communication protocol**, which is a set of rules that governs how information is exchanged. Web pages use the communication protocol **HTTP**, short for **Hypertext Transfer Protocol**, so all Web page URLs begin with the letters "http". Other Internet resources use different communication protocols. Following the communication protocol, there is typically a separator, such as a colon and two slashes (://). The exact separator depends on the Internet resource. The rest of the URL identifies the location of the document or resource on the Internet. Figure 2-31 interprets a Web page with the URL

```
http://www.mwu.edu/course/info.html#majors
```

Figure 2-31	INTERPRETING PARTS OF A URL
PART OF URL	**INTERPRETATION**
http://	The communication protocol
www.mwu.edu	The Internet host name for the computer storing the document
/course/info.html	The pathname and filename of the document on the computer
#majors	An anchor in the document

You may have noticed that many URLs don't seem to have any path or file information (such as *www.course.com*). By convention, if the path and filename are left off the URL, the browser searches for a file named "index.html" or "index.htm" in the root folder of the Web server; this file is often the home page of the Web site. Note that the path can be expressed in relative or absolute terms.

Before you walk Stephen through the task of creating the final link for his Web page, you take the time to show him how to create links to other Internet resources. It is not the objective of this tutorial to teach you about these resources in detail, but rather to show you how to reference them in your HTML files.

Linking to FTP Servers

FTP servers can store files that Internet users can download, or transfer, to their computers. **FTP**, short for **File Transfer Protocol**, is the communications protocol these file servers use to transfer information. URLs for FTP servers follow the same format as those for Web pages, except that they use the FTP protocol rather than the HTTP protocol: ftp://ftp.hostname. For example, to create a link to the FTP server located at *ftp.microsoft.com*, you use the following HTML code:

```
<a href="ftp://ftp.microsoft.com">Microsoft FTP server</a>
```

In this example, clicking the text "Microsoft FTP server" navigates the user to the Microsoft FTP server page as shown in Figure 2-32. Note that different browsers can display the contents of the FTP site in different ways. Figure 2-32 shows what it might look like with Internet Explorer.

Figure 2-32   FTP SERVER AT FTP.MICROSOFT.COM

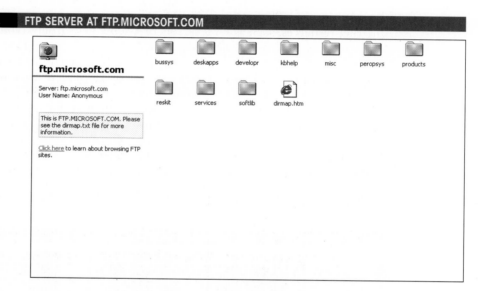

Linking to Usenet News

Usenet is a collection of discussion forums called **newsgroups** that let users exchange messages with other users on a wide variety of topics. The URL for a newsgroup is news:newsgroup. To access the surfing newsgroup alt.surfing, you place this line in your HTML file:

```
<a href="news:alt.surfing">Go to the surfing newsgroup</a>
```

When you click a link to a newsgroup, your computer starts your newsgroup software and accesses the newsgroup. For example, if you have the Outlook Newsreader program installed, clicking the link opens the window shown in Figure 2-33.

Figure 2-33   **ACCESSING THE ALT.SURFING NEWSGROUP**

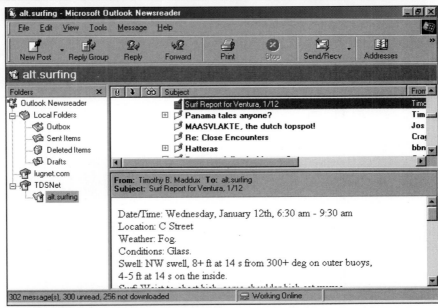

Linking to E-mail

Many Web designers include their e-mail addresses on their Web pages so that users who access the page can send feedback. You can identify e-mail addresses as hypertext links. When a user clicks the e-mail address, the browser starts a mail program and automatically inserts the e-mail address into the "To" field of the outgoing message. The URL for an e-mail address is mailto:*e-mail_address*. To create a link to the e-mail address davis@mwu.edu, for example, enter the following code into your document:

```
<a href="mailto:davis@mwu.edu">davis@mwu.edu</a>
```

If a user on the Web clicks the text davis@mwu.edu and has Microsoft Outlook installed as the default e-mail program, the window shown in Figure 2-34 is displayed.

Figure 2-34   **MAIL MESSAGE WINDOW**

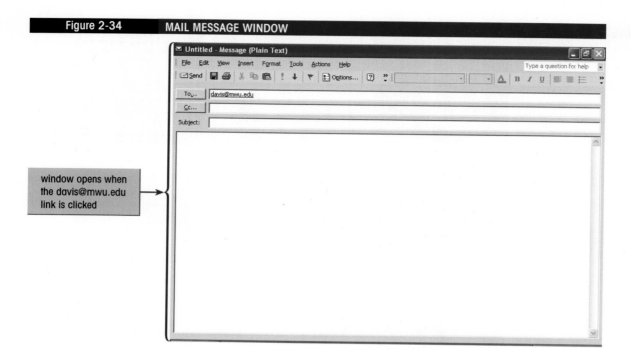

window opens when the davis@mwu.edu link is clicked

Adding an E-mail Link to Stephen's Chemistry Page

The last thing Stephen wants you to add to his Web pages is a link to his e-mail address. With this link, students and their parents can quickly send him messages via the Internet.

Stephen placed his e-mail address on his Contact page. You need to designate that text as a link so that when a user clicks it, an e-mail program window opens similar to the one shown in Figure 2-34.

To add an e-mail link to Stephen's Contact page:

1. Using your text editor, open **contact.htm**. You can close **chem.htm**.

2. Delete the text "My address is sdube@eps.ab.ca." located near the bottom of the file in the e-mail section.

   Students no longer need to know what Stephen's e-mail address is, because the link will insert it automatically into the "To" field in the mail message window.

3. After the text "…receiving the e-mail.", press the **Enter** key to create a blank line, and then type the following code:

   ```
   <a href="mailto:sdube@eps.edmonton.ab.ca">Click here</a>
   to send me an e-mail.
   ```

   Be sure to leave the closing </p> tag intact.

4. Save your changes to **contact.htm**.

5. Using your Web browser, open **contact.htm**.

6. Scroll to the bottom of the page. The link should look like the one shown in Figure 2-35.

Figure 2-35	BROWSER SHOWING LINK TO STEPHEN'S E-MAIL ADDRESS

the address itself is in the code for the mailto: URL

E-mail

E-mail is a great way to reach me. I answer e-mails from students and parents within one school day of receiving the e-mail. Click here to send me an e-mail.

TROUBLE? Some browsers do not support the mailto: URL. If you use a browser other than Netscape Navigator or Internet Explorer, check to see if it supports this feature.

7. Click the **Click here** hypertext link to Stephen's e-mail address. An e-mail message window opens, similar to the one in Figure 2-36.

Figure 2-36	TESTING STEPHEN'S E-MAIL LINK

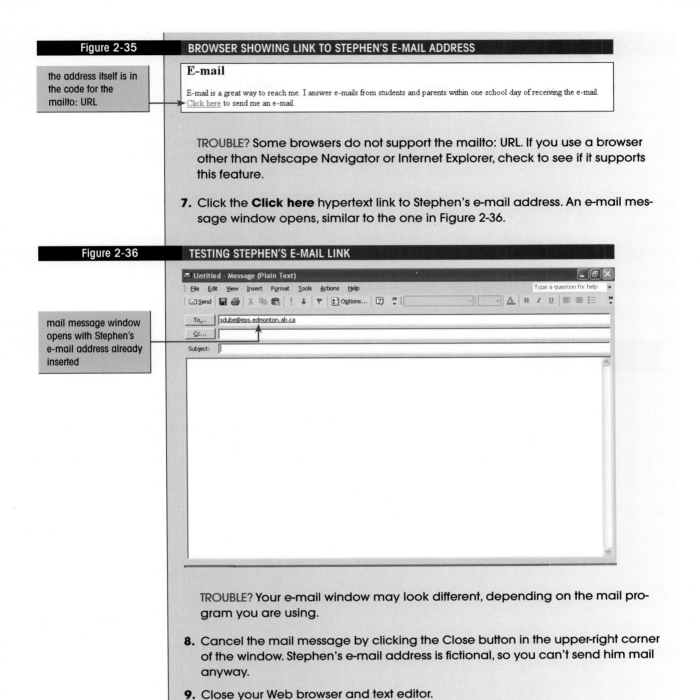

mail message window opens with Stephen's e-mail address already inserted

TROUBLE? Your e-mail window may look different, depending on the mail program you are using.

8. Cancel the mail message by clicking the Close button in the upper-right corner of the window. Stephen's e-mail address is fictional, so you can't send him mail anyway.

9. Close your Web browser and text editor.

You show Stephen the final version of the three Web pages you have been collaborating on. He's thrilled with the results. You explain to him that the next step is to contact an Internet service provider and transfer the files to an account on that provider's server. When that's done, Stephen's Web pages become available online to anyone with Internet access.

Session 2.3 QUICK CHECK

1. What's the difference between an absolute path and a relative path?

2. Refer to Figure 2-26. If the current file is parks.htm in the tutorial.02/case1/extra folder, what are the relative pathnames for the four other files?

3. What tag would you enter to link the text "White House" to the URL *http://www.whitehouse.gov*? Have this link displayed in a new browser window named "GovWin".

4. What tag would you enter to link the text "Washington" to the FTP server at *ftp.uwash.edu*?

5. What tag would you enter to link the text "Boxing" to the newsgroup *rec.sports.boxing.pro*?

6. What tag would you enter to link the text "President" to the e-mail address president@whitehouse.gov?

REVIEW ASSIGNMENTS

Stephen would like you to add a few more items to his chemistry Web pages. Since the main Chemistry page is quite long, he wants to add a link at the bottom of the page so that users can easily return to the top of the page. Additionally, in the Chemistry Classes section, he'd like to add a phrase to the Advanced Placement Chemistry course, "click for AP resources," that links to an anchor in the Links page. He's added links to some pages that will be especially helpful for AP Chemistry students. Finally, in the Appointments section, he would like the text "I can meet with you" to link to his Contact page so that students can quickly reach him for help. The final page is shown in Figure 2-37.

Figure 2-37

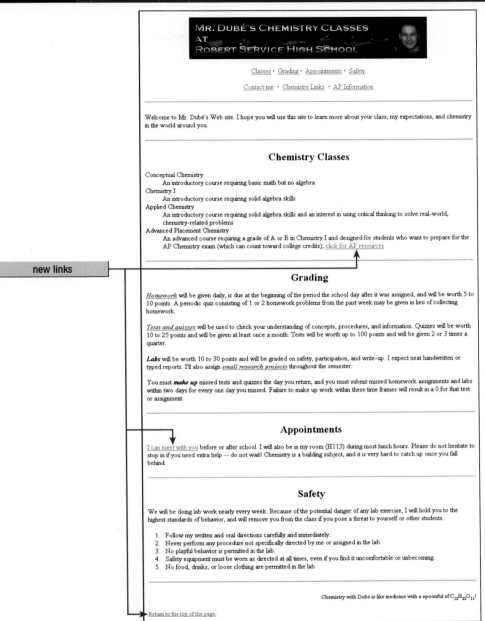

new links

1. Using your text editor, open the **chem2txt.htm** file located in the review folder in the tutorial.02 folder on your Data Disk.

2. Save the file as **chem2.htm** in the review folder on your data disk.

3. Add an anchor tag around the image file at the top of the page (**dube.jpg**), and give the anchor the name "top."

4. After the HTML line at the bottom of the page containing Stephen's "spoonful of sugar" sentence, and just before the </body> tag, type a new paragraph with the line "Return to the top of the page."

5. Use the <small> tag to format the sentence you entered in Step 4 with smaller text.

6. Create a hyperlink using the text you entered in Step 4 and pointing to the "top" anchor you created in Step 3.

7. In the Chemistry Classes list, locate the Advanced Placement Chemistry list item. After the phrase in parentheses, but before the closing </p> tag, enter the text

```
; click for AP resources
```

so that the semicolon immediately follows the closing parenthesis, with no space between.

8. Change the phrase "click for AP resources" to a hyperlink pointing to the "ap" anchor in the Links page. You'll create this anchor shortly.

9. In the Appointments section, change the phrase "I can meet with you" to a hyperlink pointing to **contact2.htm**.

10. Save **chem2.htm**.

11. Using your text editor, open **cont2txt.htm**, located in the review folder of the tutorial.02 folder on your Data Disk, and save it as **contact2.htm**. You can close **chem2.htm**.

12. Using your text editor, open **link2txt.htm**, located in the review folder of the tutorial.02 folder on your Data Disk, and save it as **links2.htm**. You can close **contact2.htm**.

13. In the **links2.htm** file, add the "ap" anchor to the heading "AP Resources," and then save **links2.htm**.

14. Using your browser, view **chem2.htm**, and compare it to Figure 2-37. (Make sure you open **chem2.htm** from the review folder of the tutorial.02 folder.)

15. Verify that all of the new links work correctly.

16. Using your text editor, fix any errors if necessary.

17. When you are satisfied with the results, use your browser to print **chem2.htm**, **contact2.htm**, and **links2.htm**.

18. Using your text editor, print **chem2.htm**, **contact2.htm**, and **links2.htm**.

19. Close your text editor.

CASE PROBLEMS

Case 1. Rock Hotel You are the Marketing Manager for the Rock Hotel, located in Green River, Utah. The hotel's owner has asked you to create a Web page listing nearby attractions, with a hyperlink for each attraction. You decide to first organize the links with appropriate <h2> headings, and then add the links. You have chosen a logo and background, provided on your Data Disk in the following files: **grrock.jpg** and **grback.jpg**.

Figure 2-38 lists the URLs you need to include in the page, and Figure 2-39 shows the page you'll create.

Figure 2-38

ATTRACTION	URL
Canyonlands National Park	http://www.nps.gov/cany/
Arches National Park	http://www.nps.gov/arch/
Capitol Reef National Park	http://www.nps.gov/care/
Green River State Park	http://parks.state.ut.us/parks/www1/gree.htm
Adventure Bound River Expeditions	http://www.raft-utah.com
Way Out West Tours	http://www.wayoutwesttours.com
Fly Fishing the Green River	http://quickbyte.com/greenriver/
City of Green River	http://www.greenriver-utah.com
Emery County	http://www.emerycounty.com/

Figure 2-39

1. Using your text editor, create a new document.

2. Enter the <html>, <head>, and <body> tags to identify different sections of the page.

3. Save the file as **rock.htm** in the case1 folder of the tutorial.02 folder on your Data Disk.

4. Within the head section, insert a <title> tag with the text "Green River Attractions".

5. With the <body> tag and background attribute, add the background image **grback.jpg**, located in the case1 folder of the tutorial.02 folder on your Data Disk.

6. Within the body section, create a centered level 2 heading containing the image file, **grrock.jpg**, located in the tutorial.02/case1 folder.

7. Below the level 2 heading, insert another level 2 heading with the text "Attractions Near Green River's Rock Hotel" as shown in Figure 2-39.

8. After the second level 2 heading, create three level 3 headings with the text "Nearby State and National Parks", "Tour Companies", and "City and County" as shown in Figure 2-39.

9. Below each heading, create an unordered list of the appropriate Web site names shown in the left column of Figure 2-38. The first four sites go under the first heading, the second three go under the second heading, and the last two sites go under the third heading.

10. Link each Web site name with its URL, shown in the right column of Figure 2-38. Because these are external links, use the target attribute to have the pages open in a new window. Use the same target name "SiteWin" for each link so the pages all open in a single separate window.

11. Save the file in your text editor.

12. View the file with your Web browser, compare it to Figure 2-39, testing the links, and then return to your text editor to fix any errors.

13. When you are satisfied with the result, print the page and close your browser.

14. Print a copy of the file from your text editor, and then close your text editor.

Case 2. Western College for the Arts You are a graduate assistant in the Music Department who has been assigned the task of creating Web pages for topics in classical music. Previously, you created a Web page that showed the different sections of the fourth movement of Beethoven's Ninth Symphony. Now that you've learned to link multiple HTML files together, you have created pages for all four movements.

The four Web pages are in the case2 folder of the tutorial.02 folder on your Data Disk. Their names are: **move1a.htm**, **move2a.htm**, **move3a.htm**, and **move4a.htm**. You'll rename them **move1.htm**, **move2.htm**, **move3.htm**, and **move4.htm**, so that the originals remain intact. Figure 2-40 shows the Web page for the third movement.

Figure 2-40

Beethoven's Ninth Symphony

🖝 **The Third Movement** 🖝

Sectional Form

1. A-Section
2. B-Section
3. A-Section varied
4. B-Section
5. Interlude
6. A-Section varied
7. Coda

View the Classical Net Home Page.

You now need to link the pages. You've already placed graphic elements—the hands pointing to the previous or next movement of the symphony—in each file. You decide to mark each image as a hypertext link that navigates the user to the previous or next movement.

1. Using your text editor, open **move1a.htm**, **move2a.htm**, **move3a.htm**, and **move4a.htm**, and save the files as **move1.htm**, **move2.htm**, **move3.htm**, and **move4.htm** in the tutorial.02/case2 folder on your Data Disk.

2. Within each of the HTML files you created in Step 1, edit the inline images **right.jpg** and **left.jpg** so that the **right.jpg** inline image is a hyperlink pointing to the next movement in the symphony, and **left.jpg** points to the previous movement in the symphony.

3. Within each of the four HTML files, change the text "View the Classical Net Home page." to a hyperlink pointing to the URL *http://www.classical.net/*. Use the target attribute and the target name "classic_site" so the page opens in a new browser window.

4. Save all four HTML files.

5. Using your Web browser, open the pages and verify that all of the links work as you expect them to.

6. Using your text editor, print each page and then close the program.

7. Using your Web browser, print each page and then close the browser.

Case 3. Diamond Health Club, Inc. You work for Diamond Health Club, a family-oriented health club in Seattle, Washington that has been serving active families for 25 years. You've been asked to help create a Web site describing the club, its classes, and its membership options. There are three pages: the main page describing the club, a page listing classes offered, and a page describing the various membership options. You need to add links within the main page and add other links connecting the pages. The completed main page is shown in Figure 2-41.

Figure 2-41

Diamond Health Club

Your Source for Year-Round, Fun Family Health

Amenities · Staff · Links

At Diamond Health Club, you can stay healthy year-round and have fun doing it! We offer something for everyone.

Amenities

- 2 workout rooms
- 2 swimming pools
  - o Olympic size pool with at least 3 laps always open
  - o warm 3-foot deep pool perfect for therapeutic swimming (also open for children's open swim and lessons)
- gymnasium with full size basketball court
- private men's, women's, and family locker rooms
- on-site child care
- weight management programs
- personal training

Staff

Ty Stoven, General Manager, ext. 300

Yosef Dolen, Assistant Manager, ext 301

Sue Myafin, Child Care, ext 302

James Michel, Health Services, ext 303

Ron Chi, Membership, ext 304

Marcia Lopez, Classes, ext 305

To contact our staff members, click the appropriate name to send an e-mail, or call 404-555-4874 and dial the extension above.

Links

Check out our great classes, for everyone from children and teens to adults and seniors.

We have the right membership option for you!

- Individual – day-time or all hours
- Family – with or without child care
- Punch cards – try the Club or give a healthy gift!

---

1. Using your text editor, open **clubtxt.htm, classtxt.htm,** and **membtxt.htm** in the tutorial.02/case3 folder of your Data Disk, and then save the files as **club.htm, classes.htm,** and **members.htm** in the case3 folder.

2. Using your text editor, open **club.htm** and add anchor names to the three <h3> headings ("Amenities", "Staff", and "Links"). Use the anchor names amen, staff, and links.

3. Link the text at the top of the page (located just below the image) to the anchors you created in Step 2.

4. Link each of the names (do not include the titles or phone extensions) in the Staff section to the appropriate e-mail address, using "first initial_last name@dmond-health.com" as a template, so the first link would be to TStoven@dmond-health.com.

5. In the Links section, link the word "classes" to **classes.htm**, and then change the text "children", "teens", "adults", and "seniors" to links pointing to the child, teen, adult, and sen anchors in **classes.htm**. You'll create the anchors in a moment.

6. In the last bulleted list item in the Links section, change the text "Individual", "Family", and "Punch cards" to links pointing to the ind, fam, and punch anchors in the **members.htm** file. You'll create the anchors in a moment.

7. Save your changes to **club.htm**.

8. Using your text editor, open **classes.htm**. Create anchors for each of the <h2> headings with the names sen, adult, teen, and child.

9. Change the text "Return to Main page" at the top of the page to a hyperlink pointing to **club.htm**, and the text "Membership Options" to a link pointing to the **members.htm** file.

10. Near the top of the page, change the text "e-mail Marcia Lopez" to a link pointing to the e-mail address MLopez@dmond-health.com. Save your changes to **classes.htm**.

11. Using your text editor, open **members.htm** and create anchors to the three <h2> headings with the names ind, fam, and punch.

12. Change the text "Return to Main page" at the top of the page to a hyperlink pointing to **club.htm**, and the text "Classes for Everyone" to a link pointing to **classes.htm**.

13. Change the text "e-mail Ron Chi" to a link pointing to the e-mail address RChi@dmond-health.com. Save your changes.

14. Using your Web browser, open **club.htm** and verify that all of your links work correctly.

15. When you've fixed any errors, use your Web browser to print each of the three Web pages, and then close the program.

16. Using your text editor, print each of the three pages and then close the program.

Case 4. Create Your Own Home Page Now that you've completed this tutorial, you are ready to create your own Web page. The page should include information about you and your interests. If you like, you can create a separate page devoted entirely to one of your favorite hobbies. Be sure to include the following elements:

- section headings
- bold and/or italic fonts
- paragraphs
- an ordered, unordered, or definition list
- an inline image that is either a link or the destination of a link
- links to some of your favorite Internet pages; have these open in a single secondary window
- a hypertext link that moves the user from one section of your page to another

1. Create a file called **myweb.htm** in the case4 folder of the tutorial.02 folder on your Data Disk, and then enter HTML code to set up the document.

2. Add heading and character attribute tags to make your Web page readable and attractive.

3. Test your code as you develop your home page by viewing **myweb.htm** in your browser.

4. Insert images you think will enhance your page.

5. Use at least one image as either a link or the destination of a link.

6. Use your Web browser to explore other Web pages. Record the URLs of pages that you like, and list them in your document. Then create links to those URLs. Remember to make them all appear in a single new browser window.

7. When you finish entering and checking your code, save and print **myweb.htm**, and then close your text editor.

8. View the final version in your browser, print the Web page, and then close your browser.

QUICK | CHECK ANSWERS

Session 2.1

1. <a name="csu">Colorado State University</a>

2. <a href="#csu">Universities</a>

3. Anchor tags should be placed within style tags such as the <h3> heading tag.

4. <a name="photo"> <img src="photo.jpg"></a>

5. <a href="#links"> <img src="button.jpg"></a>

6. True. Anchor names are case-sensitive.

Session 2.2

1. Storyboarding is diagramming a series of related Web pages, taking care to identify all hypertext links between the various pages. Storyboarding is an important tool in creating Web sites that are easy to navigate and understand.

2. A linear structure is one in which Web pages are linked from one to another in a direct chain. Users can go to the previous page or the next page in the chain, but not to a page in a different section of the chain.

3. A hierarchical structure is one in which Web pages are linked from general to specific topics. Users can move up and down the hierarchy tree.

4. It distinguishes the file name from the anchor name.

5. <a href="sports.htm">Sports info</a>

6. <a href="sports.htm#bball">Basketball news</a>

Session 2.3

1. An absolute path gives the location of a file on the computer's hard disk. A relative path gives the location of a file relative to the active Web page.

2. ../../index.htm

   ../../tutorial/chem.htm

   ../tutorial/links.htm

   ../rock.htm

3. <a href="http://www.whitehouse.gov" target="GovWin">White House</a>

4. <a href="ftp://ftp.uwash.edu">Washington</a>

5. <a href=news:rec.sports.boxing.pro>Boxing</a>

6. <a href=mailto:president@whitehouse.gov>President</a>

New Perspectives on

CREATING WEB PAGES
WITH HTML

3rd Edition

Read **This Before You Begin**

To the Student

Data Disks

To complete the Level II tutorials, Review Assignments, and Case Problems, you need four Data Disks. Your instructor will either provide you with these Data Disks or ask you to make your own.

If you are making your own Data Disks, you will need **four** blank, formatted high-density disks. You will need to copy a set of files and/or folders from a file server, standalone computer, or the Web onto your disks. Your instructor will tell you which computer, drive letter, and folders contain the files you need. You could also download the files by going to **www.course.com** and following the instructions on the screen.

The information below shows you the Data Disks you need so that you will have enough disk space to complete all the tutorials, Review Assignments, and Case Problems:

Data Disk 2

Write this on the disk label:
Data Disk 1: HTML Tutorial 3

Put these folders on the disk:
tutorial.03/tutorial
tutorial.03/review
tutorial.03/case1
tutorial.03/case2
tutorial.03/case3
tutorial.03/case4

Data Disk 2

Write this on the disk label:
Data Disk 2: HTML Tutorial 4

Put these folders on the disk:
tutorial.04/tutorial
tutorial.04/review
tutorial.04/case1
tutorial.04/case2
tutorial.04/case3
tutorial.04/case4

Data Disk 3

Write this on the disk label:
Data Disk 3: HTML Tutorial 5 and Review Assignment

Put these folders on the disk:
tutorial.05/tutorial
tutorial.05/review

Data Disk 4

Write this on the disk label:
Data Disk 4: HTML Tutorial 5 Case Problems

Put these folders on the disk:
tutorial.05/case1
tutorial.05/case2
tutorial.05/case3
tutorial.05/case4

When you begin each tutorial, Review Assignment, or Case Problem, be sure you are using the correct Data Disk. Refer to the "File Finder" chart at the back of this text for more detailed information on which files are used in which tutorials. See the inside front cover of this book for more information on Data Disk files, or ask your instructor or technical support person for assistance.

Using Your Own Computer

If you are going to work through this book using your own computer, you need:

- **Computer System** A text editor and a Web browser (preferably Netscape Navigator or Internet Explorer, versions 4.0 or higher) must be installed on your computer. If you are using a non-standard browser, it must support frames and HTML 4.0 or higher.

- **Data Disks** You will not be able to complete the tutorials or exercises in this book using your own computer until you have your Data Disks.

Visit Our World Wide Web Site

Additional materials designed especially for you are available on the World Wide Web. Go to **www.course.com/ NewPerspectives**.

To the Instructor

The Data Disk Files are available on the Instructor's Resource Kit for this title. Follow the instructions in the Help file on the CD-ROM to install the programs to your network or standalone computer. For information on creating Data Disks, see the "To the Student" section above.

You are granted a license to copy the Data Files to any computer or computer network used by students who have purchased this book.

In this tutorial you will:

- Learn how HTML handles color

- Create a color scheme for a Web page

- Work with font sizes, colors, and types

- Place a background image on a Web page

- Define colors for a Web page and for specific characters

- Learn about different image file formats

- Control the placement and appearance of images on a Web page

- Work with client-side image maps

DESIGNING A WEB PAGE

Working with Fonts, Colors, and Graphics

CASE

Arcadium Amusement Park

Arcadium is a new amusement park located in northern Georgia. The park contains a wealth of rides, including roller coaster, water rides, go-kart racetracks, and gentler rides more appropriate for young children. Tom Calloway is the director of advertising for the park. In addition to radio, newspaper, and television spots, Tom is also overseeing the development of the park's Web site. He has asked you to join his Web site development team.

The content of the site has already been determined. Tom wants you to concentrate on the site's design. He wants the design to convey a sense of fun and excitement to the reader. The Web pages you create should be colorful and should include a variety of images and even animation, if possible. Tom has provided some of the graphic files you'll need to complete the site's design.

The park is scheduled to open in three months, so Tom is very anxious to see your first draft.

In this session you'll explore how HTML handles and defines color, and you'll learn how to add color to text and to the background of a Web page. You'll also work with different fonts and type sizes. Finally, you'll learn how to create a background image for a Web page.

Working with Color in HTML

The grand opening of the park is rapidly approaching, and Tom has called you to discuss the appearance of the park's Web page. As you can see in Figure 3-1, a copywriter has written the text of the site's home page.

Figure 3-1   THE ARCADIUM WEB PAGE

Arcadium

Georgia's Newest and Best Amusement Park

Exciting adventures await you at **Arcadium**, Georgia's family fun center. The park is located 5 miles northwest of Derby - close to many of Georgia's scenic wonders. Arcadium supports over 70 rides, including some of the state's most exciting roller coasters and water rides. There's also plenty of fun for the younger kids. The park provides two separate kiddie pools and special rides for the kids.

Arcadium is open seven days a week:

- April 1 to Memorial Day weekend: 10am to 5pm
- Memorial Day weekend through Labor Day weekend: 9am to 11pm
- Labor Day weekend to October 31: 10am to 5pm
- November 1 to March 31: closed

Arcadium is easy on your budget. Compare our low daily rates to the big chain parks. Special off-season and large group rates are available.

Water Park

Arcadium's water rides constitute a park within the park. You can experience the thrill of the *Big Dipper*, Arcadium's 10-story-high water slide. Or enjoy the twisting, curving ride of Arcadium's underground water ride, the *Black Hole*. For a ride gentler on the stomach, take a few laps on the *Lazy River* in a one-, two-, or four-person inner tube. No day is complete without a visit of one of our two wavepools.

Fun Rides

Enjoy some of the most exciting roller coaster rides in the area. Start off with the *Dragon*, our double looping roller coaster more than 12 stories high. Get a great view of the park from the *Skywheel*, a 120-foot-high gondola capable of holding up to 115 people. The *Missouri Breaks* will get your heart pumping at speeds of greater than 55 mph and forces up to 2.8 g's.

Vroooom

Put yourself behind the wheel for a change, by enjoying one of our three go-kart tracks. For those with a little more aggression, you can take it out on our bumper car or bumper boat tracks. All rides support the highest safety standards in the industry.

Arcadium • Hwy 12, Exit 491 • Derby, GA 20010 • 1 (800) 555-5431

Tom is satisfied with the page's content, but he wants you to work on the design of the page. He'd like you to add a colorful background or background image to the page for visual interest, modify the appearance of some of the text, and add the Arcadium logo and photographs of people enjoying themselves at the park. Tom wants this Web page to be as eye-catching as possible, which is why he has contacted you for this job.

You decide to start this project by working on an overall color scheme for the page. The first step is to learn how to select colors using HTML. If you've worked with illustration or desktop publishing applications, you've probably made your color choices without much difficulty due to the WYSIWYG (What you see is what you get) graphical user interface those programs employ. Selecting color with HTML is somewhat less intuitive because HTML is a text-based language, requiring you to define your colors in textual terms.

HTML identifies a color in one of two ways: either by the color's name or by color values. Both methods have their advantages and disadvantages. You'll first learn about identifying a color by its name.

Using Color Names

There are 16 basic **color names** that are recognized by all versions of HTML. These color names are shown in Figure 3-2.

Figure 3-2	THE 16 BASIC COLOR NAMES

Aqua	Gray	Navy	Silver
Black	Green	Olive	Teal
Blue	Lime	Purple	White
Fuchsia	Maroon	Red	Yellow

As long as you keep to this fundamental list of colors, you can rely on these color names to create a color scheme that can be accurately displayed across different browsers and operating systems.

However, a list of only 16 colors is limiting to Web designers. In response to this need, Netscape and Internet Explorer began to support an extended list of color names in early versions of their browsers. Figure 3-3 shows a partial list of these additional color names. The extended color name list allows you to create color schemes with greater color variation. A more complete list is provided in Appendix A, "HTML Color Names."

Figure 3-3	PARTIAL LIST OF EXTENDED COLOR NAMES

Blueviolet	Gold	Orange	Seagreen
Chocolate	Hotpink	Paleturquoise	Sienna
Darkgoldenrod	Indigo	Peachpuff	Snow
Firebrick	Mintcream	Salmon	Tan

One practical problem with using a color name list is that, while it's easy to specify a blue background, "blue" might not be specific enough for the purposes of your design. How do you specify a background of "light blue with a touch of green"? To do so, you would have to look through a long list of color names before discovering that "Paleturquoise" is close to the color you want. Even so, some users might try to access your page with older browsers that do not support the long list of color names. Your page might end up being unreadable on those browsers.

When you want to have more control and more choices regarding the colors in your Web page, you need to specify colors using color values.

Using Color Values

A **color value** is a numerical expression that precisely describes a color. To better understand how HTML uses numbers to represent colors, it will help to review some of the basic principles of color theory and how they relate to the colors displayed by your monitor.

Any color can be thought of as a combination of three primary colors: red, green, and blue. You are probably familiar with the color diagram shown in Figure 3-4, in which the colors yellow, magenta, cyan, and white are produced by adding the three primary colors. By varying the intensity of each primary color, you can create almost any color and any shade of color that you want. This principle allows your computer monitor to combine pixels of red, green, and blue light to create the array of colors you see on your screen.

Figure 3-4	ADDING THE THREE PRIMARY COLORS

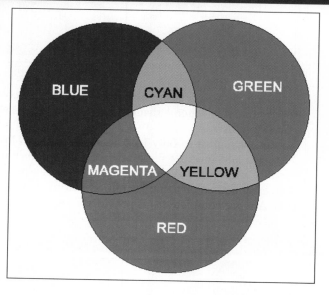

Software programs, such as your Web browser, define color mathematically. The intensity of each of the three colors (RGB) is assigned a number from 0 (absence of color) to 255 (highest intensity). In this way, 255^3, or more than 16.7 million, distinct colors can be defined. Each color is represented by a triplet of numbers, called an **RGB triplet**, based on the strength of its **R**ed, **G**reen, and **B**lue components. For example, white has a triplet of (255,255,255), indicating that red, green, and blue are equally mixed at the highest intensity. Yellow has the triplet (255,255,0) because it is an equal mixture of red and green with no presence of blue. In most programs, you make your color choices with visual clues, usually without being aware of the underlying RGB triplet. Figure 3-5 shows a typical dialog box in which you would make color selections based on the appearance of the color, rather than on the RGB values.

| Figure 3-5 | A TYPICAL COLORS DIALOG BOX |

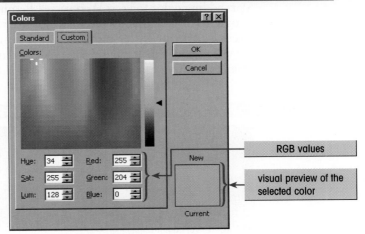

HTML requires that such color values be entered as hexadecimals. A **hexadecimal** is a number based on base-16 mathematics rather than base-10 mathematics that we use every day. In base 10 counting, you use combinations of 10 characters (0 through 9) to represent numerical values, whereas hexadecimals include six extra characters: A (for 10), B (for 11), C (for 12), D (for 13), E (for 14), and F (for 15). For values above 15, you use a combination of the 16 characters; 16 is expressed as "10," 17 is expressed as "11," and so forth. To represent a number in hexadecimal terms, you convert the value to multiples of 16 plus a remainder. For example, 21 is equal to (16 x 1) + 5, so its hexadecimal representation is 15. The number 255 is equal to (16 x 15) + 15, or FF in hexadecimal format (remember that F = 15 in hexadecimal). In the case of the number 255, the first F represents the number of times 16 goes into 255 (which is 15), and the second F represents the remainder of 15.

Once you know the RGB triplet of a color you want to use in your Web page, you need to convert that triplet to the hexadecimal format and express it in a single string of six characters. For example, the color yellow has the RGB triplet (255,255,0) and is represented by the hexadecimal string FFFF00. Figure 3-6 shows the RGB triplets and hexadecimal equivalents for the 16 basic color names presented earlier.

| Figure 3-6 | COLOR NAMES, RGB TRIPLETS, AND HEXADECIMAL VALUES |

Color Name	RGB Triplet	Hexadecimal	Color Name	RGB Triplet	Hexadecimal
Aqua	(0,255,255)	00FFFF	Navy	(0,0,128)	000080
Black	(0,0,0)	000000	Olive	(128,128,0)	808000
Blue	(0,0,255)	0000FF	Purple	(128,0,128)	800080
Fuchsia	(255,0,255)	FF00FF	Red	(255,0,0)	FF0000
Gray	(128,128,128)	808080	Silver	(192,192,192)	C0C0C0
Green	(0,128,0)	008000	Teal	(0,128,128)	008080
Lime	(0,255,0)	00FF00	White	(255,255,255)	FFFFFF
Maroon	(128,0,0)	800000	Yellow	(255,255,0)	FFFF00

At this point you might be wondering if you have to become a math major before you can start adding color to your Web pages! Because of the popularity of the Web, most graphics programs display the hexadecimal value of the colors in their color selection dialog boxes. Web page designers can also rely on tools, such as the ones shown in Figure 3-7, to generate the hexadecimal values that HTML requires for specific colors. Once you've chosen your colors, you can use the code generated by these tools in your HTML document.

Figure 3-7	COLOR SELECTION RESOURCES AVAILABLE ON THE WEB

TITLE	URL
ColorMix	http://www.colormix.com/
Palette Man	http://www.paletteman.com/
Two4U's Color Page	http://www.two4u.com/color/
ZSPC Super Color Chart	http://www.zspc.com/color/index-e.html

However you decide to work with color in your Web pages, it's important to understand how HTML handles color, if for no other reason than to be able to interpret the HTML source code of the pages you explore on the Web.

Specifying a Color Scheme for Your Page

After reviewing the issues surrounding color and HTML, you are ready to add color to the Web page that Tom has given you. Web browsers have a default color scheme that they apply to the background and text of the pages they retrieve. In most cases, the default scheme involves black text on a white or gray background, with hypertext links highlighted in purple and blue. When you want to use different colors than these, you need to modify the attributes of the page, defined within the <body> tag.

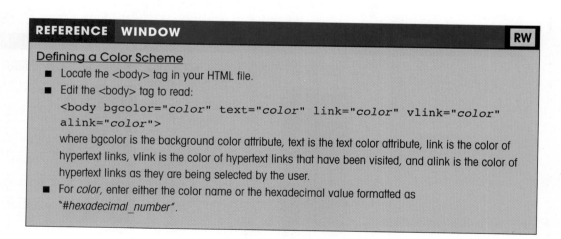

REFERENCE WINDOW   **RW**

Defining a Color Scheme
■ Locate the <body> tag in your HTML file.
■ Edit the <body> tag to read:
   `<body bgcolor="color" text="color" link="color" vlink="color" alink="color">`
   where bgcolor is the background color attribute, text is the text color attribute, link is the color of hypertext links, vlink is the color of hypertext links that have been visited, and alink is the color of hypertext links as they are being selected by the user.
■ For color, enter either the color name or the hexadecimal value formatted as "#hexadecimal_number".

In your work with HTML, you've used the <body> tag to identify the section of the HTML file containing the content that users see in their browsers. The <body> tag can also be used to indicate the colors on your page. The syntax for controlling a page's color scheme through the <body> tag is:

```
<body bgcolor="color" text="color" link="color" vlink="color"
alink="color">
```

Here, the bgcolor attribute sets the background color, the text attribute controls text color, the link attribute defines the color of hypertext links, the vlink attribute defines the color of links that have been visited by the user, and the alink attribute determines the color of an active hyperlink (the color of the link as it is clicked by the user). The value of *color* will be either one of the accepted color names or the color's hexadecimal value. If you use the hexadecimal value, you must preface the hexadecimal string with the pound symbol (#) and enclose the string in double or single quotation marks. For example, the HTML tag to create a background color with the hexadecimal value FFC088 is:

```
<body bgcolor="#FFC088">
```

After viewing various color combinations, Tom has decided that he'd like you to use a color scheme consisting of dark blue text on a light blue background. He also wants the hypertext links and active hypertext links to be red with visited links displayed in dark blue. Using color values obtained from a Web design application, Tom wants to use the RGB triplet of (220, 240, 255) for the background color. This color has the hexadecimal value of "#DCF0FF". You'll use color names for the colors of the other items on the Web page.

To change the color scheme of the Arcadium Web page:

1. Using your text editor, open **arcatxt.htm** from the tutorial.03/tutorial folder on your Data Disk, and then save the file in the same folder as **arcadium.htm**.

2. Within the <body> tag at the top of the file, type **bgcolor="#CDF0FF" text="darkblue" link="red" vlink="darkblue" alink="red"**.

   Your HTML code should look like Figure 3-8.

Figure 3-8	MODIFIED <BODY> TAG

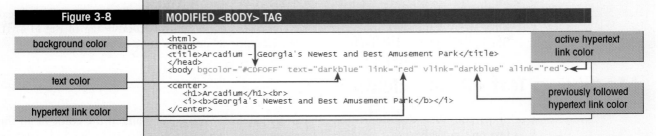

3. Save your changes to arcadium.htm, but leave the text editor open. You'll be revising this file throughout this session.

4. Using your Web browser, open the arcadium.htm file. See Figure 3-9.

Figure 3-9   **THE ARCADIUM PAGE WITH THE NEW COLOR SCHEME**

Arcadium

Georgia's Newest and Best Amusement Park

Exciting adventures await you at **Arcadium**, Georgia's family fun center. The park is located 5 miles northwest of Derby - close to many of Georgia's scenic wonders. Arcadium supports over 70 rides, including some of the state's most exciting roller coasters and water rides. There's also plenty of fun for the younger kids. The park provides two separate kiddie pools and special rides for the kids.

Arcadium is open seven days a week:

- April 1 to Memorial Day weekend: 10am to 5pm
- Memorial Day weekend through Labor Day weekend: 9am to 11pm
- Labor Day weekend to October 31: 10am to 5pm
- November 1 to March 31: closed

Arcadium is easy on your budget. Compare our low daily rates to the big chain parks. Special off-season and large group rates are available.

Water Park

Arcadium's water rides constitute a park within the park. You can experience the thrill of the *Big Dipper*, Arcadium's 10-story-high water slide. Or enjoy the twisting, curving ride of Arcadium's underground water ride, the *Black Hole*. For a ride gentler on the stomach, take a few laps on the *Lazy River* in a one-, two-, or four-person inner tube. No day is complete without a visit of one of our two wavepools.

Fun Rides

Enjoy some of the most exciting roller coaster rides in the area. Start off with the *Dragon*, our double looping roller coaster more than 12 stories high. Get a great view of the park from the *Skywheel*, a 120-foot-high gondola capable of holding up to 115 people. The *Missouri Breaks* will get your heart pumping at speeds of greater than 55 mph and forces up to 2.8 g's.

Vroooom

Put yourself behind the wheel for a change, by enjoying one of our three go-kart tracks. For those with a little more aggression, you can take it out on our bumper car or bumper boat tracks. All rides support the highest safety standards in the industry.

Arcadium • Hwy 12, Exit 491 • Derby, GA 20010 • 1 (800) 555-5431

The Arcadium Web page now has dark blue text on a light blue background. Hypertext links are red and dark blue. By adding the color scheme to the <body> tag of the HTML file, you've superseded the browser's default color scheme with one of your own.

Modifying **Text with the <font> Tag**

Specifying the text color in the <body> tag of your Web page changed the color of all the text on the Web page. Occasionally you may want to change the color of individual words or characters. This is an effective way to make specific sections of text stand out. HTML allows you to use the <font> tag with specific sections of text to override the color specified in the <body> tag.

REFERENCE   WINDOW   **RW**

<u>Modifying Text Appearance with the \<font> Tag</u>
- Using your text editor, locate the text you want to modify.
- Insert the \<font> tag as follows:
  `<font size="size" color="color" face="face"> text </font>`
  where *size* is the actual size of the text or the amount by which you want to increase or decrease the text size; *color* is the color name or color value you want to apply to the text; and *face* is the name of the font you want to use for the text.

You've worked with some character tags that allow you to bold or italicize individual characters. The \<font> tag gives you even more control by allowing you to specify the color, the size, and even the font to be used for the text on your Web page. The syntax for the \<font> tag is:

`<font size="size" color="color" face="face"> text </font>`

The \<font> tag has three attributes: size, color, and face. Your primary concern right now is to use the \<font> tag to change text color, but it's worthwhile exploring the other attributes of the tag at this time.

Changing the Font Size

The size attribute of the \<font> tag allows you to specify the font size of the text. The size value can be expressed in either absolute or relative terms. For example, if you want your text to have a size of 2, you enter size="2" in the \<font> tag. On the other hand, if you want to increase the font size by 2 relative to the surrounding text, you enter size="+2" in the tag. What is the value "size" in absolute terms? Remember that in HTML we define things such as font size in a fairly general way, allowing the browser to render the page. This means that text formatted with size 7 font in one browser might be slightly different in size than the same text in another browser. Figure 3-10 provides a representation of the various font sizes for a typical browser.

Figure 3-10	EXAMPLES OF DIFFERENT FONT SIZES

This is size 1 text
This is size 2 text
This is size 3 text
This is size 4 text
This is size 5 text
This is size 6 text
This is size 7 text

For comparison, text formatted with the <h1> tag corresponds to bold, size 6 text; the <h2> tag is equivalent to bold, size 5 text, and so forth. Figure 3-11 presents a complete comparison of header tags and font sizes.

Figure 3-11	EXAMPLES OF HEADING TAGS AND FONT SIZES

TAG	FORMAT
<h1>	Size 6, Bold
<h2>	Size 5, Bold
<h3>	Size 4, Bold
<h4>	Size 3, Bold
<h5>	Size 2, Bold
<h6>	Size 1, Bold
Normal text (no <h*i*> tag)	Size 3, Not Bold

So, if you use the attribute size="+1" to increase the size of text enclosed within an <h3> tag, the net effect will be to produce text that is size 5 and bold. The largest value for the size attribute supported by browsers is 7. Note that font sizes in HTML do not correspond to point sizes that you may be familiar with if you have experience in graphic design.

Changing the Font Color

The color attribute of the <font> tag allows you to change the color of individual characters or words. Just as you did when defining color in the <body> tag, you specify the color in the <font> tag by using either an accepted color name or the color value. For example, to change the color of the word "Arcadium" to the hexadecimal color value 8000C0, you would enter the following HTML tag:

```
<font color="#8000C0"> Arcadium</font>
```

The text surrounding the word "Arcadium" is still formatted in the color scheme specified in the <body> tag. If there is no color specified in the <body> tag, the default colors of the Web browser are used.

Changing the Font Face

The final attribute of the <font> tag we're going to examine is the face attribute. You use the face attribute to specify a particular font for a section of text. The introduction of this attribute in HTML 4.0 (although it was supported early on by Internet Explorer 1.0 and Netscape 3.0) was a bit of a departure from earlier versions of HTML, in which the browser alone determined the font used in the Web page. With the face attribute you can override the browser's font choice. For this to work, you must either specify a font that is installed on the user's computer or use one of the following five generic font names: serif, sans-serif, monospace, cursive, and fantasy. The exact depiction of these fonts depends on what fonts have been installed on the user's computer. Figure 3-12 shows some of the possible ways each of these generic fonts could be displayed.

Figure 3-12	EXAMPLES OF GENERIC FONTS

Generic Names	Font Samples		
serif	defg	defg	defg
sans-serif	defg	defg	defg
monospace	defg	defg	defg
cursive	defg	defg	defg
fantasy	DEFG	DEFG	defg

within each generic font there can be a wide range of appearances

Because you have no way of knowing which fonts have been installed on the user's computer, the face attribute allows you to specify a list of potential font names. The browser tries to use the first font in the list; if that fails, it will try the second font, and so on until the list is exhausted. It's a good idea to have a generic font name as the last item in the list so that if the browser cannot find any of the specific fonts, it will still have the generic font to fall back on.

For example, to display the word "Arcadium" in a sans-serif, you could enter the following HTML tag:

```
<font face="Arial, Helvetica, sans-serif">Arcadium</font>
```

In this example, each of the three fonts is a sans-serif font. The browser first tries to display the word "Arcadium" using the Arial font. If the user's computer doesn't have that font installed, the browser tries to apply the Helvetica font, and after that it will use whatever generic sans-serif font is available.

Now that you've learned how to use the face attribute of the <font> tag, you decide to change some of the headings in the Web page to a sans-serif font.

To change the appearance of some of the page headings:

1. Return to **arcadium.htm** in your text editor.

2. Locate the h3 heading for the Water Park, located halfway through the document.

3. Enclose the heading within the <font> tag as follows:

   <font face="Arial, Helvetica, sans-serif">Water Park</font>

4. Enclose the h3 headings for the Fun Rides and Vroooom headings within the same set of <font> tags. Figure 3-13 shows the revised code for arcadium.htm.

5. Save your changes to arcadium.htm.

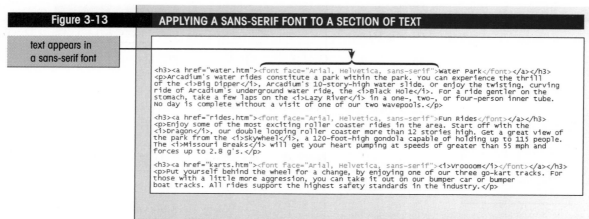

Figure 3-13   **APPLYING A SANS-SERIF FONT TO A SECTION OF TEXT**

text appears in a sans-serif font

```
<h3><a href="water.htm"><font face="Arial, Helvetica, sans-serif">Water Park</font></a></h3>
<p>Arcadium's water rides constitute a park within the park. You can experience the thrill
of the <i>Big Dipper</i>, Arcadium's 10-story-high water slide. Or enjoy the twisting, curving
ride of Arcadium's underground water ride, the <i>Black Hole</i>. For a ride gentler on the
stomach, take a few laps on the <i>Lazy River</i> in a one-, two-, or four-person inner tube.
No day is complete without a visit of one of our two wavepools.</p>

<h3><a href="rides.htm"><font face="Arial, Helvetica, sans-serif">Fun Rides</font></a></h3>
<p>Enjoy some of the most exciting roller coaster rides in the area. Start off with the
<i>Dragon</i>, our double looping roller coaster more than 12 stories high. Get a great view of
the park from the <i>Skywheel</i>, a 120-foot-high gondola capable of holding up to 115 people.
The <i>Missouri Breaks</i> will get your heart pumping at speeds of greater than 55 mph and
forces up to 2.8 g's.</p>

<h3><a href="karts.htm"><font face="Arial, Helvetica, sans-serif"><i>Vroooom</i></font></a></h3>
<p>Put yourself behind the wheel for a change, by enjoying one of our three go-kart tracks. For
those with a little more aggression, you can take it out on our bumper car or bumper
boat tracks. All rides support the highest safety standards in the industry.</p>
```

6. Open arcadium.htm in your Web browser. Figure 3-14 shows the new Arcadium page with the sans-serif headings.

Figure 3-14   **HEADINGS IN A SANS-SERIF FONT**

Water Park

Arcadium's water rides constitute a park within the park. You can experience the thrill of the *Big Dipper*, Arcadium's 10-story-high water slide. Or enjoy the twisting, curving ride of Arcadium's underground water ride, the *Black Hole*. For a ride gentler on the stomach, take a few laps on the *Lazy River* in a one-, two-, or four-person inner tube. No day is complete without a visit of one of our two wavepools.

Fun Rides

Enjoy some of the most exciting roller coaster rides in the area. Start off with the *Dragon*, our double looping roller coaster more than 12 stories high. Get a great view of the park from the *Skywheel*, a 120-foot-high gondola capable of holding up to 115 people. The *Missouri Breaks* will get your heart pumping at speeds of greater than 55 mph and forces up to 2.8 g's.

Vroooom

Put yourself behind the wheel for a change, by enjoying one of our three go-kart tracks. For those with a little more aggression, you can take it out on our bumper car or bumper boat tracks. All rides support the highest safety standards in the industry.

Using the <font> Tag to Specify Color

As you can see, the <font> tag gives you significant control over the appearance of individual blocks of text. Tom wants the subtitle of the page, "Georgia's Newest and Best Amusement Park," to stand out on the page. To accomplish this, you'll format the line of text to be red using the <font> tag.

To change the color of the page's subtitle:

1. Return to arcadium.htm in your text editor.

2. Insert the <font> tag around the park's motto as follows:

    <font color="red">Georgia's Newest and Best Amusement Park</font>

    The arcadium.htm file should now appear as shown in Figure 3-15.

3. Save your changes to arcadium.htm.

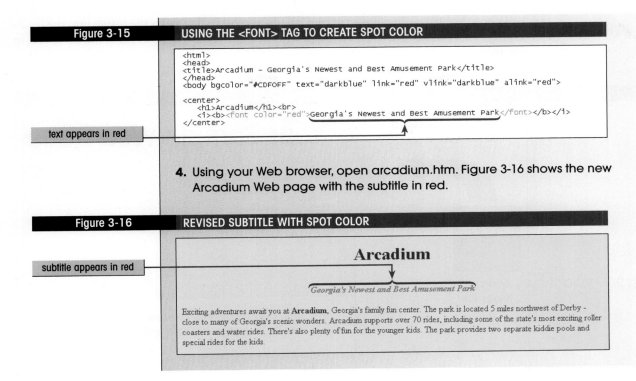

Figure 3-15   **USING THE <FONT> TAG TO CREATE SPOT COLOR**

```
<html>
<head>
<title>Arcadium - Georgia's Newest and Best Amusement Park</title>
</head>
<body bgcolor="#CDFOFF" text="darkblue" link="red" vlink="darkblue" alink="red">

<center>
    <h1>Arcadium</h1><br>
    <i><b><font color="red">Georgia's Newest and Best Amusement Park</font></b></i>
</center>
```

text appears in red

4. Using your Web browser, open arcadium.htm. Figure 3-16 shows the new Arcadium Web page with the subtitle in red.

Figure 3-16   **REVISED SUBTITLE WITH SPOT COLOR**

subtitle appears in red

Arcadium

Georgia's Newest and Best Amusement Park

Exciting adventures await you at **Arcadium**, Georgia's family fun center. The park is located 5 miles northwest of Derby - close to many of Georgia's scenic wonders. Arcadium supports over 70 rides, including some of the state's most exciting roller coasters and water rides. There's also plenty of fun for the younger kids. The park provides two separate kiddie pools and special rides for the kids.

You show the revised page to Tom and he likes the new subtitle color. However, he feels that the background needs some enhancement. He's seen Web pages that use images for backgrounds, and he'd like you to try something similar for this project.

Inserting a Background Image

Another attribute of the <body> tag is the background attribute. With this attribute you can use an image file for the background of your Web page. The syntax for inserting a background image is:

```
<body background="URL">
```

where *URL* is the location and filename of the graphic file you want to use for the background of the Web page. For example, to use an image named "bricks.gif" as your background image, you would use the tag:

```
<body background="bricks.gif">
```

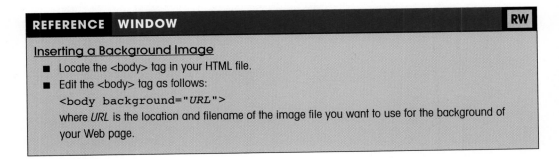

REFERENCE WINDOW   **RW**

Inserting a Background Image
- Locate the <body> tag in your HTML file.
- Edit the <body> tag as follows:
  ```
  <body background="URL">
  ```
  where *URL* is the location and filename of the image file you want to use for the background of your Web page.

When the browser retrieves your image file, it repeatedly inserts the image into the background, in a process called **tiling**, until the entire display window is filled up, as shown in Figure 3-17.

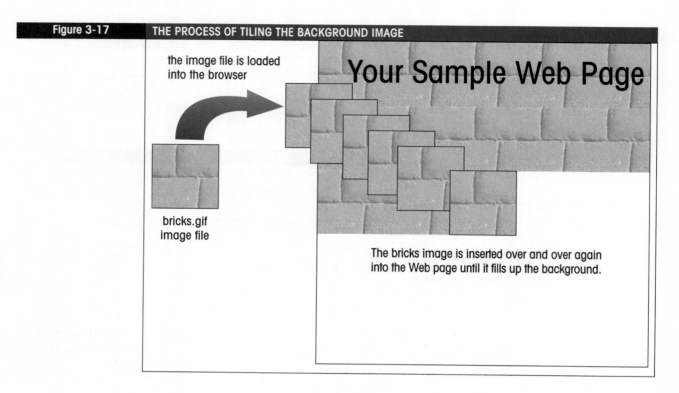

Figure 3-17   THE PROCESS OF TILING THE BACKGROUND IMAGE

the image file is loaded into the browser

Your Sample Web Page

bricks.gif image file

The bricks image is inserted over and over again into the Web page until it fills up the background.

In choosing a background image, you should remember the following:

- Use an image that will not detract from the text on the Web page, making it hard to read.
- Do not use a large image file (more than 20 kilobytes). Large and complicated backgrounds will increase the time it takes a page to load.
- Be sure to take into consideration how an image file looks when it is tiled in the background.

Figure 3-18 shows some examples of well-designed and poorly designed Web page backgrounds.

Figure 3-18	WEB PAGE BACKGROUNDS

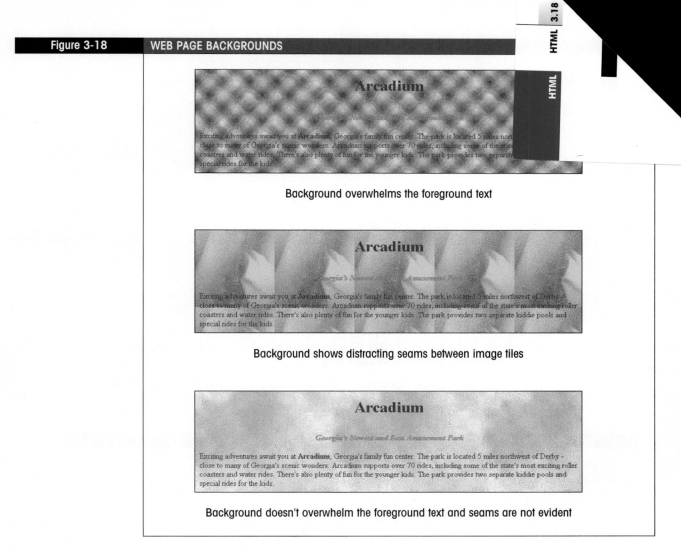

Background overwhelms the foreground text

Background shows distracting seams between image tiles

Background doesn't overwhelm the foreground text and seams are not evident

There are many collections of background images available on the Web. The only restriction is that you cannot sell or distribute the images in a commercial product. Figure 3-19 provides a list of some of these collections. Finding the right background image is a process of trial and error. You won't know for certain whether a background image works well until you actually view it in a browser.

Figure 3-19	SOURCE OF WEB BACKGROUNDS

TITLE	URL
Absolute Backgrounds Textures Archive	http://www.grsites.com/textures/
Free Backgrounds	http://www.free-backgrounds.com/
Texture Station	http://www.nepthys.com/textures/
WebGround	http://www.ip.pt/webground/

After searching, Tom has found a background image he thinks will work well for the Arcadium Web site. The image, **clouds.jpg**, is shown in Figure 3-20.

Figure 3-20   **CLOUDS.JPG WEB BACKGROUND**

The next step is to replace the light blue background of the Arcadium Web page with the Clouds image that Tom has selected.

To add clouds.jpg to the background:

1. Return to arcadium.htm in your text editor

2. Modify the <body> tag, replacing the bgcolor attribute with:
background="clouds.jpg"

The revised <body> tag should now appear as shown in Figure 3-21.

3. Save your changes to arcadium.htm.

Figure 3-21   **ENTERING CLOUDS.JPG AS THE BACKGROUND**

setting the image file for the page's background

```
<html>
<head>
<title>Arcadium - Georgia's Newest and Best Amusement Park</title>
</head>
<body background="clouds.jpg" text="darkblue" link="red" vlink="darkblue" alink="red">

<center>
    <h1>Arcadium</h1><br>
    <i><b><font color="red">Georgia's Newest and Best Amusement Park</font></b></i>
</center>
```

4. Reload arcadium.htm in your web browser.

Figure 3-22 shows the new background for the Arcadium page.

Figure 3-22   **THE ARCADIUM PAGE WITH THE CLOUDS.JPG BACKGROUND**

Arcadium

Georgia's Newest and Best Amusement Park

Exciting adventures await you at **Arcadium**, Georgia's family fun center. The park is located 5 miles northwest of Derby - close to many of Georgia's scenic wonders. Arcadium supports over 70 rides, including some of the state's most exciting roller coasters and water rides. There's also plenty of fun for the younger kids. The park provides two separate kiddie pools and special rides for the kids.

Tom is pleased with the impact of the new background. He notes that the size of the image file is not too large (only about 3 kilobytes) and that it does not show any obvious seams between the image tiles. Also, the background does not overwhelm the content of the Web page.

Extensions to the <font> and <body> Tags

Both Netscape and Internet Explorer support some attributes for the <font> and <body> tags that are not part of the specifications from the World Wide Web Consortium (W3C). Netscape supports the following two extensions to the <font> tag:

```
<font point-size="size" weight="boldness">
```

where *size* is the point size of the font and *boldness* is a measure of the weight or boldness of the font. The point-size attribute operates the same way that point sizes work in word processing and graphic design applications. This attribute provides Web designers with greater control over font sizes than can be obtained by using the size attribute. Values for the weight attribute range from 100 to 900 in increments of 100, with 900 being the heaviest, or "most bold" font. For example, to display text in a 12 point font with a weight of 700, you would use the following <font> tag:

```
<font point-size="12" weight="700">
```

Both of these attributes are supported only by Netscape 4.0 or higher. They are not supported by Internet Explorer, so you should not rely on them if you intend your Web page to be viewed by browsers other than Netscape 4.0 or higher.

Internet Explorer does not support any extensions for the <font> tag, but it does support the following additional attributes for the <body> tag:

```
<body bgproperties="properties" bottommargin="value"
leftmargin="value" rightmargin="value" topmargin="value">
```

where the bgproperties attribute is used to determine whether the background image can scroll along with the page, and the bottommargin, leftmargin, rightmargin, and topmargin attributes specify the size of the margin between the Web page and the edge of the browser window in pixels. If bgproperties attribute is set to the value "fixed", the background image will not scroll with the page. Any other value for this attribute will cause the background to scroll (the default behavior). Both of these attributes are supported by Internet Explorer 4.0 or above. They are not supported by Netscape.

Deprecated Tags

The <font> tag and the attributes of the <body> tag discussed in this session have both been **deprecated** by the W3C, which means that they are considered to be outdated by newer methods. Web page authors are encouraged to use other approaches, such as cascading style sheets, to format the appearance of their Web pages. However, in practical terms, most of the deprecated tags and attributes are still supported by the major browsers. Indeed, many applications that generate HTML code will include deprecated tags like the <font> tag.

In time, tags like the <font> tag will be completely replaced, but for now they are still a heavily used tool of the Web page author. As you review the source code of other Web documents (an excellent way to learn HTML) you will run across these deprecated tags, and it's important to understand what they do. Moreover, if you need to design a Web page that supports older browsers, you may have to use those tags and attributes that have been deprecated in the latest HTML specifications.

In the next session, you'll learn more about handling graphics with HTML as you add inline images to the Arcadium Web page.

Session 3.1 QUICK CHECK

1. What are the two ways of specifying a color in an HTML file? What are the advantages and disadvantages of each?

2. What HTML tag would you use in your HTML file to use a color scheme of red text on a gray background, with hypertext links displayed in blue, and previously visited hypertext links displayed in yellow?

3. What HTML tag would you use to format the words "Major Sale" in red, with a font of size 5 larger than the surrounding text?

4. What HTML tag would you use to display the text "Major Sale" in the Times New Roman font and, if that font is not available, in the MS Serif font?

5. What HTML tag would you use to define "stars.gif" as the background image for a Web page?

6. Name three things you should avoid when choosing a background image for your Web page.

SESSION 3.2

In this session you'll learn about different image file formats and how you can use them to add special effects to your Web page. You'll also explore the advantages and disadvantages of each format. Finally, you'll learn how to control the size, placement, and appearance of inline images on your Web page.

Having added color to the Arcadium Web page, you now turn to the task of adding images in order to make the Web page more interesting to tourists. The two image file formats supported by most Web browsers are GIF and JPEG. Choosing the appropriate image format is an important part of Web page design. You must balance the goal of creating an interesting and attractive page against the need to keep the size of your page small and easy to retrieve. Each file format has its advantages and disadvantages, and you will probably use a combination of both formats in your Web page designs. First, let's look at the advantages and disadvantages of using GIF image files.

Working with GIF Files

GIF (Graphics Interchange Format) is the most commonly used image format on the Web, being compatible with virtually all browsers. GIF files are limited to displaying 256 colors, so they are more often used for graphics requiring fewer colors, such as clip art images, line art, logos, and icons. Images that require more color depth, such as photographs, can appear grainy when saved as GIF files.

There are actually two GIF file formats: GIF87 and GIF89a. The **GIF89a** format, the newer standard, includes enhancements such as interlacing, transparent colors, and animation. You'll explore these enhancements now and learn how to use them in your Web page design.

Interlaced and Noninterlaced GIFs

Interlacing refers to the way the GIF file is saved by the graphics software. Normally, with a **noninterlaced GIF** the image is saved one line at a time, starting from the top of the graphic and moving downward. Figure 3-23 shows how a noninterlaced GIF appears as it is slowly retrieved by the Web browser. If the graphic is large, it might take several minutes for the entire image to appear, which can frustrate the visitors to your Web page.

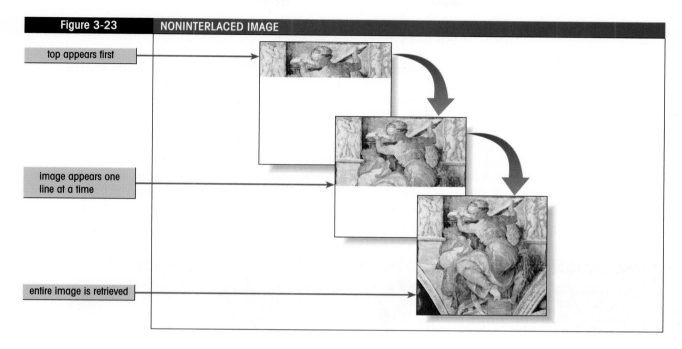

Figure 3-23 NONINTERLACED IMAGE

top appears first

image appears one line at a time

entire image is retrieved

With **interlaced GIFs**, the image is saved and retrieved "stepwise." For example, every fifth line of the image might appear first, followed by every sixth line, and so forth through the remaining rows. As shown in Figure 3-24, the effect of interlacing is that the image starts out as a blurry representation of the final image, then gradually comes into focus–unlike the noninterlaced image, which is always a sharp image as it's being retrieved, although an incomplete one.

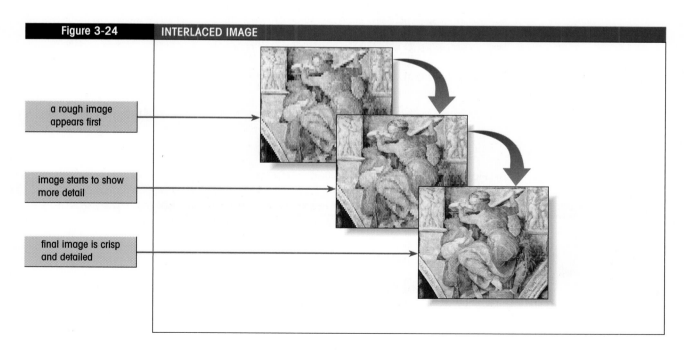

Figure 3-24 INTERLACED IMAGE

a rough image appears first

image starts to show more detail

final image is crisp and detailed

Interlacing is an effective format if you have a large graphic and want to give users a preview of the final image as it loads. They get an immediate idea of what the image looks like and can decide whether to wait for it to come into focus. The downside of interlacing is that it increases the size of the GIF file by anywhere from 3 to 20 kilobytes, depending on the image.

Transparent GIFs

Another enhancement of the GIF89a format is the ability to use transparent colors. A **transparent color** is a color from the image that is not displayed when the image is viewed in an application. In place of a transparent color, the browser will display whatever is on the page background, whether that is white, a background color, or a background image.

The process by which you create a transparent color depends on the graphics software you are using. Many applications include the option to designate a transparent color when saving the image, while other packages include a transparent color tool, which you use to click the color from the image that you want saved as transparent.

Tom has saved the Arcadium logo in the GIF89a format. He wants you to replace the text heading from arcadium.htm with the logo. The logo, saved as **aclogo1.gif**, is shown in Figure 3-25.

| Figure 3-25 | THE ACLOGO1.GIF FILE |

the green background will be transparent when displayed in the browser

When the logo was created, the green background color was designated as transparent. This means that when you insert the graphic into your Web page, the background image you inserted in the previous session will show through in places where green now appears. To see how this works, you'll replace the text heading with the logo.

To insert the logo in your HTML file:

1. Using your text editor, open the **arcadium.htm** file that you worked on in the last session.

2. Navigate to the top of the page and replace the entire h1 heading with the <img> tag.

   ```
   <img src="aclogo1.gif">
   ```

   Figure 3-26 shows the modified code for arcadium.htm.

| Figure 3-26 | REPLACING THE HEADING TEXT WITH A GRAPHIC LOGO |

tag for the logo image file

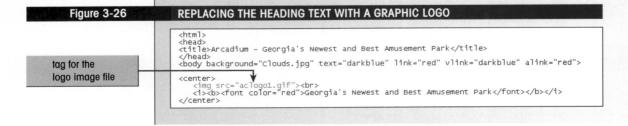

```
<html>
<head>
<title>Arcadium - Georgia's Newest and Best Amusement Park</title>
</head>
<body background="Clouds.jpg" text="darkblue" link="red" vlink="darkblue" alink="red">

<center>
    <img src="aclogo1.gif"><br>
    <i><b><font color="red">Georgia's Newest and Best Amusement Park</font></b></i>
</center>
```

3. Save your changes to arcadium.htm.

4. Using your Web browser, open arcadium.htm.

The browser displays the revised page with the logo, as shown in Figure 3-27.

Figure 3-27	ARCADIUM LOGO DISPLAYED IN THE WEB PAGE

logo background
is transparent

Note that the background image is visible beneath the logo in those locations
where the green background appeared in the original image.

Transparent GIFs can be used as layout tools to help Web page designers to place elements on a Web page. To accomplish this, a GIF is created that is one pixel in size, with the color of the pixel specified as transparent. This type of image is sometimes referred to as a **spacer**. A Web designer can then size the spacer image in order to position objects in specific locations on the page. Using the height and width attributes, you can place another object at any coordinate within the page. For example, to position an object 100 pixels from the top of the page, insert the spacer at the top of the page and assign it a height of 100 pixels. Place your object directly after the spacer in the HTML file. Because the spacer is transparent, it will appear that the object has been placed, magically, 100 pixels from the page's top margin. You'll have a chance to work with spacers in a case problem at the end of the tutorial.

Animated GIFs

One of the most popular uses of GIFs is to create animated images. Compared to video clips, animated GIFs are easier to create and smaller in size. An **animated GIF** is composed of several images that are displayed one after the other in rapid succession. Animated GIFs are an effective way to compose slide shows or to simulate motion. Figure 3-28 provides a list of programs available on the Web that you can use to create your own animated GIFs.

Figure 3-28	ANIMATED GIF PROGRAMS

TITLE	URL
AniMagic	http://www.rtlsoft.com
Gif Construction Set	http://www.mindworkshop.com
Gif.glf.giF	http://www.peda.com
GIFMation	http://www.boxtopsoft.com/GIFmation/
ImageMagik	http://www.imagemagick.org/
Xara	http://www.xara.com/products/

Most animated GIF software allows you to control the rate at which the animation plays (as measured by frames per second) and to determine the number of times the animation is repeated before stopping. You can also set the animation to repeat without stopping. You can combine individual GIF files into a single animated file and create special transitions between images.

If you don't want to take the time to create your own animated GIFs, many animated GIF collections are available on the Web. Figure 3-29 lists a few of them.

Figure 3-29	ANIMATED GIF COLLECTIONS
TITLE	**URL**
Animated GIFs	http://www.webdeveloper.com/animations/
Animation Express	http://www.animationexpress.co.uk/
Animation Factory	http://www.animfactory.com/
Animation Library	http://www.animationlibrary.com/
Web Animation Library	http://webwizards.hypermart.net/

Because an animated GIF is typically larger than a static GIF image, the use of animated GIFs can greatly increase the size of your Web page. You should also be careful not to overwhelm the user with animated images. Animated GIFs can quickly become a source of irritation to the user once the novelty has worn off, especially because there is no way for the user to turn them off! As with other GIF files, animated GIFs are limited to 256 colors. This makes them ideal for small icons and logos, but not for photographic images.

To see whether an animated GIF enhances the appearance of your Web page, you'll replace the existing Arcadium logo with an animated version.

To insert the animated logo in your HTML file:

1. Return to **arcadium.htm** in your text editor.

2. Replace "aclogo1.gif" in the <img> tag at the top of the document with the filename "**aclogo2.gif**".

3. Save your changes to arcadium.htm and open the file using your Web browser.

The revised Web page now shows a moving train of cars on the roller coaster. Note that animated GIFs, like static GIFs, can use transparent colors. Early browser versions may not support animated GIFs. If a user tries to access your Web page with a browser that does not support animated GIFs, a static image of the first frame of the animation is displayed.

The GIF Controversy

The future of GIFs as a preferred file format on the World Wide Web is in doubt. The problem is that GIFs employ an image compression method known as **Lempel-Ziv-Welch**, or **LZW**. When the GIF format became hugely popular, CompuServe released the format as a free and open file specification, meaning that people could create and distribute GIFs without purchasing the rights from CompuServe. Between 1987 and 1994, GIF became the most popular image format on the Internet, and later, on the World Wide Web. However, the LZW compression method at the heart of the GIF format is patented by the Unisys Corporation. In 1994, Unisys and CompuServe announced that software developers would have to pay a license fee to continue to use LZW compression. This included developers of GIFs.

Because the Web relies so heavily on free and open standards, the possibility that GIFs would be licensed caused an uproar. Unisys is not asking for any licenses for GIFs themselves, but only for software that incorporates the LZW algorithm. Most commercial programs that create GIF files already have a GIF/LZW license from Unisys, so users and Web authors creating GIF files with these programs do not need to worry about getting a separate license.

Still, uncertainty about the patent issue and how Unisys might try to enforce its patent in the future has caused many in the Web community to move away from GIFs as a preferred file format. In its place, a new file format called **PNG (portable network graphics)** has been offered. PNG files use a free and open file format and can display more colors than GIFs. However, PNGs cannot be used for animated graphics. PNGs do allow transparent colors, but not all browsers support this feature. The PNG format may eventually replace GIFs as the primary image type of the World Wide Web, but for the moment, to ensure compatibility across the widest range of browsers, GIFs are still the preferred standard. A detailed summary of this issue and its history can be found in the article "The GIF Controversy: A Software Developer's Perspective" at http://cloanto.com/users/mcb/19950127giflzw.html.

To provide more flexibility for the Web page author, Internet Explorer and Netscape have expanded the types of graphic formats they can display. Internet Explorer can display graphic files in the BMP format, while Netscape can display XPM and XBM files. Be aware that if you use one of these formats, your image might not be viewable in all browsers or browser versions.

Working **with JPEG Files**

The other main image file format is the JPEG format. **JPEG** stands for **Joint Photographic Experts Group**. JPEGs differ from GIFs in several ways. In the JPEG format you can create images that use the full 16.7 million colors available in the color palette. Because of this, JPEG files are most often used for photographs and images that cover a wide spectrum of color.

Another feature of JPEG files is that their image compression algorithm yields image files that are usually (though not always) smaller than their GIF counterparts. For example, in the previous session you used the JPEG file **clouds.jpg** as your background image. The size of that file was only 3.53 KB. If that image were converted to a GIF file, the file size would increase to 43.6 KB. There are situations in which the GIF format creates a smaller and better-looking image—such as when the image has large sections covered with a single color—but as a general rule, JPEGs are smaller.

You can control the size of a JPEG by controlling the degree of image compression applied to the file. Increasing the compression reduces the file size, but it might do so at the expense of image quality. Figure 3-30 shows the effect of compression on a JPEG file. As you can see, the increased compression cuts the file size to one-tenth that of the original, but the resulting image is less well-defined than the image with low compression.

| Figure 3-30 | THE EFFECTS OF COMPRESSION ON JPEG FILE SIZE AND QUALITY |

minimal compression: file size = 84.3 KB

moderate compression: file size = 20.7 KB

medium compression: file size = 14.2 KB

heavy compression: file size = 8.6 KB

By testing different compression levels with your image editing software, you can reduce the size of your JPEG files while maintaining an attractive image. Note that a smaller file size does not always mean that your page will load faster. The browser has to decompress the JPEG image when it retrieves it, and for a heavily compressed image this can take more time than retrieving and displaying a less compressed file.

There are some other differences between JPEGs and GIFs. You cannot use transparent colors or animation with JPEG files. A JPEG format called **progressive JPEG** does allow JPEG files to be interlaced. However, not all design applications and Web browsers support progressive JPEGs.

Tom wants you to add an image of a roller coaster ride to the Arcadium Web page. The photo has been saved as a JPEG file named **ride.jpg** on your Data Disk. You will insert the image below the title and date on the Web page.

To insert the roller coaster image in your Web page:

1. Return to **arcadium.htm** in your text editor.

2. Locate the paragraph that begins "Exciting adventures await you at" and then insert the following <img> tag after the <p> tag:

   `<img src="ride.jpg">`

   Figure 3-31 shows how the revised HTML code should look.

Figure 3-31	ADDING THE RIDE.JPG IMAGE TO THE ARCADIUM PAGE

```
<p><img src="ride.jpg">Exciting adventures await you at
<b>Arcadium</b>, Georgia's family fun center. The park is located 5 miles
northwest of Derby - close to many of Georgia's scenic wonders. Arcadium supports over 70 rides,
including some of the state's most exciting roller coasters and water rides. There's also
plenty of fun for the younger kids. The park provides two separate kiddie pools and special
rides for the kids.</p>
```

3. Save your changes to the file and reload the file using your Web browser. Figure 3-32 shows the revised page with the newly inserted JPEG image.

Figure 3-32	RIDE INLINE IMAGE

TROUBLE? If the image appears blurry or grainy, it could be because your monitor is capable of displaying only 256 colors, and not the full palette of 16.7 million colors.

Controlling **Image Placement and Size**

You show Tom the progress you've made on the Web page. Although he's pleased with the image of the ride, he doesn't like how the image is positioned on the page. With the current design, there is a large blank space between the park logo and the first paragraph. Tom wonders if you could control the way text flows around the image so that there is less blank space. You can, using the align attribute of the <img> tag.

REFERENCE WINDOW | **RW**

Aligning Text Around an Image

- Locate the <img> tag for the inline image.
- Edit the <img> tag as follows:

  `<img src="URL" align="alignment">`

  where *URL* is the location and filename of the image file, and *alignment* specifies how surrounding text is aligned with the image. The possible values for alignment are "absbottom", "absmiddle", "baseline", "bottom", "left", "middle", "right", "texttop", or "top". Only "left" and "right" cause the surrounding text to wrap around the graphic image, while the remaining alignment options place the image in line with the surrounding text.

Controlling Image Alignment

As you know, the align attribute can be used to control the alignment of paragraph tags. The align attribute fulfills a similar function in the <img> tag. The syntax for the align attribute is:

`<img src="URL" align="alignment">`

where *URL* is the location and filename of the graphic file, and *alignment* indicates how you want the image aligned in relation to the surrounding text. Figure 3-33 describes the possible values of the align attribute.

Figure 3-33	ALIGNMENT OPTIONS
ALIGN=	**DESCRIPTION**
absbottom	Aligns the bottom of the object with the absolute bottom of the surrounding text. The absolute bottom is equal to the baseline of the text minus the height of the largest descender in the text.
absmiddle	Aligns the middle of the object with the middle of the surrounding text. The absolute middle is the mid-point between the absolute bottom and text top of the surrounding text.
baseline	Aligns the bottom of the object with the baseline of the surrounding text.
bottom	Aligns the bottom of the object with the bottom of the surrounding text. The bottom is equal to the baseline minus the standard height of a descender in the text.
left	Aligns the object to the left of the surrounding text. All preceding and subsequent text flows to the right of the object.
middle	Aligns the middle of the object with the surrounding text.
right	Aligns the object to the right of the surrounding text. All subsequent text flows to the left of the object.
texttop	Aligns the top of the object with the absolute top of the surrounding text. The absolute top is the baseline plus the height of the largest ascender in the text.
top	Aligns the object to the right of the surrounding text. All subsequent text flows to the left of the object.

The seven align values—absbottom, absmiddle, baseline, bottom, middle, texttop, and top—place the image in line with the surrounding text. The distinctions between absbottom and bottom, absmiddle and middle, and texttop and top, are subtle. In most cases you can simply use bottom, middle, and top to align the image with the bottom, middle, and top of the surrounding text.

The align values left and right do not place the image in line with the surrounding text; instead, the image is aligned with either the left or right margin of the Web page, and the text is wrapped around the image.

Figure 3-34 shows the effect of each of these alignment options on text surrounding the roller coaster image.

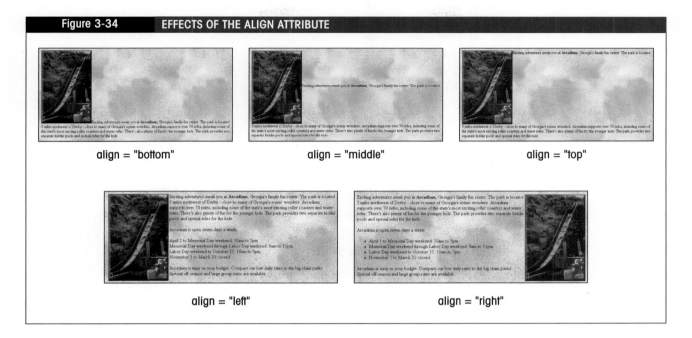

Figure 3-34   EFFECTS OF THE ALIGN ATTRIBUTE

align = "bottom"   align = "middle"   align = "top"

align = "left"   align = "right"

Tom would like you to align the ride.jpg image with the right margin of the Web page so that the text wraps around the left edge of the image.

To align the image on the right margin of the Web page:

1. Within the <img> tag for the ride.jpg image, insert the attribute: **align="right"**.

2. Save your changes to the file and reload it in your Web browser.

The image is now aligned with the right margin of the page, and the text wraps around the image.

Controlling Vertical and Horizontal Space

Wrapping the text around the image has solved one problem: the large blank space has been removed. However, a second problem has surfaced. There's not enough space separating the image and the opening paragraph, which makes the page appear crowded. You can increase the horizontal and vertical space around the image with the hspace and vspace attributes, as follows:

```
<img src="URL" vspace="value" hspace="value" >
```

The hspace (horizontal space) attribute indicates the amount of space to the left and right of the image. The vspace (vertical space) attribute controls the amount of space above and below the image.

REFERENCE WINDOW   RW

Increasing the Space Around an Image

- Add the following attributes to the <img> tag:

  hspace="*value*" vspace="*value*"

  where the hspace attribute indicates the amount of space to the left or the right of the image, and the vspace attribute indicates the amount of space above or below the image. All space values are measured in pixels.

You decide to set the horizontal space to 15 pixels and the vertical space to 5 pixels.

To increase the space around the ride image:

1. Return to **arcadium.htm** in your text editor.

2. Within the <img> tag for ride.jpg, add the following attributes and values: **hspace="15" vspace="5"**.

Your revised <img> tag should appear as shown in Figure 3-35.

Figure 3-35   **USING THE HSPACE AND VSPACE ATTRIBUTES**

set the horizontal space around the image to 15 pixels and the vertical space to 5 pixels

```
<p><img src="ride.jpg" align="right" hspace="15" vspace="5">Exciting adventures await you at
<b>Arcadium</b>, Georgia's family fun center. The park is located 5 miles
northwest of Derby – close to many of Georgia's scenic wonders. Arcadium supports over 70 rides,
including some of the state's most exciting roller coasters and water rides. There's also
plenty of fun for the younger kids. The park provides two separate kiddie pools and special
rides for the kids.</p>
```

3. Save your changes to the file and reload it in your Web browser.

As shown in Figure 3-36, the revised page shows increased space between the image and the surrounding text and appears less crowded.

Figure 3-36	INCREASING THE SPACE AROUND THE RIDE IMAGE

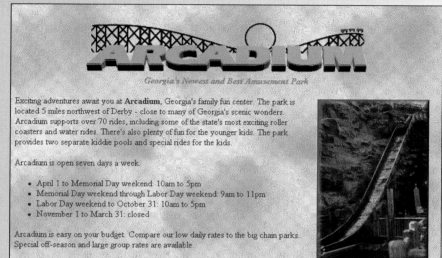

Controlling Image Size

Another set of attributes for the <img> tag are the height and width attributes. Height and width attributes instruct the browser to display an image at a specific size. These attributes can be used to increase or decrease the size of the image on your page. The syntax for setting the height and width attributes is:

```
<img src="URL" height="value" width="value">
```

where *value* is the height or width of the image either in pixels or as a percentage of the page's height or width.

REFERENCE	WINDOW	RW

Specifying the Size of an Inline Image
- Add the following attributes to the <img> tag:
  `height="value" width="value"`
  where the height and width attributes specify the dimensions of the image as measured in pixels or as a percentage of the height or width of the Web page.

Generally, if you want to decrease the size of an image, you should do so using an image editing application so that the file size is reduced as well as the dimensions of the image. Changing the size of the image within the <img> tag does not affect the file size, it merely makes the image look smaller without improving the performance of the Web page. It is a good idea to specify the height and width of an image even if you're not trying to change the dimensions. Why? Because of the way browsers work with inline images. When a browser encounters an inline image, it calculates the image size and then uses this information to format the page. If you include the dimensions of the image, the browser does not have to perform that calculation, and the page is displayed, or loaded, that much faster. You can obtain the height and width of an image as measured in pixels using an image editing application such as Adobe Photoshop.

The logo image, aclogo.gif, is 517 pixels wide by 119 pixels high, and the roller coaster image, ride.jpg, is 201 pixels wide by 300 pixels high. Add this information for each of the <img> tags in the document.

To specify the width and height of the two images:

1. Return to **arcadium.htm** in your text editor.

2. Within the <img> tag for the aclogo2.gif graphic, add the following attributes and values: **width="517" height="119"**.

3. Within the <img> tag for the ride.jpg image, add the following attributes and values: **width="201" height="300"**.

   The revised arcadium.htm file should appear as shown in Figure 3-37.

Figure 3-37 | **INCREASING THE SPACE AROUND THE RIDE IMAGE**

```
<html>
<head>
<title>Arcadium - Georgia's Newest and Best Amusement Park</title>
</head>
<body background="clouds.jpg" text="darkblue" link="red" vlink="darkblue" alink="red">

<center>
    <img src="aclogo2.gif" width="517" height="119"><br>
    <i><b><font color="red">Georgia's Newest and Best Amusement Park</font></b></i>
</center>

<p><img src="ride.jpg" align="right" hspace="15" vspace="5" width="201" height="300">Exciting adventures await you at
<b>Arcadium</b>, Georgia's family fun center. The park is located 5 miles
northwest of Derby - close to many of Georgia's scenic wonders. Arcadium supports over 70 rides,
including some of the state's most exciting roller coasters and water rides. There's also
plenty of fun for the younger kids. The park provides two separate kiddie pools and special
rides for the kids.</p>
```

4. Save your changes to arcadium.htm and reload it in your Web browser.

5. Confirm that the layout is the same as the last time you viewed the page because you have not changed the dimensions of the inline images; you've simply included their dimensions in the HTML file.

Using the alt Attribute

Another attribute available with the <img> tag is the alt attribute. The alt attribute allows you to specify text to display in place of your inline images, either temporarily or for the entire time a viewer has your page loaded. Alternate image text is important because it allows users who have nongraphical browsers to know the content of your images. Alternate image text also appears as a placeholder for the image while the page is loading. This can be particularly important for users accessing your page through a slow dial-up connection.

REFERENCE WINDOW | **RW**

Specifying Alternate Text for an Inline Image

■ Add the following attribute to the <img> tag:

   alt="*alternate text*"

   where *alternate text* is the text that nongraphical browsers will display in place of the image.

The syntax for specifying alternate text is:

```
<img src="URL" alt="alternate text">
```

Because you replaced the heading text with the Arcadium logo, you decide it would be a good idea to place the text of the logo into the alt attribute for users who are not using graphical browsers.

To insert alternate image text into your Web page:

1. Return to **arcadium.htm** in your text editor.

2. Within the <img> tag for the Arcadium logo image, insert the text:
alt="Arcadium Amusement Park".

Figure 3-38 shows the revised <img> tag.

Figure 3-38	SPECIFYING ALTERNATIVE TEXT FOR AN INLINE IMAGE

```
<html>
<head>
<title>Arcadium - Georgia's Newest and Best Amusement Park</title>
</head>
<body background="clouds.jpg" text="darkblue" link="red" vlink="darkblue" alink="red">

<center>
    <img src="aclogo2.gif" width="517" height="119" alt="Arcadium Amusement Park"><br>
    <i><b><font color="red">Georgia's Newest and Best Amusement Park</font></b></i>
</center>
```

3. Save your changes to the file and close your text editor.

General Tips for Working with Color and Images

You've completed much of the layout for the Arcadium Web page. When working with color and images, keep in mind that the primary purpose of the page is to convey information. "A picture is worth a thousand words," and if an image can convey an idea quickly, by all means use it. If an image adds visual interest to your page and makes the user interested in what you have to say, include it. However, always be aware that overusing images can make your page difficult to read and cumbersome to display. With that in mind, this section provides some tips to remember as you design your Web pages.

Reduce the Size of Your Pages

You should strive to make your page quick and easy to retrieve; particularly for users with dial-up connections. A user with a 56Kbps dial-up modem can retrieve information at a rate of about 7 kilobytes per second. If you have 100 Kilobytes of information on your page, that user will wait, on average, 15 to 20 seconds to see the page in its entirety. To get a feeling how long that can be, sit quietly and patiently count to 20. When users are used to quick responses from their computers, 20 seconds can seem like a long time. That's a problem when a user is a potential customer whose business you don't want to lose. A general rule of thumb is that the total size of the images on your Web page should be no more than 40 to 50 kilobytes. There are several ways to achieve this:

- Reduce the size of the images using an image editing application; don't simply reduce the height and width of the image with the <img> tag
- Experiment with different image file types. Is the file size smaller with the JPEG format or the GIF? Can you compress an image without losing image quality?

- Use **thumbnails**—reduced versions of your images. Place the thumbnail image within a hypertext link to the larger, more detailed image, so that clicking the reduced image loads the higher-quality image. This gives users who want to view the better image the option to do so. Note that the thumbnail has to be a different, smaller file than the original image. If you simply use the height and width attributes to reduce the original image file, you won't be saving your browser any time in rendering the page.

- Reuse your images. If you are creating a Web presentation containing several pages, consider using the same background image for each page. Once a browser has retrieved the image file for the background, it stores the image locally on the user's computer and can quickly display it again. This can also give your Web site a consistent look and feel.

Finally, you can provide an alternate, text-only version of your Web page for those users who are either using a text-based browser or want to quickly load the information stored on your page without viewing inline images.

Manage Your Colors

Color can add a lot to your page, but it can also detract from it. Make sure that you have enough contrast between the text and the background. In other words, don't put dark text on a dark background or light text on a light background. Color is handled differently on different browsers, so you should try to view your page in most of the popular browsers. Certainly you should check to see how Netscape Navigator and Internet Explorer render your page before going live to the Web.

You should also check to see how your Web page is displayed on monitors with different color depth capabilities. Your monitor might be capable of displaying 24-bit color (millions), but users viewing your page might not be so lucky. View your page with your display set to 8-bit color to see how it is rendered. When an image that contains millions of colors (JPEGs) or a GIF image that contains custom colors is displayed on an 8-bit monitor, the browser goes through a process called **dithering**, in which the colors in the image are converted to a fixed palette. As shown in Figure 3-39, dithered images can sometimes appear grainy. Even if your computer is capable of displaying full-color images, you might want to consider creating all your images in 256 colors to control, and if possible eliminate, the effects of dithering.

Figure 3-39	IMAGE DITHERING

original image   dithered image

To completely eliminate dithering, some Web designers recommend that you use the Safety Palette. The **Safety Palette**, also referred to as the **browser-safe palette**, **web palette**, or **216 color palette**, is a collection of 216 colors that display consistently on different browsers and operating systems.

By limiting your color selections to the colors of the Safety Palette, you can be assured that your images will appear the same to all users regardless of the browser they are using. You can search the Web and find several pages devoted to the use of the Safety, or browser-safe, Palette.

The only reason to use a Safety Palette of 216 colors is to accommodate those in your audience who have 8-bit (256 color) systems. Given the growth of 24-bit (millions of colors) color systems, this is rapidly becoming less of an issue for Web designers.

You're finished working with the inline images on your Web page. You've learned about the different image formats supported by most browsers and their advantages and disadvantages. You've also seen how to control the appearance and placement of images on your Web page. In the next session, you'll learn how to create an image that links to other Web pages.

Session 3.2 QUICK CHECK

1. List three reasons for using the GIF image format instead of the JPEG format.

2. List three reasons for using the JPEG image format instead of the GIF format.

3. What HTML tag would you use to display the alternate text "MidWest University" in place of the image mwu.jpg?

4. What HTML tag would you use to align mwu.jpg with the top of the surrounding text?

5. What HTML tag would you use to place the surrounding text on the left side of mwu.jpg?

6. What HTML tag would you use to increase the horizontal and vertical space around mwu.jpg to 10 pixels?

7. The mwu.jpg image is 120 pixels wide by 85 pixels high. Using this information, what would you enter into your HTML file to increase the speed at which the page is rendered by the browser?

8. What is dithering? What is the Safety Palette?

SESSION 3.3

In this session you'll learn about different types of image maps, and you'll create an image map and test it for the Arcadium Web site.

Understanding **Image Maps**

Tom has reviewed your Arcadium Web page and is pleased with the progress you're making. He's decided that the page should also include a park map so that visitors can easily find their way to all of the different attractions.

Tom wants the map to be interactive so that, for example, when a user clicks the section of the map on roller coaster rides a page describing the roller coaster rides at Arcadium is displayed. Figure 3-40 shows how these links work on the map.

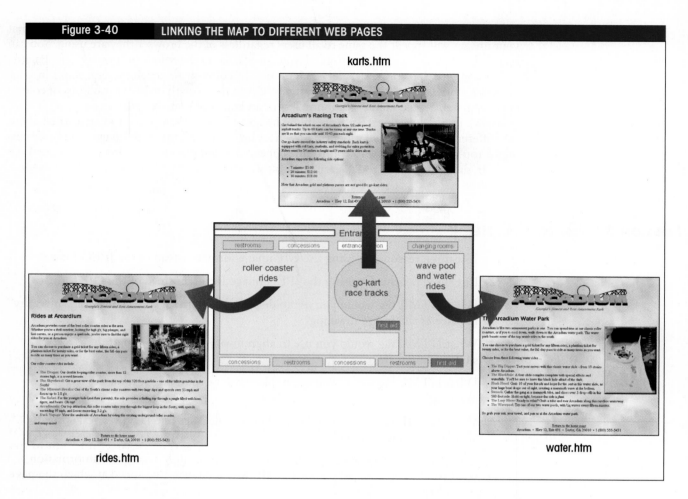

Figure 3-40   LINKING THE MAP TO DIFFERENT WEB PAGES

To use a single image to access multiple targets, you must set up hotspots within the image. A **hotspot** is a defined area of the image that acts as a hypertext link. Any time a user clicks within a hotspot, the hypertext link is activated.

Hotspots are defined through the use of **image maps**, which list the positions of all hotspots within a particular image. As a Web designer, you can use two types of image maps: server-side image maps and client-side image maps. Each has advantages and disadvantages.

Server-Side Image Maps

In a **server-side image map**, the image map is stored on the Web server (see Figure 3-41). When a user clicks a hotspot, the coordinates where the user clicked are sent to a program running on the server. The program uses the coordinates to determine which hotspot was clicked and then activates the corresponding hypertext link.

Figure 3-41   **SERVER-SIDE IMAGE CROP**

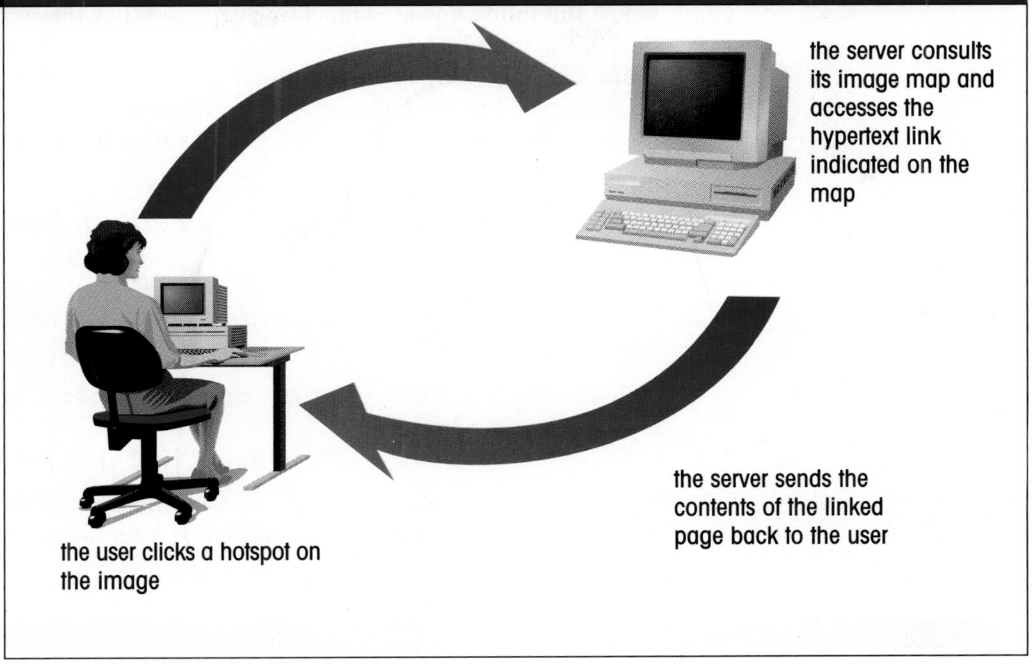

the server consults its image map and accesses the hypertext link indicated on the map

the user clicks a hotspot on the image

the server sends the contents of the linked page back to the user

Server-side image maps are supported by most graphical browsers, but there are some limitations to their use. Because a program on the server must process the image map, you cannot test your HTML code using local files. Additionally, server-side image maps can be slow to operate, since every time a user clicks the inline image, the request is sent to the Web server for processing. With most Web browsers, the target of a hypertext link is indicated in the browser's status bar, providing valuable feedback to the user. This is not the case with hotspots of a server-side image map. Because it is the server and not the Web browser that handles the hotspots, no feedback is given to the user regarding the location of the hotspots and their targets.

Client-Side Image Maps

With a **client-side image map**, you insert the image map into the HTML file, and the Web browser locally processes the image map. Because all of the processing is done locally, and not on the Web server, you can easily test your Web pages using the HTML files stored on your computer. Another advantage of client-side image maps is that they tend to be more responsive than server-side maps, because the information does not have to be sent over the network or dial-up connection. Finally, when a user moves the pointer over the inline image, the browser's status bar displays the target of each hotspot. The downside of client-side image maps is that older browsers do not support them. This is much less of a problem than it once was, so you can now use client-side image maps with confidence.

As you become more experienced with HTML, you may want to support both server-side and client-side image maps in your Web pages. For the purposes of this tutorial, you'll concentrate solely on client-side image maps.

The first step in creating the image map is to add the park map image to the Arcadium Web page. In addition to the image, you'll add a note that describes what the user should do to activate hypertext links within the image map. This note should appear directly above the image. To achieve this, you can use the <br> tag, which creates a line break and forces the following image or text to appear on its own line.

The clear attribute is often used within the <br> tag to create the effect of starting a paragraph below the inline image. The clear attribute starts the next line at the first point at which the page margin is clear of text or images. For example, using <br clear="left"> starts the next line when the left page margin is clear.

In this case, you'll use just the <br> tag to force the park map image to appear directly below the text describing how to activate the hypertext links in the image map.

To add the park map image to arcadium.htm:

1. Using your text editor, open **arcadium.htm**.

2. At the bottom of the file, directly above the <hr> tag, enter the following HTML code:

```
<h5 align="center"> Click each location for a list of
attractions <br>
<img src="parkmap.gif" width="520" height="309"> </h5>
```

The <br> tag creates a line break, causing the parkmap.gif image to be displayed directly below the explanatory text. Your revised file should appear as shown in Figure 3-42.

Figure 3-42   INSERTING THE PARK MAP IMAGE

```
<h5 align="center">Click each location for a list of attractions<br>
<img src="parkmap.gif" width="520" height="309"></h5>

<hr>

<center>
 Arcadium  &#149;  Hwy 12, Exit 491  &#149; 
 Derby, GA 20010  &#149; 1 (800) 555-5431
</center>

</body>
</html>
```

the <br> tag creates a line break

3. Save your changes to the file and reload it in your Web browser.

Figure 3-43 shows the park map image as it appears in the Web page.

Figure 3-43   PARK MAP IMAGE AS IT APPEARS IN THE BROWSER

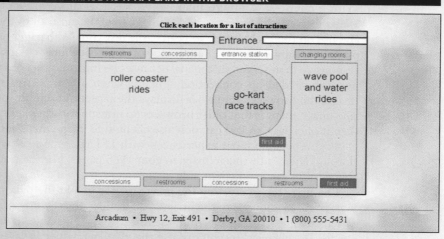

Your next task is to convert parkmap.gif to an image map.

Defining Image Map Hotspots

To create the image map, you could open the image in an image editing application and record the coordinates of the points corresponding to the hotspot boundaries. However, this is a difficult and time-consuming procedure. Instead, a Web designer typically uses a special program that determines the image map coordinates. Most image map programs generate the coordinates for hotspots as well as the necessary HTML code. There are several programs available for this purpose, some of which are listed in Figure 3-44.

Figure 3-44	PROGRAMS FOR CREATING IMAGE MAPS	

TITLE	URL
CompuPic Pro	http://www.photodex.com/products/pro/
Image Mapper	http://www.coffeecup.com/mapper/
LiveImage	http://www.mediatec.com/
MapEdit	http://www.boutell.com/mapedit/
Visual Imagemapper	http://www.sofasitters.net/imagemap/

To help you understand the syntax of image maps better, you'll be given the coordinates and then use that information to create your own HTML code.

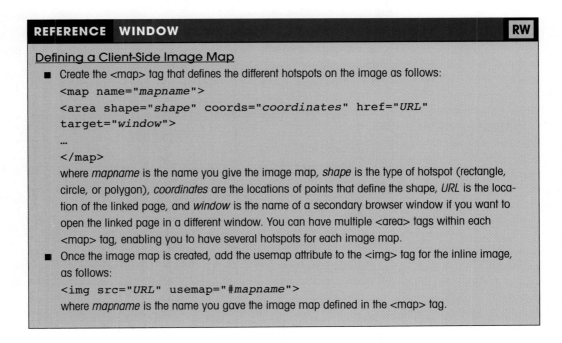

REFERENCE WINDOW   **RW**

Defining a Client-Side Image Map
- Create the <map> tag that defines the different hotspots on the image as follows:

```
<map name="mapname">
<area shape="shape" coords="coordinates" href="URL"
target="window">
...
</map>
```

where *mapname* is the name you give the image map, *shape* is the type of hotspot (rectangle, circle, or polygon), *coordinates* are the locations of points that define the shape, *URL* is the location of the linked page, and *window* is the name of a secondary browser window if you want to open the linked page in a different window. You can have multiple <area> tags within each <map> tag, enabling you to have several hotspots for each image map.
- Once the image map is created, add the usemap attribute to the <img> tag for the inline image, as follows:

```
<img src="URL" usemap="#mapname">
```

where *mapname* is the name you gave the image map defined in the <map> tag.

The general syntax for an image map tag is:

```
<map name="mapname">
<area shape="shape" coords="coordinates" href="URL"
target="window">
</map>
```

The <map> tag gives the name of the image map. Within the <map> tag, you use the <area> tag to specify the areas of the image that act as hotspots. You can include as many <area> tags within the <map> tags as you need for the image map.

The shape attribute refers to the shape of the hotspot. It has three possible values: "rect" for a rectangular hotspot, "circle" for a circular hotspot, and "poly" or " Polygon" for irregularly-shaped polygon hotspots.

In the coords attribute, you enter coordinates to specify the location of the hotspot. The values you enter depend on the shape of the hotspot. As you'll see, you need to enter different coordinates for a rectangular hotspot than you would for a circular one. Coordinates are expressed as a point's distance in pixels from the left and the top edges of the image. For example, the coordinates (123,45) refer to a point 123 pixels from the left edge and 45 pixels down from the top. If the coordinates of your <area> tags overlap, the browser uses the first tag in the list for the hotspot.

In the href attribute you enter the location of the page opened by the hotspot. In the target attribute, you can specify the name of a secondary browser window in which to open the linked page. You can use the value "nohref" in place of a URL if you do not want the hotspot to activate a hypertext link. This is a useful technique when you are first developing your image map, without all the hypertext links in place. The <area> tag then acts as a placeholder until the time when you have the hypertext links ready for use.

REFERENCE   WINDOW   **RW**

<u>Defining Image Map Hotspots</u>

■ Within the <map> tag, enter the code for the type of hotspot(s) and the coordinates.
   The syntax for a rectangular hotspot is:

```
<area shape="rect" coords="x_left, y_upper, x_right, y_lower"
href="URL" target="window">
```

   where *x_left, y_upper* are the coordinates of the upper-left corner of the rectangle, and *x_right, y_lower* are the coordinates of the lower-right corner.
   The syntax for a circular hotspot is:

```
<area shape="circle" coords="x_center, y_center, radius"
href="URL" target="window">
```

   where *x_center, y_center* is the center of the circle, and *radius* is the circle's radius.
   The syntax for a polygonal hotspot is:

```
<area shape="polygon" coords="x1, y1, x2, y2, x3, y3, … "
href="URL" target="window">
```

   where *x1, y1, x2, y2, x3, y3,* … are the coordinates of the vertices of the polygon.

Before creating your <area> tags, you'll add the <map> tag to arcadium.htm and assign the name "ParkMap" to the image map.

To insert the <map> tag:

1. Return to **arcadium.htm** in your text editor.

2. Navigate to the bottom of the file and enter the following directly above the </body>tag:

```
<map name="ParkMap">
</map>
```

With the <map> tag in place, you must next determine the hotspot areas for the image. Tom wants the image map to include hotspots for the roller coaster rides (a polygonal hotspot), the go-kart track (a circular hotspot), and the water park (a rectangular hotspot). You'll start by creating the rectangular hotspot for the water park.

Creating a Rectangular Hotspot

Two points define a rectangular hotspot: the upper-left corner and the lower-right corner. These points for the waterpark hotspot are located at (384,61) and (499,271). In other words, the upper-left corner is 384 pixels to the left and 61 pixels down from the left and top edges of the image, and the lower-right corner is 499 pixels to the left and 271 pixels down. The hotspot links to water.htm, a Web page that contains information on all the rides in the water park.

To insert the waterpark <area> tag:

1. Insert a blank line between the opening and closing <map> tags you just entered. The blank line is necessary only to make your code more readable.

2. Type the following code in the blank line:

```
<area shape="rect" coords="384,61,499,271"
href="water.htm">
```

Note that the coordinates are entered as a series of four numbers separated by commas. Because this is a rectangular hotspot, HTML expects that the first two numbers represent the coordinates for the upper-left corner of the rectangle, and the second two numbers indicate the location of the lower-right corner.

Next you'll enter the <area> tag for the go-kart race track, a circular hotspot.

Creating a Circular Hotspot

The coordinates required for a circular hotspot differ from those of a rectangular hotspot. A circular hotspot is defined by the location of its center and its radius. The circle representing the go-kart racing area hotspot is centered at the coordinates (307,137), and it has a radius of 66 pixels. The hotspot is a hypertext link to karts.htm.

To insert the go-kart <area> tag:

1. Insert a blank line directly above the waterpark <area> tag.

2. Type the following in the new blank line:

```
<area shape="circle" coords="307,137,66"
href="karts.htm">
```

The final hotspot you need to define is for the roller coaster rides. Because of its irregular shape, you need to create a polygonal hotspot.

Creating a Polygonal Hotspot

To create a polygonal hotspot, you enter the coordinates for each vertex in the shape.

The coordinates for the vertices of the roller coaster hotspot are shown in Figure 3-45. The link for this hotspot is rides.htm.

Figure 3-45   COORDINATES FOR THE ROLLER COASTER HOTSPOT

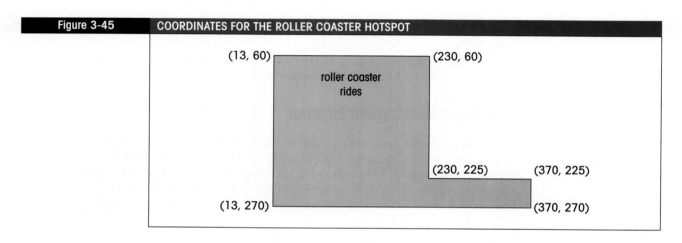

With the coordinate information in hand, you can create the final <area> tag for your image map.

To insert the roller coaster <area> tag:

1. Insert a blank line directly above the go-kart <area> tag.

2. Type the following in the new blank line:

```
<area shape="polygon" coords="13,60,13,270,370,270,370,
225,230,225,230,60" href="rides.htm">
```

Figure 3-46 shows the completed list of <area> tags for the ParkMap image map. Compare these values with the values you entered to confirm that you entered them correctly.

Figure 3-46   PARKMAP IMAGE MAP AND HOTSPOTS

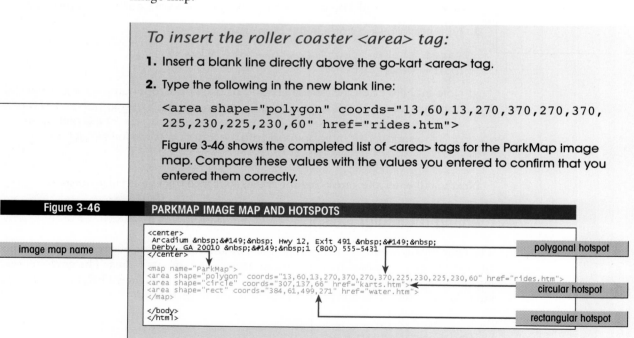

With all of the <area> tags in place, you're finished defining the image map. Your next task is to instruct the browser to use the ParkMap image map with the inline image. Then you'll test the image to confirm that it works properly.

Using an Image Map

The final step in adding an image map to a Web page is to add the usemap attribute to the <img> tag for the image map graphic. The usemap attribute tells the browser the name of the image map to associate with the inline image. The syntax for adding the usemap attribute is:

```
<img src="URL" usemap="#mapname">
```

Here, *mapname* is the name assigned to the name attribute in the <map> tag. Note that you have to place a pound sign (#) before the image map name. You named your image map ParkMap and you inserted the image into your Web page. Now you have to add the usemap attribute to the <img> tag to associate parkmap.gif with the ParkMap image map.

To assign the ParkMap image map to parkmap.gif and test the image map:

1. Navigate to the parkmap.gif <img> tag.

2. Add the following attribute to the tag: **usemap="#ParkMap"**.

The completed <img> tag should appear as shown in Figure 3-47.

Figure 3-47	PARKMAP IMAGE MAP AND HOTSPOTS

```
<h5 align="center">Click each location for a list of attractions<br>
<img src="parkmap.gif" width="520" height="309" usemap="#ParkMap"></h5>

<hr>

<center>
 Arcadium  &#149;  Hwy 12, Exit 491  &#149; 
 Derby, GA 20010  &#149; 1 (800) 555-5431
</center>

<map name="ParkMap">
<area shape="polygon" coords="13,60,13,270,370,270,370,225,230,225,230,60" href="rides.htm">
<area shape="circle" coords="307,137,66" href="karts.htm">
<area shape="rect" coords="384,61,499,271" href="water.htm">
</map>

</body>
</html>
```

name of image to use

properties of image map

3. Save your changes to the file and reload arcadium.htm in your Web browser.

4. Scroll to the park map image, positioning your mouse pointer over the image.

Note that the pointer changes to a hand when it is positioned over a hotspot, and the status bar displays the URL for that particular hotspot. See Figure 3-48.

| Figure 3-48 | PARKMAP IMAGE MAP AND HOTSPOTS |

Click each location for a list of attractions

Entrance

| restrooms | concessions | entrance station | changing rooms |

roller coaster rides

wave pool and water rides

go-kart race tracks

first aid

| concessions | restrooms | concessions | restrooms | first aid |

pointer changes to a hand as it passes over a hot spot

Arcadium • Hwy 12, Exit 491 • Derby, GA 20010 • 1 (800) 555-5431

TROUBLE? If your image does not have a red border around it, don't worry. The border is created by some browsers and not others and is discussed in the following section.

5. Click anywhere within the roller coaster rides section of the map.
The Web browser opens a Web page describing the different rides at the Arcadium theme park.

6. Click the **Back** button in your Web browser to return to the Arcadium Web page.

7. Test the other hotspots in the image map to confirm that they navigate to the appropriate Web pages.

8. When you're finished testing the hotspots, return to the Arcadium Web page.

With some browsers, you'll notice that an image map is displayed with a red border. Where did this border come from? Some browsers use the border to identify the image as a hypertext link. The border color is red because that is the color you specified earlier for hypertext links. You can remove that border using the <img> tag's border attribute.

Using the border Attribute

The border attribute specifies the size of the border surrounding your inline images. The syntax for setting the border width is:

```
<img src="URL" border="value">
```

where *value* is the width of the border in pixels. An inline image that does not contain hypertext links to other documents will, by default, not have a border. However, if the image does contain hypertext links, some browsers create a two-pixel-wide border. If you want to either create or remove a border, you can do so by specifying the appropriate border width.

Tom thinks that the map would look better without a border, so you'll remove it from the image by specifying a border width of 0 pixels. Even if your browser did not display a red border, you should complete the following steps for those browsers that do add borders around image maps.

To remove the border from the ParkMap graphic:

1. Return to **arcadium.htm** in your text editor.

2. Locate the <img> tag for the park map and insert the attribute **border="0"**.

3. Save your changes to the file, and then close the file and your text editor.

4. Open **arcadium.htm** in your Web browser and verify that the border is not displayed around the park map.

5. Close your Web browser.

Tom reviews the completed Arcadium page. He's pleased with the work you've done and will get back to you with any changes he wants you to make. For now you can close your browser and text editor.

Figure 3-49 shows the finished Web page of the Arcadium amusement park.

Figure 3-49 | **COMPLETED ARCADIUM WEB PAGE**

Georgia's Newest and Best Amusement Park

Exciting adventures await you at **Arcadium**, Georgia's family fun center. The park is located 5 miles northwest of Derby - close to many of Georgia's scenic wonders. Arcadium supports over 70 rides, including some of the state's most exciting roller coasters and water rides. There's also plenty of fun for the younger kids. The park provides two separate kiddie pools and special rides for the kids.

Arcadium is open seven days a week:

- April 1 to Memorial Day weekend: 10am to 5pm
- Memorial Day weekend through Labor Day weekend: 9am to 11pm
- Labor Day weekend to October 31: 10am to 5pm
- November 1 to March 31: closed

Arcadium is easy on your budget. Compare our low daily rates to the big chain parks. Special off-season and large group rates are available.

Water Park

Arcadium's water rides constitute a park within the park. You can experience the thrill of the *Big Dipper*, Arcadium's 10-story-high water slide. Or enjoy the twisting, curving ride of Arcadium's underground water ride, the *Black Hole*. For a ride gentler on the stomach, take a few laps on the *Lazy River* in a one-, two-, or four-person inner tube. No day is complete without a visit of one of our two wavepools.

Fun Rides

Enjoy some of the most exciting roller coaster rides in the area. Start off with the *Dragon*, our double looping roller coaster more than 12 stories high. Get a great view of the park from the *Skywheel*, a 120-foot-high gondola capable of holding up to 115 people. The *Missouri Breaks* will get your heart pumping at speeds of greater than 55 mph and forces up to 2.8 g's.

Vroooom

Put yourself behind the wheel for a change, by enjoying one of our three go-kart tracks. For those with a little more aggression, you can take it out on our bumper car or bumper boat tracks. All rides support the highest safety standards in the industry.

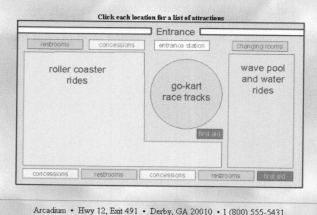

Click each location for a list of attractions

Arcadium • Hwy 12, Exit 491 • Derby, GA 20010 • 1 (800) 555-5431

You've done an effective job enhancing the Arcadium Web page with images. You've seen how to create an image map so that a single image can provide links to multiple Web pages. You've also learned about some of the design issues and challenges involved in adding images to a Web page, and how to choose the correct file type for a particular image. Using the knowledge you've gained, you're ready to work on new design challenges that Tom has in store for you.

Session 3.3 Quick Check

1. What is a hotspot? What is an image map?

2. What are the two types of image maps? List the advantages and disadvantages of each.

3. What HTML tag would you use to define a rectangular hotspot with the upper-left edge of the rectangle at the point (5,20) and the lower-right edge located at (85,100) and with oregon.htm displayed when the hotspot is activated?

4. What HTML tag would you use for a circular hotspot centered at (44,81) with a radius of 23 pixels to be linked to la.htm?

5. What HTML tag would you use for a hotspot that connects the points (5,10), (5,35), (25,35), (30,20), and (15,10) and that you want linked to hawaii.htm?

6. What HTML tag would you use to assign an image map named States to westcoast.gif?

7. What HTML tag would you use to increase the border around westcoast.gif to 5 pixels?

REVIEW ASSIGNMENTS

Tom has come back to you with some more changes and additions he wants made to the Arcadium Web pages. The park has a new area called the Toddler Park, specially designed for very young children. Tom needs you to revise the hotspots for the new park map, and he also needs you to design a Web page for the toddler park. Figure 3-50 shows a preview of the toddler page you'll create.

| Figure 3-50 |

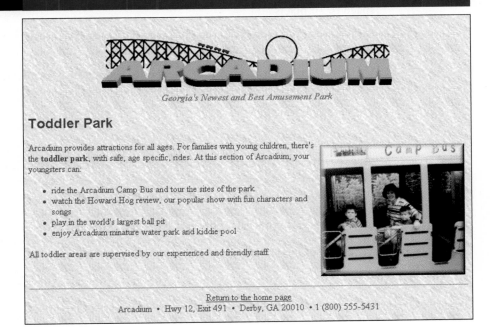

To complete this task:

1. Using your text editor, open **arcatxt2.htm** located in the tutorial.03/review folder of your Data Disk and save it as **arca2.htm**.

2. At the bottom of the file, before the </body> tag, create an image map named pmap2 with the following hotspots:

   ■ a polygonal hotspot for **rides.htm**. The coordinates of the polygon's vertices are: (13, 54), (13, 245), (294, 245), (294, 204), (184, 204), and (184, 54).

   ■ a circular hotspot for **karts.htm**. The circle is centered at the coordinate (246,125) and has a radius of 59 pixels.

   ■ a polygonal hotspot for **water.htm**. The coordinates of the polygon's vertices are: (310,55), (310, 246),(503, 246), (503, 186), (423, 186), and (423, 55).

   ■ a rectangular hotspot for **toddler.htm**. The coordinates of the rectangle's corners are (428, 55) and (502, 182).

3. Associate the **pmap2.jpg** image with the image map. Set the size of the image border to 0 pixels.

4. Save your changes to the file, and print the code.

5. Using your text editor, open **toddtxt.htm** and save it as **toddler.htm**.

6. Use **wall.jpg** for the background of the Web page. Set the link color to blue. Set the text, previously followed links, and active link color to dark red.

7. Replace the h1 heading with the **aclogo1.gif** image and display the text "Arcadium" for browsers that don't support inline graphics.

8. Change the font of the Toddler Park heading to the following font list: Arial, Helvetica, and sans-serif.

9. At the top of the Toddler Park paragraph, insert **toddler.jpg** and align it with the right margin of the page. Set the width of the graphic to 250 pixels and the height to 234 pixels. Set the horizontal space around the graphic to 5 pixels and the vertical space to 10 pixels.

10. Above the <hr> tag, modify the <br> tag so that the line break clears any object on the right margin of the page.

11. Using your text editor, save your changes to toddler.htm. Print the HTML code.

12. Using your Web browser, open **arca2.htm**. Verify that the image map works properly and opens all four files.

13. Hand in your files and printouts to your instructor.

Case 1. Midwest University Center for Diversity. Stewart Findlay is a project coordinator for the Midwest University Center for Diversity. He is currently working on a Web site highlighting the words and deeds of minorities in America. He's asked you to help develop a page on Martin Luther King, Jr. The page shows an excerpt from one of Dr. King's speeches, along with a photo of Dr. King. Stewart has created the text for the page, but he needs your help in improving the page's design. Figure 3-51 shows a preview of the page you'll create in this assignment.

Figure 3-51

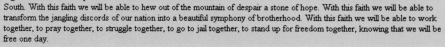

Martin Luther King, Jr.

I have a dream that one day this nation will rise up and live out the true meaning of its creed: "We hold these truths to be self-evident: that all men are created equal." I have a dream that one day on the red hills of Georgia the sons of former slaves and the sons of former slaveowners will be able to sit down together at a table of brotherhood. I have a dream that one day even the state of Mississippi, a desert state, sweltering with the heat of injustice and oppression, will be transformed into an oasis of freedom and justice. I have a dream that my four children will one day live in a nation where they will not be judged by the color of their skin but by the content of their character. I have a dream today.

I have a dream that one day the state of Alabama, whose governor's lips are presently dripping with the words of interposition and nullification, will be transformed into a situation where little black boys and black girls will be able to join hands with little white boys and white girls and walk together as sisters and brothers. I have a dream today. I have a dream that one day every valley shall be exalted, every hill and mountain shall be made low, the rough places will be made plain, and the crooked places will be made straight, and the glory of the Lord shall be revealed, and all flesh shall see it together. This is our hope. This is the faith with which I return to the South. With this faith we will be able to hew out of the mountain of despair a stone of hope. With this faith we will be able to transform the jangling discords of our nation into a beautiful symphony of brotherhood. With this faith we will be able to work together, to pray together, to struggle together, to go to jail together, to stand up for freedom together, knowing that we will be free one day.

This will be the day when all of God's children will be able to sing with a new meaning, "My country, 'tis of thee, sweet land of liberty, of thee I sing. Land where my fathers died, land of the pilgrim's pride, from every mountainside, let freedom ring." And if America is to be a great nation, this must become true. So let freedom ring from the prodigious hilltops of New Hampshire. Let freedom ring from the mighty mountains of New York. Let freedom ring from the heightening Alleghenies of Pennsylvania! Let freedom ring from the snowcapped Rockies of Colorado! Let freedom ring from the curvaceous peaks of California! But not only that; let freedom ring from Stone Mountain of Georgia! Let freedom ring from Lookout Mountain of Tennessee! Let freedom ring from every hill and every molehill of Mississippi. From every mountainside, let freedom ring.

When we let freedom ring, when we let it ring from every village and every hamlet, from every state and every city, we will be able to speed up that day when all of God's children, black men and white men, Jews and Gentiles, Protestants and Catholics, will be able to join hands and sing in the words of the old Negro spiritual, "Free at last! free at last! thank God Almighty, we are free at last!"

Created by the Midwest University Center for Diversity

To complete this task:

1. Using your text editor, open **kingtext.htm** in the tutorial.03/case1 folder of your Data Disk and save it as **king.htm**.

2. Change the background color of the Web page to tan.

3. Format the h1 heading so it appears in one of the following fonts: Arial, Helvetica, or sans-serif.

Explore

4. Change the color of the heading to the RGB triplet (73, 111, 197). Note that you will need to convert this RGB triplet to a hexadecimal value using one of the resources mentioned in this tutorial.

5. At the top of the first paragraph, insert the image **mlk.gif** and align it with the right margin of the Web page. Set the dimensions of the image to 336 pixels wide by 400 pixels high. Set the horizontal and vertical space around the image to 5 pixels.

6. Replace the letter "I" in the first line of the Dr. King's speech with **i.gif** and align the image with the left margin of the Web page.

7. Display the closing sentence of Dr. King's speech using the same color you used for the Web page heading. Set the font size to 4.

Explore
8. Replace the <hr> tag at the bottom of the page with **line.gif** and set the width of the image to 100% of the Web page width. Set the height of the image to 3 pixels.

9. Display the text below the line in the same color you used for the Web page heading.

10. Save your changes and print a copy of the HTML code.

11. Using your Web browser, open **king.htm** and verify that you've changed the design correctly.

12. Hand in your printouts and files to your instructor.

Case 2. Kelsey's Diner. You've been asked to create an online menu for Kelsey's Diner, a well-established restaurant in Worcester, Massachusetts, so that patrons can order carryout dishes via the Web. Cindy Towser is the manager and she has provided you with a text file that contains the current carryout breakfast menu. She wants you to spice it up with an effective color scheme and some images. She also wants you to create hypertext links to the lunch and dinner carryout menus. A preview of the page that you'll create is shown in Figure 3-52.

Figure 3-52

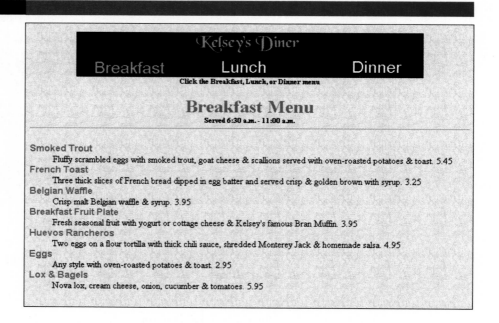

To create the Web menu for Kelsey's Diner:

1. Using your text editor, open **breaktxt.htm** from the tutorial.03/case2 folder on your Data Disk, and save it as **breakfst.htm** in the same folder.

2. Use **tan.jpg** for the background of the Web page.

3. Insert **breakfst.jpg** at the top of the page within a set of <h5> heading tags and center the image on the page. Directly below the image, after a line break, insert the text "Click the Breakfast, Lunch, or Dinner menu" (within the <h5> tags used for the inline image).

Explore
4. Change the text of the title "Breakfast Menu" to green, and increase the point size of the text by three.

5. For the name of each dish in the menu, make the text boldface, change the color of the text to green, and specify that the text should appear in either the Arial, Helvetica, or sans-serif font (in that order).

6. At the bottom of the page, insert an image map named Menu. The image map should have three rectangular hotspots. The first hotspot has the coordinates (20,40) and (156,77) and points to **breakfst.htm**; the second has coordinates at (241,40) and (336,77) and points to **lunch.htm**; the third has coordinates at (464,40) and (568,77) and points to **dinner.htm**. Apply this image map to **breakfst.jpg** and set the border width of the image to 0 pixels.

7. Repeat Steps 2 through 6 with **lunchtxt.htm**, but place **lunch.jpg** at the top of the page and save the file as **lunch.htm**.

8. Repeat Steps 2 through 6 with **dinnrtxt.htm**, but place **dinner.jpg** at the top of the page and save the file as **dinner.htm**.

9. Using your Web browser, open **breakfst.htm** and test the hypertext links. Verify that the pages look correct and that the inline image changes to reflect the change in the menu.

10. Using your text editor, print the source code for all three files.

11. Hand in your printouts and files to your instructor.

Case 3. Pixal Digital Products, Inc.   PDP, Inc. is a leading manufacturer and distributor of digital cameras. You've been hired by Plant Manager Maria Sanchez to work on the Web site for PDP.

Maria would like you to develop a **splash screen**, an opening Web page that provides some animation and visual interest to the reader. Maria suggests that you use an animation that displays the Pixal logo on the Web page. A PDP designer has already created the animated GIF file that Maria would like to use. The animated GIF image is to be centered and offset 250 pixels from the top margin of the Web page. Figure 3-53 shows a preview of how Maria wants the splash screen to look.

Figure 3-53

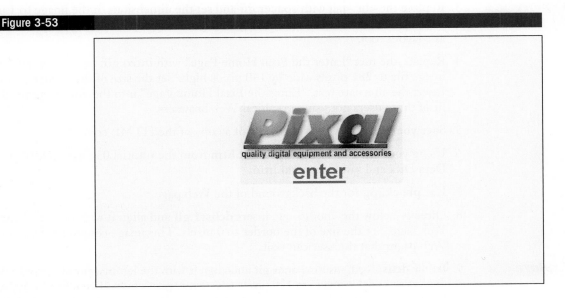

When users click on the logo in the splash screen, Maria would like the browser to display the home page of the PDP Web site. She has created text for the home page and three other Web pages describing Pixal's DC100, DC250, and DC500 digital cameras. Figure 3-54 shows a preview of one of the Web pages you'll create for Maria.

Figure 3-54

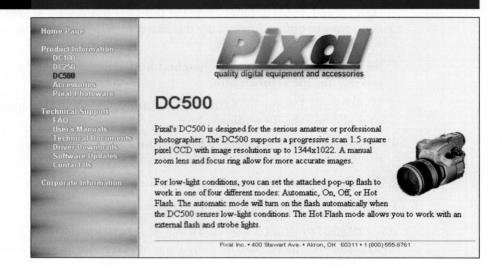

To create a Web page for PDP, Inc.:

1. Using your text editor, open **introtxt.htm** located in the tutorial.03/case3 folder of your Data Disk and save it as **intro.htm**.

Explore

2. Set the background color of the page to ivory. Instead of using the color name, use the hexadecimal value for the ivory color as listed in Appendix A.

Explore

3. Replace the <br> tag with **spacer.gif** and set the dimensions of the image to 1 pixel wide by 250 pixels high. Note that **spacer.gif** is a transparent image, 1 pixel in size, used as a layout tool.

4. Replace the text "Enter the Pixal Home Page" with **intro.gif**. Set the dimensions of the image file to 281 pixels wide by 140 pixels high. Set the size of the border to 0 pixels. Insert the alternate text, "Enter the Pixal Home Page" into the <img> tag for the benefit of those users not using graphical Web browsers.

5. Save your changes to intro.htm. Print a copy of the HTML code.

6. Using your text editor, open **pixaltxt.htm** from the tutorial.03/case3 folder of your Data Disk and save it as **pixal.htm**.

7. Use **pback.jpg** for the background of the Web page.

8. Directly below the <body> tag, insert **dclist1.gif** and align it with the left margin of the Web page. Set the size of the border to 0 pixels. This image contains a menu of Pixal Web pages that the user can visit.

Explore

9. Below **dclist1.gif**, insert **spacer.gif** and align it with the left margin of the page. Set the dimensions of this image to 120 pixels wide by 90 pixels high. The effect of this spacer image is to position the company name precisely 120 pixels to the right of the page menu.

10. Replace the entire h2 heading (include the opening and closing <h2> tags), "Pixal Digital Products," with the **plogo.jpg** image. Set the dimensions of the image to 281 pixels wide by 96 pixels high. Specify the alternate text "Pixal Digital Products" for this image.

Explore

11. Below **plogo.jpg**, insert another **spacer.gif** image. Align this spacer with the left margin of the Web page, and set the dimensions of the spacer image to 20 pixels wide by 400 pixels high. The effect of this spacer is to position the paragraph text precisely 20 pixels to the right of the page menu.

12. Scroll to the bottom of the file and replace the <hr> tag with the inline image **red.jpg**. Set the dimensions of the inline image to 1 pixel in height and 100% of the width of the Web page.

13. Display the company name, address, and phone number at the bottom of the page in an Arial, Helvetica, or sans-serif font. Set the color of this text to blue and the font size to 1.

14. Create an image map named dcpages with the following hotspots:

    ■ a rectangular hotspot for **pixal.htm** with the coordinates (1, 1) and (81, 15)
    ■ a rectangular hotspot for **dc100.htm** with the coordinates (23, 50) and (64, 62)
    ■ a rectangular hotspot for **dc250.htm** with the coordinates (23, 64) and (64, 79)
    ■ a rectangular hotspot for **dc500.htm** with the coordinates: (23, 81) and (64, 95)

15. Apply the dcpages image map to **dclist1.gif**, located at the top of the page.

16. Using your text editor, save your changes to pixal.htm and print the HTML code.

17. Using your text editor, open **dc100txt.htm** and save it as **dc100.htm**.

18. Apply the same design to this file as you applied to **pixal.htm**, with the following additions:

    ■ Change the image file for the page menu to **dclist2.gif**.
    ■ Display the h1 heading, DC100, in an Arial, Helvetica, or sans-serif font and specify the color as blue.
    ■ Insert **dc100.jpg** into the first paragraph and align it with the right margin of the Web page.

19. Using your text editor, save your changes to dc100.htm and print the HTML code.

20. Using your text editor, open **dc250txt.htm** and save it as **dc250.htm**. Apply the same design to this page as you applied to **dc100.htm**, except use **dclist3.gif** for the menu on the Web page, and insert **dc250.jpg** into the first paragraph of the page. Save your changes and print the HTML code.

21. Using your text editor, open **dc500txt.htm** and save it as **dc500.htm**. Apply the same design to this page as you applied to the other two product pages, except use **dclist4.gif** for the menu on the Web page, and insert **dc500.jpg** into the first paragraph of the page. Save your changes and print the HTML code.

22. Open **intro.htm** with your Web browser and view the Pixal Web site. Verify that all hotspots work correctly and that the page design resembles the design shown in Figure 3-57.

23. Hand in your printouts and files to your instructor.

Case 4. Tri-State Realty. Tri-State Realty is in the process of putting its listings on the World Wide Web. You've been asked to create some Web pages for its Web site. The marketing manager at Tri-State has provided you with the information for your first Web page: a property listing located at 22 North Shore Drive.

"This is a must see. Large waterfront home overlooking Mills Lake. It comes complete with three bedrooms, a huge master bedroom, hot tub, family room, large office or den, and three-car garage. Wood boat ramp. Great condition!"

In addition, the owners have included the following main selling points that they want featured on the Web page:

- 2900 sq. feet
- 15 years old
- updated electrical, plumbing, and heating systems
- central air conditioning
- near school, park, and shopping center
- nice, quiet neighborhood
- asking price: $280,000

Finally, you've been given the following files to complete your task that are located in the case4 subfolder of the tutorial.03 folder on your Data Disk:

- **house.jpg**, which contains a photo of the property; size is 243x163
- **tristate.gif**, the company logo; size is 225x100
- **listings.gif**, an image showing the various listing categories; size is 600x100
- **tsback.gif**, the background image used on all Tri-State Web pages

Using this information, you'll create a Web page for the property at 22 North Shore Drive. The design of the page is up to you, but it should include the following:

- an appropriately titled heading
- a paragraph describing the house
- a list of the main points of interest
- the photo of the house, the logo, and the image of the different listing categories
- the background image for the background on all the Web pages you design
- at least one example of a color other than the color specified in the <body> tag or default browser colors
- at least one example of a font displaying a different face and size from the surrounding text
- alternate text for the logo and house photo images
- height and width information for all inline images
- the listings image converted to an image map, with the following hotspots (target files are blank, except for some placeholder text):
  - rectangular hotspot at (5,3) (182,44) that points to **newhome.htm**
  - rectangular hotspot at (12,62) (303,95) that points to **mansions.htm**
  - rectangular hotspot at (210,19) (374,60) that points to **business.htm**
  - rectangular hotspot at (375,1) (598,44) that points to **family.htm**
  - rectangular hotspot at (378,61) (549,96) that points to **apartmnt.htm**
  - appropriately labeled hypertext links that point to the same files as indicated in the image map
  - your name, as Web designer, in italics

Save the page as **tristate.htm** in the tutorial.03/case4 folder, and then print a copy of your page and the HTML code. Close your Web browser and your text editor when you're finished.

QUICK | CHECK ANSWERS

Session 3.1

1. Color names and color values. Color names are easier to work with, but the color name may not exist for exactly the color you want to use. Also your color name may not be supported by all browsers. Color values allow you to precisely describe a color, but they can be difficult to work with.

2. <body bgcolor="gray" text="red" link="blue" vlink="yellow">

3. <font color="red" size="+5">Major Sale</font>

4. <font face="Times New Roman, MS Serif">Major Sale</font>

5. <body background="stars.gif">

6. Overwhelming the page's text, using a large image file that will make the page take longer to load, and using an image that displays visible seams.

Session 3.2

1. Use GIF when you want to use transparent colors, when you want to use an animated image, and when your image has 256 colors or less.

2. Use JPEG for photographic images, for images that contain more than 256 colors, to reduce file size through compression, and to avoid the problem of the legal issues of using GIFs.

3. <img src="mwu.jpg" alt="MidWest University">

4. <img src="mwu.jpg" align="top">

5. <img src="mwu.jpg" align="right">

6. <img src="mwu.jpg" hspace="10" vspace="10">

7. <img src="mwu.jpg" height="85" width="120">

8. When an image with many colors is displayed on a monitor that does not support all those colors, the monitor will attempt to approximate the appearance of those colors by "dithering". The Safety Palette, or browser-safe palette, is a palette of 216 colors that display consistently on different browsers and operating systems.

Session 3.3

1. A hotspot is a defined area of the image that acts as a hypertext link. An image map lists the coordinates on the image that define the boundaries of the hotspots.

2. Server-side and client-side. The server-side is the older, more accepted method of creating image maps and relies on the Web server to interpret the image map and create the hypertext link. The client-side image map is newer and is not supported by some older browsers. Because the user's browser interprets the image map, the image map is interpreted more quickly; it can be tested on the local machine, and information about various hotspots appear in the status bar of the Web browser.

3. <area shape="rect" coords="5,20,85,100" href="oregon.htm">

4. <area shape="circle" coords="44,81,23" href="la.htm">

5. <area shape="poly" coords="5,10,5,35,25,35,30,20,15,10" href="hawaii.htm">

6. <img src="westcoast.gif" usemap="#States">

7. <img src="westcoast.gif" border="5">

In this tutorial you will:

- Create a text table

- Create a table using the <table>, <tr>, and <td> tags

- Create table headers and captions

- Control the appearance of a table and table text

- Create table cells that span several rows or columns

- Use nested tables to enhance page design

- Learn about Internet Explorer extensions for use with tables

DESIGNING A WEB PAGE WITH TABLES

Creating a News Page

CASE

The Park City Gazette

Park City, Colorado, is a rural mountain community located near a popular national park. The town's primary attraction is tourism as visitors from around the world come to Park City to enjoy its natural beauty, hike and climb in the national park, and ski at the many area resorts. During the busy tourist season, the population of Park City can triple in size.

Kevin Webber is the editor of the weekly Park City Gazette. Kevin knows that the newspaper is a valuable source of information for tourists as well as year-round residents, and he would like to publish a Web edition.

He has approached you about designing a Web site for the paper. He would like the design of the Web site to have the same look and feel as the printed Gazette, which has been published for over 100 years. The Gazette has a classic and traditional design and a large and loyal readership.

In order to implement the design that Kevin is looking for, you'll need to learn how to work with tables in HTML.

SESSION 4.1

In this session you'll learn how to add tables to a Web page, starting with simple text tables and progressing to graphical tables, and you'll learn the advantages of each approach. You'll also learn how to define table rows, cells, and headings with HTML tags. Finally, you'll add a caption to your table and learn how to control the caption's placement on a Web page.

Tables on the World Wide Web

Kevin has his first assignment for you. The annual Front Range Marathon in Boulder has just been run, and a local woman, Laura Blake, won the women's open division. Kevin wants you to place the marathon story on the Web. With the story, he would like to see a table that lists the top three male and female finishers. Kevin presents you with a table of the race results shown in Figure 4-1.

Figure 4-1   **MARATHON RESULTS**

GROUP	RUNNER	TIME	ORIGIN
Men	1. Peter Teagan	2:12:34	San Antonio, Texas
Men	2. Kyle Wills	2:13:05	Billings, Montana
Men	3. Jason Wu	2:14:28	Cutler, Colorado
Women	1. Laura Blake	2:28:21	Park City, Colorado
Women	2. Kathy Lasker	2:30:11	Chicago, Illinois
Women	3. Lisa Peterson	2:31:14	Seattle, Washington

A table can be stored on a Web page either in a text or a graphical format. A **text table**, like the one shown in Figure 4-2, contains only text, evenly spaced on the Web page in rows and columns. Text tables use only standard word processing characters, so cell borders and lines must be created using such characters as hyphens or equal signs.

Figure 4-2   **A TEXT TABLE**

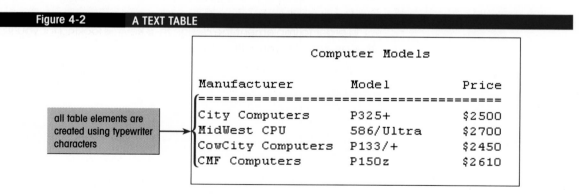

all table elements are created using typewriter characters

A **graphical table**, as shown in Figure 4-3, is displayed using graphical elements to distinguish the table components. You can include such design elements as background colors and colored borders with shading. You can also control the size of individual table cells and align text within those cells. You can even create cells that span several rows or columns.

Figure 4-3   **A GRAPHICAL TABLE**

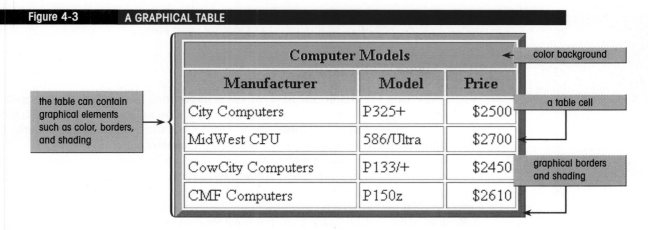

Although graphical tables are more flexible and attractive than text tables, there are some situations when you'll want to use a text table. Some browsers, such as the text-based Lynx browser used on many UNIX systems, can display only text characters. Also, working with the tags for graphical tables can be complicated and time-consuming. For these reasons, you might want to create two versions of your Web page: one that uses only text elements and text tables, and another that takes advantage of graphical elements. Due to the wide variety of Gazette readers, this is the approach Kevin suggests that you take. First you'll create a text table of the marathon results, and then you'll work on the graphical version of the table.

Creating a Text Table

Information for the text table version of the race results page has been created for you and is stored on your Data Disk as racetxt1.htm. To begin, you'll open this text file and save it with a new name.

To open racetxt1.htm and save it with a new name:

1. Using your text editor, open **racetxt1.htm** from the tutorial.04/tutorial folder on your Data Disk.

2. Save the file as **race1.htm** in the same folder.

Figure 4-4 shows a preview of the page as it is displayed in a browser.

Figure 4-4   **THE RACE1 PAGE**

Local Woman Wins Marathon

Park City native, **Laura Blake**, won the 27th Front Range Marathon over an elite field of the best long distance runners in the country. Laura's time of 2 hr. 28 min. 21 sec. was only 2 minutes off the women's course record set last year by Sarah Rawlings. Kathy Lasker and Lisa Peterson finished second and third, respectively. Laura's victory came on the heels of her performance at the NCAA Track and Field Championships, in which she placed second running for Colorado State.

In an exciting race, **Peter Teagan** of San Antonio, Texas, used a finishing kick to win the men's marathon for the second straight year, in a time of 2 hr. 12 min. 34 sec. Ahead for much of the race, Kyle Wills of Billings, Montana, finished second, when he could not match Teagan's finishing pace. Jason Wu of Cutler, Colorado, placed third in a very competitive field.

This year's race through downtown Boulder boasted the largest field in the marathon's history, with over 9500 men and 6700 women competing. Race conditions were perfect with low humidity and temperatures that never exceeded 85°.

The page consists of an article that Kevin has written about the marathon. You'll place the race results table between the first and second paragraphs.

Using Fixed-Width Fonts

When you create a text table, the font you use is important. A text table relies on spaces and the characters that fill those spaces to create its column boundaries. To accomplish this, you need to use a **fixed-width**, or **mono-space**, font so that the columns align properly. Fixed-width fonts use the same amount of space for each character.

Most typeset documents, including the one you're reading now, use **proportional fonts**. Proportional fonts assign a different amount of space for each character depending on the width of that character. For example, since the character "m" is wider than the character "l," a proportional font assigns it more space.

Because of the variable spacing, proportional fonts are more visually attractive, and typically easier to read, than fixed-width fonts. However, proportional fonts are less suitable for text tables. The distinction between fixed-width and proportional fonts is important. If you use a proportional font in a text table, the varying width of the characters and the spaces between characters can cause errors when the page is rendered in the user's browser. Figure 4-5 shows how a text table that uses a proportional font loses alignment when the font size is increased or decreased.

Figure 4-5   COLUMN ALIGNMENT PROBLEMS WITH PROPORTIONAL FONTS

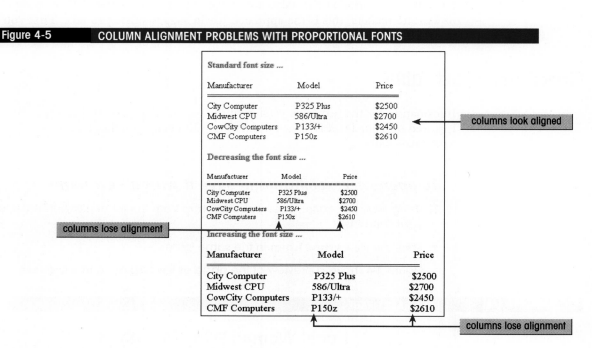

By contrast, the table shown in Figure 4-6 uses fixed-width fonts. Note that the columns remain aligned regardless of font size.

Figure 4-6   **COLUMN ALIGNMENT WITH FIXED-WIDTH FONTS**

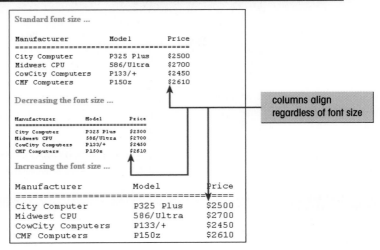

Different browsers and operating systems may use different font sizes to display your page's text, so you should always use a fixed-width font to ensure that the columns in your text tables remain in alignment.

Using the <pre> Tag

Remember that HTML ignores blank spaces, blank lines, and tabs. However, to control the appearance of a text table, you need to use spaces and other characters for alignment. You can use the <pre> tag to display preformatted text, which is text formatted in ways that HTML would otherwise not recognize. Any text formatted with the <pre> tag retains any spaces or lines you want to display on your Web page. The <pre> tag also displays text using a fixed-width font, which makes it effective for building text tables.

REFERENCE WINDOW   **RW**

Creating a Text Table Using the <pre> Tag
- Before the table, insert the tag <pre>.
- Enter the table text, aligning the columns of the table by inserting blank spaces as needed.
- Immediately following the table, insert the tag </pre> to turn off the preformatted text tag.

You'll use the <pre> tag to enter the table data from Figure 4-1 into race1.htm. When you use this tag, you insert blank spaces by pressing the spacebar to align the columns of text in the table.

To create a text table using the <pre> tag:

1. Place the insertion point in the blank line located between the first and second paragraphs of Kevin's article.

2. Type **<pre>** and press the **Enter** key to create a blank line.

3. Type **Group** and press the spacebar 4 times.

4. Type **Runner** and press the spacebar 15 times.

5. Type **Time** and press the spacebar 10 times.

6. Type **Origin** and press the **Enter** key to create a blank line.

7. Underline each heading (Group, Runner, Time, Origin) using the equal sign symbol (see Figure 4-7) and press the **Enter** key.

8. Complete the table by entering the information from Figure 4-1 about the runners, their times, and their places of origin. Place a blank line between the men's and women's results, and align each entry with the left edge of the column headings.

9. Below the women's results, type **</pre>** to turn off the preformatted text tag. Figure 4-7 shows the complete preformatted text as it appears in the file.

Figure 4-7	TEXT TABLE CREATED WITH THE <PRE> TAG

```
<p>
Park City native, <b>Laura Blake</b>, won the 27<sup>th</sup> Front Range Marathon
over an elite field of the best long distance runners in the country. Laura's
time of 2 hr. 28 min. 21 sec. was only 2 minutes off the women's course record
set last year by Sarah Rawlings. Kathy Lasker and Lisa Peterson finished second
and third, respectively. Laura's victory came on the heels of her performance at
the NCAA Track and Field Championships, in which she placed second running for
Colorado State.
</p>
<pre>
Group      Runner              Time           Origin
=====      ======              ====           ======
Men        1. Peter Teagan     2:12:34        San Antonio, Texas
Men        2. Kyle Wills       2:13:05        Billings, Montana
Men        3. Jason Wu         2:14:28        Cutler, Colorado

Women      1. Laura Blake      2:28:21        Park City, Colorado
Women      2. Kathy Lasker     2:30:11        Chicago, Illinois
Women      3. Lisa Peterson    2:31:14        Seattle, Washington
</pre>
<p>
In an exciting race, <b>Peter Teagan</b> of San Antonio, Texas, used a finishing
kick to win the men's marathon for the second straight year, in a time of
2 hr. 12 min. 34 sec. Ahead for much of the race, Kyle Wills of Billings, Montana,
finished second, when he could not match Teagan's finishing pace. Jason Wu of
Cutler, Colorado, placed third in a very competitive field.
</p>
```

text will appear in the browser as it appears here

10. Save your changes to race1.htm and close the file.

11. Using your Web browser, open **race1.htm**. Figure 4-8 displays the page as it appears in the browser.

Figure 4-8	TEXT TABLE AS IT APPEARS IN THE BROWSER

Local Woman Wins Marathon

Park City native, **Laura Blake**, won the 27th Front Range Marathon over an elite field of the best long distance runners in the country. Laura's time of 2 hr. 28 min. 21 sec. was only 2 minutes off the women's course record set last year by Sarah Rawlings. Kathy Lasker and Lisa Peterson finished second and third, respectively. Laura's victory came on the heels of her performance at the NCAA Track and Field Championships, in which she placed second running for Colorado State.

```
Group      Runner              Time           Origin
=====      ======              ====           ======
Men        1. Peter Teagan     2:12:34        San Antonio, Texas
Men        2. Kyle Wills       2:13:05        Billings, Montana
Men        3. Jason Wu         2:14:28        Cutler, Colorado

Women      1. Laura Blake      2:28:21        Park City, Colorado
Women      2. Kathy Lasker     2:30:11        Chicago, Illinois
Women      3. Lisa Peterson    2:31:14        Seattle, Washington
```

table text appears in a fixed width font

In an exciting race, **Peter Teagan** of San Antonio, Texas, used a finishing kick to win the men's marathon for the second straight year, in a time of 2 hr. 12 min. 34 sec. Ahead for much of the race, Kyle Wills of Billings, Montana, finished second, when he could not match Teagan's finishing pace. Jason Wu of Cutler, Colorado, placed third in a very competitive field.

This year's race through downtown Boulder boasted the largest field in the marathon's history, with over 9500 men and 6700 women competing. Race conditions were perfect with low humidity and temperatures that never exceeded 85°.

By using the <pre> tag, you've created a text table that can be displayed by all browsers, and you've ensured that the columns will retain their alignment no matter what font the browser is using.

You show the completed table to Kevin. He's pleased with your work and would like you to create a similar page using a graphical table. To create that table, you'll start by studying how HTML defines table structures.

Defining a Table Structure

Creating graphical tables with HTML can be a complicated process because a lot of information is required to define the layout and appearance of a table. The first step is to specify the table structure: the number of rows and columns, the location of column headings, and the placement of a table caption. Once the table structure is in place, you can start entering data into the table.

The contents for the graphical table have been created for you and stored on your Data Disk, as racetxt2.htm. The first step is to open the file using your text editor and save it with a new name.

> *To open racetxt2.htm and save it with a new name:*
>
> **1.** Using your text editor, open **racetxt2.htm** from the tutorial.04/tutorial folder on your Data Disk and save it as **race2.htm** in the same folder.
>
> Figure 4-9 shows a preview of the page as it appears in the browser. Note that Kevin has added more graphical features to this page because he intends it to be viewed by graphical Web browsers.

Figure 4-9	THE RACE2 PAGE

Local Woman Wins Marathon

Park City native, **Laura Blake**, won the 27th Front Range Marathon over an elite field of the best long distance runners in the country. Laura's time of 2 hr. 28 min. 21 sec. was only 2 minutes off the women's course record set last year by Sarah Rawlings. Kathy Lasker and Lisa Peterson finished second and third, respectively. Laura's victory came on the heels of her performance at the NCAA Track and Field Championships, in which she placed second running for Colorado State.

In an exciting race, **Peter Teagan** of San Antonio, Texas, used a finishing kick to win the men's marathon for the second straight year, in a time of 2 hr. 12 min. 34 sec. Ahead for much of the race, Kyle Wills of Billings, Montana, finished second, when he could not match Teagan's finishing pace. Jason Wu of Cutler, Colorado, placed third in a very competitive field.

This year's race through downtown Boulder boasted the largest field in the marathon's history, with over 9500 men and 6700 women competing. Race conditions were perfect with low humidity and temperatures that never exceeded 85°.

Using the <table>, <tr>, and <td> Tags

Graphical tables are enclosed within a two-sided <table> tag that identifies the start and ending of the table structure. Each row of the table is indicated using a two-sided <tr> (for table row) tag. Finally, within each table row, a two-sided <td> (for table data) tag indicates the presence of individual table cells. The general syntax of a graphical table is therefore:

```
<table>
     <tr>
             <td> First Cell </td>
             <td> Second Cell </td>
```

```
          </tr>
          <tr>
                  <td> Third Cell </td>
                  <td> Fourth Cell </td>
          </tr>
    </table>
```

This example creates a table with two rows and two columns. Figure 4-10 shows the layout of a table with this HTML code.

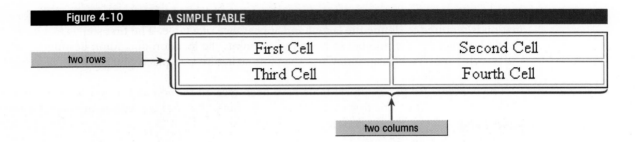

Figure 4-10   **A SIMPLE TABLE**

two rows

| First Cell | Second Cell |
| Third Cell | Fourth Cell |

two columns

REFERENCE WINDOW   **RW**

Defining Table Structure with HTML

- Enter the <table> and </table> tags to identify the beginning and end of the table.
- Enter <tr> and </tr> tags to identify the beginning and end of each table row.
- Enter <td> and </td> tags to identify the beginning and end of each table cell.
- Enter <th> and </th> tags to identify text to be table headers.

You may have noticed that there is no HTML tag for table columns. In the original HTML specifications, the number of columns is determined by how many cells are inserted within each row. For example, if you have four <td> tags in each table row, that table has four columns. Later versions of HTML have provided increased support for controlling the appearance of table columns. You'll learn about those tags later in the tutorial.

Let's return to the table that Kevin outlined in Figure 4-1. His table requires seven rows and four columns. The first row contains column titles; the remaining six rows display the table's data. HTML provides a special tag for column titles, which you'll learn about shortly. For now you'll create the table structure for the table data.

To create the structure for the race results table:

1. Place the insertion point in the blank line between the first and second paragraphs of Kevin's article.

2. Type **<table>** to identify the beginning of the table structure, and then press the **Enter** key.

3. Type the entries for the first row of the table as follows:

```
<tr>
  <td></td>
  <td></td>
```

```
   <td></td>
   <td></td>
</tr>
```

Note that you do not need to indent the <td> tags or place them on separate lines, but you may find it easier to interpret your code if you do so.

4. Press the **Enter** key and then repeat Step 3 five times to create the six rows of the table. You might want to use the copy and paste function of your text editor to save time.

5. Press the **Enter** key and then type **</table>** to complete the code for the table structure. See Figure 4-11.

Figure 4-11	STRUCTURE OF THE RACE RESULTS TABLE

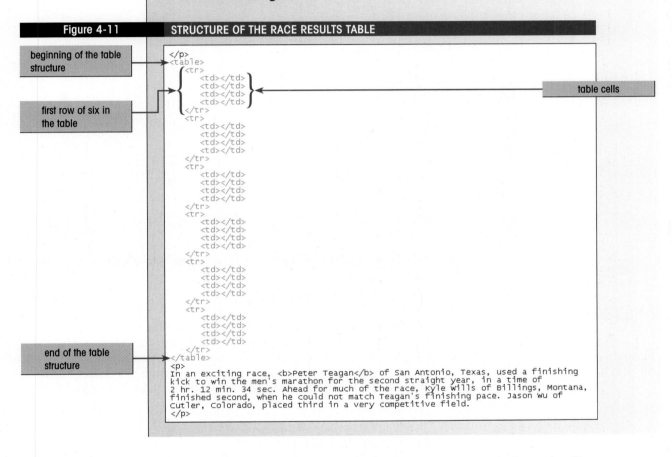

beginning of the table structure

first row of six in the table

table cells

end of the table structure

```
</p>
<table>
  <tr>
      <td></td>
      <td></td>
      <td></td>
      <td></td>
  </tr>
  <tr>
      <td></td>
      <td></td>
      <td></td>
      <td></td>
  </tr>
  <tr>
      <td></td>
      <td></td>
      <td></td>
      <td></td>
  </tr>
  <tr>
      <td></td>
      <td></td>
      <td></td>
      <td></td>
  </tr>
  <tr>
      <td></td>
      <td></td>
      <td></td>
      <td></td>
  </tr>
  <tr>
      <td></td>
      <td></td>
      <td></td>
      <td></td>
  </tr>
</table>
<p>
In an exciting race, <b>Peter Teagan</b> of San Antonio, Texas, used a finishing
kick to win the men's marathon for the second straight year, in a time of
2 hr. 12 min. 34 sec. Ahead for much of the race, Kyle Wills of Billings, Montana,
finished second, when he could not match Teagan's finishing pace. Jason Wu of
Cutler, Colorado, placed third in a very competitive field.
</p>
```

With the table structure in place, you're ready to add the text for each cell.

To insert the table text:

1. Locate the first <td> tag in the table structure and type **Men** between the opening and closing <td> tags.

2. Within the next three <td> tags, type the remaining entries for the first row of the table as follows:

```
<td>1. Peter Teagan</td>
<td>2:12:34</td>
<td>San Antonio, Texas</td>
```

3. Continue entering the text for the cells for the remaining five rows of the table. Figure 4-12 shows the completed text for the body of the table.

Figure 4-12   COMPLETED TABLE TEXT

```
<table>
    <tr>
        <td>Men</td>
        <td>1. Peter Teagan</td>
        <td>2:12:34</td>
        <td>San Antonio, Texas</td>
    </tr>
    <tr>
        <td>Men</td>
        <td>2. Kyle Wills</td>
        <td>2:13:05</td>
        <td>Billings, Montana</td>
    </tr>
    <tr>
        <td>Men</td>
        <td>3. Jason Wu</td>
        <td>2:14:28</td>
        <td>Cutler, Colorado</td>
    </tr>
    <tr>
        <td>Women</td>
        <td>1. Laura Blake</td>
        <td>2:28:21</td>
        <td>Park City, Colorado</td>
    </tr>
    <tr>
        <td>Women</td>
        <td>2. Kathy Lasker</td>
        <td>2:30:11</td>
        <td>Chicago, Illinois</td>
    </tr>
    <tr>
        <td>Women</td>
        <td>3. Lisa Peterson</td>
        <td>2:31:14</td>
        <td>Seattle, Washington</td>
    </tr>
</table>
```

With the text for the body of the table entered, the next step is to add the column headings.

Creating Headings with the <th> Tag

Instead of the <td> tag, HTML provides the <th> tag for the table headings. The difference between the <th> and <td> tags is that text formatted with the <th> tag is centered within the cell and displayed in a boldface font. The <th> tag is most often used for column headings, but you can use it for any cell that you want to contain centered boldfaced text.

In the race results table, Kevin has specified a single row of table headings. You'll enter them using the <th> tag.

To insert the table headings:

1. Place the insertion point after the <table> tag and press the **Enter** key to create a blank line.

2. Type the following HTML code and content:

```
<tr>
    <th>Group</th>
    <th>Runner</th>
    <th>Time</th>
    <th>Origin</th>
</tr>
```

Figure 4-13 shows the <th> tags as they appear in your file.

Figure 4-13	ADDING TABLE HEADINGS TO THE TABLE

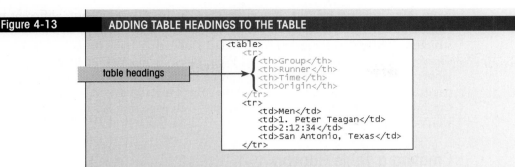

table headings

```
<table>
    <tr>
        <th>Group</th>
        <th>Runner</th>
        <th>Time</th>
        <th>Origin</th>
    </tr>
    <tr>
        <td>Men</td>
        <td>1. Peter Teagan</td>
        <td>2:12:34</td>
        <td>San Antonio, Texas</td>
    </tr>
```

3. Using your text editor, save your changes to race2.htm.

4. Using your Web browser, open **race2.htm**. The table is shown in Figure 4-14.

Figure 4-14	RACE RESULTS TABLE AS DISPLAYED IN THE BROWSER

table headings appear bold and centered over their columns

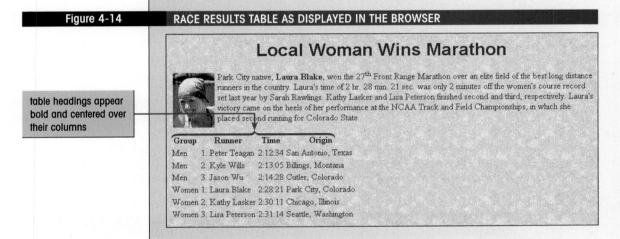

Note that the text in cells formatted with the <th> tag is bold and centered above each table column.

Identifying the Table Heading, Body, and Footer

HTML allows you to identify the different parts of your table using the <thead>, <tbody>, and <tfoot> tags, which are used for the table's heading, body, and footer, respectively. These tags do not format the table, but they do contain collections of rows called **row groups**. The general syntax for these tags is:

```
<table>
    <thead>
        <tr>heading information ...
    </thead>
    <tfoot>
        <tr>footer  information ...
    </tfoot>
    <tbody>
        <tr>first group of table rows ...
    </tbody>
    <tbody>
        <tr>second group of table rows ...
    </tbody>
...
</table>
```

Note that a single table can contain several <tbody> tags to identify different parts of the table. The <thead> and <tfoot> sections *must* appear before any <tbody> sections in the table structure. These tags are most often used in a table that draws its data from an external data source, or for tables that span several Web pages. By identifying which rows belong to the table's header or footer, the browser can be made to repeat those sections across multiple pages, while changing the contents of the table's main body. Not all browsers support this capability, and since it does not apply to the Web page that Kevin wants you to design, we won't use these tags in the table.

Creating a Table Caption

HTML allows you to specify a caption for your table. The syntax for creating a caption is:

```
<caption align="alignment">caption text</caption>
```

where *alignment* indicates the caption placement.

- A value of "bottom" centers the caption below the table.
- A value of "top" or "center" centers the caption above the table.
- Values of "left" or "right" place the caption above the table to the left or right.

Only Internet Explorer supports all caption values. Netscape supports only the "top" and "bottom" values. Because the <caption> tag works only with tables, the tag must be placed within the table structure.

Captions are shown as normal text without special formatting, but you can format the caption by embedding the caption text within other HTML tags. For example, placing the caption text within a pair of <b> and <i> tags causes the caption to display as bold and italic.

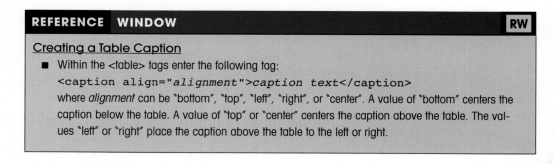

REFERENCE WINDOW   **RW**

Creating a Table Caption
- Within the <table> tags enter the following tag:
  ```
  <caption align="alignment">caption text</caption>
  ```
  where *alignment* can be "bottom", "top", "left", "right", or "center". A value of "bottom" centers the caption below the table. A value of "top" or "center" centers the caption above the table. The values "left" or "right" place the caption above the table to the left or right.

Kevin asks you to add the caption "Race Results" above the table, centered and bold.

To add the caption to the race results table:

1. Return to **race2.htm** in your text editor.

2. Insert the following code below the <table> tag (see Figure 4-15):

```
<caption align="top"><b>Race Results</b></caption>
```

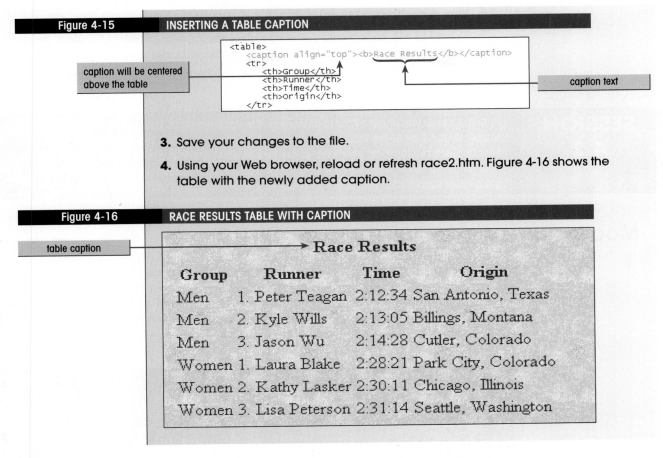

Figure 4-15	INSERTING A TABLE CAPTION

caption will be centered above the table

```
<table>
    <caption align="top"><b>Race Results</b></caption>
    <tr>
        <th>Group</th>
        <th>Runner</th>
        <th>Time</th>
        <th>origin</th>
    </tr>
```

caption text

3. Save your changes to the file.

4. Using your Web browser, reload or refresh race2.htm. Figure 4-16 shows the table with the newly added caption.

Figure 4-16	RACE RESULTS TABLE WITH CAPTION

table caption

Race Results

Group	Runner	Time	Origin
Men	1. Peter Teagan	2:12:34	San Antonio, Texas
Men	2. Kyle Wills	2:13:05	Billings, Montana
Men	3. Jason Wu	2:14:28	Cutler, Colorado
Women	1. Laura Blake	2:28:21	Park City, Colorado
Women	2. Kathy Lasker	2:30:11	Chicago, Illinois
Women	3. Lisa Peterson	2:31:14	Seattle, Washington

You've completed your work with the initial structure of the race results table. Kevin is pleased with your progress, but he would like you to make some improvements in the table's appearance. In the next session, you'll learn how to modify the appearance and placement of your table and the text contained in it.

Session 4.1 QUICK CHECK

1. What are the two kinds of tables you can place in a Web page? What are the advantages and disadvantages of each?

2. What is the difference between a proportional font and a fixed-width font? Which should you use in a text table, and why?

3. What HTML tag would you use to create a text table?

4. Define the purpose of the following HTML tags in defining the structure of a table:

   ```
   <tr>
   <td>
   <th>
   ```

5. How do you specify the number of rows in a graphical table? How do you specify the number of columns?

6. How does the <th> tag differ from the <td> tag?

7. What HTML code would you use to place the caption "Product Catalog" below a table? Where must this HTML code be placed in relation to the <table> and </table> tags?

SESSION 4.2

In this session you'll learn how to customize the appearance of your tables, including how to specify the size of the table and the space between and within the cells. You'll learn how to place the table on your Web page, how to align the text within the table, and also how to merge several cells into a single cell. Finally, this session shows you how to create a color scheme for your table by modifying the background and border colors.

Modifying the Appearance of a Table

After viewing the race results table in the browser, Kevin notes that the text is displayed with properly aligned columns, but the lack of gridlines and borders makes the table difficult to read. Kevin asks you to enhance the table's design by adding borders, gridlines, and a background color. He also wants you to control the placement and size of the table. HTML provides tags and attributes to do all of these things.

REFERENCE WINDOW   **RW**

Changing a Table's Appearance

- To add a table border, use the attribute:
  `border="value"`
  where *value* is the width of the table border in pixels. If you insert the border attribute but do not specify a value for it, the browser will display a table border 1 pixel wide.
- To specify the size of the border around individual table cells, use the attribute
  `cellspacing="value"`
  where *value* is the width of the cell border in pixels. The default cell spacing value is 2 pixels.
- To specify the size of the gap between the cell text and the surrounding cell border, use the attribute:
  `cellpadding="value"`
  where *value* is the size of the gap in pixels. The default cell padding value is 1 pixel.

You'll begin enhancing the race results table by adding a table border.

Adding a Table Border

By default, browsers display tables without table borders. You can create a table border by adding the border attribute to the <table> tag. The syntax for creating a table border is:

```
<table border="value">
```

where *value* is the width of the border in pixels. The size attribute is optional; if you don't specify a size, but simply insert the border attribute without a value, the browser creates a table border 1 pixel wide. Figure 4-17 shows the effect on a table's border when the border size is varied. Note that only the outside border is affected by the border attribute; the internal gridlines are not affected. You'll see how to change the size of these gridlines later on.

Figure 4-17 | **TABLES WITH DIFFERENT BORDER VALUES**

```
A B          A B          A B          A B
C D          C D          C D          C D

0 pixels     1 pixel      5 pixels     10 pixels
```

Kevin wants a wide border around the race results table, so you'll format the table with a 5-pixel-wide border.

To insert a table border:

1. Using your text editor, open **race2.htm**, if it is not currently open.

2. Locate the <table> tag, and within the tag, type **border="5"**. See Figure 4-18.

Figure 4-18 | **ADDING A 5-PIXEL BORDER TO THE RACE RESULTS TABLE**

```
<table border="5">
    <caption align="top"><b>Race Results</b></caption>
    <tr>
        <th>Group</th>
        <th>Runner</th>
        <th>Time</th>
        <th>Origin</th>
    </tr>
```

3. Save your changes to race2.htm.

4. Using your Web browser, reload or refresh race2.htm. Figure 4-19 shows the new border.

Figure 4-19 | **RACE RESULTS TABLE WITH A BORDER VALUE OF 5**

Race Results

Group	Runner	Time	Origin
Men	1. Peter Teagan	2:12:34	San Antonio, Texas
Men	2. Kyle Wills	2:13:05	Billings, Montana
Men	3. Jason Wu	2:14:28	Cutler, Colorado
Women	1. Laura Blake	2:28:21	Park City, Colorado
Women	2. Kathy Lasker	2:30:11	Chicago, Illinois
Women	3. Lisa Peterson	2:31:14	Seattle, Washington

You've modified the outside border of the table, and now Kevin would like you to change the width of the gridlines within the table. He feels that the table would look better if the interior borders were less prominent.

Controlling Cell Spacing

The cellspacing attribute controls the amount of space inserted between table cells. The syntax for specifying the cell spacing is:

```
<table cellspacing="value">
```

where *value* is the width of the interior borders in pixels. The default cell spacing is 2 pixels. Figure 4-20 shows how different cell spacing values affect a table's appearance.

Figure 4-20   **TABLES WITH DIFFERENT CELL SPACING VALUES**

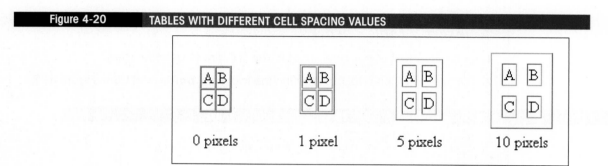

Kevin has decided that he wants the width of the borders between individual table cells to be as small as possible, so you'll decrease the width to 0 pixels. This will not remove the border between the cells. As long as you have a border around the entire table, there will be gridlines separating individual table cells, but it will reduce the interior border width to a minimal size. This is because the interior border includes a drop shadow, and even if cell spacing is set to 0, the drop shadow remains to give the effect of an interior border.

To change the cell spacing:

1. Return to **race2.htm** in your text editor.

2. Type **cellspacing="0"** within the <table> tag, as shown in Figure 4-21.

Figure 4-21   **SETTING THE CELL SPACING TO 0 PIXELS**

```
<table border="5" cellspacing="0">
    <caption align="top"><b>Race Results</b></caption>
    <tr>
        <th>Group</th>
        <th>Runner</th>
        <th>Time</th>
        <th>Origin</th>
    </tr>
```

3. Save your changes to the file.

4. Using your Web browser, reload or refresh race2.htm. The new cell spacing is shown in Figure 4-22. Note that the line that separates the cells has been reduced, but not eliminated. Compare Figure 4-19 with Figure 4-22.

Figure 4-22	RACE RESULTS TABLE WITH A CELLSPACING VALUE OF 0

Race Results

Group	Runner	Time	Origin
Men	1. Peter Teagan	2:12:34	San Antonio, Texas
Men	2. Kyle Wills	2:13:05	Billings, Montana
Men	3. Jason Wu	2:14:28	Cutler, Colorado
Women	1. Laura Blake	2:28:21	Park City, Colorado
Women	2. Kathy Lasker	2:30:11	Chicago, Illinois
Women	3. Lisa Peterson	2:31:14	Seattle, Washington

Kevin feels that the race results table is too crowded. He would like you to increase the space between the table text and the surrounding gridlines. You can do this by increasing the amount of cell padding in the table.

Defining Cell Padding

To control the space between the table text and the cell borders, add the cellpadding attribute to the table tag. The syntax for this attribute is:

```
<table cellpadding="value">
```

where *value* is the distance from the table text to the cell border, as measured in pixels. The default cell padding value is 1 pixel. Figure 4-23 shows the effect of changing the cell padding value for a table.

Figure 4-23	TABLES WITH DIFFERENT CELL PADDING VALUES

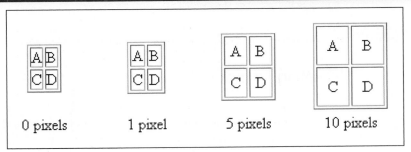

It is easy to confuse the terms cell spacing and cell padding. Just remember that cell spacing refers to the space between the cells, and cell padding refers to the space within the cells. You need to increase the amount of space within your table cells because the default value of 1 pixel is too small and results in crowded text. You'll increase the cell padding to 4 pixels to satisfy Kevin's request.

To increase the amount of cell padding:

1. Return to **race2.htm** in your text editor.

2. Type the attribute **cellpadding="4"** within the <table> tag, as shown in Figure 4-24.

Figure 4-24   **SETTING THE CELL PADDING TO 4 PIXELS**

```
<table border="5" cellspacing="0" cellpadding="4">
    <caption align="top"><b>Race Results</b></caption>
    <tr>
        <th>Group</th>
        <th>Runner</th>
        <th>Time</th>
        <th>Origin</th>
    </tr>
```

3. Save your changes to the file, and then reload **race2.htm** in your Web browser. Figure 4-25 shows the table with the increased amount of cell padding.

Figure 4-25   **RACE RESULTS TABLE WITH A CELLPADDING VALUE OF 4**

Race Results

Group	Runner	Time	Origin
Men	1. Peter Teagan	2:12:34	San Antonio, Texas
Men	2. Kyle Wills	2:13:05	Billings, Montana
Men	3. Jason Wu	2:14:28	Cutler, Colorado
Women	1. Laura Blake	2:28:21	Park City, Colorado
Women	2. Kathy Lasker	2:30:11	Chicago, Illinois
Women	3. Lisa Peterson	2:31:14	Seattle, Washington

By increasing the cell padding, you added needed space to the table.

Creating Frames and Rules

Two additional table attributes introduced in HTML 4.0 are the frame and rule attributes. As you've seen, when borders are displayed, they surround the entire table, and gridlines are automatically applied between cells. With the frame and rule attributes you can control how borders and gridlines are applied to the table.

The frame attribute allows you to determine which sides of the table will have borders. The syntax is:

```
<table frame="type">
```

where *type* is either "box" (the default), "above", "below", "hsides", "vsides", "lhs", "rhs", or "void". Figure 4-26 describes each of these options.

Figure 4-26   **VALUES OF THE FRAME ATTRIBUTE**

FRAME VALUE	DESCRIPTION
"box"	Border is drawn around all four sides of the table
"above"	Border is drawn only above the table
"below"	Border is drawn only below the table
"hsides"	Border is drawn on the top and bottom sides of the table (the horizontal sides)
"lhs"	Border is drawn only on the left-hand side
"rhs"	Border is drawn only on the right-hand side
"vsides"	Border is drawn on the left and right sides of the table (the vertical sides)
"void"	No border is drawn around the table

Figure 4-27 shows the effect of each of these values on the table grid. The frames attribute is supported by Internet Explorer version 4.0 and above. It is supported by Netscape version 6.2, but not by earlier versions of Netscape.

Figure 4-27   **EFFECT OF DIFFERENT FRAME VALUES**

A	B	C
D	E	F
G	H	I

frame="box"

A	B	C
D	E	F
G	H	I

frame="above"

A	B	C
D	E	F
G	H	I

frame="below"

A	B	C
D	E	F
G	H	I

frame="hsides"

A	B	C
D	E	F
G	H	I

frame="lhs"

A	B	C
D	E	F
G	H	I

frame="rhs"

A	B	C
D	E	F
G	H	I

frame="vsides"

A	B	C
D	E	F
G	H	I

frame="void"

The rules attribute lets you control how the table gridlines are drawn. The syntax of this attribute is:

```
<table rules="type">
```

where *type* is either "all", "rows", "cols", or "none". Figure 4-28 shows the effect of each of the attribute values on a table.

Figure 4-28   **EFFECT OF DIFFERENT RULES VALUES**

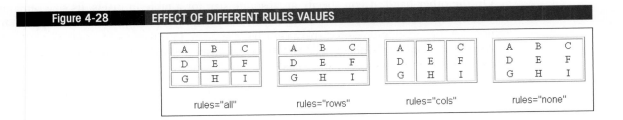

A	B	C
D	E	F
G	H	I

rules="all"

A	B	C
D	E	F
G	H	I

rules="rows"

A	B	C
D	E	F
G	H	I

rules="cols"

A	B	C
D	E	F
G	H	I

rules="none"

The rules attribute is supported by Internet Explorer version 4.0 and above. It is not supported by any versions of Netscape.

Working with Table and Cell Size

Unless you specify differently, the size of a table is determined by the text it contains in its cells. By default, HTML places text on a single line. As you add text in a cell, the width of the column and the table expands to the edge of the page while keeping text on a single line unless you've inserted a line break, paragraph, or heading tag within the cell. Once the page edge is reached, the browser reduces the size of the remaining columns to keep the text to a single line. The browser wraps the text to a second line within the cell only when it can no longer increase the size of the column and table or decrease the size of the remaining columns. As more text is added, the height of the table expands to accommodate the additional text.

To gain control over what your table looks like, it is important to manually define the size of the table cells and the table as a whole.

REFERENCE WINDOW **RW**

Choosing Table and Cell Size

- Limit your table size to approximately 600 pixels to prevent the table from expanding beyond the viewing area of many browsers.
- Specify a cell width, either absolute or relative, for all of your table cells, so that you can be sure that the table will be rendered accurately in the browser.
- Test the appearance of your Web page under several different monitor resolutions, from 640 x 480 on up.

Defining the Table Size

The syntax for specifying the table size is:

```
<table width="size" height="size">
```

where *size* is the width and height of the table as measured in pixels or as a percentage of the display area. If you want your table to fill the entire width of the display area, regardless of the resolution of the user's monitor, set the width attribute to 100%. Note that the percent value should be placed within double quotation marks (use width="100%" not width=100%). Similarly, to create a table whose height is equal to the entire height of the display area, enter the attribute height="100%".

On the other hand, if you specify an absolute size for a table in pixels, its size remains constant, regardless of the browser or monitor settings used. If you use this approach, remember that some monitors display your page at a resolution of 640 by 480 pixels. If it's important that the table not exceed the browser's display area, you should specify a table width of less than 610 pixels to allow space for other window elements such as scroll bars.

Specifying a Table Size

■ To create a table of a specific size, enter the following attributes to the <table> tag:

`width="value" height="value"`

where *value* is the table's height or width, either in pixels or as a percentage of the browser's display area.

Kevin feels that the race results table appears too crowded and would like you to increase its width to 500 pixels. This will ensure that the table will not extend beyond the display area, but it will also provide more room in the table cells if you want to insert additional text. You don't need to specify the height of the table, because the table's height expands if additional race entries are added.

To specify the width of the race results table:

1. Return to **race2.htm** in your text editor.

2. Type **width="500"** within the <table> tag, as shown in Figure 4-29.

Figure 4-29   **SETTING THE WIDTH OF THE RACE RESULTS TABLE TO 500 PIXELS**

```
<table border="5" cellspacing="0" cellpadding="4" width="500">
    <caption align="top"><b>Race Results</b></caption>
    <tr>
        <th>Group</th>
        <th>Runner</th>
        <th>Time</th>
        <th>Origin</th>
    </tr>
```

3. Save your changes to the file and then reload it in your Web browser. Figure 4-30 shows the revised page with the table width increased to 500 pixels.

Figure 4-30   **RACE RESULTS TABLE WITH A WIDTH OF 500 PIXELS**

Park City native, **Laura Blake**, won the 27th Front Range Marathon over an elite field of the best long distance runners in the country. Laura's time of 2 hr. 28 min. 21 sec. was only 2 minutes off the women's course record set last year by Sarah Rawlings. Kathy Lasker and Lisa Peterson finished second and third, respectively. Laura's victory came on the heels of her performance at the NCAA Track and Field Championships, in which she placed second running for Colorado State.

Race Results

Group	Runner	Time	Origin
Men	1. Peter Teagan	2:12:34	San Antonio, Texas
Men	2. Kyle Wills	2:13:05	Billings, Montana
Men	3. Jason Wu	2:14:28	Cutler, Colorado
Women	1. Laura Blake	2:28:21	Park City, Colorado
Women	2. Kathy Lasker	2:30:11	Chicago, Illinois
Women	3. Lisa Peterson	2:31:14	Seattle, Washington

Now that you've set the width of the table, you can set the width of individual cells and columns.

Defining Cell and Column Sizes

To set the width of an individual cell, add the width attribute to either the <td> or <th> tags using the syntax:

```
width="value"
```

where *value* can be expressed either in pixels or as a percentage of the table width. For example, a width value of 30% displays a cell that is 30% of the total width of the table. To create a cell that is always 35 pixels wide, you enter width="35" within the <td> or <th> tag. Whether you enter a pixel value or a percentage depends on whether you're trying to create a table that will be a specific size or fill a relative space.

Specifying a width for an individual cell does not guarantee that the cell will be that width when displayed in the browser. The reason for this is that the cell is part of a column containing other cells. If another cell in the column is set to a different width or expands because of the text in it, the widths of all cells in the column change accordingly. Setting a width for one cell guarantees only that the cell width will not be less than that value. If you want to ensure that the cells do not change in size, you must set the width of all the cells in the column to the same value.

The height attribute can also be used in the <td> or <th> tags to set the height of individual cells. Like the width attribute, the height attribute is expressed either in pixels or as a percentage of the height of the table. If you include more text than can be displayed within that height value you specify, the cell expands to display the additional text. For this reason, the height value is seldom used.

Kevin notices that the Group column is slightly wider than it needs to be. He suggests that you reduce the size of the column to 50 pixels. To accomplish this, you need only add the width attribute to the <th> tag of the first column.

To set a column width for the Group column:

1. Using your text editor, open **race2.htm** if it is not currently open.

2. Type the attribute **width="50"** within the <th> tag for the Group column.

3. Save your changes to race2.htm.

4. Using your Web browser, reload **race2.htm**.

   Note that the first column is narrower than before.

Next you'll work with the alignment of a table and the text it contains.

Aligning a Table and Its Contents

By default, a browser places a table on the left margin of a Web page, with surrounding text placed above and below the table. Kevin would like the table to be placed so that surrounding text wraps around it. He likes the way the text wraps around the photo of Laura Blake, and he wants the table to have a similar appearance.

Aligning a Table on the Web Page

To align a table with the surrounding text, use the align attribute as follows:

```
align="alignment"
```

where *alignment* equals "left", "right", or "center". The align attribute is similar to the align attribute used with the <img> tag, except that images have more alignment options. As with inline images, using left or right alignment places the table on the margin of the Web page and wraps surrounding text to the side. Center alignment places the table in the horizontal center of the page, but does not allow text to wrap around it.

The align attribute is available only with browsers that support HTML 3.2 or later. Earlier browsers ignore the align attribute, placing the table on the left margin of the Web page without text wrapping.

REFERENCE   WINDOW   **RW**

Aligning a Table on the Page

■ To align a table on a Web page, use the align attribute within the <table> tag as follows:
```
align="alignment"
```
where *alignment* is either "left", "right", or "center". Using a value of "left" or "right" places the table on the left or right margin of the Web page and wraps the text around the table. Using a value of "center" centers the table on the page and does not wrap text around the table.

Kevin wants the race results table to be placed on the right margin of the Web page.

To align the race results table to the right margin:

1. Return to **race2.htm** in your text editor.

2. Type the attribute **align="right"** within the <table> tag as shown in Figure 4-31.

Figure 4-31   **ALIGNING THE RACE RESULTS TABLE WITH THE PAGE'S RIGHT MARGIN**

```
<table border="5" cellspacing="0" cellpadding="4" width="500" align="right">
    <caption align="top"><b>Race Results</b></caption>
    <tr>
        <th width="50">Group</th>
        <th>Runner</th>
        <th>Time</th>
        <th>Origin</th>
    </tr>
```

3. Save your changes to the file and then reload it in your Web browser.

The race results table is now displayed on the right margin of the Web page as shown in Figure 4-32.

Figure 4-32   **RIGHT-ALIGNED RACE RESULTS TABLE**

Local Woman Wins Marathon

 Park City native, **Laura Blake**, won the 27th Front Range Marathon over an elite field of the best long distance runners in the country. Laura's time of 2 hr. 28 min. 21 sec. was only 2 minutes off the women's course record set last year by Sarah Rawlings. Kathy Lasker and Lisa Peterson finished second and third, respectively. Laura's victory came on the heels of her performance at the NCAA Track and Field Championships, in which she placed second running for Colorado State.

In an exciting race, **Peter Teagan** of San Antonio, Texas, used a finishing kick to win the men's marathon for the second straight year, in a time of 2 hr. 12 min. 34 sec. Ahead for much of the race, Kyle Wills of Billings, Montana, finished second, when he could not match Teagan's finishing pace. Jason Wu of Cutler, Colorado, placed third in a very competitive field.

This year's race through downtown Boulder boasted the largest field in the

Race Results

Group	Runner	Time	Origin
Men	1. Peter Teagan	2:12:34	San Antonio, Texas
Men	2. Kyle Wills	2:13:05	Billings, Montana
Men	3. Jason Wu	2:14:28	Cutler, Colorado
Women	1. Laura Blake	2:28:21	Park City, Colorado
Women	2. Kathy Lasker	2:30:11	Chicago, Illinois
Women	3. Lisa Peterson	2:31:14	Seattle, Washington

marathon's history, with over 9500 men and 6700 women competing. Race conditions were perfect with low humidity and temperatures that never exceeded 85°.

Aligning the Contents of a Table

By default cell text is placed in the middle of the cell, aligned with the cell's left edge. By using the align and valign attributes, you can specify the text's horizontal and vertical placement. Figure 4-33 shows how the combination of the align and valign attributes can affect the position of the cell text in relation to the cell borders.

Figure 4-33   **VALUES OF THE ALIGN AND VALIGN ATTRIBUTES**

align="left" valign="top"		
	align="left" valign="middle"	
		align="left" valign="bottom"
align="center" valign="top"		
	align="center" valign="middle"	
		align="center" valign="bottom"
align="right" valign="top"		
	align="right" valign="middle"	
		align="right" valign="bottom"

After reviewing the table, Kevin decides that the values in the Time column would look better if they were right-aligned. Because of the way HTML works with table columns, if you want to align the text for a single column, you must apply the align attribute to every cell in that column.

To right-align the Time column values:

1. Return to **race2.htm** in your text editor.

2. Type the attribute **align="right"** within each <td> tag in the Time column. Figure 4-34 shows the revised HTML code.

Figure 4-34   RIGHT-ALIGNING THE VALUES IN THE TIME COLUMN

```
<table border="5" cellspacing="0" cellpadding="4" width="500" align="right">
    <caption align="top"><b>Race Results</b></caption>
    <tr>
        <th width="50">Group</th>
        <th>Runner</th>
        <th>Time</th>
        <th>Origin</th>
    </tr>
    <tr>
        <td>Men</td>
        <td>1. Peter Teagan</td>
        <td align="right">2:12:34</td>
        <td>San Antonio, Texas</td>
    </tr>
    <tr>
        <td>Men</td>
        <td>2. Kyle wills</td>
        <td align="right">2:13:05</td>
        <td>Billings, Montana</td>
    </tr>
    <tr>
        <td>Men</td>
        <td>3. Jason Wu</td>
        <td align="right">2:14:28</td>
        <td>Cutler, Colorado</td>
    </tr>
    <tr>
        <td>women</td>
        <td>1. Laura Blake</td>
        <td align="right">2:28:21</td>
        <td>Park City, Colorado</td>
    </tr>
    <tr>
        <td>women</td>
        <td>2. Kathy Lasker</td>
        <td align="right">2:30:11</td>
        <td>Chicago, Illinois</td>
    </tr>
    <tr>
        <td>women</td>
        <td>3. Lisa Peterson</td>
        <td align="right">2:31:14</td>
        <td>Seattle, washington</td>
    </tr>
</table>
```

3. Save your changes to the file and reload it in your Web browser. The race times should now be aligned with the right edge of the Time column. See Figure 4-35.

Figure 4-35   RACE RESULTS TABLE WITH TIME VALUES RIGHT-ALIGNED

| | | **Race Results** | | |
Group	Runner	Time	Origin
Men	1. Peter Teagan	2:12:34	San Antonio, Texas
Men	2. Kyle Wills	2:13:05	Billings, Montana
Men	3. Jason Wu	2:14:28	Cutler, Colorado
Women	1. Laura Blake	2:28:21	Park City, Colorado
Women	2. Kathy Lasker	2:30:11	Chicago, Illinois
Women	3. Lisa Peterson	2:31:14	Seattle, Washington

You can also use the align and valign attributes with the <tr> tag to align all the text within a single row in the same manner as you did with columns.

Spanning **Rows and Columns**

Kevin has reviewed your table and would like to make a few more changes. He feels that repeating the group information for each row in the table is redundant and wonders if you can merge several cells into a single cell. He draws a proposed layout for the table, which is displayed in Figure 4-36.

| Figure 4-36 | KEVIN'S PROPOSED TABLE LAYOUT |

	Runner	Time	Origin
Men	1. Peter Teagan	2:12:34	San Antonio, Texas
	2. Kyle Wills	2:13:05	Billings, Montana
	3. Jason Wu	2:14:28	Cutler, Colorado
Women	1. Laura Blake	2:28:21	Park City, Colorado
	2. Kathy Lasker	2:30:11	Chicago, Illinois
	3. Lisa Peterson	2:31:14	Seattle, Washington

To merge several cells into one, you need to create a **spanning cell**, which is a cell that occupies more than one row or column in a table. Figure 4-37 shows a table of opinion poll data in which some of the cells span several rows and/or columns.

| Figure 4-37 | EXAMPLE OF SPANNING CELLS |

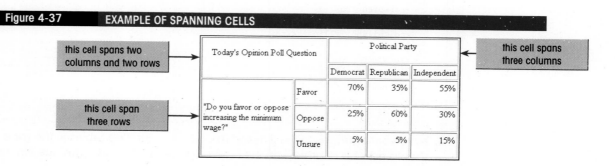

Spanning cells are created by inserting the rowspan and colspan attributes in a <td> or <th> tag. The syntax for these attributes is:

```
rowspan="value" colspan="value"
```

where *value* is the number of rows or columns that the cell spans in the table. The direction of the spanning is downward and to the right of the cell containing the rowspan and colspan attributes. For example, to create a cell that spans two columns in the table, you enter the <td> tag as:

```
<td colspan="2">
```

For a cell that spans two rows, the tag is:

```
<td rowspan="2">
```

and to span two rows and two columns at the same time, the tag is:

```
<td rowspan="2" colspan="2">
```

The important thing to remember when you have a cell that spans several rows or columns is that you must adjust the number of cell tags used in the table row. For example, if a row has five columns, but one of the cells in the row spans three columns, you only need three <td> tags within the row: two <td> tags for the cells that occupy a single column and the third for the cell spanning three rows.

When a cell spans several rows, the rows below the spanning cell must also be adjusted. Consider the table, shown in Figure 4-38, with three rows and four columns. The first cell in the first row is a spanning cell that spans three rows. You need four <td> tags for the first row, but only three <td> tags for rows two and three. This is because the spanning cell from row one occupies the cells that would normally appear in rows two and three.

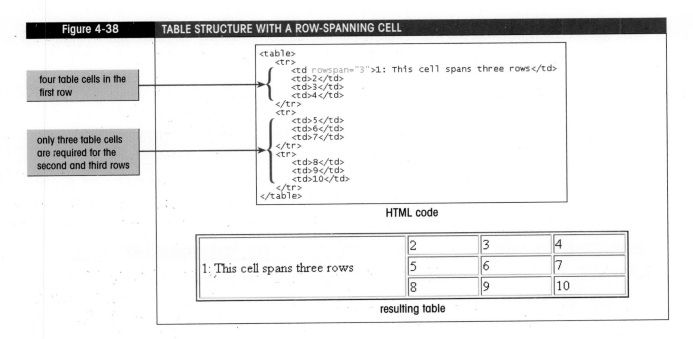

Figure 4-38   **TABLE STRUCTURE WITH A ROW-SPANNING CELL**

four table cells in the first row

only three table cells are required for the second and third rows

```
<table>
   <tr>
      <td rowspan="3">1: This cell spans three rows</td>
      <td>2</td>
      <td>3</td>
      <td>4</td>
   </tr>
   <tr>
      <td>5</td>
      <td>6</td>
      <td>7</td>
   </tr>
   <tr>
      <td>8</td>
      <td>9</td>
      <td>10</td>
   </tr>
</table>
```

HTML code

1: This cell spans three rows	2	3	4
	5	6	7
	8	9	10

resulting table

REFERENCE WINDOW   **RW**

Creating a Spanning Cell

- To create a cell that spans several columns, enter the colspan attribute within the <td> or <th> tag as follows:

  `colspan="value"`

  where *value* is the number of columns to be spanned.

- To create a cell that spans several rows, enter the rowspan attribute as follows:

  `rowspan="value"`

  where *value* is the number of rows to be spanned.

To make the changes that Kevin has requested, delete the table heading for the Group column, and then span the Runner table heading across two columns.

To create a cell that spans two columns:

1. Return to **race2.htm** in your text editor.

2. Delete the **Group** table heading, including both the opening and closing <th> tags.

3. Type the attribute **colspan="2"** within the <th> tag for the Runner table heading.

Next, you'll delete the second and third occurrences of the "Men" and "Women" cells in the table, keeping only the first occurrences. You'll also span those two cells over three rows of the table.

To span two cells over three rows:

1. Insert the attribute **rowspan="3"** in the first <td> tag that contains the text "Men".

2. Delete the next two <td> tags that contain the text "Men".

3. Insert the attribute **rowspan="3"** in the first <td> tag that contains the text "Women".

4. Delete the next two <td> tags that contain the text "Women". Figure 4-39 shows the revised table structure.

Figure 4-39	ADDING SPANNING CELLS TO THE RACE RESULTS TABLE

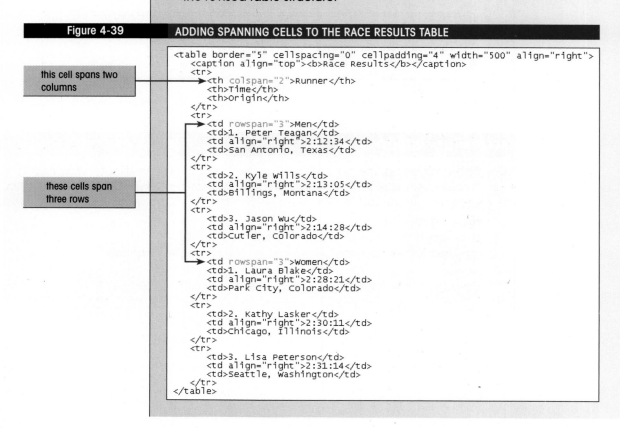

this cell spans two columns

these cells span three rows

```
<table border="5" cellspacing="0" cellpadding="4" width="500" align="right">
   <caption align="top"><b>Race Results</b></caption>
   <tr>
      <th colspan="2">Runner</th>
      <th>Time</th>
      <th>Origin</th>
   </tr>
   <tr>
      <td rowspan="3">Men</td>
      <td>1. Peter Teagan</td>
      <td align="right">2:12:34</td>
      <td>San Antonio, Texas</td>
   </tr>
   <tr>
      <td>2. Kyle Wills</td>
      <td align="right">2:13:05</td>
      <td>Billings, Montana</td>
   </tr>
   <tr>
      <td>3. Jason Wu</td>
      <td align="right">2:14:28</td>
      <td>Cutler, Colorado</td>
   </tr>
   <tr>
      <td rowspan="3">Women</td>
      <td>1. Laura Blake</td>
      <td align="right">2:28:21</td>
      <td>Park City, Colorado</td>
   </tr>
   <tr>
      <td>2. Kathy Lasker</td>
      <td align="right">2:30:11</td>
      <td>Chicago, Illinois</td>
   </tr>
   <tr>
      <td>3. Lisa Peterson</td>
      <td align="right">2:31:14</td>
      <td>Seattle, Washington</td>
   </tr>
</table>
```

5. Save your changes to race2.htm and reload it in your Web browser. Figure 4-40 shows the revised table.

| Figure 4-40 | RACE RESULTS TABLE WITH SPANNING CELLS |

The text in the two cells that span three rows is centered vertically, but Kevin feels it would look better if it were placed at the top of those cells. You can do this using the valign attribute that was discussed earlier.

To align the text with the top of the spanning cell:

1. Return to **race2.htm** in your text editor.

2. Type the attribute **valign="top"** within the <td> tag for the Men and Women spanning cells that you edited in the last set of steps.

Applying a Color Scheme to a Table

Kevin is pleased with the structure you've created for the race results table. He does have some concern that the table may be difficult to read due to the color scheme and would like you to apply a different one. He would like you to apply colors to the table background and to the table cells.

Applying a Background Color

Table elements support the same bgcolor attribute that can be applied to an entire Web page. You can specify a background color for all of the cells in a table, all of the cells in a row, or for individual cells, by adding the bgcolor attribute to either the <table>, <tr>, <td>, or <th> tags as follows:

```
<table bgcolor="color">
<tr bgcolor="color">
<td bgcolor="color">
<th bgcolor="color">
```

where *color* is either a color name or hexadecimal color value. Note that you cannot set a background color for a column with a single attribute; to set the background color for an entire column, you must define the background color for each cell in that column.

The color defined for a cell overrides the color defined for a row, and the color defined for a row overrides the color defined for a table. Keep this hierarchy in mind as you develop color schemes for tables.

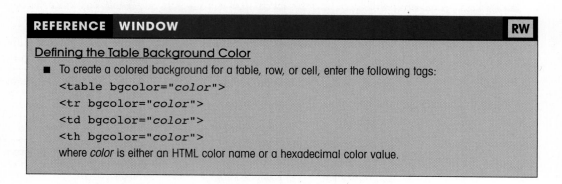

REFERENCE WINDOW   **RW**

<u>Defining the Table Background Color</u>

■ To create a colored background for a table, row, or cell, enter the following tags:

```
<table bgcolor="color">
<tr bgcolor="color">
<td bgcolor="color">
<th bgcolor="color">
```

where *color* is either an HTML color name or a hexadecimal color value.

After considering many different colors, Kevin tells you to change the color of the table cells to white, the table heading to yellow, the cell containing the text "Men" to light blue, and the cell containing the text "Women" to light green.

To apply a color scheme to the table:

1. Type the attribute **bgcolor="white"** within the <table> tag.

2. Type the attribute **bgcolor="yellow"** within the <tr> tag for the table heading.

3. Type the attribute **bgcolor="lightblue"** within the <td> tag for the cell containing the text "Men".

4. Type the attribute **bgcolor="lightgreen"** within the <td> tag for the cell containing the text "Women". Figure 4-41 shows the revised HTML code for the table.

Figure 4-41   **SPECIFYING TABLE, ROW, AND CELL COLORS**

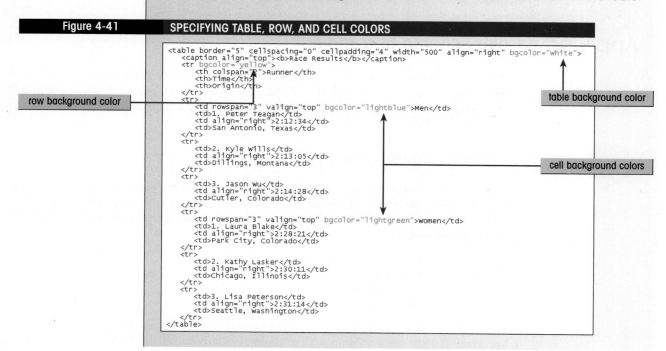

```
<table border="5" cellspacing="0" cellpadding="4" width="500" align="right" bgcolor="white">
  <caption align="top"><b>Race Results</b></caption>
  <tr bgcolor="yellow">
    <th colspan="2">Runner</th>
    <th>Time</th>
    <th>Origin</th>
  </tr>
  <tr>
    <td rowspan="3" valign="top" bgcolor="lightblue">Men</td>
    <td>1. Peter Teagan</td>
    <td align="right">2:12:34</td>
    <td>San Antonio, Texas</td>
  </tr>
  <tr>
    <td>2. Kyle Wills</td>
    <td align="right">2:13:05</td>
    <td>Billings, Montana</td>
  </tr>
  <tr>
    <td>3. Jason Wu</td>
    <td align="right">2:14:28</td>
    <td>Cutler, Colorado</td>
  </tr>
  <tr>
    <td rowspan="3" valign="top" bgcolor="lightgreen">Women</td>
    <td>1. Laura Blake</td>
    <td align="right">2:28:21</td>
    <td>Park City, Colorado</td>
  </tr>
  <tr>
    <td>2. Kathy Lasker</td>
    <td align="right">2:30:11</td>
    <td>Chicago, Illinois</td>
  </tr>
  <tr>
    <td>3. Lisa Peterson</td>
    <td align="right">2:31:14</td>
    <td>Seattle, Washington</td>
  </tr>
</table>
```

row background color

table background color

cell background colors

Figure 4-46 | APPLYING A BACKGROUND IMAGE TO A TABLE, ROW, AND CELL

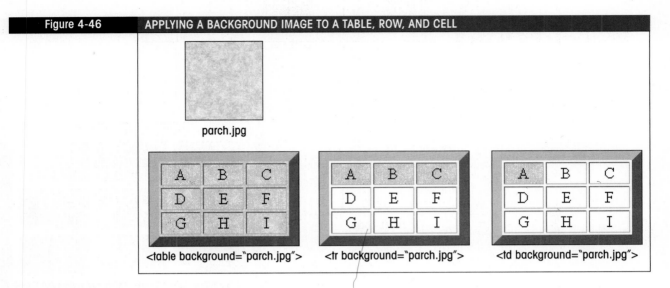

Note that certain browser versions may not support the use of background images in tables.

Working with Column Groups

Thus far, you've formatted columns by manipulating the attributes of individual cells within a column. HTML 4.0 supports tags that allow you to manipulate the features of entire columns and groups of columns. This feature is currently only supported by Internet Explorer 4.0 or above, and not at all by Netscape. Therefore it shouldn't be used if your page is to be viewed by multiple browsers and browser versions.

To define a column, add the following tag to the top of the table structure:

```
<col span="value">
```

where *value* is the number of columns in the group. The <col> tag supports many of the attributes you've applied to tables, rows, and cells, including the align, bgcolor, valign, and width attributes. Figure 4-47 shows an example of the <col> tag used to format the appearance of entire table columns.

Figure 4-47 USING THE <COL> TAG

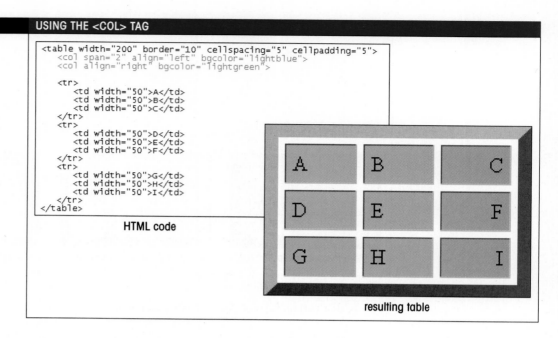

```
<table width="200" border="10" cellspacing="5" cellpadding="5">
    <col span="2" align="left" bgcolor="lightblue">
    <col align="right" bgcolor="lightgreen">

    <tr>
        <td width="50">A</td>
        <td width="50">B</td>
        <td width="50">C</td>
    </tr>
    <tr>
        <td width="50">D</td>
        <td width="50">E</td>
        <td width="50">F</td>
    </tr>
    <tr>
        <td width="50">G</td>
        <td width="50">H</td>
        <td width="50">I</td>
    </tr>
</table>
```

HTML code

resulting table

In this example, setting the span attribute to "2" modifies the first <col> tag and the first two table columns. The second <col> tag modifies the appearance of the third column.

Another way of grouping columns is by using the <colgroup> tag. The syntax of the <colgroup> tag is:

```
<colgroup span="value">
       columns
</colgroup>
```

where *value* is the number of columns in the group, and *columns* are definitions for individual columns within the group (defined using the <col> tag.) Figure 4-48 shows an example of a column group used to center the text of all columns in the table. Background colors for the individual columns are specified using a series of <col> tags.

Figure 4-48 USING THE <COLGROUP> TAG

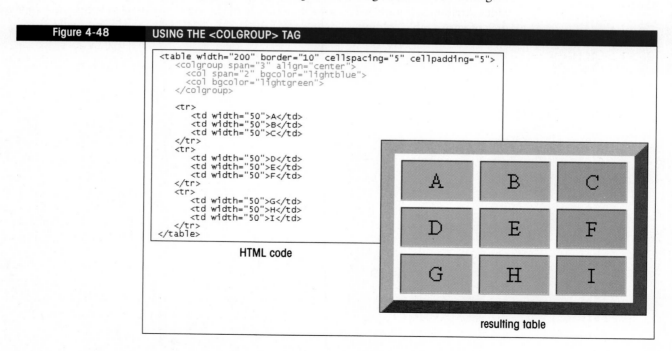

```
<table width="200" border="10" cellspacing="5" cellpadding="5">
    <colgroup span="3" align="center">
        <col span="2" bgcolor="lightblue">
        <col bgcolor="lightgreen">
    </colgroup>

    <tr>
        <td width="50">A</td>
        <td width="50">B</td>
        <td width="50">C</td>
    </tr>
    <tr>
        <td width="50">D</td>
        <td width="50">E</td>
        <td width="50">F</td>
    </tr>
    <tr>
        <td width="50">G</td>
        <td width="50">H</td>
        <td width="50">I</td>
    </tr>
</table>
```

HTML code

resulting table

In the event of a conflict between the attributes in the <col> and <colgroup> tags, the <col> tag attributes take precedence.

You've completed your work on the race results table and the story that Kevin wanted you to work on. In the next session, you'll use tables to create a layout for this story and other features of the Park City Gazette.

Session 4.2 QUICK CHECK

1. What HTML code would you use to create a table with a 5-pixel-wide outside border, a 3-pixel-wide border between table cells, and 4 pixels of padding between the cell text and the cell border?

2. What HTML code would you use to align text with the top of a table heading cell?

3. What HTML code would you use to center all of the text within a given row?

4. What are the two ways of expressing table width? What are the advantages and disadvantages of each?

5. What HTML code would you use to create a table that fills half the width of the browser's display area, regardless of the resolution of the user's monitor?

6. What HTML code would you use to set the width of a cell to 60 pixels? Will this keep the cell from exceeding 60 pixels in width? Will this keep the cell from being less than 60 pixels wide? How can you guarantee that the cell width will be exactly 60 pixels?

7. What HTML code would you use to set the background color of your table to yellow? What are some limitations of this code?

8. What HTML code would you use to create a cell that spans three rows and two columns?

SESSION 4.3

In this session you'll work with tables to create a newspaper-style layout for a Web page. You'll learn how to create comments for your HTML document to assist in the design process. You'll also learn how to nest one table within another, and how to format the text within table cells using the <font> tag.

Designing a Page Layout with Tables

In the first two sessions, you used the <table> tag to create a table of products that was part of a larger Web page. In practice, however, HTML tables are most often used to define the layout of an entire Web page. If you want to design a page that displays text in newspaper-style columns, or separates the page into distinct sections, you'll find tables an essential and useful tool. One of the most useful features of tables is that you can use any of the HTML layout tags you've learned so far for individual table cells. For example, you can format your cell text as an h1 heading, or the cell can store an unordered list of bulleted items. You can even nest one table inside another.

Kevin is satisfied with the layout of the article on the marathon results. He now wants you to create a newspaper-style Web page for the entire Gazette. The Web page will contain the Gazette logo, a list of links to other pages, and a few articles, one of which is the race results article you've been working on. Figure 4-49 displays the layout that Kevin has created.

Figure 4-49   KEVIN'S DESIGN SKETCH FOR THE GAZETTE HOME PAGE

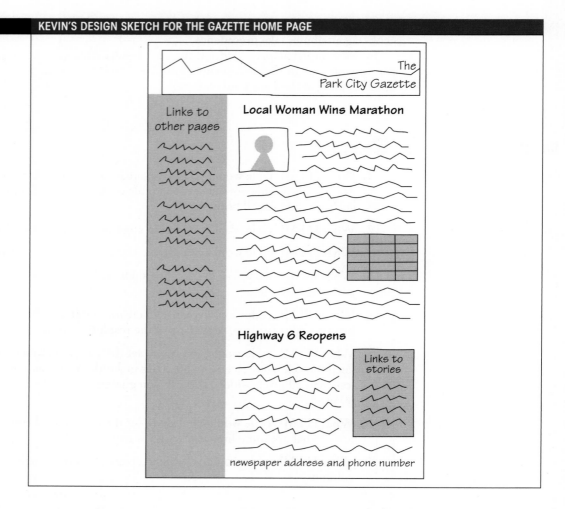

One way to lay out the page specified in Kevin's sketch is to create two tables, one nested inside the other. The outer table, shown in Figure 4-50, consists of four cells that are contained in two columns and three rows. The first cell, containing the Gazette logo, occupies the first row of the table and spans two columns. The second cell, displaying the list of links, occupies one column and spans the remaining two rows. The articles and newspaper address are placed in the remaining two cells, each occupying a single row and column.

You'll set the width of the table to 620 pixels to ensure that the entire Web page can be viewed by monitors with resolutions as low as 640 x 480 pixels. The first column's width will be set to 120 pixels. The second column, containing the articles and the paper's address, will be 500 pixels wide.

Figure 4-50 **TABLE LAYOUT OF THE GAZETTE HOME PAGE**

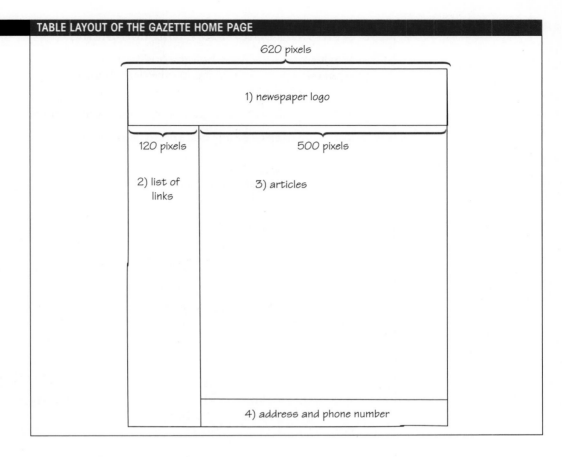

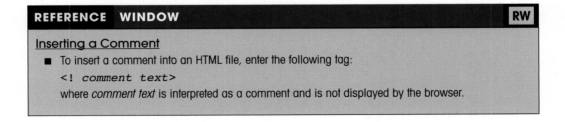

Creating the Outer Table

Kevin has created the initial part of the file for the front page, setting the page background and text color. Your job is to create the table structure displayed in Figure 4-50.

HTML code for pages like this one can be long and complex. **Comment tags** can aid you and others viewing your HTML file by describing the different sections of the code. The syntax for creating a comment tag is:

```
<! comment text>
```

where *comment text* is the text that you want to insert into the comment. Any text appearing within the comment tag is ignored by the browser and not displayed in the page.

REFERENCE WINDOW   **RW**

Inserting a Comment
- To insert a comment into an HTML file, enter the following tag:
```
<! comment text>
```
where *comment text* is interpreted as a comment and is not displayed by the browser.

To create the outer table and comments:

1. If you took a break after the previous session, use your text editor to open **page1txt.htm** located in the tutorial.04/tutorial folder of your Data Disk and save it as **page1.htm**.

2. Enter the following code in a new line immediately following the <body> tag:

```
<table width="620" cellpadding="5">
<tr>
 <td colspan="2">
 <!-- Newspaper logo -->
 </td>
</tr>

<tr>
 <td width="120" rowspan="2" valign="top">
 <!— List of links —>
 </td>
 <td width="500" valign="top">
 <!-- Articles -->
 </td>
</tr>

<tr>
 <td width="500" valign="top" align="center">
 <!-- Newspaper address -->
 </td>
</tr>

</table>
```

Figure 4-51 displays what page1.htm should look like.

| Figure 4-51 | TABLE STRUCTURE OF THE PAGE1 WEB PAGE |

```
<html>
<head>
<title>The Park City Gazette</title>
</head>
<body background="parch2.jpg" text="#524020" link="#524020" vlink="#524020" alink="#524020">
<table width="620" cellpadding="5">

<tr>
 <td colspan="2">
 <!-- Newspaper logo -->
 </td>
</tr>

<tr>
 <td width="120" rowspan="2" valign="top">
 <!-- List of links -->
 </td>

 <td width="500" valign="top">
 <!-- Articles -->
 </td>
</tr>

<tr>
 <td width="500" valign="top" align="center">
 <!-- Newspaper address -->
 </td>
</tr>

</table>
</body>
</html>
```

Note that in three of the cells of this outer table, you've set the vertical alignment to top, rather than using the default value of middle. This is because the cells in this table act as newspaper columns. The tables in this layout don't display any borders.

Now you place the Gazette logo, pclogo.jpg, on the Web page.

To insert the logo in a table cell:

1. Insert the code **<img src="pcglogo.jpg" alt="The Park City Gazette">** immediately after the comment <!--- Newspaper logo --->.

2. Save your changes to page1.htm and open the file in your Web browser. Your page should appear as shown in Figure 4-52.

Figure 4-52   **INITIAL CONTENTS OF PAGE1**

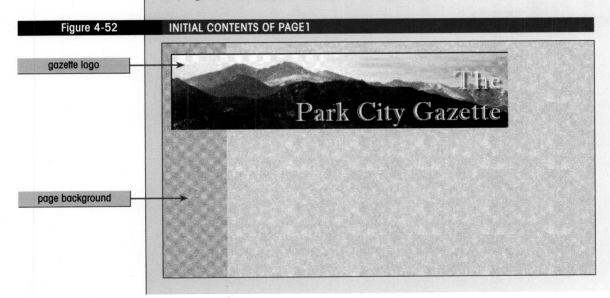

gazette logo

page background

Next you'll insert the list of links into the second table cell. The contents of this cell have been created for you and stored in a file named links.htm. You'll copy the information from that document and paste into the table cell. If you don't know how to copy and paste with your text editor, ask your instructor or technical support person for assistance.

To insert the contents of the links.htm file:

1. Using your text editor, open **links.htm** from the tutorial.04/tutorial folder of your data disk.

2. Copy the HTML code within the <body> tags of links.htm, but do *not* include the opening and closing <body> tags.

3. Close links.htm and return to **page1.htm** in your text editor.

4. Paste the HTML code you copied from links.htm directly after the comment tag, <!-- List of links --> as shown in Figure 4-53.

Figure 4-53   **INSERTING THE CONTENTS OF LINKS.HTM**

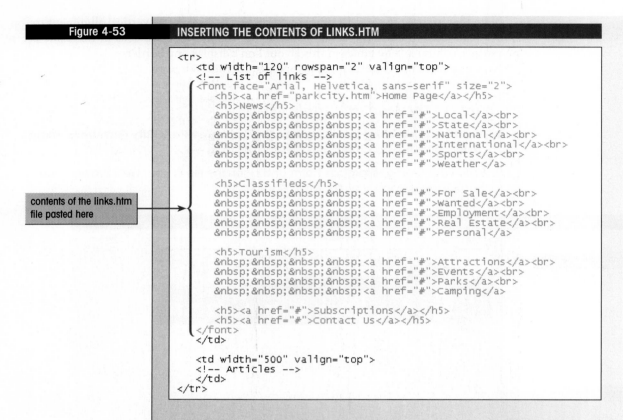

contents of the links.htm
file pasted here

```
<tr>
    <td width="120" rowspan="2" valign="top">
    <!-- List of links -->
    <font face="Arial, Helvetica, sans-serif" size="2">
        <h5><a href="parkcity.htm">Home Page</a></h5>
        <h5>News</h5>
            <a href="#">Local</a><br>
            <a href="#">State</a><br>
            <a href="#">National</a><br>
            <a href="#">International</a><br>
            <a href="#">Sports</a><br>
            <a href="#">Weather</a>

        <h5>Classifieds</h5>
            <a href="#">For Sale</a><br>
            <a href="#">Wanted</a><br>
            <a href="#">Employment</a><br>
            <a href="#">Real Estate</a><br>
            <a href="#">Personal</a>

        <h5>Tourism</h5>
            <a href="#">Attractions</a><br>
            <a href="#">Events</a><br>
            <a href="#">Parks</a><br>
            <a href="#">Camping</a>

        <h5><a href="#">Subscriptions</a></h5>
        <h5><a href="#">Contact Us</a></h5>
    </font>
    </td>

    <td width="500" valign="top">
    <!-- Articles -->
    </td>
</tr>
```

5. Save your changes to page1.htm and reload it in your Web browser. Figure 4-54 shows the current state of the home page of the Park City Gazette.

Figure 4-54   **PAGE1 WITH LINKS**

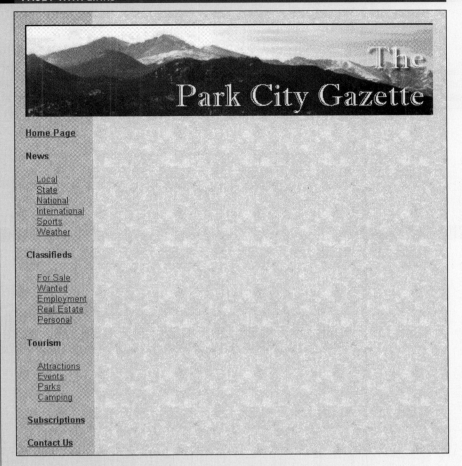

TROUBLE? At this point, the links on this page point to page1.htm and are acting as placeholders. Kevin will add the actual links as more work is done on the Gazette's Web site.

The next piece of the outer table you'll add is the newspaper address and phone number located at the bottom of the page. The content for this cell has been created for you, stored in the address.htm file.

To insert the contents of address.htm into a table:

1. Using your text editor, open **address.htm** from the tutorial.04/tutorial folder of your data disk.

2. Copy the HTML code within the <body> tags of address.htm, not including the opening and closing <body> tags.

3. Close address.htm and return to **page1.htm** in your text editor.

4. Paste the HTML code you copied from address.htm directly after the comment tag, <!-- Newspaper address --> as shown in Figure 4-55.

Figure 4-55   INSERTING THE CONTENTS OF ADDRESS.HTM

contents of the
address.htm file
pasted here

```
<tr>
   <td width="500" valign="top" align="center">
   <!-- Newspaper address -->
   <img src="brline.gif" width="500" height="3">
   <font face="Arial, Helvetica, sans-serif" size="1">
      Park City Gazette  &#149; 
      801 Elkhart Avenue  &#149; 
      Park City, CO  80511  &#149; 
      1 (800) 555-2918
   </font>
   </td>
</tr>
```

5. Save your changes to page1.htm and reload it in your Web browser. See Figure 4-56.

Figure 4-56   PAGE1 WITH THE NEWSPAPER ADDRESS

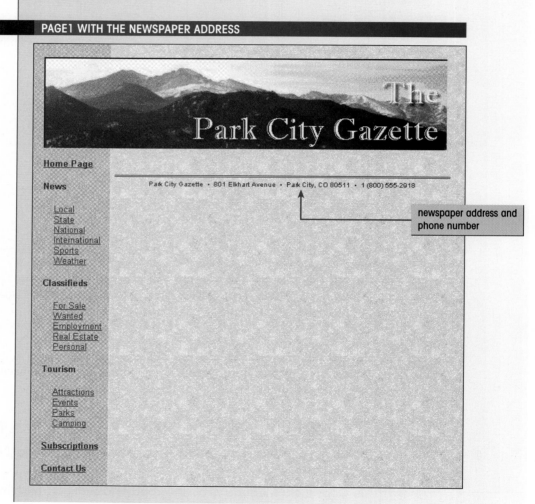

newspaper address and
phone number

At this point, you've populated all of the table cells with information except one, the articles cell. Essentially, the articles cell is the only cell with content that changes on a weekly basis. When Kevin wants to update this Web page, he need only edit the contents of a single cell. Therefore, it makes sense to separate the articles content from the rest of the front page by placing it in a separate cell.

Creating the Nested Table

Kevin has decided on the stories he wants you to use for today's front page articles. The main story is the results of the marathon, and another story concerns the reopening of Highway 6 (one of Park City's main roads over the Continental Divide). He also wants the Web page to have a sidebar with links to some of the other important stories and features of the day. In Figure 4-57, Kevin has sketched a layout to assist you with the design of the Web page.

Figure 4-57	DESIGN SKETCH FOR TODAY'S ARTICLES

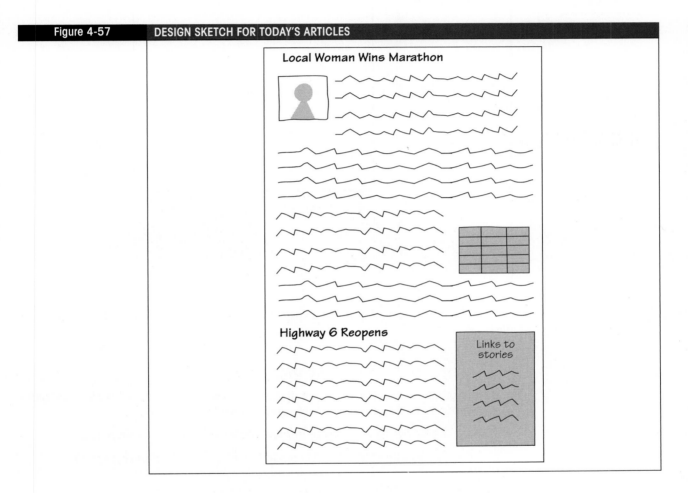

This material is best organized in a second table, an outline of which is shown in Figure 4-58. The width of this table is 500 pixels, since it has to match the width assigned to the third cell from Figure 4-50. The first cell contains the marathon story and spans two columns. The second cell, 300 pixels wide, contains the Highway 6 story. The third cell contains a list of links to other stories and is 200 pixels wide. For this third cell, you'll use the parch3.jpg graphic for a background image.

Figure 4-58   **TABLE LAYOUT OF TODAY'S ARTICLES**

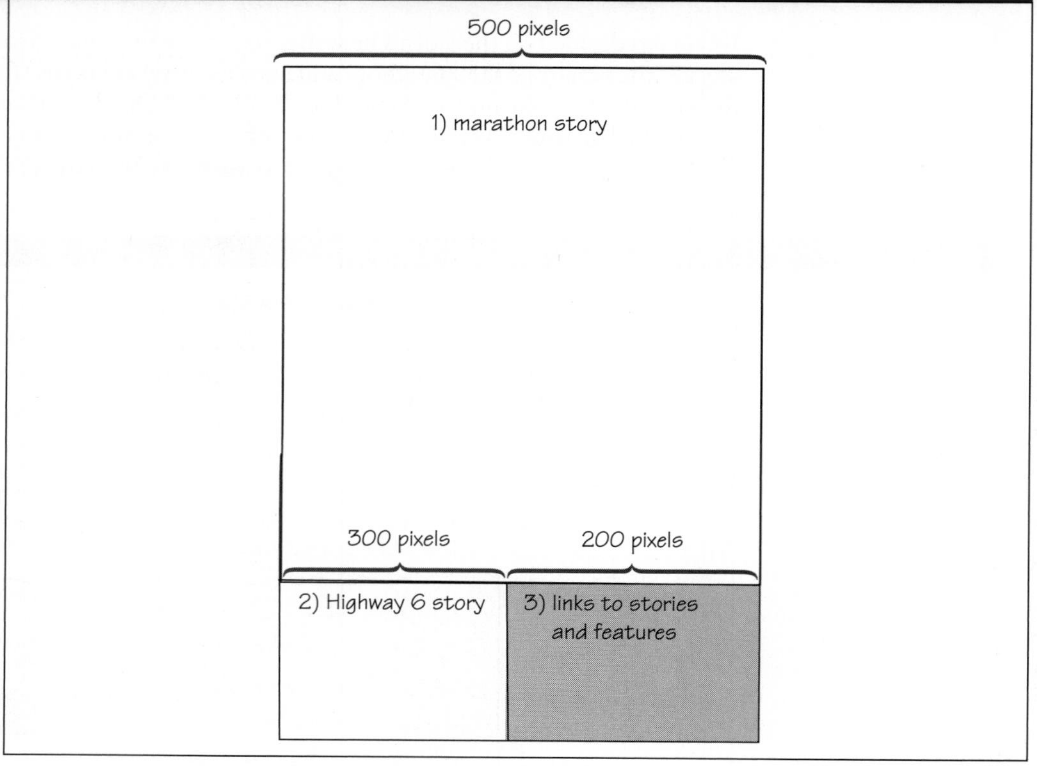

Kevin has begun creating the Web page for this table, artcltxt.htm, and you can open that file now.

To create the outer table and comments:

1. Using your text editor, open **artcltxt.htm** located in the tutorial.04/tutorial folder of your Data Disk and save it as **articles.htm** in the same folder.

2. Type the following HTML code immediately following the <body> tag:

```
<table width="500" cellpadding="5" cellspacing="5">
<tr>
  <td colspan="2" valign="top">
  <!-- Marathon story -->
  </td>
</tr>

<tr>
  <td width="300" valign="top">
  <!-- Highway story -->
  </td>

  <td width="200" valign="top" background="parch3.jpg">
  <!-- Features -->
  </td>
</tr>

</table>
```

Figure 4-59 displays what articles.htm should look like.

Figure 4-59	TABLE STRUCTURE OF THE ARTICLES WEB PAGE

```
<html>
<head>
<title>Today's Headlines</title>
</head>

<body background="parch.jpg" text="#524020" link=""#524020" vlink="#524020" alink="#524020">
<table width="500" cellpadding="5" cellspacing="5">

<tr>
   <td colspan="2" valign="top">
   <!-- Marathon story -->
   </td>
</tr>

<tr>
   <td width="300" valign="top">
   <!-- Highway story -->
   </td>

   <td width="200" valign="top" background="parch3.jpg">
   <!-- Features -->
   </td>
</tr>

</table>
</body>

</html>
```

3. Save your changes to the file.

The next step is to copy the code for the marathon article that you created in race2.htm and paste it in the first cell of the table. You will also have to edit some of the contents of this material to fit the size of the cell.

To insert the contents of race2.htm into the first cell:

1. Using your text editor, open **race2.htm** from the tutorial.04/tutorial folder of your Data Disk.

2. Copy the HTML code within the <body> tags of race2.htm, but do *not* include the <body> tags themselves.

3. Close the file and return to **articles.htm** in your text editor.

4. Paste the HTML code you copied from race2.htm directly after the comment tag <!-- Marathon story--> as shown in Figure 4-60. Save your changes to articles.htm.

Figure 4-60	INSERTING THE CONTENTS OF RACE2.HTM

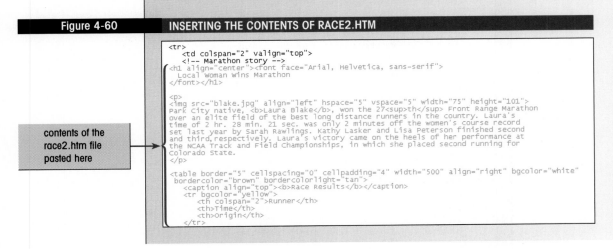

contents of the race2.htm file pasted here

```
<tr>
   <td colspan="2" valign="top">
   <!-- Marathon story -->
<h1 align="center"><font face="Arial, Helvetica, sans-serif">
  Local Woman Wins Marathon
</font></h1>

<p>
<img src="blake.jpg" align="left" hspace="5" vspace="5" width="75" height="101">
Park City native, <b>Laura Blake</b>, won the 27<sup>th</sup> Front Range Marathon
over an elite field of the best long distance runners in the country. Laura's
time of 2 hr. 28 min. 21 sec. was only 2 minutes off the women's course record
set last year by Sarah Rawlings. Kathy Lasker and Lisa Peterson finished second
and third, respectively. Laura's victory came on the heels of her performance at
the NCAA Track and Field Championships, in which she placed second running for
Colorado State.
</p>

<table border="5" cellspacing="0" cellpadding="4" width="500" align="right" bgcolor="white"
  bordercolor="brown" bordercolorlight="tan">
   <caption align="top"><b>Race Results</b></caption>
   <tr bgcolor="yellow">
      <th colspan="2">Runner</th>
      <th>Time</th>
      <th>Origin</th>
   </tr>
```

One problem you have with the current layout is that the total width of the article is limited to 500 pixels, yet the race results table alone is 500 pixels. In order to make the text wrap around the results table, you need to reduce the width of the table. Kevin suggests a new width of 300 pixels. However, with a smaller table, the text entries no longer fit as neatly into the individual cells. One solution is to use the <font> tag to reduce the size of the text in the table.

It would be convenient if you could apply the <font> tag to all of the text in the table at once, but the <font> tag cannot be applied that way. In order to change the size of the table text, you need to insert a <font> tag into each cell. You decide to set the size of the caption, table headings, and the Men and Women cells to size "2", and all other text in the table to size "1". You may find the following steps easier to complete by using the copy and paste feature of your text editor.

To change the size of the text in the race results table:

1. Within articles.htm, locate the **<table>** tag for the race results table and change the width of the table from "500" to **"300"**.

   Please refer to Figure 4-61 as you enter the code specified in the following steps.

2. Insert the tag **<font size="2">** immediately before the <b> tag in the table caption, and then insert a closing **</font>** tag immediately after the closing </b> tag in the table caption.

3. Enclose the text for all of the table headings in **<font size="2">** tags.

4. Locate the table cell containing the text "Men", and enclose that text with the **<font size="2">** tag.

5. Locate the table cell containing the text "Women", and enclose that text with the **<font size="2">** tag.

6. Enclose the remaining text in the race results table with the **<font size="1">** tags. Figure 4-61 shows the revised code for the table.

Figure 4-61 — CHANGING THE FONT SIZE IN THE RACE RESULTS TABLE

```html
<table border="5" cellspacing="0" cellpadding="4" width="300" align="right" bgcolor="white"
  bordercolor="brown" bordercolorlight="tan">
  <caption align="top"><font size="2"><b>Race Results</b></font></caption>
  <tr bgcolor="yellow">
    <th colspan="2"><font size="2">Runner</font></th>
    <th><font size="2">Time</font></th>
    <th><font size="2">Origin</font></th>
  </tr>
  <tr>
    <td rowspan="3" valign="top" bgcolor="lightblue"><font size="2">Men</font></td>
    <td><font size="1">1. Peter Teagan</font></td>
    <td align="right"><font size="1">2:12:34</font></td>
    <td><font size="1">San Antonio, Texas</font></td>
  </tr>
  <tr>
    <td><font size="1">2. Kyle Wills</font></td>
    <td align="right"><font size="1">2:13:05</font></td>
    <td><font size="1">Billings, Montana</font></td>
  </tr>
  <tr>
    <td><font size="1">3. Jason Wu</font></td>
    <td align="right"><font size="1">2:14:28</font></td>
    <td><font size="1">Cutler, Colorado</font></td>
  </tr>
  <tr>
    <td rowspan="3" valign="top" bgcolor="lightgreen"><font size="2">Women</font></td>
    <td><font size="1">1. Laura Blake</font></td>
    <td align="right"><font size="1">2:28:21</font></td>
    <td><font size="1">Park City, Colorado</font></td>
  </tr>
  <tr>
    <td><font size="1">2. Kathy Lasker</font></td>
    <td align="right"><font size="1">2:30:11</font></td>
    <td><font size="1">Chicago, Illinois</font></td>
  </tr>
  <tr>
    <td><font size="1">3. Lisa Peterson</font></td>
    <td align="right"><font size="1">2:31:14</font></td>
    <td><font size="1">Seattle, Washington</font></td>
  </tr>
</table>
```

7. Save your changes to articles.htm and reload it in your Web browser. Figure 4-62 shows the current appearance of the page.

Figure 4-62   **ARTICLES PAGE WITH THE MARATHON STORY**

Local Woman Wins Marathon

Park City native, **Laura Blake**, won the 27th Front Range Marathon over an elite field of the best long distance runners in the country. Laura's time of 2 hr. 28 min. 21 sec. was only 2 minutes off the women's course record set last year by Sarah Rawlings. Kathy Lasker and Lisa Peterson finished second and third, respectively. Laura's victory came on the heels of her performance at the NCAA Track and Field Championships, in which she placed second running for Colorado State.

In an exciting race, **Peter Teagan** of San Antonio, Texas, used a finishing kick to win the men's marathon for the second straight year, in a time of 2 hr. 12 min. 34 sec. Ahead for much of the race, Kyle Wills of Billings, Montana, finished second, when he could not match Teagan's finishing pace.

Race Results

	Runner	Time	Origin
Men	1. Peter Teagan	2:12:34	San Antonio, Texas
	2. Kyle Wills	2:13:05	Billings, Montana
	3. Jason Wu	2:14:28	Cutler, Colorado
Women	1. Laura Blake	2:28:21	Park City, Colorado
	2. Kathy Lasker	2:30:11	Chicago, Illinois
	3. Lisa Peterson	2:31:14	Seattle, Washington

Jason Wu of Cutler, Colorado, placed third in a very competitive field.

This year's race through downtown Boulder boasted the largest field in the marathon's history, with over 9500 men and 6700 women competing. Race conditions were perfect with low humidity and temperatures that never exceeded 85°.

TROUBLE? It's easy to make a mistake in the set of steps outlined here. Make sure that each <font> tag is placed *inside* the <td>, <th>, or <caption> tags and that you've included the closing </font> tag within each cell. Another possible source of error is to neglect to include a closing double quotation mark around the attribute values. Carefully compare your HTML code to the code shown in Figure 4-61.

Next you need to insert the article about the reopening of Highway 6 in the second table cell. The text for this file has been created for you and is in highway.htm.

To insert the contents of highway.htm in the second table cell:

1. Open **highway.htm** from the tutorial.04/tutorial folder of your Data Disk in your text editor.

2. Copy the HTML code contained between the <body> tags of highway.htm.

3. Close highway.htm and open **articles.htm** with your text editor if it is not currently open.

4. Paste the copied HTML code into articles.htm immediately after the comment tag, <!-- Highway story--> as shown in Figure 4-63.

Figure 4-63	INSERTING THE CONTENTS OF HIGHWAY.HTM

contents of the
highway.htm file
pasted here

```
<tr>
  <td width="300" valign="top">
  <!-- Highway story -->
  <h3 align="center"><font face="Arial, Helvetica, sans-serif">Highway 6 Reopens</font></h3>

  <p>Highway 6 will reopen this Friday, May 3<sup>rd</sup>, after a final safety
  inspection. A late blizzard delayed road crews, marking this as one of the
  latest dates for the highway's reopening on record.</p>

  <p>Rising to an elevation of 12,351 feet at Grace Pass, Highway 6 is a main link
  between Park City and Lake Elton. The reopening of the road is one of the annual signs
  that summer is near and the tourist season will soon be upon us!</p>
  </td>

  <td width="200" valign="top" background="parch3.jpg">
  <!-- Features -->
  </td>
</tr>
```

5. Save your changes to articles.htm and reload it in your Web browser (see Figure 4-64).

Figure 4-64   ARTICLES PAGE WITH THE HIGHWAY STORY

Local Woman Wins Marathon

Park City native, **Laura Blake**, won the 27th Front Range Marathon over an elite field of the best long distance runners in the country. Laura's time of 2 hr. 28 min. 21 sec. was only 2 minutes off the women's course record set last year by Sarah Rawlings. Kathy Lasker and Lisa Peterson finished second and third, respectively. Laura's victory came on the heels of her performance at the NCAA Track and Field Championships, in which she placed second running for Colorado State.

In an exciting race, **Peter Teagan** of San Antonio, Texas, used a finishing kick to win the men's marathon for the second straight year, in a time of 2 hr. 12 min. 34 sec. Ahead for much of the race, Kyle Wills of Billings, Montana, finished second, when he could not match Teagan's finishing pace.

Jason Wu of Cutler, Colorado, placed third in a very competitive field.

Race Results

	Runner	Time	Origin
Men	1. Peter Teagan	2:12:34	San Antonio, Texas
	2. Kyle Wills	2:13:05	Billings, Montana
	3. Jason Wu	2:14:28	Cutler, Colorado
Women	1. Laura Blake	2:28:21	Park City, Colorado
	2. Kathy Lasker	2:30:11	Chicago, Illinois
	3. Lisa Peterson	2:31:14	Seattle, Washington

This year's race through downtown Boulder boasted the largest field in the marathon's history, with over 9500 men and 6700 women competing. Race conditions were perfect with low humidity and temperatures that never exceeded 85°.

Highway 6 Reopens

Highway 6 will reopen this Friday, May 3rd, after a final safety inspection. A late blizzard delayed road crews, marking this as one of the latest dates for the highway's reopening on record.

Rising to an elevation of 12,351 feet at Grace Pass, Highway 6 is a main link between Park City and Lake Elton. The reopening of the road is one of the annual signs that summer is near and the tourist season will soon be upon us!

The final piece you'll add to articles.htm is the code for the links to stories and features. The code for this cell is stored in features.htm.

To insert the contents of features.htm in a table cell:

1. Using your text editor, open **features.htm** from the tutorial.04/tutorial folder.

2. Copy the HTML code located between the <body> tags of the file.

3. Close features.htm and return to **articles.htm** in your text editor.

4. Paste the copied HTML code directly after the comment tag <!-- Features --> as shown in Figure 4-65.

Figure 4-65	INSERTING THE CONTENTS OF FEATURES.HTM

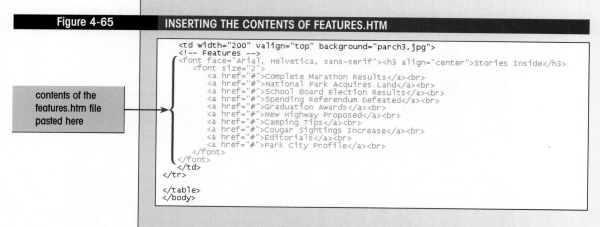

contents of the features.htm file pasted here

```
<td width="200" valign="top" background="parch3.jpg">
<!-- Features -->
<font face="Arial, Helvetica, sans-serif"><h3 align="center">Stories Inside</h3>
   <font size="2">
      <a href="#">Complete Marathon Results</a><br>
      <a href="#">National Park Acquires Land</a><br>
      <a href="#">School Board Election Results</a><br>
      <a href="#">Spending Referendum Defeated</a><br>
      <a href="#">Graduation Awards</a><br>
      <a href="#">New Highway Proposed</a><br>
      <a href="#">Camping Tips</a><br>
      <a href="#">Cougar Sightings Increase</a><br>
      <a href="#">Editorials</a><br>
      <a href="#">Park City Profile</a><br>
   </font>
</font>
</td>
</tr>

</table>
</body>
```

5. Save your changes to articles.htm and reload the file in your Web browser. The completed page appears in Figure 4-66.

Figure 4-66   **COMPLETED ARTICLES PAGE**

Local Woman Wins Marathon

 Park City native, **Laura Blake**, won the 27th Front Range Marathon over an elite field of the best long distance runners in the country. Laura's time of 2 hr. 28 min. 21 sec. was only 2 minutes off the women's course record set last year by Sarah Rawlings. Kathy Lasker and Lisa Peterson finished second and third, respectively. Laura's victory came on the heels of her performance at the NCAA Track and Field Championships, in which she placed second running for Colorado State.

In an exciting race, **Peter Teagan** of San Antonio, Texas, used a finishing kick to win the men's marathon for the second straight year, in a time of 2 hr. 12 min. 34 sec. Ahead for much of the race, Kyle Wills of Billings, Montana, finished second, when he could not match Teagan's finishing pace. Jason Wu of Cutler, Colorado, placed third in a very competitive field.

Race Results

	Runner	Time	Origin
Men	1. Peter Teagan	2:12:34	San Antonio, Texas
	2. Kyle Wills	2:13:05	Billings, Montana
	3. Jason Wu	2:14:28	Cutler, Colorado
Women	1. Laura Blake	2:28:21	Park City, Colorado
	2. Kathy Lasker	2:30:11	Chicago, Illinois
	3. Lisa Peterson	2:31:14	Seattle, Washington

This year's race through downtown Boulder boasted the largest field in the marathon's history, with over 9500 men and 6700 women competing. Race conditions were perfect with low humidity and temperatures that never exceeded 85°.

Highway 6 Reopens

Highway 6 will reopen this Friday, May 3rd, after a final safety inspection. A late blizzard delayed road crews, marking this as one of the latest dates for the highway's reopening on record.

Rising to an elevation of 12,351 feet at Grace Pass, Highway 6 is a main link between Park City and Lake Elton. The reopening of the road is one of the annual signs that summer is near and the tourist season will soon be upon us!

Stories Inside

Complete Marathon Results
National Park Acquires Land
School Board Election Results
Spending Referendum Defeated
Graduation Awards
New Highway Proposed
Camping Tips
Cougar Sightings Increase
Editorials
Park City Profile

Combining the Outer and Inner Tables

It's now time to place the code from articles.htm into page1.htm. You'll use the same copy and paste techniques that you've used to populate the other table cells.

To insert the contents of articles.htm into page1.htm:

1. Return to **articles.htm** in your text editor.

2. Copy the HTML code between the <body> tags.

3. Close articles.htm and open **page1.htm** using your text editor if it is not currently open.

4. Paste the copied HTML code from Step 2 directly after the comment tag <! -- Articles --> as shown in Figure 4-67.

Figure 4-67	INSERTING THE CONTENTS OF ARTICLES.HTM INTO PAGE1.HTM

```
        <h5><a href="#">Subscriptions</a></h5>
        <h5><a href="#">Contact Us</a></h5>
    </font>
    </td>

    <td width="500" valign="top">
    <!-- Articles -->
<table width="500" cellpadding="5" cellspacing="5">

<tr>
    <td colspan="2" valign="top">
    <!-- Marathon story -->
<h1 align="center"><font face="Arial, Helvetica, sans-serif">
 Local Woman Wins Marathon
</font></h1>

<p>
<img src="blake.jpg" align="left" hspace="5" vspace="5" width="75" height="101">
Park City native, <b>Laura Blake</b>, won the 27<sup>th</sup> Front Range Marathon
over an elite field of the best long distance runners in the country. Laura's
time of 2 hr. 28 min. 21 sec. was only 2 minutes off the women's course record
set last year by Sarah Rawlings. Kathy Lasker and Lisa Peterson finished second
and third, respectively. Laura's victory came on the heels of her performance at
the NCAA Track and Field Championships, in which she placed second running for
Colorado State.
</p>
```

contents of the articles.htm file pasted here

5. Save your changes to page1.htm and reload it in your Web browser. Figure 4-68 shows the final appearance of the front page of the Park City Gazette.

Figure 4-68   COMPLETED GAZETTE FRONT PAGE

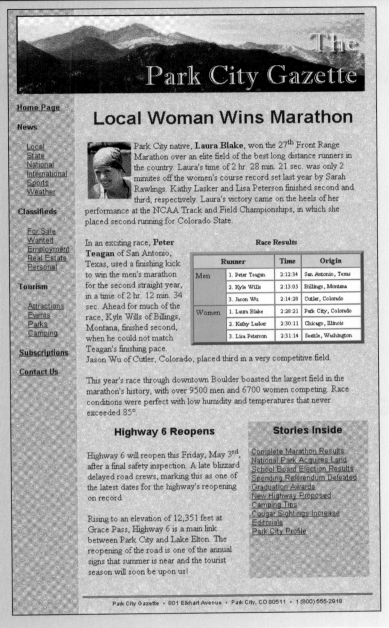

You've finished designing the Park City Gazette's front page. Using tables, you've managed to create an interesting and attractive layout. The process you followed used several principles you should keep in mind as you gain experience as a Web designer:

1. Diagram the layout before you start writing the HTML code.

2. Create the text for various columns and cells in separate files to be inserted later.

3. Create the table structure for the outer table first, and then gradually work inward.

4. Insert comment tags to identify the different sections of a Web page.

5. Indent the code for the various levels of nested tables, to make your code easier to read.

6. Test and review your code as you proceed to catch errors early in the design process.

REFERENCE WINDOW   **RW**

Using Tables to Control Page Layout

- Use cell padding and cell spacing to keep your columns from being too crowded.
- Add background colors to table cells to provide visual interest and variety.
- Use the valign="top" attribute in cells containing articles, to ensure that the text flows from the top down.
- Use row spanning to vary the size and starting point of articles within your columns. Having all articles start and end within the same row creates a static layout that can be difficult to read.
- If possible, avoid using more than three columns of text. Too many columns can make column widths too narrow and make the text hard to read.

You show the final version of the Web page to Kevin and he's pleased you were able to create a Web page that closely resembles his original design sketch. He decides to use this layout for future issues of the Gazette. As he compiles new articles, he may look for your help in providing design assistance.

Session 4.3 QUICK | CHECK

1. What HTML code would you use to create a 2 × 2 table nested inside the upper-left cell of another 2 × 2 table?

2. What HTML code is used to insert the comment "Nested table starts here"?

3. If you wanted to change the font color of all cells in a table to red, how would you enter the HTML code?

4. What HTML code would you use to insert the text "Headlines" into a table cell in an h1 heading with an Arial, Helvetica, or sans-serif font?

5. What is the first thing you should do when creating a table layout?

REVIEW ASSIGNMENTS

Kevin has another page of the Park City Gazette to place on the Web site. Cougar sightings have recently increased in the Park City area, causing great concern for both local residents and tourists. Kevin has written an article describing the sightings and providing safety tips for effectively handling a cougar encounter. Kevin has also created a table, shown in Figure 4-69, listing local cougar sightings for the last six months. Kevin would like you to include this table with his article.

Figure 4-69

LOCATION	APRIL	MAY	JUNE	JULY	AUGUST	TOTAL
Park City	0	2	1	3	4	10
Riley	2	1	1	3	2	9
Dixon	0	2	3	1	4	10
TOTAL	2	5	5	7	10	29

The articles should employ the same layout you designed for the paper's front page. Figure 4-70 shows a preview of the Web page you'll create for Kevin.

Figure 4-70

The Park City Gazette

Home Page

News

Local
State
National
International
Sports
Weather

Classifieds

For Sale
Wanted
Employment
Real Estate
Personal

Tourism

Attractions
Events
Parks
Camping

Subscriptions

Contact Us

Cougar Sightings Increase

Cougar sightings have increased 40% in the Park City area according to a report released yesterday by the state DNR. In the last month alone, there were ten sightings in Park City and the surrounding communities of Riley and Dixon. This compares to only twelve sightings for the entire spring of last year.

Reasons for the growing number of cougar sightings include increasing encroachment by people into former wildlife habitats and new wildlife regulations that result in decreasing numbers of elk and deer being taken by hunters. Cougars may be wandering into developed areas, following the herds.

DNR spokesman Steve Tasker asks residents to call the DNR report line at 555-6981 if they believe they have seen a cougar or any large predator animal. Two fatalities have already occurred in the west this year from cougar attacks.

If You Encounter a Cougar

Stop, stand tall, and don't run. A cougar's instinct is to chase.

Try to appear larger than the cougar by raising your arms.

Back away slowly, always keeping eye contact.

If the cougar displays aggressive behavior, shout and wave your arms. Convince the cougar that you are not prey, but a potential danger.

In the case of an attack, stay on your feet and fight back aggressively.

Cougar Sightings This Year

Location	Jan	Feb	Mar	Apr	May	TOTAL
Park City	0	2	1	3	4	10
Riley	2	1	1	3	2	9
Dixon	0	2	3	1	4	10
TOTAL	2	5	5	7	10	29

Park City Gazette · 801 Elkhart Avenue · Park City, CO 80511 · 1 (800) 555-2918

To complete this task:

1. Using your text editor, open **sighttxt.htm** located in the tutorial.04/review folder of your Data Disk and save it as **sighting.htm**.

2. Below the last paragraph in the story, insert a table with the following attributes:
   - The table should be 300 pixels wide with a 7-pixel-wide border.
   - The cell spacing should be set to 0 pixels. The cell padding should be set to 2 pixels.
   - The table should have a white background. The color of the table border should be brown. The light border color should be tan.
   - The table should be centered on the page.

Explore

3. Apply gridlines to the rows of the table only (HINT: Use the rules attribute).

4. Insert the caption "Cougar Sightings This Year" in a bold font above the table.

5. Insert the table entries shown in Figure 4-69. Create the cells in the table's first row using the <th> tag. Give the table headings and the table's first row a pink background. Display the text, "TOTAL", in the last row of the first column in a bold font.

6. Right-align all numeric values in the table.

7. Save your changes to sighting.htm and print the HTML code.

8. Using your text editor, open **art2txt.htm** and save it as **article2.htm**.

9. Below the <body> tag, insert a table that is 500 pixels wide with a cell spacing value of 3 and a cell padding value of 5.

10. Create a cell on the first row of the table that spans two columns, and identify this cell with the comment "Cougar headline". Within this cell, insert a centered h1 heading that contains the text "Cougar Sightings Increase". Display the headline in an Arial, Helvetica, or sans-serif font.

11. In the second row of the table, insert a cell that is 300 pixels wide and spans two rows. Vertically align the text of this cell with the cell's top border. Identify this cell with the comment "Cougar story". Insert the contents of the **sighting.htm** file (excluding the <body> tags) into this cell.

12. Also in the table's second row, insert a cell that is 200 pixels wide. Identify this cell with the comment "Cougar photo". Display the image, cougar.jpg, in the cell.

13. In the table's third row, insert a cell that is 200 pixels wide, has a red background, and align the cell text with the cell's top border. Insert the comment "Cougar tips" for this cell. Insert the contents of the **tips.htm** file (excluding the <body> tags) into this cell.

14. Save your changes to article2.htm and print the HTML code.

15. Using your text editor, open **page2txt.htm** and save it as **page2.htm**.

16. Locate the Articles cell in the main table of this file (it will be the third cell). Insert the contents of **article2.htm**. Save your changes to the file and view its contents with your Web browser.

17. Hand in your files and printouts to your instructor.

CASE PROBLEMS

Case 1. dHome, Inc. dHome is one of the nation's leading manufacturers of geodesic dome houses. Olivia Moore, the director of advertising for dHome, has hired you to work on the company's Web site. She has provided you with all of the text you need for the Web page, and your job is to design the page's layout. Olivia would like each page in the Web site to display the company logo, a column of links, a footer displaying additional hypertext links, and another footer displaying the company's address and phone number. In the center of the page, she would like you to place the appropriate text for the topic of that particular Web page. Figure 4-71 shows a preview of the company's Web page.

Figure 4-71

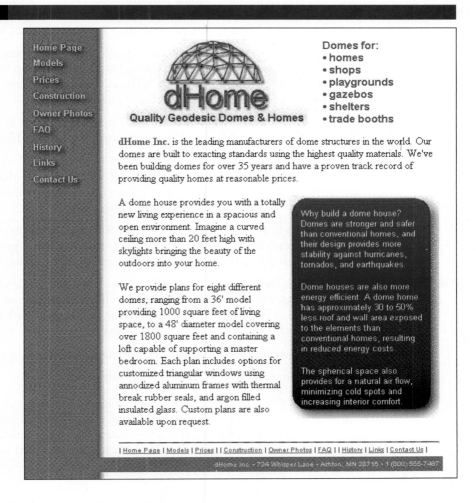

To create the dHome Web page:

1. Using your text editor, open **introtxt.htm** from the tutorial.04/case1 folder of your Data Disk and save it as **intro.htm**.

2. Between the first and the second paragraphs, create a table 224 pixels wide and 348 pixels high. Set the cell padding and cell spacing values to zero. Align the table with the right margin of the Web page.

Explore

3. The table should have a single row with three columns. The first cell should be 20 pixels wide, using the **back3.jpg** file for its background.

4. The second cell should be 200 pixels wide, using the **back4.jpg** file as a background. Insert the contents of the uses.htm file into this cell.

5. The third cell should be 30 pixels wide and use the **back4.jpg** file as its background.

6. Save your changes to intro.htm and print the file.

7. Using your text editor, open **dhometxt.htm** and save it as **dhome.htm**.

8. Within the file, create a table 620 pixels wide with a cell padding of 5 and a cell spacing of zero.

9. The first row of the table should have three cells. The first cell should be 120 pixels wide and span 3 rows. Within this cell, insert the **links.jpg** image, aligning it with the cell's top border. Identify this cell with the comment tag "List of links".

10. The second cell should be 300 pixels wide. Within this cell insert the company's logo, found in the dhome.jpg file. Align the logo with the cell's top border. For non-graphical browsers, provide the alternate text "dHome Quality Geodesic Domes & Homes". Identify this cell with the comment tag "Company logo".

11. The third cell should be 200 pixels wide. Insert the contents of the textbox.htm file into this cell. Align the text of the cell with the cell's top border. Identify the cell with the comment "Text box".

12. In the table's second row, create a single cell 500 pixels wide that spans two columns. Insert the contents of the intro.htm file into this cell. Align the text with the top of the cell. Identify the cell with the comment "Intro text".

13. In the table's third row, create another cell 500 pixels wide that spans two columns. Within this cell, insert the contents of the footer.htm file, aligning the contents with the top of the cell. Identify the contents of this cell with the comment "Footer".

Explore

14. In the fourth and last row of the table, create a cell 620 pixels wide and 15 pixels high, that spans three columns. Use **back2.jpg** as the background image for the cell. Insert the contents of the **address.htm** file into the cell, aligned with the cell's right border. Identify the cell with the comment, "Address".

15. Save your changes to the file, and print the final version of the code.

16. Hand in your printouts and files to your instructor.

Case 2. Chamberlain Civic Center. The Chamberlain Civic Center of Chamberlain, Iowa, is in the process of designing a Web page to advertise its events and activities. Stacy Dawes, the director of the publicity, has asked you to create a Web page describing the events in February shown in the following list. Ticket prices are provided in parentheses.

- Every Sunday, the Carson Quartet plays at 1 p.m. ($8)
- February 1, 8 p.m.: Taiwan Acrobats ($16/$24/$36)
- February 5, 8 p.m.: Joey Gallway ($16/$24/$36)
- February 7–8, 7 p.m.: Joey Gallway ($24/$36/$64)
- February 10, 8 p.m.: Jazz Masters ($18/$24/$32)
- February 13, 8 p.m.: Harlem Choir ($18/$24/$32)
- February 14, 8 p.m.: Chamberlain Symphony ($18/$24/$32)
- February 15, 8 p.m.: Edwin Drood ($24/$36/$44)
- February 19, 8 p.m.: The Yearling ($8/$14/$18)

- February 21, 8 p.m.: An Ellington Tribute ($24/$32/$48)
- February 22, 8 p.m.: Othello ($18/$28/$42)
- February 25, 8 p.m.: Madtown Jugglers ($12/$16/$20)
- February 28, 8 p.m.: Robin Williams ($32/$48/$64)

Figure 4-72 shows a preview of the Web page you'll create for Stacy.

Figure 4-72

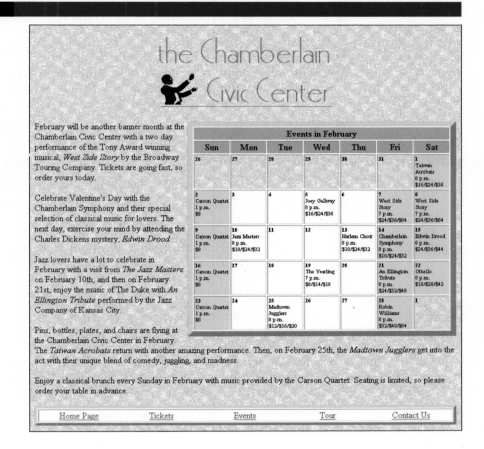

To create the CCC calendar:

1. Using your text editor, open **febtxt.htm** from the tutorial.04/case2 folder of your Data Disk and save it as **feb.htm**.

2. Below the first <p> tag, insert a table with the following attributes:

   - The table should be aligned with the right margin of the Web page.
   - The table border should be 10 pixels wide. The color of the table border should be red and pink.
   - The background color of the table should be white.

Explore 3. Within the table, create a column group spanning seven columns. These columns represent the seven days of the week in the calendar table. Set the width of the columns to 60 pixels and align the text in the column group with the top of each cell.

Explore 4. Within the column group, assign the first column a background color of pink. Assign a background color of white to the next four columns, and assign a background color of pink to the last two columns.

5. In the table's first row, create a heading that spans seven columns. Insert the text "Events in February" centered horizontally within the cell. Make the background color light blue.

6. In the table's second row, insert the following table headings: "Sun", "Mon", "Tue", "Wed", "Thu", "Fri", and "Sat". Make the background color light blue.

7. The next five rows contain the individual days from the calendar, each placed in a separate table cell. Format the dates as follows:

   ■ The font size of each cell should be "1". (HINT: Enclose the contents of the cell in a <font> tag.)

   ■ Display the day of the month on its own line, formatted with a boldfaced font.

   ■ If there is an event for that date, display the name of the event on one line, the time the event takes place on the second line, and the ticket price on a third line. Separate one line from another using the <br> tag.

   ■ If the date is not in the month of February, use the back.jpg image as the cell's background.

Explore 8. At the bottom of the Web page, insert a table with the following attributes:

   ■ The width of the table should be 100% of the width of the Web page.

   ■ The table should have a 5-pixel-wide border in red and pink.

   ■ The background color of the table should be white.

Explore 9. The bottom table should contain a single row with five columns. Make the width of each cell 20% of the width of the table. Enter the following text into the five cells: "Home Page", "Tickets", "Events", "Tour", and "Contact Us". Make each entry a hypertext link that, for the moment, points to the current file.

Explore 10. Use the <col> tag to horizontally center the contents of five cells in the bottom table.

Explore 11. Remove all gridlines from the bottom table. (HINT: Use the rules attribute.)

12. Save your changes to the file and print your HTML code. Using your Web browser, verify that the table displays correctly. Note that Netscape users will not see the results of creating a column group or removing the gridlines from the bottom table.

13. Hand in your printouts and files to your instructor.

Case 3. Dunston Retreat Center. The Dunston Retreat Center, located in northern Wisconsin, offers weekends of quiet and solitude for all who visit. The center, started by a group of Trappist monks, has grown in popularity over the last few years as more people have become aware of its services. The director of the center, Benjamin Adams, wants to advertise the center on the Internet and has asked you to create a Web site for the center. The Web site includes a welcome message from Benjamin Adams, a list of upcoming events, a letter from one of the center's guests, and a description of the current week's events. The Web page you'll create is shown in Figure 4-73.

Figure 4-73

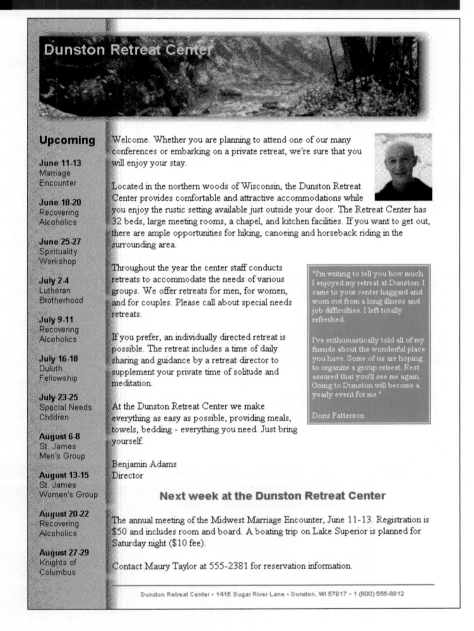

To create the Dunston Retreat Center Web page:

1. Using your text editor, open **welctxt.htm** located in the tutorial.04/case3 folder of your Data Disk and save it as **welcome.htm**.

2. At the top of the third paragraph, insert a table with the following attributes:

   - Align the table with the page's right margin
   - The table's border and cell padding should be 5 pixels
   - The border color should be white. The table background should be equal to the hexadecimal color value 8080FF.

3. Within the table insert a single cell 180 pixels wide, with the text aligned with the top of the cell. Insert the contents of the **letter.htm** file into the cell.

4. Save your changes to welcome.htm and print the code.

5. Using your text editor, open **dunsttxt.htm** and save it as **dunston.htm**.

6. Create a table 620 pixels wide with cell spacing and cell padding values of 5 within the file.

7. In the first row of the table, insert a single cell two columns wide containing the image **dlogo.jpg**. Center the contents of the cell.

8. The second row of the table should contain two cells. The first cell should be 100 pixels wide, spanning three rows. It should contain the contents of the events.htm file, aligned with the cell's top border.

9. The second cell should be 520 pixels wide. It should contain the contents of **welcome.htm** that you just created and be aligned with the top border of the cell.

10. In the third row of the table, insert a single cell 520 pixels wide containing the contents of **next.htm**, and align the text with the top of the cell.

11. The table's fourth row contains a single cell 520 pixels wide. In this cell, insert the contents of **address.htm** and center it horizontally within the cell.

12. Save your changes to the file and print the HTML code. Open the file in your Web browser and verify that the layout displays correctly.

13. Hand in your files and printouts to your instructor.

Case 4. TravelWeb E-ZineMagazine. TravelWeb provides useful material to online subscribers. You have joined the staff of TravelWeb, which publishes travel information and tips, and you have been asked to work on the layout for the Web page. You've been given files that you should use in creating the page that are listed and described in Figure 4-74.

Figure 4-74

FILE	DESCRIPTION
luxair.txt	Article about LuxAir reducing airfares to Europe
photo.txt	Article about the Photo of the Week
ppoint.jpg	Large version of the Photo of the Week (320 x 228)
ppoint2.jpg	Small version of the Photo of the Week (180 x 128)
toronto.txt	Article about traveling to Toronto
twlinks.htm	Links to other TravelWeb pages (list version)
twlinks2.htm	Links to other TravelWeb pages (table version)
twlogo.jpg	Image file of the TravelWeb logo (425 x 105)
yosemite.txt	Article about limiting access to Yosemite National Park
yosemite.jpg	Image file of Yosemite National Park (112 x 158)

To create a Web page for TravelWeb:

1. Use the files listed in Figure 4-74 to create a newspaper-style page. All of these files are stored in the tutorial.04/case4 folder on your Data Disk. The page should include several columns, but the number, size, and layout of the columns is up to you.

2. Use all of the files on the page, with the following exceptions: use only one of the two files twlinks.htm or twlinks2.htm, and use only one of the two image files ppoint.jpg or ppoint2.jpg. Note that not all of the links on this Web page point to existing files.

3. Use background colors to give the Web page an attractive and interesting appearance.

4. Include comment tags to describe the different parts of your page layout.

5. Save your page as **tw.htm** in the tutorial.04/case4 folder.

6. Print a copy of the Web page and the HTML code.

QUICK | CHECK ANSWERS

Session 4.1

1. Text tables and graphical tables. Text tables are supported by all browsers and are easier to create. The graphical table is more difficult to create but provides the user with a wealth of formatting options.

2. A proportional font assigns different widths to each character based on the width of the character. A fixed-width font assigns the same width to each character regardless of width.

3. The <pre> tag

4. The <table> tag identifies the beginning of a table. The <tr> tag identifies the start of a table row. The <td> tag identifies individual table cells, and the <th> tag identifies table cells that act as table headings.

5. The number of rows in a table is determined by the number of <tr> tags. The number of columns is equal to the largest number of <td> and <th> tags within a single table row.

6. Text within the <th> tag is automatically bolded and centered within the table cell.

7. <caption align="bottom">Product Catalog</caption>

   Place this tag anywhere between the <table> and </table> tags.

Session 4.2

1. <table border="5" cellspacing="3" cellpadding="4">

2. <td valign="top">

   or

   <th valign="top">

3. <tr align="center">

4. In pixels or as a percentage of the display area. Use pixels if you want to control the size of the table. Use percentages if you want your table to adapt to the user's monitor resolution.

5. <table width="50%">

6. <td width="60">

   or

   <th width="60">

   This keeps the cell from exceeding 60 pixels in width. The only way to guarantee that all cells will be exactly 60 pixels wide is to set the width of all cells in that table column to 60 pixels.

7. <table bgcolor="yellow">

   This attribute is not supported by earlier browsers.

8. <td rowspan="3" colspan="2">

   or

   <th rowspan="3" colspan="2">

Session 4.3

1. <table

```
<tr>
        <td>
        <table><tr><td></td><td></td></tr>
               <tr><td></td><td></td></tr>
        </table>
        </td>
        <td></td>
</tr>
<tr>
        <td></td>
        <td></td>
</tr>
</table>
```

2. <! Nested table starts here>

3. Separate <font> tags would have to be placed within each table cell.

4. <td><h1><font face="Arial, Helvetica, sans-serif">Headlines</font></h1></td>

5. Diagram the layout.

USING FRAMES IN A WEB SITE

Using Frames to Display Multiple Web Pages

CASE

The Yale Climbing School

One of the most popular climbing schools and touring agencies in Colorado is the Yale Climbing School (YCS). Located in Vale Park, outside Rocky Mountain National Park, YCS specializes in teaching beginning and advanced climbing techniques. The school also sponsors several tours, leading individuals on some of the most exciting, challenging, and picturesque climbs in North America. The school has been in business for 15 years and, in that time, it has helped thousands of people experience the mountains in ways they never thought possible.

Yale Climbing School has a lot of competition from other climbing schools and touring groups in the area. Debbie Chen is the owner of the school and is always looking for ways to market her programs and improve the visibility of the school. Early on, she decided to use the Internet and the World Wide Web as a means of promoting the school, and she has already created many Web pages.

Debbie has seen other Web sites use frames to display several Web pages in a single browser window. She feels that frames would be a good way to highlight all that the school has to offer potential students. She asks you to help develop a frame-based Web site for the YCS.

SESSION 5.1

In this session you'll create a Web site that contains frames. You'll use the HTML tags that control the placement and appearance of frames, and you'll learn how to specify a source document for each frame and how to nest one set of frames inside another.

Introducing Frames

Typically, as a Web site grows in size and complexity, each page is dedicated to a particular topic or group of topics. One page might contain a list of hypertext links, another page might display contact information for the company or organization, and another page might describe the business philosophy. As more pages are added to the site, the designer might wish for a way to display information from several pages at the same time.

One solution is to duplicate that information across the Web site, but that presents problems as well. It requires a great deal of time and effort to repeat (or copy and paste) the same information over and over again. Also, each time a change is required, you need to repeat your edit for each page in the site—a process that could easily result in error.

Such considerations contributed to the creation of frames. A **frame** is a section of the browser window capable of displaying the contents of an entire Web page. Figure 5-1 shows an example of a browser window containing two frames. The frame on the left displays the contents of a Web page containing a list of hypertext links. The frame on the right displays a Web page with product information.

Figure 5-1   **EXAMPLE OF FRAMES**

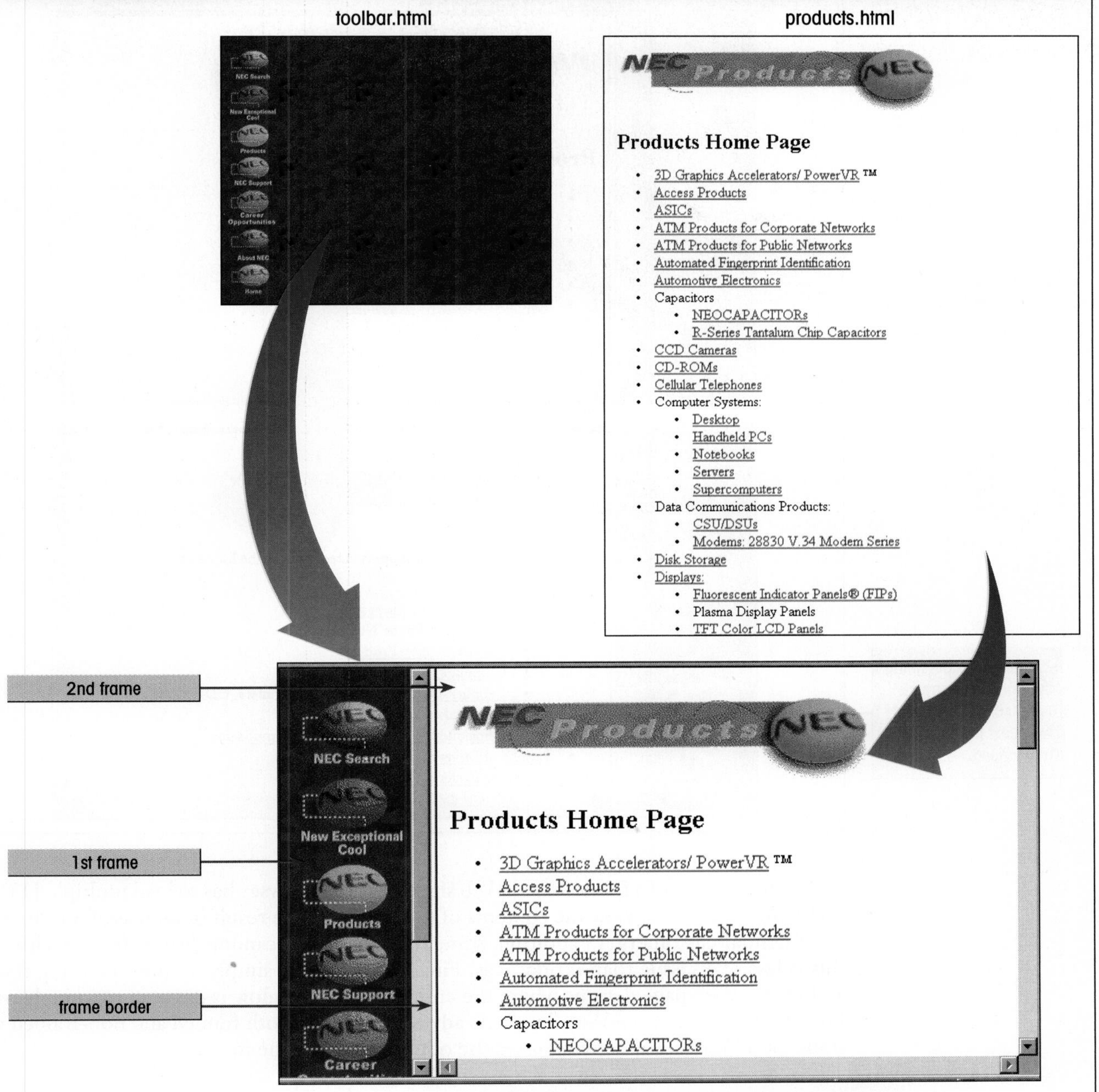

Both files are joined into a single page using frames

This example illustrates a common use of frames: displaying a table of contents in one frame, while showing individual pages from the site in another. Figure 5-2 illustrates how a list of hypertext links can remain on the screen while the user navigates through the contents of the site. An advantage for the designer is that the list of links can be easily updated because it is stored on only one page.

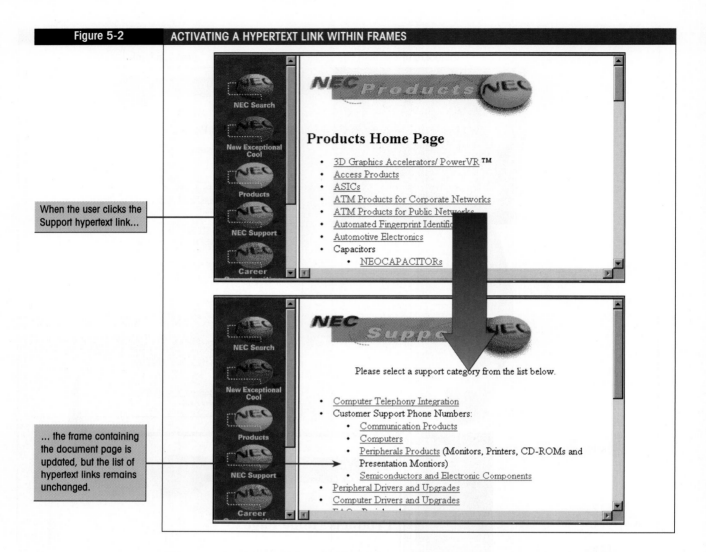

Figure 5-2   ACTIVATING A HYPERTEXT LINK WITHIN FRAMES

When the user clicks the Support hypertext link...

... the frame containing the document page is updated, but the list of hypertext links remains unchanged.

A consequence of a frame-based Web site is that the browser has to load multiple HTML files before a user can view the contents of the site. This can result in increased waiting time for potential customers. In addition, some older browsers cannot display frames, although this is less of an issue than it once was. Finally, some users simply do not like using frames and prefer Web page designs where the entire browser window is devoted to a single page. For these reasons, some Web designers advocate creating both framed and non-framed versions for a Web site and giving users the option of which one to use.

Planning **Your Frames**

Before you start creating your frames, it is a good idea to plan their appearance and how they are to be used. There are several issues to consider:

- What information will be displayed in each of the frames?
- How do you want the frames placed on the Web page? What is the size of each frame?
- Which frames will be static, that is, always showing the same content?
- Which frames will change in response to hypertext links being clicked?
- What Web pages will users first see when they access the site?
- Should users be permitted to resize the frames to suit their needs?

As you progress with your design for the Web site for the Yale Climbing School, you'll consider each of these questions. Debbie has already created the Web pages for the YCS Web site. Figure 5-3 describes the different Web pages you'll work with in this project.

Figure 5-3	DOCUMENTS AT THE YCS WEB SITE	
TOPIC	**FILENAME**	**CONTENT**
Biographies	staff.htm	Links to biographical pages of the YCS staff
Home page	home.htm	The YCS home page
Lessons	lessons.htm	Climbing lessons offered by the YCS
Logo	head.htm	A page containing the company logo
Philosophy	philosoph.htm	Statement of the YCS's business philosophy
Table of contents	links.htm	Links to the YCS pages
Tours	diamond.htm	Description of the Diamond climbing tour
Tours	eldorado.htm	Description of the Eldorado Canyon tour
Tours	grepon.htm	Description of the Petit Grepon climbing tour
Tours	kieners.htm	Description of the Kiener's Route climbing tour
Tours	lumpy.htm	Description of the Lumpy Ridge climbing tour
Tours	nface.htm	Description of the North Face climbing tour

Debbie has organized the pages by topic, such as tour descriptions, climbing lessons, and company philosophy. Two of the files, links.htm and staff.htm, do not focus on a particular topic but contain hypertext links to other YCS Web pages. How should this material for YCS be organized on the Web site, and what information should the user see first?

Debbie has considered these questions carefully and has sketched a layout that illustrates how she would like the frames to be organized. See Figure 5-4.

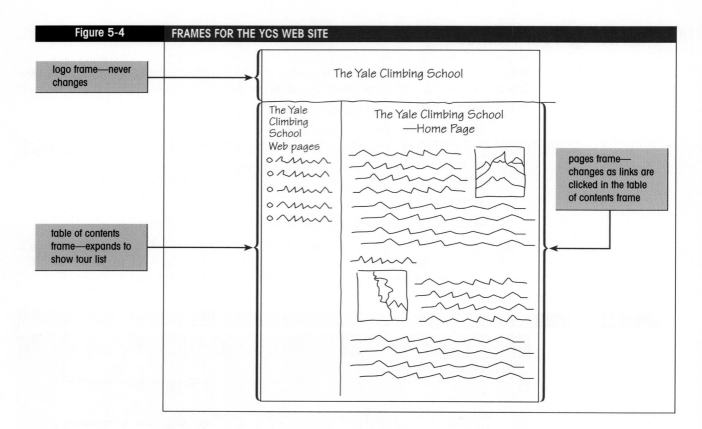

Figure 5-4 — FRAMES FOR THE YCS WEB SITE

logo frame—never changes

table of contents frame—expands to show tour list

The Yale Climbing School

The Yale Climbing School Web pages

The Yale Climbing School —Home Page

pages frame— changes as links are clicked in the table of contents frame

Debbie would like you to create three frames. The top frame displays the school's logo and address. The frame on the left displays a list of the Web pages at the YCS Web site. Finally, the frame on the lower-right displays the content of those pages.

Your first task is to enter the HTML code for the frame layout Debbie has described.

Creating a Frame Layout

The general syntax for creating an HTML file with frames is:

```
<html>
<head>
<title>Page Title</title>
</head>
<frameset>
    Frame Definitions
</frameset>
</html>
```

In this code, the <frameset> tag is used to store the definitions of the various frames in the file. These definitions will typically include the size and location of the frames, as well as the Web pages the frames display.

Note that the code does not include an opening and closing <body> tag. The reason for this is that this HTML file displays the contents of other Web pages; technically, it is not a Web page. Later in the tutorial, we'll explore situations where you would include a <body> tag in order to support browsers that do not display frames. For now, we'll concentrate on defining the appearance and content of the frames.

Specifying Frame Size and Orientation

To create a frame layout, you use the rows and cols attributes of the <frameset> tag. The rows attribute creates a row of frames, while the cols attribute creates a column of frames. You cannot use both attributes within a single <frameset> tag. You must choose to lay out your frames in either rows or columns (see Figure 5-5).

Figure 5-5	FRAMES DEFINED IN EITHER ROWS OR COLUMNS

Frames laid out in columns

The first frame	The second frame	The third frame

Frames laid out in rows

The first frame

The second frame

The third frame

The syntax for creating a row or column frame layout is:

```
<frameset rows="row height 1, row height 2, row height 3,
. . .">
```

or

```
<frameset cols="column width 1, column width 2, column
width 3, . . .">
```

where *row height* is the height of each row, and *column width* is the width of each column. There is no limit to the number of rows or columns you can specify for a frameset.

Row and column sizes can be specified in three ways: in pixels, as a percentage of the total size of the frameset, or by an asterisk (*). The asterisk instructs the browser to allocate any unclaimed space in the frameset to the particular row or column. For example, the tag <frameset rows="160,*"> creates two rows of frames. The first row has a height of 160 pixels, and the height of the second row is equal to whatever space remains in the display area. You can combine the three methods. The tag <frameset cols="160,25%,*"> lays out the frames in the columns shown in Figure 5-6. The first column is 160 pixels wide, the second column is 25% of the width of the display area, and the third column covers whatever space is left.

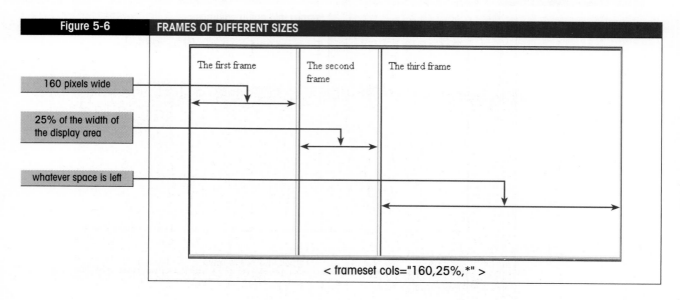

Figure 5-6   **FRAMES OF DIFFERENT SIZES**

160 pixels wide

25% of the width of the display area

whatever space is left

The first frame   The second frame   The third frame

< frameset cols="160,25%,*" >

It is a good idea to specify at least one of the rows or columns of your <frameset> tag with an asterisk to ensure that the frames fill up the screen regardless of a user's monitor settings. You can also use multiple asterisks. In that case, the browser divides the remaining display space equally among the frames with the asterisks. For example, the tag <frameset rows="*,*,*"> creates three rows of frames with equal heights.

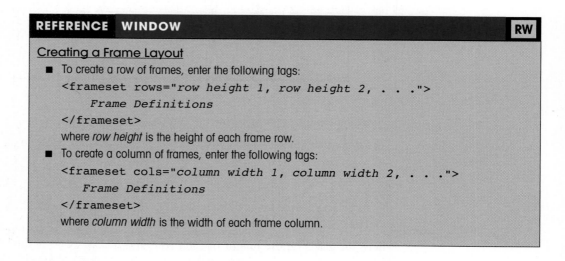

REFERENCE WINDOW   **RW**

<u>Creating a Frame Layout</u>
- To create a row of frames, enter the following tags:
  ```
  <frameset rows="row height 1, row height 2, . . .">
      Frame Definitions
  </frameset>
  ```
  where *row height* is the height of each frame row.
- To create a column of frames, enter the following tags:
  ```
  <frameset cols="column width 1, column width 2, . . .">
      Frame Definitions
  </frameset>
  ```
  where *column width* is the width of each frame column.

Debbie has created an HTML file that she wants you to edit in order to create the frame layout she's described.

To edit Debbie's file:

1. Using your text editor, open **yaletxt.htm** from the tutorial.05/tutorial folder on your Data Disk.

2. Save the file in the same folder as **yale.htm**.

The first set of frames you'll create for the Yale Climbing School page has two rows. The top row is used for the company logo, and the second row is used for the remaining content of the Web page. A frame that is 85 pixels high should provide enough space to display the logo. The rest of the display area is occupied by the second row.

To create the first set of frames:

1. Create a blank line directly below the </head> tag in yale.htm.

2. Insert the following HTML code:

```
<frameset rows="85,*">
</frameset>
```

This code specifies a height of 85 pixels for the top row and allocates the remaining space to the second row. Figure 5-7 shows the revised yale.htm file.

Figure 5-7	CREATING TWO ROWS OF FRAMES

tag creates two rows of frames: the first 85 pixels high and the second occupying the remaining display area

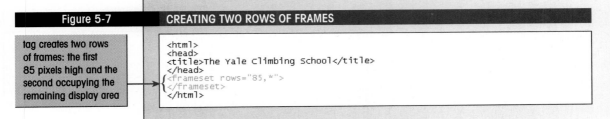

```
<html>
<head>
<title>The Yale Climbing School</title>
</head>
<frameset rows="85,*">
</frameset>
</html>
```

The initial frame layout is now defined, and you'll augment this design later to include the third frame as Debbie has specified. For now, you need to specify the source for the two frame rows that you have created.

Specifying a Frame Source

To specify a source for a frame, use the <frame> tag with the syntax:

```
<frame src="URL">
```

where *URL* is the filename and location of the page that you want to load. You must insert the <frame> tag between the opening and closing <frameset> tags.

REFERENCE WINDOW	RW

Specifying the Source for a Frame
- To specify the source for the content of a frame, enter the following HTML code:
```
<frame src="URL">
```
where *URL* is the filename and location of the page that you want to display in the frame.

The company logo is to be displayed in the top frame. Figure 5-8 provides you with a preview of the logo and its placement.

Figure 5-8   YALE.HTML CONTAINING THE YCS LOGO

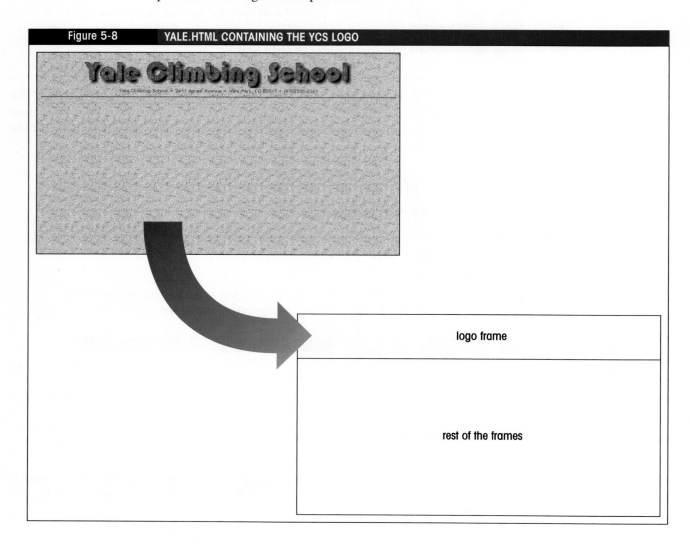

To define the YCS logo as a frame source:

1. Insert a blank line after the opening <frameset> tag line.

2. Type the following HTML code (see Figure 5-9):

```
<!-- Company Logo -->
<frame src="head.htm">
```

Figure 5-9   INSERTING A FRAME FOR THE HEAD.HTM FILE

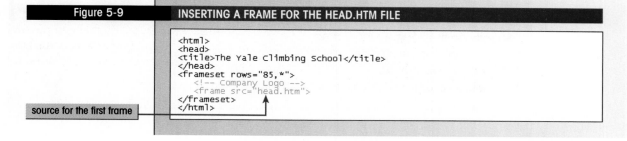

```
<html>
<head>
<title>The Yale Climbing School</title>
</head>
<frameset rows="85,*">
    <!-- Company Logo -->
    <frame src="head.htm">
</frameset>
</html>
```

source for the first frame

> Because this is the first <frame> tag, the browser displays head.htm in the first frame row. Note that using the comment tag and indenting the <frame> tag a few spaces helps make your HTML code easier to follow and interpret.

You have successfully specified the source for the first row, but what about the second row? Looking at Debbie's sketch in Figure 5-4, you notice that the second row contains two additional frames. So rather than specify a source for the second row, you need to create another set of frames.

Nesting <frameset> Tags

A frameset is defined by rows or columns, but not both. To create frames using both rows *and* columns, one frameset must be nested inside another. When you use this technique, the interpretation of the rows and cols attributes changes slightly. For example, a row height of 25% does not mean 25% of the display area, but rather 25% of the height of the frame into which that row has been inserted (or nested).

Debbie wants the second row of your current frame layout to contain two frames in separate columns. The first column displays a table of contents, and the second column displays a variety of YCS documents. You'll specify a width of 140 pixels for the first column, and whatever remains in the display area will be allotted to the second column.

To create the second set of frames:

1. Create a blank line immediately below the <frame> tag line that you just inserted.

2. Type the following HTML code:

```
<!-- Nested Frames -->
<frameset cols="140,*">
</frameset>
```

Your file should appear as shown in Figure 5-10. It is not necessary to indent the code as shown in the figure, but it makes the code easier to read and interpret.

| Figure 5-10 | CREATING A NESTED SET OF FRAMES IN THE SECOND FRAME ROW |

two columns of frames nested in the second frame row

```
<html>
<head>
<title>The Yale Climbing School</title>
</head>
<frameset rows="85,*">
   <!-- Company Logo -->
   <frame src="head.htm">
   <!-- Nested Frames -->
   <frameset cols="140,*">
   </frameset>
</frameset>
</html>
```

Next, you'll specify the sources for the two frames in the frameset. The frame in the first column displays the contents of links.htm. The Yale Climbing School home page, home.htm, is displayed in the second frame. Figure 5-11 shows the content of these two pages and their placement on the Web page.

Figure 5-11   LINK.HTM AND HOME.HTM PAGES

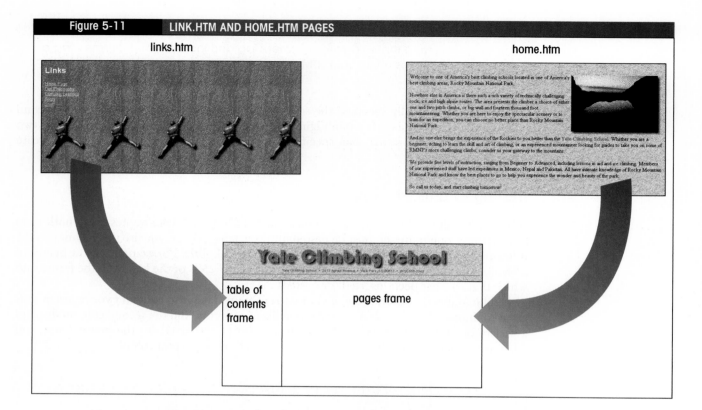

To insert the sources for the two frames:

1. Create a blank line immediately below the nested <frameset> tag you just inserted.

2. Type the following HTML code:

```
<!-- List of YCS Links -->
<frame src="links.htm">
<!-- YCS Home Page -->
<frame src="home.htm">
```

Figure 5-12 shows the code for the two new frames. It is not necessary to indent the code as shown in the figure, but it can make the code easier to read and interpret.

Figure 5-12   SOURCES FOR THE TWO FRAMES IN THE SECOND ROW

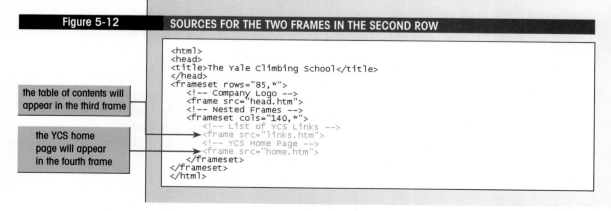

3. Save your changes to the file.

4. Using your Web browser, open **yale.htm**. Figure 5-13 shows how the Web page looks at this point.

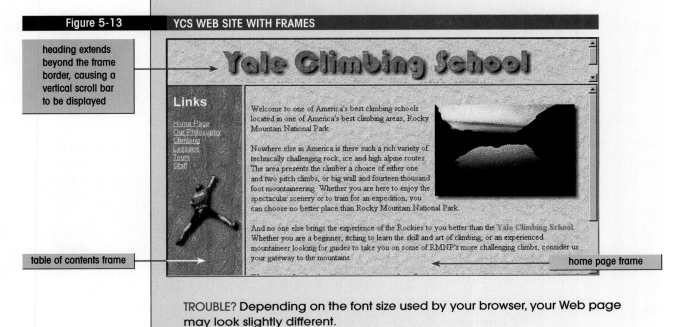

| Figure 5-13 | YCS WEB SITE WITH FRAMES |

heading extends beyond the frame border, causing a vertical scroll bar to be displayed

table of contents frame

home page frame

TROUBLE? Depending on the font size used by your browser, your Web page may look slightly different.

The browser window displays three Web pages from the YCS Web site. However, the design of the frame layout could use some refinement. Notice that the address information has been cut off in the logo frame. Because not all of the contents of this page fit into the frame, scroll bars have been added to the frame. Scroll bars do not appear in the links frame, because the entire list of links is visible. Debbie doesn't mind the appearance of scroll bars for the school's home page—she realizes that entire page won't fit into the frame—but she doesn't want scroll bars for the frame containing the school's logo and address.

Controlling **the Appearance of Your Frames**

You can control three attributes of a frame: scroll bars, the size of the margin between the source document and the frame border, and whether or not the user is allowed to change the size of the frame.

REFERENCE WINDOW   **RW**

Modifying the Appearance of Frames

- To control the appearance of scroll bars in a frame, add the scrolling attribute to the frame tag as follows:

```
<frame src="URL" scrolling="scrolling">
```

where *scrolling* can be either "yes" (scroll bars) or "no" (no scroll bars). If you do not specify the scrolling attribute, scroll bars appear only when the content of the frame source cannot fit within the boundaries of the frame.

- To control the amount of space between the frame source and the frame boundary, add the marginwidth and/or the marginheight attributes to the frame tag:

```
<frame src="URL" marginwidth="value" marginheight="value">
```

where the width and height *value* is expressed in pixels. The margin width is the space to the left and right of the frame source. The margin height is the space above and below the frame source. If you do not specify a margin height or width, the browser assigns dimensions based on the content of the frame source.

- To keep users from resizing frames, add the noresize attribute to the frame tag:

```
<frame src="URL" noresize>
```

The first attribute you'll work with is the scroll bar attribute.

Controlling the Appearance of Scroll Bars

By default, scroll bars are displayed when the content of the source page cannot fit within the frame. You can override this setting using the scrolling attribute. The syntax for this attribute is:

```
<frame src="URL" scrolling="scrolling">
```

where *scrolling* can either be "yes" (to always display scroll bars) or "no" (to never display scroll bars). If you don't specify a setting for the scrolling attribute, the browser displays scroll bars when necessary.

Debbie feels that scroll bars are inappropriate for the logo frame, and she wants to ensure that they are never displayed for that frame. Therefore, you need to add the scrolling="no" attribute to the <frame> tag. However, Debbie does want scroll bars for the other two frames, as needed, so the default value for this frame is sufficient. Note that if you are using Netscape you need to close and then open the file for the changes to the frames to take effect. If you simply click the Reload button, your changes are not displayed. This is not the case with Internet Explorer 3.0 and above, in which you can view changes to the page by clicking the Refresh button.

To remove the scroll bars from the logo frame:

1. Return to **yale.htm** in your text editor.

2. Within the <frame> tag in the logo frame, enter the attribute **scrolling="no"**, as shown in Figure 5-14.

Figure 5-14	REMOVING THE SCROLL BARS FROM THE LOGO FRAME

set the scrolling attribute to "no" to remove the scroll bars

```
<frameset rows="85,*">
   <!-- Company Logo -->
   <frame src="head.htm" scrolling="no">
   <!-- Nested Frames -->
   <frameset cols="140,*">
      <!-- List of YCS Links -->
      <frame src="links.htm">
      <!-- YCS Home Page -->
      <frame src="home.htm">
   </frameset>
</frameset>
```

3. Save your changes to yale.htm and reload it in your Web browser. Note that if you are using Netscape you might have to close and then open yale.htm for the changes to take effect.

Although the scroll bars for the logo frame have been removed, you still cannot see all of the text that is contained in head.htm. This problem can be corrected by modifying the frame margins.

When working with frames, keep in mind that you should remove scroll bars from a frame only when you are convinced that the entire Web page will be visible in the frame. To do this, you should view your Web page using several different monitor settings. Few things are more irritating to Web site visitors than to discover that some content is missing from a frame with no scroll bars available to reveal the missing content.

With that in mind, your next task is to solve the problem of the missing text from the logo frame. To do so, you need to modify the internal margins of the frame.

Controlling Frame Margins

When your browser retrieves the frame's Web page, it determines the amount of space between the content of the page and the frame border. Occasionally the browser sets the margin between the border and the content too large. Generally, you want the margin to be big enough to keep the source's text or images from running into the frame's borders. However, you do not want the margin to take up too much space, because you typically want to display as much of the source as possible.

You've already noted that the margin height for the logo frame is too large, and this has shifted some of the text beyond the border of the frame. To fix this problem, you need to specify a smaller margin for the frame so that the logo can move up and allow all of the text to be displayed in the frame.

The syntax for specifying margins for a frame is:

```
<frame src="URL" marginheight="value" marginwidth="value">
```

where, marginheight is the amount of space, in pixels, above and below the content of the page in the frame, and marginwidth is the amount of space to the left and right of the page. You do not have to specify both the margin height and width. However, if you specify only one, the browser assumes that you want to use the same value for both. Setting margin values is a process of trial and error as you determine what combination of margin sizes looks best.

To correct the problem with the logo frame, you'll decrease its margin size to 0 pixels. This setting will allow the entire page to be displayed within the frame. Also, to keep the home page from running into the borders of its frame, you'll set the frame's margin width to 10 pixels, and Debbie wants you to decrease the frame's margin height to 0 pixels. The links frame margin does not require any changes.

To set the margin sizes for the frames:

1. Return to the **yale.htm** file in your text editor.

2. Within the <frame> tag for the logo frame, enter the attribute **marginheight="0"**. This will, by default, set both the margin height and the margin width to 0.

3. Within the <frame> tag for the home page frame, enter the attributes **marginheight="0" marginwidth="10"**.

   Figure 5-15 shows the revised HTML code for yale.htm.

Figure 5-15	SPECIFYING THE MARGIN SIZES FOR THE FRAMES

height of the margin text for the logo frame will be 0 pixels

height of the margin for the home page will be 0 pixels and the width of the margin will be 10 pixels

```
<frameset rows="85,*">
   <!-- Company Logo -->
   <frame src="head.htm" scrolling="no" marginheight="0">
   <!-- Nested Frames -->
   <frameset cols="140,*">
      <!-- List of YCS Links -->
      <frame src="links.htm">
      <!-- YCS Home Page -->
      <frame src="home.htm" marginheight="0" marginwidth="10">
   </frameset>
</frameset>
```

4. Save your changes to yale.htm and reload or refresh it in your Web browser. The revised frames are shown in Figure 5-16.

Figure 5-16	YCS WEB SITE WITH RESIZED FRAME MARGINS

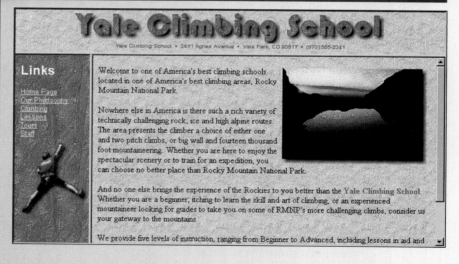

Debbie is satisfied with the changes you've made to the Web page. Your next task is to "lock in" the sizes and margins for each frame on the page to prevent users from resizing the frames.

Controlling Frame Resizing

By default, users can resize frame borders in the browser by simply dragging a frame border. However, some Web designers prefer to freeze, or lock, frames, so that users cannot resize them. This insures that the Web site displays as the designer intended. Debbie would like you to do this for the YCS Web site. The syntax for controlling frame resizing is:

```
<frame src="URL" noresize>
```

The noresize attribute is included within the <frame> tag to prevent users from modifying the sizes of your frames. You'll add this attribute now to all the frames in yale.htm.

To prevent the frames in the YCS Web site from being resized:

1. Return to **yale.htm** in your text editor.

2. Within each of the three <frame> tags in the file, add the attribute **noresize**.

3. Save your changes to yale.htm and reload it in your Web browser.

4. Verify that the frames are now "locked in" and cannot be resized by the user.

You're ready to take a break from working on the YCS Web site. Debbie is pleased with the progress you've made to the site, although there are a few things left to accomplish before your work is complete. For example, you haven't specified how the targets of the site's hypertext links should be displayed. You'll deal with this question and others in the next session.

Session 5.1 QUICK CHECK

1. What are frames, and why are they useful in displaying and designing a Web page?

2. Why is the <body> tag unnecessary for pages that contain frames?

3. What HTML code do you use to create three rows of frames with the height of the first row set to 200 pixels, the height of the second row set to 50% of the display area, and the height of the third row set to occupy the remaining space?

4. What HTML code do you use to specify home.htm as a source for a frame?

5. What HTML code do you use to remove the scroll bars from the frame for home.htm?

6. What HTML code do you use to set the size of the margin above and below the home.htm frame to 3 pixels?

7. What is the size of the margins to the right and left of the frame in Question 6?

8. What code would you use to prevent users from moving the frame borders in home.htm?

SESSION 5.2

In this session you'll learn how hypertext links work within frames, and you'll control which frame displays the source of an activated hypertext link. You'll also learn how to create a Web page that can be used by browsers that support frames and browsers that don't. Finally, you'll examine some extensions to the <frame> and <frameset> tags, and you'll learn how to create internal frames using the <iframe> tag.

Working with Frames and Hypertext Links

Now that you've created frames for the Yale Climbing School Web site, you're ready to work on the hypertext links for the Web page. The table of contents page contains the following five hypertext links (see Figure 5-17):

- The Home Page link points to home.htm
- The Our Philosophy link points to philosph.htm
- The Climbing Lessons link points to lessons.htm
- The Tours link points to tours.htm
- The Staff link points to staff.htm

Figure 5-17	PAGES IN THE YCS WEB SITE

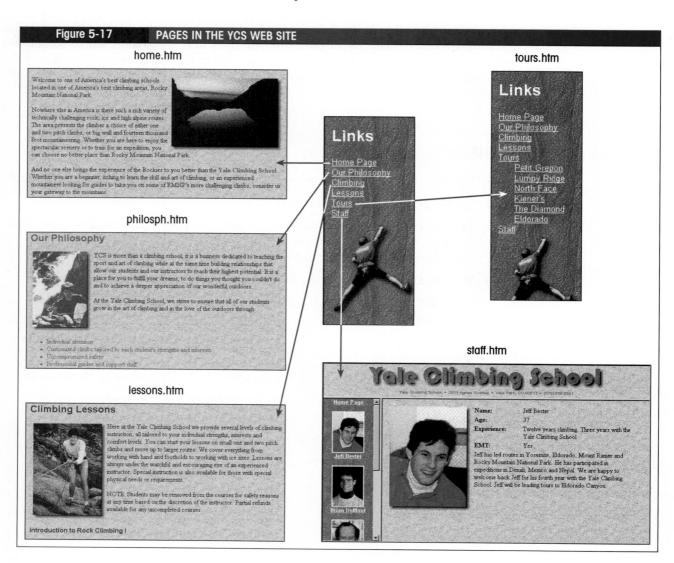

By default, clicking a hypertext link within a frame opens the linked file inside the same frame. However, this is not the way Debbie wants each of the hypertext links to work. She wants:

- the Home, Our Philosophy, and Climbing Lessons pages to display in the bottom-right frame
- the Tours page to display in the table of contents frame
- the Staff page to occupy the entire browser window

When you want to control the behavior of hyperlinks in a framed page, there are two required steps: you need to give each frame on the page a name, and then point each hypertext link to one of the named frames.

REFERENCE WINDOW   **RW**

<u>Retrieving a Page in a Specific Frame</u>

- Assign a name to the frame by editing the <frame> tag as follows:

  `<frame src="URL" name="frame_name">`

  where *frame_name* is a single word you choose to describe the content and purpose of the frame.
- Edit the <a> tag for the hyperlink, specifying a target for the link as follows:

  `<a href="URL" target="frame_name">`

  where *frame_name* is the name you assigned to the frame.
- To use the same target for all links in a page, insert the <base> tag between the file's <head> and </head> tags as follows:

  `<base target="frame_name">`
- All links on the page direct their output to the frame specified by "*frame_name*".

Assigning a Name to a Frame

To assign a name to a frame, add the name attribute to the frame tag. The syntax for this attribute is:

`<frame src="URL" name="frame_name">`

where *frame_name* is any single word you assign to the frame. Case is important in assigning names: "information" is considered a different name than "INFORMATION."

You'll name the three frames in the YCS Web site: "logo," "links," and "pages."

To assign names to the frames:

1. Using your text editor, open **yale.htm** if it is not currently open.

2. Within the tag for the logo frame, enter the attribute **name="logo"**.

3. Within the tag for the links frame, enter the attribute **name="links"**.

4. Within the tag for the home page frame, enter the attribute **name="pages"**.

   Figure 5-18 shows the revised code for yale.htm.

Figure 5-18   ASSIGNING A NAME TO EACH FRAME

```
<frameset rows="85,*">
   <!-- Company Logo -->
   <frame src="head.htm" scrolling="no" marginheight="0" noresize name="logo">
   <!-- Nested Frames -->
   <frameset cols="140,*">
      <!-- List of YCS Links -->
      <frame src="links.htm" noresize name="links">
      <!-- YCS Home Page -->
         <frame src="home.htm" marginheight="0" marginwidth="10" noresize name="pages">
   </frameset>
</frameset>
```

5. Save your changes to yale.htm.

Now that you've named the frames, the next task is to specify the "pages" frame as the target for the Home Page, Our Philosophy, and Climbing Lessons hyperlinks, so that clicking each of these links opens the corresponding file in the home page frame.

Specifying a Link Target

Previously you may have used the target attribute to open a page in a new browser window. You can also use the target attribute to open a page in a specific frame. The syntax for this is:

```
<a href="URL" target="frame_name">
```

where *frame_name* is the name you've assigned to a frame on your Web page. In this case, the target name for the frame you need to specify is "documents." To change the targets for the links, edit the <a> tags in links.htm. You'll start by editing only the <a> tags pointing to the Home Page, Our Philosophy, and Climbing Lessons pages. These are the hyperlinks to be displayed in the "pages" frame of yale.htm. You'll work with the other hyperlinks later.

To specify the targets for the hypertext links:

1. Using your text editor, open **links.htm** from the tutorial.05/tutorial folder on your Data Disk.

2. Within the <a> tag for the Home Page, Our Philosophy, and Climbing Lessons hypertext links, enter the attribute **target="pages"**. The revised code is shown in Figure 5-19.

Figure 5-19   ASSIGNING A TARGET TO A HYPERTEXT LINK

```
<html>
<head>
<title>Yale Climbing School Links</title>
</head>
<body background="wall2.jpg" text="white" link="white" vlink="white" alink="white">
<font face="Arial, Helvetica, sans-serif" color="white">
<h2>Links</h2>
<font size="2"><b>
<a href="home.htm" target="pages">Home Page</a><br>
<a href="philosph.htm" target="pages">Our Philosophy</a><br>
<a href="lessons.htm" target="pages">Climbing Lessons</a><br>
<a href="tours.htm">Tours</a><br>
<a href="staff.htm">Staff</a>
</b></font>
</body>
</html>
```

the Web page will appear in the pages frame

3. Save your changes to links.htm.

TROUBLE? If you need to return to the original version of the file, you can open linkstxt.htm in the tutorial.05/tutorial folder of your Data Disk.

Now test the first three hyperlinks in the list.

4. Using your Web browser, open **yale.htm**

5. Click the **Our Philosophy** link in the Links frame. The Our Philosophy Web page should display in the lower-right frame. See Figure 5-20.

Figure 5-20	ASSIGNING A TARGET TO A HYPERLINK

TROUBLE? If the Our Philosophy page displays in the left frame instead, you may need to close and open yale.htm for your changes to take effect.

6. Click the **Home Page** and **Climbing Lessons** links, verifying that the links are working properly and the pages are displaying in the "pages" frame.

There are occasions when a page contains dozens of hypertext links that should all open in the same frame. It would be tedious to insert target attributes for each link. Fortunately, HTML provides a way to specify a target frame for all the hypertext links within a single page.

Using the <base> Tag

The <base> tag is used within the <head> tags of your HTML file and is used to specify global options for the page. One of the attributes of the <base> tag is the target attribute, which identifies a default target for all of the hypertext links in a page. The syntax for this attribute is:

```
<base target="frame_name">
```

where *frame_name* is the name of the target frame. The <base> tag is useful when your page contains a lot of hypertext links that all point to the same target. Rather than adding the target attribute to each <a> tag, you can enter the information once with the <base> tag.

You can still use the <base> tag even if your file contains links that point to a different target than the one specified in the <base> tag. The target in the <a> tag overrides any target specified in the <base> tag.

To see how the <base> tag works, you'll use it to indicate that the "pages" frame is the default target for all hyperlinks in the links.htm file.

To specify a default target using the <base> tag:

1. Return to **links.htm** in your text editor.

2. Delete the **target="pages"** attributes within the <a> tags that you previously entered.

3. Insert the line **<base target="pages">** directly above the </head> tag, as shown in Figure 5-21.

Figure 5-21	SPECIFYING A DEFAULT TARGET FOR ALL HYPERTEXT LINKS

the target of all links will be the page frame

```
<html>
<head>
<title>Yale Climbing School Links</title>
<base target="pages">
</head>
<body background="wall2.jpg" text="white" link="white" vlink="white" alink="white">
<font face="Arial, Helvetica, sans-serif" color="white">
<h2>Links</h2>
<font size="2"><b>
<a href="home.htm" target="pages">Home Page</a><br>
<a href="philosph.htm" target="pages">Our Philosophy</a><br>
<a href="lessons.htm" target="pages">Climbing Lessons</a><br>
<a href="tours.htm">Tours</a><br>
<a href="staff.htm">Staff</a>
</b></font>
</body>
</html>
```

4. Save your changes to links.htm.

5. Using your Web browser, reload or refresh yale.htm. Verify that the links for the Home, Our Philosophy, and Climbing Lessons pages still work correctly.

   TROUBLE? If any of the hyperlinks do not work correctly, check the frame name and target name to verify that they match exactly, both in spelling and in the use of uppercase and lowercase letters.

So far you've worked with the first three hypertext links in the list. The remaining two links require different targets.

Using Reserved Target Names

The remaining two tags in the list of hypertext links point to a list of the tours offered by the Yale Climbing School (tours.htm) and to a staff information page, respectively. The tours.htm file does not contain information about individual tours; instead, it is an expanded table of contents of YCS Web pages, some of which are devoted to individual tours. Each tour has its own Web page, as shown in Figure 5-22.

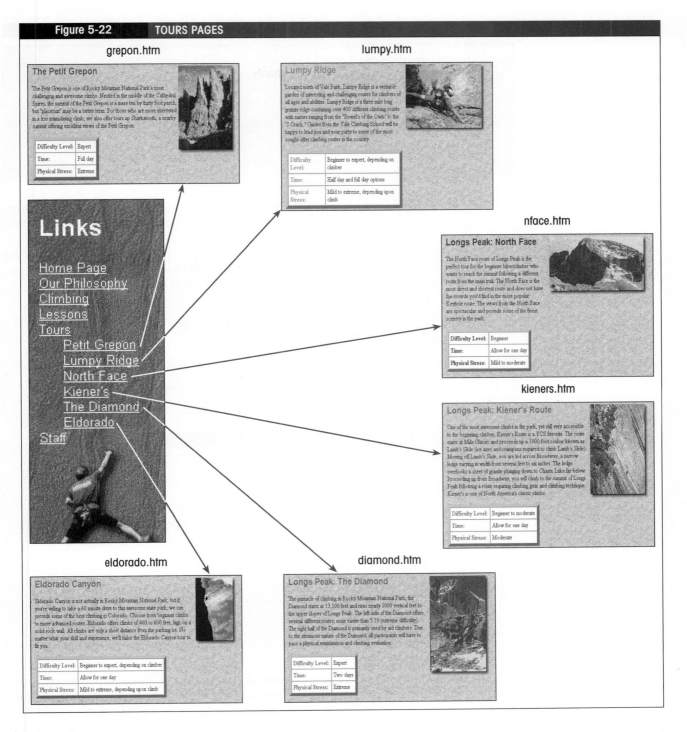

Figure 5-22   TOURS PAGES

Debbie wants tours.htm to display in the links frame in order to give the effect of expanding the table of contents whenever a user clicks the Tours hypertext link. You can specify Links (the name of the frame) as the target. However, there is another way to do this using reserved target names.

Reserved target names are special names that can be used in place of a frame name as the target. They are useful in situations where the name of the frame is unavailable, when you want the page to appear in a new window, or when you want the page to replace the current browser window. Figure 5-23 describes the reserved target names.

Figure 5-23 **RESERVED TARGET NAMES**

RESERVED TARGET NAME	DESCRIPTION
_blank	Loads the document into a new browser window
_self	Loads the document into the same frame or window that contains the hypertext link tag
_parent	In a layout of nested frames, loads the document into the frame that contains the frame with the hyperlink tag
_top	Loads the document into the full display area, replacing the current frame layout

All reserved target names begin with the underscore character (_) to distinguish them from other target names. Note that reserved target names are case-sensitive, so you must enter them in lowercase.

Because Debbie wants the contents of tours.htm to display in the links frame, you can use the reserved target name, _self, which overrides the target specified in the <base> tag and instructs the browser to open the page in the same frame that contains the hypertext link.

To use the reserved target name to specify the target for the Tours link:

1. Return to **links.htm** in your text editor.

2. Enter the attribute **target=_self** within the <a> tag for the Tours hypertext link. See Figure 5-24.

Figure 5-24 **USING THE _SELF TARGET NAME IN THE LINKS.HTM FILE**

```
<html>
<head>
<title>Yale Climbing School Links</title>
<base target="pages">
</head>
<body background="wall2.jpg" text="white" link="white" vlink="white" alink="white">
<font face="Arial, Helvetica, sans-serif" color="white">
<h2>Links</h2>
<font size="2"><b>
<a href="home.htm" target="pages">Home Page</a><br>
<a href="philosph.htm" target="pages">Our Philosophy</a><br>
<a href="lessons.htm" target="pages">Climbing Lessons</a><br>
<a href="tours.htm" target=_self>Tours</a><br>
<a href="staff.htm">Staff</a>
</b></font>
</body>
</html>
```

page will appear in the frame containing the hypertext link

3. Save your changes to links.htm.

The tours.htm Web page is an expanded table of contents for Web pages containing information about specific tours. Debbie wants each of these pages to display in the "pages" frame. To do this, you specify the "pages" frame as the default hyperlink target in tours.htm. The tours.htm file also contains a hyperlink that takes the user back to links.htm. You should specify _self as the target for this hyperlink.

To modify tours.htm as you did links.htm:

1. Using your text editor, open **tours.htm** from the tutorial.05/tutorial folder on your Data Disk.

2. Insert the tag **<base target="pages">** directly above the </head> tag. This code displays the individual tour pages in the "pages" frame when a user clicks any of the tour hyperlinks.

3. Enter the attribute **target=_self** within the <a> tag that points to links.htm. The original table of contents, links.htm, displays in the Links frame. See Figure 5-25.

Figure 5-25	REVISED TOURS.HTM FILE

```
<html>
<head>
<title>Yale Climbing School Links</title>
<base target="pages">
</head>
<body background="wall3.jpg" text="white" link="white" vlink="white" alink="white">
<font face="Arial, Helvetica, sans-serif" color="white">
<h2>Links</h2>
<font size="2"><b>
<a href="home.htm">Home Page</a><br>
<a href="philosph.htm">Our Philosophy</a><br>
<a href="lessons.htm">Climbing Lessons</a><br>
<a href="links.htm" target=_self>Tours</a><br>
      <a href="grepon.htm">Petit Grepon</a><br>
      <a href="lumpy.htm">Lumpy Ridge</a><br>
      <a href="nface.htm">North Face</a><br>
      <a href="kieners.htm">Kiener's</a><br>
      <a href="diamond.htm">The Diamond</a><br>
      <a href="eldorado.htm">Eldorado</a><br>
<a href="staff.htm">Staff</a>
</b></font>
</body>
</html>
```

4. Save your changes to tours.htm.

   TROUBLE? If you need to revert back to the original version of tours.htm for any reason, it is saved in the tutorial.05/tutorial folder of your Data Disk as tourstxt.htm

5. Reload **yale.htm** in your Web browser.

6. Verify that the Tours link works as you intended. As you click on the link, the table of contents list should alternately collapse and expand. In addition, click on the individual tour pages links to verify that they display correctly in the "pages" frame. See Figure 5-26.

Figure 5-26	VIEWING A TOUR PAGE

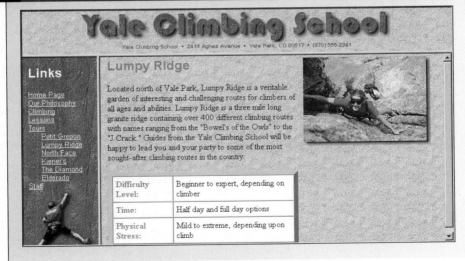

The technique employed here is commonly used for tables of contents that double as hypertext links. Clicking the Tours hypertext link gives the effect that the list is expanding and contracting, but what is actually happening is that one table of contents file is being replaced by another.

The final link you need to create points to a Web page of staff biographies. Debbie asked another employee to produce the contents of this Web page, and the results are shown in Figure 5-27.

Figure 5-27   STAFF WEB PAGE

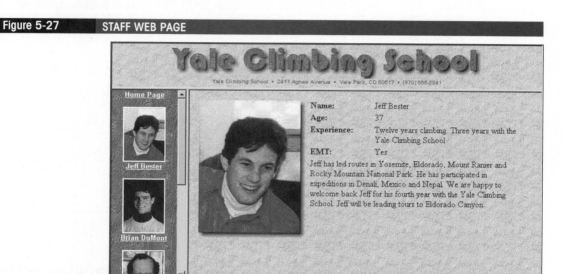

As you can see, this Web page also uses frames. How can this Web page be displayed within your frame layout? If you specify the "pages" frame as the target, the result will be a series of nested frame images as shown in Figure 5-28.

Figure 5-28   A NESTED FRAME LAYOUT

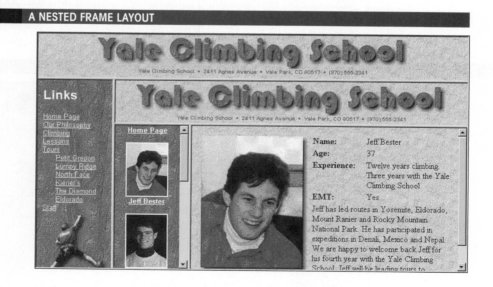

This is not what Debbie wants. She wants the Staff Web page to load into the full display area, replacing the frame layout with its own layout. To target a link to the full display area, you use the _top reserved target name. The _top target is often used when a framed page is accessed from another. It's also used when you are linking to pages that lie outside your Web site altogether.

For example, a link to the Colorado Tourism Board Web site should not display within a frame on the YCS Web site for two reasons. First, once you go outside your Web site, you lose control of the frame layout, and you could easily end up with nested frame images. The second reason is that such a design could easily confuse users, making it appear as if the Colorado Tourism Board is a component of the Yale Climbing School.

To specify the target for the Staff link:

1. Return to **links.htm** in your text editor.

2. Enter the attribute **target=_top** within the <a> tag for the Staff link. See Figure 5-29.

| Figure 5-29 | REVISED LINKS.HTM PAGE USING THE _TOP RESERVED TARGET NAME |

```
<html>
<head>
<title>Yale Climbing School Links</title>
<base target="pages">
</head>
<body background="wall2.jpg" text="white" link="white" vlink="white" alink="white">
<font face="Arial, Helvetica, sans-serif" color="white">
<h2>Links</h2>
<font size="2"><b>
<a href="home.htm" target="pages">Home Page</a><br>
<a href="philosph.htm" target="pages">Our Philosophy</a><br>
<a href="lessons.htm" target="pages">Climbing Lessons</a><br>
<a href="tours.htm" target=_self>Tours</a><br>
<a href="staff.htm" target=_top>Staff</a>
</b></font>
</body>
</html>
```

3. Save your changes to links.htm.

Because tours.htm also acts as a detailed table of contents, you should edit the hypertext link to the Staff page in that file. This way, a user can click the Staff hypertext link from both the table of contents with the expanded list of tours and the original table of contents.

To edit tours.htm:

1. Return to **tours.htm** in your text editor.

2. Enter the attribute **target=_top** within the <a> tag for the Staff link.

3. Save your changes to tours.htm.

4. Using your Web browser, reload **yale.htm**. Verify that the Staff link now opens the Staff page and replaces the existing frame layout with its own. Be sure to test the Staff link from both the original table of contents and the table of contents with the expanded list of tours.

   TROUBLE? If the Staff link does not work properly, verify that you used lowercase letters for the reserved target name.

Debbie has viewed all the hypertext links on the YCS Web site and is quite satisfied with the results. However, she wonders what would happen if a user with an older browser encountered the page. Is there some way to accommodate browsers that don't support frames? Yes, by using the <noframes> tag.

Using the <noframes> Tag

To allow your Web site to be viewable using browsers that do not support frames, as well as by those that do, you can use the <noframes> tag to create a section of your HTML file containing code for browsers incapable of viewing frames. The general syntax for the <noframes> tag is:

```
<html>
<head>
<title>Page Title</title>
</head>
<frameset>
      Frame Definitions
</frameset>
<noframes>
<body>
      Page Layout
</body>
</noframes>
</html>
```

When a browser that supports frames processes this code, it ignores everything within the <noframes> tags and concentrates solely on the code within the <frameset> tags. When a browser that doesn't support frames processes this HTML code, it doesn't know what to do with the <frameset> and <noframes> tags, so it ignores them. However it does know how to render whatever appears within the <body> tags. This way, both types of browsers are supported within a single HTML file. Note that when you use the <noframes> tag, you must include <body> tags.

REFERENCE WINDOW   **RW**

Supporting Frame-Blind Browsers
- Create a version of your page that does not use frames.
- In the framed version of the page, insert the following tags:
  ```
  <noframes>
  </noframes>
  ```
- Copy the HTML code between the <body> tags, including both the <body> and </body> tags, from the nonframed version of the page.
- Paste the HTML code between the <noframes> and </noframes> tags in the framed version of the page.

The Yale Climbing School has been using the nonframed Web site displayed in Figure 5-30 for several years.

Figure 5-30   **FRAMELESS VERSION OF THE YCS WEB SITE**

If you want this Web page to display for frame-blind browsers but still use your framed version, copy the HTML code, including the <body> tags, from the source code of the non-framed Web page and place it within a pair of <noframes> tags in the framed Web page, yale.htm.

To insert support for frame-blind browsers:

1. Using your text editor, open **yale.htm**.

2. Create a blank line immediately above the </html> tag.

3. Enter the following HTML code:

```
<!-- Noframes version of this page -->
<noframes>
</noframes>
```

4. Save your changes to the file.

   Next copy the code from the noframe page into yale.htm.

5. Using your text editor, open **noframes.htm** from the tutorial.05/tutorial folder on your Data Disk.

6. Copy the HTML code between the opening and closing <body> tags. Be sure to include both the opening and closing <body> tags in your copy selection.

7. Return to **yale.htm** in your text editor.

8. Create a blank line immediately below the <noframes> tag.

9. Paste the text you copied from noframes.htm in the blank line you created below the <noframes> tag. Figure 5-31 shows the beginning and end of the revised code.

Figure 5-31 | INSERTING THE NOFRAMES CODE INTO THE YALE.HTM FILE

```
<frameset rows="85,*">
    <!-- Company Logo -->
    <frame src="head.htm" scrolling="no" marginheight="0" noresize name="logo">
    <!-- Nested Frames -->
    <frameset cols="140,*">
        <!-- List of YCS Links -->
        <frame src="links.htm" noresize name="links">
        <!-- YCS Home Page -->
        <frame src="home.htm" marginheight="0" marginwidth="10" noresize name="pages">
    </frameset>
</frameset>
<!-- Noframes version of this page -->
<noframes>
<body background="wall.jpg" link="white" vlink="white" alink="white">
<table width="620" cellpadding="5">
<tr>
```

```
        <p>We provide five levels of instruction, ranging from Beginner to
        Advanced, including lessons in aid and ice climbing. Members of our
        experienced staff have led expeditions in Mexico, Nepal and Pakistan.
        All have intimate knowledge of Rocky Mountain National Park and know the
        best places to go to help you experience the wonder and beauty of the
        park.</p>
        <p>So call us today, and start climbing tomorrow!</p>
    </td>
</tr>
</table>

</body>
</noframes>
</html>
```

10. Save your changes to yale.htm.

To test your Web page, use a browser that does not support frames. You can obtain early versions of Netscape Navigator and Internet Explorer from their respective Web sites. Note that the table structure of the frameless page closely matches the frame layout you created. In this case, the first row is a single cell that spans two columns and displays the company logo, and the second row contains the list of links in the first cell and the home page text in the second cell.

Another way of supporting browsers that do not display frames is to create a Web page that contains links to the framed and nonframed versions of your Web site. A user with an older browser can thereby avoid the frames. This technique also provides users with the option of not viewing frames, even though their browsers have the ability to. Some people just don't like frames.

Working with Frame Borders

There are additional attributes you can apply to the <frame> tag that allow you to change border size and appearance. For example, you can remove borders from your frames to free up more space for text and images, or you can change the color of the frame border so that it matches or complements the color scheme for your Web site.

Setting the Border Color

To change the color of a frame's border, use the bordercolor attribute. The attribute can be applied either to an entire set of frames, using the <frameset> tag, or to individual frames, using the <frame> tag. The syntax for this attribute is:

```
<frameset bordercolor="color">
```

or

```
<frame bordercolor="color">
```

where *color* is either a color name or a color value. Applying the bordercolor attribute to the <frameset> tag affects all of the frames and nested frames within the set. If you apply the bordercolor attribute to a single <frame> tag, that particular color of the border changes in Internet Explorer, but in Netscape Navigator, all of the frame borders change. It is important to remember that when you apply these types of tags and attributes to your Web page, you should always view the page using different browsers and, if possible, browser versions.

Debbie asks you to test the bordercolor attribute on the YCS Web site by changing the color of the frame borders to brown.

To change the frame border color:

1. Return to **yale.htm** in your text editor.

2. Enter the attribute **bordercolor="brown"** within the initial <frameset> tag.

3. Save your changes to the file, and then reload it in your Web browser. Figure 5-32 shows the frames with a brown border.

Figure 5-32	WEB SITE WITH BROWN FRAME BORDER

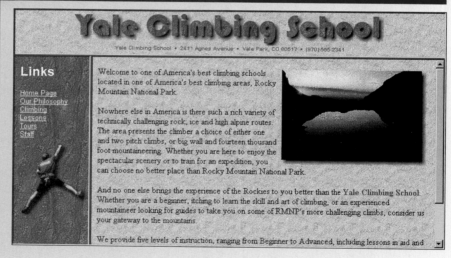

Setting the Border Width

Another way of modifying frame borders is to change their widths using the border attribute. Unlike the bordercolor attribute, this attribute can be used only in the <frameset> tag, and not in individual <frame> tags. The syntax for the border attribute is:

```
<frameset border="value">
```

where *value* is the width of the frame borders in pixels.

To see how this attribute affects the appearance of your Web page, Debbie asks you to use it to remove the frame borders by setting the width to 0 pixels.

To change the size of the frame borders:

1. Return to **yale.htm** in your text editor.

2. Delete the bordercolor attribute that you entered in the previous set of steps. You don't need this attribute because you're going to remove the frame borders entirely.

3. Enter the **attribute border="0"** within the first <frameset> tag. See Figure 5-33.

Figure 5-33	REMOVING THE FRAME BORDERS

setting the width of the frame border to zero has the effect of removing the border

```
<frameset rows="85,*" border="0">
    <!-- Company Logo -->
    <frame src="head.htm" scrolling="no" marginheight="0" noresize name="logo">
    <!-- Nested Frames -->
    <frameset cols="140,*">
        <!-- List of YCS Links -->
        <frame src="links.htm" noresize name="links">
        <!-- YCS Home Page -->
        <frame src="home.htm" marginheight="0" marginwidth="10" noresize name="pages">
    </frameset>
</frameset>
```

4. Save your changes to yale.htm and then reload it in your Web browser. As shown in Figure 5-34, the frame borders have been removed from the page.

5. Close any YCS files that may still be open.

Figure 5-34 | **THE YCS WEB SITE WITHOUT FRAME BORDERS**

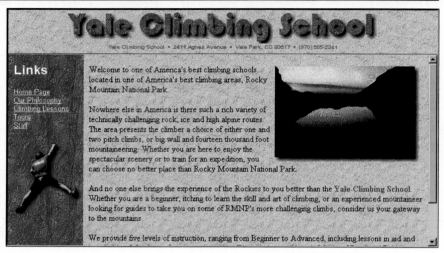

By removing the borders, you've created more space for the text and images in each of the Web pages. You've also created the impression of a "seamless" Web page. Some Web designers prefer not to show frame borders in order to give the illusion of having a single Web page rather than three separate ones, while other Web designers believe that hiding frame borders can confuse users as they navigate the Web site.

You can create a similar effect by using the frameborder attribute. Adding frameborder="no" to a <frameset> tag removes the borders from the frames in your page. Internet Explorer also supports the framespacing attribute, which has the same effect as the border attribute. Note that Netscape does not support this attribute.

Creating **Floating Frames**

Another way of using frames is to create a floating frame. Introduced by Internet Explorer 3.0 and added to the HTML 4.0 specifications, a **floating frame**, or **internal frame**, is displayed as a separate box or window within a Web page. The frame can be placed within a Web page in much the same way as an inline image. The syntax for a floating frame is:

```
<iframe src="URL" frameborder="option">
</iframe>
```

where *URL* is the name and location of the file you want to display in the floating frame and the frameborder attribute determines whether the browser displays a border ("yes") or not ("no") around the frame.

In addition to these attributes, you can use some of the other attributes you used with fixed frames, such as the marginwidth, marginheight, and name attributes. Figure 5-35 describes some of the other attributes associated with the <iframe> tag.

Figure 5-35	ATTRIBUTES OF THE <IFRAME> TAG
ATTRIBUTE	**DESCRIPTION**
align="*alignment*"	How the frame is aligned with the surrounding text (use "left" or "right" to flow text around the inline frame.)
border="*value*"	The size of the border around the frame, in pixels
frameborder="*type*"	Specifies whether to display a border ("yes") or not ("no")
classid="*URL*"	The class identifier of the object
height="*value*" width="*value*"	The height and width of the frame, in pixels
hspace="*value*" vspace="*value*"	The horizontal and vertical space around the frame, in pixels
marginheight="*value*" marginwidth="*value*"	The size of the internal margins of the frame, in pixels
name="*text*"	The name of the frame
scrolling="*type*"	Specifies whether the frame can be scrolled ("yes") or not ("no")
src="*URL*"	The location and filename of the page displayed in the frame

Debbie is interested in floating frames, and she would like you to create a staff page that employs this technique.

To create a floating frame:

1. Using your text editor, open **iftxt.htm** from the tutorial.05/tutorial folder of your Data Disk.

2. Save the file as **iframe.htm**.

3. Immediately following the </center> tag, insert the following HTML code. See Figure 5-36.

```
<iframe width="400" height="250" align="right"
hspace="5" src="bios.htm">
</iframe>
```

Figure 5-36	CREATING A FLOATING FRAME

```
<html>
<head>
<title>The YCS Staff</title>
</head>
<body background="wall.jpg">

<center><img src="logo.jpg" alt="The Yale Climbing School"><br>
<font face="Arial, Helvetica, sans-serif" size="1" color="green"><b>
 Yale Climbing School  &#149; 
 2411 Agnes Avenue  &#149; 
 Vale Park, CO 80517  &#149; 
 (970) 555-2341
</b></font>
<hr width="100%">
</center>

<iframe width="400" height="250" align="right" hspace="5" src="bios.htm">
</iframe>

<h1><font face="Arial, Helvetica, sans-serif" color="brown">Staff</font></h1>
The staff at the Yale Climbing School is here to help with all of your climbing needs.
All of our instructors are fully qualified with years of climbing and teaching experience.
Scroll through the biographies at the right for more information.
</body>
</html>
```

html code to create a floating frame

4. Save your changes to iframe.htm and close the file.

5. Open iframe.htm in your Web browser. Figure 5-37 shows the resulting Web page.

Figure 5-37   VIEWING A FLOATING FRAME

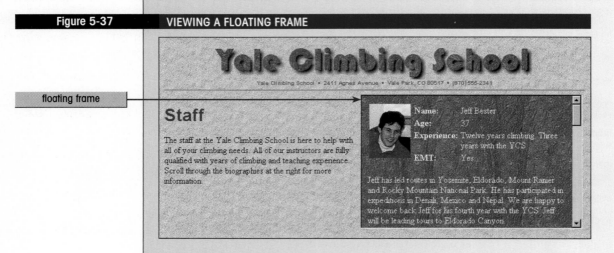

floating frame

TROUBLE? If you're running Netscape version 4.7 or earlier, you will not see the floating frame displayed in Figure 5-37.

6. Use the scroll bars in the floating frame to view the entire list of staff biographies.

7. Close your Web browser.

If you want to use floating frames in your Web page, you must make sure that your users are running at least Internet Explorer 3.0 or Netscape 6.2. Users of other browsers and browser versions might not be able to view floating frames.

You've completed your work for Debbie and the Yale Climbing School. Using frames, you've created an interesting presentation that is both attractive and easy to navigate. Debbie is pleased and will get back to you if she needs any additional work done.

Session 5.2 QUICK CHECK

1. When you click a hypertext link inside a frame, in what frame will the Web page appear by default?

2. What HTML code would you use to assign the name "Address" to a frame with the document source address.htm?

3. What HTML code would you use to direct a hypertext link to a frame named "News"?

4. What HTML code would you use to point a hypertext link to the document "sales.htm" with the result that the sales.htm file is loaded into the entire display area, overwriting any frames in the process?

5. What HTML code would you use to direct all hypertext links in a document to the "News" target?

6. Describe what you would do to make your Web page readable by browsers that support frames and by those that do not.

7. What HTML tag would you use to set the frame border color of every frame on the page to red?

8. What HTML tag would you use to set the frame border width to 5 pixels?

REVIEW ASSIGNMENTS

Debbie has asked you to revise the layout for the YCS Web site. She would like links for all of the Web pages to display in separate frames so that users can always click a link for a specific page or collection of pages no matter where they are in the Web site. Figure 5-38 shows a preview of the frames you'll create for the Yale Climbing School.

To implement Debbie's suggestions:

Figure 5-38

You'll create the following files for the YCS Web site:

- tlist.htm—contains a list of links to the tour pages
- slist.htm—contains a list of links to staff bios
- tours2.htm—a frame layout displaying YCS tours
- staff2.htm—a frame layout displaying YCS staff bios
- tourlink.htm—a Web page containing a link to tour2.htm
- staflink.htm—a Web page containing a link to staff2.htm
- head2.htm—a Web page containing the company logo and links to three pages
- yale2.htm—a frame layout displaying all of the YCS Web pages

To create the YCS Web site:

1. Using your text editor, open **tlisttxt.htm** from the tutorial.05/review folder of your Data Disk and save it as **tlist.htm**.

2. Define "Tours" as the default target for links in this file.

3. Save your changes to **tlist.htm** and close the file.

4. Using your text editor, open **slisttxt.htm** and save it as **slist.htm**. Set "Bios" as the default target for links on this page. Save your changes and close the file.

5. Using your text editor, open **tourstxt.htm** and save it as **tours2.htm**. In the **tours2.htm** file do the following:

   - Create a frame layout consisting of two columns of frames. The first frame should be 140 pixels wide, the second frame should occupy the remaining space.
   - Make the frame borders 5 pixels wide and brown in color.
   - The source for the first frame should be the **tlist.htm** file.
   - The source for the second frame should be the **grepon.htm** file. Assign the frame the name "Tours".
   - Do not allow users to resize either frame in the frameset.
   - Add comments describing the contents of each frame.

6. Save your changes and close the file.

7. Using your text editor, open **stafftxt.htm** and save it as **staff2.htm**.

   - In staff2.htm create a frame layout containing two columns. Make the first frame 140 pixels wide; the second frame should occupy the remaining space.
   - Make the frame borders 5 pixels wide and brown in color
   - The first frame should have a margin height of 1 pixel and a margin width of 10 pixels. The source for this frame should be the slist.htm file.
   - Display the contents of the bester.htm file in the second frame. Name the frame "Bios". You do not have to specify a margin height or width.
   - Do not allow users to resize either frame.
   - Add comments describing the two frames.

8. Save your changes to staff2.htm and close the file.

9. Using your text editor, open **tltxt.htm** and save it as **tourlink.htm**. Set the target of the hyperlinks in this file to the target name "docs". Save your changes and close the file.

10. Open **sltxt.htm** in your text editor and save it as **staflink.htm**. Set the target of the hyperlinks to the target name "docs". Save your changes and close the file.

11. Open **headtxt.htm** in your text editor and save it as **head2.htm**. Once again, point the target of the hyperlinks to the "docs" target name. Close the file, saving your changes.

12. Open **yale2txt.htm** in your text editor and save the file as **yale2.htm**.

   ■ In yale2.htm create a frame layout containing three rows of frames. The first frame should be 85 pixels high, the third frame should be 30 pixels high, and the middle frame should occupy the remaining space.

   ■ Make the frame borders brown, 5 pixels in width. Do not allow users to resize the frames.

   ■ Display **head2.htm** in the first frame. Set the margin height to 0 pixels.

   ■ Display the contents of the **home.htm** file in the second frame and name the frame "docs". Set the second frame's margin height to 0 pixels and the margin width to 10 pixels.

   ■ Insert a frameset containing three columns into the third frame. The first and third columns of the nested frameset should be 100 pixels wide; the second column should occupy the remaining space. Use **staflink.htm** as the source for the first frame, **footer.htm** as the source for the second frame, and **tourlink.htm** as the source for the third frame. Set the margin width and height of each frame to 5 pixels. Make the frame borders brown and 5 pixels wide. Do not allow users to resize the frames.

13. For browsers that don't support frames, insert the contents of **noframes.htm** into yale2.htm.

14. Save your changes to yale2.htm and close the file.

15. Open **yale2.htm** in your Web browser, and verify that you can view all of the Web pages in the YCS Web site in the appropriate frames.

16. Hand in the files used by this Web site to your instructor.

CASE PROBLEMS

Case 1. Doc-Centric Copiers Located in Salt Lake City, Doc-Centric is one of the nation's leading manufacturers of personal and business copiers. The annual shareholders' convention in Chicago is approaching, and the general manager, David Edgars, wants you to create an online report for the convention participants. The report will run off a computer located in the convention hall and will be accessible to everyone. David feels that creating a Web presentation to run locally on the computer is the best way of presenting the sales data. Using hyperlinks between various reports will enable Doc-Centric Copiers to make a wealth of information available to shareholders in an easy-to-use format. Most of the Web pages have been created for you. Your job is to display that information using frames. A preview of the layout you'll create is shown in Figure 5-39.

Figure 5-39

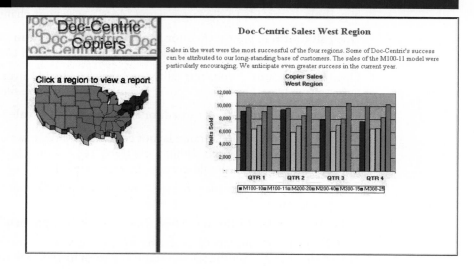

You'll use the following files in the Doc-Centric Web presentation:

- dcc.htm, a frame layout of all of the Doc-Centric Web pages
- dccmw.htm, a page describing sales data for the Midwest region
- dccne.htm, a page describing sales data for the Northeast region
- dccs.htm, a page describing sales data for the South region
- dccw.htm, a page describing sales data for the West region
- head.htm, a page with the company logo
- map.htm, a page with a map of the company's sales regions
- report.htm, a page welcoming shareholders to the convention

To create the Doc-Centric Copiers sales presentation:

1. Using your text editor, open **dcctxt.htm** from the tutorial.05/case1 folder on your Data Disk, and save it as **dcc.htm** in the same folder.

2. Create a frame layout with the following design documents:

- The layout contains two columns with a blue frame border, 10 pixels in width. The first frame should be 240 pixels wide. The second frame should occupy the remaining space in the design window.
- Create two rows of nested frames in the first frame. The first row should be 75 pixels high; the second row should fill up the remaining space. Display the contents of the **head.htm** file in the first row. Display the contents of the **map.htm** file in the second row. Name the first frame "logo", the second frame "usmap".
- In the second frame, display the contents of the report.htm file. Name the frame "reports".
- Add comments describing the contents of the various frames.

3. Using your text editor, open **maptxt.htm** and save it as **map.htm**.

4. Direct each link in the map.htm file to the reports target, so that the pages will appear in the reports frame. Save your changes and close the file.

5. Using your text editor, open **headtxt.htm** and save it as **head.htm**. Direct the hyperlinks in this file to the reports target. Close the file, saving your changes.

6. Use your Web browser to view dcc.htm. What improvements could be made to the page? What should be removed?

7. Return to **dcc.htm** in your text editor and reduce the margin for the logo frame to 1 pixel. Reduce the margin width for the usmap frame to 1 pixel, and change that frame's margin height to 30 pixels.

8. Remove scroll bars from both the logo and usmap frames.

9. View the Web page again to verify that the problems you identified in Step 6 have been resolved.

10. Return to dcc.htm in your text editor, and lock the size of the frames to prevent users from changing the frame sizes.

Explore   11. Using your Web browser, reload **dcc.htm** and test the image map in the usmap frame. Verify that each of the four sales reports is correctly displayed in the reports frame. Click the company logo in the upper-left frame and verify that it redisplays the opening page in the reports frame.

12. Print a page displaying one of the sales reports. Print a copy of the dcc.htm and map.htm files.

13. Hand in your files and printouts to your instructor.

Case 2. Browyer Realty   Linda Browyer is the owner of Browyer Realty, a real estate company in Minnesota. She's asked you to help her design a Web page for the listings in her book. Linda envisions a Web page that displays basic information about a listing, including the owner's description. She would like to have several photos of the listing on the page, but rather than cluttering up the layout with several images, she would like users to be able to view different images by clicking a link on the page. Linda wants the images to open within the listing page, not in a separate Web page. Figure 5-40 shows a preview of the page you'll create for Linda.

Figure 5-40

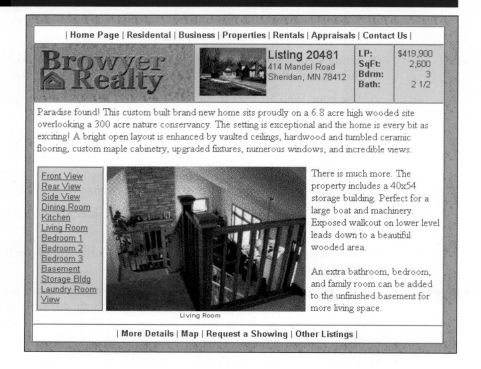

To create this page you'll create a floating frame that displays Web pages containing different photos of the listing. There are 13 pages you'll display in the floating frame, named img01.htm, img02.htm, and so forth.

To create the Browyer Realty listing:

1. Using your text editor, open **listtxt.htm** from the tutorial.05/case2 folder of your Data Disk in your text editor and save it as **listing.htm**.

Explore

2. Directly above the paragraph beginning with the line, "There is much more...," insert a floating frame with the following attributes:

- The source of the frame is the img01.htm file.
- The name of the frame is "images".
- The frame is aligned with the left margin of the page.
- The frame is 300 pixels wide and 240 pixels high.
- The frame's margin width and height are 0 pixels.
- There is no frame border.

3. Insert a comment above the floating frame indicating its purpose in the Web page.

4. Change each of the 13 entries in the list of photos to a hypertext link. Direct the first entry to img01.htm, the second entry to img02.htm, and so forth.

5. Display the 13 hypertext links you created in the previous step in the "images" floating frame.

6. Save your changes to the file.

7. Using your Web browser, open **listing.htm**. Verify that each link displays a different photo and photo caption in the Web page and that the rest of the page remains unchanged.

8. Hand in the files for this Web site to your instructor.

Case 3. SkyWeb Astronomy Dr. Andrew Weiss of Central Ohio University maintains an astronomy page for his students called SkyWeb. In his Web site he discusses many aspects of astronomy and observing. One of the pages he wants your help with involves the Messier catalog, a list of deep sky objects of particular interest to astronomers and amateur observers.

Dr. Weiss wants his page to contain a slide show of various Messier objects, displaying both a photo of the object and a text box describing the object's history and features. He wants his users to be able to click a forward or backward button to move through the slide show. The rest of the Web page remains unchanged as users view the presentation. Figure 5-41 shows a preview of the page that Dr. Weiss wants to create.

Figure 5-41

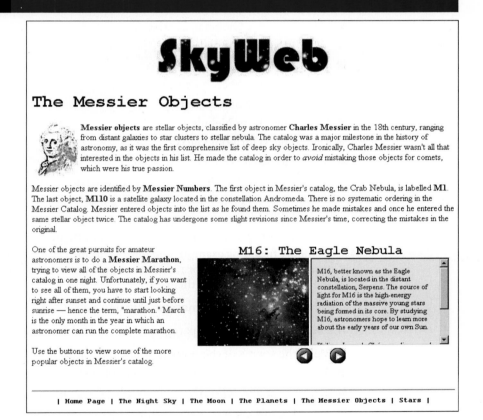

To create a presentation like this, you'll need to insert one floating frame inside of another. Dr. Weiss has created the text you need for the Web site. Your job is to create the frames needed to complete the Web page.

To create the SkyWeb Web page:

1. Using your text editor, open **mxxtxt.htm** from the tutorial.05/case3 folder of your Data Disk and save it as **m01.htm**.

Explore

2. The m01.htm file displays an image of the Messier object M1 and also contains a text box describing this stellar object. Replace the title and heading for the Web page with the text "M1: The Crab Nebula".

3. Replace the inline image mxx.jpg with the image m01.jpg

4. Replace the inline image mxxdesc.jpg with a floating frame of the same dimensions, displaying the contents of the file m01desc.htm

5. Direct the hypertext link for the Previous button located at the bottom of the page to the file **m57.htm**. Note that you'll create this file later.

6. Direct the hypertext link for the Next button to the file m13.htm—another file you'll create shortly.

7. Save your changes to **m01.htm**.

8. With m01.htm as a guide, use your text editor to create similar Web pages for the other eight Messier objects. Save the files as **m13.htm**, **m16.htm**, **m20.htm**, **m27.htm**, **m31.htm**, **m42.htm**, **m51.htm**, and **m57.htm**. The titles and headings for these pages are:

   - M13: Hercules Globular Cluster
   - M16: The Eagle Nebula
   - M20: The Trifid Nebula
   - M27: The Dumbbell Nebula
   - M31: The Andromeda Galaxy
   - M42: The Orion Nebula
   - M51: The Whirlpool Galaxy
   - M57: The Ring Nebula

   The floating frame for each page should point to the file containing descriptive text on the Messier object. For example, the floating frame for the m13.htm file should display the m13desc.htm file and so forth.

   The Previous and Next buttons in each page should point to the previous and next Messier object files. For example, the buttons in m27.htm should point to m20.htm and m31.htm. The Next button for m57.htm should point to m01.htm. Save your changes to all the files, and then close them.

9. Using your text editor, open **messtxt.htm** and save it as **messier.htm**.

10. At the beginning of the third paragraph, insert a floating frame.

   - Make the source of the floating frame m01.htm.
   - Align the frame with the right margin of the page.
   - Make the frame 460 pixels wide by 240 pixels high.
   - Make the margin width and height 0 pixels.
   - Set the horizontal space around the frame to 5 pixels.
   - There should be no border around the frame.

11. Insert a comment before the floating frame describing its purpose.

12. Save your changes to messier.htm and close the file.

13. Open messier.htm in your Web browser. Click the Previous and Next buttons and verify that you can navigate through the list of Messier objects without disturbing the rest of the Web page. Verify that you can use the scroll bars around the description box to view descriptions of each object.

14. Hand in the files for this Web site to your instructor.

Case 4. Warner Peripherals, Inc. Warner Peripherals, a company located in Tucson, makes high-quality peripherals for computers. The company is an industry leader and has been delivering innovative technical solutions to consumers for more than 20 years. Its most popular products include the SureSave line of tape drives and the SureRite line of disk drives. You've been asked to consolidate several Web pages describing these products into a single Web presentation using frames. The files shown in Figure 5-42 are available for your use.

Figure 5-42

FILE	DESCRIPTION
drive15l.htm	Description of the 15L SureRite hard drive
drive20m.htm	Description of the 20M SureRite hard drive
drive33m.htm	Description of the 33M SureRite hard drive
drive60s.htm	Description of the 60S SureRite hard drive
tape800.htm	Description of the 800 SureSave tape backup drive
tape3200.htm	Description of the 3200 SureSave tape backup drive
tape9600.htm	Description of the 9600 SureSave tape backup drive
wlogo.htm	An Web page containing the Warner Peripherals logo

To create the Warner Peripherals Web presentation:

1. Create a table of contents page that includes hypertext links to the files listed in Figure 5-42. The design of this Web page is up to you. Save this page as **wtoc.htm** in the tutorial.05/case4 folder of your Data Disk.

2. In the same folder, create a file named **warner.htm** that consolidates the logo page, table of contents page, and product description pages into a single page, using frames. Include comment tags in the file describing each element of the page.

3. Test your Web page and verify that each link works properly and appears in the correct frame.

4. Print a copy of the page and the HTML code.

5. Save your work and close your Web browser and text editor.

QUICK | CHECK ANSWERS

Session 5.1

1. Frames are windows appearing within the browser's display area, each capable of displaying the contents of a different HTML file.

2. Because there is no page body. Instead, the browser displays the <body> tags from other pages.

3. <frameset rows="2, 50%,*">

4. <frame src="home.htm">

5. <frame src="home.htm" scrolling="no">

6. <frame src="home.htm" marginheight="3">

7. 3 pixels

8. <frame src="home.htm" noresize>

Session 5.2

1. The frame containing the hypertext link

2. <frame src="address.htm" name="Address">

3. <a href="*URL*" target="News">

4. <a href="sales.htm" target=_top>

5. Place the tag <base target="News"> in the <head> section of the HTML file

6. Create a section starting with the <noframes> tag. After the <noframes> tag enter a <body> tag to identify the text and images you want frame-blind browsers to display. Complete this section with a </body> tag followed by a </noframes> tag.

7. <frameset bordercolor="red">

8. <frameset borderwidth="5">

New Perspectives on

CREATING WEB PAGES
WITH HTML

3rd Edition

Read This Before You Begin

To the Student

Data Disks

To complete the Level III tutorials, Review Assignments, Case Problems, and Additional Case Problems, you need ten Data Disks. Your instructor will either provide you with these Data Disks or ask you to make your own.

If you are making your own Data Disks, you will need ten blank, formatted high-density disks. You will need to copy a set of files and/or folders from a file server, standalone computer, or the Web onto your disks. Your instructor will tell you which computer, drive letter, and folders contain the files you need. You could also download the files by going to www.course.com and following the instructions on the screen.

The information below shows you the Data Disks you need so that you will have enough disk space to complete all the tutorials, Review Assignments, and Case Problems:

Data Disk 1

Write this on the disk label:
Data Disk 1: HTML Tutorials 6 and 7
Put these folders on the disk:

tutorial.06/tutorial	tutorial.06/case3	tutorial.07/case1
tutorial.06/review	tutorial.06/case4	tutorial.07/case2
tutorial.06/case1	tutorial.07/tutorial	tutorial.07/case3
tutorial.06/case2	tutorial.07/review	tutorial.07/case4

Data Disk 2

Write this on the disk label:
Data Disk 2: HTML Tutorials 8 and 9
Put these folders on the disk:

tutorial.08/tutorial	tutorial.08/case3	tutorial.09/case1
tutorial.08/review	tutorial.08/case4	tutorial.09/case2
tutorial.08/case1	tutorial.09/tutorial	tutorial.09/case3
tutorial.08/case2	tutorial.09/review	tutorial.09/case4

Data Disk 3

Write this on the disk label:
Data Disk 3: HTML Tutorial 10 Tutorial
Put this folder on the disk:
tutorial.10/tutorial

Data Disk 4

Write this on the disk label:
Data Disk 4: HTML Tutorial 10 Review Assignment
Put this folder on the disk:
tutorial.10/review

Data Disk 5

Write this on the disk label:
Data Disk 5: HTML Tutorial 10 Case Problem 1
Put this folder on the disk:
tutorial.10/case1

Data Disk 6

Write this on the disk label:
Data Disk 6: HTML Tutorial 10 Case Problem 2
Put this folder on the disk:
tutorial.10/case2

Data Disk 7

Write this on the disk label:
Data Disk 7: HTML Tutorial 10 Case Problem 3
Put this folder on the disk:
tutorial.10/case3

Data Disk 8

Write this on the disk label:
Data Disk 8: HTML Tutorial 10 Case Problem 4
Put this folder on the disk:
tutorial.10/case4

Data Disk 9

Write this on the disk label:
Data Disk 9: HTML Additional Cases 1 and 2
Put these folders on the disk:

tutorial.add/case1	tutorial.add/case2

Data Disk 10

Write this on the disk label:
Data Disk 10: HTML Additional Case 3
Put this folder on the disk:
tutorial.add/case3

When you begin each tutorial, Review Assignment, or Case Problem, be sure you are using the correct Data Disk. Refer to the "File Finder" chart at the back of this text for more detailed information on which files are used in which tutorials. See the inside front cover of this book for more information on Data Disk files, or ask your instructor or technical support person for assistance.

Using Your Own Computer

If you are going to work through this book using your own computer, you need:

- **Computer System** A text editor and a Web browser (preferably Netscape Navigator or Internet Explorer, versions 4.0 or higher) must be installed on your computer. If you are using a non-standard browser, it must support frames and HTML 4.0 or higher.
- **Data Disks** You will not be able to complete the tutorials or exercises in this book using your own computer until you have your Data Disks.

Visit Our World Wide Web Site

Additional materials designed especially for you are available on the World Wide Web. Go to www.course.com/NewPerspectives.

To the Instructor

The Data Disk Files are available on the Instructor's Resource Kit for this title. Follow the instructions in the Help file on the CD-ROM to install the programs to your network or standalone computer. For information on creating Data Disks, see the "To the Student" section above.

You are granted a license to copy the Data Files to any computer or computer network used by students who have purchased this book.

OBJECTIVES

In this tutorial you will:

- Learn about CGI scripts

- Review the various parts of an online form

- Create form elements

- Create a hidden field on a form

- Work with form attributes

- Learn how to send data from a form to a CGI script

- Learn how to send form information without using CGI scripts

CREATING WEB PAGE FORMS

Designing a Product Registration Form

CASE

Creating a Registration Form for LanGear

LanGear, located in Farley, South Dakota, is a leading manufacturer of network hardware and software. The company has already established a presence on the World Wide Web with a Web site describing the company's products and its corporate philosophy. Now LanGear would like to build on that presence by creating interactive pages to allow customers to give feedback online.

Susan Gorski, customer support director for LanGear, would like to have a Web page for customer registration. She's aware that fewer than 10% of the registration cards included with the product packaging are returned to the company, and she feels that this low response could be improved with a Web registration system. Susan has asked you to help her create such a registration Web page. To do so, you'll need to learn how to create HTML forms and how to use these forms to record information for the company.

SESSION 6.1

In this session you'll learn some of the fundamentals for creating forms with HTML. You'll learn how forms interact with CGI scripts to transfer information from a Web browser to the Web server. You'll also create your first form element, a text box. Finally, you'll attach a form label to the text boxes you create.

Working with CGI Scripts

Susan has been thinking about how she wants the product registration form to appear, keeping in mind that the company plans to use the form to record customer information. Susan decides to model the form on the registration cards already packaged with LanGear's products. Because a long form would discourage customers from completing it, Susan wants the form to be brief and focused on the information the company is most interested in. She has provided you with a sketch of her idea, shown in Figure 6-1.

Figure 6-1	SUSAN'S PROPOSED REGISTRATION FORM

The form collects contact information for each customer, information on which product the customer purchased and when, what network operating system the customer uses, and how the customer uses the product. There is also a place for customers to enter comments.

With this registration form, Susan hopes to collect information to help LanGear better understand its customers and their needs.

Before you can create the form, you need to understand how forms are interpreted and processed on the Web. Although HTML supports tags that allow you to create forms like the one shown in Figure 6-1, it does not process that information. To do that, you need a **CGI (Common Gateway Interface) script** running on the Web server that receives data from the form and uses it to perform a set of tasks. Figure 6-2 illustrates how a Web page form interacts with a CGI script.

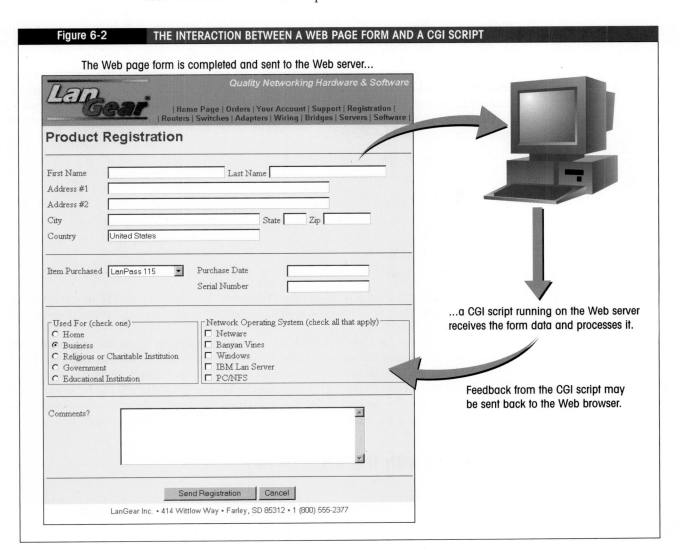

Figure 6-2   THE INTERACTION BETWEEN A WEB PAGE FORM AND A CGI SCRIPT

The introduction of CGI scripts represented a dramatic change in how the Web was perceived and used. By giving users access to programs that react to user input, the Web became a more dynamic environment where companies and customers could interact with each other. Among the many things CGI scripts made possible are:

- online databases containing customer information
- catalogues for ordering and purchasing items online
- databases containing product support information
- determining the number of times a Web page has been accessed

- server-side image maps
- message boards for online discussion forums
- e-mail for discussion groups

Because CGI scripts run on the Web server, Web page designers may not be able to create or edit them. In some cases, a programmer creates the scripts offered by the Web server and provides the designer with their specifications, indicating what input the scripts expect and what output they create.

Internet service providers (ISPs) and universities may provide CGI scripts that their customers and students can use on their Web sites, but which they cannot directly access or modify.

There are several reasons to restrict direct access to CGI scripts. The primary reason is that when you run a CGI script, you are actually running a program directly on the server. Mindful of the security risks that computer hackers can present and the drain on system resources caused by large numbers of programs running simultaneously, system administrators are understandably careful to maintain strict control over their servers and systems.

CGI scripts can be written in a variety of different computer languages. Some of the most commonly used languages are:

- AppleScript
- ASP
- C/C++
- Perl
- TCL
- the UNIX shell
- Visual Basic

Which language is used depends on the Web server. Check with your ISP or system administrator to find out how CGI scripts are used on your server and what rights and privileges you have in working with them.

The programmers at LanGear have created a script to retrieve the data from the registration form and e-mail the results to one of Susan's assistants. The information can then be extracted from the e-mail message and entered into the company's registration database. You will not have access to the CGI scripts on the Web server, so you'll just be working with the HTML end of this process. After Susan uploads the page to the company's Web server, others will test the page and the script to verify that the information is passed on correctly.

Starting an Online Form with the <form> Tag

Now that you're familiar with how CGI scripts interact with Web page forms, you can begin to work on the registration form that Susan wants you to create. As shown in Figure 6-3, the form contains the following elements, called **control elements**, which are commonly used in Web page forms:

- **text boxes** for text and numerical entries
- **selection lists** for long lists of options, usually appearing in a **drop-down list box**
- **radio buttons**, also called **option buttons**, to select a single option from a predefined list
- **check boxes** to specify an item as either present or absent
- **groups boxes** to organize form elements
- **text areas** for extended entries that can include several lines of text
- **buttons** that can be clicked to start processing the form

Figure 6-3   **FORM COMPONENTS**

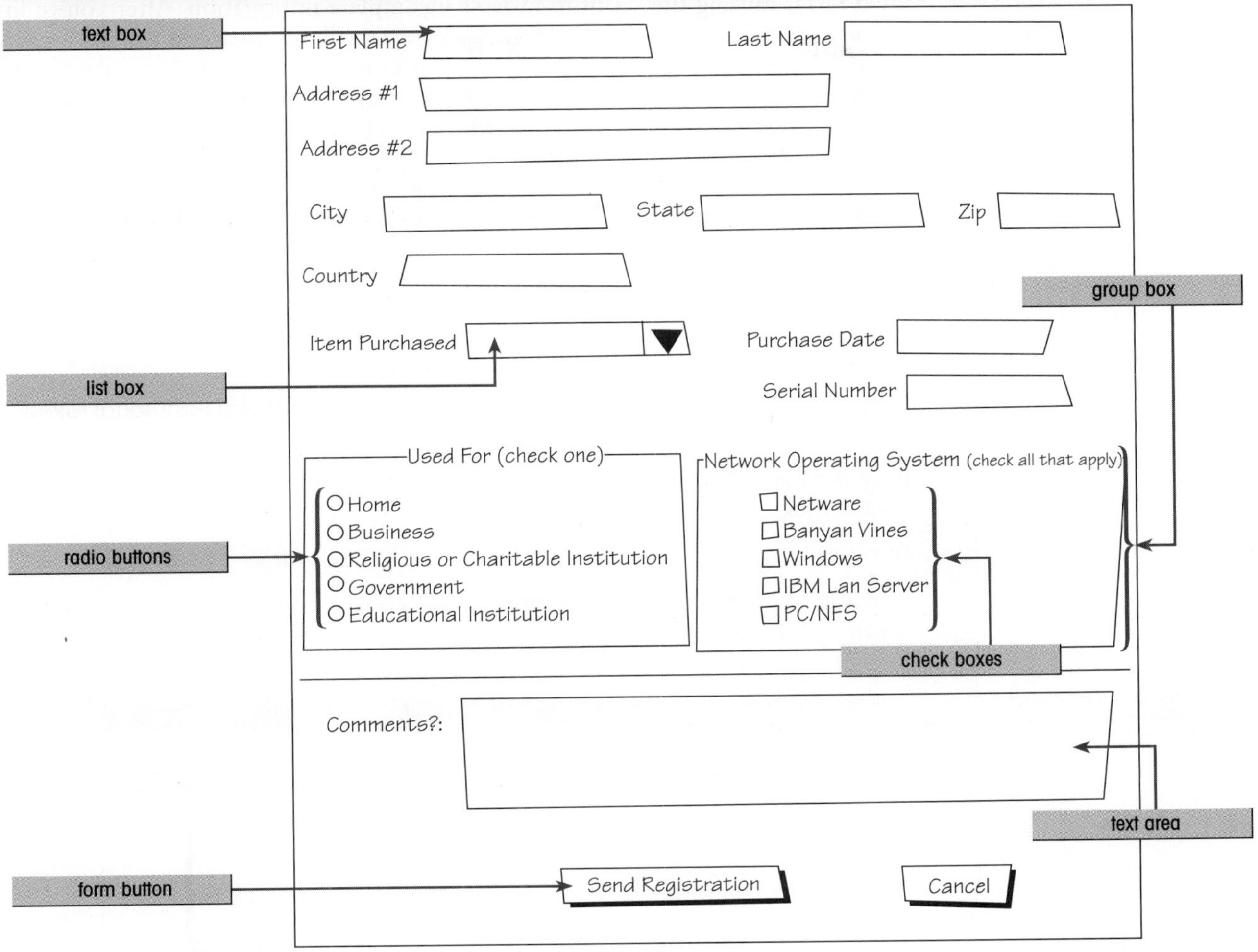

Each control element in which the user can enter information is called a **field**. Information entered into a field is called the **field value**, or simply the **value**. In some fields, users are free to enter anything they choose. Other fields, such as selection lists, limit the user to a predefined list of options.

Before you can create any fields, you must first indicate to the browser that the Web page contains fields. You do this using the <form> tag. The <form> tag identifies the beginning and end of a form, in the same way that the <table> tag defines the beginning and end of a graphical table. A single page can include several different forms, but you cannot nest one form inside another, as you can with tables. The general syntax of the <form> tag is:

```
<form attributes>
     form elements and layout tags
</form>
```

Between the <form> and </form> tags, you place the various tags for each of the fields in the form. You can also specify the form's appearance using standard HTML tags. For example, you can place a selection list within a table or place a text box alongside an <h2> heading.

The <form> tag includes attributes that control how the form is processed, including information on what CGI script to use, how the data is to be transferred to the script, and so forth. When you first begin designing your form, you can leave these attributes out. One good reason for doing so is to prevent you from accidentally running the CGI script on an unfinished form, causing the script to process incomplete information. After you've finalized the form's appearance, you can add the necessary attributes to access the CGI script.

Because a single Web page can contain multiple forms, the <form> tag includes the name attribute, allowing you to identify each form on the page. The name attribute is also needed for programs that retrieve values from the form. You'll name the form for the LanGear Web page "reg".

Susan has already started work on the design for the Web page. To ensure that different form elements align properly on the page, Susan wants you to use table elements for the layout of the form. Though not necessary, using tables in your form can make the form easier to read and use.

To open Susan's Web page:

1. Using your text editor, open **regtxt.htm** located in the tutorial.06/tutorial folder of your Data Disk and save it as **register.htm**.

2. Type the following code: **<form name="reg">** immediately below the <body> tag.

3. Scroll to the bottom of the file and locate the </body> tag

4. Type the code **</form>** directly above the </body> tag. Figure 6-4 shows the revised code for register.htm.

Figure 6-4	ADDING THE <FORM> TAG

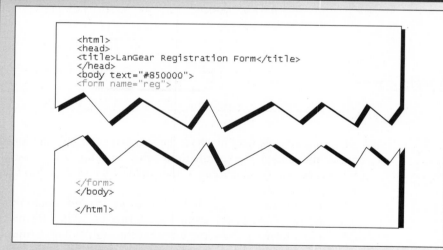

```
<html>
<head>
<title>LanGear Registration Form</title>
</head>
<body text="#850000">
<form name="reg">




</form>
</body>

</html>
```

In order to make it easier to work with the layout, Susan has divided the form into five sections: contact information, product information, usage information, comments, and buttons. As shown in Figure 6-5, these sections are separated from each other with a horizontal line. Structuring a form in this fashion can make it easier to identify the different sections.

Figure 6-5   **LAYOUT OF THE REGISTRATION FORM**

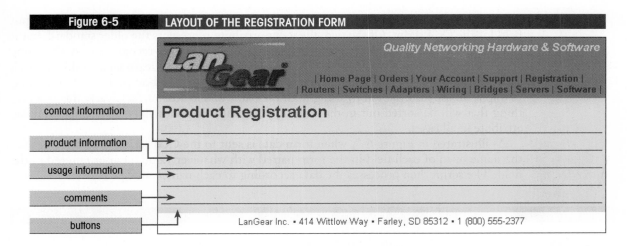

The first part of the form will contain text boxes displaying contact information for each LanGear customer.

Working with Text Boxes

Text boxes, like most form controls, are created using the <input> tag. The general syntax is:

```
<input type="type" name="name" id="id">
```

where *type* specifies the type of input field.

HTML supports 10 input types, described in Figure 6-6. To create a text box, you would enter the tag:

```
<input type="text">
```

or you could simply not include the type attribute, and the Web browser assumes, by default, that you want to create a text box. You'll learn about the other types shown in Figure 6-6 as you progress with the creation of Susan's registration form.

Figure 6-6   **INPUT TYPES**

TYPE	DESCRIPTION	
type="button"	Display a button that can be clicked to perform an action from a script	button
type="checkbox"	Display a check box	✔
type="file"	Display a browse button to locate and select a file	Browse...
type="hidden"	Create a hidden field, not viewable on the form	
type="image"	Display an inline image that can be clicked to perform an action from a script	
type="password"	Display a text box that hides text entered by the user	********
type="radio"	Display a radio (option) button	◉
type="reset"	Display a button that resets the form when clicked	reset
type="submit"	Display a button that submits the form when clicked	submit
type="text"	Display a text box that displays text entered by the user	LanGear

The name and id attributes of the <input> tag serve the same purpose: to identify the input field for the CGI script. Of the two, the name attribute represents the older standard, but it is deprecated in HTML 4.01. However, some CGI scripts still recognize only the name attribute. The newest standards use the id attribute, and as you'll learn later in this tutorial, the id attribute is required if your form contains form labels. The bottom line is that it's best to duplicate the information by using both the name and id attributes. Clearly this is something that will be sorted out in the coming years with the id attribute replacing the name attribute in all cases.

As illustrated in Figure 6-7, when form data is sent to the CGI script, the script receives the name or id of each field in the form paired with whatever value the user entered in the field. The script then processes the data according to each name/value pair.

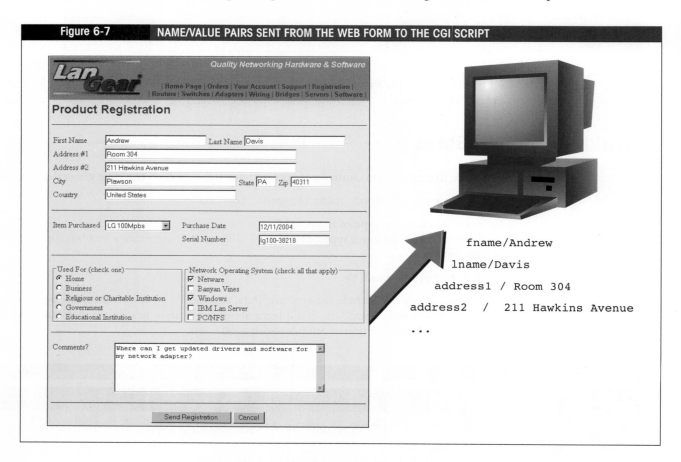

Figure 6-7   NAME/VALUE PAIRS SENT FROM THE WEB FORM TO THE CGI SCRIPT

Note that the value you enter for the name attribute is not necessarily the "name" you see next to a form element. In Figure 6-7, the value for the name attribute of the first address line is "address1," but the label associated with the text box is "Address #1." The latter is what users see on their Web browsers, and the former is sent to the CGI script. The two can be the same, but they don't have to be.

Some CGI scripts require a particular field or group of fields. For example, a CGI script whose purpose is to e-mail form values to another user might require a field named "email" that contains the e-mail address of the recipient. Before using a CGI script, you should check the documentation for any requirements and then design your form accordingly.

Finally, be aware that case is important in field names. A field named "email" might not be interpreted by the CGI script in the same way as a field named "EMAIL."

Creating a Text Box
- To create a text box, use the following HTML code:

```
<input name="name" id="id" value="value" size="value"
maxlength="value">
```
where the *name* and *id* attributes identify the field, the *value* attribute assigns a default value to the text box, the *size* attribute defines the width of the text box in number of characters, and the *maxlength* attribute defines the maximum number of characters allowed in the field.

The first part of the registration form relates to customer contact information. Each field in this section is a text box. Because text boxes are blank and do not contain any accompanying text, you need to insert a text description, such as "First Name", adjacent to each box so that the user knows what to enter. In Susan's form you are also using a table to control the layout of the form, so the appropriate row and cell tags are required as well.

To insert the text boxes on the form:

1. Type the following code within the <td> tags and immediately following the "Contact Information" comment tag as shown in Figure 6-8.

```
<table width="100%">
    <tr>
        <td width="100">
            First Name
        </td>
        <td>
            <input type="text" name="fname" id="fname">
            Last Name
            <input type="text" name="lname" id="lname">
        </td>
    </tr>
    <tr>
        <td width="100">
            Address #1
        </td>
        <td>
            <input type="text" name="address1" id="address1">
        </td>
    </tr>
    <tr>
        <td width="100">
            Address #2
        </td>
        <td>
            <input type="text" name="address2" id="address2">
        </td>
    </tr>
    <tr>
        <td width="100">
            City
```

```
        </td>
        <td>
          <input type="text" name="city" id="city">
          State
          <input type="text" name="state" id="state">
          ZIP
          <input type="text" name="zip" id="zip">
        </td>
    </tr>
    <tr>
        <td width="100">
          Country
        </td>
        <td>
          <input type="text" name="country" id="country">
        </td>
    </tr>
    </table>
```

Figure 6-8 | INSERTING CONTACT INFORMATION INTO THE FORM

```html
<!-- Contact Information -->
<tr>
   <td valign="top" colspan="2">
      <table width="100%">
      <tr>
         <td width="100">
            First Name
         </td>
         <td>
            <input type="text" name="fname" id="fname">
            Last Name
            <input type="text" name="lname" id="lname">
         </td>
      </tr>
      <tr>
         <td width="100">
            Address #1
         </td>
         <td>
            <input type="text" name="address1" id="address1">
         </td>
      </tr>
      <tr>
         <td width="100">
            Address #2
         </td>
         <td>
            <input type="text" name="address2" id="address2">
         </td>
      </tr>
      <tr>
         <td width="100">
            City
         </td>
         <td>
            <input type="text" name="city" id="city">
            State
            <input type="text" name="state" id="state">
            Zip
            <input type="text" name="zip" id="zip">
         </td>
      </tr>
      <tr>
         <td width="100">
            Country
         </td>
         <td>
            <input type="text" name="country" id="country">
         </td>
      </tr>
      </table>
   </td>
</tr>
<tr>
   <td colspan="2">
      <hr color="#850000" size="1">
   </td>
</tr>
```

2. Save your changes to the file.

3. Using your Web browser, open **register.htm** (see Figure 6-9). Note that by using a table, you've created a uniform appearance for the registration form by vertically aligning the leftmost text boxes in each row.

TROUBLE? Depending on your Web browser and browser version, your Web page may look different from the one shown in Figure 6-9.

Figure 6-9 **TEXT BOXES**

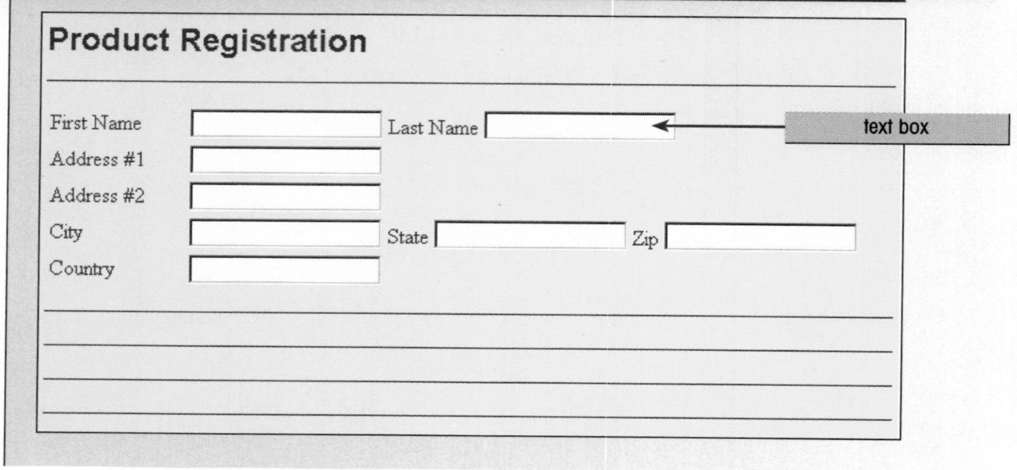

Product Registration

First Name	[ ]	Last Name	[ ] ←	text box
Address #1	[ ]		
Address #2	[ ]		
City	[ ]	State [ ]	Zip [ ]
Country	[ ]		

Controlling the Size of a Text Box

By default, all text boxes are 20 characters wide. This may be appropriate for the first and last name fields, but it's not necessary for an item like the zip code. The syntax for changing the size of a text box is:

```
<input size="value">
```

where *value* is the size of the text box in characters.

After reviewing the form, Susan decides that the size of both the fname field and the lname field should be increased to 30 characters to allow for longer names. Similarly, the address1 and address2 fields should be increased to 60 characters each to allow for street numbers and street names. The state field can be reduced to a size of three characters, and the size of the zip code field can be reduced to 10 characters. Finally, the city and country fields can be set to a width of 40 characters each.

To specify the size of the text boxes:

1. Return to **register.htm** in your text editor.

2. Type the attribute **size="30"** for the fname and lname <input> tags.

3. Type the attribute **size="60"** for the address1 and address2 <input> tags.

4. Type the attribute **size="3"** for the state <input> tag.

5. Type the attribute **size="10"** for the zip <input> tag.

6. Type the attribute **size="40"** for the city and country <input> tags.

   Figure 6-10 shows the revised code.

Figure 6-10 SETTING THE WIDTH OF TEXT BOXES

```
<tr>
    <td valign="top" colspan="2">
    <table width="100%">
    <tr>
        <td width="100">
            First Name
        </td>
        <td>
            <input type="text" name="fname" id="fname" size="30">
            Last Name
            <input type="text" name="lname" id="lname" size="30">
        </td>
    </tr>
    <tr>
        <td width="100">
            Address #1
        </td>
        <td>
            <input type="text" name="address1" id="address1" size="60">
        </td>
    </tr>
    <tr>
        <td width="100">
            Address #2
        </td>
        <td>
            <input type="text" name="address2" id="address2" size="60">
        </td>
    </tr>
    <tr>
        <td width="100">
            City
        </td>
        <td>
            <input type="text" name="city" id="city" size="40">
            State
            <input type="text" name="state" id="state" size="3">
            Zip
            <input type="text" name="zip" id="zip" size="10">
        </td>
    </tr>
    <tr>
        <td width="100">
            Country
        </td>
        <td>
            <input type="text" name="country" id="country" size="40">
        </td>
    </tr>
    </table>
    </td>
</tr>
```

7. Save your changes to the file, and then reload it in your browser. Figure 6-11 shows the form's revised appearance. Note that Netscape users may have to close and open register.htm for the changes to the Web form to take effect.

Figure 6-11	SETTING THE WIDTH OF TEXT BOXES

Product Registration

text box width set to 30 characters

First Name _____ Last Name _____ ←

Address #1 _____

Address #2 _____

City _____ State ____ Zip ____

Country _____

Setting the Maximum Length for Text Input

Setting the width of a text box does not limit the number of characters the box can hold. If a user tries to enter text longer than the box's width, the text scrolls to the left. The user cannot see the entire text, but all of it is sent to the CGI script for processing.

There are times when you want to limit the number of characters a user can enter. The syntax for setting the maximum length for field input is:

```
<input maxlength="value">
```

where *value* is the maximum number of characters that can be stored in the field. For example, if you have a Social Security Number field, you know that only nine characters are needed. You can prevent users from entering more than nine characters by inserting the attribute maxlength="9" into the <input> tag.

For the registration form, Susan wants to limit the width of the zip code field to five characters.

To specify the maximum length for the zip field:

1. Return to **register.htm** in your text editor.

2. Type the attribute **maxlength="5"** within the <input> tag for the zip field. See Figure 6-12.

Figure 6-12	SETTING THE MAXIMUM LENGTH FOR A TEXT BOX

no more than 5 characters are allowed in this text box

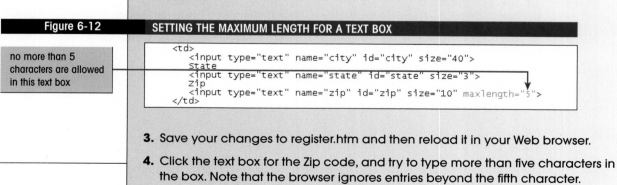

```
<td>
   <input type="text" name="city" id="city" size="40">
   State
   <input type="text" name="state" id="state" size="3">
   Zip
   <input type="text" name="zip" id="zip" size="10" maxlength="5">
</td>
```

3. Save your changes to register.htm and then reload it in your Web browser.

4. Click the text box for the Zip code, and try to type more than five characters in the box. Note that the browser ignores entries beyond the fifth character.

Setting a Default Value for a Field

If most people enter the same value into a field, it may make sense to define a default value for a field. Default values can save time and increase accuracy for users of your Web site. To define a default value, use the following syntax:

```
<input value="value">
```

here *value* is the default text or number that is displayed in the field. In the case of a text box, the default value is the value that appears in the text box when the form is initially opened.

Because domestic sales account for over 80% of LanGear's income, Susan wants the country field on the registration form to have a default value of "United States".

To set the default value for the country field:

1. Return to **register.htm** in your text editor.

2. Type **value="United States"** in the <input> tag for the country field as shown in Figure 6-13.

Figure 6-13	DEFINING A DEFAULT VALUE FOR A FIELD

default value

```
<tr>
    <td width="100">
        Country
    </td>
    <td>
        <input type="text" name="country" id="country" size="40" value="United States">
    </td>
</tr>
```

3. Save your changes to the file and then reload it in your Web browser. Verify that the text "United States" is displayed in Country text box.

If customers from countries other than the United States use this Web form, they can remove the default value by selecting the text and pressing the Delete key.

Creating a Password Field

In some instances users won't want information they enter into a text box to be displayed. For example, one part of your form might prompt the user for a credit card number. If so, you would like to prevent the card number from being displayed on the computer monitor, as a security measure. You can accomplish this with a password field. A **password field** is a text box in which the characters typed by the user are displayed as bullets or asterisks. The syntax for creating a Password field is:

```
<input type="password">
```

Using a password field should not be confused with having a secure connection between the Web client and the Web server. The password itself is not encrypted, so it is still possible for someone to intercept the information as it is being sent from your Web browser to the CGI script. The password field only acts as a mask for the field entry as it is entered. Susan does not need you to specify any Password fields for the registration form.

Working with Form Labels

So far, you've entered text alongside the text boxes to indicate the purpose of the text box to the user. For example, you can enter "Last Name" next to a text field where the user should type his or her last name. HTML allows you to formally link a label with an associated text element for scripting purposes. The syntax for creating a form label is:

```
<label for="id">label text</label>
```

where *id* is the value of the id attribute for a field on the form, and *label text* is the text of the label. Note that you must bind the label to the id attribute of the field and not the name attribute.

Labels can simplify the data entry process by allowing a user to click on either the control element or the element's label to enter data. Labels have the added advantage that users can write scripts to modify their content for interactive forms. While the <label> tag is part of the HTML 4.0 specifications, it is not currently supported by Netscape. The Netscape browser, and versions of the Internet Explorer browser prior to 4.0, ignore the <label> tag but still display the label text.

To add labels to the registration form:

1. Return to **register.htm** in your text editor.

2. Locate the field name "First Name" and enclose the text **"First Name"** within a set of opening and closing <label> tags.

3. Type the attribute **for="fname"** within the opening label tag. See Figure 6-14.

Figure 6-14	CREATING A LABEL FOR THE FNAME FIELD

value of the id attribute for the first name field

```
<td width="100">
    <label for="fname">First Name</label>
</td>
```

4. Enclose the rest of the field names in <label> tags with the for attribute in each <label> tag pointing to the value of the corresponding control element's id attribute.

   Figure 6-15 shows the revised code.

5. Close your text editor, saving you changes to register.htm.

Figure 6-15	CREATING LABELS FOR THE REMAINING FIELDNAMES

```
<tr>
    <td width="100">
        <label for="fname">First Name</label>
    </td>
    <td>
        <input type="text" name="fname" id="fname" size="30">
        <label for="lname">Last Name</label>
        <input type="text" name="lname" id="lname" size="30">
    </td>
</tr>
<tr>
    <td width="100">
        <label for="address1">Address #1</label>
    </td>
    <td>
        <input type="text" name="address1" id="address1" size="60">
    </td>
</tr>
<tr>
    <td width="100">
        <label for="address2">Address #2</label>
    </td>
    <td>
        <input type="text" name="address2" id="address2" size="60">
    </td>
</tr>
<tr>
    <td width="100">
        <label for="city">City</label>
    </td>
    <td>
        <input type="text" name="city" id="city" size="40">
        <label for="state">State</label>
        <input type="text" name="state" id="state" size="3">
        <label for="zip">Zip</label>
        <input type="text" name="zip" id="zip" size="10" maxlength="5">
    </td>
</tr>
<tr>
    <td width="100">
        <label for="country">Country</label>
    </td>
    <td>
        <input type="text" name="country" id="country" size="40" value="United States">
    </td>
</tr>
</table>
```

Before going on to other tasks, you'll test the registration form by entering some test values in it. Press the Tab key to move between text boxes. To move to the previous text box, press the Tab key while holding down the Shift key. Typically, pressing the Enter key submits the form, but because you have not created a submit button for the form yet, pressing the Enter key does nothing at this point.

To test your form:

1. Reload **register.htm** in your Web browser.

2. Enter sample text in the form fields, pressing Tab to move from one text box to the next.

3. Test the operation of the filed labels by clicking them. Clicking a label in Internet Explorer places the cursor in the text box associated with the label .

4. After you have tested the form, close your Web browser.

You've completed working on the first part of the registration form and you've learned how forms and CGI scripts work together to allow Web designers to collect information from users. You've also learned how to create simple text boxes using the <input> tag and create field labels associated with those text boxes. In the next session, you'll learn other uses for the <input> tag by adding new fields to the form, including: a selection list, radio buttons, and check boxes.

Session 6.1 QUICK CHECK

1. What is a CGI script?

2. What is the purpose of the <form> tag?

3. What HTML tag would you use to create a text box with the name "Phone"?

4. What HTML attribute would you use to create a Phone text box that is 10 characters in length?

5. What HTML attribute would you use to limit entry to the Phone text box to no more than 10 characters?

6. What HTML tag would you use to create a text box named "Subscribe" with a default value of "yes"?

7. How would you prevent the contents of a text box from being displayed on the user's computer screen?

8. What HTML code would you use to insert the text "Date of Birth" as a field label associated with the control element id "dob"?

SESSION 6.2

In this session you'll learn how to create selection lists that allow users to select single or multiple options from a drop-down list box. You'll also create radio buttons for selecting single option values, and you'll create check boxes for selecting one or more items in a list. You'll also see how to enclose multiple fields within a single element called a group box. Finally, you'll create text areas for entering extended comments and memos.

Creating a Selection List

The next section of the registration form focuses on collecting information about the product that the customer has purchased and how the customer intends to use it. The first field you'll create in this section records the product name. Figure 6-16 displays the products that Susan wants you to include in the registration form.

Figure 6-16   LANGEAR PRODUCTS

ITEM GROUP	ITEM
Routers	LanPass 115
	LanPass 125
	LanPass 250
Switches	FastSwitch 200
	FastSwitch 400
Adapters	LG 10Mpbs
	LG 10Mpbs/w
	LG 100Mpbs
	LG 100Mpbs/w

Because the products constitute a predefined list of values for the product name, Susan wants this information displayed with a selection list. A **selection list** is a list box from which a user selects a particular value or set of values. Selection lists are a good idea when there is a fixed set of possible responses; they help prevent spelling mistakes and erroneous entries.

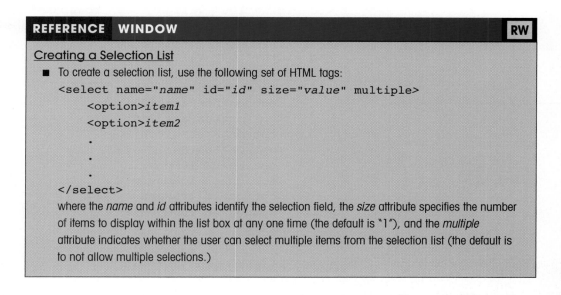

Using the `<select>` and `<option>` Tags

You create a selection list using the `<select>` tag, and you specify individual selection items with the `<option>` tag. The general syntax for the `<select>` and `<option>` tags is:

```
<select name="name" id="id">
    <option>item1
    <option>item2
    .
    .
    .
</select>
```

where the *name* and *id* attributes identify the selection field and each `<option>` tag represents an individual item in the selection list. The text in the selection list is indicated by the text in *item1*, *item2*, and so forth. Note that the `<option>` tag is a one-sided tag.

Enter the list of LanGear products into a selection list on the form:

1. Using your text editor, open **register.htm**.

2. Type the following HTML code within the <td> tag located immediately following the "Product Information" comment tag:

```
<table width="100%">
<tr>
   <td width="100" valign="top" rowspan="2">
      <label for="item">Item Purchased</label>
   </td>
   <td width="150" valign="top" rowspan="2">
      <select name="item" id="item">
         <option>LanPass 115
         <option>LanPass 125
         <option>LanPass 250
         <option>FastSwitch 200
         <option>FastSwitch 400
         <option>LG 10Mpbs
         <option>LG 10Mpbs/w
         <option>LG 100Mpbs
         <option>LG 100Mpbs/w
      </select>
   </td>
```

Figure 6-17 shows the revised HTML code.

Figure 6-17 CREATING A SELECTION LIST

```
<!-- Product Information -->
<tr>
   <td valign="top" colspan="2">
   <table width="100%">
   <tr>
      <td width="100" valign="top" rowspan="2">
         <label for="item">Item Purchased</label>
      </td>
      <td width="150" valign="top" rowspan="2">
         <select name="item" id="item">
               <option>LanPass 115
               <option>LanPass 125
               <option>LanPass 250
               <option>FastSwitch 200
               <option>FastSwitch 400
               <option>LG 10Mpbs
               <option>LG 10Mpbs/w
               <option>LG 100Mpbs
               <option>LG 100Mpbs/w
         </select>
      </td>
   </td>
</tr>
<tr>
   <td colspan="2">
      <hr color="#850000" size="1">
   </td>
</tr>
```

selection list field name

items in the selection list

3. Next, add text boxes for two other fields that record the date of purchase and the serial number for the product. Add the following code below the code you just inserted. See Figure 6-18.

```
<td width="150" valign="top">
   <label for="date">Purchase Date</label>
</td>
<td valign="top">
   <input type="text" name="date" id="date" size="20">
</td>
```

```
      </tr>
      <tr>
        <td width="150" valign="top">
           <label for="snumber">Serial Number</label>
        </td>
        <td valign="top">
           <input type="text" name="snumber" id="snumber"
size="20">
        </td>
      </tr>
      </table>
```

Figure 6-18   **ADDING TEXT BOXES FOR DATE OF PURCHASE AND SERIAL NUMBER**

```
<table width="100%">
<tr>
    <td width="100" valign="top" rowspan="2">
        <label for="item">Item Purchased</label>
    </td>
    <td width="150" valign="top" rowspan="2">
        <select name="item" id="item">
            <option>LanPass 115
            <option>LanPass 125
            <option>LanPass 250
            <option>FastSwitch 200
            <option>FastSwitch 400
            <option>LG 10Mpbs
            <option>LG 10Mpbs/w
            <option>LG 100Mpbs
            <option>LG 100Mpbs/w
        </select>
    </td>
    <td width="150" valign="top">
        <label for="date">Purchase Date</label>
    </td>
    <td valign="top">
        <input type="text" name="date" id="date" size="20">
    </td>
</tr>
<tr>
    <td width="150" valign="top">
        <label for="snumber">Serial Number</label>
    </td>
    <td valign="top">
        <input type="text" name="snumber" id="snumber" size="20">
    </td>
</tr>
</table>
```

4. Save your changes to register.htm and reload the file in your browser. The form now contains the selection list. Note that the first item in the list, LanPass 115, is displayed in the selection list box.

5. Click the **Item Purchased** list arrow to verify that the products you entered with the <option> tags are displayed. See Figure 6-19.

| Figure 6-19 | USING THE ITEM PURCHASED SELECTION LIST |

Product Registration

First Name _____ Last Name _____

Address #1 _____

Address #2 _____

City _____ State ____ Zip ____

Country [United States]

Item Purchased [LanPass 115 ▼]   Purchase Date _____

| LanPass 115 |
| LanPass 125 |
| LanPass 250 |
| FastSwitch 200 |
| FastSwitch 400 |
| LG 10Mpbs |
| LG 10Mpbs/w |
| LG 100Mpbs |
| LG 100Mpbs/w |

Serial Number _____

Wittlow Way • Farley, SD 85312 • 1 (800) 555-2377

TROUBLE? Your selection list might look slightly different depending on your browser and browser version.

Modifying the Appearance of a Selection List

HTML provides several attributes you can use to modify the appearance and behavior of selection lists and selection options. By default, the <select> tag displays one option from the selection list, along with a list arrow to view additional selection options. You can change the number of options displayed by modifying the size attribute. The syntax of the size attribute is:

```
<select size="value">
```

where *value* is the number of items that the selection list displays in the form. By specifying a value greater than 1, you change the selection list from a drop-down list box to a list box with a scroll bar that allows a user to scroll through the selection options. If you set the size attribute to be equal to the number of options in the selection list, the scroll bar is either not displayed or is dimmed. See Figure 6-20.

| Figure 6-20 | SELECTION LISTS WITH DIFFERENT SIZE VALUES |

Susan likes the product selection list as it is, so you don't have to specify a different value for the size attribute.

Making Multiple Selections

Users are not limited to a single selection from a selection list. Adding the multiple attribute to the <select> tag allows multiple selections from a list. The syntax for this attribute is:

```
<select multiple>
```

A common method to make multiple selections from a selection list is to hold down a specific key while you make the selections. With the Windows operating system, multiple selections can be made as follows:

- For noncontiguous selections, press and hold the Ctrl key while you make your selections.
- For a contiguous selection, select the first item, press and hold the Shift key, and then select the last item in the range. The two items you selected and all the items between them are selected.

If you decide to use a multiple selection list in a form, be aware that the form sends a name/value pair to the CGI script for each option the user selects from the list. This requires the CGI script to be able to handle a single field with multiple values. Check and verify that your CGI scripts are designed to handle this before using a multiple selection list.

Working with Option Values

By default, a form sends the values that are displayed in the selection list to the CGI script. In your form, if the user selects the first option from the selection list, the text string "LanPass 115" is sent to the CGI script. Sometimes you may want to send an abbreviation or code to the CGI script instead of the entire text string. For example, you may display descriptive text for each option in the selection list to help users make an informed choice, but only an abbreviated version is required for your records. You can specify the value that is sent to the CGI script with the value attribute. The following HTML code sends the value "1" to the CGI script if the LanPass 115 is selected, the value "2" if the LanPass 125 is selected, and so forth:

```
<option value="1">LanPass 115
<option value="2">LanPass 125
<option value="3">LanPass 250
<option value="4">FastSwitch 200

. . .
```

You can also specify which item in the selection list is selected, or highlighted, when the form is initially displayed. The first option in the list is highlighted by default, but you can specify a different value using the selected attribute. In the following HTML code, the LanPass 250 is the option that is initially selected when the user first encounters the selection list field on the form, even though it is not the first item in the list.

```
<option>LanPass 115
<option>LanPass 125
<option selected>LanPass 250
<option>FastSwitch 200
. . .
```

Susan doesn't need to change the default selection in the form, but she would like to group the options in the selection list according to item type.

Working with Option Groups

In its current state, the item names are grouped together in a single list. Susan feels that it would be easier for customers to locate a specific item if they were grouped by item type. This is particularly true if she expands the list by adding more items.

The most recent releases of HTML allow you to organize selection lists into distinct groups called **option groups**. The syntax for creating an option group is:

```
<optgroup label="label">
    <option>item1a
    <option>item2a
. . .
</optgroup>
<optgroup label="label">
    <option>item1b
    <option>item2b
. . .
</optgroup>
. . .
```

where *label* is the label assigned to the option group. The text for the label appears in the selection list above each group of items but is not a selectable item from the list.

Susan would like you to create three option groups labeled "Routers", "Switches", and "Adapters" for this selection list.

To create option groups for the selection list

1. Return to **register.htm** in your text editor.

2. Type the code: **<optgroup label="Routers">** immediately above the <option> LanPass 115 tag.

3. Type the following code immediately following the option item, "LanPass 250":

```
</optgroup>
<optgroup label="Switches">
```

4. Type the following the two lines immediately following the option item "FastSwitch 400":

```
</optgroup>
<optgroup label="Adapters">
```

5. Type the following code immediately following the option item "LG 100Mpbs/w":

```
</optgroup>
```

Figure 6-21 shows the revised code.

Figure 6-21   CREATING OPTION GROUPS

a single option group →

option group label

```
<select name="item" id="item">
<optgroup label="Routers">
    <option>LanPass 115
    <option>LanPass 125
    <option>LanPass 250
</optgroup>
<optgroup label="Switches">
    <option>FastSwitch 200
    <option>FastSwitch 400
</optgroup>
<optgroup label="Adapters">
    <option>LG 10Mpbs
    <option>LG 10Mpbs/w
    <option>LG 100Mpbs
    <option>LG 100Mpbs/w
</optgroup>
</select>
```

6. Save your changes to the file and then reload it in your Web browser. As show in Figure 6-22, the selection list items are now grouped by type.

Figure 6-22   OPTION GROUPS

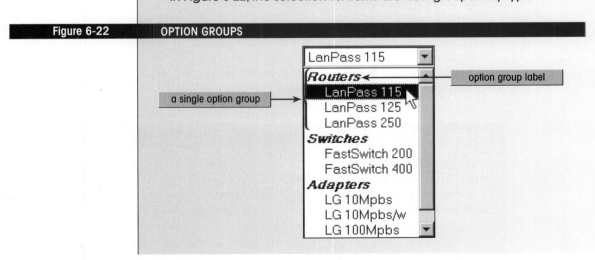

a single option group →

option group label

Note that versions of Internet Explorer and Netscape prior to 6.0 display the selection list without the group labels.

Working with Radio Buttons

Radio buttons are similar to selection lists in that they display a list of choices from which a user makes a selection. Unlike selection list items, only one radio button can be selected at a time. The syntax to create a radio button is:

```
<input type="radio" name="name" id="id" value="value">
```

where the *name* identifies the field containing the radio button, the *id* attribute identifies the specific option, and the *value* attribute indicates the value sent to the CGI script if that radio button is selected by the user. The id attribute is only required if you intend to use a field label with the radio button.

You *must* include the name attribute because it groups distinct radio buttons together, so that selecting one radio button in the group automatically deselects all of the other radio buttons in that group. Like the text boxes you created earlier, the <input> tag does not create any text for the radio button. In order for users to understand the purpose of the radio button, you must insert descriptive text next to the button. If you enclose that text within a label tag, the user can select the radio button by clicking either the button or the label.

Figure 6-23 shows an example of HTML code that creates radio buttons for party affiliations.

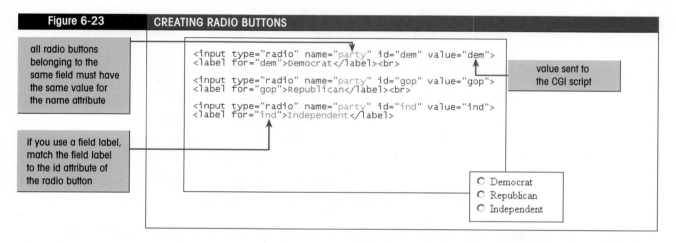

Figure 6-23   CREATING RADIO BUTTONS

all radio buttons belonging to the same field must have the same value for the name attribute

if you use a field label, match the field label to the id attribute of the radio button

```
<input type="radio" name="party" id="dem" value="dem">
<label for="dem">Democrat</label><br>

<input type="radio" name="party" id="gop" value="gop">
<label for="gop">Republican</label><br>

<input type="radio" name="party" id="ind" value="ind">
<label for="ind">Independent</label>
```

value sent to the CGI script

○ Democrat
○ Republican
○ Independent

Note that in this sample code, the value sent to the CGI script does not match the field label. If the user selects the Republican radio button, the value "gop" is sent to the CGI script paired with the field name "party."

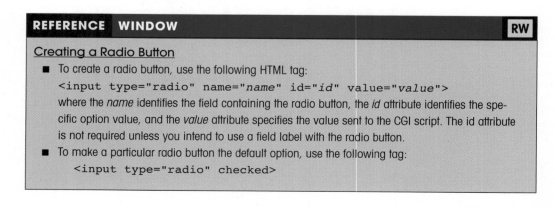

REFERENCE WINDOW   **RW**

Creating a Radio Button
- To create a radio button, use the following HTML tag:
  ```
  <input type="radio" name="name" id="id" value="value">
  ```
  where the *name* identifies the field containing the radio button, the *id* attribute identifies the specific option value, and the *value* attribute specifies the value sent to the CGI script. The id attribute is not required unless you intend to use a field label with the radio button.
- To make a particular radio button the default option, use the following tag:
  ```
  <input type="radio" checked>
  ```

Susan has indicated that she would like you to create radio buttons for product usage on the registration form. The name of the field is "use" and it has five possible options:

- home
- business
- religious or charitable institution
- government
- educational institution

To create radio buttons for the use field:

1. Return to **register.htm** in your text editor.

2. Type the following code within the opening and closing <td> tags as shown in Figure 6-24:

```
<table width="100%">
<tr>
    <td valign="top">
        <input type="radio" name="use" id="home"
value="home">
        <label for="home">Home</label><br>

        <input type="radio" name="use" id="bus" value="bus">
        <label for="bus">Business</label><br>

        <input type="radio" name="use" id="char"
value="char">
        <label for="char">Religious or Charitable
Institution</label><br>

        <input type="radio" name="use" id="gov" value="gov">
        <label for="gov">Government</label><br>

        <input type="radio" name="use" id="edu" value="edu">
        <label for="edu">Educational Institution</label>
    </td>
</tr>
</table>
```

Figure 6-24   ADDING RADIO BUTTONS TO THE REGISTER.HTM FORM

```
<!-- Usage Information -->
<tr>
   <td valign="top" colspan="2">
   <table width="100%">
   <tr>
      <td valign="top">
         <input type="radio" name="use" id="home" value="home">
         <label for="home">Home</label><br>

         <input type="radio" name="use" id="bus" value="bus">
         <label for="bus">Business</label><br>

         <input type="radio" name="use" id="char" value="char">
         <label for="char">Religious or Charitable Institution</label><br>

         <input type="radio" name="use" id="gov" value="gov">
         <label for="gov">Government</label><br>

         <input type="radio" name="use" id="edu" value="edu">
         <label for="edu">Educational Institution</label>
      </td>
   </tr>
   </table>
   </td>
</tr>
<tr>
   <td colspan="2">
      <hr color="#850000" size="1">
   </td>
</tr>
```

3. Save your changes to register.htm and then reload it in your Web browser. See Figure 6-25.

4. Click each radio button. Note that as you click one button, the previously selected button is deselected.

5. If you are using Internet Explorer, click the button labels to verify that this has the same effect as clicking the button itself.

Figure 6-25   RADIO BUTTONS IN THE REGISTRATION FORM

- ○ Home
- ○ Business
- ○ Religious or Charitable Institution
- ○ Government
- ○ Educational Institution

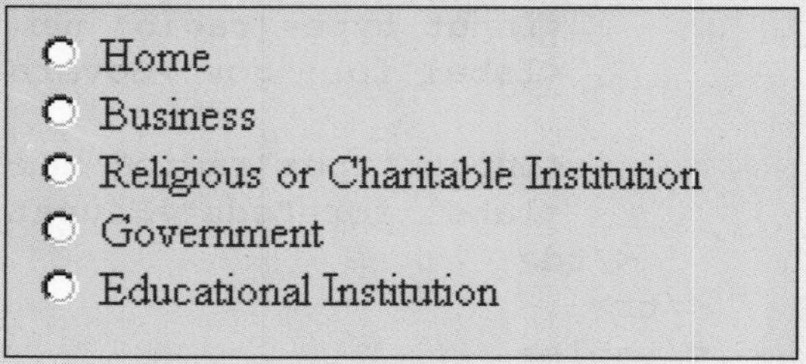

TROUBLE? If clicking one radio button fails to deselect another, check the names you've assigned to each button and verify that they are identical and that the cases (uppercase and lowercase) match.

Note that when you first open the registration form, none of the radio buttons is selected. Susan informs you that most LanGear products are used by businesses, and she would like this option set as the default in the Web page form. You can do this by adding the checked attribute to the <input> tag for that particular radio button. The code to make the Business radio button the default option would be:

```
<input type="radio" name="use" id="bus" value="bus" checked>
```

To edit the radio button:

1. Return to **register.htm** in your text editor.

2. Following the syntax shown previously, type "**checked**" within the <input> tag for the Business radio button.

3. Save your changes to register.htm and then reload it in your Web browser. Verify that the Business radio button is selected by default.

When should you use radio buttons, and when should you use a selection list? Generally, if you have a long list of options, you should use a selection list. If you want to allow users to select more than one option, you should use a selection list with the multiple attribute. If you have a short list of options, and only one option is allowed at a time, you should use radio buttons.

Creating a Group Box

Susan notices that there is no label for the entire collection of radio buttons. You could insert a text string into the form for this purpose, but another approach is to enclose the radio buttons in a **group box**. A group box is a box placed around a set of fields that indicates that they belong to a common group. The syntax for creating a group box is:

```
<fieldset>
     <legend align="align">legend text</legend>
        collection of fields
</fieldset>
```

where the <legend> tag is used to display a legend on the group box, and *legend text* specifies the text for that legend. The align attribute specifies where the legend is placed in the box. The possible align values are "top" (the default), "bottom", "left", and "right". In practical terms, browsers only support the "top" and "right" options at the time of this writing. Figure 6-26 shows an example of a group box applied to a set of radio buttons.

Figure 6-26   **CREATING A GROUP BOX LEGEND**

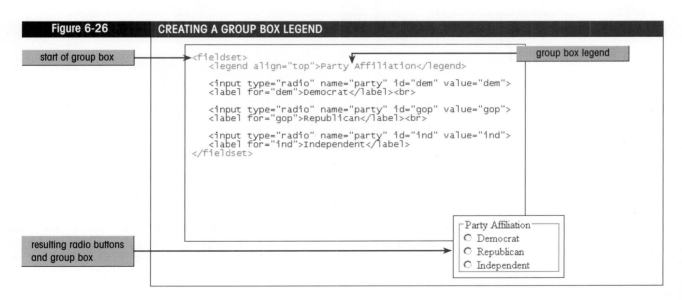

start of group box

group box legend

```
<fieldset>
    <legend align="top">Party Affiliation</legend>

    <input type="radio" name="party" id="dem" value="dem">
    <label for="dem">Democrat</label><br>

    <input type="radio" name="party" id="gop" value="gop">
    <label for="gop">Republican</label><br>

    <input type="radio" name="party" id="ind" value="ind">
    <label for="ind">Independent</label>
</fieldset>
```

resulting radio buttons and group box

```
┌─Party Affiliation────────
│  ○ Democrat
│  ○ Republican
│  ○ Independent
```

Now that you've seen how to create a group box, apply one to the radio buttons on the registration form.

To create a group box:

1. Return to **register.htm** in your text editor.

2. Type the following code immediately above the <input> tag for the "home" radio button:

```
<fieldset>
<legend align="top">Used For (check one)</legend>
```

3. Type the following code after the Educational Institution label:

```
</fieldset>
```

See Figure 6-27.

Figure 6-27   **CREATING A GROUP BOX FOR THE USED RADIO BUTTONS**

```
<fieldset>
<legend align="top">Used For (check one)</legend>
<input type="radio" name="use" id="home" value="home">
<label for="home">Home</label><br>

<input type="radio" name="use" id="bus" value="bus" checked>
<label for="bus">Business</label><br>

<input type="radio" name="use" id="char" value="char">
<label for="char">Religious or Charitable Institution</label><br>

<input type="radio" name="use" id="gov" value="gov">
<label for="gov">Government</label><br>

<input type="radio" name="use" id="edu" value="edu">
<label for="edu">Educational Institution</label>
</fieldset>
```

4. Save your changes to the file and then reload it in your Web browser. See Figure 6-28.

Figure 6-28   **RADIO BUTTONS WITHIN A GROUP BOX**

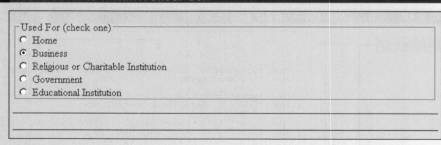

There is no attribute to control the size of the group box. The box's height will be large enough to accommodate the fields and labels in the field set. The width is the width of whatever space remains on the Web page. If you wish to set the width to a specific value, you can place the group box in a table cell and then set the width of the cell.

An important point to remember about group boxes is that they cannot extend across table cells; all of the fields in the field set must be placed within a single cell.

Working **with Check Boxes**

The next type of input field you'll create in the registration form is a check box. A check box is either selected or not, but unlike radio buttons, there is only one check box per field. Check boxes are created using the following syntax:

```
<input type="checkbox" name="name" id="id" value="value">
```

where the name and id attributes identify the check box, and the value attribute specifies the value that is sent to the CGI script when the check box is selected. For example, the following code assigns the value "democrat" to the party field if the check box is selected.

```
<input type="checkbox" name="party" value="democrat">
```

As with text boxes and radio buttons, the <input> tag for a check box does not display any text. You add text or a label next to the <input> tag to describe the purpose of the check box.

Check boxes are not selected by default. To change this, you can add the checked attribute to the <input> tag.

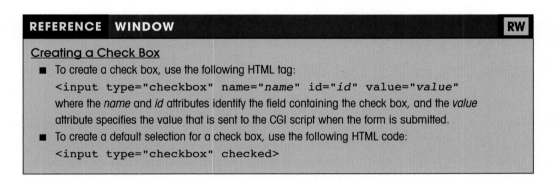

REFERENCE   WINDOW   **RW**

Creating a Check Box
■ To create a check box, use the following HTML tag:
```
<input type="checkbox" name="name" id="id" value="value"
```
where the *name* and *id* attributes identify the field containing the check box, and the *value* attribute specifies the value that is sent to the CGI script when the form is submitted.
■ To create a default selection for a check box, use the following HTML code:
```
<input type="checkbox" checked>
```

There are a total of five check boxes that Susan wants you to add to the form. The check boxes are for users to indicate what network operating systems they are running with the LanGear product. Susan is tracking five network operating systems: Netware, Banyan Vines, Windows, IBM Lan Server, and PC/NFS. Even though you'll arrange these check boxes together on the form, each one is associated with a different field. This is different than the radio buttons you just created, where all are associated with the use field.

To add check boxes to your form:

1. Return to **register.htm** in your text editor.

2. Type the following code immediately following the </td> tag for the radio buttons (see Figure 6-29):

```
<td valign="top">
    <input type="checkbox" name="nw" id="nw" value="yes">
    <label for="nw">Netware</label><br>

    <input type="checkbox" name="bv" id="bv" value="yes">
    <label for="bv">Banyan Vines</label><br>

    <input type="checkbox" name="win" id="win" value="yes">
    <label for="win">Windows</label><br>
```

```
<input type="checkbox" name="ibm" id="ibm" value="yes">
<label for="ibm">IBM Lan Server</label><br>

<input type="checkbox" name="pcnfs" id="pcnfs"
value="yes">
<label for="pcnfs">PC/NFS</label>
</td>
```

Figure 6-29   **ADDING CHECK BOXES TO THE REGISTER.HTM FORM**

```
        <input type="radio" name="use" id="edu" value="edu">
        <label for="edu">Educational Institution</label>
        </fieldset>
    </td>
    <td valign="top">
        <input type="checkbox" name="nw" id="nw" value="yes">
        <label for="nw">Netware</label><br>

        <input type="checkbox" name="bv" id="bv" value="yes">
        <label for="bv">Banyan Vines</label><br>

        <input type="checkbox" name="win" id="win" value="yes">
        <label for="win">Windows</label><br>

        <input type="checkbox" name="ibm" id="ibm" value="yes">
        <label for="ibm">IBM Lan Server</label><br>

        <input type="checkbox" name="pcnfs" id="pcnfs" value="yes">
        <label for="pcnfs">PC/NFS</label>
    </td>
</tr>
</table>
```

3. Save your changes to register.htm and then reload it in your Web browser.

4. Click the different check boxes in the form. Note that you can click either the check box or the label associated with the check box to select and deselect the field. See Figure 6-30.

Figure 6-30   **CHECK BOXES IN THE REGISTRATION FORM**

☐ Netware
☐ Banyan Vines
☐ Windows
☐ IBM Lan Server
☐ PC/NFS

Susan likes the check boxes, but she would like you to enclose the check boxes within a group box.

To enclose the check boxes in a group box:

1. Return to **register.htm** in your text editor.

2. Type the following code immediately above the <input> tag for the Netware check box:

```
<fieldset>
    <legend align="top">Network Operating System (check all
    that apply)</legend>
```

3. Type the closing tag **</fieldset>** below the <label> tag for the PC/NFS label (see Figure 6-31).

Figure 6-31   CREATING A GROUP BOX FOR THE OPERATING SYSTEM CHECK BOXES

```
<fieldset>
<legend align="top">Network Operating System (check all that apply)</legend>
<input type="checkbox" name="nw" id="nw" value="yes">
<label for="nw">Netware</label><br>

<input type="checkbox" name="bv" id="bv" value="yes">
<label for="bv">Banyan Vines</label><br>

<input type="checkbox" name="win" id="win" value="yes">
<label for="win">Windows</label><br>

<input type="checkbox" name="ibm" id="ibm" value="yes">
<label for="ibm">IBM Lan Server</label><br>

<input type="checkbox" name="pcnfs" id="pcnfs" value="yes">
<label for="pcnfs">PC/NFS</label>
</fieldset>
```

4. Save your changes to the file and then reload it in your Web browser. See Figure 6-32.

Figure 6-32   GROUP BOXES FOR THE RADIO BUTTONS AND CHECK BOXES

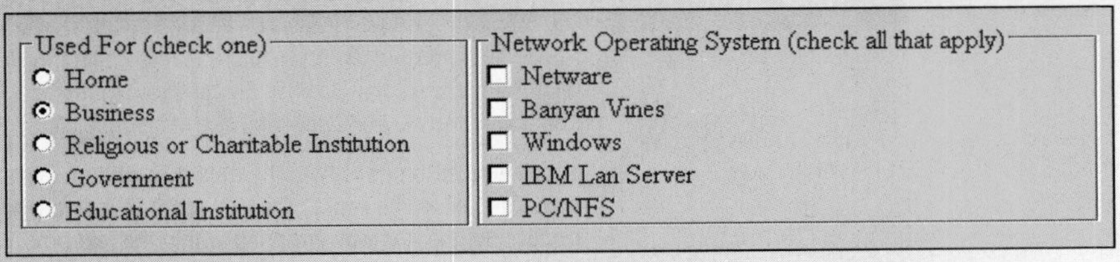

Creating a Text Area

The next section of the registration form allows users to enter comments about the products they've purchased. Because these comments will likely contain several lines of text, a text box would be too small. To create a larger text area for the text box, use the tag:

```
<textarea name="name" id="id" rows="value" cols="value">
default text </textarea>
```

where the rows and cols attributes define the dimensions of the text box. The rows attribute indicates the number of lines in the text box, though some early browser versions show more lines than indicated by the rows attribute, and the cols attribute specifies the number of characters in each line. Though not required, you can specify default text that will appear in the text box when the form is initially displayed. Figure 6-33 shows an example of a text area with default text.

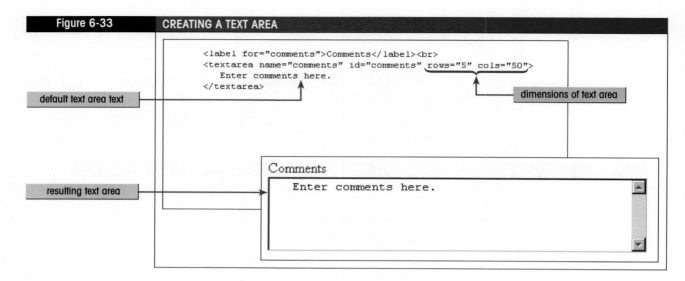

Figure 6-33   CREATING A TEXT AREA

```
<label for="comments">Comments</label><br>
<textarea name="comments" id="comments" rows="5" cols="50">
   Enter comments here.
</textarea>
```

default text area text

dimensions of text area

resulting text area

Comments

Enter comments here.

Note that unlike the <input> tag, <textarea> is a two-sided tag, which means that it has an opening tag, <textarea>, and a closing tag, </textarea>. You need to include the </textarea> tag even if you don't specify default text.

The text you enter in a text area wraps to the next line when it exceeds the width of the box. You can control how your browser wraps text to a new line using the wrap attribute. Figure 6-34 describes the three possible wrap options.

Figure 6-34   WRAP ATTRIBUTE VALUES

WRAP VALUE	DESCRIPTION
wrap="off"	All the text is displayed on a single line, scrolling to the left if the text extends past the width of the box. Text goes to the next row in the box only if the Enter key is pressed. The text is sent to the CGI script in a single line.
wrap="soft"	Text wraps automatically to the next row when it extends beyond the width of the text box. The text is still sent to the CGI script in a single line without any information about how the text was wrapped within the text box.
wrap="hard"	Text wraps automatically to the next row when it extends beyond the width of the text box. When the text is sent to the CGI script, the line-wrapping information is included, allowing the CGI script to work with the text exactly as it appears in the text box.

Typically, you'll set the value of the wrap attribute to either "soft" or "hard" to allow text to wrap within the text box. The difference between these two options lies in how the text is sent to the CGI script. The "hard" setting preserves any line wrapping that takes place in the text box and the "soft" setting does not. Review the documentation for the CGI script to determine whether one method is preferred over the other. If no value for the wrap attribute is specified, a value of "soft" is used.

REFERENCE   WINDOW   **RW**

<u>Creating a Text Area</u>

■ To create a text area for extended text entry, use the following tag:

```
<textarea name="name" id="id" rows="value" cols="value">default
  text</textarea>
```

where the *default text* is the text that is displayed in the text area (this is optional), and the *rows* and *cols* attribute specifies the number of lines in the text area and the number of characters in each line.

■ To control how text wraps in a text area, add the attribute wrap="*option*" to the <textarea> tag, where *option* is "off", "soft", or "hard". The "off" option removes line wrapping. The "soft" option turns line wrapping on (the default), but does not send line-wrapping information to the Web server. The "hard" option turns line wrapping on and also sends this information to the Web server.

For the comments field, use the <textarea> tag with the wrap attribute set to "soft" so that the user's comments wrap to the next line in the box. The size of the text area is 6 lines high and 50 characters wide, which Susan thinks should be enough for the typed comments.

To add a text area text box to the registration form:

1. Return to **register.htm** in your text editor.

2. Type the following code within the opening and closing <td> tags immediately below the "Comments" comment tag (see Figure 6-35):

```
<table width="100%">
<tr>
   <td width="120" valign="top">
      <label for="comments">Comments?</label>
   </td>
   <td valign="top">
      <textarea name="comments" id="comments" rows="6"
cols="50" wrap="soft">
      </textarea>
   </td>
</tr>
</table>
```

| Figure 6-35 | ADDING A TEXT AREA TO THE REGISTER.HTM FORM |

```
<!-- Comments -->
<tr>
   <td valign="top" colspan="2">
   <table width="100%">
   <tr>
      <td width="120" valign="top">
         <label for="comments">Comments?</label>
      </td>
      <td valign="top">
         <textarea name="comments" id="comments" rows="6" cols="50" wrap="soft">
         </textarea>
      </td>
   </tr>
   </table>
   </td>
</tr>
<tr>
   <td colspan="2">
      <hr color="#850000" size="1">
   </td>
</tr>
```

3. Save your changes to register.htm and reload it in your Web browser.

4. Test the text-wrapping feature by typing the following text in the comments field (see Figure 6-36):

I'm very pleased with my purchase of the LG 100Mpbs/w wireless network adapter. How do I obtain updates to the driver and software?

Figure 6-36	TEXT AREA

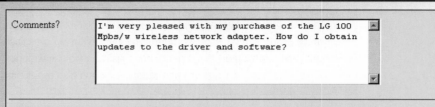

Note that the text box includes a vertical scroll bar so that a user can scroll to see the hidden text if needed.

TROUBLE? Depending on your Web browser, your Comments text box may look slightly different from the one shown in Figure 6-36.

You've created the last input field for the registration form. Using HTML you've added text boxes, a selection list, radio buttons, check boxes, and a text area to your form. In the next session, you'll learn how to set up your form to work with a CGI script.

Session 6.2 QUICK CHECK

1. What HTML tag would you use to create a selection list with a field named State and with the options California, Nevada, Oregon, and Washington?

2. How would you modify the HTML tag in Question 1 to allow more than one state to be selected from the list?

3. What HTML tag would make Oregon the default selection in Question 1?

4. What HTML code would you use to place the options from Question 1 in an option group named "West Coast"?

5. What HTML tag would you use to create a series of radio buttons for a field named State with the options California, Nevada, Oregon, and Washington? Place the radio buttons in a group box with the legend "West Coast".

6. How would you modify the HTML tag in Question 5 to send the number 1 to the CGI script if the user selects California, 2 for Nevada, 3 for Oregon, and 4 for Washington?

7. What HTML tag would you use to create a check box field named California? If you don't specify otherwise, what value is sent to the CGI script if the check box is selected?

8. What HTML tag would you use to create a text box field named Memo that is 5 rows high and 30 columns wide and has the default text "Enter notes here."?

9. What attribute would you add to the HTML tag in Question 8 to cause the Memo text to wrap to the next row and send the text-wrapping information to the CGI script?

SESSION 6.3

In this session you'll learn how to create submit and reset buttons to either send your form to a CGI script or reset it to its initial state. You'll learn how to create image fields and to work with form attributes to control how your form is submitted to the CGI script. You'll also learn how to process form data without using a CGI script. Finally, the session ends with a discussion about how to access specific control elements in your form.

Creating Form Buttons

Up to now, all of your control elements have been input fields of some kind. Another type of control element is one that performs an action. In forms, this is usually done with a button. Buttons can be clicked to run programs, submit forms, or reset the form to its original state.

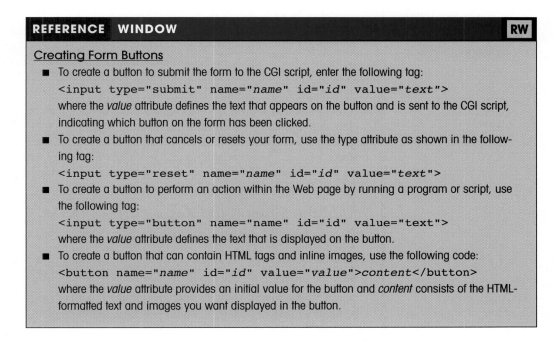

REFERENCE WINDOW   RW

Creating Form Buttons

■ To create a button to submit the form to the CGI script, enter the following tag:

```
<input type="submit" name="name" id="id" value="text">
```
where the *value* attribute defines the text that appears on the button and is sent to the CGI script, indicating which button on the form has been clicked.

■ To create a button that cancels or resets your form, use the type attribute as shown in the following tag:

```
<input type="reset" name="name" id="id" value="text">
```

■ To create a button to perform an action within the Web page by running a program or script, use the following tag:

```
<input type="button" name="name" id="id" value="text">
```
where the *value* attribute defines the text that is displayed on the button.

■ To create a button that can contain HTML tags and inline images, use the following code:

```
<button name="name" id="id" value="value">content</button>
```
where the *value* attribute provides an initial value for the button and *content* consists of the HTML-formatted text and images you want displayed in the button.

Creating a Push Button

One type of button, called a **push button**, is created using the <input> tag as follows:

```
<input type="button" value="text">
```

where *text* is the text that appears on the button. By themselves, push buttons perform no actions in the Web page. To create an action for a push button, you have to write a script or program that runs automatically when the button is clicked. In later tutorials, you'll learn how to write and attach such programs to push buttons.

Creating Submit and Reset Buttons

Two other kinds of buttons are submit and reset buttons. A **submit button** is a button that submits the form to the CGI script for processing. A **reset button** resets the form to its original (default) values. The syntax for creating these two buttons is:

```
<input type="submit" value="text">
<input type="reset" value="text">
```

where the value attribute defines the text that appears on the button.

You can also specify name and value attributes for push, submit, and reset buttons, although these attributes are not required. You would use these attributes when the form contains multiple buttons and a program that processes the form needs to distinguish one button from the others. For example, a Web page advertising a shareware program might include three buttons: one used to download the program from the company's Web site, another used to retrieve additional information about the product, and the third to cancel the form. The HTML tags for such buttons are displayed in Figure 6-37.

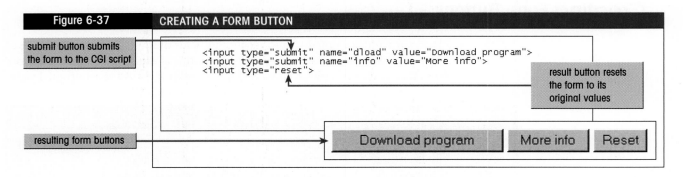

| Figure 6-37 | CREATING A FORM BUTTON |

submit button submits the form to the CGI script

```
<input type="submit" name="dload" value="Download program">
<input type="submit" name="info" value="More info">
<input type="reset">
```

result button resets the form to its original values

resulting form buttons

Download program   More info   Reset

This form has two submit buttons for submitting the form, but the CGI script responds differently depending on which button is used.

Susan wants the registration form to include both a submit and a reset button. The submit button, labeled "Send Registration," sends the form data to the CGI script. The reset button, labeled "Cancel," cancels the form and resets the fields to their default values.

To add the Submit and Reset buttons to the registration form:

1. Using your text editor, open **register.htm**.

2. Type the following lines of code within the opening and closing <td> tags located near the Buttons comment tag (see Figure 6-38):

```
<input type="submit" value="Send Registration">
<input type="reset" value="Cancel">
```

| Figure 6-38 | ADDING FORM BUTTONS TO THE REGISTER.HTM FORM |

```
<!-- Buttons -->
<tr>
    <td valign="top" colspan="2" align="center">
        <input type="submit" value="Send Registration">
        <input type="reset" value="Cancel">
    </td>
</tr>
```

3. Save your changes to register.htm and then reload it in your Web browser. Figure 6-39 shows the completed registration form, including the two buttons you just created.

Figure 6-39	THE COMPLETED REGISTRATION FORM

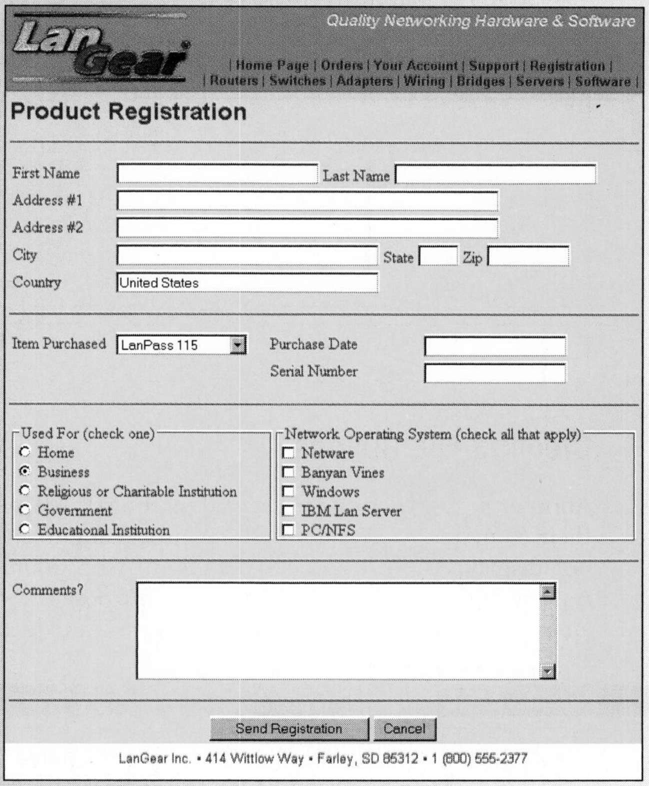

TROUBLE? Depending on which browser you're using, your registration form may appear slightly different from the one shown in Figure 6-39.

4. Test the Cancel button by entering test values into the form and then clicking the Cancel button. The form should return to its initial state.

TROUBLE? If the Cancel button doesn't work, check the HTML code for the button and verify that you've entered the code correctly. The Send Registration button does not perform a function yet, because you have not identified the CGI script to receive the form data.

Creating Buttons with the <button> Tag

Buttons created with the <input> tag do not allow the Web page designer to control the appearance of the button, other than specifying the text for the button label. For greater artistic control over the appearance of the button, use the <button> tag. The syntax of the <button> tag is:

```
<button name="name" value="value" type="option">
   button text and HTML tags
</button>
```

where the name and value attributes specify the name of the button and the value sent to a CGI script, and the type attribute specifies the button type (submit, reset, or button). The default value for the type attribute is "button". Note that within the <button> tags you can place whatever HTML tags you wish to format the button's appearance. This includes inline images. Figure 6-40 shows how to create a button that contains formatted text and an inline image.

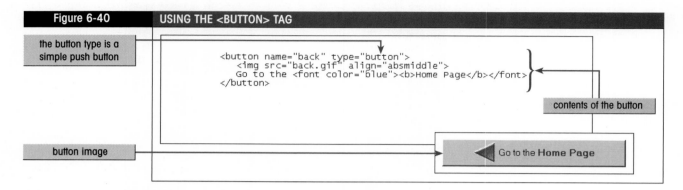

| Figure 6-40 | USING THE <BUTTON> TAG |

the button type is a simple push button

```
<button name="back" type="button">
    <img src="back.gif" align="absmiddle">
    Go to the <font color="blue"><b>Home Page</b></font>
</button>
```

contents of the button

button image

◄ Go to the **Home Page**

Creating File Buttons

Another type of button introduced in HTML 4.0 is a file button, used to select files so that their contents can be submitted for processing to a CGI script. The contents of the file are not displayed—only the file's location. A programmer can then use that information to retrieve the file and use it for whatever purpose is required by the script. Figure 6-41 shows an example of using the file button to return the location of a file named "report.doc."

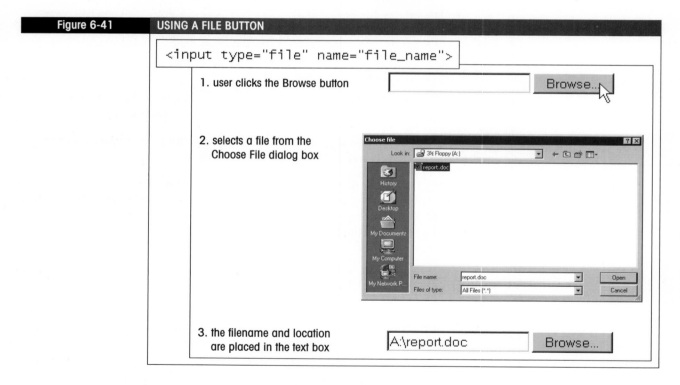

| Figure 6-41 | USING A FILE BUTTON |

```
<input type="file" name="file_name">
```

1. user clicks the Browse button

Browse...

2. selects a file from the Choose File dialog box

3. the filename and location are placed in the text box

A:\report.doc   Browse...

Note that the text box and the Browse button are created for you. You cannot change the label for the browse button, but you can increase the size of the text box by using the size attribute in the <input> tag.

Creating **Image Fields**

Another control element you can use in your Web form is the inline image. Inline images can act like submit buttons so that when the user clicks the image, the form is submitted. The syntax for this type of control element is:

```
<input type="image" src="URL" name="text" value="text">
```

where *URL* is the filename and location of the inline image, the name attribute assigns a name to the field, and the value attribute assigns a value to the image. When the form is submitted to the CGI script, the coordinates of where the user clicked are attached to the image's name and value in the format: name.x_coordinate, value.y_coordinate. For example, suppose your Web page contains the following inline image form element:

```
<input type="image" src="usamap.gif" name="usa" value="state">
```

If we assume that a user loads your page and clicks the inline image at the coordinates (15,30), the Web page sends the field name and x coordinate, usa.15, paired with the field value and y coordinate, state.30, to the CGI script. Once the CGI script receives this data, the action it performs depends on where the user clicked within the image. See Figure 6-42.

Figure 6-42	USING AN IMAGE CONTROL WITH A CGI SCRIPT

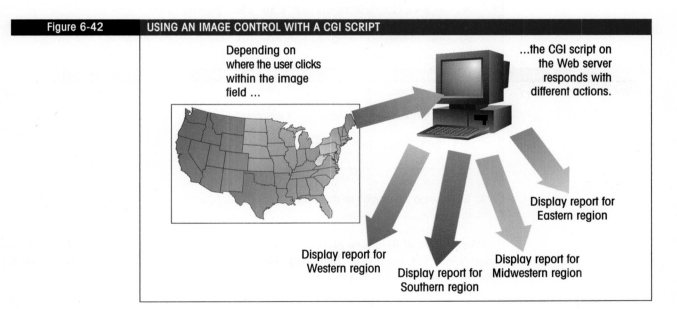

You are not required to include any inline image controls or file buttons in your Web page form for this project.

Working **with Hidden Fields**

Susan is pleased with the final appearance of the registration form. She shows the code for the form to Warren Kaughman, one of the programmers at LanGear and the person responsible for the CGI script that you'll be using. Warren notices only one thing missing from the code: the e-mail address of Susan's assistant, who is to receive the registration forms via e-mail. Warren's CGI script requires that the form include the e-mail address of the recipient.

Unlike the other fields you've created so far, this field has a predefined value that users of the Web form should not be able to change. In fact, the e-mail address of Susan's assistant should not even be displayed on the form. To accomplish this, you need to use a **hidden field**, which is added to the form but not displayed in the Web page. The syntax for creating a hidden field is:

```
<input type="hidden" name="name" value="value">
```

You've learned from Warren that the name of the e-mail field should be "email", and you know from Susan that the e-mail address of her assistant is adavis@langear.com (note that this is a fictional address used for the purposes of this tutorial.) Now that you know both the field name and the field value, you can add the hidden field to the registration form.

Because the field is hidden, you can place it anywhere between the opening and closing <form> tags. A common practice is to place all hidden fields in one location, usually at the beginning of the form, to make it easier to read and interpret your HTML code. You should also include a comment describing the purpose of the field.

To add the hidden field to the registration form:

1. Return to **register.htm** in your text editor.

2. Type the following code directly below the <form> tag (see Figure 6-43):

```
<!-- e-mail address of the recipient -->
<input type="hidden" name="email" value="adavis@langear.
com">
```

| Figure 6-43 | ADDING A HIDDEN FIELD TO THE REGISTRATION FORM |

```
<html>
<head>
<title>LanGear Registration Form</title>
</head>
<body text="#850000">
<form name="reg">
<!-- e-mail address of the recipient -->
<input type="hidden" name="email" value="adavis@langear.com">
```

3. Save your changes to the file.

With the email field now placed in the registration form, you'll return to the first tag you entered into this document, the <form> tag, and insert the attributes needed for it to inteact with the LanGear CGI script.

Working **with Form Attributes**

You've added all the elements needed for the form. Your final task is to specify where to send the form data and how to send it. You do this by adding the following attributes to the <form> tag:

```
<form action="URL" method="option" enctype="text">
```

where the *URL* specifies the filename and location of the CGI script that processes the form, the method attribute specifies how your Web browser sends data to the CGI script, and the enctype attribute specifies the format of the data stored in the form's field. Let's examine the method and enctype attributes in more detail.

There are two possible values for the method attribute: "get" or "post". The "get" method (the default) packages the form data by appending it to the end of the URL specified in the action attribute. The "post" method sends form data in a separate data stream, allowing the

Web server to receive the data through what is called "standard input." Because it is more flexible, the "post" method is considered the preferred way of sending data to a Web server. It is also safer, because some Web servers limit the amount of data sent via the "get" method and will truncate the URL, cutting off valuable information.

Don't be concerned if you don't completely understand the difference between using "get" and "post." Your Internet service provider can provide the necessary information about which of the two methods you should use in your <form> tag.

The exact meaning of the enctype attribute is a technical issue that goes beyond the scope of this tutorial. The default enctype value is "application/x-www-form-urlencoded," so if you do not specify an encoding value, this is the one the Web server assumes is used for your data. Another enctype value that is often used is "multipart/form-data," which allows the form to send files to the Web server along with any form data. The most basic way of encoding data is to use "text/plain," which encodes the data as simple text. This is most often used with the mailto action, which you'll learn about shortly. In most cases, the documentation for the CGI script will tell you how the data should be encoded.

Finally, another attribute you might use with the <form> tag is the target attribute. You can use the target attribute to send form data to a different window or frame. This is not a concern with the registration form, so you do not have to worry about the target attribute.

Now that you've been introduced to the issues involved in sending form data to a CGI script, you are ready to make some final modifications to register.htm. Warren tells you that the CGI script that processes the form is located at the URL *http://www.langear.com/cgi/mailer* (a fictional address) and uses the "post" method. You do not have to specify a value for the enctype attribute.

To add the attributes to the <form> tag:

1. Using your text editor, type the following attributes within the <form> tag in **register.htm** (see Figure 6-44):

```
action="http://www.langear.com/cgi/mailer" method="post"
```

Figure 6-44   SPECIFYING WHERE AND HOW TO SEND FORM DATA

```
<html>
<head>
<title>LanGear Registration Form</title>
</head>
<body text="#850000">
<form name="reg" action="http://www.langear.com/cgi/mailer" method="post">
<!-- e-mail address of the recipient -->
<input type="hidden" name="email" value="adavis@langear.com">
```

2. Save your changes to register.htm and close the file and your text editor.

You've finished the registration form, and Warren places a copy of register.htm in a folder on the company's Web server. From there it can be fully tested to verify that the CGI script and the form work properly, and that the form data is e-mailed to Susan's assistant.

To allow you to see how this form works once it's installed on a Web server along with the appropriate CGI script, a modified version of it has been placed on the Web at the following URL:

http://www.careys.com/langear/register_test.htm

If you have a connection to the Web, you can open this page and test the form and the CGI script.

To test the registration form:

1. Using your Web browser, open the URL **http://www.careys.com/langear/register_test.htm**.

   A modified version of the page that you created in this tutorial is displayed.

2. Type (*your e-mail address*) in the E-mail text box in the first field of the form.

   Note that unlike the form you created, this form e-mails the form data to the e-mail address you enter.

3. Enter contact information for yourself in the appropriate fields.

4. Complete the rest of the form, using test entries of your own choosing.

5. Click the **Click to Register** button. Your Web browser presents a page, an example of which is shown in Figure 6-45, displaying the name of each field in the form and the value you've assigned to it. At the same time, the CGI script formats a mail message to be sent to the address you entered in Step 2.

Figure 6-45   TEST REGISTRATION FORM VALUES

LanGear Test Registration Form Values

Below is what you submitted to adavis@langear.com on Thursday, March 11, 2004 at 15:33:57

address1: Room 634

address2: 211 Hawkins Avenue

city: Lawrence

comments: How do I access the internal settings of the router?

country: United States

date: 2/14/2004

fname: Andrew

item: LanPass 250

lname: Davis

nw: yes

snumber: LG100-78711

state: WI

use: edu

win: yes

zip: 53701

You should soon receive a message in your mailbox that looks like the page shown in Figure 6-45.

TROUBLE? If you don't receive an e-mail message within a few hours, either there is a problem with your mail server, causing a delay in the posting of the message, or you may have mistyped your e-mail address on the registration form. You should try again, carefully checking your e-mail address in the form.

REFERENCE WINDOW   RW

Creating Web Page Forms
- Form elements will differ between browsers, so be sure to view your form on different browsers and different browser versions to ensure that the form displays correctly in all situations.
- Label all text boxes clearly and concisely.
- Use horizontal lines, tables, and line breaks to separate topical groups from one another. Number your elements to give your form an organized structure.
- Use radio buttons, check boxes, and selection lists whenever possible to control the user's entries. Use text boxes only in situations where a specified list of options is unavailable.
- Let users know the correct format for the text in a text box by inserting default text (for example, inserting the text string "mm/dd/yyyy" in a Date text box indicates the date format to be used).
- Use selection lists for items with several possible options. Use radio buttons for items with fewer options. Use check boxes for items with only two options (yes/no).
- Use password fields for any text boxes that contain sensitive or confidential information (for example, credit card numbers and passwords).

Using the "mailto" Action

So far in working with Susan's registration file, you have built a form to use Warren's e-mail CGI script. There is, however, a way to send form information via e-mail without using a CGI script: you can use the "mailto" action. This action accesses the user's own e-mail program and uses it to mail form information to a specified e-mail address, bypassing the need for using CGI scripts on a Web server. The syntax of the "mailto" action is:

```
<form action="mailto:e-mail_address" method="post" enctype=
"text/plain">
```

where *e-mail_address* is the e-mail address of the recipient of the form. Because the "mailto" action does not require a CGI script, you can avoid some of the problems associated with coordinating your page with a program running on the Web server. One disadvantage of this action is that not all browsers support it. For example, versions of Internet Explorer earlier than 4.0 and Netscape Navigator 3.0 do not. Another concern is that messages sent via the "mailto" action are not encrypted for privacy. Also, the recipient's e-mail address is revealed to the user. For example, Susan's assistant's e-mail address would be revealed to LanGear customers.

When you click the submit button on a form using the "mailto" action, your mail program receives the content for the mail message from your Web browser. Depending on how your system is configured, either you will have a chance to edit the mail message further, or it will be automatically sent to the e-mail address specified by the creator of the form without allowing you to intervene.

Figure 6-46 shows an e-mail message that the "mailto" action generated for the registration form you completed in this tutorial. Note that the format of your mail message may look different depending on your browser and e-mail software.

Figure 6-46	MAIL MESSAGE CREATED USING THE "MAILTO" ACTION

```
From: Andrew Davis [adavis@langear.com]
Sent: Thursday, March 11, 2004 1:10 PM
To: adavis@langear.com
Subject: Form posted from Microsoft Internet Explorer.

email=adavis@langear.com
fname=Andrew
lname=Davis
address1=Room 634
address2=211 Hawkins Avenue
city=Lawrence
state=WI
zip=53701
country=United States
item=FastSwitch 400
date=2/14/2004
snumber=3983493
use=edu
nw=yes
win=yes
comments=How do I access the internal settings of the router?
```

Note that if you don't specify the "text/plain" value for the enctype attribute, the mail message is sent anyway, but it contains symbols that require a special program to decode.

Specifying the Tab Order

Typically, users navigate through a Web form using the Tab key, which moves the cursor from one field to another in the order that the field tags are entered into the HTML file.

You can also specify the tab order by adding the tabindex attribute to any control element in your form. With each element assigned a tab index number, the cursor moves through the fields from the lowest index number to the highest. For example, to assign the tab index number "1" to the fname field from the registration form, you enter the code:

```
<input name="fname" tabindex="1">
```

If you assign to a field the tab index number "0", that field is tabbed to go in the order that it appears in the file, as if you had not used a tab index. Fields with negative tab indexes are omitted from the tab order entirely.

Web page designers can use tab index numbers in their forms without worrying about older browsers that do not support this new standard. Browsers that do not support this feature simply ignore the tabindex attribute and continue to tab to the fields in the order that they appear in the HTML file.

Specifying an Access Key

Another way of accessing elements in your form is with an access key. An **access key** is a single key that you type in conjunction with the Alt key for Windows users or the Command key for Macintosh users, to jump to one of the control elements in the form. To create an access key, add the accesskey attribute to any of the control elements discussed in this tutorial. To create an access key for the lname field, enter the following code:

```
<input name="lname" accesskey="l">
```

If a user types Alt+l (or Command+l for Macintosh users), the control element for the lname field is selected. Note that you must use letters that are not reserved by your browser. For example, Alt+f is used by Internet Explorer to access the File menu. If you do use an access key, you should provide some visual clues about the key's existence. The accepted method is to underline the character corresponding to the access key. For example, in the previous code, you might display the lname label as "Last Name".

Susan does not need you to work with the tabbing order for this form or to create any access keys. You'll have a chance to work with these attributes in the case problems at the end of the tutorial.

You're now finished working with forms and form attributes. The page you created for Susan has been stored on the company's Web server. She is reviewing the Web page with her assistant and will inform you if you need to make any changes to your work.

Session 6.3 QUICK CHECK

1. What tag would you use to create a submit button with the label "Send Form"?

2. What HTML tag would you use to create a reset button with the label "Cancel Form"?

3. What HTML tag would you use to create an image field named Sites for sites.gif with the value attribute GotoPage?

4. What HTML tag would you use to create a hidden field named Subject with the field value "Form Responses"?

5. You need to have your form work with a CGI script located at *http://www.j_davis.com/cgi-bin/post-query*. The method the Web server uses is the "get" method. What should the <form> tag be to correctly access this CGI script?

6. You want to use the "mailto" action to send your form to the e-mail address walker@j_davis.com. What is the appropriate <form> tag to enter?

7. What HTML code would you use to assign the access key, n, to the FirstName field?

REVIEW ASSIGNMENTS

Susan and her assistant are pleased with the work you've done on the registration form, and they would like you to create a new form for users who experience technical support problems. To receive support, users need to provide their e-mail addresses, the product they're working with, information about their computing environment, and a statement describing the trouble they're having with their equipment. Some customers have support contracts with LanGear that entitle them to particular support services. Susan would like the form to have a check box to indicate whether the customer has such a contract. The form also needs a text box in which the customer can enter a service contract number.

Susan has created the layout for the page and much of the text. She needs you to enter the various control elements for the form. Figure 6-47 shows a preview of the form you'll create for Susan.

Figure 6-47

To create the tech support form:

1. Using your text editor, open **suptxt.htm** from the tutorial.06/review folder on your Data Disk and save it as **support.htm**.

2. Insert a <form> tag directly after the <body> tag and name the form "support_form". Assign the fictional URL "http://www.langear.com/cgi/mailer" to the form's action. Form data is submitted using the "post" method and is encoded as "text/plain". Insert a closing </form> tag directly before the closing </body> tag.

3. When the form is completed it should be sent to the support department. To do this, Susan needs you to insert a hidden field named "recipient" with a value of "techsup-port@langear.com". Place this field directly after the <form> tag.

4. In the second table cell below the Customer Name comment, create a text box with the name and id set to "cust_name". Set the size of the text box to 50 characters. Change the text "Your name:" to a label that is connected to the cust_name field.

5. Similarly, create text boxes 50 characters wide for the Customer Phone Number and Customer E-mail sections of the document. Assign "cust_phone" as the name and id for the customer phone number text box, and assign "cust_mail" as the name and id for the customer e-mail text box. Change the text, "Your phone #:" and "Your E-mail address:" to labels that are connected to their respective fields.

6. In the table cell below the "Check for Support Contract" comment, create a checkbox that has "contract" for its name and id. Assign the value "yes" to this field if it is clicked by the user.

7. In the table row with the "Support Contract" comment tag, create a text box 50 characters wide in the second cell. Assign the text box the name and id "cid". Change the text "Contract ID:" to a label that is connected to the cid field.

8. In the second cell of the row located below the "Product" comment, create a selection list with the products and option groups you created for register.htm. Assign this selection list the name and id "item". Change the text "Product:" from the preceding table cell into a label connected to the item field.

9. In the second cell of the table row containing the "Operating System" comment, create another selection list with the field name "os". The os field should contain the following entries:

   - Windows 98
   - Windows 2000
   - Windows XP
   - Windows NT
   - Macintosh
   - UNIX
   - Linux
   - OS/2

   Create two option groups for the os selection list. The first, named "Windows", contains the four Windows operating systems; the second, named "Others", contains the remaining four operating systems. Change the text "Your operating system:" to a label that is connected to the os field.

10. Locate the table row containing the "Memory Options" comment tag. In the second cell below this comment, create a group box that contains three radio buttons. These radio buttons allow users to specify the amount of memory on their computer. Each radio button should belong to a field named "memory".

11. The first radio button should have the id "mem1" and the value "1". Insert the label text "0-64MB" to the right of the radio button. Insert a line break and create the second radio button with the id "mem2" and the value "2". To the right of this radio button insert the label text "65-256MB". Insert another line break and create the third radio button with the id "mem3" and the value "3". The text label for this radio button is "+257MB". Make sure each radio button label is connected to its radio button.

Explore 12. Locate the table row containing the comment tag "Message." In the second cell below this comment tag, create a text area box that is 8 rows high and 40 columns wide. The field has the name and id "message." The text area box contains the default text "Enter your tech support question here." Change the text "Message to Tech Support:" to a label that is connected to the message field.

Explore 13. In the table cell below the "Submit Button" comment, create a Submit button that contains the image mail.gif. The button contains the text "Submit Your Question" in a blue, bold font and is aligned with the middle of the image mail.gif. Set the vertical space around the image to 5 pixels.

Explore 14. Create a reset button in the table cell below the comment "Reset Button." This button contains the cancel.gif image and is aligned with the middle of this image. Set the vertical space around the image to 5 pixels. The button displays the text "Reset the Form" in a red, bold font.

15. Save your changes to support.htm, print the revised code, and close the file.

16. Using your Web browser, open support.htm and verify that all control elements and labels work correctly. You do not have to submit the form, but verify that the reset button works correctly. Print the resulting form.

17. Hand in your printouts and files to your instructor.

CASE PROBLEMS

Case 1. The Fitness Factory The Fitness Factory is a new online store that specializes in exercise equipment. Carl Evans is the sales director for the company, and he has asked for your help in developing a customer order form that has the following elements:

- billing address
- shipping address
- credit card information

Carl wants you to include a check box where customers can choose to have their order mailed to the billing address (the usual situation). He also wants the form to have three buttons: one to return the customer to a page listing the items in their "shopping cart," another to submit their order, and a third to reset the order form. You are not responsible for programming any of these buttons; Carl has assigned that job to a Web page programmer who will write the CGI scripts for you.

Carl also wants you to control how the tab key navigates through the form. He would like the shipping address field to be skipped initially in the tabbing order, so that users will go from the billing address fields directly to the payment information fields.

The layout and most of the text for the Web page have been created for you. Your job is to create the required control elements and fields.

A preview of the page you'll create for Carl is shown in Figure 6-48.

Figure 6-48

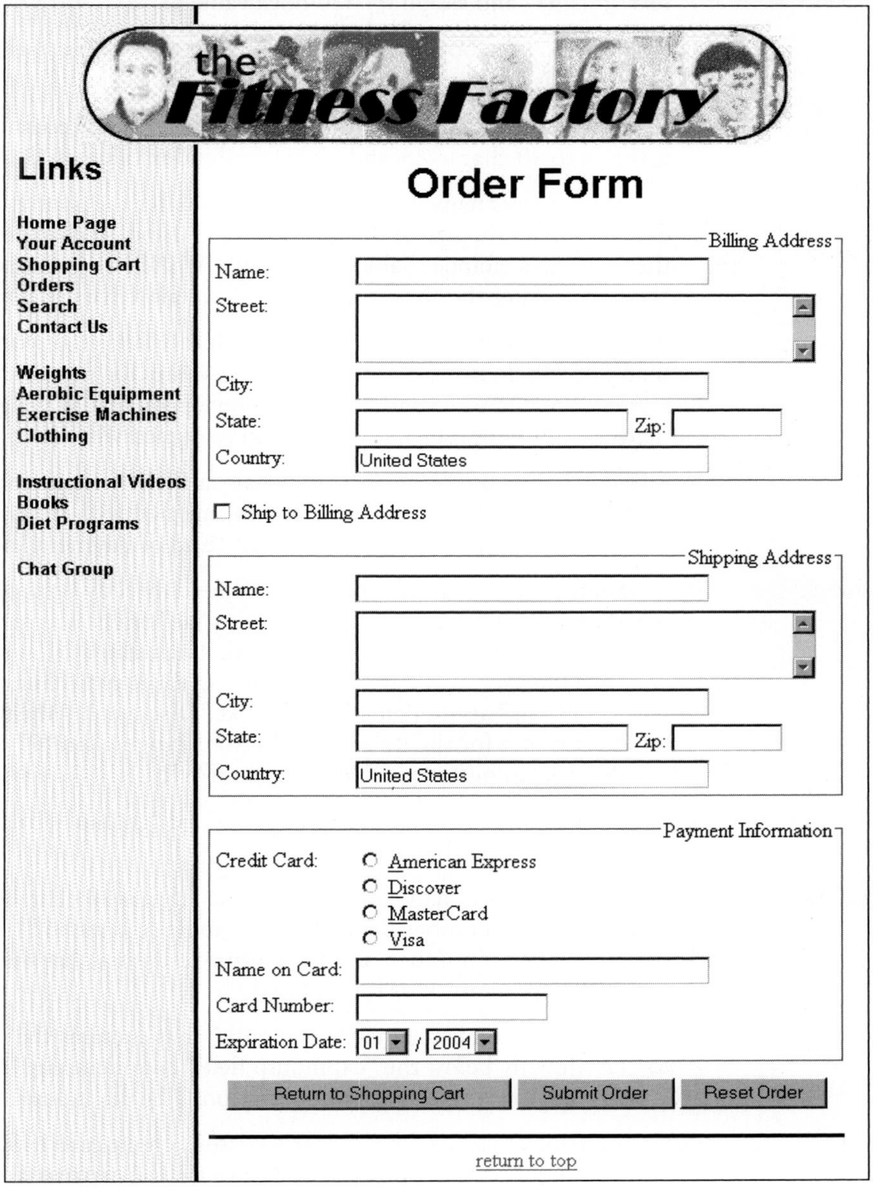

To create the order form:

1. Using your text editor, open **ordertxt.htm** located in the tutorial.06/case1 folder and save it as **order.htm**.

2. Directly after the <body> tag, create a form with the name "order_form". You do not need to specify any actions or methods for this form. Insert the closing form tag directly before the closing </body> tag located at the bottom of the file.

3. Locate the "Billing Address Field" comment and insert tags below this comment to create a group box with the legend "Billing Address". Align the legend with the right side of the group box. The group box extends to the comment "End of Billing Address Fields" located further down in the file.

Explore

4. After the "bname field" comment, insert a text box that has 40 characters. Name the text "bname" and assign it a tabindex value of "1".

5. Insert a text area box named "bstreet" after the "bstreet field" comment tag. The text area box has 3 rows and 40 columns. Give the field a tabindex value of "2".

6. Insert a text box named "bcity" after the "bcity field" comment tag. Set the size of the text box to 40 characters and give it a tabindex value of "3".

7. Insert text boxes named "bstate" and "bzip" after the appropriate comment tags in the document. Set the size of the text boxes to 30 and 10 characters, respectively, and assign the text boxes tabindex values of "4" and "5". Add a 40-character-wide text box named "bcountry" after the "bcountry field" comment. Give this element a tabindex value of "6".

8. Apply the same layout to the shipping address fields that you did for the billing address fields, except do not specify any tabindex values for these fields, and modify the field names to match the comments tags. The legend text of the group box surrounding these fields is "Shipping Address Fields" and is aligned with the right side of the group box.

9. Directly below the "Payment Information Fields" comment tag, create a group box with the legend "Payment Information" aligned with the right edge of the box. The group box extends to the comment tag "End of Payment Information Fields".

Explore

10. Create four radio buttons for the ccard field directly below the "ccard field" comment tag. The value of the first radio button is "ae" and is accompanied by the text "American Express" with the letter "A" underlined. The radio button has the tabindex value "8" and uses the accesskey "a". The remaining three radio buttons have values of "dis", "mc", and "vis" accompanied by the text "Discover", "MasterCard", and "Visa". The tabindex values for the three radio buttons range from "9" to "11". The access keys for the three radio buttons are "d", "m", and "v".

11. Create a text box, 40 characters wide, named "cname" directly below the comment tag "cname field". Set the tabindex to "12".

Explore

12. Create a password field named "cnumber" that is 20 characters wide directly below the comment tag "cnumber field". Set the tabindex value to "13". This field contains the user's credit card number, and Carl wants to ensure that that information is not displayed on the monitor as it is entered.

13. Create a selection list named "expmonth" that contains the range of numbers from "01" to "12" directly below the "expmonth field" comment tag. This selection list is used by Carl to obtain expiration date information. The tab index for this field is set to "14".

14. Create a selection list for the year the user's credit card expires directly below the "expyear field" comment tag. The values for the expyear field range from "2004" to "2010". Set the tabindex value to "15".

15. Create three form buttons directly below the comment tag "form buttons". The first button is a simple push button with the value "Return to Shopping Cart". The second button is a submit button with the value "Submit Order". The third button is a reset button with the value "Reset Order". The tabindex values for the three buttons are 16 through 18.

16. Save your changes to order.htm, print the revised code, and close the file.

17. Using your Web browser, open order.htm. Test the tabbing order in the form. Verify that the shipping address fields are skipped over when you tab. Test the operation of the access keys by pressing Alt+a, Alt+d, Alt+m, and Alt+v to select the American Express, Discover, MasterCard, and Visa option buttons, respectively. Note that Macintosh users use the command ke instead of the Alt key. Print the Web page.

18. Hand in your printouts and files to your instructor.

Case 2. DeLong Enterprises, Inc. DeLong Enterprises, a manufacturer of computer components, is establishing a corporate intranet to put news and information online for their
employees. One item that Dolores Crandall, a payroll manager, would like to put online is
travel expense forms. Dolores has asked you for help with this project.

The travel expense form requires a DeLong employee to provide information about the
business trip and to itemize various travel deductions. A preview of the form you'll create
is shown in Figure 6-49.

Figure 6-49

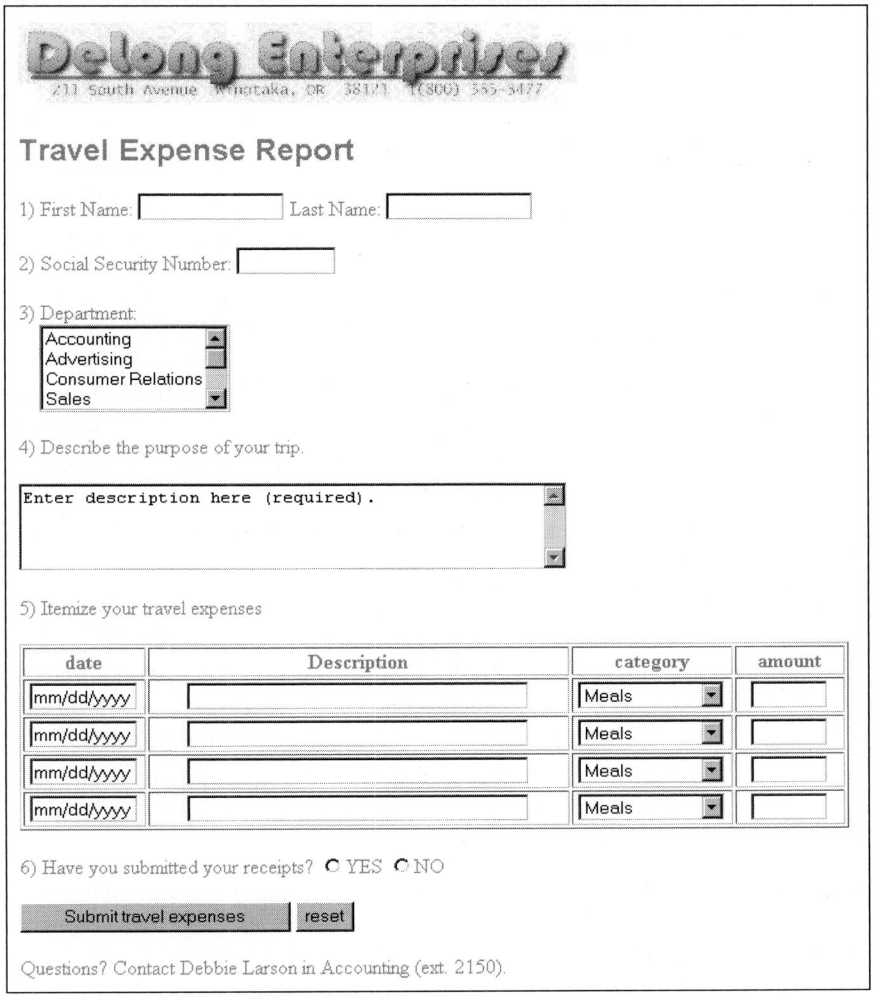

To create the travel expense form:

1. Using your text editor, open **dltxt.htm** from the tutorial.06/case2 folder of your Data
   Disk and save it as **delong.htm**.

2. Type an opening and closing <form> tag within the body of the Web page and name the
   form "travel".

3. Insert text boxes for the first and last name of employees in item 1 of the form. Assign
   these fields the names "first" and "last". Set the size of both text boxes to 15 characters.

4. Create a password text box for the Social Security number in item 2 of the form. Set the width and maximum length of the text box to 9 characters and name the field "ssnum".

Explore

5. Create a list box for the list of departments in item 3. Insert the following options into the list box:

- Accounting
- Advertising
- Consumer Relations
- Sales
- Management
- Payroll
- Quality Control
- R&D

Set "dept" as the field name for the list box, and display four items in the list box at a time.

6. Create a text area field for the trip description in item 4. The text area field is 4 rows high and 50 columns wide. Set "desc" as the field name. Define "Enter description here (required)." as the default text.

7. In item 5, insert the following form elements in each row of the table, except the header row.

- In the first column, insert a text box with the field name "date" and a size of 10 characters. Specify "mm/dd/yyyy" as the default text.
- In the second column, insert a text box 40 characters long with the field name "description".
- In the third column, insert a selection list with the field name "category" and include the following options in the list: Meals, Miscellaneous, Registration, and Transportation.
- In the fourth column, insert a text box named "amount" 6 characters wide.

8. Create a pair of radio buttons for item # 6. Name both fields "receipt". Assign the first radio button the value "yes" and the second button the value "no". Insert the text "YES" next to the first radio button and the text "NO" next to the second button.

9. Below item # 6 insert two form buttons. The first button is a submit button with the value "Submit travel expenses." The second button is a reset button with the default value "Reset".

Explore

10. Design the form so that it sends a plain text e-mail message to the e-mail address "dcrandall@delongent.com". Note that your instructor may provide you with a different e-mail address, since this is a fictional address.

11. Save your changes to delong.htm.

12. Using your Web browser, reload or refresh delong.htm. Print a copy of the completed Web page and the corresponding HTML code.

13. Hand in your printouts and files to your instructor.

Case 3. Park City Gazette   Kevin Webber, the editor of the Park City Gazette of Park City, Colorado, has asked for your help in developing a subscription page for his Web site. The page includes a form where customers can enter the length of the subscription they want to purchase, their mailing address, and credit card information. Kevin has already created much of the layout and text for the form, and your job is to add the fields and control elements for the form. A preview of the subscription Web page you'll create for Kevin is shown in Figure 6-50.

Figure 6-50

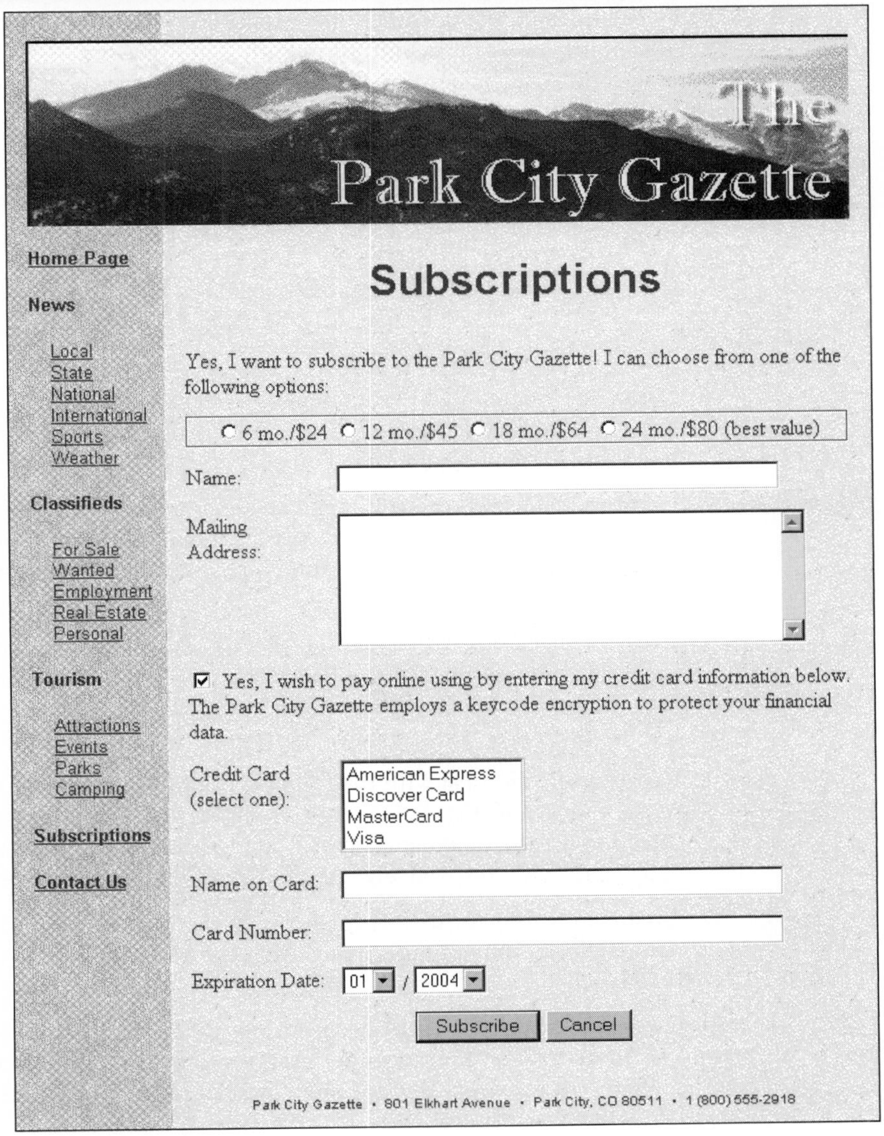

Kevin would like the results of the form mailed to the e-mail address of the Gazette business manager : *pcg_business@parkcitygazette.com*. You'll use a plain text format for the mail message.

To create the subscription Web page:

1. Using your text editor, open **subtxt.htm** located in the tutorial.06/case3 folder of your Data Disk and save it as **subscrib.htm**.

2. Create a form named "subscription" directly below the <body> tag. The form uses the "mailto" action pointing to the e-mail address *pcg_business@parkcitygazette.com*. The text of the mail message is encoded using text/plain. Note that your instructor may provide you with a different e-mail address, since this is a fictional address and cannot be tested.

3. Type the closing form tag directly before the closing </body> tag.

4. Scroll through the document to locate the "Subscription Form" comment tag. From this point, insert radio buttons directly below the comment tag "Subscription Plan Radio Buttons." There are four radio buttons with the following text:

   - 6 mo./$24
   - 12 mo./$45
   - 18 mo./$64
   - 24 mo./$80 (best value)

   The field name for the four radio buttons is "splan", and the button values are "6", "12", "18", and "24", respectively. Enclose the radio buttons in a group box, but do not specify a legend for the group box.

5. Below the "Name Field" comment tag, insert a text box 50 characters wide. The name and id of the field is "name". Change the text of the preceding table cell "Name:" to a label that is connected to the "name" field.

Explore

6. Create a text area box 6 rows high and 40 columns wide below the "Address Field" comment tag. The name and id of the control element is "address", and text wrapping is set to "hard". Change the text of the preceding cell "Mailing Address:" to a label connected to the "address" field.

7. Create a check box with a name and id of "cardcb" below the "Card Checkbox" comment tag. The purpose of this check box is to verify that customers wish to pay for the subscription online. Make the check box selected by default, and change the text that follows the check box to a label connected to the "cardcb" field.

8. Create a selection list with the following options: American Express, Discover Card, MasterCard, and Visa below the "Credit Card List Box" comment tag. Assign this selection list the field name "ccard", and make the values of the four options "ae", "dis", "mc", and "vis", respectively. Set the size of the list box to "4".

9. Create a text box for the cardname field with a width of 50 characters below the "card-name field" comment tag. Change the text of the preceding cell "Name on Card:" to a field label.

10. Create a text box for users to enter their credit card numbers, and name the field "cardnum". It is important that users' credit card numbers are not displayed on the screen as they are entered. Change the text of the preceding cell "Card Number:" to a label for the cardnum field.

11. Create a list for the months and years of the expiration dates below the "expmonth list box" and "expyear list box" comment tags. Name the two fields "expmonth" and "expyear". The selection list displays the values "01" though "12" and "2004" through "2010", respectively.

12. Create submit and reset buttons below the comment tag "form buttons". The submit button displays the text "Subscribe". The reset button displays the text "Cancel".

13. Save your changes to subscrib.htm.

14. Open subscrib.htm in your Web browser and verify that all of the controls are working properly. If you were provided with a real e-mail address to use, complete the form and submit the form to the address.

15. Print a copy of the Web page form.

16. Hand in your printouts and files to your instructor.

Case 4. *Millennium Computers*   You are employed at Millennium Computers, a discount mail-order company specializing in computers and computer components. You've been asked by your supervisor, Sandy Walton, to create an order form Web page so that customers can purchase products online. Your order form is for computer purchases only. There are several options for customers to consider when purchasing computers from Millennium:

- Processor speed: 1.5 GHz, 1.9 GHz, 2.5 GHz, 3.2 GHz
- Memory: 64 MB, 128 MB, 256 MB, or 512 MB
- Drive size: 15 GB, 30 GB, or 60 GB
- Monitor size: 15-inch, 17-inch, 19-inch, or 21-inch
- CD-ROM: 24x, 32x, 48x, 64x, or 72x

Create Sandy's order form using the following guidelines. The design of the Web page is up to you:

1. Create text boxes for the customer's first and last name, phone number, credit card number, and credit card expiration date. Make sure the credit card information does not display on the screen.

2. Using selection boxes or radio buttons, create fields in the form for the different component options.

3. Insert a check box asking whether the customer wants to be placed on the Millennium Computers mailing list.

4. Place three buttons on the form: a Submit button to send the order, a Reset button to reset the page, and a second Submit button to request that a Millennium Computers representative call the customer. Use the values "Send", "Cancel", and "Call Me" for the three buttons.

5. Name the form "c_order", submit the form using the "post" method, and set up the form to use the CGI script located at *http://www.mill_computers.com*. Note that this is a fictional URL.

6. Save your changes and save the file as computer.htm in the tutorial.06/case4 folder on your Data Disk. Print a copy of your HTML code from your text editor and the Web page from your Web browser.

7. Hand in all printouts and files to your instructor.

QUICK CHECK ANSWERS

Session 6.1

1. A CGI script is any program or set of commands running on the Web server that receives data from the Web page and then processes that data to perform a certain task.

2. The <form> tag identifies the beginning and end of a form.

3. <input name="Phone">

4. <input name="Phone" size="10">

5. <input name="Phone" size="10" maxlength="10">

6. <input name="Subscribe" value="Yes">

7. Set the value of the type attribute to "password".

8. <label for="dob">Date of Birth</label>

Session 6.2

1. <select name="State">

```
<option>California
<option>Nevada
<option>Oregon
<option>Washington
</select>
```

2. Change the <select> tag to <select multiple>

3. <option selected>Oregon

4. Place the selection list within a two-sided <fieldset> tag. After the opening <fieldset> tag, insert the tag: <legend>West Coast</legend>

5. <fieldset>

```
<legend>West Coast</legend>
<input type="radio" name="State" value="California">
California
<input type="radio" name="State" value="Nevada">Nevada
<input type="radio" name="State" value="Oregon">Oregon
<input type="radio" name="State" value="Washington">
Washington
</fieldset>
```

6. <input type="radio" name="State" value="1">California

```
<input type="radio" name="State" value="2">Nevada
<input type="radio" name="State" value="3">Oregon
<input type="radio" name="State" value="4">Washington
```

7. <input type="checkbox">California

   A value of "on" is sent to the CGI script.

8. <textarea rows="5" cols="30" name="Memo">Enter notes here.</textarea>

9. wrap="hard"

Session 6.3

1. <input type="submit" value="Send Form">
2. <input type="reset" value="Cancel Form">
3. <input type="img" name="Sites" src="sites.gif" value="GotoPage">
4. <input type="hidden" name="Subject" value="Form Responses">
5. <form method="get" action="http://www.j_davis.com/cgi-bin/post-query">
6. <form action="mailto:walker@j_davis.com" enctype="text/plain">
7. accesskey="n"

OBJECTIVES

In this tutorial you will:

- Learn about the history and theory of cascading style sheets

- Create inline styles, embedded styles, and style sheets

- Understand style precedence and style inheritance

- Use cascading style sheets to format paragraphs, lists, and headings

- Design a style for hypertext links in their four conditions

- Define document content with the class and id attributes and create styles for them

- Mark document content with the <div> and <span> tags and create styles for them

- Use cascading style sheets to design page layout

WORKING WITH CASCADING STYLE SHEETS

Designing a Style for a Web Site at Maxwell Scientific

CASE

Maxwell Scientific

Maxwell Scientific is a mail-order firm that sells science kits and science education products to schools and educators. The Maxwell marketing team plans to put portions of its catalog on its Web site and provide people with the ability to purchase items online. The Web site includes product information, comments, and scientific articles.

Chris Todd leads the Web development team at Maxwell Scientific, and she has asked you to assist in the Web design process. You'll start by designing the pages that describe Maxwell Scientific products. However, because the Web site will eventually contain a large number of pages, she wants your work to be easily scaled to the entire site. To make the Web design project more efficient, Chris suggests you use cascading style sheets. Chris has seen other Web sites use style sheets to make their Web sites more flexible, easier to maintain, and more aesthetically interesting.

In this session you'll learn about the history and theory of cascading style sheets. You'll also learn how to create inline styles, embedded styles, and external style sheets. Finally, you'll study how styles are applied to a wide range of tags in your Web site and how the styles are cascaded through the structure of nested tags on your Web pages.

Introduction to Cascading Style Sheets

At Maxwell Scientific, each scientific discipline has a Web page devoted to it. To make the project manageable, you'll limit yourself to only two of those Web pages: Astronomy and Chemistry.

Chris asks you to open the Astronomy Web page to become familiar with the basic structure of these documents.

To open the Astronomy page:

1. Using your text editor, open **astrotxt.htm** from the tutorial.07/tutorial folder of your Data Disk.

2. Save the file as **astro.htm**.

Figure 7-1 shows the current Web page. Chris explains that this sample page displays many of the elements you'll see throughout the Maxwell product Web pages:

- The Maxwell Scientific logo
- A list of links to other product pages
- A heading identifying the particular discipline for that Web page
- An introductory paragraph
- A science column authored by an in-house science writer
- A list of products, including monthly specials
- Selected quotes from satisfied customers
- Contact information for Maxwell Scientific

Figure 7-1   MAXWELL SCIENTIFIC'S ASTRONOMY PAGE

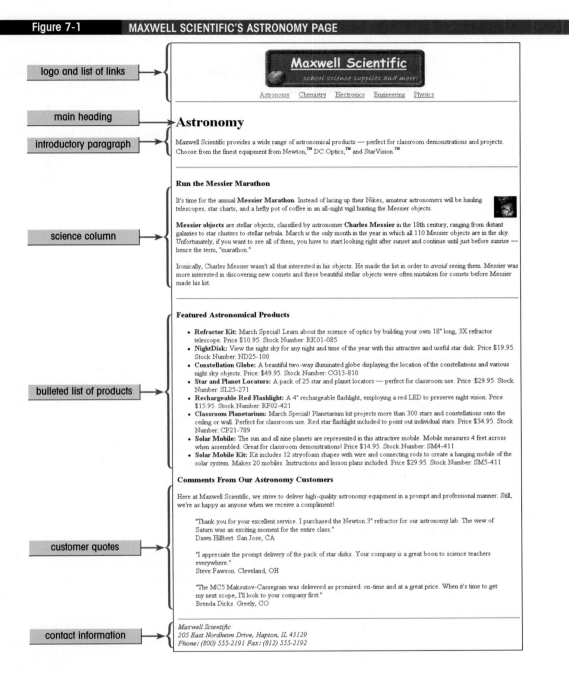

logo and list of links

main heading

introductory paragraph

science column

bulleted list of products

customer quotes

contact information

Because the content of the Maxwell Scientific Web pages changes from day to day, any design you create should focus more on these common elements than on the specific content of each page. Ideally, the design you create for the astronomy page should be easily applied to the other pages in the Web site, allowing the site to maintain a consistent look. Moreover, if Chris needs you to change the design in the future, you'll want to be able to do that without having to edit each individual page. How can you accomplish all of this with HTML?

HTML and Page Layout

Early versions of HTML had little support for Web page design. The philosophy, after all, was to use basic text files that could be quickly downloaded, and to rely on Web browsers to format much of the document's appearance. This approach meant that the application of tags might differ between browsers and operating systems. Some browsers might represent h1 headings with a 20-point font, others might use a 24-point font. The simplicity of HTML tags made creating Web pages easier and made pages load faster, but it came at the cost of limiting design options. As HTML evolved and the Web became more popular, Web designers looked for ways to control their pages' appearance in order to deliver more visually interesting documents. This has been accomplished primarily in three ways:

- Using HTML extensions created by different browsers
- Converting text to images
- Using tables to control page layout

Though innovative, there are drawbacks to each of these approaches. The extensions to HTML introduced by individual browsers provide Web designers with more choices in layout and design. Some extensions, like inline frames, have been embraced in the latest HTML specifications. Overuse of extensions has also led to a confusing array of standards, forcing the Web page designer either to create costly workarounds trying to support different browsers and browsers versions or to limit the audience to only those with the correct browser.

The second approach, converting text to images, has several benefits. For example, rather than worry whether a browser supports a particular font, you can convert text to an inline image for the browser to display. Similarly, one can create text boxes using inline images, which can be placed in specific locations on the Web page. A problem with this approach is that too many images on a Web page can adversely affect how fast the page downloads for users. Additionally, it can be time consuming to make changes to inline graphics.

Finally, tables have become a significant design tool for Web designers, though not without its cost. When tables were introduced, no one thought of them as a layout tool. However, tables have proven to be the most popular way of defining page layout, even though they can make HTML files more complicated to write and to interpret.

History and Support of CSS

One principle of design theory is to separate, as much as possible, the content of a document from its design. For example, what if you want to display all h1 headings in a red, 24 point, bold, Arial font? Because the tags that specify these attributes are intertwined with the content in HTML, you must locate all of the occurrences of the <h1> tag and modify each one individually. For a Web site containing dozens of pages, this is a daunting task to say the least.

One way around this problem is to create a **style** defining the appearance of a document element. Instead of relying on Web browsers to determine the appearance of h1 headings, a style would define this for the browser. When the browser loads the document, it retrieves both the element and the element's style. The collection of styles for a Web page or Web site is known as a **style sheet**.

Like HTML, style sheets use a common language and syntax. The main style sheet standard is **Cascading Style Sheets (CSS)**. CSS has been developed by the World Wide Web Consortium, the same organization that develops specifications for HTML. The first CSS standard, **CSS1**, was released in 1996, and a second standard, **CSS2**, was released in 1998. The latest standard, **CSS3**, is being developed at the time of this writing. CSS is designed to augment HTML, not replace it. As you'll see, CSS provides several tools not available with standard HTML.

Browser support for CSS is uneven. Internet Explorer introduced style sheets in version 3.0 and provides support for the CSS1 standard with version 4.0. Later versions of Internet Explorer have improved support for CSS1, though there are still bugs in the implementation of Internet Explorer. Netscape's support for CSS1 has been spotty due in part to Netscape's decision to push its own style sheet language over CSS. When using cascading style sheets, one must be careful to test the Web page on a variety of browsers and browser versions, especially if styles use some features of CSS2.

For more information about the compliance of browsers with CSS1 and CSS2, and for information about the standards themselves, you can access the Web sites shown in Figure 7-2.

Figure 7-2	WEB SITES WITH INFORMATION ON CASCADING STYLE SHEETS

WEB SITE	URL
CSS Pointers Group	http://css.nu/
RichInStyle Bug List	http://www.richinstyle.com/bugs
WebReview	http://www.webreview.com/style/css1/charts/mastergrid.shtml
World Wide Web Consortium	http://www.w3.org/Style/CSS/

Style Types

There are three ways of employing CSS in your Web pages:

- **Inline styles** in which styles are added to each tag within the HTML file. The style affects that particular tag but does not affect other tags in the document.
- **Embedded** or **global styles** applied to an entire HTML file, allowing the Web designer to modify the appearance of any tag in the document.
- **Linked** or **external style sheets** placed in an external file and linked with pages in the Web site, allowing the Web designer to modify the appearance of tags in several documents.

Which approach you choose depends on your Web site's design. If you need to format just a single section in your Web page, you'd probably use an inline style. If you need to modify all instances of a particular element in a Web page, you'll use an embedded or global style. Finally, if you need to control the style for an entire Web site, you'll use a linked style sheet. You may also use a combination of all three approaches.

Using **Inline Styles**

To create an inline style, you add the style attribute to the HTML tag using the following syntax:

```
<tag style="style declarations">
```

where *tag* is the name of the tag (h1, h2, etc.) and *style declarations* are the styles you'll define for that particular tag. Note that the style declaration must be enclosed within double quotation marks.

A style declaration consists of attribute names that specify such features as the font size, color, and font type, followed by a colon and then the value of the attribute. Multiple attributes can be used as long as you separate each one by a semicolon. The general syntax for the style declaration is therefore:

```
attribute1:value1; attribute2:value2; …
```

A common mistake is to forget the semicolon that separates the attributes. If this semicolon is missing, your browser may not display any of your style changes.

REFERENCE WINDOW	RW

Creating an Inline Style

■ Within the tag that you want to apply the inline style to, insert the attribute:

`style="style declaration"`

where the *style declaration* defines the style, following the general form:

`attribute1:value1; attribute2:value2; …`

where *attribute1* is the name of a particular style attribute, and *value1* is the value the style applies to that attribute.

Chris would like to see the first h1 heading in the astro.htm file be a gold sans-serif font. This is done with the following code (you'll learn where these attribute names and values come from later):

```
<h1 style="color:gold; font-family:sans-serif">
```

Add this code to astro.htm now.

To change the style for the first <h1> tag:

1. Scroll through astro.htm until you locate the first occurrence of the <h1> tag.

2. Type **style="color:gold; font-family:sans-serif"** within the <h1> tag. See Figure 7-3.

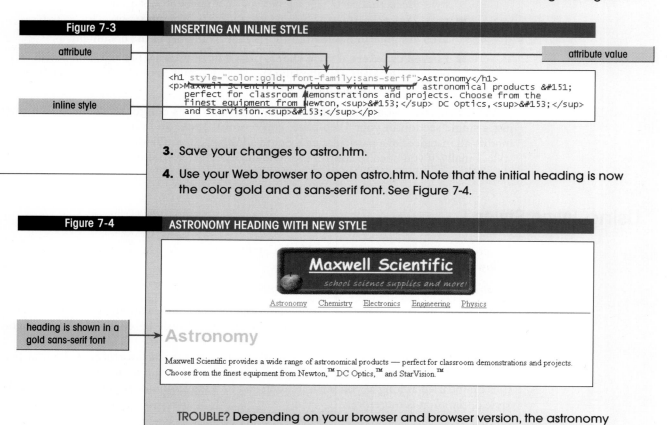

Figure 7-3   **INSERTING AN INLINE STYLE**

attribute   attribute value

inline style

```
<h1 style="color:gold; font-family:sans-serif">Astronomy</h1>
<p>Maxwell Scientific provides a wide range of astronomical products &#151;
   perfect for classroom demonstrations and projects. Choose from the
   finest equipment from Newton, <sup>&#153;</sup> DC Optics, <sup>&#153;</sup>
   and StarVision. <sup>&#153;</sup></p>
```

3. Save your changes to astro.htm.

4. Use your Web browser to open astro.htm. Note that the initial heading is now the color gold and a sans-serif font. See Figure 7-4.

Figure 7-4   **ASTRONOMY HEADING WITH NEW STYLE**

heading is shown in a gold sans-serif font

TROUBLE? Depending on your browser and browser version, the astronomy heading may look slightly different from the one shown in Figure 7-4.

Creating **an Embedded Style**

Chris would like to see the style you used for the astronomy heading applied to other h1 headings. To do that you could insert inline styles into other <h1> tags, but a more efficient way is to create an embedded style for all h1 headings. To do that, you insert a <style> tag within the head section of your HTML file. Within the <style> tag, enclose the style declarations you need for the entire Web page. The syntax of an embedded style is:

```
<style type="style sheet language">
    style declarations
</style>
```

Here, *style sheet language* identifies the type of style language used in the document. There are several style languages available, but the most common language, and the default, is "text/css" for use with CSS.

REFERENCE WINDOW   **RW**

Creating an Embedded Style
- Within the head section of your HTML file, insert the following HTML code:

```
<style type="style sheet language">
    style declarations
</style>
```
where *style sheet language* is the language of your cascading style sheets. If no language is specified, the default value "text/css" is used.
- To enter a *style declaration*, use the following syntax:

```
selector {attribute1:value1; attribute2:value2; …}
```
where *selector* identifies an element in your document, *attribute1* is the first style attribute and *value1* is the value assigned to the first attribute, and so forth.

Selectors and Declarations

Style declarations within the <style> tags obey the following syntax:

```
selector {attribute1:value1; attribute2;value2; …}
```

where *selector* identifies an element in your document, such as a heading or paragraph, and the attributes and values within the curly braces indicate the styles applied to all the occurrences of that element. This collection of attributes and values is also referred to as the declaration of the selector. For example, to display all h1 headings in the HTML document using a gold sans-serif font, you could use the following embedded style:

```
<style>
    h1 {color: gold; font-family: sans-serif}
</style>
```

In this example, "h1" is the selector and the text enclosed in the braces is the declaration. Note that the type attribute was not included within the <style> tag. This is because "text/css" is the default style language, and unless you specify a different style language, you don't need to enter the type attribute. Also, since you are using the <style> tags, you don't need to include double quotes around the attributes and attribute values as you did for inline styles.

Try adding this embedded style to astro.htm now.

To insert an embedded style:

1. Return to **astro.htm** in your text editor.

2. Delete the inline style you created for the initial <h1> tag.

3. Navigate to the top of the file and enter the following text directly above the </head> tag:

```
<style>
h1 {color:gold; font-family:sans-serif}
</style>
```

4. Figure 7-5 shows the revised file.

Figure 7-5	DEFINING A GLOBAL STYLE

embedded or global
style for all h1 headings

```
<html>
<head>
<title>Astronomical products at Maxwell Scientific</title>
<style>
    h1 {color:gold; font-family:sans-serif}
</style>
</head>
<body>
```

5. Save your changes to the file and reload it in your Web browser. Because you applied a global style to all h1 text, the "Astronomy" heading should appear in a gold sans-serif font even though you removed the inline style.

   TROUBLE? If the main heading is not displayed in the gold sans-serif font, check the syntax of the style declaration you entered in astro.htm.

Grouping Selectors

You can apply the same declaration to a group of selectors by including all of the selector names separated by commas. Chris would like to see all headings formatted in a gold sans-serif font. You can do this using the following style declaration:

```
<style>
    h1, h2, h3, h4, h5, h6 {color:gold; font-family:sans-serif}
</style>
```

Modify astro.htm so that all heading tags use the same color and font family.

To apply a declaration to a group of selectors:

1. Return to **astro.htm** in your text editor.

2. Modify the style declaration for the <h1> tag, changing the selector to **h1, h2, h3, h4, h5, h6** as shown in Figure 7-6.

Figure 7-6	APPLYING A STYLE TO A GROUP OF SELECTORS

```
<style>
    h1, h2, h3, h4, h5, h6 {color:gold; font-family:sans-serif}
</style>
```

3. Save your changes and reload it in your Web browser.

Figure 7-7 shows a portion of the revised Web page. Note that all headings are now displayed in a gold sans-serif font.

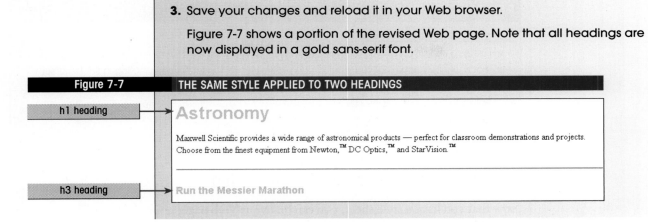

| Figure 7-7 | THE SAME STYLE APPLIED TO TWO HEADINGS |

h1 heading → Astronomy

Maxwell Scientific provides a wide range of astronomical products — perfect for classroom demonstrations and projects. Choose from the finest equipment from Newton,™ DC Optics,™ and StarVision.™

h3 heading → Run the Messier Marathon

Even though you used the same style for all heading tags, there were still some differences in how the browser displayed text formatted with these tags. Most notably, the styles did not affect the relative sizes of the text. Text formatted with the <h1> tag is still in a larger font than text formatted with the <h2> tag. This is because you haven't explicitly defined the size of heading text, so that attribute is left to the browser's internal style rules.

Using an External Style Sheet

The final task that Chris wants you to complete is to create styles that apply to an entire Web site. Chris wants all headings on the Web site to be formatted in a gold sans-serif font. To do this you'll first create a text file containing your style declarations, and then you'll create a link to that file in each page of the Web site.

To create an external style sheet:

1. Using your text editor, create a new document.

2. Type the following code in the new file:

```
h1, h2, h3, h4, h5, h6 {color:gold; font-family:
sans-serif}
```

3. Save your document as **mws.css** in the tutorial.07/tutorial folder of your Data Disk.

Most style sheets have the extension ".css", though this is not a requirement. Also note that within a style sheet, you don't need <style> tags, just the style declarations.

The simple file you just created is a style sheet even though it only contains a single line of code. Most style sheets, of course, have many selectors and declarations.

<u>Creating a Linked Style Sheet</u>
- Create a text file containing the style definitions that you want to apply to the pages on the Web site.
- For each Web page that you want to apply the styles to, insert the following tag in the head section of the HTML file:

```
<link href="URL" rel="stylesheet" type="text/css">
```
where *URL* is the URL or filename of the style sheet.

Linking to Style Sheets with the <link> Tag

Now that you have a style sheet, you can link your Web page, or pages, to it. This is accomplished by adding a <link> tag to the head section of your HTML file. The general syntax for using the <link> tag is as follows:

```
<link href="URL" rel="relation_type" type="link_type">
```

where *URL* is the URL of the linked document, *relation_type* establishes the relationship between the linked document and the Web page, and *link_type* indicates the language used in the linked document. In order to link to a style sheet, the value of the rel attribute should be "stylesheet" and the value of the type attribute should be "text/css". To link to a style sheet named "mws.css", the <link> tag would be:

```
<link href="mws.css" rel="stylesheet" type="text/css">
```

Add this tag to astro.htm.

To link to the mws.css style sheet:

1. Return to **astro.htm** in your text editor.

2. Because you don't need it anymore, delete the style declaration between the <style> and </style> tags in the head section of the HTML file, but keep both the <style> and </style> tags, because you'll be using them later.

3. Insert the following code directly above the opening <style> tag :

```
<link href="mws.css" rel="stylesheet" type="text/css">
```

4. Save your changes to astro.htm and reload it in your Web browser to verify that the headings still appear in a gold sans-serif font.

To apply this style sheet to other pages in the Web site, simply add the <link> tag to each HTML file. Try this with the Chemistry page.

To add the MWS style sheet to the Chemistry page:

1. Using your text editor, open **chemtxt.htm** from the tutorial.07/tutorial folder of your Data Disk and save it as **chem.htm**.

2. Insert the following code directly before the </head> tag. You can either type the code as it appears here or copy it from astro.htm if you prefer.

```
<link href="mws.css" rel="stylesheet" type="text/css">
```

3. Open **chem.htm** in your Web browser. As shown in Figure 7-8, the page now employs the same h1 style used by the Astronomy page.

| Figure 7-8 | THE CHEMISTRY PAGE |

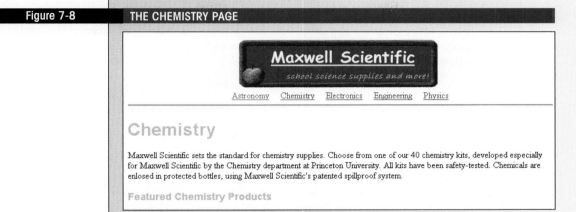

Chris points out that once the final version for the external style sheet is determined, you can modify the design of any of the pages in the Maxwell Scientific Web site by simply adding a <link> tag pointing to the mws.css style sheet.

Linking to Style Sheets with @import

Another way to link to a style sheet is to use the @import command, which accesses the style sheet definitions from another file. To use @import with your styles, you enclose the @import command within the embedded <style> tags as follows:

```
<style>
   @import url(stylesheet.css);
   style declarations
</style>
```

where *stylesheet.css* is the URL of the style sheet file. If you want to access a style sheet from within another style sheet, simply add the @import command to your style sheet file:

```
@import url(stylesheet.css);
styles
```

The advantage of this approach is that it allows you to easily combine different style sheets. For example, Maxwell Scientific can create a style sheet named "basic.css" that contains general style rules for all pages in the Web site. A second style sheet, designed for only the product pages, would combine the basic.css rules with product page styles as follows:

```
@import url(basic.css);
styles specific to the product pages …
```

The @import command provides greater flexibility than the <link> tag when working with multiple style sheets, but it has limited browser support. Unless you have a compelling reason to use @import, you are probably better off using the <link> tag.

Resolving Style Precedence

You've now used three different methods to create and apply styles to your Web site. What would happen if you used all three methods in the same Web page and mistakenly used different formatting for the same content? How does your Web browser determine how to apply the various styles? In cases where the styles conflict, precedence is determined in the following order:

1. An inline style overrides any embedded style or external style sheet.

2. An embedded style overrides an external style sheet.

3. An external style sheet overrides the internal style rules set by the Web browser.

4. Any style attributes left undefined by an inline style, an embedded style, or an external style sheet are left to the Web browser.

For example, if you specify the h1 heading "Astronomy" in astro.htm to display in a blue sans-serif font, this style definition overrides any conflicting style declaration for h1 headings in the embedded style or the external style sheet.

Note that precedence is only an issue when styles conflict (using gold sans-serif versus blue sans-serif, for example.) If styles don't conflict, then browsers merge the different styles.

To illustrate this concept, Chris suggests that you modify the external style sheet so that all headings display in a sans-serif font, but font color is determined by the embedded styles within each page. She would like the Astronomy page headings to display in gold and the Chemistry page headings to display in red.

To modify the styles for the Web site:

1. Return to **mws.css** in your text editor and edit the style definition line, deleting the color attribute so that it reads as follows:

```
h1, h2, h3, h4, h5, h6 {font-family:sans-serif}
```

2. Save your changes to mws.css.

3. Using your text editor, open **astro.htm** and enter the following code between the <style> and </style> tags:

```
h1, h2, h3, h4, h5, h6 {color: gold}
```

4. Save your changes to astro.htm.

5. Using your text editor, open **chem.htm** and insert the following code after the <link> tag:

```
<style>
    h1, h2, h3, h4, h5, h6 {color: red}
</style>
```

6. Save your changes to chem.htm.

7. Reload chem.htm in your Web browser. Figure 7-9 shows the current state of this page.

| Figure 7-9 | THE CHEMISTRY PAGE WITH EMBEDDED STYLES AND AN EXTERNAL STYLE SHEET |

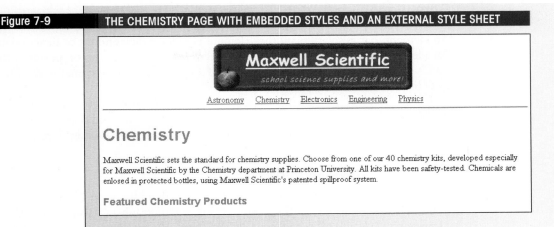

The Chemistry page now displays headings in a red sans-serif font, combining the style rules from the Chemistry page's embedded style and the mws.css style sheet.

As a change is made to a style at one level, the changes are cascaded through to the other levels (hence the term, cascading style sheets). If you change the font from sans-serif to Times Roman in the mws.css style sheet, the change is cascaded through the embedded and inline styles, changing the font to Times Roman in every case where a different font has not already been specified.

As you define more styles for your Web site, you need to keep track of the inline, embedded, and external style sheets to correctly predict the impact that style changes have on the appearance of each page.

Working **with Style Inheritance**

Web pages invariably have elements placed within other elements. For example, a Web page might have a bold tag, <b>, placed within a paragraph tag, <p>, to create boldface text within the paragraph. The paragraph tag is likewise placed within the <body> tag. You can display this relationship using a tree diagram like the one shown in Figure 7-10.

| Figure 7-10 | SAMPLE TREE STRUCTURE OF HTML ELEMENTS |

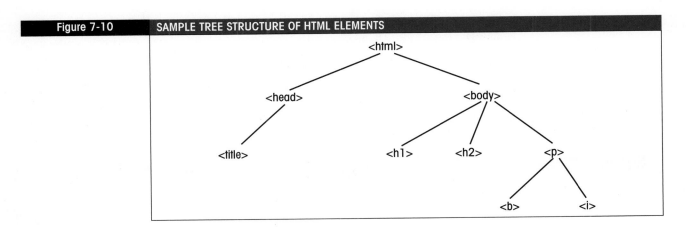

Parent and Descendant Elements

An element that lies within another element is called a **descendant** or **descendant element**. An element that contains another element is called the **parent** or **parent element**. The <body> tag is perhaps the prime example of a parent, because it contains all of the other tags used to format the content of your page.

Using the principle of **inheritance**, styles defined for each parent tag are transferred to its descendants. If Figure 7-10 represents all of the elements and their relationships in a particular HTML file, you could change the font color of every element in the Web page using the following style definition:

```
h1, h2, p {color: blue}
```

and all of the h1, h2, and paragraph text displays in a blue font. Note that any boldface or italic text using the <b> and <i> tags within a paragraph tag also inherit the color blue. However, as you add more tags to your Web page, the tree structure becomes more complex and the style declarations can become long and unwieldy. A simpler approach is to define a style for the <body> tag. You could set all font color to blue using the style definition:

```
body {color: blue}
```

Because all elements are descendants of the body element, all the text in the page is displayed in blue.

You can override this inheritance by specifying a different style for the element's descendants. For example, consider the following style definitions:

```
body {color: blue}
h1, h2 {color: green}
```

These definitions specify all text in the Web page to be displayed in a blue font except the h1 and h2 headings, and any descendants of the h1 and h2 elements, which are displayed in green. Note that the order in which you enter these style definitions does not matter. Web browsers resolve the style definitions based on the underlying tree structure. Still, it is considered good practice to enter your style definitions in an order that follows the tree hierarchy.

Chris suggests that you change the default font color in the Maxwell Scientific pages to green, but leave the current headings as gold.

To specify a default font color for the Maxwell Scientific Web site:

1. Return to **mws.css** in your text editor.

2. Insert the following code directly before the style definitions for the h1–h6 tags:

   ```
   body {color:green}
   ```

   Figure 7-11 shows the revised file.

| Figure 7-11 | CHANGING THE BODY TEXT COLOR TO GREEN |

```
body {color:green}
h1, h2, h3, h4, h5, h6 {font-family: sans-serif}
```

3. Save your changes to mws.css.

4. Return to your Web browser and reload astro.htm. Figure 7-12 shows the new version of the Web page with a green font color except for the headings, which are displayed in gold.

| Figure 7-12 | REVISED FONT COLOR IN THE ASTRONOMY PAGE |

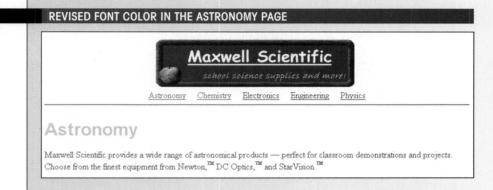

Contextual Selectors

You can use the tree structure concept to better control how your styles are applied to your Web page. Consider the structure of the tags shown in Figure 7-13.

| Figure 7-13 | TREE STRUCTURE WITH TWO <B> TAG LOCATIONS |

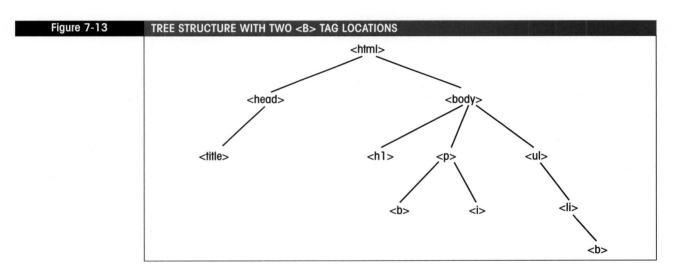

A <b> tag appears in two locations: within the <p> tag and within the <li> tag. You want to display the boldface text within the <li> tag in a blue font, but you want all other occurrences of bold text to remain unchanged. If you use the following style declaration:

```
b {color: blue}
```

all boldface text is displayed in blue, including text that does not lie within <li> tags. To restrict the application of this style, you use a contextual selector, indicating the context in which the style is to be applied. For example, the declaration:

```
li b {color: blue}
```

indicates that any boldface text that lies within an <li> tag is displayed as blue. Any boldface text located elsewhere in the Web page is not affected by this style.

Cascading Style Sheet provide ways of fine-tuning the context in which the selector is applied. If you want to apply a style only to the direct descendant of a parent element, use the syntax:

```
e1 > e2
```

where *e1* and *e2* are the names of HTML elements and *e2* is directly below the *e1* in the hierarchy of elements in the document. For example, you could use the declaration:

```
li > b {color: blue}
```

to apply a blue font to boldface text within the <li> tag as long as the <b> tag is a direct descendant of the <li> tag. This would not work, however, for the following code:

```
<li>This month's <i><b>specials</b></i>
```

because the <i> tag lies between the <li> and <b> in the hierarchy of elements.

If two elements follow each other in the document, the syntax for this group of elements would be:

```
e1 + e2
```

where *e1* is the first element and *e2* is the element that follows. The following declaration:

```
h1+h2 {color: blue}
```

applies a blue color to h1 and h2 headings that follow each other in the document. The following code satisfies those conditions:

```
<h1>Astronomy</h1>
<h2>Monthly Specials</h2>
```

but this code does not:

```
<h1>Astronomy</h1>
    <p>Welcome to the Maxwell Scientific Astronomy page.</p>
<h2>Monthly Specials</h2>
```

Note that not all browsers support contextual selectors, and you should always test your page using various browsers and browser versions.

You've completed your work on applying styles to the Maxwell Scientific Web site. In the next session, you'll learn about more attributes with which to control styles.

Session 7.1 QUICK | CHECK

1. What do the acronyms CSS1 and CSS2 refer to?

2. What are inline styles, embedded styles, and linked style sheets? Which would you use to create a set of styles for an entire Web site?

3. What style would you use to change the color of all text found within the paragraph tag <p> to blue?

4. What style would you use to change the color of both the h1 and h2 headings to yellow?

5. What style would you use to change the color of boldface text within your paragraphs to red? Will boldface text located elsewhere be affected by your style?

6. What tag would you use to link to the external style sheet "basicstyle.css"? Where should you place this tag in your HTML file?

7. If a style sheet sets the color of h1 headings to blue, and an embedded style in the Web page sets the h1 color to green, what color is displayed in the Web browser and why?

SESSION 7.2

In this session you'll learn more about the CSS language. You'll learn about specific attributes that you can use with styles to modify the appearance of fonts, including font size and alignment. You'll learn how to use styles to work with colors and background images. Finally, you'll use style attributes to create and format lists.

Setting Font and Text Attributes

In the last session you learned how to apply styles to the Maxwell Scientific Web site. To keep things simple, you worked with only two attributes: font color and font family. Now you're ready to learn more about the style language of CSS and how to create additional styles. You'll start by examining the font-family attribute more closely.

Using Font Families

The font-family attribute allows you to choose a font face for use in your Web page. CSS works with two types of font faces: specific and generic. A **specific font** is a font such as Arial, Garamond, or Times New Roman that is actually installed on a user's computer. A **generic font** is a general description of a font, allowing the operating system to determine which installed font best matches it. CSS supports five generic font types: serif, sans-serif, monospace, cursive, and fantasy. Figure 7-14 shows examples of each generic type. Note that for each generic font there can be a wide range of designs.

Figure 7-14	GENERIC FONTS

Generic Names	Font Samples		
serif	defg	defg	defg
sans-serif	defg	defg	defg
monospace	defg	defg	defg
cursive	*defg*	*defg*	*defg*
fantasy	**DEFG**	**DEFG**	**defg**

within each generic font there can be a wide range of appearances

REFERENCE WINDOW   **RW**

<u>Choosing a Font Family</u>
- To choose a font family for a Web page element, use the style:

  `font-family:font1, font2 ...`

  where *font1*, *font2*, and so forth are either specific or generic font names. Generic font names must be serif, sans-serif, monospace, cursive, or fantasy.

One issue with generic fonts is that you cannot be sure which specific font the Web browser uses to display your text. Figure 7-14 shows a range of possible fonts used with each of the generic types. Whenever possible, it is a good idea to use specific fonts. To do this effectively, you can provide the Web browser with several fonts to choose from. Browsers that don't have access to the font you specified as your first choice may have your second or third choice available. List specific font names first, followed by a generic font name for the browser to use if none of the specific fonts can be found. Separate the font names by commas as shown in the following style declaration:

`body {font-family: Times Roman, Century Schoolbook, serif}`

This declaration instructs the browser to display body text in a Times Roman font. If that font cannot be found, the browser looks for Century Schoolbook, and if that font is also missing, the browser uses whatever serif font is available.

In your earlier work, you specified only the generic sans-serif font for heading text. Now that you've seen how to more effectively use the font-family attribute, Chris suggests that you augment your earlier style, allowing the browser to first search for the Arial font and then for Helvetica before resorting to the generic font.

To modify the font-family attribute for the heading text:

1. Using your text editor, open the **mws.css** style sheet.

2. Change the style for the h1–h6 tags to:

   `h1, h2, h3, h4, h5, h6 {font-family: Arial, Helvetica, sans-serif}`

3. Save your changes to mws.css.

4. Using your Web browser, reload astro.htm and chem.htm. Depending on the fonts installed on your computer, you may notice a slight change in the appearance of the heading text.

Managing Font Size

Chris has other suggestions to improve the design of the Web page. At the bottom of each page is address information formatted with the <address> tag. By default, text formatted with this tag is displayed in normal-sized type, italicized, and aligned with the left edge of the Web page. Chris doesn't like this style and has several changes to propose. First of all, she wants the address information to take up less space on the Web page by reducing the font size of the text.

A common method for specifying font sizes with HTML is to use the size attribute of the <font> tag. While useful for simple formatting, the size attribute limits you to only seven font sizes, 1 through 7, and the Web browser determines what the precise sizes are when displayed. Depending on how browsers are configured, two browsers can display font sizes quite differently, leaving an important aspect of your design out of your control.

REFERENCE WINDOW **RW**

<u>Specifying a Font Size</u>

■ To specify a font size for an element, use the style:

`font-size: size`

where *size* can either be a unit of length (specified as mm, cm, in, pt, pc, em, or ex), a keyword (xx-small, x-small, small, medium, large, x-large, xx-large), a percentage of the font size of the parent element, or a keyword describing the size relative to the parent element (larger or smaller).

In CSS, you use the font-size attribute to manage font sizes. Font sizes can be expressed:

■ as a unit of length

■ with a keyword description

■ as a percentage of the parent element

■ with a keyword expressing the size relative to the font size of the parent element

If you choose to express size as a unit of length, you can use absolute units or relative units. Because absolute and relative units come up a lot in CSS, it's worthwhile to spend some time understanding them.

Absolute units define the font size based on one of the following standard units of measurement: mm (millimeter), cm (centimeter), in (inch), pt (point), and pc (pica.) For comparison, there are 72 points in an inch, 12 points in a pica, and 6 picas in an inch. Size values can be whole numbers (0, 1, 2 …) or decimals (0.5, 1.6, 3.9 …). If you want your h1 headings to be 1/2 inch in size, you can use any of the following styles (note that you should not insert a space between the size value and the unit abbreviation):

```
h1 {font-size: 0.5in}
h1 {font-size: 36pt}
h1 {font-size: 3pc}
```

These measurement units are useful if you intend to have users print the Web page on standard 8 1/2 x 11 sheets of paper. They don't work as well in the browser window, where the size of the user's monitor and resolution are unknown. For example, a 1/2-inch heading on a 14-inch monitor has a very different impact than the same size heading on a 21-inch monitor.

To overcome this problem, you can use a **relative unit**, one that expresses the font size relative to a size of a standard character. There are two standard typesetting characters, referred to as "em" and "ex." The **em unit** is equal to the width of the capital letter "M" in the browser's default font size. The **ex unit** is equal to the height of a small "x" in the default font (see Figure 7-15.)

Figure 7-15 **THE EM AND EX UNITS**

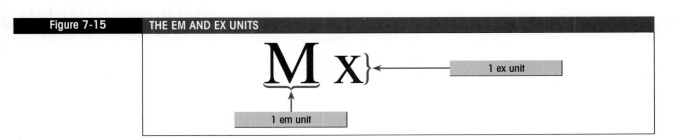

Of these two units, the em unit is more useful for page design, because 1 em is equal to the browser's default font size for body text. This is true no matter what font is being used (unlike the ex unit, whose size changes based on the font face being used). For example, if the Web browser displays body text in a 12-point font, the following style:

```
h1 {font-size: 2em}
```

makes all h1 headings twice the default font size, or 24 points. As with absolute units, you can specify fractional values for the em and ex units. Unlike the absolute units, em and ex units are **scalable** in that they retain their relative proportions regardless of the monitor size or resolution.

The final unit of measurement we'll examine is the **pixel**, entered with the unit abbreviation "px". To set the size of your h1 headings to 20 pixels, use the style:

```
h1 {font-size: 20px}
```

Pixels give you the greatest control over size, because a pixel is the smallest element recognized by the monitor, but they should be used with some caution. Text that is 10 pixels high may be perfectly readable at a monitor resolution of 640 x 480, but it can become unreadable if your user's monitor is set to 1024 x 768.

If you are uncomfortable dealing with units of length, you can use one of the seven descriptive keywords: xx-small, x-small, small, medium, large, x-large, or xx-large. These keywords correspond to the seven values of the size attribute in the <font> tag. For example, to format an h1 heading with the largest font size, you can use either the HTML command:

```
<h1><font size="7">Your Heading Text</font></h1>
```

or the style:

```
h1 {font-size: xx-large}
```

If you want the size of certain text to be expressed relative to the size of the parent element, you can do so using percentage values. In the following set of style definitions, the size of boldface type has been increased to 150% of the size of its parent element. Since the body text is 12 points, boldface body text is displayed as 18-point type.

```
body {font-size: 12pt}
b {font-size: 150%}
```

Figure 7-16 shows the impact of such a style definition on boldface text in a Web page. Note that the style has the same impact within a heading, since the heading is the parent element, and the boldface text is increased to 150% of the surrounding heading text.

Figure 7-16   EXPRESSING FONT SIZE AS A PERCENTAGE OF THE PARENT TAG

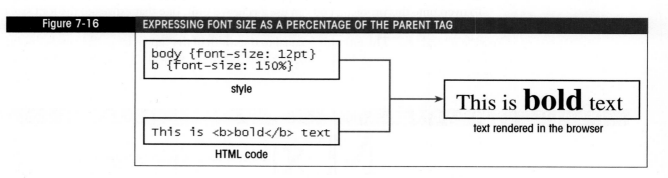

Lastly, you can express a font size using the keywords "larger" and "smaller," which makes the font one size larger or smaller than the size of the parent element. For example, to make the h2 heading one size larger than the body text, you could use the following style:

```
body {font-size: medium}
h2 {font-size: larger}
```

Note that you could have achieved the same effect by using the keyword "large" for the h2 style.

Armed with an almost-dizzying array of possible font size values, you're ready to apply your knowledge to the <address> tag in the Astronomy page. Recall that Chris wanted this font to be smaller. You decide to reduce the font to 0.6 em, or 60% of the size of normal body text.

To decrease the font size of the <address> tag:

1. Return to the **mws.css** style sheet in your text editor.

2. Insert the following code at the bottom of the file:

```
address {font-size: 0.6em}
```

3. Save your changes to mws.css.

4. Reload astro.htm and chem.htm in your Web browser. Scroll to the bottom of each page, verifying that the address information has been reduced in size as shown in Figure 7-17.

| Figure 7-17 | REDUCING THE SIZE OF THE ADDRESS TEXT |

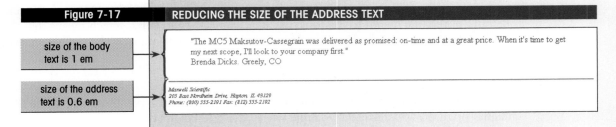

size of the body text is 1 em

size of the address text is 0.6 em

"The MC5 Maksutov-Cassegrain was delivered as promised: on-time and at a great price. When it's time to get my next scope, I'll look to your company first."
Brenda Dicks. Greely, CO

Maxwell Scientific
205 East Nordheim Drive, Hapton, IL 49129
Phone: (800) 555-2191 Fax: (812) 555-2192

Specifying Word, Letter, and Line Spacing

In addition to controlling font sizes, you can use CSS font attributes to control the spacing between letters, words, and lines of text. To set the space between individual letters, you use the letter-spacing attribute, with the syntax:

```
letter-spacing: size
```

where *size* can either have the value "normal", which allows the browser to determine the letter spacing based on the font being used, or a number expressed in the same measuring units used to describe font size (inches, millimeters, centimeters, em units, etc.). To set the letter spacing for text in a paragraph to 0.5 em, use the style:

```
p {letter-spacing: 0.5em}
```

Using the letter-spacing attribute to stretch a word over an E X T E N D E D space is one way of adding flair and impact to your design. Another technique is to change the spacing between individual words. This is achieved with the word-spacing attribute:

```
word-spacing: size
```

where *size* is either equal to "normal", to allow the browser to set the word spacing, or to a specific length using the standard units of measure. Modifying the space between words is not done often, but you can do it with CSS if you need to.

Finally, you can use the line-height attribute to modify the vertical space between lines of text. Graphic designers may know this spacing as leading. The line-height attribute specifies the minimum distance between the baselines of adjacent lines. Figure 7-18 shows how the line height relates to the font size. Note that the line height is usually larger than the font size to leave additional space between lines of text.

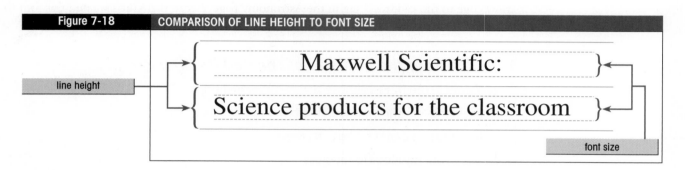

Figure 7-18   COMPARISON OF LINE HEIGHT TO FONT SIZE

To set the line height, use the style:

```
line-height: size
```

where *size* is either a specific length, a percentage of the font size, or a number representing the ratio of the line height to the font size. The standard ratio is 1.2, which means that the line height is 1.2 times the font size. If you wanted your paragraphs to be double-spaced, you would enter the style definition:

```
p {line-height: 2}
```

A common typographic technique is to create titles with large fonts and small line heights. Figure 7-19 shows an example where the line height is actually smaller than the font size. This treatment can give the title greater impact than it would have with more space between the two lines.

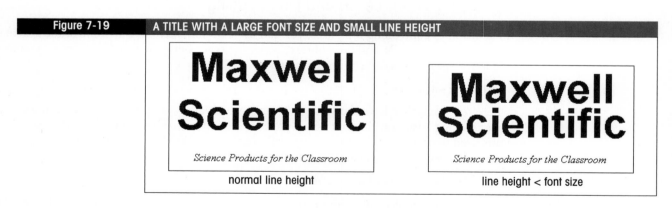

Figure 7-19   A TITLE WITH A LARGE FONT SIZE AND SMALL LINE HEIGHT

REFERENCE   WINDOW   **RW**

Controlling Letter, Word, and Line Spacing

- To define the space between individual letters, use the style:

  `letter-spacing: size`

  where *size* is the amount of space between letters.
- To define the space between individual words, use the style:

  `word-spacing: size`

  where *size* is the space between individual words.
- To define the vertical space between lines of text, use the style:

  `line-height: size`

  where *size* is either the specific length between the baseline of the lines, a percentage of the font size of the text in the lines, or a number representing the ratio of the line height to the font size.

Setting Font Styles and Weights

Chris feels that the address information with the smaller font size is difficult to read. Perhaps it would help if the text weren't in italics. Note that text formatted with the <address> tag uses italics by default. Font styles are controlled by the font-style attribute, which has three possible values: normal, italic, or oblique.

REFERENCE   WINDOW   **RW**

Controlling Font Appearance and Weight

- To specify the appearance for your font, use the style:

  `font-style: style_type`

  where *style_type* is either normal, italic, or oblique.
- To control the weight of your fonts, use the style:

  `font-weight: weight`

  where *weight* is either a value ranging from 100 (lightest) to 900 (heaviest) in intervals of 100, a keyword describing the weight of the font (normal or bold), or a keyword that describes the weight relative to the weight of the parent element (lighter or bolder).

The italic and oblique styles are similar in appearance though there can be small differences depending on the font. Versions of Netscape prior to 6.0 do not support the oblique attribute value.

Since you want to remove the italics from the address information, you can add the font-style: normal attribute to your style sheet. This overrides the default italic setting in the <address> tag.

To remove italics from the <address> tag:

1. Return to the **mws.css** style sheet in your text editor.

2. Insert the style **; font-style: normal** in the declaration for the <address> tag, as shown in Figure 7-20.

Figure 7-20	APPLYING THE NORMAL FONT STYLE

```
body {color: green}
h1, h2, h3, h4, h5, h6 {font-family: Arial, Helvetica, sans-serif}
address {font-size: 0.6em; font-style: normal}
```

3. Save your changes to mws.css and reload astro.htm and chem.htm in your Web browser. Verify that the address information is no longer displayed in italics on both pages.

TROUBLE? If the text has not changed in appearance as a result of your edits, return to your style sheet to ensure that you placed a semicolon between the attributes.

You may be wondering why "bold" was not included as one of the font-style values. This is because CSS considers "bold" to be an aspect of the font's weight, or line thickness. Font weights can be expressed as an absolute number ranging in intervals of 100, going from 100 (the lightest) up to 900 (the heaviest or "most bold"). While this is good in theory, most fonts do not support nine different font weights. For most fonts, you can assume that a weight of 400 corresponds to normal text, a weight of 700 can be used for bold text, and 900 for "extra" bold text. For light text, you can try a weight of 100, but for many fonts you won't notice a difference between the 100 and 400 weight.

You can also use the keywords "normal" and "bold" in place of a weight value, or you can express the font weight relative to the parent tag by using the keywords "bolder" or "lighter." For example, in HTML all headings are boldface, so the <b> tag has no effect within an <h2> tag. This is not true with CSS, where you can use the bolder attribute to get bolder text, as shown below:

```
h2 {font-weight: 700}
b {font-weight: bolder}
```

If these style definitions are applied to a Web page, h2 text formatted with the <b> tag will be bolder or thicker in appearance than the surrounding heading text. How noticeable the difference is depends on the Web browser and the type of font used.

Aligning Text Horizontally and Vertically

In looking over the current design of the Astronomy page, you decide that the address information would look better if centered on the bottom of the page. To do this with CSS, you use the text-align attribute:

text-align: *alignment*

where *alignment* can be left, center, right, or justify. Setting the text-align value to "justify" stretches the text, extending it from the left to the right margin, but in actual practice not all browsers interpret the "justify" value in this way. Some browsers will ignore this attribute value altogether.

To center the address information:

1. Return to the **mws.css** style sheet in your text editor.

2. Add the following attribute to the address tag style **; text-align: center**, as shown in Figure 7-21.

Figure 7-21 | **APPLYING THE CENTER TEXT-ALIGN STYLE**

```
body {color: green}
h1, h2, h3, h4, h5, h6 {font-family: Arial, Helvetica, sans-serif}
address {font-size: 0.6em; font-style: normal; text-align: center}
```

3. Save your changes to mws.css and then reload astro.htm and chem.htm using your Web browser. The address text is now centered.

REFERENCE WINDOW   **RW**

Controlling Text Alignment

■ To specify the horizontal alignment of your text, use the style:

   `text-align: ` *alignment*

   where *alignment* is either left, center, right, or justify.

■ To control the vertical alignment of text and images relative to the baseline of the parent element, use the style:

   `vertical-align: ` *alignment*

   where *alignment* equals one of the following keywords: baseline, bottom, middle, sub, super, text-bottom, text-top, or top, or is expressed as a distance or percentage that the element is raised or lowered relative to the height of the parent element.

CSS also allows you to vertically align elements such as text and images relative to the surrounding text. The syntax for setting the vertical alignment is:

`vertical-align: ` *alignment*

where *alignment* has one of the keyword values shown in Figure 7-22.

Figure 7-22 | **VALUES OF THE VERTICAL ALIGNMENT ATTRIBUTE**

ATTRIBUTE VALUE	DESCRIPTION
baseline	Aligns the element with the baseline
bottom	Aligns the bottom of the element with the bottom of the lowest element (text or image) in the line
middle	Aligns the element in the middle of the text
sub	Aligns the element as a subscript
super	Aligns the element as a superscript
text-bottom	Aligns the element with the font's bottom
text-top	Aligns the element with the top of the tallest letter
top	Aligns the element with the top of the tallest element (text or image) in the line

Figure 7-23 shows an example of each vertical-align value. Baseline is the default value for vertical alignment.

Figure 7-23 | **EXAMPLES OF THE VERTICAL ALIGNMENT VALUES**

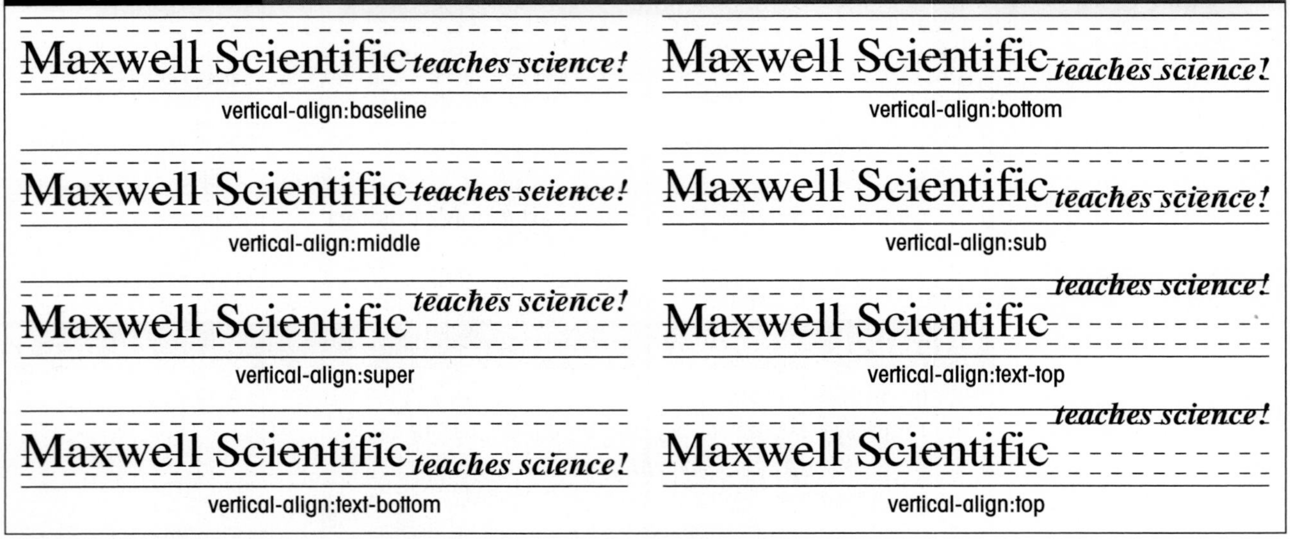

Maxwell Scientific *teaches science!*
vertical-align:baseline

Maxwell Scientific *teaches science!*
vertical-align:bottom

Maxwell Scientific *teaches science!*
vertical-align:middle

Maxwell Scientific *teaches science!*
vertical-align:sub

Maxwell Scientific *teaches science!*
vertical-align:super

Maxwell Scientific *teaches science!*
vertical-align:text-top

Maxwell Scientific *teaches science!*
vertical-align:text-bottom

Maxwell Scientific *teaches science!*
vertical-align:top

In place of the keywords, you can also enter a distance or percentage that an element is raised relative to the surrounding text. A positive value or percentage raises the element above the surrounding text, and a negative value or percentage lowers the element. For example, the style:

```
vertical-align: 50%
```

raises the element by half of the line height of the surrounding text, while the style

```
vertical-align: -50%
```

lowers the element by half of the line height.

Indenting Text

CSS allows you to indent the first line of a paragraph. The syntax for creating an indentation is:

```
text-indent: indentation
```

where *indentation* is either the length, in either absolute or relative units, of the indentation or a percentage of the width of the paragraph. For example, an indentation value of 5% indents the first line by 5% of the width of the paragraph, while an indentation value of 2em indents the first line by 2 em units. The length and percentage values also can be negative, which extends the first line to the left by the specified value or percentage, and then indents the rest of the lines in the paragraph. This particular effect, called a **hanging indent**, works sporadically on many browsers, so you should be sure to test your style sheet thoroughly if you intend to create a hanging indent in your Web page.

Special Text Attributes

CSS provides three attributes for special text effects: text-decoration, text-transform, and font-variant. As shown in Figure 7-24, the text-decoration attribute can be used to underline your text or place a line over or through your text. You can also make your text blink on and off using the text-decoration:blink attribute.

Figure 7-24 | **VALUES OF THE TEXT-DECORATION ATTRIBUTE**

Maxwell Scientific teaches science
text-decoration:none

Maxwell Scientific teaches science
text-decoration:underline

Maxwell Scientific teaches science
text-decoration:overline

~~Maxwell Scientific teaches science~~
text-decoration:line-through

REFERENCE WINDOW   **RW**

Formatting Your Text with Special Attributes

- To decorate your text, use the style:

    `text-decoration:` *decoration*

    where *decoration* equals blink, line-through, overline, underline, or none.

- To change the case of the font, use the style:

    `text-transform:` *transform*

    where *transform* equals capitalize, lowercase, uppercase, or none.

- To display a variant of the font's appearance, use the style:

    `font-variant:` *variant*

    where *variant* equals small-caps or none.

The text-transform attribute can be used to capitalize the first letter of each word in a paragraph, display the text in all capital letters, or display the text in all lowercase letters. Figure 7-25 shows the effect of the various text-transform values.

Figure 7-25 | **VALUES OF THE TEXT-TRANSFORM ATTRIBUTE**

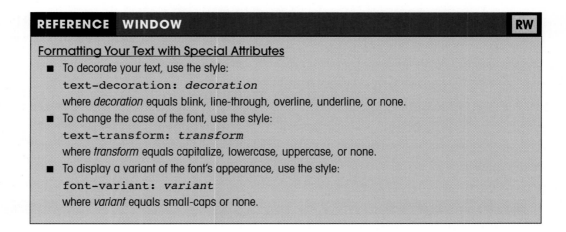

Maxwell Scientific teaches science
text-transform:none

Maxwell Scientific Teaches Science
text-transform:capitalize

MAXWELL SCIENTIFIC TEACHES SCIENCE
text-transform:uppercase

maxwell scientific teaches science
text-transform:lowercase

Finally, you can use the font-variant command to create small caps. Small caps are capital letters that are the same size as lowercase letters. Figure 7-26 shows an interesting effect that can be achieved using the style on your text.

`font-variant: small-caps`

Netscape does not support the font-variant attribute in versions prior to 6.0.

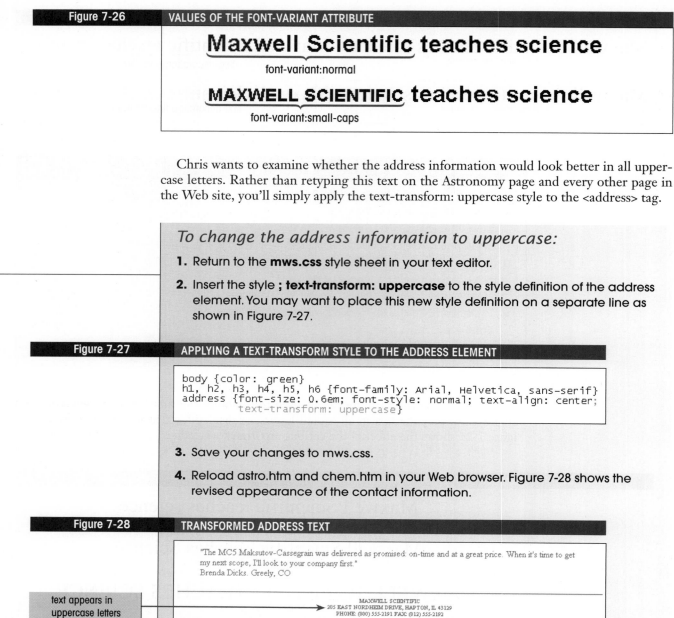

Figure 7-26   VALUES OF THE FONT-VARIANT ATTRIBUTE

Maxwell Scientific teaches science

font-variant:normal

MAXWELL SCIENTIFIC teaches science

font-variant:small-caps

Chris wants to examine whether the address information would look better in all upper-case letters. Rather than retyping this text on the Astronomy page and every other page in the Web site, you'll simply apply the text-transform: uppercase style to the <address> tag.

To change the address information to uppercase:

1. Return to the **mws.css** style sheet in your text editor.

2. Insert the style **; text-transform: uppercase** to the style definition of the address element. You may want to place this new style definition on a separate line as shown in Figure 7-27.

Figure 7-27   APPLYING A TEXT-TRANSFORM STYLE TO THE ADDRESS ELEMENT

```
body {color: green}
h1, h2, h3, h4, h5, h6 {font-family: Arial, Helvetica, sans-serif}
address {font-size: 0.6em; font-style: normal; text-align: center;
         text-transform: uppercase}
```

3. Save your changes to mws.css.

4. Reload astro.htm and chem.htm in your Web browser. Figure 7-28 shows the revised appearance of the contact information.

Figure 7-28   TRANSFORMED ADDRESS TEXT

"The MC5 Maksutov-Cassegrain was delivered as promised: on-time and at a great price. When it's time to get my next scope, I'll look to your company first."
Brenda Dicks. Greely, CO

text appears in uppercase letters →

MAXWELL SCIENTIFIC
205 EAST NORDHEIM DRIVE, HAPTON, IL 43129
PHONE: (800) 555-2191 FAX: (812) 555-2192

Chris examines the address text and is happy with the final style you selected for the address tag element. You won't need to make any more changes to the address information.

The Font Attribute

You can pool many of the individual text and font attributes you've learned about so far into a single attribute, called the font attribute. The syntax for the font attribute is:

```
font: font-style font-variant font-weight font-size/
line-height font-family
```

where *font-style*, *font-variant*, and so forth are the values for font and text style attributes you've learned about in this session. The font attribute provides an efficient way for you to define multiple attributes. For example, the following two style forms are equivalent:

```
h2 {font-style: italic; font-variant: small-caps;
font-weight: bold;
    font-size: 3em; line-height: 0.8em;
    font-family: Times Roman, serif }

h2 {font: italic small-caps bold 3em/0.8em Times Roman,
serif}
```

The font attribute requires that you specify the font size, font variant, and font weight (in that order) while the other font attributes are optional. If you don't include a font attribute, your browser assigns the normal or standard value for the element.

Working with Color and Background

You can now turn your attention to the color and background choices you'll make for the Maxwell Scientific Web site. In Session 1, you worked with color names by changing the body text to green and the heading text to gold. Now you're ready to examine the syntax of the color attribute in considerable detail.

The Color Attribute

There are many ways of defining color with CSS. As you saw in Session 1, you can use color names to specify color; CSS works with most of the color names supported by HTML.

Another way to specify color in CSS is to use RGB color values. You can enter the hexadecimal form of the color value just as you did with HTML, or you can enter the RGB color values directly (yeah, no more hexadecimals!) For example, to change the body text color to teal, you can use any of the following styles:

```
body {color: teal}
body {color: #008080}
body {color: rgb(0,128,128)}
body {color: rgb(0%, 50%, 50%)}
```

Remember that RGB color values range from 0 to 255, so specifying a color percentage of 50% for green and blue is close to a color value of 128.

You decide that the gold color used for the headings in astro.htm is too light. After reviewing possible color choices, you decide that a brownish gold with a color value corresponding to RGB values of (153,102,6) would be more appealing. Because this is an embedded style, you'll make your changes to astro.htm.

> ### To revise the color of headings in the Astronomy page:
>
> **1.** Return to **astro.htm** in your text editor.
>
> **2.** Change the color of the h1–h6 headings from gold to **rgb(153,102,6)** as shown in Figure 7-29.

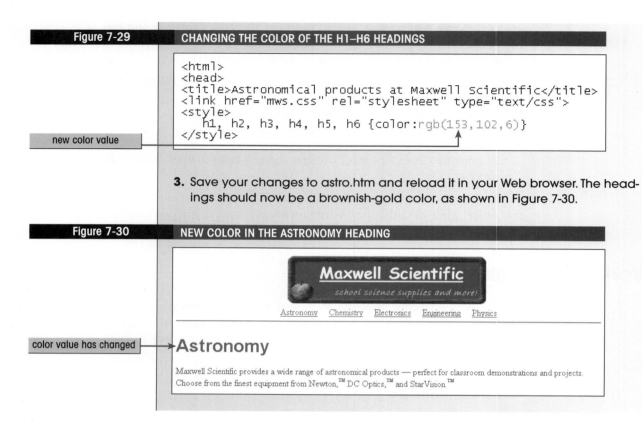

Figure 7-29 | **CHANGING THE COLOR OF THE H1–H6 HEADINGS**

```
<html>
<head>
<title>Astronomical products at Maxwell Scientific</title>
<link href="mws.css" rel="stylesheet" type="text/css">
<style>
    h1, h2, h3, h4, h5, h6 {color:rgb(153,102,6)}
</style>
```

new color value

3. Save your changes to astro.htm and reload it in your Web browser. The headings should now be a brownish-gold color, as shown in Figure 7-30.

Figure 7-30 | **NEW COLOR IN THE ASTRONOMY HEADING**

Maxwell Scientific
school science supplies and more!

Astronomy   Chemistry   Electronics   Engineering   Physics

color value has changed → **Astronomy**

Maxwell Scientific provides a wide range of astronomical products — perfect for classroom demonstrations and projects. Choose from the finest equipment from Newton,™ DC Optics,™ and StarVision.™

Working with Background Color

By default, elements take on the background color of their parent element. In most cases this will be the background color of the Web page. To change the background color of almost any element in your Web page, you can use the background-color style.

Chris wants you to try this approach with the customer comments that are displayed on the product pages. Each comment has been formatted with the <blockquote> tag. Chris suggests that you apply a silver background to all of the quotes in your Web site.

To change the background color of the customer quotes:

1. Return to the **mws.css** style sheet in your text editor.

2. Add the following style declaration to the bottom of the file (see Figure 7-31):

```
blockquote {background-color: silver}
```

Figure 7-31 | **APPLYING A BACKGROUND COLOR**

```
body {color: green}
h1, h2, h3, h4, h5, h6 {font-family: Arial, Helvetica, sans-serif}
address {font-size: 0.6em; font-style: normal; text-align: center;
        text-transform: uppercase}
blockquote {background-color: silver}
```

3. Save your changes to the file.

4. Reload astro.htm and chem.htm in your Web browser. As shown in Figure 7-32, both pages now display the customer comments with a silver background.

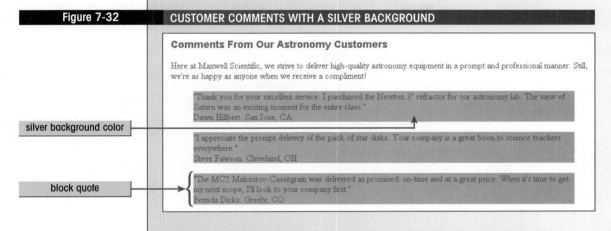

Figure 7-32 | CUSTOMER COMMENTS WITH A SILVER BACKGROUND

Comments From Our Astronomy Customers

Here at Maxwell Scientific, we strive to deliver high-quality astronomy equipment in a prompt and professional manner. Still, we're as happy as anyone when we receive a compliment!

"Thank you for your excellent service. I purchased the Newton 3" refractor for our astronomy lab. The view of Saturn was an exciting moment for the entire class."
Dawn Hilbert, San Jose, CA

silver background color →

"I appreciate the prompt delivery of the pack of star disks. Your company is a great boon to science teachers everywhere."
Steve Fawson, Cleveland, OH

block quote →

"The MC5 Maksutov-Cassegrain was delivered as promised: on-time and at a great price. When it's time to get my next scope, I'll look to your company first."
Brenda Dicks, Greely, CO

TROUBLE? If you're using Netscape, the background color may only cover the text in the blockquote. With Internet Explorer, the background color is applied to the entire block of text.

Working with Background Images

Almost any element on the page can also be displayed with its own background image. The background image has four attributes:

- the source of the image file
- how the image is repeated in the background
- where the image is placed on the background
- whether the image scrolls with the display window

To specify which file you want to use for a background, use the syntax:

```
background-image: url(URL)
```

where *URL* is the location of the image file. Figure 7-33 demonstrates how you can apply this style to the <b> tag to create an interesting design for a section of boldface text.

Figure 7-33 | APPLYING A BACKGROUND IMAGE TO AN ELEMENT

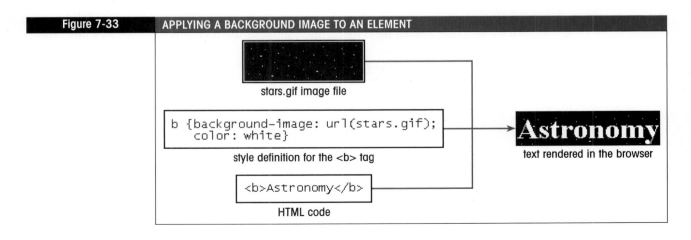

stars.gif image file

```
b {background-image: url(stars.gif);
   color: white}
```

style definition for the <b> tag

Astronomy

text rendered in the browser

```
<b>Astronomy</b>
```

HTML code

By default, background images are tiled both horizontally and vertically behind the element until the entire element is filled. You can control the way the tiling occurs using the background-repeat style attribute. The background-repeat attribute has four possible values, discussed in Figure 7-34. Examples of each attribute value are shown in Figure 7-35.

Figure 7-34	VALUES OF THE BACKGROUND-REPEAT ATTRIBUTE

BACKGROUND-REPEAT	DESCRIPTION
repeat	The image is tiled both horizontally and vertically until the entire background of the element is covered.
repeat-x	The image is tiled only horizontally across the width of the element.
repeat-y	The image is tiled only vertically across the height of the element.
no-repeat	The image is not repeated at all.

Figure 7-35	EXAMPLES OF THE BACKGROUND-REPEAT VALUES

background image

background-image:repeat

background-image:repeat-x

background-image:repeat-y

background-image:no-repeat

Background images are placed in the upper-left corner of their element, and then repeated (if tiling is being used) from there. You can move the background image to a different location using the background-position style attribute. The background-position attribute has two values: the first indicates the distance from the left edge of the element, and the second indicates the distance from the element's top edge. These values can be expressed as a percentage of the display area, in units of length, or with keywords.

For example, the style:

```
p {background-image:url(logo.gif); background-position:
10% 20%}
```

places logo.gif at a point 10% to the right and 20% down from the upper-left corner of the paragraph. Similarly, the style:

```
p {background-image:url(logo.gif); background-position:
2cm 5cm}
```

places logo.gif 2 centimeters to the right and 5 centimeters down from the upper-left corner of the paragraph. If you enter one attribute value, the browser applies that value to the horizontal position and vertically centers the image.

For a more general description of image position, you can use a combination of the six keywords: left, center, right (for the horizontal position), and top, center, bottom (for the vertical position). Figure 7-36 shows how these keywords relate to the percentage values. Unlike percentages and units of length, you do not need to place keywords in any particular order. The browser interprets the background position (top, right) the same way it interprets (right, top). Note that Netscape prior to version 6.0 does not support the background-position attribute.

| Figure 7-36 | BACKGROUND-POSITION KEYWORDS AND PERCENTAGES |

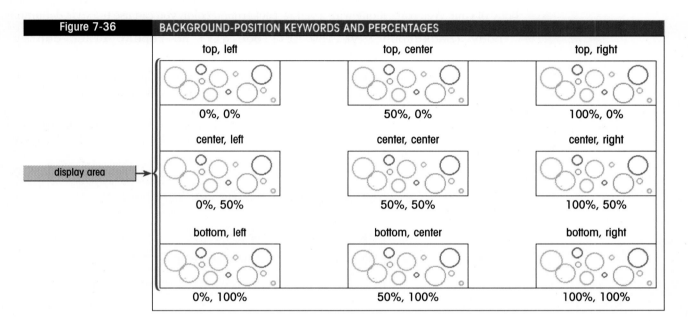

By default, background images move along with the background of the page as the user scrolls through the Web page. You can change this with the background-attachment attribute. The syntax of this style is:

```
background-attachment: attach
```

where *attach* is either "scroll," to scroll the image along with the element, or "fixed, which places the image in a fixed place in the browser's display window, preventing it from moving even if the user scrolls down through the Web page. The background-attachment attribute is not supported by Netscape prior to version 6.0.

Fixed background images are often used to create the impression of a **watermark**, a term that refers to a translucent graphic impressed into the very fabric of the paper and used in specialized stationery.

If you use a background image that employs a transparent color, you can combine the background-color and background-image attributes to create a new image. For example, the style:

```
body {background-color: yellow;
      background-image: url(logo.gif) }
```

displays logo.gif on the background, and anywhere that a transparent color appears in the logo, the background color yellow will shine through.

The Background Attribute

Like the font attribute discussed earlier, you can combine all of the various attributes for backgrounds into one attribute, called the background attribute. The syntax for the background attribute is:

```
background: background-color background-image
background-repeat
    background-attachment background-position
```

Where *background-color*, *background-image*, etc., are the values for the various background attributes. For example, to center the nonrepeating image file logo.gif as a fixed image in the body of your Web page, along with a yellow background color, you can use the style definition:

```
body {background: yellow url(logo.gif) no-repeat fixed center
center}
```

You do not have to enter all of the attribute values for the background attribute, but the ones you do specify should follow the order indicated by the syntax. Failure to do this can lead to unpredictable results with some browsers.

At Maxwell Scientific, Web designers are asked to place a watermark with the word "DRAFT" on every Web page that is in the design process. The watermark has been created for you as the image file draft.jpg.

To insert the draft watermark to the background of the Web pages:

1. Return to the **mws.css** style sheet in your text editor.

2. Add the following attribute to the body style (see Figure 7-37):

   ```
   ; background: white url(draft.jpg) no-repeat fixed
   center center
   ```

Figure 7-37	USING THE BACKGROUND STYLE ATTRIBUTE

```
body {color: green;
      background: white url(draft.jpg) no-repeat fixed center center}
h1, h2, h3, h4, h5, h6 {font-family: Arial, Helvetica, sans-serif}
address {font-size: 0.6em; font-style: normal; text-align: center;
        text-transform: uppercase}
blockquote {background-color: silver}
```

Note that with these attributes, draft.jpg is placed in the center of the display window, it is not tiled, and it does not scroll.

3. Save your changes to mws.css.

4. Reload astro.htm and chem.htm in your Web browser. As shown in Figure 7-38, the draft watermark has been added. Note that as you scroll through the display window, the watermark remains in the center of the browser window.

Figure 7-38	VIEWING THE DRAFT WATERMARK

draft watermark fixed in the center of the browser window →

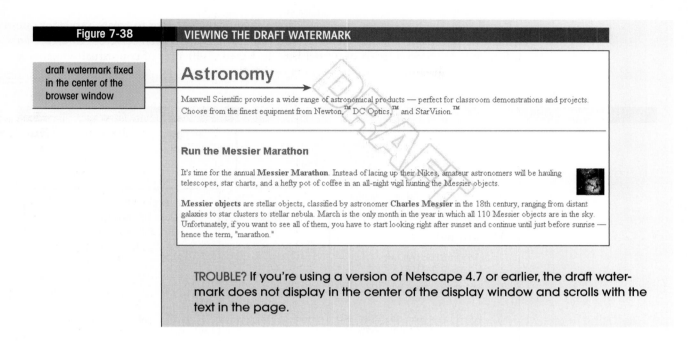

TROUBLE? If you're using a version of Netscape 4.7 or earlier, the draft watermark does not display in the center of the display window and scrolls with the text in the page.

Working with List Styles

CSS provides more control over the appearance and behavior of ordered, unordered, and definition lists than does HTML, allowing you to specify the types of labels attached to list items and how to position the labels with respect to the label text.

Choosing a List Style Type

The list-style-type attribute allows you to choose the type of label to display alongside text formatted with the <ul>, <ol>, or <li> tags. Figure 7-39 shows the possible values of the list-style-type attribute.

Figure 7-39	VALUES OF THE LIST-STYLE-TYPE ATTRIBUTE

ATTRIBUTE VALUE	THE WEB BROWSER DISPLAYS
disc (the default)	•
circle	o
square	☐
decimal	1, 2, 3, …
decimal-leading-zero	01, 02, 03, …
lower-roman	i, ii, iii, …
upper-roman	I, II, III, …
lower-alpha	a, b, c, …
upper-alpha	A, B, C, …

Recall from the first session that you can use a contextual selector to create a style for one element nested inside another element. You can also use contextual selectors to create an outline style for several levels of nested lists. In Figure 7-40 a set of contextual selectors is used to create an outline style for different outline levels.

Figure 7-40	CREATING A NESTED OUTLINE STYLE

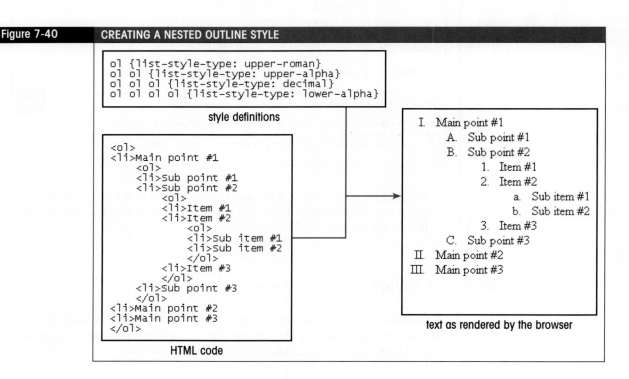

```
ol {list-style-type: upper-roman}
ol ol {list-style-type: upper-alpha}
ol ol ol {list-style-type: decimal}
ol ol ol ol {list-style-type: lower-alpha}
```

style definitions

```
<ol>
<li>Main point #1
    <ol>
    <li>sub point #1
    <li>sub point #2
        <ol>
        <li>Item #1
        <li>Item #2
            <ol>
            <li>sub item #1
            <li>sub item #2
            </ol>
        <li>Item #3
        </ol>
    <li>Sub point #3
    </ol>
<li>Main point #2
<li>Main point #3
</ol>
```

HTML code

```
 I.  Main point #1
     A.  Sub point #1
     B.  Sub point #2
              1.  Item #1
              2.  Item #2
                      a.  Sub item #1
                      b.  Sub item #2
              3.  Item #3
     C.  Sub point #3
II.  Main point #2
III. Main point #3
```

text as rendered by the browser

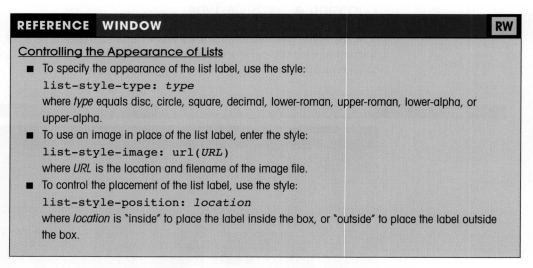

REFERENCE   WINDOW   **RW**

Controlling the Appearance of Lists

- To specify the appearance of the list label, use the style:

  `list-style-type: type`

  where *type* equals disc, circle, square, decimal, lower-roman, upper-roman, lower-alpha, or upper-alpha.
- To use an image in place of the list label, enter the style:

  `list-style-image: url(URL)`

  where *URL* is the location and filename of the image file.
- To control the placement of the list label, use the style:

  `list-style-position: location`

  where *location* is "inside" to place the label inside the box, or "outside" to place the label outside the box.

Using a List Style Image

If you want to use a label not included in the list-style-type values, you can create your own with an image file and the list-style-image attribute. The syntax for applying this attribute is:

```
list-style-image: url(URL)
```

where *URL* is the location and the filename of the image file. This attribute is not supported by Netscape version 4.7 or earlier. Because of this, it's a good idea to include the list-style-type attribute along with the list-style-image attribute. This way, if a browser doesn't support this attribute, or if the image file is not available, the browser displays whatever label is indicated by the list-style-type attribute.

Defining the List Style Position

List items are treated by CSS as if they have an invisible box around them. In reality, other HTML elements have this attribute, too, and you'll learn more about it in the next session. The labels for the list items can be placed either outside or inside this box (see Figure 7-41). The syntax for specifying the location of the list item label is:

```
list-style-position: location
```

where *location* is either "inside" or the default value, "outside."

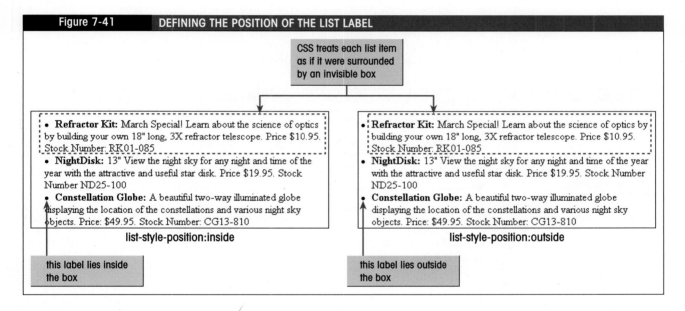

Figure 7-41   **DEFINING THE POSITION OF THE LIST LABEL**

The List-Style Attribute

You can combine all of these attributes into the list-style attribute. The syntax for this style is:

```
list-style: list-style-type list-style-image list-style-position
```

where *list-style-type*, *list-style-image*, and *list-style-position* are the attribute values for each of the individual list style attributes.

Chris wants you to use this attribute to revise the products list. In place of bullets, she wants you to display the apple.jpg image outside the box. Since some earlier browser versions do not support the use of images as list bullets, you'll also specify a list style type, replacing the bullet with an open circle for use with those browsers.

To define a style for the product list:

1. Return to the **mws.css** style sheet in your text editor.

2. Insert the following style definition at the bottom of the file (see Figure 7-42).

```
ul {list-style: circle url(apple.jpg) outside}
```

Figure 7-42	DEFINING THE APPEARANCE OF THE LIST LABEL

label displays as a circle unless the browser supports the use of graphical bullets

labels are placed outside the rectangular box

```
body {color: green;
      background: white url(draft.jpg) no-repeat fixed center center}
h1, h2, h3, h4, h5, h6 {font-family: Arial, Helvetica, sans-serif}
address {font-size: 0.6em; font-style: normal; text-align: center;
         text-transform: uppercase}
blockquote {background-color: silver}
ul {list-style: circle url(apple.jpg) outside}
```

3. Save your changes to mws.css.

4. Reload astro.htm and chem.htm in your Web browser. The list item bullets have been replaced with an image of an apple, as shown in Figure 7-43.

Figure 7-43	REPLACING THE LIST LABEL WITH AN IMAGE

Featured Astronomical Products

apple.jpg image

- **Refractor Kit:** March Special! Learn about the science of optics by building your own 18" long, 3X refractor telescope. Price $10.95. Stock Number: RK01-085
- **NightDisk:** View the night sky for any night and time of the year with this attractive and useful star disk. Price $19.95. Stock Number: ND25-100
- **Constellation Globe:** A beautiful two-way illuminated globe displaying the location of the constellations and various night sky objects. Price: $49.95. Stock Number: CG13-810

TROUBLE? If you are using Netscape version 4.7 or earlier, your labels display as open circles.

Chris likes the look of the new style, and she has only one suggestion. She wants the name of each product to display in dark red. Currently the product name is in boldface type. You can use the color attribute to change the boldface type to a dark red, but you don't want to change boldface type everywhere it occurs on the Web page. To accomplish your task, you must use a contextual selector for text formatted with the <b> tag nested within the <ul> tag.

To display the product names in dark red:

1. Return to the **mws.css** style sheet in your text editor.

2. Insert the following code at the bottom of the file:

```
ul b {color: rgb(155,0,0)}
```

3. Save your changes to mws.css.

4. Reload astro.htm and chem.htm in your Web browser. As shown in Figure 7-44, the product names are a dark red color that matches the color of the apple.

Figure 7-44   CHANGING THE COLOR OF BOLDFACED TEXT WITHIN AN UNORDERED LIST

Featured Astronomical Products

- **Refractor Kit:** March Special! Learn about the science of optics by building your own 18" long, 3X refractor telescope. Price $10.95. Stock Number: RK01-085
- **NightDisk:** View the night sky for any night and time of the year with this attractive and useful star disk. Price $19.95. Stock Number: ND25-100
- **Constellation Globe:** A beautiful two-way illuminated globe displaying the location of the constellations and various night sky objects. Price: $49.95. Stock Number: CG13-810

boldfaced text

You've made a lot of changes to the style sheet for Maxwell Scientific. In the next session, you'll use CSS to format hypertext links and to work with the layout of your Web pages.

Session 7.2 QUICK CHECK

1. What style would you use to change the font of a block quote to Times Roman, or if Times Roman is not available, to change to a serif font?

2. What style would you use to set the size of paragraph text to 12-point type?

3. What is the difference between an absolute unit and a relative unit? What are the two relative units supported by CSS?

4. What style would you use to underline all your headings and display the heading text in uppercase letters?

5. What style would you use to center your paragraph text and display it in boldface italics?

6. What style would you use to display your unordered lists with the lists.gif background image centered in the background?

7. What style would you use to display your ordered lists with an integer label?

SESSION 7.3

In this session you'll format hypertext links on your Web page, and you'll learn how to create a "rollover" effect for them. You'll work with CSS classes and pseudo-classes, and you'll see how to use the <div> and <span> tags to create containers for blocks of text. Finally, you'll learn how to format block-level elements in order to format the layout of your Web page.

Formatting Hypertext Links

The next area Chris wants you to focus on is the hypertext links that are located at the top of each product page. In the future, you'll be adding more product categories, and she wants you to reduce the size of the hypertext font so that additional text will fit on a single line. She also wants you to format the hypertext links so that when a mouse passes over the text, they change appearance, thus indicating that the text is a link.

First, you'll change the text formatted with the <a> tag to green, with a font size of 0.65 em.

To modify the font size of the hypertext links:

1. Using your text editor, open **mws.css**.

2. Insert the following code at the bottom of the file:

```
a {font-size: 0.65em; color: green}
```

3. Save your changes to mws.css.

4. Reload astro.htm and chem.htm in your browser and verify that the font size has been reduced and the font color is changed.

You can use all of the CSS attributes that you learned in the last session on hypertext. Some Web designs do away with the default style of underlining hypertext. Instead, these designs display hypertext links in a different color from normal text but with no underline. The following style is one way to accomplish this:

```
a {text-decoration: none}
```

Note that setting the value of the text-decoration attribute to none removes the underlining. Hypertext also has an additional attribute that normal text doesn't have: the condition of the hypertext link itself. A hypertext link can be in one of four states:

- The link's target has already been visited by the user.
- The link's target has never been visited by the user.
- The link is currently being clicked by the user.
- The user's mouse pointer is hovering over the link.

Typically, Web browsers provide a visual clue for each of these states, such as a different color for visited links, and a different shape for the pointer when it is hovering over a link. CSS provides a different selector for each condition. The general syntax is:

```
a:visited {styles for previously visited targets}
a:link {styles for targets that have never been visited}
a:active {styles for links that are currently being clicked}
a:hover {styles when the mouse cursor is hovering over the
link}
```

You can use a variety of CSS attributes to create a different style for each condition. For example, to change the color of previously visited targets to red, and that of targets that have never been visited to green, use the styles:

```
a:visited {color:red}
a:link {color:green}
```

Chris wants the hypertext links to change in appearance when the pointer passes over them. This is called a **rollover effect**. Try this now by adding the a:hover selector to your style sheet and creating a style that displays the hypertext link in red uppercase letters.

To create the rollover effect:

1. Return to the **mws.css** style sheet in your text editor.

2. Insert the following code at the bottom of the file (see Figure 7-45):

```
a:hover {color:red; text-transform:uppercase}
```

Figure 7-45	CREATING A ROLLOVER EFFECT

```
body {color: green;
      background: white url(draft.jpg) no-repeat fixed center center}
h1, h2, h3, h4, h5, h6 {font-family: Arial, Helvetica, sans-serif}
address {font-size: 0.6em; font-style: normal; text-align: center;
         text-transform: uppercase}
blockquote {background-color: silver}
ul {list-style: circle url(apple.jpg) outside}
ul b {color: rgb(155,0,0)}
a {font-size: 0.65em; color: green}
a:hover {color: red; text-transform: uppercase}
```

style when the mouse pointer is positioned over the hypertext link

3. Save your changes to the file.

4. Reload astro.htm and chem.htm in your browser and verify that as you pass your pointer over the hypertext links, the text changes color, case, and weight (see Figure 7-46).

Figure 7-46	VIEWING A ROLLOVER EFFECT

text changes to red uppercase letters when the mouse pointer is positioned over it

TROUBLE? If you are running Netscape version 4.7 or earlier, the rollover effect does not display.

Note that Internet Explorer supports all four of the conditions for hypertext; Netscape, through version 4.7, does not support the hover condition.

Working with ids and Classes

The preceding example of adding the rollover effect demonstrates a feature of CSS called a pseudo-class. A **pseudo-class** is a classification of an element based on its status or its use. In this case, the status was the condition of the hypertext link. The element itself, a hypertext link with the pointer located over it, is called a **pseudo-element**. CSS2 introduces additional pseudo-classes, including the first-line pseudo-class and the first-letter pseudo-class, which are used for formatting the first line and first letter of a block of text, respectively. For example, if you wish to display the first line of your paragraphs in uppercase, you can create the following style definition:

```
p:first-line {text-transform: uppercase}
```

Similarly, you can increase the size of the first letter of your paragraphs by using this pseudo-class style:

```
p:first-letter {font-size: 200%}
```

After applying these two styles, your paragraphs would look like the one shown in Figure 7-47.

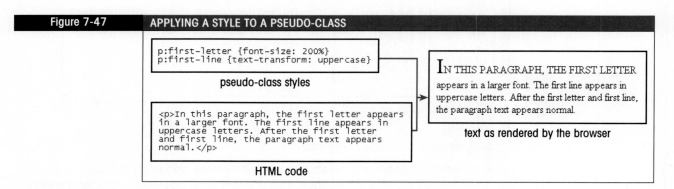

Figure 7-47   APPLYING A STYLE TO A PSEUDO-CLASS

```
p:first-letter {font-size: 200%}
p:first-line {text-transform: uppercase}
```
pseudo-class styles

```
<p>In this paragraph, the first letter appears
in a larger font. The first line appears in
uppercase letters. After the first letter
and first line, the paragraph text appears
normal.</p>
```
HTML code

IN THIS PARAGRAPH, THE FIRST LETTER appears in a larger font. The first line appears in uppercase letters. After the first letter and first line, the paragraph text appears normal.

text as rendered by the browser

The Class Attribute

Many browsers do not support the first-letter and first-line pseudo-classes yet. The only pseudo-classes widely supported are the four hypertext link conditions. However, you can create your own customized classes by adding the class attribute to your HTML tags. The syntax for creating a class is:

```
<tag class="class_name">
```

where *tag* is the HTML tag and *class_name* is the name of the class. For example, to create a class named "FirstHeading" for the first h1 heading in the Astronomy page, use the following tag in your HTML file:

```
<h1 class="FirstHeading">Astronomy</h1>
```

Once a class has been created, you can apply a style specific to that class with the declaration:

```
tag.class_name {style attributes and values}
```

where *tag* is the HTML tag and *class_name* is the name of the class you created. Figure 7-48 demonstrates this approach by creating an underline style for the h1 heading with the class name "FirstHeader." This technique is useful when you have multiple Web pages in which you want the first heading in each page to be formatted in the same way.

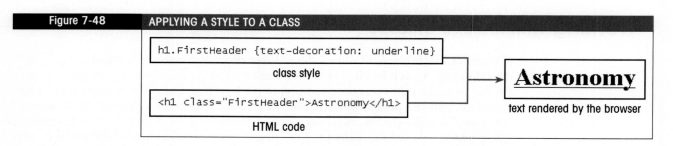

Figure 7-48   APPLYING A STYLE TO A CLASS

```
h1.FirstHeader {text-decoration: underline}
```
class style

```
<h1 class="FirstHeader">Astronomy</h1>
```
HTML code

Astronomy

text rendered by the browser

If the same class name is used for several different types of tags, you would omit the tag name from the style declaration, following the syntax:

```
.class_name {style attributes and values}
```

For example, the following headings both use the same class name:

```
<h1 class="NewHeading">Astronomical Products</h1>
<h2 class="NewHeading">Comments</h2>
```

If you want to display both of these headings in italics, you can apply the style to the class, using the statement:

```
.NewHeading {font-style: italic}
```

and this style applies to any tag with the class="NewHeading" attribute.

Class names cannot contain blank spaces, and they are case-sensitive. The class name "FirstHeading" is different from the class name "firstheading."

The id Attribute

Closely related to the class attribute is the id attribute, which applies an id to a specific element in the document. Unlike the class attribute, the id attribute must be unique; there cannot be more than one tag with the same id value. The syntax for creating an id is:

```
<tag id="id_name">
```

where *tag* is the HTML tag and *id_name* is an id name assigned to the tag. To apply a style to an id, use the style declaration:

```
#id_name {style attributes and values}
```

The class and id attributes are useful HTML features that you can use with CSS to define styles for specific content in your Web page without having to use inline styles.

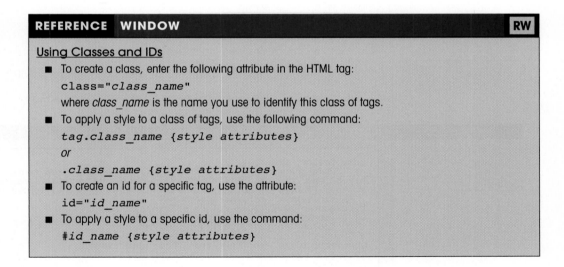

REFERENCE   WINDOW   **RW**

Using Classes and IDs
- To create a class, enter the following attribute in the HTML tag:
  ```
  class="class_name"
  ```
  where *class_name* is the name you use to identify this class of tags.
- To apply a style to a class of tags, use the following command:
  ```
  tag.class_name {style attributes}
  ```
  or
  ```
  .class_name {style attributes}
  ```
- To create an id for a specific tag, use the attribute:
  ```
  id="id_name"
  ```
- To apply a style to a specific id, use the command:
  ```
  #id_name {style attributes}
  ```

Each month, Maxwell Scientific offers special deals on selected merchandise. Chris would like to see these products displayed in a different color in the product list. You can do this quickly and easily by creating a class named "Special" for those products. There are two specials in the Astronomy page to highlight with this method.

To create a class of special products:

1. Using your text editor, open **astro.htm**.

2. Insert the attribute **class="Special"** within the <li> tag for "Refractor Kit."

3. Insert the attribute **class="Special"** within the <li> tag for "Classroom Planetarium." See Figure 7-49.

Figure 7-49   CREATING A CLASS FOR MONTHLY SPECIALS

monthly special

```
<li class="Special"><b>Refractor Kit: </b>March Special! Learn about the science of optics
        by building your own 18" long, 3X refractor telescope. Price $10.95.
        Stock Number: RK01-085
<li><b>NightDisk: </b>View the night sky for any night and time of the
        year with this attractive and useful star disk. Price $19.95.
        Stock Number: ND25-100
<li><b>Constellation Globe: </b>A beautiful two-way illuminated globe
        displaying the location of the constellations and various night sky
        objects. Price: $49.95. Stock Number: CG13-810
<li><b>Star and Planet Locators: </b>A pack of 25 star and planet locators &#151;
        perfect for classroom use. Price :$29.95. Stock Number: SL25-271
<li><b>Rechargeable Red Flashlight: </b>A 4" rechargeable flashlight,
        employing a red LED to preserve night vision. Price $15.95.
        Stock Number: RF02-421
<li class="Special"><b>Classroom Planetarium: </b>March Special! Planetarium kit projects
        more than 300 stars and constellations onto the ceiling or wall.
        Perfect for classroom use. Red star flashlight included to point
        out individual stars. Price $34.95. Stock Number: CP21-789
```

4. Save your changes to the file.

Now that you've created the class, you can define a style for it in your style sheet. You decide to display the monthly specials in a boldface blue font.

To define the special products style:

1. Return to the **mws.css** style sheet in your text editor.

2. At the bottom of the file, insert the new style (see Figure 7-50):

   ```
   li.Special {color: blue; font-weight:bold}
   ```

Figure 7-50   DEFINING THE MONTHLY SPECIAL STYLE

```
body {color: green;
        background: white url(draft.jpg) no-repeat fixed center center}
h1, h2, h3, h4, h5, h6 {font-family: Arial, Helvetica, sans-serif}
address {font-size: 0.6em; font-style: normal; text-align: center;
        text-transform: uppercase}
blockquote {background-color: silver}
ul {list-style: circle url(apple.jpg) outside}
ul b {color: rgb(155,0,0)}
a {font-size: 0.65em; color: green}
a:hover {color: red; text-transform: uppercase}
li.Special {color: blue; font-weight: bold}
```

3. Save your changes to mws.css.

4. Reload astro.htm in your browser. Figure 7-51 shows the revised appearance of the products on special.

Figure 7-51 | **MONTHLY SPECIALS AS RENDERED BY THE WEB BROWSER**

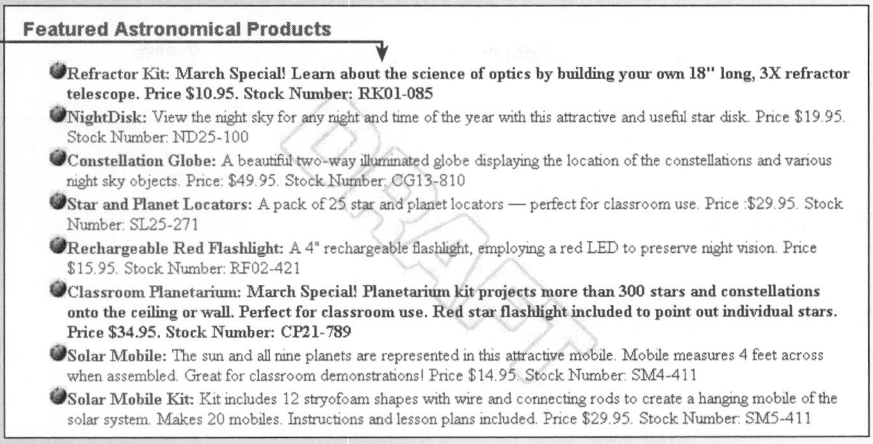

monthly special

Featured Astronomical Products

- **Refractor Kit: March Special!** Learn about the science of optics by building your own 18" long, 3X refractor telescope. **Price $10.95. Stock Number: RK01-085**
- **NightDisk:** View the night sky for any night and time of the year with this attractive and useful star disk. Price $19.95. Stock Number: ND25-100
- **Constellation Globe:** A beautiful two-way illuminated globe displaying the location of the constellations and various night sky objects. Price: $49.95. Stock Number: CG13-810
- **Star and Planet Locators:** A pack of 25 star and planet locators — perfect for classroom use. Price :$29.95. Stock Number: SL25-271
- **Rechargeable Red Flashlight:** A 4" rechargeable flashlight, employing a red LED to preserve night vision. Price $15.95. Stock Number: RF02-421
- **Classroom Planetarium: March Special!** Planetarium kit projects more than 300 stars and constellations onto the ceiling or wall. Perfect for classroom use. Red star flashlight included to point out individual stars. **Price $34.95. Stock Number: CP21-789**
- **Solar Mobile:** The sun and all nine planets are represented in this attractive mobile. Mobile measures 4 feet across when assembled. Great for classroom demonstrations! Price $14.95. Stock Number: SM4-411
- **Solar Mobile Kit:** Kit includes 12 stryofoam shapes with wire and connecting rods to create a hanging mobile of the solar system. Makes 20 mobiles. Instructions and lesson plans included. Price $29.95. Stock Number: SM5-411

TROUBLE? If you are using Netscape version 4.7 or earlier, the monthly special text is not changed by the Special style, but the open circle in the bulleted list will change color to match the color of the headings.

Working with Container Elements

The next design element that Chris wants you to work on is the science article. Chris would like the science article to be reduced in size, aligned with the right margin of the display window, and to have a different background color from the rest of the page. In addition, she would like the rest of the text on the page to flow around the science article.

Even though the science article consists of several elements, including a heading, three paragraphs, and an inline image, Chris wants it to be treated as a single entity. To do this, she can enclose the contents of the science article in a **container** that identifies the start and ending points of the article. HTML supports two types of container tags: <span> and <div>.

The <div> Tag

The <div> tag is used to group blocks of text such as paragraphs, block quotes, headings, or lists. Collectively, these text blocks are known as **block-level elements**. To enclose a block-level element within a div container, you use the syntax:

```
<div> block-level elements </div>
```

Note that the <div> tag does not actually format the block-level elements; it merely groups them as a unit. For this reason, the <div> tag always includes either a class or id attribute that identifies that group. Figure 7-52 shows an example in which a heading and a paragraph have been enclosed in a <div> container. A style is assigned to the container and formats both the heading and the paragraph as white text on a blue background.

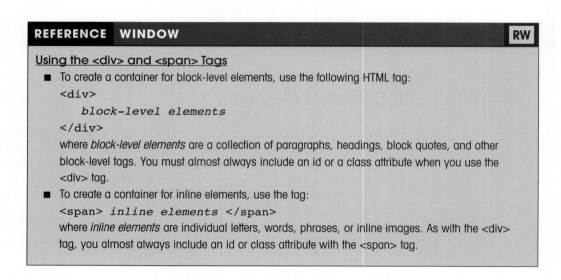

Figure 7-52   USING THE <DIV> TAG

```
#intro {color: white; background-color: blue}
```
div style

```
<div id="intro">

<h1>Astronomy</h1>

<p>Maxwell Scientific provides a wide range of astronomical
products, perfect for classroom demonstrations and
projects. Choose from the finest equipment from Newton,
<sup>&#153;</sup> DC Optics,<sup>&#153;</sup> and
StarVision.<sup>&#153;</sup></p>

</div>
```
HTML code

Astronomy

Maxwell Scientific provides a wide range of astronomical products, perfect for classroom demonstrations and projects. Choose from the finest equipment from Newton,™ DC Optics,™ and StarVision.™

text as rendered by the browser

REFERENCE WINDOW   RW

Using the <div> and <span> Tags

■ To create a container for block-level elements, use the following HTML tag:

```
<div>
    block-level elements
</div>
```

where *block-level elements* are a collection of paragraphs, headings, block quotes, and other block-level tags. You must almost always include an id or a class attribute when you use the <div> tag.

■ To create a container for inline elements, use the tag:

```
<span> inline elements </span>
```

where *inline elements* are individual letters, words, phrases, or inline images. As with the <div> tag, you almost always include an id or class attribute with the <span> tag.

The <span> Tag

The <span> tag is used to contain **inline elements** such as individual letters, words, phrases, or inline images. Typically, inline elements appear within block-level elements. The syntax for the <span> container is:

```
<span> inline elements </span>
```

You almost always include an id or class attribute with the <span> tag. Figure 7-53 shows an example of how the <span> tag can be used to format a selection of text within a paragraph. Note that a <div> tag is used to format the entire paragraph.

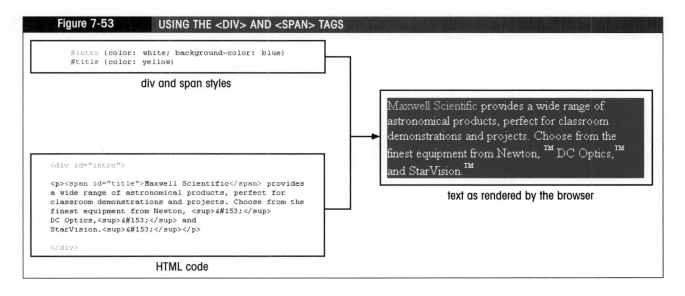

Figure 7-53   USING THE <DIV> AND <SPAN> TAGS

```
#intro {color: white; background-color: blue}
#title {color: yellow}
```

div and span styles

```
<div id="intro">

<p><span id="title">Maxwell Scientific</span> provides
a wide range of astronomical products, perfect for
classroom demonstrations and projects. Choose from the
finest equipment from Newton, <sup>&#153;</sup>
DC Optics,<sup>&#153;</sup> and
StarVision.<sup>&#153;</sup></p>

</div>
```

HTML code

Maxwell Scientific provides a wide range of astronomical products, perfect for classroom demonstrations and projects. Choose from the finest equipment from Newton, ™ DC Optics,™ and StarVision. ™

text as rendered by the browser

Chris suggests that you enclose the contents of the science article on the Astronomy page in a <div> tag with the class name "article" and create a style that assigns a light brown background color with a color value of (252,221,163).

To use the <div> tag in the Astronomy page:

1. Return to **astro.htm** in your text editor.

2. Locate the <hr> tag directly before the <h3> tag for the "Run the Messier Marathon" heading and replace the <hr> tag with the following code:

   <div class="article">

3. Locate the next occurrence of the <hr> tag above the <h3> tag for the "Feature Astronomical Products" heading and replace the <hr> tag with a **</div>** tag, then save your changes. See Figure 7-54.

Figure 7-54   CREATING A CONTAINER FOR THE SCIENCE ARTICLE

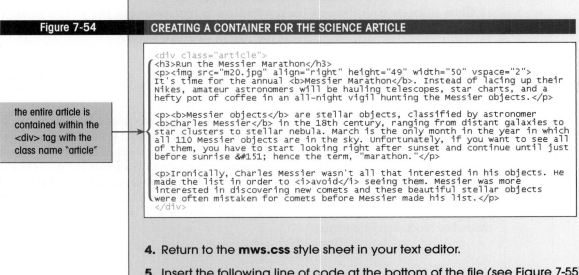

```
<div class="article">
<h3>Run the Messier Marathon</h3>
<p><img src="m20.jpg" align="right" height="49" width="50" vspace="2">
It's time for the annual <b>Messier Marathon</b>. Instead of lacing up their
Nikes, amateur astronomers will be hauling telescopes, star charts, and a
hefty pot of coffee in an all-night vigil hunting the Messier objects.</p>

<p><b>Messier objects</b> are stellar objects, classified by astronomer
<b>Charles Messier</b> in the 18th century, ranging from distant galaxies to
star clusters to stellar nebula. March is the only month in the year in which
all 110 Messier objects are in the sky. Unfortunately, if you want to see all
of them, you have to start looking right after sunset and continue until just
before sunrise &#151; hence the term, "marathon."</p>

<p>Ironically, Charles Messier wasn't all that interested in his objects. He
made the list in order to <i>avoid</i> seeing them. Messier was more
interested in discovering new comets and these beautiful stellar objects
were often mistaken for comets before Messier made his list.</p>
</div>
```

the entire article is contained within the <div> tag with the class name "article"

4. Return to the **mws.css** style sheet in your text editor.

5. Insert the following line of code at the bottom of the file (see Figure 7-55).

   div.article {background-color: rgb(252,221,163)}

Figure 7-55 | **SETTING A BACKGROUND COLOR FOR THE SCIENCE ARTICLE**

```
body {color: green;
      background: white url(draft.jpg) no-repeat fixed center center}
h1, h2, h3, h4, h5, h6 {font-family: Arial, Helvetica, sans-serif}
address {font-size: 0.6em; font-style: normal; text-align: center;
         text-transform: uppercase}
blockquote {background-color: silver}
ul {list-style: circle url(apple.jpg) outside}
ul b {color: rgb(155,0,0)}
a {font-size: 0.65em; color: green}
a:hover {color: red; text-transform: uppercase}
li.Special {color: blue; font-weight: bold}
div.article {background-color: rgb(252,221,163)}
```

6. Save your changes to mws.css and then reload astro.htm in your browser. The entire content of the science article should now have a light brown background as shown in Figure 7-56.

Figure 7-56 | **SCIENCE ARTICLE WITH LIGHT BROWN BACKGROUND COLOR**

Astronomy

Maxwell Scientific provides a wide range of astronomical products — perfect for classroom demonstrations and projects. Choose from the finest equipment from Newton,™ DC Optics,™ and StarVision.™

Run the Messier Marathon

It's time for the annual **Messier Marathon**. Instead of lacing up their Nikes, amateur astronomers will be hauling telescopes, star charts, and a hefty pot of coffee in an all-night vigil hunting the Messier objects.

Messier objects are stellar objects, classified by astronomer **Charles Messier** in the 18th century, ranging from distant galaxies to star clusters to stellar nebula. March is the only month in the year in which all 110 Messier objects are in the sky. Unfortunately, if you want to see all of them, you have to start looking right after sunset and continue until just before sunrise — hence the term, "marathon."

Ironically, Charles Messier wasn't all that interested in his objects. He made the list in order to *avoid* seeing them. Messier was more interested in discovering new comets and these beautiful stellar objects were often mistaken for comets before Messier made his list.

Chris is happy with the new background color, but she would like you to make some additional changes to the appearance and placement of the science article. To do that, you'll need to learn more about block-level elements and how CSS can help you format them.

Formatting Block-Level Element Boxes

So far, your work with CSS has been focused on the design of various page elements. Now it's time to examine the other important use of CSS, page layout. With CSS, you can control the layout of a Web page by manipulating the size and location of block-level elements. You learned earlier with the list-style-position attribute that CSS treats list items as if they were grouped together as a box. In reality, CSS treats all block-level elements this way. This is a powerful feature of CSS because you can move elements around on the page, apply borders, set the internal margins for a box, etc. Here are a few of the HTML tags that can be treated as block-level elements:

- <h1> – <h6> tags
- <p> tag
- <blockquote> and <address> tags

- <ul>, <ol>, and <dl> list tags
- <li>, <dt>, or <dd> tags (individual list items)
- <div> tag
- <body> tag
- <hr> tag
- <img> tag

CSS2 introduced many features for manipulating these boxes. Unfortunately, only the most recent browser versions support these styles, so you'll focus your attention on the features that are commonly supported by older browsers.

Parts of the Block-Level Element Box

Figure 7-57 shows a diagram of a block-level element (a paragraph) with the key features of the box that surrounds it. There are three elements:

- **margin** between the box and the parent element
- **border** of the box
- **padding**, which is the space between the box around the block-level element and the border

CSS provides attributes you can use to control the appearance and behavior of each of these elements.

Figure 7-57	FEATURES OF BLOCK-LEVEL ELEMENTS

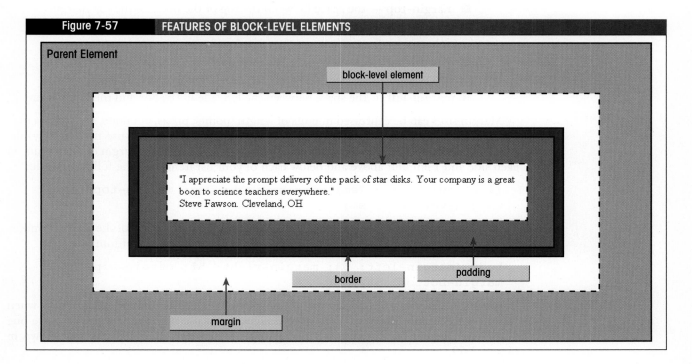

Your entire Web page can be thought of as a series of nested boxes. For example, list items created with the <li> tag are block-level elements, each with its own box. Each of these boxes exists inside the box created by its parent element—either the <ul> or <ol> tag. The list is placed within a box defined for its parent, the Web page. Figure 7-58 shows some of the boxes in the Astronomy page.

Figure 7-58   SOME BLOCK-LEVEL ELEMENTS IN THE ASTRONOMY PAGE

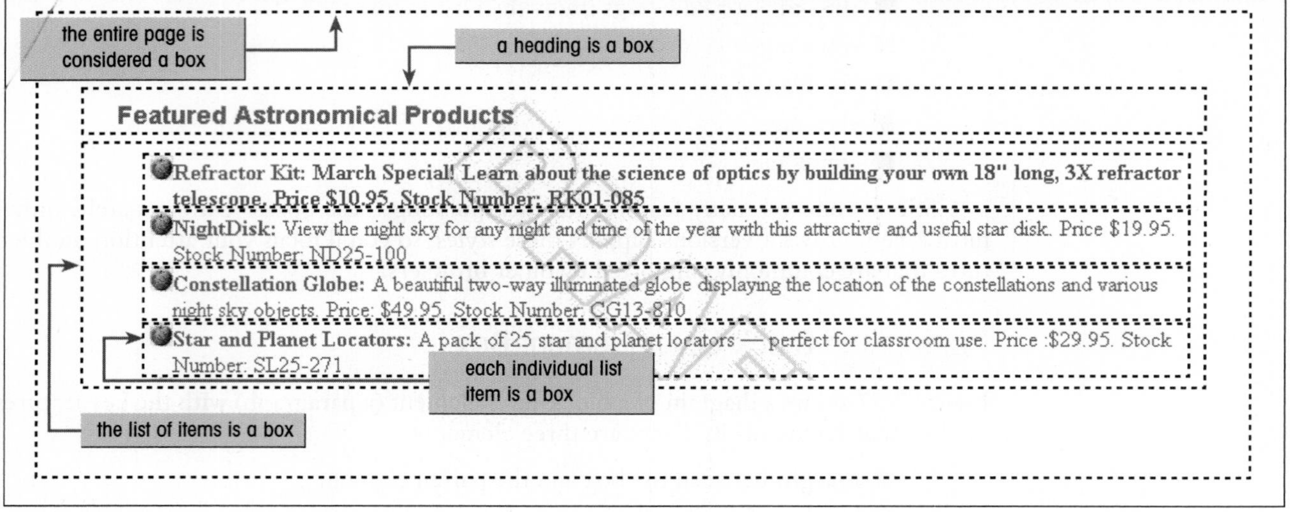

Controlling Margins

The margin is the space between the block-level element and the parent element. There are four attributes that control the margin size:

- **margin-top** — the space between the top of the box and the top margin
- **margin-right** — the space between the right side of the box and the right margin
- **margin-bottom** — the space between the bottom of the box and the bottom margin
- **margin-left** — the space between the left side of the box and the left margin

Margin sizes can be expressed in units of length (points, pixels, em units, etc.) or as a percentage of the width of the parent element box. Alternately, you can use the "auto" value, which allows the browser to determine the margin size. To create a margin of 2 em units on each side and 1 em unit above and below each of your list items, use the following style:

```
li {margin-left: 2em; margin-right: 2em; margin-top: 1em;
margin-bottom: 1 em}
```

If you want the size of the margins of the Web page body to be 5% of the display window (the parent element of the <body> tag), enter the following style definition:

```
body {margin-left: 5%; margin-right: 5%; margin-top: 5%;
margin-bottom: 5%}
```

A margin size also can be negative, although this can lead to unpredictable results when viewed with certain browsers. Web page designers can use negative margins to place one block-line element on top of another, creating an "overlay" effect like the one shown in Figure 7-59.

Figure 7-59   **CREATING AN OVERLAY EFFECT**

Astronomy *Physi*
Biology *Electron*
lysics Chemistry
Astron

Maxwell Scientific

original page

```
.title {margin-top: -100px}
```

style

```
<center>
    <img src="logo.gif">
    <h1 class="title">Maxwell Scientific</h1>
</center>
```

HTML code

Astronomy *Physi*
Biology *Electron*
Maxwell Scientific
lysics Chemistry
Astron

final page with the heading moved up

The four margin attributes can be combined into a single attribute with the syntax:

```
margin: margin-top margin-right margin-bottom margin-left
```

where *margin-top, margin-right, margin-bottom, margin-left* are the top, right, bottom, and left margin values. If you only include three values in the combined attribute, they are applied in the following order: top, right, bottom, and the browser sets the left margin to match the right margin; if two values are specified, they are applied to the top and right margins, and the browser sets the bottom and left margins to match the top and right margins, respectively. If only one value is entered, the browser applies the value to all four margins.

Setting Padding Size

Padding refers to the amount of space between the element and its border. Four attributes are used to control the size of the element's padding:

- padding-top
- padding-right
- padding-bottom
- padding-left

One difference to keep in mind is that when padding is expressed as a percentage, it is the percentage of the width of the block-level element rather than the parent element, as is the case for margins.

Formatting the Border

CSS provides a variety of attributes for managing the box's border width, border color, and border style. These attributes can be applied to all four borders at once, or you can work with individual borders. Figure 7-60 summarizes the various border attributes.

Figure 7-60	DIFFERENT BORDER ATTRIBUTES

BORDER ATTRIBUTE	DESCRIPTION
border-top-width	Specifies the width of the top border
border-right-width	Specifies the width of the right border
border-bottom-width	Specifies the width of the bottom border
border-left-width	Specifies the width of the left border
border-width	Specifies the width of any or all of the borders
border-top-color	Specifies the color of the top border
border-right-color	Specifies the color of the right border
border-bottom-color	Specifies the color of the bottom border
border-left-color	Specifies the color of the left border
border-color	Specifies the color of any or all of the borders
border-top-style	Specifies the line style of the top border
border-right-style	Specifies the line style of the right border
border-bottom-style	Specifies the line style of the bottom border
border-left-style	Specifies the line style of the left border
border-style	Specifies the line style of any or all of the borders

Border widths can be expressed using units of length or with the keywords thin, medium, or thick. The border color can be defined using color names or color values. As for the border style, there are nine different styles that can be applied to the border. Figure 7-61 shows an example of each one.

Figure 7-61	EXAMPLES OF BORDER-STYLE VALUES

For example, if you want to place a double border around a block-level element, you would use the style declaration:

```
border-style: double;
```

You can combine all of the border attributes into a single style declaration. The syntax is:

```
border: border-width border-style border-color;
```

To create a 5-point blue dotted border, you would use either of these style declarations:

```
border-width: 5pt; border-style: dotted; border-color: blue
```

or

```
border: 5pt dotted blue;
```

The syntax for formatting individual borders is:

```
border-top: border-width border-style border-color;
```

```
border-right: border-width border-style border-color;
```

```
border-bottom: border-width border-style border-color;
```

```
border-left: border-width border-style border-color;
```

So, if you want to insert a thick black solid line beneath a block-level element, you could do so with the style declaration:

```
border-bottom: thick solid black
```

As you can see, there are a variety of ways border styles can be expressed. It is important to know, however, that support for this declaration is inconsistent across browser types and versions. As always, you should make sure that any border declarations you use are supported by the browsers that your audience uses.

Chris wants you to create and format a box around the science article on the Messier marathon, found on the Astronomy page. Chris wants the padding around the article to be 0.5 em on each side of the box. The article should have a solid border 2 pixels wide.

To create the style for the science article:

1. Return to the **mws.css** style sheet in your text editor.

2. Add the following style attributes to the div.article element (see Figure 7-62):

   ```
   ;padding: 0.5em; border-style: solid; border-width: 2px
   ```

Figure 7-62   SPECIFYING THE PADDING AND BORDER ATTRIBUTES

```
body {color: green;
      background: white url(draft.jpg) no-repeat fixed center center}
h1, h2, h3, h4, h5, h6 {font-family: Arial, Helvetica, sans-serif}
address {font-size: 0.6em; font-style: normal; text-align: center;
        text-transform: uppercase}
blockquote {background-color: silver}
ul {list-style: circle url(apple.jpg) outside}
ul b {color: rgb(155,0,0)}
a {font-size: 0.65em; color: green}
a:hover {color: red; text-transform: uppercase}
li.special {color: blue; font-weight: bold}
div.article {background-color: rgb(252,221,163);
             padding: 0.5em; border-style: solid; border-width: 2px}
```

3. Save your changes to mws.css and then reload astro.htm in your browser. The science article is now displayed in a box as shown in Figure 7-63.

Figure 7-63   THE REVISED SCIENCE ARTICLE

Astronomy

Maxwell Scientific provides a wide range of astronomical products — perfect for classroom demonstrations and projects. Choose from the finest equipment from Newton,™ DC Optics,™ and StarVision.™

Run the Messier Marathon

It's time for the annual **Messier Marathon**. Instead of lacing up their Nikes, amateur astronomers will be hauling telescopes, star charts, and a hefty pot of coffee in an all-night vigil hunting the Messier objects.

Messier objects are stellar objects, classified by astronomer **Charles Messier** in the 18th century, ranging from distant galaxies to star clusters to stellar nebula. March is the only month in the year in which all 110 Messier objects are in the sky. Unfortunately, if you want to see all of them, you have to start looking right after sunset and continue until just before sunrise — hence the term, "marathon."

Ironically, Charles Messier wasn't all that interested in his objects. He made the list in order to *avoid* seeing them. Messier was more interested in discovering new comets and these beautiful stellar objects were often mistaken for comets before Messier made his list.

TROUBLE? If you're using Netscape version 4.7 or earlier, the color of both the article text and the border will be black.

Resizing **and Moving Block-Level Boxes**

For the most part, Chris likes the way the new text box for the science article looks. She now wants you to reduce the width of the box and align it with the right margin of the display window so that it appears as a sidebar.

Formatting the Width and Height of Block-Level Boxes

To change the width of a box, you use the width attribute. Box width can be expressed in terms of absolute or relative units of length, or as a percentage of the width of the parent element. For example, the style:

```
body {width: 75%}
```

reduces the width of the Web page body to 75% of the width of the browser's display area. The width attribute is seldom used except with text boxes and inline images. One problem is that for many elements, results can be unpredictable with some browsers. Also, note that the width value you set is not the width of the document content. The actual width is what is left after you subtract the margin, border, and padding for the element.

The height attribute sets the height of the element. Heights can be expressed in absolute or relative lengths, but not percentages. Typically, you won't set the height of a block-level element because problems can arise when the amount of text in the element exceeds the height allowed. When this occurs, browsers may introduce a scrollbar or other device to allow you to view the hidden text. More often, however, browsers may ignore the style, or worse, truncate the extra text. For these reasons, the height attribute is usually applied to inline images and little else.

Using the Float Attribute

When your browser renders a Web page, it positions the block-level elements one after another on the page, with the exact positions determined by the element's width, margin, and padding. CSS allows you to place each block-level element in a specific location on the Web page. This is good in theory, but in actual practice, the results can be subject to error.

When you position objects on the page, you need to test the page very carefully, under different browsers, browser versions, and operating systems.

REFERENCE WINDOW   **RW**

Floating a Block-Level Element

- To float a block-level element, use the style declaration:

  `float: margin`

  where *margin* indicates the margin of the parent element to be aligned with the floating element. Possible values of margin are "right" and "left".

- To prevent a floating element from appearing alongside a block-level element, insert the following style declaration into the nonfloating element:

  `clear: margin`

  where *margin* can be "right", "left", or "both", to leave the right, left, or both margins clear, respectively.

There are so many attributes and techniques for managing page layout that the topic deserves a chapter all to itself. However, you'll concentrate on one of the simpler tools: the float attribute. The float attribute works like the align="left" or align="right" attributes used with the <img> tags. It places the block-level element on the left or right margin of the parent element. As shown in Figure 7-64, when the browser encounters the float attribute, it moves the element over to whatever margin the Web author has specified and then brings the next block-level element up. The text in that element is wrapped around the floating element.

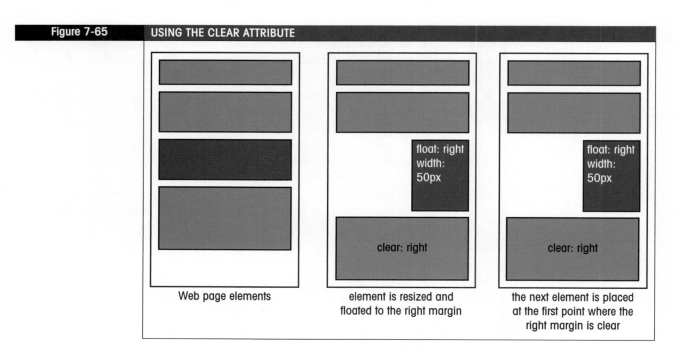

Figure 7-64   FLOATING A BLOCK-LEVEL ELEMENT

float: right
width:
50px

float: right
width:
50px

| Web page elements | one element is resized and floated on the right margin | the next element is moved up and wrapped around the floating element |

You can prevent other elements from wrapping around the floating element by adding the clear attribute to the element below the floating element. When the value of the clear attribute is set to "right," the browser displays the element on the page at the point where the right margin is clear. See Figure 7-65. Other possible values for the clear attribute are "left" and "both" (for both margins).

Figure 7-65   USING THE CLEAR ATTRIBUTE

float: right
width:
50px

float: right
width:
50px

clear: right

clear: right

| Web page elements | element is resized and floated to the right margin | the next element is placed at the first point where the right margin is clear |

You decide to resize the science article, setting the width to 250 pixels. You'll also float the article against the right margin, but you'll allow the remaining block-level elements to wrap around the article.

To resize and float the science article:

1. Return to the **mws.css** style sheet in your text editor.

2. Add the following attributes to the style declaration for the div.article selector (see Figure 7-66):

```
; width: 250px; float: right
```

Figure 7-66	FINAL FORM OF THE MWS STYLE SHEET

```
body {color: green;
      background: white url(draft.jpg) no-repeat fixed center center}
h1, h2, h3, h4, h5, h6 {font-family: Arial, Helvetica, sans-serif}
address {font-size: 0.6em; font-style: normal; text-align: center;
         text-transform: uppercase}
blockquote {background-color: silver}
ul {list-style: circle url(apple.jpg) outside}
ul b {color: rgb(155,0,0)}
a {font-size: 0.65em; color: green}
a:hover {color: red; text-transform: uppercase}
li.special {color: blue; font-weight: bold}
div.article {background-color: rgb(252,221,163);
             padding: 0.5em; border-style: solid; border-width: 2px;
             width: 250px; float: right}
```

3. Save your changes to mws.css and close your text editor. You've completed your work on the style sheet.

4. Use your browser to reload astro.htm. Figure 7-67 shows the completed version of the Astronomy Web page.

Figure 7-67 | **FINAL ASTRONOMY PAGE**

Astronomy Chemistry Electronics Engineering Physics

Astronomy

Maxwell Scientific provides a wide range of astronomical products — perfect for classroom demonstrations and projects. Choose from the finest equipment from Newton,™ DC Optics,™ and StarVision.™

Featured Astronomical Products

- **Refractor Kit: March Special! Learn about the science of optics by building your own 18" long, 3X refractor telescope. Price \$10.95. Stock Number: RK01-085**
- **NightDisk:** View the night sky for any night and time of the year with this attractive and useful star disk. Price \$19.95. Stock Number: ND25-100
- **Constellation Globe:** A beautiful two-way illuminated globe displaying the location of the constellations and various night sky objects. Price: \$49.95. Stock Number: CG13-810
- **Star and Planet Locators:** A pack of 25 star and planet locators — perfect for classroom use. Price :\$29.95. Stock Number: SL25-271
- **Rechargeable Red Flashlight:** A 4" rechargeable flashlight, employing a red LED to preserve night vision. Price \$15.95. Stock Number: RF02-421
- **Classroom Planetarium: March Special! Planetarium kit projects more than 300 stars and constellations onto the ceiling or wall. Perfect for classroom use. Red star flashlight included to point out individual stars. Price \$34.95. Stock Number: CP21-789**
- **Solar Mobile:** The sun and all nine planets are represented in this attractive mobile. Mobile measures 4 feet across when assembled. Great for classroom demonstrations! Price \$14.95. Stock Number: SM4-411
- **Solar Mobile Kit:** Kit includes 12 stryofoam shapes with wire and connecting rods to create a hanging mobile of the solar system. Makes 20 mobiles. Instructions and lesson plans included. Price \$29.95. Stock Number: SM5-411

Comments From Our Astronomy Customers

Here at Maxwell Scientific, we strive to deliver high-quality astronomy equipment in a prompt and professional manner. Still, we're as happy as anyone when we receive a compliment!

"Thank you for your excellent service. I purchased the Newton 3" refractor for our astronomy lab. The view of Saturn was an exciting moment for the entire class."
Dawn Hillbert. San Jose, CA

"I appreciate the prompt delivery of the pack of star disks. Your company is a great boon to science teachers everywhere."
Steve Fawson. Cleveland, OH

"The MC5 Maksutov-Cassegrain was delivered as promised: on-time and at a great price. When it's time to get my next scope, I'll look to your company first."
Brenda Dicks. Greely, CO

Run the Messier Marathon

It's time for the annual **Messier Marathon**. Instead of lacing up their Nikes, amateur astronomers will be hauling telescopes, star charts, and a hefty pot of coffee in an all-night vigil hunting the Messier objects.

Messier objects are stellar objects, classified by astronomer **Charles Messier** in the 18th century, ranging from distant galaxies to star clusters to stellar nebula. March is the only month in the year in which all 110 Messier objects are in the sky. Unfortunately, if you want to see all of them, you have to start looking right after sunset and continue until just before sunrise — hence the term, "marathon."

Ironically, Charles Messier wasn't all that interested in his objects. He made the list in order to *avoid* seeing them. Messier was more interested in discovering new comets and these beautiful stellar objects were often mistaken for comets before Messier made his list.

MAXWELL SCIENTIFIC
205 EAST NORDHEIM DRIVE, HAPTON, IL 43129
PHONE: (800) 555-2191 FAX: (812) 555-2192

TROUBLE? Depending on your browser, monitor resolution, and monitor size, the position and size of the science article may differ from the one shown in Figure 7-67.

5. Close your Web browser.

As shown in Figure 7-67, the science article now floats on the right margin and the rest of the page wraps around it. With the style sheet you created, you can easily apply this effect to other Web pages by enclosing any block of text within a set of <div> tags with the Article class name, and then linking the HTML file to your style sheet.

Chris is pleased with the current design. She'll show the two pages you designed to other members of the Web site group and get back to you with any changes she may want to make.

Session 7.3 QUICK CHECK

1. What style would you use to change your hypertext to white text on a red background whenever the pointer is positioned over the link?

2. What HTML code would you use to assign a block of text the class name "Report"?

3. What HTML code would you use to assign a single word the id name "Author"?

4. What is a block-level element? What is an inline element? Give examples of each.

5. What style declaration would you use to change the margin around your block quote elements to 10 pixels?

6. What style declaration would you use to create a dashed border around your block quotes?

7. What style declaration would you use to float your block quotes against the left margin of the Web page?

REVIEW ASSIGNMENTS

Chris has received feedback on the design of your Web pages from the other members of the Web site team at Maxwell Scientific. They like the way you've used style sheets to create an overall design, but there are some style changes they'd like you to make.

Also, the physics, engineering, and electronics Web pages have been written, so one of your tasks is to apply the style sheet to those pages. In addition, Chris would like you to continue giving each products page a distinct heading color. Finally, she wants you to insert the watermark image review.jpg on each page to indicate that these Web pages are going back to the Web site team for final review once you're finished. Figure 7-68 shows a preview of one of the Web pages you'll create for Chris.

Figure 7-68

Electronics

When you need quality electronic kits, think first of Maxwell Scientific. Our kits will provide your students with a wide variety of interesting and fun projects. Remember, every kit comes with a teacher's manual and a packet of professionally-designed lesson plans.

Featured Electronics Products

- **Burglar Alarm Kit:** Your students can build their own burglar alarms with this board-mounted horn and LED indicator. Requires a 6-volt DC battery (not included.) Price $5.95 Stock Number: EL1-001
- **Crystal Radio Kit:** Teach the principles of radios and electronics with this special radio kit. *No batteries required.* Price $5.95 Stock Number: EL1-002
- **Microphone Kit:** Build a simple RF transmitter. Sounds are picked up by a miniature microphone and then transmitted to an FM radio. Price $9.95 Stock Number: EL1-003
- **Binary Counter Kit:** Teach electronics and the principles of binary mathematics with this fun and interesting kit. Binary counts can be displayed with Maxwell Scientific's Decimal Display Kit. Price $9.95 Stock Number: EL1-004
- **Strobe Light Kit:** Use the enclosed xenon strobe tube to create your own strobe light. Adult supervision required. Price $19.95 Stock Number: EL2-001
- **Electronics Lab:** Explore the fun of electronics with this lab kit. The kit contains instructions for over 100 different projects. Lesson plans included. Price $59.95 Stock Number: EL3-017
- **Advaned Electronics Lab:** Explore more of the world of electronics with this kit for advanced users. Features over 300 different projects with lesson plans and a teacher's guide. Price $129.95 Stock Number: EL5-001
- **Circuit Board:** Students can learn the fundamentals of electronics and circuits with this circuit board. Comes with double-ole switch, 2 DC motors, 2 lights, jumper wires, and clamp-type connectors. Price $59.95. Stock Number: EL3-010

Oersted's Lucky Lecture

At the beginning of the nineteenth century, electricity and magnetism had been seen as two entirely different forces. This all changed thanks to Hans Christian Oersted's lucky lecture.

Orested had been using a strong battery in one of his lectures, and as he concluded his talk he placed a current-carrying wire over a compass. To his surprise, the compass begain to move quickly from the north direction to the east directon, as if it were in the presence of an intense magnetic field. Oersted reversed the flow of the electric current and the compass promptly began pointing west.

As soon as Oersted announced his discovery, physicists all over Europe duplicated the experiment and quickly realized that electricity and magnetism were two aspects of the same force. Today we refer to this force as *electromagnetism*, thanks, in part, to Oersted's lucky lecture.

Comments From Our Electronics Customers

No other area of our business has received as much praise as electronics. We take great pride in providing you with quality teaching materials at a great price. It seems from your comments, that you've noticed.

"There are a lot of electronic lab kits available to the science teacher. I've found Maxwell Scientific's kits to be, without question, the best."
Ryan Knight, Carson, ME

"Your lab kits are simply the best."
Maria Larson, Oak Park, IL

"I appreciate the support you give to teachers. When I had a few questions about the Binary Counter Kit, your staff was able to give me the answers I needed."
Tom Thomas, Grand Island, NE

MAXWELL SCIENTIFIC
205 EAST NORDHEIM DRIVE, HAPTON, IL 43129
PHONE: (800) 555-2191 FAX: (812) 555-2192

To make the design changes to the Web site:

1. Using your text editor, open the files **physicstxt.htm**, **engtxt.htm**, and **electtxt.htm** located in the tutorial.07/review folder of your Data Disk. Save the three files as **physics.htm**, **eng.htm**, and **elect.htm**, respectively, in the same folder.

2. Using your text editor, open **mwsptxt.css** located in the tutorial.07/review folder on your Data Disk, and save it as **mwsp.css**.

3. Change the font color for headings in the Engineering Web page to blue, in the Electronics page to teal, and in the Physics page to the rgb color value (158, 160, 224).

4. Replace the horizontal lines surrounding the science articles in the Electronics and Physics pages with a <div> container that has the class name "sciarticle."

5. Locate the product specials in the Engineering, Electronics, and Physics Web pages and add the attribute class="special" to the appropriate <li> tags.

6. Link the three Web pages to the mwsp.css style sheet.

7. Set the page background color for all three Web pages to white. Use the review.jpg image as a background image for all three Web pages. Set the image in the background so that it doesn't scroll with the rest of the page, and place the image in the center of the page, both horizontally and vertically. Do not tile the image.

8. For each page, reduce the font size of the customer comments to 0.8 em, and display the comment text, customer name, and customer location in italics.

9. Change the style of hypertext links so that they are displayed in a background color with the RGB value of (128,128,128) in a white font, with no underlining. Set the size of the hypertext to 1 em unit and the font to Arial, Helvetica, and then any other generic sans-serif font. If the mouse pointer is positioned over the link, the font color changes to yellow.

Explore   10. Create the illusion of a 3-D box around the science articles by changing the width of the top and left borders to 1 pixel and the width of the right and bottom borders to 4 pixels.

Explore   11. Create a new class named "scititle" for the title of science articles. Display the science article titles centered within a white box with a solid black border 1 pixel wide.

12. Save your changes to all of the files.

13. Print your style sheet and the HTML code for the five Web pages.

14. Open each of the five Web pages in your Web browser and print each one.

15. Hand in your files and printouts to your instructor.

CASE PROBLEMS

Case 1. The Stuff Shop   You've been asked to create an opening page for The Stuff Shop, an online store for buying, selling, and trading of used merchandise, antiques, and rare collectibles. Sandy Baxter, who leads the Web development team, wants a crisp and bold style for the opening screen. Figure 7-69 shows a preview of the page you'll create for her. Because she wants a different style for the rest of the pages in the Web site, you won't work with an external style sheet. All styles are either inline or embedded.

Figure 7-69

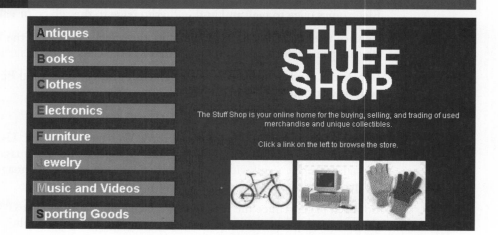

To format the opening page for The Stuff Shop:

1. Using your text editor, open **stufftxt.htm** located in the tutorial.07/case1 folder of your Data Disk, and save it as **stuff.htm** in the same folder.

2. Using an embedded style, change the background color of the Web page to black, the font color to white, and the font family to Arial, Helvetica, or, if those fonts are missing, sans-serif.

3. Using the <div> tag, enclose the list of product categories at the beginning of the document in a container and give the container the class name "leftbox".

4. Format the style of the leftbox so that it floats against the left margin of the Web page. The width of the left box should be 30% of the width of the display area.

5. Each product category is formatted as an h5 heading. Change the style so that each h5 heading has a background color of red and the amount of padding to the left of the heading is 5 pixels.

6. The text for each product category acts as a hypertext link. Modify the style of hypertext links in the document so that the links are displayed in a white font, with a size of 20 pixels. Remove the underlining from the hypertext links. If a pointer is positioned over the hypertext link, the font color changes to yellow.

Explore

7. Use an inline style and the <span> tag to change the color of the first letter of each product category. The color of the first letters is as follows:

   - Antiques = black
   - Books = blue
   - Clothes = teal
   - Electronics = lime
   - Furniture = maroon
   - Jewelry = aqua
   - Music and Videos = silver
   - Sporting Goods = navy

8. Use the <div> tag to enclose the title "The Stuff Shop" within another container and name the container "rightbox".

9. Center the contents of the rightbox. Assign the text a font weight of 900. Change the font size to 60 pixels and the line height to 40 pixels.

10. Below the rightbox, change the style of the block quote. Center the contents of the block quote and change the font size to 12 pixels.

11. Save your changes to stuff.htm.

12. Using your browser, reload or refresh stuff.htm to verify the changes. (Note to users of Netscape 4.7 or earlier: The red boxes you create are not all the same width, and the color of the hypertext link does not change when the pointer is positioned over the link.)

13. Print out your HTML file and the corresponding Web page.

14. Hand in your printouts and files to your instructor.

Case 2. Willet Creek Golf Course   You've been asked to create a Web site for the Willet Creek Golf Course. A portion of the Web site is a preview of each of the 18 holes complete with distances and shot recommendations. The current Web pages are stored in 18 files named h01txt.htm, h02txt.htm, and so on, through h18txt.htm. You decide to create an external style sheet so that you can easily edit and update the appearance of these 18 Web pages. A preview of one of the Web pages you'll create is shown in Figure 7-70.

Figure 7-70

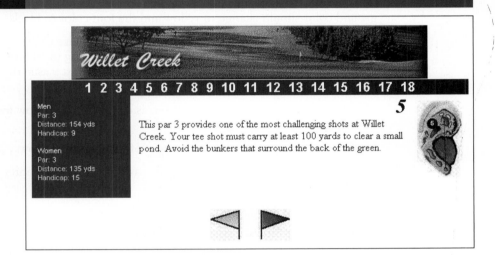

To format course information for the Willet Creek Web site:

1. Use your text editor to open **h01txt.htm** through **h18txt.htm** located in the tutorial.07/ case2 folder of your Data Disk and save them as **h01.htm** through **h18.htm** in the same folder.

2. For each page, enclose the list of hypertext links at the top of the file within a set of <div> tags with the class name "holelist".

   ■ For each page, enclose the information on the hole's par value, distance, and handicap for men and women within a set of <div> tags with the class name "holestats".

   ■ For each page, replace the pair of <center> tags that enclose the hypertext links at the bottom of the file with a set of <div> tags with the class name "flags".

3. Using your text editor, create an external style sheet named **willet.css** and link each of the 18 Web pages to the style sheet. You may want to use copy and paste to save typing and reduce the possibility of errors.

4. Change the body style for the Web site by setting the size of the left and right margins to 10 pixels.

5. Display the body text in either an Arial, Helvetica, or sans-serif font.

6. Set the background color of the Web page body to white.

7. Display all paragraph text in a Times Roman or serif font. Set the width of the top margin of your paragraphs to 0 pixels.

8. Display all h1 headings right-aligned, in an italic Times Roman or serif font. Set the margin around your h1 headings to 0 pixels.

9. Display all hypertext links on the Web pages without an underline.

10. Set the width of the holelist box to 100% of the display area. The margin width is 1 pixel on top and 0 pixels everywhere else. The size of the border is 1 pixel. The background color and the border color are both displayed with the RGB values (53,43,48). The text in the holelist box is centered.

11. Display all hypertext links within the holelist box in a white boldface font and 1.25 em units in size. If the pointer is positioned over one of these hypertext links, the background color should change to yellow and the font color to black.

12. Set the width of the holestats box to 150 pixels. Set the size of the right margin to 10 pixels. Set the bottom padding to 25 pixels and all other padding to 10 pixels. Set the box background color to the RGB value (53,43,48). Display all text within the box in a white font and 0.7 em units in size.

13. All boldface text within the holestats box is displayed in a yellow font with a normal font weight.

14. Float the holestats box on the left margin of the display window.

15. Display the flags box only when the left margin is clear, and center any text or images within the box.

16. Using your text editor, save your changes to willet.css.

17. Using your Web browser, open **h01.htm** and verify that your changes match what is shown in Figure 7-71. Use the hypertext links to move through the rest of the Web site either by clicking hole numbers at the top of the page or by clicking the forward and backward flags located at the bottom. Verify that a rollover effect is seen when you position the pointer over the list of hole numbers. Note to users of Netscape 4.7 or earlier: There is a vertical gap between the holelist and holestats boxes. There also is a white border around your list of hypertext links, and there is no rollover effect when you position the pointer over the hole numbers.

18. Using your text editor, print the contents of the willet.css style sheet and the HTML code for the first hole of the Willet Web site.

19. Using your Web browser, print all 18 Web pages.

Explore 20. Using your Web browser, print the **h01.txt** Web page and compare this printout with the printout for the h01 Web page that takes advantage of the Willet style sheet you created. How could you have created the same kind of Web page without using style sheets? How easy would it have been to do this for all 18 Web pages? What are some effects you could not have created without using CSS?

21. Hand in your printouts and files to your instructor.

Case 3. Chamberlain Civic Center Stacy Dawes, the director of publicity for the Chamberlain Civic Center, has asked you to modify the style of several event calendar Web pages. The events for each calendar have been created, but the tables have not yet been formatted.

Style sheets can be used to format the appearance and layout of tables. This can be a great timesaver, since without style sheets a Web page author would have to insert <font> tags into each table cell to format the cell's text. CSS treats tables, table rows, and table cells as block-level elements, so many of the style attributes you've applied to other block-level elements can also be applied to table elements.

Stacy would like each calendar table to float alongside the right edge of the Web page. The table headings appear in a sans-serif font on a light blue background. Each entry in the calendar table contains a hypertext link to a Web page containing detailed information about the events of that day. Stacy wants these entries to be underlined only when the user's mouse is positioned over the text. She would like all weekend events displayed with a pink background, weekday and Sunday events displayed with a white background, and events from the previous or next month displayed with a textured background. The date is displayed in a boldface font on a light blue background.

At the top of each page, there is a list of links embedded in a table. Stacy would like each cell in this table to have a 3-D border and the table itself to have a solid red bottom border. Figure 7-71 shows a preview of one of the Web pages you'll create for the CCC.

Figure 7-71

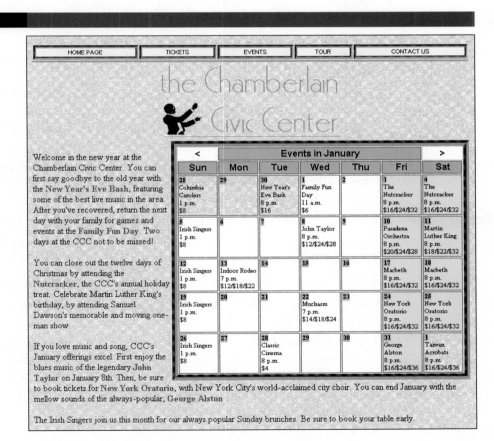

To format the CCC events calendar:

1. Using your text editor, open **jantxt.htm**, **febtxt.htm**, and **martxt.htm** from the tutorial.07/case3 folder of your Data Disk and save them as **jan.htm**, **feb.htm**, and **mar.htm**.

Explore   2. Within the jan.htm file, locate the table at the top of the page that contains a list of links to other CCC Web pages. Assign this table the id value "links". (*Hint*: Add the id attribute to the <table> tag.)

3. Locate the table containing the calendar of events for January and assign this table the id name "calendar".

Explore   4. In the first table row, assign the first table heading (containing the < character) the class name "prev". Assign the third table heading (containing the > character) the class name, "next". (*Hint:* Add the class attribute to the <th> tag.)

5. Navigate through the remaining table cells. If the table cell corresponds to a date from the previous month, assign the cell the class name "prev". If the table cell corresponds to a date from the next month, assign the cell the class name "next". If the cell corresponds to a weekend date, assign the cell the class name "weekend".

6. Within the head section for the Web page, create a link to the style sheet **calendar.css** (you'll create this file shortly).

7. Save your changes to jan.htm and close the file.

8. Repeat steps 2 through 7 for **feb.htm** and **mar.htm**.

9. Use your text editor to create a new file on your Data Disk and name it **calendar.css**.

10. Within calendar.css, enter a style declaration to set the background image of the Web page body to **back.jpg**.

   ■ Enter a style declaration to display boldfaced text in blue.

   ■ Enter a style declaration to remove underlining from hypertext links on the Web page.

   ■ Enter a style declaration to display hypertext links in a black font, regardless of the state of the hypertext link.

   ■ Enter a style declaration to if the mouse pointer is positioned over a hypertext link, the text appears in a red font with underlining.

Explore   11. Within calendar.css, create a style declaration for the links table, setting the width of the table to 100% of the display area, and apply a solid red bottom border to the table that is 3 pixels wide.

Explore   12. For the cells within the links table, set the background color to ivory.

13. Center the text within each cell. Make the font size 8 points. Display the cell text in an Arial, Helvetica, or sans-serif font. Change the text to uppercase letters.

14. Apply a 5-point red border to each cell, displayed in the groove style.

15. Float the calendar table on the right edge of the Web page. Give the calendar table a 10-point red border in the groove style.

16. Apply a light blue background to table headings within the calendar table (those cells created using the <th> tag). Display the text of table headings in an Arial, Helvetica, or sans-serif font. Apply a solid 1-pixel-wide blue border to the headings.

17. If the calendar table heading belongs to the "next" or "prev" class, remove the border and set the background color to white.

Explore   18. For those table cells within the calendar table (those cells created with the <td> tag), apply the following styles:

   ■ Make each cell 65 pixels wide.

   ■ Set the background color to white.

- Set the size of the text in the cell to 8 points, and align the text with the top of the cell (*Hint:* use the vertical-align style attribute).
- Surround each cell with a 1-pixel-wide solid blue border.
- Display boldfaced text within these cells in a black font with a light blue background.
- If the table cell belongs to the "next" or "prev" class, use **back.jpg** for the cell's background image.
- If the table cell belongs to the "weekend" class, set the background color to pink.

19. Print the code for the calendar.css file, and then close it Using your text editor, save your changes to calendar.css, print it, and then close the file.

20. Using your Web browser, open **jan.htm** and verify that the layout and appearance of the two tables matches that shown in Figure 7-71. (*Note:* If you are running Netscape 4.7 or Internet Explorer 4.0, you will not see the style design shown in Figure 7-71). Position the mouse pointer over the entries in the two tables and verify that the hypertext link text changes to a red font and is underlined.

21. Click the **>** cell to move to the February calendar and then to the March calendar. Verify that the appropriate styles have been applied to these Web pages as well.

22. Hand in your files and printouts to your instructor.

Case 4. Midwest University Music Department You've been hired by the music department at Midwest University to create Web pages for a new course on opera. The instructor, Faye Dawson, has provided you information on five different composers: Mozart, Verdi, Puccini, Bizet, and Wagner. She wants a separate Web page for each composer, but there needs to be a common style for all five Web pages. Professor Dawson has provided you with the following items:

- an image of each composer
- a list of operas by each composer
- a short biography for each composer

The opera lists and biographies are in text files on your Data Disk. For example, the file containing Mozart's operas is **mozartlist.txt**, the Mozart biography is **mozartbio.txt**, the image of Mozart is **mozart.jpg**. Information for other composers follows a similar naming convention. Feel free to use any additional material that is available to you.

Using this information, create a Web site consisting of five different Web pages. The actual design of the site is up to you, but it must contain the following features.

- The names of the five Web pages must be: **bizet.htm, mozart.htm, puccini.htm, verdi.htm**, and **wagner.htm**.
- Each Web page must have at least one example of an embedded style.
- Each Web page must be linked to a style sheet named **opera.css** that contains styles applied to the entire site.
- You must have at least one example of a style modifying the body element of your Web pages.
- You must have at least one example of a style that defines a font family and font size.
- You must use the <div> or <span> tags at least once in your Web site, with styles defined for either a class or id name.
- You must show at least one example of a floating box, with a value defined for the margin, the border, and the padding.

■ You must place hypertext links to the other Web pages on each page, and you must define a style for your hypertext links, including a special style for the link when the pointer is positioned over the link.

■ When you're finished, print your HTML code and the resulting Web pages.

QUICK CHECK ANSWERS

Session 7.1

1. CSS1 and CSS2 are the first and second standards developed for the application of Cascading Style Sheets.

2. Inline styles are styles that are added to a specific tag within an HTML file. An embedded style is a style defined for a group of tags within the HTML file. A linked style sheet is a separate text file containing the styles used for one or more Web pages.

3. p {color: blue}

4. h1, h2 {color: yellow}

5. p b {color :red}

   This style affects only boldface text located within a <p> tag.

6. <link href="basicstyle.css" rel="stylesheet" type="text/css">

   This tag should be placed within the head section of the HTML file.

7. Green, because embedded styles override linked style sheets when there is a conflict in the style declarations.

Session 7.2

1. blockquote {font-family: Times Roman, serif}

2. p {font-size: 12pt}

3. Absolute units, such as inches, centimeters, and millimeters, retain their sizes for any monitor resolutions. Relative units are scalable, and they change size based on the monitor resolution. There are two relative units: em and ex.

4. h1, h2, h3, h4, h5, h6 {text-decoration: underline; text-transform: uppercase}

5. p {text-align: center; font-weight: bold; font-style: italic}

6. ul {background-image: url(list.gif); background-position: center center}
   or
   ul {background: url(list.gif) center center}

7. ol {list-style-type: decimal}
   ol {list-style-type: decimal-leading-zero}

Session 7.3

1. a:hover {color: white; background-color: red}

2. <div class="report">text block </div>

3. <span id="author">single word</span>

4. Block-level elements are elements that enclose blocks of text, such as paragraphs, block quotes, headings, or lists. Individual letters, words, or phrases that appear within block-level elements are known as inline elements.

5. margin: 10px

6. border-style: dashed

7. float: left

OBJECTIVES

In this tutorial you will:

- Learn about the features of JavaScript

- Send output to a Web page

- Work with variables and data

- Work with expressions and operators

- Create a JavaScript function

- Work with arrays and conditional statements

- Learn about program loops

PROGRAMMING WITH JAVASCRIPT

Creating a Programmable Web Page for North Pole Novelties

CASE

Calculating Shopping Days for North Pole Novelties

North Pole Novelties (NPN), located in Seton Grove, Minnesota, is a gift shop specializing in toys, decorations, and other items for the holiday season. Founded in 1968 by David Watkins, NPN is one of the largest holiday supply stores in the country, with over 300 employees serving customers from around the world.

Because December 25 is the "red letter" day for North Pole Novelties, the store is always aware of the number of shopping days remaining until Christmas and wants its customers to be aware of this, too.

With this in mind, Andrew Savatini, director of marketing, wants the company's home page to display the number of days remaining until Christmas. To accomplish this, the Web page must be updated daily to reflect the correct number of days left until the big day. Although the company could assign someone the task of manually changing the Web page each morning, it would be more efficient and reliable if the update could be performed automatically by a program running on the Web page itself.

Andrew has asked you to create such a program. To do this, you'll have to learn how to write and run programs in **JavaScript**, a programming language specifically designed for Web pages.

SESSION 8.1

In this session, you'll learn about the development and features of JavaScript. You'll also learn how to insert a JavaScript program into an HTML file and how to hide that program from older browsers that don't support JavaScript. Finally, you'll write a simple JavaScript program to send customized output to a Web page.

Introduction to JavaScript

In your work with HTML so far, you've created static Web pages, whose content and layout did not change. Beginning with this tutorial, you'll learn how to create Web pages whose content and layout can be modified through the use of specialized programs or scripts run when the browser initially opens the page.

Server-side and Client-side Programs

In Tutorial 6, you learned how to access CGI scripts that we run from the Web server. There are some disadvantages to this approach. The user must be connected to the Web server to run the CGI script, only the programmer can create or alter the script, and the Web server's system administrator can place limitations on how users access the script. Such an approach also poses problems for the system administrator, who has to be concerned about users continually accessing the server and potentially overloading the system.

Issues like those highlighted previously led to the development of programs, or scripts, that could be run from the Web browser (the client), as illustrated in Figure 8-1.

Figure 8-1	SERVER-SIDE AND CLIENT-SIDE PROGRAMMING

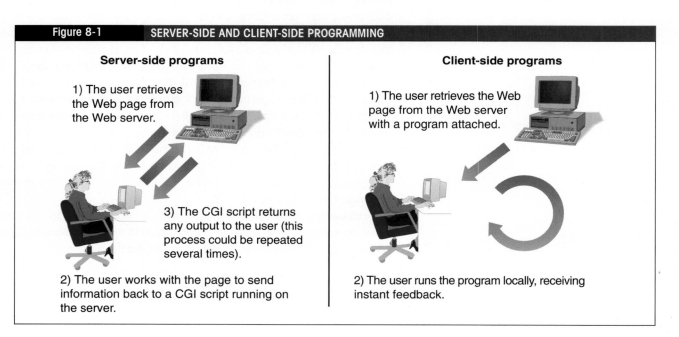

Server-side programs

1) The user retrieves the Web page from the Web server.

3) The CGI script returns any output to the user (this process could be repeated several times).

2) The user works with the page to send information back to a CGI script running on the server.

Client-side programs

1) The user retrieves the Web page from the Web server with a program attached.

2) The user runs the program locally, receiving instant feedback.

Client-side programs solve many of the problems associated with server-side scripts. Computing is distributed over the Web so that no one server is overloaded with programming requests. A client-side program can be tested locally without first uploading it to a Web server. Client-side programs are also likely to be more responsive to the user, because the user does not have to wait for data to be sent over the Internet to the Web server.

However, client-side programs can never completely replace CGI scripts. If you need to run a search form or process a purchase order, that type of job must be run from a central server, because only the server contains the database needed to complete those types of operations.

The Development of Java and JavaScript

As with many computing innovations, client-side programming came from some unexpected sources. In the early 1990s, programmers at Sun Microsystems envisioned a day when common appliances and devices, such as refrigerators, toasters, and garage door openers, would be networked and controllable using a single operating system. The programmers began development on such an operating system and based it on a language called **Oak**. Oak was extremely reliable and flexible, but unfortunately, the project did not succeed. However, Oak worked so well that Sun Microsystems saw its potential for use on the Internet. Oak was modified in 1995 and renamed **Java**.

Sun Microsystems also developed a product called **HotJava**, which ran programs written in the Java language. HotJava was a **Java interpreter**, which means it can interpret and run Java programs. The idea was that Java programs would run inside Java interpreters, and because Java interpreters could be created for different operating systems, users could run Java on the UNIX, Windows, DOS, and Macintosh operating systems. Just as Web pages are platform-independent, so was Java.

The advantages of Java were immediately apparent and success soon followed. Netscape incorporated a Java interpreter into Netscape Navigator version 2.0, making HotJava unnecessary for Netscape users. Microsoft wasted little time including its own Java interpreter with Internet Explorer version 3.0.

A Web browser that has a Java interpreter runs the program locally on the user's computer, freeing up the Web server for other purposes (Figure 8-2).

Figure 8-2	APPLETS AND JAVA INTERPRETERS

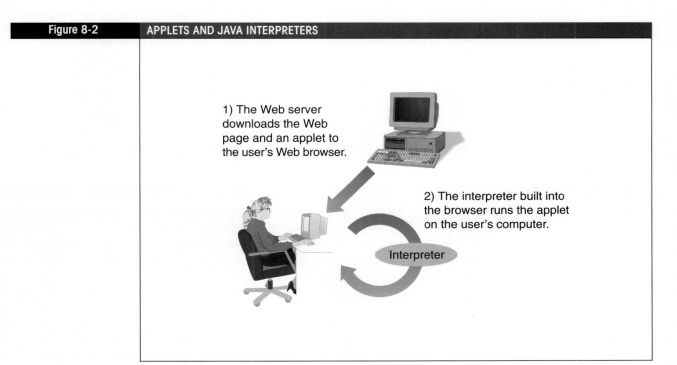

1) The Web server downloads the Web page and an applet to the user's Web browser.

2) The interpreter built into the browser runs the applet on the user's computer.

Interpreter

A problem with Java was that nonprogrammers found it difficult to learn and use. Users also needed access to the Java Developer's Kit (JDK) in order to create a Java program and then compile it. **Compiling** is the process by which a program is converted from a text file of code into an executable file called an **applet**.

To simplify this complex process, a team of developers from Netscape and Sun Microsystems created a subset of Java called **JavaScript**. There are several important differences between Java and JavaScript. Users don't need to work with a developer's kit to compile a JavaScript program, and JavaScript commands can be inserted directly into an HTML file rather than being placed in a separate program file. This saves the Web browser from having to download a separate file when the Web page is accessed. JavaScript may not be as powerful a computing language as Java, but it is simpler to use, and it meets the needs of most users who want to create programmable Web pages.

Figure 8-3 highlights some of the key differences between Java and JavaScript.

Figure 8-3	COMPARISON OF JAVA AND JAVASCRIPT	
JAVA	**JAVASCRIPT**	
Complicated	Easy to learn and use	
Requires the JDK (Java Developer's Kit) to create applets	No developer's kit required	
Programs must be saved as separate files and compiled before they can be run	Scripts are written directly into the HTML file and require no compiling	
Powerful; used for complex tasks	Used for relatively simple tasks	

Through the years, JavaScript has undergone several revisions. Internet Explorer actually supports a slightly different version of JavaScript called **JScript**. Essentially, JScript is identical to JavaScript, but there are some JavaScript commands not supported in JScript, and vice versa. For this reason, you should, as always, test your JavaScript programs on a variety of Web browsers. Although it is tempting to use commands available in the latest JavaScript or JScript versions, your programs might not run on older browsers.

Because of all these competing versions and revisions, the responsibility for the development of a scripting standard has been transferred to an international body called the **European Computer Manufacturers Association (ECMA)**. The standard developed by the ECMA is called **ECMAScript**, though browsers still refer to it as JavaScript. The latest version is **ECMA-262**, which is supported by the major browsers, though there are still a few areas of the standard that have not been implemented.

Figure 8-4 lists the versions of JavaScript or JScript and the corresponding browser support.

Figure 8-4	VERSIONS OF JAVASCRIPT AND JSCRIPT	
VERSION	**BROWSER**	**YEAR**
JavaScript 1.0	Netscape Navigator 2.0	1995
JScript 1.0	Internet Explorer 3.0	1996
JavaScript 1.1	Netscape Navigator 3.0	1996
JavaScript 1.2	Netscape Navigator 4.0	1997
JScript 3.0	Internet Explorer 4.0	1997
JavaScript 1.3	Netscape Navigator 4.5	1998
JScript 5.0	Internet Explorer 5.0	1999
JavaScript 1.5	Netscape Navigator 6.0	2001

Other client-side programming languages are also available to Web page designers, such as the Internet Explorer scripting language, **VBScript**. However, because of the nearly universal support for JavaScript, you'll use this language for your work with North Pole Novelties.

Running **JavaScript**

Your task is to use JavaScript to create a Web page that displays the days remaining until Christmas on the company's home page. Figure 8-5 shows the layout of the home page.

Figure 8-5	NORTH POLE NOVELTIES HOME PAGE

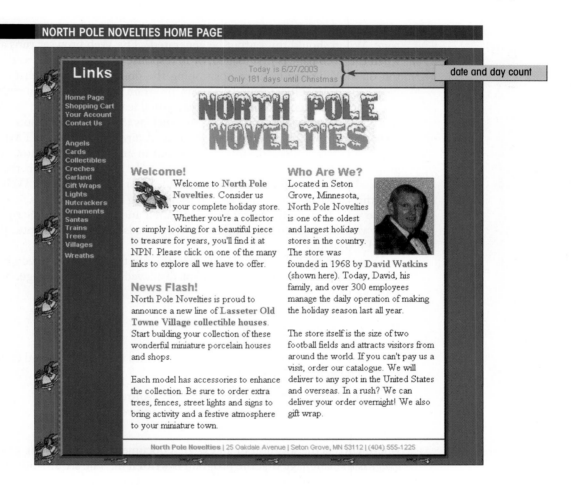

date and day count

The information shown in Figure 8-5 has been explicitly entered into the HTML file and, therefore, works only if the date is June 27, 2003. Andrew wants a program that works for any date. Furthermore, if the current date falls between December 25 and December 31, he wants the page to display the text "Happy Holidays from North Pole Novelties" instead of the day count.

Before you begin writing a program, it's a good idea to outline the main tasks you want the program to perform. In this case, the tasks are as follows:

> ☐ 1) Learn how to display text on a Web page using JavaScript
> ☐ 2) Display date values on a Web page
> ☐ 3) Calculate the number of days between the test date and December 25th
> ☐ 4) If the date is December 25th or later (through December 31st), display a
>   greeting message; otherwise, display the number of days remaining until Christmas

Your first task is to create and run a JavaScript program that sends output to your Web page. When should this output be generated? The Web browser runs a JavaScript program when the Web page is first loaded, or in response to an event such as the user clicking a button on a Web page form or positioning the pointer over a hypertext link. In the case of North Pole Novelties, your JavaScript program will run automatically when the browser loads the Web page. In the next tutorial, you'll learn how to create JavaScript programs that run in response to user-initiated events, such as the clicking of a button.

JavaScript programs can either be placed directly into the HTML file or they can be saved in external files. Placing the program in an external file allows you to hide the program code from the user, whereas source code placed directly in the HTML file can be viewed by anyone. However, an external file must be stored on the Web server, which means that the server has the added task of transferring both the Web page and the JavaScript file to the user. Generally, the more complicated and larger the JavaScript program, the more likely you are to place it in an external file. In this tutorial you'll enter the code directly into the HTML file.

When you place JavaScript code directly into the HTML file, you need some way of distinguishing it from text that you want displayed on the Web page. You do this using the <script> tag.

Using the <script> Tag

The <script> tag is a two-sided tag that identifies the beginning and end of a client-side program. The general syntax for this tag is:

```
<script src="URL" language="language">
        Script commands and comments
<script>
```

where *URL* is the location of an external document containing the program code, and *language* is the language that the program is written in. The src attribute is required only if the program is placed in a separate file. The language attribute is needed so that the browser knows which interpreter to use with the client-side program code. The default language value is "JavaScript." Note that Internet Explorer interprets "JavaScript" as being identical to "JScript." If you omit the language attribute, the browser assumes that the program is written in JavaScript.

<u>Inserting a Client-Side Program</u>

■ To insert a client-side program into an HTML file, use the following syntax:

```
<script src="URL" language="language">
        Script commands and comments
</script>
```

where *URL* is the location of the file containing the programming commands, if you choose to store the program in an external file, and the language attribute is the programming language of the client-side program. To create a JavaScript program, set the language attribute to "JavaScript" or omit the language attribute, and the Web browser assumes that JavaScript is the programming language by default.

Your program can be placed anywhere within the HTML file. Many programmers favor placing their programs between <head> tags in order to separate the programming code from the Web page content and layout, while others prefer placing programs within the body of the Web page at the location where the program output is generated and displayed. In this tutorial, you'll do a little of both.

Hiding Your Script from Older Browsers

Older browsers that do not support JavaScript can present a problem for Web designers. If such browsers encounter JavaScript commands, they may display the program code as part of the Web page body. To avoid this problem, you can hide the script from these browsers using comment tags.

You've already used comment tags in your HTML files to provide additional information regarding your HTML code. JavaScript supports similar comment tags, using a set of double slashes (//) at the beginning of a line that instructs the browser to ignore the line and not interpret it as a JavaScript command.

By combining the HTML comment tag and JavaScript comment symbols, you can hide your JavaScript program from browsers that don't support the <script> tag. The syntax for doing this is as follows:

```
<script language="JavaScript">
<!-- Hide from non-JavaScript browsers
    JavaScript commands
// Stop hiding from older browsers -->
</script>
```

When a Web browser that doesn't support scripts encounters this code, it ignores the <script> tag, as it does any tag it doesn't recognize. The next line it sees is the start of the HTML comment tag, which doesn't close until the > symbol in the second-to-last line. So, everything in the JavaScript program is ignored. The final </script> tag is similarly ignored by the older browser.

A browser that supports JavaScript recognizes the <script> tag and ignores any HTML tags found between the <script> and </script> tags. Therefore, in this example, it bypasses the comment tag in the second line and processes the JavaScript program as written. The JavaScript comment (starting with the // symbol) in the second-to-last line is there to help other users understand and interpret your code.

Having seen the basic structure of a JavaScript program, you're ready to insert the necessary code into the North Pole Novelties home page. Your first task will be to delete the

HTML tags that contain the 6/27/2003 date information because you'll replace that information with a program that works for any date, not just June, 27, 2003.

To begin creating your programmable Web page:

1. Using your text editor, open **npntxt.htm** from the tutorial.08/tutorial folder on your Data Disk, and save the file as **npn.htm** in the same folder.

2. Scroll through the file until you locate the HTML comment tag, "<--- Days until Christmas --->".

3. Delete the following code:

```
Today is 6/27/2003<br>
Only 181 days until Christmas
```

4. Insert the following code in place of the code you just deleted (it's a good idea to indent the new code to make the code easier to interpret):

```
<script language="JavaScript">
    <!-- Hide from non-JavaScript browsers
    // Stop hiding -->
</script>
```

Your file should appear as shown in Figure 8-6. At this point, no date information would display on the Web page if opened with a browser.

Figure 8-6	INSERTING A JAVASCRIPT PROGRAM INTO AN HTML FILE

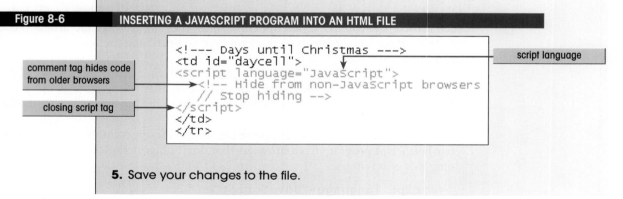

5. Save your changes to the file.

With the <script> tags and comments in place, your next task is to write a JavaScript program that sends output to the Web page. Because you haven't yet learned how to determine the current date or calculate the number of days between the current date and December 25, this program is limited to displaying a simple text string.

Sending Output to a Web Page

JavaScript provides two methods to display text on a Web page: the document.write() and document.writeln() method. The syntax for these commands is:

```
document.write("text");
document.writeln("text");
```

where *text* is a string of characters for display on the Web page. The following method shows how to display the text "Only 45 days until Christmas" in the Web page:

```
document.write("Only 45 days until Christmas");
```

The document.write() and document.writeln() methods reflect the object-oriented nature of the JavaScript language. Here, "document" is an object (the page that your Web browser is accessing), and "write()" or "writeln()" are actions that can be applied to the document. You'll learn more about objects and methods in the next tutorial. For now, when the term "method" is used, understand that it means an action applied to something existing on your Web page or in your Web browser.

Most of the time you'll use the document.write() method. The document.writeln() method differs from document.write()in that it attaches a carriage return to the end of each text string sent to the Web page. This becomes relevant only when the text string is formatted with the <pre> tag for which the browser recognizes the existence of carriage returns.

REFERENCE WINDOW **RW**

Sending Output to a Web Page

- To display text on your Web page, use the following JavaScript commands:

```
document.write("text");
```

or

```
document.writeln("text");
```

where *text* is the text and HTML tags to be sent to your Web page. The document.write() and document.writeln() methods are identical, except that the document.writeln() method attaches a carriage return to the text. This difference is important only if you are formatting the text using the <pre> tag.

You're not limited to displaying text; you can also include HTML tags in the text string to format the text and to insert images. For example, the following command displays the text "News Flash!" formatted with the <h3> header tag:

```
document.write("<h3>News Flash!</h3>");
```

The text string specified by the document.write() method can be enclosed within either double or single quotation marks. This allows you to write a text string that includes attribute values. Consider the following JavaScript command:

```
document.write('<td class="calendar_head" colspan="7">');
```

This command writes the table cell tag:

```
<td class="calendar_head" colspan="7">;
```

to the Web page. Alternately, you can display single quotation marks by enclosing your text string within double quotation marks.

There are some syntax issues you should be aware of with JavaScript. Most JavaScript commands and names are case-sensitive. You can use the command "document.write()", but you cannot replace that command with "Document.Write()" without JavaScript generating an error message.

Note that each JavaScript command line ends with a semicolon to separate it from the next command line in the program. In some situations, the semicolon is optional, but it is a good idea to use it to make your code easier to follow and interpret.

Now that you've learned the basics for the document.write() method, you'll add it to a JavaScript program. Because this is your first program, you'll only have it display the number of days until Christmas, assuming that the current date is December 15, 2003.

To display text on your Web page with JavaScript:

1. Insert the following two commands directly below the line "<!--- Hide from non-JavaScript browsers":

```
document.write("Today is 12/15/2003<br>");
document.write("Only 10 days until Christmas");
```

Note that the text you're sending to the Web page includes the <br> tag to create a line break between the date and the number of days until Christmas. Figure 8-7 shows the revised file.

| Figure 8-7 | USING JAVASCRIPT TO DISPLAY TEXT ON A WEB PAGE |

```
<!--- Days until Christmas --->
<td id="daycell">
<script language="JavaScript">
   <!-- Hide from non-JavaScript browsers
   document.write("Today is 12/15/2003<br>");
   document.write("Only 10 days until Christmas");
   // Stop hiding -->
</script>
</td>
</tr>
```

2. Save your changes to npn.htm and then open it in your Web browser. The browser displays the date and days information you inserted into your JavaScript program.

   TROUBLE? If you receive a JavaScript error message, close the Error Message dialog box and return to your text editor. Compare the code you entered to the code shown in the steps. Minor errors, such as omitting a quotation mark, can cause your program to fail.

| REFERENCE WINDOW | RW |

Tips for Writing a JavaScript Program
- Use comments extensively to document your program and its features. Comments help you and others better understand the program code.
- Use indented text where appropriate to make your code easier to read and interpret.
- Be careful how you use uppercase and lowercase letters in your code, because most JavaScript commands and names are case-sensitive.
- Enclose your JavaScript commands within HTML comment tags to hide your JavaScript code from older browsers that do not support JavaScript.
- Test your JavaScript program using a variety of browsers and browser versions. Some browsers might not support the commands you have written.

You've completed your first JavaScript program! True, the program does little more than display text you could have entered directly with HTML, but it's a program you'll build on over the following sessions to complete the more sophisticated tasks required to meet Andrew's goals for the North Pole Novelties Web page.

Session 8.1 QUICK CHECK

1. What is a client-side program? What is a server-side program?

2. Describe two differences between Java and JavaScript.

3. What are the two ways JavaScript can be run from a Web page?

4. What HTML tags would you use to indicate the beginning and end of a JavaScript program?

5. Why should you place your JavaScript commands within an HTML comment tag?

6. What JavaScript command would you use to place the text "Avalon Books", formatted with the h1 heading style, into your Web page?

SESSION 8.2

In this session you'll learn some of the fundamentals of the JavaScript language. You'll learn how to create variables and how to work with different data types. You'll also learn about expressions and operators and how to use them to change variable values. Finally, you'll create your own JavaScript function and use it in a program.

Working with Variables and Data

In the previous session you learned how to insert text into your Web page using the document.write() method. Because you specified the text explicitly, the program did no more than what could have been accomplished by placing the text directly in the HTML file. The next task on your list for the North Pole Novelties home page is to have your program determine the current date and then display that information on the Web page.

● 1) Learn how to display text on a Web page using JavaScript
○ 2) Display date values on a Web page
○ 3) Calculate the number of days between the test date and December 25th
○ 4) If the date is December 25th or later (through December 31st), display a greeting message; otherwise, display the number of days remaining until Christmas

---

To do this, you need to create a JavaScript variable. A **variable** is a named element in a program that stores information. Variables are useful because they can store information created in one part of your program and use that information in another. For example, you can create a variable named "Year" to store the value of the current year, and then use the Year variable at different locations in your program.

To assign the value 2003 to the variable "Year", enter the following JavaScript command:

```
Year=2003;
```

With the Year variable assigned a value, you can use the document.write() method to display this value on the Web page, as follows:

```
document.write(Year);
```

This code displays the text "2003" on the Web page. You can also combine text with the variable value by using a plus symbol (+), as shown in the following example:

```
document.write("The year is " + Year);
```

This command displays the text "The year is 2003" on the Web page.

In the program you're creating for Andrew, you won't explicitly enter the date information. Instead, your program determines the current date and year for you and stores that information in a variable so that you can use it later in the program. For now, you'll learn about variables by entering a fixed value.

The following restrictions apply to your variable names:

- The first character must be either a letter or an underscore character (_).
- The remaining characters can be letters, numbers, or underscore characters.
- Variable names cannot contain spaces.
- You cannot use words that JavaScript has reserved for other purposes. For example, you cannot name a variable "document.write".

Variable names are case-sensitive. A variable named "Year" is different from a variable named "YEAR". If your JavaScript program isn't working properly, it may be because you did not match the uppercase and lowercase letters.

Types of Variables

JavaScript supports four different types of variables:

- numeric variables
- string variables
- Boolean variables
- null variables

A **numeric variable** can be any number, such as 13, 22.5, or -3.14159. Numbers also can be expressed in scientific notation: for example, 5.1E2 for the value 5.1×10^2, or 510. A **string variable** is any group of characters, such as "Hello" or "Happy Holidays!" Strings must be enclosed within either double or single quotation marks, but not both; the string value 'Hello' is acceptable, but the string value "Hello' is not. **Boolean variables** are variables that accept one of two values, either true or false. They are most often used in programs that have to act differently based on different conditions. For example, one can create a Boolean variable to determine whether the user is running the Netscape browser or not. If the value of this Boolean variable is true, the program would run differently for Netscape users than otherwise. Finally, a **null variable** is a variable that has no value at all. This happens when you've created a variable in the program, but have not assigned it a value yet. Once a value has been assigned to a variable, it falls into one of the three previous data types.

Declaring a Variable

Before you can use a variable in your program, you need to create it; also known as **declaring a variable**. You declare a variable in JavaScript using the **var** command or by assigning the variable a value. Any of the following commands is a legitimate way of creating a variable named "Month":

```
var Month;
var Month = "December";
Month = "December";
```

The first command creates the variable without assigning it a value, while the second and third commands both create the variable and assign it a value.

It's considered good programming style to include the var command whenever you create a variable. Doing so helps you keep track of the variables the program uses and also makes it easier for others to read and interpret your code. Many Web designers place all of their variable declarations at the beginning of the program along with comments describing the purpose of each variable in the program.

REFERENCE WINDOW **RW**

Declaring a JavaScript Variable
- You can create (declare) variables with any of the following JavaScript commands:
```
var variable;
var variable = value;
variable = value;
```
where *variable* is the name of the variable, and *value* is the initial value of the variable. The first command creates the variable without assigning it a value; the second and third commands both create the variable and assign it a value.

You need to create the following variables for your JavaScript program:

- **Today** — containing information about the current date and time
- **ThisDay** — storing the current day of the month
- **ThisMonth** — storing a number indicating the current month
- **ThisYear** — storing a number indicating the current year
- **DaysLeft** — storing the number of days until December 25

To add variables to the JavaScript program:

1. Using your text editor, open **npn.htm**.

2. Insert the following JavaScript code directly below the "<!--- Hide from non-JavaScript browsers" line (see Figure 8-8):

```
var Today;
var ThisDay;
var ThisMonth;
var ThisYear;
var DaysLeft;
```

Figure 8-8   **DECLARING JAVASCRIPT VARIABLES**

variable declarations →

```
<!--- Days until Christmas --->
<td id="daycell">
<script language="JavaScript">
   <!-- Hide from non-JavaScript browsers
  var Today;
  var ThisDay;
  var ThisMonth;
  var ThisYear;
  var DaysLeft;
   document.write("Today is 12/15/2003<br>");
   document.write("Only 10 days until Christmas");
   // Stop hiding -->
</script>
</td>
</tr>
```

Now that you've declared the variables, you need to use the JavaScript date methods to calculate the variable values.

Working **with Dates**

In your program for North Pole Novelties, you'll be working with dates as you calculate the number of days remaining until December 25. JavaScript does not provide a date data type as some other programming languages do. However, it does allow you to create a **date object**, which is an object containing date information. There are two ways to create a date object:

```
variable = new Date("month, day, year, hours:minutes:
seconds")
```

or

```
variable = new Date(year, month, day, hours, minutes,
seconds)
```

where *variable* is the name of the variable that contains the date information, and *month*, *day*, *year*, *hours*, *minutes*, and *seconds* indicate the date and time. In the previous example, the keyword **new** indicates that you're creating a new object. Note that in the first command form you specify the date using a text string, and in the second command form you use values. Both of the following commands creates a variable named "SomeDay" corresponding to a date of June 15, 2003, and a time of 2:35 p.m.:

```
SomeDay = new Date("June, 15, 2003, 14:35:00");
SomeDay = new Date(2003, 5, 15, 14, 35, 0);
```

In this example, you may have noticed a couple of interesting things regarding how JavaScript handles dates. First, when you specify the month with values rather than a text string, you must subtract 1 from the month number. This is because JavaScript numbers the months 0 for January through 11 for December. So, in the second command, the date for June 15 is expressed as (2003, 5, 15 ...) and not as (2003, 6, 15 ...) as you might have expected. Also note that hours are expressed in military (24-hour) time (14:35 rather than 2:35 P.M.).

If you omit the hours, minutes, and seconds values, JavaScript assumes that the time is 0 hours, 0 minutes, and 0 seconds. If you omit both the date and time information, JavaScript returns the current date and time, which it gets from the system clock on the user's computer.

The following command creates a variable named "Today" that contains information about the current date and time:

```
Today = new Date();
```

This command is eventually what you'll want to use in your program.

REFERENCE WINDOW **RW**

Creating a Date and Time Variable

- To store a date and time in a variable, use the following JavaScript command:

  `variable = new Date("month, day, year, hours:minutes:seconds")`

  or

  `variable = new Date(year, month, day, hours, minutes, seconds)`

  For example, the following commands create a date and time variable named DayVariable, representing the same date and time:

  `DayVariable = new Date("April, 4, 2003, 16:40:00");`

  `DayVariable = new Date(2003, 3, 4, 16, 40, 0);`

- Use the following command to return the current date and time:

  `variable = new Date();`

Now that you've seen how to store date and time information in a variable, you can add that feature to the JavaScript program. Eventually, you'll want to set the Today variable to whatever the current date is. For now, use the date, October 15, 2003, so that a single date is discussed throughout this tutorial.

To enter a value for the Today variable:

1. Return to **npn.htm** in your text editor.

2. Change the line that declares the Today variable from "var Today;" to:

   `var Today=new Date("October 15, 2003");`

3. Save your changes to the file.

Retrieving the Day Value

The Today variable has all the date and time information that you need, but unfortunately, it's not in a form that is very useful to you. The problem is that JavaScript stores dates and times as the number of milliseconds since 6 P.M. on December 31, 1969. All of the JavaScript date and time functions are numerical calculations of these hidden numbers. Fortunately, you don't have to do the calculations that translate those numbers into dates. Instead, you can use some of the built-in JavaScript date methods to do the calculations for you. For each part of the date that you want displayed in your Web page, or used in a calculation, you need a date method to retrieve its value.

For example, you want the ThisDay variable to store the day of the month. To get that information, you apply the **getDate()** method to your date variable. The general syntax of this method is:

```
DayValue = DateObject.getDate()
```

where *DayValue* is the name of a variable that contains the day of the month, and *DateObject* is a date object or a date variable that contains the complete date and time information. To apply this method to the Today variable, you would use the command:

```
ThisDay = Today.getDate();
```

and then day of month would be stored in the ThisDay variable. If the current date is October 15, 2003, then the ThisDay variable would have the value "15".

REFERENCE WINDOW | **RW**

__Retrieving Date and Time Values__
- To retrieve the year value from a date object, use the command:
  `Year = DateObject.getYear();`
- To retrieve the month value from a date and time variable named *DateObject,* use the command:
  `Month = DateObject.getMonth();`
- To retrieve the day of the month value from a date and time variable named *DateObject,* use the command:
  `Day = DateObject.getDate();`
- To retrieve the day of the week value from a date and time variable named *DateObject,* use the command:
  `DayofWeek = DateObject.getDay();`

Retrieving the Month Value

A similar method exists for extracting the value of the current month. This method is named **getMonth()**. Note that because JavaScript starts counting the months with 0 for January, you may want to add 1 to the month number returned by the getMonth() method. The following JavaScript code extracts the current month number, increases it by 1, and stores it in a variable named ThisMonth:

```
ThisMonth = Today.getMonth()+1;
```

For a date of October 15, the ThisMonth variable would have a value of "10".

Retrieving the Year Value

The final date method you'll be using in your program is the getFullYear () method. As the name suggests, the **getFullYear()** method extracts the year value from the date variable. The following code shows how you would store the value of the current year in a variable you name ThisYear:

```
ThisYear = Today.getFullYear();
```

If the date stored in the Today variable is October 15, 2003, the value of the getFullYear variable is "2003".

Why is the method name getFullYear(), and not simply, getYear()? There is a getYear() method, but the limitation with this method is that it returns only the last two digits of the year for years prior to 2000. For example, instead of 1999, a date of 99 would be returned. As shown in Figure 8-9, you run into difficulty once you get beyond the year 1999.

Figure 8-9	VALUES OF THE GETYEAR() METHOD FROM 1998 TO 2001

YEAR	GETYEAR() VALUE
1998	98
1999	99
2000	2000
2001	2001

The getYear() date method returns a value of 2000 for year 2000, so if you use it to calculate the number of years between 1998 and 2000, you would come up with an answer of 1902 years! This is a classic example of a Y2K bug that caused so much concern in the late 1990s with the new millennium approaching. The getFullYear() date method was introduced in JavaScript 1.3 to correct this problem, and it is supported by Netscape 4.5 and Internet Explorer 4.0 and above. So even though there is a getYear() date method, you should not use it if your program is calculating a difference in dates before and after the year 2000. In this program, we'll use the getFullYear() date method.

Most of the date methods you can use with JavaScript are shown in Figure 8-10.

Figure 8-10	DATE METHODS

METHOD	DESCRIPTION	VALUE
In the following examples, assume that the variable Today stores the date object: Date("April, 8, 2004, 12:25:28")		
Today.getSeconds()	Retrieves the seconds from the date	28
Today.getMinutes()	Retrieves the minutes from the date	25
Today.getHours()	Retrieves the hour from the date	12
Today.getDate()	Retrieves the day of the month from the date	8
Today.getDay()	Retrieves the day of the week from the date (0=Sunday, 1=Monday, 2=Tuesday, 3=Wednesday, 4=Thursday, 5=Friday, 6=Saturday)	4
Today.getMonth()	Retrieves the month from the date (0=January, 1=February, ...)	3
Today.getFullYear()	Retrieves the four digit year number from the date	2004
Today.getTime()	Retrieves the time value, as expressed in milliseconds since December 31, 1969, 6 P.M.	1,081,445,128,000

Now that you've learned how to extract date information, you are ready to modify your JavaScript program to work with the Today variable. Remember, eventually you'll set up the program to use whatever the current date is, but for now, you'll use October 15, 2003 to test the program.

To calculate the day, month, and year values:

1. Return to **npn.htm** in your text editor.

2. Modify the variable declarations for the ThisDay, ThisMonth, and ThisYear variables, so they read as follows:

```
var ThisDay=Today.getDate();
var ThisMonth=Today.getMonth()+1;
var ThisYear=Today.getFullYear();
```

To display this date information in your Web page, use the command:

```
document.write("Today is "+ThisMonth+"/"+ThisDay+"/"+ThisYear
+"<br>");
```

If the current date is October 15, 2003, JavaScript displays the following text:

```
Today is 10/15/2003
```

You haven't calculated the value of the DaysLeft variable yet. At this point, you'll set this value equal to "999". You'll learn how to calculate the true value shortly.

To display the day, month, and year values:

1. Modify the variable declaration for the DaysLeft variable to read:

```
var DaysLeft=999;
```

2. Replace the first document.write() command with the:

```
document.write("Today is "+ThisMonth+"/"+ThisDay+"/
"+ThisYear+"<br>");
```

3. Replace the second document.write() command with:

```
document.write("Only "+DaysLeft+" days until Christmas"
);
```

When entering this code, be sure to carefully note the placement of the double quotation marks and uppercase and lowercase letters. Your complete code should appear as shown in Figure 8-11.

Figure 8-11	RETRIEVING DATE INFORMATION WITH JAVASCRIPT

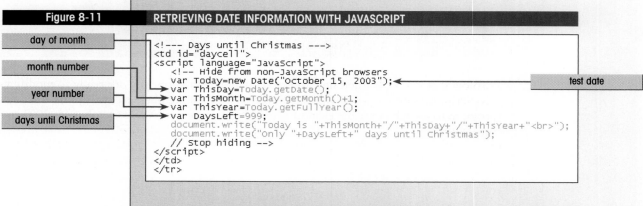

```
<!--- Days until Christmas --->
<td id="daycell">
<script language="JavaScript">
    <!-- Hide from non-JavaScript browsers
    var Today=new Date("October 15, 2003");          ← test date
    var ThisDay=Today.getDate();                      ← day of month
    var ThisMonth=Today.getMonth()+1;                 ← month number
    var ThisYear=Today.getFullYear();                 ← year number
    var DaysLeft=999;                                 ← days until Christmas
    document.write("Today is "+ThisMonth+"/"+ThisDay+"/"+ThisYear+"<br>");
    document.write("Only "+DaysLeft+" days until Christmas");
    // Stop hiding -->
</script>
</td>
</tr>
```

4. Save your changes to the file, and then open npn.htm in your Web browser. The revised page should appear as shown in Figure 8-12.

Figure 8-12 DISPLAYING THE DATE VALUES

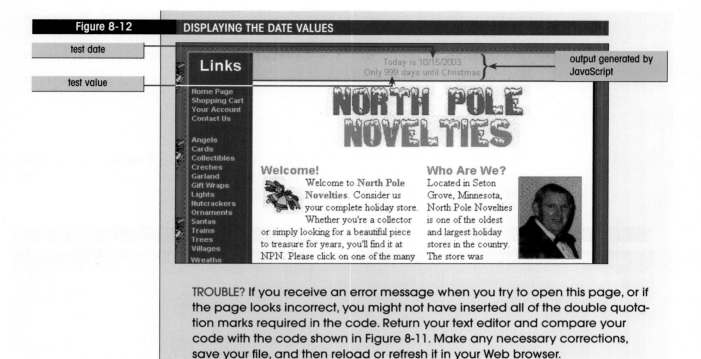

test date

test value

output generated by JavaScript

TROUBLE? If you receive an error message when you try to open this page, or if the page looks incorrect, you might not have inserted all of the double quotation marks required in the code. Return your text editor and compare your code with the code shown in Figure 8-11. Make any necessary corrections, save your file, and then reload or refresh it in your Web browser.

You've completed the second item on your task list, displaying date information on the Web page.

1) Learn how to display text on a Web page using JavaScript
2) Display date values on a Web page
3) Calculate the number of days between the test date and December 25th
4) If the date is December 25th or later (through December 31st), display a greeting message; otherwise, display the number of days remaining until Christmas

Your next step is to take those date values and use them to calculate the days remaining until December 25. To do this, you must learn how to work with expressions, operators, and functions.

Working with Expressions and Operators

Expressions are JavaScript commands that assign values to your variables. You've already worked with several expressions in your JavaScript program. For example, you used the expression, DaysLeft=999, to assign the value 999 to the DaysLeft variable. Expressions are created using variables, values, and **operators** (elements that perform actions within the expression). One of the most commonly used operators is the **+ operator**, which performs the action of adding or combining two elements. You used the plus operator in your program with the following command:

```
var ThisMonth = Today.getMonth()+1;
```

to increase the value returned by the getMonth() method by 1. You also used the + operator to combine text strings:

```
document.write("Only " + DaysLeft + " days until Christmas");
```

In both of these examples, the plus operator combines two or more values or elements to create a single value or element.

Arithmetic Operators

The + operator belongs to a group of operators called **arithmetic operators**, which perform simple mathematical calculations. Figure 8-13 lists some of the arithmetic operators and gives examples of how they work.

Figure 8-13	ARITHMETIC OPERATORS	
OPERATOR	**DESCRIPTION**	**EXAMPLE**

+	Adds two values together	var Men = 20;
		var Women = 25;
		var TotalPeople = Men + Women;

−	Subtracts one value from another	var Price = 1000;
		var Expense = 750;
		var Profit = Price - Expense;

*	Multiplies two values together	var Width = 50;
		var Length = 25;
		var Area = Width*Length;

/	Divides one value by another	var People = 50;
		var TotalCost = 200;
		var CostperPerson = TotalCost/People;

%	Shows the remainder after dividing one value by another	var TotalEggs = 64;
		var CartonSize = 12;
		var EggsLeft = TotalEggs % CartonSize;

++	Increases a value by 1 (unary operator)	var Eggs = 12; var BakersDozen = Eggs++;
- -	Decreases a value by 1 (unary operator)	var Eggs = 12; var EggsIfOneIsBroken = Eggs- -;
−	Changes the sign of a value (unary operator)	var MyGain = 50; var YourLoss = − MyGain;

Some of the arithmetic operators in Figure 8-13 are also known as **binary operators** because they work on two elements in an expression. There are also **unary operators**, which work on only one variable. Unary operators include: the increment (++), decrement (--), and negation (-) operators. The **increment operator** can be used to increase the value of a variable by 1. In the following code, an increment operator is used to increase the value of the x variable by one. Thus, after both commands are run, the value of the x variable is 100 and the value of the y variable is 101.

```
x = 100;
y = x++;
```

You do not always have to assign the value of one variable to another. For example, the following code:

```
x++;
```

increases the value of the x variable by 1. If the original value of the x variable is 100, this command increases its value by 1 to 101.

The decrement operator has the opposite effect, reducing the value of a variable by 1. The following JavaScript code assigns the value 100 to the x variable and 99 to the y variable:

```
x = 100;
y = x--;
```

Finally, the negation operator changes the sign of a variable, as in the following example:

```
x = -100;
y = -x;
```

In this example, the value of the x variable is -100, and the value of the y variable is opposite that, or 100.

Assignment Operators

Expressions assign values using **assignment operators**. The most common assignment operator is the equals (=) sign. JavaScript provides additional assignment operators that manipulate elements in an expression and assign values within a single operation. One of these is the += operator. In JavaScript, the following two expressions create the same result:

```
x = x + y;
x += y
```

In both expressions, the value of the x variable is added to the value of the y variable and then the new variable is stored back into the x variable.

An assignment operator also can be used with numbers to increase a variable by a specific amount. For example, to increase the value of the x variable by 2, you can use either of the following two expressions:

```
x = x + 2;
x += 2
```

A common use of the += operator is to create extended text strings. In this case, the operator appends one text string to another. For example, if you have a text string that covers several lines, you may find it difficult to store that text in a variable using a single command. However, you can do so in the following manner:

```
quote = "To be or not to be. ";
quote +="That is the question. ";
quote +="Whether tis nobler of the mind to suffer the slings
and arrows of outrageous fortune, ";
quote +="Or to take arm against a sea of troubles";
quote +="And by opposing end them. ";
...
```

Continuing in this fashion, the quote variable eventually contains the complete text of Hamlet's soliloquy, but it does so using a series of short, simple expressions rather than one long and cumbersome expression. This technique is often used to store large sections of HTML code. The code for an entire Web page could be created in this fashion. Other assignment operators are discussed in Figure 8-14.

Figure 8-14	ASSIGNMENT OPERATORS
OPERATOR	**DESCRIPTION**
=	Assigns the value of the variable on the right to the variable on the left (x = y)
+=	Adds the two variables and assigns the result to the variable on the left (equivalent to x = x + y)
−=	Subtracts the variable on the right from the variable on the left and assigns the result to the variable on the left (equivalent to x = x − y)
*=	Multiplies the two variables together and assigns the result to the variable on the left (equivalent to x = x*y)
/=	Divides the variable on the left by the variable on the right and assigns the result to the variable on the left (equivalent to x = x/y)
%=	Divides the variable on the left by the variable on the right and assigns the remainder to the variable on the left (equivalent to x = x % y)

As you can see, once you master the syntax, assignment operators allow you to create expressions that are both efficient and compact. As you start learning JavaScript, you might prefer using the longer form for such expressions. However, if you study the code of other JavaScript programmers, you will certainly encounter programs that make substantial use of assignment operators to reduce program size.

The Math Object and Math Methods

Another way of performing a calculation is to use one of the JavaScript built-in Math methods. These methods are applied to an object called the **Math object**. The syntax for applying a Math method is:

```
value = Math.method(variable);
```

where *method* is the method you'll apply to a variable, and *value* is the resulting value. For example, to calculate the absolute value of a variable named NumVar, you use the "abs" method as follows:

```
AbsValue = Math.abs(NumVar);
```

and the value of the AbsValue variable is set to the absolute value of the NumVar variable. Figure 8-15 lists some additional math methods supported by JavaScript.

Figure 8-15	MATH METHODS
MATH METHOD	**DESCRIPTION**
Math.abs(*number*)	Returns the absolute value of *number*
Math.sin(*number*)	Calculates the sine of *number*, where *number* is an angle expressed in radians
Math.cos(*number*)	Calculates the cosine of *number*, where *number* is an angle expressed in radians
Math.round(*number*)	Rounds *number* to the closet integer
Math.ceil(*number*)	Rounds *number* up to the next highest integer
Math.floor(*number*)	Rounds *number* down to the next lowest integer
Math.random()	Returns a random number between 0 and 1

As you probably guessed, case is important with JavaScript commands. You must type "Math" (with an uppercase M) instead of "math" when using these commands.

Creating **JavaScript Functions**

You can use all of the JavaScript expressions and operators to create your own customized functions. A **function** is a series of commands that performs an action or calculates a value. A function consists of the **function name**, which identifies it; **parameters**, which are values used by the function; and a set of commands that are run when the function is used. Not all functions require parameters. The general syntax of a JavaScript function is:

```
function function_name(parameters){
    JavaScript commands
}
```

where *function_name* is the name of the function, *parameters* are the values sent to the function, and *JavaScript commands* are the actual commands and expressions used by the function. Note that curly braces   } are used to mark the beginning and end of the commands in the function. The group of commands set off by the curly braces is called a **command block** and, as you'll see, command blocks exist for other JavaScript structures in addition to functions.

Function names, like variable names, are case-sensitive. XMASDAYS and XmasDays are different function names. The function name must begin with a letter or underscore (_) and cannot contain any spaces.

There is no limit to the number of function parameters that a function may contain. The parameters must be placed within parentheses, following the function name, and the parameters must be separated by commas.

REFERENCE WINDOW   **RW**

Creating and Using a JavaScript Function

- To create a user-defined function, use the following syntax:

```
function function_name(parameters){
    JavaScript commands
}
```

   where *function_name* is the name of the function, *parameters* are the parameters of the function and are separated by commas, and the opening and closing braces enclose the *JavaScript commands* used by the function.

- To run, or call, a user-defined function, use the following command:

```
function_name(values);
```

   where *function_name* is the name of the function, and *values* are the values substituted for each of the function parameters.

Performing an Action with a Function

To see how a function works, consider the following function, which displays a message with the current date:

```
function ShowDate(date) {
    document.write("Today is " + date + "<br>");
}
```

In this example, the function name is ShowDate, and it has one parameter, date. There is one line in the function's command block, which displays the current date along with a text string. To run a function, you insert a JavaScript command containing the function name and any parameters it requires. This process is known as **calling** a function. To call the ShowDate function, enter the following commands:

```
var Today = "3/25/2003";
ShowDate(Today);
```

In this example, the first command creates a variable named "Today" and assigns it the text string, "3/25/2003". The second command runs the ShowDate function, using the value of the Today variable as a parameter. The result of calling the ShowDate function is that the following sentence is displayed on the Web page:

Today is 3/25/2003

Returning a Value from a Function

You can also use a function to calculate a value. This is achieved by placing a **return** command along with a variable or value, at the end of the function command block. Consider the following Area function:

```
function Area(Width, Length) {
    var Size = Width*Length;
    return Size;
}
```

Here, the Area function calculates the area of a rectangular region and places the value in a variable named "Size". The value of the Size variable is returned by the function. A simple JavaScript program that uses this function might appear as follows:

```
var x = 8;
var y = 6;
var z = Area(x,y);
```

The first two commands assign the values 8 and 6 to the x and y variables, respectively. The values of both of these variables are then sent to the Area function, corresponding to the Width and Length parameters. The Area function uses these values to calculate the area, which it then returns, assigning that value to the z variable. As a result of these commands, 48 is assigned to the value of the z variable.

Placing a Function in an HTML File

Where you place a function in the HTML file is important. The function definition must be placed before the command that calls the function. If you try to call a function before it is defined, you might receive an error message from the browser. Although not a requirement, one programming convention is to place all of the function definitions used in the Web page between the <head> and </head> tags. This ensures that each function definition has been read and interpreted before being called by the JavaScript commands in the body of the Web page. When the browser loads the HTML file containing a function, the browser bypasses the function without executing it. The function is executed only when called by another JavaScript command.

If you plan to use your functions in several Web pages, you can place the function in a separate file and access the function from each Web page. To access the externally located function, insert the following command in the head section of the HTML file:

```
<script src="URL" language="JavaScript"></script>
```

Where *URL* is the filename and location of the external file containing the functions. Once you've done this, any function defined in the external file can be used anywhere within the Web page. It's common practice for JavaScript programmers to create libraries of functions located in external files to be easily accessible to many Web pages.

Create the XmasDays Function

You now have all of the information you need to create your own function, the XmasDays function. The function has only one parameter, CurrentDay, which contains the current date. The function returns one value, the number of days between the current date and December 25 of the current year. The function has three variables:

- **XYear**: The current year
- **XDay**: The date of Christmas. The initial value of this variable is the date "December 25, 2003."
- **DayCount**: The number of days between current date and December 25. This is the value that is returned by the function.

The initial command block of the XmasDays function looks as follows:

```
function XmasDays(CurrentDay) {
   var XYear=CurrentDay.getFullYear();
   var XDay=new Date("December, 25, 2003");
}
```

These commands set the initial values of the XYear and XDay variables. However, the function needs to change the value of the XDay variable from December, 25, 2003 to December 25 of the current year. After all, it might not be 2003! This is done using the JavaScript **setFullYear()** method. The command looks as follows:

```
XDay.setFullYear(XYear);
```

If the current year is actually 2004, the date stored in the XDay variable changes from "December 25, 2003" to "December 25, 2004". Figure 8-16 shows other JavaScript functions that allow you to set or change the values of date objects.

| Figure 8-16 | SETTING DATE VALUES |

METHOD	DESCRIPTION
DateObject.setSeconds(seconds)	Set the seconds value of the DateObject to seconds
DateObject.setMinutes(minutes)	Set the minutes value of the DateObject to minutes
DateObject.setHours(hours)	Set the hours value of the DateObject to hours
DateObject.setDate(date)	Set the day of the month value of the DateObject to date
DateObject.setMonth(month)	Set the month value of the DateObject to month
DateObject.setFullYear(year)	Set the full year (four digit) value of the DateObject to year
DateObject.setTime(time)	Set the time of the DateObject to time, which is the number of milliseconds since December 31, 1969 at 6 P.M.

Next, the function needs to calculate the time difference between December 25 and the current date. This would be:

```
var DayCount=XDay - CurrentDay;
```

There's a problem. Remember that JavaScript stores date information in terms of milliseconds. Taking the difference between these two dates calculates the number of milliseconds before Christmas. This is hardly the information you want to display on your Web page. To make it a more meaningful statistic, you must convert this value into days by dividing the difference by the number of milliseconds in one day. This would then be:

```
var DayCount=(XDay - CurrentDay)/(1000*60*60*24);
```

because there are 1000 milliseconds in a second, 60 seconds in a minute, 60 minutes in an hour, and 24 hours in one day.

There is one more issue. When the user displays the Web page, it's unlikely that it will be precisely a whole number of days before Christmas. It's more likely that it will be a certain number of days, plus a fraction of a day before Christmas. Andrew doesn't want that fractional part displayed. You'll remove the fractional part by rounding the value of DayCount to the nearest day using the round Math method. The command is:

```
DayCount = Math.round(DayCount);
```

The complete XmasDays function looks as follows:

```
function XmasDays(CurrentDay) {
   var XYear=CurrentDay.getFullYear();
   var XDay=new Date("December, 25, 2003");
   XDay.setFullYear(XYear);
   var DayCount=(XDay-CurrentDay)/(1000*60*60*24);
   DayCount=Math.round(DayCount);
return DayCount;
}
```

Now that you see what the XmasDays function looks like, you'll insert it into the npn.htm file. Following standard practice, you'll place the code for this function between the <head> and </head> tags. Once again, you must place this JavaScript code within a set of <script> tags.

To insert the XmasDays function into npn.htm:

1. Return to **npn.htm** in your text editor.

2. Insert the following lines of code directly below the <title> tag located at the beginning of the HTML file:

```
<script language="JavaScript">
<!-- Hide from non-JavaScript browsers
function XmasDays(CurrentDay) {
   var XYear=CurrentDay.getFullYear();
   var XDay=new Date("December, 25, 2003");
   XDay.setFullYear(XYear);
   var DayCount=(XDay-CurrentDay)/(1000*60*60*24);
   DayCount=Math.round(DayCount);
return DayCount;
}
// Stop hiding -->
</script>
```

Figure 8-17 shows the revised head section of npn.htm.

Figure 8-17	THE XMASDAYS FUNCTION

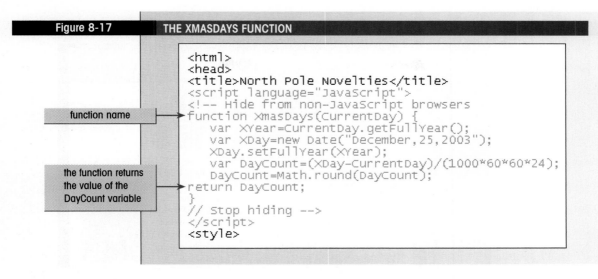

function name

the function returns
the value of the
DayCount variable

```
<html>
<head>
<title>North Pole Novelties</title>
<script language="JavaScript">
<!-- Hide from non-JavaScript browsers
function XmasDays(CurrentDay) {
    var XYear=CurrentDay.getFullYear();
    var XDay=new Date("December,25,2003");
    XDay.setFullYear(XYear);
    var DayCount=(XDay-CurrentDay)/(1000*60*60*24);
    DayCount=Math.round(DayCount);
return DayCount;
}
// Stop hiding -->
</script>
<style>
```

Next, you have to insert a command into npn.htm to run this function. Recall that you previously set the value of the DaysLeft variable to 999 to act as a placeholder. You'll replace that command with one that calls the XmasDay function using the Today variable. The DaysLeft variable is then set to whatever value is returned by the XmasDays function.

To call the XmasDays function:

1. Scroll through npn.htm to the line "var DaysLeft = 999;" and replace this line of code with:

   var DaysLeft=XmasDays(Today);

   Figure 8-18 shows the revised code.

Figure 8-18	CALLING THE XMASDAYS FUNCTION

```
<!--- Days until Christmas --->
<td id="daycell">
<script language="JavaScript">
    <!-- Hide from non-JavaScript browsers
    var Today=new Date("October 15, 2003");
    var ThisDay=Today.getDate();
    var ThisMonth=Today.getMonth()+1;
    var ThisYear=Today.getFullYear();
    var DaysLeft=XmasDays(Today);
    document.write("Today is "+ThisMonth+"/"+ThisDay+"/"+ThisYear+"<br>");
    document.write("Only "+DaysLeft+" days until Christmas");
    // Stop hiding -->
</script>
</td>
</tr>
```

the value of the DaysLeft variable is set to the value returned by the XmasDays function

2. Save your changes to npn.htm.

3. Reload npn.htm in your Web browser. As shown in Figure 8-19, the Web page now shows that there are 71 days between the test date of October 15 and December 25.

| Figure 8-19 | **DAYS UNTIL CHRISTMAS IN THE NPN WEB PAGE** |

TROUBLE? If you receive an error message or if your Web page shows an incorrect value, check your use of uppercase and lowercase letters, and verify that each JavaScript command ends with a semicolon.

You've completed the XmasDays function. Andrew plans to test the Web page you've created and get back to you with any suggestions or changes he wants to make.

Session 8.2 QUICK CHECK

1. What are the four data types supported by JavaScript?

2. What command would you use to store the current date in a variable named Now?

3. What command would you use to extract the current day of the month from the Now variable and store it in a variable called Tdate?

4. If the current month is September, what value would be returned by the getMonth( ) method?

5. Define the following terms:

   Expression

   Operator

   Binary operator

   Unary operator

6. List two commands you could use to take the variable *x*, increase its value by 1, and store the result in a variable named *y*.

7. Provide the general syntax of a JavaScript function.

SESSION 8.3

In this session you'll learn how to add decision-making capabilities to your JavaScript program through the use of conditional statements. You'll also learn how to create and use arrays, and finally, you'll be introduced to program loops in order to run a command block repeatedly.

Working with Conditional Statements

Now that you've created a function that calculates the number of days until Christmas using a test date, you and Andrew take a look at how you've progressed through the list of tasks that you started with.

1) Learn how to display text on a Web page using JavaScript
2) Display date values on a Web page
3) Calculate the number of days between the test date and December 25th
4) If the date is December 25th or later (through December 31st), display a greeting message; otherwise, display the number of days remaining until Christmas

The only task remaining is to have the Web page display a greeting message in place of the day count from December 25 through December 31. To do this, you need to create a conditional statement.

A **conditional statement** is one that runs only when specific conditions are met. There are many types of conditional statements, but the one most often used is the If statement. An If statement has the following general syntax:

```
if (condition) {
     JavaScript Commands
}
```

where *condition* is an expression that is either true or false. If the condition is true, the *JavaScript Commands* in the command block are executed. If the condition is not true, then no action is taken.

Comparison, Logical, and Conditional Operators

To create a condition in JavaScript, you need one of three types of operators: comparison operators, logical operators, or conditional operators. A **comparison operator** compares the value of one element with that of another. This creates a **Boolean expression** that is either true or false. Here are two examples of Boolean expressions:

```
x < 100;
y == 20;
```

In the first example, if x is less than 100, this expression returns the value *true*; however, if x is 100 or greater, the expression is *false*. In the second example, the y variable must have an exact value of 20 for the expression to be true. Note that this comparison operator uses a double equal sign (==) rather than a single one. The single equal sign is an assignment operator and is not used for making comparisons (a very easy mistake to make!). Figure 8-20 lists some of the other comparison operators used in JavaScript.

Figure 8-20	COMPARISON OPERATORS

OPERATOR	DESCRIPTION
==	Returns true if variables are equal (x = y)
!=	Returns true if variables are not equal (x != y)
>	Returns true if the variable on the left is greater than the variable on the right (x > y)
<	Returns true if the variable on the left is less than the variable on the right (x < y)
>=	Returns true if the variable on the left is greater than or equal to the variable on the right (x >= y)
<=	Returns true if the variable on the left is less than or equal to the variable on the right (x <= y)

A **logical operator** connects two or more Boolean expressions. One such operator is the && operator, which returns a value of true only if all of the Boolean expressions are true. For example, the following expression is true only if x is less than 100 and y is equal to 20:

```
(x < 100) && (y == 20);
```

Figure 8-21 lists some of the logical operators used by JavaScript.

Figure 8-21	LOGICAL OPERATORS

OPERATOR	DESCRIPTION	EXAMPLE
In the following examples, assume that x = 20 y = 25		
&&	Returns true when both expressions are true.	(x == 20) && (y == 25) returns true (x == 20) && (y == 20) returns false
||	Returns true when either expression is true.	(x == 20) || (y == 20) returns true (x == 25) || (y == 20) returns false
!	Returns true if the expression is false and false if the expression is true.	! (x == 20) returns false ! (x == 25) returns true

Finally, a **conditional operator** tests whether a specific condition is true and returns one value if the condition is true and a different value if the condition is false. The syntax of the conditional operator is:

```
(condition) ? value1: value2
```

where *condition* is the condition being tested, *value1* is the value returned by the operator if the condition is true, and *value2* is the value if the condition is false. For example, the following statement:

```
message = (mail == "Yes") ? "You have mail": "No mail";
```

tests whether the mail variable is equal to the value "Yes". If it is, the message variable has the value "You have mail"; otherwise the message variable has the value "No mail".

<u>Using Conditional Statements</u>
- To create a command block that runs only if a certain condition is met, use the following syntax:

```
if (condition) {
        JavaScript Commands
}
```
where *condition* is an expression that is either true or false. If condition is true, the command block is run. If the value is false, the command block is skipped.
- To choose between two command blocks, use the following syntax:

```
if(condition) {
        JavaScript Commands if true
} else
        JavaScript Commands if false
}
```

Using an If Statement

Let's see how these operators work in an If statement. The following is an example of an If statement that controls what text is sent to the Web page:

```
if (Day=="Friday") {
    document.write("The weekend is almost here!");
}
```

In this example, if the Day variable is equal to "Friday", the text string "The weekend is almost here!" is sent to the Web page. If Day is not equal to "Friday", then no action is taken.

Using an If...Else Statement

The If statement runs a set of commands if the condition is true, but it does nothing if the condition is false. There are occasions when you may want the If statement to run for one set of commands if the condition is true and another set of commands if the condition is false. This is done using an If...Else statement. The general syntax is:

```
if (condition) {
        JavaScript Commands if true
} else
        JavaScript Commands if false
}
```

where *condition* is an expression that is either true or false, and one set of commands is run if the expression is true, and another is run if the expression is false. The following is an example of an If...Else statement:

```
if (Day=="Friday") {
document.write("The weekend is almost here!");
} else
document.write("It's not Friday yet");
}
```

In this example, the text "The weekend is almost here!" is generated if Day equals "Friday"; otherwise, the text "It's not Friday yet" appears.

If...Else structures can also be nested within each other. Here is an example of a nested structure:

```
if (Day=="Friday") {
    document.write("The weekend is almost here!");
} else
    if(Day=="Monday")
        document.write("Time for another work week");
    } else
        document.write("It's not Friday yet");
    }
}
```

In this example, the text "The weekend is almost here!" appears if the day is Friday. If the day is Monday, the text "Time for another work week" appears. On days other than Friday and Monday, the text "Hello" is generated.

You have a similar situation in the North Pole Novelties home page. If the current date is before December 25, Andrew wants the page to display the number of days until Christmas as calculated by the XmasDays function; otherwise, if the date is between December 25 and December 31, it displays a holiday greeting.

You can distinguish between the two situations by creating an If...Else statement that looks at the value returned by the XmasDays function. If that value is positive, then the current date is before December 25, and the page displays the number of days left in the holiday season. On the other hand, if the value is 0 or negative, then the current date is December 25 or later in the year, and a holiday message is displayed. The code to perform this is as follows:

```
if (DaysLeft > 0) {
    document.write("Only " + DaysLeft + " days until
Christmas");
} else
    document.write("Happy Holidays from North Pole Novelties")
;
}
```

You need to insert these statements into npn.htm, replacing the previous document.write() method you used to display the number of days until Christmas.

To create an If...Else structure:

1. Using your text editor, open **npn.htm**.

2. Replace the line 'document.write("Only " + DaysLeft + " days until Christmas");' with the following code:

```
if (DaysLeft > 0) {
    document.write("Only "+DaysLeft+" days until Christmas
");
} else {
document.write("Happy Holidays from North Pole Novelties"
);
}
```

Indent the various lines of your program to make it easier to read. The revised code should appear as shown in Figure 8-22.

Figure 8-22	USING AN IF ... ELSE CONDITIONAL STATEMENT

```
<!--- Days until Christmas --->
<td id="daycell">
<script language="JavaScript">
   <!-- Hide from non-JavaScript browsers
   var Today=new Date("October, 15, 2003");
   var ThisDay=Today.getDate();
   var ThisMonth=Today.getMonth()+1;
   var ThisYear=Today.getFullYear();
   var DaysLeft=xmasDays(Today);
   document.write("Today is "+ThisMonth+"/"+ThisDay+"/"+ThisYear+"<br>");
   if (DaysLeft > 0) {
      document.write("only "+DaysLeft+" days until Christmas");
   } else {
      document.write("Happy Holidays from North Pole Novelties");
   }
   // Stop hiding -->
</script>
</td>
</tr>
```

command that is run for dates prior to December 25

command that is run for dates between December 25 and December 31

3. Save your changes to npn.htm and then open the file in your Web browser. The page displays the text "Only 71 days until Christmas" because the date specified in the Today variable is still October 15, 2003.

4. Return to npn.htm in your text editor.

5. Change the date of the Today variable to **"December, 28, 2003"**.

6. Save your changes to npn.htm and reload the file in your Web browser. As shown in Figure 8-23, the page now displays the Happy Holidays greeting.

Figure 8-23	DISPLAYING A SPECIAL HOLIDAY GREETING

You've completed all of the tasks on your list. Now you must turn your attention to some of the things Andrew wants you to change.

● 1) Learn how to display text on a Web page using JavaScript

● 2) Display date values on a Web page

● 3) Calculate the number of days between the test date and December 25th

● 4) If the date is December 25th or later (through December 31st), display a greeting message; otherwise, display the number of days remaining until Christmas

Using Arrays

Andrew has received feedback on your Web page. While everyone likes the Christmas Day countdown feature, many feel that the date format is uninviting. Instead of displaying:

Today is 10/15/2003

The reviewers would rather see:

Today is October 15

Unfortunately, there are no built-in JavaScript methods to display dates in this format, but you can create your own. One approach is to create a series of conditional statements based on the value of the ThisMonth variable, and display a different text string for each month. That would require 12 nested If...Else statements. Fortunately, there is an easier way to display the desired text using arrays.

REFERENCE WINDOW   **RW**

Creating and Populating an Array

- To create an array variable, use the command:

  ```
  var variable = new Array();
  ```
  where *variable* is the name of the array variable.

- To populate the array with values, use the command:

  ```
  variable[i]=value;
  ```
  where *variable* is the name of the array variable, *i* is the *i*th element of the array, and *value* is the value of the *i*th element.

or

  ```
  var variable = new Array(content);
  ```
  where *content* is a list of the array elements enclosed in quotes and separated by commas.

An **array** is an ordered collection of values referenced by a single variable name. The syntax for creating an array variable is:

```
var variable = new Array(size);
```

where *variable* is the name of the array variable and *size* is the number of elements in the array. Specifying a size for an array is optional. If you don't specify a size, JavaScript increases the size of the array as you add more elements. The code for creating an array named "Month" is:

```
var Month = new Array();
```

Once an array is created, you create values for each individual element in the array. To create values for the Month array, use the following commands:

```
Month[1] = "January";
Month[2] = "February";
Month[3] = "March";
Month[4] = "April"
Month[5] = "May";
Month[6] = "June";
Month[7] = "July";
```

```
Month[8] = "August";
Month[9] = "September"
Month[10] = "October";
Month[11] = "November";
Month[12] = "December";
```

These commands create 12 new elements in the Month array. Each element is identified by its index, which is an integer displayed between brackets. For example, the element "August" has an index value of 8 in the Month array. The first element in any array has an index value of 0, the second item has an index value of 1, and so on. In the Month array, there are actually thirteen total elements. The first element, Month[0], is not shown and has a null value. This is because you want the index number to match the month number. It seems counterintuitive to assign December an index value of 11, though the program could be written that way.

A more efficient way of populating an array is to specify the array contents in the new Array() statement. In this form, the syntax is:

```
var variable = new Array(contents);
```

where *contents* are the array elements enclosed in quotes and separated by commas. For example, the following statement creates an array of the names of the seven days of the week:

```
var WDay=new Array('Sun', 'Mon', 'Tue', 'Wed', 'Thu', 'Fri',
'Sat');
```

The value of WDay[0] would be 'Sun', WDay[1] would be 'Mon', and so forth.

You can use a variable in place of an index number. For example, if the variable "i" has the value 5, then:

```
WDay[i]
```

is equal to the value of WDay[5], which is 'Fri'.

You decide to use arrays in creating a function named "MonthTxt". The function has one parameter, "MonthNumber", which is the number of a month that the function uses to return the name of the corresponding month. Here's the code for the function:

```
function MonthTxt (MonthNumber) {
   var Month = new Array();
   Month[1]="January";
   Month[2]="February";
   Month[3]="March";
   Month[4]="April"
   Month[5]="May";
   Month[6]="June";
   Month[7]="July";
   Month[8]="August";
   Month[9]="September"
   Month[10]="October";
   Month[11]="November";
   Month[12]="December";
return Month[MonthNumber];
}
```

If you run the command MonthTxt(10), the function will return the value "October", which is what Andrew's colleagues want to see in the Web page.

To create the MonthTxt function:

1. Return to **npn.htm** in your text editor.

2. Insert the code for the new function MonthTxt directly after the XmasDays function (see Figure 8-24):

```
function MonthTxt (MonthNumber) {
    var Month = new Array();
    Month[1]="January";
    Month[2]="February";
    Month[3]="March";
    Month[4]="April";
    Month[5]="May";
    Month[6]="June";
    Month[7]="July";
    Month[8]="August";
    Month[9]="September";
    Month[10]="October";
    Month[11]="November";
    Month[12]="December";
return Month[MonthNumber];
}
```

| Figure 8-24 | CREATING THE MONTHTXT FUNCTION |

```
<script language="JavaScript">
<!-- Hide from non-JavaScript browsers
function XmasDays(CurrentDay) {
    var XYear=CurrentDay.getFullYear();
    var XDay=new Date("December,25,2003");
    XDay.setFullYear(XYear);
    var DayCount=(XDay-CurrentDay)/(1000*60*60*24);
    DayCount=Math.round(DayCount);
return DayCount;
}
function MonthTxt (MonthNumber) {
    var Month=new Array();
    Month[1]="January";
    Month[2]="February";
    Month[3]="March";
    Month[4]="April";
    Month[5]="May";
    Month[6]="June";
    Month[7]="July";
    Month[8]="August";
    Month[9]="September";
    Month[10]="October";
    Month[11]="November";
    Month[12]="December";
return Month[MonthNumber];
}
// Stop hiding -->
</script>
```

Next, you'll use the value of the ThisMonth variable to call this function and then store the results in a new variable named "MonthName." You'll then display the name of the month on the Web page, along with the day of the month.

To call the MonthTxt function and display the results:

1. Return to **npn.htm** in your text editor.

2. Locate the document.write() command that displays the current date in the main body of the HTML file, and insert the new commands directly above the command you located.

```
var MonthName=MonthTxt(ThisMonth);
document.write("Today is "+MonthName+" "+ThisDay+"<br>");
```

Note the blank space to be inserted between the MonthName variable and the ThisDay variable. This prevents the name of the month from running into the day of the month.

3. Delete the **document.write()** command that displayed the current date in the old style. Your code should look like Figure 8-25.

Figure 8-25	CALLING THE MONTHTXT FUNCTION

determine the name of the current month

display the name of the month and the day in the Web page

```
<script language="JavaScript">
    <!-- Hide from non-JavaScript browsers
    var Today=new Date("December, 28, 2003");
    var ThisDay=Today.getDate();
    var ThisMonth=Today.getMonth()+1;
    var ThisYear=Today.getFullYear();
    var DaysLeft=XmasDays(Today);
    var MonthName=MonthTxt(ThisMonth);
    document.write("Today is "+MonthName+" "+ThisDay+"<br>");
    if (DaysLeft > 0) {
        document.write("only "+DaysLeft+" days until Christmas");
    } else {
        document.write("Happy Holidays from North Pole Novelties");
    }
    // Stop hiding -->
</script>
```

4. Save your changes to npn.htm.

5. Reload npn.htm in your Web browser. As shown in Figure 8-26, the new date style appears on the Web page.

Figure 8-26	DATE DISPLAYED IN THE NEW STYLE

Before showing the Web page to Andrew for his final approval, you need to remove the test date and allow the page to use the current date (whatever that might be). Remember that if you don't specify a date value, the current date and time are used. You'll make this change to npn.htm now.

To use the current date in the North Pole Novelties Web page:

1. Return to **npn.htm** in your text editor.

2. Change the line 'var Today=new Date("December, 28, 2003")' to:

```
var Today=new Date();
```

3. Save your changes to npn.htm and then close your text editor.

4. Reload npn.htm in your browser, and verify that the correct date and days until December 25 are shown.

   You've completed your work with the JavaScript program. Figure 8-27 shows the code for the main portion of your program.

Figure 8-27	FINAL JAVASCRIPT COMMANDS

```
<script language="JavaScript">
   <!-- Hide from non-JavaScript browsers
   var Today=new Date();
   var ThisDay=Today.getDate();
   var ThisMonth=Today.getMonth()+1;
   var ThisYear=Today.getFullYear();
   var DaysLeft=xmasDays(Today);
   var MonthName=MonthTxt(ThisMonth);
   document.write("Today is "+MonthName+" "+ThisDay+"<br>");
   if (DaysLeft > 0) {
      document.write("Only "+DaysLeft+" days until Christmas");
   } else {
      document.write("Happy Holidays from North Pole Novelties");
   }
   // Stop hiding -->
</script>
```

5. Close your Web browser.

Working with Loops

In the future, Andrew may have additional JavaScript programs he wants you to run. He suggests that you learn about the other types of programs you can create. He notes that the JavaScript code you created for North Pole Novelties is designed to run once every time the Web is either opened or refreshed with a browser. However, programming often involves code that does not run just once, but is repeated until a particular condition has been fulfilled.

To provide the program with this capability, you use a program loop. A **program loop** is a set of instructions that is executed repeatedly. There are two types of loops: loops that repeat a set number of times before quitting and loops that repeat as long as a certain condition is met. You create the first type of loop using a For statement.

<u>Creating Program Loops</u>

- To create a For loop, use the following syntax:

```
for (start; condition; update) {
    JavaScript Commands
}
```

where *start* is an expression defining the starting value of the For loop's counter, *condition* is a Boolean expression that must be true for the loop to continue, and *update* is an expression defining how the counter changes as the For loop progresses.

- To create a While loop, use the following syntax:

```
while (condition) {
    JavaScript Commands
}
```

where *condition* is a Boolean expression that halts the While loop when its value becomes false.

The For Loop

The For loop allows you to create a group of commands to be executed a set number of times through the use of a **counter** that tracks the number of times the command block has been run. You set an initial value for the counter, and each time the command block is executed, the counter changes in value. When the counter reaches a value above or below a certain stopping value, the loop ends. The general syntax of the For loop is:

```
for (start; condition; update) {
    JavaScript Commands
}
```

where *start* is the starting value of the counter, *condition* is a Boolean expression that must be true for the loop to continue, and *update* specifies how the counter changes in value each time the command block is executed. Like a function, the command block in the For loop is set off by curly braces { }. Figure 8-28 shows an example of a For loop used to write a row of table cells.

Figure 8-28	CREATING A FOR LOOP

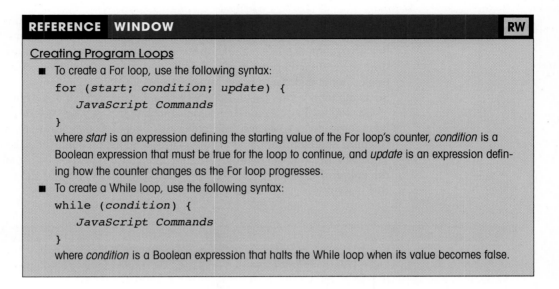

```
<table border>
<tr>
<script>
    for (num = 1; num <=4; num++) {
        document.write("<td>"+num+"</td>");
    }
</script>
</tr>
</table>
```

For loop

1 2 3 4

resulting table

The num variable is the counter in this example, starting with an initial value of 1. As long as the value of num is less than or equal to 4, the condition for running the loop is met, but when num exceeds 4, the loop stops. Finally, the expression "num++" indicates that each time the command block is run, the value of the num variable increases by 1. As you learned earlier in the discussion of arithmetic operators, this is an example of an increment operator. So as the loop is run, the num variable has the values 1, 2, 3, and finally, 4.

For loops can be nested inside one another. Figure 8-29 shows code used to write a table containing three rows and four columns. There are two counter variables in this example: rownum and colnum. The rownum variable loops through the values 1, 2, and 3. For each value of rownum, the colnum variable takes on the values 1, 2, 3, and 4. For each value of the colnum variable, a table cell is written. For each value of the rownum variable, a table row is written.

Figure 8-29	NESTING A FOR LOOP

```
<table border>
<script>
for (rownum = 1; rownum <=3; rownum++) {
    document.write("<tr>");
    for (colnum = 1; colnum <=4; colnum++) {
        document.write("<td>" + rownum + "," + colnum + "</td>");
    }
    document.write("</tr>");
}
</script>
</table>
```

nested For loop

1,1	1,2	1,3	1,4
2,1	2,2	2,3	2,4
3,1	3,2	3,3	3,4

resulting table

The For loop is not limited to incrementing the value of the counter by 1. Figure 8-30 shows examples of other ways of incrementing the counter in a For loop.

Figure 8-30	SPECIFYING COUNTER VALUES IN A FOR LOOP	

FOR LOOP	COUNTER VALUES
for (i = 1; i <= 5; i++)	i = 1, 2, 3, 4, 5
for (i = 5; i > 0; i--)	i = 5, 4, 3, 2, 1
for (i = 0; i <= 360; i += 60)	i = 0, 60, 120, 180, 240, 300, 360
for (i = 2; i <= 64; i *= 2)	i = 2, 4, 8, 16, 32, 64

The While Loop

Similar to the For loop, the While loop runs a command group as long as a specific condition is met, but it does not employ any counters. The general syntax of the While loop is:

```
while (condition) {
    JavaScript Commands
}
```

where *condition* is a Boolean expression that can be either true or false. As long as the condition is true, the commands in the command block are executed. Figure 8-31 shows how you can create a set of table cells using a While loop.

Figure 8-31	CREATING A WHILE LOOP

```
<table border>
<tr>
<script>
    var num = 1;
    while (num <= 4) {
        document.write("<td>"+num+"</td>");
        num++;
    }
</script>
</tr>
</table>
```

While loop

```
1 2 3 4
```

resulting table

Note that this particular While loop produces the same results as does the sample For loop discussed earlier. The num variable starts with a value of 1 and is increased by 1 each time the command block is run. The loop ends when the condition that num should be less than or equal to 4 is no longer true.

As with For loops, While loops can be nested inside one another (see Figure 8-32).

Figure 8-32	NESTING A WHILE LOOP

```
<table border>
<script>
var rownum = 1;
var colnum = 1;
while (rownum <=3) {
   document.write("<tr>");
   while (colnum <=4) {
      document.write("<td>" + rownum + "," + colnum + "</td>");
      colnum++;
   }
   document.write("</tr>");
   colnum = 1;
   rownum++;
}
</script>
</table>
```

nested While loop

1,1	1,2	1,3	1,4
2,1	2,2	2,3	2,4
3,1	3,2	3,3	3,4

resulting table

For loops and While loops share many of the same characteristics; which one you use is often a matter of personal preference. Generally, a While loop is used for conditions that don't yield themselves to using counter variables.

You've completed your study of JavaScript. Andrew has received the final version of your Web page and the JavaScript programs you created. He has viewed the page with his Web browser and is thrilled that it works so well. He'll review the Web page with his colleagues and get back to you with any final modifications they might suggest.

Session 8.3 QUICK CHECK

1. What code would you use to display the text "Welcome back to school!" if the value of the MonthName variable is "September"?

2. What code would you use to display the text "Welcome back to school!" if MonthName equals "September," or the text "Today's Headlines" if the month is not September?

3. What code would you use to display the text "Welcome back to school!" if MonthName equals September, "Summer's here!" if the MonthName equals June, or "Today's headlines" for other months?

4. What is an array? What command would you use to create an array named Colors?

5. The Colors array contains five values: Red, Green, Blue, Black, and White. What commands would you use to insert these values into the array? How many elements are in this array?

6. What is a program loop? Name the two types of program loops supported by JavaScript.

7. What code would you use to run the command document.write("News Flash!
"); five times?

8. What values will the counter variable *i* take in the following For loop?

```
for (i=5; i<=25; i+=5)
```

REVIEW ASSIGNMENTS

Andrew has extensively tested your Web page and shown it to other employees at North Pole Novelties. As a result, they would like you to make two changes to the Web page:

■ Include the day of the week in the date information. In other words, instead of displaying, "Today is October 15", display "Today is Monday, October 15".

■ Change the message for December 24 so that it reads "Last day for Christmas shopping." Keep the other messages the same.

To make these changes:

1. Using your text editor, open **npntxt2.htm** in the tutorial.08/review folder of your Data Disk, and save it as **npn2.htm** in the same folder.

2. Create a new function named WeekDayTxt and insert it directly after the MonthTxt function, but before the "// Stop hiding —>" comment within the <script> tags. The function has one parameter named WeekDayNumber.

3. Within the WeekDayTxt function, create an array named WeekDay. Populate the elements of the WeekDay array with the days of the week; that is, WeekDay[1]="Sunday" and so on.

4. Use the value of the WeekDayNumber parameter as the index and have WeekDayTxt function return the value of WeekDay[WeekDayNumber].

Explore   5. In npn2.htm, locate the section that displays the current date and holiday message. Create a new variable named "ThisWeekDay" that calculates the day of the week for the Now variable. Add one to this value so that if the day of the week is Sunday, ThisWeekDay has a value of 1, and so forth.

Explore   6. Call the WeekDayTxt function using the value of ThisWeekDay, and determine the day of the week. Store this value in a new variable named "WeekDayName".

7. Revise the document.write() method so that it displays the day of the week followed by a comma, and then the month name and the day of the month.

Explore   8. Delete the current If...Else statement, and replace it with a set of nested If...Else statements that display text using the following conditions:

■ If DaysLeft > 1, display the number of days until Christmas.

■ If DaysLeft = 1, display "Last day for Christmas shopping". (*Hint:* be sure to use == and not = as your comparison operator.)

■ Else, display "Happy Holidays from North Pole Novelties".

9. Using your Web browser, view your Web page with the following test dates and print a copy of each test.

   ■ August 12, 2003
   ■ December 24, 2003
   ■ December 31, 2003

10. Print a copy of your JavaScript code for both the WeekDayTxt function and the revised script to display the daily messages.

11. Hand in your printouts and files to your instructor.

CASE PROBLEMS

Case 1. Kelsey's Diner   Kelsey's Diner has made its dinner menu available on the World Wide Web. The only item missing from the menu is the chef's nightly special. Each day of the week, there is a different special. Rather than updating the page every day, or including a cumbersome list of all the specials, the manager would like you to use JavaScript to display the special that is available on any particular day. The daily specials follow. The names of the specials are italicized. A description accompanies each special.

   ■ Sunday: *Chicken Burrito Amigo*. Chicken with mushrooms, onions, and Monterey Jack cheese wrapped in a flour tortilla. 9.95
   ■ Monday: *Chicken Tajine*. Chicken baked with garlic, olives, capers, and prunes. 8.95
   ■ Tuesday: *Pizza Bella*. Large pizza with pesto, goat cheese, onions, and mozzarella cheese. 8.95
   ■ Wednesday: *Salmon Filet*. Grilled salmon with a spicy curry sauce and baked potato. 9.95
   ■ Thursday: *Greek-style Shrimp*. Shrimp, feta cheese, and tomatoes simmered in basil and garlic. 9.95
   ■ Friday: *All-you-can-eat fish*. Deep-fried cod with baked potato and rolls. 9.95
   ■ Saturday: *Prime Rib*. 12-oz cut with baked potato, rolls, and dinner salad. 12.95

You'll write a program to create a variable with the current date, and extract from the date the day of the week, using the getDay() method. Using the day of the week value, you'll create two functions, DishName and DishDesc, which returns the name of the daily special and a description of the daily special, respectively. You'll place these text strings in the appropriate places on the Web page. Your finished Web page should look like the Sunday menu shown in Figure 8-33.

Figure 8-33

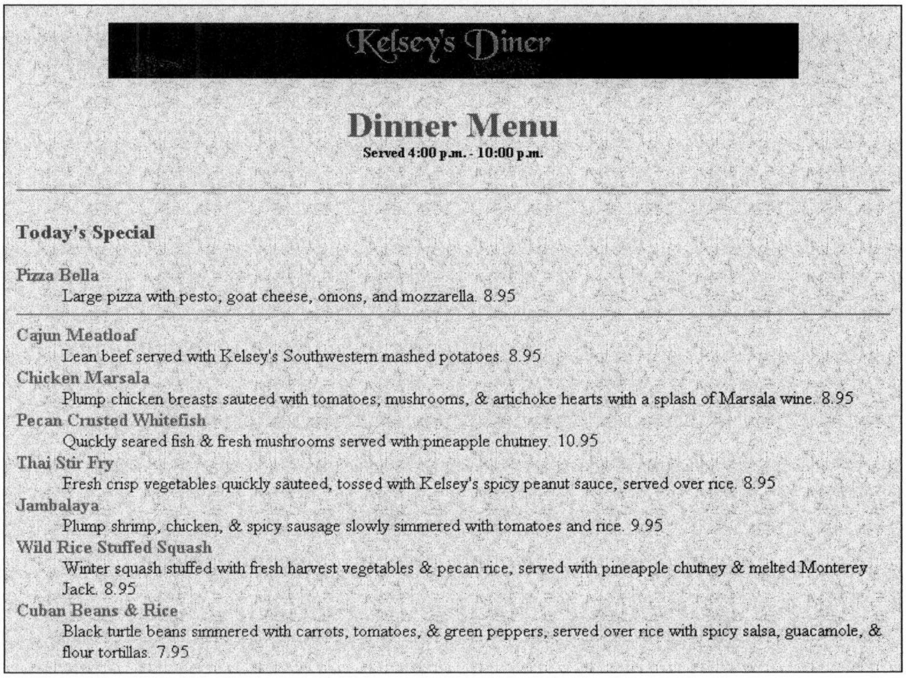

To create the daily dinner menu:

1. Using your text editor, open **menutxt.htm** from the tutorial.08/case1 folder on your Data Disk, and save it as **menu.htm** in the same folder.

2. Insert <script> tags for the functions you'll be creating in the head section of the HTML file. Add an HTML comment tag and a JavaScript comment line to hide the script from older browsers.

3. Create a new function named DishName with a single parameter, Day within the <script> tags.

4. Create an array variable named DName within the DishName function. Populate the array with the names of the nightly dish specials as follows: for Sunday let DName[0]="Chicken Burrito Amigo", and so on.

5. Using the value of the Day parameter as the index variable, instruct the DishName function to return the value of DName[Day].

6. Create another function named DishDesc below the DishName function that contains the single parameter, Day.

7. Create an array variable named DDesc within the DishDesc function. Populate the array with the descriptions of the nightly dish specials. Use the same index numbering that you used for the DishName function. That is, for Sunday let DDesc[0]="Chicken with mushrooms, onions, and Monterey Jack in flour tortilla. 9.95", and so on. Using the value of the Day parameter as the index variable, have the DishDesc function return the value of DDesc[Day].

8. Navigate to the <script> tags already entered in the body of the document. Within the first set of <script> tags, enter a command line to retrieve the current date information and save it to a variable named Today.

9. Using the getDay() method, extract the day of the week number from the Today variable and save it as a variable named WeekDay.

10. Use the document.write() method to display the value of DishName(WeekDay) on your Web page.

11. Navigate to the second <script> tag in the body of the Web page and enter another command line to retrieve the current date information and save it to a variable named Today. As before, extract the day of the week number from this variable and save it in the WeekDay variable.

12. Use the document.write() method to display the value of DishDesc(WeekDay) on your Web page.

13. Test your JavaScript program for the dates September 16, 2003, through September 22, 2003.

14. Print the resulting Web pages for each test date.

15. Restore your Web page so that it uses the current date.

16. Save and print a copy of menu.htm.

17. Hand in your printouts and files to your instructor.

Case 2. Madison State College Professor Stewart Templeton of the Humanities Department at Madison State College has created a Web site devoted to the works of Mark Twain. One of the Web pages in the site is dedicated to Mark Twain's quotations. Stewart would like you to help him with the Web page by creating a JavaScript program to display random quotes from the legendary author and humorist. He has provided you with a Web page and a list of five quotes to work with. You must use these components to create a function, MQuote, to display one of the quotes on the Web page.

JavaScript includes a Math method for generating random numbers, but it only can create a random number between 0 and 1. You can convert the random number it generates to an integer between 0 and *n*, where *n* is the upper range of the integers, using the JavaScript command:

```
Rnum = Math.round(Math.random()*n)
```

In this function, the random number is multiplied by *n* and then, using the Math.round method, that value is rounded to the nearest integer. Rnum is therefore restricted to integer values between 0 and *n*.

You'll use this command with *n* set to 5, to select which one of the five quotes to be shown on the Web page. The Mark Twain quotes Stewart wants you to use are:

- "I smoke in moderation, only one cigar at a time."
- "Be careful of reading health books, you might die of a misprint."
- "Man is the only animal that blushes or needs to."
- "Clothes make the man. Naked people have little or no influence on society."
- "One of the most striking differences between a cat and a lie is that a cat has only nine lives."

A preview of the Web page you'll create is shown in Figure 8-34.

Figure 8-34

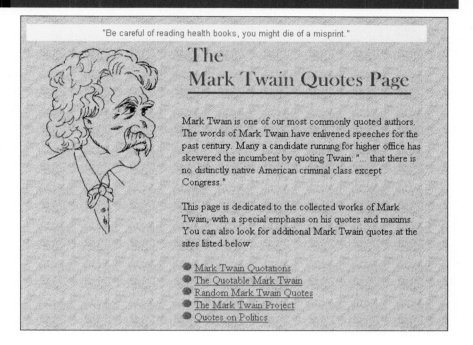

To create the Mark Twain random quotes function:

1. Using your text editor, open **twaintxt.htm** from the tutorial.08/case2 folder of your Data Disk and save it as **twain.htm**.

2. Navigate to the <script> tags located in the head section of the document and create a function named MQuote that contains the single parameter, Qnum.

Explore
3. Within the MQuote function, create an array named Quotes that contains five elements. The first element Quotes[0] contains the text "'I smoke in moderation, only one cigar at a time.'" Note that the double quotation marks of the statement are enclosed within single quotation marks; this allows the double quotation marks to be part of the text that is displayed on the page. Set the next four elements in the array to include the remaining quotes in the list.

4. Using the value of the Qnum parameter as the index variable, have the MQuote function return the value of Quotes[Qnum].

Explore
5. Directly below the MQuote function, but still within the <script> tags, create a second function named RandInt. The function has one parameter, Size, and one variable, Rnum. Set Rnum equal to a random integer between 0 and Size. Return the value of Rnum.

6. Scroll through the body of the twain.htm file until you locate the <script> tags. Within the <script> tags, create a variable named RandValue, and set the value of the variable by calling the RandInt function with a value of 4.

7. Create a variable named QuoteText, and set its value by calling the MQuote function using the RandValue variable as a parameter.

8. Using the document.write() method, display the value of QuoteText on your Web page.

9. Save your changes to twain.htm.

10. Using your Web browser, reload twain.htm several times and verify that the quotations are displayed randomly each time you reload or refresh the Web page.

11. Print a copy of the page as it appears in your Web browser.

12. Print a copy of the source code for the MQuote and RandInt functions you created.

13. Hand in your printouts and files to your instructor.

Explore

Case 3. Butler Community Center Beth Heurtzel is the director of the Butler Community Center in Butler, Utah. One of her jobs is to organize the calendar of events for the center and to publish that information on the center's Web site. Beth would like the ability to place a monthly calendar on the Web page along with a list of events for that month.

To do this, you'll create a JavaScript function named "calendar" that creates a table displaying a monthly calendar with a specified data highlighted. For example, if the user inserts the function:

```
calendar("February, 8, 2004")
```

into the HTML code, the browser displays the monthly calendar for February 2004 with the date, February 8, highlighted. Furthermore, Beth would like the option to replace the date with the text "today" as follows:

```
calendar("today")
```

which instructs the browser to display the calendar for the current month and to highlight today's date.

You'll save this function in a separate file so that it can be used by Beth for other Web pages as well. The appearance of the table is determined from a Cascading Style Sheet (CSS). The calendar table has five elements you can modify with the style sheet.

- The calendar table, identified with the id name "calendar"
- The calendar heading, where the month and year are displayed, identified with the id name "calendar_head"
- The calendar headings, which display the names of the seven weekdays, identified with the class name "calendar_weekdays"
- The individual table cells, which display the days of the month, identified with the class name "calendar_dates"
- The highlighted date in the calendar, identified with the id name "calendar_today"

Beth has already created a style sheet that formats these elements: calendar.css. She has also created the Web page that she wants the calendar to appear in. Your job is to create the calendar() function, save it in a file, and apply it to Beth's Web page. A preview of the completed Web page with the calendar highlighting the date, April 8, 2004, is shown in Figure 8-35.

Figure 8-35

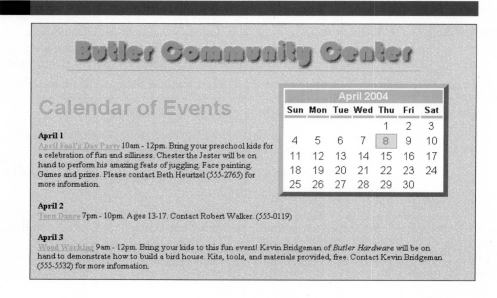

To create the calendar() function:

1. Using your text editor, open a new blank file. Save the file as **calendar.js** in the tutorial.08/case3 folder of your Data Disk.

2. Within the file, insert a function named calendar() that has a single parameter named "caldate". The caldate parameter stores the date the user wants highlighted in the calendar.

3 Within the command block of the calendar() function, create an array named "MonthName" that stores the names of the twelve months. The first element in the array, MonthName[0] should have a value of "January". Complete the rest of the array similarly.

4. Create an array, "DayName", that stores the three letter abbreviations of the seven weekday names, staring with DayName[0] = "Sun".

5. After the DayName array, create a date object variable named Calendar_Day. If the value of the caldate parameter is equal to "today", set Calendar_Day equal to the current date and time; otherwise, set Calendar_Day equal to the date specified by the caldate parameter. (Hint: use the command: Calendar_Day = new Date(caldate)).

6. Use the getDate(), getMonth(), and getFullYear() methods to extract the day of the month, month number, and four-digit year from the Calendar_Day variable. Store these values in variables named ThisDay, ThisMonth, and ThisYear, respectively.

7. Use the document.write() method to write the following tags to the Web page:

```
<table id="calendar">
<tr>
<th id="calendar_head" colspan="7">Month, Year </th>
</tr>
```

where *Month, Year* is the name of the month and the four-digit year. (Hint: Use MonthName[ThisMonth] to display the name of the month; use the ThisYear variable to display the year value.)

Explore

8. Create a For loop that writes a table row containing seven table heading cells. The For loop should generate the following HTML code:

```
<tr>
<th class="calendar_weekdays">Sun</th>
<th class="calendar_weekdays">Mon</th>
<th class="calendar_weekdays">Tue</th>
<th class="calendar_weekdays">Wed</th>
<th class="calendar_weekdays">Thu</th>
<th class="calendar_weekdays">Fri</th>
<th class="calendar_weekdays">Sat</th>
</tr>
```

(*Hint*: Within the For loop, use the DayName[index] array element, where index is the counter variable ranging in value from 0 to 6.)

The next part of the calendar() function creates the first row of dates. The first row of the calendar should contain empty table cells up to the first day of the month, after which the table cells should display the day number. To do this, the function must determine on which day of the week the month starts.

9. Use the setDate() method to change the date of the Calendar_Day variable to the first day of the month (Hint: Use setDate(1).) Use the getDay() method to calculate the day of the week for this new date. Store this value in a variable named week_day.

10. Use a For loop to generate the following HTML code:

```
<tr>
<td></td>
<td></td>
...
```

where the number of empty table cells is one less than the value of the week_day variable (*Hint*: use a counter variable that starts with a value of zero and increases by 1. Run the loop as long as the counter variable is less than the value of the week_day variable. Within each loop, write an empty cell using the document.write() method.)

The next part of the calendar() function populates the calendar with cells containing the days of the month. To do this you need two variables: cellcount and day. The cellcount variable counts the number of cells that have date numbers in them. The day variable records the day of the month for the current table cell.

11. Create the cellcount and day variables, setting their initial values to one.

Explore ▶ 12. Create a While loop with the condition that the value of the cellcount variable must be equal to the value of the day variable (remember to use the == comparison operator!). Within the While loop's command block perform the following tasks:

- If the value of the week_day variable = 0 (which means that the day in the calendar is a Sunday), generate the following HTML tag:

```
<tr>
```

to start a new table row in the calendar:

- Then, test whether the value of the day variable equals the value of the ThisDay variable (which means that the day in the calendar is equal to the date specified by the user). If it does, generate the following HTML code:

```
<td class="calendar_dates" id="calendar_today">Day</td>
```

where *Day* is value of the day variable; otherwise, generate the HTML code:

```
<td class="calendar_dates">Day</td>
```

- Finally, test whether the value of the week_day variable = 6 (which means that the day in the calendar is a Saturday), if it does, generate the HTML code:

```
</tr>
```

to complete the table row.

- After the writing the HTML code previously shown, increase the value of the cellcount variable by 1 to move to the next cell in the table.

- Use the setDate() method to change the day stored in the Calendar_Day variable to the value of the cellcount variable. This has the effect of moving the date in the Calendar_Day variable forward one day.

- Use the getDay() method to determine the day of the week for the new date stored in the Calender_Day variable and store this value in the week_day variable.

- Use the getDate() method to extract the day of month from the Calendar_Day variable, and store this value in the day variable.

Note that the cellcount and day variables will always have the same value until you exceed the number of days in the current month. At that point, the cellcount variable will continue to increase, but the day variable will drop back to "1" (since the Calendar_Day variable will have moved to the first day of the next month). Since the two variables will no longer be equal at this point, the While loop will end, and the function will stop writing table cells.

13. After the command block for the While loop, generate the following HTML code:

```
</tr></table>
```

to close out the table row and the table.

14. Print the code for **calendar.js**, and then save your changes and close the file.

15. Using your text editor, open **bcctxt.htm** from the tutorial.08/case3 folder of your Data Disk and save it as **bcc.htm**.

16. Above the </head> tag, insert the opening and closing <script> tags, linking this Web page to calendar.js.

17. Directly above the h1 heading "Calendar of Events", insert a second set of opening and closing <script> tags. Within these <script> tags, run the calendar() function. Use an initial value of "April, 8, 2004" for the date, and be sure to enclose the value in quotes.

18. Save your changes to bcc.htm and open it in your Web browser. Verify that it shows the monthly calendar for April, 2004 with the 8th highlighted. (*Note*: If you are running Netscape 4.7 or Internet Explorer 5.0, you will see the calendar, but it will not be formatted as shown in Figure 8-35.)

If the function doesn't work at all, check your code in calendar.js. Common sources for coding problems are:

- using different uppercase and lowercase letters for the same variable name
- forgetting the opening or closing curly braces { } around the If, For, or While command blocks
- forgetting the opening or closing quotes with the document.write() method
- using the = symbol rather than the == when comparing one variable to another in the While loop or the If statement.

19. Return to bcc.htm in your text editor. Change the value from "April, 8, 2004" to the text string, "today". Save your changes and reload bcc.htm in your Web browser. Verify that it shows the calendar for the current month and that the current date is highlighted in the calendar.

20. Print the code for bcc.htm.

21. Hand in your printouts and files to your instructor.

Case 4. Generating the Safety Palette Chloe MacDonald runs a Web site that contains information on Web page design. One of the issues she wants to highlight on her site is the safety palette. The safety palette is a palette of colors that are designed to be accurately rendered by all browsers, regardless of operating system or platform. Colors in the safety palette are limited to the following six hexadecimal values for their red, green, and blue components: 00, 33, 66, 99, CC, and FF. Thus, a color value of #33CC00 belongs to the safety palette, but a value of #33CC22 does not. The total number of colors in the palette is 6x6x6 or 216 colors.

Chloe would like her Web page to display each of the 216 colors along with their hexadecimal color values. She could create a table that has 216 cells with different background colors, but that would be time-consuming, and she feels that she might easily make a typing error as she created the Web page.

Instead, she would like your help in using JavaScript to generate the safety palette. She has already created a Web page that describes the palette. She needs you to write the JavaScript program. The design and layout of the page is up to you. One possible solution is displayed in Figure 8-36.

Figure 8-36

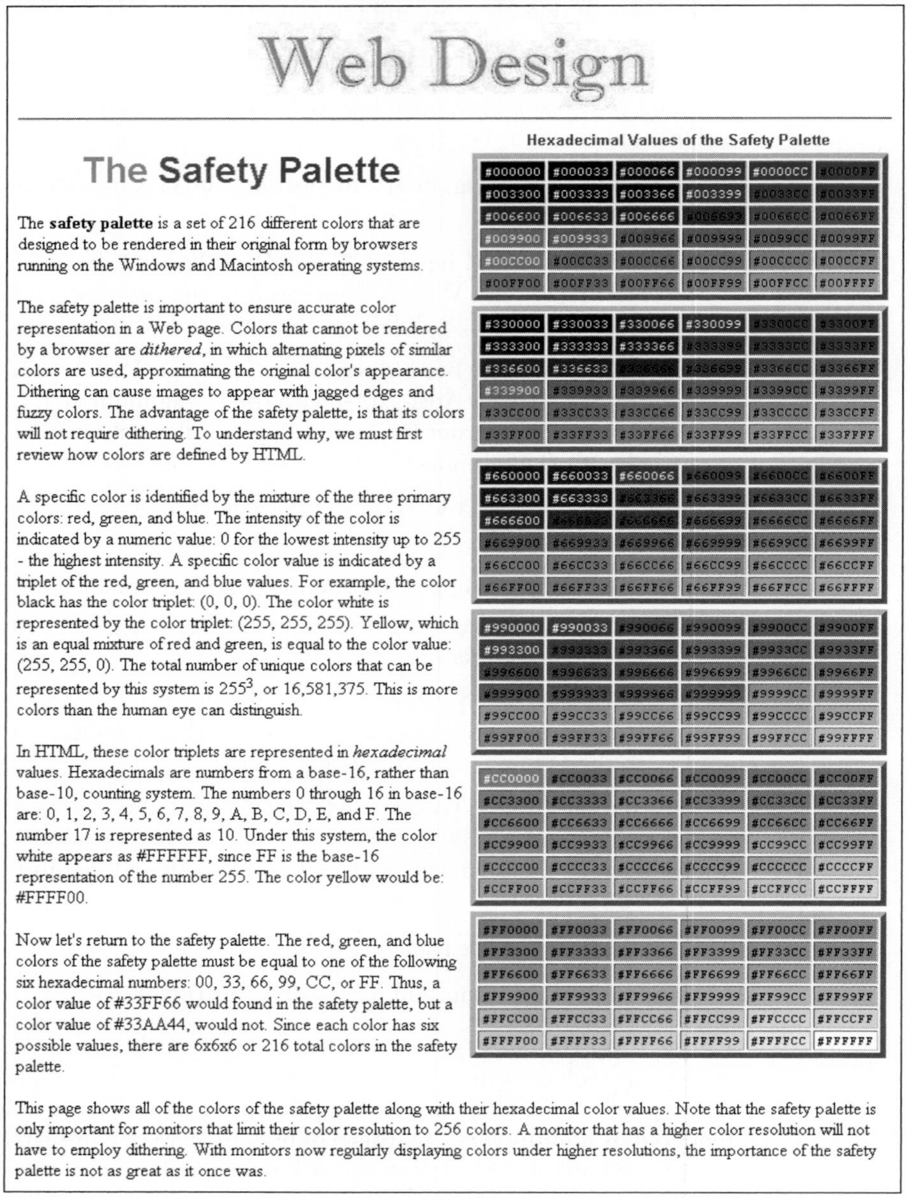

Web Design

The Safety Palette

The **safety palette** is a set of 216 different colors that are designed to be rendered in their original form by browsers running on the Windows and Macintosh operating systems.

The safety palette is important to ensure accurate color representation in a Web page. Colors that cannot be rendered by a browser are *dithered*, in which alternating pixels of similar colors are used, approximating the original color's appearance. Dithering can cause images to appear with jagged edges and fuzzy colors. The advantage of the safety palette, is that its colors will not require dithering. To understand why, we must first review how colors are defined by HTML.

A specific color is identified by the mixture of the three primary colors: red, green, and blue. The intensity of the color is indicated by a numeric value: 0 for the lowest intensity up to 255 - the highest intensity. A specific color value is indicated by a triplet of the red, green, and blue values. For example, the color black has the color triplet: (0, 0, 0). The color white is represented by the color triplet: (255, 255, 255). Yellow, which is an equal mixture of red and green, is equal to the color value: (255, 255, 0). The total number of unique colors that can be represented by this system is 255^3, or 16,581,375. This is more colors than the human eye can distinguish.

In HTML, these color triplets are represented in *hexadecimal* values. Hexadecimals are numbers from a base-16, rather than base-10, counting system. The numbers 0 through 16 in base-16 are: 0, 1, 2, 3, 4, 5, 6, 7, 8, 9, A, B, C, D, E, and F. The number 17 is represented as 10. Under this system, the color white appears as #FFFFFF, since FF is the base-16 representation of the number 255. The color yellow would be: #FFFF00.

Now let's return to the safety palette. The red, green, and blue colors of the safety palette must be equal to one of the following six hexadecimal numbers: 00, 33, 66, 99, CC, or FF. Thus, a color value of #33FF66 would found in the safety palette, but a color value of #33AA44, would not. Since each color has six possible values, there are 6x6x6 or 216 total colors in the safety palette.

This page shows all of the colors of the safety palette along with their hexadecimal color values. Note that the safety palette is only important for monitors that limit their color resolution to 256 colors. A monitor that has a higher color resolution will not have to employ dithering. With monitors now regularly displaying colors under higher resolutions, the importance of the safety palette is not as great as it once was.

To generate the safety palette, follow these guidelines:

1. Using your text editor, open **colortxt.htm** from the tutorial.08/case4 folder of your Data Disk and save it as **color.htm**.

2. Within color.htm, create a JavaScript program to generate the safety palette table. One way of creating the safety palette table is as follows:

- Create an array named "colors" containing the 6 allowed color values: 00, 33, 66, 99, CC, and FF.
- Create three nested If loops using the following structure:

```
for (i = 0; i <= 5; i++) {
    for (j = 0; j <= 5; j++) {
        for (k = 0; k <= 5; k++) {
        }
    }
}
```

- Within the innermost For loop, write table cells that have a background color equal to the color value, #color[i]color[j]color[k]
- Within the middle For loop, write tags to start and end each table row.
- Within the outer loop, write tags to create and close the table.

3. Each cell in the safety palette table should contain text indicating the color value of the cell's background color.

4. If the text cannot be read, for example, black text on a dark background, modify the JavaScript program to change the color of the text for that cell to a lighter color to better display on the Web page.

5. Save your changes to colors.htm and print the HTML code.

6. Open colors.htm in your Web browser and verify that all 216 colors are displayed in the safety palette table.

7. Hand in your printouts and files to your instructor.

Quick | Check Answers

Session 8.1

1. A client-side program is a program that is run on the user's computer, usually with a Web browser. A server-side program is run off of the Web server.

2. Java can be more difficult to learn than JavaScript. Java requires a development kit to create executable applets; JavaScript does not. Java programs must be compiled; JavaScript programs are scripts that can be run without compiling. Java is the more powerful of the two languages.

3. A JavaScript program is run by the Web browser either in the process of rendering the HTML file or in response to an event, such as the user clicking a Submit button or positioning the pointer on a hyperlink.

4. <script> and </script>

5. To prevent older browsers that do not support JavaScript from displaying the JavaScript commands on the Web page.

6. document.write("<h1>Avalon Books</h1>")

Session 8.2

1. numbers, strings, Boolean, and null values

2. var Now = new Date();

3. var Tdate = Now.getDate();

4. 8

5. Expressions are JavaScript commands that assign values to your variables. Operators are elements that perform actions within an expression. Binary operators work on two elements in an expression. Unary operators work on only a single expression element.

6. Y = X + 1; Y = X++;

7. function *function_name*(*parameters*) {

   ```
   JavaScript commands
   }
   ```

Session 8.3

1. if(Month=="September") {

   ```
     document.write("Welcome back to school!");
   }
   ```

2. if(Month=="September") {

   ```
     document.write("Welcome back to school!");
   } else {
         document.write("Today's headlines");
   }
   ```

3. if(Month=="September")

   ```
     document.write("Welcome back to school!");
   } else {
     if(Month="June") {
       document.write("Summer's here!")
     } else {
       document.write("Today's headlines");
     }
   }
   ```

4. An array is an ordered collection of values referenced by a single variable name.

   ```
   var Colors = new Array();
   ```

5. Colors[1]="Red";
   Colors[2]="Green";
   Colors[3]="Blue";
   Colors[4]="Black";
   Colors[5]="White";

6. A loop is a set of instructions that is executed repeatedly. There are two types of loops: loops that repeat a set number of times before quitting (For loops) and loops that repeat until a certain condition is met (While loops.)

7. for(i=1; i<=5; i++) {

   ```
     document.write("News Flash!<br>");
   }
   ```

8. 5, 10, 15, 20, 25

OBJECTIVES

In this tutorial you will:

- Learn about form validation

- Study the object-based nature of the JavaScript language

- Work with objects, properties, methods, and events of your Web page

- Create a program to calculate a value

- Copy a value into a form field

- Extract a value from a selection list and radio button

- Display a message box to the user

- Control a form submission

WORKING
WITH JAVASCRIPT
OBJECTS AND EVENTS

Enhancing Your Forms with JavaScript

CASE

GPS-ware

GPS-ware is a company that specializes in mapping and global positioning software and hardware. The company is in the planning stages for making its products available online. Carol Campbell is heading the development effort and has asked for your help in creating an order form Web page.

A GPS-ware employee has created the form and input fields for the page, but the form lacks the tools to assist the customer in submitting a valid order. Carol would like the form to calculate the total cost of the customer's order, including purchase price, sales tax, and a shipping fee. The form should also verify that the customer has provided the necessary information before the order information is submitted to the Web server for processing.

To add this functionality to the order form, you'll need to create JavaScript programs that validate the completed order form, alerting the customer to any problems.

SESSION 9.1

In this session you'll learn about the principle of form validation. You'll also see how validation applies to the objects found on a Web page form. Finally, you'll learn about the object-based nature of the JavaScript language and explore the principles of objects, properties, and methods.

Understanding Form Validation

You have a meeting with Carol to discuss the order form she's created. Although you won't be working with the form immediately, you have to learn more about JavaScript. First, you'll open it and view it with your Web browser.

To open the order form for the GPS-ware Web site:

1. Using your text editor, open **ordertxt.htm** from the tutorial.09/tutorial folder of your Data Disk and save it as **order.htm**.

2. Open order.htm in your Web browser. Figure 9-1 shows the current state of the Web page form.

| Figure 9-1 | THE GPS-WARE ORDER FORM |

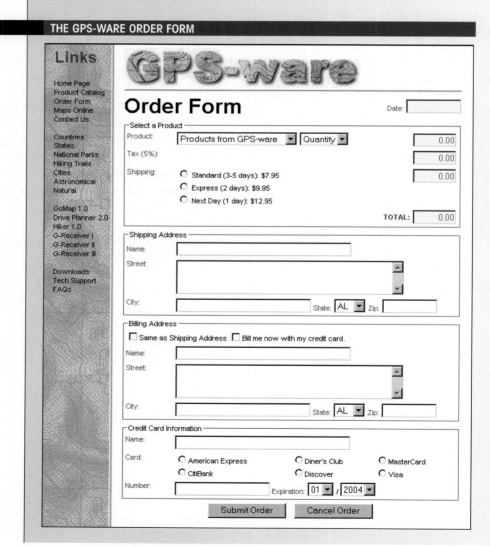

TROUBLE? If you're using the Netscape browser, your form may look different from the form shown in the figure.

3. Scroll through the form and examine its structure. Enter some test data to become familiar with the form's layout and content.

TROUBLE? You cannot enter data in either the date field or any of the fields that display the cost of the product, tax, or shipping. Carol has disabled these fields, and their values can only be set using JavaScript, as you'll see later.

The order form is divided into four sections. In the top section, customers select the products and quantities of the items they want to order. Carol wants the form to calculate the cost of those items and then display that value in a text box located in the upper-right portion of the page. Each purchase is subject to a 5% sales tax, so the form should calculate this value as well and display it in the second text box. Customers can choose one of three shipping options: standard ($7.95), express ($9.95), or next day ($12.95). The cost of shipping appears in the third text box. Finally, as users make purchase options, Carol wants the fourth text box to display the total cost of the order.

The second section is where customers enter their shipping address, and the third section is where customers enter the billing address. Carol has provided a check box for users to click if the shipping address and the billing address are the same. If users do select this check box, Carol wants you to create a program that copies all of the shipping data into the corresponding fields in the billing section.

Some users pay online using a credit card. Carol has also provided a check box for this option. If a user selects this check box, Carol wants the cursor to jump to the fourth section, where credit card information is entered.

When the form is submitted, Carol wants a JavaScript program to test the form's validity. Specifically, she wants your program to verify that:

- One of the three shipping methods has been selected
- If the credit card payment method is selected, all of the credit card information has been entered. A CGI script will be used later to verify that the credit card information is accurate.

If these two conditions are not met, she wants the program to alert the user to that fact and then return the user to the uncompleted form.

Carol's criteria are examples of **form validation**, a process by which the server or the browser checks form entries and, where possible, eliminates errors. On the Web, validation can occur on the client side or the server side. As shown in Figure 9-2, with **server-side validation**, the form is sent to the Web server for checking. If an error is found, the user is notified and asked to resubmit the form. In **client-side validation**, the form is checked as the user enters the information, and immediate feedback is provided if the user makes a mistake. Carol wants to use client-side validation for her form. Form validation is a critical aspect of data entry. A properly designed form reduces the possibility of faulty data being entered.

Figure 9-2   **SERVER-SIDE AND CLIENT-SIDE VALIDATION**

Server-side validation

1) The user submits the form to the Web server.

2) The Web server validates the user's responses and, if necessary, returns the form to the user for correction.

3) After correcting any errors, the user resubmits the form to the Web server for another validation.

Client-side validation

1) The user submits the form, and validation is performed on the user's computer.

2) After correcting any errors, the user submits the form to the Web server.

A powerful use of JavaScript is to provide client-side validation. With a script built into the Web page form, you can provide immediate feedback to users as they enter data. Client-side validation can reduce the network traffic between users and the Web server. Your first step is to learn how JavaScript can be used to manipulate elements on your Web page when the page is initially loaded and in response to events initiated by the user. You'll need to understand the object-based nature of JavaScript and how it can be used to control the behavior of the Web page, the form on the Web page, and even the Web browser itself.

Working with JavaScript Objects

JavaScript is an **object-based language**, which means that the language is based on manipulating objects by modifying an object's properties or by applying methods to an object. That definition might sound complex, but the concept is simple. **Objects** are items that have a defined existence. Each object has **properties** that describe its appearance, purpose, or behavior. Each object has **methods**, which are actions that can be performed with the object or to it.

Consider the example of an oven in your kitchen. The oven is an object. It has certain properties, such as model name, age, size, and temperature. There are certain methods you can perform with the oven object, such as turning on the grill or the self-cleaner. Some of these methods change the properties of the oven, such as the oven's temperature when you're preheating it.

Similarly, your Web browser has its own set of objects, properties, and methods. The Web browser itself is an object, and the page you're viewing is an object. If the page contains frames, each frame is an object, and if the page contains a form, the form and any fields it contains are objects.

These objects have properties. The browser object has a property that indicates its type, such as Netscape or Internet Explorer, or its version. You can apply different methods to the browser: you can open it, close it, reload its contents, or move back and forth in its history list.

Now that you know how to think of your Web browser and Web pages in terms of objects, properties, and methods, let's see how this applies to writing a JavaScript program.

Understanding JavaScript Objects and Object Names

In JavaScript, each object is identified by an **object name**. Figure 9-3 lists some of the many objects available in JavaScript and their corresponding object names. For example, when you want to use JavaScript to manipulate the current window, you use the object name "window." Operations that affect the current Web page use the "document" object name.

| Figure 9-3 | SOME JAVASCRIPT OBJECTS AND THEIR OBJECT NAMES |

OBJECT	JAVASCRIPT OBJECT NAME
The browser window	window
A frame within the browser window	frame
The history list containing the Web pages the user has already visited in the current session	history
The Web browser being run by the user	navigator
The URL of the current Web page	location
The Web page currently shown in the browser window	document
A hypertext link on the current Web page	link
A target or anchor on the current Web page	anchor
A form on the current Web page	form

The object name can also be based on the name assigned to the object by the user. You've now seen many HTML tags that use the name attribute, such as the <form>, <frame>, and <input> tags. For example, Carol's order form starts with the following tag:

```
<form name="order" method="post">
```

so you can refer to this specific form using the object name, "order", in your JavaScript program.

Introducing the Document Object Model

JavaScript arranges objects in a **document object model** or **DOM**. The DOM defines the logical structure of objects and the way an object is accessed and manipulated. The document object model can be thought of as a hierarchy moving from the most general object to the most specific. Figure 9-4 shows a section of the entire DOM. The full DOM would be a much larger figure.

Figure 9-4   **A PART OF THE DOCUMENT OBJECT MODEL**

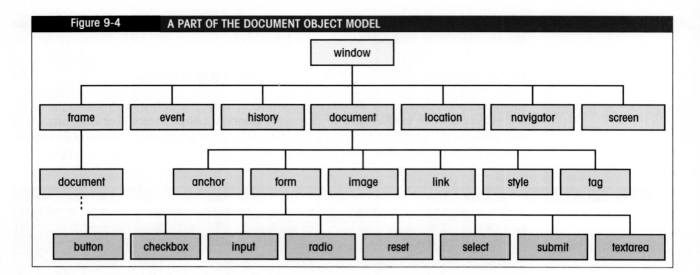

The topmost object in the hierarchy is the window object, which contains the other objects in the list, such as the current frame, history list, and the Web page document. The Web page document contains its own set of objects, including links, anchors, and forms. Within each form are form objects, such as input boxes, radio buttons, or selection lists.

In some situations, you'll need to include this hierarchy when referring to an object. You can do that by dividing each object name with periods and including the objects in the object name, starting at the top of the hierarchy and moving down. For example, for Carol's form, the order form is part of the document object, which falls within the window object. The complete object reference for the form is:

```
window.document.order
```

In most cases, you can omit the window object name from the hierarchy, and JavaScript assumes that it is there. A simpler reference to the order form is:

```
document.order
```

When working with objects on Web page forms, such as the form you'll be developing for Carol, you should include the entire hierarchy of object names, except for the window object. Some browsers cannot interpret the object names without the complete hierarchy.

Each of the fields in Carol's order form has been given a name as displayed in Figure 9-5.

Figure 9-5 | **FIELD NAMES IN THE ORDER FORM**

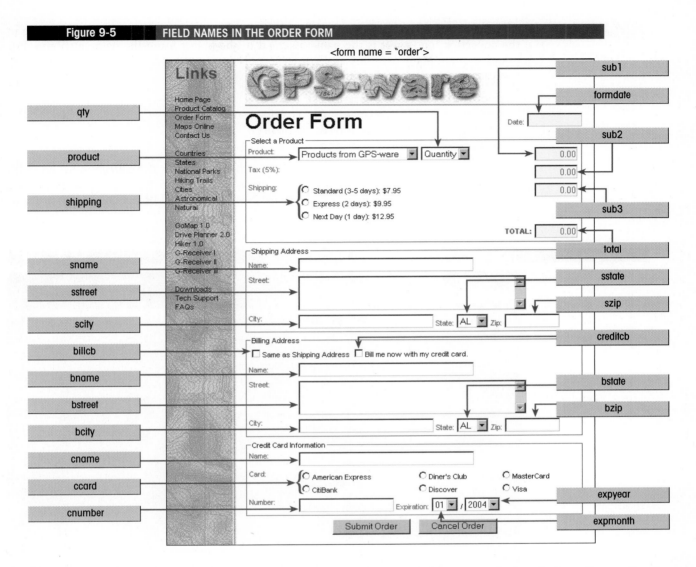

To refer to a particular field, you attach the field name to the JavaScript reference for the form. For example, Carol wants the current date to be displayed in the formdate field. Therefore, the JavaScript object reference for this field is:

```
document.order.formdate
```

Other fields from the order form can be similarly referenced. There is another way to reference an object and that is with an object collection.

Object Collections

An **object collection** is an array of all objects of a particular type, such as all of the hypertext link for a single document or all of the elements within a single form. An item from an object collection can be referenced in one of three ways:

```
collection[i]
collection["name"]
collection.name
```

where *collection* is the JavaScript name of the collection, *i* is an index number of the item in the collection, and *name* is the name assigned to the object using the name attribute. For example, the first element in Carol's order form is named "formdate". To refer to this item, you can use any of the following object names:

```
document.order.elements[0]
document.order.elements["formdate"]
document.order.elements.formdate
document.order.formdate
```

Note that index numbering starts with '0', so the first item in the collection has an index number of '0', the second has an index of '1', and so forth. Figure 9-6 lists some of the more commonly used JavaScript object collections. Note that not all object collections are supported by all browsers or browser versions.

| Figure 9-6 | SOME JAVASCRIPT OBJECT COLLECTIONS |

COLLECTION	DESCRIPTION	BROWSER SUPPORT NETSCAPE	IE
document.all	All HTML elements in the document		4.0
document.anchors	All anchor elements in the document	3.0	3.0
document.applets	All Java applets in the document. The applet must be started before being recognized as part of the DOM	3.0	3.0
document.embeds	All embedded objects in the document	3.0	4.0
document.*form*.elements	All of the elements in the form named *form*		
document.forms	All forms in the document	2.0	3.0
document.frames	All internal frames in the document		4.0
document.images	All inline images in the document	2.0	3.0
document.links	All hypertext links in the document	2.0	3.0
document.plugins	All plug-ins in the document		4.0
document.scripts	All scripts (created with the <script> tag) in the document		4.0

Now that you've seen how JavaScript assigns object names to various objects and collections, you'll next look at how you can use JavaScript to change the properties of those objects.

Working with Object Properties

Each object in JavaScript has properties associated with it. The number of properties depends on the particular object; some objects have only a few properties, while others have many. As with object names, certain keywords identify properties. A partial list of objects and their properties is shown in Figure 9-7.

Figure 9-7 | **JAVASCRIPT OBJECTS AND PROPERTIES**

OBJECT	PROPERTY NAME	DESCRIPTION
window	defaultStatus	The default message displayed in the window's status bar
	frames	An array of all the frames in the window
	length	The number of frames in the window
	name	The target name of the window
	status	A priority or temporary message in the window's status bar
frame	document	The document displayed within the frame
	length	The number of frames within this frame
	name	The target name of the frame
history	length	The number of entries in the history list
navigator	appCodeName	The code name of the browser
	appName	The name of the browser
	appVersion	The version of the browser
location	href	The URL of the location
	protocol	The protocol (HTTP, FTP, etc.) used by the location
document	bgColor	The background color of the page
	fgColor	The color of text on the page
	lastModified	The date the document was last modifie
	linkColor	The color of hypertext links on the page
	title	The title of the page
link	href	The URL of the hypertext link
	target	The target window of the hypertext link (if specified)
anchor	name	The name of the anchor
form	action	The action attribute of the <form> tag
	length	The number of elements in the form
	method	The method attribute of the <form> tag
	name	The name of the form

There are several ways of working with properties. You can change the value of a property, store the property's value in a variable, or test whether the property equals a specified value in an If...Then expression.

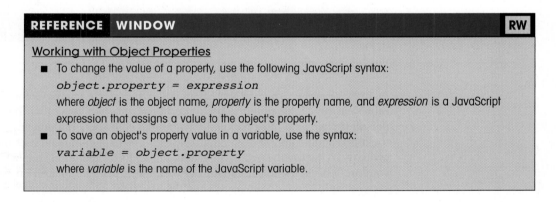

REFERENCE WINDOW | **RW**

Working with Object Properties
- To change the value of a property, use the following JavaScript syntax:

  `object.property = expression`

  where *object* is the object name, *property* is the property name, and *expression* is a JavaScript expression that assigns a value to the object's property.
- To save an object's property value in a variable, use the syntax:

  `variable = object.property`

  where *variable* is the name of the JavaScript variable.

Modifying a Property's Value

The syntax for changing the value of a property is:

```
object.property = expression
```

where *object* is the JavaScript name of the object you want to manipulate, *property* is a property of that object, and *expression* is a JavaScript expression that assigns a value to the property. Figure 9-8 shows how you can use objects and properties to modify your Web page and Web browser.

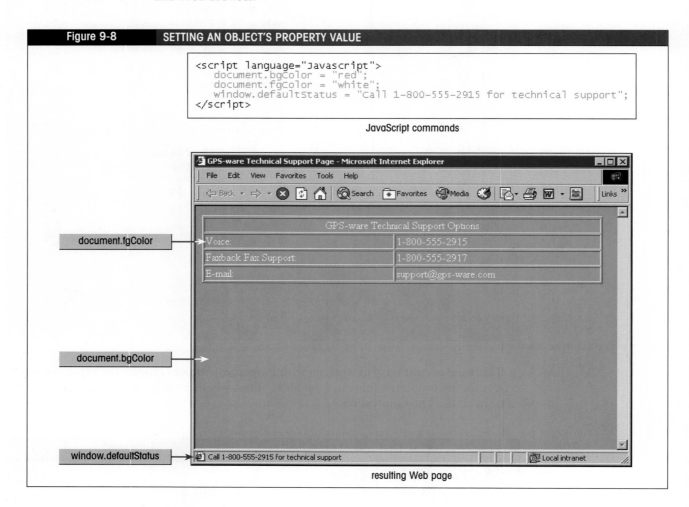

| Figure 9-8 | SETTING AN OBJECT'S PROPERTY VALUE |

```
<script language="Javascript">
    document.bgColor = "red";
    document.fgColor = "white";
    window.defaultStatus = "Call 1-800-555-2915 for technical support";
</script>
```

JavaScript commands

resulting Web page

In this example, the first JavaScript command, document.bgColor="red", modifies the current Web page, changing the background color to red. Note that this overrides the browser's default background color. Similarly, the second command, document.fgColor="white", changes the foreground color, or text color, to white. The final command uses the window.defaultStatus property to display the text "Call 1-800-555-2915 for technical support" in the status bar of the window. This is the default status bar text, but it can be replaced on occasion with other text, such as the URL of a Web page when the user interacts with a hypertext link.

Not all properties can be changed. Some properties are **read-only**, which means that you can read the property value, but you cannot modify it. One such property is the appVersion property of the navigator object, which identifies the version number of your Web browser. Although it would be nice to upgrade the version of your browser by running a simple JavaScript command, you're not allowed to change this value. Figure 9-9 shows how you can use JavaScript to display additional read-only information about your browser.

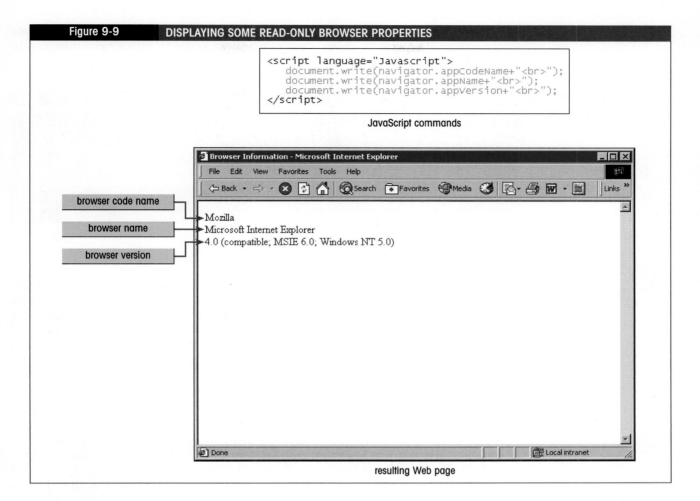

Figure 9-9   DISPLAYING SOME READ-ONLY BROWSER PROPERTIES

```
<script language="Javascript">
    document.write(navigator.appCodeName+"<br>");
    document.write(navigator.appName+"<br>");
    document.write(navigator.appversion+"<br>");
</script>
```

JavaScript commands

browser code name

browser name

browser version

Mozilla
Microsoft Internet Explorer
4.0 (compatible; MSIE 6.0; Windows NT 5.0)

resulting Web page

In this example, the values of the appCodeName, appName, and appVersion properties are used to display the browser code name, browser name, and browser version on the Web page. You might use this information to help you design Web pages that contain HTML extensions that are only supported by specific browsers or browser versions as follows. A JavaScript program could first test to see whether the user is running one of those browsers before inserting the tags into the Web page.

Assigning a Property to a Variable

Although you cannot change the value of read-only properties, you can assign a value to a variable in your JavaScript program. The syntax for assigning a property to a variable is:

variable = object.property

where *variable* is the variable name, *object* is the name of the object, and *property* is the name of its property. Figure 9-10 shows three examples of property values being assigned to JavaScript variables:

Figure 9-10	ASSIGNING PROPERTY VALUES TO VARIABLES	

COMMAND	DESCRIPTION
PageColor=document.bgColor;	Assign the background color of the page to the PageColor variable.
FrameNumber=window.length;	Store the number of frames in the window in the variable FrameNumber.
BrowserName=navigator.appName;	Save the name of the browser in the variable BrowserName.

Using Properties in Conditional Expressions

A final situation where you might need to work with properties is a conditional statement that changes how the Web page behaves based on the value of an object property. You'll use this technique later when adding form validation to Carol's registration form. The following JavaScript code shows how you can incorporate object properties into a simple conditional expression:

```
if(document.bgColor=="black") {
    document.fgColor="white";
} else {
    document.fgColor="black";
}
```

In this example, JavaScript first checks the background color of the Web page. If the background color is black, JavaScript changes the color of the text on the page to white, using the fgColor property of the page. If the background color is not black, then the text color is changed to black. As you can see, using objects, properties, and conditional statements provides you with great deal of control over the appearance of your Web page.

Working with Object Methods

Another way of controlling your Web page is to use methods. Remember that **methods** are either actions that objects perform or actions you apply to objects.

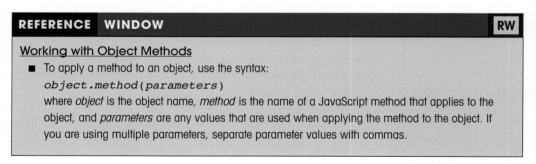

REFERENCE WINDOW | RW

Working with Object Methods
- To apply a method to an object, use the syntax:
  object.*method*(*parameters*)
  where *object* is the object name, *method* is the name of a JavaScript method that applies to the object, and *parameters* are any values that are used when applying the method to the object. If you are using multiple parameters, separate parameter values with commas.

The syntax for applying a method to an object is:

object.*method*(*parameters*);

where *object* is the name of the object, *method* is the method to be applied, and *parameters* are any values used in applying the method to the object. If you are using multiple parameters, you should separate values with commas. One of the most commonly used methods is the write() method applied to the document object, which sends text to the Web page document. Figure 9-11 shows three examples of objects and methods:

Figure 9-11	EXAMPLES OF JAVASCRIPT OBJECTS AND METHODS

COMMAND	DESCRIPTION
history.back();	Make the browser go back to the previously viewed page in the browser's history list.
form.submit();	Submit the form to the CGI script.
document.write("Thank you");	Write the text "Thank you" in the document.

Figure 9-12 lists some additional JavaScript objects and some of the methods associated with them. A more complete list of objects, properties, and methods is included in Appendix G. For now, you have a sufficient understanding of JavaScript object-based design and how useful it can be in designing your Web pages and controlling your Web browser.

Figure 9-12	JAVASCRIPT OBJECTS AND THEIR METHODS	

OBJECT NAME	METHOD NAME	DESCRIPTION
window	alert(*message*) close() prompt(*message, default_text*) scroll(*x, y*)	Displays a dialog box with a message in the window Closes the window Displays a dialog box prompting the user for information Scrolls to the (x,y) coordinate in the window
frame	alert(*message*) close() prompt(*message, default_text*)	Displays a dialog box with a message in the frame Closes the frame Displays a dialog box prompting the user for information
history	back() forward()	Returns to the previous page in the history list Goes to the next page in the history list
location	reload()	Reloads the current page
document	write(*string*) writeln(*string*)	Writes text and HTML tags to the current document Writes text and HTML tags to the current document on a new line
form	reset() submit()	Resets the form Submits the form

In the next session, you'll learn how JavaScript can be used to respond to user-initiated events as you modify Carol's registration form.

Session 9.1 QUICK CHECK

1. What is the difference between server-side validation and client-side validation?

2. Define the following terms: object, property, and method.

3. What object reference would you use for a check box named "join" located in a form named "enroll"?

4. What command changes the text color on a Web page to blue?

5. What command assigns the value of the page's text color to a variable named tcolor?

6. What command would you use to reset a form named "enroll"?

SESSION 9.2

In this session, you'll learn how to use event handlers to run JavaScript programs in response to specific events. You'll also learn how to insert values into input fields and how to navigate from one field to another. This session also shows you how to create a calculated field that is updated as values in the form change. Finally, you'll learn how to extract values from selection lists and radio buttons.

Managing Events

Now that you've studied some of the principles of programming with JavaScript, you're ready to look at the specifics of Carol's proposed changes to the order form. The following is a checklist of changes Carol wants you to make.

> ☐ 1) Automatically enter the current date in the formdate field, and move the cursor to the next field in the form.
>
> ☐ 2) Calculate the total cost of the customer's purchase based on the cost and quantity of the item, the sales tax, and the cost of shipping.
>
> ☐ 3) If the shipping address is the same as the billing address, copy the shipping address information into the billing address fields.
>
> ☐ 4) If the user is paying with a credit card, move the user to the credit card fields.
>
> ☐ 5) Check that the form has been properly filled out before allowing it to be submitted to the CGI script.

Your first task is to ensure that the current date is automatically entered into the formdate field whenever the Web page is opened by a browser. To do this, you'll need to work with events. An **event** is a specific occurrence within the Web browser. It can be as simple as opening up a Web page or as detailed as positioning the mouse pointer over a location on that page. Events are an important part of JavaScript programming because with them, you can write scripts that run in response to the actions of the user, even after the Web page has been opened.

Working with Event Handlers

Events are controlled in JavaScript using **event handlers** that specify what actions the browser takes in response to an event. Event handlers are created as attributes added to the HTML tag in which the event is triggered. The general syntax is:

```
<tag onevent = "JavaScript commands;">
```

where *tag* is the name of the HTML tag, *onevent* is the name of the event that occurs within the tag, and *JavaScript commands* are the commands the browser runs in response to the event.

JavaScript provides a wealth of event handlers, a few of which are described in Figure 9-13 and Appendix G.

| Figure 9-13 | JAVASCRIPT EVENT HOLDERS |

CATEGORY	EVENT HANDLER	DESCRIPTION	NETSCAPE	IE
Window and Document events	onload	The browser has completed loading the document.	2.0	3.0
	onunload	The browser has completed unloading the document.	2.0	3.0
	onabort	The transfer of an image has been aborted.	3.0	4.0
	onerror	An error has occurred in the JavaScript program.	3.0	4.0
	onmove	The user has moved the browser window.	4.0	3.0
	onresize	The user has resized the browser window.	4.0	4.0
	onscroll	The user has moved the scrollbar.		4.0
Form events	onfocus	The user has entered an input field.	2.0	3.0
	onblur	The user has exited an input field.	2.0	3.0
	onchange	The content of an input field has changed.	2.0	3.0
	onselect	The user has selected text in an input or textarea field.	2.0	3.0
	onsubmit	A form has been submitted.	2.0	3.0
	onreset	The user has clicked the Reset button.	3.0	4.0
Keyboard and Mouse events	onkeydown	The user has pressed a key.	4.0	4.0
	onkeyup	The user has released a key.	4.0	4.0
	onkeypress	The user has pressed and released a key.	4.0	4.0
	onclick	The user has clicked the mouse button.	2.0	3.0
	ondblclick	The user has double-clicked the mouse button.	4.0	4.0
	onmousedown	The user has pressed the mouse button.	4.0	4.0
	onmouseup	The user has released the mouse button.	4.0	4.0
	onmousemove	The user has moved the mouse pointer.	4.0	4.0
	onmouseover	The user has moved the mouse pointer over an element.	2.0	3.0
	onmouseout	The user has moved the mouse pointer out from an element.	3.0	4.0

| REFERENCE | WINDOW | RW |

Calling an Event Handler

■ To invoke an event handler, use the JavaScript syntax:

```
<tag onevent = "JavaScript commands;">
```

where *tag* is the HTML tag in which the event occurs, *onevent* is the name of the event, and *JavaScript commands* are the commands the browser runs in response to the event.

Figure 9-14 shows an example of the onclick event handler used with a collection of radio buttons. When the user clicks a radio button, the click event is initiated and the onclick event handler instructs the browser to run a JavaScript command to change the background color of the Web page. Note that the JavaScript commands invoked in this way do not require <script> tags, but they must be placed within a pair of single or double quotation marks within the tag. You can enter several commands with this method, separating one command line from another with a semicolon. However, when you have several JavaScript commands to run, the standard practice is to place them in a function, which can be called using a single command line.

Figure 9-14	USING THE ONCLICK EVENT HANDLER

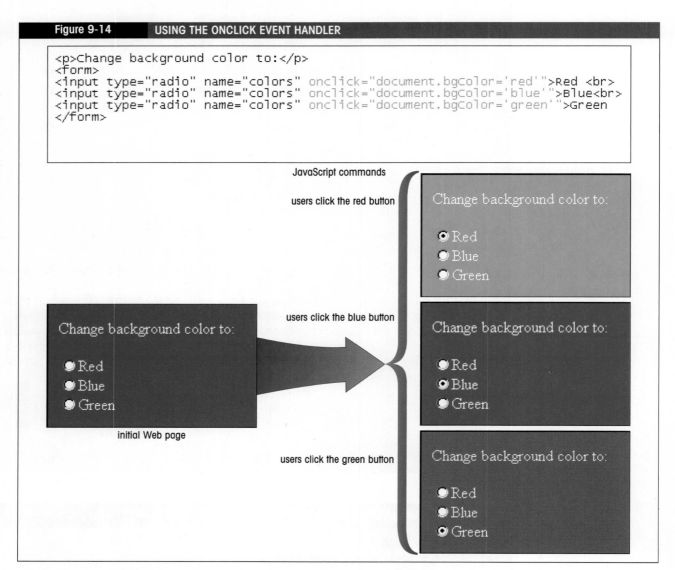

Events often take place in rapid succession. Consider the example shown in Figure 9-15. A user presses the Tab key to navigate to an input field, types a value into the field, and then presses the Tab key again to move to the next input field. One of the first events associated with the input field is the **focus** event as the input field becomes the active field in the form. The **change** event initiates notes that the value of the field has been changed. Finally, the **blur** event occurs as the focus leaves the field, going to a different field in the form. There are other events occurring during this scenario as well. The **keypress**, **keyup**, and **keydown** events continuously occur as the user tabs into fields, types a new value, and then tabs out. Each of these events can be captured using an event handler applied to the correct object in the Web page.

Figure 9-15	EVENTS INITIATED BY THE USER DURING DATA ENTRY

Event

Name: [|] Focus

1) The user tabs into an input field.

Name: [Ian Thompson|] Change

2) The user changes the field's value then tabs out of the field.

Name: [Ian Thompson] Blur

3) The user has left the field, and the change in the field's value has been noted.

The event handlers listed in Figure 9-14 do not apply to all JavaScript objects. For example, the onload event handler only works with form objects. Generally, Internet Explorer and Netscape 6.0 can apply event handlers to most HTML tags. Versions of Netscape prior to 6.0 apply event handlers to a smaller number of HTML tags. Appendix H provides a fuller description of browser support for the event handlers and the HTML tags they apply to. Because this is an area where there can be big differences between browsers and browser versions, you should always test your Web page with a variety of browsers and browser versions, especially if the Web page relies on JavaScript functions to operate correctly.

Running JavaScript Commands as Hypertext Links

If you want to run a command in response to the click event, an easy way of doing this is to create a hyperlink around the object to receive the mouse click. The syntax for doing this is:

```
<a href="javascript:JavaScript commands">Hypertext</a>
```

where *JavaScript commands* are the commands you want to run when the text link *Hypertext* is clicked by the user. For example, the following code changes the Web page's background color to red when the hypertext "Change background to red" is clicked.

```
<a href="javascript:document.bgcolor= 'red';">
  Change background to red
</a>
```

One advantage of this technique is that you can apply it to objects that might not support the onclick event handler in all browsers or browser versions.

Using the onload Event Handler

Now that you've learned how to work with events, you are ready to tackle the first task in Carol's list: insert the current date into the formdate field of the order form.

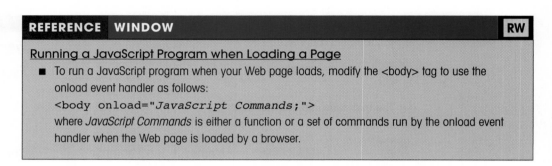

You want to insert the current date when the Web page is first loaded by the browser. The event handler for loading the Web page is the **onload** event hander. This handler is associated with the document object and must be placed in the <body> tag of the HTML file. When the browser encounters the load event, it runs the startform() function that you'll create momentarily.

To add the onload event handler to Carol's form:

1. Using your text editor, open **order.htm** from the tutorial.09/tutorial folder of your Data Disk.

2. Insert the attribute **onload="startform()"** in the <body> tag. See Figure 9-16.

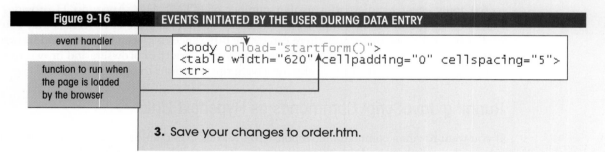

| Figure 9-16 | EVENTS INITIATED BY THE USER DURING DATA ENTRY |

event handler

function to run when the page is loaded by the browser

```
<body onload="startform()">
<table width="620" cellpadding="0" cellspacing="5">
<tr>
```

3. Save your changes to order.htm.

Now you need to create the startform() function, which serves two purposes: first, it enters the current date into the Date field, and second, it moves the cursor to the next field in the order form.

The startform() function relies on another JavaScript function named todaytxt(), which has been created for you in order.htm. The code for the todaytxt() function is as follows:

```
function todaytxt() {
var Today=new Date();
return Today.getMonth()+1+"/"+Today.getDate()+"/"+Today.getFullYear();
}
```

This function contains JavaScript commands that you should be familiar with. It uses the date object and extracts the current day, month, and year, and then combines those values in a text string, displaying the current date in the format dd/mm/yyyy. One of the purposes of the startform() function is to retrieve this text string and display it in the formdate field of the order form. The code for the startform() function is therefore:

```
function startform() {
    document.order.formdate.value=todaytxt();
}
```

Note that this function inserts the text string into the formdate field by changing the value property of that field; it does not use the document.write() method you used in the previous tutorial.

To add the startform() function to order.htm:

1. Locate the <script> tag in order.htm.

2. Enter the following commands directly below the closing bracket of the todaytxt() function:

```
function startform() {
    document.order.formdate.value=todaytxt();
}
```

Your file should look like Figure 9-17.

| Figure 9-17 | CREATING THE STARTFORM() FUNCTION |

```
function startform() {
    document.order.formdate.value=todaytxt();
}
</script>
</head>

<body onload="startform()">
<table width="620" cellpadding="0" cellspacing="5">
<tr>
```

3. Save your changes to order.htm and reload the file in your Web browser. Your Web page should now show the current date in the Date field. See Figure 9-18.

| Figure 9-18 | CURRENT DATE INSERTED INTO THE ORDER FORM |

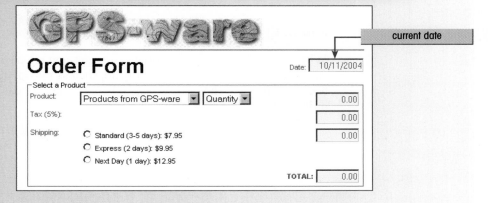

TROUBLE? Note that your date is different from the one shown in the figure. If your browser displays an error message, return to your text editor and verify that you have entered the code exactly as shown in the steps.

The "value" property is one of many properties you can associate with input boxes such as the formdate field. Additional properties and methods that can be associated with fields are shown in Figure 9-19.

| Figure 9-19 | PROPERTIES, METHODS, AND EVENT HANDLERS OF INPUT FIELDS |

PROPERTY	DESCRIPTION	IE	NETSCAPE
defaultvalue	Default value of the field	3.0	2.0
maxlength	Maximum number of characters in the field	4.0	6.0
name	The name of the field	3.0	2.0
size	The width of the field in characters	4.0	6.0
type	The type of input field	4.0	3.0
value	The value of the input field	3.0	2.0
METHOD	**DESCRIPTION**	**IE**	**NETSCAPE**
blur()	Remove the focus from the field	3.0	2.0
focus()	Give focus to the field	3.0	2.0
select()	Select the field	3.0	2.0
EVENT HANDLER	**DESCRIPTION**	**IE**	**NETSCAPE**
onfocus()	Run when the field receives the focus	3.0	2.0
onblur()	Run when the field loses the focus	3.0	2.0
onchange()	Run when the value of the field changes	3.0	2.0

This function performs one of the two jobs it needs to; it displays the date in the formdate field. Carol also wants the function to move the cursor to the next field in the form. To accomplish this, you need to learn how to make JavaScript not only respond to an event, but initiate one.

Initiating Events with JavaScript

When you use JavaScript to initiate an event, you are instructing the Web page to perform an action that a user would normally do, such as moving the cursor to a specific field in the form. Figure 9-20 shows three examples of JavaScript commands that initiate events in the order form.

Figure 9-20	INITIATING AN EVENT WITH JAVASCRIPT

COMMAND	DESCRIPTION
document.order.product.focus()	Move the cursor to the product field in the order form.
document.order.product.blur()	Move the cursor out of the product field.
document.order.submit()	Submit the order form for processing.

Additional events you can emulate in your forms are shown in Figure 9-21.

Figure 9-21	EVENTS INITIATED BY THE USER DURING DATA ENTRY

OBJECT	EVENT METHODS
button	click()
check box	click()
document	clear()
form	reset(), submit()
frames	blur(), close(), focus()
input box	focus(), blur(), select()
radio button	click()
reset button	click()
submit button	click()
text area box	focus(), blur(), select()
window	blur(), close(), focus()

REFERENCE   WINDOW   RW

Moving Between Input Fields
- To instruct the cursor to move to a specific field on your Web page form, use the JavaScript command:
  `document.form.field.focus();`
  where *form* is the name of the Web page form, and *field* is the name of the field that the cursor moves to.
- To have the cursor move from a field on your Web page form, use the JavaScript command:
  `document.form.field.blur();`
  where the blur() method removes the cursor from the specified input field.

You need to add a command to the startform() function that places the cursor in the next field in the order form, which in this case is the product field. The command to move the cursor to the product field is:

```
document.order.product.focus();
```

To revise the startform() function:

1. Return to **order.htm** in your text editor.

2. Locate the startform() function at the beginning of the file, and then add the following command to the end of the command block:

```
document.order.product.focus();
```

See Figure 9-22.

| Figure 9-22 | MOVING THE FOCUS TO THE PRODUCT FIELD |

```
function startform() {
    document.order.formdate.value=todaytxt();
    document.order.product.focus();
}
</script>
</head>

<body onload="startform()">
<table width="620" cellpadding="0" cellspacing="5">
<tr>
```

the product field receives the focus of the cursor after the current date is entered in the formdate field

3. Save your changes to order.htm, and reload the file in your Web browser.

TROUBLE? If you're using Netscape version 4.7 or earlier, you may need to close the file and open it again for the changes to take effect; clicking the Reload or Refresh button may not be sufficient.

When the page is reloaded, the product field should be selected. You can verify this by looking to see if the list box is highlighted.

You've completed the first task on your list for Carol.

1) Automatically enter the current date in the formdate field, and move the cursor to the next field in the form.

2) Calculate the total cost of the customer's purchase based on the cost and quantity of the item, the sales tax, and the cost of shipping.

3) If the shipping address is the same as the billing address, copy the shipping address information into the billing address fields.

4) If the user is paying with a credit card, move the user to the credit card fields.

5) Check that the form has been properly filled out before allowing it to be submitted to the CGI script.

For the next task, you'll work on calculating the cost of a customer's order based on product purchased, quantity, sales tax, and shipping costs.

Creating a Calculated Field

The total cost of the order is divided into three subtotals and stored in fields named sub1, sub2, and sub3.

- The sub1 field displays the cost of the selected product multiplied by the number of items ordered.
- The sub2 field displays the sales tax, which is 5% of the value of the sub1 field.
- The sub3 field displays the cost of the selected shipping method.

The order form needs to run the following formula each time the user changes the product, quantity, or shipping method:

```
total = sub1 + sub2 + sub3
```

JavaScript treats the values of input fields as text strings. This means you cannot simply add the value of the three input fields together because JavaScript will append the text strings rather than adding their numeric values. For example, if sub1="100", sub2="5", and sub3="10", then the formula

```
sub1 + sub2 + sub3
```

returns the text string "100510" (adding the three text strings together). To convert a text string to a numeric value, you must use the **eval()** function as follows:

```
eval(sub1)+eval(sub2)+eval(sub3)
```

which returns the value 115.

An important thing to remember about calculating values: *JavaScript does not round off the values to nice digits.* Instead, JavaScript displays calculated values to several digits. This is a problem for Carol, since she wants the total order cost calculated in dollars and cents. It would certainly be confusing to the customer to be told that she owes $45.78129 dollars!

To solve this problem, the following function has been added to order.htm:

```
function dollars(n) {

  n = eval(n);

  n = Math.round(n*100)/100;

  return (n == Math.round(n)) ? n += ".00" :
         (n*10 == Math.round(n*10)) ? n += "0" :
         n;

}
```

The dollars() function takes a value, *n*, and rounds it to two digits to the right of the decimal point. For example, the following values are returned by the dollars() function:

```
dollars(45.78129) = 45.78
dollars(45.78859) = 45.79
dollars(45.7) = 45.70
dollars(45) = 45.00
```

You may want to take some time to review the formulas used in this function, especially the use of the Math.round() method and the conditional operator.

The function to calculate the total cost of a customer's order will, therefore, appear as follows:

```
function total_price() {
    s1 = eval(document.order.sub1.value);
    s2 = eval(document.order.sub2.value);
    s3 = eval(document.order.sub3.value);
    document.order.total.value = dollars(s1+s2+s3);
}
```

Add this function to order.htm now.

To add the total_price() function:

1. Return to **order.htm** in your text editor.

2. Add the following function directly before the closing </script> tag in the head section of the file:

```
function total_price() {
    s1 = eval(document.order.sub1.value);
    s2 = eval(document.order.sub2.value);
    s3 = eval(document.order.sub3.value);
    document.order.total.value = dollars(s1+s2+s3);
}
```

See Figure 9-23.

Figure 9-23	INSERTING THE TOTAL_COST() FUNCTION

```
function total_price() {
    s1=eval(document.order.sub1.value);
    s2=eval(document.order.sub2.value);
    s3=eval(document.order.sub3.value);
    document.order.total.value=dollars(s1+s2+s3);
}
</script>
</head>

<body onload="startform()">
<table width="620" cellpadding="0" cellspacing="5">
<tr>
```

Now that you've created the total_price() function, how should it be used? Carol wants the function to run whenever the values of the product, qty, and shipping fields are changed. Let's see how to accomplish this, first with the product and qty fields. Since both of these fields used selection lists, it will require us to learn how JavaScript handles that type of field.

Working **with** a **Selection List**

JavaScript treats a selection list as an array of option values. In the case of Carol's form, the tags that define the product list are:

```
<select name="product">
  <option value="0">Products from GPS-ware
  <option value="19.95">GoMap 1.0 ($19.95)
  <option value="29.95">Drive Planner 2.0 ($29.95)
  <option value="29.95">Hiker 1.0 ($29.95)
  <option value="149.50">G-Receiver I ($149.50)
  <option value="199.50">G-Receiver II ($199.50)
  <option value="249.50">G-Receiver III ($249.50)
</select>
```

Each option in the product selection list has a text property and a value property. The text property indicates what text is displayed in the list box, and the value property corresponds to the value attribute of the <option> tag. Figure 9-24 displays the JavaScript object references and property values for the items in the product selection list. Note that the array of selection options starts with an index value of 0.

Figure 9-24	SELECT LIST ARRAY TEXT AND VALUES

| OBJECT | OBJECT PROPERTIES | |
	.TEXT	.VALUE
document.order.product.options[0]	Products from GPS-ware	0
document.order.product.options[1]	GoMap 1.0 ($19.95)	19.95
document.order.product.options[2]	Drive Planner 2.0 ($29.95)	29.95
document.order.product.options[3]	Hiker 1.0 ($29.95)	29.95
document.order.product.options[4]	G-Receiver I ($149.50)	149.50
document.order.product.options[5]	G-Receiver II ($199.50)	199.50
document.order.product.options[6]	G-Receiver III ($249.50)	249.50

There is no value property for the selection list itself, only for the options within the list. How then do you determine the price of the product the customer selects in the order form? This is accomplished by using the **selectedIndex** property, which indicates the index number of the selected option. Once you know that information, you can use it to return the value of that option. In the following code, the index number of the selected item is stored in the item_index variable. The item_index variable is then used to determine the value of the selected item and stores that value in the item_value variable. In the same fashion, the text of the selected item is stored in the item_text variable.

```
item_index = document.order.product.selectedIndex;
item_value = document.order.product.options[item_index].value;
item_text = document.order.product.options[item_index].text;
```

Figure 9-25 shows some of the other properties and methods associated with selection lists and selection options.

Figure 9-25   SELECTION LISTS AND SELECTION OPTIONS

	PROPERTY	DESCRIPTION	IE	NETSCAPE
	length	The number of options in the list	3.0	2.0
	name	The name of the selection list	3.0	2.0
	selectedIndex	The index number of the item currently selected in the list	3.0	2.0
THE ENTIRE SELECTION LIST	**METHOD**	**DESCRIPTION**	**IE**	**NETSCAPE**
	focus()	Give focus to the selection list	3.0	2.0
	blur()	Remove focus from the selection list	3.0	2.0
	EVENT HANDLER	**DESCRIPTION**	**IE**	**NETSCAPE**
	onfocus()	Run when the selection list receives the focus	3.0	2.0
	onblur()	Run when the selection list loses the focus	3.0	2.0
	onchange()	Run when the user selects a different option from the list	3.0	2.0
	PROPERTY	**DESCRIPTION**	**IE**	**NETSCAPE**
AN OPTION FROM THE SELECTION LIST	index	The index value of the option	3.0	2.0
	selected	A Boolean value indicating whether the option has been selected	3.0	2.0
	text	The text of the option	3.0	2.0
	value	The value of the option	3.0	2.0

REFERENCE WINDOW   **RW**

Referring to Values in a Selection List

- To refer to the value of an option in a selection list, use the object and property:
  ```
  document.form.field.options[index].value
  ```
  where *form* is the name of the Web page form, *field* is the name of the selection field, and *index* is the index number of the option.
- To refer to the text of an option (the text that is shown to the user) in a selection list, use the object and property:
  ```
  document.form.field.options[index].text
  ```
- To determine the index number of the currently selected option, use the JavaScript property:
  ```
  document.form.field.selectedIndex;
  ```
  Now you have enough information to create a function to display the cost of the customer's order in the sub1 field. The function is as follows:
  ```
  function order_price() {
     item_index = document.order.product.selectedIndex;
     item_value = document.order.product.options[item_index].value;
     qty_ordered = document.order.qty.selectedIndex;
     document.order.sub1.value = dollars(item_value*qty_ordered);
     document.order.sub2.value = dollars(item_value*qty_ordered*0.05);
     total_price();
  }
  ```

The first two lines of this function are used to determine the value of the selected product. The third line determines the quantity of items ordered, which also happens be equal to the index of the document.order.qty.options array. In the fourth line, the cost of the selected item multiplied by the number of items purchased is stored in the sub1 field. Note that the command calls the dollars() function so that the value in the sub1 field is displayed to two decimal places. The fifth line in the function calculates the 5% sales tax on the cost of the item and the quantity ordered. It stores this value in the sub2 field. Finally, the last line of the function runs the total_price() function, recalculating the total cost of the order based on the new values of the sub1 and sub2 fields.

To add the order_price() function to order.htm:

1. Within **order.htm**, insert the following commands directly above the closing </script> tag:

```
function order_price() {
   item_index = document.order.product.selectedIndex;
   item_value = document.order.product.options[item_index].value;
   qty_ordered = document.order.qty.selectedIndex;
   document.order.sub1.value = dollars(item_value*qty_ordered);
   document.order.sub2.value = dollars(item_value*qty_ordered*0.05);
   total_price();
}
```

2. Locate the <select> tag for the product field and add the event handler: **onchange="order_price()"**.

3. Locate the <select> tag for the qty field and add the event handler: **onchange="order_price()"**.

Figure 9-26 highlights the revised code for order.htm.

Figure 9-26 | CREATING THE ORDER_PRICE() FUNCTION

```
function order_price() {
    item_index=document.order.product.selectedIndex;
    item_value=document.order.product.options[item_index].value;
    qty_ordered=document.order.qty.selectedIndex;
    document.order.sub1.value=dollars(item_value*qty_ordered);
    document.order.sub2.value=dollars(item_value*qty_ordered*0.05);
    total_price();
}

</script>
</head>
```

```
<!-- LIST OF GPS-WARE PRODUCTS -->
<td width="70" valign="top"><span class="fmlabel">Product:</span></td>
<td width="350" valign="top">
    <select name="product" onchange="order_price()">
    <option value="0">Products from GPS-ware
    <option value="19.95">GoMap 1.0 ($19.95)
    <option value="29.95">Drive Planner 2.0 ($29.95)
    <option value="29.95">Hiker 1.0 ($29.95)
    <option value="149.50">G-Receiver I ($149.50)
    <option value="199.50">G-Receiver II ($199.50)
    <option value="249.50">G-Receiver III ($249.50)
    </select>

<!-- QUANTITY OF ORDER -->
    <select name="qty" onchange="order_price()">
    <option>Quantity</option>
    <option>1<option>2<option>3<option>4<option>5<option>6<option>7
    <option>8<option>9<option>10
    </select>
</td>
```

4. Save your changes to order.htm and reload the file in your browser.

5. Select **Hiker 1.0 ($29.95)** from the Product list box and **2** from the Quantity list box. The value of the sub1, sub2, and total fields change to reflect the selected item and quantity (see Figure 9-27).

Figure 9-27 | CALCULATING THE COST OF AN ORDER

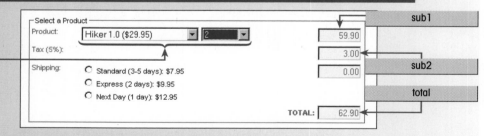

as the user selects an option, the values of the sub1, sub2, and total fields are updated

6. Select different products and quantities from the two list boxes to verify that each time you change one of these values, the values of the sub1, sub2 and total fields are updated.

Working with Radio Buttons

The final component of the total cost of an order concerns the shipping cost. There are three options: standard, express, and next day. Carol has placed these three options in radio buttons associated with the field name "shipping". The HTML tags in order.htm are as follows:

```
<input type="radio" name="shipping" value="7.95">Standard
(3-5 days): $7.95
<input type="radio" name="shipping" value="9.95">Express
(2 days): $9.95
<input type="radio" name="shipping" value="12.95">Next Day
(1 day): $12.95
```

The JavaScript reference for a radio button is:

```
document.form.field[i]
```

where *form* is the name of the Web page form, *field* is the name assigned to the radio buttons, and *i* is the index number of a specific radio button. Like all arrays, the first radio button has an index value of 0, the second button has an index value of 1, and so on. In Carol's form, the JavaScript object references for the three shipping radio buttons are:

```
document.order.shipping[0]
document.order.shipping[1]
document.order.shipping[2]
```

Figure 9-28 describes some of the properties, methods, and event handlers associated with radio buttons.

Figure 9-28	PROPERTIES, METHODS, AND EVENT HANDLERS OF RADIO BUTTONS		
PROPERTY	**DESCRIPTION**	**IE**	**NETSCAPE**
checked	A Boolean value indicating whether the radio button has been checked	3.0	2.0
name	The name of the radio button field	3.0	2.0
value	The value of radio button	3.0	2.0
METHOD	**DESCRIPTION**	**IE**	**NETSCAPE**
focus()	Give focus to the radio button	3.0	2.0
blur()	Remove focus from the radio button	3.0	2.0
click()	Click the radio button	3.0	2.0
EVENT HANDLER	**DESCRIPTION**	**IE**	**NETSCAPE**
onfocus()	Run when the radio button receives the focus	3.0	2.0
onblur()	Run when the radio button loses the focus	3.0	2.0
onclick()	Run when the radio button is clicked	3.0	2.0

For example, the values of the three shipping radio buttons can be expressed as follows in JavaScript:

```
document.order.shipping[0].value = "7.95";
document.order.shipping[1].value = "9.95";
document.order.shipping[2].value = "12.95";
```

Carol would like you to create a script that displays the shipping value of the selected radio button in the sub3 field and then updates the total cost of the order. One problem is that there is no JavaScript object that refers to the entire collection of radio buttons; thus, there is no single value property that tells us which button was selected. There are only value properties for the individual radio buttons. How then do you determine the value of the selected shipping option? You could treat each radio button as a different field and run a different function for each button, or you could use an If...Then statement to test which radio button was selected. Both approaches are needlessly complicated, and thankfully, there is an easier way: use the "this" keyword.

Using the "this" Keyword

The **"this"** keyword is a JavaScript object name that refers to the currently selected object, whatever that may be. It's particularly useful in situations where several different objects on the page might access the same function. In that situation, the "this" keyword can pass along information about the object that initiated the function. To apply this technique to the shipping field radio buttons, add the following event handlers to the three <input> tags:

```
<input type="radio" name="shipping" value="7.95"
onclick="shipping_price(this)">

<input type="radio" name="shipping" value="9.95"
onclick="shipping_price(this)">

<input type="radio" name="shipping" value="12.95"
onclick="shipping_price(this)">
```

The shipping_price() function looks like the following:

```
function shipping_price(field) {
document.order.sub3.value = dollars(field.value);
   total_price();
}
```

The "this" object passes a reference to the object that initiated the program to the shipping_price() function. That information is stored in the field variable. The value of the field variable is then formatted using the dollars() function and displayed in the sub3 field of the order form. Finally, the total_price() function is called to update the total price of the order based on the new sub3 value.

To create the shipping_price() function:

1. Return to **order.htm** in your text editor.

2. Insert the following function directly above the closing </script> tag:

```
function shipping_price(field) {
    document.order.sub3.value = dollars(field.value);
    total_price();
}
```

3. Add the event handler **onclick="shipping_price(this)"** to the three <input> tags for the shipping radio buttons (see Figure 9-29):

Figure 9-29   CREATING THE SHIPPING_PRICE() FUNCTION

```
function shipping_price(field) {
    document.order.sub3.value=dollars(field.value);
    total_price();
}

</script>
</head>
```

```
<!-- METHOD OF SHIPPING -->
<td width="70" valign="top"><span class="fmlabel">Shipping:</span></td>
<td valign="top">
    <input type="radio" name="shipping" value="7.95" onclick="shipping_price(this)">
    Standard (3-5 days): $7.95<br>
    <input type="radio" name="shipping" value="9.95" onclick="shipping_price(this)">
    Express (2 days): $9.95<br>
    <input type="radio" name="shipping" value="12.95" onclick="shipping_price(this)">
    Next Day (1 day): $12.95
</td>
```

4. Save your changes to order.htm and close your text editor.

5. Using your Web browser, reload order.htm.

6. Select **G-Receiver III ($249.50)** from the Product list box, **1** from the Quantity list box, and click the **Next Day** option button. Figure 9-30 shows the subtotals and total cost of the order.

Figure 9-30   CALCULATING THE TOTAL ORDER COST

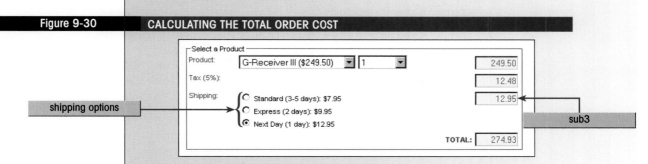

7. Continue testing your form, viewing other combinations of products, quantities, and shipping options. Verify that the cost of the order changes whenever one of these factors changes.

8. Close your Web browser.

You've successfully completed the second item in Carol's list.

> ● 1) Automatically enter the current date in the formdate field, and move the cursor to the next field in the form.
>
> ● 2) Calculate the total cost of the customer's purchase based on the cost and quantity of the item, the sales tax, and the cost of shipping.
>
> ○ 3) If the shipping address is the same as the billing address, copy the shipping address information into the billing address fields.
>
> ○ 4) If the user is paying with a credit card, move the user to the credit card fields.
>
> ○ 5) Check that the form has been properly filled out before allowing it to be submitted to the CGI script.

In the next session you'll complete your work on scripting Carol's order form, and you'll learn how to use JavaScript to submit or reset a form.

Session 9.2 QUICK CHECK

1. Define the following terms: event, event handler, and event method.

2. How would you modify an HTML file to run the function Welcome() whenever the Web page is loaded into the browser?

3. How would you modify the following HTML tag so that it runs the CheckCredit()function whenever the user exits the following input field?

```
<input name="CreditCard">
```

Use the following HTML tags to answer Quick Checks 4 through 6:

```
<form name="product">

    <select name="model">
            <option value="P220">Pentium 220
            <option value="P300">Pentium 300
            <option value="P500">Pentium 500
    </select>
</form>
```

4. What JavaScript command would you use to change the value of the first option in the selection list to "P250"?

5. What JavaScript command would you use to change the text of the first option in the selection list to "Pentium 250"?

6. What JavaScript command would you use to store the index of the option the user selected in a variable named ModelNumber?

7. What is the "this" object and how can you use it in your JavaScript programs?

8. The study form contains two input fields named weight and weight2. If the weight field contains the value "5" and the weight2 field contains the value "25", what text is returned by the following JavaScript expression?

```
document.study.weight.value + document.study.weight2.value;
```

In this session, you'll learn how to work with check boxes and how to copy values from one field to another. You'll also learn how to use JavaScript to submit or reset a Web page form. Finally, you'll learn how to create dialog boxes to display messages to the user or to prompt the user for specific information.

Working with Check Boxes

Now that you've completed work on calculating the cost of the customer's order, you'll turn to the shipping address and billing address sections. In many cases these two addresses will be the same. Carol has included a check box on the form where customers can indicate that this is in fact the case. Carol would like you to create a program that copies the shipping address information into the billing address fields if the check box is checked.

Figure 9-31 lists some of the properties, methods, and event handlers of check box objects.

Figure 9-31	PROPERTIES, METHODS, AND EVENT HANDLERS OF CHECK BOXES			
PROPERTY	**DESCRIPTION**	**IE**	**NETSCAPE**	
checked	A Boolean value indicating whether the check box has been checked	3.0	2.0	
name	The name of the check box field	3.0	2.0	
value	The value of the check box	3.0	2.0	
METHOD	**DESCRIPTION**	**IE**	**NETSCAPE**	
focus()	Give focus to the check box	3.0	2.0	
blur()	Remove focus from the check box	3.0	2.0	
click()	Click the check box	3.0	2.0	
EVENT HANDLER	**DESCRIPTION**	**IE**	**NETSCAPE**	
onfocus()	Run when the check box receives the focus	3.0	2.0	
onblur()	Run when the check box loses the focus	3.0	2.0	
onclick()	Run when the check box is clicked	3.0	2.0	

In Carol's form, the following HTML tag is used to create the check box that is checked if the shipping address and the billing address are the same.

```
<input type="checkbox" name="billcb">Same as shipping address
```

To test whether this check box has been selected, use the following JavaScript object reference:

```
document.order.billcb.checked
```

If this value is true, Carol wants your program to copy the shipping address into the billing address. The complete function looks like the following:

```
function copy_shipping() {
   if (document.order.billcb.checked) {
      document.order.bname.value=document.order.sname.value;
      document.order.bstreet.value=document.order.sstreet.value;
      document.order.bcity.value=document.order.scity.value;
      document.order.bstate.selectedIndex=document.order.sstate.selectedIndex;
      document.order.bzip.value=document.order.szip.value;
   }
}
```

Note that most of the address fields are text boxes, so you only need to copy the value of the shipping field to the corresponding billing field. The only exception is the bstate field which is a selection list containing two-letter abbreviations of the 50 states. For that field you must use the selectedIndex property to copy the index number of the selected option from the bstate field into the sstate field.

Carol wants this function to run whenever the user clicks the billcb check box.

To create the shipping_price() function:

1. Using your text editor, open **order.htm** if it is not currently open.

2. Insert the following function directly above the closing </script> tag:

```
function copy_shipping() {
    if (document.order.billcb.checked) {
document.order.bname.value=document.order.sname.value;
document.order.bstreet.value=document.order.sstreet.value;
document.order.bcity.value=document.order.scity.value;
document.order.bstate.selectedIndex=document.order.sstate.selectedIndex;
document.order.bzip.value=document.order.szip.value;
    }
}
```

3. Locate the <input> tag for the billcb field and add the event handler **onclick="copy_shipping()"**. Figure 9-32 highlights the revised code.

| Figure 9-32 | CREATING THE COPY_SHIPPING() FUNCTION |

```
function copy_shipping() {
    if (document.order.billcb.checked) {
        document.order.bname.value=document.order.sname.value;
        document.order.bstreet.value=document.order.sstreet.value;
        document.order.bcity.value=document.order.scity.value;
        document.order.bstate.selectedIndex=document.order.sstate.selectedIndex;
        document.order.bzip.value=document.order.szip.value;
    }
}

</script>
</head>
```

```
<tr>
<!-- BILLING ADDRESS FIELDS -->
<td valign="top" colspan="2">
<fieldset>
<legend>Billing Address</legend>
<table>
<tr>
    <td colspan="2">
        <input type="checkbox" name="billcb" onclick="copy_shipping()">Same as Shipping Address
        <input type="checkbox" name="creditcb">Bill me now with my credit card.
    </td>
</tr>
```

4. Save your changes to order.htm.

5. Using your Web browser, open order.htm.

6. Type the following address into the shipping address fields:

   Carol Campbell
   75 Allen Street
   Clarkston, MI 38912

7. Click the **Same as shipping address** check box, and verify that the shipping address is copied into the billing address fields (see Figure 9-33).

Figure 9-33	COPYING THE SHIPPING ADDRESS TO THE BILLING ADDRESS

select this option to copy the shipping address to the billing address

The other check box on the form, with the field name "creditcb", indicates whether the customer is paying online with a credit card. If a customer selects this check box, Carol wants the form to navigate to the credit card section, giving the cname field the focus. The function to move the customer is:

```
function use_credit() {
if (document.order.creditcb.checked) document.order.cname.focus();
}
```

To create the use_credit() function:

1. Return to **order.htm** in your text editor.

2. Add the following code directly above the closing </script> tag:

```
function use_credit() {
    if (document.order.creditcb.checked) document.order.cname.focus();
}
```

3. Locate the <input> tag for the creditcb field and add the event handler **onclick="use_credit()"**. See Figure 9-34.

Figure 9-34   CREATING THE USE_CREDIT() FUNCTION

```
function use_credit() {
    if (document.order.creditcb.checked) document.order.cname.focus();
}

</script>
</head>
```

```
<tr>
<!-- BILLING ADDRESS FIELDS -->
<td valign="top" colspan="2">
<fieldset>
<legend>Billing Address</legend>
<table>
<tr>
   <td colspan="2">
      <input type="checkbox" name="billcb" onclick="copy_shipping()">Same as Shipping Address
      <input type="checkbox" name="creditcb" onclick="use_credit()">Bill me now with my credit card.
   </td>
</tr>
```

4. Save your changes to order.htm.

5. Using your Web browser, reload order.htm.

6. Click the **Bill me now with my credit card** checkbox, and verify that the cursor navigates to the credit card section of the order form.

You've now completed four of the five tasks that Carol assigned to you. The remaining task is to create scripts to validate the form before it is submitted to a CGI script.

- 1) Automatically enter the current date in the formdate field, and move the cursor to the next field in the form.
- 2) Calculate the total cost of the customer's purchase based on the cost and quantity of the item, the sales tax, and the cost of shipping.
- 3) If the shipping address is the same as the billing address, copy the shipping address information into the billing address fields.
- 4) If the user is paying with a credit card, move the user to the credit card fields.
- 5) Check that the form has been properly filled out before allowing it to be submitted to the CGI script.

Submitting a Form

Before the form can be submitted, Carol would like you to create a program to check that the following things have been completed:

1. A product, quantity, and shipping method have been selected.

2. A complete shipping address has been entered.

3. A complete billing address or complete credit card information has been entered.

If one of these conditions is not met, Carol would like the browser to refuse the form submission and indicate to the user why the form was not submitted.

To test whether the user has selected a product, quantity, and shipping method, you can simply test whether the values in the sub1, sub2, and sub3 fields are nonzero. The JavaScript commands to do this are:

```
product_ok = true;
if (document.order.sub1.value == "0.00") product_ok = false;
if (document.order.sub2.value == "0.00") product_ok = false;
if (document.order.sub3.value == "0.00") product_ok = false;
```

The product_ok variable indicates whether the user has selected a product, quantity, and shipping method. The value of the variable is assumed to be true, and it only changes to false if the value of the sub1, sub2, or sub3 field is equal to "0.00".

A similar set of code can test whether a shipping address has been specified by the customer. In this case, we simply test whether the sname, street, scity, and szip fields are empty. The code for this is:

```
shipping_ok = true;
if (document.order.sname.value == "") shipping_ok = false;
if (document.order.sstreet.value == "") shipping_ok = false;
if (document.order.scity.value == "") shipping_ok = false;
if (document.order.szip.value == "") shipping_ok = false;
```

The test for a valid billing address is similar:

```
billing_ok = true;
if (document.order.bname.value == "") billing_ok = false;
if (document.order.bstreet.value == "") billing_ok = false;
if (document.order.bcity.value == "") billing_ok = false;
if (document.order.bzip.value == "") billing_ok = false;
```

To test whether the user has entered credit card information, we have to first check for a valid card name and number. The code to do this is as follows:

```
credit_ok = true;
if (document.order.cname.value == "") credit_ok = false;
if (document.order.cnumber.value == "") credit_ok = false;
```

Next, you need to examine each of the six radio buttons from the ccard field that indicate the type of credit card used by the customer. At least one of those radio buttons must be selected. To test for this, create a For loop that evaluates the checked property for each radio button. The code is:

```
cardchecked = false;
for (i=0; i<=5; i++) {
    if (document.order.ccard[i].checked) cardchecked=true;
}
if (cardchecked == false) credit_ok=false;
```

The cardchecked variable has an initial value of "false". It remains false unless one of the six radio buttons is checked. The final part of this command block sets the value of the credit_ok variable to "false" if the cardchecked variable is "false," indicating that no radio button was checked.

A customer can either pay with a credit card or be billed. This means either the credit card information or the billing address must be complete. We can test this as follows:

```
payment_ok = (credit_ok || billing_ok);
```

Recall that the || symbol represents the "or" operator. Thus, if credit_ok is true or billing_ok is true, the value of the payment_ok variable is true. As long as the customer has completed the credit information correctly or the billing address information correctly, the payment information has been completed correctly.

Finally, you need to test whether all three sections of the form have been properly completed. We'll store this value in the form_ok variable as follows:

```
form_ok = (product_ok && shipping_ok && payment_ok);
```

The && symbol stands for the "and" operator; so the form_ok variable is true only if the product_ok, shipping_ok, and payment_ok variables are true. In other words, if the customer has selected a product correctly, entered a complete shipping address, and completed the payment information, the form is valid. The complete command block looks like the following:

```
function checkform() {
product_ok = true;
if (document.order.sub1.value == "0.00") product_ok =
false;
if (document.order.sub2.value == "0.00") product_ok =
false;
if (document.order.sub3.value == "0.00") product_ok =
false;

   shipping_ok = true;
if (document.order.sname.value == "") shipping_ok = false;
if (document.order.sstreet.value == "") shipping_ok =
false;
if (document.order.scity.value == "") shipping_ok = false;
if (document.order.szip.value == "") shipping_ok = false;
   billing_ok = true;
if (document.order.bname.value == "") billing_ok = false;
if (document.order.bstreet.value == "") billing_ok =
false;
if (document.order.bcity.value == "") billing_ok = false;
if (document.order.bzip.value == "") billing_ok = false;

   credit_ok = true;
if (document.order.cname.value == "") credit_ok = false;
if (document.order.cnumber.value == "") credit_ok = false;
   cardchecked = false;
   for (i=0; i<=5; i++) {
      if (document.order.ccard[i].checked) cardchecked=true;
   }
if (cardchecked == false) credit_ok=false;

payment_ok = (credit_ok || billing_ok);

form_ok = (product_ok && shipping_ok && payment_ok);
}
```

This is a lot of code, so you should take some time to review this function to ensure that you understand its different components.

To create the checkform() function:

1. Return to **order.htm** in your text editor.

2. Add the following code directly above the closing </script> tag (see Figure 9-35):

```
function checkform() {
    product_ok = true;
    if (document.order.sub1.value == "0.00") product_ok = false;
    if (document.order.sub2.value == "0.00") product_ok = false;
    if (document.order.sub3.value == "0.00") product_ok = false;

    shipping_ok = true;
    if (document.order.sname.value == "") shipping_ok = false;
    if (document.order.sstreet.value == "") shipping_ok = false;
    if (document.order.scity.value == "") shipping_ok = false;
    if (document.order.szip.value == "") shipping_ok = false;

    billing_ok = true;
    if (document.order.bname.value == "") billing_ok = false;
    if (document.order.bstreet.value == "") billing_ok = false;
    if (document.order.bcity.value == "") billing_ok = false;
    if (document.order.bzip.value == "") billing_ok = false;

    credit_ok = true;
    if (document.order.cname.value == "") credit_ok = false;
    if (document.order.cnumber.value == "") credit_ok = false;
    cardchecked = false;
    for (i=0;  i<=5;  i++) {
        if (document.order.ccard[i].checked) card checked= true;
    }
    if (cardchecked == false) credit_ok=false;

    payment_ok = (credit_ok || billing_ok);

    form_ok = (product_ok && shipping_ok && payment_ok);
    }
```

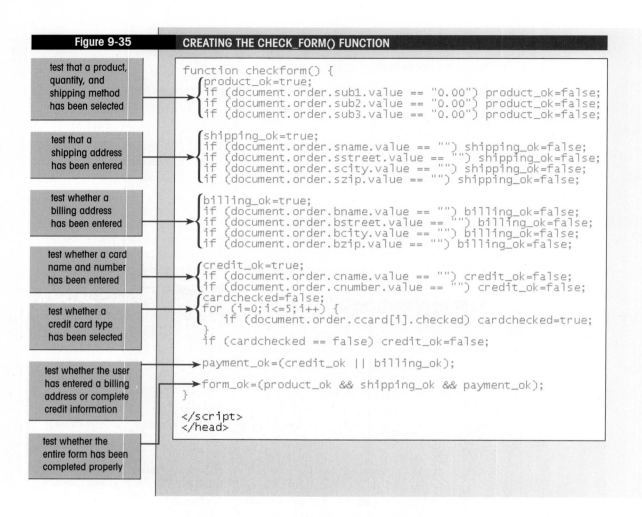

| Figure 9-35 | CREATING THE CHECK_FORM() FUNCTION |

test that a product, quantity, and shipping method has been selected

test that a shipping address has been entered

test whether a billing address has been entered

test whether a card name and number has been entered

test whether a credit card type has been selected

test whether the user has entered a billing address or complete credit information

test whether the entire form has been completed properly

```
function checkform() {
    product_ok=true;
    if (document.order.sub1.value == "0.00") product_ok=false;
    if (document.order.sub2.value == "0.00") product_ok=false;
    if (document.order.sub3.value == "0.00") product_ok=false;

    shipping_ok=true;
    if (document.order.sname.value == "") shipping_ok=false;
    if (document.order.sstreet.value == "") shipping_ok=false;
    if (document.order.scity.value == "") shipping_ok=false;
    if (document.order.szip.value == "") shipping_ok=false;

    billing_ok=true;
    if (document.order.bname.value == "") billing_ok=false;
    if (document.order.bstreet.value == "") billing_ok=false;
    if (document.order.bcity.value == "") billing_ok=false;
    if (document.order.bzip.value == "") billing_ok=false;

    credit_ok=true;
    if (document.order.cname.value == "") credit_ok=false;
    if (document.order.cnumber.value == "") credit_ok=false;
    cardchecked=false;
    for (i=0;i<=5;i++) {
        if (document.order.ccard[i].checked) cardchecked=true;
    }
    if (cardchecked == false) credit_ok=false;

    payment_ok=(credit_ok || billing_ok);

    form_ok=(product_ok && shipping_ok && payment_ok);
}

</script>
</head>
```

The checkform() function is run when the user submits the form for processing.

Controlling Form Submission

When a user completes a form and then clicks the submit button, a submit event is initiated. JavaScript provides the onsubmit event handler that allows you to run a program in response to this action. Because the Submit event is associated with the form object, you must place the event handler within the <form> tag. There is one important difference between this event handler and others that you've used so far in this form. The onsubmit event handler must be able to override the act of submitting the form if the form fails a validation test. The syntax for doing this is:

```
<form onsubmit="return function();">
```

where *function* is the name of the function that validates your form. In addition to anything else the function does, it must return a value of true or false. If the value is true, the form is submitted. If the value is false, the submission is canceled, and the user is returned to the form (hopefully to correct the problem). Note the keyword *return* in this syntax. If you do not include the return keyword, the browser submits the form whether or not it passes the validation test.

To add the onsubmit event handler to the order form:

1. Return to **order.htm** in your text editor.

2. Go to the <form> tag located a third of the way down the file and insert the event handler: **onsubmit= "return checkform()"** within the <form> tag.

   The checkform() function must also be modified to return the value of the form_ok variable that indicates whether or not the form was completed properly.

3. Navigate to the last line of the checkform() function and insert the following command directly above the closing curly brace (see Figure 9-36):

   ```
   return form_ok;
   ```

Figure 9-36   **USING THE ONSUBMIT EVENT HANDLER**

```
    form_ok=(product_ok && shipping_ok && payment_ok);

    return form_ok;
}

</script>
</head>
```

```
<!-- START OF ORDER FORM -->
<form name="order" method="post" onsubmit="return checkform()">
<td>
<h1 style="margin-bottom:0px">Order Form</h1>
</td>
```

4. Save your changes to order.htm and reload it in your Web browser to test the validation function.

5. Select **GoMap 1.0 ($19.95)** from the Product list box, **1** from the Quantity list box, and click the **Standard** shipping option button.

6. Click the **Submit Order** button on the bottom of the order form.

   Because you have not entered shipping or payment information, you should be returned to the form, but all of the choices you made for the product, quantity, and shipping method should still be entered. This is a visual clue that the form was not submitted. Submitted forms return to their initial state.

7. Enter the following shipping address:

   **Carol Campbell
   75 Allen Street
   Clarkston, MI 38912**

8. Click the **Same as Shipping Address** check box to copy the shipping address into the billing address fields.

9. Click the **Submit Order** button.

   Because all relevant information has now been entered into the order form, the form is submitted and all fields returned to their initial state.

TROUBLE? If your browser does not respond in the manner described in steps 6 and 9, you may have made a mistake when entering the checkform() function. Return to your text editor and compare your code with the code shown in Figure 9-35. Common mistakes include misspelling variable names, using an uppercase letter when a lowercase letter is required, and forgetting a closing quote.

You show the form to Carol, and she is pleased with the validity check. However, she would like you to display a message to the user to indicate that the form was not properly completed. You'll accomplish this by displaying a customized dialog box.

Creating a Dialog Box

JavaScript supports three types of dialog boxes: alert, prompt, and confirm. An **alert dialog box** displays a message, usually alerting the user to a problem. The **prompt dialog box** displays both a message and a text box. The **confirm dialog box** displays a message along with OK and Cancel buttons. The syntax for creating these dialog boxes is:

```
alert("message");
prompt("message", "default");
confirm("message");
```

where *message* is the text displayed in the dialog box, and *default* is the default text for the prompt dialog box. Figure 9-37 shows examples of these dialog boxes. Note that different browsers display their dialog boxes with subtle differences, but all dialog boxes share the common features of a title bar, default value, OK button, and Cancel button.

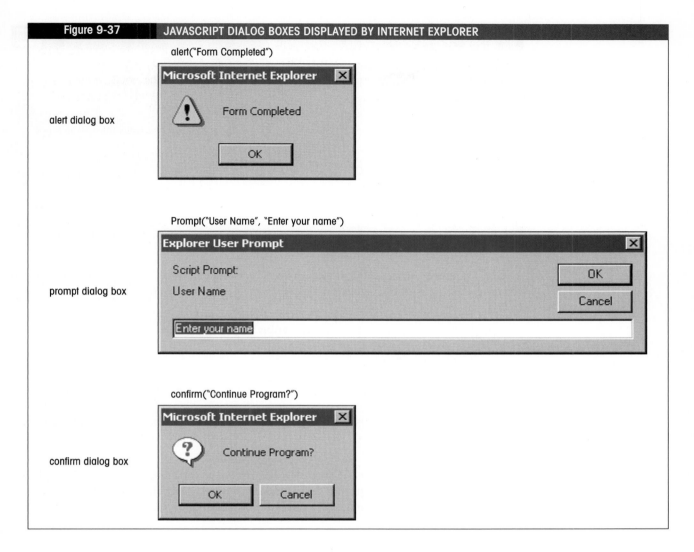

Figure 9-37 | JAVASCRIPT DIALOG BOXES DISPLAYED BY INTERNET EXPLORER

alert("Form Completed")

alert dialog box

Prompt("User Name", "Enter your name")

prompt dialog box

confirm("Continue Program?")

confirm dialog box

You can store the response of the user for both the prompt and the confirm dialog boxes. The syntax is:

variable = prompt("*message*", "*default*");

variable = confirm("*message*");

where *variable* is a variable that stores the user's response. In the case of the prompt dialog box, this is the contents of the text box. For the confirm dialog box, *variable* has a value of true if the user clicks the OK button and false if the user clicks the Cancel button.

REFERENCE WINDOW	RW

Displaying a JavaScript Dialog Box

■ To create a dialog box that alerts the user to an issue or problem, use the JavaScript command

```
alert("message");
```

where *message* is the message that will appear in the dialog box.

■ To create a dialog box that prompts the user for input inside of a text box, enter the command

```
prompt("message", "default");
```

where *default* is the default text that initially displays in the text box.

■ To create a dialog box that alerts the user and contains an OK button and a Cancel button, use the command

```
confirm("message");
```

Carol suggests that you add an alert dialog box to the checkform() function, indicating to the user what parts of the order form were omitted. The code to do this is:

```
if (form_ok) {
alert("Your order has been submitted");
} else {
   if (product_ok == false) alert("Select a product,
quantity, and shipping method");
   if (shipping_ok == false) alert("Enter a shipping address"
);
   if (payment_ok == false) alert("Enter a billing address or
 credit card");
}
```

This code first tests whether the form has been successfully completed. If so, it displays a dialog box informing the customer that the order has been submitted. If not, it displays up to three dialog boxes indicating to the user the source, or sources, of trouble.

To add alert dialog boxes to the checkform() function:

1. Return to **order.htm** in your text editor.

2. Insert the following code directly before the "return form_ok;" command in the checkform() function (see Figure 9-38):

```
if (form_ok) {
alert("Your order has been submitted");
} else {
   if (product_ok == false) alert("Select a product,
quantity, and shipping method");
   if (shipping_ok == false) alert("Enter a shipping
address");
   if (payment_ok == false) alert("Enter a billing
address or credit card");
}
```

Figure 9-38	CREATING ALERT DIALOG BOXES

```
    form_ok=(product_ok && shipping_ok && payment_ok);

    if (form_ok) {
        alert("Your order has been submitted")
    } else {
        if (product_ok==false) alert("Select a product, quantity, and shipping method");
        if (shipping_ok==false) alert("Enter a shipping address");
        if (payment_ok==false) alert("Enter a billing address or credit card");
    }

    return form_ok;
}

</script>
</head>
```

3. Save your changes to order.htm and reload it in your Web browser.

   TROUBLE? If a message indicates that the page cannot be refreshed without resending the information, click the Retry button.

4. Click the **Submit Order** button before entering any information into the form. Your browser displays the alert dialog box shown in Figure 9-39.

Figure 9-39	DISPLAYING AN ALERT DIALOG BOX

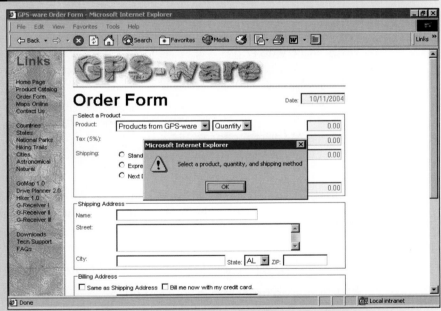

5. Click the **OK** button three times.

6. Complete the form, entering all required information.

7. Click the **Submit Order** button. The browser displays an alert box indicating that the form has been submitted.

Resetting a Form

There is one more issue to consider with the order form. A user who wants to reset the form can press the Cancel Order button, which sets all of the fields in the form to their default values, but is this what Carol wants? Not exactly. Recall that the first action this form takes is to insert the current date into the formdate field. This action runs whenever the Web page is loaded. Unfortunately, resetting a form does not load the page, which means the date is not automatically reinserted into the formdate field.

To do this, you'll use JavaScript to reload the page. This has the effect of resetting all field values and rerunning the startform() function that inserts the current date. To reload the page, use the **location object**, the JavaScript object that references the current page in the browser. One of the methods associated with the location object is the reload() method, which reloads the current page. The syntax is simply

```
location.reload();
```

If you want to use JavaScript to load a different page, the command is

```
location="URL";
```

where URL is the address of the Web page you want to display in the browser.

REFERENCE WINDOW   **RW**

Loading a Web Page
- To load a Web page in your browser, use the JavaScript command
  ```
  location = "URL"
  ```
  where URL is the address of the Web page you want to load.
- To reload the current page in your Web browser, use the command
  ```
  location.reload();
  ```

To control the reset event, use the onreset event handler and apply it to the <form> tag. Do this now to instruct the browser to reload the Web page when the reset button is clicked.

To modify the action of the reset button:

1. Return to **order.htm** in your text editor.

2. Locate the <form> tag and add the following event handler: **onreset="location.reload()"** (see Figure 9-40).

Figure 9-40   **SPECIFYING AN ACTION FOR THE FORM RESET**

```
<!-- START OF ORDER FORM -->
<form name="order" method="post" onsubmit="return checkform()" onreset="location.reload()">
<td>
<h1 style="margin-bottom:0px">Order Form</h1>
</td>
```

3. Save your changes to order.htm and exit your text editor.

4. Using your Web browser, reload order.htm.

5. Enter some text in the form, and then click the **Cancel Order** button at the bottom of the form. Verify that the page reloads properly and that the fields reset to their default values. Additionally, the current date should be inserted into the formdate field, and the Product list box should be selected.

TROUBLE? If a message indicates that the page cannot be refreshed without resending the information, click the Retry button.

6. Close your Web browser.

REFERENCE   WINDOW   **RW**

Form Validation Tips
- Include informative labels for your input fields so that users know ahead of time what values are appropriate to enter in each field.
- Use check boxes, selection lists, and radio buttons as often as possible, rather than text input boxes, to control which values the users are allowed to enter.
- Create JavaScript functions that test values entered into your input boxes. If a value should be entered only within a defined range, create a function that rejects values outside that range.
- Ensure that any alert or prompt dialog boxes you create are clear and concise, informing users of the precise nature of the error and what they should do to fix it.
- Perform a second validation at the time the form is submitted to confirm that appropriate data values have been entered in all fields.

You've completed your work on Carol's order form. Using JavaScript, you've been able to make the form easier to work with and have provided some validation checks to inform customers of problems *before* the form is sent to the CGI script. Carol will take some time to review and test the form and plans to get back to you with any changes or new projects.

Session 9.3 QUICK CHECK

1. A form named survey contains a check box named female. What JavaScript expression would you use to reference whether or not the female check box has been selected?

2. If you want to run the validate() function when your Web page form is submitted, what event handler should you add to the <form> tag? Assume that the purpose of the validate function is to cancel form submission if there was a mistake in filling out the form.

3. If you want to run the restart() function when your Web page form is reset, what event handler should you add to the <form> tag?

4. What command would you use to create an alert box containing the message, "Thank You"?

5. What command would you use to create a prompt box containing the message, "Enter your age"? Assume that there is no default text. Store the user's response in a variable named "age".

6. What command would you use to create a confirm box containing the message, "Do you wish to continue?"? Store the user's response in variable named "continue".

7. What command would you use to load a Web page with the URL *http://www.gps-ware.com*?

REVIEW ASSIGNMENTS

After reviewing the order form, Carol has made a few changes. Rather than displaying products in a list box, Carol would like the product names to appear in a table. This allows customers to purchase more than one product at a time. Also, instead of displaying the quantity of the order in a selection list, Carol wants that information placed into an input field so that customers can specify quantities greater than 10.

GPS-ware is also moving away from billing customers. Instead, all transactions are paid for with credit cards. Carol has removed the billing address section from the order form. Figure 9-41 shows the layout of the new order form.

Figure 9-41

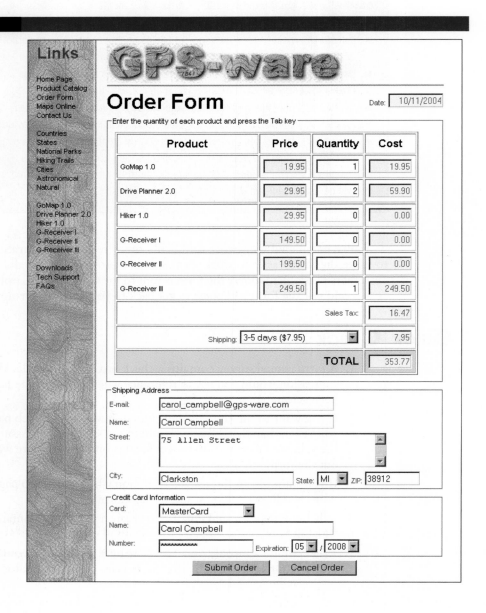

Carol wants you to create the following additions to the order form:

■ When a customer opens the form, the current date is placed in the formdate field, and the quantity input box for the GoMap 1.0 product is selected.

■ When a customer enters new quantity values in the Quantity column, the subtotals and total order cost are updated.

■ When a customer selects a shipping method, the total price of the order is updated.

■ When the form is submitted, it checks that at least one product and shipping method have been selected and that all address and credit card information has been entered.

■ If the Cancel Order button is clicked, the Web page is reloaded.

To revise the order form:

1. Using your text editor, open **ordertxt2.htm** from the tutorial.09/review folder of your Data Disk and save it as **order2.htm**.

Explore

2. Within the <script> tags at the top of the file, create a function named "loadform()" that displays the current date in the formdate field and then moves the cursor focus to the qty1 field and selects it. Hint: Apply both the focus() and select() methods to the qty1 input box, and run the loadform() function when the page is loaded by the browser.

3. Below the loadform() function, insert a function named total_price that calculates the sum of the numeric values of the sub1 through sub8 fields.

4. Below the total_price function, create a function named tax_price() that adds the values of the sub1 through sub6 fields and then multiples that total by 0.05. Use the dollars() function to display this value rounded to two decimal places.

Explore

5. Below the tax_price() function, create a function named sub_price() that calculates the order cost for a selected item in the Product table. The function line for the sub_price() function should appear as:

```
function sub_price(pricename, qtyname, subname)
```

Here, the pricename parameter is a field on the form that contains the price of an item. The qtyname parameter is a field on the form that stores the quantity ordered of that item. The subname parameter is the form field that stores the cost (price × quantity) of the item.

Within this function do the following:

Explore

■ Store the value of the pricename field in a variable named "pricevalue". *Hint:* Use the JavaScript object reference eval(document.order.elements[pricename]).

■ Store the value of the qtyname field in a variable named "qtyvalue". *Hint:* Use the JavaScript object eval(document.order.elements[qtyname]).

■ Change the value of the document.order.elements[subname] object to pricevalue multiplied by qtyvalue (be sure to round this value to two decimal places using the dollars() function.)

■ Run the tax_price() function to update the total sales tax on the order.

■ Run the total_price() function to update the total price of the order.

Explore

6. Locate the <input> tag for the qty1 field. Run the following function when this tag encounters the blur() event:

```
sub_price('price1', 'qty1', 'sub1');
```

Create similar event handlers for the qty2 through qty6 input fields.

7. Below the sub_price() function, create a function named shipping_price() that does the following:
   - Retrieve the value of the selected option in the shipping field and store that value in the sub8 field of the form.
   - Run the total_price() function to update the total price of the order.

8. Add an onchange event handler to the shipping field in the form to run the shipping_price() function whenever the user changes the selected shipping method.

9. Below the shipping_price() function, insert a function named checkform() that does the following:
   - Create a variable named purchase_ok that checks whether the purchase information has been entered correctly. Set the initial value of purchase_ok to true. Change the value of this variable to false only if the value of the sub8 or total field is equal to "0.00". *Hint:* Remember to use the == comparison operator rather than the = operator to compare values.
   - Create a variable named address_ok that checks whether complete shipping information has been entered. Set the initial value of address_ok to "true". Change the value to "false" only if the email, name, street, city, or zip field is equal to "".
   - Create a variable named credit_ok that checks whether complete credit card data has been entered. The initial value of the credit_ok variable is "true". Change the value of this variable to "false" only if the ccard, cname, or cnumber field is equal to "".
   - Create a variable named form_ok that is true only if purchase_ok, address_ok, and credit_ok are all true.
   - If form_ok is true (which means that the form has been correctly completed), display an alert box with the message, "Order Submitted"; otherwise display the alert "You must select a product and shipping method" if product_ok is "false," display the alert "You must complete all address fields" if address_ok is "false," and diisplay the alert "You must complete all credit card fields" if credit_ok is "false."
   - Return the value of the form_ok function.

10. Add an onsubmit event handler to the <form> tag that uses the checkform() function to validate the completed form.

11. Add an onreset event handler to the <form> tag that reloads the Web page when the form is reset.

12. Save your changes to order2.htm and reload or refresh the page in your Web browser.

13. Test the form, verifying that it correctly updates the total cost of the order and correctly validates the form when the Submit Order button is clicked.

14. Print out order2.htm and hand in your files and printouts to your instructor.

CASE PROBLEMS

Case 1. Monroe Public Library. The Monroe Public Library has added Web access for its patrons. To make it easier for new users to access particular Web pages, the library has employed you to create custom Web pages for different topics. One of these custom Web pages contains links to various government Web sites.

Because there are so many hypertext links, your supervisor, Denise Kruschev, thinks the best approach is for the list of hyperlinks to be contained within selection list boxes. Denise envisions users clicking a site within a selection list, which would open the Web page they selected.

Denise has created the Web page shown in Figure 9-42. Your job is to use JavaScript to open up the Web pages as specified by the options in the selection lists.

Figure 9-42

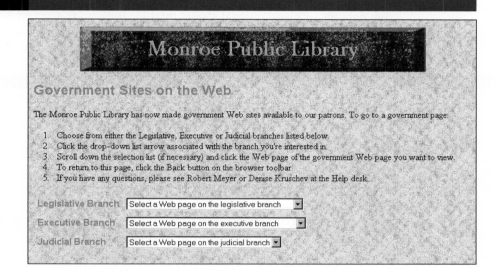

To finish the Monroe Public Library government Web page:

1. Using your text editor, open **mpltxt.htm** from the tutorial.09/case1 folder of your Data Disk and save it as **mpl.htm**.

2. Scroll through **mpl.htm**. Note that the values of the selection options are all URLs and that the text in the selection list consists of descriptions of the Web pages.

3. Insert an event handler within the <select> tag for each of the three selection lists that runs the function jump_to_link(this) whenever the value of the selection list changes.

Explore ▶ 4. Create a JavaScript function named jump_to_link(weblist) within the head section of **mpl.htm**. Within this function, create a variable named url_number that is equal to the selectedIndex property of the weblist variable.

   ■ Set the location object equal to the value of the selected option in the weblist field. Hint: The selected option has the object name weblist.options[url_number].

   ■ Run the function jump_to_link(this) whenever a user selects an item from one of the three selection lists in the form.

Explore ▶ ■ For the first option of each of the three selection lists, there is an <a> tag but no URL is specified. Change this by creating a URL to those <a> tags that runs a JavaScript command to reload the Web page.

   ■ Save and print mpl.htm.

   ■ Using your Web browser, open **mpl.htm** and click the "Department of Education" option in the Executive Branch selection list to verify that the appropriate Web page loads with your browser.

   ■ Close your Web browser and your text editor.

   ■ Hand in your files and printouts to your instructor.

Case 2. Games Etc. Games Etc. is an innovative and fun-loving company that specializes in games and puzzles. The company also has a Web site with several free online games. Pete Burdette, the coordinator for Web site development, has asked you to join his team.

Pete's first project for you is to program a Web page on magic squares. Magic squares are square grids of sequential numbers arranged so that the sums of the rows, columns, and the two main diagonals are equal.

Pete is working on a Web page where users can enter numbers into a 3x3 empty grid, trying to complete a magic square containing the numbers 1 through 9. The values in each row, column, or main diagonal should total 15. If users are successful, Pete wants the page to display a congratulatory message. Figure 9-43 shows a preview of the page you'll create with one possible solution to the magic square problem.

Figure 9-43

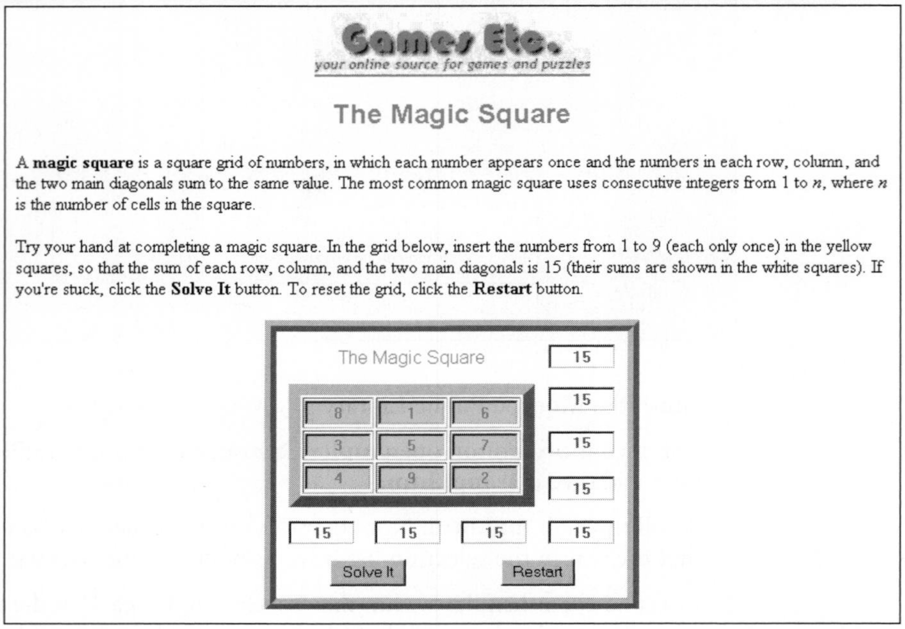

Pete has created the content of the page and he has placed the cells of the magic square in a table. Each of those cells contains an input field into which users can enter a single-digit number. Pete has labeled these input fields as shown in Figure 9-44:

Figure 9-44

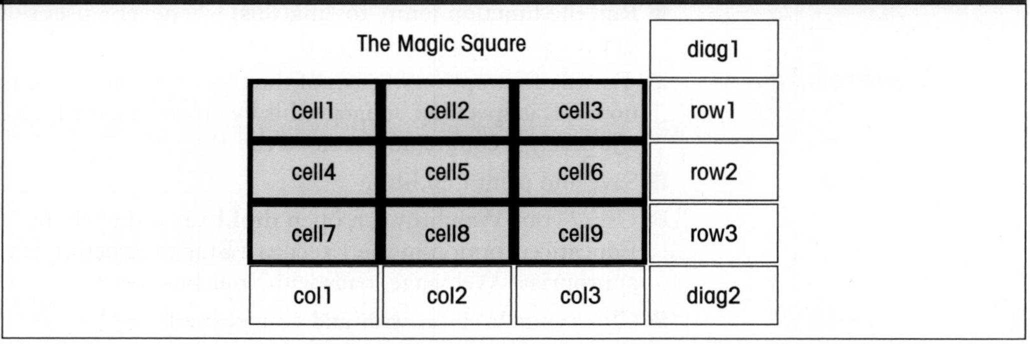

The numbers in the magic square are stored in the fields cell1 through cell9. The row1 through row3 fields display the current totals of the first cell rows. The col1 through col3 fields display the totals of the first three columns. The diag1 field displays the total of the ascending diagonal (cell7+cell5+cell3), and the diag2 field displays the total of the descending diagonal (cell1+cell5+cell9). Pete wants these totals to be updated whenever a user changes one of the values in the cell1 through cell9 fields.

If a user cannot solve the problem, Pete has included a form button that will present the solution displayed in Figure 9-43. Users need to be able to reset the square by clicking the Restart button. Pete's file also includes a function named valid_square() that determines whether the square contains duplicate integers. You'll use this function as part of a validation check on the user's solution.

To program the magic square:

1. Using your text editor, open **magictxt.htm** from the tutorial.09/case2 folder of your Data Disk, and save it as **magic.htm**.

Explore ▸ 2. Create a function named test_square() that does the following:

- Creates a variable named magic that tests whether the current values in the table constitute a magic square. Set the initial value of the magic variable to true.

- If any of the input fields, row1 through row3, col1 through col3, diag1, or diag2 does not equal "15", change the value of the magic variable to false. *Hint:* Use the != comparison operator.

- If the value returned by the valid_square() function is false, change the value of the magic variable to false. Hint: Use the condition: valid_square()==false.

- If the value of the magic variable is still true, display a dialog box with the message, "Puzzle Completed!!", otherwise do nothing.

3. Create a function named sum() that calculates the row, column, and main diagonal totals and then stores those values in the appropriate input fields in the form. After performing these calculations, it should run the test_square() function, testing whether the square is magic.

Explore ▸ 4. Add event handlers to the cell1 through cell9 input fields to run the sum() function whenever a user changes the value of any of these fields.

5. Create a function named solve() that inserts the solution values shown in Figure 9-43 into the cell1 through cell9 input fields and then runs the sum() function.

6. Add an event handler to the Solve It button to run the solve() function when the button is clicked.

7. Add an event handler to the Restart button to reload the page when the button is clicked.

8. Add an onload event handler to the Web page to (a) set the focus() of the cursor to the cell1 field and (b) select the contents of the cell1 field.

Explore ▸ 9. Add an event handler to the cell9 field so that when that field loses the cursor focus, the focus is given to the cell1 field. This keeps the cursor within one of the nine cell fields of the magic square.

10. Save magic.htm and print the file.

11. Using your Web browser, open **magic.htm**. Enter the digits 1 through 9 in the magic square and verify that the row, column, and diagonal totals are updated correctly. Insert the values from Figure 9-43 into the square to verify that a congratulatory message is

displayed once the magic square is complete. Test the Solve It and Restart buttons to verify that they function properly.

12. Hand in your printouts and files to your instructor.

Case 3. Programming the Safety Color Palette.   Chloe MacDonald has approached you again to ask for your help in developing a Web page describing the safety palette (for a description of the safety palette, see Case Problem 4 from Tutorial 8). She would like you to develop a Web page where users can select hexadecimal color values from a set of list boxes. Chloe wants the background and text colors of the page to change in response to the user's choices. Figure 9-45 shows a preview of the page you'll create.

Figure 9-45

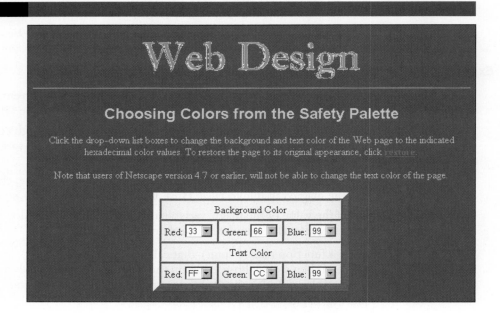

Versions of Netscape earlier than 6.0 cannot change the text color after the Web page has been loaded. For those users, Chloe wants you to add a JavaScript function that tests what kind of browser a user is using to access the page, and if the browser is Netscape, to display a warning message.

To create the Color Picker Web page:

1. Using your text editor, open **colortxt.htm** from the tutorial.09/case3 folder of your Data Disk and save it as **color.htm**.

Explore   2. Create the test_browser() function in the head section of the HTML file. Instruct the function to test whether the browser is Netscape. If it is, display an alert dialog box containing the message, "Users of Netscape version 4.7 and earlier can only change the background color." *Hint:* Use the navigator.appName property to determine the name of the browser.

3. Set the test_browser() function to run whenever the browser loads the Web page.

Explore   4. Create a function named apply_color() that does the following:

■ Create variables named back_red_index, back_green_index, and back_blue_index, which are equal to the index numbers of the selected options from the backred, backgreen, and backblue selection lists in the colors form.

- ■ Create variables named text_red_index, text_green_index, and text_blue_index equal to the index numbers of the selected options from the textred, textgreen, and textblue selection lists in the colors form.
- ■ Store the text of the selected color values in variables named back_red, back_green, back_blue, text_red, text_green, and text_blue. Hint: Use the text property of the options object.
- ■ Create a variable named backcolor equal to the pound symbol (#) combined with the values of the back_red, back_green, and back_blue variables.
- ■ Create a variable named textcolor equal to the pound symbol (#) combined with the values of the text_red, text_green, and text_blue variables.
- ■ Change the background color of the document to the color value stored in the backcolor variable. *Hint:* Use the bgColor property of the document object.
- ■ Change the text color of the document to the color value stored in the textcolor variable. *Hint:* Use the fgColor property of the document object.

5. Run the apply_color() function whenever the user changes the selected item in any of the six list boxes on the Web page.

6. Change the boldfaced word "restore" located in the paragraph at the top of the file to a hypertext link that runs a JavaScript command to reload the current page.

7. Save your changes to color.htm and print the HTML code using your text editor.

Explore

8. Using a Netscape Web browser, open **color.htm** and verify that the warning message is issued. Alternately, open **color.htm** using Internet Explorer to verify that no warning message is displayed.

9. Using Internet Explorer, test your Web page for the following color combinations. Netscape users running version 4.7 or earlier can only test changes to the background color.

- ■ Background = "#CC33CC" Text="#FFFFFF"
- ■ Background = "#3300CC" Text ="#FFCCCC"
- ■ Background = "#333300" Text = "#FFFFCC"

10. Click the Restore hypertext link in the paragraph at the top of the page, and verify that it reloads the page and restores the background color to white and the text color to black.

11. Hand in your printouts and files to your instructor.

Case 4. Frontier Savings and Loan. The mortgage finance officers at Frontier Savings and Loan have asked you to create a mortgage calculator that customers can use to estimate monthly mortgage payments. Your project manager, Lisa Drummond, explains that the Web page should contain a form in which the customer enters the loan amount, the number of monthly payments, and the yearly interest rate, and then clicks a button to see what the monthly payment and total payments for the loan would be. You need JavaScript to accomplish this task. A function named Monthly(), which is used to calculate the monthly payment, follows:

```
function Monthly(I, N, S) {
      // I = yearly interest rate;
      // N = number of monthly payments;
      // S = loan amount;
return (S*I/12*Math.pow(I/12+1,N))/(Math.pow(I/12+1,N)-1);
}
```

The Monthly() function takes three parameter values: the yearly interest rate (I), the total number of monthly payments (N), and the amount of the loan (S). With these parameters, the function returns the value of the monthly payment for the loan.

Note that this function uses the Math.pow() method, which calculates the value of a base value raised to an exponent; for example:

```
Math.pow(a, n) = an
```

Once you know the value of the monthly payment, the total amount paid is simply the monthly payment multiplied by the total number of payments. Using the Monthly() function, you'll complete the rest of the Web page for Frontier Savings and Loan. Figure 9-46 shows one possible solution to this assignment.

Figure 9-46

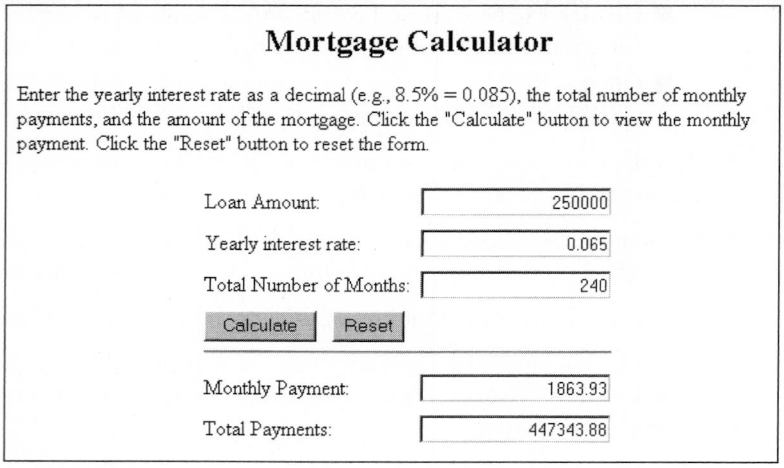

Mortgage Calculator

Enter the yearly interest rate as a decimal (e.g., 8.5% = 0.085), the total number of monthly payments, and the amount of the mortgage. Click the "Calculate" button to view the monthly payment. Click the "Reset" button to reset the form.

Loan Amount:	250000
Yearly interest rate:	0.065
Total Number of Months:	240

[Calculate] [Reset]

| Monthly Payment: | 1863.93 |
| Total Payments: | 447343.88 |

To create the mortgage calculator Web page:

1. Using your text editor, create a file named **mortgage.htm** in the tutorial.09/case4 folder of your Data Disk.

2. Create a form that contains the following fields (the layout of the form is up to you):
   - Five input fields used for the loan amount, yearly interest rate, number of payments, monthly payment amount, and total payment.
   - Two buttons: one labeled Calculate (used to calculate the monthly and total payments) and the other labeled Reset (used to reset the form).

3. Insert the Monthly() function shown earlier within the head section of **mortgage.htm**.

4. Create a function named ShowVal() that extracts the values in the interest rate, number of payments, and loan amount fields and calls the Monthly() function with those values to determine the monthly payment. Hint: Don't forget to use the eval function when extracting field values. Use the results of the Monthly() function to determine the total amount of payments to the bank. Place the results of your two calculations in the appropriate fields on your form.

5. Add an event handler to the Calculate button that runs the ShowVal() function when this button is clicked.

6. The Monthly() function requires that the interest rate be a number between 0 and 1. Create a function named CheckInterest() that checks to see if the interest rate is greater than 0 and less than 1. If it is not, the CheckInterest() function displays a message to the user and returns the user to the interest rate field.

7. Add an event handler to the interest rate field that calls the CheckInterest() function whenever the user leaves the field.

8. Insert the <h2> heading "Mortgage Calculator", along with a paragraph describing the purpose of the Web page and how to use the calculator, at the top of the Web page, located before the calculator.

9. Save your changes to mortgage.htm, and print the HTML code and JavaScript commands you created.

10. Open **mortgage.htm** in your Web browser. Test your mortgage calculator with the following values, and print the resulting Web pages:

   ■ loan = 100000, interest rate = 0.085, number of payments = 300
   ■ loan = 100000, interest rate = 0.10, number of payments = 300
   ■ loan = 100000, interest rate = 0.085, number of payments = 360

11. Hand in your printouts and files to your instructor.

QUICK | CHECK ANSWERS

Session 9.1

1. In server-side validation, the user input is checked on the Web server, usually via a CGI script. In client-side validation, user input is checked within the Web browser on the user's computer.

2. Objects are items that exist in a defined space such as the Web page, Web browser, form, or table. Properties describe an object's appearance, purpose, or behavior. Methods are actions that can be performed with an object or on an object.

3. document.enroll.join

4. document.fgColor= "blue";

5. document.fgColor=tcolor;

6. document.enroll.reset();

Session 9.2

1. An event is a specific action that triggers the browser to run a block of JavaScript commands. An event handler is code added to an HTML tag that is run whenever a particular event occurs. An event method is a method applied to a JavaScript object that emulates the occurrence of an event.

2. Edit the <body> tag to read: <body onload="Welcome();">

3. <input name=CreditNumber onBlur="CheckCredit();">

4. document.product.model.options[0].value=P250;

5. document.product.model.options[0].text="Pentium 250";

6. var ModelNumber = document.product.model.selectedIndex;

7. It refers to the currently selected object. You can use the "this" object to write programs that can be applied to several objects on the page.

8. "525"

Session 9.3

1. document.survey.female.checked
2. onsubmit = "return validate()"
3. onreset = "restart()"
4. alert("Thank You")
5. age = prompt("Enter your age")
6. continue = confirm("Do you wish to continue?")
7. location = "http://www.gps-ware.com"

OBJECTIVES

In this tutorial you will:

- Work with external and embedded multimedia files

- Learn about the principles of sound and video clips

- Work with the <embed> tag to enhance a Web page with sound and video

- Provide tags for browsers that do not support embedded objects

- Learn how to create a background sound with Internet Explorer

- Use the <applet> tag to add a Java applet to a Web page

- Create a scrolling marquee with the <marquee> tag

CREATING A MULTIMEDIA WEB PAGE

Enhancing a Page with Sound, Video, and Java Applets

CASE

The Mount Rainier Newsletter

Mount Rainier dominates the skyline for much of the state of Washington, and Mount Rainier National Park is a popular vacation spot for travelers to the Northwest from all over the world. The park publishes a monthly newsletter, Mount Rainier News, which is distributed to visitors at each park entrance. The newsletter contains information on upcoming events, tips on park trails and enjoying nature, and information on campsites and lodging. In recent years, the newsletter has also been published on the World Wide Web so travelers can conveniently obtain park news before they arrive. The Web page contains all the information available in the printed version, as well as links to other sites on the Web about Mount Rainier and the surrounding communities of Sunrise, Longmire, and Paradise.

Tom Bennett, the editor of Mount Rainier News, has been looking at other newsletter sites on the Web and has noticed how multimedia elements like sound, video, and animation are being used to add interest and information to those pages. Tom has asked you to add multimedia elements to the Mount Rainier News Web page in an effort to make it more appealing. The current Web page features stories on an upcoming folk festival and a new attraction at the Paradise visitors' center. Tom would like you to locate sound and video clips that can be used to enhance those stories.

SESSION 10.1

In this session you'll learn about the attributes of external and embedded media and how to add sound to a Web page. You'll examine how sound can be saved in a sound file, and you'll learn how to reduce the size of a sound file to maximize page performance. You'll create a hypertext link to a sound clip and embed the sound clip within a Web page. Finally, you'll see how Internet Explorer allows you to specify a background sound for your Web page.

Working with Multimedia

One of the most popular and useful features of the World Wide Web is the ability to transfer information through the use of sound and video. When creating Web pages that include these elements, you have to consider several factors, not the least of which is the issue of bandwidth. **Bandwidth** is a measure of the amount of data that can be sent through a communications circuit each second. Bandwidth values range from slow connections—such as phone lines, which can transfer data at a rate of 58.6 kbps—to high-speed direct network connections capable of transferring data at several megabytes per second. Large sound and video files cause the most trouble for users with low-bandwidth connections. One of the primary goals when using multimedia is to create media clips that are compact in size without sacrificing quality.

As shown in Figure 10-1, multimedia can be added to a Web page in one of two ways: as external media or inline media. With external media, the sound or video file is accessed through a hypertext link. Inline media clips are placed into the Web page itself as embedded objects. An advantage of using an external file is that users are not required to retrieve the multimedia clip, but only do so if they want to. This is useful in situations where a user has a low-bandwidth connection and wants the choice of whether or not to take the time to download a large multimedia file. An embedded media clip works like an inline image and can be played within the Web page itself. Because the clip appears within the Web page, you can supplement it with other material on the page. For example, descriptive text can appear alongside an embedded video clip. A downside of using inline media is that the user is forced to wait for the clip to be retrieved by the browser. If the user has a low-bandwidth connection, this can be a major inconvenience.

Figure 10-1	INLINE AND EXTERNAL MEDIA

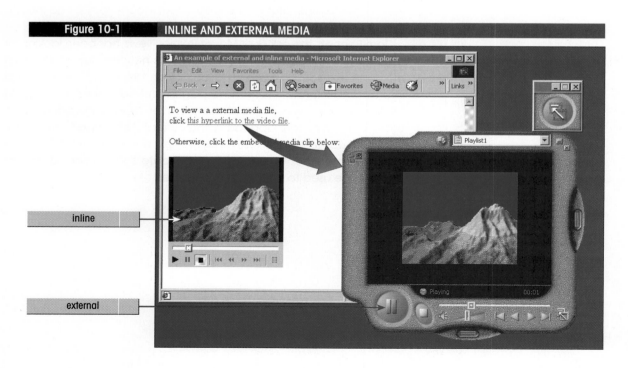

inline

external

You ask Tom whether he wants to use inline or external media with the Mount Rainier News Web page. Tom directs you to create two versions of the page: one using inline media and the other using external media. One page, which you'll name rainier.htm, uses external media and is intended for users with low-bandwidth Internet connections, such as phone lines. The second page, rainier2.htm, uses inline media and is available to users at the park headquarters who can access the Web page using a high-speed connection.

The version of the newsletter you'll work with is shown in Figure 10-2. In addition to a table of links to other Web sites, the page contains three news articles. One is the current weather forecast, located at the top of the page. The second is an article about the upcoming folk festival at Sunrise. The third article describes MRIM, the Mount Rainier Interactive Map, recently installed at the Paradise visitors' center.

Figure 10-2	THE MOUNT RAINIER NEWS WEB PAGE

Your first task is to add a sound clip to the article on the Sunrise Folk Festival, but before you can do that, you need to learn a little more about sound files.

Understanding **Sound Files**

In order to work with sound clips, it is helpful to understand some of the issues involved in converting a sound from the analog form we hear with our ears to the digital form that is stored in files on our computers. Consider the simple sound wave shown in Figure 10-3. There are two components to the sound wave: amplitude and frequency. The **amplitude** is the height of the sound wave, and it relates to the loudness of the sound—the higher the amplitude, the louder the sound. The **frequency** is the speed at which the sound wave moves, and it relates to the sound pitch. Sounds with high frequency have higher pitches.

Figure 10-3	A SIMPLE SOUND WAVE

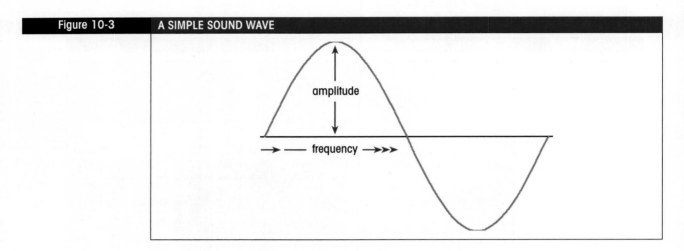

Sampling Rate and Sample Resolution

A sound wave is a continuous function. To convert it to a form that can be stored as a digital sound file, your computer must record measurements of the sound at discrete moments in time. Each measurement is called a **sample**. The number of samples taken per second is called the **sampling rate**. The sampling rate is measured in kilohertz (KHz). The most commonly used sampling rates are 11 KHz, 22 KHz, and 44 KHz. As shown in Figure 10-4, a higher sampling rate means that more samples are taken per second, resulting in a digital sound that more closely matches the analog sound. The trade-off in increasing the sampling rate is that it increases the size of the sound file.

Figure 10-4   **APPROXIMATING A SOUND WAVE WITH DIFFERENT SAMPLING RATES**

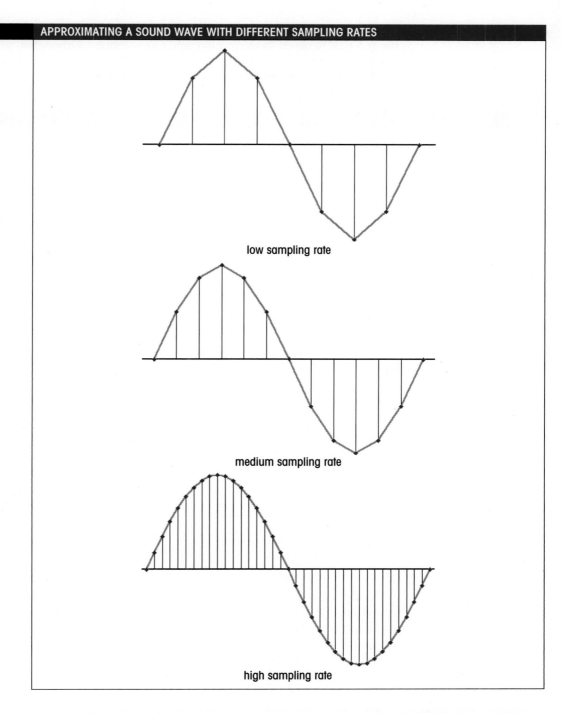

low sampling rate

medium sampling rate

high sampling rate

A second factor in converting a sound to a digital form is the sample resolution. **Sample resolution** indicates the precision in measuring the sound within each sample. There are three commonly used sample resolution values: 8-bit, 16-bit, and 32-bit. As shown in Figure 10-5, increasing the sample resolution creates a digital sound file that represents the analog sound more accurately but, once again, results in a larger file. For most applications, saving sound files at the 16-bit resolution provides a good balance of sound quality and file size.

A final choice for you to make is determining the number of channels to use. Typically, the choice is between stereo or monaural (mono) sound, although in some special situations you may want to add extra channels. Stereo provides a richer sound than mono, but at the expense of approximately doubling the size of the sound file.

Figure 10-5	APPROXIMATING A SOUND WAVE AT DIFFERENT SAMPLE RESOLUTIONS

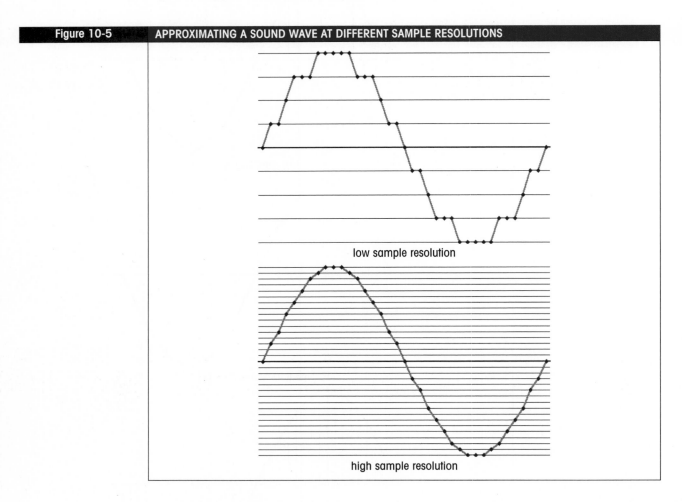

low sample resolution

high sample resolution

Figure 10-6 shows how sampling rate, sample resolution, and channel size relate to sound quality in terms of everyday objects. Your telephone provides the poorest sound quality, and this is a reflection of the low sampling rate and sample resolution as well as the monaural sound. A CD or DAT player provides much higher sound quality at a higher sampling rate and sample resolution. These players also support stereo sound, and in some cases, additional sound channels.

Figure 10-6	SAMPLING RATE AND SAMPLE RESOLUTION AS RELATED TO SOUND QUALITY

SAMPLING RATE AND SAMPLE RESOLUTION	SOUND QUALITY
8 KHz, 8-bit, mono	Telephone
22 KHz, 16-bit, stereo	Radio
44 KHz, 16-bit, stereo	CD
48 KHz, 16-bit, stereo	DAT

To create a sound file, you need a computer with a sound card, speakers, a microphone, and sound-editing software. There are several sound editors available on the Web. In addition to modifying the sampling rate, sample resolution, and number of channels, these sound editors allow you to add special sound effects, remove noise, and give you the ability to copy and paste sounds from one sound file to another. Figure 10-7 lists some of the sound editors available to you.

Figure 10-7	SOUND EDITING SOFTWARE ON THE WEB	
TITLE	**URL**	**DESCRIPTION**
CoolEdit	http://www.syntrillium.com	Sound editing software for Windows
Shareware Music Machine	http://www.hitsquad.com/smm/	Links to audio software on the Web
Sonic Control	http://www.soniccontrol.com/	Links to audio software on the Web
The Sonic Spot	http://www.sonicspot.com	Links to audio software on the Web

Sound File Formats

Several different sound formats are in use on the Web. The various formats are used by different operating systems and provide varying levels of sound quality and sound compression, which is the ability to reduce the size of the digital sound file. Figure 10-8 lists some of the sound file formats that might be used for the Sunrise Folk Festival sound clip.

Figure 10-8	SOUND FILE FORMATS
FORMAT	**DESCRIPTION**
AIFF/AIFC	Audio Interchange File Format. Sound files with this format usually have an .aiff or .aif filename extension. AIFF was developed by Apple for use on the Macintosh operating system. AIFF sound files can be either 8 bit or 16 bit, can be mono or stereo, and can be recorded at several different sampling rates.
AU	Also called μlaw (mu-law) format. Sound files with this format usually have an .au filename extension. One of the oldest sound formats, it is primarily used on UNIX workstations. AU sound files have 8-bit sample resolutions, use a sampling rate of 8 KHz, and are recorded in mono.
MIDI	Musical Instrument Digital Interface. MIDI files cannot be used for general sound recording like other sound formats, but are limited to synthesizers and music files. The MIDI format represents sound by recording each note's pitch, length, and volume. MIDI files tend to be much smaller in size than other sound formats.
MPEG	Moving Pictures Expert Group. A format primarily used for video clips, though occasionally MPEGs are used for audio files. MPEG files are usually small due to the MPEG file compression algorithm. Because of their small size, MPEGs are most often used for transferring whole music recordings. The most recent MPEG standard is MP3.
RealAudio	Another popular sound format on the Web, RealAudio files are designed for real-time playing over low- to high-bandwidth connections. RealAudio files tend to be much smaller than AU or VAV files, but the sound quality is usually not as good.
SND	The SND format is used primarily on the Macintosh operating system for creating system sounds. This format is not widely supported on the Web.
WAV	WAV sound files were developed for the Windows operating system and are one of the most common sound formats on the Web. WAV files can be recorded in 8-bit or 16-bit sample resolutions, in stereo or mono, and under a wide range of sampling rates. WAV sound files usually have the .wav filename extension.

WAV is one of the most common sound formats on the Web. Support for this format is built into the Microsoft Windows operating system and both of the leading browsers. If your users primarily work on Macintosh systems, you should consider using either AIFF or SND files. Web sites designed primarily for UNIX workstations often use the AU sound format.

However, *the* most common sound file format on the Web today is undoubtedly **MP3**, a version of the MPEG format that compresses audio files with minor impact on sound quality. One of the reasons for its popularity is that it is an open standard, allowing for greater innovation from developers creating MP3-related software. MP3 also has no security features, making it easier for users to share MP3 files and to attach them to e-mail messages. This ease of sharing was one of the factors that led to copyrighted material being encoded in MP3 format. For larger sound files, such as recordings of complete songs or even concerts, MPEG is the preferred sound format because of its ability to greatly compress the size of the sound file. Since its introduction, MP3 has expanded past the confines of the Web and is readily available in portable music players and car stereos. Users can also convert their MP3 files into WAV format files and burn them onto CDs.

Sound formats are generally classified into two types: nonstreaming and streaming. A **nonstreaming** sound format must be completely downloaded by the user before it can be played. This requirement creates lengthy delays because users have to download whole files before listening to them. When multimedia elements were first added to Web pages, all media was nonstreaming. In response to the desire to be able to listen to sound in "real time." RealAudio introduced **streaming media** in which media clips, including both sound and video, are processed in a steady and continuous stream as they are downloaded by the browser. Rather than waiting to hear a sound file, users of streaming media can listen to the sound almost immediately. This makes streaming media ideal for broadcasting up-to-the-minute news and sporting events. The success of streaming media depends in part on the speed and quality of the connection. A low-bandwidth connection can result in a sound recording that has frequent breaks, because the connection cannot keep up with the speed of the sound clip. In addition to RealAudio, MP3, WAV, and most other sound formats can now be streamed.

Another popular sound format is the MIDI format. **MIDI, or Musical Instrument Digital Interface**, is a standard for synthesizers and sound cards. This format reduces sound to a series of values that describe the pitch, length, and volume of each note. Because MIDI is a widely supported standard, sounds created on one synthesizer can be played and manipulated on another synthesizer, or sound-editing software can be used to manipulate the MIDI files, creating new sounds and sound effects. An additional advantage of MIDI files is that they are much smaller than other sound formats. A MIDI composition that lasts several minutes is less than 20 KB in size. A similar file in WAV format would be several megabytes in size. However, the MIDI format is limited to music and cannot be used for general sounds, such as speech.

If you don't want to create your own sound clips, many sites on the Web maintain archives of sound clips that you can download. A few of these sites are listed in Figure 10-9. Be aware that some sound clips have copyright restrictions.

Figure 10-9	SOUND ARCHIVES ON THE WEB		
WEB SITE	**URL**	**DESCRIPTION**	
Broadcast.com	http://www.broadcast.com	A collection of live and archived recordings that use streaming media	
Historic sound clips	http://www.webcorp.com/sounds/	Sound clips from historical figures and events in history	
MP3.com	http://www.mp3.com	Resource for news and information about MP3s, including links to MP3 archives	
MSU Voice Library	http://www.lib.msu.edu/vincent/	Selections from the G. Robert Vincent Voice library at Michigan State University	
Planet MIDI	http://www.planetz.net/midi/	An archive of MIDI files, broken down by categories	
Sound America	http://www.soundamerica.com	An archive of almost 30,000 sound clips broken down into categories	

Tom has created three sound files from last year's Folk Festival in the WAV, AU, and MP3 format and saved them as mountain.wav, mountain.au, and mountain.mp3, respectively. The files range in size from 211 kilobytes for the WAV and AU files to 342 kilobytes for the MP3 file. Tom doesn't want the sound files to be much larger than this so that users can easily retrieve them. The files are stored on your Data Disk.

Linking to a Sound File

Now that you have the sound clips, you're ready to create rainier.htm. Recall that rainier.htm is the Web page to be accessed by users with low-bandwidth connections and that it uses hypertext links to access media files. Because media clips tend to be large, it's a good idea to include information about their format and size in your Web page. This gives users some idea of how long it takes to retrieve the clip before initiating the download.

To create a link to Folk Festival sound files:

1. Use your text editor to open **raintxt.htm** from the tutorial.10/tutorial folder of your Data Disk, and save it as **rainier.htm** in the same folder.

2. Insert the following code directly below the last paragraph of the article on the Sunrise Folk Festival. Note that it is a good idea to indent the code to make it easier to read.

```
<p>Click below to listen to the sounds of <i>Adams &
Davis</i>from last year's folk festival:</p>
<blockquote>
    <a href="mountain.mp3">Wild Mountain Thyme Full Clip
(342K - MP3)</a><br>
    <a href="mountain.wav">Wild Mountain Thyme Partial
Clip (211K - WAV)</a><br>
    <a href="mountain.au">Wild Mountain Thyme Partial Clip
 (211K - AU)</a>
</blockquote>
```

Figure 10-10 displays the revised text of rainier.htm.

Figure 10-10	LINKING TO THE SOUND FILES

```
<p>Click below to listen to the sounds of <i>Adams & Davis</i> from last year's
folk festival.</p>
<blockquote>
    <a href="mountain.mp3">Wild Mountain Thyme Full Clip (342K - MP3)</a><br>
    <a href="mountain.wav">Wild Mountain Thyme Partial Clip (211K - WAV)</a><br>
    <a href="mountain.au">Wild Mountain Thyme Partial Clip (211K - AU)</a>
</blockquote>

<!--- ARTICLE ABOUT THE MOUNT RAINIER INTERACTIVE MAP --->
<h2><img src="mrim.jpg" align="left" hspace="5" vspace="1">
Visitors Prepare to Meet MRIM</h2>
```

3. Save your changes to rainier.htm.

Now that you've inserted a hypertext link to the sound clip, you can test the link. What happens when you do so depends on how your system and browser have been configured. When your browser encounters a link to an external file, like a sound file, it checks to see if there is a program installed on your system designed to handle that type of file. Such programs are called **helper applications** because they help the browser to interpret and present the file. Different users have different helper applications installed on their systems. As you've seen, there are many different sound editors, and similarly, there are many different sound players. In the latest versions of Netscape and Internet Explorer, you may be prompted to play the sound clip from within the browser. If the browser does not find a helper application and cannot play the sound clip itself, the browser might display an error message and prompt you to download one from the Web.

In the following steps, you'll test your newly created hypertext link. These steps assume that you have an application on your system that is capable of playing MP3 files. However, you might have a completely different application installed on your system. If so, you should use that instead. If necessary, check with your instructor or technical support person to determine which player is installed on your system. If no player has been installed, you'll need to download a player to hear the sound clip.

To test the hypertext link to mountain.mp3:

1. Open **rainier.htm** in your Web browser.

2. Click the hypertext link **Wild Mountain Thyme Full Clip (342K - MP3)** located on the Web page. As shown in Figure 10-11, the browser opens a separate application to play the sound file. Note that you may need to click a play button to play the sound clip.

   TROUBLE? If you are asked to choose whether to open the file or save it, choose to open the sound file. If you are asked to play the sound clip in its own window, you may do that as well.

Figure 10-11   **PLAYING THE MOUNTAIN.MP3 CLIP**

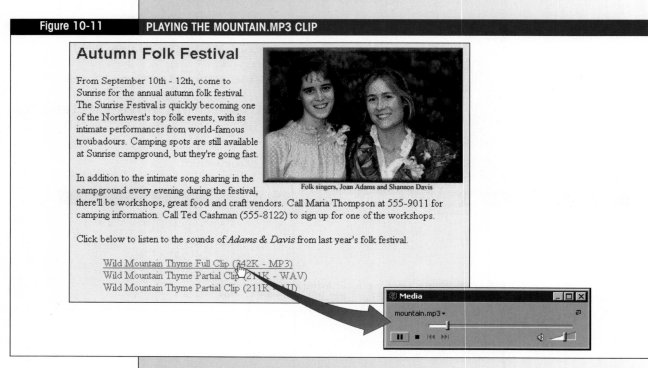

3. After listening to the sound file, close the media player playing the sound clip.

Now that you've created a hypertext link to the mountain sound clip, repeat this process to create the second version of the page. This time, instead of creating a hypertext link to the sound file, embed the clip in the Web page.

Embedding a Sound File

A sound clip placed directly into a Web page is one example of an embedded object. An **embedded object** is any media clip, file, program, or other object that can be run or viewed from within the Web page. To use embedded objects, the browser must support them and must have access to the appropriate plug-in applications. **Plug-ins** are programs that enable the browser to work with an embedded object. When the browser encounters an embedded object, it loads the appropriate plug-in plus any controls needed to manipulate the object. For example, a sound file plug-in might place controls on the Web page that enable the user to play the sound clip, pause it, rewind it, or change the volume. Because the object is embedded, these controls are displayed as part of the Web page.

One problem with plug-ins is that they require users to download and install additional software before being able to view the Web page. When presented with this choice, many users choose not to view the Web page rather than take the time to do this.

There are many plug-ins available for embedded sound clips. Netscape provides the LiveAudio and Winamp media player. Internet Explorer provides the ActiveMovie media player and the Windows Media player. You can also use third-party plug-ins, such as RealPlayer. Since sound has become such a useful feature on the World Wide Web, your Web browser probably supports one or more of these plug-ins.

Using the <embed> Tag

To embed a sound clip into a Web page, use the <embed> tag. The syntax of the <embed> tag is:

```
<embed src="URL" width="value" height="value" align="value"
autostart="startvalue">
```

where *URL* is the filename and location of the embedded object, and the height and width attributes define the size of the embedded object on the Web page. You might think it strange to define the width and height of an embedded sound clip, but these attributes refer to the size of the object and the object's controls. You need to define a size large enough to display the necessary controls for the user to play the media clip.

The align attribute defines how text wraps around the embedded clip. Like inline images, text can wrap to the left, right, top, or bottom of the clip. The default is for text to flow beneath the embedded clip. Netscape also supports the border, vspace, and hspace attributes, but Internet Explorer does not. Note that the <embed> clip is not part of the HTML 4.01 specifications. However, since both major browsers support it, it has seen widespread use.

The autostart attribute is used to determine whether or not the browser starts the embedded clip automatically when the Web page is loaded. Enter a value of autostart="true" to start the clip automatically and autostart="false" to leave it to the user to manually play the sound clip. The default behavior for playing an embedded clip varies among browsers. Some browsers play the clip automatically by default, others will not. To be sure, it's a good idea to use the autostart attribute.

REFERENCE WINDOW | **RW**

Embedding a Media Clip

■ To embed a sound or video clip on your Web page, use the following HTML tags:

```
<embed src="URL" width="value" height="value" align="value"
autostart="startvalue">
```

where *URL* is the filename and location of the object to be embedded, and the width and height attributes are used to define the size of the embedded object on your Web page. The align attribute defines how text flows around the clip, with the default being "bottom". Set autostart to "true" to play the clip when the browser loads the page. Set autostart to "false" to leave it up to the user to play the clip. Netscape also supports the hspace, vspace, and border attributes, which control the amount of space between the clip and the surrounding text.

Having learned how to create an embedded object, you'll now create the rainier2.htm file. Remember that rainier2.htm is the Web page installed at the visitor center and accessed directly by the user through a high-speed connection, so Tom feels comfortable with embedding the media clip directly into the Web page. For this page, you'll embed the mountain.mp3 file. If your browser and operating system do not support the MP3 format, you can substitute either the mountain.wav or mountain.au file.

To embed a sound clip:

1. Return to **raintxt.htm** in your text editor and save it as **rainier2.htm** in the same folder.

2. Insert the following code directly after the article on the Sunrise Folk Festival (substitute mountain.wav or mountain.au if your system supports that format):

```
<p>Listen to the sounds of <i>Adams & Davis</i> from
last year's festival:</p>
 <blockquote>
        <embed src="mountain.mp3" width="145" height="60"
 autostart="false">
</blockquote>
```

See Figure 10-12.

Figure 10-12	INSERTING AN EMBEDDED SOUND CLIP

embedded sound clip

width and height of
sound clip controls

```
<p>Listen to the sounds of <i>Adams & Davis</i> from last year's festival:</p>
<blockquote>
    <embed src="mountain.mp3" width="145" height="60" autostart="false">
</blockquote>

<!--- ARTICLE ABOUT THE MOUNT RAINIER INTERACTIVE MAP --->
<h2><img src="mrim.jpg" align="left" hspace="5" vspace="1">
Visitors Prepare to Meet MRIM</h2>
```

sound clip does not
play automatically

Note that when inserting the embedded sound clip you did not need to specify the clip's size, as you did earlier with the hypertext link. This is because the sound clip is downloaded to the user's browser, whether the user wants it or not. The height and width values were picked to give enough space to show the controls of the embedded player. When you embed your own media clips in the future, you'll probably need to test various height and width values to find a size that looks right. Also, you set the autostart value to "false" to allow the users to play the clip at a time of their own choosing.

3. Save your changes to the file and then close your text editor.

4. Open rainier2.htm in your Web browser. As shown in Figure 10-13, the page loads with the controls for the embedded sound clip shown on the page.

| Figure 10-13 | **PLAYING AN EMBEDDED SOUND CLIP** |

Autumn Folk Festival

From September 10th - 12th, come to Sunrise for the annual autumn folk festival. The Sunrise Festival is quickly becoming one of the Northwest's top folk events, with its intimate performances from world-famous troubadours. Camping spots are still available at Sunrise campground, but they're going fast.

In addition to the intimate song sharing in the campground every evening during the festival, there'll be workshops, great food and craft vendors. Call Maria Thompson at 555-9011 for camping information. Call Ted Cashman (555-8122) to sign up for one of the workshops.

Folk singers, Joan Adams and Shannon Davis

Listen to the sounds of *Adams & Davis* from last year's festival:

embedded sound clip and controls (your controls may differ)

TROUBLE? If you do not see any controls for the sound clip on your Web page, it may be because your browser does not support embedded objects, or you might have mistyped the name of the sound file. Return to your text editor and verify that your code matches the code shown in Figure 10-12. If you are still having trouble, talk to your instructor.

5. If necessary, click the play button on the embedded object to start playing the sound clip.

TROUBLE? If necessary, consult the documentation for your browser or plug-in to learn how to work with the sound clip, or ask your instructor or technical support person for assistance.

Using the <bgsound> Tag

With version 3.0, Internet Explorer introduced a tag for playing background sounds on your Web page. The syntax of the <bgsound> tag is:

```
<bgsound src="URL" balance="value" loop="value"
volume="value">
```

where *URL* is the filename and location of the sound file, the balance attribute defines how the sound should be balanced between the computer's left and right speakers, the loop attribute defines how many times the sound clip is played in the background, and the volume attribute indicates the volume of the background sound. The value of the balance attribute can range from -10,000 up to 10,000. Similarly, the value of the volume attribute ranges from 0 (muted) up to 10,000. The loop attribute can be either an integer (1, 2, 3, ...) or "infinite" if you want the sound clip to be played continuously. The default loop value is 1.

For example, to set mountain.mp3 to play once in the background when rainier2.htm is loaded, insert the following tag anywhere in the file:

```
<bgsound src="mountain.mp3" loop="1">
```

Because this is a background sound, no control or object is displayed on the Web page; therefore, a user cannot stop the sound from playing, pause it, or rewind it. Since the user has little control over the sound, the <bgsound> tag should be used with caution. You should also set the loop value to "1" or a small number, because playing the sound clip over and over again can be irritating to users.

REFERENCE WINDOW   **RW**

<u>Creating a Background Sound</u>

- To create a background sound, use the following tag for Internet Explorer browsers:

  `<bgsound src="URL" balance="value" loop="value" volume="value">`

  where *URL* is the filename and location of the sound file, the balance attribute defines how the sound should be balanced between the computer's left and right speakers, the loop attribute defines how many times the sound clip should be played in the background, and the volume attribute indicates the volume of the background sound. To play a background sound continuously, set the value of the loop attribute to "infinite".

- To create a background sound with the <embed> tag, use the HTML tag:

  `<embed src="URL" width="0" height="0" autostart="true">`

The <bgsound> tag is not supported by Netscape and is ignored by that browser. You should keep this in mind when deciding whether or not to use the <bgsound> tag on your Web page. You can create an effect similar to that produced by the <bgsound> tag by inserting an embedded sound clip on your Web page, setting its width and height attributes to 0, and having the clip start when the page is loaded. For example, to insert a background sound clip with Netscape, use the following HTML tag:

```
<embed src="mountain.mp3" width="0" height="0"
autostart="true">
```

The sound clip starts, but because it is 0 pixels wide and 0 pixels high, it does not appear on the Web page.

You've finished adding sound to the Mount Rainier newsletter page. You show your work to Tom, and he approves of both files you've created. In the next session, you'll learn about various video file formats and how to insert them into your Web pages.

Session 10.1 QUICK CHECK

1. Describe two ways of adding sound to your Web page.

2. Define the following terms: bandwidth, sampling rate, and sample resolution.

3. What sound file formats would you use on an intranet composed exclusively of Macintosh computers?

4. What tag would you use to allow users to access music.mp3 as an external sound clip?

5. What is an embedded object? What two things must a browser have to use an embedded object?

6. What tag would you use to allow users to access the sound file music.mp3 as an embedded object?

7. What tag would you use to have music.mp3 played once in the background when the page is loaded by Internet Explorer? How about Netscape?

SESSION 10.2

In this session you'll work with both an external and an inline video clip. You'll learn about different video formats and how to use them to control the size of your video files. You'll also work with the <embed> tag to include a video clip in the rainier2.htm Web page. Finally, you'll learn about an extension to the <img> tag that allows you to create inline images that also work as inline video clips.

Working with Video Files

Tom's next task for you is to add a video clip to the Web page taken from the Mount Rainier Interactive Map, which was recently installed at the Paradise visitors' center. This video clip shows a simulated flyby of Mount Rainier.

Displaying video is one of the most popular uses of the Web. Video files can be exciting and provide lots of information. At the same time, video files can be very large and difficult to work with. Depending on the format, a single video clip, no more than 30 seconds in length, can be as large as 10MB.

You can create video files with a video capture board installed on your computer to record images from a camcorder, television, or VCR. You can also create video clips using computer animation software. In either case, creating a video file can be a time-consuming process as you try to balance the desire to create an interesting and visually attractive clip against the need to create a compact file. To create and work with video files, you can install some of the video editors listed in Figure 10-14.

Figure 10-14	VIDEO-EDITING SOFTWARE		
WEB SITE	**URL**		**OPERATING SYSTEM**
iMovie	http://www.apple.com/imovie		Macintosh
Kino	http://www.schirmacher.de/arne/kino/		Linux
Pinnacle Studio 7	http://www.pinnaclesys.com		Windows
Video Factory	http://www.sonicfoundry.com		Windows
Video Studio	http://www.ulead.com		Windows
VideoWave	http://www.mgisoft.com/		Windows

Frame Rates and Codecs

A video file is composed of frames, where each **frame** represents a single image. When the video file is played, each frame is shown in sequence, giving the illusion of motion. The number of frames shown in each unit of time is called the **frame rate** and is expressed as frames per second (fps). Working with the frame rate is one way to control the size and quality of your video file. A video file with a high frame rate has a smooth playback, but at the expense of taking up a lot of disk space. For comparison, VHS videotape renders video at the speed of 30 fps, and video files that match this frame rate are usually quite large. You can reduce the frame rate to reduce the size of the file. When you do so, you're not slowing down the video; instead, you're reducing the number of frames shown each second and thereby reducing the total number of frames in the file. For example, instead of using 30 frames in one second of video, you might be using only 15. The overall duration of the video clip remains the same, but the size of the file is reduced.

Another way of controlling the size of the video file is by compressing each frame. The image is compressed when stored in the file. Then, as the video clip is played, the image is decompressed. The technique of compressing and decompressing video frames is a called a **codec** (for compression/decompression). There are many different codecs, each with its own advantages and disadvantages. Your video editor usually allows you to choose the codec for your video file. You'll need to experiment to determine which codec provides the best file compression without sacrificing video quality. You can also reduce the size of your video files by simply reducing the size of the video frames. A frame size of 160 pixels wide by 120 pixels high is considered standard on the Web, but you can reduce this size if you find that your video file is too large. Changing the video from color to grayscale can also reduce the size of the file. If your video clip contains a sound track, you can reduce the sampling rate, sample resolution, or the number of channels to further reduce the size of the video file. Each of these techniques is available to you in your video-editing software.

Video File Formats

Video on the Web typically appears in one of five formats: ASF, AVI, MPEG, QuickTime, or RealVideo. Figure 10-15 describes each of these formats.

Figure 10-15	VIDEO FILE FORMATS
FORMAT	**DESCRIPTION**
ASF	Advanced Streaming Format. Developed by Microsoft to eventually replace the AVI video format, ASF employs streaming media technology to provide live video over low- and high-bandwidth connections.
AVI	Audio Video Interleave. AVI is the standard video format for Windows. AVI files can have a resolution no larger than 320 × 240 pixels with a frame rate no faster than 30 fps, which means that AVI files cannot be used for full-screen, full-motion video. However, AVI files require no special hardware, making AVI one of the standard video formats for the Web.
MPEG	Moving Pictures Group. The MPEG format allows for high compression of the video file, resulting in smaller files sizes. There are two MPEG formats: MPEG-1 and MPEG-2. MPEG-1 files have a maximum resolution of 352 × 240 pixels at 30 fps. MPEG-2 files can be displayed at a maximum resolution of 1280 × 720 pixels with a frame rate of 60 fps, making MPEG-2 files appropriate for full-screen, full-motion video. Special software is required to create and play MPEG files.
QuickTime	Developed by Apple Computer for the Macintosh, QuickTime movies can also be played in Windows if the user has installed the proper software and drivers (available free from *http://www.quicktime.apple.com*.) Because of its popular support, QuickTime is also a Web standard for video files.
RealVideo	Developed by RealNetworks, RealVideo uses streaming media technology to provide live video over low- and high-bandwidth connections. Video quality is usually poorer than what can be achieved using nonstreaming video.

Which format should you use for your Web page? The answer depends in part on who your audience is. The QuickTime format was developed for Macintosh users, but QuickTime players exist for other operating systems, such as QuickTime for Windows. Therefore, QuickTime might be the format with the most cross-platform support. On the other hand, support for AVI is built into Windows, and cross-platform support might not be that important, given that the Windows platform controls 80% of the computer market. Video players for MPEG files are also available for all operating systems. Most of these formats are now available as streaming media, so users can view the video clips as they are retrieved off the Web. In order to ensure that your video clips can reach the maximum audience, many developers recommend that you make the clip available in several different formats.

Tom has an excerpt from the Mount Rainier Interactive Map—a three-second video clip that simulates a flyby of the summit at 14,000 feet. Using video-editing software, you and Tom save the video clip in AVI format under a variety of sizes and frame rate settings, shown in Figure 10-16.

Figure 10-16   FILE SIZES OF THE MRIM VIDEO CLIP

| FRAME RATE | FRAME SIZE (IN PIXELS) | |
	200 X 167	400 X 334
5 fps	187 KB	595 KB
10 fps	371 KB	719 KB
15 fps	671 KB	745 KB
20 fps	890 KB	974 KB
25 fps	917 KB	969 KB

The size of this video clip ranges from just under 1MB to 187KB. As you can see from the figure, there is no easy way of predicting what the size of the video clip will be under varying conditions. You must experiment to find the best setting for your needs. After viewing the different clips, you and Tom decide to use the smallest video clip (187KB in size). Tom saves the clip as mrim.avi. Tom also uses his video editor to convert this file to QuickTime format and saves the file as mrim.mov. The size of this file is 215KB. Tom gives you both of these clips, which are on your Data Disk, and asks you to add hypertext links to rainier.htm that point to these files.

Linking to a Video File

You follow the same procedure to link to a video clip as you did to link to a sound clip. Once again, you should include information about the size of each video file so that users can determine whether or not they want to retrieve the clip. You'll place the hypertext links to the video clip files at the bottom of rainier.htm.

To create hypertext links to mrim.avi and mrim.mov:

1. Using your text editor, open **rainier.htm** from the tutorial.10/tutorial folder of your Data Disk.

2. Locate the last paragraph of the article on the Mount Rainier Interactive Map.

3. Insert the following code directly below the paragraph:

```
<p>Preview a clip from the Mount Rainier Interactive
Map.</p>
<blockquote>
     <a href="mrim.avi">Summit Flyby (187K -
 AVI)</a><br>
     <a href="mrim.mov">Summit Flyby (215K - MOV)</a>
</blockquote>
```

The revised code is shown in Figure 10-17.

Figure 10-17	INSERTING HYPERTEXT LINKS TO VIDEO FILES

```
<p>MRIM uses state-of-the-art computer animation combined with
data from geological satellites to help you explore places you might
never visit on foot. The results of your journey are displayed on a
large screen monitor - perfect for group presentations or individual
explorations. Contact Doug LeCourt at Paradise for more information.</p>

<p>Preview a clip from the Mount Rainier Interactive Map.</p>
<blockquote>
    <a href="mrim.avi">Summit Flyby (187K - AVI)</a><br>
    <a href="mrim.mov">Summit Flyby (215K - MOV)</a>
</blockquote>

</body>
</html>
```

4. Save your changes to the file.

As you discovered earlier with sound files, different browsers respond in different ways to hypertext links to video clips. Both Internet Explorer and Netscape are capable of displaying AVI and MOV files directly within the browser without the use of plug-ins. In this case, when a user clicks a hypertext link for a video file, the clip is shown in its own Web page. The user can start the clip either by clicking a control that appears with the clip or by clicking the image if no controls appear. If no controls appear, the user can also right-click the image to view a shortcut list of commands, such as Pause, Stop, and Rewind.

On other browsers, a plug-in is activated when the user clicks the hypertext link, making the video clip play in a separate window. With this in mind, you'll test the hypertext links you created to discover if your browser supports video files, and if so, how.

To test your video file hypertext links:

1. Open **rainier.htm** with your Web browser.

2. Click the hypertext links to the AVI and MOV files you just created. Depending on their configurations, your computer and browser might be able to display only one of the video files. If so, verify that the video clip works. Figure 10-18 shows a sample of how one user might access the mrim.avi video clip.

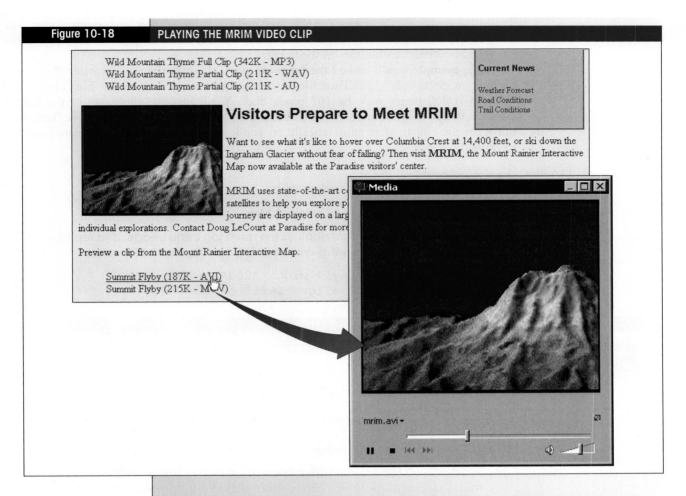

Figure 10-18 | **PLAYING THE MRIM VIDEO CLIP**

TROUBLE? It's possible that your browser has not been set up to handle video. You might see a dialog box informing you of this fact when you click the AVI or MOV hypertext link. The dialog box may also give you the option of downloading the necessary software from the Internet. If you are working on a computer on a campus network, you should talk to your instructor or technical resource person before installing any software from the Web.

TROUBLE? If you are asked to choose whether to open the file or save it, choose to open the video file.

3. After viewing the video, close the media player displaying the video clip.

Now that you've created a hypertext link to the video clips, your next task is to modify the rainier2 Web page by placing the video clip within the page itself.

Embedding a Video File

To embed a video file, you can use the <embed> tag, just as you did to embed the sound file in the previous session. You must specify a source for the embedded video clip with the src attribute and a size for the clip using the height and width attributes. The object's height and width should be large enough to display any controls needed to operate the clip.

Typically, you decide the size of a clip by trial and error. In addition to these attributes, you can also specify whether or not you want the clip to start when the page is loaded by entering autostart="true" within the <embed> tag.

In this example, you'll embed the mrim.avi video clip into the rainier2.htm file. If your browser supports only QuickTime files, you can substitute the mrim.mov file. The size of this clip is 200 pixels wide by 167 pixels high. You'll increase the value of the height attribute to 200 to accommodate the embedded object's video clip controls. Also, Tom does not want the clip to start automatically, so you'll set the value of the autostart attribute to "false."

To embed the mrim video clip:

1. Using your text editor, open **rainier2.htm**.

2. Locate the <img> tag that displays the mrim.jpg inline image, and replace the <img> tag with the following <embed> tag (see Figure 10-19):

```
<embed src="mrim.avi" width="200" height="200"
autostart="false" align="left" hspace="5">
```

Figure 10-19	INSERTING AN EMBEDDED VIDEO CLIP

replace the inline image with an embedded clip

```
<!--- ARTICLE ABOUT THE MOUNT RAINIER INTERACTIVE MAP --->
<h2>
<embed src="mrim.avi" width="200" height="200" autostart="false" align="left" hspace="5">
Visitors Prepare to Meet MRIM</h2>

<p>Want to see what it's like to hover over Columbia Crest at 14,400 feet,
or ski down the Ingraham Glacier without fear of falling? Then visit
<b>MRIM</b>, the Mount Rainier Interactive Map now available at the
Paradise visitors' center.</p>
```

3. Save your changes to the file.

4. Open rainier2.htm in your Web browser. As shown in Figure 10-20, the inline image is now replaced with an embedded video clip along with controls for operating the clip.

Figure 10-20	PLAYING AN EMBEDDED VIDEO CLIP

embedded video clip and controls (your controls may differ)

TROUBLE? Depending on your browser and its configuration, your Web page may look different from the one shown in Figure 10-20. The size of the embedded clip may display differently or it may have different controls than the ones shown in the figure.

5. Start the video clip by either clicking the play button or clicking the video clip itself. See the documentation for your plug-in or browser for more details on how to start the clip.

Using the <noembed> Tag

Older browsers don't support embedded objects such as the mrim video clip. If you still want to support those older browsers, you can use the <noembed> tag.

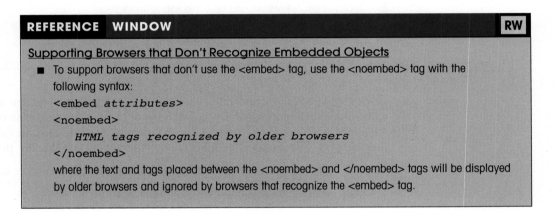

REFERENCE WINDOW   **RW**

<u>Supporting Browsers that Don't Recognize Embedded Objects</u>

■   To support browsers that don't use the <embed> tag, use the <noembed> tag with the following syntax:

```
<embed attributes>
<noembed>
    HTML tags recognized by older browsers
</noembed>
```

where the text and tags placed between the <noembed> and </noembed> tags will be displayed by older browsers and ignored by browsers that recognize the <embed> tag.

The <noembed> tag works like the <noframe> tag did for frames, by providing a way to support older browsers that don't recognize the <embed> tag. The general syntax of the <noembed> tag is:

```
<embed attributes>
<noembed>
    HTML tags recognized by older browsers
</noembed>
```

A browser that recognizes the <embed> tag embeds the object on the Web page listed in the first line of code. It recognizes the <noembed> tags and ignores any text that lies within them. An older browser, on the other hand, ignores the <embed> and <noembed> tags because it doesn't recognize them, but it runs whatever tags are entered between the <noembed> tags.

Tom would like you to use the <noembed> tag for any browser that views rainier2.htm that is unable to support embedded objects.

To use the <noembed> tag:

1. Return to **rainier2.htm** in your text editor.

2. Insert the following code directly beneath the <embed> tag for the embedded video clip (see Figure 10-21):

```
<noembed>
    <img src="mrim.jpg" align="left" hspace="5"
vspace="1">
</noembed>
```

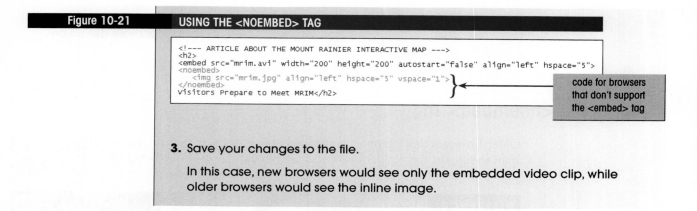

Figure 10-21   **USING THE <NOEMBED> TAG**

```
<!--- ARTICLE ABOUT THE MOUNT RAINIER INTERACTIVE MAP --->
<h2>
<embed src="mrim.avi" width="200" height="200" autostart="false" align="left" hspace="5">
<noembed>
   <img src="mrim.jpg" align="left" hspace="5" vspace="1">
</noembed>
Visitors Prepare to Meet MRIM</h2>
```

code for browsers that don't support the <embed> tag

3. Save your changes to the file.

In this case, new browsers would see only the embedded video clip, while older browsers would see the inline image.

Using the dynsrc Attribute

If your users have Internet Explorer version 3.0 and above, you can take advantage of some additional attributes for the <img> tag. One of these is the dynsrc attribute, which stands for "dynamic source." This attribute allows you to specify a video clip that is associated with an inline image. For example, an inline image that was inserted using the following <img> tag:

```
<img src="mrim.jpg" align="right" hspace="5" vspace="1">
```

You could replace this tag with the following:

```
<img dynsrc="mrim.avi" src="mrim.jpg" align="right"
hspace="5" vspace="1">
```

The result of the new tag is that Internet Explorer displays mrim.jpg as an inline image, but if the user clicks the image, the browser plays mrim.avi. Using this tag allows you to display a GIF or JPEG image as a "preview" of the inline video clip.

There are other attributes of the <img> tag that you can use along with the dynsrc attribute. These include the controls attribute, the loop attribute, and the start attribute. You can use the controls attribute to specify whether to include VCR-like controls beneath the video clip, include the word "controls" in the <img> tag to insert the controls, or omit this attribute to remove them. Use the loop attribute to specify the number of times the video is played; loop can be either an integer or the word "infinite" that allows the clip to be played without stopping. Use the start attribute to control how the video clip is started. Enter start="fileopen" in the <img> tag to start the clip when the browser opens the file, enter start="mouseover" to start the clip when the user moves the mouse over the image, and omit the start attribute to start the clip when the image is clicked by the user.

Because the dynsrc attribute and its associated attributes are supported only by Internet Explorer, if you use these attributes you will probably have to supplement your HTML code with the <embed> tag to allow other browsers to use the embedded video clip.

One way of doing this is to create a JavaScript program to test whether the user is running Internet Explorer, and if so, you can have JavaScript insert an <img> tag with the dynsrc attribute. If the user is not running Internet Explorer, JavaScript inserts an <embed> tag. Sample code for doing this is:

```
<script>
var btype = navigator.appName;
if (btype == "Microsoft Internet Explorer") {
   document.write('<img src="mrim.jpg"dynsrc="mrim.avi">');
} else {
```

```
      document.write('<embed src="mrim.avi">');
}
</script>
```

Note that this code uses the navigator object, which refers to the current browser, and the appName attribute, which contains the name of the current browser. You can supplement this code by adding the height, width, and other attributes to the tags created by the document.write() methods.

REFERENCE WINDOW   **RW**

Tips for Using Multimedia in Your Web Page
- Avoid embedding large files on your Web page if it is to be used by users with slow Internet connections. Use hypertext links instead.
- Indicate the size of the media clip when creating a hypertext link so that users know how large the file is before committing to downloading it.
- Provide different media formats for your users. For example, provide MP3, WAV, and AU versions of your audio files. Provide AVI, QuickTime, and RealVideo versions of your video files.
- Test your media clips on different browsers and browser versions.

This concludes your work with external and embedded video clips. In the next session, you'll supplement the rainier2 page by adding a Java applet to display a scrolling window of current news and reports.

Session 10.2 QUICK | CHECK

1. Define the following terms: frame, frame rate, and codec.

2. Name three ways of reducing the size of a video file.

3. What tag would you use to allow users to access the movie.mov video clip as an external video clip?

4. What tag would you use to allow users to access the movie.mov video clip as an embedded object?

5. What HTML tag would you use to run the tag you created in Question 3 for older browsers, and the tag you created in Question 4 for new browsers?

6. If your users are running Internet Explorer, how would you modify the tag <img src="movie.jpg"> to allow it to run the video file "movie.mov" whenever the user places the mouse over the inline image?

7. What are the limitations of the tag you created in Question 6?

SESSION 10.3

In this session you'll work with Java applets to create a scrolling marquee. You'll learn how Java applets are stored in .class files and how to access those files from your Web page. You'll also control a Java applet by specifying parameter values for it. Next, you'll learn how to create a scrolling marquee using one of the HTML extensions supported by Internet Explorer. Finally, you'll learn about the <object> tag, which can be used to create another type of embedded object.

Introducing Java Applets

Tom has reviewed your work with sound and video and has only one more task for you. The top of the Mount Rainier News Web page contains a table that shows the current weather forecast for the area. Tom would like to expand the forecast to include two-day predictions. Doing so presents a challenge, because including more text in the box pushes the articles further down the page. Tom would like to avoid this because he wants users to see as much of the newsletter as possible without scrolling. An effective solution is to retain the current box size and have the text automatically scroll, as it does in theatre marquees. Tom has seen scrolling text in other Web pages and knows that it requires the use of a Java applet.

Understanding Applets and .class Files

As you learned in Tutorial 8, the Java computing language was developed to allow users to run programs from within their Web browsers rather than on the Web server. Each Java program is called an **applet**. You can find Java applets for stock market tickers, games, animations, and other utilities. Unlike JavaScript, a Java applet is not inserted into your HTML file, but it is an external file that is downloaded and executed by your browser. The applet itself is displayed as an embedded object on your Web page in an **applet window**. You can specify the size and position of the applet window as it is displayed on your Web page. Some applets, however, can appear outside of your browser, in separate windows that can be resized, minimized, and placed on the desktop.

Many Java applets are available on the Web; sometimes they are free and sometimes you have to pay for them. Figure 10-22 lists a few of the more popular sources for Java applets.

Figure 10-22	JAVA APPLET ARCHIVES ON THE WEB	
TITLE	**URL**	
Applets from Sun	http://java.sun.com/applets/	
Free Java Applets	http://www.free-applets.com/	
Java Boutique	http://www.javaboutique.com/	
Java Corner	http://sunsite.berkeley.edu/Java/res/applets.htm	
Java Review Service	http://www.jars.com/	

To write your own Java applet, you need a Java Developer's Kit (JDK). You can download a free copy of the Java Developer's Kit from the Sun Microsystems Java Web site located at *http://www.java.sun.com*. There are also commercial JDKs that provide easy-to-use graphical tools and menus to help you create your Java applets quickly and easily. Once you have the JDK, be prepared to hit the books to learn the Java computing language. It is similar to JavaScript, but it is a more complicated and powerful language.

After you write the code for a Java program, you save the source code as a file with the four-letter extension .java. This file is then changed, in a process called **compiling**, into an **executable file** that can run by itself without the JDK. The executable filename has the four-letter extension .class and is called a **.class file**. Some Java applets may require several .class files. Class files are different from the other program files you have on your computer. Unlike an .exe or .com file, which is run by your operating system, a class file can be run only from within a Java interpreter. In most cases, the Java interpreter is your Web browser. This feature is what allows the same Java applet to be run under Windows or on a Macintosh, as long as the browser supports Java.

Working with the <applet> and <param> Tags

Once you've located a Java applet or written one of your own, you use the <applet> tag to insert the applet into your Web page. The <applet> tag identifies the .class file used by the applet and allows you to specify any parameters required by the applet. The general syntax of the <applet> tag is:

```
<applet code="file">
    <param>
   <param>
  . . .
    <param>
</applet>
```

where *file* is the filename of the Java applet. The <param> tags are used for any parameters required by the applet. Documentation is usually supplied with the applet to specify which parameters, if any, are required. The syntax of the <param> tag is:

```
<param name="text" value="value">
```

where the name attribute identifies the name of the parameter required by the applet, and *value* is the value you'll give the parameter.

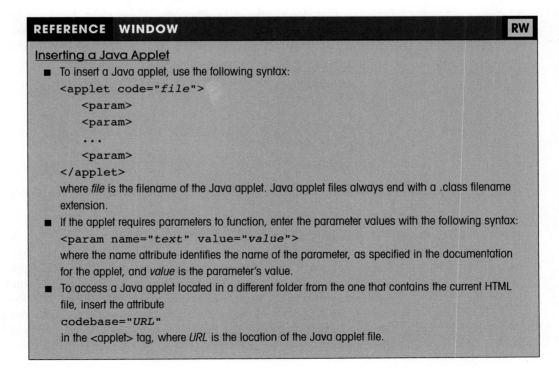

REFERENCE WINDOW   **RW**

Inserting a Java Applet

- To insert a Java applet, use the following syntax:
  ```
  <applet code="file">
      <param>
      <param>
      ...
      <param>
  </applet>
  ```
  where *file* is the filename of the Java applet. Java applet files always end with a .class filename extension.
- If the applet requires parameters to function, enter the parameter values with the following syntax:
  ```
  <param name="text" value="value">
  ```
  where the name attribute identifies the name of the parameter, as specified in the documentation for the applet, and *value* is the parameter's value.
- To access a Java applet located in a different folder from the one that contains the current HTML file, insert the attribute
  ```
  codebase="URL"
  ```
  in the <applet> tag, where *URL* is the location of the Java applet file.

Some of the other attributes supported by the <applet> tag are shown in Figure 10-23.

Figure 10-23	ATTRIBUTES OF THE <APPLET> TAG

ATTRIBUTE	DESCRIPTION
align="*alignment*"	Specifies how the surrounding text is aligned with the applet
alt="*text*"	A text string that is displayed in place of the applet before the browser has finished loading the applet
codebase="*URL*"	The location of the .class file, if different from the Web page
code="*file*"	The filename of the .class file
height="*value*"	The height of the embedded applet in pixels
hspace="*value*"	The horizontal space between the embedded applet and the surrounding text, in pixels
name="*text*"	The name of the applet
vspace="*value*"	The vertical space between the embedded applet and the surrounding text, in pixels
width="*value*"	The width of the embedded applet in pixels

One attribute you may often use is the codebase attribute, which enables you to run an applet placed in a different location than your Web page. Placing your applets in a central location allows you to maintain only one copy of each applet, rather than copies for each Web page. This makes it easier for you to manage your collection of applets. Another aspect of the codebase attribute is that it allows you to run someone else's Java applet from that person's Web server. However, this practice is discouraged and, in some cases, is a violation of copyright laws. If you want to use someone else's Java applet in your own Web page, you should first obtain permission and retrieve the .class file before placing it on your Web server.

In addition to inserting <param> tags between the opening and closing <applet> tags, you can also insert other HTML tags and text. This is often done for the benefit of older browsers that don't support Java applets. These older browsers ignore the <applet> and <param> tags and instead display the text you specify. New browsers that support Java applets ignore that text. For example, if you use the following structure in your HTML file:

```
<applet code="file">
   <param>
   <param>
   ...
   <h3>To fully enjoy this page, upgrade your browser to
support Java</h3>

</applet>
```

the browser displays the applet, or if it's an older browser, the message to upgrade.

Inserting a Java Applet into a Web Page

Tom has located a Java applet for you to use in rainier2.htm. The applet allows you to specify several lines of text to be scrolled, or rolled, vertically through a window, similar to the way credits are rolled after a movie. The name of the .class file is CreditRoll.class, and it is located on your Data Disk. Tom read through the documentation that accompanied the applet and determined that the CreditRoll.class file uses the parameters shown in Figure 10-24.

Figure 10-24	PARAMETERS OF THE CREDITROLL APPLET
PARAMETER NAME	**DESCRIPTION**
BGCOLOR	The background color of the applet window, expressed as a color value
FADEZONE	The text in the applet window fades in and out as it scrolls. This parameter sets the size of the area in which the text fades (in pixels).
TEXTCOLOR	The color value of the text in the applet window
FONT	The font used for the scrolling text in the applet window
TEXTx	Each line of text in the applet window requires a separate TEXTx parameter, where x is the line number. For example, the parameter TEXT1 sets the text for the first line in the applet window, TEXT2 sets the text for the second line in the applet window, and so forth.
URL	If the applet window is clicked, it opens the Web page specified in this URL parameter.
REPEAT	Specifies whether the text in the applet window is repeated. Setting this parameter's value to "yes" causes the text to scroll continuously.
SPEED	The speed at which the text scrolls, expressed in pixels per 1/100 of a second
VSPACE	The space between each line of text, in pixels
FONTSIZE	The point size of the text in the applet window

After considering how he wants the weather information to appear, Tom asks you to use the parameter values shown in Figure 10-25. These values create a marquee box with dark purple text on a white background. The box includes eight lines of text, including two blank lines, that provide a two-day weather forecast. The text is set to scroll continuously, and the size of the applet window is 400 pixels wide by 60 pixels high.

Figure 10-25	VALUES FOR THE CREDITROLL APPLET
PARAMETER NAME	**PARAMETER VALUE**
BGCOLOR	FFFFFF (white)
FADEZONE	20
TEXTCOLOR	663366 (dark purple)
FONT	ARIAL
TEXTx	TODAY'S WEATHER FORECAST TODAY...Partly sunny. TONIGHT...Partly cloudy. Showers with sleet. TUESDAY...Rain heavy at times. Snow likely. WEDNESDAY...Clearing. Click to view the Weather Page.
URL	http://www.nps.gov/mora/current/weather.htm
REPEAT	yes
SPEED	100
VSPACE	3
FONTSIZE	12

Now that you know the value of the parameters, you are ready to replace the static box containing the weather information with a window containing the CreditRoll applet. Because there is a lot of text involved in inserting this applet, a text file, credits.txt, has been prepared for you containing the code for the parameter values.

To insert the CreditRoll applet:

1. Using your text editor, open **credits.txt** from the tutorial.10/tutorial folder of your Data Disk.

2. Copy all of the text in the file and then close the file.

3. Using your text editor, open **rainier2.htm**.

4. Locate the <div class="weather"> tag located midway through the file.

5. Delete all of the text between the opening and closing <div> tags.

6. Paste the text you copied from credits.txt between the opening and closing <div> tags.

   The revised code in rainier2.htm should appear as shown in Figure 10-26. Take some time to study the HTML code you just inserted. Note that blank lines are indicated in the values for the TEXT2 and TEXT7 parameters by the empty space allotted to those values.

Figure 10-26	INSERTING THE CREDITROLL APPLET AND PARAMETER VALUES

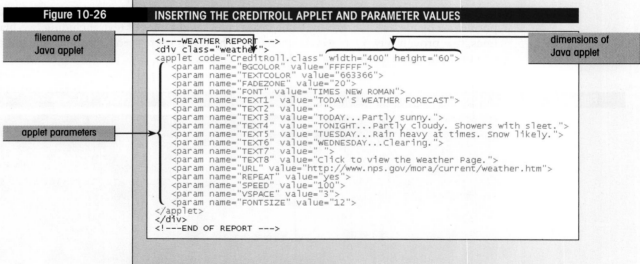

filename of Java applet

dimensions of Java applet

applet parameters

```
<!---WEATHER REPORT -->
<div class="weather">
<applet code="CreditRoll.class" width="400" height="60">
    <param name="BGCOLOR" value="FFFFFF">
    <param name="TEXTCOLOR" value="663366">
    <param name="FADEZONE" value="20">
    <param name="FONT" value="TIMES NEW ROMAN">
    <param name="TEXT1" value="TODAY'S WEATHER FORECAST">
    <param name="TEXT2" value=" ">
    <param name="TEXT3" value="TODAY...Partly sunny.">
    <param name="TEXT4" value="TONIGHT...Partly cloudy. Showers with sleet.">
    <param name="TEXT5" value="TUESDAY...Rain heavy at times. Snow likely.">
    <param name="TEXT6" value="WEDNESDAY...Clearing.">
    <param name="TEXT7" value=" ">
    <param name="TEXT8" value="Click to view the weather Page.">
    <param name="URL" value="http://www.nps.gov/mora/current/weather.htm">
    <param name="REPEAT" value="yes">
    <param name="SPEED" value="100">
    <param name="VSPACE" value="3">
    <param name="FONTSIZE" value="12">
</applet>
</div>
<!---END OF REPORT --->
```

7. Save your changes to the file.

8. Open rainier2.htm in your Web browser. With the large number of embedded objects and the Java applet, this Web page may take a while to load. After the page loads, you should see the weather forecast scrolling in the window at the top of the Web page. Figure 10-27 shows the CreditRoll applet as it is displayed on the Web page.

Figure 10-27 | THE CREDITROLL APPLET IN ACTION

text fades as it leaves the applet window

text scrolls vertically

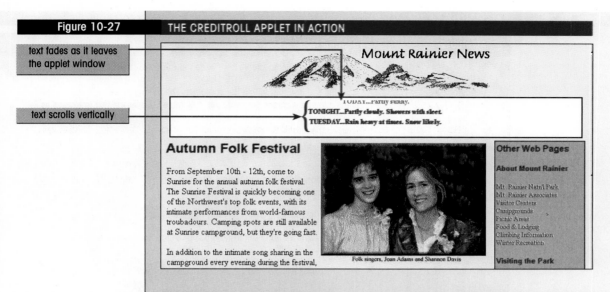

TROUBLE? If your browser has trouble accessing the CreditRoll applet, check the <applet> and <param> tags for any errors or misspellings. If you are running an early version of Netscape, you may have to exit from your browser, restart Netscape, and then reopen rainier2.htm for the applet to run properly.

Using the Internet Explorer <marquee> Tag

If you don't want to use an applet to create a box with scrolling text, and you know that users accessing your Web page are using Internet Explorer 3.0 or above, you can take advantage of the Internet Explorer <marquee> tag to create a theatre-style marquee. The general syntax of the <marquee> tag is:

```
<marquee attributes>Marquee Text</marquee>
```

where *Marquee Text* is the text that appears in the marquee box. Browsers that do not support the <marquee> tag will simply display the entire marquee text without any scrolling. Figure 10-28 describes some of the attributes of the <marquee> tag.

Figure 10-28	ATTRIBUTES OF THE <MARQUEE> TAG

ATTRIBUTE	DESCRIPTION
begin="*value*"	The time (in seconds) before beginning the marquee. The default is "0"
behavior="*type*"	How the text behaves within the container. The default value of "scroll" causes the text to scroll across the container, "alternate" causes the text to reverse its direction when it reaches the container's edge, "slide" stops the text once it reaches the end of the container.
bgcolor="*color*"	The background color of the container
direction="*type*"	The direction of the text movement (options are "left", "right", "down", or "up"). The default is "left".
end="*value*"	The time (in seconds) before ending the marquee.
height="*value*" width="*value*"	The height and width of the marquee container, in pixels.
hspace="*value*" vspace="*value*"	The horizontal and vertical space around the marquee container, in pixels.
loop="*value*"	The number of times the marquee will play. A value of "0" or "-1" will cause the marquee to play without stopping. The default is "-1".
scrollamount="*value*"	The distance, in pixels, that the text moves each time the marquee is redrawn. The default is "6".
scrolldelay="*value*"	The delay, in milliseconds, between subsequent redrawings of the marquee. The default is "85".

For example, to approximate the behavior of the CreditRoll applet, enter the following code with the <marquee> tag:

```
<marquee bgcolor="#FFFFFF" scrolldelay="10"
        scrollamount="1" direction="up"
        width="400" height="60">
   <div style="color: #663366; font-size:12pt;
        text-align:center; font-family: Times New Roman">
      TODAY'S WEATHER FORECAST<br><br>
      TODAY ... Partly sunny.<br>
      TONIGHT ... Partly cloudy. Showers with sleet.<br>
      TUESDAY ... Rain heavy at times. Snow likely.<br>
      WEDNESDAY ... Clearing.<br><br>
      <a href="http://www.nps.gov/mora/weather.htm">
         Click to view the Weather Page.
      </a>
   </div>
</marquee>
```

REFERENCE WINDOW   RW

<u>Creating a Marquee with Internet Explorer</u>

■ To create a marquee for Internet Explorer browsers, use the following HTML tag:

`<marquee>`*Marquee Text*`</marquee>`

where *Marquee Text* is the text that will scroll from right to left across the box.

■ To control the appearance and size of the marquee, insert the following attributes into the `<marquee>` tag:

`bgcolor="`*color*`" width="`*value*`" height="`*value*`"`

where the bgcolor attribute controls the background color of the marquee box, and the width and height attributes define the dimensions of the box.

■ To control the placement of the marquee with the surrounding text, use the attributes:

`hspace="`*value*`" vspace="`*value*`"`

where the hspace and vspace attributes define the amount of horizontal and vertical space in pixels around the box.

■ To control the behavior of text within the marquee, use the attributes:

`behavior="`*type*`" direction="`*type*`" loop="`*value*`"`

where behavior is either "scroll" (to scroll the text across the box), "slide" (to slide the text across the box and stop), or "alternate" (to bounce the text back and forth across the box). The direction attribute, defining the direction the text moves, is "left" (the default), "right", "down", or "up". The loop attribute determines how often the text moves across the box and is either an integer or "infinite".

■ To control the speed of the text within the marquee, use the attributes:

`scrollamount="`*value*`" scrolldelay="`*value*`"`

where scrollamount is the amount of space, in pixels, that the text moves each time it advances across the page, and scrolldelay is the amount of time, in milliseconds, between text advances.

You should show restraint in using the `<marquee>` tag. Like animated GIFs, marquees can distract your users from other elements on your Web page if used too often. As you can imagine, a continuous marquee can quickly become a nuisance.

Because the `<marquee>` tag is only supported by Internet Explorer, you decide against using it in rainier2.htm.

Tom would like you to learn about one final tag, the `<object>` tag, before concluding your work with multimedia Web pages. Again, because the `<object>` tag is supported only by Internet Explorer, you'll learn about it without implementing it in your newsletter for Tom. Therefore, you can close your text editor and your browser at this time.

To close your work:

1. Close your Web browser.

2. Return to your text editor and close rainier2.htm.

Using the <object> Tag

There are four types of embedded objects that can exist on your Web page:

- sound clips
- video clips
- applets
- images

In order to deal with these objects in a consistent way, HTML 4.0 introduced the <object> tag, which is used for any embedded object. The <object> tag replaces the <img>, <embed>, and <applet> tags, but for now you may still need to use those tags to be compatible with older browsers. Netscape, in particular, does not support the <object> tag through version 4.7. The general syntax for the <object> tag is:

```
<object data="URL" type="type" classid="URL" codebase="URL">
     <param parameter name and value>
     <param parameter name and value>
     ...
     Text and tags that are displayed by browsers that don't
support the <object> tag
</object>
```

where the data attribute is used to indicate the source of the data for the embedded object, similar to the src attribute in the <embed> tag; the type attribute indicates the type of data to be embedded (enclosed in quotes); the classid attribute identifies the class of object being embedded; and the codebase attribute indicates the location of the source data, if it differs from the location of the Web page, similar to the codebase attribute of the <applet> tag. A partial list of the attributes associated with the <object> tag is shown in Figure 10-29.

Figure 10-29	ATTRIBUTES OF THE <OBJECT> TAG
ATTRIBUTE	**DESCRIPTION**
align="*alignment*"	How the object is aligned with surrounding text
border="*value*"	The size of the border around the object, in pixels
classid="*URL*"	The class identifier of the object
code="*URL*"	The location pointing to the object's code or class
codebase="*URL*"	The location where the object is implemented
codetype="*type*"	The content type of the object specified by classid attribute
data="*type*"	The data type of the object, used when the classid attribute is missing
height="*value*" width="*value*"	The height and width of the object, in pixels
hspace="*value*" vspace="*value*"	The horizontal and vertical space around the object, in pixels
standby="*text*"	Text to display while waiting for the browser to load the object
type="*type*"	The data type of the object

Specifying the Type Value

Some of the attributes of the <object> tag require further explanation. Let's start with the type attribute. You express the type attribute in terms of the MIME data type. The **MIME (Multipurpose Internet Mail Extension)** data type was developed to allow e-mail messages to include nontext objects such as sound and video files. Later, MIME was adapted for use on the World Wide Web. Each MIME data type has a name associated with it. Figure 10-30 lists the MIME names for some of the objects you'll embed in your Web pages.

Figure 10-30	SOME MIME DATA TYPES				

IMAGE		AUDIO		VIDEO	
TYPE	**MIME NAME**	**TYPE**	**MIME NAME**	**TYPE**	**MIME NAME**
GIF	image/gif	AIFF	audio/aiff	ASF	video/x-ms-af
JPG	image/jpeg	AU	audio/basic	AVI	video/m-msvideo
		MIDI	audio/mid	MPEG	video/mpeg
		MP3	audio/mpeg	QuickTime	video/quicktime
		WAV	audio/wav		

If you don't specify a value for the type attribute, the Web browser may have difficulty rendering the Web page. If the browser doesn't support the MIME data type, it will not download the object from the Web server. In the case of large object files, this can save valuable time.

For example, to embed mrim.avi using the <object> tag rather than the <embed> tag, use the following code:

```
<object data="mrim.avi"
type="video/x-msvideo" height="200" width="200"></object>
```

Note that in this example, the type attribute value is "video/x-msvideo", which is the MIME data type for AVI files. Similarly, you can replace this <img> tag:

```
<img src="logo.gif" alt="Mount Rainier News">
```

with the following <object> tag:

```
<object data="logo.gif" type="image/gif">
     Mount Rainier News
</object>
```

Note that by treating the inline image as an embedded object, you specify alternate text between the <object> and </object> tags.

Specifying the classid Value

The classid attribute provides information to the browser on how the object is to be implemented on the Web page. For inline images, sound files, and video files, you don't need to specify a value for the classid attribute. However, for Java applets, the classid attribute takes the place of the data attribute. The syntax for embedding a Java applet within the <object> tag is:

```
<object classid="java: filename">
     <param>
```

```
        <param>
        . . .
</object>
```

To insert the CreditRoll applet with the <object> tag, use the following code:

```
<object classid="java:CreditRoll.class" width="400"
height="60">
        <param>
        <param>
        . . .
</object>
```

using all of the <param> tags as you did for the <applet> tag.

ActiveX controls require the classid attribute along with the <object> tag to use them in your Web pages. ActiveX controls can be inserted into your document with the following classid attribute value:

```
<object classid="clsid:class_identifier">
        <param>
        <param>
        . . .
</object>
```

where *class_identifier* is a complex text string that identifies the ActiveX control for the browser. For example, the class identifier for the ActiveX control that displays a label is:

99B42120-6EC7-11CF-A6C7-00AA00A47DD2

ActiveX controls can add a lot to your Web pages, and Microsoft supports a large library of controls. To help you work with them, and to determine their class ID strings, you can refer to the online library at *http://msdn.microsoft.com/library/*.

Nesting <object> Tags

One additional advantage of the <object> tag is that you can nest one <object> inside another. This is useful in situations where you want to give the browser alternatives for displaying an embedded object. For example, if you have multiple versions of the mrim video file, the following code provides the browser with four options for playing the video clip:

```
<object data="mrim.mpg" type="video/mpeg">
    <object data="mrim.mov" type="video/quicktime">
        <object data="mrim.avi" type="video/x-msvideo">
            <img src="mrim.jpg">
        </object>
    </object>
</object>
```

In this example, the browser first tries to display the MPEG version. If it can't support that video format, it tries the QuickTime version and then the AVI format. If the browser can't display any of these video formats, it displays an inline still image. To accomplish the same thing with the <embed> tag would require writing a special JavaScript program.

The <object> tag shows great promise for expanding the capability of HTML in handling embedded objects. In fact, HTML 4.01 deprecates the <embed> tag, preferring Web designers to use the <object> tag. However, you will probably have to wait for browser support to catch up with the <object> tag's potential before using it in your Web pages, or at least provide workarounds for users with older browsers.

Satisfied with the condition of both the rainier.htm and rainer2.htm pages, you present them to Tom for his approval. He is impressed by the use of sound and video in the newsletter and is happy with how the CreditRoll applet allows him to enter an almost unlimited amount of weather information without altering the layout of the page. He wants to examine the Web pages more closely and will contact you later with any requests for changes.

Session 10.3 QUICK | CHECK

1. What is compiling?

2. How does a .class file differ from other executable files you might find on your computer?

3. What tag would you use to insert the Java applet StockTicker.class into your Web page?

4. What tag would you use to remotely access the applet StockTicker.class if it is located at the URL **http://www.wstreet.com**?

5. The StockTicker.class applet has two parameters. The URL parameter identifies the URL of a Web resource containing stock data, and the TIME parameter specifies the time lag, in seconds, between stock market updates. If URL="http://www.stockinfo.com" and TIME=60, what HTML tags would you add to use these values?

6. In Internet Explorer, what tag would you use to create a scrolling marquee containing the text "Stock Information" in white letters on a black background?

7. What attribute or attributes would you add to the tag in Question 6 to instruct the text to scroll once from the left side of the marquee to the right and then stop?

8. What <object> tag would you use to insert a video file named "rainier.mov" with a width of 150 pixels and a height of 100 pixels into your Web page? What is a limitation of embedding the video file in this way?

REVIEW ASSIGNMENTS

Tom has returned with two additional multimedia clips that he would like you to use in the Mount Rainier News Web page. One is a sound clip that includes samples from performers from the previous year's Sunrise Folk Festival and has been saved in MP3, WAV, and AU formats. The second multimedia clip is a video clip with a new excerpt from the Mount Rainier Interactive Map. There are two versions of this video clip: mrim2.avi and mrim2.mov. You'll create two versions of the newsletter: one with hypertext links to external files and the other with embedded media clips. Tom also wants you to add a background sound to the Web page with embedded media clips. The background sound is based on a short sound file that welcomes users to Mount Rainier.

Tom would also like you to modify the behavior of the CreditRoll applet. He thinks that the text scrolls too slowly and would like you to increase the scrolling speed. He wants the fade-zone area set to 1 and would like to have the text of the applet window changed to black.

To implement Tom's changes to the Mount Rainier News Web page:

1. Using your text editor, open **raintxt2.htm** from the tutorial.10/review folder on your Data Disk, and save it as **rainier3.htm** in the same folder.

2. Insert hypertext links to song.mp3, song.wav, and song.au directly below the article describing the Sunrise Folk Festival. Be sure to include the name of the piece, À la Claire Fontaine, file formats, and the size of the sound files, in kilobytes.

3. Insert a hypertext link pointing to mrim2.avi and mrim2.mov directly below the paragraph describing the Mount Rainier Interactive Map. Include the description "Mount Rainier Flyby - East Ridge", the file format of each video file, and the size of the files in kilobytes.

4. Save your changes to the file and then open it in your Web browser. Verify that all of the hypertext links work correctly.

5. Using your text editor, open **raintxt2.htm** and save it as **rainier4.htm**.

6. Insert an embedded clip with the song.mp3, song.wav, or song.au file (depending on what format your system supports) directly below the paragraph on the folk festival. Set the size of the embedded object to 145 by 60 pixels, and set the autostart value to "false."

7. Replace the mrim2.jpg inline image with either the mrim2.avi or mrim2.mov video clip (depending on what your system supports). Set the size of the embedded video clip to 200 by 200 pixels, and set the autostart value to "false." For users whose browsers do not support embedded objects, display the mrim2.jpg image.

Explore ▶ 8. Embed the audio file welcome.mp3, welcome.wav, or welcome.au at the bottom of the document with a width and height of 0 pixels and set the autostart value to "true."

Explore ▶ 9. Replace the weather forecast information at the top of the page with a scrolling marquee created with the CreditRoll applet. Set the parameters of the applet as follows:

- Set the value of the SPEED parameter to 120.
- Set the FADEZONE value to 1.
- Change the TEXTCOLOR parameter to black. Hint: The applet's specifications require you to use the hexadecimal color value for black, not the color name.
- Set the rest of the parameters to those used earlier for rainier2.htm that you created in the tutorial.

10. Save your changes to the file.

11. Using your Web browser, open **rainier4.htm** and verify that the embedded links and Java applet work correctly. Also, verify that the background sound file plays correctly.

12. Hand in your files to your instructor.

CASE PROBLEMS

Case 1. Lincoln Museum. Maria Kalski is the director of public relations for the Lincoln Museum of Natural History located in Lincoln, Iowa. Maria wants to overcome the idea that museums are boring, stuffy places, so she has asked you to help liven up the museum's Web page. You've accomplished this by adding some fun graphics and fonts. Maria likes the revised page, but she would also like you to add some video and sound clips. She provides you with some multimedia files that she wants added to the Web site. She wants you to create a hypertext link to the video file, a clip of a dinosaur coming to life in a museum, and she wants the sound file to be added to the background of the Web page and played once each time the Web page is loaded by the browser. The final version of your Web page is shown in Figure 10-31.

Figure 10-31

To create the Lincoln Museum of Natural History Web page:

1. Using your text editor, open **lmnhtxt.htm** from the tutorial.10/case1 folder of your Data Disk, and save it as **lmnh.htm**.

2. Locate the word "movie" in the final paragraph of the page and change this text to a hypertext link that points to either dino.avi or dino.mov, depending on which video format your system supports. Specify the video format and video file size in the text of the hypertext link.

3. Navigate to the bottom of the file and insert <script> tags for a JavaScript program directly after the image map.

Explore

4. Using the JavaScript program presented earlier in the tutorial as a model, write a program that uses the appName attribute to determine which browser is displaying the Web page. If the browser is Microsoft Internet Explorer, then use the document.write() method to create a background sound using the Internet Explorer <bgsound> tag. Use dino.wav as the sound source (you may use dino.au instead, if that is what your system supports).

5. If the browser is not Internet Explorer, then use the document.write() method to create an embedded sound clip with dino.wav or dino.au as the source. Set the dimensions of the embedded sound clip to 0 by 0 and play the sound clip each time the Web page is loaded by the browser.

6. Save your changes to the file, print the file, and close your text editor.

7. Open **lmnh.htm** in your Web browser and verify that the hypertext link displays the video clip and that the sound clip plays automatically when the Web page loads.

Explore

8. If you have access to both Netscape and Internet Explorer, open the Web page in both browsers and verify that the background sound is played each time.

9. Print a copy of your HTML file and hand it in to your instructor.

Case 2. Madison State College. Professor Debra Li of the Madison State College English department has asked you to help her create a Web page devoted to the works of the poet Robert Frost. With your help, a Web page has been created with a short biography of the poet and the complete text of two of his works. Professor Li would like to add interest to the page by inserting sound clips of the two poems so that her students can listen to Frost's poetry as well as read it.

She also wants you to create hypertext links to Frost pages on the Web. She's located a Java applet that creates a set of graphical buttons that act as hypertext links. Professor Li thinks this applet would also make her page more interesting. The Java applet uses the button.class file and has the parameters shown in Figure 10-32 (note that parameter names are in lowercase and should be enclosed in double quotes):

Figure 10-32	
PARAMETER NAME	**DESCRIPTION**
"buttons"	The number of buttons in the set
"color"	The color of all the buttons in the set
"direction"	The orientation of the set of buttons (0=vertical orientation, 1=horizontal orientation)
"border width"	The width of the borders of the buttons, in pixels
"f_size"	The point size of the text labels on each button
"f_color"	The color value of the button labels
"f_color2"	The color value of the button labels when the mouse passes over the button or when the button is clicked
"f_offset"	The space between the button labels and the button borders, in pixels
"font"	The font face of the button labels; can be either TimesRoman, Helvetica, or Courier
"label x"	The label for each button; use the "label 0" parameter for the first button's label, "label 1" for the second button's label, and so forth
"link x"	The URL that each button links to; use the "link 0" parameter for the first button's hyperlink, "link 1" for the second button's hyperlink, and so forth

A preview of the page you'll create for Professor Li is shown in Figure 10-33.

Figure 10-33

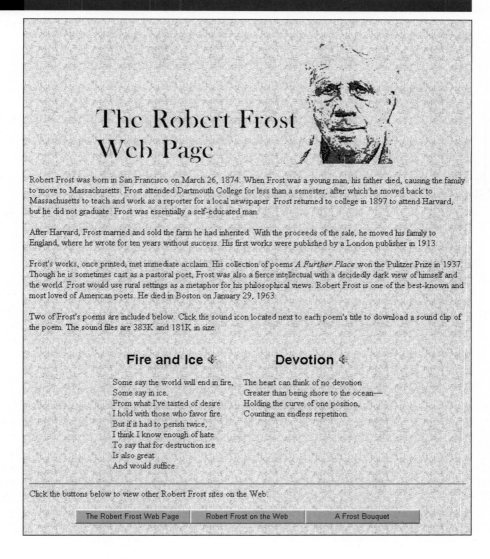

To create the Robert Frost Web page:

1. Using your text editor, open **rftxt.htm** from the tutorial.10/case2 folder of your Data Disk and save it as **rf.htm**.

2. Insert the inline image sound.gif directly after the title of the Fire and Ice poem located in the table at the bottom of the page. Align the image with the bottom of the surrounding text; set the horizontal space to 3 pixels and the image border to 0 pixels.

3. Change the Sound image to a hypertext link that points to the fireice.mp3, fireice.wav, or fireice.au sound file, depending on which format your browser supports.

4. Repeat Steps 2 and 3 for the Devotion poem located in the first row and second column of the table. Instruct the Sound image to point to the devotion.mp3, devotion.wav, or devotion.au sound file.

5. Indicate the size of the two sound files at the end of the last paragraph before the table.

6. Insert the Java applet that calls the button.class file at the bottom of the rf.htm file, within the <p align="center"> and </p> tags. Set the size of the applet to 600 by 26.

7. Specify the following parameters for the applet:

   ■ There are three buttons.
   ■ Color value of the buttons is "C0C0C0".
   ■ Buttons are oriented horizontally on the page.
   ■ Button border width is 3 pixels.
   ■ Font size of the button labels is 13.
   ■ Color of the button labels is "000000" ("FFFFFF" when clicked).
   ■ There are 4 pixels between the button labels and the button borders.
   ■ Font face is Helvetica.
   ■ Label of the first button is "The Robert Frost Web Page", and it points to *http://www.robertfrost.org/*.
   ■ Label of the second button is "Robert Frost on the Web", and it points to *http://www.amherstcommon.com/walking_tour/frost.html*.
   ■ Label of the third button is "A Frost Bouquet", and it points to *http://www.lib.virginia.edu/exhibits/frost/home.html*.

8. Print the HTML tags for the Java applet and save and close rf.htm.

9. View the page in your Web browser, and test the three links to the other Frost pages as well as the links to the two sound clips. Note that the button.class applet will only work on pages viewed locally. You cannot run the button.class applet from a Web server.

10. Print a copy of the Web page from your Web browser.

Case 3. Franklin High School. Fractals are geometric objects discovered by mathematicians, which closely model the sometimes chaotic world of nature. Mr. Doug Hefstadt, a mathematics teacher at Franklin High School in Monroe, Illinois, has just begun a unit on fractals for his senior math class. He's used the topic of fractals to construct a Web page to be placed on the school network, and he needs your help to complete the Web page. He has a video clip of a fractal that he wants placed on the Web page as well as a Java applet that allows students to interactively explore the Mandelbrot set, a type of fractal object. He wants your assistance in putting these two objects on his Web page. A preview of the page you'll create is shown in Figure 10-34.

Figure 10-34

A *fractal* is a geometric object that retains its complexity under any level of magnification. Many fractals are *self-similar* in that the fractal image is infinitely repeated on a smaller scale as one "zooms" into the object. The most famous of the fractal objects is the *Mandelbrot Set* named after its discoverer, Benoit B. Mandelbrot. As you can see in the accompanying images, the Mandelbrot Set, a bug-shaped object, appears again and again as one magnifies the image.

View a Fractal Movie

Fractals are not simply an abstract geometric concept. Fractals appear everywhere in nature: from the irregular shape of a coastline to the outlines of trees, clouds, and mountains. The application of fractal geometry to science and physics has allowed mathematicians and physicists to describe phenomena that had, until recently, eluded description.

Fractals have also been used in image processing. Mathematician Michael F. Barnsley has applied fractal mathematics to the compression of digital photographs and video images. Because of their beauty, fractals are a popular source of computer art as well.

Ready to explore your own fractals? Great. Use the Java applet below. To improve the resolution of the fractal image, change the value in the drop-down list box (a value of 1 is the most precise; 10 is the least,) and click the *Redraw* button. To magnify a particular section of the fractal, click the *Zoom In* button and drag a rectangle over the section you want to magnify. To switch between the Mandelbrot Set and the Julia Set (another type of fractal, closely related to the Mandelbrot Set) click the *Switch [M <-> J]* button, and then click a spot on the Mandelbrot Set. This applet is generously provided by James Henstridge.

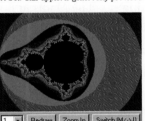

Exploring Fractals · Fractory · Fractals and Fractal Art · Fractals on the Web

To create the Fractal page:

1. Using your text editor, open **fracttxt.htm** from the tutorial.10/case3 folder of your Data Disk and save it as **fractal.htm**.

2. Insert the video clip mandel.avi, or mandel.mov if your system requires that video format, within the <div> tag containing the id name "movie".

3. Set the size of the video clip to 104 pixels wide by 120 pixels high. The clip should not start automatically.

4. Beneath the embedded video clip, use the <noembed> tags to insert a hypertext link to mandel.avi, or mandel.mov, in order to support older browsers that cannot display embedded objects. Be sure to indicate the size of the video file alongside the hypertext link.

5. Insert a Java applet for Mandel.class within the <div> section at the bottom of the file with the id name "applet".

6. Set the size of the applet to 250 by 210 pixels.

Explore

7. For browsers that do not support Java applets, display the text, "Your browser does not support Java applets."

8. Using your text editor, save, print, and close fractal.htm.

9. Open the Web page in your Web browser and verify that the video plays correctly. Test the Fractal applet.

10. Print a copy of your Web page and close the Web browser.

11. Hand in your printouts and files to your instructor.

Case 4. Madison Boy Choir.   The Madison Boy Choir is one of the premier boy choirs in the United States. Rachel Dawes, the choir director, has asked you to help create a Web site that contains a sound clip and a video clip of the choir. You need to create two Web pages for Rachel: one that contains hypertext links to the media clips and another in which the clips are embedded in the page. She also wants the page with the embedded clips to contain a scrolling marquee that displays upcoming events for the choir.

The design of the Web site is up to you, but you can use the following files in creating the page:

- **concert.rm**   A RealMedia video clip of the choir
- **CreditRoll.class** The scrolling marquee applet
- **folksong.mp3**   An MP3 clip of the boy choir
- **mbc.jpg**   A photo of the choir
- **mbcinfo.txt**   General information about the choir
- **mbclogo.jpg**   The Madison Boy Choir logo
- **schedule.txt**   The choir's schedule of upcoming events

To complete this assignment

1. Create a file named **mbc1.htm** in the tutorial.10/case4 folder of the Data Disk.

2. The mbc1.htm file should contain information about the choir, the choir logo, photo, and schedule of upcoming events.

3. Include hypertext links to the concert.rm and folksong.mp3 media clips.

4. View the contents of mbc1.htm in your Web browser. Verify that it works properly.

5. Create a file named **mbc2.htm** in the tutorial.10/case4 folder of your Data Disk.

6. Along with the other choir information, embed the concert.rm and folksong.mp3 media clips. Ensure that your Web page provides access to the media files for those users running browsers that do not support embedded clips.

7. Display the schedule of upcoming events in a scrolling marquee.

8. Using your Web browser, open mbc2.htm and verify that the embedded clips work properly.

9. Hand in your files to your instructor.

LAB ASSIGNMENTS

Multimedia brings together text, graphics, sound, animation, video, and photo images. In this lab, you'll learn how to apply multimedia and have the opportunity to see what it might be like to design some aspects of multimedia projects.

1. Click the Steps button to learn about multimedia development. As you proceed through the Steps, answer the Quick Check questions. After you complete the Steps, you'll see a Quick Check Report. Follow the instructions on the screen to print this report.

2. In Explore, browse through the STS-79 Multimedia Mission Log. How many videos are included in the Multimedia Mission Log? The image on the Mission Profile page is a vector drawing. What happens when you enlarge it?

3. Listen to the sound track on Day 3. Is this a WAV file or a MIDI file? Why do you think so? Is this a synthesized sound or a digitized sound? Listen to the sound track on page 8. Can you tell if this is a WAV file or a MIDI file?

4. Suppose you were hired as a multimedia designer for a multimedia series on targeting fourth- and fifth-grade students. Describe the changes you would make to the Multimedia Mission Log so it would be suitable for these students. Also, include a sketch showing a screen from your revised design.

5. When you view the Mission Log on your computer, do you see palette flash? Why or why not? If you see palette flash, list the images that flash.

6. Multimedia can be effectively applied to encyclopedias, atlases, and animated story-books; to computer-based training for foreign languages, first aid, or software applications; to games and sports simulations; to business presentations; to personal albums, scrapbooks, and baby books; to product catalogs and Web pages. Suppose you were hired to create one of these projects. Write a one-paragraph description of the project you would be creating. Describe some of the multimedia elements you would include. For each element, indicate its source and whether you would need to obtain permission for its use. Finally, sketch a screen or two showing your completed project.

QUICK CHECK ANSWERS

Session 10.1

1. You can add sound by either embedding a sound clip into the Web page or providing a hypertext link to a sound file.

2. Bandwidth is a measure of the amount of data that can be sent through a communications circuit each second. The number of samples taken per second from a sound source is called the sampling rate. Sample resolution indicates the precision in measuring the sound within each sample.

3. MP3, AIFF, AIFC, or SND

4. <a href="music.mp3">

5. An embedded object is any media clip, file, program, or other object that can be run or viewed from within the Web page. First, the browser must be able to support the <embed> tag, and then it must have a plug-in or add-on installed to work with the object.

6. `<embed src="music.mp3">`

7. `<bgsound src="music.mp3" loop="1">` In Netscape, you can use the tag:
   `<embed src="music.mp3" width="0" height="0" autostart="true">`

Session 10.2

1. A frame is an individual image in a video file. The number of frames displayed in each unit of time is called the frame rate. The technique of compressing and decompressing video frames is a called codec (for compression/decompression).

2. Reducing the size of each frame, reducing the frame rate, compressing the file via the codec, reducing the size of the sound track by changing the sample size or sampling rate, or reducing the color depth of the images in the video file.

3. `<a href="movie.mov">`

4. `<embed src="movie.mov">`

5. `<embed src="movie.mov"><noembed>`   `<a href="movie.mov"></noembed>`

6. `<img src="movie.jpg" dynsrc="movie.mov" start="mouseover">`

7. It may not be supported by browsers other than Internet Explorer.

Session 10.3

1. Compiling is a process that changes a file into an executable file—that is, a file that runs by itself without requiring additional software.

2. It must be run within a Java interpreter, such as your Web browser.

3. `<applet code="StockTicker.class">`

4. `<applet code="StockTicker.class" codebase="http://www.wstreet.com">`

5. `<param name="URL" value="http://www.stockinfo.com">`
   `<param name="TIME" value="60">`

6. `<font color="#FFFFFF">`
      `<marquee bgcolor="#000000">Stock Information</marquee>`
   `</font>`

7. `direction="left" behavior="slide"`

8. `<object data="rainier.mov" height="100" width="150" type="video/quicktime">`
   This tag is not supported by some browsers.

OBJECTIVES

In this case you will:

- Paste text into a Web page formatted with tables

- Create hypertext link anchors and link to anchors on other Web pages

- Insert a registered trade-mark symbol, using a special character code

- Create form elements for a product order form

- Create a JavaScript program to calculate the total cost of an order

CREATING A COMPANY WEB SITE

FrostiWear Winter Clothes

FrostiWear is a retail mail-order company that specializes in winter clothing and gear. Recently, the company created a Web site to advertise its wares on the World Wide Web. Part of the Web site allows customers to order products online.

Susan Crawford, the director of the company's Internet Advertising Division, has asked you to create three Web pages for the company's line of gloves and mittens. She's provided you with a list of popular products that she would like you to add to the company's Web site. Later, after she approves your work, she'll ask you to add the complete company line, over 35 styles of gloves and mittens, to the Web site.

Susan wants the Web pages you create to match the established style of the company's Web site. She gives you a file, frosti.txt, containing one of the standard page layouts. You'll use this layout as a guide for two of the pages she wants you to create. These are:

- **gloves.htm**: a page containing an overview of FrostiWear's glove and mitten products
- **gproduct.htm**: a page with specific information on the four products that Susan wants you to add to the site

Susan also wants you to create a third page, gorder.htm, which contains an order form for the company's glove and mitten products. This page should be based on the company's standard form, which is saved in the order.txt file. Your form should calculate the total cost of the order. In addition, FrostiWear provides a 5% discount (rounded to the nearest dollar) for customers who have a FrostiWear Club card. Your form should take the discount into account when calculating the total. If the customer is not a FrostiWear Club member, the form should display a message inviting the customer to join.

To complete these pages, Susan gives you image files of the glove products, the logo, and a background, and text files containing product specifications and descriptions. Figure AC1-1 and Figure AC1-2 list the files you'll be working with.

Figure AC1-1	TEXT FILES FOR THE FROSTIWEAR WEB SITE
FILENAME	**DESCRIPTION**
arctic.txt	Description of the ArcticBlast glove
fLg.txt	Description of the Fingerless Glove
frosti.css	Stylesheet for the FrostiWear Web site
frosti.htm	FrostiWear home page
frosti.txt	Basic layout of all FrostiWear Web pages
gloves.txt	Overview of the line of FrostiWear gloves and mittens
gmitt.txt	Description of the Glomitt glove/mitt combination product
order.txt	Standard layout for FrostiWear's online order forms
pfm.txt	Description of the PolyFleece mitt

Figure AC1-2	GRAPHIC FILES FOR THE FROSTIWEAR WEB SITE
FILENAME	**DESCRIPTION**
arcticb.jpg	Image of the ArcticBlast glove
blueline.jpg	Background image, to be used on all Web pages except the online order form page
fless.jpg	Image of the Fingerless Glove
flogo.jpg	FrostiWear company logo, to be included on all Web pages
glomitt.jpg	Image of the Glomitt glove/mitt combination product
gloves.jpg	Image to be used in the Glove Overview Web page
polyflce.jpg	Image of the PolyFleece mitt
sweaters.jpg	Image displayed on the FrostiWear home page

To create Web pages for the FrostiWear Web site:

1. Start your text editor and open **frosti.txt** in the case1 subfolder of the tutorial.add folder on your Data Disk, and then save as **gloves.htm** in the same folder.
2. Change the title of the Web page to "FrostiWear Gloves."
3. Within the second table cell, after the "Enter Page text here" comment, insert the **gloves.jpg** inline image, aligned with the right cell margin.

4. Below the inline image, but within the table cell, insert the contents of **gloves.txt** (you might want to use the copy and paste features of your text editor to do this). Format the paragraph title as a h1 header. Separate one paragraph from another using paragraph marks.

Explore

5. After the first occurrence of each of the three words PolyFleece, ArcticBlast, and Gore-Tex, insert the registered trademark symbol ® as a superscript.

6. Change the following text to hypertext links (each item, except the last, appears in the second paragraph; the last item appears in the third paragraph):
   - "Fingerless Gloves" linked to the FLess anchor in the gproduct.htm file
   - "PolyFleece mitts" linked to the PolyF anchor in the gproduct.htm file
   - "Glomitt" linked to the Glomitt anchor in the gproduct.htm file
   - "ArcticBlast Gore-Tex mitts" linked to the ArcticBlast anchor in the gproduct.htm file
   - "online order form" linked to the gorder.htm file

7. Save the gloves.htm file and preview it in your Web browser. Your Web page should be similar to the one shown in Figure AC1-3 (your browser might render the page slightly differently). Print your Web page.

Figure AC1-3   THE GLOVES AND MITTS PAGE

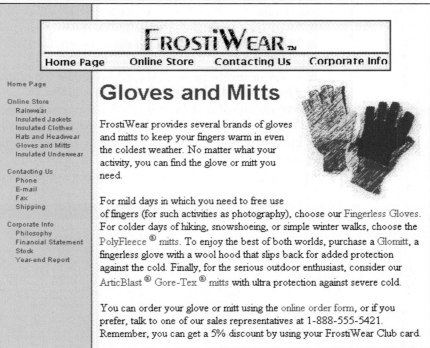

8. Open the **frosti.txt** template file in your text editor and save it as **gproduct.htm**.

9. Change the Web page title to "FrostiWear Glove Products."

10. In the second table cell below the "Enter page text here" comment, insert the **fless.jpg** image, aligned with the right cell margin.

11. Below the image, insert the contents of the **flg.txt** file, which describes the Fingerless Glove.

12. Format the text you inserted by displaying the title as an h1 heading header, and insert an anchor named "FLess" at the beginning of the h1 header. Place paragraph tags around the paragraph describing the fingerless glove.

13. Below the paragraph, insert the product specification table shown in Figure AC1-4. Create a row of table headers and set the width of the first table column to 150 pixels, and set the width of the second column to 300 pixels. Set the border width of the table to 2 pixels.

Figure AC1-4 — **TABLE OF FINGERLESS GLOVES PRODUCT SPECIFICATIONS**

SPECIFICATION	DESCRIPTION
Product ID	G725
Color	Burgundy, Red, Black, Gray
Size	Small, Medium, Large, XLarge
Price	$28.00

14. Below the table, enter additional text from the files for the three remaining products. Use the files **pfm.txt**, **gmitt.txt**, and **arctic.txt**. Format those sections in the same way you formatted the Fingerless Gloves section, and include the appropriate inline image and product information table for each item. Make the following changes to each section:

For PolyFleece mitts:
- Insert an anchor named "PolyF" at the beginning of the section.
- In the product specification table, the Product ID is G726, and the price is $38.00.

For Glomitts:
- Insert an anchor named "Glomitt" at the beginning of the section.
- The Product ID is G727, and the price is $18.00.

For ArcticBlast mitts:
- Insert an anchor named "ArcticBlast" at the top of the section.
- The Product ID is G728, and the price is $98.00.

Explore 15. Insert the registered trademark symbol as a superscript after the first occurrence (other than in headers) of the words: PolyFleece, ArcticBlast, and Gore-Tex on the page.

16. Link the text "Order online." to gorder.htm (each of the four times this text occurs on the page).

17. Open the page in your Web browser. Your page should look similar to the one shown in Figure AC1-5.

Figure AC1-5 — **THE GLOVE PRODUCTS PAGE**

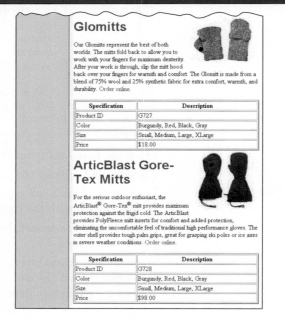

18. Verify that each of the four product hypertext links you created in the gloves.htm file navigates to the appropriate location in the gproduct.htm page. Print a copy of your page as it appears in your Web browser.

19. Open **order.txt** and save it as **gorder.htm**.

20. Change the text "Product Order Form" in the page's title and heading to "Gloves and Mitts Order Form." Change the text "Product page" in the initial paragraph to "Gloves and Mitts page," and link it to gloves.htm.

21. Within the Order form, change the Brand selection list so that it displays the names of the four glove brands along with their prices. Set the value of each of the four options in the selection list to the price of the glove or mitt.

22. Enter options for the Size and Color selection lists, based on the table entries in the gproduct.htm page.

Explore ▶ 23. Within the head section of the gorder.htm file, create a JavaScript function named "Calculate()." The Calculate() function should do the following:

   ■ Determine the value (price) of the selected brand (*Hint*: First determine the selected index in the Brand selection list, and then use this information to determine the value of the option corresponding to that index).

   ■ Multiply the brand's price by the quantity ordered. Store this value in a variable named "Subtotal."

   ■ Determine the customer discount and store it in a variable named "Discount." The discount should be either 0 or, if the customer is a FrostiWear card holder, it should be equal to Math.round(0.05*Subtotal).

   ■ Subtract Discount from Subtotal and store the result in a variable named "Total."

   ■ Store the subtotal value in the subtotal input box, the discount value in the discount input box, and the total value in the total input box.

24. Modify the Calculate Total button so that it runs the Calculate() function when clicked.

Explore ▶ 25. Modify the form so that if the customer is not a FrostiWear Club member, an alert box appears with the text "You can enjoy additional savings with a FrostiWear Club card" when the customer submits the order.

26. Using your Web browser, open **gorder.htm**. Your Web page should look similar to the one shown in Figure AC1-6.

Figure AC1-6   THE GLOVES AND MITTS ORDER FORM

FrostiWear™

Home Page   Online Store   Contacting Us   Corporate Info

Gloves and Mitts Order Form

Go to the Gloves and Mitts page to learn more about our products and styles.

1) I am a FrostiWear Club Member* ☐ Club ID: `FC-#####`

2) Brand: `Fingerless Gloves ($28)` ▼

3) Gender: `Male` ▼

4) Size: `Small` ▼

5) Color: `Burgundy` ▼

6) Quantity: `0`

Subtotal: `0`

Discount: `0`

Total: `0`

[Calculate Total]   [Add to Shopping Cart]   [Reset Form]

*FrostiWear Club members receive a 5% discount on all merchandise (rounded to the nearest dollar amount).

27. Print a copy of the Web page showing the total order cost for the following values:

- FrostiWear Club Member = yes, Brand = Glomitt, Quantity = 3
- FrostiWear Club Member = no, Brand = Fingerless Gloves, Quantity = 4
- FrostiWear Club Member = yes, Brand = ArcticBlast, Quantity = 1
- FrostiWear Club Member = no, Brand = PolyFleece Mitts, Quantity = 3

28. Open the **gloves.htm** page and verify that all of the hypertext links you created between the three pages work properly. (Links to Web pages other than the FrostiWear home page will not work.) Close your Web browser.

29. Print a copy of the HTML code for all the pages you created.

In this case you will:

- Use embedded styles and a linked style sheet to create styles for a Web site

- Insert an animated GIF to display a slide show

- Create and use an image map involving polygonal hotspots

- Insert an embedded video clip

- Provide support for older browsers that do not support inline media

CREATING A STYLE FOR A WEB SITE

CASE

Mayer Photography

Mayer Photography is a family-owned photography studio founded by Ted and Jane Mayer in 1972. They've managed to create a successful business in Elmridge, New Hampshire, and the neighboring communities. Ted recently approached you to create a Web site for his studio.

Ted envisions four Web pages for his Web site: a home page that describes the company and provides contact information for customers, a page describing the company's wedding services, a page devoted to the company's portrait services, and a final page that will describe monthly specials offered by the company. You'll name these pages mayer.htm, weddings.htm, portraits.htm, and specials.htm, respectively.

Ted has also collected four recommendations from Mayer Photography customers and he would like to include these comments on each of the four Web pages. He has provided text files containing these comments as well as the general text that he wants you to place on his Web site. He has also given you image files containing samples of his company's work. Because Mayer Photography has lately been involved in providing video services for weddings, he has also provided a video clip (in AVI and QuickTime format) that he would like you to add to the Web page describing the company's wedding services. Figure AC2-1 shows the files you'll place on each Web page.

Figure AC2-1	FILES FOR THE MAYER PHOTOGRAPHY WEB SITE	

WEB PAGE	FILES	FILE DESCRIPTIONS
Mayer.htm		
	mlogo.jpg	The company logo and list of Web pages
	slides.gif	Animated graphic
	mayer.txt	Description of Mayer Photography's services
	guitar.jpg	Image to be placed next to the description of the company's services
	comment1.txt	Comments from a satisfied customer
	comment1.jpg	Photo of the satisfied customer
Weddings.htm		
	mlogo.jpg	The company logo and list of Web pages
	slides.gif	Animated graphic
	weddings.txt	Description of Mayer Photography's wedding services
	wedding.jpg	Image to accompany the wedding services article
	comment2.txt	Comments from a satisfied wedding customer
	comment2.jpg	Image of the wedding customer
	wedding.avi	Wedding video (AVI format)
	wedding.mov	Wedding video (QuickTime format)
Portraits.htm		
	mlogo.jpg	The company logo and list of Web pages
	slides.gif	Animated graphic
	portraits.txt	Description of Mayer Photography's portrait services
	family.jpg	Image to accompany the portrait services article
	baby.jpg	Second image to accompany the portrait services article
	comment3.txt	Comments from a satisfied portrait customer
	comment3.jpg	Image of the portrait customer
Specials.htm		
	mlogo.jpg	The company logo and list of Web pages
	slides.gif	Animated graphic
	specials.txt	Description of Mayer Photography's specials and special services
	couple.jpg	Image to accompany the special services article
	comment4.txt	Comments from a satisfied customer
	comment4.jpg	Image of the satisfied customer

A preview of the first Web page you'll create, mayer.htm, is shown in Figure AC2-2. (Netscape users: the top of the initial header will not be aligned with the top of the comment box.)

Figure AC2-2   THE MAYER PHOTOGRAPHY HOME PAGE

To create Web pages for the Mayer Photography Web site:

1. Create a file named **mayer.htm** in the case2 subfolder of the tutorial.add folder on your Data Disk. Specify the title "Mayer Photography: Home Page" for the Web page.

2. At the top of the page, insert the **mlogo.jpg** file. Set the border width to 0 pixels and specify "Mayer Photography" as the alternate text. Create an image map for the logo with the following polygonal hotspot coordinates:

   - (3,83)(20,69)(40,66)(60,69)(81,83)(60,97)(40,100)(20,97) pointing to the mayer.htm file
   - (103,83)(120,69)(140,66)(160,69)(181,83)(160,97)(140,100)(120,97) pointing to the weddings.htm file (you'll create this file, along with portraits.htm and specials.htm, in a moment)
   - (203,83)(220,69)(240,66)(260,69)(281,83)(260,97)(240,100)(220,97) pointing to the portraits.htm file
   - (303,83)(320,69)(340,66)(360,69)(381,83)(360,97)(340,100)(320,97) pointing to the specials.htm file

3. Directly to the right of the logo, insert the animated GIF, **slides.gif**.

4. Insert a horizontal line below the logo and animated GIF, and then center these three elements on the Web page (as shown in Figure AC2-2).

5. Below the horizontal line, create a centered table with a width of 100% of the display area. The table should have one row of table headers, with the width of each table header set to 25% of the width of the table. Within the four table headers, insert the following centered text: "Home," "Weddings," "Portraits," and "Specials," and link the appropriate word to the files: mayer.htm, weddings.htm, portraits.htm, and specials.htm, respectively. Set the cell padding of the table to 10 pixels.

6. Below the table, insert the **comment1.jpg** image file, centered horizontally. Below the image, insert the contents of the **comment1.txt** file. Insert paragraph tags around the paragraph in text, and italicize the name of the customer and the customer's home town in a paragraph below the comment text.

7. Place the **comment1.jpg** image and the **comment1.txt** file within a pair of <div> tags with the class name, comments.

8. Below the comments element, insert the contents of the **mayer.txt** file. Add paragraph tags around each paragraph and format the titles of each paragraph as an h2 heading. Format the address information at the bottom of the column, using the <address> tag, and add line breaks after each line in the address. Insert the **guitar.jpg** image between the first and second articles, aligned with the right cell margin. Set the horizontal distance between the iamge and the surrounding text to 5 pixels.

9. Within the first article (titled "Who Are We?"), link the text "portraits, senior class photos" to the portraits.htm file. Link the text "weddings" in the same sentence to the weddings.htm file.

10. Create an embedded style for the page, setting the text color of hypertext links and all headers to brown, and the background color of the class element, comments, to brown as well.

11. Save your changes to mayer.htm file.

12. Create a style sheet named **mayer.css** in the case2 subfolder of the tutorial.add folder on your Data Disk. In the style sheet, set the background color of the page body to white and the font color to black. Also set the font face of all headers to Arial, Helvetica, and sans-serif. Reduce the size of the top margin around all headers to 0 pixels. Set the font size of any text in an Address element to 0.75em, center the address text, and set the font face to Arial, Helvetica, and sans-serif.

13. Within the mayer.css style sheet, create a style for the class element comments, such that the comment element is a box floating on the left, with a width of 175 pixels, a margin of 5 pixels, and a padding of 5 pixels. Set the font color of text in the comments element to white.

14. Save your changes to the mayer.css style sheet and print a copy of the sheet.

15. Open **mayer.htm** file in your text editor and link it to the mayer.css style sheet.

16. Save your changes to mayer.htm. Print a copy of the HTML code, and then open the page in your Web browser and print a copy of the page using your Web browser.

17. Create the **weddings.htm** page with your text editor, using the same layout you applied to the mayer.htm page and linking it to the mayer.css style sheet. Once again, the comments box should contain an image and a recommendation from a satisfied customer, and the right column should contain information on how Mayer Photography handles weddings. Use the **comment2.txt** file along with the **comment2.jpg** image for the recommendation. Use the **weddings.txt** file along with the **wedding.jpg** image for the column containing wedding information. The wedding.jpg image should be aligned with the right margin, alongside the text of the first paragraph of wedding information.

18. Use a different color style for the weddings.htm page. Instead of brown, use the rgb color values (153, 102, 255) to create a lavender color for the text links, headers, and the background of the comments box.

19. Italicize the words "Draybeck Video Services" in the paragraph on wedding videos.

20. Directly below the wedding videos paragraph, insert a centered embedded video clip using either the **wedding.avi** or **wedding.mov** file (depending on which video format your computer supports). Set the width and height of the embedded clip to 120 pixels, and set the autostart value to "false."

Explore ▷ 21. If the customer's browser does not support inline video, have the weddings.htm page display hypertext links to the wedding.avi and wedding.mov files instead. Include information on the size and format of each video clip along with the linked text.

22. Save the weddings.htm file. Your page should appear as shown in Figure AC2-3. Print a copy of the HTML code you used to create your page, and print your page with your Web browser.

Figure AC2-3 | THE MAYER PHOTOGRAPHY WEDDINGS PAGE

23. Create the portraits.htm page shown in Figure AC2-4. Apply the same layout and style choices you used in the two other pages. Use the **comment3.txt** file for the Greer family recommendation, along with the **comment3.jpg** image. Use the **portraits.txt** file for the

information on Mayer Photography portraits, along with the **family.jpg** and **baby.jpg** images. The color value of the comments box background, text links, and paragraph headings should be rgb(0,102,153). Print a copy of the HTML code for this file, along with the page with your Web browser.

Figure AC2-4   **THE MAYER PHOTOGRAPHY PORTRAITS PAGE**

Home   Weddings   Portraits   Specials

Portraits: A Cherished Gift

A well-crafted portrait is a gift you'll cherish forever. At Mayer Photography, we understand this and we strive to create portraits of unsurpassed quality. We work with you to create the portrait you deserve. You can choose between a formal studio setting or, if the mood strikes you, we can go to locations that highlight your personality and interests.

"Mayer Photography has done numerous portraits for our family. We've always been very pleased with their work and professionalism."

Paul & Sue Greer, Idaville

For Any Occasion

Whether you're interested in large group photos, family portraits, or Senior class pictures, Mayer Photography is the place to go for portraits. We offer competitive group rate pricing for organizations, businesses and students. Our highly-trained and experienced staff is ready to serve you.

24. Create the specials.htm page shown in Figure AC2-5. Use the **comment4.txt** file for the recommendation from Barbara Lee, along with the **comment4.jpg** image. Insert the text from the **specials.txt** file into the right column, along with the **couple.jpg** image. The color value of the comments box background, text links, and paragraph headings should be rgb(0,102,0).

Figure AC2-5   THE MAYER PHOTOGRAPHY SPECIALS PAGE

Home   Weddings   Portraits   Specials

Special Prices, Special People

During the month of May, Mayer Photography is reducing the price of its family portraits by 15%. If you've delayed creating that special photo, don't delay any longer, and get it at a special price. As always, Mayer Photography will offer competitive discounts for large groups and organizations.

Digital Photography

As you can see from our Web site, Mayer Photography is not shy about jumping into the computer age. If you have a PC or Macintosh, look into our scanning services. We can take your photos and convert them into graphics files suitable for desktop wallpaper or the World Wide Web. We can also use our imaging software to enhance your photos with special effects. Call us for details. You can also e-mail us at:

"I'm so pleased with their work. I call Mayer Photography on almost every special occasion."

Barbara Lee, Whitenburg

DigitPhotos@MayerPhoto.com

25. Center the e-mail address and change the e-mail address itself into a hypertext link pointing to the specified address.

26. Print both the Web page and the corresponding HTML code you created.

27. Test the hypertext links you created for this Web site, both at the bottom of the page and within the Mayer Photography logo. Verify that the links allow you to open each of the four pages you created.

28. Close your Web browser and your text editor.

OBJECTIVES

In this case you will:

- Design and create an online newsletter incorporating several Web pages

- Format your newsletter using tables, styles, special fonts, and other layout features

- Create an image map containing hotspots to each page in the Web site

- Create a JavaScript program that displays the current date

- Insert a scrolling banner Java applet that displays a list of events

- Create an online survey form containing several form elements

CREATING AN ONLINE NEWSLETTER

CASE

Twin Life Magazine*

Twin Life is a magazine created for parents of twins, triplets, and other multiple-birth children. Recently the company has decided to go online and publish parts of its monthly magazine on the World Wide Web. Elise Howard, the magazine's editor, has asked you to create a Web site for the contents of Twin Life. You've been handed a disk containing text files of the articles she wants you to add and image files she wants to have placed on the site.

Elise envisions a total of five Web pages for the site: a front page, a news page, a monthly features page, a page of special articles, and a customer survey page. Figure AC3-1 lists the files that you should use for each page of the Web site.

*Please note: All of Additional Case 3 is an Exploration Exercise.

The actual layout of the pages in the Web site is up to you, but it should incorporate the following features:

- Each Web page should have a title, and you need to specify a style for the colors of the background, text, and linked text.

- The front page should display a message with the current date, for example, "Today is 11/4/2003."

- The site should show at least one example of a font that uses the Arial, Helvetica, or Sans Serif font family and that is a different color from the surrounding text.

- The magazine's logo (twinlogo.gif) should include an image map linking to the five Web pages in the Web site. You will have to determine the coordinates for each hotspot using either your image editing software or an image map editor. In addition, each page in the site should have text links to all five pages, in order to provide support for browsers that cannot display client-side image maps.

- The pages should use tables or styles to format the layout of the different articles in the newsletter. There should be at least one example of an article that has a different background color from the rest.

- The list of upcoming events (found in the calendar.txt file) should be displayed in a scrolling window, using the CreditRoll.class Java applet. You need to determine the values of each parameter in the applet, aside from the TEXTx parameters.

- Any text in one article that refers to the contents of another article should be changed to a hypertext link pointing to that article.

- A Submit button and a Reset button should be included with the online survey form.

To create Web pages for the Twin Life Web site:

1. Using your text editor, create HTML files named **twinlife.htm**, **news.htm**, **feature.htm**, **articles.htm**, and **survey.htm**.

2. Using the list of files from the tutorial.add/case3 folder of your data disk shown in Figure AC3-1, insert the appropriate text and images into each of these Web pages (you can copy the text using the copy and paste functions of your text editor). Format the pages with an attractive layout.

Figure AC3-1   **FILES FOR THE _TWIN LIFE_ WEB SITE**

WEB PAGE	FILES	FILE DESCRIPTIONS
Front page		
	twinlogo.gif	The magazine logo
	twins.jpg	An image of twins to be used on the front page
	editor.txt	A message from the editor
	howard.jpg	An image of the editor
	staff.txt	A list of the magazine's staff
	calendar.txt	A list of upcoming events (to be displayed as scrolling text via a Java applet)
News		
	chicago.txt	An article on a convention in Chicago of mothers of multiple births
	lasker.jpg	An image of the author of the Chicago article
	rates.txt	An article on twin birth rates
	mbirths.txt	An article on the increase in multiple-birth pregnancies
Features		
	twintips.txt	Twin Tips question and answer forum
	lawson.jpg	An image of the author of Twin Tips
	deliver.jpg	Image of the month
	deliver.txt	Text to accompany the photo of the month
	recipe.txt	The recipe of the month
Articles		
	roles.txt	An article on the roles that twins play
	kerkman.jpg	An image of the author of the Roles article
	talk.txt	An article on how twins acquire speech
	kuhlman.jpg	An image of the author of the Talk article
Survey	survey.txt	The text of the online survey form

3. Open the **twinlife.htm** file in your Web browser and test each of the hypertext links you created. When satisfied with the behavior and appearance of the Web site, print a copy of each Web page as it appears in your Web browser.

4. Return to your text editor and print the HTML code for each of the five Web pages.

5. Close your Web browser and your text editor.

Web Pages & HTML

LAB ASSIGNMENTS

Web Pages & HTML It's easy to create your own Web pages. There are many software tools to help you become a Web designer. In this Lab you'll experiment with a Web authoring wizard that automates the process of creating a Web page. You'll also try your hand at working directly with HTML code.

1. Click the Steps button to activate the Web authoring wizard and learn how to create a basic Web page. As you proceed through the Steps, answer all of the Quick Check questions. After you complete the Steps, you will see a Quick Check summary Report. Follow the instructions on the screen to print this report.

2. In Explore, click the File menu, and then click New to start working on a new Web page. Use the wizard to create a Home page for a veterinarian who offers dog day-care and boarding services. After you create the page, save it on drive A or C, and print the HTML code. Your site must have the following characteristics:

   a. Title: Dr. Dave's Dog Domain
   b. Background color: Gold
   c. Image: dog.jpg
   d. Body text: Your dog will have the best care day and night at Dr. Dave's Dog Domain. Fine accommodations, good food, playtime, and snacks are all provided. You can board your pet by the day or week. Grooming services also available.
   e. Text link: "Reasonable rates" links to *www.cciw.com/np3/rates.htm*
   f. E-mail link: "For more information:" links to daveassist@drdave.com

3. In Explore, use the File menu to open the HTML document, **politics.htm**. After you use the HTML window (not the wizard) to make the following changes, save the revised page on drive A or C, and print the HTML code. Refer to the HTML Tag Reference at the end of this book for a list of HTML tags you can use.

   a. Change the title to Politics 2000.
   b. Center the page heading.
   c. Change the background color to FFE7C6 and the text color to 000000.
   d. Add a line break before the sentence "What's next?"
   e. Add a bold tag to "Additional links on this topic:".
   f. Add one more link to the "Additional links" list. The link should go to the site *http://www.elections.ca* and the clickable link should read "Elections Canada."
   g. Change the last graphic to display the image "next.gif."

4. In Explore, use the Web authoring wizard and the HTML window to create a home page about yourself. You should include at least a screenful of text, an image, an external link, and an e-mail link. Save the page on drive A, then print the HTML code. Turn in your disk and printout.

New Perspectives on

X M L

Read This Before You Begin

To the Student

Data Disks

To complete the Level I tutorials, Review Assignments, and Case Problems, you need two Data Disks. Your instructor will either provide you with these Data Disks or ask you to make your own.

If you are making your own Data Disks, you will need **two** blank, formatted high-density disks. You will need to copy a set of files and/or folders from a file server, standalone computer, or the Web onto your disks. Your instructor will tell you which computer, drive letter, and folders contain the files you need. You could also download the files by going to **www.course.com** and following the instructions on the screen.

The information below shows you the Data Disks you need so that you will have enough disk space to complete all the tutorials, Review Assignments, and Case Problems:

Data Disk 1

Write this on the disk label:
Data Disk 1: XML Tutorials 1 and 2

Data Disk 2

Write this on the disk label:
Data Disk 2: XML Tutorials 3 and 4

When you begin each tutorial, Review Assignment, or Case Problem, be sure you are using the correct Data Disk. Refer to the "File Finder" chart at the back of this text for more detailed information on which files are used in which tutorials. See the inside front cover of this book for more information on Data Disk files, or ask your instructor or technical support person for assistance.

Using Your Own Computer

If you are going to work through this book using your own computer, you need:

- **Computer System** A text editor and a Web browser (preferably Netscape Navigator or Internet Explorer, versions 4.0 or higher) must be installed on your computer. If you are using a non-standard browser, it must support frames and HTML 4.0 or higher.

- **Data Disks** You will not be able to complete the tutorials or exercises in this book using your own computer until you have your Data Disks.

Visit Our World Wide Web Site

Additional materials designed especially for you are available on the World Wide Web.
Go to **www.course.com/NewPerspectives**.

To the Instructor

The Data Disk Files are available on the Instructor's Resource Kit for this title. Follow the instructions in the Help file on the CD-ROM to install the programs to your network or standalone computer. For information on creating Data Disks, see the "To the Student" section above.

You are granted a license to copy the Data Files to any computer or computer network used by students who have purchased this book.

OBJECTIVES

In this tutorial you will:

- Learn about the history of XML

- Compare the features of XML and HTML

- Learn how XML documents are structured

- Create your own XML elements and attributes

- Link an XML document to a cascading style sheet

- Display an XML document in a Web browser

CREATING AN XML DOCUMENT

Developing an XML Document for the Jazz Warehouse

CASE

The Jazz Warehouse

The Jazz Warehouse is a store located in Kansas City specializing in jazz recordings and collectibles. The store is famous for locating hard-to-find records as well as current releases. The store has also had recent success in offering items on the World Wide Web.

Richard Brooks manages the Jazz Warehouse's Web site. When the site was first created, it was developed using standard HTML code. Since then, Richard has heard of several Web sites that are changing from HTML documents to XML documents that incorporate style sheets. Richard has learned that XML has some advantages over HTML in presenting structured content. XML is more flexible, allowing authors to create their own document tags specifically tailored to their needs. XML also supports tools that ensure any data entered into an XML document follows well-defined rules for both structure and content. This feature will make it easier for Richard to create documents that accurately reflect the Jazz Warehouse's inventory.

Richard believes that the company will eventually move from HTML to a combination of XML and style sheets, so he wants to start investigating how to display the company's recording inventory using an XML document. He has asked for your help in creating a small demonstration document for this purpose.

SESSION 1.1

In this session, you'll study the history and theory of XML as well as compare the features of XML and HTML. You'll also learn how XML documents are created and review some of the XML editors available to you. Finally, you'll learn about well-formed and valid XML documents and how XML ensures the integrity and consistency of your data.

Introducing XML

You and Richard meet to discuss how XML can help him in developing content for the Jazz Warehouse's Web site. First, Richard wants to know what XML is and how it can help his business.

XML stands for **Extensible Markup Language**. A **markup language** is a computer language that specifies the structure and content of a document by breaking the document down into a series of **elements**, where each element represents a different part of the document. The term **extensible** means that the language can be used to create a wide variety of document types by using elements tailored to each document. The following XML history lesson may help you better understand the XML of today.

A Short History of XML

XML has its roots in the Standard Generalized Markup Language (SGML). Introduced in the 1980s, SGML was used to create the general structure of markup languages. SGML can be thought of as the parent or umbrella technology for both XML and HTML (see Figure 1-1).

Figure 1-1	THE ROOTS OF XML AND HTML

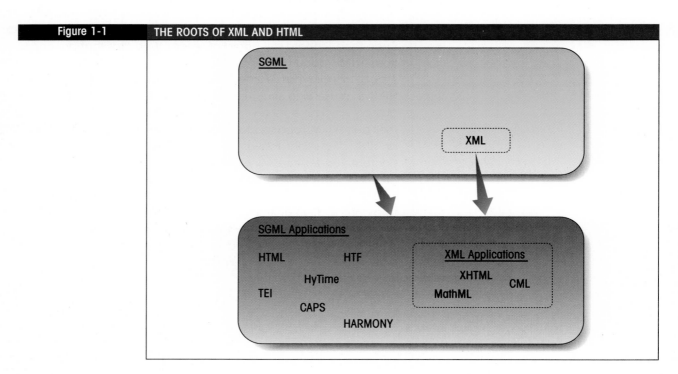

SGML is device independent and system independent, which means that it can be used with almost any type of document stored in almost any format. SGML has been the chosen vehicle for creating documents in businesses and government organizations of all sizes. For example, think of the daunting task of documenting all of the parts used in creating the space shuttle while at the same time creating a structure that shuttle engineers can use to quickly retrieve and edit that information. SGML provides tools to manage documentation projects of this magnitude.

But, there is a price to pay for this type of complex system; thus, SGML is limited to those organizations that can afford the cost and overhead of maintaining complex SGML environments. SGML is often most useful in creating applications, based on the SGML architecture, that apply to specific types of documents. The most famous of these applications is Hypertext Markup Language, or HTML, the language of the World Wide Web.

The success of the World Wide Web is due in no small part to HTML. HTML allows Web authors to easily create documents that can be displayed across different operating systems. Creating Web sites with HTML is a straight-forward process that does not require a programming background. This ease of use has made HTML popular with many different types of users. Millions of Web sites, including the Jazz Warehouse Web site, were created with HTML, and there is every indication that HTML will continue to be an important language of the Web for a long time to come.

The Limits of HTML

Despite its popularity, HTML is not without limitations and flaws, which continue to frustrate Web developers. The major problem is that people are interested in Web pages not only for their appearance but also for their content, and HTML was not designed with data content in mind. For example, if Richard wants to display information on music sold by the Jazz Warehouse, he might use the following HTML code in his Web page:

```
<H2>Kind of Blue</H2>
<H3>Miles Davis</H3>
<OL>Tracks
        <LI>So What (9:22)</LI>
        <LI>Freddie Freeloader (9:46)</LI>
        <LI>Blue in Green (5:37)</LI>
        <LI>All Blues (11:33)</LI>
        <LI>Flamenco Sketches (9:26)</LI>
</OL>
```

The HTML tags <H2>, <H3>, <OL>, and <LI> merely format the information, they do not describe it. After all, those same tags could be used in a grocery Web page:

```
<H2>HiValue Foods</H2>
<H3>Fresh Produce</H3>
<OL>Products
        <LI>Apples ($1.99/bag)</LI>
        <LI>Grapes ($1.49/bag)</LI>
        <LI>Onions ($1.99/bag)</LI>
        <LI>Red Leaf Lettuce ($0.50/bunch)</LI>
        <LI>Mushrooms ($0.79/carton)</LI>
</OL>
```

As long as your only concern is formatting, it makes no difference whether your page is about music or mushrooms. But, what if Richard wants to develop a Web application that can easily access the company's inventory of a particular recording artist? Without being able to determine whether an HTML tag refers to a CD title, music track, price, or artist, it may be difficult to locate the information. In response to this limitation, developers have added features to HTML, such as the CLASS attribute, which allow Web authors to attach descriptive information to each tag. Web authors can also make use of the <META> tag to record information about a document's contents. These additional HTML features are helpful, but they don't entirely solve the problem of effectively describing and cataloging data in an HTML document.

A second problem of HTML is that it is not extensible and, therefore, can't be modified to meet specific needs. As a result of the demands of the market and competition, the various Web browsers have developed their own unique flavors of HTML. Netscape Communicator saw a need for frames, so it introduced a version of HTML that included the <FRAMESET> and <FRAME> tags, both of which were not part of standard HTML. Internet Explorer saw a need for internal frames and introduced the <IFRAME> tag, and that innovation also represented a departure from standard HTML.

The result was a confusing mix of competing HTML standards, one for each browser and, indeed, each browser version. The innovations offered by Netscape, Internet Explorer, and others certainly increased the scope and power of HTML but did so at the expense of clarity. Web authors could not easily create Web sites without taking into account the cross-browser compatibility of the code in the Web pages.

Finally, HTML can be inconsistently applied. Some browsers require all tag attributes to be enclosed within quotes; some don't. Some browsers require all paragraphs to include an ending </P> tag; others do not. The lack of standards can make it easier to write HTML code, but it also means that code read by one browser may be rejected by another.

Partly because of the reasons outlined above, the Web was in need of a language that could more effectively handle data content, be easily customized by developers, and hold developers accountable to well-defined standards. In response to these needs, XML was created.

Exploring the Concepts Behind XML

Like HTML, XML was developed by the **W3C** (**World Wide Web Consortium**), an organization created in 1994 to develop common protocols and standards for sharing information on the World Wide Web. You can learn more about the W3C and view specifications for XML, HTML, and other languages at *http://www.w3.org*.

XML Design Goals

The W3C established ten primary design goals for XML:

1. XML must be easily usable over the Internet.

   XML was developed with the Web in mind and supports major Web protocols such as HTTP and MIME.

2. XML must support a wide variety of applications.

   Although XML was developed for the Web, it can also be used for other applications such as databases, financial transactions, and voice mail.

3. XML must be compatible with SGML.

   Because XML is a subset of SGML, many of the software tools developed for SGML can be adapted for XML.

4. It must be easy to write programs that process XML documents.

   One of HTML's greatest strengths is its simplicity. XML has tried to emulate this by making it easy for even nonprogrammers to write XML code.

5. The number of optional features in XML must be kept to the absolute minimum, ideally zero.

   SGML supports a wide range of optional features, which means that SGML software can be large and cumbersome. XML removed this aspect of SGML, which makes it a more suitable Web-development tool.

6. XML documents should be clear and easily understood by nonprogrammers.

   Like HTML, XML documents are text files. The contents of an XML document follow a logical, tree-like structure. As you'll see later, XML authors can specify element names whose meanings are intuitively clear to anyone reading the XML code.

7. The XML design should be prepared quickly.

   XML was only going to be a viable alternative to HTML if the Web community adopted it as a standard. For that to happen, W3C had to quickly settle on a design for XML before other competing standards emerged.

8. The design of XML must be exact and concise.

   XML can be easily processed by computer programs, which makes it easy for programmers to develop applications.

9. XML documents must be easy to create.

   For XML to be practical, XML documents must be as easy to create as HTML documents.

10. Terseness in XML markup is of minimal importance.

    Because of the speed in which information can be exchanged over the Internet, keeping document size small is not as important as keeping the document code understandable and easy to use.

Although XML is sometimes referred to as a markup language, it is actually more of a meta-markup language because it is a markup language that is used to create other markup languages. Unlike HTML, which is an SGML application, XML should be considered a subset of SGML—without SGML's complexity and overhead.

Comparing XML and HTML

As you can see, XML and HTML share many of the same design goals. So, how does XML differ from HTML? HTML is a language used for data presentation and formatting, whereas XML's emphasis is on data content only. Figure 1-2 shows how the same data content from the Jazz Warehouse can be encoded in both HTML and XML. The HTML code tells us that the first line should be displayed using an H2 heading, followed by an H3 heading. The document concludes with an ordered list of text.

Figure 1-2	SAMPLE HTML AND XML CODE
HTML CODE	**XML CODE**

```
<H2>Kind of Blue</H2>
<H3>Miles Davis</H3>
<OL>Tracks
  <LI>So What (9:22)</LI>
  <LI>Freddie Freeloader (9:46)</LI>
  <LI>Blue in Green (5:37)</LI>
  <LI>All Blues (11:33)</LI>
  <LI>Flamenco Sketches (9:26)</LI>
</OL>
```

```
<CDTITLE>Kind of Blue</CDTITLE>
<ARTIST>Miles Davis</ARTIST>
<CONTENTS>
  <TRACK>So What (9:22)</TRACK>
  <TRACK>Freddie Freeloader (9:46)</TRACK>
  <TRACK>Blue in Green (5:37)</TRACK>
  <TRACK>All Blues (11:33) </TRACK>
  <TRACK>Flamenco Sketches (9:26) </TRACK>
</CONTENTS>
```

HTML code describes the format of the data, but not the data content	XML code describes the data content, but not the data format

The same data encoded with XML tells us about the type of information in the document. Without knowing anything about the document, you can quickly see that this contains data on a music CD named *Kind of Blue* by the artist Miles Davis and that the CD has five tracks, starting with "So What" and concluding with "Flamenco Sketches." The document doesn't tell you anything about how this information should be rendered on a page, or even with what media the data is to be presented.

The <CDTITLE>, <ARTIST>, <CONTENTS>, and <TRACK> tags in this example do not come from any particular XML specification, rather they are custom tags that Richard could create specifically for one of his documents. Richard could create additional tags describing the selling price of the CD, the CD label, and the date the CD was recorded. Because an XML document doesn't indicate how data is to be formatted or displayed, it must be linked to a style sheet containing formatting instructions for each element.

One final point of comparison between HTML and XML: a document created with HTML has no mechanism for monitoring the document's content. If Richard neglects to include the name of the artist in an HTML document about the company's music CDs, no one will be the wiser. However, with XML one can force a document to follow a defined structure. This is done by attaching either a **document type definition** (**DTD**) or a **schema** to the XML document containing the data. Both DTDs and schema define rules for how data in the document should be structured. For example, Richard can create a DTD or schema to require his documents to list the title, the artist, a list of tracks, and the price of each CD. DTDs and schemas are not required, but they can be helpful to ensure that your XML documents follow a uniform structure. You'll learn how to create and apply DTDs and schemas in upcoming tutorials.

Creating an XML Document

Like HTML, XML documents are text files. Therefore, an XML author needs no more than a simple text editor, like Notepad, Emacs, or vi, to get started. There are more sophisticated XML editors available that may make it easier to design your document, but they are not required. Figure 1-3 lists some of the XML editors and the associated URL that are available to you today. The XML Spy application is included with this book, and you'll have a chance to work with XML Spy later on.

Figure 1-3	XML EDITORS	
XML EDITOR	**URL**	**TYPE**
Amaya	http://www.w3.org/Amaya/	Windows, UNIX
BBEdit	http://www.bbedit.com/	Macintosh
EditML Pro	http://www.editml.com/	Windows
Emilé	http://www.in-progress.com/emile/	Macintosh
Merlot	http://www.merlotxml.org/	Java
Visual XML	http://www.pierlou.com/visxml/index.html	Java
XML Pro	http://www.vervet.com/xmlpro.html	Windows
XML Spy	http://www.xmlspy.com/	Windows
XMLwriter	http://www.xmlwriter.net/	Windows

XML Parsers

After the XML document is created, it needs to be evaluated by an application known as an **XML processor** or **XML parser**. Part of the function of the parser is to interpret the document's code and verify that it satisfies all of the XML specifications for document structure and syntax. XML parsers are strict. If one tag is omitted or a character is lowercase when it should be uppercase, the parser will report an error and reject the document. This may seem excessive, but that rigidity was built into XML to correct the flaw in HTML that gave Web browsers too much discretion interpreting HTML code. The end result is that XML code accepted by the parser is sure to work the same everywhere.

Microsoft developed an XML parser called **MSXML** for its Internet Explorer browser. MSXML was introduced as an add-on for Internet Explorer version 4.0 and then was built directly into the Web browser for Internet Explorer versions 5.0 and above. The current release of MSXML is MSXML 4.0. Netscape also introduced its own XML parser, called **Mozilla**, which is available starting with version 6.0 of the browser. In addition, any of the editors listed in Figure 1-3 can process and interpret XML code.

Well-Formed and Valid XML Documents

XML documents fall into one of two categories: well-formed documents or valid documents. A **well-formed document** contains no syntax errors and satisfies the specifications for XML code as laid out by the W3C. A **valid document** is a well-formed document that also satisfies the rules laid out in the DTD or schema attached to the document. An XML parser that can verify whether an XML document is valid is called a **validating parser**. If the parser can only check for well-formedness, it is referred to as a **nonvalidating parser**. Netscape's parser is a nonvalidating parser, whereas Internet Explorer checks for both well-formedness and validity in some cases.

Richard is only concerned with creating well-formed documents for his project at the Jazz Warehouse. You'll learn how to create valid documents in upcoming tutorials.

Once the XML document is parsed, it can be displayed to the user. Figure 1-4 outlines the complete process from document creation to final presentation.

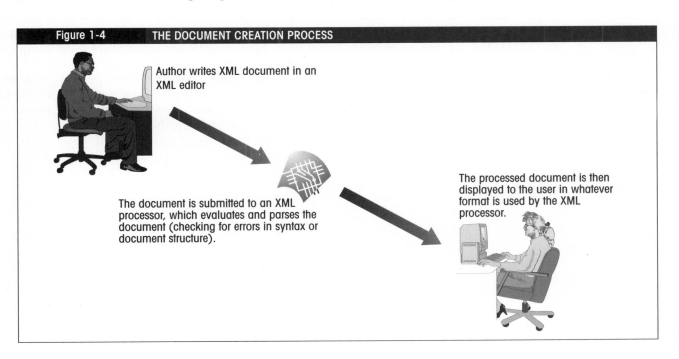

Figure 1-4   THE DOCUMENT CREATION PROCESS

Author writes XML document in an XML editor

The document is submitted to an XML processor, which evaluates and parses the document (checking for errors in syntax or document structure).

The processed document is then displayed to the user in whatever format is used by the XML processor.

Working with XML Applications

XML shares with SGML the ability to create markup languages, called **XML applications**. Several XML applications have been developed to work with specific types of documents. For example, a scientist may need to describe the chemical structure of a molecule, containing hundreds of atoms bonded to other atoms and molecules. That scientist could use the **Chemical Markup Language (CML)**, an XML application designed specifically to code molecular information. Another XML application, **MathML**, is used to display and evaluate mathematical equations. Figure 1-5 shows an example of MathML code and how that code might be displayed by an XML application that can interpret MathML code.

Figure 1-5	A MATHML EXAMPLE

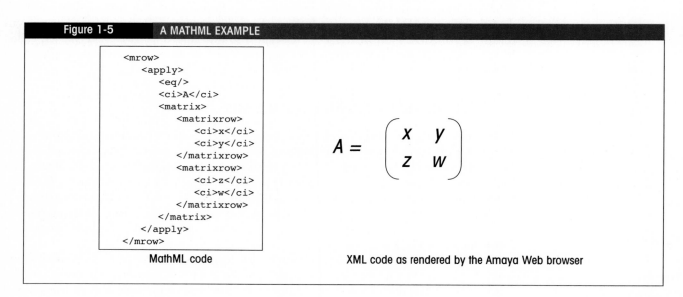

```
<mrow>
    <apply>
        <eq/>
        <ci>A</ci>
        <matrix>
            <matrixrow>
                <ci>x</ci>
                <ci>y</ci>
            </matrixrow>
            <matrixrow>
                <ci>z</ci>
                <ci>w</ci>
            </matrixrow>
        </matrix>
    </apply>
</mrow>
```

$$A = \begin{pmatrix} x & y \\ z & w \end{pmatrix}$$

MathML code

XML code as rendered by the Amaya Web browser

Each of these applications uses a defined set of tag names called a **vocabulary**. For example, the MathML code shown in Figure 1-5 has the following tag names in its vocabulary: mrow, apply, eq, ci, matrix, and matrixrow. The advantage of using a vocabulary is that it makes it easier to exchange information between different organizations and computer applications because there is a common way of referring to items.

To use one of these XML applications, you need a program that can parse the code and then display it in a useful format. For example, the mathematical equations written in MathML can be rendered using the Amaya Web browser developed by the W3C, but if you open a MathML document in either Internet Explorer or Netscape, you would see the XML code, but not the equations. Figure 1-6 lists some of the other XML applications.

Figure 1-6	XML APPLICATIONS	
XML APPLICATION	**DESCRIPTION**	**URL**
CDF	(Channel Definition Format) Permits a Web publisher to offer to automatically deliver information to PCs or other information appliances	http://www.w3.org/TR/NOTE-CDFsubmit.html
CML	(Chemical Markup Language) Used to code molecular and chemical information	http://www.xml-cml.org/
MathML	(Mathematical Markup Language) Used to present and evaluate mathematical equations	http://www.w3.org/Math/
MusicML	(Musical Markup Language) Used to display musical notation	http://www.tcf.nl/3.0/musicml/index.html
OFX	(Open Financial Exchange) Used to exchange financial data between financial institutions, businesses, and consumers via the Internet	http://www.ofx.net/
SMIL	(Synchronized Multimedia Integration Language) Used to edit interactive audiovisual presentations involving streaming audio, video, text, and any other media type	http://www.w3.org/AudioVideo/
VoiceXML	(Voice Markup Language) Used for creating audio dialogs that feature synthesized speech, digitized audio, and speech recognition	http://www.voicexml.org/

As you can see, XML can be applied to virtually any type of document. Now that you've reviewed some of the background of XML, you'll create your first XML document for the Jazz Warehouse in the next session.

Session 1.1 QUICK CHECK

1. Define the term 'extensible.' How does the concept of extensibility relate to XML?

2. What is SGML and why was SGML not used for authoring pages on the World Wide Web?

3. What is the W3C?

4. Name three limitations of HTML that led to the development of XML.

5. Is XML a markup language? Explain your answer.

6. What is a DTD? What is a well-formed XML document, and how does it differ from a valid XML document?

7. What is an XML parser?

8. What is MathML?

In this session, you'll learn how to create a simple XML document. First, you'll learn how to create a prolog, describing the document's features. Next, you'll learn how to describe the document using comments. This session will also show you how to create your own XML elements, and you'll learn how those elements should be structured within your document. Finally, you'll learn how to create attributes for the document's elements.

Exploring the Structure of an XML Document

Now that you are familiar with the history and theory of XML, you are ready to create your first XML document. XML documents consist of three parts: the prolog, the document body, and the epilog. The **prolog** is optional, providing information about the document itself. The **document body** contains the document's content in a hierarchical tree structure. An optional **epilog** contains any final comments or processing instructions.

Creating the Prolog

A prolog consists of four parts in the following order:

1. XML declaration
2. miscellaneous statements or comments
3. document type declaration
4. miscellaneous statements or comments

The order of these parts is important. If you place the document type declaration before the XML declaration, the XML parser generates an error message. Note that none of these parts are required, but it is considered good form to include at least the XML declaration.

The XML Declaration

The XML declaration is always the first line of code in any XML document. It signals to the processor that the document is written using XML and provides information about how that code is to be interpreted by a parser. The declaration starts with the text "<?xml," which signals the parser that an XML declaration follows. The complete syntax of an XML declaration is

```
<?xml version="version number" encoding="encoding type"
standalone="yes|no" ?>
```

where *version number* is the version of the XML specification being used in the document. The default, and only, value for the version declaration is "1.0." The *encoding type* value identifies the character codes used in the document. Because different languages use different encoding schemes, this declaration allows XML to support different languages. The default encoding scheme is the English language scheme, "UTF-8." Finally, the standalone attribute indicates whether the document has any links to external files. A standalone value of "yes" indicates that the document is self-contained, and a value of "no" indicates that the XML processor must include external files when it parses the document. Note that the version number, encoding type, and standalone value must be enclosed in either double or single quotation marks. A sample XML declaration might appear as follows:

```
<?xml version="1.0" encoding="UTF-8" standalone="yes" ?>
```

This declaration indicates that the XML version is 1.0, the UTF-8 (English language) encoding scheme is being used, and the document is self-contained. You could also enter the XML declaration

```
<?xml version="1.0" ?>
```

and the processor would apply the default encoding scheme and standalone values.

It is important to remember that *XML code is case sensitive*. You cannot change the code to uppercase letters, as follows:

```
<?XML VERSION="1.0" ENCODING="UTF-8" STANDALONE="YES" ?>
```

without the parser rejecting the document. Nor can you drop the quotation marks around the values in the declaration. An XML declaration of

```
<?xml version=1.0 encoding=UTF-8 standalone=no ?>
```

also results in an error. This is a critical difference from HTML, which provides the author more latitude in entering code and does not distinguish between uppercase and lowercase letters.

REFERENCE   WINDOW   **RW**

Creating an XML Declaration

■ To create the XML declaration, enter the following code in the first line of the XML document:

```
<?xml version="version number" encoding="encoding type"
standalone="yes|no" ?>
```

where *version number* is the version of the XML specification being used in the document, *encoding type* identifies the character codes used in the document, and the standalone attribute indicates whether the XML parser needs to access external files when parsing the document.

Now that you've seen how to structure an XML declaration, you can start creating your first XML document by writing the prolog.

To create the prolog:

1. Place your Data Disk in drive A (or wherever your floppy drive is located).

TROUBLE? If you don't have a Data Disk, you need to get one. Your instructor will either give you one or ask you to make your own. See the Read This Before You Begin page at the beginning of these tutorials for instructions. Your instructor may also direct you to save your data files onto a network drive or a local hard drive.

2. Using a text editor, open a new document.

TROUBLE? Your instructor may direct you to use an XML editor. If you don't know how to use your text or XML editor, talk to your instructor or technical resource person.

3. Type the following line of code into your document:

```
<?xml version="1.0" encoding="UTF-8"
standalone="yes" ?>
```

4. Save your document as **Jazz.xml** in the Tutorial.01X/Tutorial folder of your Data Disk, but do not close your text editor.

TROUBLE? Windows Notepad automatically assigns the ".txt" extension to text files. To specify the ".xml" extension, type "Jazz.xml" in the File name box, click "All Files" from the Save as Type drop-down list box, and then click the save button.

TROUBLE? If you use a word processor like Microsoft Word, you must save the document as a text file and not in the word processor's native format.

Inserting Comments

After the XML declaration, you can enter comments or miscellaneous statements that may be required by the document. You'll learn about processing instructions in the next session.

Comments may appear anywhere in the XML document. It's a good idea to insert a comment somewhere in the prolog (after the XML declaration) to provide additional information about what the document will be used for and how it was created. Comments are ignored by the processor and do not affect the document's content or structure.

The syntax for a comment is

```
<!-- comment text -->
```

where *comment text* is the text of the comment. Note that XML comments have the same syntax as HTML comments.

To add a comment to an XML document:

1. In your text editor, insert the following line *below* the XML declaration you just entered:

```
<!-- This document contains data on Jazz Warehouse
special offers -->
```

2. Save your changes to the Jazz.xml document.

You are finished working with the prolog for now. It is now time to focus your attention on the content of Richard's document.

Working with Elements and Attributes

Elements are the basic building blocks of XML files, containing the data content of the document. XML supports two kinds of elements: closed and empty (or open). A **closed element** has the following syntax:

```
<element_name>Content</element_name>
```

where *element_name* is the name given to the closed element, and *Content* represents the content of the element. For example, Richard could store the name of the artist as follows:

```
<Artist>Miles Davis</Artist>
```

There are a few important points to remember about closed elements.

- Element names are case sensitive.
- Element names must begin with a letter or the underscore character (_) and may not contain blank spaces (e.g., you cannot name an element "First Name," but you can name it "First_Name").
- Element names cannot begin with the letters "xml" because those characters are reserved for special XML commands.
- The name of the element's closing tag must match the name in the opening tag.

For example, the following element text results in an error because the starting tag is capitalized and the ending tag is not:

```
<ARTIST>Miles Davis</artist>
```

Elements can be nested within each other. Elements that are placed within other elements are called **child elements**. In the following example, the CD element contains multiple occurrences of a child element named "TRACK:"

```
<CD>Kind of Blue
     <TRACK>So What (9:22)</TRACK>
     <TRACK>Freddie Freeloader (9:46)</TRACK>
     <TRACK>Blue in Green (5:37)</TRACK>
     <TRACK>All Blues (11:33) </TRACK>
     <TRACK>Flamenco Sketches (9:26) </TRACK>
</CD>
```

Elements must either be placed side-by-side or nested. You cannot have a child element overlapping the opening and closing tags of its parent. This set of XML code

```
<CD>Kind of Blue <ARTIST>Miles Davis</CD></ARTIST>
```

results in an error message because the CD element is closed before the ARTIST element. Think of the parent element as a container that must completely contain all of its child elements.

```
<CD>Kind of Blue <ARTIST>Miles Davis</ARTIST></CD>
```

XML is much more rigorous than HTML in this regard because many Web browsers accept HTML files with improperly nested elements.

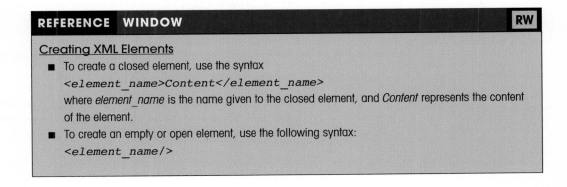

REFERENCE WINDOW   **RW**

Creating XML Elements

- To create a closed element, use the syntax

  `<element_name>Content</element_name>`

  where *element_name* is the name given to the closed element, and *Content* represents the content of the element.
- To create an empty or open element, use the following syntax:

  `<element_name/>`

The Root Element

The nesting concept applies to the entire XML document. All elements must be nested within a single **document** or **root element**. There can be only one root element. The following XML document is in error because the elements are not nested within a single root element:

```
<?xml version="1.0" ?>
<CD>Kind of Blue
        <TRACK>So What (9:22)</TRACK>
        <TRACK>Freddie Freeloader (9:46)</TRACK>
        <TRACK>Blue in Green (5:37)</TRACK>
        <TRACK>All Blues (11:33) </TRACK>
        <TRACK>Flamenco Sketches (9:26) </TRACK>
</CD>
<CD>Cookin'
        <TRACK>My Funny Valentine (5:57)</TRACK>
        <TRACK>Blues by Five (9:53)</TRACK>
        <TRACK>Airegin (4:22)</TRACK>
        <TRACK>Tune-Up (13:03)</TRACK>
</CD>
```

However, if a single root element, such as <ARTIST>, is added, the XML document is not in error.

```
<?xml version="1.0" ?>
<ARTIST>Miles Davis
   <CD>Kind of Blue
        <TRACK>So What (9:22)</TRACK>
        <TRACK>Freddie Freeloader (9:46)</TRACK>
        <TRACK>Blue in Green (5:37)</TRACK>
        <TRACK>All Blues (11:33) </TRACK>
        <TRACK>Flamenco Sketches (9:26) </TRACK>
   </CD>
   <CD>Cookin'
        <TRACK>My Funny Valentine (5:57)</TRACK>
        <TRACK>Blues by Five (9:53)</TRACK>
        <TRACK>Airegin (4:22)</TRACK>
        <TRACK>Tune-Up (13:03)</TRACK>
   </CD>
</ARTIST>
```

In addition to text and nested elements, comments can be placed within elements.

```
<CD>Cookin' <!-- Live Recording --> </CD>
```

Note that the comment must follow the same syntax used for comments placed in the document's prolog. Also, the comment must be placed entirely within the element's tags. The following code is in error because the ending </CD> tag occurs before the ending comment tag, -->:

```
<CD>Cookin' <!-- Live Recording </CD> -->
```

Empty Elements

An **open** or **empty element** is an element that contains no content. Empty element tags are comprised of the element name followed by a forward slash and ending with a right-angle bracket. The syntax for an empty element is

```
<element_name/>
```

where *element_name* is the name of the empty element. Note that empty elements consist of a single tag—there is no opening and closing tag. An equivalent way of expressing an empty element is as follows:

```
<element_name></element_name>
```

HTML supports a collection of empty elements, such as the <HR> tag for horizontal lines or the <IMG> tag used for inline graphics. In XHTML (the version of HTML based on XML specifications) these tags are represented as <HR /> and <IMG />.

Empty elements contain no content, so why use them in an XML document? One reason is to mark certain sections of the document for the XML parser. Richard might want to use an empty element to distinguish one group of CD titles from another.

Empty elements usually contain attributes that provide information to the XML parser that is not displayed in the document.

Element Attributes

An **attribute** describes a feature or characteristic of an element. The syntax for adding an attribute to an element is

```
<element_name attribute="value"> … </element_name>
```

or in the case of an empty attribute

```
<element_name attribute="value" />
```

Here, *attribute* is the name given to the attribute and *value* is the attribute's value. Attribute values are text strings and thus must always be enclosed within either single or double quotes. For example, if Richard wants to include the length of each music track as an attribute of the <TRACK> element, he could enter the following code:

```
<TRACK length="9:22">So What</TRACK>
```

Because they're considered text strings, attribute values may contain spaces and almost any character other than angle brackets (< and >). You can choose any name for the attribute subject to the following constraints:

- The attribute must begin with a letter or underscore (_).
- Spaces are not allowed in attribute names.
- Attribute names should not begin with the text string "xml."
- An attribute name can only appear once in the same starting tag.

Finally, as in all of XML, attribute names are case sensitive. Attributes are often used to provide additional information about an element to the XML parser that processes the document.

REFERENCE WINDOW   RW

Adding an Attribute to an Element

■ To add an attribute to an element use the syntax

  `<element_name attribute="value"> … </element_name>`

or

  `<element_name attribute="value" />`

  where *attribute* is the name given to the attribute and *value* is the attribute's value.

It's not always clear when to use attribute values instead of inserting the information within a set of element tags. Some argue that attributes should never be used because they add to the document's complexity and the information would be better placed within an element. Generally, it's best to use attributes only for that information that is processed by the XML parser and does not need to be viewed.

Adding Elements to an XML Document

Now that you've reviewed some of the features of XML elements, you'll use these elements in an XML document. Richard would like information on the CDs, shown in Figure 1-7, added to the Jazz.xml file that describes the company's monthly specials.

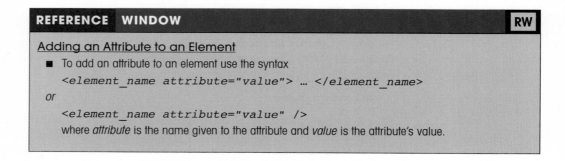

Figure 1-7	JAZZ WAREHOUSE CDS	
CD TITLE	**ARTIST**	**TRACKS**
Kind of Blue	Miles Davis	So What (9:22) Freddie Freeloader (9:46) Blue in Green (5:37) All Blues (11:33) Flamenco Sketches (9:26)
Cookin'	Miles Davis	My Funny Valentine (5:57) Blues by Five (9:53) Airegin (4:22) Tune-Up (13:03)
Blue Train	John Coltrane	Blue Train (10:39) Moment's Notice (9:06) Locomotion (7:11) I'm Old Fashioned (7:55) Lazy Bird (7:03)

Richard has decided to use elements named <CD>, <ARTIST>, and <TRACK> to contain the information displayed in Figure 1-7. The length of each track needs to be stored as an attribute of the <TRACK> element. He would like you to add a <TITLE> element that describes the contents of the document. Finally, all of this information is to be contained within a single root element named <SPECIALS>.

To add these elements to the XML document:

1. Open the **Jazz.xml** document from the Tutorial.01X/Tutorial folder on your Data Disk in your text editor. Figure 1-8 shows the current state of the document.

Figure 1-8   PROLOG OF RICHARD'S DOCUMENT

```
<?xml version="1.0" encoding="UTF-8" standalone="yes" ?>
<!-- This document contains data on Jazz Warehouse special offers -->
```

2. Below the comment line, insert a blank line and then the following XML code:

```
<SPECIALS>
<TITLE>Monthly Specials at the Jazz Warehouse</TITLE>
   <CD>Kind of Blue
       <ARTIST>Miles Davis</ARTIST>
       <TRACK length="9:22">So What</TRACK>
       <TRACK length="9:46">Freddie Freeloader</TRACK>
       <TRACK length="5:37">Blue in Green</TRACK>
       <TRACK length="11:33">All Blues</TRACK>
       <TRACK length="9:26">Flamenco Sketches</TRACK>
   </CD>
   <CD>Cookin'
       <ARTIST>Miles Davis</ARTIST>
       <TRACK length="5:57">My Funny Valentine</TRACK>
       <TRACK length="9:53">Blues by Five</TRACK>
       <TRACK length="4:22">Airegin</TRACK>
       <TRACK length="13:03">Tune-Up</TRACK>
   </CD>
   <CD>Blue Train
       <ARTIST>John Coltrane</ARTIST>
       <TRACK length="10:39">Blue Train</TRACK>
       <TRACK length="9:06">Moment's Notice</TRACK>
       <TRACK length="7:11">Locomotion</TRACK>
       <TRACK length="7:55">I'm Old Fashioned</TRACK>
       <TRACK length="7:03">Lazy Bird</TRACK>
   </CD>
</SPECIALS>
```

Figure 1-9 shows the revised Jazz.xml file.

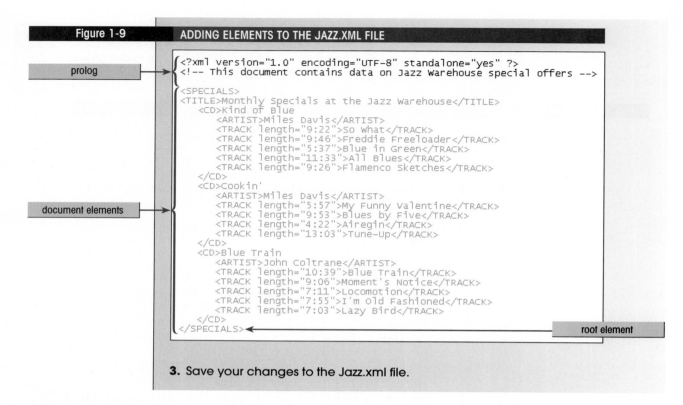

Figure 1-9 ADDING ELEMENTS TO THE JAZZ.XML FILE

prolog

document elements

root element

```
<?xml version="1.0" encoding="UTF-8" standalone="yes" ?>
<!-- This document contains data on Jazz Warehouse special offers -->

<SPECIALS>
<TITLE>Monthly Specials at the Jazz Warehouse</TITLE>
    <CD>Kind of Blue
        <ARTIST>Miles Davis</ARTIST>
        <TRACK length="9:22">So What</TRACK>
        <TRACK length="9:46">Freddie Freeloader</TRACK>
        <TRACK length="5:37">Blue in Green</TRACK>
        <TRACK length="11:33">All Blues</TRACK>
        <TRACK length="9:26">Flamenco Sketches</TRACK>
    </CD>
    <CD>Cookin'
        <ARTIST>Miles Davis</ARTIST>
        <TRACK length="5:57">My Funny Valentine</TRACK>
        <TRACK length="9:53">Blues by Five</TRACK>
        <TRACK length="4:22">Airegin</TRACK>
        <TRACK length="13:03">Tune-Up</TRACK>
    </CD>
    <CD>Blue Train
        <ARTIST>John Coltrane</ARTIST>
        <TRACK length="10:39">Blue Train</TRACK>
        <TRACK length="9:06">Moment's Notice</TRACK>
        <TRACK length="7:11">Locomotion</TRACK>
        <TRACK length="7:55">I'm Old Fashioned</TRACK>
        <TRACK length="7:03">Lazy Bird</TRACK>
    </CD>
</SPECIALS>
```

3. Save your changes to the Jazz.xml file.

You've entered the CD information that Richard has requested; but now he has some additional information for you to work with. He wants you to enter the selling price of each CD on special. Because the Jazz Warehouse has a sizable customer base in Great Britain, the XML document needs to record the selling price in both U.S. dollars ($) and British pounds (£). Figure 1-10 displays the cost of the CDs in each currency.

Figure 1-10 SALES PRICE FOR JAZZ WAREHOUSE CDS

CD TITLE	SELLING PRICE (U.S. $)	SELLING PRICE (G.B. £)
Kind of Blue	$11.99	£8.39
Cookin'	$7.99	£5.59
Blue Train	$8.99	£6.29

To accomplish this additional step, Richard needs to know how to include the £ symbol into his XML document to represent British pounds.

Using **Character References**

Sometimes, you may need to include a character not found on your keyboard, such as the copyright symbol, registered trademark symbol, or the symbol for the British pound.

REFERENCE WINDOW **RW**

Inserting Character References

■ To insert special characters into an XML document, use the following form:

&#*character*;

where *character* is a character reference number or name from the ISO/IEC character set.

To insert characters into your XML document not available on a keyboard, you use a **character reference**. The syntax for a character reference is

&#*character*;

where *character* is a character reference number or name from the ISO/IEC character set. The **ISO/IEC character set** is an international numbering system for referencing characters from virtually any language. If you've used HTML, this will be familiar to you because character references in XML work the same as characters references in HTML. Figure 1-11 shows a few of the commonly used character reference numbers, and the appendix contains character reference numbers for the first 256 characters in the ISO/IEC character set. Note that not all characters have both reference numbers and names.

Figure 1-11	XML CHARACTER REFERENCES		
SYMBOL	**CHARACTER REFERENCE**	**CHARACTER NAME**	**DESCRIPTION**
©	&#169;		Copyright symbol
®	&#174;		Registered trademark
™	&#153;		Trademark symbol
<	&#60;	&lt;	Less than symbol
>	&#62;	&gt;	Greater than symbol
&	&#38;	&amp;	Ampersand
"	&#22;	&quot;	Double quote
'	&#27;	&apos;	Apostrophe (single quote)
£	&#163;		Pound sign
€	&#128;		Euro Sign
¥	&#165;		Yen sign

The character reference for the £ symbol is £. Use this character reference now to add British currency information to the Jazz.xml document.

To insert price information into the document:

1. After the first occurrence of <ARTIST>Miles Davis</ARTIST> in the Jazz.xml file, insert the following code:

```
<PRICEUS>US: $11.99</PRICEUS>
<PRICEUK>UK: &#163;8.39</PRICEUK>
```

2. After the second occurrence of `<ARTIST>Miles Davis</ARTIST>`, insert the following code:

```
<PRICEUS>US: $7.99</PRICEUS>
<PRICEUK>UK: &#163;5.59</PRICEUK>
```

3. After the `<ARTIST>John Coltrane</ARTIST>` line, insert the following code:

```
<PRICEUS>US: $8.99</PRICEUS>
<PRICEUK>UK: &#163;6.29</PRICEUK>
```

Figure 1-12 shows the revised Jazz.xml file.

Figure 1-12   **INSERTING A CHARACTER REFERENCE**

```
<SPECIALS>
<TITLE>Monthly Specials at the Jazz Warehouse</TITLE>
   <CD>Kind of Blue
      <ARTIST>Miles Davis</ARTIST>
      <PRICEUS>US: $11.99</PRICEUS>
      <PRICEUK>UK: &#163;8.39</PRICEUK>
      <TRACK length="9:22">So What</TRACK>
      <TRACK length="9:46">Freddie Freeloader</TRACK>
      <TRACK length="5:37">Blue in Green</TRACK>
      <TRACK length="11:33">All Blues</TRACK>
      <TRACK length="9:26">Flamenco Sketches</TRACK>
   </CD>
   <CD>Cookin'
      <ARTIST>Miles Davis</ARTIST>
      <PRICEUS>US: $7.99</PRICEUS>
      <PRICEUK>UK: &#163;5.59</PRICEUK>
      <TRACK length="5:57">My Funny Valentine</TRACK>
      <TRACK length="9:53">Blues by Five</TRACK>
      <TRACK length="4:22">Airegin</TRACK>
      <TRACK length="13:03">Tune-Up</TRACK>
   </CD>
   <CD>Blue Train
      <ARTIST>John Coltrane</ARTIST>
      <PRICEUS>US: $8.99</PRICEUS>
      <PRICEUK>UK: &#163;6.29</PRICEUK>
      <TRACK length="10:39">Blue Train</TRACK>
      <TRACK length="9:06">Moment's Notice</TRACK>
      <TRACK length="7:11">Locomotion</TRACK>
      <TRACK length="7:55">I'm Old Fashioned</TRACK>
      <TRACK length="7:03">Lazy Bird</TRACK>
   </CD>
</SPECIALS>
```

character reference

4. Save your changes to Jazz.xml.

A common mistake in XML documents is to forget that the ampersand symbol (&) is interpreted by the XML processor as a character reference and not as a character. For example, the following code

```
<ARTIST>Miles Davis & John Coltrane</ARTIST>
```

will result in an error message after the XML parser fails to find a character reference number for the & symbol. To avoid this problem, you need to use the & or & character reference for the ampersand symbol:

```
<ARTIST>Miles Davis &amp; John Coltrane</ARTIST>
```

Character references are often used to store the text of HTML code within an XML element. For example, to store the HTML tag <img src="Logo.gif"> in an element named HTMLCODE, you need to use character references to reference the < and > symbols contained in the HTML tag. The following code accomplishes this:

```
<HTMLCODE>&#60;img src="Logo.gif"&#62;</HTMLCODE>
```

Note that you can't use

```
<HTMLCODE><img src="Logo.gif"></HTMLCODE>
```

because the XML processor attempts to interpret the <IMG> tag as a tag and *not* part of the document's content.

Working **with CDATA Sections**

Sometimes, an XML document needs to store large blocks of text containing the < and > symbols (think of writing a tutorial about HTML in an XML document!). In that case, it would be cumbersome to replace all of the < and > symbols with < and > character references. The code itself will be difficult to read.

Instead of using character references, you can place large blocks of text into a CDATA section. A **CDATA section** is a large of block text that the XML processor interprets only as text. The syntax for creating a CDATA section is as follows:

```
<![CDATA[
    Text Block
]]>
```

A CDATA section:

- ■ may contain most markup characters, such as <, >, and &, and those characters will be interpreted by the XML parser as text and not markup commands
- ■ may be placed anywhere that text occurs in the document, such as between opening and closing element tags
- ■ cannot be nested within one another
- ■ cannot be empty

The only sequence of symbols that may not occur within a CDATA section is "]]>" because the XML parser interprets this text string as a marker ending the CDATA section.

In the following example, a CDATA section is used to store several HTML tags within an element named HTMLCODE:

```
<HTMLCODE>
    <![CDATA[
        <h1>The Jazz Warehouse</h1>
        <h2>Your Online Store for Jazz Music</h2>
    ]]>
</HTMLCODE>
```

The HTML code in this example is treated by the XML processor as simple text and not as code. In general, it is a good idea to place any large block of text within a CDATA section to protect yourself from inadvertently inserting a character that will be misinterpreted by the XML processor (such as the ampersand symbol).

Richard would like you to insert a message element into the Jazz.xml file that describes the purpose and content of the document. You decide to use a CDATA section for this task.

To create a CDATA section:

1. After the <TITLE> tag near the top of the Jazz.xml file, insert the following lines of code:

```
<MESSAGE>
<![CDATA[
    Here are some of the latest specials from the Jazz
Warehouse.
    Please note that all Miles Davis & John Coltrane CDs
will be
    on sale for the month of March.
]]>
</MESSAGE>
```

Figure 1-13 shows the updated Jazz.xml file.

Figure 1-13	INSERTING A CDATA SECTION

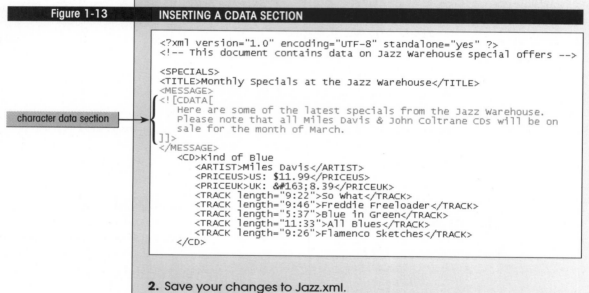

character data section

```
<?xml version="1.0" encoding="UTF-8" standalone="yes" ?>
<!-- This document contains data on Jazz Warehouse special offers -->

<SPECIALS>
<TITLE>Monthly Specials at the Jazz Warehouse</TITLE>
<MESSAGE>
<![CDATA[
    Here are some of the latest specials from the Jazz Warehouse.
    Please note that all Miles Davis & John Coltrane CDs will be on
    sale for the month of March.
]]>
</MESSAGE>
    <CD>Kind of Blue
        <ARTIST>Miles Davis</ARTIST>
        <PRICEUS>US: $11.99</PRICEUS>
        <PRICEUK>UK: &#163;8.39</PRICEUK>
        <TRACK length="9:22">So What</TRACK>
        <TRACK length="9:46">Freddie Freeloader</TRACK>
        <TRACK length="5:37">Blue in Green</TRACK>
        <TRACK length="11:33">All Blues</TRACK>
        <TRACK length="9:26">Flamenco Sketches</TRACK>
    </CD>
```

2. Save your changes to Jazz.xml.

3. Close your text editor.

Congratulations! You've completed your work on Richard's XML document. In the next session, you'll learn how to display the document in a Web browser.

Session 1.2 QUICK CHECK

1. What are the three parts of an XML document?

2. What XML declaration would you enter to specify that your XML document supports version 1.0, uses the ISO-8859-1 encoding scheme, and contains links to other documents?

3. What XML code would you enter to insert the comment "Values extracted from the JW database" into your XML document?

4. Why is the following code in error?

```
<Title>Kind of Blue</title>
```

5. Why is the following code in error?

```
<CD TITLE>Kind of Blue</CD TITLE>
```

6. What is the root element?

7. What is an empty element? Why would you need an empty element in your XML document?

8. Name two ways to insert the ampersand (&) symbol into the content of your XML document.

SESSION 1.3

In this session, you'll display Richard's XML document in a Web browser. You'll study how Internet Explorer and Netscape differ in displaying XML documents, and you'll learn how those browsers can "catch" syntax errors. Finally, you'll learn how to link an XML document to a cascading style sheet through the use of a processing instruction.

Displaying an XML Document in a Web Browser

You've entered all of the elements for Richard's document, and now he would like to be able to view it. Just like HTML files, XML documents can be opened in either Internet Explorer or Netscape Navigator. Both browsers contain XML parsers to verify that the document is well formed. If a syntax error is found, an error message is displayed instead of the document's contents.

If there are no syntax errors, Internet Explorer displays the document's contents including all markup tags. The various parts of the document are color coded, making it easier to read and interpret. Internet Explorer also displays the document in an expandable/collapsible outline format that allows you to hide nested elements. Netscape does not provide these options. Instead, Netscape displays the contents of the document, but not the tags. Nor does it provide the ability to hide and then redisplay nested elements.

To display the Jazz.xml file in a Web browser:

1. Start your Web browser and open the **Jazz.xml** file located in the Tutorial.01X/Tutorial folder of your Data Disk.

Figure 1-14 shows the contents of the file in both Internet Explorer 6.0 and Netscape 6.2. Note that the character reference you used for the British pound (£) shows up as a £ when the page is processed by the browsers.

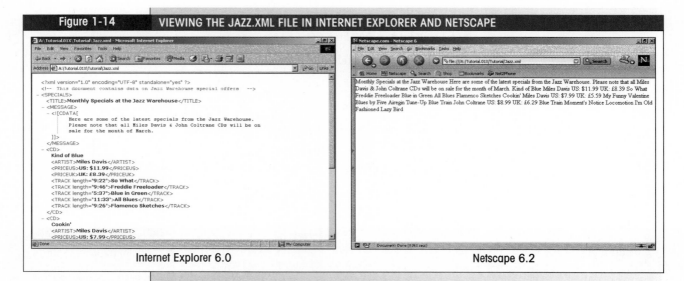

Figure 1-14	VIEWING THE JAZZ.XML FILE IN INTERNET EXPLORER AND NETSCAPE

Internet Explorer 6.0   Netscape 6.2

2. If you are running Internet Explorer, click the **minus (–)** symbols in front of the <CD> tags.

   Internet Explorer collapses content and the elements nested within the <CD> tags (see Figure 1-15).

Figure 1-15	HIDING NESTED ELEMENTS IN INTERNET EXPLORER

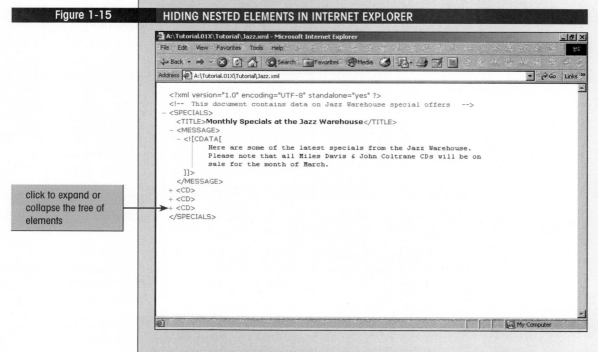

click to expand or collapse the tree of elements

3. Click the **plus (+)** symbols to expand the content and display the contents of the <CD> elements.

Having viewed the XML files with a Web browser, Richard would like to see how these browsers check for errors. He asks that you intentionally introduce an error into the Jazz.xml file to verify that the error will be identified by the browser.

To test for errors in the XML document:

1. Open the **Jazz.xml** file in your text editor.

2. Change the last line of the file from </SPECIALS> to </**Specials**>.

   This change violates the rule that all elements must have a starting and ending tag. The <SPECIALS> tag at the top of the Jazz.xml file has no corresponding ending </SPECIALS> tag because XML is case sensitive.

3. Save your changes to Jazz.xml.

4. Return to your Web browser.

5. If you are running Internet Explorer, click **View** and **Refresh** on the menu bar. If you are running Netscape, click **View** and **Reload**.

   Both browsers display error messages instead of the document's content (see Figure 1-16).

Figure 1-16	TESTING FOR ERRORS USING INTERNET EXPLORER AND NETSCAPE

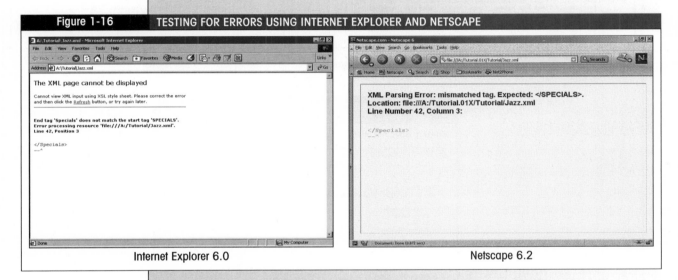

Internet Explorer 6.0   Netscape 6.2

6. Return to the Jazz.xml file in your text editor and change </Specials> back to </**SPECIALS**>.

Netscape does not validate XML documents, and Internet Explorer only validates XML documents against DTDs; though both test for well-formedness. If your document needs to be validated against a schema, you will need to use one of the XML editors or parsers available on the Web. This will be discussed in Tutorials 3 and 4.

Linking **to a Style Sheet**

Richard appreciates your work on the XML document. At this point he's concerned about the appearance of the document in the two browsers. Richard would like to share this type of information with other users and place it on the World Wide Web, but first he needs to have the data formatted—especially for users of the Netscape browser!

The easiest way to turn an XML document into a formatted document is to link the document to a style sheet. The XML document and the style sheet are then combined by the XML processor to display a single formatted document (see Figure 1-17).

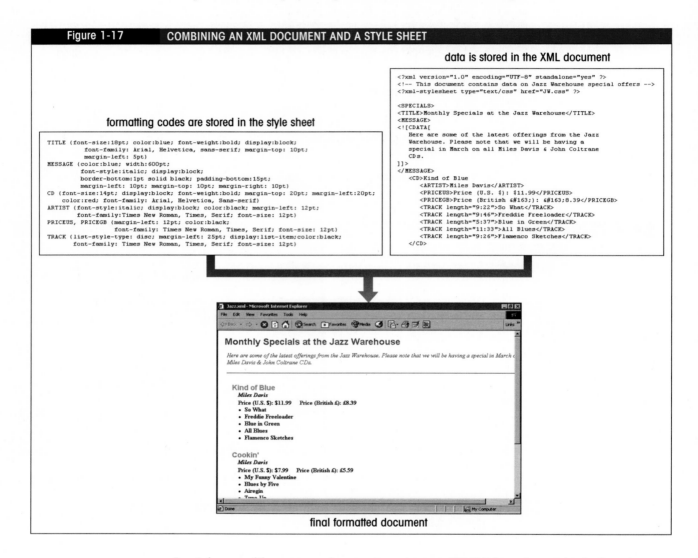

Figure 1-17   COMBINING AN XML DOCUMENT AND A STYLE SHEET

It might seem like extra work to separate content (XML) from format (style sheets), especially when HTML combines both in a single document. However, there are some significant benefits to this approach:

- Separating content from format allows you to concentrate on the appearance of the document without having to worry about content, and to record the document's content without having to bother with the formatting questions.

- Different style sheets can be applied to the same XML document, allowing the author to tailor different style sheets for specific needs. In fact, because XML documents are device independent, the same document can be applied to different devices using the appropriate style sheet and XML processor.

- Any changes made to the style sheets are automatically reflected in any Web page based on the style sheet.

There are two main style sheet languages that are used with XML documents on the World Wide Web. **Cascading Style Sheets (CSS)** is an older standard developed for use with HTML. CSS is supported by most browsers and is relatively easy to learn and use. **Extensible Stylesheet Language (XSL)** is a newer standard. XSL is more powerful than CSS, but it is not as easy to use, nor does it have the same degree of browser support as CSS does to date.

Applying a Style to an Element

For Richard's needs, you decide to apply a cascading style sheet to the document. CSS creates styles using the following syntax:

```
selector {attribute1:value1; attribute2:value2; …}
```

where *selector* identifies an element (or a set of elements with each element separated by commas) from the XML document; and *attribute* and *value* are the style attributes and attribute values to be applied to the element. For example, to display the text of the ARTIST element in a red boldface type, you would enter the following style declaration in a cascading style sheet:

```
ARTIST {color:red; font-weight: bold}
```

CSS supports many different style attributes, and there is a great deal of flexibility in specifying to which elements a particular declaration is applied. It is not the purpose of this book to teach you CSS.

Creating Processing Instructions

Once you have created a style sheet, you create a link from the XML document to the style sheet through the use of a processing instruction. A **processing instruction** is a command that provides instructions to the XML parser. Processing instructions have the general form

```
<?target instruction ?>
```

where *target* identifies the application (or object) to which the processing instruction is directed, and *instruction* is information that the document will pass on to the parser for processing. For example, the processing instruction to access and link the contents of the XML document to a style sheet is

```
<?xml-stylesheet type="style" href="sheet" ?>
```

where *style* is the type of style sheet the XML processor will be accessing and *sheet* is the name and location of the style sheet. Here, "xml-stylesheet" is the processing instruction's target and everything else within the tag are processing instructions that identify the type and location of the style sheet. For a cascading style sheet, *style* should be "text/css".

REFERENCE WINDOW **RW**

Attaching an XML Document to a Style Sheet
- To attach an XML document to a cascading style sheet, insert the following command within the XML document's prolog:
```
<?xml-stylesheet type="text/css" href="sheet" ?>
```
where sheet is the name and location of the style sheet file.

The Jazz Warehouse has a cascading style sheet that Richard wants you to apply to the Jazz.xml file. The style sheet, shown in Figure 1- 18, is stored in the JW.css file.

Figure 1-18	JW.CSS STYLE SHEET

```
TITLE {display:block; font-size:18pt; color:blue; font-weight:bold;
       font-family: Arial, Helvetica, sans-serif;
       margin-top: 10pt; margin-left: 5pt}

MESSAGE {display:block; width:500pt; color:blue; font-style:italic;
         border-bottom:1pt solid black; padding-bottom:15pt;
         margin-left: 10pt; margin-top: 10pt; margin-right: 10pt}

CD {display:block; font-size:14pt;color:red; font-weight:bold;
    font-family: Arial, Helvetica, Sans-serif;
    margin-top: 20pt; margin-left:20pt}

ARTIST {display:block; font-size: 12pt; color:black; font-style:italic;
        font-family:Times New Roman, Times, Serif;
        margin-left: 12pt}

PRICEUS, PRICEUK {color:black; font-size: 12pt;
                  font-family: Times New Roman, Times, Serif;
                  margin-left: 12pt}

TRACK {display:list-item; font-size: 12pt; color:black; list-style-type: disc;
       font-family: Times New Roman, Times, Serif;
       margin-left: 25pt}
```

To link the JW.css style sheet to the Jazz.xml file:

1. Open **Jazz.xml** if not already open.

2. Below the comment in the prolog, insert the following processing instruction (see Figure 1-19):

   `<?xml-stylesheet type="text/css" href="JW.css" ?>`

Figure 1-19	ACCESSING A STYLE SHEET

processing instruction to access the JW.css style sheet

```
<?xml version="1.0" encoding="UTF-8" standalone="yes" ?>
<!-- This document contains data on Jazz Warehouse special offers -->
<?xml-stylesheet type="text/css" href="JW.css" ?>

<SPECIALS>
<TITLE>Monthly Specials at the Jazz Warehouse</TITLE>
<MESSAGE>
<![CDATA[
   Here are some of the latest specials from the Jazz Warehouse.
   Please note that all Miles Davis & John Coltrane CDs will be on
   sale for the month of March.
]]>
</MESSAGE>
```

3. Close Jazz.xml, saving your changes.

4. Open **Jazz.xml** in your Web browser.

   Figure 1-20 shows the contents of the Jazz.xml file with JW.css applied to the file's contents.

   TROUBLE? If you are viewing this file using Internet Explorer 5.5 or earlier, the music tracks are not displayed in a bulleted list.

| Figure 1-20 | THE JAZZ.XML DOCUMENT FORMATTED WITH THE JW.CSS STYLE SHEET |

Monthly Specials at the Jazz Warehouse

Here are some of the latest specials from the Jazz Warehouse. Please note that all Miles Davis & John Coltrane CDs will be on sale for the month of March.

Kind of Blue
Miles Davis
US: $11.99   UK: £8.39
- So What
- Freddie Freeloader
- Blue in Green
- All Blues
- Flamenco Sketches

Cookin'
Miles Davis
US: $7.99   UK: £5.59
- My Funny Valentine
- Blues by Five
- Airegin
- Tune-Up

Blue Train
John Coltrane
US: $8.99   UK: £6.29
- Blue Train
- Moment's Notice
- Locomotion
- I'm Old Fashioned
- Lazy Bird

You show Richard the formatted document and he tells you that it's just what he is looking for. Richard will show your work to the other members of his Web team, and they'll get back to you if they need more documents created in the future.

Session 1.3 QUICK CHECK

1. What will happen if you try to display an XML document with syntax errors in either Internet Explorer or Netscape?

2. What will happen if you try to display an XML document that is not valid (but is well formed) in either Internet Explorer or Netscape?

3. How do Internet Explorer and Netscape differ in how they display XML documents?

4. What CSS style declaration would you enter to display the TITLE element in a bold font?

5. What is a processing instruction?

6. What XML code would you enter to display the current document using the Standard.css cascading style sheet?

REVIEW ASSIGNMENTS

Richard has returned with another document that he wants you to convert to XML. This document contains a list of hard-to-find recordings that the Jazz Warehouse has recently acquired. Richard has saved the information in a text file and needs you to edit the document and add the appropriate element tags. He also would like you to display the document using the JW2.css style sheet, which he is also providing.

To complete this task:

1. Using your text editor, open **Rare.txt**, located in the Tutorial.01X/Review folder of your Data Disk. Save the document as **Rare.xml**.

2. Create a prolog at the top of the document, indicating that this is an XML document using the UTF-8 encoding scheme and that it is a standalone document.

3. Below the XML declaration, insert the following comment: "Jazz collectibles, recently acquired."

4. Enclose the document content in a root element named "rare."

5. Create an element named "title" for the title of the document, "Rare Jazz Collectibles."

6. Create an element named "subtitle" for the subtitle "New Offerings."

7. There are five new recordings that the Jazz Warehouse needs to include in this document. Each recording contains the following information:

   ■ name of the artist
   ■ name of the album
   ■ year the album was released
   ■ album label
   ■ condition of the album
   ■ selling price of the album in dollars
   ■ selling price of the album in pounds

   Enter element tags for each of these items using the following element names: artist, record, year, label, condition, priceus, and priceuk.

8. Richard was not able to type the symbol for British pounds in his original text document. Instead he used a capital "L." Replace these with a character reference to the British pound, £.

Explore 9. At the bottom of the file is a message to record collectors. Enclose this message in a CDATA section and place it within an element named "message."

10. Add a processing instruction to the document's prolog, to attach the document to the JW2.css style sheet.

11. Print the contents of Rare.xml and save your changes.

12. Open **Rare.xml** in your Web browser and print the page.

13. Hand in your files and printouts to your instructor.

CASE PROBLEMS

Case 1. Jackson Electronics Located in Santa Fe, NM, Jackson Electronics is a privately held manufacturer of consumer digital products such as scanners, printers, and digital cameras. Originally founded by Pete Jackson in 1948 as an office supply store, Jackson Electronics has thrived over the years with innovative thinking and effective use of cutting-edge technology. Alison Greely is one of the webmasters for the Jackson Electronics Web site. Her primary responsibility is to maintain information on the frequently asked questions (FAQs) section of the site. Alison would like to convert her documents into XML format and has asked for your help. She has given you a text file containing FAQs for two of Jackson Electronics' products: the ScanMaster scanner and the DigiCam digital camera. She would like this text file converted to an XML document and then linked to a cascading style sheet.

To complete this task:

1. Using your text editor, open **FAQ.txt**, located in the Tutorial.01X\Cases folder of your Data Disk. Save the document as **FAQ.xml**.

2. Create a prolog at the top of the document, indicating that this is an XML document using version 1.0 of XML.

3. After the XML declaration, insert the following comment: "ScanMaster and DigiCam FAQ."

4. Enclose the document's title, "Jackson Electronics Products," in a set of <title> tags.

5. Set the document's subtitle, "Frequently Asked Questions," as a subtitle element.

6. Set each question in the document as a question element.

7. Set each answer in the document as an answer element, and place the text of each answer within a CDATA section.

8. Set the two product name titles as product elements.

9. Enclose the entire document content within a root element named "FAQ."

10. Add a processing instruction to the prolog to direct the XML processor to access the FAQ.css style sheet when it loads this document.

11. Print your XML code and then close the FAQ.xml document, saving your changes.

12. Open the **FAQ.xml** document in your Web browser. Print the page that the browser generates. Note that FAQ text will not wrap to a new line for users of Netscape 6.21.

13. Hand in your files and printouts to your instructor.

Case 2. Midwest University One of the original Federal Land Grant Universities, Midwest University now includes several world-class undergraduate and graduate programs. Professor David Teagarden is a member of the award-winning English department at MU. And, he is working on a Web site devoted to the work and life of William Shakespeare. He has created a document detailing the acts and scenes of *Hamlet* and has asked your help in placing this data in XML form.

To complete this task:

1. Start your text editor and open the **Hamlet.txt** file, located in the Tutorial.01X/Cases folder of your Data Disk. Save the document as **Hamlet.xml**.

2. Create a prolog at the top of the document, indicating that this is an XML document using version 1.0 of XML. You do not need to include any other information in the XML declaration.

3. Enclose the entire document content in a root element named "Play."

4. Place the title of the play in a root element named "Title".

5. Add an attribute to the Title element named "type." Set the value of the type attribute to "Tragedy."

6. Place the summary of the place in a CDATA section within an element named "Summary."

Explore

7. Place all of the information about each act of the play within an element named "Act." Place the name of each act (Act 1, Act 2, and so forth) within an element named "Act_Number."

Explore

8. Place all of the information about each scene of the play within an element named "Scene." Place the name of each scene (Scene i, Scene ii, and so forth) within an element named "Scene_Number." Place the location of each scene within an element named "Location."

9. Create a processing instruction to access the Plays.css style sheet when a Web browser accesses this document.

10. Print your XML code and save your changes.

11. Open the **Hamlet.xml** document in your Web browser. Print the pages as they are rendered by the browser.

12. Hand in your printouts and files to your instructor.

Case 3. Biotech, Inc. Located in Dallas, TX, BI was created in March of 1998 as a result of the merger of four smaller biotechnology research concerns. Linda Abrahams is a human resource representative for Biotech, Inc. Most recently, she has been entering employee data into an XML document and is running into a few problems. When she opened the document in her Web browser, the browser reported several syntax errors. Linda doesn't know how to solve the problem and has sought your help in cleaning up her code.

To complete this task:

1. Start your text editor and open the **Staff1.xml** file, located in the Tutorial.01X/Cases folder of your Data Disk. Save the document as **Staff2.xml**.

2. Open the **Staff2.xml** file in your Web browser.

Explore

3. The Web browser will report syntax errors with the document. Using the information from the browser, locate and fix the errors. (*Note*: Both Internet Explorer and Netscape will report only one error at a time. After you fix one error, the browsers will then display the next error in the file—if one exists.)

4. Once you've fixed all of the syntactical errors, link the Staff2.xml document to the Staff.css cascading style sheet.

5. Add a gender attribute to each Employee element in the document. Set the value of the gender attribute to "male" for male employees and "female" for female employees.

6. Print the final code for the Staff2.xml file.

7. Reopen the Staff2.xml file in your Web browser and print the resulting Web page. Note that Netscape 6.21 does not render this page correctly.

8. Hand in your printouts and files to your instructor.

Case 4. Delton Mutual Life Brian Carlson is an accounts manager for Delton Mutual Life and has created a text document containing personnel information for all the accounts in his portfolio. He would like your help in converting his text file to an XML document and then displaying that information in a Web page.

To complete this task:

1. Using the contents of Accounts.txt, create an XML document named **Accounts.xml** saved to the Tutorial.01X/Cases folder of your Data Disk.

2. The Accounts.xml file should contain the following items:

   ■ The root element of the document should be named "Accounts." The Accounts element should contain multiple occurrences of a child element named "Client."

   ■ The Client element should have five child elements: Name, Address, Phone, E-mail, and Account_Total.

   ■ The Client element should have a single attribute named "ID," containing the customer ID number of each person (customer ID numbers begin with the letters "CS" followed by four digits).

   ■ The Name element should contain two child elements named "First" and "Last," storing the first and last names of each person in Brian's accounts list.

   ■ The Address element should contain the following child elements: Street, City, State, and Zip, which contain the individual parts of the client's address.

   ■ The Phone element should contain the client's phone number.

   ■ The E-mail element should contain the client's e-mail address.

   ■ The Account_Total element should contain the current amount of money each client has invested with Delton Mutual Life.

3. Within the document's prolog, insert a comment describing the purpose of the document. Include your name and the date in the comment text.

4. Attach the Accounts.xml file to a cascading style sheet named "Delton.css."

5. Print the code for the Accounts.xml document.

6. Open **Accounts.xml** in your Web browser and print the page generated by the browser.

7. Hand in your printouts and files to your instructor.

QUICK | CHECK ANSWERS

Session 1.1

1. Extensible means that the language can be used to create a wide variety of document types by using elements tailored to each document. XML allows the author to create markup tags that are specific for each document type.

2. SGML stands for Standard Generalized Markup Language and was used to develop HTML, the language of the Web. However, SGML was too complicated and required too much overhead to be the language of Web page design.

3. The W3C is an organization created in 1994 to develop common protocols and standards for sharing information on the World Wide Web.

4. HTML is not "data aware," HTML does not impose rigid standards for syntax, and HTML is not easily extended to different document types.

5. No, XML is a meta-markup language used for developing other markup languages.

6. DTD stands for Document Type Definition and is used to create rules governing the structure and content of an XML document. A well-formed XML document has to satisfy the syntax of XML; a valid document has to be well formed and also satisfy the rules of the DTD or schema.

7. an application that interprets XML code, verifying that it satisfies all of the XML specifications for document structure and syntax

8. an XML application designed to work with mathematical documents

Session 1.2

1. the prolog, body, and epilog

2. `<?xml version="1.0" encoding="ISO-8859-1" standalone="yes" ?>`

3. `<!-- Values extracted from the JW database -->`

4. The case of the opening and closing tags does not match.

5. There is a blank space in the element name.

6. The element at the top of the document hierarchy; all other elements in the document are children of the root element

7. An empty element contains no content, though it might contain one or more attributes whose values might be used by the XML parser.

8. using a CDATA section or using the & or & character reference

Session 1.3

1. Both browsers will report an error.

2. The browsers will display the contents of the XML document without reporting the error.

3. Internet Explorer displays the hierarchical structure and content of the document. Netscape only displays the content of the document.

4. TITLE {font-weight:bold}

5. A processing instruction is a command that provides instructions to the XML parser.

6. `<?xml-stylesheet type="text/css" href="Standard.css" ?>`

In this tutorial you will:

- Work with XML fields, records, and recordsets

- Create a data island in a Web page

- Bind XML elements to HTML tags

- Navigate through a collection of XML records

- Display XML data in a Web table

- Work with hierarchical recordsets

BINDING XML DATA WITH INTERNET EXPLORER

Creating a Staff Directory for Freezing Point Refrigerators

CASE

Freezing Point Refrigerators

Freezing Point is an online company that manufactures and sells refrigerators and other kitchen appliances. To make information easily accessible to its employees, the company maintains an intranet with Web pages containing a wide variety of corporate information.

Catherine Davis is a personnel manager at Freezing Point and has been assigned the job of putting the staff directory on the company's intranet. Her Web page needs to include each employee's name, department, position, phone number, years of service, and job status, as well as a picture of each employee.

Catherine has stored all of the information in an XML document, but she needs a way to put that information into her Web page. She doesn't want to re-enter all of that information into an HTML file because doing so would be time consuming and there's a possibility she would make an error in transferring the data. Catherine also doesn't want to edit the HTML file every time employee information changes, which is frequently. Catherine knows there is a way to display XML data in a formatted Web page. She finds this an attractive option because then she would only need to maintain the XML document. Catherine can format the Web page herself, but she needs your help to place XML data into the Web page.

**SESSION
2.1**

In this session, you'll learn how to interpret XML documents in terms of fields, records, and recordsets. You'll also examine how to reference an XML document by adding a data island to a Web page. Finally, this session explores how to bind HTML tags to specific XML elements in order to display the contents of an XML element in a Web page.

Using XML as a Data Source

So far, you've worked with XML to store your data, but you haven't used that data in an application. In this tutorial, you'll learn how to attach data from an XML document to a Web page. This technique involves **data binding** where the Web page's content is drawn from a data source (see Figure 2-1).

Figure 2-1	DATA BINDING

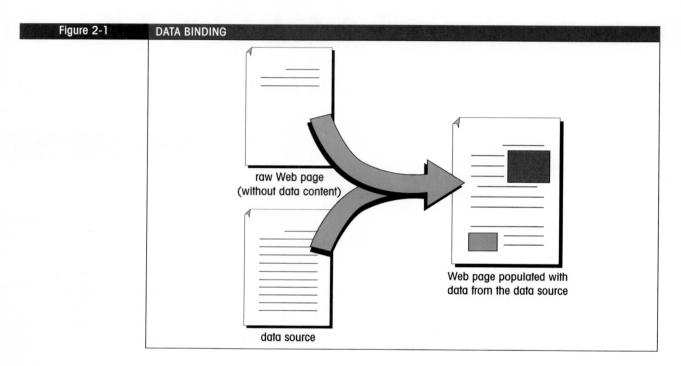

raw Web page
(without data content)

Web page populated with
data from the data source

data source

One of the advantages of data binding is that it frees the data from the format in which it is displayed. This means that the same data source can be combined with several different Web pages, without forcing the Web page designer to re-enter that data (see Figure 2-2). It also makes it easier to design the Web page because the designer only has to be concerned with the appearance of the page, not with its content.

Figure 2-2   **BINDING THE SAME DATA SOURCE WITH SEVERAL WEB PAGES**

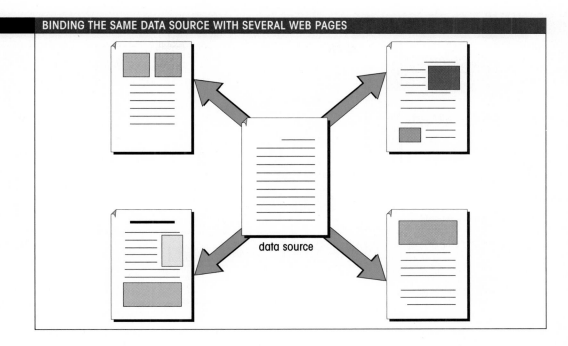

data source

Data binding can be used with a wide variety of possible data sources, from complex databases to simple text files. In Catherine's case, her data source is an XML document containing information about the employees at Freezing Point.

Catherine has already created a draft of the Web page she wants to use for the staff directory. In place of actual employee data, Catherine has inserted placeholder text that you'll replace later with actual employee data.

To open Catherine's Web page:

1. Using your text editor, open **FP1text.htm** located in the Tutorial.02X/Tutorial folder of your Data Disk.

2. Save the file as **FP1.htm**.

3. Using Internet Explorer, open and view **FP1.htm**. See Figure 2-3.

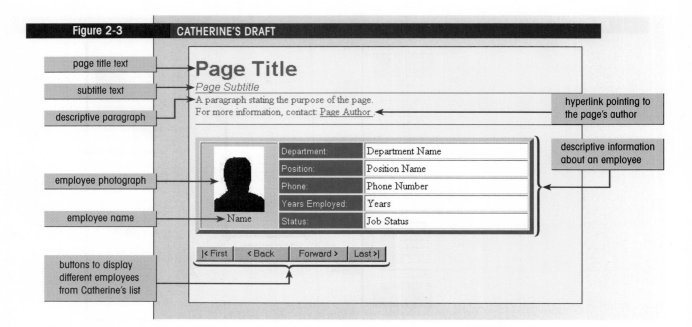

Figure 2-3   CATHERINE'S DRAFT

Catherine's Web page contains the following elements that need to be populated with data:

- page title
- page subtitle
- paragraph describing the purpose and content of the page
- hyperlink pointing to the e-mail address of the Web page designer
- table containing each employee's name, photo, department, position, phone number, years of service, and job status

The data that Catherine wants to use in this Web page comes from two XML documents: FPInfo.xml and Emp1.xml. The FPInfo.xml document contains general information about Freezing Point Refrigerators. The Emp1.xml document contains information about specific employees. Figure 2-4 shows a preview of how you'll use these documents to create a final Web page displaying information about the company and its employees.

Figure 2-4 | **USING DATA BINDING TO CREATE A FINAL WEB PAGE**

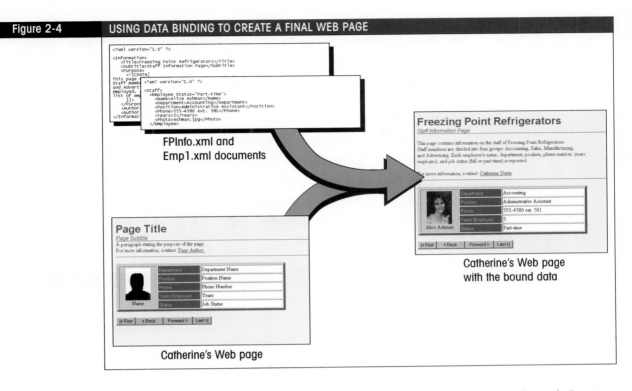

FPInfo.xml and
Emp1.xml documents

Catherine's Web page
with the bound data

Catherine's Web page

The techniques you'll use to populate these items with data work only with Internet Explorer version 5.0 and above. Netscape does not support the data-binding techniques employed by Internet Explorer.

Before we can apply data binding to Catherine's Web page, we first need to look at how data sources are organized.

Understanding Fields, Records, and Recordsets

Data in a data source is organized by fields, records, and recordsets. A **field** is an element that contains a single item of information, such as the employee's last name or age. A collection of these fields is called a **record**. Finally, a collection of records is called a **recordset**. Figure 2-5 displays the contents of an XML document in terms of fields, records, and recordsets.

Figure 2-5 | **FIELDS, RECORDS, AND RECORDSETS**

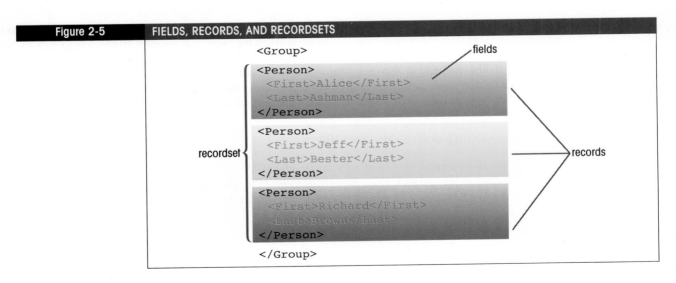

This particular document contains a single recordset, which stores three records, with each record containing two fields named "First" and "Last." The Person element in Figure 2-5 is sometimes called a **record element** because it contains a single record. The First and Last elements are **field elements** because they store field data (in this case, the person's first and last name).

Recordsets are divided into two classes: simple and hierarchical. A **simple recordset** satisfies the following properties:

■ There is a single root element containing a series of records of the same type.

■ Each record contains the same number of field elements.

■ Each field contains character data only.

The other type of recordset is a **hierarchical recordset**, which contains a collection of recordsets nested inside of each other. Figure 2-6 shows an example of a simple and hierarchical recordset.

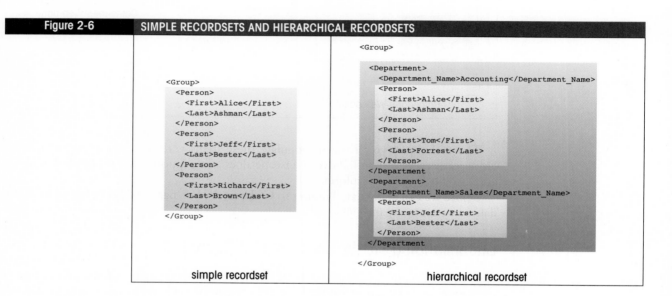

Figure 2-6	SIMPLE RECORDSETS AND HIERARCHICAL RECORDSETS

```
<Group>
  <Person>
    <First>Alice</First>
    <Last>Ashman</Last>
  </Person>
  <Person>
    <First>Jeff</First>
    <Last>Bester</Last>
  </Person>
  <Person>
    <First>Richard</First>
    <Last>Brown</Last>
  </Person>
</Group>
```
simple recordset

```
<Group>
  <Department>
    <Department_Name>Accounting</Department_Name>
    <Person>
      <First>Alice</First>
      <Last>Ashman</Last>
    </Person>
    <Person>
      <First>Tom</First>
      <Last>Forrest</Last>
    </Person>
  </Department>
  <Department>
    <Department_Name>Sales</Department_Name>
    <Person>
      <First>Jeff</First>
      <Last>Bester</Last>
    </Person>
  </Department>
</Group>
```
hierarchical recordset

The hierarchical recordset shown on the right in Figure 2-6 contains two simple recordsets. The outer recordset contains two records on the departments at Freezing Point Refrigerators, with each record containing two fields: Department_Name and Person. The inner recordset contains information on the employees within those departments. Each Person record contains two fields: First and Last. There is no limit to the number of nested recordsets a single document may contain.

The distinction between simple and hierarchical recordsets is important because Internet Explorer uses different data binding techniques depending on the form of the recordset. We'll start by using data binding with a simple recordset.

Working with Data Islands

The first step in data binding is to attach the Web page to a recordset. This attached data is called a **data island**. Data islands can either be external files or code entered directly into the HTML file. The syntax to create a data island from an external file is

```
<xml id="id" src="URL"></xml>
```

where *id* is the id name assigned to the data island, and *URL* is the filename and location of the external XML file. For example, to create a data island named "Company" attached to Company.xml, you enter the following code into your HTML file:

```
<xml id="Company" src="Company.xml"></xml>
```

To insert a data island directly into the HTML file, use the syntax

```
<xml id="id">
    xml code
</xml>
```

where *xml code* is the content of an XML document. The following code illustrates how a data island is placed directly into an HTML file:

```
<html>
<body>
    <xml id="staff">
        <?xml version="1.0"?>
        <Group>
          <Person>
            <First>Alice</First>
            <Last>Ashman</Last>
          </Person>
          <Person>
            <First>Jeff</First>
            <Last>Bester</Last>
          </Person>
          <Person>
            <First>Richard</First>
            <Last>Brown</Last>
          </Person>
        </Group>
    </xml>
contents of the HTML file
</body>
</html>
```

Note that you have to include all of the features of a well-formed XML document, including the XML declaration and the root element.

It's generally not useful to insert the XML code directly into the HTML file. After all, the whole philosophy of XML is to separate data content from data formatting. By placing her data in a separate document, Catherine can update her staff listings and company information without editing the Web page itself. Similarly, she can edit the appearance of her Web page without having to worry about data content.

REFERENCE WINDOW   **RW**

Creating a Data Island

- To create a data island for data stored in an XML document, add the following tag to the HTML file:

  ```
  <xml id="id" src="URL"></xml>
  ```

  where *id* is the id name assigned to the data island, and *URL* is the filename and location of the XML file.

- To create a data island for XML data entered directly into the HTML file, use the following code:

  ```
  <xml id="id">
      xml code
  </xml>
  ```

  where *xml code* is the content of an XML document.

How Data Islands Are Stored

When Internet Explorer creates a data island (from an internal or external source) from an XML document, the XML parser built into Internet Explorer reads and stores the data island as a **Data Source Object** or **DSO**. The DSO handles all of the interaction between the Web page and the data island, supplying the values from the data island for each element in the Web page. More than that, one can write program code to control the actions of the DSO, such as specifying which records are displayed in the Web page at any one time. If the XML document is not well formed or valid, Internet Explorer will not create a DSO. Unfortunately, it will not report the source of the problem to the user. This differs from how Internet Explorer handles poorly formed XML documents viewed directly within the browser.

It is also important to note that the DSO is created only once for each session. If the contents of the data source are modified after Internet Explorer creates the DSO, those changes are not reflected in the Web page until the next time the page is opened or refreshed.

Creating a Data Island

You'll start your work on Catherine's Web page by creating a data island, attaching her Web page to the contents of the FPInfo.xml file. Recall that this file contains information about the company and the nature of Catherine's Web page. Figure 2-7 displays the contents of the FPInfo.xml file.

Figure 2-7   THE CONTENTS OF THE FPINFO.XML DOCUMENT

```
<?xml version="1.0" ?>

<Information>
    <Title>Freezing Point Refrigerators</Title>
    <Subtitle>Staff Information Page</Subtitle>
    <Purpose>
        <![CDATA[
This page contains information on the staff of Freezing Point Regrigerators.
Staff members are divided into four groups: Accounting, Sales, Manufacturing,
and Advertising. Each employee's name, department, position, phone number, years
employed, and job status (full or part-time) is reported. To move through the
list of employees, click the buttons below the table at the bottom of the page.
        ]]>
    </Purpose>
    <Author>Catherine Davis</Author>
    <Author_Email>mailto:cdavis@freezingpoint.com</Author_Email>
</Information>
```

The FPInfo.xml file contains one record and five fields: Title, Subtitle, Purpose, Author, and Author_Email. Catherine wants you to create a data island for the contents of this file named "Page_Info."

To create the data island:

1. Using your text editor, return to FP1.htm and insert a blank line following the <body> tag, and insert the following HTML code (see Figure 2-8):

   ```
   <xml id="Page_Info" src="FPInfo.xml"></xml>
   ```

Figure 2-8	CREATING A DATA ISLAND

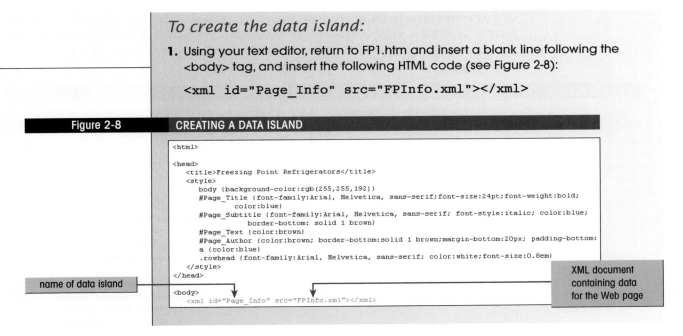

name of data island

XML document containing data for the Web page

```
<html>
<head>
   <title>Freezing Point Refrigerators</title>
   <style>
      body {background-color:rgb(255,255,192)}
      #Page_Title {font-family:Arial, Helvetica, sans-serif;font-size:24pt;font-weight:bold;
            color:blue}
      #Page_Subtitle {font-family:Arial, Helvetica, sans-serif; font-style:italic; color:blue;
            border-bottom: solid 1 brown}
      #Page_Text {color:brown}
      #Page_Author {color:brown; border-bottom:solid 1 brown;margin-bottom:20px; padding-bottom:
      a {color:blue)
      .rowhead {font-family:Arial, Helvetica, sans-serif; color:white;font-size:0.8em)
   </style>
</head>

<body>
   <xml id="Page_Info" src="FPInfo.xml"></xml>
```

The next step is to bind the elements contained in the FPInfo.xml document to specific tags in the HTML file.

Binding **XML Elements to HTML Tags**

Catherine wants to bind the XML elements to HTML tags as described below (see Figure 2-9).

- Bind the Title field to the Web page title.
- Bind the Subtitle field to the Web page subtitle.
- Bind the Purpose field to the description paragraph of the Web page.
- Bind the Author field to the name of the Web page designer.
- Bind the Author_Email field to the target of the author hyperlink.

Figure 2-9	BINDING XML ELEMENTS TO THE WEB PAGE

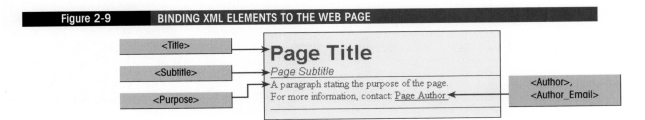

The syntax for binding an HTML tag to a data field is

```
<tag datasrc="#id" datafld="field">
```

where *tag* is the name of the HTML tag, *id* is the name of the data island, and *field* is the name of the field in the data source. Note that the name of the data island must have the # symbol as a prefix.

Different HTML tags employ the value of the data field in different ways. As shown in Figure 2-10, performing data binding with the <span> tag has the effect of placing the contents of the element between the opening and closing <span> tags. Alternately, binding an XML element to an <a> tag replaces the <a> tag's href attribute with the value of the bound element. This has the effect of changing the target of a hyperlink but not the text of the link itself.

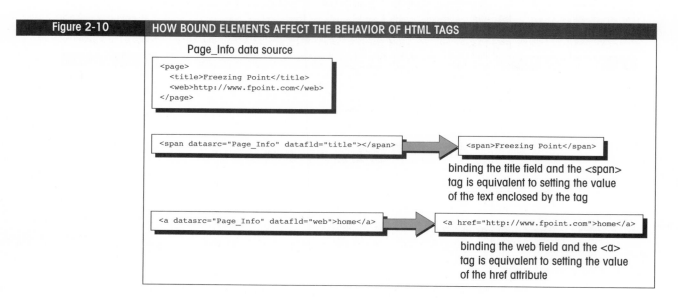

Figure 2-10   HOW BOUND ELEMENTS AFFECT THE BEHAVIOR OF HTML TAGS

Not every HTML tag supports data binding. Figure 2-11 lists the HTML tags that allow for bound data and indicates how the value of the bound field is attached to the tag.

Figure 2-11   HTML TAGS THAT SUPPORT DATA BINDING IN INTERNET EXPLORER

HTML ITEM	BOUND ELEMENT
hyperlink	`<a href="bound element value">`
Java applet	`<applet param="bound element value">`
button	`<button>bound element value</button>`
div container	`<div>bound element value</div>`
frame	`<frame src="bound element value">`
internal frame	`<iframe src="bound element value">`
inline image	`<img src="bound element value">`
checkbox	`<input type="checkbox" checked="bound element value">`
hidden field	`<input type="hidden" value="bound element value">`
password field	`<input type="password" value="bound element value">`
radio button	`<input type="radio" checked="bound element value">`
text field	`<input type="text" value="bound element value">`
label	`<label>bound element value</label>`
marquee	`<marquee>bound element value</marquee>`
list box item	`<option>bound element value</option>`
span container	`<span>bound element value</span>`
text area	`<textarea>bound element value</textarea>`

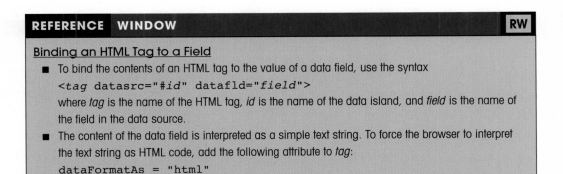

<u>Binding an HTML Tag to a Field</u>

- To bind the contents of an HTML tag to the value of a data field, use the syntax

  `<tag datasrc="#id" datafld="field">`

  where *tag* is the name of the HTML tag, *id* is the name of the data island, and *field* is the name of the field in the data source.
- The content of the data field is interpreted as a simple text string. To force the browser to interpret the text string as HTML code, add the following attribute to *tag*:

  `dataFormatAs = "html"`

Now that you've seen how to bind HTML tags and XML elements, you are ready to bind the contents of the FPInfo document to Catherine's Web page.

To bind XML elements to HTML tags:

1. In FP1.htm, locate the <div> tag for the page title. Remove the placeholder text displayed between the opening and closing <div> tags, and add the following attributes to the <div> tag (see Figure 2-12):

   `datasrc="#Page_Info" datafld="Title"`

Figure 2-12   BINDING A TAG TO THE TITLE ELEMENT

data source of the bound element

bound element

placeholder text is deleted

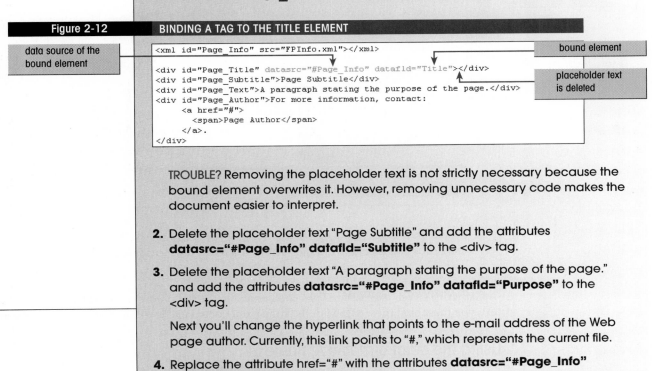

```
<xml id="Page_Info" src="FPInfo.xml"></xml>

<div id="Page_Title" datasrc="#Page_Info" datafld="Title"></div>
<div id="Page_Subtitle">Page Subtitle</div>
<div id="Page_Text">A paragraph stating the purpose of the page.</div>
<div id="Page_Author">For more information, contact:
    <a href="#">
      <span>Page Author</span>
    </a>.
</div>
```

TROUBLE? Removing the placeholder text is not strictly necessary because the bound element overwrites it. However, removing unnecessary code makes the document easier to interpret.

2. Delete the placeholder text "Page Subtitle" and add the attributes **datasrc="#Page_Info" datafld="Subtitle"** to the <div> tag.

3. Delete the placeholder text "A paragraph stating the purpose of the page." and add the attributes **datasrc="#Page_Info" datafld="Purpose"** to the <div> tag.

   Next you'll change the hyperlink that points to the e-mail address of the Web page author. Currently, this link points to "#," which represents the current file.

4. Replace the attribute href="#" with the attributes **datasrc="#Page_Info" datafld="Author_Email"**.

   Finally, bind the name of the page's author to the Author element.

5. Delete the placeholder text "Page Author" and add the attributes **datasrc="#Page_Info" datafld="Author"** to the <div> tag. Figure 2-13 shows the revised HTML code.

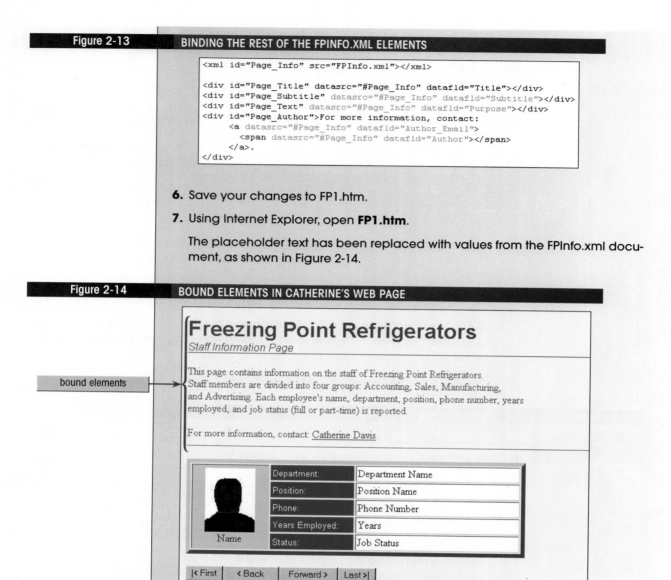

Figure 2-13 — BINDING THE REST OF THE FPINFO.XML ELEMENTS

```
<xml id="Page_Info" src="FPInfo.xml"></xml>

<div id="Page_Title" datasrc="#Page_Info" datafld="Title"></div>
<div id="Page_Subtitle" datasrc="#Page_Info" datafld="Subtitle"></div>
<div id="Page_Text" datasrc="#Page_Info" datafld="Purpose"></div>
<div id="Page_Author">For more information, contact:
      <a datasrc="#Page_Info" datafld="Author_Email">
        <span datasrc="#Page_Info" datafld="Author"></span>
      </a>.
</div>
```

6. Save your changes to FP1.htm.

7. Using Internet Explorer, open **FP1.htm**.

The placeholder text has been replaced with values from the FPInfo.xml document, as shown in Figure 2-14.

Figure 2-14 — BOUND ELEMENTS IN CATHERINE'S WEB PAGE

Freezing Point Refrigerators
Staff Information Page

This page contains information on the staff of Freezing Point Refrigerators. Staff members are divided into four groups: Accounting, Sales, Manufacturing, and Advertising. Each employee's name, department, position, phone number, years employed, and job status (full or part-time) is reported.

For more information, contact: Catherine Davis.

bound elements

	Department:	Department Name
	Position:	Position Name
	Phone:	Phone Number
	Years Employed:	Years
Name	Status:	Job Status

| \|< First | < Back | Forward > | Last >\| |

8. Move the mouse pointer over the hyperlink for Catherine Davis and verify that the status bar displays the URL *mailto:cdavis@freezingpoint.com*.

Catherine's Web page still has placeholder text in the staff information table. To replace that text, you must bind those tags with the Emp1.xml document. You'll do that in the next session.

Using the dataFormatAs Attribute

By default, the contents of an XML element are interpreted by Internet Explorer as literal text. However, there may be situations where you wish to store HTML code in an XML element. For example, rather than using two elements for the author name and e-mail address, you could have included both pieces in a single element using a CDATA section:

```
<name>
  <![CDATA[
    <a href="mailto:cdavis@freezingpoint.com">
```

```
Catherine Davis</a>
  ]]>
</name>
```

However, if Catherine bound this element to an HTML tag, as follows:

```
Questions? Contact <span datasrc="#Page_Info" datafld="name">
</span>
```

Internet Explorer would still interpret contents as literal text and *not* render the text as a hyperlink. The contents would be displayed in the Web browser as follows:

```
Questions? Contact <a href="mailto:cdavis@freezingpoint.com">
Catherine Davis</a>
```

To get around this problem, you can specify that Internet Explorer interpret the content of an element as HTML code rather than literal text by using the dataFormatAs attribute. The syntax is

```
dataFormatAs="type"
```

where *type* is either "text" (the default) or "html". In Catherine's case, she would need to change her code to

```
Questions? Contact <span datasrc="#Page_Info" datafld="name"
dataFormatAs="html"></span>
```

for Internet Explorer to display the author's name as a hyperlink.

Note that only the following HTML tags support the dataFormatAs attribute: <button>, <div>, <label>, <marquee>, and <span>.

Using the $TEXT Field

Up to this point, you've used field names to reference specific elements in the XML document. The DSO also creates an pseudo field named "$Text." The **$Text** field contains the character data from all of the fields in a record, not including attribute values. For example, the value of the $Text field for the following record is "Alice Ashman", taking its value from the values of both the First and Last fields.

```
<Person>
  <First>Alice</First>
  <Last>Ashman</Last>
</Person>
```

If Catherine wanted to bind an HTML tag to the entire contents of this record, she could use an HTML tag such as:

```
The employee's name is <span datasrc="#Page_Info" datafld=
"$Text"></span>.
```

and the Web page would be rendered as

```
The employee's name is Alice Ashman.
```

The $Text field name is useful when you need to work with all of the field values as a single text string. It is also useful for binding element attributes to HTML tags, as you'll see later in the tutorial.

You've successfully completed the first stage of working with Catherine's Web page. In the next session, you'll bind more elements to her document and you'll learn how to display multiple records in a single page.

To close your work:

1. Exit Internet Explorer.

2. Close FP1.htm and exit your text editor.

Session 2.1 QUICK CHECK

1. Define the following terms:
   a. data binding
   b. field
   c. record
   d. recordset

2. What is the difference between a simple recordset and a hierarchical recordset?

3. What is a data island?

4. What HTML code would you enter to create a data island named CompInfo that is connected to the Company.xml file?

5. What HTML code would you enter to bind a <span> tag to the CName field in the CompInfo data island?

6. How is the bound element's content manifested in the <IMG> tag?

7. What is the $Text field?

SESSION 2.2

In this session, you'll learn how to use data binding with element attributes. You'll also see how to work with XML documents that contain multiple records. Finally, you'll learn to work with the recordset object in order to navigate through a collection of records within a single Web page.

Examining Multiple Records

In the last session, you learned how to bind data from a single record to a Web page. However, Catherine's staff directory involves several records, so there is some additional work that needs to be done. She has stored the data in an XML file named Emp1.xml. Take a moment to view the contents of Emp1.xml now.

To view the Emp1.xml document:

1. Using your text editor, open **Emp1.xml**.

2. Scroll through the document and examine the structure and content of the document. A portion of the file is displayed in Figure 2-15.

Figure 2-15	BOUND ELEMENTS IN CATHERINE'S WEB PAGE

```
<?xml version="1.0" ?>
<Staff>
   <Employee Status="Part-time">
      <Name>Alice Ashman</Name>
      <Department>Accounting</Department>
      <Position>Administrative Assistant</Position>
      <Phone>555-4580 ext. 581</Phone>
      <Years>5</Years>
      <Photo>Ashman.jpg</Photo>
   </Employee>
   <Employee Status="Full-time">
      <Name>Jeff Bester</Name>
      <Department>Sales</Department>
      <Position>Sales Manager</Position>
      <Phone>555-4580 ext. 411</Phone>
      <Years>3</Years>
      <Photo>Bester.jpg</Photo>
   </Employee>
   <Employee Status="Full-time">
      <Name>Richard Brown</Name>
      <Department>Manufacturing</Department>
      <Position>Shop Manager</Position>
      <Phone>555-4580 ext. 193</Phone>
      <Years>15</Years>
      <Photo>Brown.jpg</Photo>
   </Employee>
```

3. Close the file, being sure not to save any changes.

The document contains a recordset with 20 records—one for each employee. Catherine has entered the following fields for each employee record:

- **Name**: employee's full name
- **Department**: department in which the employee works
- **Position**: employee's job title
- **Phone**: employee's phone number
- **Year**: number of years the employee has worked for the company
- **Photo**: filename of an image file

In addition, the Employee record element has an attribute named "Status," indicating whether the employee works full or part time. Figure 2-16 shows how each of these items fits into the layout of Catherine's Web page.

Figure 2-16	BINDING XML ELEMENTS TO THE STAFF TABLE

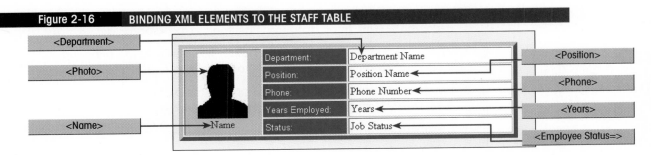

You'll start by binding the field elements, using the techniques covered in the last session.

To bind the elements to Catherine's document:

1. Using your text editor, open **FP1.htm** if it is not currently open.

2. Below the <xml> tags to create the Page_Info data island, enter the following HTML code, as shown in Figure 2-17:

```
<xml id="Staff_Info" src="Emp1.xml"></xml>
```

Figure 2-17	CREATING THE STAFF_INFO DATA ISLAND

```
<body>
    <xml id="Page_Info" src="FPInfo.xml"></xml>
    <xml id="Staff_Info" src="Emp1.xml"></xml>

    <div id="Page_Title" datasrc="#Page_Info" datafld="Title"></div>
    <div id="Page_Subtitle" datasrc="#Page_Info" datafld="Subtitle"></div>
    <div id="Page_Text" datasrc="#Page_Info" datafld="Purpose"></div>
    <div id="Page_Author">For more information, contact:
        <a datasrc="#Page_Info" datafld="Author_Email">
          <span datasrc="#Page_Info" datafld="Author"></span>
        </a>.
    </div>
```

Now bind the XML elements from the Emp1.xml file to tags in the HTML file.

3. Scroll through the HTML document to the table section and replace the src="Photo.jpg" attribute with the attributes **datasrc="#Staff_Info" datafld="Photo"**, as shown in Figure 2-18.

Figure 2-18	BINDING THE PHOTO ELEMENT TO AN <IMG> TAG

the Photo element contains the filename of a graphic file

```
<table border="6" bordercolordark="blue" bordercolorlight="#CCCCFF" cellpadding="2">
  <tr><td rowspan="5" align="center" width="110" bgcolor="#CCCCFF">
        <img datasrc="#Staff_Info" datafld="Photo"><br>
        <span>Name</span>
      </td>
      <td width="120" bgcolor="blue">
        <span class="rowhead">Department:</span>
      </td>
      <td width="240" bgcolor="white">
        <span>Department Name</span>
      </td>
  </tr>
```

4. Delete the "Name" placeholder text and add the attributes **datasrc="#Staff_Info" datafld="Name"** to the <span> tag.

5. Delete the "Department Name" placeholder text and add the attributes **datasrc="#Staff_Info" datafld="Department"** to the <span> tag.

6. Delete the "Position Name" placeholder text and add the attributes **datasrc="#Staff_Info" datafld="Position"** to the <span> tag.

7. Delete the "Phone Number" placeholder text and add the attributes **datasrc="#Staff_Info" datafld="Phone"** to the <span> tag.

8. Delete the "Years" placeholder text and add the attributes **datasrc="#Staff_Info" datafld="Years"** to the <span> tag.

The revised table is displayed in Figure 2-19.

Figure 2-19 **BINDING THE REMAINING ELEMENTS**

```
<table border="6" bordercolordark="blue" bordercolorlight="#CCCCFF" cellpadding="2">
  <tr><td rowspan="5" align="center" width="110" bgcolor="#CCCCFF">
        <img datasrc="#Staff_Info" datafld="Photo"><br>
        <span datasrc="#Staff_Info" datafld="Name"></span>
      </td>
      <td width="120" bgcolor="blue">
        <span class="rowhead">Department:</span>
      </td>
      <td width="240" bgcolor="white">
        <span datasrc="#Staff_Info" datafld="Department"></span>
      </td>
  </tr>
  <tr><td width="120" bgcolor="blue">
        <span class="rowhead">Position:</span>
      </td>
      <td width="240" bgcolor="white">
        <span datasrc="#Staff_Info" datafld="Position"></span>
      </td>
  </tr>
  <tr><td width="120" bgcolor="blue">
        <span class="rowhead">Phone:</span>
      </td>
      <td width="240" bgcolor="white">
        <span datasrc="#Staff_Info" datafld="Phone"></span>
      </td>
  </tr>
  <tr><td width="120" bgcolor="blue">
        <span class="rowhead">Years Employed:</span>
      </td>
      <td width="240" bgcolor="white">
        <span datasrc="#Staff_Info" datafld="Years"></span>
      </td>
  </tr>
  <tr>
      <td width="120" bgcolor="blue">
        <span class="rowhead">Status:</span>
      </td>
      <td width="240" bgcolor="white">
        <span>Job Status</span>
      </td>
  </tr>
</table>
<br>
```

TROUBLE? Don't worry that we haven't created a data bind for the value of the Status attribute yet. You will accomplish that in the next set of exercises.

9. Save your changes to FP1.htm.

10. Using Internet Explorer, open and verify that your Web page matches the one shown in Figure 2-20.

Figure 2-20 **STAFF_INFO DATA DISPLAYED IN THE WEB PAGE**

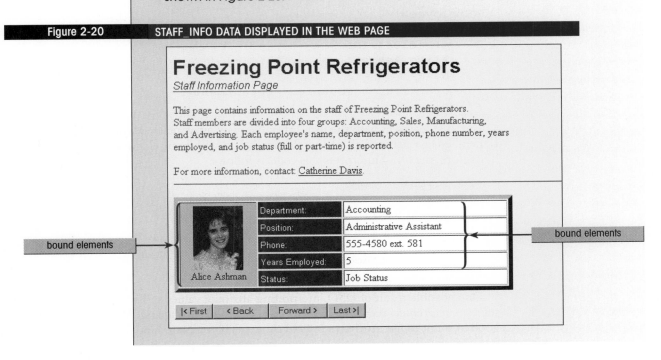

bound elements

bound elements

After reviewing the revised Web page with Catherine, she's pleased with its appearance. However, she notices that the job status has not been included yet. You'll take on that challenge next.

Binding to an XML Attribute

Attributes, like the Status attribute of the Employee element, are treated by the DSO as fields. If the attribute is part of a record element, it's easy to bind attribute values to a Web page. For example, the following code, which has an ID attribute as part of the Employee element,

```
<Employee ID="E304">
   <Name>Alice Ashman</Name>
   <Department>Accounting</Department>
</Employee>
```

is interpreted by the DSO as

```
<Employee>
   <ID>E304</ID>
   <Name>Alice Ashman</Name>
   <Department>Accounting</Department>
</Employee>
```

Attributes become more complicated when they're part of a field element, as in the following set of code:

```
<Employee>
   <Name ID="E304">Alice Ashman</Name>
   <Department>Accounting</Department>
</Employee>
```

In this case, the attribute is still treated by the DSO as a field element, and the field element containing the attribute becomes a record element. A DSO treats the above code as follows:

```
<Employee>
   <Name>
      <ID>E304</ID>
      Alice Ashman
   </Name>
   <Department>Accounting</Department>
</Employee>
```

But, that leaves us with the text "Alice Ashman" unassociated with a field. The trick is to remember to reference all of the character data within an element using the $Text field. Therefore, the DSO interprets this code as follows:

```
<Employee>
   <Name>
      <ID>E304</ID>
      <$Text>Alice Ashman</$Text>
   </Name>
   <Department>Accounting</Department>
</Employee>
```

One possible result of DSO interpreting attribute values is that it treats a simple recordset as a hierarchical recordset, which can complicate the data binding. For this reason, it's a good idea not to use attributes in field elements if you plan to do data binding.

In Catherine's document, the Status attribute is part of the Employee record element, not one of the field elements, so you can interpret it as a separate field.

To bind the attribute value:

1. Using your text editor, open **FP1.htm** if it is not currently open.

2. Locate and delete the "Job Status" placeholder text and add the following attributes to the <span> tag: **datasrc="#Staff_Info" datafld="Status"** (see Figure 2-21).

Figure 2-21	BINDING THE <SPAN> TAG TO THE STATUS ATTRIBUTE

```
<tr>
    <td width="120" bgcolor="blue">
        <span class="rowhead">Status:</span>
    </td>
    <td width="240" bgcolor="white">
        <span datasrc="#Staff_Info" datafld="Status"></span>
    </td>
</tr>
</table>
<br>
```

3. Save your changes to FP1.htm.

4. Using Internet Explorer, refresh the contents of FP1.htm. The Web page now displays the job status information, as shown in Figure 2-22.

Figure 2-22	DATA VALUES FROM THE FIRST RECORD

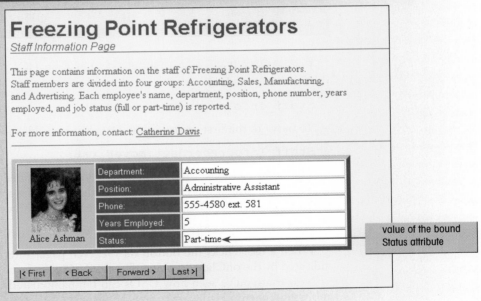

Working **with the Data Source Object**

Most HTML tags can only display field values one record at a time. You see an example of this in Catherine's Web page, which only displays information on the first employee. However, Catherine wants to be able to navigate through the contents of her staff directory.

To do this, you can take advantage of data-access technology supported by Microsoft called **ActiveX Data Objects** or **ADO**. ADO allows you to work with the Data Source Object by either applying a **method** (a command to perform an operation on an object) or changing one of the **properties** or characteristics of the DSO. Let's first examine how to apply a method to the Data Source Object.

Applying a Method to a Data Source Object

The syntax for applying a method to a DSO is

```
id.recordset.method
```

where *id* is the name of the data island in your Web document and *method* is the name of a method supported by ADO. There are several methods that can be applied to DSOs, but we're only going to concentrate on those that allow us to navigate through the records in the recordset. These methods are listed in Figure 2-23.

Figure 2-23	RECORDSET METHODS

RECORDSET METHODS	DESCRIPTION
id.recordset.moveFirst()	Move to the first record in the *id* recordset
id.recordset.movePrevious()	Move to the previous record
id.recordset.moveNext()	Move to the next record
id.recordset.moveLast()	Move to the last record in the *id* recordset
id.recordset.move(*i*)	Move to record number *i* in the *id* recordset (record numbering starts with the number 0)

For example, if you want to display the last record in a DSO whose id is "Staff_Info," run the following method:

```
Staff_Info.recordset.moveLast()
```

To move to the first record in the Data Source Object, use the method

```
Staff_Info.recordset.moveFirst()
```

The other methods listed in Figure 2-23 can be applied in a similar way.

There are several ways to run these methods, but the simplest is to assign the method to the onClick event handler of a <button> element, as shown below:

```
<button onClick="Staff_Info.recordset.moveLast()">
```

When a user clicks the button on the Web page, Internet Explorer runs the command indicated by the onClick event handler, displaying the last record in the Staff_Info recordset.

Now that you've seen how DSOs can be manipulated using methods, you are ready to apply these methods to Catherine's Web page.

To assign a recordset method:

1. Using your text editor, open **FP1.htm** if it is not currently open.

2. Locate the first occurence of the <button> tag (the First button). Within the <button> tag, enter the text **onClick="Staff_Info.recordset.moveFirst()"**, as shown in Figure 2-24.

Figure 2-24	ENTERING THE MOVEFIRST() METHOD

```
<button onClick="Staff_Info.recordset.moveFirst()">
   |&lt; First
</button>
<button>
     &lt; Back   
</button>
<button>
   Forward &gt;
</button>
<button>
   Last &gt;|
</button>
</body>
</html>
```

> move to the first record
> in the recordset when
> this button is clicked

3. Locate the second occurrence of the <button> tag (the Back button). Within the <button> tag, enter the text **onClick="Staff_Info.recordset.movePrevious()"**.

4. Locate the third occurrence of the <button> tag (the Forward button). Within the <button> tag, enter the text **onClick="Staff_Info.recordset.moveNext()"**.

5. Locate the last occurrence of the <button> tag (the Last button). Within the <button> tag, enter the text **onClick="Staff_Info.recordset.moveLast()"**.

Figure 2-25 shows the completed onClick commands for all four buttons.

Figure 2-25	ENTERING THE REMAINING RECORDSET METHODS

```
<button onClick="Staff_Info.recordset.moveFirst()">
   |&lt; First
</button>
<button onClick="Staff_Info.recordset.movePrevious()">
     &lt; Back   
</button>
<button onClick="Staff_Info.recordset.moveNext()">
   Forward &gt;
</button>
<button onClick="Staff_Info.recordset.moveLast()">
   Last &gt;|
</button>
</body>
</html>
```

> move to the
> previous record

> move to the next record

> move to the last record

6. Save your changes to FP1.htm.

7. Using Internet Explorer, open **FP1.htm** and verify that the four buttons located below the table allow you to move through the records in the recordset. Figure 2-26 displays the contents of the last record.

Figure 2-26	THE LAST RECORD IN THE RECORDSET

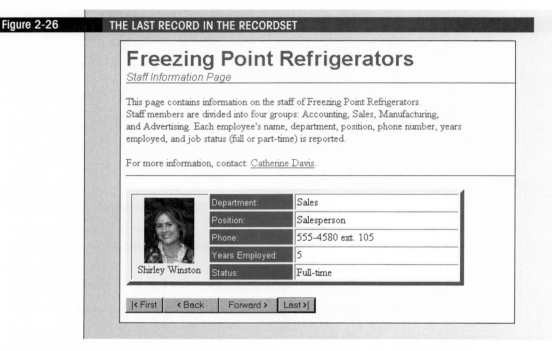

Working with Data Source Object Properties

Catherine is thrilled with your work and the button feature. However, she did discover one small problem that needs to be addressed. When she navigated to the last button and clicked the Forward button, the Web page displayed a blank record with a missing inline image.

You explain to Catherine that this is the result of the Web page trying to access a record that doesn't exist. Catherine understands your explanation but is concerned that users will find this effect disconcerting. She would like you to revise the page to prohibit users from moving outside the boundaries of the recordset.

To do this, you need to determine which record the user is currently viewing, which is accomplished by working with the properties of the Data Source Object. DSO properties are described with the syntax

    id.recordset.*property*

where *property* is one of the Data Source Object properties supported by the ADO. Just as there were DSO methods, there are many DSO properties that allow programmers to develop sophisticated data-access pages. In this tutorial, we'll concentrate on those properties that work with the location of the current record. These properties are described in Figure 2-27.

Figure 2-27	RECORDSET PROPERTIES

RECORDSET PROPERTIES	DESCRIPTION
id.recordset.BOF	Indicates whether the current record position is before the first record in the recordset
id.recordset.EOF	Indicates whether the current record position is after the last record in the recordset
id.recordset.Index	Returns the index number of the current record
id.recordset.RecordCount	Returns the total number of records in the recordset

Two properties are of most use to you: the BOF (beginning of file) property and the EOF (end of file) property. Both properties return a value of *true* if a user moves off the edge of the recordset. Otherwise they return the value *false*. To prevent the page from attempting to display a record before the first one in the recordset, add the following command to the Back button:

```
if (Staff_Info.recordset.BOF) Staff_Info.recordset.moveFirst()
```

The code uses the "if" command to first test whether the page is trying to display a record occurring before the first record in the recordset, which would of course be an empty record. If that is the case, the Web page displays the first record in the recordset.

Similarly, to prevent the page from attempting to display a record beyond the last record in the recordset, add the following command to the Forward button:

```
if (Staff_Info.recordset.EOF) Staff_Info.recordset.moveLast()
```

With this code, the last record is displayed if a user attempts to access a record that occurs after the last record in the recordset.

To modify the features of the Back and Forward buttons:

1. Using your text editor, open **FP1.htm** if it is not currently open.

2. Locate the <button> tag for the Back button.

3. After the movePrevious() method, type a semi-colon (;), and then type the following command, as shown in Figure 2-28:

```
if (Staff_Info.recordset.BOF) Staff_Info.recordset.move
First()
```

| Figure 2-28 | TESTING WHETHER THE CURRENT RECORD POSITION IS BEFORE THE FIRST RECORD |

if the current record is before the first record in the recordset...

...move back to the first record

```
<button onClick="Staff_Info.recordset.moveFirst()">
  |&lt; First
</button>
<button onClick="Staff_Info.recordset.movePrevious();
          if (Staff_Info.recordset.BOF) Staff_Info.recordset.moveFirst()">
    &lt; Back   
</button>
<button onClick="Staff_Info.recordset.moveNext()">
  Forward &gt;
</button>
<button onClick="Staff_Info.recordset.moveLast()">
  Last &gt;|
</button>
</body>
</html>
```

commands must be separated by a semi-colon and the commands must be enclosed in quotes

The semicolon separates one command from another. Note also that you have to enclose both commands within the set of quotation marks.

4. After the moveNext() method in the <button> tag for the Forward button, type a semicolon followed by the command

```
if (Staff_Info.recordset.EOF) Staff_Info.recordset.moveLast()
```

See Figure 2-29.

Figure 2-29

TESTING WHETHER THE CURRENT RECORD POSITION IS AFTER THE LAST RECORD

```
<button onClick="Staff_Info.recordset.moveFirst()">
   |&lt; First
</button>
<button onClick="Staff_Info.recordset.movePrevious();
              if (Staff_Info.recordset.BOF) Staff_Info.recordset.moveFirst()">
     &lt; Back   
</button>
<button onClick="Staff_Info.recordset.moveNext();
              if (Staff_Info.recordset.EOF) Staff_Info.recordset.moveLast()">
   Forward &gt;
</button>
<button onClick="Staff_Info.recordset.moveLast()">
   Last &gt;|
</button>
</body>
</html>
```

5. Save your changes to FP1.htm and use Internet Explorer to refresh FP1.htm.

6. Within the browser, click the **< Back** button and verify that you cannot display a record before the first record in the recordset.

7. Click the **Last>|** button followed by the **Forward >** button to verify that you cannot display a record after the last record in the recordset.

You've completed your work on FP1.htm and Catherine is impressed with the way that you handled this latest challenge.

To complete your work:

1. Exit from Internet Explorer and your text editor.

In the next session, you'll continue to work with Catherine's employee data, learn how to display multiple records in a single table, and learn how to work with hierarchical recordsets.

Session 2.2 QUICK CHECK

1. In general, how does the DSO object treat an element attribute?

2. Describe how the DSO treats an attribute that is part of a field element.

3. What command would you use to display the last record from a data island named "Cinfo"?

4. What command would you use to display the previous record from the CInfo recordset?

5. What command would you use to display a record with the index number "5" from the CInfo recordset?

6. What recordset property indicates whether the current record is past the last record in the recordset?

7. What recordset property returns the index number of the current recordset?

SESSION 2.3

In this session, you'll display multiple records within a single table using data table binding. You'll also learn how to segment your recordset into pages and how to navigate from page to page. Finally, you'll explore how to create and work with hierarchical recordsets.

Working with Table Binding

The tags you worked with in the last session had the limitation of displaying a single value at a time. Catherine wants to create a page where she can view all of the staff records at a glance, without having to scroll through several pages of records.

As you will see in this session, this can be done using **table data binding**, in which each record is displayed in a different row of a table. The syntax for binding a recordset to a table is

```
<table datasrc="#id">
  <tr>
    <td><span datafld="field1"></span></td>
    <td><span datafld="field2"></span></td>
  </tr>
</table>
```

where *id* is the name of the data island and *field1*, *field2*, etc., are the fields from the recordset. Even though the fields are bound to a single tag in the table, the browser repeats the field value for each record in the recordset to automatically add as many rows to the table as there are records. The difference between this table and the table you worked on in the last session is that the datasrc attribute is placed in the <table> tag and the datafld attributes are placed in individual table cells. The <td> tag doesn't support data binding, so you must enclose the text of each table cell using the <span> tag, or any other tag that supports data binding (see Figure 2-11).

Catherine has put together another draft of a page she would like you to develop. As shown in Figure 2-30, she wants the table placed on the right margin of the Web page. Currently, the Web page displays a single sample row, but when you're finished, the Web page will display content from all of the records in the XML document.

Figure 2-30	CATHERINE'S NEW PAGE

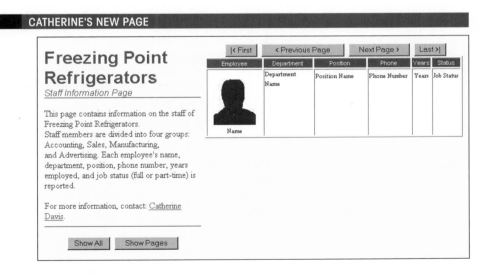

Note that the Web page also contains buttons to display the table by pages. You'll learn about pages and how to use them later in the session.

Binding Data to a Table

- To bind data to an HTML table, use the general form

```
<table datasrc="#id">
  <tr>
    <td><span datafld="field1"></span></td>
    <td><span datafld="field2"></span></td>
  </tr>
</table>
```

where *id* is the name of the data island and *field1*, *field2*, etc., are the fields from the recordset.

Catherine has already inserted <xml> tags in her HTML file to connect the document to the FPInfo and Emp1 XML documents. Your job is to bind the cells in the table to the appropriate fields in those XML documents.

To bind the table to an XML document:

1. Using your text editor, open **FP2text.htm**, located in the Tutorial.02X/Tutorial folder of your Data Disk.

2. Save the file as **FP2.htm**.

   As before, the staff information has been placed in a data island named "Staff_Info". Reference this data island in the <table> tag.

3. Locate the <table> tag, and insert the attribute **datasrc="#Staff_Info"**, as shown in Figure 2-31.

Figure 2-31   SPECIFYING THE DATASRC FOR THE TABLE

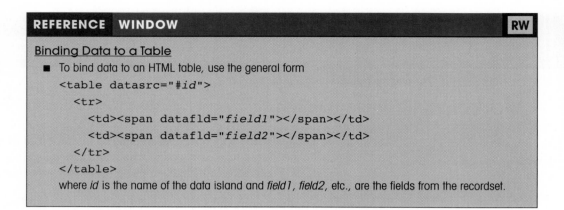

```
<table width="460" border="1" datasrc="#Staff_Info">
  <thead>
    <th bgcolor="blue" width="100"><span class="colhead">Employee</span></th>
    <th bgcolor="blue" width="90"><span class="colhead">Department</span></th>
    <th bgcolor="blue" width="100"><span class="colhead">Position</span></th>
    <th bgcolor="blue" width="80"><span class="colhead">Phone</span></th>
    <th bgcolor="blue" wdith="30"><span class="colhead">Years</span></th>
    <th bgcolor="blue" width="50"><span class="colhead">Status</span></th>
  </thead>
```

4. Locate the <img> tag in the table's first cell and replace the src="Photo.jpg" attribute with the attribute **datafld="Photo"**.

5. Delete the "Name" placeholder text and add the attribute **datafld="Name"** to the <span> tag.

6. Continue through the rest of the table, deleting the placeholder text for Department Name, Position Name, Phone Number, Years, and Job Status, and add datafld attributes to the corresponding <span> tags that point to the Department, Position, Phone, Years, and Status fields. Figure 2-32 shows the revised code.

Figure 2-32	SPECIFYING THE DATASRC FOR THE TABLE

```html
<table width="460" border="1" datasrc="#Staff_Info">
  <thead>
    <th bgcolor="blue" width="100"><span class="colhead">Employee</span></th>
    <th bgcolor="blue" width="90"><span class="colhead">Department</span></th>
    <th bgcolor="blue" width="100"><span class="colhead">Position</span></th>
    <th bgcolor="blue" width="80"><span class="colhead">Phone</span></th>
    <th bgcolor="blue" wdith="30"><span class="colhead">Years</span></th>
    <th bgcolor="blue" width="50"><span class="colhead">Status</span></th>
  </thead>
  <tr><td align="center" bgcolor="white">
      <img datafld="Photo"><br>
      <span class="celltext" datafld="Name"></span>
    </td>
    <td valign="top" bgcolor="white">
      <span class="celltext"datafld="Department"></span>
    </td>
    <td valign="top" bgcolor="white">
      <span class="celltext" datafld="Position"></span>
    </td>
    <td valign="top" bgcolor="white">
      <span class="celltext" datafld="Phone"></span>
    </td>
    <td valign="top"  align="center" bgcolor="white">
      <span class="celltext" datafld="Years"></span>
    </td>
    <td valign="top" bgcolor="white">
      <span class="celltext" datafld="Status"></span>
    </td>
  </tr>
</table>
```

7. Save your changes to FP2.htm.

8. Using Internet Explorer, open **FP2.htm**.

   Figure 2-33 displays the completed page with all of the records from the Emp1.xml document inserted into the table.

Figure 2-33	VIEWING THE RECORDS IN A SINGLE TABLE

records from the
Staff_Info recordset

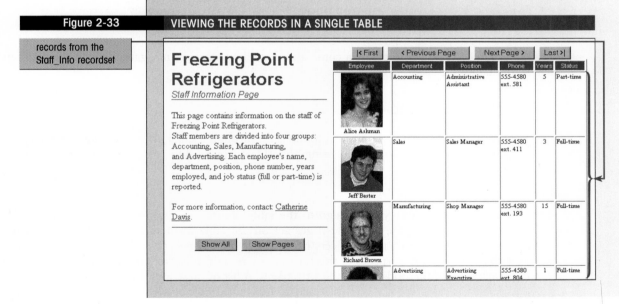

Working with Table Pages

Catherine realizes that as she adds more records to her XML document, the table in the Web page becomes increasingly long and unwieldy. With that in mind, Catherine would like to give users the option of limiting the number of records displayed at any one time to three. They could then move forward or backward through the recordset, three records at a time. This technique of breaking up the recordset into manageable chunks is called **paging**.

Specifying the Page Size

To create a table page, the first step is to add the **dataPageSize** attribute to the <table> tag. The syntax for this attribute is

```
dataPageSize="number"
```

where *number* is the number of records you want displayed in a single page. Add this attribute to the <table> tag now.

To define a page size:

1. Return to FP2.htm in your text editor.

2. Insert the attribute **dataPageSize="3"** for the <table> tag, as shown in Figure 2-34.

Figure 2-34   SPECIFYING A PAGE SIZE FOR THE TABLE

```
<table width="460" border="1" datasrc="#Staff_Info" datapagesize="3">
    <thead>
        <th bgcolor="blue" width="100"><span class="colhead">Employee</span></th>
        <th bgcolor="blue" width="90"><span class="colhead">Department</span></th>
        <th bgcolor="blue" width="100"><span class="colhead">Position</span></th>
        <th bgcolor="blue" width="80"><span class="colhead">Phone</span></th>
        <th bgcolor="blue" wdith="30"><span class="colhead">Years</span></th>
        <th bgcolor="blue" width="50"><span class="colhead">Status</span></th>
    </thead>
```

3. Save your changes to FP2.htm.

4. Using Internet Explorer, open **FP2.htm** and verify that only the first three records are displayed in the Web page.

The next step is to create a command that allows users to navigate through the pages in the table.

Navigating a Table Page

Before you can write a command to navigate through a table page, you must first assign a unique identifier to the table using the ID attribute. The syntax for assigning an ID attribute is

```
<table id="id">
```

where *id* is the name you'll assign to the table object. This step is necessary because the commands to navigate the table pages act on the table itself and not the recordset. Like Data Source Objects, table objects have a long list of properties and methods associated with them. For the purposes of this tutorial, we're only going to concern ourselves with the properties and methods associated with pages. A list of these is shown in Figure 2-35.

Figure 2-35   TABLE METHODS AND PROPERTIES

TABLE METHODS AND PROPERTIES	DESCRIPTION
id.firstPage()	Display the first page in the *id* table
id.previousPage()	Display the previous page in the table
id.nextPage()	Display the next page in the table

Figure 2-35	TABLE METHODS AND PROPERTIES (CONTINUED)	

TABLE METHODS AND PROPERTIES	DESCRIPTION
id.lastPage()	Display the last page in the table
id.dataPageSize=*n*	Set the number of pages in the *id* table to *n* pages

To run these commands, you can add the command to the onClick event handler of a <button> tag as you did for the buttons in Catherine's other page. For example, to move to the last page in a data table named "StaffTable," you enter the attribute

```
onClick="StaffTable.lastPage()"
```

Complete the following steps to add the appropriate table methods to the four buttons located above the table in Catherine's Web page.

To add the table methods to Catherine's Web page:

1. Return to FP2.htm in your text editor.

2. Assign the attribute **id="StaffTable"** to the <table> tag to give an ID name to the data table.

3. Locate the <button> tag for the "First" button and insert the attribute **onClick="StaffTable.firstPage()"**.

4. Locate the <button> tag for the "Previous" button and insert the attribute **onClick="StaffTable.previousPage()"**.

5. Locate the <button> tag for the "Next" button and insert the attribute **onClick="StaffTable.nextPage()"**.

6. Finally, locate the <button> tag for the "Last" button and insert the attribute **onClick="StaffTable.lastPage()"**.

Figure 2-36 shows the revised HTML code.

Figure 2-36	ENTERING THE PAGE METHODS

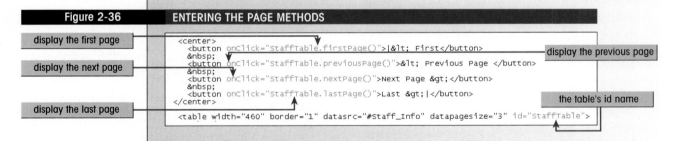

```
<center>
   <button onClick="StaffTable.firstPage()">|&lt; First</button>
    
   <button onClick="StaffTable.previousPage()">&lt; Previous Page </button>
    
   <button onClick="StaffTable.nextPage()">Next Page &gt;</button>
    
   <button onClick="StaffTable.lastPage()">Last &gt;|</button>
</center>

<table width="460" border="1" datasrc="#Staff_Info" datapagesize="3" id="StaffTable">
```

display the first page
display the next page
display the last page
display the previous page
the table's id name

7. Save your changes to FP2.htm.

8. Using Internet Explorer, reload **FP2.htm** and click the First, Previous Page, Next Page, and Last buttons to verify that they navigate you through the pages of the table as you expected.

Catherine also wants to provide users with the option of switching between a view of all records in the table and a view that displays the table by pages. To do this, you add a command to the button to change the dataPageSize attribute of the table. To show all of the records in the recordset, you must set the value of the page size to a very high value and then instruct the browser to move to the first page in the table. The complete command to accomplish this task is

```
onClick="StaffTable.dataPageSize=999999;StaffTable.firstPage()"
```

To restore the page size to three, use the command

```
onClick="StaffTable.dataPageSize=3"
```

Catherine has two buttons for this purpose located in the bottom left corner of the Web page. Modify these buttons now to solve Catherine's problem.

To modify the buttons:

1. Using your text editor, open **FP2.htm** if it is not currently open.

2. Locate the Show All <button> tag, and insert the text **onClick="StaffTable.dataPageSize=999999; StaffTable.firstPage()"**.

3. Locate the Show Pages <button> tag, and insert the attribute **onClick="StaffTable.dataPageSize=3"** with the <button tag>. Figure 2-37 shows the revised HTML code.

Figure 2-37	CHANGING THE DATAPAGESIZE

set the dataPageSize to an extremely large value and then display the first (and only) page

set the dataPageSize value to 3

```
<div id="Page_Title" datasrc="#Page_Info" datafld="Title"></div>
<div id="Page_Subtitle" datasrc="#Page_Info" datafld="Subtitle"></div>
<div id="Page_Text" datasrc="#Page_Info" datafld="Purpose"></div>
<div id="Page_Author">For more information, contact:
    <a datasrc="#Page_Info" datafld="Author_Email">
        <span datasrc="#Page_Info" datafld="Author"></span>
        </a>.
</div>

<center>
    <button onClick="StaffTable.dataPageSize=999999; StaffTable.firstPage()">Show All</button>
     
    <button onClick="StaffTable.dataPageSize=3">Show Pages</button>
</center>
</div>
```

4. Save your changes to FP2.htm.

5. Reload **FP2.htm** in Internet Explorer and verify that you can switch between a page view and a view of all records by clicking the Show Page and Show All buttons.

Working with Hierarchical Recordsets

Catherine has created another XML document, named Emp2.xml, which organizes employees by departments. Figure 2-38 shows a tree diagram of the elements in her document.

Figure 2-38   **LAYOUT OF THE EMP2.XML DOCUMENT**

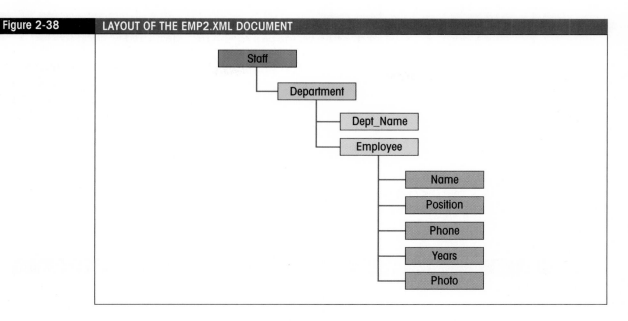

Up to this point, you've worked with simple recordsets where each record contains a fixed number of fields and is made up exclusively of character data. The layout displayed in Figure 2-38 shows a hierarchical recordset in which the Employee field contains not character data, but a record of fields describing each employee.

The syntax for binding a nested record to a table is

```
<table datasrc="#id" datafld="record">
  <tr>
    <td><span datafld="field1"></span></td>
    <td><span datafld="field2"></span></td>
  </tr>
</table>
```

where *id* is the name of the data island, *record* is the name of the field that contains the nested record, and *field1*, *field2*, etc., are fields within the nested record. Note that the main difference between this table format and the table format for a simple recordset is that you must include the name of the record element in the <table> tag. For example, to bind the Employee fields displayed in Figure 2-38 to a table, you create a table as follows:

```
<table datasrc="#Staff_Info" datafld="Employee">
  <tr>
    <td><span datafld="Name"></span></td>
    <td><span datafld="Position"></span></td>
    <td><span datafld="Phone"></span></td>
    . . .
  </tr>
</table>
```

If the recordset contains several levels of nested recordsets, you must include several levels of nested tables to match. For example, the layout shown in Figure 2-39 would be matched by the series of nested tables shown below.

```
<table datasrc="#id" datafld="record1">
  <tr>
  <td><table datasrc="#id" datafld="record2">
```

```
        <tr>
          <td><table datasrc="#id" datafld="record3">
                <tr>
                  <td><span datafld="field1"></span></td>
                  <td><span datafld="field2"></span></td>
                  <td><span datafld="field3"></span></td>
                </tr>
              </table>
          </td>
        </tr>
        </table>
    </td>
    </tr>
  </table>
```

Figure 2-39	SEVERAL LAYERS OF NESTED RECORDS

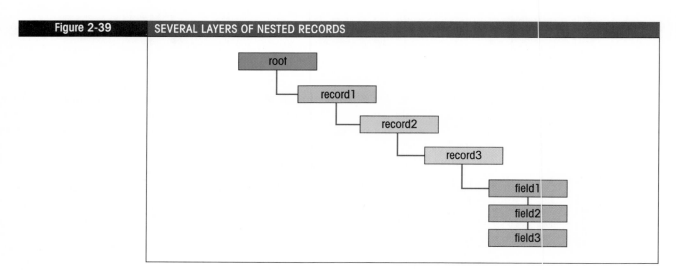

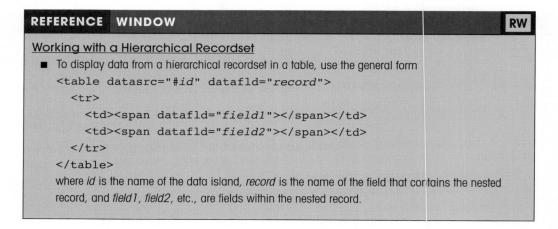

REFERENCE   WINDOW   RW

Working with a Hierarchical Recordset
■ To display data from a hierarchical recordset in a table, use the general form

```
<table datasrc="#id" datafld="record">
  <tr>
    <td><span datafld="field1"></span></td>
    <td><span datafld="field2"></span></td>
  </tr>
</table>
```

where *id* is the name of the data island, *record* is the name of the field that contains the nested record, and *field1*, *field2*, etc., are fields within the nested record.

Catherine has assembled one last draft of a Web page. This time, her Web page is based on the layout of the Emp2.xml document. Figure 2-40 shows the type of page she has in mind.

Figure 2-40	DRAFT OF CATHERINE'S FINAL WEB PAGE

employee information is grouped by department

With this page, employee information is grouped by department. The table displays information on all employees for a given department. To navigate from the current department to the next one in the recordset, Catherine wants users to be able to click the Next Department button located in the bottom left corner of the Web page.

To bind data to Catherine's page:

1. Using your text editor, open **Emp2.xml** from the Tutorial.02X/Tutorial folder on your Data Disk. Scroll through the document, noting the document structure, the name of the various elements, and the content of each element.

2. Close the file without saving any changes.

3. Using your text editor, open **FP3text.htm** and save the file as **FP3.htm**.

4. Locate the <xml> tag that created the data island for the FPInfo.xml document. Below it insert an <xml> tag to create a data island named "Staff_Info" that connects to the Emp2.xml document:

   ```
   <xml id="Staff_Info" src="Emp2.xml"></xml>
   ```

5. Locate the placeholder text, "Department Name," and add the following attribute to its <span> tag. Delete the placeholder text.

   ```
   datasrc="#Staff_Info" datafld="Dept_Name"
   ```

6. Locate the <table> tag and insert the following attributes:

   ```
   datasrc="#Staff_Info" datafld="Employee"
   ```

7. Following the same process you used for Catherine's other Web pages, delete all of the placeholder text in the table and add datafld attributes, binding the tags to the contents of the Emp2.xml document. To assist you, Figure 2-41 shows the revised code for this file, highlighted in red.

Figure 2-41 | BINDING TO A HIERARCHICAL RECORDSET

```
<body>
  <xml id="Page_Info" src="FPInfo.xml"></xml>
  <xml id="Staff_Info" src="Emp2.xml"></xml>

  <div id="Page_Data">

    <div id="Page_Title" datasrc="#Page_Info" datafld="Title"></div>
    <div id="Page_Subtitle" datasrc="#Page_Info" datafld="Subtitle"></div>
    <div id="Page_Text" datasrc="#Page_Info" datafld="Purpose"></div>
    <div id="Page_Author">For more information, contact:
      <a datasrc="#Page_Info" datafld="Author_Email">
        <span datasrc="#Page_Info" datafld="Author"></span>
      </a>.
    </div>
    <button>
      Next Department
    </button>
  </div>

  <center>
    <span id="DName" datasrc="#Staff_Info" datafld="Dept_Name"></span><br>
  </center>

  <table width="460" border="1" datasrc="#Staff_Info" datafld="Employee">
    <thead>
      <th bgcolor="blue" width="100"><span class="colhead">Employee</span></th>
      <th bgcolor="blue" width="100"><span class="colhead">Position</span></th>
      <th bgcolor="blue" width="80"><span class="colhead">Phone</span></th>
      <th bgcolor="blue" wdith="30"><span class="colhead">Years</span></th>
      <th bgcolor="blue" width="50"><span class="colhead">Status</span></th>
    </thead>
    <tr><td align="center" bgcolor="white">
        <img datafld="Photo"><br>
        <span class="celltext" datafld="Name"></span>
      </td>
      <td valign="top" bgcolor="white">
        <span class="celltext" datafld="Position"></span>
      </td>
      <td valign="top" bgcolor="white">
        <span class="celltext" datafld="Phone"></span>
      </td>
      <td valign="top" align="center" bgcolor="white">
        <span class="celltext" datafld="Years"></span>
      </td>
      <td valign="top" bgcolor="white">
        <span class="celltext" datafld="Status"></span>
      </td>
    </tr>
  </table>

</body>
```

8. Save your changes to FP3.htm.

9. Using Internet Explorer, open **FP3.htm** and verify that it shows information on employees from the Accounting department, as shown in Figure 2-42.

| Figure 2-42 | | **EMPLOYEES FROM THE ACCOUNTING DEPARTMENT** |

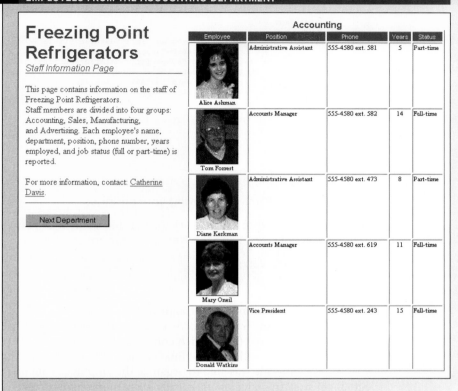

To show employee data from other departments, you move to the next record in the department recordset. Because this is the topmost recordset in the hierarchy, you can use the following command to accomplish this:

```
Staff_Info.recordset.moveNext()
```

There is only one button in Catherine's Web page to navigate through the recordset, so when users reach the last record, Catherine would like them sent back to the first record. The following code is used to add the desired functionality to the Next Department button:

```
Staff_Info.recordset.moveNext();
if (Staff_Info.recordset.EOF) Staff_Info.recordset.moveFirst()
```

To customize the Next Department button:

1. Return to FP3.htm in your text editor.

2. Locate the <button> tag for the Next Department button and insert the following code within the <button> tag (see Figure 2-43):

```
onClick="Staff_Info.recordset.moveNext();
  if (Staff_Info.recordset.EOF) Staff_Info.recordset.move
First()"
```

| Figure 2-43 | INSERTING A COMMAND TO MOVE TO THE NEXT DEPARTMENT |

```
<div id="Page_Data">

  <div id="Page_Title" datasrc="#Page_Info" datafld="Title"></div>
  <div id="Page_Subtitle" datasrc="#Page_Info" datafld="Subtitle"></div>
  <div id="Page_Text" datasrc="#Page_Info" datafld="Purpose"></div>
  <div id="Page_Author">For more information, contact:
    <a datasrc="#Page_Info" datafld="Author_Email">
      <span datasrc="#Page_Info" datafld="Author"></span>
    </a>.
  </div>
  <button onClick="Staff_Info.recordset.moveNext();
              if (Staff_Info.recordset.EOF) Staff_Info.recordset.moveFirst()">
    Next Department
  </button>
</div>
```

3. Close the FP3.htm file, saving your changes.

4. Reload **FP3.htm** in Internet Explorer and verify that you can move through the recordset by clicking the Next Department button.

5. Close your Web browser.

Note that as you moved through the department recordset, the list of employees was automatically changed to the correct department. This is because as you moved to the next record, the Employee field, which contains the nested record, was also changed.

Catherine is pleased with the final version of her staff Web page. By using a hierarchical recordset, Catherine was able to organize the employee data in a reasonable and useful way. She'll get back to you if she needs any more work done on this issue.

Session 2.3 QUICK CHECK

1. Where should you put the datasrc attribute if you want to use table binding?

2. What is paging?

3. How do you set the size of a table to five pages?

4. A table object has the name "PTable." What command would you use to display the last page in the table?

5. What command would you use to change the page size of PTable to six?

6. How do you display a hierarchical recordset in a table?

REVIEW ASSIGNMENTS

Catherine has been using the staff page you've designed for a few weeks now. Her associates at Freezing Point Refrigerators have seen her work and would like to use data binding with some of their XML documents. Jason Lewis maintains a Web page describing the various refrigerators sold by the company. He would like to bind the contents of this page with some of his XML documents.

Jason has collected the following information on each refrigerator model: the model name, the selling price, the refrigerator's cubic capacity, the refrigerator's dimensions, whether the model is energy efficient or not, and whether the freezer unit is located above or side-by-side with the main unit. Jason has also organized the refrigerator models into two types: those that are designed to fit into cabinet spaces and those that are freestanding.

Jason has created three XML documents named SInfo.xml, Refg1.xml, and Refg2.xml. The SInfo.xml document contains information about the company that Jason wants to include in any Web page he creates. The Refg1.xml document contains data on individual refrigerator models in a simple recordset. The Refg2.xml document contains a hierarchical recordset in which the models are divided based on whether they are cabinet style or freestanding.

Jason would like to create the following three Web pages from these documents: Inv1.htm, Inv2.htm, and Inv3.htm. The purpose of these pages is similar to the three pages that Catherine created for her staff directory. The Inv1.htm Web page should display each refrigerator model in a separate page. The Inv2.htm page should display all of the refrigerator models in a single table that can be broken into individual pages. The Inv3.htm page should display the model data broken down by model type.

Jason has already created the basic format for these three pages. He needs your help in binding those pages with the contents of his XML documents and inserting commands to navigate through the records in the recordsets.

To complete this task:

1. Using your text editor, open and review the contents of the **Refg1.xml** and **Refg2.xml** documents, located in the Tutorial.02X/Review folder of your Data Disk. Take some time to become familiar with their contents and the document structure. Close the documents without saving any changes.

2. Using your text editor, open **Invtxt1.htm** from the Tutorial.02X/Review folder and save the file as **Inv1.htm**.

3. Create two data islands. The first, named "Sinfo," should point to the contents of the SInfo.xml file. The second, named "Ref_Info," should point to the contents of the Refg1.xml file.

4. Bind the text of the page's title, subtitle, and purpose with the contents of the Title, Subtitle, and Purpose fields in the SInfo data island. Bind the target of the author's hyperlink to the value of the Author_Email field of the SInfo data island. Bind the text of the author's name to the Author field.

5. Within the table describing an individual refrigerator model, bind the following items to fields in the Ref_Info data island:

   - Bind the inline image to the Photo field.
   - Bind the model type to the MType field.
   - Bind the price of the refrigerator to the Price field.
   - Bind the capacity and dimensions of the refrigerator to the Capacity and Dimensions fields.
   - Bind the energy efficiency and freezer location to the Energy and Freezer fields.

6. Add the following commands to the buttons located at the bottom of the page:

   - If the user clicks the First or Last buttons, display the first or last records in the Ref_Info recordset.

- If the user clicks the Next button, display the next record in the Ref_Info recordset, unless this causes the Data Source Object to move off the edge of the recordset.
- If the user clicks the Previous button, display the previous records in the Ref_Info recordset, unless this would cause the Data Source Object to move off the edge of the recordset.

7. Save your changes to Inv1.htm. Open the file in your Internet Explorer browser and verify that you can scroll though the contents of the Ref_Info data island by clicking the buttons on the Web page.

8. Using your text editor, open the **Invtxt2.htm** file from the Tutorial.02X/Review folder and save the file as **Inv2.htm**. Create data islands named "Sinfo" and "Ref_Info" for the SInfo.xml and Refg1.xml documents.

9. Bind the page's title, subtitle, purpose, author name, and author hyperlink to the appropriate fields in the SInfo data island.

10. Set the data page size for the table to 4. Bind the contents of the table to the appropriate fields in the Ref_Info data island.

11. Add the following commands to the buttons on the page:

- If the user clicks the First, Previous Page, Next Page, or Last Page buttons, display the first, previous, next, or last page of records in the table.
- If the user clicks the Show All button, set the data page size to an extremely high number.
- If the user clicks the Show Pages button, set the data page size to 4.

12. Save your changes to Inv2.htm. Open the file in your Internet Explorer browser and verify that you can view the records in the Ref_Info recordset by pages.

13. Using your text editor, open **Invtxt3.htm** from the Tutorial.02X/Review folder and save the file as **Inv3.htm**. Create data islands named "Sinfo" and "Ref_Info2" for the SInfo.xml and Refg2.xml documents.

14. Bind the page's title, subtitle, purpose, author name, and author hyperlink to the appropriate fields in the SInfo data island. Bind the model type text to the MType field in the Ref_Info2 data island. Bind contents of the table to the appropriate fields in the Ref_Info2 data island.

Explore 15. Edit the Cabinet Refrigerators radio button so that it displays the first record in the Ref_Info2 data island.

Explore 16. Edit the Freestanding Refrigerators radio button so that it displays the last record in the Ref_Info2 data island.

17. Save your changes to Inv3.htm. Open the file in your Internet Explorer browser and verify that you can view the different model types in the recordset by clicking the appropriate radio button.

18. Print out the contents of Inv1.htm, Inv2.htm, and Inv3.htm. Hand in your printouts and files to your instructor.

CASE PROBLEMS

Case 1. Online Electronics, Inc. Brett Keyes is a product manager for Online Electronics (OE), an Internet superstore. He's working on a Web page that lists OE car stereo products. Brett has already created a draft of the Web page, and the product list is stored in an XML document named OE.xml. He needs your help in binding the data to the Web page.

Figure 2-44 shows the structure of Brett's XML document. The XML document is organized in the form of a hierarchical recordset. The top level indicates the car stereo type. Brett has organized the car stereos into four distinct groups: CD players/receivers for less than $200 and greater than $200, and cassette tape players selling for less than $50 and greater than $50. For each car stereo, Brett has recorded a product ID (PID), the stereo's manufacturer, the name of the product, and the product's selling price.

Figure 2-44

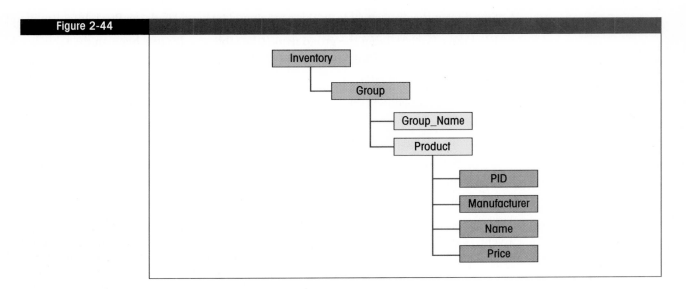

Brett would like this hierarchical recordset displayed within a single table with the information on each individual car stereo nested within that stereo's product group. Figure 2-45 shows a preview of the page you'll create.

Figure 2-45

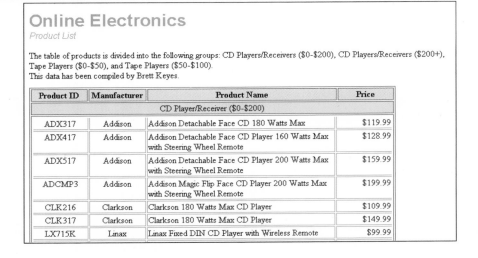

Online Electronics
Product List

The table of products is divided into the following groups: CD Players/Receivers ($0-$200), CD Players/Receivers ($200+), Tape Players ($0-$50), and Tape Players ($50-$100).
This data has been compiled by Brett Keyes.

Product ID	Manufacturer	Product Name	Price
CD Player/Receiver ($0-$200)			
ADX317	Addison	Addison Detachable Face CD 180 Watts Max	$119.99
ADX417	Addison	Addison Detachable Face CD Player 160 Watts Max with Steering Wheel Remote	$128.99
ADX517	Addison	Addison Detachable Face CD Player 200 Watts Max with Steering Wheel Remote	$159.99
ADCMP3	Addison	Addison Magic Flip Face CD Player 200 Watts Max with Steering Wheel Remote	$199.99
CLK216	Clarkson	Clarkson 180 Watts Max CD Player	$109.99
CLK317	Clarkson	Clarkson 180 Watts Max CD Player	$149.99
LX715K	Linax	Linax Fixed DIN CD Player with Wireless Remote	$99.99

Brett also has an XML document named OETitles.xml that contains some of the page titles and introductory text he wants to display in the document.

To complete this task:

1. Using your text editor, open **OETitles.xml** and **OE.xml** from the Tutorial.02X/Cases folder of your Data Disk. Take some time to view these documents, becoming familiar with their content and structure. Close both files without saving any changes to them.

2. Using your text editor, open **OEInvtxt.htm** located in the Tutorial.02X/Cases folder. Save the file as **OEInv.htm**.

3. Create two data islands named "Page_Info" and "Prod_Info" that point to the OETitles.xml and OE.xml files, respectively.

4. Bind the page's title, subtitle, and introduction to the Title, Subtitle, and Intro fields of the Page_Info data island.

5. Specify that the product table on this page should be bound with the Prod_Info data island.

6. Bind the row containing the group name (the table row located beneath the table heading) to the contents of the Group_Name field.

Explore 7. Bind the embedded table to the Prod_Info data island and the Product field.

8. Within the embedded table, bind each cell to the appropriate fields in the Prod_Info data island.

9. Save your changes to the file.

10. Using Internet Explorer, open **OEInv.htm** and verify that it shows information on all of the car stereo products divided into Brett's four groups.

11. Print OEInv.htm, and hand in your files and printouts to your instructor.

Case 2. Central High School Class Reunion Committee. Cindy Carlson works for Special Events, a company that promotes and organizes parties, reunions, receptions, and other special events. Cindy has been developing a class reunion Web page for Central High School. Cindy's idea is to have several computer terminals located at the class reunion site allowing participants to access online information about the party and their classmates.

Cindy has already collected information about the participants of a class reunion for Central High School, and she's stored that data in an XML document named CHList.xml. The structure of the XML document is shown in Figure 2-46.

Figure 2-46

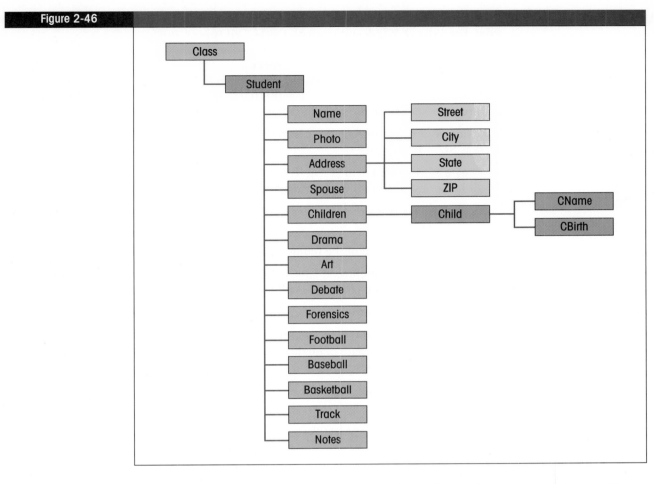

Cindy's document is organized in a hierarchical recordset with several nested levels. Her document includes information on each student's name, address, and children; activities they were involved with in school; special notes about their high school experiences; and a current photo. Figure 2-47 shows a preview of the page that Cindy wants you to create.

Figure 2-47

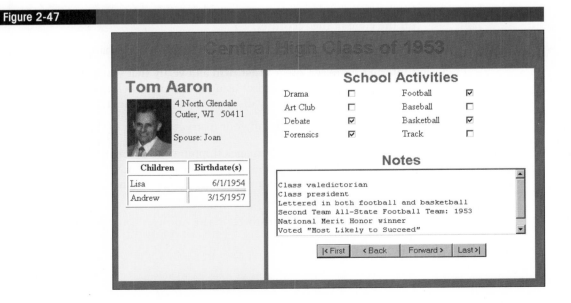

Cindy has already created a draft of the Web page, but she needs your help in binding the contents of her XML document with the HTML file.

To complete this task:

1. Using your text editor, open **CHList.xml** from the Tutorial.02X/Cases folder of your Data Disk. Take some time to view this file to become familiar with its content and structure. Close the file without saving any changes.

2. Using your text editor, open **SListtxt.htm** from the Tutorial.02X/Cases folder and save it as **SList.htm**.

3. Create a data island named "Stud_Info" that points to the CHList.xml file. Assume that all fields described in the following steps belong to this data source.

4. Locate the <div> tag that contains the participant's name and bind the contents of this tag to the SName field.

5. Bind the inline image of the reunion participant to the Photo field.

6. Bind the participant's Street, City, State, and ZIP fields to the embedded table in the SList.htm document. (*Hint*: You will have to bind this data as a hierachical recordset.)

7. Bind the Spouse field to the <span> tag containing the spouse's name.

Explore   8. Bind the CName and CBirth fields to the embedded table listing the children of each participant and their date of birth. (*Hint*: You will have to bind this data as a hierachical recordset with two nesting levels.)

Explore   9. Bind the checkboxes in the table to the Drama, Football, Art, Baseball, Debate, Basketball, Forensics, and Track fields.

Explore   10. Bind the Notes text area to the Notes field.

11. Add the following commands to the buttons at the bottom of the page:

   ■ If the user clicks the First or Last buttons, display the first or last records in the Stud_Info recordset.

   ■ If the user clicks the Next button, display the next record in the Stud_Info recordset unless this would cause the Data Source Object to move off the edge of the recordset.

   ■ If the user clicks the Previous button, display the previous records in the Stud_Info recordset unless this would cause the Data Source Object to move off the edge of the recordset.

12. Using your text editor, print the revised code, and save your changes to the SList.htm file.

13. Using Internet Explorer, open **SList.htm** and verify that you can properly scroll through the records in the recordset using the navigation buttons and that all values from the data source are properly displayed in the document.

14. Hand in your printouts and files to your instructor.

Case 3. AutoMaze, Inc. David Hansen manages shipping and receiving for AutoMaze, an auto parts superstore. The company stores shipping manifests in XML documents and then makes them accessible to employees via the company's intranet. David is exploring ways to bind the XML data to a Web page.

He has a sample shipping manifest stored in the AutoOrd.xml file. The structure of this file is shown in Figure 2-48.

Figure 2-48

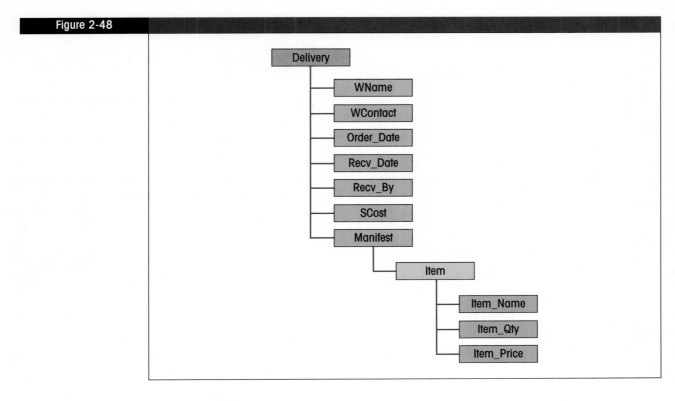

A preview of the Web page you'll create for David is shown in Figure 2-49. David has already created a draft of this page; your job will be to insert the data binding.

Figure 2-49

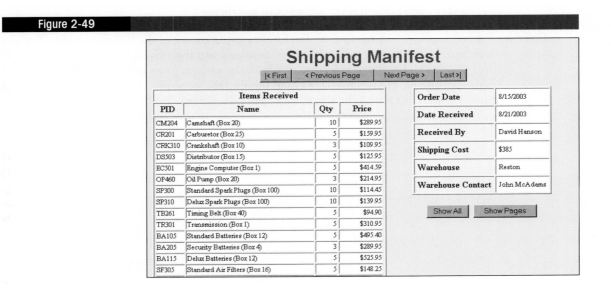

To complete this task:

1. Using your text editor, open **AutoOrd.xml** from the Tutorial.02X/Cases folder of your Data Disk. Take some time to view this file to become familiar with its content and structure. Close the file without saving any changes.

2. Using your text editor, open **AMtxt.htm** from the Tutorial.02X/Cases folder and save it as **AM.htm**.

3. Create a data island named "Order_Info" that points to the AutoOrd.xml file. All of the fields described in the following steps belong to this data source.

Explore

4. The first nested table in the file is used to display the items on the shipping manifest. Bind the outer table to the Manifest field. Bind the inner table to the Item field. Bind the cells of the inner table to the corresponding fields in the nested recordset from the AutoOrd.xml file. Set the id name of the inner table to "Orders". Set the page size of the inner table to six records.

5. The second table on the right edge of the Web page displays descriptive information about the shipping manifest. Bind each of the items in this table to the corresponding fields in the data source.

6. Add commands to the first set of four buttons to move to the first, previous, next, and last page of the Orders table.

7. Add commands to the second set of buttons to show all pages in the Orders table or to reset the page size of the Orders table back to six.

8. Print the AM.htm file, and close the file, saving your changes.

9. Using Internet Explorer, open **AM.htm** and verify that you can use the buttons on the page to navigate as you expected through the pages in the Orders table.

10. Hand in your file and printouts to your instructor.

Case 4. Travel Scotland Touring Co. Ian Findlay is the owner of the touring agency Travel Scotland, Inc., which organizes tours to Scotland and the British Isles for travelers from all over the world. He stores information about the various tours offered by his agency in an XML document. He needs your help in binding the data from his document to a Web page. Figure 2-50 shows the structure of Ian's document, tour.xml.

Figure 2-50

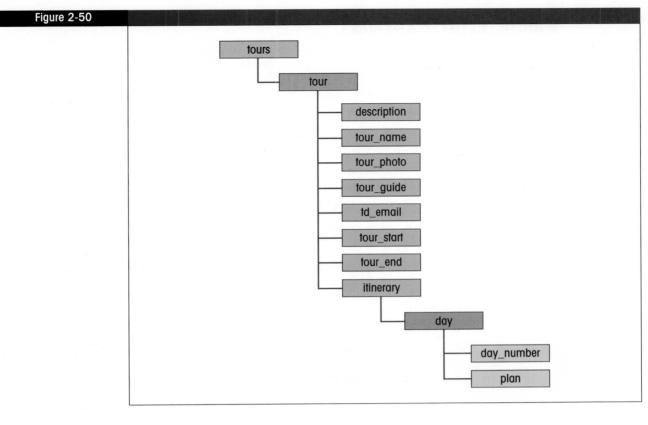

The description field contains a CDATA section of HTML code that Ian wants you to insert directly into the document. The itinerary field contains a nested recordset describing the events of each day of the tour. There are four tours in his file: the Lake District tour, the Hebrides tour, the Highland tour, and the Castles of Scotland tour. Ian has not created a Web page for his data yet. He has left the design up to you.

To complete this task:

1. Using your text editor, create a Web page named **Scotland.htm** to be stored in the Tutorial.02X/Cases folder of your Data Disk.

2. The Web page should display information about a single tour at a time, and the itinerary for each tour should be displayed as a table in the Web page.

3. The page should display an image from the selected tour (the image source file is indicated in the photo field).

4. The page should display a hyperlink to the e-mail address of the tour guide (found in the td_email field).

Explore 5. The information from the description field should be displayed in the Web page using the HTML formatting codes indicated in the tour.xml document.

6. The rest of the tour information should be displayed elsewhere in the Web page.

7. The page should include navigation buttons to move through the tours in the XML document.

8. When you are finished, print out the code for Scotland.htm and then view the page using Internet Explorer to verify that you can view information about the different Travel Scotland tours as you intended.

9. Hand in your printouts and files to your instructor.

QUICK CHECK ANSWERS

Session 2.1

1. **a.** Data binding is a technique in which the Web page's content is drawn from a data source.

   b. A field is an element that contains a single item of information.

   c. A record is a collection of fields.

   d. A recordset is a collection of records.

2. A hierarchical recordset can contain nested recordsets. A simple recordset cannot.

3. A data island is the data attached to a Web page through the process of data binding.

4. `<xml id="CompInfo" src="Company.xml"></xml>`

5. `<span datasrc="#CompInfo" datafld="CName"></span>`

6. as the value of the src attribute

7. The $Text field contains the character data from all of the fields in a record, not including attribute values.

Session 2.2

1. as a field

2. The field element becomes a record element with the attribute becoming one of the fields of the record element. The text in the field can only be accessed through the $Text field name.

3. `CInfo.recordset.moveLast()`

4. `CInfo.recordset.movePrevious()`

5. `CInfo.recordset.move(5)`

6. EOF

7. Index

Session 2.3

1. within the <table> tag

2. the process by which a table is divided into groups of records called pages

3. Include the dataPageSize="5" attribute in the table tag.

4. `PTable.lastPage()`

5. `PTable.dataPageSize=6`

6. If the recordset contains several levels of nested recordsets, you must include several levels of nested tables to match.

OBJECTIVES

In this tutorial you will:

- Create a Document Type Definition
- Learn how to declare elements
- Work with nested elements
- Learn how to declare attributes
- Create parsed and unparsed entities
- Learn how to validate an XML document

CREATING A VALID XML DOCUMENT

Working with a Document Type Definition

CASE

Pixal Digital Products

Pixal Digital Products sells imaging hardware and software such as scanners, digital cameras, copiers, and digital tablets to individual consumers and businesses. Kristin Laughlin is the customer service manager at Pixal, and part of her job is to record information on Pixal's customers, including the individual orders they make.

Kristin is starting to use XML to record this information and has already created several XML documents containing information on customers and their orders. Eventually, Kristin wants to bind the data in the XML documents with a Web page. Kristin knows that her document needs to be well formed, following the rules of XML syntax exactly, but she would also like her document to follow certain rules regarding content. For example, every customer entered into her document must have a name, phone number, and address. Every customer order must contain a complete list of the items purchased, including the date they were ordered. In XML terms, she wants to create documents that are both well formed and valid. Kristin has asked for your help to create a valid document that adheres to both the rules of XML and the rules she has set up for the document's content and structure.

SESSION 3.1

In this tutorial, you'll learn how XML can be used to create a valid document. You'll explore how to create and use internal and external document type definitions (DTDs). You'll also learn how to create element declarations to indicate which elements are valid in the document. Finally, you'll learn how to specify your document's structure, indicating which, and how many, elements are nested inside other elements.

Creating a Valid Document

In the last tutorial, you learned how to bind the contents of your XML document with an HTML file in order to publish the document to the Web or a corporate intranet in a useful way. In this and the following tutorials, you'll explore how XML documents can be validated to prevent errors in their content or structure.

You meet with Kristin to discuss the information she's collecting on Pixal's customers. To keep things to a manageable size, Kristin has limited her document to a subset of only three customers. Figure 3-1 shows the information she's entered for those customers.

Figure 3-1   CUSTOMER INFORMATION COLLECTED BY KRISTIN

Customer		Orders		Item	Qty.	Price
Name:	Mr. David Lynn	OrderID:	OR10311	DCT3Z	1	559.95
CustID:	Cust201	Date:	8/1/2004	SM128	1	199.95
Type:	home			RCL	2	29.95
Address:	211 Fox Street	OrderID:	OR11424	BCE4L	1	59.95
	Greenville, NH 80021	Date:	9/14/2004			
Phone:	(315) 555-1812					
E-mail:	dylnn@nhs.net					
Name:	Mrs. Jean Kaufmann	OrderID:	OR10899	WBC	1	59.99
CustID:	Cust202	Date:	8/11/2004			
Type:						
Address:	411 East Oak Avenue			RCA	2	5.95
	Cashton, MI 20401					
Phone:	(611) 555-4033					
E-mail:	JKaufmann@cshweb.com					
Name:	Adservices	OrderID:	OR11201	SCL4C	3	179.99
CustID:	Cust203	Date:	9/15/2004			
Type:	business					
Address:	55 Washburn Lane					
	Creighton, UT 98712					
Phone:	(811) 555-2987					
E-mail:						

For each customer, Kristin has recorded customer name, customer ID, type (home or business), address, phone number, and e-mail address. Note that she was not able to determine the customer type for Mrs. Jean Kaufmann or an e-mail address for Adservices.

Each customer has made one or more separate orders. For each order, Kristin has recorded an order ID number and the date the order was placed. Finally, within each order, Kristin has entered the items purchased, the quantity of each item, and the price.

She's already placed this information in an XML document. Open this file now.

To open Kristin's document:

1. Use your text editor to open the **Ordertxt.xml** document located in the Tutorial.03X/Tutorial folder of your Data Disk.

2. Save the file as **Orders.xml**.

Figure 3-2 displays the contents of the Orders.xml document for the first customer.

Figure 3-2   **THE FIRST CUSTOMER IN THE ORDERS.XML DOCUMENT**

```
<Customers>
    <Customer CustID="Cust201" CustType="home">
        <Name Title="Mr.">David Lynn</Name>
        <Address>
            <![CDATA[
            211 Fox Street
            Greenville, NH 80021
            ]]>
        </Address>
        <Phone>(315) 555-1812</Phone>
        <E-mail>dlynn@nhs.net</E-mail>
        <Orders>
            <Order OrderID="OR10311" OrderBy="Cust201">
                <Order_date>8/1/2004</Order_date>
                <Items>
                    <Item ItemPrice="599.95">DCT3Z</Item>
                    <Item ItemPrice="199.95">SM128</Item>
                    <Item ItemPrice="29.95" ItemQty="2">RCL</Item>
                </Items>
            </Order>
            <Order OrderID="OR11424" OrderBy="Cust201">
                <Order_date>9/14/2004</Order_date>
                <Items>
                    <Item ItemPrice="59.95">BCE4L</Item>
                </Items>
            </Order>
        </Orders>
    </Customer>
```

3. Examine the contents of Kristin's document. In particular, compare the elements entered in the document with the table in Figure 3-1.

Note that some of the elements in Kristin's document, like Name and Phone, can appear only once for each customer, whereas others, like Order and Item, can appear multiple times. The E-mail element appears to be optional: two customers have an e-mail address and one does not. Some of the attributes also appear to be optional. There is no need for the Title attribute when the customer is a company, nor has Kristin included an ItemQty attribute when the number of items ordered is one.

Kristin has created the diagram shown in Figure 3-3 to better illustrate the structure of the elements and attributes. Optional elements are indicated by dotted lines. Note that Kristin requires there be at least one order per customer. Also, each order needs to contain at least one item. Optional attributes are surrounded by square brackets. There are two optional attributes in the document: Title associated with the Name element and ItemQty associated with the Item element.

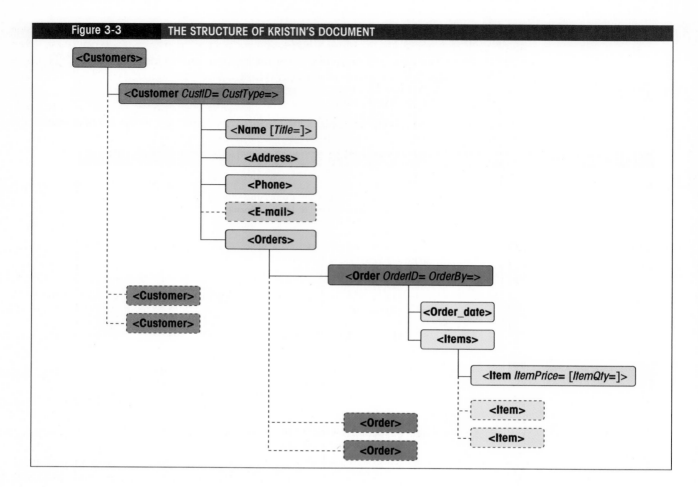

Figure 3-3 **THE STRUCTURE OF KRISTIN'S DOCUMENT**

The document structure is important to Kristin. As information is stored in this document, it is important that customer information include the address and phone number for each customer, the items ordered, and the date the order was placed. In XML terms, this means that her documents have to be not only well formed but also valid. XML documents can be validated using either DTDs (Document Type Definitions) or schemas. In this tutorial, we'll explore how to create and use DTDs.

Declaring a DTD

Used in conjunction with an XML parser that supports data validation, a DTD can be used to:

- ensure that all required elements are present in the document
- prevent undefined elements from being used in the document
- enforce a specific data structure on the document
- specify the use of element attributes and define their permissible values
- define default values for attributes
- describe how the parser should access non-XML or nontextual content

There can only be one DTD per XML document. To create a DTD, you must first enter a document type declaration into the XML document. Despite their similarity in names, a document type declaration is different than a document type definition. A document type definition is the collection of rules or declarations that define the content and structure of the document. A **document type declaration** attaches those rules to the document's content.

When we speak of the DTD, it should be understood that this refers to the document type definition and not the declaration. For brevity, the document type declaration is often referred to as the **DOCTYPE declaration** for reasons you'll soon understand. There can only be one DOCTYPE declaration in an XML document, and it must be placed before any document content.

Although there can also be only one DTD, the DTD can be divided into two parts: an internal subset and an external subset. The **internal subset** is a set of declarations placed in the same file as the document content, whereas the **external subset** is located in a separate file.

The DOCTYPE declaration for an internal subset is

```
<!DOCTYPE root
[
   declarations
]>
```

where *root* is the name of the document's root element, and *declarations* are the statements that comprise the DTD. If the name of the *root* attribute doesn't match the name of the document's root element, the XML parser will report an error and stop processing the document.

For external subsets, the DOCTYPE declaration takes two possible forms, one that uses a SYSTEM location and one that uses a PUBLIC location. The syntax of the declarations are

```
<!DOCTYPE root SYSTEM "URL">
```

or

```
<!DOCTYPE root PUBLIC "identifier" "URL">
```

where *root* is once again the document's root element, *identifier* is a text string that tells an application how to locate the external subset, and *URL* is the location and filename of the external subset. The PUBLIC location form is used when the DTD has to be limited to an internal system or when the XML document is part of an old SGML application. If the application can't locate the external subset from the public identifier, it uses the location and file specified by the URL. The SYSTEM location form doesn't include a public identifier; instead it simply specifies the name and location of the external subset through the "*URL*" value. In practice, unless your application requires a public identifier, you can and should use the SYSTEM location form.

Finally, a DOCTYPE declaration can indicate both an external and an internal subset. The syntax for this declaration is as follows:

```
<!DOCTYPE root SYSTEM "URL"
[
  declarations
]>
```

or

```
<!DOCTYPE root PUBLIC "identifier" "URL"
[
   declarations
]>
```

There are some advantages to using an internal DTD. By placing the DTD within the document, you can compare the DTD to the document's content without having to switch between files. However, the real power of XML comes from an external DTD that can be shared among many documents written by different authors. A common DTD forces those documents to use the same elements, attributes, and document structure.

If a document contains both an internal and external subset, the internal subset has precedence over the external subset if there is conflict between the two. This is useful when an external subset is shared among several documents. The external subset would define some basic rules for all of the documents, and the internal subset would define those rules that are specific to each document (see Figure 3-4).

| Figure 3-4 | COMBINING AN EXTERNAL AND INTERNAL DTD SUBSET |

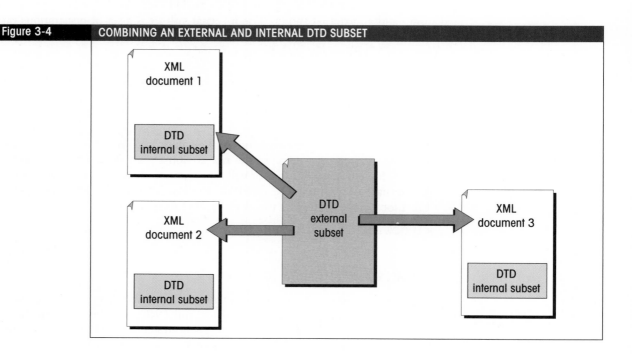

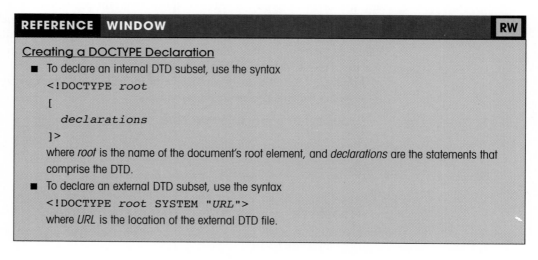

REFERENCE WINDOW   **RW**

Creating a DOCTYPE Declaration

- To declare an internal DTD subset, use the syntax

```
<!DOCTYPE root
[
   declarations
]>
```

  where *root* is the name of the document's root element, and *declarations* are the statements that comprise the DTD.
- To declare an external DTD subset, use the syntax

```
<!DOCTYPE root SYSTEM "URL">
```

  where *URL* is the location of the external DTD file.

Writing the Document Type Declaration

Kristin decides to add the DTD directly to the Orders.xml document so she can compare the DTD to the document's actual contents.

To create the document type declaration:

1. Below the XML declaration, enter the following comment line, followed by a blank line:

```
<!-- document type declaration follows -->
```

2. Next, insert the following lines below the comment:

```
<!DOCTYPE Customers
[

]>
```

Remember that "Customers" is the root element of Kristin's document and therefore must be the *root* attribute of the DOCTYPE declaration.

Figure 3-5 displays the revised code for the Orders.xml document.

Figure 3-5	INSERTING AN INTERNAL DTD SUBSET

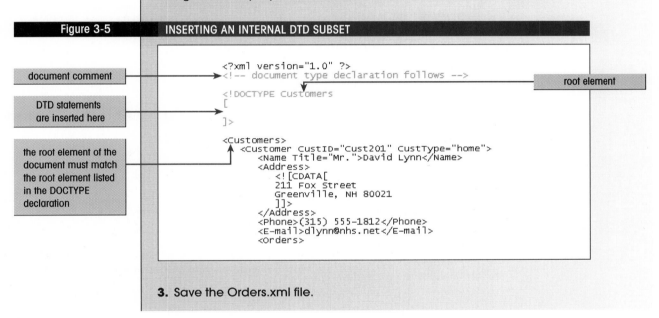

document comment

DTD statements are inserted here

the root element of the document must match the root element listed in the DOCTYPE declaration

root element

```
<?xml version="1.0" ?>
<!-- document type declaration follows -->

<!DOCTYPE Customers
[

]>

<Customers>
    <Customer CustID="Cust201" CustType="home">
        <Name Title="Mr.">David Lynn</Name>
        <Address>
            <![CDATA[
            211 Fox Street
            Greenville, NH 80021
            ]]>
        </Address>
        <Phone>(315) 555-1812</Phone>
        <E-mail>dlynn@nhs.net</E-mail>
        <Orders>
```

3. Save the Orders.xml file.

Now that you've created the document type declaration, you're ready to define the structure of Kristin's document.

Declaring **Document Elements**

In a valid document, every element used in the document must be declared in the DTD. An **element type declaration** specifies the name of the element and indicates what kind of content the element can contain. It can even specify the order in which elements appear in the document. The syntax of an element declaration is

```
<!ELEMENT element content-model>
```

where *element* is the name of the element. The element name is case sensitive, so if the element name is Products in the declaration, it must be entered as Products in the XML document. Element names cannot contain any spaces or reserved symbols such as "<" or ">."

The *content-model* specifies what type of content the element contains. Generally, elements contain either text or other elements. For example, in Kristin's document, the Name element contains a text string identifying the name of the customer. The Customer element contains five elements (Name, Address, Phone, E-mail, and Orders). We refer to the Customer element in this case as the **parent element** and the five elements it contains as **child elements**.

DTDs define five different types of element content:

- **Any elements**. There are no restrictions on the element's content.
- **Empty elements**. The element cannot store any content.
- **Character data**. The element can only contain a text string.
- **Elements**. The element can only contain child elements.
- **Mixed**. The element contains both a text string and child elements.

Let's investigate each of these types in more detail.

ANY Content

The most general type of content model is ANY, which allows the declared element to store any type of content. The syntax for declaring that an element can contain anything is as follows:

```
<!ELEMENT element ANY>
```

For example, the following declaration in the DTD

```
<!ELEMENT Products ANY>
```

would allow the Products element to take any of the following forms in the XML document:

```
<Products>SLR100 Digital Camera</Products>
<Products/>

<Products>
      <Name>SLR100</Name>
      <Type>Digital Camera</Name>
</Products>
```

Allowing an element to contain any type of content has limited use in document validation. After all, the idea behind validating a document is to enforce a particular set of rules on the elements and their content.

EMPTY Content

The EMPTY content model is reserved for elements that store no content. The syntax for an empty element declaration is as follows:

```
<!ELEMENT element EMPTY>
```

The following element declaration

```
<!ELEMENT IMG EMPTY>
```

would only allow the following forms for the IMG element:

```
<IMG></IMG>
```

or

```
<IMG />
```

Attempting to add content to any empty element results in the parser rejecting the document as invalid.

Character Content

Elements that can store only text strings are declared as follows:

```
<!ELEMENT element (#PCDATA)>
```

The keyword, #PCDATA, stands for "parsed-character data." **Parsed-character data** is any well-formed text string. Most text strings are well formed, except those that contain symbols reserved by XML, such as "<," ">," or "&."

Child elements are not allowed with this declaration. For example, if the DTD declares the Name element as follows:

```
<!ELEMENT Name (#PCDATA)>
```

this would be a valid use of the Name element:

```
<Name>Lea Ziegler</Name>
```

but this would not be:

```
<Name>
    <First>Lea</First>
    <Last>Ziegler</Last>
</Name>
```

REFERENCE WINDOW   RW

Declaring Elements

- To declare that an element may contain any type of content, use
  ```
  <!ELEMENT element ANY>
  ```
  where *element* is the name of the element in the XML document.
- To declare that an element must be empty, use the following:
  ```
  <!ELEMENT element EMPTY>
  ```
- To declare that an element can only contain text, use the following:
  ```
  <!ELEMENT element (#PCDATA)>
  ```
- To declare that an element can only contain child elements, use the following:
  ```
  <!ELEMENT element (child_elements)>
  ```
  where *child_elements* is a list of the elements contained by the parent element.
- To declare that an element can contain text or child elements, use the following:
  ```
  <!ELEMENT element (#PCDATA | child1 | child2 | ...)*>
  ```
  where *child1*, *child2*, and so forth are elements contained by the parent element.

Working with Element Content

The most complicated element declaration is for elements that contain child elements. The syntax for declaring that an element contains only child elements is

```
<!ELEMENT element (child elements)>
```

where *child elements* is a list of child elements. The simplest content model would consist of a single child associated with a parent element. For example, the declaration

```
<!ELEMENT Customer (Phone)>
```

indicates that the Customer element can contain only one child element, named Phone. There are no exceptions. The following document is invalid because the Customer element contains two child elements:

```
<Customer>
    <Name>Lea Ziegler</Name>
    <Phone>Great 555-2819</Phone>
</Customer>
```

Additionally, you cannot repeat the same child element more than once with this declaration. The child element can only appear as many times as it is listed in the content model. The following code is invalid because it contains the Phone element twice and it's only listed once in the declaration:

```
<Customer>
    <Phone>555-3187</Phone>
    <Phone>555-8917</Phone>
</Customer>
```

For more complicated lists, DTDs allow XML authors to define sequences or choices of child elements.

Element Sequences and Choices

A **sequence** is a list of elements that follow a defined order. The syntax of the sequence model is

```
<!ELEMENT element (child1, child2, ...)>
```

where *child1*, *child2*, etc., represent the sequence of child elements within the parent element. The order of the child elements in the XML document must match the order defined in the element declaration. For example, the following element declaration defines a sequence of three child elements for the Customer parent element:

```
<!ELEMENT Customer (Name, Phone, E-mail)>
```

Under this declaration, the following document is valid:

```
<Customer>
    <Name>Lea Ziegler</Name>
    <Phone>(813) 555-8931</Phone>
    <E-mail>LZiegler@tempmail.net</E-mail>
</Customer>
```

But, the following document is not valid because the sequence doesn't match the defined order, even though the elements and their content are identical:

```
<Customer>
    <Name>Lea Ziegler</Name>
    <E-mail>LZiegler@tempmail.net</E-mail>
    <Phone>(813) 555-8931</Phone>
</Customer>
```

A sequence can also be applied to the same child element. The declaration

```
<!ELEMENT Customer (Phone, Phone, Phone)>
```

indicates that the Customer element should contain three child elements named Phone. Note that the number of child elements in the document must match the number in the element declaration. You could not use this particular declaration with only two child elements.

Specifying a Sequence or Choice of Child Elements

- To specify that child elements in an element declaration should appear in a defined order, enter the following code into an element declaration:

  `<!ELEMENT element (child1, child2, ...)>`

  where *child1, child2*, etc., represent the sequence of child elements within the parent element.

- To specify a choice of child elements for the parent element, use the element declaration

  `<!ELEMENT element (child1 | child2 | ...)>`

  where *child1, child2*, etc., are the possible child elements of the parent element.

The other way of listing child elements, **choice**, presents a set of possible child elements. The syntax of the choice model is

`<!ELEMENT element (child1 | child2 | ...)>`

where *child1*, *child2*, etc., are the possible child elements of the parent element. For example, the following declaration allows the Customer element to contain either the Name element or the Company element:

`<!ELEMENT Customer (Name | Company)>`

Therefore, either of these documents is valid:

```
<Customer>
    <Name>Lea Ziegler</Name>
</Customer>
```

or

```
<Customer>
    <Company>VTech Productions</Company>
</Customer>
```

But, you cannot have both the Name and the Company element because the choice model allows only one of the child elements.

Choice and sequence models can be combined and used together. The following declaration indicates that the Customer element must have three child elements:

`<!ELEMENT Customer ((Name | Company), Phone, E-mail)>`

The first must be either Name or Company, and the next two must be Phone and E-mail, in that order. With this declaration, either of the following sample documents is valid:

```
<Customer>
    <Name>Lea Ziegler</Name>
    <Phone>(813) 555-8931</Phone>
    <E-mail>LZiegler@tempmail.net</E-mail>
</Customer>
```

or

```
<Customer>
    <Company>VTech Productions</Company>
    <Phone>(813) 555-8931</Phone>
    <E-mail>LZiegler@tempmail.net</E-mail>
</Customer>
```

So far, all of the content models have limited the number of child elements to one. However, Kristin needs to be able to enter several Customer elements as child elements to the Customers element. To accomplish this, modifying symbols will be used.

Modifying Symbols

Modifying symbols are symbols appended to the content model, indicating the number of occurrences of each element. There are three modifying symbols: a question mark (?), a plus sign (+), and an asterisk (*). Figure 3-6 describes the meaning of each symbol.

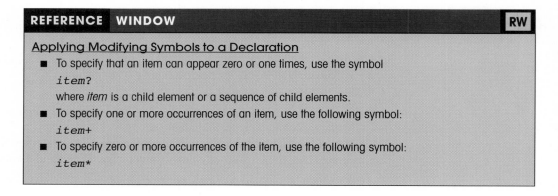

Figure 3-6	MODIFYING SYMBOLS

MODIFYING SYMBOL	DESCRIPTION
?	Allow zero or one of the item
+	Allow one or more of the item
*	Allow zero or more of the item

For example, the + symbol allows the document to contain one or more of the specified item, so the following declaration allows one or more Name elements to be placed within the Customer element:

```
<!ELEMENT Customer (Name+)>
```

REFERENCE WINDOW   RW

Applying Modifying Symbols to a Declaration
- To specify that an item can appear zero or one times, use the symbol
  item?
  where *item* is a child element or a sequence of child elements.
- To specify one or more occurrences of an item, use the following symbol:
  item+
- To specify zero or more occurrences of the item, use the following symbol:
  *item**

Modifying symbols can also be applied within sequences or choices. The following declaration allows the Customer element to contain zero or one E-mail elements, and one or more Order elements. The other child elements in the sequence (Name, Address, and Phone) can only appear once.

```
<!ELEMENT Customer (Name, Address, Phone, E-mail?, Order+)>
```

The three modifying symbols can also modify entire element sequences or choices. This is done by placing the character immediately following the closing parenthesis of the sequence or choice. When applied to a sequence, the modifying symbol is used to repeat the sequence. For example, the declaration

```
<!ELEMENT Order (Order_date, Items)+>
```

allows the child element sequence (Order_date, Items) to be included one or more times.

When applied to a choice model, the modifying symbols allow for multiple combinations of each child element. For example, the declaration

```
<!ELEMENT Customer (Name | Company)+>
```

allows any of the following lists of child elements:

```
Name
Company
Name, Company
Name, Name, Company
Name, Company, Company
```

The only requirement is that the combined total of Name and Company child elements be greater than zero.

Working with Mixed Content

As the name implies, an element with **mixed content** contains both character data and child elements. The syntax for declaring mixed content is as follows:

```
<!ELEMENT element (#PCDATA | child1 | child2 | ...)*>
```

Note that this form applies the * modifying symbol to a choice of character data or elements. This means that the parent element can contain character data or any number of the specified child elements, or it can contain no content at all. For example, the declaration

```
<!ELEMENT Title (#PCDATA | Subtitle)*>
```

allows the Title element to contain any of the following:

```
<Title>The Importance of Being Earnest</Title>
<Title>The Importance of Being Earnest
    <Subtitle>A Trivial Comedy for Serious People</Subtitle>
</Title>

<Title>The Importance of Being Earnest
    <Subtitle>A Trivial Comedy for Serious People</Subtitle>
    <Subtitle>by Oscar Wilde</Subtitle>
</Title>
```

Mixing character data and child elements restricts your ability to control the structure of your document. You can only specify the names of the child elements. You cannot constrain the order in which those child elements appear or control the number of occurrences for each element. For this reason, it is better not to work with mixed content if you want a tightly structured document.

Inserting Element Declarations into a DTD

Now that you've reviewed the syntax of element declarations, you are ready to create element declarations for all of the elements in Kristin's document. It is often best to work from the top level of the document's structure and proceed down through each child element. As we proceed through each element declaration, compare the declaration with Kristin's diagram, shown earlier in Figure 3-3.

To insert element declarations into Kristin's document:

1. The top-most element in Kristin's document is the Customers element that can contain one or more occurrences. Insert the following element declaration between the opening and closing bracket of the DOCTYPE declaration (see Figure 3-7):

```
<!ELEMENT Customers (Customer+)>
```

Figure 3-7	INSERTING THE ELEMENT DECLARATION FOR THE CUSTOMERS ELEMENT

```
<?xml version="1.0" ?>
<!-- document type declaration follows -->

<!DOCTYPE Customers
[
    <!ELEMENT Customers (Customer+)>
]>
```

the Customers element must contain one or more child elements named "Customer"

2. The Customer element has five child elements: Name, Address, Phone, E-mail, and Orders. Remember that the E-mail element is optional. Add the following element declaration directly below the Customers declaration:

```
<!ELEMENT Customer (Name, Address, Phone, E-mail?,
  Orders)>
```

3. The Name, Address, Phone, and E-mail elements can only contain character data. Add the following declarations below the Customer declaration:

```
<!ELEMENT Name (#PCDATA)>
<!ELEMENT Address (#PCDATA)>
<!ELEMENT Phone (#PCDATA)>
<!ELEMENT E-mail (#PCDATA)>
```

4. Next, add the declaration for the Orders element, which must contain at least one occurrence of the Order element:

```
<!ELEMENT Orders (Order+)>
```

5. Each Order element has two child elements: Order_date and Items. Add the following declaration below the Orders declaration:

```
<!ELEMENT Order (Order_date, Items)>
```

6. The Items element contains one or more occurrences of the Item element. Add the following declaration for the Items element:

```
<!ELEMENT Items (Item+)>
```

7. Finally, both the Order_date and Item elements contain only character data. Add the following declarations to the document.

```
<!ELEMENT Order_date (#PCDATA)>
<!ELEMENT Item (#PCDATA)>
```

Your complete list of element declarations should resemble Figure 3-8.

Figure 3-8	ELEMENT DECLARATIONS IN THE ORDERS.XML FILE

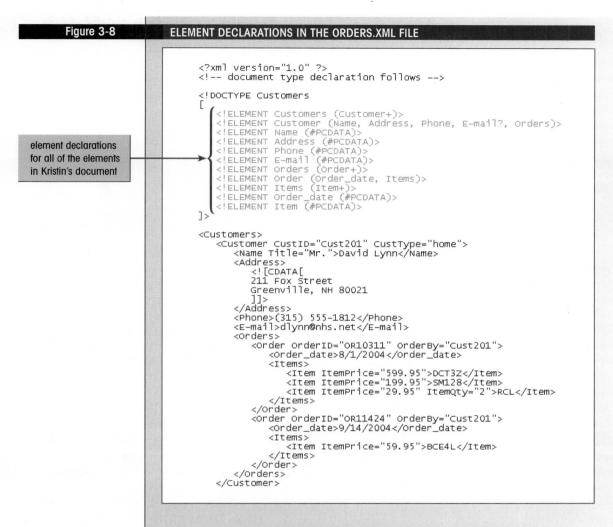

element declarations for all of the elements in Kristin's document

```
<?xml version="1.0" ?>
<!-- document type declaration follows -->

<!DOCTYPE Customers
[
   <!ELEMENT Customers (Customer+)>
   <!ELEMENT Customer (Name, Address, Phone, E-mail?, Orders)>
   <!ELEMENT Name (#PCDATA)>
   <!ELEMENT Address (#PCDATA)>
   <!ELEMENT Phone (#PCDATA)>
   <!ELEMENT E-mail (#PCDATA)>
   <!ELEMENT Orders (Order+)>
   <!ELEMENT Order (Order_date, Items)>
   <!ELEMENT Items (Item+)>
   <!ELEMENT Order_date (#PCDATA)>
   <!ELEMENT Item (#PCDATA)>
]>

<Customers>
   <Customer CustID="Cust201" CustType="home">
      <Name Title="Mr.">David Lynn</Name>
      <Address>
         <![CDATA[
         211 Fox Street
         Greenville, NH 80021
         ]]>
      </Address>
      <Phone>(315) 555-1812</Phone>
      <E-mail>dlynn@nhs.net</E-mail>
      <Orders>
         <Order OrderID="OR10311" orderBy="Cust201">
            <Order_date>8/1/2004</Order_date>
            <Items>
               <Item ItemPrice="599.95">DCT3Z</Item>
               <Item ItemPrice="199.95">SM128</Item>
               <Item ItemPrice="29.95" ItemQty="2">RCL</Item>
            </Items>
         </Order>
         <Order OrderID="OR11424" orderBy="Cust201">
            <Order_date>9/14/2004</Order_date>
            <Items>
               <Item ItemPrice="59.95">BCE4L</Item>
            </Items>
         </Order>
      </Orders>
   </Customer>
```

8. Save your changes to Orders.xml and close your text editor.

You've successfully defined a structure for Kristin's document by specifying exactly what content each element in her document can contain. In the next session, you'll learn how to do the same with the attributes in her document.

Session 3.1 QUICK | CHECK

1. What code would you enter to connect your document to a DTD stored in the file "Books.dtd" (assume that the name of the root element is Inventory)?

2. What declaration would you enter for an element named "Book" that can contain any content?

3. What declaration would you enter for an empty element named "Video"?

4. What declaration would you enter for an element named "Book" that can contain only character text?

5. What declaration would you enter for an element named "Book" that contains a single child element named "Author"?

6. What declaration would you enter for an element named "Book" that contains one or more child elements named "Author"?

7. What declaration would you enter to allow the Book element to contain either character text or child elements named "Author" and "Title"?

SESSION 3.2

In this session, you'll work with element attributes. You'll learn how to declare an attribute list and how to specify the type of content that can be stored in an attribute. You'll also learn how to specify a default value for an attribute and indicate whether that attribute is required or optional.

Declaring **Element Attribute**

In the last session, you defined the structure of Kristin's document by declaring the names of all of the elements in her document and indicating what type of content each could contain. However, for Kristin's document to be valid, you must also declare all of the attributes associated with those elements.

In Figure 3-9, Kristin has described all of the attributes she intends to use in her document, indicating whether the attribute is required and what, if any, default values are assumed for the attribute.

Figure 3-9	ELEMENT ATTRIBUTES IN KRISTIN'S DOCUMENT			
ELEMENT	**ATTRIBUTES**	**DESCRIPTION**	**REQUIRED?**	**DEFAULT VALUE(S)**
Customer	CustID	Customer ID number	Yes	none
	CustType	Customer type	No	"home" or "business"
Name	Title	Title associated with the customer's name	No	"Mr.", "Mrs.", or "Ms."
Order	OrderID	Order ID number	Yes	none
	OrderBy	ID of the customer making the order	Yes	none
Item	ItemID	Item ID number	Yes	none
	ItemPrice	Item price	Yes	none
	ItemQty	Quantity of the item ordered	Yes	"1"

To enforce these attribution properties on Kristin's document, you must add an **attribute-list declaration** to the document's DTD. The attribute-list declaration accomplishes the following:

- lists the names of all of the attributes associated with a specific element
- specifies the data type of the attribute
- indicates whether the attribute is required or optional
- provides a default value for the attribute, if necessary

The syntax for declaring a list of attributes is

```
<!ATTLIST element attribute1 type1 default1
                  attribute2 type2 default2
                  attribute3 type3 default3 ... >
```

where *element* is the name of the element associated with the attributes, *attribute* is the name of an attribute, *type* is the attribute's data type, and *default* indicates whether the attribute is required or implied, and whether it has a fixed or a default value.

In practice, declarations for elements with multiple attributes are easier to interpret if the attribute declaration is defined separately rather than in one long declaration. An equivalent form in the DTD would be as follows:

```
<!ATTLIST element attribute1 type1 default1>
<!ATTLIST element attribute2 type2 default2>
<!ATTLIST element attribute3 type3 default3>
...
```

The XML parser combines the different statements into a single attribute declaration. If the processor encounters more than one declaration for the same attribute, it ignores the second statement. Attribute-list declarations can be located anywhere within the document type declaration, although it is easier to work with attribute declarations that are located adjacent to the declaration for the element with which they're associated.

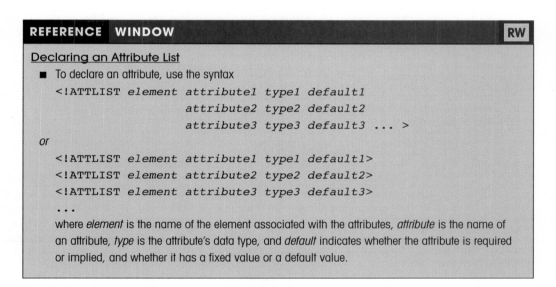

REFERENCE WINDOW   **RW**

Declaring an Attribute List
- To declare an attribute, use the syntax

```
<!ATTLIST element attribute1 type1 default1
                  attribute2 type2 default2
                  attribute3 type3 default3 ... >
```
or
```
<!ATTLIST element attribute1 type1 default1>
<!ATTLIST element attribute2 type2 default2>
<!ATTLIST element attribute3 type3 default3>
...
```
where *element* is the name of the element associated with the attributes, *attribute* is the name of an attribute, *type* is the attribute's data type, and *default* indicates whether the attribute is required or implied, and whether it has a fixed value or a default value.

Working with Attribute Types

All attribute values are text strings, but you can control what type of text is used with the attribute. As shown in Figure 3-10, attribute values can be placed into three general categories: string, enumerated, and tokenized. Each of these categories gives you varying degrees of control over the attribute's content. Let's investigate these categories in greater detail.

Figure 3-10	CATEGORIES OF ATTRIBUTE VALUES

ATTRIBUTE VALUE	DESCRIPTION
String type	The attribute value can be any text string
Enumerated	The attribute value must be selected from a list of possible values
Tokenized	The attribute value must be a valid XML name

String Types

String types are the simplest form for the attribute value. The content of an attribute that is declared as a string type is ignored by the XML parser, which means that string types can contain blank spaces and any character except those reserved by XML (e.g.,<, >, and & characters), even symbols that are not part of ASCII text. To declare an attribute value as string type, use the following attribute type:

```
attribute CDATA
```

For example, the following statement indicates that the CustID attribute of the Customer element can contain simple text strings with few restrictions on its content:

```
Customer CustID CDATA
```

Any of the following attribute values are allowed under this declaration:

```
<Customer CustID="Cust259">
<Customer CustID="J. B. Browne">
<Customer CustID="β100z"
```

When Kristin needs to put more restrictions on attribute values, she can declare the attribute as either an enumerated type or a tokenized type.

Enumerated Types

One attribute whose value Kristin needs to restrict is the CustType attribute in the Customer element. Kristin uses the CustType attribute to indicate whether the customer is making purchases for business or home use. Because these are the only two possibilities, Kristin can limit the values of the CustType attribute to either "home" or "business." Attributes that are limited to a set of possible values are **enumerated types**. The general form of an enumerated type is

```
attribute (value1 | value2 | value3 | ...)
```

where *value1*, *value2*, etc., are allowed values for specified attributes. Because Kristin wants to limit the value of the CustType attribute to either "home" or "business," she can include the following type in her declaration:

```
Customer CustType (home | business )>
```

Under this declaration, any document that uses a CustType value that is not "home" or "business" is rejected by the XML parser as invalid.

Another type of enumerated attribute is a **notation**. The notation associates the value of the attribute with a <!NOTATION> declaration located elsewhere in the DTD. You'll learn about <!NOTATION> declarations in the next session. Notations are primarily used when the XML document contains references to documents written in formats other than XML. The notation provides information to the XML parser as to how it should handle the non-XML data. The notation type has the following syntax:

```
NOTATION (notation1 | notation2 | notation3 | ...)
```

where *notation1*, *notation2*, etc., are valid notation values defined in a <NOTATION> declaration.

REFERENCE WINDOW   **RW**

<u>Declaring Attribute Types</u>
- To declare an attribute value as a simple text string, use the type
  attribute CDATA
  where *attribute* is the name of the attribute.
- To declare the attribute as an enumerated type, use
  attribute (value1 | value2 | value3 | ...)
  where *value1*, *value2*, etc., are allowed values for specified attributes.
- To declare the attribute as a tokenized type, use
  attribute token
  where *token* indicates the type of token in use. DTDs support the following token types: ID, IDREF, IDREFS, NMTOKEN, NMTOKENS, ENTITY, and ENTITIES.

Tokenized Types

Tokenized types are text strings that follow certain rules for format and content. The syntax for declaring an attribute as a tokenized type is

```
attribute token
```

where *token* is the type of token being applied to the attribute. There are seven tokenized types, described in Figure 3-11.

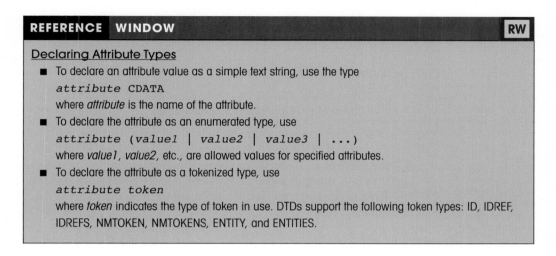

Figure 3-11	ATTRIBUTE TOKENS
TOKENIZED TYPE	**DESCRIPTION**
ID	Used to create a unique identifier for an attribute
IDREF	Used to allow an attribute to reference the ID attribute from another element
IDREFS	A list of ID references, separated by blank spaces
NMTOKEN	A name token whose value is restricted to a valid XML name
NMTOKENS	A list of name token references, separated by blank spaces
ENTITY	A reference to an external file, usually one containing non-XML data
ENTITIES	A list of entity references, separated by blank spaces

For example, the **ID** token is used with attributes that require unique values. In Kristin's document, the Customer element contains the CustID attribute, which stores a unique ID for each customer. For Kristin to prevent users from entering the same CustID value for different customers, she defines the attribute type for the CustID attribute as follows:

```
Customer CustID ID
```

Under this declaration, the following elements are valid:

```
<Customer CustID="Cust021"> ... </Customer>
<Customer CustID="Cust022"> ... </Customer>
```

but the following elements are not because the customer ID values are duplicated for different customers:

```
<Customer CustID="Cust021"> ... </Customer>
<Customer CustID="Cust021"> ... </Customer>
```

Once an attribute value is declared in the document, other attribute values can link to it using the IDREF token. An attribute declared as an **IDREF** type must have a value equal to the value of an ID attribute located somewhere in the same document.

The Order element in Kristin's document has an attribute named OrderBy so that Kristin can store the ID of the customer who made the order. She specifies the attribute type as follows:

```
Order OrderBy IDREF
```

When the XML parser encounters this attribute, it searches the XML document for ID values that match the value of the OrderBy attribute. For example, an Order element has the following OrderBy attribute value:

```
<Order OrderBy="Cust021">
```

unless there is another element in the document that has an ID value equal to "Cust021." Note that you cannot specify *which* attribute has the value to which the IDREF type should match.

To create a reference to multiple ID values, you use the **IDREFS** token type. Kristin might want to do this if she were to list all of the orders made by a certain customer as an attribute, as in the following sample code:

```
<Customer Orders="OR3413 OR3910 OR5310"> ... </Customer>
```

```
<Order OrderID="OR3413">...</Order>
<Order OrderID="OR3910">...</Order>
<Order OrderID="OR5310">...</Order>
```

In this case, the attribute types of the Orders and OrderID attributes are defined as follows:

```
Customer Orders IDREFS
Order OrderID ID
```

As with the IDREF token type, all of the IDs listed in an IDREFS token type must be found in an ID attribute located somewhere in the file, or the parser will reject the document as invalid.

The **NMTOKEN** type is used with character data whose values must be valid XML names. This constraint makes them less flexible than string types. The main difference between the NMTOKEN type and a simple text string defined with the CDATA type is that text strings defined as NMTOKEN attributes cannot contain blank spaces. If Kristin wants to make sure that an attribute value is always a single word, she would use the NMTOKEN type in preference to the CDATA type. An attribute that contains a list of name tokens, each separated by a blank space, can be defined using the **NMTOKENS** token type.

Finally, the **ENTITY** and **ENTITIES** token types are used for attribute values that reference unparsed entities. You'll learn more about entities in the next session.

Working **with Attribute Defaults**

The final part of an attribute declaration is the attribute default. There are four possible defaults: #REQUIRED, #IMPLIED, a default value, and a fixed default value. Figure 3-12 describes each of these attribute defaults.

Figure 3-12	ATTRIBUTE DEFAULTS

ATTRIBUTE DEFAULT	DESCRIPTION
#REQUIRED	The attribute must appear with every occurrence of the element.
#IMPLIED	The attribute is optional.
"*default*"	The attribute is optional. If an attribute value in not specified, a validating XML parser will supply the *default* value.
#FIXED "*default*"	The attribute is optional. If an attribute value is specified, it *must* match the *default* value.

Earlier, in Figure 3-9, Kristin outlined the properties for the attributes in her document. Note that the CustType attribute is required for every Customer element. That being the case, Kristin can use an attribute default as shown below:

```
<!ATTLIST Customer CustID ID #REQUIRED>
```

On the other hand, Kristin is not always able to determine whether a customer represents a home or business, so she uses the #IMPLIED attribute default for the CustType attribute. This is what the complete attribute declaration looks like:

```
<!ATTLIST Customer CustType (home | business) #IMPLIED>
```

If an XML parser encounters a Customer element without a CustType attribute, it won't invalidate the document but will instead assume a blank value for the attribute.

Another attribute from Kristin's document is the ItemQty attribute, which indicates the quantity of each item on the order. The ItemQty is optional, but Kristin wants the XML parser to assume a value of "1" for this attribute if it's missing from the Item element. The complete attribute declaration is as follows:

```
<!ATTLIST Item ItemQty CDATA "1">
```

For this attribute default to work, the XML parser must be capable of interpreting the DTD and validating the document. Not all XML parsers have this capability. This issue will be discussed later.

The last type of attribute default is the #FIXED default, which fixes the attribute to a specified value. If you omit the attribute from the element, the XML parser supplies the default value, and if you include the attribute, you must make the attribute value equal to the default or the document will be invalid. Note that you can't use the #FIXED form with an ID attribute because ID attributes need to have unique values for each element in the document.

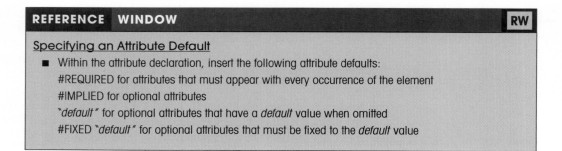

Creating and Applying Attribute Declarations

Now that you've reviewed the syntax of attribute declarations, you can create attribute-list declarations for the elements in Kristin's document. You'll place each attribute declaration into the DOCTYPE declaration right below the declaration for the element that contains the attribute.

```
<!ATTLIST Order OrderID ID #REQUIRED>
<!ATTLIST Order OrderBy IDREF #REQUIRED>
```

The attribute declarations are written as follows:

```
<!ATTLIST Item ItemPrice CDATA #REQUIRED>
<!ATTLIST Item ItemQty CDATA "1">
```

Now that you know the attribute declarations, you can add them to Kristin's document.

To insert the attribute declarations:

1. Use your text editor to open the **Orders.xml** document from the Tutorial.03X/Tutorial folder on your Data Disk.

2. Below the Customer element declaration in the DTD, insert the following attribute declarations to define the properties of the CustID and CustType attributes, which are both associated with the Customer element:

```
<!ATTLIST Customer CustID ID #REQUIRED>
<!ATTLIST Customer CustType (home | business) #IMPLIED>
```

Title is the only attribute for the Name element. It's an optional element that can have one of three possible values: Mr., Mrs., or Ms.

3. Insert the following code below the element declaration:

```
<!ATTLIST Name Title (Mr. | Mrs. | Ms.) #IMPLIED>
```

There are two attributes associated with the Order element. The OrderID attribute assigns a required ID number to the order, and the OrderBy attribute indicates the ID of the customer who submitted the order.

4. Add the following attribute declarations below the Order element declaration:

```
<!ATTLIST Order OrderID ID #REQUIRED>
<!ATTLIST Order OrderBy IDREF #REQUIRED>
```

Finally, there are two attributes for the Item element: ItemPrice and ItemQty. ItemPrice is a required attribute that records the price of the item. ItemQty is an optional element that records the quantity of items ordered. The default value is "1".

5. Insert the following code beneath the Item element declaration:

```
<!ATTLIST Item ItemPrice CDATA #REQUIRED>
<!ATTLIST Item ItemQty CDATA "1">
```

Figure 3-13 shows the revised contents of the Orders.xml file.

Figure 3-13 | **INSERTING ATTRIBUTE-LIST DECLARATIONS**

attribute declaration →

```
<?xml version="1.0" ?>
<!-- document type declaration follows -->

<!DOCTYPE Customers
[
   <!ELEMENT Customers (Customer+)>
   <!ELEMENT Customer (Name, Address, Phone, E-mail?, Orders)>
   <!ATTLIST Customer CustID ID #REQUIRED>
   <!ATTLIST Customer CustType (home | business) #IMPLIED>
   <!ELEMENT Name (#PCDATA)>
   <!ATTLIST Name Title (Mr. | Mrs. | Ms.) #IMPLIED>
   <!ELEMENT Address (#PCDATA)>
   <!ELEMENT Phone (#PCDATA)>
   <!ELEMENT E-mail (#PCDATA)>
   <!ELEMENT Orders (Order+)>
   <!ELEMENT Order (Order_date, Items)>
   <!ATTLIST Order OrderID ID #REQUIRED>
   <!ATTLIST Order OrderBy IDREF #REQUIRED>
   <!ELEMENT Items (Item+)>
   <!ELEMENT Order_date (#PCDATA)>
   <!ELEMENT Item (#PCDATA)>
   <!ATTLIST Item ItemPrice CDATA #REQUIRED>
   <!ATTLIST Item ItemQty CDATA "1">
]>
```

6. Save your changes to Orders.xml and leave the file and your text editor open.

Congratulations, you've created a DTD that declares all of the elements and attributes in the document, but how do you know that all of your hard work has resulted in a valid XML document? It's possible that you've forgotten to declare an element or attribute, or you may have made a simple typing mistake. How do you test for validity?

Validating **Documents with XML Spy**

To test for validity, your XML parser must be able to validate your XML document against the rules you set up in the DTD. The Web is an excellent source for validating parsers. A partial list is displayed in Figure 3-14.

Figure 3-14	XML-VALIDATING PARSERS

VALIDATING PARSER	URL
MSXML	http://msdn.microsoft.com/library/
Oracle	http://technet.oracle.com/tech/xml/content.html
ProjectX	http://java.sun.com/xml/index.html
Xerces	http://xml.apache.org/xerces-j/
XML4J	http://www.alphaworks.ibm.com/tech/xml4j
XML Spy	http://link.xmlspy.com
XP	http://jclark.com/xml/xp/index.html

The CD that accompanies this book contains an evaluation copy of XML Spy. XML Spy can test your document for being well formed as well as valid. To install XML Spy, review the material in the appendix at the end of this book. If you have any problems installing XML Spy, contact your instructor or technical resource person.

To start XML Spy:

1. Click the **Start** button on your Taskbar, point to **Programs**, point to **XML Spy Suite**, and click **XML Spy IDE** from the menu.

   TROUBLE? Your system may be configured with the XML Spy program located in a different folder or menu. Contact your instructor if you are having problems locating or starting XML Spy.

2. Click the **File** menu and then click **Open**.

3. Select the **Orders.xml** file, located in the Tutorial.03X/Tutorial folder of your Data Disk and click the **Open** button.

   With XML Spy, you can organize all of the files related to your XML document into projects. Information about the different aspects of the project is placed in separate panes in the XML Spy window. There is a pane that lists all of the files involved in your project and another pane, named Info, that provides information about the project. There are other panes that list the elements, attributes, and entities in your XML project. The contents of Orders.xml are displayed in the document pane.

   TROUBLE? By default, XML Spy verifies that your document is both well formed and valid when the document is opened. If you receive a message indicating an error in the file, you may have made a typing mistake when entering the DTD. The error message gives you a clue as to the nature of the error. Review the steps that follow to learn how to interpret and correct validation errors, and then return to Orders.xml and try to correct the mistake.

4. Click the **Maximize** button 🔲 on the document pane to maximize its appearance within XML Spy. See Figure 3-15.

   TROUBLE? Your screen may appear slightly different depending on how XML Spy is configured on your computer.

Figure 3-15   **XML SPY WINDOW**

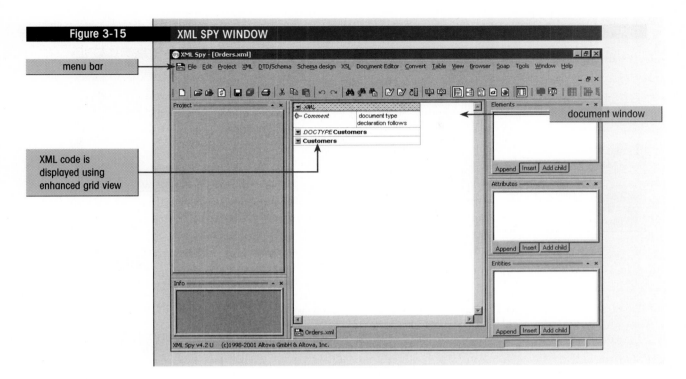

By default, XML Spy opens documents in **enhanced grid view**, which shows the hierarchical structure of an XML document as a set of nested containers. The containers can be expanded or contracted to get a clear picture of the document's structure and content. For this example, though, we'll view the contents of the document as a text file.

To view the document as a text file:

1. Click **View** on the menu bar.

2. Click **Text view**.

   Depending on your monitor's resolution, there may be line wrap in the text, making it difficult to read. You can increase the amount of horizontal space given to the document window by dragging the borders of the document window to the left or right.

3. Move the mouse pointer over the left edge of the document pane until the pointer changes to a ╫. Drag the border to the left, increasing the width of the window (see Figure 3-16).

Figure 3-16   XML SPY WINDOW

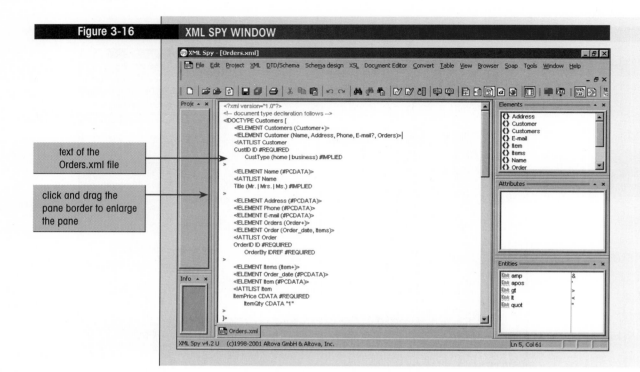

text of the Orders.xml file

click and drag the pane border to enlarge the pane

Next, test the document for being both well formed and valid. Typically, XML Spy runs these tests whenever you open an XML document, but it's good practice to see how to do this manually.

To test Orders.xml:

1. Click **XML** on the menu bar, and then click **Check well-formedness**.

2. XML Spy reports that the file is well formed and indicates that you should validate the document against its DTD.

3. Click **XML** on the menu bar, and then click **Validate**.

   XML Spy returns the message that the file is valid (see Figure 3-17).

Figure 3-17	XML SPY REPORTS THAT THE FILE IS VALID

```
<?xml version="1.0"?>
<!-- document type declaration follows -->
<!DOCTYPE Customers [
        <!ELEMENT Customers (Customer+)>
        <!ELEMENT Customer (Name, Address, Phone, E-mail?, Orders)>
        <!ATTLIST Customer
        CustID ID #REQUIRED
            CustType (home | business) #IMPLIED
>
        <!ELEMENT Name (#PCDATA)>
        <!ATTLIST Name
        Title (Mr. | Mrs. | Ms.) #IMPLIED
>
        <!ELEMENT Address (#PCDATA)>
        <!ELEMENT Phone (#PCDATA)>
        <!ELEMENT E-mail (#PCDATA)>
        <!ELEMENT Orders (Order+)>
        <!ELEMENT Order (Order_date, Items)>
        <!ATTLIST Order
        OrderID ID #REQUIRED
            OrderBy IDREF #REQUIRED
>
        <!ELEMENT Items (Item+)>
        <!ELEMENT Order_date (#PCDATA)>
        <!ELEMENT Item (#PCDATA)>
        <!ATTLIST Item
        ItemPrice CDATA #REQUIRED
```

This file is valid.

OK

Orders.xml

Note that you can also run the well-formedness and validity tests by pressing the F7 and F8 keys on your keyboard or by clicking the ✅ and ✅ buttons on the XML Spy toolbar.

Though the file is valid, it is a good learning experience to place a few intentional errors into the XML code to see how validation errors are reported. You can edit the contents of Orders.xml directly in the document pane.

To make Orders.xml invalid:

1. Locate the element declaration for the E-mail element near the top of the document. Select the name "E-mail" and change the name in the element declaration to "Mail."

2. Click the ✅ button to validate the file.

3. XML Spy reports that the file is not valid because the E-mail element is undefined. It also highlights the section in the document where it encountered an error. See Figure 3-18.

Figure 3-18 | **XML SPY REPORTS THAT THE FILE IS INVALID**

```
<?xml version="1.0"?>
<!-- document type declaration follows -->
<!DOCTYPE Customers [
    <!ELEMENT Customers (Customer+)>
    <!ELEMENT Customer (Name, Address, Phone, E-mail, Orders)>
    <!ATTLIST Customer
    CustID ID #REQUIRED
        CustType (home | business) #IMPLIED
    >
    <!ELEMENT Name (#PCDATA)>
    <!ATTLIST Name
    Title (Mr. | Mrs. | Ms.) #IMPLIED
    >
    <!ELEMENT Address (#PCDATA)>
    <!ELEMENT Phone (#PCDATA)>
    <!ELEMENT Mail (#PCDATA)>
    <!ELEMENT Orders (Order+)>
    <!ELEMENT Order (Order_date, Items)>
    <!ATTLIST Order
    OrderID ID #REQUIRED
        OrderBy IDREF #REQUIRED
    >
    <!ELEMENT Items (Item+)>
    <!ELEMENT Order_date (#PCDATA)>
    <!ELEMENT Item (#PCDATA)>
    <!ATTLIST Item
    ItemPrice CDATA #REQUIRED
```

which results in an error because the E-mail child element has no corresponding element declaration

the name in the element declaration is changed from "E-mail" to "Mail"

This file is not valid:
DTD/Schema error - element 'E-mail' is undefined

Revalidate

Orders.xml

4. Click **Edit** and then click **Undo** to remove your edit, restoring the document back to its original condition.

5. Click the **Revalidate** button located at the bottom of the document pane to re-evaluate the file.

    XML Spy reports that the file is once again valid.

    TROUBLE? If you still get an error message, examine the reason for the error and then make the necessary corrections.

    After confirming that Order.xml is a valid XML document, close XML Spy.

6. Click **File** and then click **Exit**. Click the **Yes** button to save your changes.

Nice work! You've completed the exercises for declaring and defining the attributes of the elements in Kristin's document. In the next session, you'll create and work with entities and binary data.

Session 3.2 QUICK CHECK

1. What attribute declaration would you enter to create an optional text string attribute named "Title" for an element named "Book"?

2. The Play element has a required attribute named "Type," which can have one of four possible values: Romance, Tragedy, History, and Comedy. Enter the appropriate attribute declaration.

3. What is the main difference between an attribute with the CDATA type and one with the NMTOKEN type?

4. The Book element has a required ID attribute named "ISBN." Enter the appropriate attribute declaration.

5. An Author element has an optional attribute named "BooksBy," which contains the ISBN numbers of the books the author has written. If ISBN is an ID attribute for another element in the document, what declaration would you use for the BooksBy attribute?

6. The Book element has an optional attribute named "InStock" that can have the value "yes" or "no." The default value is "yes." What is the declaration for the InStock attribute?

SESSION 3.3

In this session, you'll learn how to create and work with entities, and, specifically, you'll learn how to work with general entities to store long text strings containing data and elements. You'll also review how to create parameter entities to store elements and attributes. Finally, you'll learn how to use unparsed entities to include binary data, such as image files and multimedia clips, in your XML documents.

Working with Entities

Until this point, you've worked with data that has been entered directly into an XML document. As you will see, this is not always the case. In fact, one of the strengths of XML is that a document's content can be stored in multiple files and in multiple formats. These storage units are called **entities**. The most fundamental entity is the XML document itself, known as the **document entity**, but entities can refer to other items as well, including:

- a text string
- a DTD
- an element or attribute declaration
- an external file containing character or binary data

Entities can be declared in a DTD. The syntax for declaring an entity depends on how the entity is classified. There are three factors involved in classifying an entity: 1) the content of the entity, 2) how the entity is constructed, and 3) where the definition of the entity is located. Let's consider each of these factors now.

An entity that is part of an XML document's content is called a **general entity**. General entities are often used as placeholders for text strings that the author wants to repeat throughout the document or in other documents. For example, Kristin can create a general entity declaration to store the company's address and phone number. Rather than retyping this information for every document that needs it, she can reference the declarations. If this information changes, Kristin only has to change it in one location rather than several. An entity that is not part of the document's content is called a **parameter entity**. Parameter entities are used to store the various declarations found in a DTD. Those declarations can then be shared among multiple documents.

If the entity is constructed using well-formed XML text, it is a **parsed entity**. The company's address and phone number would be one such example. If the entity is constructed from non-XML data, it is an **unparsed entity**. A graphic image file would be an example of an unparsed entity.

Finally, if the entity can be defined with a text string within the document's DTD, it's an **internal entity**. If the definition relies on the content of an external file, particularly a non-XML file, it's an **external entity**. Figure 3-19 summarizes these categories.

Figure 3-19	CLASSIFYING ENTITIES		
ENTITY CLASSIFICATIONS			**DESCRIPTION**
What does the entity refer to?	General vs. Parameter		General entities are used only with the contents of an XML document. Parameter entities are used only with contents of a DTD.
How is the entity constructed?	Parsed vs. Unparsed		Parsed entities consist entirely of well-formed XML content. Unparsed entities are constructed from non-XML data, including nontext data.
Where is the entity located?	Internal vs. External		An internal entity is defined within a declaration in the document's DTD. An external entity is defined in an external file.

You'll start your work on entity declarations by learning how to declare a general parsed entity.

Working with General Parsed Entities

Like elements and attributes, general entities are declared within the DTD of a document. The syntax for declaring a general internal entity is

```
<!ENTITY entity "value">
```

where *entity* is the name you've assigned to the entity and *value* is the general entity's value. The entity name follows the same rules that apply to all XML names: there can be no blank spaces in the name and the name must begin with either a letter or underscore. The entity value itself must be well-formed XML text. This can be a simple text string, or it can be a text string containing XML tags.

For example, an entity named "Pixal" can be created to store the company's official name:

```
<!ENTITY Pixal "Pixal Digital Products">
```

Note that XML tags can be included as part of the general entity's value, as in the following declaration:

```
<!ENTITY Pixal "<Company>Pixal Digital Products</Company>" >
```

If you do include an XML tag in the entity's value, you must include both the opening and closing tag for the document to be valid.

Inserting a General Entity

Once a general entity has been declared in the DTD, it can be referenced anywhere within the XML document. The syntax for inserting a general entity reference is

```
&entity;
```

where *entity* is the name in the entity declaration. For example, to insert the Pixal entity into a document, use the following text string:

```
<Title>This is the home page of &Pixal;.</Title>
```

The XML parser interprets the contents of the Title element as

```
<Title>This is the home page of Pixal Digital Products.</Title>
```

substituting the value of the entity for the entity reference.

You may have noticed a similarity between inserting general entities and inserting character references that were discussed in the first tutorial. A character reference is actually a special case of a general entity called a **predefined entity**. The five predefined entities are: < > ' &quote; and &amp.

Because of the way entities are inserted into XML documents, you cannot include the & symbol as part of the entity's value. The XML parser interprets the & symbol as a reference to another entity and attempts to resolve the reference. You also cannot use the % symbol, which, as you'll learn later, is the symbol used for inserting parameter entities.

Declaring a General External Entity

General entities can also refer to values located in external files. The advantage of an external entity is that it can be accessed by several XML documents, and, if the entity is modified, those documents automatically reflect that change. The syntax for declaring a general external entity is

```
<!ENTITY  entity SYSTEM "URL" >
```

where *URL* indicates the location of the file containing the entity data. For example, an author working with a collection of articles located at *www.newsflash.com* can access those external entities using the following declaration:

```
<!ENTITY  headlines SYSTEM "http://www.newsflash.com/
stories.xml" >
```

In this example, an entity named "headlines" retrieves its value from the document, stories.xml, located at *http://www.newsflash.com.*The external file can contain only text to be inserted directly into an element, such as character data or nested elements. If the stories.xml file contains the following text:

```
<Head>Stocks Surge</Head>
<Summary>The NYSE Composite Index rose 15 points yesterday in
heavy trading with 616,891,000 shares traded (details to
follow.)
</Summary>
<Head>Presidential Trip</Head>
<Summary>The President left on his European trip this
morning. He will address the British Parliament Wednesday
afternoon (details to follow.)
</Summary>
```

the news summaries could then be inserted into XML document using the following entity reference:

```
<News>
    &headlines;
</News>
```

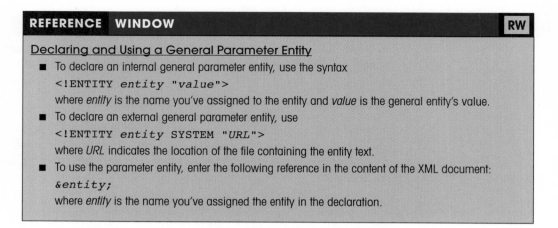

REFERENCE WINDOW   **RW**

<u>Declaring and Using a General Parameter Entity</u>
■ To declare an internal general parameter entity, use the syntax

   `<!ENTITY entity "value">`

   where *entity* is the name you've assigned to the entity and *value* is the general entity's value.
■ To declare an external general parameter entity, use

   `<!ENTITY entity SYSTEM "URL">`

   where *URL* indicates the location of the file containing the entity text.
■ To use the parameter entity, enter the following reference in the content of the XML document:

   `&entity;`

   where *entity* is the name you've assigned the entity in the declaration.

Creating and Applying General Parsed Entities

Kristin's colleagues at Pixal are developing other XML documents to be published on their web site. They decided that it will be more efficient to have certain information located in a shared document so that multiple XML authors can reference the same file. To do this, a document named Items.dtd has been created that contains entity declarations for several products. The entity names represent abbreviations for the products sold by Pixal, and the entity values are extended descriptions of the products. The contents of the file are shown in Figure 3-20.

Figure 3-20   **ENTITIES DECLARED IN THE ITEMS.DTD FILE**

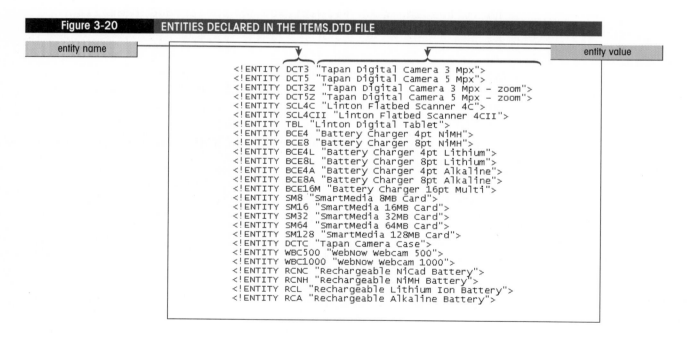

entity name   entity value

```
<!ENTITY DCT3 "Tapan Digital Camera 3 Mpx">
<!ENTITY DCT5 "Tapan Digital Camera 5 Mpx">
<!ENTITY DCT3Z "Tapan Digital Camera 3 Mpx - zoom">
<!ENTITY DCT5Z "Tapan Digital Camera 5 Mpx - zoom">
<!ENTITY SCL4C "Linton Flatbed Scanner 4C">
<!ENTITY SCL4CII "Linton Flatbed Scanner 4CII">
<!ENTITY TBL "Linton Digital Tablet">
<!ENTITY BCE4 "Battery Charger 4pt NiMH">
<!ENTITY BCE8 "Battery Charger 8pt NiMH">
<!ENTITY BCE4L "Battery Charger 4pt Lithium">
<!ENTITY BCE8L "Battery Charger 8pt Lithium">
<!ENTITY BCE4A "Battery Charger 4pt Alkaline">
<!ENTITY BCE8A "Battery Charger 8pt Alkaline">
<!ENTITY BCE16M "Battery Charger 16pt Multi">
<!ENTITY SM8 "SmartMedia 8MB Card">
<!ENTITY SM16 "SmartMedia 16MB Card">
<!ENTITY SM32 "SmartMedia 32MB Card">
<!ENTITY SM64 "SmartMedia 64MB Card">
<!ENTITY SM128 "SmartMedia 128MB Card">
<!ENTITY DCTC "Tapan Camera Case">
<!ENTITY WBC500 "WebNow Webcam 500">
<!ENTITY WBC1000 "WebNow Webcam 1000">
<!ENTITY RCNC "Rechargeable NiCad Battery">
<!ENTITY RCNH "Rechargeable NiMH Battery">
<!ENTITY RCL "Rechargeable Lithium Ion Battery">
<!ENTITY RCA "Rechargeable Alkaline Battery">
```

To use these entities in the Orders.xml file, you need to create a reference to the Items.dtd file. At this point, it may be helpful for you to review the external DTD discussion in the first session of this tutorial.

To create a reference to the Items.dtd file:

1. Using your text editor, open the **Orders.xml** document located in the Tutorial.03X/Tutorial folder of your Data Disk.

2. Locate the document type declaration at the top of the file, and insert the text **SYSTEM "Items.dtd"**, as shown in Figure 3-21.

Figure 3-21 **CONNECTING TO THE ITEMS.DTD FILE**

```
<?xml version="1.0"?>
<!-- edited with XML Spy v4.2 U (http://www.xmlspy.com) by Kristin Laughlin (Pixal) -->
<!-- document type declaration follows -->
<!DOCTYPE Customers SYSTEM "Items.dtd" [
  <!ELEMENT Customers (Customer+)>
  <!ELEMENT Customer (Name, Address, Phone, E-mail?, Orders)>
  <!ATTLIST Customer
  CustID ID #REQUIRED
    CustType (home | business) #IMPLIED
>
```

Note that adding the URL for the Items.dtd document changes the DTD of the Orders.xml document from a purely internal DTD to a DTD combining both internal and external subsets.

To display the entity values in her document, Kristin must replace the product abbreviations with entity references. For example, the first customer, David Lynn, purchased a DCT3Z, also known as the Tapan Digital Camera 3 Mpx - Zoom Model. To display the full product name, replace the item name with the following entity reference:

&DCT3Z;

The XML parser automatically inserts the entity's value. You can now add entity references for some additional Pixal products.

To add entity references:

1. Locate the first item name in the Orders.xml document, and change DCT3Z to **&DCT3Z;**

2. Locate the second item name, SM128, and change the item name to **&SM128;**

3. Continue through the rest of the document and insert an ampersand (&) before, and a semi-colon after, each item. There are a total of seven items in the document. Figure 3-22 shows the revised Orders.xml file with the modified items highlighted in red.

Figure 3-22 | CHANGING PRODUCT DESCRIPTIONS TO ENTITY REFERENCES

```
<Customers>
  <Customer CustID="Cust201" CustType="home">
    <Name Title="Mr.">David Lynn</Name>
    <Address><![CDATA[
        211 Fox Street
        Greenville, NH 80021
        ]]></Address>
    <Phone>(315) 555-1812</Phone>
    <E-mail>dlynn@nhs.net</E-mail>
    <Orders>
      <Order OrderID="OR10311" OrderBy="Cust201">
        <Order_date>8/1/2004</Order_date>
        <Items>
          <Item ItemPrice="599.95">&DCT3Z;</Item>
          <Item ItemPrice="199.95">&SM128;</Item>
          <Item ItemPrice="29.95" ItemQty="2">&RCL;</Item>
        </Items>
      </Order>
      <Order OrderID="OR11424" OrderBy="Cust201">
        <Order_date>9/14/2004</Order_date>
        <Items>
          <Item ItemPrice="59.95">&BCE4L;</Item>
        </Items>
      </Order>
    </Orders>
  </Customer>
  <Customer CustID="Cust202">
    <Name Title="Mrs.">Jean Kaufmann</Name>
    <Address><![CDATA[
        411 East Oak Avenue
        Cashton, MI  20401
        ]]></Address>
    <Phone>(611) 555-4033</Phone>
    <E-mail>JKaufmann@cshweb.com</E-mail>
    <Orders>
      <Order OrderID="OR10899" OrderBy="Cust202">
        <Order_date>8/11/2004</Order_date>
        <Items>
          <Item ItemPrice="59.99">&WBC500;</Item>
          <Item ItemPrice="5.95" ItemQty="2">&RCA;</Item>
        </Items>
      </Order>
    </Orders>
  </Customer>
  <Customer CustID="Cust203" CustType="business">
    <Name>AdServices</Name>
    <Address><![CDATA[
        55 Washburn Lane
        Creighton, UT  98712
        ]]></Address>
    <Phone>(811) 555-2987</Phone>
    <Orders>
      <Order OrderID="OR11201" OrderBy="Cust203">
        <Order_date>9/15/2004</Order_date>
        <Items>
          <Item ItemPrice="179.99" ItemQty="3">&SCL4C;</Item>
        </Items>
      </Order>
    </Orders>
  </Customer>
</Customers>
```

4. Save your changes to Orders.xml.

Now, check to see whether the entity references are resolved in the entity values by an XML parser. You can check this using the Internet Explorer browser.

To view the entity values:

1. Using Internet Explorer, open **Orders.xml**. Figure 3-23 shows how Internet Explorer resolves the entity references and displays the entity values when it renders the document.

| Figure 3-23 | ENTITY VALUES AS RENDERED BY THE INTERNET EXPLORER BROWSER |

```
<Customers>
    <Customer CustID="Cust201" CustType="home">
        <Name Title="Mr.">David Lynn</Name>
        <Address>
            <![CDATA[
            211 Fox Street
            Greenville, NH 80021
            ]]>
        </Address>
        <Phone>(315) 555-1812</Phone>
        <E-mail>dlynn@nhs.net</E-mail>
        <Orders>
            <Order OrderID="OR10311" OrderBy="Cust201">
                <Order_date>8/1/2004</Order_date>
                <Items>
                    <Item ItemPrice="599.95">&DCT3Z;</Item>
                    <Item ItemPrice="199.95">&SM128;</Item>
                    <Item ItemPrice="29.95" ItemQty="2">&RCL;</Item>
                </Items>
            </Order>
```

entity reference

Orders.xml document

```
- <Customers>
  - <Customer CustID="Cust201" CustType="home">
      <Name Title="Mr.">David Lynn</Name>
    - <Address>
      - <![CDATA[
               211 Fox Street
               Greenville, NH 80021

        ]]>
      </Address>
      <Phone>(315) 555-1812</Phone>
      <E-mail>dlynn@nhs.net</E-mail>
    - <Orders>
      - <Order OrderID="OR10311" OrderBy="Cust201">
          <Order_date>8/1/2004</Order_date>
        - <Items>
            <Item ItemPrice="599.95">Tapan Digital Camera 3 Mpx - zoom</Item>
            <Item ItemPrice="199.95">SmartMedia 128MB Card</Item>
            <Item ItemPrice="29.95" ItemQty="2">Rechargeable Lithium Ion Battery</Item>
          </Items>
        </Order>
```

resolved entity value

Orders.xml document as viewed in Internet Explorer

TROUBLE? If you open the file using a Netscape browser, the entity references are not resolved.

2. Close your browser and return to your text editor.

Working with Parameter Entities

The other type of entity is the parameter entity, which is used to store the content of a DTD. Parameter entities are declared using a form similar to general entities. For internal parameter entities, the syntax is

```
<!ENTITY % entity "value">
```

where *entity* is the name of the parameter entity and *value* is a text string of the entity's value. For external parameter entities, the syntax is

```
<!ENTITY % entity SYSTEM "URL">
```

where *URL* is the URL of the file containing the entity's value.

To reference a parameter entity, you use the syntax

```
%entity;
```

where *entity* is the name assigned to the parameter entity. Parameter entity references can only be placed where a declaration would normally occur, such as an internal or external DTD. You *cannot* insert a parameter entity reference within the content of the XML document. The following example shows how to create a parameter entity for a collection of elements and attributes:

```
<!ENTITY % books
    "<!ELEMENT Book (Title, Author)>
     <!ATTLIST Book Pages CDATA #REQUIRED>
     <!ELEMENT Title (#PCDATA)>
     <!ELEMENT Author (#PCDATA)>"
>
```

The books parameter entity stores three element declarations named "Book," "Title," and "Author," and an attribute list named "Pages." To reference these declarations, you include the statement

```
%books;
```

as a separate line in a DTD.

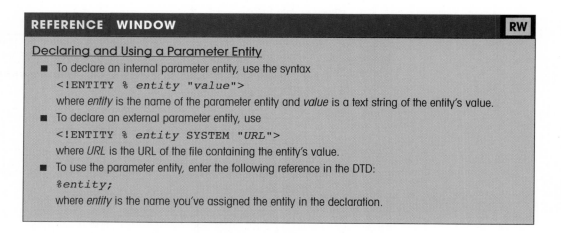

It's not a practical strategy to use parameter entities with an internal DTD because it adds an extra step without saving any time or effort.

However, an external parameter entity can overcome XML's limit of one DTD per document by combining declarations from multiple DTDs (see Figure 3-24).

Figure 3-24	USING PARAMETER ENTITIES TO COMBINE MULTIPLE DTDS

```
<!ELEMENT Book (Title, Author)>
<!ATTLIST Book Pages CDATA #REQUIRED>
<!ELEMENT Title (#PCDATA)>
<!ELEMENT Author (#PCDATA)>
```
Book.dtd

```
<!ELEMENT Magazine (Name)>
<!ATTLIST Magazine Publisher CDATA #REQUIRED>
<!ELEMENT Name (#PCDATA)>
```
Magazine.dtd

```
<!ENTITY % Books SYSTEM "Book.dtd">
<!ENTITY % Mags SYSTEM "Magazine.dtd">
%Books;
%Mags;
```

```
<!ELEMENT Book (Title, Author)>
<!ATTLIST Book Pages CDATA #REQUIRED>
<!ELEMENT Title (#PCDATA)>
<!ELEMENT Author (#PCDATA)>
<!ELEMENT Magazine (Name)>
<!ATTLIST Magazine Publisher CDATA #REQUIRED>
<!ELEMENT Name (#PCDATA)>
```

DTD contains parameter entities to two external documents   which the XML parser resolves into element and attribute declarations

Working with Unparsed Entities

So far, all of your work with Kristin has focused on character and parsed data. For an XML document to reference either binary data, such as images or video clips, or character data that is not well formed, you need to create an unparsed entity. Because the XML parser cannot work with this type of data directly, the unparsed entity includes instructions for how the unparsed entity needs be treated.

Declaring a Notation

The first step in using unparsed entities is to declare a **notation** identifying a resource that can handle the unparsed data. For example, to include a sound clip or image in the XML document, you must identify a sound- or image-editing application that can work with data in that format. The syntax for declaring a notation is

```
<!NOTATION notation SYSTEM "URL">
```

where *notation* is the notation's name and *URL* indicates the location of the resource. For example, the following declaration creates a notation named "audio" that points to the sound-editing application Recorder.exe.

```
<!NOTATION audio SYSTEM "Recorder.exe">
```

Once a notation has been declared, you declare an unparsed entity that instructs the XML parser to associate the data to the notation. The syntax of this declaration is

```
<!ENTITY entity SYSTEM "URL" NDATA notation>
```

where *entity* is the name you'll assign to the entity, *URL* is the location of the unparsed data, and *notation* is the name of the notation that handles the data. The following declaration takes unparsed data in the form of an audio file and assigns it to an unparsed entity named "Theme:"

```
<!ENTITY Theme SYSTEM "Overture.wav" NDATA audio>
```

The notation in this example is the audio notation that points to the Recorder.exe file. It's important to understand precisely what this declaration does and does not accomplish. It does *not* tell the Recorder.exe application to run the Overture.wav sound file. It merely identifies for the XML parser what resource is capable of handling the unparsed data.

> **REFERENCE WINDOW**   **RW**
>
> Declaring an Unparsed Entity
> - To declare an unparsed entity, first you must declare a notation (a resource that the XML parser should access for the unparsed data), using the syntax
>   ```
>   <!NOTATION notation SYSTEM "URL">
>   ```
>   where *notation* is the notation's name and *URL* indicates the location of the resource.
> - To associate an unparsed entity with a notation, use
>   ```
>   <!ENTITY entity SYSTEM "URL" NDATA notation>
>   ```
>   where *entity* is the name you'll assign to the entity, *URL* is the location of the unparsed data, and *notation* is the name of the notation that handles the data.

Using Unparsed Entities in Attributes

Unparsed entities are often used as attribute values, especially for image files. The following DTD shows the structure of a very simple document. It has a root element named "Page" with a single child element named "Image." The Image element contains an entity attribute named "source." The DTD also contains a notation named "BMP" pointing to the Paint.exe file, which is an image-editing application. Finally, an unparsed entity has been declared for the Logo.bmp graphics file telling the XML processor which application can work with that particular image file.

```
<!DOCTYPE Page
[
    <!ELEMENT Page (Image)>
    <!ELEMENT Image EMPTY>
    <!ATTLIST Image Source ENTITY #REQUIRED>
    <!NOTATION BMP SYSTEM "Paint.exe">
    <!ENTITY Logo SYSTEM "Logo.bmp" NDATA BMP>
]
>
```

The XML author can put these declarations together in the following document:

```
<Page>
  <Image Source="Logo" />
</Page>
```

When this document is opened by the XML parser, the parser is able to interpret the Source attribute of the Image element to know which application is responsible for processing the unparsed data contained in the Logo.bmp file. Currently, Kristin doesn't have any unparsed data for her document, but in the future, she may want to include image files of products in the Pixal product line.

Working with Conditional Sections

When you're creating a new DTD, it's useful to be able to try out different combinations of declarations. Rather than rewriting the DTD each time a change is made, you divide the DTD into two sections. One section contains declarations that will be interpreted by the parser, and the other contains declarations that the parser will ignore. As you experiment with the structure of your DTD, you can move declarations from one section to another without losing the code.

The syntax for creating a section is

```
<![keyword
    declarations
]]>
```

where *keyword* is equal to INCLUDE (for a section of declarations that you want the parser to interpret) or IGNORE (for the declarations that you want the parser to pass over). For example, the following code creates two sections of declarations:

```
<![IGNORE
    <!ELEMENT Magazine (Name)>
    <!ATTLIST Magazine Publisher CDATA #REQUIRED>
    <!ELEMENT Name (#PCDATA)>
]]>
<![INCLUDE
    <!ELEMENT Book (Title, Author)>
    <!ATTLIST Book Pages CDATA #REQUIRED>
    <!ELEMENT Title (#PCDATA)>
    <!ELEMENT Author (#PCDATA)>
]]>
```

The parser processes the declarations involving the Book element, but it ignores the declarations involving the Magazine element.

The DTD can contain multiple IGNORE and INCLUDE sections. One effective way of handling multiple IGNORE sections is to create a parameter entity that defines whether those sections should be included or not, and use the value of the entity as the keyword for the conditional section. For example, the following UseFullDTD entity has a value of "IGNORE," which causes the conditional section that follows to be ignored by the XML parser:

```
<!ENTITY % UseFullDTD "IGNORE">
<![ %UseFullDTD [
    <!ELEMENT Magazine (Name)>
    <!ATTLIST Magazine Publisher CDATA #REQUIRED>
    <!ELEMENT Name (#PCDATA)>
]]>
```

By changing the value of the UseFullDTD from "IGNORE" to "INCLUDE," any conditional section that uses that entity reference will be added to the document's DTD. Thus, the XML author can switch multiple sections in the DTD off and on by editing a single line in the file.

You've completed your work on Kristin's document. You can close the file now.

To complete your work:

1. Return to your text editor and close Orders.xml document.

Session 3.3 QUICK CHECK

1. What is the difference between a general entity and a parameter entity?

2. What is the difference between a parsed entity and an unparsed entity?

3. What declaration would you enter to store the text string "<Title>Hamlet</Title>" as an entity named "Play"? What command would you enter to reference this entity in a document?

4. What declaration would you enter to store the contents of the Plays.xml file as an entity named "Plays"?

5. What code would you enter to store the contents of the Plays.dtd file as a parameter entity named "Works"?

6. What is a notation?

7. How would you store the image file "Shakespeare.gif" in an entity named "Portrait"? Assume that this entity is using a notation named "Paint".

REVIEW ASSIGNMENTS

Kristin has two additional documents that she needs your help on. One document describes Pixal's software products and the other describes its hardware offerings. In the software XML document, each product is contained in an element named "Software." The Software element has three child elements: Title, Company, and SPrice. The Title element has two attributes: first is SID (software ID), and second is OS, which indicates the operating system being used.

In the hardware XML file, each product is contained within an element named "Hardware." The Hardware element has three child elements: Model, Manufacturer, and MPrice. In addition, the Model element has the following attributes: MID, hardware ID, Category, and an optional attribute, SBundle, which identifies software bundled with a hardware item.

Figure 3-25 shows a diagram of the two documents.

Figure 3-25

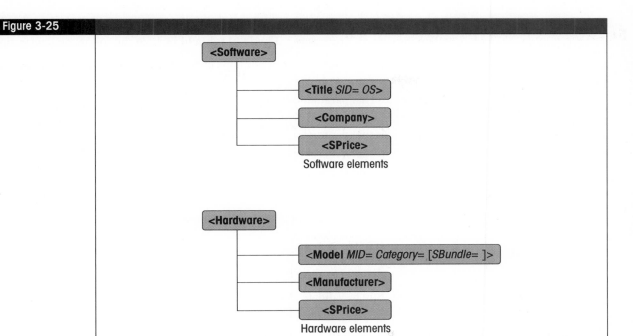

<Software>
<Title *SID= OS*>
<Company>
<SPrice>
Software elements

<Hardware>
<Model *MID= Category= [SBundle=]*>
<Manufacturer>
<SPrice>
Hardware elements

From these two documents, she wants to create a master document that contains a complete inventory of software and hardware products. As you did with the Orders document, it is important to enforce a document structure to ensure that information recorded in these documents is valid.

In the case problems that follow, some of the XML documents contain intentional errors. Part of your job is to find and correct those errors using DTDs.

To complete this task:

1. Using your text editor, open **Pixaltxt.xml**, which is located in the Tutorial.03X/Review folder of your Data Disk.

2. Save the document as **Pixal.xml**. Similarly, create a copy of the SWListtxt.xml file, saving it as **SWList.xml**, and a copy of the HWListtxt.xml file, saving it as **HWList.xml**. Review the contents of these files to get familiar with the structure of the documents involved and the type of content contained in each element and attribute.

3. Using your text editor, create a new file, name it **SW.dtd**, and save it in the Tutorial.03X/Review folder. Create element declarations for all of the software elements.

4. Within SW.dtd, create attribute list declarations for all of the attributes associated with the software elements. The SID attribute should be treated as an ID type. The OS attribute should be treated as an enumerated type, constrained to the following values: Macintosh, Windows, UNIX, or Other.

5. Using your text editor, create a file named **HW.dtd**. Create element declarations for all of the hardware elements.

6. Create attribute list declarations for all of the attributes associated with the hardware elements. Your attribute declarations should fulfill the following conditions:

   ■ The MID attribute should be declared as an ID token.
   ■ The Category attribute should be declared as an enumerated type, constrained to the following values: Camera, Scanner, or Tablet.
   ■ The SBundle attribute should be optional and treated as an ID reference token.

Explore ⟩ 7. Using your text editor, open the **Pixal.xml** file and insert an internal DTD for a root element named "Inventory." The DTD should include the following declarations:

- ■ an Inventory element that contains a choice of multiple child elements named "Hardware" and "Software" (*Hint:* Use a modifying symbol.)
- ■ an external parameter entity named sw_decl that points to the contents of the SW.dtd file you created earlier
- ■ an external parameter entity named hw_decl to point to the HW.dtd file
- ■ an external general entity named sw_list to point to the SWList.xml file
- ■ an external general entity named hw_list to point to the HWList.xml file

Explore ⟩ 8. Insert the sw_decl and hw_decl entity references into the document's DTD.

Explore ⟩ 9. Below the DTD, insert the body of the document. The document's body should include the Inventory root element. Within the root element, insert entity references for the sw_list and hw_list general entities.

10. Save your changes to the Pixal.xml file.

Explore ⟩ 11. Use XML Spy to validate Pixal.xml. If any errors are reported, make your corrections to the SWList.xml and HWList.xml files.

12. Print the contents of all of the files you created in this project.

13. Hand in your files and printouts to your instructor.

CASE PROBLEMS

Case 1. Professional Basketball Association Kurt Vaughn works for the Professional Basketball Association (PBL) and is responsible for coordinating information and statistics for the PBL's many developmental leagues. Part of Kurt's job is to maintain a document that lists the starting lineup for each team as well as providing individual player statistics. Kurt has asked for your help in creating XML documents that maintain a consistent document structure. He has a sample document describing six teams from the Eastern Developmental League (EDL). The document lists the five starting players on each team, including the following statistics about each player: PPG (points per game), RPG (rebounds per game), and Assists (assists per game). Figure 3-26 shows a tree diagram of the document structure. Note that PPG, RPG, and Assists attributes are all optional.

Figure 3-26

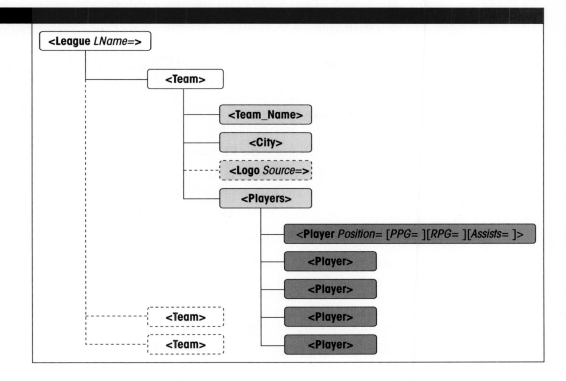

The document also contains an element that stores information about graphic files of team logos. The Logo element is optional. Any DTD that you create for this document will also need to work with the unparsed data contained in these graphic files.

To complete this task:

1. Using your text editor, open the **EDLtxt.xml** file, located in the Tutorial.03X/Cases folder of your Data Disk. Save the document as **EDL.xml**. Take some time to review the elements and attributes of the document.

2. Using your text editor, create a document named **DL.dtd**.

3. In the DL.dtd document, create a DTD, declaring elements shown in Figure 3-26. In addition to the document structure, the declarations should include the following:

   ■ The League element must contain one or more child elements named "Team."
   ■ The LName attribute must be a CDATA type.
   ■ The Team_Name and City elements must contain character data.
   ■ The optional Logo element should be empty, but it should have an entity attribute named "Source." The attribute is required.
   ■ The Players element should contain exactly five child elements named "Player."
   ■ Each Player element should contain only character data. The Player element has one required attribute named "Position," which must have the value Center, Forward, or Guard. The Player element can also have three optional elements named "PPG," "RPG," and "Assists," containing character data.

Explore 4. Also within the DTD, declare a notation named "Graphics" that references the Paint.exe application.

5. Save the DL.dtd file.

6. Within the EDL.xml file, create a mixed DTD. The DTD should reference the DL.dtd file.

Explore

7. Within the internal DTD for the EDL.xml file, create three unparsed entities. Each entity should reference the Graphics notation you created in the DL.dtd file. The first entity should be named "Tigers" and should reference the Tigers.bmp file. The second entity, named "Raiders," should reference the Raiders.bmp file. Finally, the third entity should be named "Storm" and should reference the Storm.bmp file.

8. Save your changes to the EDL.xml file.

9. Test the EDL.xml file using XML Spy. Correct any reported errors to make the document valid. If you have access to a different XML parser, you may use that as well.

10. Print out the code for the DL.dtd and EDL.xml files.

11. Hand in your files and printouts to your instructor.

Case 2. Web News Service, Inc. Alan Li works for the Web News Service, Inc. (WNS) and is responsible for entering daily news items. WNS publishes stories about national and international events, sports, entertainment, and leisure. Each news story is accompanied by a headline, a synopsis, and a reference to a file that contains the complete report. Some news stories are accompanied by image files.

Because of your growing reputation as an XML guru, Alan has asked you to help him store this information using a series of XML documents. The system that you two develop must be easy to update and maintain. Toward this objective, he has decided to place the DTDs in external files. In fact, he's already created one external DTD file for the image files, images.dtd, and another for the full text reports, full_text.dtd. Mr. Li is currently on a much-deserved vacation, and he needs you to create a DTD for the news story synopsis and for a document that displays all of the current stories.

To complete this task:

1. Using your text editor, open **newstxt.xml**, located in the Tutorial.03X/Cases folder of your Data Disk. Save the document as **news.xml**. Review the contents of this document, making careful note of the document's structure and content before proceeding.

2. Using your text editor, create a file named **stories.dtd**. The file needs to contain the following declarations:

   ■ An element named "story" containing four child elements named "headline," "synopsis," "full_text," and "image." The image child element can appear any number of times, but the rest of the child elements can appear only once.

   ■ The story element has a required attribute named "category" that must be one of the following values: national, international, sports, entertainment, leisure, or weather.

   ■ Another attribute of the story element is an optional attribute named "byline." It contains only character data.

   ■ The headline and synopsis elements should contain only character data.

   ■ The full_text and image elements should both be empty elements.

   ■ The full_text element has a entity attribute named "ref." The attribute is required.

   ■ The image element has a required entity attribute named "src."

3. Save the contents of the stories.dtd file.

4. Using your text editor, create a file named **WNS.xml**. This file will display all of the new stories from the other documents.

5. Create an internal DTD for WNS.xml. The DTD should contain the following items:

   ■ a root element named "News_Feed" that contains a single child element named "stories"

   ■ the stories element can occur zero or more times within the News_Feed element

   ■ a parameter entity declaration named "stories," pointing to the stories.dtd file

   ■ a parameter entity declaration named "images," pointing to the images.dtd file

   ■ a parameter entity declaration named "full_text," pointing to the full_text.dtd file

   ■ a general entity declaration named "news," pointing to the news.xml file

   ■ entity references for the stories, images, and full_text entities

6. Create the document body, containing a root element named "News_Feed."

7. Within the News_Feed element, insert an entity reference to the news entity.

8. Save your changes to the WNS.xml file.

9. Use XML Spy to verify that the WNS.xml document is valid. Correct any errors reported by the validator.

10. Print out the contents of all of the documents used in this project.

11. Hand in your printouts and files to your instructor.

Case 3. Freelance Programmer Linda Sanchez is a freelance programmer and is currently working on a checking account application. Having read how XML documents can be read by a wide variety of applications, she is considering using XML to store checking account records for her current project.

She's asked for your help in putting together a document of checking account transactions. She has already entered the elements and attributes, but she needs your help in making the document valid. Figure 3-27 shows the structure of her document.

Figure 3-27

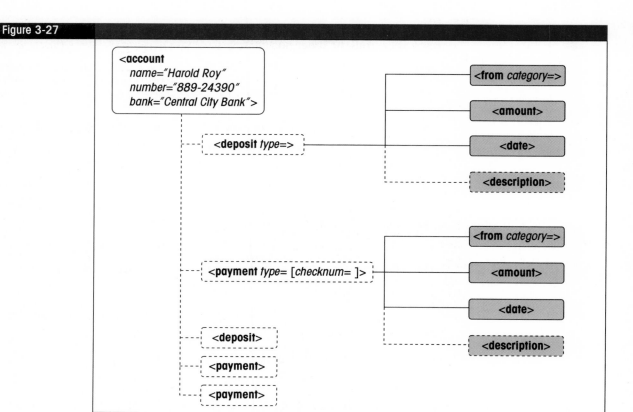

To complete this task:

1. Using your text editor, open the **accounttxt.xml** file, located in the Tutorial.03X/Cases folder of your Data Disk. Save the document as **account.xml**.

2. Take some time to review the contents of the account.xml file, noting the order of the elements and their attributes.

3. Using your text editor, create a file named **checking.dtd** in the Tutorial.03X/Cases folder.

4. Within the checking.dtd file, declare the following elements:

   ■ the account element containing two child elements named "payment" and "deposit," which can occur multiple times in any order

   ■ the deposit element that contains the child elements named "from," "amount," "date," and "description;" the description element is optional

   ■ the payment element that contains the child elements named "to," "amount," "date," and an optional description element

   ■ the from, to, amount, date, and description elements, which contain character data only

5. Add the following attributes to the DTD:

   ■ The account element should have three character data attributes: name, number, and bank. The value of the name attribute must be fixed as "Harold Roy." The value of the number attribute is fixed as "899-24390." The value of the bank attribute is fixed as "Central City Bank."

   ■ The deposit element has one required attribute named "type." The type attribute is limited to the following values: direct, cash, transfer, or check.

- The payment element has a required element named "type" limited to the values atm, check, transfer, or withdrawal. A second attribute of the payment element, named "checknum," is optional, and is treated as an ID token.

- The from element has one required attribute named "category," which must be equal to either income, savings, check, or cash.

- The to element has an optional attribute named "category" that must be equal to one of the following values: utilities, entertainment, food, clothing, cash, or other.

6. Declare a general parsed entity in the DTD named "employer" that stores the text string "Net World."

7. Save your changes to checking.dtd.

8. Return to the account.xml file in your text editor. Create an external DTD that references the checking.dtd file you just created.

9. Replace the text string "Net World" in the first checking transaction with a reference for the employer entity stored in checking.dtd.

10. Save your changes to the account.xml file.

11. Use XML Spy to validate the account.xml file for errors. Fix any errors reported.

12. Print the code of the files you created.

13. Hand in your printouts and files to your instructor.

Case 4. The Lighthouse Charitable Trust. Sela Voight is the Membership Coordinator for The Lighthouse, a charitable organization located in central Kentucky. One of her responsibilities is to maintain a membership list of people in the community who have contributed to The Lighthouse. Members can be in one of three categories: Platinum, Gold, and Premium. The categories assist Sela in defining her fund-raising goals and strategies to reach those goals.

Currently, most of the data that Sela has compiled resides in text files. To be a more effective fundraiser, she wants to convert this data into an XML document and wants to ensure that the resulting document follows some specific guidelines.

To complete this task:

1. Using the data stored in the Members.txt file in the Tutorial.03X/Cases folder of your Data Disk, create an XML document named **List.xml**.

2. The membership data from the Members.txt file should be organized into elements. The appearance of the document is up to you, but it should include the following features:

   - a root element named "List"
   - each member contained within an element named "Member"
   - Member containing the following child elements: Name, Address, Phone, E-mail, Contribution, and Notes; the E-mail and Notes elements are optional child elements, occurring no more than once
   - the Member element containing an attribute named "Level" to identify the level—Platinum, Gold, or Premium—for each member

3. Create a external DTD stored in LHouse.dtd. The DTD should contain declarations for the document structure you applied to List.xml.

4. Test the List.xml file and verify its validity and then print the completed code.

5. Hand in your completed assignment to your instructor.

QUICK CHECK ANSWERS

Session 3.1

1. `<!DOCTYPE Inventory SYSTEM "Books.dtd">`
2. `<!ELEMENT Book ANY>`
3. `<!ELEMENT Video EMPTY>`
4. `<!ELEMENT Book (#PCDATA)>`
5. `<!ELEMENT Book (Author)>`
6. `<!ELEMENT Book (Author+)>`
7. `<!ELEMENT Book (#PCDATA | Author | Title)*>`

Session 3.2

1. `<!ATTLIST book Title CDATA #IMPLIED>`
2. `<!ATTLIST Play Type (Romance | Tragedy | History | Comedy) #REQUIRED>`
3. NMTOKEN types cannot contain blank spaces.
4. `<!ATTLIST Book ISBN ID #REQUIRED>`
5. `<!ATTLIST Author BooksBy IDREF #IMPLIED>`
6. `<!ATTLIST Book InStock (yes | no) "yes">`

Session 3.3

1. General entities are used only with the contents of an XML document. Parameter entities are used only with contents of a DTD.
2. Parsed entities consist entirely of well-formed XML content. Unparsed entities are constructed from non-XML data, including nontext data.
3. `<!ENTITY Play "<Title>Hamlet</Title>">`
   `&Play;`
4. `<!ENTITY Plays SYSTEM "Plays.xml">`
5. `<!ENTITY % Works "<!ENTITY % Works SYSTEM "Plays.dtd">`
6. A notation is a resource that an XML parser uses to handle unparsed data.
7. `<!ENTITY Portrait SYSTEM "Shakespeare.gif" NDATA Paint>`

OBJECTIVES

In this tutorial you will:

- Learn to create and apply namespaces

- Learn about schemas and schema dialects

- Create simple type declarations

- Create complex type declarations

- Learn how different schemas are structured

- Derive customized data types

- Annotate a schema and attach it to an instance document

WORKING
WITH NAMESPACES
AND SCHEMAS

Creating a Patient Report Document

CASE

University Hospital

Allison Grant is a project coordinator at the Clinical Cancer Center of the University Hospital. Her job is to coordinate the various research projects at the center. Allison wants to use XML to record data on the different studies and the patients enrolled in them. She then plans to use these XML documents to create Web pages for the hospital network, which investigators can use to view relevant information on patients and studies. Allison is new to XML and has sought out your help in a couple of areas.

On occasion, Allison needs to combine data from different sources into a single XML document. For example, the data from one document describing a study may need to be combined with data from another document describing individual patients. Allison would like to discuss with you how best to combine data from two XML documents.

A second issue involves data integrity. Accuracy is important to Allison. She needs to know that the data she enters is error free. For example, some of the studies have age criteria. Allison would like to be able to confirm that any patient she enters matches the age criteria for that study. Allison knows that DTDs cannot fulfill this function because they have a limited range of data types and provide no way to deal with numeric data. Allison has heard that schemas may be able to give the kind of control over data quality that she requires and would like you to help her implement them.

SESSION 4.1

In this session, you'll learn how to add namespaces to an XML document, and you'll see how namespaces can help you avoid "name collisions" when combining information from several documents. You'll also learn how namespaces can be applied to elements and attributes, and the consequences of using namespaces in the document's DTD.

Working with Namespaces

It is common practice to create several XML documents, with each document focused on one particular topic. This practice, however, can create significant challenges when information from different sources needs to be merged into a common document. One common problem is **name collision**, where elements from two or more documents share the same name. Figure 4-1 shows an example in which the Name element is used to store the name of a book in one document, while in another document, it stores the name of an author. When data from the two documents is combined, the Name element is used in two different contexts. The structure of the two Name elements is also different: in the Book document it stores text and in the Author document it contains two child elements.

Figure 4-1	NAME COLLISION

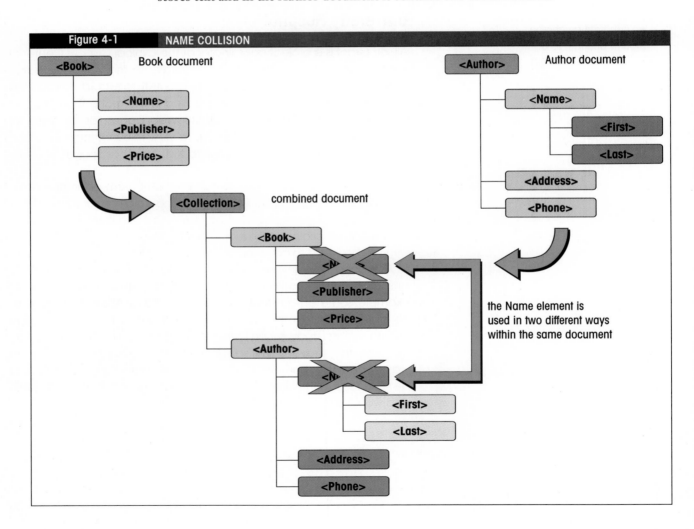

Such is the situation that Allison has with two of her XML documents. One document contains information on the clinical studies taking place at the hospital. Another document stores information on patients enrolled in those studies. Allison has combined data from both documents into a single file. Open that combined document now.

To open Allison's document:

1. Using your text editor, open **UHosptxt.xml** located in the Tutorial.04X/Tutorial folder of your Data Disk.

2. Save the file as **UHosp.xml**. Figure 4-2 shows a diagram of the structure of the UHosp.xml file. Take some time to study the document, comparing the code to the diagram.

Figure 4-2	LAYOUT OF THE UHOSP.XML DOCUMENT

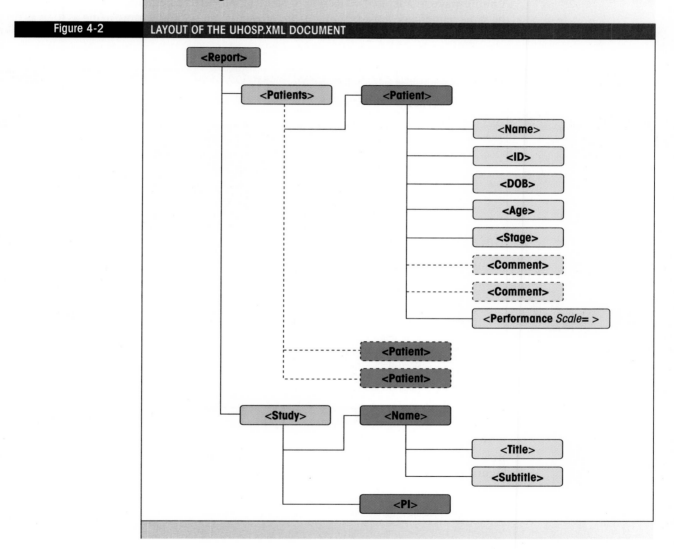

Note that there is a collision in Allison's document between the use of the Name element as a container for a patient's name and for storing information about the name of the study. As long as Allison is not concerned with validation, such collisions are not a problem. The content of her documents only needs to be well-formed. However, if she tried to validate this document, she would run into trouble because of the different ways the Name element is being used.

For a single author working on a small number of documents involving only a handful of elements, it is a relatively easy task to prevent name collisions. One simply ensures that each element has a unique name. However, in large organizations with several authors working to maintain hundreds of XML documents with thousands of element names, it is a nearly impossible job to avoid name collision. Allison doesn't have the ability to edit the original Patient and Study documents to rename their elements. Nor does she want to rename the elements in her combined document because she would then have to maintain two sets of element names: one for the individual documents and one for the combined document. There is a third way to solve this problem: namespaces.

Declaring a Namespace in the Document Prolog

A **namespace** is a defined collection of element and attribute names. Names that belong to the same namespace must be unique, but elements can share the same name as long as they reside in different namespaces (see Figure 4-3).

Figure 4-3	USING NAMESPACES TO AVOID NAME COLLISION

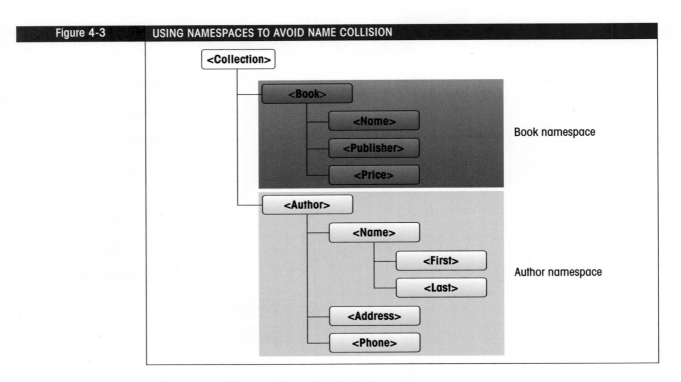

In Allison's case, it would make sense to create one namespace for all of the elements and attributes associated with patients, and another namespace for the clinical studies (see Figure 4-4).

Figure 4-4 THE PATIENT AND STUDY NAMESPACES

```xml
<?xml version="1.0" ?>

<Report>

    <Patients>
        <Patient>
            <Name>Cynthia Dibbs</Name>
            <ID>MR890-041-02</ID>
            <DOB>1945-05-22</DOB>
            <Age>58</Age>
            <Stage>II</Stage>
            <Performance Scale="Karnofsky">0.81</Performance>
        </Patient>
        <Patient>
            <Name>Karen Wilkes</Name>
            <ID>MR771-121-10</ID>
            <DOB>1959-02-24</DOB>
            <Age>44</Age>
            <Stage>II</Stage>
            <Comment>Dropped out of study.</Comment>
            <Performance Scale="Karnofsky">0.84</Performance>
        </Patient>
        <Patient>
            <Name>Olivia Sanchez</Name>
            <ID>MR701-891-05</ID>
            <DOB>1958-08-14</DOB>
            <Age>45</Age>
            <Stage>I</Stage>
            <Comment>Possibly Stage I/II</Comment>
            <Comment>Karnofsky performance rating unavailable.</Comment>
            <Performance Scale="Bell">0.89</Performance>
        </Patient>
        <Patient>
            <Name>Alice Russell</Name>
            <ID>MR805-891-08</ID>
            <DOB>1952-09-14</DOB>
            <Age>51</Age>
            <Stage>II</Stage>
            <Performance Scale="Karnofsky">0.76</Performance>
        </Patient>
        <Patient>
            <Name>Brenda Browne</Name>
            <ID>MR815-741-03</ID>
            <DOB>1964-04-25</DOB>
            <Age>39</Age>
            <Stage>I</Stage>
            <Performance Scale="Karnofsky">0.88</Performance>
        </Patient>
    </Patients>

    <Study>
        <Name>
            <Title>Tamoxifen Breast Cancer Study</Title>
            <Subtitle>Randomized Phase 3 Clinical Trial</Subtitle>
        </Name>
        <PI>Dr. Diane West</PI>
    </Study>

</Report>
```

patient namespace

Study namespace

Before they can be applied, namespaces must first be declared. A namespace can either be declared in the document's prolog or as an element attribute. The syntax for declaring a namespace in the prolog is

```
<?xml:namespace ns="URI" prefix="prefix"?>
```

where *URI* is a Uniform Resource Identifier that assigns a unique name to the namespace, and *prefix* is a string of letters that associates each element or attribute in the document with the declared namespace. For example, the following code declares a namespace with the prefix "pat" and the URI, "http://uhosp/patients/ns".

```
<?xml:namespace ns="http://uhosp/patients/ns" prefix="pat"?>
```

The URI looks like a Web address, but it's not. Before proceeding further with namespaces, URIs need a bit of explanation.

A Few Words About URIs, URLs, and URNs

A **Uniform Resource Identifier**, or **URI**, is a text string that identifies either a physical or an abstract resource. A physical resource would be a resource that one could access or work with, such as a file, a Web page, or an e-mail address. One type of URI is a URL, which is used to identify actual resources on the Internet. An abstract resource is a resource that doesn't have any physical existence, and the URI in this case is simply an identifier, much like an ID. Though it may look like an Internet address, an abstract resource doesn't actually reference an existing file or resource. The URI in the above sample code,

```
http://uhosp/patients/ns
```

is simply a text identifier. There is no Web page located at this address.

Actually, any unique text string can work as a namespace identifier, but there is good reason for using URIs. If the XML document is to be shared on the Web, the XML author needs to make sure that the document's namespace name will be unique. One way of doing this would be to have an organization register namespaces in the same way that Internet addresses are registered. However, because we already have a registry of unique Internet addresses, it makes sense to expand that system to encompass abstract references.

Another proposed type of URI is the URN or Universal Resource Name. A **URN** is a persistent resource identifier, which means that the user only needs to know the name of a resource, and one or more agencies retrieve the nearest copy of the resource, no matter where it is located. URNs take the following form:

```
urn:NID:NSS
```

where *NID* is the namespace identifier and *NSS* is the namespace-specific string. The *NID* tells us how to interpret the *NSS*. For example, the following URN is used to uniquely identify the ISBN number of a book:

```
urn:isbn:0-619-01969-7
```

The use of URNs with namespaces is still in its early stages, but URNs may eventually become the preferred way of expressing namespace names.

Declaring and Applying a Namespace

■ To declare a namespace in the document's prolog, use the following declaration:

```
<?xml:namespace ns="URI" prefix="prefix"?>
```

where *URI* is a Uniform Resource Identifier that assigns a unique name to the namespace, and *prefix* is the namespace prefix.

■ To declare a namespace within an element, add the following attribute to the element:

```
xmlns:prefix="URI"
```

■ To associate an element with a namespace, insert the namespace prefix before the element name as follows:

```
<prefix:element>
   content
</prefix:element>
```

■ To create a default namespace, do not include the *prefix* in the namespace declaration.

Applying a Namespace to an Element

Once a namespace has been declared and its URI specified, it can be applied to individual elements and attributes within the document. This is done by inserting the namespace prefix before each element name that belongs to the namespace. The general form is

```
<prefix:element>
   content
</prefix:element>
```

where *prefix* is the namespace prefix and *element* is the **local part** of the element name. Prefixed names are called **qualified names**. An element name lacking a namespace prefix is referred to as **unqualified name**.

Allison could adapt her element names to namespaces using the following code:

```
<?xml:namespace ns="http://uhosp/patients/ns" prefix="pat"?>
<?xml:namespace ns="http://uhosp/studies/ns" prefix="std"?>
<Report>
  <pat:Patients>
    <pat:Patient>
      <pat:Name>Cynthia Dibbs</pat:Name>
      <pat:ID>MR890-041-02</pat:ID>
      <pat:DOB>1945-05-22</pat:DOB>
      <pat:Age>58</pat:Age>
      <pat:Stage>II</pat:Stage>
      <pat:Performance Scale="Karnofsky">0.81</pat:
       Performance>
    </pat:Patient>

  ...

  <std:Study>
     <std:Name>Tamoxifen Breast Cancer Study</std:Name>
     <std:ID>CP2004-05-01</std:ID>
     <std:Director>Dr. Diane West</std:Director>
  </std:Study>
</Report>
```

In this sample code, there is no collision between the Name and ID elements because they belong to different namespaces. Moreover, from the prefixes, it is clear which element is associated with which namespace. In this example, each element name except Report is a qualified element name.

Declaring a Namespace as an Element Attribute

The more common way of declaring a namespace is to add the xmlns attribute to an element. The syntax is

```
xmlns:prefix="URI"
```

where *prefix* and *URI* are the prefix and URI for the namespace. Once a namespace is declared in this fashion, the namespace is made available to that element and to any of its child elements. The following code shows how to apply the namespace "http://uhosp/patients/ns namespace" to the Patient element and all of its child elements:

```
<pat:Patients xmlns:pat="http://uhosp/patients/ns">
  <Patient>
    <Name>Cynthia Dibbs</Name>
    <ID>MR890-041-02</ID>
    <DOB>1945-05-22</DOB>
    <Age>58</Age>
    <Stage>II</Stage>
    <Performance Scale="Karnofsky">0.81</Performance>
  </Patient>

...

</pat:Patients>
```

Note that the "pat" prefix was only added to the Patients element name. Even though the other elements in this sample code lack the prefix, the XML parser still considers them part of the Patients namespace because they inherit the namespace of their parent element, Patients. The lack of a namespace prefix does make them unqualified elements, however.

The most common way of declaring a namespace is to add it as an attribute of the document's root element. This method places all document elements in that namespace because all elements are children of the root element.

Declaring a Default Namespace

To avoid using namespace prefixes, you can specify a **default namespace** by omitting the prefix in the namespace declaration. The element containing the namespace attribute and all of its child elements are assumed to be part of the default namespace unless a different namespace is explicitly defined for one of those elements. The Patients namespace is applied to all of the elements in the following sample code, even though none of the elements are qualified:

```
<Patients xmlns="http://uhosp/patients/ns">
  <Patient>
    <Name>Cynthia Dibbs</Name>
    <ID>MR890-041-02</ID>
    <DOB>1945-05-22</DOB>
    <Age>58</Age>
    <Stage>II</Stage>
    <Performance Scale="Karnofsky">0.81</Performance>
```

```
    </Patient>

...

    </Patients>
```

Using Namespaces with Attributes

Like elements, attributes can become qualified by adding the namespace prefix to the attribute name as follows:

```
prefix:attribute="value"
```

There are two important rules to remember regarding attribute names:

- No element may contain two attributes with the same name, whether the attribute name is qualified or not.
- No element may contain two qualified attribute names with the same local part, pointing to identical namespaces, even if the prefixes are different.

Under these rules, the two elements in the following document would be considered invalid:

```
<Document
    xmlns:pat1="http:/uhosp/patients/ns"
    xmlns:pat2="http:/uhosp/patients/ns">

    <Name pat1:att1="1" pat1:att1="2" />
    <Name pat1:att1="1" pat2:att1="2" />
</Document>
```

The first element is invalid because the attribute names are identical and XML doesn't allow duplicate attributes within the same element. The second element is invalid because although the attribute names are different, their local parts are identical and their prefixes point to the same namespace.

A final important point to remember about attribute names is that an unqualified attribute name does not explicitly belong to any namespace, even if a default namespace has been declared for the document. This means that even if the element belongs to a namespace, the attribute does not, unless the attribute name is qualified by adding a namespace prefix. Generally, assigning a namespace to an attribute is not necessary unless you intend to use two attributes with the same name within a single element. In that case, to avoid name collision, they must be assigned to different namespaces and have different prefixes.

Creating a Namespace

After reviewing the material on namespaces, Allison decides that she needs to include namespaces in her document to avoid the problem of name collision. She has asked for your help in editing the document to ensure it is done correctly.

Allison wants to assign all of the patient data to a default namespace with the URI http://uhosp/patients/ns using the prefix "pat." She wants to assign all of the study data to a namespace with the URI "http://uhosp/studies/ns" and a namespace prefix of "std." You decide to declare the namespaces as attributes of the Patients and Study elements.

To create the two namespaces:

1. In the UHosp.xml file, add the following attribute to the Patients element: **xmlns:pat="http://uhosp/patients/ns"**.

2. Add the following attribute to the Study element: **xmlns:std="http://uhosp/studies/ns"**.

   To avoid confusion, you decide to make all of the elements in the Study namespace qualified elements. You'll leave the elements in the Patient namespace unqualified, aside from the opening and closing Patients tag.

3. Change the opening and closing tags of the Patients element from Patients to **pat:Patients**.

4. Change the opening and closing tags of the Study element from Study to **std:Study**.

5. Make all of the child elements of the std:Study element qualified elements by inserting the "std" namespace prefix.

   Figure 4-5 displays the revised XML code for UHosp.xml.

Figure 4-5 | **DECLARING NAMESPACES**

```
<pat:Patients xmlns:pat="http://uhosp/patients/ns">              Patient namespace
    <Patient>                                                    declaration
        <Name>Cynthia Dibbs</Name>
        <ID>MR890-041-02</ID>
        <DOB>1945-05-22</DOB>
        <Age>58</Age>
        <Stage>II</Stage>
        <Performance Scale="Karnofsky">0.81</Performance>
    </Patient>
    <Patient>
        <Name>Karen Wilkes</Name>
        <ID>MR771-121-10</ID>
        <DOB>1959-02-24</DOB>
        <Age>44</Age>
        <Stage>II</Stage>
        <Comment>Dropped out of study.</Comment>
        <Performance Scale="Karnofsky">0.84</Performance>
    </Patient>
    <Patient>
        <Name>Olivia Sanchez</Name>
        <ID>MR701-891-05</ID>
        <DOB>1958-08-14</DOB>
        <Age>45</Age>
        <Stage>I</Stage>
        <Comment>Possibly Stage I/II</Comment>
        <Comment>Karnofsky performance rating unavailable.</Comment>
        <Performance Scale="Bell">0.89</Performance>
    </Patient>
    <Patient>
        <Name>Alice Russell</Name>
        <ID>MR805-891-08</ID>
        <DOB>1952-09-14</DOB>
        <Age>51</Age>
        <Stage>II</Stage>
        <Performance Scale="Karnofsky">0.76</Performance>
    </Patient>
    <Patient>
        <Name>Brenda Browne</Name>
        <ID>MR815-741-03</ID>
        <DOB>1964-04-25</DOB>
        <Age>39</Age>
        <Stage>I</Stage>
        <Performance Scale="Karnofsky">0.88</Performance>           Study namespace
    </Patient>                                                       declaration
</pat:Patients>

<std:Study xmlns:std="http://uhosp/studies/ns">
    <std:Name>
        <std:Title>Tamoxifen Breast Cancer Study</std:Title>
        <std:Subtitle>Randomized Phase 3 Clinical Trial</std:Subtitle>
    </std:Name>
    <std:PI>Dr. Diane West</std:PI>
</std:Study>
```

namespace prefix

6. Save your changes to UHosp.xml.

Now that you've inserted namespaces into the document, Allison wants to validate it with a DTD from an external subset. She has already created the DTD, but she's not sure how to modify it for use with namespaces.

Working with Namespaces and DTDs

Documents containing namespaces must adhere to the same rules for XML validity that documents without namespaces must follow. Each element and attribute appearing in the document must be included in the DTD, even if it belongs to a namespace that is not the default namespace. Namespace prefixes must also appear in the DTD for the document. For example, if a text element named "ID" becomes a qualified element with the namespace prefix "pat," it must appear in the DTD as follows:

```
<!ELEMENT pat:ID (#PCDATA)>
```

In essence, the XML parser considers the prefix, the separating colon, and the local part as a single entity.

Something else to consider is if you use the xmlns attribute to declare a namespace, you need to include this attribute in the DTD, declared as a fixed value. For example, if you have the following element in your document:

```
<pat:Patients xmlns:pat="http://uhosp/patients/ns">
```

you need to declare it in the DTD as follows:

```
<!ATTLIST pat:Patients xmlns:pat CDATA #FIXED
"http://uhosp/patients/ns">
```

Qualified attribute names also need to include the namespace prefix in any declaration in the DTD.

Allison would like you to adapt her DTD file for use with the namespaces you created.

To edit the DTD and link it to an XML document:

1. Use your text editor to open the **UHDTDtxt.dtd** document located in the Tutorial.04X/Tutorial folder of your Data Disk.

2. Save the file as **UHDTD.dtd**.

   Figure 4-6 displays the current contents of UHDTD.dtd file.

Figure 4-6	UHDTD.DTD

```
<!ELEMENT Report (Patients, Study)>

<!ELEMENT Patients (Patient+)>
<!ELEMENT Patient (Name, ID, DOB, Age, Stage, Comment*, Performance)>
<!ELEMENT Name (#PCDATA)>
<!ELEMENT ID (#PCDATA)>
<!ELEMENT DOB (#PCDATA)>
<!ELEMENT Age (#PCDATA)>
<!ELEMENT Stage (#PCDATA)>
<!ELEMENT Comment (#PCDATA)>
<!ELEMENT Performance (#PCDATA)>
<!ATTLIST Performance Scale (Karnofsky | Bell) #REQUIRED>

<!ELEMENT Study (Name, PI)>
<!ELEMENT Name (Title, Subtitle)>
<!ELEMENT Title (#PCDATA)>
<!ELEMENT Subtitle (#PCDATA)>
<!ELEMENT PI (#PCDATA)>
```

3. Change the name of the Patients element to **pat:Patients** wherever it appears in the DTD.

4. Change the name of the Study element to **std:Study** wherever it appears in the DTD.

5. Make all of the names of the child elements of the Study element into qualified element names by adding the "std" namespace prefix to each element name.

6. Add the attribute declarations for the two namespaces to the DTD by inserting the following two lines of code at the end of the DTD:

```
<!ATTLIST pat:Patients xmlns:pat CDATA #FIXED
"http://uhosp/patients/ns">
<!ATTLIST std:Study xmlns:std CDATA #FIXED
"http://uhosp/studies/ns">
```

Figure 4-7 displays the contents of the revised DTD. Save your changes and close the file.

Figure 4-7	ADDING NAMESPACE INFORMATION TO THE DTD

namespace prefixes must be included in the DTD

the xmlns attribute that assigns the namespace must be declared as a fixed character data

```
<!ELEMENT Report (pat:Patients, std:Study)>

<!ELEMENT pat:Patients (Patient+)>
<!ELEMENT Patient (Name, ID, DOB, Age, Stage, Comment*, Performance)>
<!ELEMENT Name (#PCDATA)>
<!ELEMENT ID (#PCDATA)>
<!ELEMENT DOB (#PCDATA)>
<!ELEMENT Age (#PCDATA)>
<!ELEMENT Stage (#PCDATA)>
<!ELEMENT Comment (#PCDATA)>
<!ELEMENT Performance (#PCDATA)>
<!ATTLIST Performance Scale (Karnofsky | Bell) #REQUIRED>

<!ELEMENT std:Study (std:Name, std:PI)>
<!ELEMENT std:Name (std:Title, std:Subtitle)>
<!ELEMENT std:Title (#PCDATA)>
<!ELEMENT std:Subtitle (#PCDATA)>
<!ELEMENT std:PI (#PCDATA)>

<!ATTLIST pat:Patients xmlns:pat CDATA #FIXED "http://uhosp/patients/ns">
<!ATTLIST std:Study xmlns:std CDATA #FIXED "http://uhosp/studies/ns">
```

7. Close the UHDTD.dtd file, saving your changes, and then open **UHosp.xml** using your text editor. After the first line, insert the following document type declaration (see Figure 4-8):

```
<!DOCTYPE Report SYSTEM "UHDTD.dtd">
```

Figure 4-8	APPLYING THE REVISED DTD TO ALLISON'S DOCUMENT

```
<?xml version="1.0" ?>
<!DOCTYPE Report SYSTEM "UHDTD.dtd">
<Report>
```

8. Save your changes and close UHosp.xml.

In general, there are a number of issues and practical concerns that prevent namespaces and DTDs from working particularly well together. For example, there is no way to associate a specific DTD with namespace. What this means to XML authors is that a new DTD must be created each time two or more documents are combined into a single document. If you're in the habit of combining data from several different sources, like Allison is, this can be a frustrating use of your time. For this and other reasons, the use of namespaces is a controversial topic of discussion among some XML developers. Many developers would prefer a system where namespaces and data validation could more easily coexist.

One possible solution to this dilemma is the use of schemas, which will be discussed in the next two sessions.

Session 4.1 QUICK CHECK

1. What is a namespace and why are namespaces important?

2. What is a qualified element name?

3. How would you declare a namespace with the URI "http://ns.doc/book" and the prefix "Book" in the prolog of your document?

4. How would you declare the namespace from the previous question as an attribute of an element named "Work"?

5. How do you create a default namespace?

6. How are qualified elements represented in a DTD?

SESSION 4.2

In this session, you'll learn about schemas, their history, and their different dialects. You'll create a schema and use it to declare the features and properties of the elements and attributes in an XML document. Finally, you'll learn how to attach a schema to a document.

Introducing Schemas

Having completed your work on combining the content of the Study and Patients documents into a single XML file, Allison now wants you to look at the contents of the Patients document alone. Allison is particularly concerned that the data entered into that document is valid. Currently, she is doing validation with DTDs but feels that they are inadequate for her needs.

The use of DTDs as a validation tool is due largely to the fact that XML is an offshoot of SGML. SGML was originally designed for text-based documents such as reports and technical manuals. As long as the data content is limited to simple text, DTDs work well for validation. However, XML is being used for a wider range of document types, and there are several limitations that have prompted XML developers to explore alternatives to DTDs.

One of these limitations was discussed in the last session—the inability of DTDs to work well with namespaces. In an environment with hundreds of XML documents, it is extremely time consuming to create and manage a separate DTD for each combination of documents. Another complaint about DTDs is the lack of data types. For example, if Allison wants to record each patient's age, she can declare an Age element, but she cannot specify in the DTD that the Age element contain only numbers, or numbers within a specified range of values. She can create a Date element, but the DTD won't have the tools to ensure that only dates are entered into the document. DTDs simply do not have the control over the data that Allison requires.

A DTD is also limited in its ability to enforce a structure on mixed content. A DTD can specify that an element contain both text and child elements, but it cannot control the sequence or number of each child element. There are workarounds, but they can be complicated to implement.

Finally, DTDs use a different syntax from XML called **Extended Backus Naur Form** (**EBNF**). This means that an application that validates an XML document must be able to work with not only the syntax of XML but also EBNF. XML authors also have to be conversant with both syntaxes.

Because XML stands for *Extensible* Markup Language, why not use XML itself to describe the structure of XML documents? This is the idea behind schemas.

Schemas and DTDs

A **schema** is an XML document that defines the content and structure of one or more XML documents. To avoid confusion, the XML document containing the content is called the **instance document** because it represents a specific instance of the structure defined in the schema.

Figure 4-9 outlines some of the important differences between schemas and DTDs.

Figure 4-9 — COMPARING SCHEMAS AND DTDS

SCHEMAS	DTDS
Written in XML	Written in Extended Backus Naur Form (EBNF)
Multiple, competing schema standards	One single DTD standard
Not supported by all validating parsers	Supported by all validating parsers
Supports over 44 data types	Supports ten data types
Users can create customized data types	Users cannot create customized data types
Easily handles mixed content	Cannot easily handle mixed content
Schemas can be attached to namespaces	DTDs cannot be attached to namespaces
Does not support entities	Supports entities

Schemas have a number of advantages over DTDs. For one, the XML parser only needs to understand XML, and thus all of the tools used to create the instance document can be applied to designing the schema. Schemas also support more data types, including data types for numbers and dates. The only content supported by DTDs involves text or child elements.

So if schemas are so useful, why do we need DTDs at all? First of all, DTDs represent an older standard for XML documents and are, therefore, more widely supported. It will still be a few years before schemas entirely replace DTDs for document validation. DTDs can also do a few things that schemas cannot, such as create entities. Therefore, we need to view schemas and DTDs as complementary approaches. In some cases, an XML document might use both a schema and a DTD.

Schema Dialects

Unlike DTDs, there is not a single form of the schema. Instead, several schema "dialects" have been developed in the XML language. Each dialect has distinct advantages and disadvantages, and a few of these dialects are listed in Figure 4-10.

Figure 4-10	SCHEMA DIALECTS	
SCHEMA	**DESCRIPTION**	**URL**
DDML	DDML (Document Definition Markup Language) is a schema language for XML documents, encoding the logical (as opposed to physical) content of DTDs in an XML document. It is also known as XSchema.	http://www.w3.org/TR/NOTE-ddml
RELAX	The RELAX (Regular Language for XML) schema is based on a Japanese national schema standard.	http://www.xml.gr.jp/relax
RELAX NG	The RELAX NG schema combines the RELAX and NG schema specifications.	http://www.oasis-open.org/committees/relax-ng/
Schematron	The Schematron schema represents documents using a tree pattern, allowing support for those document structures that might be difficult to represent in more traditional schema languages.	http://www.ascc.net/xml/resource/schematron/schematron.html
TREX	The TREX (Tree Regular Expressions) schema specifies a pattern for the structure and content of an XML document, identifying a class of XML documents that match the pattern.	http://www.thaiopensource.com/trex/
XDR	The XDR (XML-Data Reduced) schema is developed and supported by Microsoft, in particular Microsoft's Internet Explorer browser. XDR is sometimes referred to as XML-Data.	http://www.ltg.ed.ac.uk/~ht/XMLData-Reduced.htm
XML-Schema	XML-Schema, created by the W3C Schema Working Group, is a large specification designed to handle a broad range of document structures. It is also referred to as XSD.	http://www.w3.org/XML/Schema

Please note that support for a particular schema depends solely on the XML parser being used for validation. Before applying any of the schemas listed in Figure 4-10, you will have to verify the level of support offered by your application for that particular schema. The two most prominent dialects are XML Schema and XDR.

XML Schema, developed by the W3C in March of 2001, represents the closest thing to a schema standard. Because the specifications for XML Schema are so new, not all applications support all of its aspects. However, due to the influence associated with the W3C and its specifications, it is certain that most XML parsers will eventually support XML Schema.

Microsoft's schema, XDR, was the first schema to be developed. As such, XDR is supported by most of Microsoft's XML-aware applications—most notably Internet Explorer. It should be noted that Microsoft is moving toward supporting both XDR and XML Schema. Internet Explorer version 5.5 and above supports both schema dialects.

The focus of this tutorial is primarily on the XML Schema dialect, though many of the concepts involved with XML Schema can be applied to the other schema dialects as well. You can convert your DTD files to XML Schema files using the dtd2xs converter, available at *http://www.w3.org/XML/Schema*. Also, for XML developers who need to work with both XML Schema and XDR, Microsoft provides a tool to convert XML Schema files into the XDR format. You can access this converter at: *http://msdn.microsoft.com/downloads/default.asp?url=/downloads/topic.asp?url=/msdn-files/028/000/072/topic.xml*.

Starting a Schema File

DTDs can be divided into internal or external subsets. This is not the case with schemas. A schema is always placed in a separate XML document that is referenced by the instance document. A schema file written in the XML Schema dialect typically ends with the .xsd file extension. XDR schemas are usually stored in files with the .xdr file extension.

Before you start creating the schema, though, you should open and save Allison's Patients document.

To open Allison's document:

1. Using your text editor, open **Pattxt.xml** located in the Tutorial.04X/Tutorial folder of your Data Disk.

2. Save the file as **Patient.xml**.

   Note that the data is this file is the same as the data in the UHosp.xml document, except that there are no study elements and the root element is now Patients rather than Report.

Allison has also created a table describing the types of rules she would like to see applied to the data in this document. For example, she wants to ensure that a number is entered for the patient's age rather than a text string. Figure 4-11 describes the contents of each element and attribute in Allison's document.

Figure 4-11	ELEMENTS AND ATTRIBUTES OF THE PATIENT DOCUMENT
ELEMENTS	**DESCRIPTION**
Patients	The root element of Allison's document
Patient	The element that stores information about each individual patient (Name, ID, DOB, Stage, and Performance)
Name	The patient's name
ID	The patient's medical record number in the format MR###-###-##
DOB	The patient's date of birth in the format YYYY-MM-DD
Age	The patient's age (must be 21 or older)
Stage	The stage of the patient's breast cancer (must be either I or II)
Performance	A measure of the patient's health (must be a number between 0 and 1)
Comment	Optional comments providing additional information about the patient
ATTRIBUTES	
Scale	A required attribute of the Performance element indicating the type of performance measure; the attribute value must be equal to either "Karnofsky" or "Bell"

Creating a Schema
- Create an XML document with a root element named schema.
- The contents of the schema file should match the following general format:

```
<xsd:schema xmlns:xsd="http://www.w3.org/2001/XMLSchema">
    document specifications
</xsd:schema>
```

where *document specifications* are schema elements that declare the properties and contents of the data in the instance document.

Now that you've seen the structure of Allison's document, you can begin creating the schema to match it.

To create the schema file:

1. Open a new blank file in your text editor.

   Because schemas are XML documents, they follow the same structure as other XML documents: they must have a prolog and a root element, and must begin with the xml tag.

2. Type **<?xml version="1.0" encoding="UTF-8"?>** in the first line of document.

   Add a comment to describe the purpose of this file.

3. Below the prolog, enter the following line:

   ```
   <!-- Schema for breast cancer patient data -->
   ```

   Because this file will be using the XML Schema, save it with the .xsd file extension.

4. Save the file as **PSchema1.xsd** to the Tutorial.04X/Tutorial folder of your Data Disk.

Next you insert the document's root element. In XML Schema, the root element is named "schema." Also, the schema element must contain a namespace declaration that tells the XML parser that the elements in this document are written in XML Schema form. The URI of the XML Schema namespace is *http://www.w3.org/2001/XMLSchema*. An XML Schema document is therefore constructed as follows:

```
<xsd:schema xmlns:xsd="http://www.w3.org/2001/XMLSchema">
    document specifications
</xsd:schema>
```

where *document specifications* is the XML code that we'll use to define the content of the instance document.

By convention, the prefix "xsd" or "xs" is assigned to the XML Schema namespace, though such a prefix is not required. One could define the XML Schema namespace as the default namespace for the document or use a different prefix altogether. However, the xsd prefix does serve a useful role as a visual reminder that this is an XML Schema document and not a generic XML file.

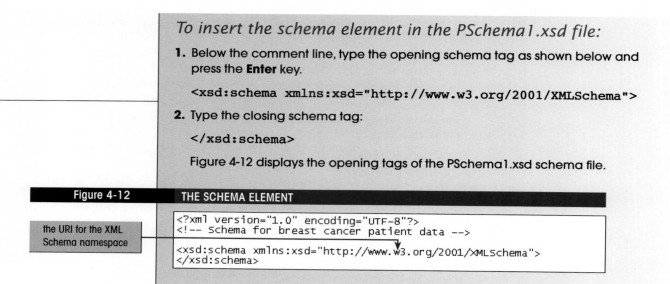

To insert the schema element in the PSchema1.xsd file:

1. Below the comment line, type the opening schema tag as shown below and press the **Enter** key.

   ```
   <xsd:schema xmlns:xsd="http://www.w3.org/2001/XMLSchema">
   ```

2. Type the closing schema tag:

   ```
   </xsd:schema>
   ```

   Figure 4-12 displays the opening tags of the PSchema1.xsd schema file.

Figure 4-12	THE SCHEMA ELEMENT

the URI for the XML Schema namespace

```
<?xml version="1.0" encoding="UTF-8"?>
<!-- Schema for breast cancer patient data -->

<xsd:schema xmlns:xsd="http://www.w3.org/2001/XMLSchema">
</xsd:schema>
```

Note that the schema tags are case sensitive. You cannot use the element name "Schema" (with an initial capital letter) in place of "schema." You are now ready to insert declarations for the elements and attributes for Allison's XML document.

Working with Simple Types

XML Schema recognizes two categories of element types: complex and simple. A **complex type** element is an element that has one or more attributes, or is the parent to one or more child elements. A **simple type** element contains only character data and has no attributes (see Figure 4-13).

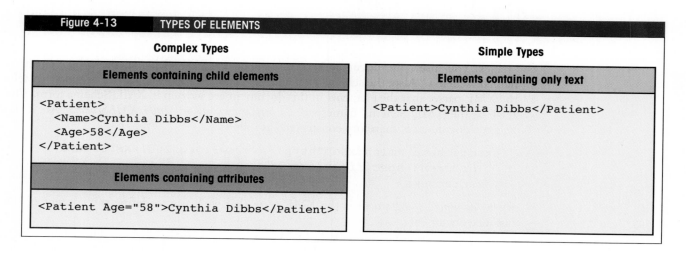

Figure 4-13	TYPES OF ELEMENTS

Complex Types

Elements containing child elements

```
<Patient>
  <Name>Cynthia Dibbs</Name>
  <Age>58</Age>
</Patient>
```

Elements containing attributes

```
<Patient Age="58">Cynthia Dibbs</Patient>
```

Simple Types

Elements containing only text

```
<Patient>Cynthia Dibbs</Patient>
```

In Allison's XML document, both the Patients and Patient elements represent complex types because they contain child elements. The Performance element is also a complex type because it has the Scale attribute. All of the other elements in her XML document are simple types because they contain only text.

To declare a simple type element in XML Schema, use the general syntax

```
<element name="name" type="type"/>
```

where *name* is the name of the element in the instance document and *type* is the data type of the element. This declaration uses an empty element tag because it doesn't enclose any content in the schema file.

Note that we have not included the namespace prefix in the syntax for the element. If a namespace prefix is used with the XML Schema namespace, then any XML Schema tags must be qualified with the namespace prefix. For example, if the namespace prefix for the schema is xsd, a simple type element declaration would have to be qualified as follows:

```
<xsd:element name="name" type="xsd:type"/>
```

Note that both the tag name and the attribute name must be qualified.

The syntax for the rest of the XML Schema elements in this tutorial will not include the namespace prefix, but be aware that you will have to include the prefix in the actual schema documents you create.

Understanding Data Types

XML Schema supports two categories of data types: built-in and user-derived. A **built-in data type** is part of the XML Schema specifications and is available to all XML Schema authors. A **user-derived data type** is created by the XML Schema author for specific data values in the instance document. You'll learn how to create user-derived data types in the next session.

XML Schema divides its built-in data types into two classes: primitive and derived. A **primitive data type** or **base type** is one of 19 fundamental data types that are not defined in terms of other types. A **derived data type** is a collection of 25 data types that the XML Schema developers created based on the 19 primitive types. Figure 4-14 provides a schematic diagram of all 44 built-in data types.

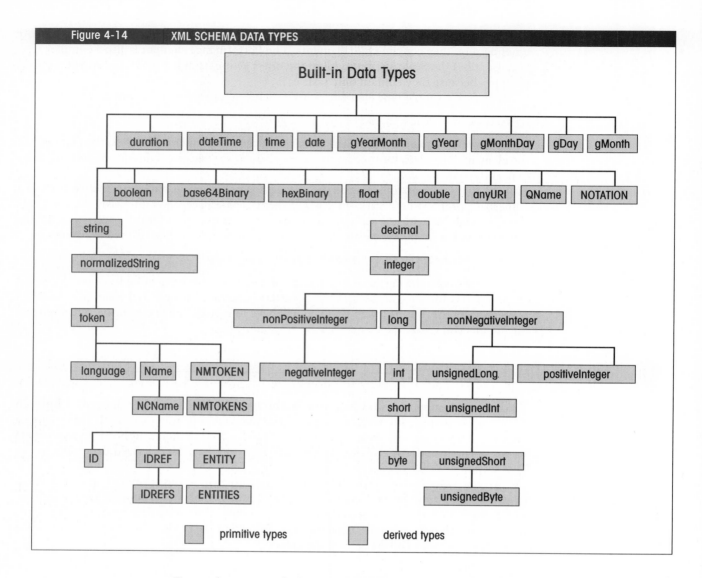

Figure 4-14   XML SCHEMA DATA TYPES

From the point of view of the XML author, the distinction between primitive and derived built-in types makes little difference because both are supported by XML Schema. Figure 4-15 describes a few of the more commonly used built-in data types.

Figure 4-15	A PARTIAL DESCRIPTION OF XML SCHEMA DATA TYPES	
DATA TYPE	**DESCRIPTION**	**EXAMPLES**
string	Any legal XML text string	Cynthia Dibbs
decimal	A decimal number of arbitrary precision	3.14, 5.9E–10, 0, 7.0
integer	An arbitrarily large or small integer	0, 10, –10
positiveInteger	An integer strictly greater than zero	10
nonNegativeInteger	An integer greater than or equal to zero	0, 10
negativeInteger	An integer strictly less than zero	–10
nonPositiveInteger	An integer less than or equal to zero	0, –10
boolean	A value representing a binary outcome (0, 1, true, or false)	0, 1, true, false
date	A date in the format CCYY-MM-DD where CC represents the century, YY represents the year, MM represents the month, and DD represents the day	2003-04-01
ID, IDREF, ENTITY, ENTITIES, NMTOKEN, NMTOKENS	Derived data types based on the original DTD data types for attribute values	

For example, Allison's XML document contains an Age element that she wants to limit to only positive integers. To do that, she could declare the Age element in her schema as follows:

```
<element name="Age" type="positiveInteger"/>
```

Note that XML Schema treats dates in a way that you might not be familiar with. In XML Schema, dates are displayed starting with the year and, reading left to right, continuing on with month and day with each unit separated by dashes. The date July 4, 1776 would be written as 1776-07-04 (leading zeroes must be included for both months and days).

Finally, all of the data types you used with your DTDs are also supported by XML Schema. The important difference is that the DTD data types are only used with attribute values, whereas XML Schema allows these data types to be applied to both attribute values and element content.

You can learn more about the wealth of built-in data types by accessing the W3 data type specifications page at *http://www.w3.org/TR/xmlschema-2/*.

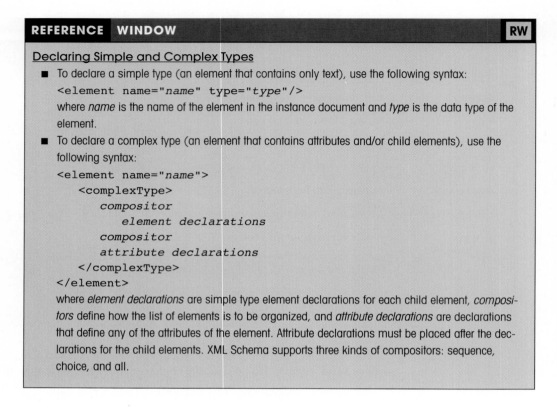

Working with Complex Types

A complex type element contains one or more attributes or is the parent to one or more child elements. For these types of elements, the general syntax is as follows:

```
<element name="name">
   <complexType>
      compositor
         element declarations
      compositor
      attribute declarations
   </complexType>
</element>
```

where *name* is the name of the element in the instance document, *element declarations* are simple type element declarations for each child element, *compositors* define how the list of elements is to be organized, and *attribute declarations* are declarations that define any of the attributes of the element (you'll learn about these later). Any attribute declarations, if they exist, must be placed after the declarations for the child elements.

Working with Compositors

A **compositor** is a schema tag that defines how the list is to be treated. XML Schema supports three types of compositors: sequence, choice, and all. The **sequence compositor** forces elements in the instance document to be entered in the same order as indicated in the schema. For example, the following complex type assigns the element Address four child elements—Street, City, State, and Country:

```
<element name="Address">
   <complexType>
      <sequence>
         <element name="Street" type="string"/>
         <element name="City" type="string"/>
         <element name="State" type="string"/>
         <element name="Country" type="string"/>
      </sequence>
   </complexType>
</element>
```

An instance document that doesn't display all of these child elements or displays them in a different order would be invalid.

The **choice compositor** allows any *one* of the items in the list to be used in the instance document. In the following declaration, the Sponsor element can contain either the Parent element or the Guardian element, but not both:

```
<element name="Sponsor">
   <complexType>
      <choice>
         <element name="Parent" type="string"/>
         <element name="Guardian" type="string"/>
      </choice>
   </complexType>
</element>
```

Finally, the **all compositor** allows any of the items to appear in the instance document in any order. The following declaration allows the Family element to contain an element named "Father" and/or another named "Mother" in no particular order:

```
<element name="Family">
   <complexType>
      <all>
         <element name="Father" type="string"/>
         <element name="Mother" type="string"/>
      </all>
   </complexType>
</element>
```

Compositors can be nested inside of one another. The following declaration using choice compositors allows the instance document to display the Person or Company element followed by the Cash or Credit element:

```
<element name="Account">
   <complexType>
      <sequence>
         <choice>
            <element name="Person" type="string"/>
            <element name="Company" type="string"/>
         </choice>
         <choice>
            <element name="Cash" type="string"/>
            <element name="Credit" type="string"/>
```

```
        </choice>
      </sequence>
    </complexType>
  </element>
```

The only restriction with nesting compositors is when using the all compositor type. A complex type element can only contain one all compositor and the all compositor must appear as the first child of the complex type element. You cannot combine the all compositor with either the choice or sequence compositor.

Specifying the Occurrences of an Item

In the previous code samples, it was assumed that each element in the list appeared once and only once. This will not always be the case. In Allison's document, the Comments element can appear multiple times or not at all. To specify the number of times each element appears in the instance document, you can use the **minOccurs** and **maxOccurs** attributes.

For example, the following element declaration specifies that the Phone element appears zero to three times in the instance document:

```
<element name="Phone" type="string" minOccurs="0"
maxOccurs="3"/>
```

Note that any time the minOccurs attribute is set to 0, the declared item is optional. The maxOccurs attribute can be any positive value or have a value of "unbounded," meaning that there is no upper limit to the number of occurrences of the element. If a value is specified for the minOccurs attribute, but the maxOccurs attribute is missing, the value of the maxOccurs attribute is assumed to be equal to the value of the minOccurs attribute. Finally, if both attributes are missing, their value is assumed to be 1.

The minOccurs and maxOccurs attributes can also be used with compositors to repeat entire sequences of items. In the following code, the sequence of three child elements (FirstName, MiddleName, LastName) can be repeated countless times within the Customer element:

```
<element name="Customer">
  <complexType>
    <sequence minOccurs="1" maxOccurs="unbounded">
      <element name="FirstName" type="string"/>
      <element name="MiddleName" type="string"/>
      <element name="LastName" type="string"/>
    </sequence>
  </complexType>
</element>
```

Specifying Mixed Content

As you remember, one of the limitations of using DTDs is their inability to define mixed content, which is an element that contains both text and child elements. You can specify the child elements with a DTD, but you cannot constrain their order or number. XML Schema gives you more control over mixed content. To specify that an element contains both text and child elements, add the mixed attribute to the complexType tag. When the mixed attribute is set to the value "true," XML Schema assumes that the element contains both text and child elements. The structure of the child elements can then be defined with the conventional method. For example, the following XML content:

```
<Summary>
  Patient <Name>Cynthia Davis</Name> was enrolled on
```

```
    the <Study>Tamoxifen Study</Study> on 8/15/2003.
</Summary>
```

can be declared in XML Schema as

```
<element name="Summary">
    <complexType mixed="true">
        <sequence>
            <element name="Name" type="string"/>
            <element name="Study" type="string"/>
        </sequence>
    </complexType>
</element>
```

Note that XML Schema allows content text to appear before, between, and after any of the child elements.

Declaring an Attribute

So far, the complex types that you've examined have involved elements that contain child elements. Remember, any element that contains an attribute is also a complex type. The syntax for declaring an attribute is

```
<attribute name="name" type="type" use="use"
default="default" fixed="fixed" />
```

where *name* is the name of the attribute, *type* is the data type, *use* indicates whether the attribute is required, *default* is the attribute's default value, and *fixed* is a fixed value for the attribute. Attributes use the same collection of data types that simple type elements do.

The use attribute has three possible values:

- **required**: The attribute must always appear with the element.
- **optional**: The attribute can appear once or not at all.
- **prohibited**: The attribute cannot be used with the element.

If you fail to specify a use value in the attribute declaration, XML Schema assumes that the attribute is optional. The following attribute declaration declares the Gender attribute with a default value of female:

```
<attribute name="Gender" type="string" default="female"/>
```

An attribute must always be declared along with the element it belongs to. XML Schema will use a different structure for elements that contain content and attributes versus elements that contain only attributes. There are four possible situations:

- The element contains only attributes but no content (an empty element).

- The element contains attributes and child elements, but no text.
- The element contains attributes, text, and child elements.
- The element contains attributes and text, but no child elements.

Let's examine how to work with an empty element first.

Attributes with Empty Elements

If the element is empty, you declare the attributes using syntax similar to what you used for declaring child elements. The primary difference is that the order in which the attributes appear is not specified and therefore not placed within compositors. The syntax for declaring attributes within an empty element is as follows:

```
<complexType>
    attribute declarations
</complexType>
```

For example, the following element in the instance document:

```
<Patient ID="MR89-8901-25" Gender="female"/>
```

can be declared as

```
<element name="Patient">
    <complexType>
        <attribute name="ID" type="string"/>
        <attribute name="Gender" type="string"/>
    </complexType>
</element>
```

Note that you don't need a compositor with a list of attributes as you do with a list of child elements.

Attributes with Child Elements

If an element contains only child elements in addition to attributes, the attributes are placed after the element declarations. The following content:

```
<Patient ID="MR89-8901-25" Gender="female">
  <Name>Cynthia Dibbs</Name>
  <Age>58</Age>
</Patient>
```

can be declared as

```
<element name="Patient">
    <complexType>
        <sequence>
            <element name="Name" type="string"/>
            <element name="Age" type="positiveInteger"/>
        </sequence>
        <attribute name="ID" type="string"/>
        <attribute name="Gender" type="string"/>
    </complexType>
</element>
```

For content that contains text in addition to the child elements and attributes, insert the attribute mixed="true" into the complexType tag.

Attributes with Simple Content

For elements that contain attributes and text, but no child elements, XML Schema uses the following syntax:

```
<element name="name">
   <complexType>
      <simpleContent>
         <extension base="type">
            attribute declarations
         </extension>
      </simpleContent>
   </complexType>
</element>
```

where *type* is the data type of the element's content. The simpleContent and extension tags are important tools that XML Schema uses to derive new data types and design content models, although in this context we are only concerned with how they are used to declare attributes for elements that also contain text.

For example, the following content:

```
<Patient PID="MR-89-401-23">Cynthia Dibbs</Patient>
```

can be declared in XML as

```
<element name="Patient">
   <complexType>
      <simpleType>
         <extension base="string">
            <attribute name="PID" type="ID"/>
         </extension>
      </simpleType>
   </complexType>
</element>
```

Note that in this case, we use the ID data type for the attribute value and the string data type for the contents of the Patient element.

Now that you've seen how XML Schema can be used to declare simple types, complex types, and attributes, you are ready to complete the schema for Allison's XML document.

Inserting **Element Declarations into a Schema**

To finish a schema for Allison's document, start with the outermost element in the structure and work your way inward through all of the nested elements and attributes. The levels of element and attribute declarations in the schema correspond to the levels of parent and child elements in the instance document. With this in mind, start with the declaration for the root element of the instance document, which is Patients. As you enter the schema code, be sure to refer back to the structure of the Patients information, displayed earlier in Figure 4-2.

> *To create the declaration for the Patients element:*
>
> **1.** Verify that you are still working on the PSchema1.xsd file in your text editor.

2. Immediately following the opening schema tag, enter the opening and closing tags, as shown below, to define the element Patients. As shown in Figure 4-16, indent these lines a few spaces to offset the element tags from the surrounding schema tag. Because this is the root element, it will be defined as a complexType element.

```
<xsd:element name="Patients">
  <xsd:complexType>
    <xsd:sequence>
    </xsd:sequence>
  </xsd:complexType>
</xsd:element>
```

Figure 4-16   CREATING THE PATIENTS COMPLEX TYPE

```
<?xml version="1.0" encoding="UTF-8"?>
<!-- Schema for breast cancer patient data -->

<xsd:schema xmlns:xsd="http://www.w3.org/2001/XMLSchema">
  <xsd:element name="Patients">
    <xsd:complexType>
      <xsd:sequence>
      </xsd:sequence>
    </xsd:complexType>
  </xsd:element>
</xsd:schema>
```

Note that we must include the xsd namespace prefix for all schema tags in this document. Next, we have to insert the element declaration for the Patient element. The Patient element itself is a complexType element. Because there can be unlimited Patient elements within the root element, we have to set the value of the maxOccurs attribute to "unbounded."

3. Within the sequence tags, type the following code, once again indented a few lines (see Figure 4-17).

```
<xsd:element name="Patient" maxOccurs="unbounded">
  <xsd:complexType>
    <xsd:sequence>
    </xsd:sequence>
  </xsd:complexType>
</xsd:element>
```

Figure 4-17   CREATING THE PATIENT COMPLEX TYPE

```
<?xml version="1.0" encoding="UTF-8"?>
<!-- Schema for breast cancer patient data -->

<xsd:schema xmlns:xsd="http://www.w3.org/2001/XMLSchema">
  <xsd:element name="Patients">
    <xsd:complexType>
      <xsd:sequence>
        <xsd:element name="Patient" maxOccurs="unbounded">
          <xsd:complexType>
            <xsd:sequence>
            </xsd:sequence>
          </xsd:complexType>
        </xsd:element>
      </xsd:sequence>
    </xsd:complexType>
  </xsd:element>
</xsd:schema>
```

the Patient element can appear an unlimited number of times within the Patients element

Next, add the element declarations for the Name, ID, DOB, Age, Stage, and Comment elements. The Name, ID, Stage, and Comment elements contain text strings. The Age element should be declared as a positive integer. The DOB element should be declared using a date type. All child elements occur once, except for the Comment element, which is optional.

4. Within the sequence tags for the Patient element, enter the following schema code (see Figure 4-18):

```
<xsd:element name="Name" type="xsd:string"/>
<xsd:element name="ID" type="xsd:string"/>
<xsd:element name="DOB" type="xsd:date"/>
<xsd:element name="Age" type="xsd:positiveInteger"/>
<xsd:element name="Stage" type="xsd:string"/>
<xsd:element name="Comment" type="xsd:string"
minOccurs="0" maxOccurs="unbounded"/>
```

Figure 4-18   CREATING THE NAME, ID, DOB, AGE, STAGE, AND COMMENT ELEMENTS

```
<?xml version="1.0" encoding="UTF-8"?>
<!-- Schema for breast cancer patient data -->

<xsd:schema xmlns:xsd="http://www.w3.org/2001/XMLSchema">
  <xsd:element name="Patients">
    <xsd:complexType>
      <xsd:sequence>
        <xsd:element name="Patient" maxOccurs="unbounded">
          <xsd:complexType>
            <xsd:sequence>
              <xsd:element name="Name" type="xsd:string"/>
              <xsd:element name="ID" type="xsd:string"/>
              <xsd:element name="DOB" type="xsd:date"/>
              <xsd:element name="Age" type="xsd:positiveInteger"/>
              <xsd:element name="Stage" type="xsd:string"/>
              <xsd:element name="Comment" type="xsd:string" minOccurs="0" maxOccurs="unbounded"/>
            </xsd:sequence>
          </xsd:complexType>
        </xsd:element>
      </xsd:sequence>
    </xsd:complexType>
  </xsd:element>
</xsd:schema>
```

5. Finally, you need to declare the Performance element. Because the element has an attribute, it is also a complex type; but, it also contains decimal values, so you have to declare both the attribute type and the type of text it contains. Allison wants this to be a required attribute. To declare the Performance element and its attribute, insert the following code, as shown in Figure 4-19.

```
<xsd:element name="Performance">
  <xsd:complexType>
    <xsd:simpleContent>
      <xsd:extension base="xsd:decimal">
        <attribute name="Scale" type="xsd:string"
use="required"/>
      </xsd:extension>
    </xsd:simpleContent>
  </xsd:complexType>
</xsd:element>
```

Figure 4-19   CREATING THE PERFORMANCE ELEMENT

```
<?xml version="1.0" encoding="UTF-8"?>
<!-- Schema for breast cancer patient data -->

<xsd:schema xmlns:xsd="http://www.w3.org/2001/XMLSchema">
  <xsd:element name="Patients">
    <xsd:complexType>
      <xsd:sequence>
        <xsd:element name="Patient" maxOccurs="unbounded">
          <xsd:complexType>
            <xsd:sequence>
              <xsd:element name="Name" type="xsd:string"/>
              <xsd:element name="ID" type="xsd:string"/>
              <xsd:element name="DOB" type="xsd:date"/>
              <xsd:element name="Age" type="xsd:positiveInteger"/>
              <xsd:element name="Stage" type="xsd:string"/>
              <xsd:element name="Comment" type="xsd:string" minOccurs="0" maxOccurs="unbounded"/>
              <xsd:element name="Performance">
                <xsd:complexType>
                  <xsd:simpleContent>
                    <xsd:extension base="xsd:decimal">
                      <xsd:attribute name="Scale" type="xsd:string" use="required"/>
                    </xsd:extension>
                  </xsd:simpleContent>
                </xsd:complexType>
              </xsd:element>
            </xsd:sequence>
          </xsd:complexType>
        </xsd:element>
      </xsd:sequence>
    </xsd:complexType>
  </xsd:element>
```

declaring the
Scale attribute

6. Verify that your code matches the code in Figure 4-19. Make sure that you have used the xsd namespace prefix in all of the indicated tags and that your use of upper and lower cases in the tag and attribute names match the figures.

7. Save your changes to PSchema1.xsd.

The final step in creating the schema for Allison's document is to attach the schema to a namespace.

Attaching a Schema to a Namespace

It is not required to attach a schema to a namespace, but it does have several advantages. Both the schema and the instance document can belong to the same namespace, linking the content of the document with its validation rules. This is useful when you combine several XML documents into a single file. As we've discussed with DTDs, a new DTD has to be created for each combination of XML documents. With schemas, each part of the combined document can be associated with a different namespace and, therefore, can draw upon a different schema for validation. The schemas are combined when the data is combined (see Figure 4-20).

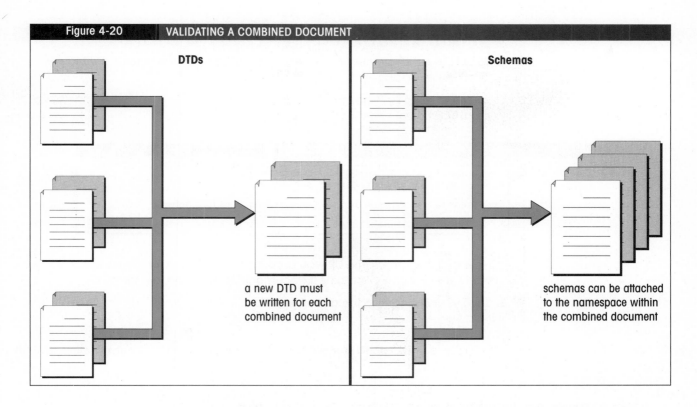

Figure 4-20 | VALIDATING A COMBINED DOCUMENT

DTDs

a new DTD must be written for each combined document

Schemas

schemas can be attached to the namespace within the combined document

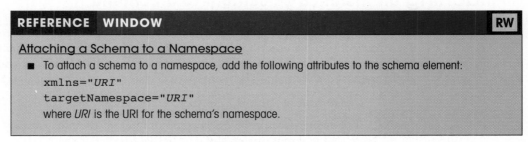

REFERENCE WINDOW | RW

Attaching a Schema to a Namespace

■ To attach a schema to a namespace, add the following attributes to the schema element:

```
xmlns="URI"
targetNamespace="URI"
```

where URI is the URI for the schema's namespace.

To associate the schema with a namespace, construct the schema element as follows:

```
<prefix:schema xmlns:prefix="http://www.w3.org/2001/
XMLSchema"
        xmlns="URI"
        targetNamespace="URI">
```

where URI is the URI for the schema's namespace. Note that the schema element has two namespaces. The first is the namespace for the W3C's XML Schema specifications; the second is a namespace for the validation rules declared in this particular schema file. To avoid confusion, the namespace for XML Schema is referred to as the XML Schema namespace, whereas the namespace for the schema file is referred to as the schema namespace. In a sense, every schema file is actually a combined document, combining the elements of the XML Schema namespace and the elements of the schema namespace.

To specify a namespace for the PSchema1.xsd file:

1. Within the schema element at the top of the file, insert the following attributes (see Figure 4-21):

   ```
   xmlns="http://uhosp/patients/ns"
   targetNamespace="http://uhosp/patients/ns"
   ```

Figure 4-21 SPECIFYING A NAMESPACE FOR A SCHEMA

```
<?xml version="1.0" encoding="UTF-8"?>
<!-- Schema for breast cancer patient data -->

<xsd:schema xmlns:xsd="http://www.w3.org/2001/XMLSchema"
            xmlns="http://uhosp/patients/ns"
            targetNamespace="http://uhosp/patients/ns">
```

Note that this is the same URI you used in the first session for the Patient elements in Allison's combined document. We'll use this fact later.

2. Save your changes to the document.

Now that you've completed the schema, you can return to the Patient.xml file and apply your schema to it.

Attaching an Instance Document to a Schema

The first step in attaching a schema to an instance document is to indicate which schema dialect is being used to validate the file. For the XML Schema dialect, this is accomplished by declaring the namespace "http://www.w3.org/2001/XMLSchema-instance" in the document's root element. The namespace declaration should appear as follows:

```
xmlns:xsi="http://www.w3.org/2001/XMLSchema-instance"
```

The namespace prefix xsi is commonly used, though you may specify a different one. Note that you must assign some namespace prefix or the XML parser will assume that you intend for the XML schema namespace to be used as the default namespace for the contents of the instance document.

Next, you indicate the name and location of the schema file. The attributes for doing this are

```
xmlns:prefix="URI"
xsi:schemaLocation="URI schema"
```

where *URI* is the namespace of the schema—the same URI you used in the schema file itself—*prefix* is a prefix for the namespace, and *schema* is the location and filename of the schema file. The complete form of the root element would therefore be as follows:

```
<prefix:root xmlns:xsi="http://www.w3.org/2001/
XMLSchema-instance"
             xmlns:prefix="URI"
             xsi:schemaLocation="URI schema">

document content

</prefix:root>
```

In Allison's document, the root element will appear as follows:

```
<pat:Patients
xmlns:xsi="http://www.w3.org/2001/XMLSchema-instance"
    xmlns:pat="http://uhosp/patients/ns"
    xsi:schemaLocation="http://uhosp/patients/
     ns PSchema1.xsd">
```

document content

```
</pat:Patients>
```

Apply this format to Allison's document now.

To apply a schema to Allison's document:

1. Return to the Patient.xml document in your text editor.

2. Within the Patients root element, insert the following attributes:

```
xmlns:xsi="http://www.w3.org/2001/XMLSchema-instance"
xmlns:pat="http://uhosp/patients/ns"
xsi:schemaLocation="http://uhosp/patients/ns PSchema1.xsd"
```

3. Add the **pat** namespace prefix to the opening and closing Patients tag.

Figure 4-22 shows the revised Patient.xml file.

Figure 4-22	ATTACHING A SCHEMA TO THE PATIENT FILE

```
<?xml version="1.0"?>
<pat:Patients xmlns:xsi="http://www.w3.org/2001/XMLSchema-instance"
              xmlns:pat="http://uhosp/patients/ns"
              xsi:schemaLocation="http://uhosp/patients/ns PSchema1.xsd">
  <Patient>
    <Name>Cynthia Dibbs</Name>
    <ID>MR890-041-02</ID>
    <DOB>1945-05-22</DOB>
    <Age>58</Age>
    <Stage>II</Stage>
    <Performance Scale="Karnofsky">0.81</Performance>
```

```
  <Patient>
    <Name>Brenda Browne</Name>
    <ID>MR815-741-03</ID>
    <DOB>1964-04-25</DOB>
    <Age>39</Age>
    <Stage>I</Stage>
    <Performance Scale="Karnofsky">0.88</Performance>
  </Patient>
</pat:Patients>
```

4. Save your changes and close the file.

Note that a schema namespace is not necessary to validate a document. It *is* necessary if you intend on combining documents. If you don't intend to attach a schema to a namespace, use the following form for your document's root element:

```
<root xmlns:xsi="http://www.w3.org/2001/XMLSchema-instance"
      xsi:noNamespaceSchemaLocation="schema">

document content

</root>
```

where *root* is the name of the document's root element and *schema* is the name and location of the schema file.

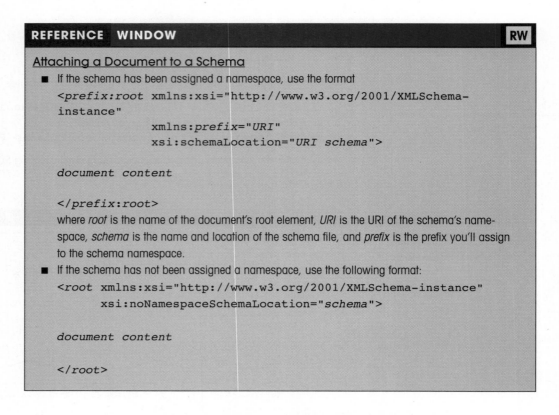

REFERENCE WINDOW   RW

Attaching a Document to a Schema

■ If the schema has been assigned a namespace, use the format

```
<prefix:root xmlns:xsi="http://www.w3.org/2001/XMLSchema-
instance"
             xmlns:prefix="URI"
             xsi:schemaLocation="URI schema">

document content

</prefix:root>
```

where *root* is the name of the document's root element, *URI* is the URI of the schema's namespace, *schema* is the name and location of the schema file, and *prefix* is the prefix you'll assign to the schema namespace.

■ If the schema has not been assigned a namespace, use the following format:

```
<root xmlns:xsi="http://www.w3.org/2001/XMLSchema-instance"
      xsi:noNamespaceSchemaLocation="schema">

document content

</root>
```

Now you can validate the Patient.xml file against the PSchema1.xsd schema file to see whether the content of Allison's document actually matches the rules she set up for it.

To validate the instance document:

1. Click the **Start** button on your Taskbar, point to **Programs**, point to **XML Spy Suite**, and click **XML Spy IDE**.

2. Click **File** on the menu bar, and then click **Open**.

3. Locate and open **Patient.xml** from the Tutorial.04X/Tutorial folder on your Data Disk.

4. Maximize the contents of the document pane and then click the **Text View** button to view the text of the file.

5. Open **PSchema1.xsd** from the Tutorial.04X/Tutorial folder, and click the **Text View** button to view the contents of the file.

6. Click the **Patient.xml** tab in the document pane.

7. Click the **Validate** button 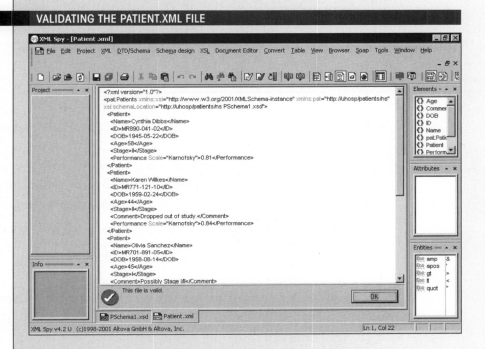 on the XML Spy toolbar.

   XML Spy returns the message that Allison's document is valid with respect to the schema she designed (see Figure 4-23).

Figure 4-23 | VALIDATING THE PATIENT.XML FILE

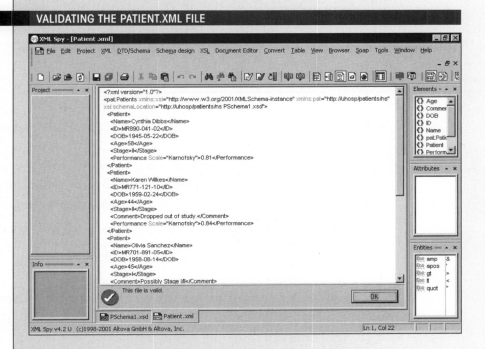

TROUBLE? If XML Spy indicates that your document is not valid, compare the code in your schema with the code shown earlier in Figure 4-19. Make sure that you have entered all of the namespaces correctly, and that namespace prefixes are used wherever necessary. Make the required changes to the PSchema1.xsd file using either your text editor, or if you prefer, the editing window in XML Spy.

TROUBLE? Based on your configuration of XML Spy, your window may look different from the one shown in Figure 4-23.

8. Once XML Spy has reported that the Patient.xml document is valid, click **File** and **Close All** to close both documents. Save any changes you may have made to the document in order to make it a valid file, but do not exit XML Spy.

Using Schemas in a Combined Document

Now that you've created a working schema for the patient data, Allison would like you to apply it to her combined document. Another schema file has already been created for you, describing the structure of the study data. The contents of this file, SSchema1.xsd, are shown in Figure 4-24. You should take some time to study the code used in this document, comparing it to the structure of the study elements shown earlier in Figure 4-2.

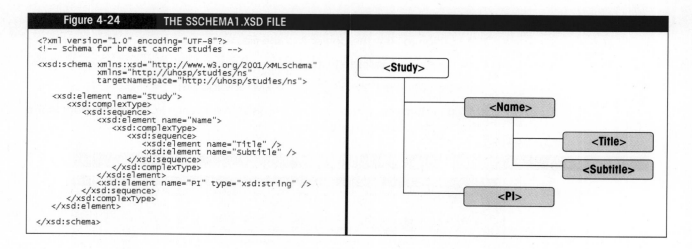

Figure 4-24   THE SSCHEMA1.XSD FILE

```
<?xml version="1.0" encoding="UTF-8"?>
<!-- Schema for breast cancer studies -->

<xsd:schema xmlns:xsd="http://www.w3.org/2001/XMLSchema"
            xmlns="http://uhosp/studies/ns"
            targetNamespace="http://uhosp/studies/ns">

   <xsd:element name="Study">
      <xsd:complexType>
         <xsd:sequence>
            <xsd:element name="Name">
               <xsd:complexType>
                  <xsd:sequence>
                     <xsd:element name="Title" />
                     <xsd:element name="Subtitle" />
                  </xsd:sequence>
               </xsd:complexType>
            </xsd:element>
            <xsd:element name="PI" type="xsd:string" />
         </xsd:sequence>
      </xsd:complexType>
   </xsd:element>

</xsd:schema>
```

To attach the schemas to the different parts of the combined document, you must do the following:

■ Add the XML Schema-instance namespace to the document's root element.

■ Assign namespaces to the different parts of the combined document.

■ Add the schemaLocation attribute to the parent element of each part.

You assigned namespaces to the different parts of the UHosp.xml file in the last session. You only need to insert the XML Schema-instance namespace to the root element and add the schemaLocation attribute to the Patients and Study elements.

To attach the two schemas to the combined document:

1. Using your text editor, open **UHosp.xml** from the Tutorial.04X/Tutorial folder on your Data Disk.

2. Delete the DOCTYPE declaration (you won't need the DTD to validate the file anymore).

3. Insert the following attribute in the Report element:

   ```
   xmlns:xsi="http://www.w3.org/2001/XMLSchema-instance"
   ```

4. Add the following attribute to the Patients element:

   ```
   xsi:schemaLocation="http://uhosp/patients/
    ns PSchema1.xsd"
   ```

5. Add a similar attribute to the Study element:

   ```
   xsi:schemaLocation="http://uhosp/studies/
    ns SSchema1.xsd"
   ```

6. Figure 4-25 shows the revised contents of the UHosp.xml file.

Figure 4-25   ATTACHING MULTIPLE SCHEMAS

```
<?xml version="1.0" ?>
<Report xmlns:xsi="http://www.w3.org/2001/XMLSchema-instance">

    <pat:Patients xmlns:pat="http://uhosp/patients/ns"
                  xsi:schemaLocation="http://uhosp/patients/ns PSchema1.xsd">
        <Patient>
            <Name>Cynthia Dibbs</Name>
            <ID>MR890-041-02</ID>
            <DOB>1945-05-22</DOB>
            <Age>58</Age>
            <Stage>II</Stage>
            <Performance Scale="Karnofsky">0.81</Performance>
        </Patient>
```

```
    <std:Study xmlns:std="http://uhosp/studies/ns"
               xsi:schemaLocation="http://uhosp/studies/ns SSchema1.xsd">
        <std:Name>
            <std:Title>Tamoxifen Breast Cancer Study</std:Title>
            <std:Subtitle>Randomized Phase 3 Clinical Trial</std:Subtitle>
        </std:Name>
        <std:PI>Dr. Diane West</std:PI>
    </std:Study>

</Report>
```

7. Save your changes to the file and close the text editor.

Now validate the file against the two schemas.

To validate the UHosp.xml file:

1. Using XML Spy, open **UHosp.xml**.

2. Maximize the contents of the document pane, and then click the **Text View** button 📄 to view the text of the file.

3. Click the **Validate** button ✅.

4. XML Spy reports that the file is valid (see Figure 4-26).

Figure 4-26   VALIDATING THE UHOSP.XML FILE

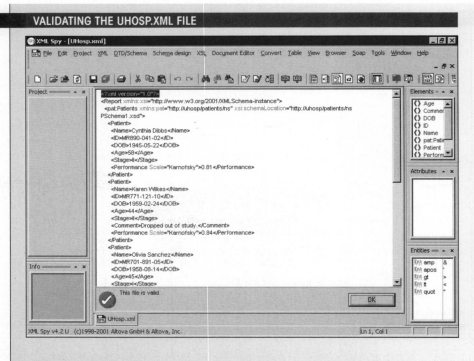

TROUBLE? If XML Spy reports that the document is invalid, check the URIs you entered for the different namespaces, and verify that you've entered the correct schema names.

5. Close XML Spy.

Allison is pleased with the work you've done applying schemas to her documents. She was particularly impressed with how she can create schemas for individual documents and then apply those schemas to a combined document.

There are still some changes that she would like to make to the XML document. For example, she would like to be able to restrict the values of some of the elements in the instance document. You'll look at this issue and some others in the next session.

Session 4.2 QUICK CHECK

1. What is a schema? What is an instance document?

2. How do schemas differ from DTDs?

3. What does the root element of an XML Schema file look like?

4. What is a simple type? What is a complex type?

5. How do you declare a simple type element named "Weight" that contains decimal data?

6. How do you declare a complex type element named "Parents" that contains two child elements named "Father" and "Mother"? (Assume that the Father and Mother elements are simple type elements containing text strings.)

7. How do you declare an attribute named "Title" that contains a text string and belongs to an element named "Book"? Assume that the Book element contains only text and no child elements.

8. What attribute would you add to the root element of an instance document to attach it to a schema file named "Schema1.xsd"? Assume that no namespace has been assigned to the schema file and that you are using the XML Schema dialect.

SESSION 4.3

In this session, you'll learn about different schema structures and the advantages and disadvantages of using them. You'll learn how to create complex types, model groups, and attribute groups. Next, you'll learn how to derive customized data types, and lists and unions of data types. You'll also work with XML Schema regular expressions to apply character patterns to element content. Finally, you'll learn how to document your completed schema file.

Structuring a Schema

There are several ways to structure a schema. The layout you applied in the last session is known as a **Russian Doll design** because it involved sets of nested declarations just like the classic Russian dolls, which are nested inside one another. Figure 4-27 illustrates the nesting of elements in PSchema1.xsd with the element levels color coded.

Figure 4-27	A RUSSIAN DOLL DESIGN

```xml
<?xml version="1.0" encoding="UTF-8"?>
<!-- Schema for breast cancer patient data -->

<xsd:schema xmlns:xsd="http://www.w3.org/2001/XMLSchema"
            xmlns="http://uhosp/patients/ns"
            targetNamespace="http://uhosp/patients/ns">
<xsd:element name="Patients">
  <xsd:complexType>
    <xsd:sequence>
      <xsd:element name="Patient" maxOccurs="unbounded">
        <xsd:complexType>
          <xsd:sequence>
            <xsd:element name="Name" type="xsd:string"/>
            <xsd:element name="ID" type="xsd:string"/>
            <xsd:element name="DOB" type="xsd:date"/>
            <xsd:element name="Age" type="xsd:positiveInteger"/>
            <xsd:element name="Stage" type="xsd:string"/>
            <xsd:element name="Comment" type="xsd:string" minOccurs="0" maxOccurs="unbounded"/>
            <xsd:element name="Performance">
              <xsd:complexType>
                <xsd:simpleContent>
                  <xsd:extension base="xsd:decimal">
                    <xsd:attribute name="Scale" type="xsd:string" use="required"/>
                  </xsd:extension>
                </xsd:simpleContent>
              </xsd:complexType>
            </xsd:element>
          </xsd:sequence>
        </xsd:complexType>
      </xsd:element>
    </xsd:sequence>
  </xsd:complexType>
</xsd:element>
</xsd:schema>
```

There are advantages and disadvantages of the Russian Doll design. On the positive side, it is easy to associate each element in the schema with the corresponding element in the instance document because the two documents are nested in the same way. However, a disadvantage is that the nesting of declarations and schema elements can be confusing and difficult to maintain. Allison's patient document has only three element levels; imagine creating a schema for an instance document with five or six levels! It would be all too easy to forget a closing tag and get lost in the maze of nested levels.

Because of this complexity, XML Schema supports other layouts that are more efficient and easier to maintain.

Working with Flat Catalogs

One of these layouts is a flat catalog. To help you understand how a flat catalog works, we first have to make a distinction between global and local components:

- **global component:** a component of the schema that is a direct child of the root schema element
- **local component:** a component nested further inside of the schema structure and not a direct child of the root schema element

The distinction is an important one. A global component can be referenced elsewhere in the schema document. A local component cannot. In a Russian Doll design, only the root element of the instance document is global, while all other element declarations are local. In the PSchema1.xsd file, only the declaration for the Patients element is global. The declarations for all the other elements are local.

In a **Flat Catalog Design**, all element declarations are made globally. The structure of the instance document is created by referencing these global element declarations at another point in the schema document. The syntax for creating a reference is

```
<element ref="name">
```

where *name* is the name of a global element.

The schema you created in the last session has been recreated in a flat catalog design. Open this new schema now.

To open the schema document:

1. Using your text editor, open **Flat.xsd** located in the Tutorial.04X/Tutorial folder of your Data Disk.

2. Scroll through the document, taking note of its structure and content (see Figure 4-28).

   The element declarations are all global; no declaration is nested inside of another. Note the use of the ref attribute to create references between one global declaration and another and between the child elements of the Patient element and their global declarations.

Figure 4-28 A FLAT CATALOG DESIGN

```xml
<?xml version="1.0" encoding="UTF-8"?>
<xsd:schema xmlns:xsd="http://www.w3.org/2001/XMLSchema">

   <xsd:element name="Name" type="xsd:string"/>
   <xsd:element name="ID" type="xsd:string"/>
   <xsd:element name="DOB" type="xsd:date"/>
   <xsd:element name="Age" type="xsd:positiveInteger"/>
   <xsd:element name="Stage" type="xsd:string"/>
   <xsd:element name="Comment" type="xsd:string"/>

   <xsd:element name="Performance">
     <xsd:complexType>
       <xsd:simpleContent>
         <xsd:extension base="xsd:decimal">
           <xsd:attribute name="Scale" type="xsd:string" use="required"/>
         </xsd:extension>
       </xsd:simpleContent>
     </xsd:complexType>
   </xsd:element>

   <xsd:element name="Patient">
     <xsd:complexType>
       <xsd:sequence>
         <xsd:element ref="Name"/>
         <xsd:element ref="ID"/>
         <xsd:element ref="DOB"/>
         <xsd:element ref="Age"/>
         <xsd:element ref="Stage"/>
         <xsd:element ref="Comment" minOccurs="0" maxOccurs="unbounded"/>
         <xsd:element ref="Performance"/>
       </xsd:sequence>
     </xsd:complexType>
   </xsd:element>

   <xsd:element name="Patients">
     <xsd:complexType>
       <xsd:sequence>
         <xsd:element ref="Patient" maxOccurs="unbounded"/>
       </xsd:sequence>
     </xsd:complexType>
   </xsd:element>

</xsd:schema>
```

reference to the Name through Comment declarations

reference to the Patient element declaration

Name through Comment element declarations

Performance element declaration

Patient element declaration

Patients element declaration

3. After you are finished studying the Flat.xsd file, close it, but leave your text editor open.

There is one more important difference between local and global components. If the schema file is attached to a namespace, globally declared elements must be explicitly qualified in the instance document, but local elements do not need to be qualified. Recall that the "pat" namespace prefix was added to the Patients element in both the Patient.xml and UHosp.xml files (see Figure 4-22 and Figure 4-25). The Patients element was the only global element in the PSchema1.xsd file and thus had to be explicitly qualified. The other elements in the schema were all local elements and did not need to be qualified. On the other hand, if a Flat Catalog schema is attached to a namespace, all of the elements in the instance document have to be qualified.

If the document is large with many elements, adding namespace prefixes to all of the element names is a big chore. There's a third layout possibility: the Venetian Blind layout. This design involves creating customized types, such as the named complex type.

Working with Named Complex Types

As you learned in the last session, elements that contain attributes or child elements are known as complex types. The complex types you worked with in the last session were **anonymous complex types** because they were associated with only one element and were not given a name. In general, any schema element not assigned a name is known as an **anonymous type**. Anonymous types must be nested within another element in order to have any context within the schema design. As you saw, this could lead to several levels of nested tags. The following declaration is an example of an anonymous complex type that describes two child elements named "FirstName" and "LastName".

```
<element name="Client">
   <complexType>
      <sequence>
         <element name="FirstName" type="string"/>
         <element name="LastName" type="string" />
      </sequence>
   </complexType>
</element>
```

Upon reflection, it seems that such FirstName/LastName pairs occur frequently in XML documents, and it would be helpful if we could store this structure rather than retyping it over and over again. We can if we name the structure, creating a **named complex type** that can be used elsewhere in the schema.

To see how this is done, we'll recreate the element declaration using a named complex type with the title "fullName".

```
<complexType name="fullName">
   <sequence>
      <element name="FirstName" type="string"/>
      <element name="LastName" type="string"/>
   </sequence>
</complexType>
```

To use this complex type in an element declaration, simply apply it to the type attribute as follows:

```
<element name="Client" type="fullName"/>
<element name="Salesperson" type="fullName"/>
```

Both the Client and the Salesperson elements have the same structure: two child elements named "FirstName" and "LastName". It doesn't matter whether we create the named complex type before or after the element declaration. The only requirement is that the named complex type must be created globally (i.e., as a direct child of the schema element). If that is done, we can use the named complex type in any element declaration in the schema.

Another way of simplifying your schema structure is with a model group.

Working with Named Model Groups

As the name suggests, a **named model group** is a collection, or group, of elements. The syntax for creating a model group is

```
<group name="name">
   element declarations
</group>
```

where *name* is the name of the model group, and *element declarations* is a collection of element declarations. The element declarations must be enclosed within a sequence, choice, or all compositor. The following code creates a model group named "fullName" that contains two elements:

```
<group name="fullName">
   <sequence>
```

```
    <element name="FirstName" type="string" />
    <element name="LastName" type="string" />
  </sequence>
</group>
```

Note that because a model group is not a simple or complex type, you must use the ref attribute within the group tag to access it in your schema. Here's how you would access the fullName group for use with an element declaration:

```
<element name="Client">
  <complexType>
    <group ref="fullName"/>
  </complexType>
</element>
```

Named model groups must be globally defined so that they can be referenced anywhere within the schema. As with named complex types, model groups are useful when your document contains element declarations or code that you want to repeat throughout the schema.

Working with Named Attribute Groups

Attributes can also be placed within **named attribute groups**. This is particularly useful for attributes that you want to use with several different elements in the schema. The syntax for a named attribute group is

```
<attributeGroup name="name">
  attribute declarations
</attributeGroup>
```

where *name* is the name of the attribute group and *attribute declarations* is a collection of attributes assigned to the group. For example, one of Allison's documents might contain the following element to identify a physician:

```
<Doctor ID="DR251" Dept="Pediatrics">
  Curt Hurley
</Doctor>
```

Both the ID and Dept attributes may need to be used in other elements. To place both of these within an attribute group named "DRInfo", you can use the following code:

```
<attributeGroup name="DRInfo">
  <attribute name="ID" type="string" use="required"/>
  <attribute name="Dept" type="string" use="required"/>
</attributeGroup>
```

To use the DRInfo attribute group with the Doctor element, create a reference within an attributeGroup tag as follows:

```
<element name="Doctor" type="deptData"/>

<complexType name="deptData">
  <simpleContent>
    <extension base="string">
      <attributeGroup ref="DRInfo"/>
    </extension>
  </simpleContent>
</complexType>
```

Note that this code not only references an attribute group, but it also uses a named complex type to simplify the declaration of the Doctor element.

Working with a Venetian Blind Layout

To design your schema in **Venetian Blind layout**, declare all of the complex elements using complex types, groups, and attribute groups. The actual element declarations are still nested within one element, but they are no longer global.

The PSchema1.xsd file has been reformatted in a Venetian Blind layout. Open the new file now.

To open the schema document:

1. Using your text editor, open **Venetian.xsd** located in the Tutorial.04X/Tutorial folder of your Data Disk.

2. Save the file as **PSchema2.xsd** and leave the file open.

3. Scroll through the document, taking note of how it uses complex types in creating the various elements of the instance document (see Figure 4-29).

There are two named complex types in this document, PatType and PerfType, and one element group named Pat_Elements. The element group is used to group the elements describing each patient. PerfType is used for storing performance information, and PatType is used for storing the patient elements. The only globally declared element is the Patients element.

Figure 4-29   **A VENETIAN BLIND LAYOUT**

```xml
<?xml version="1.0" encoding="UTF-8"?>
<!-- Schema for breast cancer patient data -->

<xsd:schema xmlns:xsd="http://www.w3.org/2001/XMLSchema"
            xmlns="http://uhosp/patients/ns"
            targetNamespace="http://uhosp/patients/ns">

  <xsd:element name="Patients">
    <xsd:complexType>
      <xsd:sequence>
        <xsd:element name="Patient" type="PatType" maxOccurs="unbounded" />
      </xsd:sequence>
    </xsd:complexType>
  </xsd:element>

  <xsd:complexType name="PatType">
    <xsd:group ref="Pat_Elements" />
  </xsd:complexType>

  <xsd:group name="Pat_Elements">
    <xsd:sequence>
      <xsd:element name="Name" type="xsd:string"/>
      <xsd:element name="ID" type="xsd:string"/>
      <xsd:element name="DOB" type="xsd:date"/>
      <xsd:element name="Age" type="xsd:positiveInteger"/>
      <xsd:element name="Stage" type="xsd:string"/>
      <xsd:element name="Comment" type="xsd:string" minOccurs="0" maxOccurs="unbounded"/>
      <xsd:element name="Performance" type="PerfType" />
    </xsd:sequence>
  </xsd:group>

  <xsd:complexType name="PerfType">
    <xsd:simpleContent>
      <xsd:extension base="xsd:decimal">
        <xsd:attribute name="Scale" type="xsd:string" use="required"/>
      </xsd:extension>
    </xsd:simpleContent>
  </xsd:complexType>

</xsd:schema>
```

Figure 4-30 summarizes the characteristics of the three schema designs. Because of its flexibility, you'll continue working on Allison's project using the Venetian Blind layout in the PSchema2.xsd file.

Figure 4-30	COMPARING SCHEMA DESIGNS	
RUSSIAN DOLL	**FLAT CATALOG**	**VENETIAN BLIND**
One single global element; all other elements are local	All elements are global	One single global element; all other elements are local
Element declarations are nested within a single global declaration	No nesting of element declarations	Element declarations are nested within a single global declaration, using named complex types and element groups
Element declarations can only be used once.	Element declarations can be reused throughout the schema	Complex types and element groups can be reused throughout the schema
If a namespace is attached to the schema, only the root element needs to be qualified in the instance document	If a namespace is attached to the schema, all elements need to be qualified in the instance document	If a namespace is attached to the schema, only the root element needs to be qualified in the instance document

Now that you've seen how to create types that describe complex elements, you'll look at how to create a data type.

Deriving New Data Types

In the previous session, you saw some of the variety and power of XML Schema data types, especially when compared to DTD data types. You are not limited to the 44 data types supported by XML Schema and can create your own. There are three components involved in deriving a new data type:

- **value space**: the set of values that correspond to the data type; for example, an integer data type consists of numbers such as 1, 2, 3, etc., but does not contain fractions or text strings
- **lexical space**: the set of textual representations of the value space; for example, the number 42 can be represented in several ways, such as 42, 42.0, or 4.2E01.
- **facets**: the properties of the data type that distinguish one data type from another; facets can include such properties as text string length or a range of allowable values; XML Schema uses one such facet to distinguish the integer data type from the positiveInteger data type

New data types are derived by manipulating the characteristics of these components. User-derived data types fall into three general categories:

- **list**: a list of values with each value in the list derived from a base type; for example, a list of integer values
- **union**: the combination of two or more data types; one such union might a combination of text strings and integers
- **restriction**: a limit placed on the facet of a base type; for example, the integer data type can be constrained to a range of values

Let's first examine how to derive a list data type.

Deriving a List Data Type

The syntax for deriving a list data type is

```
<simpleType name="name">
    <list itemType="type"/>
</simpleType>
```

where *name* is the name assigned to the list data type and *type* is the data type of the base. At the University Hospital, Allison often records patients' weekly white blood counts. A typical element containing a list of white blood cell counts can appear as follows:

```
<WBC>15.1 15.8 12.0 9.3 7.1 5.2 4.3 3.4</WBC>
```

To create a data type for this information, Allison first needs to define a list data type as follows:

```
<simpleType name="wbcList">
   <list itemType="decimal"/>
</simpleType>
```

and then she can use the wbcList data type in the declaration for the WBC element:

```
<element name="WBC" type="wbcList"/>
```

A list data type must always use a space as the delimiter. You cannot use commas or other characters.

Deriving a Union Data Type

A union data type is composed of the value and lexical spaces from any number of other data types. Each of the base types of a union data type is known as a **member type**. When a union data type is validated, the validator examines each member type in the order in which it is defined in the schema. The syntax for deriving a union data type is

```
<simpleType name="type">
    <union memberTypes="type1 type2 type3 …"/>
</simpleType>
```

where *type1*, *type2*, *type3*, etc., are the member types that comprise the union.

When compiling data on white blood cell counts, Allison may have precise counts as well as more narrative levels, such as high, normal, or low, to record in her research. As a result of this variety, the WBC element may look as follows:

```
<WBC>15.9 high 14.2 9.8 normal low 5.3</WBC>
```

Allison can create a data type for this information by combining a list type and union type. First, she creates a union data type for the union of the decimal and string types as follows:

```
<simpleType name="wbcType">
    <union memberTypes="decimal string"/>
<simpleType>
```

Next, she uses that data type to derive a list type and assigns the list type to the WBC element:

```
<simpleType name="wbcList">
    <list itemType="wbcType"/>
</simpleType>

<element name="WBC" type="wbcList"/>
```

Union data types are often used for multilingual documents in which the data content, expressed in different languages, must be validated based on a single schema.

Deriving a Restricted Data Type

The most common way of deriving a new data type is to restrict the properties of a base type. XML Schema provides twelve constraining facets for this purpose, listed in Figure 4-31.

Figure 4-31	CONSTRAINING FACETS
FACET	**DESCRIPTION**
length	Specifies the length of the datatype; for text strings, length measures the number of characters; for lists, length measures the number of items in the list
minLength	Specifies the minimum length of the datatype
maxLength	Specifies the maximum length of the datatype
pattern	Constrains the lexical space of the datatype to follow a specific pattern of characters
enumeration	Constrains the datatype to a specific set of values
maxInclusive	Specifies an upper bound for the datatype (can be used with datatypes that can be ordered, such as numbers); the upper boundary is included as a legitimate value
minInclusive	Specifies a lower bound for the datatype; the lower boundary is included
maxExclusive	Specifies an upper bound for the datatype, but the upper boundary is not included
minExclusive	Specifies a lower bound for the datatype, but the lower boundary is not included
whiteSpace	Controls the use of blanks in the lexical space; the whiteSpace facet has three values: preserve (no changes made to the content), replace (replace all tabs, carriage returns, and line feed characters with spaces), and collapse (replace all tabs, carriage returns, and line feeds, remove any opening or closing blanks, and collapse multiple blank spaces to a single blank space)
totalDigits	Constrains the value space to a maximum number of decimal places
fractionDigits	Constrains the value space to a maximum number of decimal places in the fractional part of the value

Constraining facets are applied to a base type using the syntax

```
<simpleType name="name">
   <restriction base="type">
      <facet1 value="value1" />
      <facet2 value="value2" />
      <facet3 value="value3" />
      ...
   </restriction>
</simpleType>
```

where *type* is the data type of the base type; *facet1*, *facet2*, *facet3*, etc., are constraining facets; and *value1*, *value2*, *value3*, etc., are values for each constraining facet. For example, white blood count values often fall between 0 and 20. A derived data type that enforces these boundaries could be derived as follows:

```
<simpleType name="wbcType">
   <restriction base="decimal">
      <minInclusive value="0"/>
```

```
        <maxInclusive value="20" />
    </restriction>
</simpleType>
```

```
<element name="WBC" type="wbcType"/>
```

With this derived data, the following content would be valid:

```
<WBC>12.8</WBC>
```

but these values would not be:

```
<WBC>22.5</WBC>
<WBC>-2.5</WBC>
<WBC>high</WBC>
```

REFERENCE WINDOW **RW**

Deriving New Data Types

- To derive a list data type, use the syntax

```
<simpleType name="name">
    <list itemType="type"/>
</simpleType>
```

where *name* is the name of the derived data type and *type* is the data type of the values in the list.

- To derive a union data type, use the syntax

```
<simpleType name="type">
    <union memberTypes="type1 type2 type3 …"/>
</simpleType>
```

where *type1, type2, type3,* etc., are the member types that comprise the union.

- To derive a restricted data type, use

```
<simpleType name="name">
    <restriction base="type">
        <facet1 value="value1" />
        <facet2 value="value2" />
        <facet3 value="value3" />
        ...
    </restriction>
</simpleType>
```

where *facet1, facet2, facet3,* etc., are constraining facets, and *value1, value2, value3,* etc., are values for each constraining facet.

Applying a Restricted Data Type

The more Allison learns about data types, the more she sees ways that they can help her reduce the chance of erroneous data being entered into her document. Needless to say, she will require your help with this effort. She has the following restrictions she wants to apply to the elements in her document:

- Each patient in her document must be at least 21 years of age.
- The cancer stage for each patient in her document must be either "I" or "II".
- The value of the Performance element must be between 0 and 1 (excluding 0 and 1).
- Performances must be measured on either the Karnofsky or Bell scale.

To apply these restrictions, you'll derive new data types for the Age, Stage, and Performance elements, as well as for the Scale attribute. A copy of the schema has been stored in flat catalog format for you to work with.

First, you'll derive a data type for the ageType element. This derived type sets a lower value for ages at 21 but does not set an upper boundary. Because ages are represented as positive integers, the positiveInteger type is used as the base.

To derive the ageType:

1. In the PSchema.xsd file, directly below the Pat_Elements element group, insert the following text:

```
<xsd:simpleType name="ageType">
  <xsd:restriction base="xsd:positiveInteger">
    <xsd:minInclusive value="21"/>
  </xsd:restriction>
</xsd:simpleType>
```

2. Change the data type of the Age element from "xsd:positiveInteger" to **"ageType"**. See Figure 4-32.

Figure 4-32   **CREATING THE AGETYPE DATATYPE**

```
<xsd:group name="Pat_Elements">
   <xsd:sequence>
      <xsd:element name="Name" type="xsd:string"/>
      <xsd:element name="ID" type="xsd:string"/>
      <xsd:element name="DOB" type="xsd:date"/>
      <xsd:element name="Age" type="ageType"/>
      <xsd:element name="Stage" type="xsd:string"/>
      <xsd:element name="Comment" type="xsd:string" minOccurs="0" maxOccurs="unbounded"/>
      <xsd:element name="Performance" type="PerfType" />
   </xsd:sequence>
</xsd:group>

<xsd:simpleType name="ageType">
  <xsd:restriction base="xsd:positiveInteger">
    <xsd:minInclusive value="21"/>
  </xsd:restriction>
</xsd:simpleType>
```

The next step is to create a derived type named "stageType" that constrains the value of the Stage element to either "I" or "II" and a data type named "scaleType" for the Performance element that requires values between 0 and 1.

To create the stageType and scaleType data types:

1. Below the Pat_Elements group, insert the following text:

```
<xsd:simpleType name="stageType">
  <xsd:restriction base="xsd:string">
    <xsd:enumeration value="I"/>
    <xsd:enumeration value="II"/>
  </xsd:restriction>
</xsd:simpleType>
```

2. Change the data type of the Stage element from "xsd:string" to **"stageType"**. See Figure 4-33.

Figure 4-33 CREATING THE STAGETYPE DATATYPE

```
<xsd:group name="Pat_Elements">
    <xsd:sequence>
        <xsd:element name="Name" type="xsd:string"/>
        <xsd:element name="ID" type="xsd:string"/>
        <xsd:element name="DOB" type="xsd:date"/>
        <xsd:element name="Age" type="ageType"/>
        <xsd:element name="Stage" type="stageType"/>
        <xsd:element name="Comment" type="xsd:string" minOccurs="0" maxOccurs="unbounded"/>
        <xsd:element name="Performance" type="PerfType" />
    </xsd:sequence>
</xsd:group>
<xsd:simpleType name="stageType">
    <xsd:restriction base="xsd:string">
        <xsd:enumeration value="I"/>
        <xsd:enumeration value="II"/>
    </xsd:restriction>
</xsd:simpleType>
```

3. Insert the following code below the PerfType complex type:

```
<xsd:simpleType name="scaleType">
  <xsd:restriction base="xsd:decimal">
    <xsd:minExclusive value="0"/>
    <xsd:maxExclusive value="1"/>
  </xsd:restriction>
</xsd:simpleType>
```

4. Change the data type of PerfType from "xsd:decimal" to **"scaleType"**. See Figure 4-34.

Figure 4-34 CREATING THE SCALETYPE DATATYPE

```
<xsd:complexType name="PerfType">
    <xsd:simpleContent>
        <xsd:extension base="scaleType">
            <xsd:attribute name="Scale" type="xsd:string" use="required"/>
        </xsd:extension>
    </xsd:simpleContent>
</xsd:complexType>

<xsd:simpleType name="scaleType">
    <xsd:restriction base="xsd:decimal">
        <xsd:minExclusive value="0"/>
        <xsd:maxExclusive value="1"/>
    </xsd:restriction>
</xsd:simpleType>
```

Finally, create a data type named "psType" that requires the values of the Scale attribute to be either Karnofsky or Bell.

To create the psType data type:

1. Below the PerfType complex type, insert the following:

```
<xsd:simpleType name="psType">
  <xsd:restriction base="xsd:string">
    <xsd:enumeration value="Karnofsky"/>
    <xsd:enumeration value="Bell"/>
  </xsd:restriction>
</xsd:simpleType>
```

2. Change the Scale's data type from "xsd:string" to **"psType"**, as shown in Figure 4-35.

Figure 4-35	CREATING THE PSTYPE DATATYPE

```
<xsd:complexType name="PerfType">
    <xsd:simpleContent>
        <xsd:extension base="scaleType">
            <xsd:attribute name="Scale" type="psType" use="required"/>
        </xsd:extension>
    </xsd:simpleContent>
</xsd:complexType>

<xsd:simpleType name="psType">
  <xsd:restriction base="xsd:string">
    <xsd:enumeration value="Karnofsky"/>
    <xsd:enumeration value="Bell"/>
  </xsd:restriction>
</xsd:simpleType>
```

Finally, there is one additional restriction that Allison thinks should be made to this document. She wants to create a data type for the medical record number whose values are stored in the ID element. At the hospital, medical record numbers must follow the form MR###-###-##. The schema must enforce this format in the contents of the ID element. As you will learn, you can accomplish what Allison needs using the patterns facet.

Working with Patterns

A pattern is created with a formatted text string called a **regular expression** or **regex**. XML Schema regexes are based on the same regexes used in the Perl programming language, which in turn are descendents of regexes used in the UNIX operating system. The syntax of regular expression is capable of expressing almost any kind of string format. In this tutorial, we'll just cover the basics of the regular expression syntax. You can explore this topic in more detail and learn more about the use of regular expressions with XML Schema at *http://www.w3.org/TR/xmlschema-2/#regexs*.

The basic unit of a regex is called an **atom**, which can be a single character, a group of characters, or another regex enclosed in parentheses. Let's start with a simple example using a single character. The following pattern definition forces the value of the data type to be the text string "ABC". Any other combination of letters or the use of lowercase letters would be invalid.

```
<pattern value="ABC"/>
```

By placing a range of values within a set of square brackets, a character group is created. The following pattern allows for any letter A through Z (but not a through z!):

```
<pattern value="[A-Z]"/>
```

Similarly, the following expression allows any number from 0 to 9 to be specified:

```
<pattern value="[0-9]"/>
```

Multiple ranges can be joined together to form the values of a single, if not contiguous, range. For example, the following pattern allows for any uppercase letter followed by any lowercase letter:

```
<pattern value="[A-Z][a-z]"/>
```

or two character groups can be combined into a single group as follows:

```
<pattern value="[A-Za-z]"/>
```

To specify the number of occurrences for a particular character, a **quantifier** can be appended to an atom in the regex. XML Schema supports six quantifiers, as displayed in Figure 4-36.

Figure 4-36	PATTERN QUANTIFIERS

QUANTIFIER	DESCRIPTION
?	Zero or one occurrence
*	Zero or more occurrences
+	One or more occurrences
{min, max}	Between *min* and *max* occurrences
{n}	Exactly *n* occurrences
{min, }	At least *min* occurrences

For example, to display a string of uppercase characters of any length, use the * quantifier in the following pattern:

```
<pattern value="[A-Z]*"/>
```

To allow a character string of uppercase letters no more than ten characters long, use the following pattern:

```
<pattern value="[A-Z]{0,10}"/>
```

Through the use of character ranges and quantifiers, patterns can be created for many commonly used character strings. For example, the following code creates a pattern for phone numbers, such as 555-1234:

```
<simpleType name="phoneType">
   <restriction base="string">
      <pattern value="[1-9][0-9]{2}-[0-9]{4}"/>
   </restriction>
</simpleType>
```

Note that the first digits of the phone number must be within the range of 1 through 9. This prevents phone numbers from starting with a zero in the exchange portion of the phone number.

We've only scratched the surface of what regular expressions can do. However, enough has been discussed to be able to solve Allison's request that all ID strings must be in the following format: MR###-###-##. The pattern for this expression is as follows:

```
<pattern value="MR[0-9]{3}-[0-9]{3}-[0-9]{2}"/>
```

Create a data type named "mrType" based on this expression now.

To create a data type based on a pattern:

1. Insert the following code beneath the Pat_Elements group:

```
<xsd:simpleType name="mrType">
  <xsd:restriction base="xsd:string">
    <xsd:pattern value="MR[0-9]{3}-[0-9]{3}-[0-9]{2}"/>
  </xsd:restriction>
</xsd:simpleType>
```

2. Change the type of the ID element from "xsd:string" to **"mrType"**, as shown in Figure 4-37.

Figure 4-37	CREATING THE MRTYPE DATATYPE

```
<xsd:group name="Pat_Elements">
   <xsd:sequence>
      <xsd:element name="Name" type="xsd:string"/>
      <xsd:element name="ID" type="mrType"/>
      <xsd:element name="DOB" type="xsd:date"/>
      <xsd:element name="Age" type="ageType"/>
      <xsd:element name="Stage" type="stageType"/>
      <xsd:element name="Comment" type="xsd:string" minOccurs="0" maxOccurs="unbounded"/>
      <xsd:element name="Performance" type="PerfType" />
   </xsd:sequence>
</xsd:group>

<xsd:simpleType name="mrType">
  <xsd:restriction base="xsd:string">
    <xsd:pattern value="MR[0-9]{3}-[0-9]{3}-[0-9]{2}"/>
  </xsd:restriction>
</xsd:simpleType>
```

Derived data types are a powerful and versatile feature of XML Schema. One can create a schema containing an entire library of customized data types to supplement the built-in data types supplied by XML Schema. By attaching this schema to a namespace, one can access those data types from other schema documents.

Annotating a Schema

After creating a schema, it's useful to include documentation about it. Because schemas are XML documents, you can include any information in the form of XML comments. In addition to the comments method, XML Schema provides an annotation element to store documentation regarding the schema. The syntax of the annotation element is

```
<annotation>
   <documentation>
      documentation comments
   </documentation>
   <appinfo>
      application information
   </appinfo>
</annotation>
```

The annotation element must contain at least one documentation child element or appinfo child element. The documentation element is useful for containing comments that can provide helpful information regarding the code for other XML developers.

Typically, this documentation describes the purpose and content of the schema. The appinfo element can provide information for the particular application processing the schema.

Why, you may be asking, should annotations be used rather than comments? The primary reason is that XML parsers ignore comments when they process XML documents. By putting information into a document or appinfo element, the information becomes available to the parser.

Annotations can appear at the beginning of the schema. You can also put annotations inside a specific element, attribute, simpleType, complexType, or group declaration. Allison appreciates the value of using annotations and would like you to insert an annotation at the beginning of the schema file to provide some documentation regarding the purpose of the file.

To create the annotation:

1. Insert the following code below the schema element:

```
<xsd:annotation>
  <xsd:documentation>
      This schema contains element and attribute declarations
      for the University Hospital's Breast Cancer study.
      Contact Allison Grant at 555-7832 for more information
      on the study and the creation of this schema.
  </xsd:documentation>
</xsd:annotation>
```

Figure 4-38 shows the code in the PSchema2.xsd file.

| Figure 4-38 | INSERTING AN ANNOTATION |

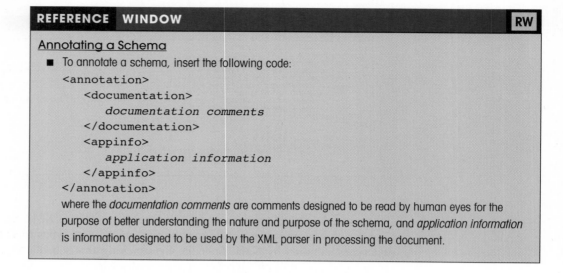

```
<?xml version="1.0" encoding="UTF-8"?>
<!-- Schema for breast cancer patient data -->

<xsd:schema xmlns:xsd="http://www.w3.org/2001/XMLSchema"
            xmlns="http://uhosp/patients/ns"
            targetNamespace="http://uhosp/patients/ns">

 <xsd:annotation>
    <xsd:documentation>
       This schema contains element and attribute declarations
       for the Unversity Hospital's Breast Cancer study.
       Contact Allison Grant at 555-7832 for more information
       on the study and the creation of this schema.
    </xsd:documentation>
 </xsd:annotation>
```

2. Save your changes and close PSchema2.xsd.

The new data types are a valuable addition to the schema. Allison suggests that you update both the Patient.xml and UHosp.xml documents to take advantage of the new schema.

To revise Allison's document:

1. Open the **Patient.xml** document in your text editor.

2. Locate the Patients element at the top of the file and change the schema location from PSchema1.xsd to **PSchema2.xsd**.

3. Close the file, saving your changes.

4. Open the UHosp.xml file in your text editor. Change the schema location for the Patients element from PSchema1.xsd to **PSchema2.xsd**.

5. Close the file and the text editor, saving your changes.

Now that you've attached a new schema to the Allison's data, she wants to validate the file. You'll do this using the Patient.xml file.

To validate the Patient.xml file:

1. Start XML Spy and open the **Patient.xml** file from the Tutorial.04X/Tutorial folder on your Data Disk. Maximize the contents of the document pane, and click the **Text View** button 📄 to view the text of the file.

2. Open **PSchema2.xsd** from the Tutorial.04X/Tutorial folder and switch to text view.

TROUBLE? XML Spy may attempt to automatically validate your document when it opens. If an error message appears, study the error message for the reason why the validation failed. Compare the code in both the Patient.xml and PSchema2.xsd files to the figures in the text.

3. Click the **Validate** button 📝 on the XML Spy toolbar to verify that the contents of the Patient.xml file fulfill Allison's validation rules.

4. Click the **OK** button.

Allison would like to confirm that any content in the document that violates the rules she set up in the schema file will be picked up by the XML parser. She asks you to test this by changing some of the values in the Patient.xml file to obvious errors.

To test the schema validation:

1. Select the value "58"—the age of Cynthia Dibbs, the first patient in Allison's document—and change the value to "**18**".

The schema for this document requires that patients must be 21 or older, thus the XML parser should flag this as an error.

2. Click the **Validate** button 📝.

XML Spy returns the error message shown in Figure 4-39, indicating that the change is not valid.

Figure 4-39   VALIDATING THE PATIENT DOCUMENT WITH AN AGE ERROR

XML Spy highlights an age value that is less than the minimum required value of 21

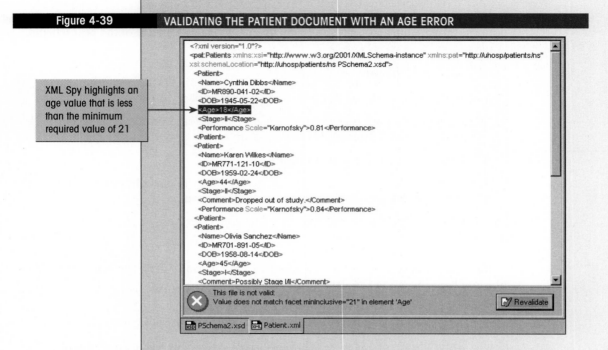

3. Click **Edit** and **Undo** to undo your change, restoring the age value to "58".

    Now test whether the pattern matching applied to the medical record number is enforced by the XML parser.

4. Change the medical record number of Cynthia Dibbs from "MR890-041-02" to "**CR890-041-02**".

    This should be an error because the schema requires all medical record numbers to be of the form MR###-###-##.

5. Click the **Validate** button.

    XML Spy returns the error message shown in Figure 4-40, indicating that the medical record number does not match the required pattern.

Figure 4-40	VALIDATING THE PATIENT DOCUMENT WITH A PATTERN ERROR

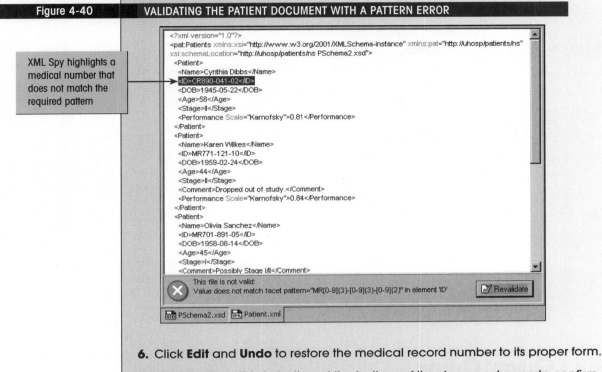

XML Spy highlights a medical number that does not match the required pattern

```
<?xml version="1.0"?>
<pat:Patients xmlns:xsi="http://www.w3.org/2001/XMLSchema-instance" xmlns:pat="http://uhosp/patients/ns"
xsi:schemaLocation="http://uhosp/patients/ns PSchema2.xsd">
  <Patient>
    <Name>Cynthia Dibbs</Name>
    <ID>CR890-041-02</ID>
    <DOB>1945-05-22</DOB>
    <Age>58</Age>
    <Stage>II</Stage>
    <Performance Scale="Karnofsky">0.81</Performance>
  </Patient>
  <Patient>
    <Name>Karen Wilkes</Name>
    <ID>MR771-121-10</ID>
    <DOB>1959-02-24</DOB>
    <Age>44</Age>
    <Stage>II</Stage>
    <Comment>Dropped out of study.</Comment>
    <Performance Scale="Karnofsky">0.84</Performance>
  </Patient>
  <Patient>
    <Name>Olivia Sanchez</Name>
    <ID>MR701-891-05</ID>
    <DOB>1958-08-14</DOB>
    <Age>45</Age>
    <Stage>I</Stage>
    <Comment>Possibly Stage I/II</Comment>
```

This file is not valid:
Value does not match facet pattern="MR[0-9]{3}-[0-9]{3}-[0-9]{2}" in element 'ID'

[✕]   [✓ Revalidate]

[XSD] PSchema2.xsd   [XML] Patient.xml

6. Click **Edit** and **Undo** to restore the medical record number to its proper form.

7. Click the **Revalidate** button at the bottom of the document pane to confirm that the Patient.xml file is now valid.

   TROUBLE? If you still get an error message, study the message for clues to the reason why the file is invalid and take the necessary measures to correct the error.

If this were a real situation, you would probably put considerably more time into testing various possible errors in the instance document. However, having seen how to test the validation procedure against two possible errors, we'll close the document.

To close your work:

1. Click **File** and **Close All** from the XML Spy menu.

2. When prompted to save your changes, click the **Yes** button.

3. Click **File** and **Exit** to exit XML Spy.

Common Schema Syntax Errors

As you write your own schemas, you may have to deal with syntax errors. Here are some of the more common mistakes:

- failure to include the XML Schema namespace prefix before each schema tag
- failure to include a closing tag for two-sided schema elements
- failure to enter simple element declarations as empty tags
- misspelling of schema elements or improper use of upper and lowercase letters
- failure to place attributes within quotation marks
- misspelling of the XML Schema namespace in either the schema or the instance document
- when the schema is attached to a namespace, forgetting to use qualified names with all global elements in the instance document

Allison is impressed. She can see that an XML parser that can validate her documents with schemas can do a lot to reduce data entry errors. She plans to enter information on the rest of the study patients into the Patient.xml document. She feels confident that the schema you designed will help ensure the quality of her work.

Session 4.3 QUICK CHECK

1. What is a flat catalog and how does it differ from a Russian Doll design?
2. What are global elements? What are local elements?
3. How do you create a named complex type? What are the advantages of named types?
4. Define the following: value space, lexical space, and facets.
5. How would you derive a data type named "counts" that contains a list of positive integers?
6. How would you derive a data type named "Status" that can be either a decimal number or a text string?
7. How would you derive a data type named "percent" that is limited to decimal numbers between 0 and 100 (including 0 and 100)?
8. How would you create a regex for social security numbers, which have the form ###-##-####?

Note: In the case problems that follow, some of the XML documents have intentional errors. Part of your job will be to find and correct those errors using schemas.

REVIEW ASSIGNMENTS

Allison has been very pleased with your work on the patient document. She has approached you with a different file to work on. This file contains information on some of the studies being done at the hospital. As before, Allison needs you to create a schema for this document to ensure that the document contains no errors and to prevent future errors when Allison adds information about other studies to the file.

Figure 4-41 shows a diagram of the elements and structure of Allison's document.

Figure 4-41

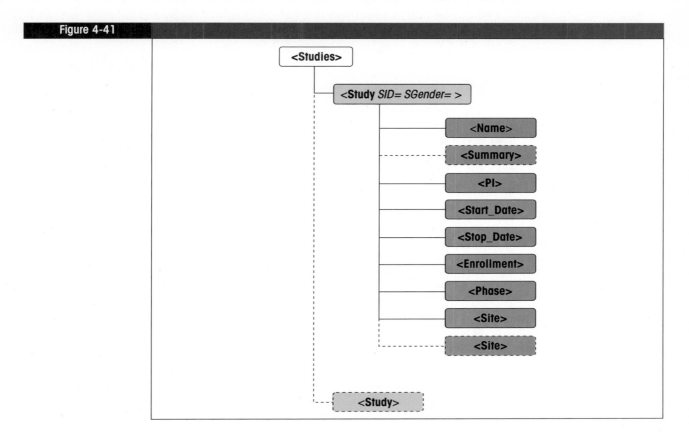

In the table in Figure 4-42, Allison has provided a description of all the elements and attributes in her document. She has also indicated which are optional and what sort of limitations she wants to place on their values.

Figure 4-42

ELEMENTS	DESCRIPTION
Studies	The root element of the document
Study	The element that stores information about each individual study
Name	The name of the study
Summary	An optional summary of the study's purpose
PI	The principal investigator on the study
Start_Date	The study's starting date
Stop_Date	The study's stopping date
Enrollment	The number of patients to be enrolled into the study
Phase	The type of study being done (Phase must be "1", "2", or "3")
Site	The hospital where the patients will be enrolled; there will be one or more sites for each study

Figure 4-42	(CONTINUED)
ATTRIBUTES	
SID	A required attribute of the Study element, providing the study's ID number; ID numbers must be in the form CCC-###-##
SGender	A required attribute of the Study element, indicating gender of patients in the study; the SGender attribute must be equal to "Female", "Male", or "All"

When you finish creating the schema, Allison wants you to attach it to her document and then to run a validity check on the document's contents. You decide to design this schema in the form of a flat catalog (you may want to refer to Figure 4-28 for guidance in laying out a flat catalog).

To complete this task:

1. Using your text editor, create a blank file named **SSchema.xsd** stored in the Tutorial.04X/Review folder of your Data Disk.

2. Add the xml declaration and root schema element to the file. Include a namespace to indicate that this is an XML Schema file. Use a namespace prefix of "xs". Do not attach the contents of the schema file to a namespace.

Explore ▷ 3. Create the following derived data types:

- a data type named "PType"; limit PType values to the integers 1, 2, or 3
- A data type named "SIDType", whose values must be an ID type following the pattern CCC-###-##
- A data type named "SGType", whose values must be one of the following text strings: "Female", "Male", or "All"

4. Declare the following simple global elements:

- the Name, Summary, PI, and Site elements, which all store a text string
- the Start_Date and Stop_Date elements, which store dates
- the Enrollment element, which stores a positive integer
- the Phase element, which stores PType data.

5. Declare a global element named "Study", which contains a sequence of the following child elements: Name, Summary, PI, Start_Date, Stop_Date, Enrollment, Phase, and Site. Specify that the Summary element may appear 0 or 1 time, and that the Site element may appear 1 or more times. (*Hint*: Use the ref attribute to reference the elements you declared in the previous step.)

6. The Study element should also have two required attributes: SID and SGender. The data type of the SID attribute should be the SIDType. The data type of the SGender attribute should be SGType.

Explore ▷ 7. Declare a global element named "Studies", which contains one or more occurrences of the Study element.

8. Save your changes to the SSchema.xsd file.

9. Open the CCCtxt.xml file from the Tutorial.04X/Review folder on your Data Disk, using your text editor. Save the file as **CCC.xml**.

10. Attach the SSchema.xsd schema to this instance document. Do not assign a namespace to the schema.

11. Open both the CCC.xml and SSchema.xsd files in XML Spy.

12. Validate the contents of the CCC.xml document, correcting any entries you find in the CCC.xml file that violate Allison's schema. Save your changes to both files once you have a valid document that satisfies the rules set out by Allison.

13. Print a copy of both the CCC.xml and SSchema.xsd files, and hand in your files and printouts to your instructor.

CASE PROBLEMS

Case 1. The Jazz Warehouse Richard Brooks is working on an inventory of the CD collection at the Jazz Warehouse. He wants to be able to validate the information he's entering to weed out any data entry errors. The structure of his XML document is shown in Figure 4-43. Figure 4-44 describes the contents and properties of each of the attributes and elements in his document. Richard would like you to create a schema based on his document and then apply that schema to some of the data he's already entered. You'll use a Russian Doll design to create your schema.

Figure 4-43

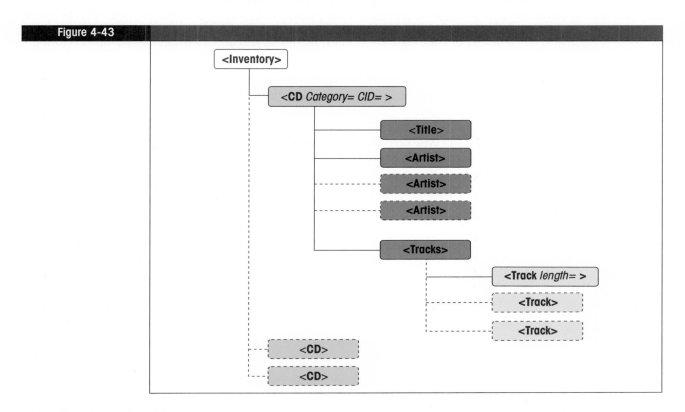

Figure 4-44

ELEMENTS	DESCRIPTION
Inventory	The root element of the document
CD	An element storing information about individual CDs
Title	The title of each CD

Figure 4-44	(CONTINUED)
ELEMENTS	**DESCRIPTION**
Artist	An element storing the name of the artist
Tracks	An element storing information about musical tracks on the CD
Track	The name of each CD track
ATTRIBUTES	
CID	A required attribute of the CD element, indicating the CD's ID number; ID numbers must be in the form JW######
Category	A required attribute of the CD element, indicating the musical category of the CD; the Category attribute must be equal to New Orleans, Swing, Bebop, or Modern

To complete this task:

1. Using your text editor, open the **JWtxt.xml file** located in the Tutorial.04X/Cases folder of your Data Disk. Save the file as **JW.xml**.

2. Using your text editor, create a blank file named **CD.xsd** in the Tutorial.04X/Cases folder of your Data Disk. Insert the initial xml declaration and opening and closing schema tags.

3. Within the opening schema tag, insert the XML Schema namespace, and assign the schema itself to the target namespace, "http://jazzwarehouse.com/schema."

Explore

4. Create the following user-derived data types as global components of your schema:

   ■ CIDType derived from the ID data type and whose values are restricted to the pattern "JW######"

   ■ CatType derived from the string data type, and whose values must be New Orleans, Swing, Bebop, or Modern

5. In a Russian Doll design, declare the following element attributes:

   ■ Declare the Inventory element as a complex type containing a sequence of one or more CD elements.

   ■ Declare the CD element to contain the following sequence of elements: Title, (one or more) Artist, and Tracks.

   ■ The CD element should also contain two required attributes: Category and CID. The Category element should contain CatType data. The CID element should contain CIDType data.

   ■ The Title and Artist elements should contain text strings.

   ■ The Tracks element should contain one or more occurrences of the Track element.

Explore

   ■ The Track element should contain a text string and an attribute named "length," which uses the time data type. (*Hint*: Use the syntax for declaring an attribute in an element with simple content.)

6. Save your changes to the CD.xsd file.

7. Return to the JW.xml file, and attach the document to the CD.xsd schema and the http://jazzwarehouse.com/schema namespace. Make sure that all global elements have qualified element names.

8. Save your changes to the JW.xml file.

9. Open JW.xml and CD.xsd in XML Spy and validate the files. Correct any entries in the JW.xml file that violate Richard's schema. Save your changes.

10. Print the contents of the JW.xml and CD.xsd files. Hand in your files and printouts to your instructor.

Case 2. Northwest Optimist Club Alicia Schaap is a board member of the Northwest Optimist Club. One of her duties is to maintain a list containing contact information for all the members. Alicia has collected information on each member's name, address, phone numbers, spouse, and children's names in an XML document. She would like to have some way of validating her data and any new data that she enters. She has asked your help in devising a schema for her document. Figure 4-45 shows a diagram of the document's structure. Figure 4-46 describes the features of each element and attribute. You decide not to attach a namespace to the schema.

Figure 4-45

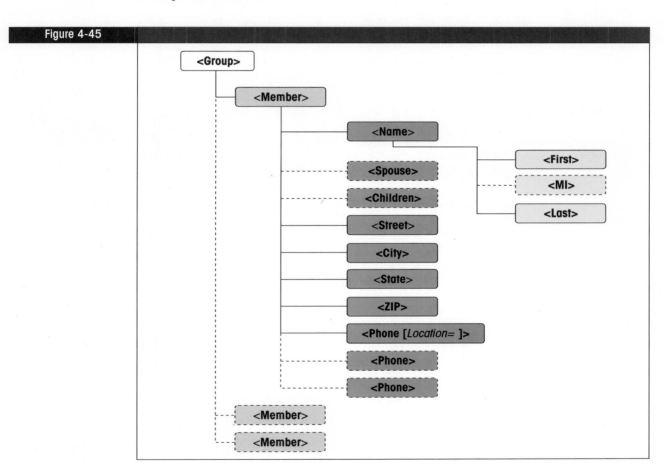

Figure 4-46

ELEMENTS	DESCRIPTION
Group	The root element of the document
Member	An element storing information about a club member
Name	An element storing information about the member's name
First	The member's first name
MI	The member's middle initial (optional)
Last	The member's last name
Spouse	The name of the member's spouse (optional)
Children	A list of the member's children (optional)
Street	The member's street address
City	The member's city of residence
State	The member's state of residence
ZIP	A 5-digit ZIP code
Phone	The member's phone number in the form ### ### - ####; a member can have one or more phone numbers
ATTRIBUTES	
Location	An optional attribute of the Phone element indicating the type of phone number; the Location attribute must be equal to home or business

To complete this task:

1. Using your text editor, open the **Listtxt.xml** file located in the Tutorial.04X/Cases folder of your Data Disk. Save the file as **List.xml**.

2. Using your text editor, create a blank file named **LSchema.xsd** in the Tutorial.04X/Cases folder of your Data Disk. Insert the initial xml declaration and opening and closing schema tags. Do not attach this schema to a target namespace.

Explore 3. Create the following user-derived data types as global items in the schema:

- LType, a text string limited to the values "home" or "business"
- PType, a text string that must follow the pattern ### ###-####
- ZIPType, a text string consisting of five integers
- CType, a list of NMTOKEN data types
- MIType, a text string that is only one character long

Explore 4. Create a complex type with the name "FullName." FullName should contain a sequence of simple elements named First, MI, and Last. Both the First and Last elements should be NMTOKEN data types. The MI element should be an optional element and be a MIType data type.

5. Declare the following elements globally:

- Name with a type = FullName
- Spouse with a data type = NMTOKEN
- Children with a data type = CType
- Street and City with string data types

■ State with a data type = NMTOKEN

■ ZIP with a data type = ZIPType

6. Globally declare a complex element named "Phone" that contains text content with the PType data type and has an optional attribute named "Location." The Location attribute should use the LType data type.

7. Globally declare a complex element named "Member," which contains the following sequence of child elements: Name, Spouse, Children, Street, City, State, Zip, and Phone. Both the Spouse and Children elements should be optional. The Phone element can occur one or more times. (*Hint*: Use the ref attribute to create a reference between the sequence of child elements and the elements you declared in Step 5.)

8. Globally declare a complex element named "Group," which contains a single child element named "Member". The Member element can occur one or more times.

9. Save your changes to LSchema.xsd file.

Explore 10. Return to the List.xml file and attach the LSchema.xsd schema to this instance document without using a namespace. Save your changes to the file.

11. Open both the List.xml and LSchema.xsd files in XML Spy. Validate the List.xml document, correcting any errors in the file that violate the rules set up by Alicia in her schema.

12. Print out the contents of the List.xml and LSchema.xsd files. Hand in your printouts and files to your instructor.

Case 3. GrillRite Grills, Inc. James Castillo manages the inventory for GrillRite Grills, one of the leading manufacturers of grills in North America. He has been using XML to record the contents of the GrillRite warehouse. James has created two documents. One document lists all of the parts in the warehouse, including the name of each part, the cost of the part, and the number in stock. Another document describes all of the fully assembled grills in the warehouse. In this document, James has recorded the name of each grill model, the selling price of the model, the number of assembled models in stock, and the parts required to assemble each model.

James would like to create schemas for both of these documents to ensure their validity. He also plans to combine information from both documents into a single file. He would like your help in creating this combined document and validating it.

Figure 4-47 shows a diagram of the structure of both documents. Figure 4-48 lists the elements and attributes of the documents and specifies any validation rules that James would like the schemas to enforce. You decide to design these schemas using a Venetian Blinds layout.

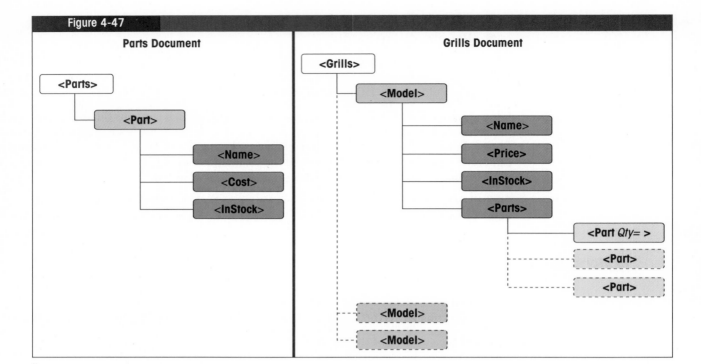

Figure 4-47

PARTS DOCUMENT ELEMENTS	DESCRIPTION
Parts	The root element of the Parts document
Part	An element storing information about a specific part
Name	The part's name
Cost	The cost of the part
InStock	The number of parts in stock
ATTRIBUTES	
None	

GRILLS DOCUMENT ELEMENTS	DESCRIPTION
Grills	The root element of the Grills document
Model	An element storing information about a specific grill model
Name	The name of the grill model
Price	The selling price of the model
InStock	The number of fully assembled grills in stock
Parts	An element storing information about the parts needed to assemble the grill model
Part	The name of each individual part (must be equal to Main Burner, Side Burner, Standard Chassis, Extended Chassis, Controls, Gas Tubing, Igniter, Main Rack, Top Rack, Side Rack, or Stand)
ATTRIBUTES	
Qty	An attribute of the Part element, indicating the number of each part used in assembling the model

Figure 4-48

To complete this task:

1. Using your text editor, open the **Partstxt.xml** file located in the Tutorial.04X/Cases folder of your Data Disk. Save the file as **Parts.xml**.

2. Use your text editor to create a blank file named **PTSchema.xsd** in your Tutorial.04X/Cases folder. Add the usual xml and schema elements to the document. Assign the schema the target namespace "http://grillrite.com/parts."

3. Create an element group named P_Elements. Within this group, create a sequence of the following elements: Name, Cost, InStock. The data type of the Name and Cost elements should be string. The InStock element should be restricted to positive integers.

4. Create a complex type named "PartType," which contains the P_Elements group.

5. Declare a global element named "Parts" that contains the child element, Part. The Part element must be present one or more times. The data type of the Part element should be PartType.

6. Save the PTSchema.xsd file and then attach the Parts.xml file to this schema and namespace. Save your changes, then open both documents in XML Spy and validate their contents.

7. With your text editor, open the Grilltxt.xml file from the Tutorial.04X/Cases folder. Save the file as **Grills.xml**.

8. Use your text editor to create a schema file named "**GRSchema.xsd**." Assign the schema to the http://grillrite.com/grills namespace.

9. Create a user-derived data type named "PartNames" that is restricted to one of the parts shown in the Grill document from Figure 4-48.

10. Create a complex type named "PartType," which is an element that contains PartNames data and has a required attribute named "Qty." The value of the Qty attribute should be a positive integer.

11. Create a complex type named "PartsType," which contains a sequence of one or more PartType elements.

12. Create a complex type named "M_Elements," which contains the following sequence of elements: Name, Price, InStock, and Parts. The Name and Price elements contain string data. The value of the InStock element should be a positive integer. The Parts element should contain the PartType complex type.

13. Declare a global element named "Grills." The Grills element should be a complex type that contains a sequence of one or more elements named "Model." The Model element should be of the type M_Elements.

14. Save the GRSchema.xsd file and then attach the Grills.xml file to this schema and namespace. Save your changes and use XML Spy to validate the contents of the file.

15. Using your text editor, create a new document named GRStock.xml that has a root element named "Stock," which contains within it the contents of both the Parts.xml and Grills.xml documents. Attach the two parts of this document to the appropriate schemas and namespaces.

16. Save the GRStock file and open it in XML Spy. Validate the contents of the file.

17. Print out the contents of the files you created for this problem. Hand in your printouts and files to your instructor.

Case 4. MediaMart Online MediaMart is an online store that specializes in selling used videos, books, and movies. Terrance Dawes, who works for MediaMart, has been given the task of putting some of their product information in XML documents. He's not very experienced with XML and would like your help in making the transfer as well as ensuring the integrity of his data. Terrance has put a small list of products into three text files named Books, Movies, and Music. Figure 4-49 describes the contents of the three files.

Figure 4-49

BOOKS	MOVIES	MUSIC
• The name of the book • The author • The genre (fiction or nonfiction) • The format (paperback or hardcover) • The price	• The name of the movie • The genre (comedy, drama, fantasy, children, musical, or family • A list of actors or actresses in the movie • The price • The year the movie was released • The format (VHS or DVD)	• The artist • The name of the work • The genre (rock, classical, opera, jazz, blues, rap, or pop) • The format (cassette or CD) • The price

To complete this task:

1. Create three XML documents named **Books.xml**, **Movies.xml**, and **Music.xml**, containing the data from the three text files. The structure of the XML documents is up to you.

Explore

2. Draw a schematic diagram of the three XML documents you created.

3. Create three schemas named **BSchema.xsd**, **MoSchema.xsd**, and **MuSchema.xsd** based on the document structure of your XML documents. The design of the schemas is up to you, but the schemas must ensure the integrity of Terrance's data, following the guidelines in Figure 4-49.

4. Include annotations in all three schemas describing the nature and purpose of the document.

5. Attach the schemas you created to your three XML documents. Validate both the XML documents and the schemas using XML Spy.

6. Combine the three XML documents into a single document named **MMart.xml**. Attach the three schemas to that single document and validate it in XML Spy.

7. Print out all of the files you created in this assignment and hand in your files and printouts to your instructor.

QUICK CHECK ANSWERS

Session 4.1

1. A namespace is a defined collection of element and attribute names. Namespaces are useful in avoiding name collisions in combined documents.

2. an element name with a namespace prefix

3. `<?xml:namespace ns="http://ns.doc/book" prefix="Book"?>`

4. `<Book:Work xmlns:Book="http://ns.doc/book">`

5. Do not specify a prefix in the namespace declaration.

6. as if the namespace prefix and the local part were the complete element name

Session 4.2

1. A schema is a collection of rules and definitions, written in XML. An instance document is the XML document that the schema is written for.

2. Schemas support namespaces and work with combined documents better than DTDs. Schemas support more data types and allow the user to easily create customized data types. Schemas are also a newer standard and are not completely supported by all XML parsers.

3. `<prefix:schema`
   `xmlns:prefix="http://www.w3.org/2001/XMLSchema">`

4. A simple type element contains only text. A complex type element contains child elements and/or attributes.

5. `<element name="Weight" type="decimal" />`

6. `<element name="Parents">`
      `<complexType>`
        `<sequence>`
          `<element name="Father" type="string" />`
          `<element name="Mother" type="string" />`
        `</sequence>`
      `</complexType>`
   `</element>`

7. `<element name="Book">`
      `<complexType>`
        `<simpleType>`
          `<extension base="string">`
            `<attribute name="Title" type="string" />`
          `</extension>`
        `</simpleType>`
      `</complexType>`
   `</element>`

8. `prefix:noNamespaceSchemaLocation="Schema1.xsd"`

Session 4.3

1. A flat catalog is a schema design in which all element declarations are global. In a Russian Doll design, only one element is global and all of the rest of the elements are nested within that one global element.

2. Global elements are elements that are direct children of the schema element and can be referenced throughout the schema file. Local elements are one or more levels below global elements and cannot be referenced by other elements.

3. by assigning a name in the <complexType> declaration; a named complexType can be used to store document structures

4. the set of values that correspond to the data type; the set of textual representations of the value space; the properties of the data type that distinguish one data type from another

5. `<simpleType name="counts">`
      `<list itemType="positiveInteger" />`
   `</simpleType>`

6. ```
<simpleType name="Status">
    <union memberTypes="decimal string" />
</simpleType>
```

7. ```
<simpleType name="percent">
   <restriction base="decimal">
      <minInclusive value="0" />
      <maxInclusive value="100" />
   </restriction>
</simpleType>
```

8. `[0-9]{3}-[0-9]{2}-[0-9]{3}`

HTML Color Names

The following is a list of HTML color names and their corresponding hexadecimal values. To view these colors, you must have a system capable of displaying at least 256 colors (8-bit). As with other aspects of Web page design, you should test these colors on a variety of browsers before using them. Different browsers may render these colors differently, or not at all. Remember, this is not a list of Web-safe, or browser safe, colors.

Extended Color Names

COLOR NAME	HEXADECIMAL VALUE	COLOR NAME	HEXADECIMAL VALUE
aliceblue	#F0F8FF	darksalmon	#E9967A
antiquewhite	#FAEBD7	darkseagreen	#8FBC8F
aqua	#00FFFF	darkslateblue	#483086
aquamarine	#70DB93	darkslategray	#2F4F4F
azure	#F0FFFF	darkturquoise	#00CED1
beige	#F5F5DC	darkviolet	#9400D3
bisque	#FFE4C4	deeppink	#FF1493
black	#000000	deepskyblue	#00BFFF
blanchedalmond	#FFEBCD	dimgray	#696969
blue	#0000FF	dodgerblue	#1E90FF
blueviolet	#8A2BE2	firebrick	#B22222
brown	#A52A2A	floralwhite	#FFFAF0
burlywood	#DEB887	forestgreen	#228B22
cadetblue	#5F9EA0	fuchsia	#FF00FF
chartreuse	#7FFF00	gainsboro	#DCDCDC
chocolate	#D2691E	ghostwhite	#F8F8FF
coral	#FF7F50	gold	#CD7F32
cornflowerblue	#6495ED	goldenrod	#DAA520
cornsilk	#FFF8DC	gray	#BEBEBE
crimson	#DC143C	green	#008000
cyan	#00FFFF	greenyellow	#ADFF2F
darkblue	#00008B	honeydew	#F0FFF0
darkcyan	#008B8B	hotpink	#FF69B4
darkgoldenrod	#B8860B	indianred	#CD5C5C
darkgray	#A9A9A9	indigo	#4B0082
darkgreen	#006400	ivory	#FFFFF0
darkkhaki	#BDB76B	khaki	#F0D58C
darkmagenta	#8B008B	lavender	#E6E6FA
darkolivegreen	#556B2F	lavenderblush	#FFF0F5
darkorange	#FF8C00	lawngreen	#7CFC00
darkorchid	#9932CC	lemonchiffon	#FFFACD
darkred	#8B0000	lightblue	#ADD8E6

COLOR NAME	HEXADECIMAL VALUE	COLOR NAME	HEXADECIMAL VALUE
lightcoral	#F08080	palegoldenrod	#EEE8AA
lightcyan	#E0FFFF	palegreen	#98FB98
lightgoldenrodyellow	#FAFAD2	paleturquoise	#AFEEEE
lightgrey	#03D3D3	palevioletred	#DB7093
lightgreen	#90EE90	papayawhip	#FFEFD5
lightpink	#FFB6C1	peachpuff	#FFDAB9
lightsalmon	#FFA07A	peru	#CD853F
lightseagreen	#20B2AA	pink	#FFC0CB
lightskyblue	#87CEFA	plum	#DDA0DD
lightslategray	#778899	powderblue	#B0E0E6
lightsteelblue	#B0C4DE	purple	#800080
lightyellow	#FFFFE0	red	#FF0000
lime	#00FF00	rosybrown	#BC8072
limegreen	#32CD32	royalblue	#4169E1
Linen	#FAF0E6	saddlebrown	#8B4513
magenta	#FF00FF	salmon	#FA8072
maroon	#800000	sandybrown	#F4A460
mediumaquamarine	#66CDAA	seagreen	#2E8B57
mediumblue	#0000CD	seashell	#FFF5EE
mediumorchid	#BA55D3	sienna	#A0522D
mediumpurple	#9370DB	silver	#C0C0C0
mediumseagreen	#3CB371	skyblue	#87CEEB
mediumslateblue	#7B68EE	slateblue	#6A5ACD
mediumspringgreen	#00FA9A	slategray	#708090
mediumturquoise	#48D1CC	snow	#FFFAFA
mediumvioletred	#C71585	springgreen	#00FF7F
midnightblue	#191970	steelblue	#4682B4
mintcream	#F5FFFA	tan	#D2B48C
mistyrose	#FFE4E1	teal	#008080
moccasin	#FFE4B5	thistle	#D8BFD8
navajowhite	#FFDEAD	tomato	#FF6347
navy	#000080	turquoise	#40E0D0
oldlace	#FDF5E6	violet	#EE82EE
olive	#808000	wheat	#F5DEB3
olivedrab	#6B8E23	white	#FFFFFF
orange	#FFA500	whitesmoke	#F5F5F5
orangered	#FF4500	yellow	#FFFF00
orchid	#DA70D6	yellowgreen	#9ACD32

HTML Character Entities

The following table lists the extended character set for HTML, also known as the ISO Latin-1 Character set. Characters can be defined by name or by numeric value. For example, to define the registered trademark symbol, ®, you can use either &reg or &#174.

Not all code names are recognized by all browsers. Some older browsers that support only the HTML 2.0 standard do not recognize the code name "&times", for instance. Code names that may not be recognized by older browsers are marked with an asterisk in the following table.

CHARACTER	CODE	CODE NAME	DESCRIPTION
	&#09		Tab
	&#10		Line feed
	&#32		Space
!	&#33		Exclamation mark
"	&#34	&quot	Double quotation mark
#	&#35		Pound sign
$	&#36		Dollar sign
%	&#37		Percent sign
&	&#38	&amp	Ampersand
'	&#39		Apostrophe
(	&#40		Left parenthesis
)	&#41		Right parenthesis
*	&#42		Asterisk
+	&#43		Plus sign
,	&#44		Comma
-	&#45		Hyphen
.	&#46		Period
/	&#47		Forward slash
0 - 9	&#48 - &#57		Numbers 0-9
:	&#58		Colon
;	&#59		Semicolon
<	&#60	&lt	Less than sign
=	&#61		Equal sign
>	&#62	&gt	Greater than sign
?	&#63		Question mark
@	&#64		Commercial at sign
A - Z	&#65 - &#90		Letters A-Z
[	&#91		Left square bracket
\	&#92		Back slash
]	&#93		Right square bracket

CHARACTER	CODE	CODE NAME	DESCRIPTION
^	&#94		Caret
_	&#95		Horizontal bar (underscore)
`	&#96		Grave accent
a - z	&#97 - &#122		Letters a-z
{	&#123		Left curly brace
|	&#124		Vertical bar
}	&#125		Right curly brace
~	&#126		Tilde
,	&#130		Comma
ƒ	&#131		Function sign (florin)
„	&#132		Double quotation mark
…	&#133		Ellipses
†	&#134		Dagger
‡	&#135		Double dagger
ˆ	&#136		Circumflex
‰	&#137		Permil
Š	&#138		Capital S with hacek
‹	&#139		Left single angle
Œ	&#140		Capital OE ligature
	&#141 - &#144		Unused
`	&#145		Single beginning quotation mark
'	&#146		Single ending quotation mark
"	&#147		Double beginning quotation mark
"	&#148		Double ending quotation mark
•	&#149		Bullet
–	&#150		En dash
—	&#151		Em dash
~	&#152		Tilde
™	&#153	&trade*	Trademark symbol
š	&#154		Small s with hacek
›	&#155		Right single angle
œ	&#156		Lowercase oe ligature
Ÿ	&#159		Capital Y with umlaut
		*	Non-breaking space
¡	&#161	&iexcl*	Inverted exclamation mark
¢	&#162	&cent*	Cent sign
£	&#163	&pound*	Pound sterling

CHARACTER	CODE	CODE NAME	DESCRIPTION
¤	&#164	&curren*	General currency symbol
¥	&#165	&yen*	Yen sign
¦	&#166	&brvbar*	Broken vertical bar
§	&#167	&sect*	Section sign
¨	&#168	&uml*	Umlaut
©	&#169	&copy*	Copyright symbol
ª	&#170	&ordf*	Feminine ordinal
«	&#171	&laquo*	Left angle quotation mark
¬	&#172	&not*	Not sign
−	&#173	&shy*	Soft hyphen
®	&#174	&reg*	Registered trademark
¯	&#175	&macr*	Macron
°	&#176	&deg*	Degree sign
±	&#177	&plusmn*	Plus/minus symbol
²	&#178	&sup2*	Superscript 2
³	&#179	&sup3*	Superscript 3
´	&#180	&acute*	Acute accent
µ	&#181	&micro*	Micro sign
¶	&#182	&para*	Paragraph sign
·	&#183	&middot*	Middle dot
¸	&#184	&cedil*	Cedilla
¹	&#185	&sup1*	Superscript 1
º	&#186	&ordm*	Masculine ordinal
»	&#187	&raquo*	Right angle quotation mark
¼	&#188	&frac14*	Fraction one-quarter
½	&#189	&frac12*	Fraction one-half
¾	&#190	&frac34*	Fraction three-quarters
¿	&#191	&iquest*	Inverted question mark
À	&#192	&Agrave	Capital A, grave accent
Á	&#193	&Aacute	Capital A, acute accent
Â	&#194	&Acirc	Capital A, circumflex accent
Ã	&#195	&Atilde	Capital A, tilde
Ä	&#196	&Auml	Capital A, umlaut
Å	&#197	&Aring	Capital A, ring
Æ	&#198	&Aelig	Capital AE ligature
Ç	&#199	&Ccedil	Capital C, cedilla
È	&#200	&Egrave	Capital E, grave accent

CHARACTER	CODE	CODE NAME	DESCRIPTION
É	&#201	&Eacute	Capital E, acute accent
Ê	&#202	&Ecirc	Capital E, circumflex accent
Ë	&#203	&Euml	Capital E, umlaut
Ì	&#204	&Igrave	Capital I, grave accent
Í	&#205	&Iacute	Capital I, acute accent
Î	&#206	&Icirc	Capital I, circumflex accent
Ï	&#207	&Iuml	Capital I, umlaut
Ð	&#208	&ETH*	Capital ETH, Icelandic
Ñ	&#209	&Ntilde	Capital N, tilde
Ò	&#210	&Ograve	Capital O, grave accent
Ó	&#211	&Oacute	Capital O, acute accent
Ô	&#212	&Ocirc	Capital O, circumflex accent
Õ	&#213	&Otilde	Capital O, tilde
Ö	&#214	&Ouml	Capital O, umlaut
×	&#215	&times*	Multiplication sign
Ø	&#216	&Oslash	Capital O slash
Ù	&#217	&Ugrave	Capital U, grave accent
Ú	&#218	&Uacute	Capital U, acute accent
Û	&#219	&Ucirc	Capital U, circumflex accent
Ü	&#220	&Uuml	Capital U, umlaut
Ý	&#221	&Yacute	Capital Y, acute accent
þ	&#222	&THORN	Capital THORN, Icelandic
ß	&#223	&szlig	Small sz ligature
à	&#224	&agrave	Small a, grave accent
á	&#225	&aacute	Small a, acute accent
â	&#226	&acirc	Small a, circumflex accent
ã	&#227	&atilde	Small a, tilde
ä	&#228	&auml	Small a, umlaut
å	&#229	&aring	Small a, ring
œ	&#230	&aelig	Small ae ligature
ç	&#231	&ccedil	Small c, cedilla
è	&#232	&egrave	Small e, grave accent
é	&#233	&eacute	Small e, acute accent
ê	&#234	&ecirc	Small e, circumflex accent
ë	&#235	&euml	Small e, umlaut
ì	&#236	&igrave	Small i, grave accent
í	&#237	&iacute	Small i, acute accent

CHARACTER	CODE	CODE NAME	DESCRIPTION
î	&#238	&icirc	Small i, circumflex accent
ï	&#239	&iuml	Small i, umlaut
ð	&#240	&eth	Small eth, Icelandic
ñ	&#241	&ntilde	Small n, tilde
ò	&#242	&ograve	Small o, grave accent
ó	&#243	&oacute	Small o, acute accent
ô	&#244	&ocirc	Small o, circumflex accent
õ	&#245	&otilde	Small o, tilde
ö	&#246	&ouml	Small o, umlaut
÷	&#247	&divide*	Division sign
ø	&#248	&oslash	Small o slash
ù	&#249	&ugrave	Small u, grave accent
ú	&#250	&uacute	Small u, acute accent
û	&#251	&ucirc	Small u, circumflex accent
ü	&#252	&uuml	Small u, umlaut
ý	&#253	&yacute	Small y, acute accent
þ	&#254	&thorn	Small thorn, Icelandic
ÿ	&#255	&yuml	Small y, umlaut

Putting a Document on the World Wide Web

Once you've completed your work on your HTML file, you're probably ready to place it on the World Wide Web for others to see. To make a file available to the World Wide Web, it must be located on a computer connected to the Web called a **Web server**.

Your **Internet Service Provider** (**ISP**)—the company or institution through which you have Internet access—usually has a Web server available for your use. Because each Internet Service Provider has a different procedure for storing Web pages, you should contact your ISP to learn its policies and procedures. Generally you should be prepared to do the following:

■ Extensively test your files with a variety of browsers and under different display conditions. Eliminate any errors and design problems before you place the page on the Web.

■ If your HTML documents have a three-letter "htm" extension, rename those files with the four-letter extension "html." Some Web servers will require the four-letter extension for all Web pages.

■ Check the hyperlinks and inline objects in each of your documents to verify that they point to the correct filenames. Verify the filenames with respect to upper and lower cases. Some Web servers distinguish between a file named "Image.gif" and one named "image.gif." To be safe, use only lowercase letters in all your filenames.

■ If your hyperlinks use absolute pathnames, change them to relative pathnames.

■ Find out from your ISP the name of the folder into which you'll be placing your HTML documents. You may also need a special user name and password to access this folder.

■ Use **FTP**, a protocol used on the Internet to transfer files, or e-mail to place your pages in the appropriate folder on your Internet Service Provider's Web server. Some Web browsers, like Internet Explorer and Netscape Navigator, have this capability built in, allowing you to easily transfer your files to the Web server.

■ Decide on a name for your site on the World Wide Web (such as "http://www.jackson_electronics.com"). Choose a name that will be easy for customers and interested parties to remember and return to.

■ If you select a special name for your Web site, you may have to register it. Registration information can be found at http://www.internic.net. Your ISP may also provide this service for a fee. Registration is necessary to ensure that any name you give to your site is unique and not already in use. Usually you will have to pay a yearly fee to use a special name for your Web site.

■ Add your site to the indexes of search pages on the World Wide Web. This is not required, but it will make it easier for people to find your site. Each search facility has different policies regarding adding information about Web sites to its index. Be aware that some will charge a fee for their services.

Once you've completed these steps, your work will be available on the World Wide Web in a form that is easy for users to access.

HTML TAGS AND ATTRIBUTES

The following list provides descriptions and browser compatibility information for the major HTML tags and attributes and is organized alphabetically. For example, a value of 4.0 in the Internet Explorer column indicates that the tag is supported by Internet Explorer 4.0 and above. Both opening and closing tags are provided when required, e.g., <table> and </table>; a single tag means that no closing tag is required. Deprecated tags are indicated as such.

You can view additional information about the latest HTML specifications at *http://www.w3.org*. Additional information about browser support for HTML tags is available at *http://www.htmlcompendium.org/*.

The following variables are used throughout this appendix:

- *Character*   A single text character
- *Color*   An HTML color name or hexadecimal color value
- *CGI Script*   The name of a CGI script on the Web server
- *Document*   The file name or URL of a file
- *List*   A list of items separated by commas, usually enclosed in double quotation marks
- *Mime-Type*   A MIME data type, such as "text/css", "audio/wav", or "video/x-msvideo"
- *Options*   Limited to a specific set of values that are shown below the attribute
- *Text*   A text string
- *URL*   The URL for a Web page or file
- *Value*   A number (usually an integer)

HTML supports six common attributes that apply to nearly all HTML tags.

COMMON ATTRIBUTES	DESCRIPTION	HTML	IE	NETSCAPE
class="Text"	The class attribute specifies the class or group to which a tag belongs.	4.0	3.0	4.0
dir="Option" (ltr | rtl)	The dir attribute indicates the text direction as related to the lang attribute. The ltr attribute value displays text from left to right; the rtl displays text from right to left.	4.0	5.5	
id="Text"	The id attribute specifies a unique identifier to be associated with each tag. Unlike the class attribute, an id value can be associated with a single tag.	4.0	3.0	4.0
lang="Text"	The lang attribute identifies the language used for the Web page content.	4.0	4.0	
style="Style Declarations"	The style attribute defines an inline style for the tag.	4.0	3.0	4.0
title="Text"	The title attribute provides information about the tag and identifies the tag for scripts.	2.0	4.0	6.0

TAGS AND ATTRIBUTES	DESCRIPTION	HTML	IE	NETSCAPE
<!-- -->	Text within the <!> tag is invisible to visitors using a browser.	2.0	1.0	1.0
<!doctype>	Specifies the Document Type Definition for a document.	2.0	2.0	1.0
<a> ... </a>	Marks the beginning and end of a hypertext link.	2.0	1.0	1.0
accesskey="Character"	Specifies an accelerator key for the element, which can be accessed by pressing the Character key along with the Alt key.	4.0	4.0	
coords="Value 1, Value 2..."	The coordinates (relative to the top left corner of the image) of the hotspot when the <a> tag is applied to an inline image. The coordinates used depend on the shape of the hotspot. Rectangle: coords="x_left, y_upper, x_right, y_lower" Circle: coords="x_center, y_center, radius" Polygon: coords="x1, y1, x2, y2, x3, y3, ..."	4.0		
href="URL"	Indicates the target filename, or URL for a hypertext link.	3.2	1.0	2.0
name="Text"	Specifies a name for the enclosed text, allowing it to be a target of a hypertext link.	2.0	1.0	1.0

TAGS AND ATTRIBUTES	DESCRIPTION	HTML	IE	NETSCAPE
rel="*Text*"	Specifies the relationship between the current page and the link specified by the href attribute.	2.0	2.0	
rev="*Text*"	Specifies a reverse relationship between the current page and the link specified by the href attribute.	2.0	2.0	
shape="*Option*" (rect | circle | polygon)	The shape of the hotspot when the <a> tag is applied to an inline image.	3.2	1.0	2.0
tabindex="*Value*"	Specifies the order for tabs in a form.	4.0	4.0	
target="*Text*"	Specifies the default target window or frame for the hypertext link.	4.0	3.0	1.0
title="*Text*"	Provides a title for the document whose address is provided by the href attribute.	2.0	2.0	
type="*Mime-Type*"	The data type of the linked document.	4.0		
<abbr> ... </abbr>	Indicates text in an abbreviated form (for example, WWW, HTTP, URL).	4.0		6.2
<acronym> ... </acronym>	Indicates a text acronym (for example, wac, radar).	3.0	4.0	6.2
<address> ... </address>	Used for information such as addresses and authorship. The text is typically italicized and indented.	2.0	1.0	1.0
<applet> ... </applet>	Supported by all Java-enabled browsers, allows Java applet in an HTML document. It has been deprecated in favor of the <object> tag in HTML 4.0.	3.2	3.0	2.0
align="*Option*" (absmiddle | | absbottom | absmiddle | baseline | bottom | center | | left | middle | right | texttop | top)	Specifies the alignment of the applet with the surrounding text.	3.2	3.0	2.0
alt="*Text*"	Specifies alternate text to be shown in place of the Java applet.	3.2	3.0	3.0
archive="*URL*"	Specifies the URL of an archive containing classes and other resources to be preloaded for use with the Java applet.	4.0		3.0
codebase="*URL*"	Specifies the base URL for the applet. If not specified, the browser uses the same location as the current document.	3.2	3.0	2.0
code="*Text*"	Specifies the name of the class file that contains the Java applet.	3.2	3.0	2.0

TAGS AND ATTRIBUTES	DESCRIPTION	HTML	IE	NETSCAPE
datafld="*Text*"	Specifies the column from a data source that supplies bound data for use with the applet.		4.0	
datasrc="*Text*"	Specifies the ID of the data source that is to be used with the applet.		4.0	
height="*Value*"	Specifies the height of the applet, in pixels.	3.2	3.0	2.0
hspace="*Value*"	Specifies the horizontal space around the applet, in pixels.	3.2	3.0	2.0
mayscript	Allows access to an applet by programs embedded in the document.	4.0		
name="*Text*"	The name assigned to the Java applet.	3.2	3.0	2.0
object="*Text*"	Specifies a resource containing a serialized representation of an applet's state. It is interpreted relative to the applet's code base. The serialized data contains the applet's class name, but not the implementation. The class name is used to retrie ve the implementation from a class file or archive.	4.0		
vspace="*Value*"	Specifies the vertical space around the applet, in pixels.	3.2	3.0	2.0
width="*Value*"	The width of the applet, in pixels.	3.2	3.0	2.0
<area>	Defines the type and coordinates of a hotspot within an image map.	3.2	2.0	1.0
coords="*Value 1, Value2…*"	The hotspot coordinates, which depend on the shape of the hotspot.	3.2	2.0	1.0
	Rectangle: coords="x_left, y_upper, x_right, y_lower" Circle: coords="x_center, y_center, radius" Polygon: coords= "x_1, y_1, x_2, y_2, x_3, y_3, …"			
href="*URL*"	Indicates the target, filename or URL to which the hotspot points.	3.2	2.0	1.0
shape="*Option*" (rect | circle | polygon)	The shape of the hotspot	3.2	2.0	1.0
target="*Text*"	Specifies the default target window or frame for the hotspot.	4.0	3.0	2.0

TAGS AND ATTRIBUTES	DESCRIPTION	HTML	IE	NETSCAPE
`<b> ... </b>`	Displays the enclosed text in bold type.	2.0	2.0	1.0
`<base>`	Allows you to specify a URL for the HTML document. It is used by some browsers to interpret relative hyperlinks.	2.0	2.0	1.0
href="*URL*"	Specifies the URL from which all relative hyperlinks are based.	2.0	2.0	4.0
target="*Text*"	Specifies the default target window or frame for every hypertext link in the document.	4.0	3.0	2.0
`<basefont>`	Specifies the default appearance of text in the document (deprecated).	3.2	2.0	1.0
color="*Color*"	The color name or value of the text.	4.0	1.0	4.0
face="*List*"	The font of the text. Multiple fonts can be specified. The browser attempts to render the text using fonts in the order specified in the list.	4.0	1.0	3.0
size="*Value*"	The size of the font in points.	3.2	2.0	1.1
`<bdo> ... </bdo>`	Overrides the current direction of text. The *dir* attribute is required.	4.0	5.0	6.2
dir="*Option*" (ltr | rtl)	Specifies the text direction, ltr (left to right), or rtl (right to left).	4.0	5.0	6.1
`<bgsound>`	Plays a background sound clip when the page is first opened.		2.0	
balance="*Value*"	Defines how the volume will be divided between two speakers, where "*Value*" is an integer between -10,000 and 10,000.		4.0	
loop="*Value*"	Specifies the number of times the sound clip is played; loop can either be a digit or infinite.		3.0	
src="*URL*"	The sound file used for the sound clip		2.0	
volume="*Value*"	Defines the volume of the background sound, where "*Value*" is an integer between 0 and 10,000.		4.0	
`<big> ... </big>`	Increases the size of the enclosed text. The exact appearance of the text depends on the browser and the default font size (deprecated).	3.2	2.0	2.0
`<blink> ... </blink>`	Instructs the enclosed text to blink on and off.		4.1	1.0
`<blockquote> ... </blockquote>`	Sets off long quotes or citations usually, by indenting the enclosed text from both margins.	2.0	1.1	1.0

TAGS AND ATTRIBUTES	DESCRIPTION	HTML	IE	NETSCAPE
<body> ... </body>	Encloses all text, images, and other elements on the Web page to be visible to the user.	2.0	1.0	1.0
alink="*Color*"	Color of activated hypertext links which are links the user has pressed with the mouse button, but has not yet released	3.2	4.1	1.1
background="*URL*"	The image file used for the Web page background	2.0	2.0	1.1
bgcolor="*Color*"	The color of the Web page background	3.2	2.0	1.1
bgproperties="fixed"	Prevents the background image from scrolling with the Web page.		2.0	
bottommargin="*Value*"	Specifies the size of the bottom margin, in pixels.		4.0	
leftmargin="*Value*"	Specifies the size of the left margin, in pixels.		2.0	
link="*Color*"	Color of all unvisited links (deprecated).	3.2	1.0	1.1
rightmargin="*Value*"	Specifies the size of the right margin, in pixels.		2.0	
scroll="*Option*" (no l yes)	Turns the scroll bars on and off (the default value is "yes").		4.0	
text="*Color*"	Color of all text in the document (deprecated).	3.2	1.0	1.1
topmargin="*Value*"	Specifies the size of the top margin, in pixels.		2.0	
vlink="*Color*"	Color of previously visited links.	3.2	1.0	1.1
<button> ... </button>	Buttons created with the <button> tag behave like buttons created with the <input> tag, but they offer more rendering possibilities.	4.0	4.1	6.1
accesskey="*Character*"	Specifies an accelerator key for the element, which can be accessed by pressing the *Character* key along with the Alt key.	4.0	4.0	6.2
disabled	Disables the button.	4.0	4.0	6.0
name="*Text*"	Specifies the button name.	4.0	5.0	6.0
value="*Text*"	Specifies the initial value of the button.	4.0	5.0	6.0
tabindex="*Value*"	Specifies the tab order in the form.	4.0	4.2	6.1
type="*Option*" (submit l reset l button)	Specifies the type of button. Setting the type to button creates a pushbutton for use with client-side scripts.	4.0	4.0	6.0

TAGS AND ATTRIBUTES	DESCRIPTION	HTML	IE	NETSCAPE
\<caption\> ... \</caption\>	Encloses the table caption.	3.0	2.0	1.1
align="*Option*" (left | right | center | top | bottom)	Specifies the alignment of the caption with respect to the table (the left, right, and center options are supported only by Internet Explorer 3.0 and above deprecated).	3.0	2.0	1.1
valign="*Option*" (top | bottom)	Specifies the vertical alignment of the caption with respect to the table.		2.0	
\<center\> ... \</center\>	Centers the enclosed text or image (deprecated).	3.2	1.0	1.0
\<cite\> ... \</cite\>	Used for citations and is usually displayed in italics.	2.0	1.0	1.0
\<code\> ... \</code\>	Used to display a sample of code. The text usually appears in a monospace font.	2.0	1.0	1.0
\<col\> ... \</col\>	Specifies the settings for a column or group of columns.	4.0	3.0	6.1
align="*Option*" (char | center | justify | left | right)	Specifies the horizontal alignment of text within a column.	4.0	4.0	
bgcolor="*Value*"	Applies a background color to all cells in the column (deprecated).		4.0	
span="*Value*"	Specifies the columns modified by the \<col\> tag.	4.0	3.0	6.1
valign="*Option*" (top | middle | bottom)	Specifies the vertical alignment of text within a column.	4.0	4.0	
width= "*Value*"	Specifies the width for each column or column group.	4.0	3.0	6.1
\<colgroup\> ... \</colgroup\>	Encloses a group of \<col\> tags, and groups columns together to set their alignment attributes.	4.0	3.1	6.1
align="*Option*" (char | center | justify | left | right)	Specifies the horizontal alignment of text within a column group.	4.0	4.1	
char="*Character*"	Specifies a character with which to align the values in the column (a period usually is used to align monetary values).	4.0		
charoff="*Value*"	Specifies the number of characters to offset the column data from the alignment character specified in the char attribute.	4.0		
span="*Value*"	Specifies the columns within the column group.	4.0	3.1	

TAGS AND ATTRIBUTES	DESCRIPTION	HTML	IE	NETSCAPE
valign="*Option*" (top | middle | bottom)	Specifies the vertical alignment of text within a column group.	4.0	4.1	
width= "*Value*"	Specifies the width of each column for the column group (deprecated).	4.0	4.1	
<dd>	Formats text to be used as definitions in a <dl> list.	2.0	1.0	1.0
<del> ... </del>	Used to indicate that text has been deleted from the document. Deleted text usually appears as strikethrough text.	3.0	4.0	6.1
cite="*URL*"	Specifies the URL for a document that has additional information about the deleted text.	4.0		
datetime="*Date*"	Specifies the date and time of the deletion.	4.0		
tabindex="*Value*"	Uses a number to identify an object's position in the tab order for keyboard navigation.		5.5	
<dfn> ... </dfn>	Used for the defining instance of a term, which is the first time the term is used. The enclosed text is usually italicized.	3.0	1.0	6.1
<div> ... </div>	Indicates a block of content for a document.	3.0	3.1	2.0
align="*Option*" (left | center | justify | right)	Horizontal alignment text options within the <div> tag.	3.0	3.0	3.0
<dl> ... </dl>	Encloses a definition list in which the <dd> definition term is left-aligned, and the <dt> relative definition is indented.	2.0	1.0	1.0
compact	Reduces the space between list items.	2.0	4.0	1.0
<dt>	Used to format the definition term in a <dl> list.	2.0	1.0	1.0
<em> ... </em>	Used to emphasize text. Typically, the enclosed text is displayed in italics.	2.0	1.0	1.0
<embed> ... </embed>	Specifies an object to be embedded in the document.		3.0	1.0
Accesskey = "*Character*"	Specifies a keyboard navigation accelerator for the element.		5.5	
autostart="*Option*" (true | false)	Specifies whether the embedded object should be started automatically when the page is loaded.		3.0	1.0
align="*Option*" (bottom | left | right | top)	Specifies the alignment of the embedded object with the surrounding text.		1.0	4.0
alt="*Text*"	Text to display if the browser cannot display the embedded object.		1.0	

TAGS AND ATTRIBUTES	DESCRIPTION	HTML	IE	NETSCAPE
border="*Value*"	The size of the border around the embedded object, in pixels.		1.0	
height="*Value*"	The height of the embedded object, in pixels.		1.0	4.0
hidden="*Option*" (true | false)	Specifies whether the embedded object is hidden or not.		4.0	
hspace="*Value*"	The amount of space to the left and right of the image, in pixels (deprecated).		4.0	
type="*Mime-Type*"	Specifies the data type of the embedded object.		4.0	
units="*Option*" (en | pixels)	Specifies the unit of measurement to be used with the embedded object.		4.0	
vspace="*Value*"	The amount of space above and below the embedded object, in pixels (deprecated).		4.0	
width="*Value*"	The width of the embedded object, in pixels.		1.0	4.0
<fieldset> ... </fieldset>	Allows designers to group form controls and labels, making it easier for users to understand the purpose of the control, and facilitating movement between fields.	4.0	4.2	6.2
accesskey="*Character*"	Specifies a keyboard navigation accelerator for the element.	4.0	5.5	
align="*Option*" (top | bottom | middle | left | right)	Specifies the alignment of the legend with respect to the field set (tag deprecated).	3.2	4.0	
<font> ... </font>	Controls the appearance of the text it encloses. Deprecated in favor of <styles>.	3.0	2.0	1.1
color="*Color*"	The color of the enclosed text.	3.0	2.0	2.0
face="*List*"	The font face of the text. Multiple font faces can be specified, separated by commas. The browser attempts to render the text in the order specified by the list.	3.0	2.0	3.0
point-size="*Value*"	Point size of the text (used with downloadable fonts).			4.0
size="*Value*"	Size of the font in points; it can be absolute or relative. Specifying a size=5 sets the font to 5 points. Specifying a size=+5 sets the font size 5 points larger than the size specified in the <basefont> tag.	3.0	2.0	4.0
weight="*Value*"	The weight of the font, ranging from 100 (the lightest) to 900 (the heaviest).			4.0

TAGS AND ATTRIBUTES	DESCRIPTION	HTML	IE	NETSCAPE
<form> … </form>	Marks the beginning and end of a Web page form.	2.0	1.0	1.0
action="*URL*"	Specifies the URL to which the contents of the form are to be sent.	2.0	1.0	1.0
autocomplete="*Option*" (yes | no)	Automatically finish filling in information the user has previously entered into an input field.		5.0	
enctype="*Text*"	Specifies the encoding type used to submit the data to the server.	2.0	1.0	1.0
hidefocus="*Option*" (true | false)	Hides focus on an element's content.		5.5	
method="*Option*" (post | get)	Specifies the method of accessing the URL indicated *in the action attribute.*	2.0	1.0	1.0
target="*Text*"	The frame or window that displays the results of the form.	4.0	3.0	2.0
<frame>	Defines a single frame within a set of frames.	4.0	3.0	2.0
bordercolor="*Color*"	Specifies the color of the frame border		4.0	3.5
frameborder="*Option*" (yes | no)	Specifies whether the frame border is visible.	4.0	3.0	3.5
hidefocus="*Option*" (true | false)	Hides focus on an element's content.		5.5	
longdesc="*URL*"	Specifies the URL of a document that contains a long description of the frame's content (used in conjunction with the title attribute).	4.0		
marginheight="*Value*"	Specifies the amount of space above and below the frame object and the frame borders.	4.0	3.0	2.0
marginwidth="*Value*"	Specifies the amount of space to the left and right of the frame object, in pixels.	4.0	3.0	2.0
name="*Text*"	Label assigned to the frame.	4.0	3.0	2.0
noresize	Prevents users from resizing the frame.	4.0	3.0	2.0
scrolling="*Option*" (yes | no | auto)	Specifies whether scroll bars are visible. ("auto" is the default and displays scroll bars as needed)	4.0	3.0	2.0
src="*URL*"	Specifies the document or URL of the object to be displayed in the frame.	4.0	3.0	2.0

TAGS AND ATTRIBUTES	DESCRIPTION	HTML	IE	NETSCAPE
<frameset> ... </frameset>	Marks the beginning and end of a set of frames.	4.0	3.0	2.0
border="*Value*"	The size of the frame borders, in pixels.		3.0	6.0
bordercolor="*Color*"	The color of the frame borders.		4.0	3.5
cols="*List*"	The size of each column in a set of frames. Columns can be specified as pixels, as a percentage of the display area, or with an asterisk (*) indicating that any remaining space be allotted to that column.	4.0	3.0	2.0
frameborder="*Option*" (yes | no)	Specifies whether the frame borders are visible.		3.0	3.5
framespacing="*Value*"	Specifies the amount of space between frames, in pixels.		3.1	
hidefocus="*Option*" (true | false)	Hides focus on the content of an element.		5.5	
rows="*List*"	The size of each row in a set of frames. Rows can be specified as pixels, as a percentage of the display area, or with an asterisk (*) indicating that any remaining space be allotted to that column.		3.0	2.0
<h1> ... </h1> <h2> ... </h2> <h3> ... </h3> <h4> ... </h4> <h5> ... </h5> <h6> ... </h6>	Used to display the six levels of text headings ranging from the largest (<h1>), to the smallest (<h6>).	2.0	1.0	1.0
align="*Option*" (left | right | center | justify)	The alignment of the heading (deprecated).	3.0	1.0	1.0
<head> ... </head>	Encloses code that provides information about the document.	2.0	1.0	1.0
<hr>	Creates a horizontal line.	2.0	1.0	1.0
align="*Option*" (left | center | right)	Alignment of the horizontal line (deprecated) (the default is "center")	3.2	1.0	1.1
color="*Color*"	Specifies a color for the line (deprecated).		3.0	
noshade	Removes 3D shading from the line (deprecated).	3.0	1.0	1.1
size="*Value*"	Specifies the thickness of the line, in pixels (deprecated).	3.2	1.0	1.1
width="*Value*"	Specified the width of the line in pixels or as a percentage of the display area (deprecated).	3.2	1.0	1.1

TAGS AND ATTRIBUTES	DESCRIPTION	HTML	IE	NETSCAPE
<html> ... </html>	Indicates the beginning and end of the HTML document.	2.0	1.0	1.0
xmlns = "*Text*"	Declares a namespace for XML-based custom tags in the document.		5.0	
<i> ... </i>	Italicizes the enclosed text.	2.0	1.0	1.0
<iframe> ... </iframe>	Allows a frame to be inserted within a block of text. Inserting an inline frame within a section of text allows you to insert one HTML document in the middle of another.	4.0	3.0	6.0
align="*Option*" (absbottom | absmiddle | baseline justify | left | middle | right | texttop)	Specifies the alignment for a floating frame (deprecated).	4.0	3.0	6.0
frameborder="*Option*" (yes | no)	Specifies whether the frame borders are visible.	4.0	3.0	6.0
height="*Value*"	Specifies the height of the floating frame, in pixels.	4.0	3.0	6.0
hspace="*Value*"	Specifies the horizontal space around the inline frame, in pixels.		3.0	
marginheight="*Value*"	Specifies the amount of space above and below the frame object and the frame borders.	4.0	3.0	6.0
marginwidth="*Value*"	Specifies the amount of space to the left and right of the frame object, in pixels.	4.0	3.0	6.0
name="*Text*"	Label assigned to the frame.	4.0	3.0	6.0
noresize	Prevents users from resizing the frame.		4.0	
scrolling="*Option*" (yes | no | auto)	Specifies whether scroll bars are visible (Auto is the default and displays scroll bars as needed).	4.0	3.0	6.0
src="*URL*"	Specifies the document or URL of the object to be displayed in the frame.	4.0	3.0	6.0
vspace="*Value*"	Specifies the vertical space around the inline frame, in pixels.		3.2	
width="*Value*"	Specifies the width of the floating frame, in pixels.	4.0	3.0	6.0
<ilayer> ... </ilayer>	Used to create an inflow layer with a relative position; it displays where it naturally would in the document.			4.0

TAGS AND ATTRIBUTES	DESCRIPTION	HTML	IE	NETSCAPE
above="*Text*"	Specifies the name of the layer to be displayed above the current layer.			4.0
background="*URL*"	Specifies the URL of the background image.			4.0
below="*Text*"	Specifies the name of the layer to be displayed below the current layer.			4.0
bgcolor="*Color*"	Specifies the background color of the layer.			4.0
clip="*top_x, left_y, bottom_x, right_y*"	Specifies the coordinates of the viewable region of the layer.			4.0
height="*Value*"	The height of the layer in pixels.			4.0
left="*Value*"	Specifies the horizontal offset of the layer, in pixels.			4.0
pagex="*Value*"	Specifies the horizontal position of the layer.			4.0
pagey="*Value*"	Specifies the vertical position of the layer.			4.0
src="*URL*"	Specifies the URL of the document displayed in the layer.			4.0
top="*Value*"	Specifies the vertical offset of the layer, in pixels.			4.0
visibility="*Option*" (hide I inherit I show)	Specifies whether the layer is hidden, shown, or inherits its visibility from the layer that contains it.			4.0
width="*Value*"	The width of the layer, in pixels			4.0
z-index="*Value*"	Specifies the stacking order of the layer relative to the other layers.			4.0
<img>	Used to insert an inline image into the document.	2.0	1.0	1.0
align="*Option*" (left I right I top I texttop I middle I absmiddle I baseline I bottom I absbottom)	Specifies the alignment of the image. Specifying an alignment of left or right aligns the image with the left or right page margin. The other alignment options align the image with surrounding text (deprecated).	2.0	1.0	1.1
alt="*Text*"	Text to display if the browser cannot display the image.	2.0	1.0	1.1
border="*Value*"	The size of the border around the image, in pixels (deprecated).	3.2	1.0	1.1
controls	Displays VCR-like controls under moving images (used in conjunction with the dynsrc attribute).		2.0	

TAGS AND ATTRIBUTES	DESCRIPTION	HTML	IE	NETSCAPE
dynsrc="*URL*"	Specifies the file of a video, AVI clip, or VRML worlds shown inside the page.		2.0	
height="*Value*"	The height of the image, in pixels.	3.0	1.0	1.1
hidefocus="*Option*" (true | false)	Hides focus on the content of an element.		5.5	
hspace="*Value*"	The amount of space to the left and right of the image, in pixels (deprecated).	3.0	1.0	1.1
ismap	Identifies the image as an image map (for use with server-side image maps).	3.0	2.0	2.0
longdesc="*URL*"	The URL of a document that contains a long description of the image (used in conjunction with the alt attribute).	4.0		
loop="*Value*"	Specifies the number of times a moving image should be played (*Value* must be either a digit or "infinite").		2.0	
lowsrc="*URL*"	A low-resolution version of an image that the browser initially displays before loading the high-resolution version.		4.1	1.0
name="*Name*"	Binds the *Name* to the image.	4.0	4.0	3.0
src="*URL*"	The source file of the inline image.	2.0	1.0	1.0
start="*Option* " (fileopen | mouseover)	Tells the browser when to start displaying a moving image file. Fileopen instructs the browser to start when the file is open; mouseover instructs the browser to start when the mouse pointer moves over the image.		2.0	
suppress="*Option*" (true | false)	Suppresses the placeholder icon and any ALT text until the image is located (if suppress="true").			4.0
tabindex="*Value*"	Uses a number to identify the object's position in the tab order for keyboard navigation.		5.5	
usemap="*#Map_Name*"	Identifies the image as an image map and specifies the name of the image map definition to use with the image (for use with client-side image maps).	3.2	1.0	2.0
vspace="*Value*"	The amount of space above and below the image, in pixels (deprecated).	3.2	1.0	1.1
width="*Value*"	The width of the image, in pixels.	3.0	1.0	1.1

TAGS AND ATTRIBUTES	DESCRIPTION	HTML	IE	NETSCAPE
<input> ... </input>	Creates an input object for use in a Web page form.	1.0	2.0	1.0
accesskey="*Character*"	Specifies an accelerator key for the element, which can be accessed by pressing the *Character* key along with the Alt key.	4.0	4.0	
align="*Option*" (left | right | top | texttop | middle | absmiddle | baseline | bottom | absbottom)	Specifies the alignment of an input image (similar to the align attribute with the <img> tag).	2.0	2.0	1.1
alt="*Text*"	Alternate text description of image buttons for browsers that do not support inline images.	4.0	4.0	
checked	Specifies that an input check box or input radio button is selected.	2.0	1.0	1.0
disabled	Disables the control.	4.0	4.0	
maxlength="*Value*"	Specifies the maximum number of characters that can be inserted into an input text box.	2.0	1.0	1.0
name="*Text*"	The label given to the input object.	2.0	1.0	1.0
readonly	Prevents the value of the control from being modified.	4.0	4.0	6.1
size="*Value*"	The visible size, in characters, of an input text box.	2.0	1.0	1.0
src="*URL*"	The source file of the graphic used for an input image object.	2.0	1.0	1.0
tabindex="*Value*"	Specifies the tab order in the form.	4.0	4.0	6.3
type="*Option*" (checkbox | hidden | image | password | radio | reset | buttonsubmit | text | file)	Specifies the type of input object.	2.0	1.0	1.0
usemap="*#Map_Name*"	Identifies the input image as an image map (similar to the usemap attribute used with the <img> tag).	4.0		2.0
value="*Value*"	Specifies the information that initially appears in the input object.	2.0	2.0	2.0
width="*Value*"	The width of the input image, in pixels		4.1	1.1
<ins> ... </ins>	Indicates that the text has been inserted into the document.	3.0	4.0	6.2
cite="*URL*"	Specifies the URL for a document that has additional information about the inserted text.		4.0	

TAGS AND ATTRIBUTES	DESCRIPTION	HTML	IE	NETSCAPE
datetime="*Date*"	Specifies the date and time of the insertion.		4.0	
<isindex>	Identifies the file as a searchable document. Deprecated in favor of <input>.	2.0	1.0	1.0
action="*CGI Script*"	Sends the submitted text to the program identified by *CGI Script*.		1.0	1.0
prompt="*Text*"	The text to be placed before the text-input field.	3.0	1.0	1.1
<label> ... </label>	Used to create labels for form controls.	4.0	4.0	6.2
accesskey="*Character*"	Specifies an accelerator key for the element, which can be accessed by pressing the *Character* key along with the Alt key.	4.0	4.0	6.2
datafld="*Text*"	Specifies the column from a data source that supplies bound data for use with the label.		4.0	6.2
dataformatas="*Option*" (text | html)	Specifies whether the data in the data source column is formatted as plain text or as HTML code.		4.0	6.2
datasrc="*Text*"	Specifies the ID of the data source that is to be used with the label.		4.0	
for="*Text*"	Indicates the name or ID of the element to which the label is applied.	4.0	4.0	6.2
<layer> ... </layer>	Used to create an inflow layer with an absolutely defined position in the document.			4.0
above="*Text*"	Specifies the name of the layer to be displayed above the current layer.			4.0
background="*URL*"	Specifies the URL of the background image			4.0
below="*Text*"	Specifies the name of the layer to be displayed below the current layer.			4.0
bgcolor="*Color*"	Specifies the background color of the layer.			4.0
clip="*top_x, left_y, bottom_x, right_y*"	Specifies the coordinates of the viewable region of the layer.			4.0
height="*Value*"	Specifies the height of the layer, in pixels.			4.0
left="*Value*"	Specifies the horizontal offset of the layer, in pixels.			4.0
pagex="*Value*"	Specifies the horizontal position of the layer.			4.0
pagey="*Value*"	Specifies the vertical position of the layer.			4.0
src="*URL*"	Specifies the URL of the document displayed in the layer.			4.0

TAGS AND ATTRIBUTES	DESCRIPTION	HTML	IE	NETSCAPE
top="*Value*"	Specifies the vertical offset of the layer, in pixels.			4.0
visibility="*Option*" (hide I inherit I show)	Specifies whether the layer is hidden, shown, or inherits its visibility from the layer that contains it.			4.0
width="*Value*"	Specifies the width of the layer, in pixels.			4.0
z-index="*Value*"	Specifies the stacking order of the layer relative to the other layers.		4.0	
<legend> ... </legend>	Allows a caption to be assigned to a fieldset (see the <fieldset> tag above).	4.0	4.0	6.2
accesskey="*Character*"	Specifies an accelerator key for the element, which can be accessed by pressing the *Character* key along with the Alt key.	4.0	4.0	6.2
align="*Option*" (top I bottom I left I right)	Specifies the position of the legend with respect to the field set.	4.0	4.0	6.2
<li>	Identifies list items in a <dir>.	2.0	1.0	1.0
<map> ... </map>	Specifies information about a client-side image map (note that it must enclose <area> tags).	3.2	1.0	1.0
name="*Text*"	The name of the image map.	3.2	1.0	2.0
<marquee> ... </marquee>	Used to create an area containing scrolling text.		2.0	
align="*Option*" (top I middle I bottom)	The alignment of the scrolling text within the marquee.		2.0	
behavior="*Option*" (scroll I slide I alternate)	Controls the behavior of the text in the marquee. scroll causes the text to repeatedly scroll across the page, slide causes the text to slide onto the page and stop at the margin, alternate causes the text to move from margin to margin.		2.0	
bgcolor="*Color*"	The background color of the marquee.		2.0	
datfld="*Text*"	The column name in the data source that is bound to the marquee.		4.0	
dataformatas="*Option*" (text I html)	Indicates the format of the bound data.		4.0	
direction="*Option*" (left I right I down I up)	The direction that the text scrolls on the page.		2.0	
height="*Value*"	The height of the marquee, either in pixels or as a percentage of the display area.		2.0	

TAGS AND ATTRIBUTES	DESCRIPTION	HTML	IE	NETSCAPE
hidefocus="Option" (true | false)	Hides focus on the content of an element.		5.5	
hspace="Value"	The amount of space to the left and right of the marquee, in pixels.		2.0	
loop="Value"	The number of times the marquee is scrolled (the "Value" must be either a digit or infinite.		2.0	
scrollamount="Value"	The amount of space between successive draws of the text in the marquee.		2.0	
scrolldelay="Value"	The amount of time between scrolling actions, in milliseconds.		2.0	
tabindex="Value"	Uses a number to identify the object's position In the tabbing order for keyboard navigation.	4.0	5.5	
truespeed="Value"	Indicates that the scrolldelay attribute value should be honored for its exact value, otherwise any value less than 60 milliseconds is rounded up.		4.0	
vspace="Value"	The amount of space above and below the marquee, in pixels.		2.0	
width="Value"	The width of the marquee, in pixels or as a percentage of the display area.		2.0	
<menu> ... </menu>	Encloses an unordered list of items, similar to a <ul> or <dir> list. Deprecated in favor of <ul>.	2.0	1.0	1.0
compact	Reduces the space between menu items.	2.0		
<meta>	Identifies information about the document not defined by other HTML tags and attributes; it can include special instructions for the Web server.	2.0	1.0	1.0
content="Text"	Contains information associated with the Name or http-equiv attributes.	2.0	2.0	1.1
http-equiv="Text"	Instructs the browser to request the server to perform different http operations.	2.0	2.0	1.1
name="Text"	The type of information specified in the content attribute.	2.0	2.0	1.1
<nobr> ... </nobr>	Prevents line breaks for the enclosed text. This tag is not often used.		1.0	1.1
<noembed> ... </noembed>	Used to display alternate content for older browsers that do not support the <embed> tag.		3.0	2.0

TAGS AND ATTRIBUTES	DESCRIPTION	HTML	IE	NETSCAPE
<noframes> ... </noframes>	Enables browsers that do not support frames to display a page that uses frames (the tag encloses the <body> tag).	4.0	3.0	2.0
<noscript> ... </noscript>	Used to enclose HTML tags for browsers that do not support client-side scripts.	4.0	3.0	3.5
<object> ... </object>	Allows designers to control whether data is rendered externally or by a program, specified by the author, that renders the data within the user agent. (Most browsers have built-in mechanisms for rendering common data types such as text, GIF images, colors, fonts, and a handful of graphic elements.	4.0	3.1	6.1
accesskey="*Character*"	Specifies an accelerator key for the object, which can be accessed by pressing the *Character* key along with the Alt key.		4.0	
archive="*URL*"	Specifies the URL of an archive containing classes and other resources that are preloaded for use with the object.	4.0		6.0
align="*Option*" (top | bottom | middle | left | right)	Specifies the alignment of the embedded object, relative to the surrounding text (deprecated).	4.0	3.0	6.1
border="*Value*"	Specifies the width of the embedded object's border, in pixels.	4.0		6.0
classid="*URL*"	Specifies the URL of the embedded object.	4.0	3.0	6.0
codebase="*URL*"	Specifies the base path used to resolve relative references within the embedded object.	4.0	3.0	6.0
codetype="*Text*"	Specifies the type of data object.	4.0	3.0	6.0
data="*URL*"	Specifies the location of data for the embedded object.	4.0	3.0	6.0
datafld="*Text*"	Specifies the column from a data source that supplies bound data for use with the object.		4.0	
datasrc="*Text*"	Specifies the ID of the data source to be used with the object.		4.0	
declare	Declares the object without installing it in the page.	4.0		
height="*Value*"	Specifies the height of the embedded object, in pixels.	4.0	3.0	6.0
hidefocus ="*Option*" (true | false)	Hides focus on the content of the element.		5.5	

TAGS AND ATTRIBUTES	DESCRIPTION	HTML	IE	NETSCAPE
hspace="*Value*"	Specifies the horizontal space around the embedded object, in pixels (deprecated).	4.0	3.0	6.0
name="*Text*"	Specifies the name of the embedded object.	4.0	3.0	6.0
standby="*Text*"	Specifies a message for the browser to display while rendering the embedded object.	4.0		
tabindex="*Value*"	Specifies the tab order of the object when it is placed in a form.	4.0	4.0	
type="*Mime-Type*"	Specifies the data type of the object.	4.0	3.0	6.0
usemap="*URL*"	The URL of the image map to be used with the object.	4.0		6.1
vspace="*Value*"	Specifies the vertical space around the embedded object, in pixels.	4.0	3.0	6.1
width="*Value*"	Specifies the width of the embedded object, in pixels.	4.0	3.0	6.1
<ol> ... </ol>	Encloses an ordered list of <li> items. Typically, ordered lists are rendered as numbered lists.	2.0	1.0	1.0
compact	Reduces the space between ordered list items.	2.0		
start="*Value*"	The value of the starting number in the ordered list (deprecated).	3.2	2.0	2.0
type="*Option*" (A | a | I | i | 1)	Specifies how ordered items are marked. A=uppercase letters, a=lowercase letters, I=uppercase Roman numerals, i=lowercase Roman numerals, and 1 (default)=digits (deprecated).	3.2	1.0	1.0
<optgroup> ... </optgroup>	Used to create a grouping of items in a selection list, as defined by the <option> tag.	4.0	6.0	6.0
disabled	Disables the group of option items.	4.0		6.0
label="*Text*"	Specifies a label for the option group.	4.0		6.0
<option> ... </option>	Used for each item in a selection list. This tag must be placed within <select> tags.	2.0	1.0	1.0
disabled	Disables the option item.	3.0	4.0	6.0
selected	The default or selected option in the selection list.	2.0	1.0	1.0
value="*Value*"	The value returned to the server when the user selects this option.	2.0	1.0	1.0

TAGS AND ATTRIBUTES	DESCRIPTION	HTML	IE	NETSCAPE
\<p> ... \</p>	Defines the beginning and end of a paragraph of text.	2.0	1.0	1.0
align="*Option*" (left | center | right)	The alignment of the paragraph text (deprecated).	3.0	1.0	1.1
\<param> ... \</param>	Specifies a set of values that may be required by an object at run-time. Any number of param elements may display in the content of an \<object> or \<applet> tag, in any order, but they must be located at the start of the content in the enclosing \<object> or \<applet> tag.	3.2	3.0	2.0
datafld="*Text*"	Specifies the column name in the data source that is bound to the parameter's value.		4.0	
dataformatas="*Option*" (text | html)	Specifies whether the data in the data source column is formatted as plain text or as HTML code.		4.0	
datasrc="*URL*"	Specifies the URL of the data source from which to draw the data.		4.0	
name="*Text*"	Specifies the name of the parameter.	3.2	3.0	2.0
value="*Text*"	Specifies the value of the parameter.	3.2	3.0	2.0
valuetype="*Option*" (data | ref | object)	Specifies the type of the value attribute.	4.0	6.0	
\<plaintext> ... \</plaintext>	Displays text in a fixed-width (monospace) font. It is supported, although inconsistently, by some early versions of Netscape.	2.0	1.0	1.0
\<pre> ... \</pre>	Retains the preformatted appearance of the text in the HTML file, including any line breaks or spaces, and is usually displayed in a fixed-width (monspace) font.	2.0	2.0	1.0
\<q> ... \</q>	Identifies the enclosed text as a short quotation.	3.0	4.0	6.2
cite="*URL*"	Specifies the URL for a document containing additional information about the quoted text.	4.0		6.2
\<rt>	Used with the \<ruby> element to create "ruby text," or annotations or pronunciation guides for words and phrases.		5.0	
\<ruby>...\</ruby>	Used with the \<rt> element to create annotations or pronunciation guides for words and phrases.	4.0	5.0	

TAGS AND ATTRIBUTES	DESCRIPTION	HTML	IE	NETSCAPE
<s> ... </s>	Displays the enclosed text with a horizontal line striking through it. Deprecated in favor of <del>.	4.0	2.0	3.0
<samp> ... </samp>	Displays text in a fixed-width font.	2.0	1.0	1.0
<script> ... </script>	Places a client-side script within a document. This element may be displayed any number of times in the head or body of an HTML document.	3.2	3.0	3.0
defer	Instructs the browser to defer executing the script.	4.0	4.0	
event="*Text*"	Specifies an event in response to which, a script should be run (this attribute must be used in conjunction with the for attribute).	4.0	4.0	
for="*Text*"	Indicates the name or ID of the element to which an event, defined by the event attribute, is applied.	4.0	4.0	
language="*Text*"	Specifies the language of the client-side script (see JavaScript for JavaScript commands).	4.0	3.0	3.0
src="*URL*"	Specifies the source of the external script file.	4.0	3.0	3.0
type="*Mime-Type*"	Specifies the data type of the scripting language (use text/javascript for JavaScript commands).	4.0	4.0	
<select> ... </select>	Encloses a set of <option> tags for use in creating selection lists.	2.0	2.0	2.0
accesskey="*Character*"	Specifies an accelerator key for the element, which can be accessed by pressing the *Character* key along with the Alt key.	4.0	4.0	
align="*Option*" (left | right | top | texttop | middle | absmiddle | baseline | bottom | absbottom)	Specifies the alignment of an input image (similar to the align option with the <img> tag)	2.0	2.0	1.1
disabled	Disables the selection list.	4.0	4.0	
hidefocus="*Option*" (true | false)	Hides focus on the content of an element.		5.5	
multiple	Allows the user to select multiple options from a selection list.	2.0	2.0	2.0
name="*Text*"	The name assigned to the selection list.	2.0	2.0	2.0
size="*Value*"	The number of visible items in the selection list.	2.0	2.0	2.0
tabindex="*Value*"	Specifies the tab order in the form.	4.0	4.0	

TAGS AND ATTRIBUTES	DESCRIPTION	HTML	IE	NETSCAPE
<small> ... </small>	Decreases the size of the enclosed text. The exact appearance of the text depends on the browser and the default font size (deprecated).	3.0	3.0	2.0
<span> ... </span>	Acts as a container for inline content.	4.0	3.0	4.0
datafld="*Text*"	Specifies the column of a data source that supplies bound data for use with the spanned text.		4.0	
dataformatas="*Option*" (text | html)	Specifies whether the data in the data source column is formatted as plain text or HTML code.		4.0	
datasrc="*Text*"	Specifies the ID of the data source that is to be used with the spanned text.		4.0	
<strike> ... </strike>	Displays the enclosed text with a horizontal line striking through it. Deprecated in favor of <del>.	3.2	2.0	3.0
<strong> ... </strong>	Used to place emphasis on the enclosed text, usually with a bold font.	2.0	1.0	1.0
<style> ... </style>	Encloses style declarations for the document.	4.0	3.0	4.0
disabled	Disables the style declarations.		4.0	
media="*Option*" (all | aural | Braille | print | projection | screen)	Specifies the destination medium for the style information.	4.0	4.0	
type="*Text*"	Defines the type of stylesheet.	3.2	3.0	4.0
_{...}	Displays the enclosed text as a subscript.	2.0	3.0	2.0
^{...}	Displays the enclosed text as a superscript.	2.0	3.0	2.0
<table> ... </table>	The <table> tag is used to identify the beginning and end of a table.	2.0	1.0	1.1
align="*Option*" (char | left | center | right)	Specifies the horizontal alignment of the table on the page (deprecated).	3.0	3.0	2.0
background= "*URL*"	Specifies a background image for the table.	3.0	4.0	
bgcolor="*Color*"	Specifies a background color for the table (deprecated).	4.0	2.0	3.0
border="*Value*"	Specifies the width of the table border, in pixels.	3.0	2.0	2.0
bordercolor="*Color*"	Specifies the color of the table border.		4.0	
bordercolordark="*Color*"	Specifies the color of the shaded edge of the table border.		2.0	
bordercolorlight="*Color*"	Specifies the color of the unshaded edge of the table border.		2.0	

TAGS AND ATTRIBUTES	DESCRIPTION	HTML	IE	NETSCAPE
cellpadding="*Value*"	Specifies the space between table cells, in pixels.	3.2	2.0	1.1
cellspacing="*Value*"	Specifies the space between cell text and the cell border, in pixels.	3.2	2.0	1.1
cols="*Value*"	Specifies the number of columns in the table.	3.0	3.1	4.2
rows="*Value*"	Specifies the number of rows that can be displayed in the table when data binding is used.	4.0	4.0	
datasrc="*URL*"	Specifies the URL of the table's data source.	4.0	3.0	6.0
frame="*Option*" (above | below | box | hsides | lhs | rhs | void | vsides)	Specifies the display of table borders: above = top border only, below = bottom border only, box = borders on all four sides, hsides = top and bottom borders, lhs = left side border, rhs = right side border, void = no borders, vsides =left and right side borders.	4.0	3.1	6.0
height="*Value*"	The height of the table, in pixels or as a percentage of the display area.		2.0	1.1
hspace="*Value*"	Specifies the horizontal space, in pixels, between the table and surrounding text.			2.0
rules="*Option*" (all | cols | none | rows)	Specifies the display of internal table borders: all = borders between every row and column, cols = borders between every column, none = no internal table borders, rows = borders between every row.	4.0	3.0	
vspace="*Value*"	Specifies the vertical space, in pixels, between the table and surrounding text.			2.0
width="*Value*"	The width of the table, in pixels or as a percentage of the display area.	3.0	2.0	1.0
<tbody> ... </tbody>	Identifies text displayed in the table body, as opposed to text in the table header, <thead> tag, or in the table footer, <tbody> tag.	4.0	4.0	6.0
align="*Option*" (char | left | center | right)	The horizontal alignment of text in the cells of the table body.	4.0	4.0	6.1
bgcolor="*Color*"	Specifies a background color for the table body.		4.0	6.1
char="*Character*"	Specifies a character with which to align the values in the column.	4.0		
charoff="*Value*"	Specifies the number of characters to offset the column data from the alignment character specified in the char attribute.	4.0		

TAGS AND ATTRIBUTES	DESCRIPTION	HTML	IE	NETSCAPE
valign="*Option*" (top | middle | bottom)	The vertical alignment of text in the cells in the table body.	4.0	4.0	6.1
<td> ... </td>	Encloses the text to display in a table cell.	2.0	2.0	1.1
abbr="*Text*"	Specifies an abbreviated name for the header cell.	4.0		
align="*Option*" (left | center | right)	Specifies the horizontal alignment of cell text.	2.0	2.0	2.0
axis="*Text*"	Specifies a name for a group of related table headers.	4.0		
background="*URL*"	Specifies a background image for the cell.	4.0	4.0	
bgcolor="*Color*"	Specifies a background color for the cell.	4.0	2.0	3.0
bordercolor="*Color*"	Specifies the color of the cell border.		2.0	
bordercolordark="*Color*"	Specifies the color of the shaded edge of the cell border.		2.0	
bordercolorlight="*Color*"	Specifies the color of the unshaded edge of the cell border.		2.0	
colspan="*Value*"	Specifies the number of columns to span the cell.	3.2	2.0	2.0
height="*Value*"	The height of the cell, in pixels or as a percentage of the display area.	3.2	2.0	2.0
nowrap	Prohibits the browser from wrapping text in the cell (deprecated).	3.0	2.0	1.1
rowspan="*Value*"	Specifies the number of rows to span the cell.	3.2	2.0	1.1
scope="*Option*" (col | colgroup | row | rowgroup)	Specifies the table cells for which the current cell provides header information. A scope value of col indicates that the cell is a header for the rest of the column, colgroup indicates that the cell is a header for the current column group, row indicates that the cell is a header for the current row, and rowgroup indicates that the cell is a he ader for the current row group.	4.0		
valign="*Option*" (top | middle | bottom)	Specifies the vertical alignment of cell text.	3.0	2.0	1.1
width= "*Value*"	The width of the cell, in pixels or as a percentage of the width of the table (deprecated).	3.2	2.0	1.1
<textarea> ... </textarea>	Creates a text box.	2.0	2.0	1.0
accesskey="*Character*"	Specifies an accelerator key for the element, which can be accessed by pressing the *Character* key along with the Alt key.	4.0	4.0	6.2

TAGS AND ATTRIBUTES	DESCRIPTION	HTML	IE	NETSCAPE
cols="*Value*"	Specifies the height of the text box, in characters.	2.0	2.0	2.0
disabled	Disables the text area.	4.0	4.0	
name="*Text*"	Specifies the name assigned to the text box.	2.0	2.0	1.0
readonly	Prevents the text area's value from being modified.	4.0	4.0	6.1
rows="*Value*"	Specifies the width of the text box, in characters.	2.0	2.0	2.0
tabindex="*Value*"	Specifies the tab order in the form.	4.0	4.0	6.3
wrap="*Option*" (off | virtual | physical)	Specifies how text is wrapped within the text box: off turns off text wrapping, virtual wraps the text but sends the text to the server as a single line, physical wraps the text and sends the text to the server as it appears in the text box.		4.0	2.0
<tfoot> … </tfoot>	Encloses footer information that is displayed in the table footer when the table prints on multiple pages.	4.0	3.0	6.1
align="*Option*" (char | center | left | right)	The horizontal alignment of the table footer.	4.0	4.0	6.1
bgcolor="*Color*"	Specifies a background color for the table footer.		4.0	6.1
char="*Character*"	Specifies a character with which to align the values in the column.	4.0	4.1	6.1
charoff="*Value*"	Specifies the number of characters to offset the column data from the alignment character specified in the char attribute.	4.0		
valign="*Option*" (top | middle | bottom)	The vertical alignment of the table footer.	4.0	4.0	6.1
<th> … </th>	Encloses the text that displays in an individual table header cell.	3.0	2.0	1.1
abbr="*Text*"	Specifies an abbreviated name for the header cell.	4.0		
align="*Option*" (center | char | left | right)	Specifies the horizontal alignment of header cell text.	3.0	2.0	1.1
background="*URL*"	Specifies a background image for the header cell.		3.1	4.3
bgcolor="*Color*"	Specifies a background color for the header cell.	4.0	2.0	3.0

TAGS AND ATTRIBUTES	DESCRIPTION	HTML	IE	NETSCAPE
bordercolor="*Color*"	Specifies the color of the header cell border.		2.0	
bordercolordark="*Color*"	Specifies the color of the shaded edge of the header cell border.		3.0	
bordercolorlight="*Color*"	Specifies the color of the unshaded edge of the header cell border.		2.0	
char="*Character*"	Specifies a character with which to align the values in the column.	4.0		
charoff="*Value*"	Specifies the number of characters to offset the column data from the alignment character specified in the char attribute.	4.0		
colspan="*Value*"	Specifies the number of columns to span the header cell.	3.0	2.0	1.1
headers="*List*"	Specifies a list of ID values that correspond to the header cells related to this cell.	4.0		
height="*Value*"	The height of the header cell, in pixels or as a percentage of the display area.	3.2	2.0	1.1
nowrap	Prohibits the browser from wrapping text in the header cell.	3.0	2.0	1.1
rowspan="*Value*"	Specifies the number of rows to span the header cell.	3.0	2.0	1.1
scope="*Option*" (col | colgroup | row | rowgroup)	Specifies the table cells for which the current cell provides header information. A scope value of col indicates that the cell is a header for the rest of the column, colgroup indicates that the cell is a header for the current column group, row indicates that the cell is a header for the current row, and rowgroup indicates that the cell is a header for the current row group.	4.0		
valign="*Option*" (top | middle | bottom)	Specifies the vertical alignment of header cell text.	3.0	2.0	1.1
width= "*Value*"	The width of the header cell in pixels or as a percentage of the width of the table.	3.2	2.0	1.1
<thead> ... </thead>	Encloses header information that is displayed in the table header when the table is printed on multiple pages.	3.0	3.0	
align="*Option*" (left | center | right)	The horizontal alignment of the table header.	4.0	4.1	6.1
bgcolor="*Color*"	Specifies a background color for the table cells within the <thead> tags.		4.0	

TAGS AND ATTRIBUTES	DESCRIPTION	HTML	IE	NETSCAPE
char="*Character*"	Specifies a character with which to align the values in the table header columns.	4.0		
charoff="*Value*"	Specifies the number of characters to offset the column data from the alignment character as specified in the char attribute.	4.0		
valign="*Option*" (top | middle | bottom)	The vertical alignment of the table header.	4.0	4.1	6.1
<title> … </title>	Specifies the text that displays in the title bar.	2.0	1.0	1.1
<tr> … </tr>	Encloses table cells within a single row.	3.0	2.0	1.1
align="*Option*" (left | center | right)	Specifies the horizontal alignment of text in a row.	3.0	2.0	1.1
bgcolor="*Color*"	Specifies a background color for the header cell.	4.0	2.0	3.0
bordercolor="*Color*"	Specifies the color of the header cell border.		2.0	
bordercolordark="*Color*"	Specifies the color of the shaded edge of the header cell border.		2.0	
bordercolorlight="*Color*"	Specifies the color of the unshaded edge of the header cell border.		2.0	
char="*Character*"	Specifies a character with which to align the Values in the table row.	4.0		
charoff="*Value*"	Specifies the number of characters to offset the column data from the alignment character as specified in the char attribute.	4.0		
valign="*Option*"	The vertical alignment of the text in the table row	3.0	2.0	2.0
<tt> … </tt>	Displays text in a fixed-width, or monospace, font.	2.0	1.0	1.0
<u> … </u>	Underlines the enclosed text. The <u> tag should be avoided because it can be confused with hypertext links, which are often underlined. Deprecated in favor of <styles>.	3.0	1.0	3.5
<ul> … </ul>	Encloses an unordered list of <li> items. Typically, unordered lists are rendered as bulleted lists.	2.0	1.0	1.0
compact	Reduces the space between unordered list items.	2.0		
Type="*Option*" (circle | disk | square)	Specifies the type of bullet used for displaying each <li> item in the <ul> list.	3.2	4.0	1.0
<var> … </var>	Used for text that represents a variable and is typically displayed in italics.	2.0	1.0	1.0

TAGS AND ATTRIBUTES	DESCRIPTION	HTML	IE	NETSCAPE
<wbr> … </wbr>	Used in conjunction with the <nobr> tag, this tag overrides tags that may preclude the use of line breaks and instructsthe browser to insert a line break if necessary. This tag is not often used.		1.0	1.0
<xmp> … </xmp>	Displays blocks of text in a fixed-width, or monospace, font. This tag is obsolete and should not be used. Deprecated in favor of the <pre> tag.	2.0	1.0	1.0

WORKING WITH XHTML

Introducing XHTML

XHTML (Extensible Hypertext Markup Language) represents the next phase in the development of markup languages for the World Wide Web. In order to understand what XHTML is and why it was created, we first have to look back at the development of the Web itself.

SGML

XHTML has its roots in the Standard Generalized Markup Language (SGML). Introduced in the 1980s, SGML was a vehicle used to create the general structure of markup languages. SGML is device-independent and system-independent, which means that it can be used with almost any type of document stored in almost any format. SGML has been widely used to create documents in businesses and government organizations of all sizes. For example, think of the daunting task of documenting all of the parts used in manufacturing the space shuttle while at the same time, creating a structure that shuttle engineers can use to quickly retrieve and edit that information. SGML provides tools to manage documentation projects of this magnitude.

But there is a price to pay to support such complex document; thus, SGML is limited to those organizations that can afford the cost and overhead of maintaining large SGML environments. SGML is most useful for creating applications, based on the SGML architecture, that apply to specific types of documents. The most famous of these applications is Hypertext Markup Language, or HTML, the language of the World Wide Web.

HTML

The success of the World Wide Web is due in no small part to HTML. HTML allows Web authors to easily create documents that can be displayed across different operating systems. Creating Web sites with HTML is a straight forward process that does not require a programming background. This ease of use has made it popular with many different types of users. Millions of Web sites have been created with HTML, and there is every indication that HTML will continue to be an important language of the Web for a long time to come.

Despite its popularity, HTML is not without limitations and flaws that continue to frustrate Web designers. The major problem is that people are interested in Web pages not only for their appearance, but also for their *content*, and HTML was not designed with data content in mind. The wide variety of HTML tags can help a Web designer describe how the page should display, but it is more difficult to use those same tags to describe what the page *is*.

In response to this limitation, developers have added features to HTML, such as the CLASS attribute, that allow Web designers to attach descriptive information to each tag. Web designers can also make use of the <meta> tag to record information about the contents of a document. These additional HTML features are helpful, but they don't entirely solve the problem of effectively describing and cataloging data in an HTML document.

A second problem of HTML is that it is not extensible and therefore can't be modified to meet specific needs. As a result of the demands of the market and competition, the various Web browsers have developed their own unique flavors of HTML. Netscape Communicator saw a need for frames, so it introduced a version of HTML that included the <frameset> and <frame> tags, both of which were not part of standard HTML. Internet Explorer saw a need for internal frames and introduced the <iframe> tag, and that innovation also represented a departure from standard HTML.

The result was a confusing mix of competing HTML standards, one for each browser and indeed, each browser version. The innovations offered by Netscape, Internet Explorer, and others certainly increased the scope and power of HTML, but they did so at the expense of clarity. Web designers could not easily create Web sites without taking into account the cross-browser compatibility of the code in the Web pages.

Finally, HTML can be inconsistently applied. Some browsers require all tag attributes to be enclosed within quotes; some don't. Some browsers require all paragraphs to include an ending </p> tag; others do not. The lack of standards can make it easier to write HTML code, but it also means that code that is read by one browser may be rejected by another. This also has an impact on the design of Web browsers. Knowing that HTML would be inconsistently applied, browser developers must increase the size and complexity of their software in order to accommodate all possible contingencies. That's a headache for the developers, but it's also a problem for consumers. In recent years the Web has branched out, leaving behind desktop computers and workstations and moving toward smaller, handheld devices. Those smaller devices limit the size of the software that can be run on them. If HTML could be made "cleaner," it would be easier for a handheld device to access the Web.

Due partly to the reasons just outlined, the Web was in need of a language that could more effectively handle data content, be easily customized by developers, but at the same time be consistent and rigid enough for developers to easily develop applications for. In response to these needs, XML was created.

XML

Like HTML, the specifications for **XML (Extensible Markup Language)** are developed by the W3C. The consortium established 10 design goals for the language that promised, among other things, that XML would be easy to develop and use, accessible to nonprogrammers, and compatible with SGML. While XML is sometimes referred to as a markup language, it is actually more of a meta-markup language because it is a markup language that is used to create other markup languages. Unlike HTML, which is an SGML application, XML should be considered a subset of SGML—without SGML's complexity and overhead. XML has been used to create a variety of markup languages, including MathML used for mathematical documents and CML for documenting chemical structures.

One of the major differences between HTML and XML is that XML documents must fulfill requirements for both syntax and content. XML documents fall into two categories: well-formed and valid. A **well-formed** XML document is one that fulfills the basic syntax of XML. A **valid** XML document is a well-formed document that, in addition, fulfills criteria defined by the user for both content and structure. For example, an XML author can control the type of data entered into an XML document and define how it is entered. This is done by attaching a **document type definition (DTD)** to the document that defines how data is stored in the document. In order to confirm that an XML document is either well-formed or valid, it must be processed with an **XML parser**. A document that is neither well-formed nor valid is rejected by the parser. XML thereby avoids the irregularity that plagues HTML, but allows XML authors some flexibility in designing their own DTDs for special needs.

XHTML

This takes us back to XHTML, which combines the features of HTML and XML. An XHTML document is actually an XML document, but the structure and content conform to what we think of as HTML. This means that an XHTML document has to be well-formed, obeying the syntax rules of XML, and valid, obeying the rules for content and structure defined by any DTD attached to the document.

There are three types of DTDs you can use with an XHTML document: the strict DTD, the transitional DTD, and the frameset DTD. The **strict DTD** is used for completely "clean" HTML documents that contain no browser-specific extensions, or deprecated elements, and which use only Cascading Style Sheets to format the Web page. The **transitional DTD** is used for documents that are designed for older browsers that may not support Cascading Style Sheets. It allows for the use of deprecated elements and formatting done directly in the HTML tags, such as using the bgcolor or text attributes within the <body> tag. The **frameset DTD** is used for files containing frames. By using one of these three DTD types, along with an XML parser, a Web designer can ensure that the file fulfills the requirements of XHTML for both syntax and content.

Working with the Syntax of XHTML

XHTML code is very similar to HTML code, although there are some important differences worth noting. Some of these differences are because XHTML demands strict adherence to its syntax. Because of this, you should be aware that code that has been accepted by your Web browser may not be accepted in XHTML.

XHTML Syntax

Figure E-1 lists some syntax rules enforced by XHTML.

Figure E-1   XHTML SYNTAX RULES

RULE	INCORRECT	CORRECT
Elements must be properly nested	<p>This text is bold</p>	<p>This text is bold</p>
Tag names must be lowercase	<P>This is a paragraph.</P>	<p>This is a paragraph.</p>
Two-sided elements must be closed	<p>First paragraph <p>Second paragraph	<p>First paragraph</p> <p>Second paragraph</p>
Empty elements must be closed	This is a line break. 	This is a line break.
Attribute names must be in lowercase	<td ALIGN="right">	<td align="right">
Attribute values must be within quotation marks	<table width=620>	<table width="620">
Attributes must include attribute values	<option selected>	<option selected="selected">

Note that XHTML uses a different form for empty tags. Empty elements must end with </>. Thus, the following empty tags:

```
<hr>
<br>
<img src="logo.gif">
```

are written in XHTML as:

```
<hr />
<br />
<img src="logo.gif" />
```

XHTML also allows Web designers to write these elements as two-sided tags containing no content, i.e.:

```
<hr></hr>
<br></br>
<img src="logo.gif"></img>
```

In reality, many browsers do not support this second form.

Another area where XHTML departs from HTML is in **attribute minimization**, in which attribute values are not required. XHTML does not allow attribute minimization. Figure E-2 lists the minimized attributes in HTML and how they should be written in XHTML.

Figure E-2	MINIMIZED ATTRIBUTES IN HTML AND XHTML

HTML	XHTML
compact	compact="compact"
checked	checked="checked"
declare	declare="declare"
readonly	readonly="readonly"
disabled	disabled="disabled"
selected	selected="selected"
defer	defer="defer"
ismap	ismap="ismap"
nohref	nohref="nohref"
noshade	noshade="noshade"
nowrap	nowrap="nowrap"
multiple	multiple="multiple"
noresize	noresize="noresize"

For example the following HTML tag:

```
<input type="radio" checked>
```

must be written in XHTML as:

```
<input type="radio" checked="checked">
```

In addition, there are other rules that involve the way elements can be nested within the same or different elements. For example, XHTML prohibits the following nested conditions:

- The <a> tag cannot contain other <a> tags.
- The <pre> tag cannot contain the following tags: <img>, <object>, <big>, <small>, <sub>, and <sup>.
- The <button> tag cannot contain the following tags: <input>, <select>, <textarea>, <label>, <button>, <form>, <fieldset>, <iframe>, and <isindex>.
- The <label> tag cannot contain other <label> tags.
- The <form> tag cannot contain other <form> tags.
- An inline element may not contain a block-level element.

Beyond these rules, there are differences in how HTML and XHTML implement certain attributes.

Using the Name and ID Attributes

HTML uses the name attribute to identify elements within an HTML document. XHTML does not support the name attribute and, instead, uses the id attribute. Thus, the following HTML tags:

```
<a name="top">
<form name="order">
<img name="logo">
<map name="parkmap">
<frame name="document">
```

are written in XHTML as:

```
<a id="top">
<form id="order">
<img id="logo">
<map id="parkmap">
<frame id="document">
```

This can create problems with older browsers that do not support replacing the name attribute with the id attribute. If you are designing Web pages to be read by older browsers, you can include both the name and id attribute, as follows:

```
<a name="top" id="top">
```

Currently, the name attribute is deprecated in XHTML 1.0, and future versions of XHTML plan to remove support for this attribute entirely.

Working with Embedded Style Sheets and Scripts

Embedded style sheets and scripts contain code that a Web browser can process, but which are not part of the XHTML specifications. If an XML parser encounters these code elements, it rejects the document for not being well-formed. XML, and therefore XHTML, allows you to create **CDATA** sections containing text that the XML parser does not process, but can be read by a Web browser. The syntax for creating an embedded style sheet or script is:

```
<style>
   <![CDATA[
       embedded style declarations
   ]]>
</style>

<script>
   <![CDATA[
       JavaScript commands and functions
   ]]>
</script>
```

Currently, many browsers do not support the method of embedded style or script commands. If you want to use XHTML, you must place your style and script commands in an external file.

The Structure of an XHTML Document

An XHTML document consists of three parts: the DOCTYPE, the Head, and the Body. The DOCTYPE section indicates which of the three XHTML DTD types (Strict, Transitional, or Frameset) is being applied to the document, the Head section includes information on the document, and the Body section includes the main content of the document. A valid XHTML document must conform to the following general structure:

```
<!DOCTYPE DTD_declaration>
<html>
<head>
<title> ... </title>
</head>
<body>
   ...
</body>
</html>
```

where *DTD_declaration* is the document type. If this structure is not conformed to, the file is rejected by the XML parser. To specify the Strict DTD, enter the following DOCTYPE declaration:

```
<!DOCTYPE html PUBLIC "-//W3C//DTD XHTML 1.0 Strict//EN"
"http://www.w3.org/TR/xhtml1/DTD/xhtml1-strict.dtd">
```

The DOCTYPE declaration for the Transition DTD is:

```
<!DOCTYPE html PUBLIC "-
//W3C//DTD XHTML 1.0 Transitional//EN"
"http://www.w3.org/TR/xhtml1/DTD/xhtml1-transitional.dtd">
```

The Frameset DTD declaration is:

```
<!DOCTYPE html PUBLIC "-//W3C//DTD XHTML 1.0 Frameset//EN"
"http://www.w3.org/TR/xhtml1/DTD/xhtml1-frameset.dtd">
```

Case distinctions are important in XHTML, so you should duplicate these DOCTYPE declarations, including the distinction between upper- and lowercase letters.

Note that you only need to include a <!DOCTYPE> declaration if you want your XHTML to be valid. The document can still be well-formed (fulfilling the basic syntax of XHTML) without it. However, in most cases, Web designers want their documents to be both well-formed and valid. Figure E-3 indicates the tags supported by the three DTDs: Strict (S), Transitional (T), and Frameset (F).

Figure E-3 **TAGS ASSOCIATED WITH XHTML DTDS**

TAG	DTD	TAG	DTD	TAG	DTD	TAG	DTD
<!-->	S,T,F	<colgroup>	S,T,F	<ins>	S,T,F	<script>	S,T,F
<!DOCTYPE>	S,T,F	<dd>	S,T,F	<isindex>	T,F	<select>	S,T,F
<a>	S,T,F	<del>	S,T,F	<kbd>	S,T,F	<small>	S,T,F
<abbr>	S,T,F	<dfn>	S,T,F	<label>	S,T,F	<span>	S,T,F
<acronym>	S,T,F	<dir>	T,F	<legend>	S,T,F	<strike>	T,F
<address>	S,T,F	<div>	S,T,F	<li>	S,T,F	<strong>	S,T,F
<applet>	T,F	<dl>	S,T,F	<link>	S,T,F	<style>	S,T,F
<area />	S,T,F	<dt>	S,T,F	<map>	S,T,F	<sub>	S,T,F
<b>	S,T,F	<em>	S,T,F	<menu>	T,F	<sup>	S,T,F
<base />	S,T,F	<fieldset>	S,T,F	<meta>	S,T,F	<table>	S,T,F
<basefont />	T,F	<font>	T,F	<noframes>	T,F	<tbody>	S,T,F
<bdo>	S,T,F	<form>	S,T,F	<noscript>	S,T,F	<td>	S,T,F
<big>	S,T,F	<frame>	F	<object>	S,T,F	<textarea>	S,T,F
<blockquote>	S,T,F	<frameset>	F	<ol>	S,T,F	<tfoot>	S,T,F
<body>	S,T,F	<h1> to <h6>	S,T,F	<optgroup>	S,T,F	<th>	S,T,F
 	S,T,F	<head>	S,T,F	<option>	S,T,F	<thead>	S,T,F
<button>	S,T,F	<hr />	S,T,F	<p>	S,T,F	<title>	S,T,F
<caption>	S,T,F	<html>	S,T,F	<param>	S,T,F	<tr>	S,T,F
<center>	T,F	<i>	S,T,F	<pre>	S,T,F	<tt>	S,T,F
<cite>	S,T,F	<iframe>	T,F	<q>	S,T,F	<u>	T,F
<code>	S,T,F	<img />	S,T,F	<s>	T,F	<ul>	S,T,F
<col>	S,T,F	<input>	S,T,F	<samp>	S,T,F	<var>	S,T,F

As XHTML evolves, support for **modularization,** where XHTML elements are broken down into smaller modules, will increase. Modularization allows alternative platforms, such as handheld devices, to load only those XHTML elements they need and makes it easier for developers to create more efficient and flexible platforms for viewing XHTML documents.

Converting **From HTML To XHTML**

At first glance, it may seem that converting to XHTML is hardly worth the effort of adhering to a strict syntax and set of supported elements. The benefits are mostly for developers because it results in a more mature standard and provides more precise control over the development of Web documents.

Fortunately, there are many tools available to make the transition from HTML to XHTML. Users can access **HTML Tidy**, a freeware utility that "cleans up" HTML files, removing coding errors, and makes them conform to XHTML standards. You can learn more about HTML Tidy at *http://tidy.sourceforge.net/*.

The W3C also supports tools to test whether your files conform to XHTML or HTML 4.01 standards. You can access their validation service at *http://validator.w3.org/*. You can use the validation service by either specifying the URL of your Web page or by uploading your HTML file to the site.

CASCADING STYLE SHEETS

This appendix describes the selectors, units, and attributes supported by Cascading Style Sheets (CSS), Internet Explorer, (IE) and Netscape. Additional information about CSS and browser support for current CSS standards can be found at these Web sites:

- http://www.w3c.org
- http://www.webreview.com
- http://builder.cnet.com

Selectors

The general form of a style declaration is:
selector {attribute1:value1; attribute2:value2; ...}

Selectors indicate which element or elements in the document are affected by the style declaration. The following table shows some of the different forms that a selector can take and the corresponding support from CSS, IE, and Netscape.

SELECTORS	DESCRIPTION	CSS	IE	NETSCAPE
*	All elements in the document	2.0	5.0	6.0
E	An element, E, in the document	1.0	3.0	4.0
E1, E2, E3, ...	A group of elements, E1, E2, E3, ... in the document	1.0	3.0	4.0
E1 E2	An element, E2, that is contained within the parent element E1	1.0	3.0	4.0
E1 > E2	An element, E2, that is the direct descendant (child) of a parent element	2.0		6.0
E:first-child	Matches element E when E is the first child of its parent			6.0
E1+E2	An element, E2, that directly follows the element, E1	2.0		6.0
#id	An element with the ID name id	1.0	3.0	4.0
E.class	An element, E, with the class name class	1.0	3.0	4.0
.class	Any element with the class name class	1.0	3.0	4.0
E[attribute]	An element, E, that contains a specified attribute	2.0		6.0
E[attribute=value]	An element, E, that contains a specified attribute with a specified value	2.0		6.0
E[attribute^=value]	An element, E, that contains a specified attribute, whose value begins exactly with the string value	3.0		6.0
E[attribute$=value]	An element, E, that contains a specified attribute, whose value ends exactly with the string value	3.0		6.0
E:root	Root element of the document	3.0		
E:nth-child(n)	An element, E, the nth child of its parent	3.0		
E:nth-last-child(n)	An element, E, the nth child of its parent, counting from the last one	3.0		
E:nth-of-type(n)	An element, E, the nth sibling of its type	3.0		
E:first-child	An element, E, first child of its parent	3.0		
E:last-child	An element, E, last child of its parent	3.0		
E:only-child	An element, E, only child of its parent	3.0		
E:empty	An element, E, that has no children	3.0		
E:target	An element, E, being the target of the referring URI	3.0		
E[attribute~=value]	An element, E, that contains a specified attribute, with part of a specified value	2.0		6.0

Units

Many attribute values have units of measurement that are used to indicate width, height, or color. The following table describes the measuring units used in CSS.

UNITS	DESCRIPTION	CSS	IE	NETSCAPE
Color	**Units of Color**			
name	A color name. There are 16 base color names recognized by all browsers: aqua, black, blue, fuchsia, gray, green, lime, maroon, navy, olive, purple, red, silver, teal, white, and yellow. Additional color names are available and are roughly equivalent to the extended HTML color names.	1.0	3.0	4.0
#rrggbb	The hexadecimal color value, where *rr* is the red value, *gg* is the green value, and *bb* is the blue value	1.0	3.0	3.0
#rgb	A compressed hexadecimal value where the *r*, *g*, and *b* values are doubled, so that, for example, #A2F = #AA22FF	1.0	3.0	3.0
rgb(*red, green, blue*)	The decimal color value, where *red* is the red value, *green* is the green value, and *blue* is the blue value	1.0	3.0	3.0
rgb(*red%, green%, blue%*)	The color value percentage, where *red%* is the percent of maximum red, *green%* is the percent of maximum green, and *blue%* is the percent of maximum blue	1.0	3.0	3.0
Length	**Units of width or height**			
em	A relative unit indicating the width and height of the capital "M" character for the default font of the browser	1.0	4.0	4.0
ex	A relative unit indicating the height of the small "x" character for the default font of the browser	1.0	4.0	6.0
px	A pixel, representing the smallest element on the monitor	1.0	3.0	3.0
in	An inch	1.0	3.0	3.0
cm	A centimeter	1.0	3.0	3.0
mm	A millimeter	1.0	3.0	3.0
pt	A point, approximately $\frac{1}{72}$ of an inch	1.0	3.0	3.0
pc	A pica, approximately $\frac{1}{12}$ of an inch	1.0	3.0	3.0
p%	The percent, *p*, of the size of the parent element	1.0	3.0	3.0
xx-small	Keyword corresponding to the size="1" attribute of the <font> tag	1.0	3.0	3.0
x-small	Keyword corresponding to the size="2" attribute of the <font> tag	1.0	3.0	3.0
small	Keyword corresponding to the size="3" attribute of the <font> tag	1.0	3.0	3.0
medium	Keyword corresponding to the size="4" attribute of the <font> tag	1.0	3.0	3.0
large	Keyword corresponding to the size="5" attribute of the <font> tag	1.0	3.0	3.0

UNITS	DESCRIPTION	CSS	IE	NETSCAPE
Length	**Units of width or height**			
x-large	Keyword corresponding to the size="6" attribute of the <font> tag	1.0	3.0	3.0
xx-large	Keyword corresponding to the size="7" attribute of the <font> tag	1.0	3.0	3.0

Attributes and Values

The following table describes the attributes and values for different types of elements. Note that in some cases, browser support can be incomplete or unreliable, even if the browser version supports the style declaration. The only sure way to verify the support of a browser for a particular style is to test it.

ATTRIBUTES AND VALUES	DESCRIPTION	CSS	IE	NETSCAPE
Boxes	**Styles applied to block-level boxes**			
border	The border attribute applies width, style, and color attributes to all four borders using the syntax {border: *border-width border-style border-color*}.	1.0	4.0	6.0
border-bottom	The border-bottom attribute is a shorthand application of the various border-bottom attributes using the syntax {border-bottom: *border-bottom-width border-style border-bottom-color*}.	1.0	4.0	6.0
border-left	The border-left attribute is a shorthand application of the various border-left attributes using the syntax {border-left: *border-left-width border-style border-left-color*}.	1.0	4.0	6.0
border-right	The border-right attribute is a shorthand application of the various border-right attributes using the syntax {border-right: *border-right-width border-style border-right-color*}.	1.0	4.0	6.0
border-top	The border-top attribute is a shorthand application of the various border-top attributes using the syntax {border-top: *border-top-width border-style border-top-color*}.	1.0	4.0	6.0
border-color	The border-color attribute is a shorthand application of the various border-color attributes using the syntax {border-color: *border-top-color border-right-color border-bottom-color border-left-color*}.	1.0	4.0	4.0
border-bottom-color	The border-bottom-color attribute controls the color of the bottom border.	1.0	4.0	6.0
color	Sets the *color* of the bottom border using a color name or color value.	1.0	4.0	6.0
border-left-color	The border-left-color attribute controls the color of the left border.	1.0	4.0	6.0
color	Sets the *color* of the left border using a color name or color value.	1.0	4.0	6.0

ATTRIBUTES AND VALUES	DESCRIPTION	CSS	IE	NETSCAPE
Boxes	**Styles applied to block-level boxes**			
border-right-color	The border-right-color attribute controls the color of the right border.	1.0	4.0	6.0
color	Sets the *color* of the right border using a color name or color value	1.0	4.0	6.0
border-top-color	The border-top-color attribute controls the color of the top border.	1.0	4.0	6.0
color	Sets the *color* of the top border using a color name or color value	1.0	4.0	6.0
border-style	The border-style attribute defines the style of border to be used for the block-level box.	1.0	4.0	4.0
dashed	Displays a dashed line	1.0	5.5	6.0
dotted	Displays a dotted line	1.0	5.5	6.0
double	Displays a double line	1.0	4.0	4.0
groove	Displays a grooved line	1.0	4.0	4.0
inset	Displays an inset line	1.0	4.0	4.0
none	Displays no line	1.0	4.0	4.0
outset	Displays an outset line	1.0	4.0	4.0
ridge	Displays a ridged line	1.0	4.0	4.0
solid	Displays a solid line	1.0	4.0	4.0
border-width	The border-width attribute is a shorthand application of the various border-width attributes using the syntax {border-width: *border-top-width border-right-width border-bottom-width border-left-width*}.	1.0	4.0	4.0
border-bottom-width	The border-bottom-width attribute controls the width of the bottom border.	1.0	4.0	4.0
length	Sets the *length* of the bottom border in absolute or relative units	1.0	4.0	4.0
thin, medium, thick	Sets the length using one of the width keywords	1.0	4.0	4.0
border-left-width	The border-left-width attribute controls the width of the left border.	1.0	4.0	4.0
length	Sets the *length* of the left border in absolute or relative units	1.0	4.0	4.0
thin, medium, thick	Sets the length using one of the width keywords	1.0	4.0	4.0
border-right-width	The border-right-width attribute controls the width of the right border.	1.0	4.0	4.0
length	Sets the *length* of the right border in absolute or relative units	1.0	4.0	4.0
thin, medium, thick	Sets the length using one of the width keywords	1.0	4.0	4.0
border-top-width	The border-top-width attribute controls the width of the top border.	1.0	4.0	4.0
length	Sets the *length* of the top border in absolute or relative units	1.0	4.0	4.0
thin, medium, thick	Sets the length using one of the width keywords	1.0	4.0	4.0
margin	The margin attribute is a shorthand application of the various margin attributes using the syntax {margin: *margin-top margin-right margin-bottom margin-left*}.	1.0	3.0	6.0

ATTRIBUTES AND VALUES	DESCRIPTION	CSS	IE	NETSCAPE
Boxes	**Styles applied to block-level boxes**			
margin-bottom	The margin-bottom attribute controls the space below the box.	1.0	3.0	6.0
length	Sets the *length* of the bottom margin in absolute units, relative units, or as a percentage of the width of the containing box	1.0	3.0	6.0
auto	Allows the browser to control the size of the bottom margin	1.0	3.0	6.0
margin-left	The margin-top attribute controls the space to the left of the box.	1.0	3.0	4.0
length	Sets the *length* of the left margin in absolute units, relative units, or as a percentage of the width of the containing box	1.0	3.0	4.0
auto	Allows the browser to control the size of the left margin	1.0	3.0	4.0
margin-right	The margin-top attribute controls the space to the right of the box.	1.0	3.0	4.0
length	Sets the *length* of the right margin in absolute units, relative units, or as a percentage of the width of the containing box	1.0	3.0	4.0
auto	Allows the browser to control the size of the right margin	1.0	3.0	4.0
margin-top	The margin-top attribute controls the space above the box.	1.0	3.0	4.0
length	Sets the *length* of the top margin in absolute units, relative units, or as a percentage of the width of the containing box	1.0	3.0	4.0
auto	Allows the browser to control the size of the top margin	1.0	3.0	4.0
padding	The padding attribute is a shorthand application of the various padding attributes using the syntax {margin: *padding-top padding-right padding-bottom padding-left*}.	1.0	4.0	4.0
padding-bottom	The padding-bottom attribute controls the space between the bottom of the content and the bottom border.	1.0	4.0	4.0
length	Sets the *length* of the bottom padding in absolute units, relative units, or as a percentage of the width of the block-level box	1.0	4.0	4.0
padding-left	The padding-top attribute controls the space between the left of the content and the left border.	1.0	4.0	4.0
length	Sets the *length* of the left padding in absolute units, relative units, or as a percentage of the width of the block-level box	1.0	4.0	4.0
padding-right	The padding-top attribute controls the space between the right of the content and the right border.	1.0	4.0	4.0
length	Sets the *length* of the right padding in absolute units, relative units, or as a percentage of the width of the block-level box	1.0	4.0	4.0
padding-top	The padding-top attribute controls the space between the top of the content and the top border.	1.0	4.0	4.0
length	Sets the *length* of the top padding in absolute units, relative units, or as a percentage of the width of the block-level box	1.0	4.0	4.0

ATTRIBUTES AND VALUES	DESCRIPTION	CSS	IE	NETSCAPE
Boxes	**Styles applied to block-level boxes**			
height	The height attribute sets the height of the block-level box.	1.0	5.0	6.0
length	Sets the *length* of the box in absolute units, relative units, or as a percentage of the height of the parent box	1.0	5.0	6.0
auto	Allows the browser to control the height of the box	1.0	5.0	6.0
width	The width attribute sets the width of the block-level box.	1.0	5.0	4.0
length	Sets the *length* of the box in absolute units, relative units, or as a percentage of the width of the parent box	1.0	5.0	4.0
auto	Allows the browser to control the width of the box	1.0	5.0	4.0
display	The display attribute specifies the element's display type.	1.0	4.0	4.0
block	Treats the element as a block-level element	1.0	5.0	6.0
inline	Treats the element as an inline element	1.0	5.0	
list-item	Treats the element as a list item	1.0		6.0
none	Does not display the element	1.0	4.0	6.0
table-header-group	Treats the element as a group of one or more rows		5.0	
table-footer-group	Treats the element as a group of one or more rows		5.0	
white-space	The white-space attribute controls how spaces, tabs, and newline characters are handled.	1.0	5.5	4.0
normal	Removes extra blank spaces and wraps lines	1.0	5.5	4.0
nowrap	Prevents line wrapping	1.0	5.5	4.0
pre	Behaves like the <pre> tag in HTML			4.0
Colors and Backgrounds	**Styles applied to element colors and element backgrounds**			
background	The background attribute is a shorthand application of background styles using the syntax {background: *background-color background-image background-repeat background-attachment background-position*}.	1.0	4.0	6.0
background-attachment	The background-attachment attribute attaches a background image to the element.	1.0	4.0	6.0
fixed	Fixes the image regardless of element scrolling	1.0	4.0	6.0
scroll	Scrolls the image with the element	1.0	4.0	6.0
background-color	The background-color attribute controls the element's background color.	1.0	3.0	4.0
color	Specifies a color name or value	1.0	3.0	4.0
transparent	Specifies the use of a transparent color	1.0	4.0	6.0
background-image	The background-image attribute specifies the element's background image.	1.0	4.0	4.0
url(*filename*)	Uses the image from the *filename* image file	1.0	4.0	4.0
none	Uses no background image	1.0	4.0	4.0

ATTRIBUTES AND VALUES	DESCRIPTION	CSS	IE	NETSCAPE
Colors and Backgrounds	**Styles applied to element colors and element backgrounds**			
background-position	The background-position attribute controls the position of the background image within the element.	1.0	4.0	6.0
x y	Places the image at the (*x*, *y*) coordinate, where *x* and *y* are measured in a unit of length	1.0	4.0	6.0
x% y%	Places the image at a point *x%* of the element's width to the right and *y%* of the element's height down	1.0	4.0	6.0
keywordx keywordy	The first keyword places the image horizontally at the top, center, or bottom; the second keyword places the image vertically at the left, center, or right.	1.0	4.0	6.0
background-repeat	The background-repeat attribute controls the tiling of the background image within the element.	1.0	4.0	4.0
no-repeat	Does not repeat the image	1.0	4.0	4.0
repeat	Repeats the image horizontally and vertically	1.0	4.0	4.0
repeat-x	Repeats the image horizontally	1.0	4.0	4.0
repeat-y	Repeats the image vertically	1.0	4.0	4.0
color	The color attribute controls the foreground color of the element.	1.0	3.0	4.0
color	Specifies a color name or value	1.0	3.0	4.0
Fonts	**Styles applied to fonts used in the document**			
font	The font attribute is a shorthand application of text and font styles using the syntax {font: *font-family font-size font-style font-weight font-variant text-tranform text-decoration*}.	1.0	4.0	4.5
font-family	The font-family attribute is used to display text in a generic or specific font.	1.0	3.0	4.0
font-name	Displays text with the *font-name* font	1.0	3.0	4.0
cursive	Uses a cursive font	1.0	4.0	6.0
fantasy	Uses a fantasy font	1.0	4.0	6.0
monospace	Uses a monospace font	1.0	3.0	4.0
serif	Uses a serif font	1.0	3.0	4.0
sans-serif	Uses a sans-serif font	1.0	3.0	4.0
font-size	The font-size attribute controls the size of the font.	1.0	3.0	4.0
value	Uses a relative length, absolute length, or a length keyword	1.0	varies	varies
font-style	The font-style attribute controls the style of the font.	1.0	3.0	4.0
normal	Uses a normal style	1.0	3.0	4.0
italic	Uses italics	1.0	4.0	4.0
oblique	Uses an oblique style	1.0	4.0	4.0
font-variant	The font-variant attribute applies a variant to the font's appearance.	1.0	4.0	6.0
normal	Displays normal text	1.0	4.0	6.0
small-caps	Displays text in small capital letters	1.0	5.0	6.0

ATTRIBUTES AND VALUES	DESCRIPTION	CSS	IE	NETSCAPE
Fonts	**Styles applied to fonts used in the document**			
font-weight	The font-weight attribute controls the weight, or boldness, of the font.	1.0	4.0	4.0
100-900	Uses a value from 100 (the lightest) to 900 (the boldest)	1.0	4.0	4.0
bold	Displays text in bold	1.0	3.0	4.0
bolder	Displays text bolder than normal	1.0	4.0	4.0
lighter	Displays text lighter than normal	1.0	4.0	4.0
normal	Displays text with normal weight	1.0	4.0	4.0
Layout	**Styles that control the layout of elements on the page**			
bottom	The bottom attribute defines the vertical coordinate for the element, relative to the lower edge. See the position attribute for the type of coordinates to be used.	2.0	4.0	6.0
y	Defines the bottom coordinate value, *y*, in absolute units, relative units, or as a percentage of the block's height	2.0		
clear	The clear attribute places the element on the page only after the left or right margin of the parent element is clear.	1.0	4.0	
both	Places the element after both margins are clear	1.0	4.0	
left	Places the element after the left margin is clear	1.0	4.0	
none	Places the element regardless of whether margins are clear	1.0	4.0	
right	Places the element after the right margin is clear	1.0	4.0	
clip	The clip attribute defines what portion of an element's rendered content is visible. By default, the clipping region has the same size and shape as the element box.	2.0	5.0	6.0
auto	Sets the clipping region to the same size as the element box	2.0	5.0	6.0
rect(*top, right, bottom, left*)	Defines the dimensions of the clipping rectangle, where *top, right, bottom*, and *left* are the offsets from the sides of the box	2.0	5.0	
float	The float attribute aligns the element with the left or right margin of the parent element, causing other elements to flow around it.	1.0	4.0	4.0
left	Aligns the element with the left margin	1.0	4.0	4.0
none	Does not align the element with either margin	1.0	4.0	4.0
right	Aligns the element with the right margin	1.0	4.0	4.0
left	The left attribute defines the horizontal coordinate for the element, relative to the left edge. See the position attribute for the type of coordinates to be used.	2.0	4.0	4.0
x	Defines the left coordinate value, *x*, in absolute units, relative units, or as a percentage of the block's width	2.0	4.0	4.0

ATTRIBUTES AND VALUES	DESCRIPTION	CSS	IE	NETSCAPE
Layout	**Styles that control the layout of elements on the page**			
overflow	The overflow attribute determines the element's behavior when the content does not fit into the element box.	2.0	5.0	6.0
auto	Allows the browser to handle the overflow region	2.0	5.0	6.0
hidden	Hides the overflow content	2.0	5.0	6.0
scroll	Provides scroll bars to view the overflow content	2.0	5.0	6.0
visible	Displays the overflow content outside the box	2.0	5.0	6.0
position	The position attribute defines the position of an element relative to other elements on the page.	2.0	4.0	6.0
absolute	Places the element at a defined position within the parent block, independent from the positions of other elements within the block	2.0	4.0	6.0
fixed	Places the element at a fixed position in the display window, not allowing the element to scroll with other elements on the page; placement is determined using absolute coordinates.	2.0		
relative	Places the element relative to its natural position in the flow of the document	2.0	4.0	6.0
static	Places the element in its natural position in the flow of the document	2.0	4.0	6.0
right	The right attribute defines the horizontal coordinate for the element, relative to the right edge. See the position attribute for the type of coordinates to be used.	2.0	4.0	
x	Defines the right coordinate value, x, in absolute units, relative units, or as a percentage of the block's width	2.0		
top	The top attribute defines the vertical coordinate for the element, relative to the upper edge. See the position attribute for the type of coordinates to be used.	2.0	4.0	4.0
y	Defines the top coordinate value, y, in absolute units, relative units, or as a percentage of the block's height	2.0	4.0	4.0
visibility	The visibility attribute determines whether an element is visible.	2.0	4.0	
hidden	Hides the element	2.0	4.0	
inherit	Inherits the visibility state from the parent element	2.0	4.0	
visible	Makes the element visible	2.0	4.0	
z-index	The z-index attribute defines how overlapping elements are to be layered on the page.	2.0	5.0	4.0
auto	Displays the layers in the order of the document flow	2.0	5.0	4.0
n	Displays the layer in the nth position with higher numbers layered above lower numbers	2.0	5.0	4.0
Lists	**Styles applied to ordered and unordered lists**			
list-style	The list-style attribute is a shorthand application of the different list style attributes using the syntax {list-style: *list-style-type list-style-image list-style-position*}.	1.0	4.0	6.0

ATTRIBUTES AND VALUES	DESCRIPTION	CSS	IE	NETSCAPE
Lists	**Styles applied to ordered and unordered lists**			
list-style-image	The list-style-image attribute is used to display an inline image as the list label.	1.0	4.0	6.0
url(*filename*)	Displays the inline image from the *filename* image file	1.0	4.0	6.0
none	Displays no inline image	1.0	4.0	6.0
list-style-type	The list-style-type attribute is used to determine the label for ordered and unordered lists.	1.0	4.0	4.0
circle	Displays an open circle label	1.0	4.0	4.0
decimal	Displays a sequence of integers (1, 2, 3, ...)	1.0	4.0	4.0
disc	Displays a black dot label	1.0	4.0	4.0
lower-alpha	Displays lowercase letters (a, b, c, ...)	1.0	4.0	4.0
lower-roman	Displays lowercase roman numerals (i, ii, iii, ...)	1.0	4.0	4.0
none	Displays no labels	1.0	4.0	4.0
square	Displays a square label	1.0	4.0	4.0
upper-alpha	Displays uppercase letters (A, B, C, ...)	1.0	4.0	4.0
upper-roman	Displays uppercase roman numerals (I, II, III, ...)	1.0	4.0	4.0
list-style-position	The list-style-position attribute places the label relative to the position of the list's block-level box.	1.0	4.0	6.0
inside	Places labels inside the box	1.0	4.0	6.0
outside	Places labels outside the box	1.0	4.0	6.0
Miscellaneous	**Miscellaneous style terms**			
/* comment */	Used for inserting a *comment* into a style sheet	1.0	3.0	4.0
! important	Specifies that the style declaration takes precedence over any conflicting style	1.0	5.0	
Text	**Styles applied to text**			
letter-spacing	The letter-spacing attribute specifies the amount of space between letters in the text.	1.0	4.0	6.0
length	Sets the *length* between letters in absolute or relative units	1.0	4.0	6.0
normal	Uses normal letter spacing	1.0	4.0	6.0
line-height	The line-height attribute controls the space between lines in a block-level element.	1.0	3.0	4.0
length	Specifies the *length* of the line height in absolute units, relative units, or as a percentage of the font size of the element	1.0	3.0	4.0
normal	Uses a normal line height	1.0	3.0	4.0
text-align	The text-align attribute controls the alignment of text within the element.	1.0	3.0	4.0
center	Centers the text	1.0	3.0	4.0
justify	Displays the text flush with the left and right margins of the element	1.0	5.0	4.0
left	Displays the text aligned with the left margin	1.0	3.0	4.0
right	Displays the text aligned with the right margin	1.0	3.0	4.0

ATTRIBUTES AND VALUES	DESCRIPTION	CSS	IE	NETSCAPE
Text	**Styles applied to text**			
text-decoration	The text-decoration attribute applies a decoration to the text's appearance.	1.0	3.0	4.0
blink	Displays blinking text	1.0		4.0
line-through	Displays the text with a line through it	1.0	3.0	4.0
none	Applies no decoration to the text	1.0	3.0	4.0
overline	Displays the text with a line over it	1.0	4.0	6.0
underline	Displays the text with a line under it	1.0	3.0	4.0
text-indent	The text-indent attribute controls the indent of the first line of a block-level element.	1.0	3.0	4.0
length	Specifies the *length* of the indent in absolute units, relative units, or as a percentage of the width of the block-level element	1.0	3.0	4.0
text-transform	The text-transform attribute transforms the appearance of the text in the element.	1.0	4.0	4.0
capitalize	Displays the text in capital letters	1.0	4.0	4.0
lowercase	Displays the text in lowercase letters	1.0	4.0	4.0
none	Applies no transformation to the text	1.0	4.0	4.0
uppercase	Displays the text in uppercase letters	1.0	4.0	4.0
vertical-align	The vertical-align attribute controls the vertical alignment of text.	1.0	4.0	6.0
baseline	Aligns the text with the baseline	1.0	4.0	6.0
bottom	Aligns the text with the bottom of the line	1.0	5.5	6.0
middle	Aligns the text with the middle of the surrounding text	1.0	5.5	6.0
sub	Aligns the text as a subscript of the surrounding text	1.0	4.0	6.0
super	Aligns the text as a superscript of the surrounding text	1.0	4.0	6.0
text-bottom	Aligns the text with the bottom of the surrounding text	1.0	5.5	6.0
text-top	Aligns the text with the top of the surrounding text	1.0	5.5	6.0
top	Aligns the text with the top of the line	1.0	5.5	6.0
p%	Vertically aligns the text at *p*% of the line height of the surrounding text	1.0		6.0
word-spacing	The word-spacing attribute specifies the amount of space between words in the text.	1.0	4.0	6.0
length	Sets the *length* between words in absolute or relative units	1.0	4.0	6.0
normal	Uses normal word spacing	1.0	4.0	6.0

Pseudo-elements and Pseudo-classes

Pseudo-elements are elements that do not exist in HTML code, but whose attributes can be set with CSS. Many pseudo-elements were introduced in CSS2 and are not widely supported by browsers.

PSEUDO-ELEMENTS	DESCRIPTION	CSS	IE	NETSCAPE
E:after {content:"*text*"}	Text content, *text*, that is inserted at the end of a block-level element *E*	2.0		
E:before {content:"*text*"}	Text content, *text*, that is inserted at the beginning of a block-level element *E*	2.0		
E:first-child	An element, *E*, that is the first child of its parent element	2.0		
E:first-letter	The first letter in the block-level element *E*	1.0		5.5
E:first-line	The first line in the block-level element *E*	1.0		5.5
E:lang(*lang*)	An element, *E*, whose contents are shown in the language *lang*	2.0		

Pseudo-classes are classes of HTML elements that define the condition or state of the element in the Web page. Many pseudo-classes were introduced in CSS2 and are not widely supported by browsers.

PSEUDO-ELEMENTS	DESCRIPTION	CSS	IE	NETSCAPE
A:active	An active link in the document	1.0	4.0	
A:hover	A link with the mouse pointer positioned over it	2.0	5.0	
A:link	An unvisited link in the document	1.0	4.0	4.0
A:visited	A visited link in the document	1.0	4.0	4.0
E:focus	An element, E, in a Web page form that has received the focus	2.0		

JAVASCRIPT
OBJECTS, PROPERTIES, METHODS, AND EVENT HANDLERS

This appendix defines some of the important JavaScript objects, properties, and methods and their compatibility with the Internet Explorer (IE) and Netscape browsers.

JAVASCRIPT ELEMENTS	DESCRIPTION	IE	NETSCAPE
Anchor	**An anchor in the document (use the anchor name)**	**4.0**	**4.0**
Properties			
accessKey	The hotkey that gives the element focus	4.0	6.0
charset	The character set of the linked document	6.0	6.0
coords	The coordinates of the object, used with the shape attribute	6.0	6.0
hreflang	The language code of the linked resource	6.0	6.0
name	The name of the anchor	4.0	4.0
nameProp	The string holding the filename portion of the URL in the href	5.0	
shape	The string defining the shape of the object	6.0	6.0
tabIndex	The numeric value that indicates the tab order for the object	4.0	6.0
text	The anchor text	4.0	4.0
type	Specifies the media type in the form of a MIME type for the link target	6.0	6.0
Methods			
blur( )	Removes focus from the element	4.0	6.0
handleEvent(*event*)	Causes the Event instance *event* to be processed	4.0	
focus( )	Gives the element focus	4.0	6.0
Applet	**A Java applet in the document**	**4.0**	**3.0**
Properties			
align	Specifies alignment, for example, "left"	4.0	6.0
alt	Specifies alternative text for the applet	6.0	
altHTML	Specifies alternative text for the applet	4.0	
archive	A list of URLs		6.0
code	The URL for the applet class file	4.0	6.0
codeBase	The base URL for the applet	4.0	6.0
height	The height of the object in pixels	4.0	6.0
hspace	The horizontal margin to the left and right of the applet	4.0	6.0
name	The name of the applet	4.0	3.0
object	The name of the resource that contains a serialized representation of the applet		

JAVASCRIPT ELEMENTS	DESCRIPTION	IE	NETSCAPE
vspace	The vertical margin above and below the applet	4.0	6.0
width	The width of the object in pixels	4.0	6.0
Area	**An area defined in an image map**	3.0	3.0
Properties			
accessKey	The hotkey that gives the element focus	4.0	6.0
alt	Alternative text to the graphic	4.0	6.0
cords	Defines the coordinates of the object	6.0	6.0
hash	The anchor name from the URL	3.0	3.0
host	The host and domain name from the URL	3.0	3.0
hostname	The hostname from the URL	3.0	3.0
href	The entire URL	3.0	3.0
pathname	The pathname from the URL	3.0	3.0
port	The port number from the URL	3.0	3.0
protocol	The protocol from the URL	3.0	3.0
search	The query portion from the URL	3.0	3.0
shape	The shape of the object, for example, "default", "rect", "circle", "poly"	4.0	6.0
tabIndex	Numeric value that indicates the tab order for the object	4.0	6.0
target	The target attribute of the <area> tag	3.0	3.0
Methods			
getSelection()	Returns the value of the current selection		3.0
Event Handlers			
onDblClick()	Runs when the area is double-clicked	4.0	4.0
onMouseOut()	Runs when the mouse leaves the area	3.0	3.0
onMouseOver()	Runs when the mouse enters the area	3.0	3.0
Array	**An array object**	3.0	3.0
Properties			
index	For an array created by a regular expression match, the zero-based index of the match in the string	5.5	4.0
input	Reflects the original string against which the regular expression was matched	5.5	4.0
length	The next empty index at the end of the array	4.0	3.0
prototype	A mechanism to add properties to an array object	3.0	3.0

JAVASCRIPT ELEMENTS	DESCRIPTION	IE	NETSCAPE
Methods			
concat(*array*)	Combines two arrays and stores the results in a third array named *array*	4.0	4.0
join(*string*)	Stores each element in a text string named *string*	3.0	3.0
pop( )	"Pops" the last element of the array and reduces the length of the array by 1	5.5	4.0
push(*arg1*, *arg2*, ...)	"Pushes" the elements in the list to the end of the array and returns the new length	5.5	4.0
reverse( )	Reverses the order of the elements in the array	3.0	3.0
shift( )	Removes the first element from an array, returns that element, and shifts all other elements down one index	5.5	4.0
slice(*array*, *begin*,*end*)	Extracts a portion of the array starting at the index number *begin* and ending at the index number *end*; the elements are then stored in *array*	4.0	4.0
sort(*function*)	Sorts the array based on the function named *function*; if *function* is omitted, the sort applies dictionary order to the array	3.0	3.0
splice(*start*,*howMany*, [*,item1*[*,item2* [*,...*]]])	Removes *howMany* elements from the array beginning at index *start* and replaces the removed elements with the *itemN* arguments (if passed). Returns an array of the deleted elements	5.5	4.0
toString( )	Returns a string of the comma-separated values of the array	4.0	3.0
unshift([Item1 [,item2[,...]]])	Inserts the items to the front of an array and returns the new length of the array	5.5	4.0
Button	**A push button in an HTML form (use the button's name)**	3.0	3.0
Properties			
accessKey	Indicates the hotkey that gives the element focus	4.0	6.0
align	Specifies the alignment of the element, for example, "right"	4.0	6.0
disabled	A Boolean indicating whether the element is disabled	4.0	6.0
enabled	Indicates whether the button has been enabled	3.0	4.0
form	The name of the form containing the button	3.0	4.0
name	The name of the button element	3.0	2.0
size	Indicates the width of the button in pixels	4.0	6.0
tabIndex	Indicates the tab order for the object	4.0	6.0

JAVASCRIPT ELEMENTS	DESCRIPTION	IE	NETSCAPE
type	The value of the type attribute for the <button> tag	4.0	3.0
value	The value of the button element	3.0	2.0
Methods			
blur()	Removes focus from the button	3.0	3.0
click()	Emulates the action of clicking the button	3.0	2.0
focus()	Gives focus to the button	4.0	4.0
Event Handlers			
onBlur	Runs when the button loses the focus	3.0	3.0
onClick	Runs when the button is clicked	3.0	2.0
onFocus	Runs when the button receives the focus	4.0	4.0
onMouseDown	Runs when the mouse button is pressed	3.0	2.0
onMouseUp	Runs when the mouse button is released	3.0	2.0
Checkbox	**A check box in an HTML form**	3.0	2.0
Properties			
accessKey	Indicates the hotkey that gives the element focus	4.0	6.0
align	Specifies the alignment of the element, for example, "right"	4.0	6.0
checked	Indicates whether the check box is checked	3.0	2.0
defaultChecked	Indicates whether the check box is checked by default	3.0	2.0
disabled	Boolean indicating whether the element is disabled	4.0	6.0
enabled	Indicates whether the check box is enabled	3.0	4.0
form	The name of the form containing the check box	3.0	4.0
height	The height of the checkbox in pixels	5.0	
name	The name of the check box element	3.0	2.0
size	Indicates the width of the button in pixels	4.0	6.0
status	Boolean indicating whether the checkbox is currently selected	4.0	
tabIndex	Indicates the tab order for the object	4.0	6.0
type	The value of the type attribute for the <input> tag	4.0	3.0
value	The value of the check box element	3.0	2.0
width	Width of the check box in pixels	5.0	
Methods			
blur()	Removes the focus from the check box	3.0	3.0
click()	Emulates the action of clicking on the check box	3.0	2.0
focus()	Gives focus to the check box	4.0	4.0

JAVASCRIPT ELEMENTS	DESCRIPTION	IE	NETSCAPE
Event Handlers			
onBlur	Runs when the check box loses the focus	4.0	3.0
onClick	Runs when the check box is clicked		
onFocus	Runs when the check box receives the focus	4.0	4.0
Date	**An object containing information about a specific date or the current date. Dates are expressed either in local time or in UTC (Universal Time Coordinates), otherwise known as Greenwich Mean Time**	3.0	2.0
Methods			
getDate()	Returns the day of the month, from 1 to 31	3.0	2.0
getDay()	Returns the day of the week from 0 to 6 (Sunday = 0, Monday = 1, etc.)	3.0	2.0
getFullYear()	Returns the year portion of the date in four-digit format	4.0	4.0
getHours()	Returns the hour in military time from 0 to 23	3.0	2.0
getMilliseconds()	Returns the number of milliseconds	4.0	4.0
getMinutes()	Returns the minute from 0 to 59	3.0	2.0
getMonth()	Returns the value of the month from 0 to 11 (January = 0, February = 1, etc.)	3.0	2.0
getSeconds()	Returns the seconds	3.0	2.0
getTime()	Returns the date as an integer representing the number of milliseconds since December 31, 1969 at 18:00:00	3.0	2.0
getTimezoneOffset()	Returns the difference between the local time and Greenwich Mean Time in minutes	3.0	2.0
getYear()	Deprecated. Returns the number of years since 1900. For example, 1996 is represented by '96'—this value method is inconsistently applied after the year 1999)	3.0	2.0
getUTCDate()	Returns the UTC getDate() value	4.0	4.0
getUTCDay()	Returns the UTC getDay() value	4.0	4.0
getUTCFullYear()	Returns the UTC getFullYear() value	4.0	4.0
getUTCHours()	Returns the UTC getHours() value	4.0	4.0
getUTCMilliseconds()	Returns the UTC getMilliseconds() value	4.0	4.0
getUTCMinutes()	Returns the UTC getMinutes() value	4.0	4.0
getUTCMonth()	Returns the UTC getMonth() value	4.0	4.0
getUTCSeconds()	Returns the UTC getSeconds() value	4.0	4.0

JAVASCRIPT ELEMENTS	DESCRIPTION	IE	NETSCAPE
getUTCTime()	Returns the UTC getTime() value	4.0	4.0
getUTCYear()	Returns the UTC getYear() value	4.0	4.0
setDate(*date*)	Sets the day of the month to the value specified in *date*	3.0	2.0
setFullYear(*year*)	Sets the year to the four digit value specified in *year*	4.0	4.0
setHours(*hour*)	Sets the hour to the value specified in *hour*	3.0	2.0
setMilliseconds(*milliseconds*)	Sets the millisecond value to *milliseconds*	4.0	4.0
setMinutes(*minutes*)	Sets the minute to the value specified in *minutes*	3.0	2.0
setMonth(*month*)	Sets the month to the value specified in *month*	3.0	2.0
setSeconds(*seconds*)	Sets the second to the value specified in *seconds*	3.0	2.0
setTime(*time*)	Sets the time using the value specified in *time*, where *time* is a variable containing the number of milliseconds since December 31, 1969, at 18:00:00	3.0	2.0
setYear(*year*)	Sets the year to the value specified in *year*	3.0	2.0
toDateString()	Returns a date as a string value	5.5	
toLocaleDateString()	Returns a date as a string value	5.5	
toTimeString()	Returns a time as a string value	5.5	
toGMTString()	Converts the current date to a text string in Greenwich Mean Time	3.0	2.0
toLocaleString()	Converts a date object's date to a text string, using the date format the Web browser is set up to use	3.0	2.0
toSource	String representing the source code of the object		4.0
toString()	String representation of a Date object	4.0	2.0
toUTCString()	Date converted to string using UTC	4.0	4.0
UTC()	Milliseconds since December 31, 18:00:00, using UTC	3.0	2.0
UTC(*date*)	Returns *date* in the form of the number of milliseconds since December 31, 1969, 18:00:00 for Universal Coordinated Time	3.0	2.0
setUTCDate(*date*)	Applies the setDate() method in UTC time	4.0	4.0
setUTCFullYear(*year*)	Applies the setFullYear() method in UTC time	4.0	4.0
setUTCHours(*hour*)	Applies the setHours() method in UTC time	4.0	4.0
setUTCMilliseconds(*milliseconds*)	Applies the setMilliseconds() method in UTC time	4.0	4.0
setUTCMinutes(*minutes*)	Applies the setMinutes() method in UTC time	4.0	4.0
setUTCMonth(*month*)	Applies the setMonth() method in UTC time	4.0	4.0
setUTCSeconds(*seconds*)	Applies the setSeconds() method in UTC time	4.0	4.0
setUTCTime(*time*)	Applies the setTime() method in UTC time	4.0	4.0
setUTCYear(*year*)	Applies the setYear() method in UTC time	4.0	4.0

JAVASCRIPT ELEMENTS	DESCRIPTION	IE	NETSCAPE
dir	**A directory listing element in the document**	4.0	6.0
Properties			
compact	A Boolean indicating whether the listing should be compacted	6.0	6.0
div	**A <div> (block container) element in the document**	4.0	6.0
Properties			
align	Alignment of the element	4.0	6.0
document	**An HTML document (child of Window)**	3.0	2.0
Properties			
alinkColor	The color of active hypertext links in the document	3.0	2.0
all[ ]	An array of each of the HTML tags in the document	4.0	
anchors[ ]	An array of the anchors in the document	3.0	3.0
applets[ ]	An array of the applets in the document	3.0	3.0
attributes[ ]	A collection of attributes for the element		6.0
bgColor	The background color of the document	3.0	2.0
body	Reference to the <body> element object of the document	3.0	6.0
charset	A string containing the character set of the document	4.0	
characterSet	A string containing the character set of the document		6.0
childNodes[ ]	A collection of child nodes of the object	5.0	6.0
classes.*class.tag.style*	Deprecated. The *style* associated with the element in the document with the class name *class* and the tag name *tag*		4.0
cookie	A text string containing the document's cookie values	3.0	2.0
designMode	Specifies whether design mode is on or off	5.0	
dir	A string holding the text direction of text enclosed in the document	5.0	6.0
doctype	Reference to the DocumentType object for the document	6.0	6.0
documentElement	Reference to the root node of the document object hierarchy	5.0	6.0
domain	The domain of the document	4.0	3.0
embeds	An array of the embedded objects in the document	4.0	3.0
expando	A Boolean dictating whether instance properties can be added to the object	4.0	

JAVASCRIPT ELEMENTS	DESCRIPTION	IE	NETSCAPE
fgColor	The text color used in the document	3.0	2.0
firstChild	Reference to the first child node of the element, if one exists	5.0	6.0
form	A form within the document (the form itself is also an object)	3.0	2.0
forms	An array of the forms in the document	3.0	2.0
ids.*id.tag.style*	Deprecated. The *style* associated with the element in the document with the id name *id* and the tag name *tag*		4.0
implementation	An object with method *hasFeature(feature, level)* that returns a Boolean indicating if the browser supports the feature given in the string *feature* at the DOM level passed in the string *level*.	6.0	6.0
lastChild	Reference to the last child node of the element, if one exists	5.0	6.0
lastModified	The date the document was last modified	3.0	2.0
layers	An array of layer objects		4.0
linkColor	The color of hypertext links in the document	3.0	2.0
links	An array of the links within the document.	3.0	2.0
localName	A string indicating the "local" XML name for the object		6.0
location	The URL of the document	3.0	2.0
media	The media for which the document is intended	5.5	
nextSibling	Reference to next sibling of the node		6.0
nodeName	A string containing the name of the node, the name of the tag to which the object corresponds		6.0
nodeValue	A string containing value within the node		6.0
ownerDocument	Reference to the Document in which the element is contained		6.0
parentNode	Reference to the parent of the object		6.0
parentWindow	Reference to the window that contains the document		6.0
previousSibling	Reference to the previous sibling of the node		6.0
protocol	A string containing the protocol used to retrieve the document. Its full name		4.0
referrer	The URL of the document containing the link that the user accessed to get to the current document	3.0	2.0
security	A string that contains information about the document's certificate		5.5
styleSheets[ ]	Collection of styleSheets in the document	4.0	6.0

JAVASCRIPT ELEMENTS	DESCRIPTION	IE	NETSCAPE
tags.*tag.style*	The *style* associated with the tag name *tag*		4.0
title	The title of the document	3.0	2.0
URL	The URL of the document	3.0	2.0
vlinkColor	The color of followed hypertext links	3.0	2.0
XMLDocument	Reference to the top-level node of the XML DOM exposed by the document	5.0	
XSLDocument	Reference to the top-level node of the XSL DOM exposed by the document	5.0	

Methods

JAVASCRIPT ELEMENTS	DESCRIPTION	IE	NETSCAPE
addEventListener(whichEvent, handler, direction)	Instructs the object to execute the function *handler* whenever an event of the type stated in *whichEvent* occurs. *Direction* is a Boolean telling which phase to fire; use true for capture and false for bubbling		6.0
appendChild(newChild)	Appends *newChild* to the end of the node's childNodes[ ] list	5.0	6.0
attachEvent(whichHandler, theFunction)	Attaches the function *theFunction* as a handler specified by the string *whichHandler*	5.0	
clear()	Clears the contents of the document window	3.0	2.0
cloneNode(cloneChildren)	Clones the node and returns the new clone	5.0	6.0
close()	Closes the document stream	3.0	2.0
createAttribute(name)	Return a new attribute node of a name given by string *name*	6.0	6.0
createComment(data)	Returns a new comment node with the text given by *data*	6.0	6.0
createElement(tagName)	Returns a new element object that corresponds to *tagName*	4.0	6.0
createEventObject([eventObj])	Creates and returns a new *Event* instance to pass to *fireEvent()*	5.5	
createStyleSheet([url [,index]])	Creates a new styleSheet object from the Stylesheet at the URL in the string *url* and inserts it into the document at index *index*	4.0	
createTextNode(data)	Returns a new text node with value given by *data*	5.0	6.0
detachEvent(whichHandler, theFunction)	Instructs the object to stop executing *theFunction* as a handler given the string *whichHandler*	5.0	
dispatchEvent(event)	Causes *event* to be processed by the appropriate handler. Is used to redirect events		6.0
fireEvent(handler [, event])	Fires the event handler given by *handler*	5.5	
focus()	Gives focus to the document and fires *onfocus* handler	5.5	

JAVASCRIPT ELEMENTS	DESCRIPTION	IE	NETSCAPE
getElementById(id)	Returns the element with *id* (or *name*) that is equal to *id*	5.0	6.0
getElementByName(name)	Gets a collection of elements with *id* (or *name*) that is equal to *name*	5.0	6.0
getElementByTagName(tagname)	Gets a collection of elements corresponding to *tagname*	5.0	6.0
getSelection()	Returns the selected text from the document		4.0
hasAttributes()	Returns a Boolean showing if any attributes are defined for the node		6.0
hasChildNodes()	Returns a Boolean showing if the node has children	5.0	6.0
insertBefore(newChild, refChild)	Inserts the node *newChild* in front of *refChild* in the *childNodes*[ ] list of *refChild*'s parent node	5.0	6.0
isSupported(feature [, version])	Returns a Boolean showing which feature and version identified in the arguments are supported		6.0
normalize()	Merges adjacent text nodes in the subtree rooted at this element	6.0	6.0
open()	Opens the document stream	3.0	2.0
recalc([forceAll])	If *forceAll* is *true*, all dynamic properties are reevaluated	5.0	
removeChild(oldChild)	Removes *oldChild* from the node's children and returns a reference to the removed node	5.0	6.0
removeEventListener (whichEvent, handler, direction)	Removes the function *handler* for the event declared in *whichEvent* for the phase stated in the Boolean *direction*		6.0
replaceChild(newChild, oldChild)	Replaces the node's child node *oldChild* with the node *newChild*	5.0	6.0
setActive()	Sets the document as the current element but does not give it focus	5.5	
write()	Writes to the document window	3.0	2.0
writeln()	Writes to the document window on a single line (used only with preformatted text)	3.0	2.0
Event Handlers			
onClick	Runs when the document is clicked	3.0	2.0
onDblClick	Runs when the document is double-clicked	3.0	2.0
onKeyDown	Runs when a key is pressed down	3.0	2.0
onKeyPress	Runs when a key is initially pressed	3.0	2.0
onKeyUp	Runs when a key is released	3.0	2.0
onLoad	Runs when the document is initially loaded	3.0	2.0
onMouseDown	Runs when the mouse button is pressed down	3.0	2.0

JAVASCRIPT ELEMENTS	DESCRIPTION	IE	NETSCAPE
onMouseUp	Runs when the mouse button is released	3.0	2.0
onUnLoad	Runs when the document is unloaded	3.0	2.0
Error	**This object gives information about the error that occurred during runtime**	5.0	6.0
Properties			
description	Describes the nature of the error	5.0	6.0
lineNumber	The line number that generated the error	6.0	
number	The numeric value of the Microsoft-specific error number	5.0	
File, FileUpload	**A file upload element in an HTML form (use the FileUpload box's name)**	3.0	2.0
Properties			
accessKey	Indicates the hotkey that gives the element focus	4.0	6.0
disabled	A Boolean signifying if the element is disabled	4.0	6.0
form	The form object containing the FileUpload box	3.0	2.0
name	The name of the FileUpload box	3.0	2.0
size	The width in pixels	4.0	6.0
tabIndex	A numeric value of the width in pixels	4.0	6.0
type	The type attribute of the FileUpload box	3.0	2.0
value	The pathname of the selected file in the FileUpload box 3.0	2.0	
Methods			
blur()	Removes the focus from the FileUpload box	4.0	3.0
focus()	Gives the focus to the FileUpload box	4.0	3.0
handleEvent(*event*)	Invokes the event handler for the specified *event*	4.0	3.0
select()	Selects the input area of the FileUpload box	3.0	2.0
Event Handlers			
onBlur	Runs when the focus leaves the FileUpload box	4.0	3.0
onChange	Runs when the value in the FileUpload box is changed	4.0	3.0
onFocus	Runs when the focus is given to the FileUpload box	4.0	3.0
Form	**An HTML form (use the form's name)**	3.0	2.0
Properties			
acceptCharset	Specifies a list of character encodings for input data to be accepted by the server processing the form	5.0	6.0

JAVASCRIPT ELEMENTS	DESCRIPTION	IE	NETSCAPE
action	The location of the CGI script that receives the form values	3.0	2.0
autocomplete	Specifies whether form autocompletion is on or off	5.0	
elements[ ]	An array of elements within the form	3.0	2.0
encoding	The type of encoding used in the form	3.0	2.0
enctype	Specifies the MIME type of submitted data		6.0
length	The number of elements in the form	3.0	2.0
method	The type of method used when submitting the form	3.0	2.0
name	The name of the form	3.0	2.0
target	The name of window into which CGI output should be directed	3.0	2.0
Methods			
handleEvent(*event*)	Invokes the event handler for the specified *event*	4.0	3.0
reset()	Resets the form	3.0	2.0
submit()	Submits the form to the CGI script	3.0	2.0
urns(urn)	Retrieves a collection of all elements to which the behavior of string *urn* is attached	5.0	
Event Handlers			
onReset	Runs when the form is reset	4.0	3.0
onSubmit	Runs when the form is submitted	3.0	2.0
Frame	**A frame window (use the frame's name)**	3.0	2.0
Properties			
document	The current document in the frame window	3.0	2.0
frames	An array of frames within the frame window	3.0	2.0
length	The length of the frames array	3.0	2.0
name	The name of the frame	3.0	2.0
parent	The name of the window that contains the frame	3.0	2.0
self	The name of the current frame window	3.0	2.0
top	The name of the topmost window in the hierarchy of frame windows	3.0	2.0
window	The name of the current frame window	3.0	2.0
Methods			
alert(*message*)	Displays an Alert box with the text string *message*	3.0	2.0

JAVASCRIPT ELEMENTS	DESCRIPTION	IE	NETSCAPE
blur()	Removes the focus from the frame	4.0	3.0
clearInterval(*ID*)	Cancels the repeated execution *ID*	4.0	4.0
clearTimeout(*ID*)	Cancels the delayed execution *ID*	4.0	4.0
confirm(*message*)	Displays a Confirm box with the text string *message*	3.0	2.0
open(*URL, name, features*)	Opens a URL in the frame with the name *name* and a feature list indicated by *features*	3.0	2.0
print()	Displays the Print dialog box	4.0	4.0
prompt(*message, response*)	Displays a Prompt dialog box with the text string *message* and the default value *response*	3.0	2.0
setInterval(*expression, time*)	Runs an *expression* after *time* milliseconds	4.0	4.0
setTimeout(*expression, time*)	Runs an *expression* every *time* milliseconds	4.0	4.0
Event Handlers			
onBlur	Runs when the focus is removed from the frame	4.0	4.0
onFocus	Runs when the frame receives the focus	4.0	4.0
onMove	Runs when the frame is moved	4.0	4.0
onResize	Runs when the frame is resized	4.0	4.0
h1…h6	**Heading level element in the document**	4.0	6.0
Properties			
align	The alignment of the element, for example, "right"	4.0	6.0
head	**Corresponds to the <head> element in the document**	4.0	6.0
Properties			
profile	A list of the URLs for data properties and legal values	6.0	6.0
hidden	**A hidden field on an HTML form (use the name of the hidden field)**	3.0	2.0
Properties			
form	The name of the form containing the hidden field	3.0	2.0
name	The name of the hidden field	3.0	2.0
type	The type of the hidden field	4.0	3.0
value	The value of the hidden field	3.0	2.0
history	**An object containing information about the Web browser's history list**	3.0	2.0
Properties			
current	The current URL in the history list	4.0	3.0

JAVASCRIPT ELEMENTS	DESCRIPTION	IE	NETSCAPE
length	The number of items in the history list	3.0	2.0
next	The next item in the history list	4.0	3.0
previous	The previous item in the history list	3.0	2.0
Methods			
back()	Navigates back to the previous item in the history list	3.0	2.0
forward()	Navigates forward to the next item in the history list	3.0	2.0
go(*location*)	Navigates to the item in the history list specified by the value of *location*. The *location* variable can be either an integer or the name of the Web page	3.0	2.0
hr	**A horizontal rule element in the document**	4.0	6.0
Properties			
align	Alignment of the object, for example, "right"	4.0	6.0
color	The color of the rule	4.0	
noShade	A Boolean indicating that the rule is not to be shaded	4.0	6.0
size	The size (height) of the rule in pixels	4.0	6.0
width	The width of the rule in pixels	4.0	6.0
html	**Corresponds to the <html> element in the document**	4.0	6.0
Properties			
version	The DTD version for the document	6.0	6.0
iframe	**An inline frame element in the document**	4.0	6.0
Properties			
align	The alignment of the object, for example, "right"	4.0	6.0
allowTransparency	A Boolean specifying whether the background of the frame can be transparent	5.0	
border	The width of the border around the frame	4.0	
contentDocument	The Document that corresponds to the content of this frame		6.0
contentWindow	The Window that corresponds to this frame	5.0	
frameBorder	String of "0" (no border) or "1" (show border)	4.0	6.0
height	The height of the frame in pixels	4.0	6.0
longdesc	The URL of a long description for the frame	6.0	6.0
marginHeight	Vertical margins in pixels	4.0	6.0
marginWidth	Horizontal margins in pixels	4.0	6.0

JAVASCRIPT ELEMENTS	DESCRIPTION	IE	NETSCAPE
name	The name of the frame	4.0	6.0
width	The width of the frame in pixels	4.0	6.0
image	**An inline image (use the name assigned to the image)**	4.0	3.0
Properties			
align	Specifies the alignment of the object, for example, "left", "right", "center"	4.0	6.0
alt	A string containing alternative text for the image	4.0	6.0
border	The width of the image border in pixels	4.0	3.0
complete	A Boolean value that indicates whether the image has been completely loaded by the browser	4.0	3.0
height	The height of the image in pixels	4.0	3.0
hspace	The horizontal space around in the image in pixels	4.0	3.0
isMap	A Boolean indicating whether the image is a server-side image map	4.0	6.0
longDesc	The URL for a more detailed description of the image	6.0	6.0
loop	An integer indicating how many times the image is to loop when activated	4.0	
lowSrc	Specifies a URL for a lower resolution image to display		6.0
lowsrc	The value of the lowsrc property of the <img> tag	4.0	3.0
name	The name of the image	4.0	3.0
nameProp	Indicates the name of the file given in the *src* attribute of the <img>	5.0	
src	The URL of the image	4.0	3.0
style	Reference to the inline *Style* object for the element	4.0	4.0
useMap	Contains a URL to use as a client-side image map	4.0	6.0
vspace	The vertical space around an image in pixels	4.0	3.0
width	The width of the image in pixels	4.0	3.0
Methods			
handleEvent(*event*)	Invokes the event handler for the specified *event*	4.0	4.0
Event Handlers			
onAbort	Runs when the image load is aborted	4.0	3.0
onError	Runs when an error occurs while loading the image	4.0	3.0
onKeyDown	Runs when a key is pressed down	4.0	3.0

JAVASCRIPT ELEMENTS	DESCRIPTION	IE	NETSCAPE
onKeyPress	Runs when a key is pressed	4.0	4.0
onKeyUp	Runs when a key is released	4.0	4.0
onLoad	Runs when the image is loaded	4.0	3.0
implementation	**Information about the DOM technologies the browser supports (child of Document)**	6.0	6.0
Methods			
hasFeature(feature [, version])	A Boolean indicating if the browser supports the feature at the DOM level given in version.	6.0	6.0
label	**A form field label in the document**	4.0	6.0
Properties			
accessKey	Indicates the hotkey that gives the element focus	4.0	6.0
form	The Form that encloses the label	4.0	6.0
layer	**A document layer (use the name of the layer) Deprecated in favor of the standard <div> element**	4.0	
Properties			
above	The layer above the current layer		4.0
background	The background image of the layer		4.0
below	The layer below the current layer		4.0
bgColor	The background color of the layer		4.0
clip.bottom, clip.height, clip.left,	The size and position of the layer's clipping area clip.right, clip.top, clip.width		4.0
document	The document containing the layer		4.0
name	The value of the *name* or *id* attribute for the layer		4.0
left	The *x*-coordinate of the layer		4.0
pageX	The *x*-coordinate relative to the document		4.0
pageY	The *y*-coordinate relative to the document		4.0
parentLayer	The containing layer		4.0
siblingAbove	The layer above in the zIndex		4.0
siblingBelow	The layer below in the zIndex		4.0
src	The URL of the layer document		4.0
top	The *y*-coordinate of the layer		4.0
visibility	The state of the layer's visibility		4.0
zIndex	The zIndex value of the layer		4.0

JAVASCRIPT ELEMENTS	DESCRIPTION	IE	NETSCAPE
Methods			
handleEvent(*event*)	Invokes the event handler for the specified *event*		4.0
load(*source, width*)	Loads a new URL into the layer from *source* with the specified *width*		4.0
moveAbove(*layer*)	Moves the layer above *layer*		4.0
moveBelow(*layer*)	Moves the layer below *layer*		4.0
moveBy(*x, y*)	Moves the x pixels in the x-direction, and y pixels in the y-direction		4.0
moveTo(*x, y*)	Moves the upper-left corner of the layer to the specified (x, y) coordinate		4.0
moveToAbsolute(*x, y*)	Moves the layer to the specified coordinate (x, y) within the page		4.0
resizeBy(*width, height*)	Resizes the layer by the specified *width* and *height*		4.0
resizeTo(*width, height*)	Resizes the layer to the specified *height* and *width*		4.0
Event Handlers			
onBlur	Runs when the focus leaves the layer		4.0
onFocus	Runs when the layer receives the focus		4.0
onLoad	Runs when the layer is loaded		4.0
onMouseOut	Runs when the mouse leaves the layer		4.0
onMouseOver	Runs when the mouse hovers over the layer		4.0
legend	**A <legend> (fieldset caption) element in the document**	4.0	6.0
Properties			
accessKey	Indicates the hotkey	4.0	6.0
align	Specifies the alignment of the element, for example, "right"	4.0	6.0
form	The Form in which the element is enclosed	4.0	6.0
link	**A link within an HTML document (use the name of the link)**	3.0	2.0
Properties			
accessKey	Indicates the hotkey that gives the element focus	4.0	6.0
charset	The character set of the linked document	6.0	6.0
coords	Defines the coordinates of the object	6.0	6.0
disabled	A Boolean indicating whether the element is disabled	4.0	6.0
hash	The anchor name from the link's URL	3.0	2.0

JAVASCRIPT ELEMENTS	DESCRIPTION	IE	NETSCAPE
host	The host from the link's URL	3.0	2.0
hostname	The hostname from the link's URL	3.0	2.0
href	The link's URL	3.0	2.0
hreflang	Indicates the language code of the linked resource	6.0	6.0
media	The media the linked document is intended for		6.0
nameProp	Holds the filename portion of the URL in the *href*	5.0	
pathname	The path portion of the link's URL	3.0	2.0
port	The port number of the link's URL	3.0	2.0
protocol	The protocol used with the link's URL	3.0	2.0
search	The search portion of the link's URL	3.0	2.0
target	The target window of the hyperlinks	3.0	2.0
text	The text used to create the link	4.0	4.0
type	Specifies the media type in the form of a MIME type for the link target	6.0	6.0

Methods

handleEvent(*event*)	Invokes the event handler for the specified *event*	4.0	4.0

Event Handlers

onClick	Runs when the link is clicked	3.0	2.0
onDblClick	Runs when the link is double-clicked	4.0	4.0
onKeyDown	Runs when a key is pressed down	4.0	4.0
onKeyPress	Runs when a key is initially pressed	4.0	4.0
onKeyUp	Runs when a key is released	4.0	4.0
onMouseDown	Runs when the mouse button is pressed down on the link	4.0	4.0
onMouseOut	Runs when mouse moves away from the link	4.0	4.0
onMouseOver	Runs when the mouse hovers over the link	4.0	4.0
onMouseUp	Runs when the mouse button is released	4.0	4.0

location	**The location of the document**	3.0	2.0

Properties

hash	The location's anchor name	3.0	2.0
host	The location's hostname and port number	3.0	2.0
href	The location's URL	3.0	2.0
pathname	The path portion of the location's URL	3.0	2.0
port	The port number of the location's URL	3.0	2.0
protocol	The protocol used with the location's URL	3.0	2.0

JAVASCRIPT ELEMENTS	DESCRIPTION	IE	NETSCAPE
Methods			
Assign(url)	Assigns the URL in the string *url* to the object	3.0	2.0
reload()	Reloads the location	4.0	3.0
replace(*URL*)	Loads a new location with the address *URL*	4.0	3.0
map	**Corresponds to a <map> (client-side image Map) element in the document**	4.0	6.0
Properties			
Areas[ ]	A collection of *areas* enclosed by the object	4.0	6.0
Name	String holding the name of the image map	4.0	6.0
Math	**An object used for advanced mathematical calculations**	3.0	2.0
Properties			
E	The value of the base of natural logarithms (2.7182...)	3.0	2.0
LN10	The value of the natural logarithm of 10	3.0	2.0
LN2	The value of the natural logarithm of 2	3.0	2.0
LOG10E	The base 10 logarithm of E	3.0	2.0
LOG2E	The base 2 logarithm of E	3.0	2.0
PI	The value of pi (3.1416...)	3.0	2.0
SQRT1_2	The square root of ½	3.0	2.0
SQRT2	The square root of 2	3.0	2.0
Methods			
abs(*number*)	Returns the absolute value of *number*	3.0	2.0
acos(*number*)	Returns the arc cosine of *number* in radians	3.0	2.0
asin(*number*)	Returns the arc sine of *number* in radians	3.0	2.0
atan(*number*)	Returns the arc tangent of *number* in radians	3.0	2.0
atan2()	Returns the arc tangent of the quotient of its arguments	3.0	2.0
ceil(*number*)	Rounds *number* up to the next highest integer	3.0	2.0
cos(*number*)	Returns the cosine of *number,* where *number* is an angle expressed in radians	3.0	2.0
exp(*number*)	Raises the value of E (2.7182...) to the value of *number*	3.0	2.0
floor(*number*)	Rounds *number* down to the next lowest integer	3.0	2.0
log(*number*)	Returns the natural logarithm of *number*	3.0	2.0
max(*number1, number2*)	Returns the greater of *number1* and *number2*	3.0	2.0

JAVASCRIPT ELEMENTS	DESCRIPTION	IE	NETSCAPE
min(*number1, number2*)	Returns the lesser of *number1* and *number2*	3.0	2.0
pow(*number1, number2*)	Returns the value of *number1* raised to the power of *number2*	3.0	2.0
random()	Returns a random number between 0 and 1	3.0	2.0
round(*number*)	Rounds *number* to the closest integer	3.0	2.0
sin(*number*)	Returns the sine of *number,* where *number* is an angle expressed in radians	3.0	2.0
sqrt(*number*)	Returns the square root of *number*	3.0	2.0
tan(*number*)	Returns the tangent of *number,* where *number* is an angle expressed in radians	3.0	2.0
toString(*number*)	Converts *number* to a text string	3.0	2.0
menu	**A <menu> (menu list) element in the document**	**4.0**	**6.0**
Properties			
compact	A Boolean signifying whether the list should be compacted	6.0	6.0
navigator	**An object representing the browser currently in use**	**3.0**	**2.0**
Properties			
appCodeName	The code name of the browser	3.0	2.0
appName	The name of the browser	3.0	2.0
appVersion	The version of the browser	3.0	2.0
cookieEnabled	A Boolean signifying whether persistent cookies are enabled	4.0	6.0
language	The language of the browser	4.0	4.0
mimeTypes	An array of the MIME types supported by the browser	4.0	4.0
oscpu	A string containing the operating system		6.0
platform	The platform on which the browser is running	4.0	4.0
plugins	An array of the plug-ins installed on the browser	4.0	3.0
preference	Allows a signed script to get and set certain Navigator preferences		4.0
userAgent	The user-agent text string sent from the client to the Web server	3.0	2.0
Methods			
javaEnabled()	Indicates whether the browser supports Java	4.0	3.0
plugins.refresh()	Checks for newly installed plug-ins	4.0	3.0
taintEnabled()	Specifies whether data tainting is enabled	5.5	3.0

JAVASCRIPT ELEMENTS	DESCRIPTION	IE	NETSCAPE
Option	**An option from a selection list (use the name of option or the index value from the options array)**	3.0	2.0
Properties			
defaultSelected	A Boolean indicating whether the option is selected by default	4.0	3.0
disabled	A Boolean indicating whether the element is disabled	4.0	6.0
index	The index value of the option	3.0	2.0
label	Alternate text for the option as specified in the *label* attribute		6.0
selected	A Boolean indicating whether the option is currently selected	3.0	2.0
text	The text of the option as it appears on the Web page	3.0	2.0
value	The value of the option	3.0	2.0
param	**Corresponds to an occurrence of a \<param\> element in the document**	4.0	6.0
Properties			
name	The name of the parameter	4.0	6.0
type	The type of the value when *valueType* is "ref"	6.0	6.0
value	The value of the parameter	6.0	6.0
valueType	Provides more information about how to interpret value. Usually "data", "ref", or "object"	6.0	6.0
Password	**A password field in an HTML form (use the name of the password field)**	3.0	2.0
Properties			
defaultValue	The default password	3.0	2.0
name	The name of the password field	3.0	2.0
type	The type value of the password field	3.0	2.0
value	The value of the password field	3.0	2.0
Methods			
focus()	Gives the password field the focus	3.0	2.0
blur()	Leaves the password field	3.0	2.0
select()	Selects the password field	3.0	2.0

JAVASCRIPT ELEMENTS	DESCRIPTION	IE	NETSCAPE
Event Handlers			
onBlur	Runs when the focus leaves the password field	3.0	2.0
onFocus	Runs when the password field receives the focus	3.0	2.0
plugin	**A plug-in object in the Web page**	**4.0**	**3.0**
Properties			
description	The description of the plug-in	4.0	3.0
filename	The plug-in filename	4.0	3.0
length	The number of MIME types supported by the plug-in	4.0	3.0
name	The name of the plug-in	4.0	3.0
popup	**A popup window object created by using the createPopup() method in IE**	**5.5**	
Properties			
document	Reference to the window's Document	5.5	
isOpen	A Boolean indicating if the window is open	5.5	
Radio	**A radio button in an HTML form (use the radio button's name)**	**3.0**	**2.0**
Properties			
accessKey	Indicates the hotkey that gives the element focus	4.0	6.0
align	A string specifying the alignment of the element, for example, "right"	4.0	6.0
alt	Alternative text for the button		6.0
checked	A Boolean indicating whether a specific radio button has been checked	3.0	2.0
defaultChecked	A Boolean indicating whether a specific radio button is checked by default	3.0	2.0
defaultValue	The initial value of the button's *value* attribute	3.0	6.0
disabled	A Boolean indicating whether the element is disabled	4.0	6.0
form	The name of the form containing the radio button	3.0	2.0
name	The name of the radio button	3.0	2.0
type	The type value of the radio button	4.0	3.0
value	The value of the radio button	3.0	2.0
Methods			
blur()	Gives the radio button the focus	3.0	2.0
click()	Clicks the radio button	3.0	2.0

JAVASCRIPT ELEMENTS	DESCRIPTION	IE	NETSCAPE
focus()	Gives focus to the radio button	3.0	2.0
handleEvent(*event*)	Invokes the event handler for the specified *event*	4.0	4.0
Event Handlers			
onBlur	Runs when the focus leaves the radio button	3.0	2.0
onClick	Runs when the radio button is clicked	3.0	2.0
onFocus	Runs when the radio button receives the focus	3.0	2.0
RegExp	**An object used for searching regular expressions**	4.0	4.0
Properties			
global	Specifies whether to use a global pattern match	4.0	4.0
ignoreCase	Specifies whether to ignore case in the search string	4.0	4.0
input	The search string	4.0	4.0
lastIndex	Specifies the index at which to start matching the next string	4.0	4.0
lastMatch	The last matched characters	4.0	4.0
lastParen	The last parenthesized substring match	4.0	4.0
leftContext	The substring preceding the most recent match	4.0	4.0
multiline	Specifies whether to search on multiple lines	4.0	4.0
rightContext	The substring following the most recent match	4.0	4.0
source	The string pattern	4.0	4.0
Methods			
compile()	Compiles a regular search expression	4.0	4.0
exec(*string*)	Executes the search for a match to *string*	4.0	4.0
test(string)	Tests for a match to string	4.0	4.0
Reset	**A reset button in an HTML form (use the name of the reset button)**	3.0	2.0
Properties			
accessKey	Indicates the hotkey that gives the element focus	4.0	6.0
align	Specifies the alignment of the element, for example, "right"	4.0	6.0
alt	Alternative text for the button		6.0
defaultValue	Contains the initial value of the button	3.0	6.0
disabled	A Boolean indicating whether the element is disabled	4.0	6.0

JAVASCRIPT ELEMENTS	DESCRIPTION	IE	NETSCAPE
form	The name of the form containing the reset button	3.0	2.0
name	The name of the reset button	3.0	2.0
type	The type value of the reset button	4.0	3.0
value	The value of the reset button	3.0	2.0
Methods			
blur()	Removes the focus from the reset button	3.0	2.0
click()	Clicks the reset button	3.0	2.0
focus()	Gives the focus to the reset button	3.0	2.0
handleEvent(*event*)	Invokes the event handler for the specified *event*	4.0	4.0
Event Handlers			
onBlur	Runs when the focus leaves the reset button	3.0	2.0
onClick	Runs when the reset button is clicked	3.0	2.0
onFocus	Runs when the reset button receives the focus	3.0	2.0
screen	**An object representing the user's screen**	4.0	4.0
Properties			
availHeight	The height of the screen, minus toolbars or any other permanent object	4.0	4.0
availWidth	The width of the screen, minus toolbars or any other permanent object	4.0	4.0
colorDepth	The number of possible colors in the screen	4.0	4.0
height	The height of the screen	4.0	4.0
pixelDepth	The number of bits per pixel in the screen	5.0	4.0
width	The width of the screen	4.0	4.0
Script	**Corresponds to a <script> element in the document**	4.0	6.0
Properties			
charset	The character set used to encode the script	6.0	6.0
defer	A Boolean indicating whether script execution may be deferred	4.0	6.0
src	The URL of the external script	4.0	6.0
text	The contents of the script	4.0	6.0
type	The value of the type attribute	4.0	6.0

JAVASCRIPT ELEMENTS	DESCRIPTION	IE	NETSCAPE
Select	**A selection list in an HTML form (use the name of the selection list)**	3.0	2.0
Properties			
disabled	A Boolean indicating whether the element is disabled	4.0	6.0
form	The name of the form containing the selection list	3.0	2.0
length	The number of *options* in the selection list	3.0	2.0
multiple	A Boolean indicating whether multiple *options* may be selected	4.0	6.0
name	The name of the selection list	3.0	2.0
options[ ]	An array of options within the selection list. See the options object for more information on working with individual selection list options	3.0	2.0
selectedIndex	The index value of the selected option from the selection list	3.0	2.0
size	The number of options that are visible at one time	4.0	6.0
tabIndex	Numeric value that indicates the tab order for the object	4.0	6.0
type	The type value of the selection list	4.0	3.0
value	The *value* of the currently selected option	4.0	6.0
Methods			
add(element, before)	Adds the *option* referenced by the *element* to the list of options before the *option* referenced by *before*. If *before* is null, it is added at the end	5.5	6.0
blur()	Removes the focus from the selection list	3.0	2.0
focus()	Gives the focus to the selection list	3.0	2.0
handleEvent(*event*)	Invokes the event handler for the specified *event*	4.0	4.0
remove(index)	Removes the option at index *index* from the list of *options*	5.5	6.0
Event Handlers			
onBlur	Runs when the focus leaves the selection list	3.0	2.0
onChange	Runs when focus leaves the selection list and the value of the selection list is changed	3.0	2.0
onFocus	Runs when the selection list receives the focus	3.0	2.0

JAVASCRIPT ELEMENTS	DESCRIPTION	IE	NETSCAPE
String	**An object representing a text string**	**3.0**	**2.0**
Properties			
length	The number of characters in the string	3.0	2.0
Methods			
anchor(*name*)	Converts the string into a hypertext link anchor with the name *name*	3.0	2.0
big()	Displays the string using the <big> tag	3.0	2.0
blink()	Displays the string using the <blink> tag	3.0	2.0
bold()	Displays the string using the <b> tag	3.0	2.0
charAt(*index*)	Returns the character in the string at the location specified by *index*	3.0	2.0
charCodeAt(position)	Returns an unsigned integer of the Unicode value of the character at index *position*	5.5	4.0
concat(*string2*)	Concatenates the string with the second text string *string2*	4.0	4.0
fixed()	Displays the string using the <tt> tag	3.0	2.0
fontColor(*color*)	Sets the color attribute of the string	3.0	2.0
fontSize(*value*)	Sets the size attribute of the string	3.0	2.0
indexOf(*string, start*)	Searches the string, beginning at the *start* character, and returns the index value of the first occurrence of the string *string*	3.0	2.0
italics()	Displays the string using the <i> tag	3.0	2.0
lastIndexOf(*string, start*)	Searches the string, beginning at the *start* character, and locates the index value of the last occurrence of the string *string*	3.0	2.0
link(*href*)	Converts the string into a hypertext link pointing to the URL *href*	3.0	2.0
match(*expression*)	Returns an array containing the matches based on the regular expression *expression*	4.0	4.0
replace(*expression, new*)	Performs a search and replace based on the regular expression *expression* and replaces the text with *new*	4.0	4.0
search(*expression*)	Performs a search based on the regular expression *expression* and returns the index number	4.0	4.0
slice(*begin, end*)	Returns a substring between the *begin* and *end* index values; the *end* index value is optional	4.0	4.0
small()	Displays the string using the <small> tag	3.0	2.0
split(*separator*)	Splits the string into an array of strings at every occurrence of the *separator* character	4.0	4.0

JAVASCRIPT ELEMENTS	DESCRIPTION	IE	NETSCAPE
strike()	Displays the string using the <strike> tag	3.0	2.0
sub()	Displays the string using the <sub> tag	3.0	2.0
substr(*begin, length*)	Returns a substring starting at the *begin* index value and continuing for *length* characters; the *length* parameter is optional	4.0	4.0
substring(*begin, end*)	Returns a substring between the *begin* and *end* index values; the *end* index value is optional	3.0	2.0
sup()	Displays the string using the <sup> tag	3.0	2.0
toLowerCase()	Converts the string to lowercase	3.0	2.0
toUpperCase()	Converts the string to uppercase	3.0	2.0
style	**This corresponds to an instance of a <style> element in the page**	4.0	6.0
Properties			
disabled	A Boolean indicating whether the element is disabled	4.0	6.0
sheet	The styleSheet object corresponding to the element		6.0
styleSheet	The styleSheet object corresponding to the element	4.0	
type	The value of the *type* attribute for the stylesheet	4.0	6.0
Submit	**A submit button in an HTML form (use the name of the submit button)**	3.0	2.0
Properties			
accessKey	String indicating the hot key that gives the element focus	4.0	6.0
alt	Alternative text for the button	6.0	
defaultValue	The initial value of the button's *value* attribute	3.0	6.0
disabled	A Boolean indicating whether the element is disabled	4.0	6.0
form	The name of the form containing the submit button	3.0	2.0
name	The name of the submit button	3.0	2.0
tabIndex	Numeric value that indicates the tab order for the object	4.0	6.0
type	The type value of the submit button	4.0	3.0
value	The value of the submit button	3.0	2.0
Methods			
blur()	Removes the focus from the submit button	3.0	2.0
click()	Clicks the submit button	3.0	2.0

JAVASCRIPT ELEMENTS	DESCRIPTION	IE	NETSCAPE
focus()	Gives the focus to the submit button	3.0	2.0
handleEvent(*event*)	Invokes the event handler for the specified *event*	4.0	4.0
Event Handlers			
onBlur	Runs when the focus leaves the submit button	3.0	2.0
onClick	Runs when the submit button is clicked	3.0	2.0
onFocus	Runs when the submit button receives the focus	3.0	2.0
Text	**An input box from a HTML form (use the name of the input box)**	3.0	2.0
Properties			
accessKey	A string indicating the hotkey that gives the element focus	4.0	6.0
defaultValue	The default value of the input box	3.0	2.0
disabled	A Boolean indicating whether the element is disabled	4.0	6.0
form	The form containing the input box	3.0	2.0
maxLength	The maximum number of characters the field can contain	4.0	6.0
name	The name of the input box	3.0	2.0
size	The width of the field in characters	4.0	6.0
tabIndex	The numeric value that indicates the tab order for the object	4.0	6.0
type	The type value of the input box	4.0	3.0
value	The value of the input box	3.0	2.0
Methods			
blur()	Removes the focus from the input box	3.0	2.0
focus()	Gives the focus to the input box	3.0	2.0
handleEvent(*event*)	Invokes the event handler for the specified *event*	4.0	4.0
select()	Selects the input box	3.0	2.0
Event Handlers			
onBlur	Runs when the focus leaves the input box	3.0	2.0
onChange	Runs when the focus leaves the input box and the input box value changes	3.0	2.0
onFocus	Runs when the input box receives the focus	3.0	2.0
onSelect	Runs when some of the text in the input box is selected	3.0	2.0

JAVASCRIPT ELEMENTS	DESCRIPTION	IE	NETSCAPE
Textarea	**A text area box in an HTML form (use the name of the text area box)**	3.0	2.0
Properties			
accessKey	Indicates the hotkey that gives the element focus	4.0	6.0
cols	The number of columns of the input area	4.0	6.0
defaultValue	The default value of the text area box	3.0	2.0
enabled	Indicates whether a textarea field is enabled using a Boolean	3.0	3.0
form	The form containing the text area box	3.0	2.0
name	The name of the text area box	3.0	2.0
rows	The number of rows of the input area	4.0	6.0
tabIndex	Numeric value that indicates the tab order for the object	4.0	6.0
type	The type value of the text area box	4.0	3.0
value	The value of the text area box	3.0	2.0
Methods			
blur()	Removes the focus from the text area box	3.0	2.0
focus()	Gives the focus to the text area box	3.0	2.0
handleEvent(*event*)	Invokes the event handler for the specified *event*	4.0	4.0
select()	Selects the text area box	3.0	2.0
Event Handlers			
onBlur	Runs when the focus leaves the text area box	3.0	2.0
onChange	Runs when the focus leaves the text area box and the text area box value changes	3.0	2.0
onFocus	Runs when the text area box receives the focus	3.0	2.0
onKeyDown	Runs when a key is pressed down	4.0	4.0
onKeyPress	Runs when a key is pressed	4.0	4.0
onKeyUp	Runs when a key is released	4.0	4.0
onSelect	Runs when some of the text in the text area box is selected	3.0	2.0
window	**The document window**	3.0	2.0
Properties			
clipboardData	Provides access to the OS's clipboard	5.0	
defaultStatus	The default message shown in the window's status bar	3.0	2.0

JAVASCRIPT ELEMENTS	DESCRIPTION	IE	NETSCAPE
directories	A Boolean specifying whether the Netscape 6 "directories" button is visible.		6.0
document	The document displayed in the window	3.0	2.0
frameElement	The *Frame* in which the window is enclosed	5.5	
frames	An array of frames within the window (see the frames object for properties and methods applied to individual frames)	3.0	2.0
history	A list of visited URLs	4.0	3.0
innerHeight	The height of the window's display area	4.0	4.0
innerWidth	The width of the widow's display area	4.0	4.0
length	The number of frames in the window	3.0	2.0
location	The URL loaded into the window	3.0	2.0
locationbar.visible	A Boolean indicating the visibility of the window's location bar	4.0	4.0
menubar.visible	A Boolean indicating the visibility of the window's menu bar	4.0	4.0
name	The name of the window	3.0	2.0
opener	The name of the window that opened the current window	4.0	3.0
outerHeight	The height of the outer area of the window	4.0	4.0
outerWidth	The width of the outer area of the window	4.0	4.0
pageXOffset	The *x*-coordinate of the window	4.0	4.0
pageYOffset	The *y*-coordinate of the window	4.0	4.0
parent	The name of the window containing this particular window	3.0	2.0
personalbar.visible	A Boolean indicating the visibility of the window's personal bar	4.0	4.0
screen	The browser's *screen* object	4.0	6.0
screenLeft	The *x* coordinate in pixels of the left edge of the client area of the browser window	5.0	
screenTop	The *y* coordinate in pixels of the top edge of the client area of the browser window	5.0	
scrollbars.visible	A Boolean indicating the visibility of the window's scroll bars	4.0	4.0
scrollX	How far the window is scrolled to the right		6.0
scrollY	How far the window is scrolled to the down		6.0
self	The current window	3.0	2.0
status	The message shown in the window's status bar	3.0	2.0

JAVASCRIPT ELEMENTS	DESCRIPTION	IE	NETSCAPE
statusbar.visible	A Boolean indicating the visibility of the window's status bar	4.0	4.0
toolbar.visible	A Boolean indicating the visibility of the window's toolbar	4.0	4.0
top	The name of the topmost window in a hierarchy of windows	3.0	2.0
window	The current window	3.0	2.0

Methods

JAVASCRIPT ELEMENTS	DESCRIPTION	IE	NETSCAPE
alert(*message*)	Displays the text contained in *message* in a dialog box	3.0	2.0
back()	Loads the previous page in the window	4.0	4.0
blur()	Removes the focus from the window	4.0	3.0
captureEvents()	Sets the window to capture all events of a specified type	4.0	4.0
clearInterval(*ID*)	Clears the interval for *ID*, set with the SetInterval method	4.0	4.0
clearTimeout()	Clears the timeout, set with the setTimeout method	3.0	2.0
close()	Closes the window	3.0	2.0
confirm(*message*)	Displays a confirmation dialog box with the text *message*	3.0	2.0
createPopup(arg)	Creates a popup window and returns a reference to the new popup object	5.5	
disableExternalCapture	Disables external event capturing	4.0	4.0
enableExternalCapture	Enables external event capturing	4.0	4.0
find(*string, case, direction*)	Displays a Find dialog box, where *string* is the text to find in the window, *case* is a Boolean indicating whether the find is case-sensitive, and *direction* is a Boolean indicating whether the find goes in the backward direction (all of the parameters are optional)	4.0	4.0
focus()	Gives focus to the window	4.0	3.0
forward()	Loads the next page in the window	4.0	4.0
handleEvent(*event*)	Invokes the event handler for the specified *event*	4.0	4.0
moveBy(*horizontal, vertical*)	Moves the window by the specified amount in the *horizontal* and *vertical* direction	4.0	4.0
moveTo(*x, y*)	Moves the window to the *x* and *y* coordinates	4.0	4.0
open()	Opens the window	3.0	2.0
print()	Displays the Print dialog box	4.0	4.0
prompt(*message, default_text*)	Displays a Prompt dialog box with the text *message* (the default message is: *default_text*)	3.0	2.0
releaseEvents(*event*)	Releases the captured events of a specified *event*	4.0	4.0

JAVASCRIPT ELEMENTS	DESCRIPTION	IE	NETSCAPE
resizeBy(*horizontal, vertical*)	Resizes the window by the amount in the *horizontal* and *vertical* direction	4.0	4.0
resizeTo(*width, height*)	Resizes the window to the specified *width* and *height*	4.0	4.0
routeEvent(*event*)	Passes the *event* to be handled natively	4.0	4.0
scroll(*x, y*)	Scrolls the window to the *x, y* coordinate	4.0	3.0
scrollBy(*x, y*)	Scrolls the window by *x* pixels in the *x*-direction, and *y* pixels in the *y*-direction	4.0	4.0
scrollTo(*x, y*)	Scrolls the window to the *x, y* coordinate	4.0	4.0
setActive( )	Sets the window to be active but does not give it focus	5.5	
setCursor(type)	Changes the cursor to *type*		6.0
setInterval(*expression, time*)	Evaluates the *expression* every *time* milliseconds have passed	4.0	4.0
setTimeout(*expression, time*)	Evaluates the *expression* after *time* milliseconds have passed	3.0	2.0
sizeToContent( )	Resizes the window so all contents are visible		6.0
stop()	Stops the windows from loading	4.0	4.0

Event Handlers

onBlur	Runs when the window loses the focus	4.0	3.0
onDragDrop	Runs when the user drops an object on or within the window	4.0	4.0
onError	Runs when an error occurs while loading the page	4.0	3.0
onFocus	Runs when the window receives the focus	4.0	3.0
onLoad	Runs when the window finishes loading	3.0	2.0
onMove	Runs when the window is moved	4.0	4.0
onResize	Runs when the window is resized	4.0	4.0
onUnload	Runs when the window is unloaded	3.0	2.0

JAVASCRIPT
OPERATORS, SYNTACTICAL ELEMENTS, AND KEYWORDS

The following table lists some of the important JavaScript operators, keywords, and elements. It also identifies their compatibility with Microsoft Internet Explorer and Netscape Navigator browsers.

OPERATORS	DESCRIPTION	IE	NETSCAPE
Assignment	**Operators used to assign values to variables**		
=	Assigns the value of the variable on the right to the variable on the left ($x = y$)	3.0	2.0
+=	Adds the two variables and assigns the result to the variable on the left (x += y is equivalent to $x = x + y$)	3.0	2.0
-=	Subtracts the variable on the right from the variable on the left and assigns the result to the variable on the left (x-=y is equivalent to $x = x - y$)	3.0	2.0
*=	Multiplies the two variables together and assigns the result to the variable on the left (x* = y is equivalent to $x = x * y$)	3.0	2.0
/=	Divides the variable on the left by the variable on the right and assigns the result to the variable on the left (x/ = y is equivalent to $x = x / y$)	3.0	2.0
&=	Combines two expressions into a single expression (x& = y is equivalent to $x = x$ & y)	3.0	2.0
%=	Divides the variable on the left by the variable on the right and assigns the remainder to the variable on the left (x% = y is equivalent to $x = x$ % y)	3.0	2.0
Arithmetic	**Operators used for arithmetic functions**		
+	Adds two variables together ($x + y$)	3.0	2.0
-	Subtracts the variable on the right from the variable on the left ($x - y$)	3.0	2.0
*	Multiplies two variables together ($x * y$)	3.0	2.0
/	Divides the variable the left by the variable on the right (x / y)		
%	Calculates the remainder after dividing the variable on the left by the variable on the right (x % y)	3.0	2.0
++	Increases the value of a variable by 1 (x + + is equivalent to $x = x + 1$)	3.0	2.0
&	Combines two expressions (x & y)	3.0	2.0
--	Decreases the value of variable by 1 (x -- is equivalent to $x = x - 1$)	3.0	2.0
-	Changes the sign of a variable (- x)	3.0	2.0
Comparison	**Operators used for comparing expressions**		
==	Returns true when the two expressions are equal ($x == y$)	3.0	2.0
!=	Returns true when the two expressions are not equal ($x != y$)	3.0	2.0
!==	Returns true when the values of the two expressions are equal ($x !== y$)	5.0	5.0
>	Returns true when the expression on the left is greater than the expression on the right ($x > y$)	3.0	2.0
<	Returns true when the expression on the left is less than the expression on the right ($x < y$)	3.0	2.0
>=	Returns true when the expression on the left is greater than or equal to the expression on the right ($x >= y$)	3.0	2.0
<=	Returns true when the expression on the left is less than or equal to the expression on the right ($x <= y$)	3.0	2.0

OPERATORS	DESCRIPTION	IE	NETSCAPE
Conditional	**Operators used to determine values based on conditions that are either true or false**		
(condition) ? *value1 : value2*	If *condition* is true, then this expression equals *value1*, otherwise it equals *value2*		
Keywords	**JavaScript keywords are reserved by JavaScript**		
infinity	Represents positive infinity (often used with comparison operators)	5.0	4.0
this	Refers to the current object	3.0	2.0
var	Declares a variable	3.0	2.0
with	Allows the declaration of all the properties for an object without directly referencing the object each time	3.0	2.0
Logical	**Operators used for evaluating true and false expressions**		
^	The XOR (exclusive OR) operator	3.0	2.0
!	Reverses the Boolean value of the expression	3.0	2.0
&&	Returns true only if both expressions are true (also known as an AND operator)		
||	Returns true when either expression is true (also known as an OR operator)	3.0	2.0
|	Returns true if the expression is false and false if the expression is true (also known as a NEGATION operator)	3.0	2.0
Syntax	**Syntactical elements**		
;	Indicates the end of a command line	3.0	2.0
/ comments*/*	Used for inserting *comments* within a JavaScript command line	3.0	2.0
// comments	Used to create a line of *comments*	3.0	2.0

CREATING
COOKIES WITH
JAVASCRIPT

Introducing Cookies

A **cookie** is a piece of information stored in a text file that the Web browser places on a user's computer. Typically, cookies contain data to be accessed the next time the user visits a particular Web site. For example, many online stores use cookies to store address and credit card information for the user. The next time the user makes a purchase at the online store, the pertinent information can be accessed from the cookie, freeing the user from reentering this material.

Where the browser places the cookie file depends on the browser. Netscape stores cookies in a single text file named "cookie.txt." Internet Explorer stores cookies in a separate text file, typically in the Windows/Cookies folder. Browsers limit each cookie to 4 kilobytes in size, and there cannot be more than 300 cookies stored at one time on the user's computer. If the browser tries to store more than 300 cookies, the extra cookies are deleted, starting with the oldest ones.

Cookies, the Web Server, and CGI Scripts

The first implementation of cookies was with a CGI script running on a Web server. The CGI script retrieves the cookie information and performs some action based on the information in the file. The process works as follows:

1. The user accesses the Web site and sends a request to the CGI script on the Web server either by filling out an order form or by some other process that calls the CGI script.

2. The CGI script determines whether a cookie exists for the user.

3. If no cookie is detected, the Web server sends a form, or page, for a user to enter the information needed by the cookie. This information is then sent to the CGI script for processing.

4. If a cookie is found, the CGI script retrieves that information and creates a new page, or modifies the current page, based on the information contained in the cookie.

Information is exchanged using the same hypertext transfer protocol used for retrieving the contents of the Web page. This is because each transfer includes a header section that contains information about the document (such as its MIME data type), and allows for general information in the form:

field-name: field-value

It is these field-name/field-value pairs that contain information that can be stored in the user's cookie.

To store this information on the Web server, the Web programmer must add the Set-Cookie statement to the header section of the CGI script. The Set-Cookie statement is used the first time the user accesses the Web page. There are four parameters that are often set with cookies: name, expires, path, and domain. The syntax is:

```
Set-Cookie: name=text; expires=date; path=text; domain=text;
secure
```

where the name parameter defines the name of the cookie. The value of the name parameter cannot contain spaces, commas, or semicolons. The expire parameter indicates the date the information expires. If no expire parameter is included, the cookie expires when the user's browsing session ends. The path parameter indicates the URL path portion to which that cookie applies. Setting this value to "/" allows the cookie to be accessed from any folder within the Web site. The domain parameter specifies the URL domain portion to which the cookie applies (usually the domain name of the current document). Finally, the secure parameter indicates that the data should be transferred over a secure link—one that uses file encryption.

Once the initial cookie is created, the browser sends the Cookie statement in the header section of the transfer the next time the user accesses the Web page. The syntax of this statement is:

```
Cookie: name1:value1; name2;value2; ...
```

where *name1* is the first field name (whatever that might be) and *value1* is the value of the first field. There can be as many field/value pairs as needed by the Web page, as long as the total size of the cookie doesn't exceed 4 kilobytes.

Once the Web server retrieves the cookie field names and values, it is the CGI script that processes them. Because CGI programming is beyond the scope of this book, you will focus on working with cookies on the client side with JavaScript.

Working with the Cookie Property

JavaScript uses the cookie property of the document object to retrieve and update cookie information. The cookie property is simply a text string containing all of the field/value pairs used by the cookie, with each pair separated by a semicolon. To set a value for a cookie, you would use the document.cookie property as follows:

```
document.cookie='cookie1=OrderForm; expires=Mon, 08-Apr-2002
12:00:00 GMT; path="/"; secure';
```

where the cookie has the cookie1 field with the value "OrderForm". This particular cookie expires at noon on Monday, April 8, 2002. Since the path value equals "/", this cookie is accessible from any folder within the Web site. The secure property has been set, so that any transfer of information involving this cookie uses file encryption. Note that this is a long text string, with the string value enclosed in single quotation marks.

If your Web page had an online form named "Orders", you could create additional field/value pairs using the form names and values as follows:

```
document.cookie='cookie1=OrderForm;
name='+document.Orders.Name.value+';
custid=+'document.Orders.CustId.value;
```

Here, two additional fields have been added to the cookie: name and custid. The values for these fields are respectively taken from the Name field and the CustId field in the Orders form.

Reading a Cookie

One of the challenges of working with cookies in JavaScript is reading the cookie information. To do this you need to extract the appropriate information from the cookie's text string and place that information in the appropriate JavaScript variables. You can use several of JavaScript's string functions to help with this task. To start, create a function named "readCookie(fname)" where "fname" is the name of the field whose value you want to retrieve. The initial code looks as follows:

```
function readCookie(fname) {
    var cookies=document.cookie;
}
```

where the text string of the cookie is stored in the "cookies" variable. In the text string, each field name is followed by an equal sign, so you can use the indexOf( ) method (see Appendix G) to locate the occurrence of the text string "*fname=*," where *fname* is the field name you want to retrieve. You'll store this location in a variable named "startname." The command is:

```
startname=cookies.indexOf(fname+"=");
```

For example, if fname="custid" in the text string below, startname would have a value of 33, since "custid" starts with the 33rd character in the text string.

```
cookie1=OrderForm; name=Brooks; custid=20010; type=clothes
```

What if the field name is not found in the cookie? In that case, startname has a value of -1, and you can create an If...Else conditional statement to handle this contingency. To simplify things for this example, you'll assume that this is not a concern and continue.

Next you need to locate the field's value. This value is placed after the equal sign, and continues until you reach a semicolon indicating the end of the field's value, or until you reach the end of the text string. The field's value then starts one space after the first equal sign after the field's name. You'll locate the beginning of the field value using the same indexOf( ) method, and store that location in the startvalue variable. The command is:

```
startvalue=cookies.indexOf("=", startname)+1;
```

Here, you locate the text string "=", starting at the point, "startname" in the cookies text string. You add one to whatever value is returned by the indexOf( ) method. In this text string:

```
cookie1=OrderForm; name=Brooks; custid=20010; type=clothes
```

the value of the startvalue variable is 40, since the "2" in "20010" is the 40th character in the string.

Now you locate the end of the field's value, which is the first semicolon after the startvalue character. If the field is the last value in the text string, there is no semicolon at the end, so the indexOf( ) method returns a value of -1. If that occurs, you'll use the length of the text string to locate the value's end. Once again, using the indexOf( ) method, you'll store this value in the endvalue variable. The JavaScript command is:

```
endvalue=cookies.indexOf(";",startvalue);
if(endvalue==-1) {
    endvalue=cookies.length;
}
```

In the text string below, the value of the endvalue variable for the custid field is 45.

```
cookie1=OrderForm; name=Brooks; custid=20010; type=clothes
```

To extract the field's value and store it in a variable named "fvalue," use the substring( ) method (see Appendix D) as follows:

```
fvalue=cookies.substring(startvalue, endvalue);
```

where the startvalue indicates the start of the substring, and the endvalue marks the substring's end. The complete readCookie(fname) function looks as follows:

```
function readCookie(fname) {
      var cookies=document.cookie;
      var startname=cookies.indexOf(fname+"=");
      var startvalue=cookies.indexOf("=", startname)+1;
      var endvalue=cookies.indexOf(";",startvalue);
      if(endvalue==-1) {
         endvalue=cookies.length;
      }
      var fvalue=cookies.substring(startvalue, endvalue);
return fvalue;
}
```

So, in a JavaScript program, calling the following function:

```
readCookie("custid");
```

returns a value of 20010, which is the customer id value stored in the cookie file. You should review this example carefully, paying close attention to the use of the indexOf() method and the substring( ) method.

Encoding Cookies

Values in the cookie text string cannot contain spaces, semicolons, or commas. This can be a problem if you are trying to store phrases or sentences. The solution to this problem is to encode the value, using the same type of encoding scheme that is used in URLs (which also cannot contain spaces, commas, and semicolons) or in the MAILTO action. JavaScript includes the escape( ) method for encoding your text strings. Encoding replaces blank spaces, semicolons, and commas with special characters. For example, if you want to insert an Address field in your cookie that contains a street number and address, you could use the following JavaScript command:

```
document.cookie='Address='+escape(document.Orders.Address.value);
```

To read a text string that has been encoded, you use JavaScript's unescape() method. For example, you could replace the command that stores the field value in the fvalue variable in the readCookie() function with the following command:

```
var fvalue=unescape(cookies.substring(startvalue, endvalue));
```

and this command removes any encoding characters and replaces them with the appropriate spaces, semicolons, commas, and so forth.

OBJECTIVES

In this appendix you will:

- Learn how to install the XML Spy software

- Receive an evaluation key-code

- Start XML Spy and explore how to work with the Project window

- View an XML document in Enhanced Grid view

- Explore the different parts of the XML Spy window

INSTALLING AND WORKING WITH XML SPY

SESSION A1.1

In this appendix, you'll learn how to install XML Spy on your computer and how to register the software. You'll learn how to start XML Spy and work with XML Spy's Project window. You'll also explore how to view the contents of an XML document in different formats.

Introducing XML Spy

XML Spy is a family of products designed to facilitate the development of XML applications. XML Spy consists of the XML Spy IDE and the XML Spy Document Framework. The **XML Spy IDE** is an application used to develop and manage XML documents, DTDs, schemas, and XSLT style sheets. The **XML Spy Document Framework** consists of two components:

- **XSLT Designer** uses an intuitive drag-and-drop interface to automate the process of writing complex XSLT style sheets. You can also use XSLT Designer to create advanced electronic forms for use with the XML Spy Document Editor.
- **XML Spy Form Editor** is a word processor type editor that supports electronic form-based data input, graphical elements, tables, and real-time data validation using XML Schema.

In this appendix we'll concentrate on working with XML Spy IDE to create and edit simple XML documents and to perform data validation using DTDs and schemas.

Installing XML Spy

An evaluation copy of XML Spy is on the CD that accompanies this book. You can use the evaluation copy, free of charge, for 120 days after installation. If you intend to use XML Spy after the evaluation period, you can purchase the application at Altova at *http://www.xmlspy.com*.

To install XML Spy:

1. Insert the XML Spy 4.3 CD that accompanies this book into the CD drive of your computer.

2. Locate the **setup43.exe** file on the CD and double-click on it to run the program.

3. Click the **Next** button to begin the XML Spy Suite installation.

4. Click the **Browse** button to select a location for XML Spy's setup files, or click the **Next** button to accept the default installation location (C:\Program Files\Altova\Setup Files\XML Spy Suite 4.3).

5. Click the **Next** button.

6. Click the option button to accept the software license agreement and click the **Next** button.

7. Click the **Change** button to select a location for the XML Spy program files, or click the **Next** button to accept the default location (C:\Program Files\Altova\XML Spy Suite\).

8. This dialog box allows you to customize XML Spy features for your work environment. Click the checkboxes for any of the following options you want to enable, and then click the **Next** button.

   ■ Make XML Spy the default editor for your XML-related files.

   ■ Add the "Edit with XML Spy" command to Internet Explorer's menu and toolbar.

   ■ Allow XML Spy to validate HTML files under the XHTML specifications.

9. Click the **Complete** option button, and then click the **Next** button.

10. Click the **Install** button to begin the installation.

    The installation procedure can take several minutes.

11. Click the **Finish** button after the installation is complete.

    TROUBLE? Depending on your computer system, your instructor may give you more detailed instructions on how your version of XML Spy should be installed on your computer.

After the XML Spy Suite has been installed on your computer, it needs to be registered before you can use it. When you register XML Spy at the Altova Web site, you receive a key-code via e-mail. When you run XML Spy for the first time, you are prompted to enter the key-code.

To register XML Spy:

1. Click the **Start** button on your Taskbar, point to **Programs**, point to **XML Spy Suite**, and select **XML Spy IDE** from the menu.

   XML Spy displays the XML Spy Licensing Manager window shown in Figure A-1.

| Figure A-1 | XML SPY LICENSING MANAGER |

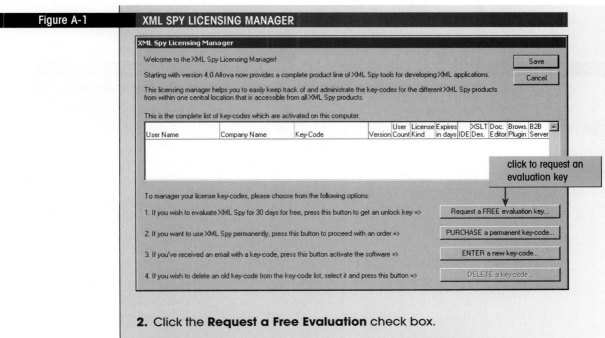

click to request an evaluation key

2. Click the **Request a Free Evaluation** check box.

XML Spy displays the dialog box as shown in Figure A-2.

3. Complete the form, being sure to include your e-mail address.

| Figure A-2 | XML SPY LICENSING MANAGER |

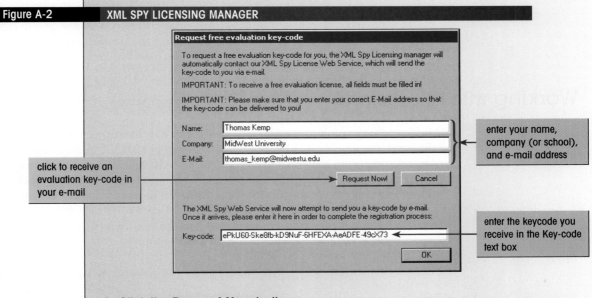

enter your name, company (or school), and e-mail address

click to receive an evaluation key-code in your e-mail

enter the keycode you receive in the Key-code text box

4. Click the **Request Now** button.

The window expands revealing a text box for you to enter your key-code. Within a few minutes, you'll receive an email from the Altova Web site with your evaluation copy key-code.

5. Enter the key-code you received in your e-mail from Altova into the Key-code text box and click the **OK** button.

TROUBLE? If XML Spy refuses to accept the key-code, verify that you've entered the key-code correctly, including upper- and lowercase letters.

Click the **Save** button to save the key-code. XML Spy IDE starts on your computer and displays the document window as shown in Figure A-3.

Figure A-3	THE OPENING XML SPY WINDOW

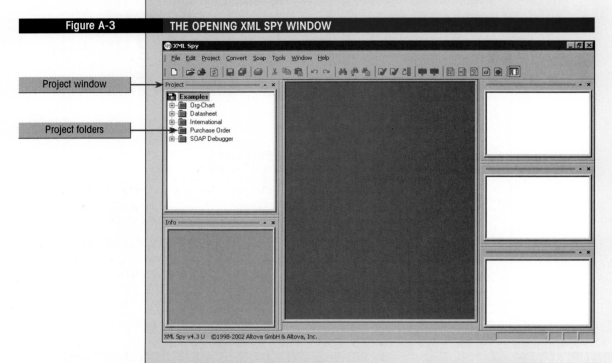

Project window

Project folders

TROUBLE? Your document window may look different than the one in Figure A-3 depending on the options you chose when you installed XML Spy.

Working with XML Projects

XML Spy allows you to organize documents into a single project. A **project** is a collection of the XML documents, DTDs, schemas, XSL and HTML files, and other supporting documents that make up a single XML application. XML Spy allows you to organize these files into separate folders and display the hierarchy of those folders in the **Project window**.

The folders displayed in the Project window represent a logical organization of your files. The folders do not necessarily represent the location of these files on your computer's hard disk, although they can. For example, you can use folders to keep common file types together such as keeping all schema files in a single folder.

To display the contents of a folder in the Project window, click the [+] box that is located in front of the folder name. Try this now, to display the contents of the Purchase Order folder.

To display the contents of the Purchase Order folder:

1. Click the **(+)** box located in front of the Purchase Order folder in the Project window.

2. Click the **(+)** box located in front of the XML Files folder.

3. XML Spy displays the contents of the XML Files folder as shown in Figure A-4. In this case the folder contains a single file, ipo.xml.

Figure A-4   **NAVIGATING THE PROJECT WINDOW**

TROUBLE? If XML Spy did not automatically open the contents of the Example project, click Open Project from the Project menu, and then open Examples.spp located in the C:\Program Files\Altova\XML Spy Suite\Examples folder.

TROUBLE? If you did not choose to install the example files when you installed XML Spy, you can continue through the remainder of the appendix, but you will be unable to perform the exercises without access to the example files.

You can use the commands in the Project menu to work with the properties of your XML project. From this menu you can:

- close, open, and save old projects, and create new projects
- add files and URLs to projects
- create new project folders
- add external folders or Web folders to projects

Additionally, you can rearrange the contents of your XML projects by dragging file icons in the Project window to other project folders.

Viewing **the Contents of an XML Document**

To view the contents of an XML document, you can either open the document with the Open command on the File menu, or you can open the file from the Project window. Because we've already accessed ipo.xml in the XML Files folder, let's view its contents.

To view the contents of an XML document:

1. Double-click the **ipo.xml** document icon located in the Project window.

   The document is displayed in a separate window.

2. Click the **Maximize** button 🔲 to expand the contents of the window to fill the available space (see Figure A-5).

Figure A-5   **DISPLAYING AN XML FILE IN ENHANCED GRID VIEW**

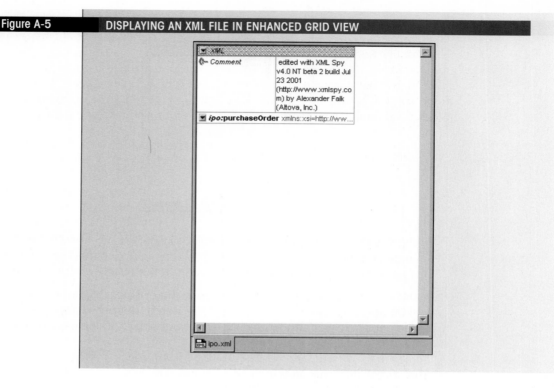

By default, XML Spy displays XML documents in **enhanced grid view**, which shows the hierarchical structure of the document through a set of nested containers. The containers can be expanded or collapsed to provide a clear picture of the document's structure. Elements that contain child elements are identified by a down arrow ▼. To close an open container, click the up arrow ▲.

To view the structure of ipo.xml:

1. Click the **down arrow** icon ▼ located in front of the ipo:purchaseOrder entry.

2. Click the **down arrow** icon ▼ located in front of the shipTo entry. The expanded structure of ipo.xml is displayed in Figure A-6.

Figure A-6   **EXPANDING THE GRID VIEW**

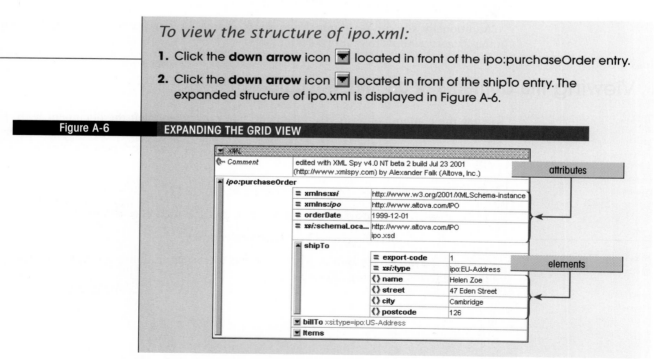

Attributes in the enhanced grid view are identified by the = symbol. Elements that contain text are indicated with a set of opening and closing brackets, < >. The attribute and element values are displayed following the attribute and element names. For example, the shipTo element, as shown in Figure A-6, contains two attributes: export-code and xsi:type. The xsi is a namespace prefix. The values of these attributes are 1 and ipo:EU-Address respectively. The shipTo element also contains four child elements: name, street, city, and postcode. A sample name and address is provided for each of these elements.

Working **with Entry Helper Windows**

If your XML document is associated with a schema or a DTD, you can use one of three entry helper windows to aid you in entering elements and attributes. The entry helper windows are stacked vertically and located to the right of the main window. The **Element Entry helper** window displays the elements that can be added at the current location in the XML document. You can choose to append an element, insert an element before the currently selected element, or add a child element to the currently selected element. Mandatory elements are identified with an exclamation point (!). Elements that can be added within the current parent element, but not at the position of the current selection, are shown in gray.

The **Attribute Entry helper** window displays the attributes that are available for the element you're currently editing. As with elements, mandatory attributes are identified with an exclamation point.

The **Entity Entry helper** window displays a list of predefined entities or parameter entities that can be used with the current XML document.

To view the contents of an entry helper window:

1. Click on the **shipTo** element located in the main window. The entire shipTo element area is highlighted.

2. XML Spy displays the attributes, elements, and entities, in their respective entry helper window, that are available within the XML document (see Figure A-7).

Figure A-7 | **ENTRY HELPER WINDOWS**

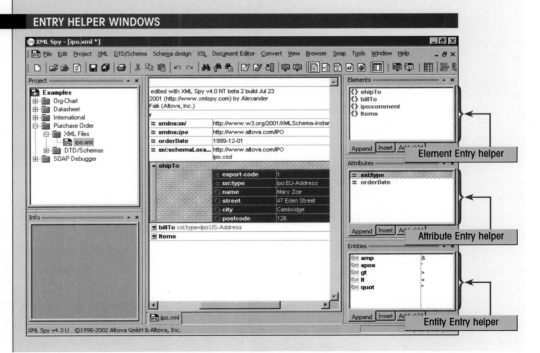

Note that the contents of both the Element Entry and the Attribute Entry helper windows are grayed out, indicating that these elements are allowed within the shipTo element, but not for the current selection.

Finally, another window you can use in developing your XML document is the Info window. The **Info** window displays information about the currently selected element or attribute in the XML document.

Now that you've explored the various parts of the XML Spy IDE, you can exit the application.

To close XML Spy IDE:

1. Click **File** and **Exit** from the XML Spy menu bar.

2. Click the **No** button when prompted to save your changes.

You can learn more about XML Spy using the online help available with the program. Also, Tutorial 3 and Tutorial 4 of this book contain examples of using XML Spy to open, edit, and validate the contents of an XML document.

TASK	PAGE #	RECOMMENDED METHOD/NOTES
ANY content, declare in a DTD	XML 3.08	Use the declaration: `<!ELEMENT element ANY>`
Attribute list, declare in a DTD	XML 3.17	See Reference Window: Declaring an Attribute List
Attribute, add to an element	XML 1.18	`<element_name attribute="value">` where *attribute* is the name of the attribute, and "*value*" is the attribute's value. A single element can have several attributes.
Attribute, declare in a schema	XML 4.25	See Reference Window: Declaring an Attribute

CDATA section, create a	XML 1.23	`<![CDATA[`
		    `Text Block`
		`]]>`
		where *Text Block* is the block of character text.

Character content, declare in a DTD	XML 3.09	Use the declaration: `<!ELEMENT element (#PCDATA)>`
Character reference, insert a	XML 1.21	See Reference Window: Inserting a Character Reference
Child elements, declare in a DTD	XML 3.09	Use the declaration: `<!ELEMENT element (child_elements)>` where *child_elements* is a list of the elements contained by *element*.
Comment, insert a	XML 1.14	`<!-- comment text -->` where *comment text* is the text of the comment.
Complex type element, declare in a schema	XML 4.22	See Reference Window: Declaring Simple and Complex Types

Condition section, create in a DTD	XML 3.38	To ignore declarations in a DTD, use the structure:
		`<![IGNORE`
		    `declarations`
		`]]>`
		To include declarations in a DTD, use the structure:
		`<![INCLUDE`
		    `declarations`
		`]]>`

Data format, apply to a bound HTML element	XML 2.12	Include the attribute: `dataformatas="format"` in the HTML element tag, where "*format*" is either "text" or "html".
Data Island, create a	XML 2.08	See Reference Window: Creating a Data Island
Data type, derive a new	XML 4.48	See Reference Window: Deriving New Data Types
Default attribute value, declare in a DTD	XML 3.22	See Reference Window: Specifying an Attribute Default
DTD, declare a	XML 3.06	See Reference Window: Creating a DOCTYPE Declaration

XML TASK REFERENCE

TASK	PAGE #	RECOMMENDED METHOD/NOTES
Element choice, declare in a DTD	XML 3.11	See Reference Window: Specifying a Sequence or Choice of Child Elements
Element sequence, declare in a DTD	XML 3.11	See Reference Window: Specifying a Sequence or Choice of Child Elements
Elements, create a closed	XML 1.14	`<element_name>Content<element_name>` where *element_name* is the name of the XML element, and *Content* is the element's content.
Elements, create a root	XML 1.16	The top level element in any XML document is the root element
Elements, create an empty	XML 1.17	`<element_name/>` where *element_name* is the name of the XML element.
Elements, declare in a DTD	XML 3.07	Use the declaration: `<!ELEMENT element content-model>` where *element* is the element's name and *content-model* specifies what type of content the element contains
EMPTY content, declare in a DTD	XML 3.08	Use the declaration: `<!ELEMENT element EMPTY>`
Entity, declare a general parameter	XML 3.32	See Reference Window: Declaring and Using a General Parameter Entity
Entity, use a	XML 3.36	See Reference Window: Declaring and Using a Parameter Entity
Enumerated attribute, declare in a DTD	XML 3.18	Use the attribute type: `attribute (value1 | value2 | value3 | ...)` where *value1*, *value2*, *value3*, and so forth are the enumerated values of the attribute
Flat Design, create	XML 4.40	Declare all elements of the instance document globally in the schema
HTML element, bind XML field to a	XML 2.11	See Reference Window: Binding an HTML Tag to a Field
Implied attribute value, declare in a DTD	XML 3.21	Use the keyword, #IMPLIED, in the attribute declaration.

List data type, derive a	XML 4.46	Use the command structure:
		`<simpleType name="name">`
		`    <list itemType="type" />`
		`</simpleType>`
		where "*name*" is the name assigned to the data type, and *type* is the data type of the base type.

Mixed content, declare in a DTD	XML 3.13	Use the declaration: `<!ELEMENT element (#PCDATA | child1 | child2 | ..)*>` where *element* is the parent element, and *child1*, *child2*, and so forth are the names of the child elements.

XML TASK REFERENCE

TASK	PAGE #	RECOMMENDED METHOD/NOTES
Mixed content, specify in a schema	XML 4.24	Add the mixed="true" attribute to a complex type element declaration
Modifying Symbols, apply to a declaration	XML 3.12	See Reference Window: Applying Modifying Symbols to a Declaration

Named attribute group, create in a schema	XML 4.43	Use the command structure:
		`<attributeGroup name="name">`
		　　　　`attribute declarations`
		`</attributeGroup>`
		where *name* is the name of the attribute group, and *attribute declarations* are the declarations for the individual attributes in the group

Named complex type, create in a schema	XML 4.22	Add the name="name" attribute to the element type declaration

Named model group, create in a schema	XML 4.42	Use the command structure:
		`<group name="name">`
		　　　　`element declarations`
		`</group>`
		where *name* is the name of the group, and *element declarations* are the declarations for the individual elements in the group

Namespace, apply to an attribute	XML 4.09	Insert the namespace prefix before the attribute name as follows: `prefix:attribute="value"`

Namespace, apply to an element	XML 4.07	Insert the namespace prefix before the element name as follows:
		`<prefix:element>`
		　　　　`content`
		`</prefix:element>`

Namespace, attach a schema to	XML 4.31	See Reference Window: Attaching a Schema to a Namespace
Namespace, declare in an element	XML 4.08	Within an element, insert the attribute: `xmlns:prefix="URI"` where *URI* is the namespace's URI, and *prefix* is the namespace prefix
Namespace, declare in document prolog	XML 4.05	Within the XML document, insert the command: `<?xml:namespace ns="URI" prefix="prefix"?>` where *URI* is the namespace's URI, and *prefix* is the namespace prefix.
Namespace, use with DTDs	XML 4.11	Use the namespace prefixes in the element and attribute declarations as if they were part of the element and attribute names.
Occurrence of an element, specify in a schema	XML 4.24	Add the minOccurs="value" maxOccurs="value" attributes to a simple type element declaration indicating the minimum and maximum times the element can occur.
Record, determine whether the current record is the first	XML 2.22	`id.recordset.BOF` where id is the name of the data island.

XML TASK REFERENCE

TASK	PAGE #	RECOMMENDED METHOD/NOTES
Record, determine whether the current record is the last	XML 2.22	`id.recordset.EOF` where *id* is the name of the data island.
Recordset, work with hierarchical	XML 2.32	See Reference Window: Working with a Hierarchical Recordset
Required attribute value, declare in a DTD	XML 3.21	Use the keyword, #REQUIRED, in the attribute declaration.

Restricted data type, derive a	XML 4.47	Use the command structure:
		`<simpleType name="name">`
		    `<restriction base="type">`
		        `<facet1 value="value1" />`
		        `<facet2 value="value2" />`
		        `<facet3 value="value3" />`
		    `</restriction>`
		`</simpleType>`
		where "*name*" is the name assigned to the data type, *facet1, facet2, facet3*, etc. are constraining facets, and *value1, value2, value3*, etc. are values for each constraining facet.

Russian Doll Design, create a	XML 4.39	Declare the root element of the instance document globally in the schema; nest all other element declarations within that declaration.
Schema ,create a	XML 4.17	See Reference Window: Creating a Schema
Schema, annotate a	XML 4.54	See Reference Window: Annotating a Schema
Schema, attach a document to a	XML 4.34	See Reference Window: Attaching a Document to a Schema
Simple type element, declare in a schema	XML 4.19	Use the command: `<element name="name" type="type"/>` where "*name*" is the name of the simple element and "*type*" is the data type.
String Attribute, declare in a DTD	XML 3.18	Use the attribute type: `attribute CDATA`
Style sheet, link to	XML 1.29	See Reference Window: Attaching an XML Document to a Style Sheet

Table pages, navigate	XML 2.28	Use the JavaScript command:
		`id.firstPage()`
		to move to the first page of the table, where *id* the name of the HTML table.
		Use:
		`id.lastPage()`
		`id.nextPage()`
		`id.previousPage()`
		to move to the last, next, and previous table page.

XML TASK REFERENCE

TASK	PAGE #	RECOMMENDED METHOD/NOTES
Table, bind XML data to a	XML 2.26	See Reference Window: Binding Data to a Table
Table, specify a page size for	XML 2.28	Include the attribute: `dataPageSize="value"` in the <table> element tag, where "*value*" is the number of rows in a single page.
Token attribute, declare in a DTD	XML 3.19	Use the attribute type: `attribute token` where *token* is one of the tokenized types.

Union data type, derive a	XML 4.46	Use the command structure:
		`<simpleType name="name">`
		`    <union memberTypes="type1 type2 type3`
		`    ..."/>`
		`</simpleType>`
		where "*name*" is the name assigned to the data type, and *type1*, *type2*, *type3*, and so forth are the different data types being united.

Unparsed entity, use a	XML 3.38	See Reference Window: Declaring a Unparsed Entity
Venetian Blind Design, create	XML 4.44	In the schema, use named complex types, model groups, and attribute groups to declare the various elements of the instance document
Web browser, display an XML document in a	XML 1.25	Open the XML document in the Web browser. Internet Explorer will show the document in a hierarchical tree. Netscape will only show the element values
XML, create a declaration	XML 1.13	See Reference Window: Creating an XML Declaration

HTML File Finder

Tutorial	Location in Tutorial	Name and Location of Data Files	Student Saves File As...	Student Creates New File
Tutorial 1	Session 1.1			
Tutorial 1	Session 1.2			chem.htm
Tutorial 1	Session 1.3	tutorial.01/tutorial/chem.htm (saved from last session) tutorial.01/tutorial/dube.jpg	chem.htm	
Tutorial 1	Review Assignments	tutorial.01/tutorial/chem.htm (saved from the Tutorial) tutorial.01/Review/dube.jpg	chem2.htm (saved in the Review folder)	
Tutorial 1	Case Problem 1	tutorial.01/case1/newborn.jpg		child.htm
Tutorial 1	Case Problem 2	tutorial.01/case2/eulertxt.htm tutorial.01/case2/euler.jpg tutorial.01/case2/pi.jpg	euler.htm	
Tutorial 1	Case Problem 3	tutorial.01/case3/frosttxt.htm tutorial.01/case3/flakes.jpg tutorial.01/case3/runner.jpg	frostrun.htm	
Tutorial 1	Case Problem 4	tutorial.01/case4/kirk.jpg		myresume.htm
Tutorial 2	Session 2.1	tutorial.02/tutorial/chemtxt.htm tutorial.02/tutorial/dube.jpg	chem.htm	
Tutorial 2	Session 2.2	tutorial.02/tutorial/conftxt.htm tutorial.02/tutorial/linktxt.htm	contact.htm links.htm	
Tutorial 2	Session 2.3	tutorial.01/tutorial/chem.htm (saved from last session) tutorial.02/tutorial/contact.htm (saved from last session) tutorial.02/tutorial/links.htm (saved from last session)	chem.htm contact.htm links.htm	
Tutorial 2	Review Assignments	tutorial.02/Review/chem2txt.htm tutorial.02/Review/cont2txt.htm tutorial.02/Review/link2txt.htm tutorial.02/Review/dube.jpg	chem2.htm contact2.htm links2.htm	
Tutorial 2	Case Problem 1	tutorial.02/case1/grback.jpg tutorial.02/case1/grrock.jpg		rock.htm
Tutorial 2	Case Problem 2	tutorial.02/case2/move1a.htm tutorial.02/case2/move2a.htm tutorial.02/case2/move3a.htm tutorial.02/case2/move4a.htm tutorial.02/case2/left.jpg tutorial.02/case2/right.jpg tutorial.02/case2/lvb1.jpg tutorial.02/case2/lvb2.jpg tutorial.02/case2/lvb3.jpg tutorial.02/case2/lvb4.jpg	move1.htm move2.htm move3.htm move4.htm	
Tutorial 2	Case Problem 3	tutorial.02/case3/clubtxt.htm tutorial.02/case3/classtxt.htm tutorial.02/case3/membtxt.htm tutorial.02/case3/aerobic.gif tutorial.02/case3/pushup.gif tutorial.02/case3/diamonds.jpg	club.htm classes.htm members.htm	
Tutorial 2	Case Problem 4			myweb.htm
Tutorial 3	Session 3.1	tutorial.03/tutorial/arcatxt.htm tutorial.03/tutorial/clouds.jpg	arcadium.htm	
Tutorial 3	Session 3.2	tutorial.03/tutorial/aradium.htm (saved from last session) tutorial.03/tutorial/aclogo2.gif tutorial.03/tutorial/ride.jpg	arcadium.htm	

HTML File Finder

Tutorial	Location in Tutorial	Name and Location of Data Files	Student Saves File As...	Student Creates New File
Tutorial 3	Session 3.3	tutorial.03/tutorial/aradium.htm (saved from last session) tutorial.03/tutorial/parkmap.gif tutorial.03/tutorial/water.htm tutorial.03/tutorial/karts.htm tutorial.03/tutorial/rides.htm	arcadium.htm	
Tutorial 3	Review Assignments	tutorial.03/review/arcatxt2.htm tutorial.03/review/toddtxt.htm tutorial.03/review/water.htm tutorial.03/review/karts.htm tutorial.03/review/rides.htm tutorial.03/review/pmap2.gif tutorial.03/review/wall.jpg tutorial.03/review/toddler.jpg	arca2.htm toddler.htm	
Tutorial 3	Case Problem 1	tutorial.03/case1/kingtxt.htm tutorial.03/case1/mlk.gif tutorial.03/case1/i.gif tutorial.03/case1/line.gif	king.htm	
Tutorial 3	Case Problem 2	tutorial.03/case2/breaktxt.htm tutorial.03/case2/lunchtxt.htm tutorial.03/case2/dinnrtxt.htm tutorial.03/case2/breakfst.jpg tutorial.03/case2/lunch.jpg tutorial.03/case2/dinner.jpg tutorial.03/case2/tan.jpg	breakfast.htm lunch.htm dinner.htm	
Tutorial 3	Case Problem 3	tutorial.03/case3/introtxt.htm tutorial.03/case3/pixaltxt.htm tutorial.03/case3/dc100txt.htm tutorial.03/case3/dc250txt.htm tutorial.03/case3/dc500txt.htm tutorial.03/case3/spacer.gif tutorial.03/case3/intro.gif tutorial.03/case3/pback.jpg tutorial.03/case3/dclist1.gif tutorial.03/case3/dclist2.gif tutorial.03/case3/dclist3.gif tutorial.03/case3/dclist4.gif tutorial.03/case3/dc100.jpg tutorial.03/case3/dc250.jpg tutorial.03/case3/dc500.jpg tutorial.03/case3/pclogo.jpg	intro.htm pixal.htm dc100.htm dc250.htm dc500.htm	
Tutorial 3	Case Problem 4	tutorial.03/case4/apartmnt.htm tutorial.03/case4/business.htm tutorial.03/case4/family.htm tutorial.03/case4/mansions.htm tutorial.03/case4/newhome.htm tutorial.03/case4/house.jpg tutorial.03/case4/listings.gif tutorial.03/case4/tristate.gif tutorial.03/case4/tsback.gif		tristate.htm
Tutorial 4	Session 4.1	tutorial.04/tutorial/racetxt1.htm tutorial.04/tutorial/racetxt2.htm tutorial.04/tutorial/blake.jpg tutorial.04/tutorial/parch.jpg	race1.htm race2.htm	
Tutorial 4	Session 4.2	tutorial.04/tutorial/race1.htm (saved from last session) tutorial.04/tutorial/blake.jpg tutorial.04/tutorial/parch.jpg	race1.htm	

HTML File Finder

Tutorial	Location in Tutorial	Name and Location of Data Files	Student Saves File As...	Student Creates New File
Tutorial 4	Session 4.3	tutorial.04/tutorial/page1txt.htm tutorial.04/tutorial/artcltxt.htm tutorial.04/tutorial/race2.htm (saved from last session) tutorial.04/tutorial/address.htm tutorial.04/tutorial/features.htm tutorial.04/tutorial/highway.htm tutorial.04/tutorial/links.htm tutorial.04/tutorial/brline.gif tutorial.04/tutorial/blake.jpg tutorial.04/tutorial/parch.jpg tutorial.04/tutorial/parch2.jpg tutorial.04/tutorial/parch3.jpg tutorial.04/tutorial/pclogo.jpg	page1.htm articles.htm	
Tutorial 4	Review Assignments	tutorial.04/review/sighttxt.htm tutorial.04/review/arttxt.htm tutorial.04/review/page2txt.htm tutorial.04/review/tips.htm tutorial.04/review/brline.gif tutorial.04/review/cougar.jpg tutorial.04/review/parch.jpg tutorial.04/review/parch2.jpg tutorial.04/review/parch3.jpg tutorial.04/review/pclogo.jpg	sighting.htm article2.htm page2.htm	
Tutorial 4	Case Problem 1	tutorial.04/case1/introtxt.htm tutorial.04/case1/dhometxt.htm tutorial.04/case1/address.htm tutorial.04/case1/footer.htm tutorial.04/case1/textbox.htm tutorial.04/case1/uses.htm tutorial.04/case1/back.jpg tutorial.04/case1/back2.jpg tutorial.04/case1/back3.jpg tutorial.04/case1/back4.jpg tutorial.04/case1/back5.jpg tutorial.04/case1/dhome.jpg tutorial.04/case1/links.jpg	intro.htm dhome.htm	
Tutorial 4	Case Problem 2	tutorial.04/case2/febtxt.htm tutorial.04/case2/ccc.gif tutorial.04/case2/back.jpg	feb.htm	
Tutorial 4	Case Problem 3	tutorial.04/case3/dunsttxt.htm tutorial.04/case3/welctxt.htm tutorial.04/case3/address.htm tutorial.04/case3/events.htm tutorial.04/case3/letter.htm tutorial.04/case3/next.htm tutorial.04/case3/adams.jpg tutorial.04/case3/back.jpg tutorial.04/case3/dlogo.jpg tutorial.04/case3/dunston.jpg	dunston.htm welcome.htm	
Tutorial 4	Case Problem 4	tutorial.04/case4/twlinks.htm tutorial.04/case4/twlinks2.htm tutorial.04/case4/luxair.txt tutorial.04/case4/photo.txt tutorial.04/case4/toronto.txt tutorial.04/case4/yosemite.txt tutorial.04/case4/ppoint.jpg tutorial.04/case4/ppoint2.jpg tutorial.04/case4/twlogo.jpg tutorial.04/case4/yosemite.jpg		tw.htm

HTML File Finder

Tutorial	Location in Tutorial	Name and Location of Data Files	Student Saves File As...	Student Creates New File
Tutorial 5	Session 5.1	tutorial.05/tutorial/yaletxt.htm tutorial.05/tutorial/bester.htm tutorial.05/tutorial/bios.htm tutorial.05/tutorial/blake.htm tutorial.05/tutorial/diamond.htm tutorial.05/tutorial/dumont.htm tutorial.05/tutorial/eldorado.htm tutorial.05/tutorial/grepon.htm tutorial.05/tutorial/head.htm tutorial.05/tutorial/home.htm tutorial.05/tutorial/jacobs.htm tutorial.05/tutorial/kieners.htm tutorial.05/tutorial/lessons.htm tutorial.05/tutorial/links.htm tutorial.05/tutorial/lumpy.htm tutorial.05/tutorial/nface.htm tutorial.05/tutorial/philosph.htm tutorial.05/tutorial/photos.htm tutorial.05/tutorial/staff.htm tutorial.05/tutorial/staford.htm tutorial.05/tutorial/tours.htm *+ 26 jpg files from the tutorial.05/tutorial folder*	yale.htm	
Tutorial 5	Session 5.2	tutorial.05/tutorial/yale.htm (saved from last session) tutorial.05/tutorial/links.htm tutorial.05/tutorial/tours.htm tutorial.05/tutorial/iftxt.htm tutorial.05/tutorial/noframes.htm *+ 18 other htm files previously listed in Session 5.1 from the tutorial.05/tutorial folder* *+ 26 jpg files from the tutorial.05/tutorial folder*	yale.htm links.htm tours.htm iframe.htm	
Tutorial 5	Review Assignments	tutorial.05/review/headtxt.htm tutorial.05/review/slisttxt.htm tutorial.05/review/sltxt.htm tutorial.05/review/stafftxt.htm tutorial.05/review/tlisttxt.htm tutorial.05/review/tourtxt.htm tutorial.05/review/tltxt.htm tutorial.05/review/yale2txt.htm *+ 18 other htm files previously listed in Session 5.1 from the tutorial.05/tutorial folder* *+ 26 jpg files from the tutorial.05/tutorial folder*	head2.htm slist.htm staflink.htm staff2.htm tlist.htm tours2.htm tourlink.htm yale2.htm	
Tutorial 5	Case Problem 1	tutorial.05/case1/dcctxt.htm tutorial.05/case1/headtxt.htm tutorial.05/case1/maptxt.htm tutorial.05/case1/dccmw.htm tutorial.05/case1/dccne.htm tutorial.05/case1/dccs.htm tutorial.05/case1/dccw.htm tutorial.05/case1/report.htm tutorial.05/case1/dcclogo.jpg tutorial.05/case1/map.jpg tutorial.05/case1/mwchart.jpg	dcc.htm head.htm map.htm	

HTML File Finder

Tutorial	Location in Tutorial	Name and Location of Data Files	Student Saves File As...	Student Creates New File
		tutorial.05/case1/nechart.jpg		
		tutorial.05/case1/schart.jpg		
		tutorial.05/case1/wchart.jpg		
Tutorial 5	Case Problem 2	tutorial.05/case2/listtxt.htm	listing.htm	
		tutorial.05/case2/img01.htm – img13.htm		
		tutorial.05/case2/back.jpg		
		tutorial.05/case2/brlogo.jpg		
		tutorial.05/case2/l20481.jpg		
		tutorial.05/case2/pback.jpg		
		tutorial.05/case2/img01.jpg – img13.jpg		
Tutorial 5	Case Problem 3	tutorial.05/case3/messtxt.htm	messier.htm	m01.htm, m13.htm, m16.htm, m20.htm, m27.htm, m31.htm, m42.htm, m51.htm, m57.htm
		tutorial.05/case3/mxxtxt.htm		
		tutorial.05/case3/m01desc.htm		
		tutorial.05/case3/m13desc.htm		
		tutorial.05/case3/m16desc.htm		
		tutorial.05/case3/m20desc.htm		
		tutorial.05/case3/m27desc.htm		
		tutorial.05/case3/m31desc.htm		
		tutorial.05/case3/m42desc.htm		
		tutorial.05/case3/m51desc.htm		
		tutorial.05/case3/m57desc.htm		
		tutorial.05/case3/lbutton.jpg		
		tutorial.05/case3/m01.jpg		
		tutorial.05/case3/m13.jpg		
		tutorial.05/case3/m16.jpg		
		tutorial.05/case3/m20.jpg		
		tutorial.05/case3/m27.jpg		
		tutorial.05/case3/m31.jpg		
		tutorial.05/case3/m42.jpg		
		tutorial.05/case3/m51.jpg		
		tutorial.05/case3/m57.jpg		
		tutorial.05/case3/messier.jpg		
		tutorial.05/case3/mxx.jpg		
		tutorial.05/case3/mxxdesc.jpg		
		tutorial.05/case3/rbutton.jpg		
		tutorial.05/case3/skyweb.jpg		
Tutorial 5	Case Problem 4	tutorial.05/case4/drive15l.htm		wtoc.htm
		tutorial.05/case4/drive20m.htm		warner.htm
		tutorial.05/case4/drive33m.htm		
		tutorial.05/case4/drive60s.htm		
		tutorial.05/case4/tape800.htm		
		tutorial.05/case4/tape3200.htm		
		tutorial.05/case4/tape9600.htm		
		tutorial.05/case4/wlogo.htm		
		tutorial.05/case4/wlogo.gif		
		tutorial.05/case4/drive15l.jpg		
		tutorial.05/case4/drive20m.jpg		
		tutorial.05/case4/drive33m.jpg		
		tutorial.05/case4/drive60s.jpg		
		tutorial.05/case4/tape800.jpg		
		tutorial.05/case4/tape3200.jpg		
		tutorial.05/case4/tape9600.jpg		
Tutorial 6	Session 6.1	tutorial.06/tutorial/regtxt.htm	register.htm	
		tutorial.06/tutorial/lglogo.jpg		
Tutorial 6	Session 6.2	tutorial.06/tutorial/register.htm (saved from last session)	register.htm	

HTML File Finder

Tutorial	Location in Tutorial	Name and Location of Data Files	Student Saves File As...	Student Creates New File
Tutorial 6	Session 6.3	tutorial.06/tutorial/register.htm (saved from last session)	register.htm	
Tutorial 6	Review Assignments	tutorial.06/review/suptxt.htm tutorial.06/review/cancel.gif tutorial.06/review/lglogo.jpg tutorial.06/review/mail.gif	support.htm	
Tutorial 6	Case Problem 1	tutorial.06/case1/ordertxt.htm tutorial.06/case1/back.jpg tutorial.06/case1/fflogo.jpg	order.htm	
Tutorial 6	Case Problem 2	tutorial.06/case2/dltxt.htm tutorial.06/case2/delong.jpg	delong.htm	
Tutorial 6	Case Problem 3	tutorial.06/case3/subtxt.htm tutorial.06/case3/pclogo.jpg tutorial.06/case3/parch2.jpg	subscrib.htm	
Tutorial 6	Case Problem 4			computer.htm
Tutorial 7	Session 7.1	tutorial.07/tutorial/astrotxt.htm tutorial.07/tutorial/chemtxt.htm tutorial.07/tutorial/elect.htm tutorial.07/tutorial/eng.htm tutorial.07/tutorial/physics.htm tutorial.07/tutorial/m20.jpg tutorial.07/tutorial/mwslogo.gif	astro.htm chem.htm	mws.css
Tutorial 7	Session 7.2	tutorial.07/tutorial/astro.htm (saved from last session) tutorial.07/tutorial/chem.htm (saved from last session) tutorial.07/tutorial/mws.css (saved from last session) tutorial.07/tutorial/elect.htm tutorial.07/tutorial/eng.htm tutorial.07/tutorial/physics.htm tutorial.07/tutorial/apple.jpg tutorial.07/tutorial/draft.jpg tutorial.07/tutorial/m20.jpg tutorial.07/tutorial/mwslogo.gif	astro.htm chem.htm mws.css	
Tutorial 7	Session 7.3	tutorial.07/tutorial/astro.htm (saved from last session) tutorial.07/tutorial/chem.htm (saved from last session) tutorial.07/tutorial/mws.css (saved from last session) tutorial.07/tutorial/elect.htm tutorial.07/tutorial/eng.htm tutorial.07/tutorial/physics.htm tutorial.07/tutorial/apple.jpg tutorial.07/tutorial/draft.jpg tutorial.07/tutorial/m20.jpg tutorial.07/tutorial/mwslogo.gif	astro.htm chem.htm mws.css	
Tutorial 7	Review Assignments	tutorial.07/review/physicstxt.htm tutorial.07/review/engtxt.htm tutorial.07/review/electtxt.htm tutorial.07/review/mwsptxt.css tutorial.07/review/astro.htm tutorial.07/review/chem..htm tutorial.07/tutorial/apple.jpg tutorial.07/tutorial/draft.jpg tutorial.07/tutorial/m20.jpg tutorial.07/tutorial/mwslogo.gif	physics.htm eng.htm elect.htm mwsp.css	

HTML File Finder

Tutorial	Location in Tutorial	Name and Location of Data Files	Student Saves File As...	Student Creates New File
Tutorial 7	Case Problem 1	tutorial.07/case1/stufftxt.htm tutorial.07/case1/const.htm tutorial.07/case1/bike.jpg tutorial.07/case1/gloves.jpg tutorial.07/case1/pc.jpg	stuff.htm	
Tutorial 7	Case Problem 2	tutorial.07/case2/h01txt.htm – h18txt.htm	h01.htm – h18.htm	willet.css
Tutorial 7	Case Problem 3	tutorial.07/case3/febtxt.htm tutorial.07/case3/jantxt.htm tutorial.07/case3/martxt.htm tutorial.07/case3/back.jpg tutorial.07/case3/ccc.gif	feb.htm jan.htm mar.htm	calendar.css
Tutorial 7	Case Problem 4	tutorial.07/case4/bizetbio.htm tutorial.07/case4/bizetlist.txt tutorial.07/case4/bizet.jpg tutorial.07/case4/mozartbio.htm tutorial.07/case4/mozartlist.txt tutorial.07/case4/mozart.jpg tutorial.07/case4/puccinibio.htm tutorial.07/case4/puccinilist.txt tutorial.07/case4/puccini.jpg tutorial.07/case4/verdibio.htm tutorial.07/case4/verdilist.txt tutorial.07/case4/verdi.jpg tutorial.07/case4/wagnerbio.htm tutorial.07/case4/wagnerlist.txt tutorial.07/case4/wagner.jpg		bizet.htm mozart.htm puccini.htm verdi.htm wagner.htm opera.css
Tutorial 8	Session 8.1	tutorial.08/tutorial/npntxt.htm tutorial.08/tutorial/const.htm tutorial.08/tutorial/bells.jpg tutorial.08/tutorial/logo.jpg tutorial.08/tutorial/watkins.jpg tutorial.08/tutorial/wrap.jpg	npn.htm	
Tutorial 8	Session 8.2	tutorial.08/tutorial/npn.htm (saved from last session) tutorial.08/tutorial/const.htm tutorial.08/tutorial/bells.jpg tutorial.08/tutorial/logo.jpg tutorial.08/tutorial/watkins.jpg tutorial.08/tutorial/wrap.jpg	npn.htm	
Tutorial 8	Session 8.3	tutorial.08/tutorial/npn.htm (saved from last session) tutorial.08/tutorial/const.htm tutorial.08/tutorial/bells.jpg tutorial.08/tutorial/logo.jpg tutorial.08/tutorial/watkins.jpg tutorial.08/tutorial/wrap.jpg	npn.htm	
Tutorial 8	Review Assignments	tutorial.08/review/npntxt2.htm tutorial.08/review/const.htm tutorial.08/review/bells.jpg tutorial.08/review/logo.jpg tutorial.08/review/watkins.jpg tutorial.08/review/wrap.jpg	npn2.htm	
Tutorial 8	Case Problem 1	tutorial.08/case1/menutxt.htm tutorial.08/case1/dinner.jpg tutorial.08/case1/tan.jpg	menu.htm	

HTML File Finder

Tutorial	Location in Tutorial	Name and Location of Data Files	Student Saves File As...	Student Creates New File
Tutorial 8	Case Problem 2	tutorial.08/case2/twaintxt.htm tutorial.08/case2/logo.gif tutorial.08/case2/paper.gif tutorial.08/case2/twain.gif tutorial.08/case2/button.gif	twain.htm	
Tutorial 8	Case Problem 3	tutorial.08/case3/bcctxt.htm tutorial.08/case3/calendar.css tutorial.08/case3/bcc.jpg tutorial.08/case3/paper.jpg	bcc.htm	calendar.js
Tutorial 8	Case Problem 4	tutorial.08/case4/colortxt.htm tutorial.08/case4/wd.jpg	color.htm	
Tutorial 9	Session 9.1	tutorial.09/tutorial/ordertxt.htm tutorial.09/tutorial/border.jpg tutorial.09/tutorial/gpsware.jpg	order.htm	
Tutorial 9	Session 9.2	tutorial.09/tutorial/order.htm (saved from last session) tutorial.09/tutorial/border.jpg tutorial.09/tutorial/gpsware.jpg	order.htm	
Tutorial 9	Session 9.3	tutorial.09/tutorial/order.htm (saved from last session) tutorial.09/tutorial/border.jpg tutorial.09/tutorial/gpsware.jpg	order.htm	
Tutorial 9	Review Assignments	tutorial.09/review/ordertxt2.htm tutorial.09/review/border.jpg tutorial.09/review/gpsware.jpg	order2.htm	
Tutorial 9	Case Problem 1	tutorial.09/case1/mpltxt.htm tutorial.09/case1/mplback.jpg tutorial.09/case1/mpllogo.jpg	mpl.htm	
Tutorial 9	Case Problem 2	tutorial.09/case2/magictxt.htm tutorial.09/case2/logo.jpg	magic.htm	
Tutorial 9	Case Problem 3	tutorial.09/case3/colortxt.htm tutorial.09/case3/wd.gif	color.htm	
Tutorial 9	Case Problem 4			mortgage.htm
Tutorial 10	Session 10.1	tutorial.10/tutorial/raintxt.htm tutorial.10/tutorial/raintxt.htm tutorial.10/tutorial/logo.gif tutorial.10/tutorial/mrim.jpg tutorial.10/tutorial/singers.jpg tutorial.10/tutorial/mountain.au tutorial.10/tutorial/mountain.mp3 tutorial.10/tutorial/mountain.wav	rainier.htm rainier2.htm	
Tutorial 10	Session 10.2	tutorial.10/tutorial/rainier.htm (saved from last session) tutorial.10/tutorial/rainier2.htm (saved from last session) tutorial.10/tutorial/logo.gif tutorial.10/tutorial/mrim.jpg tutorial.10/tutorial/singers.jpg tutorial.10/tutorial/mrim.avi tutorial.10/tutorial/mrim.mov	rainier.htm rainier2.htm	
Tutorial 10	Session 10.3	tutorial.10/tutorial/rainier.htm (saved from last session) tutorial.10/tutorial/rainier2.htm (saved from last session) tutorial.10/tutorial/logo.gif tutorial.10/tutorial/mrim.jpg	rainier2.htm	

HTML File Finder

Tutorial	Location in Tutorial	Name and Location of Data Files	Student Saves File As...	Student Creates New File
		tutorial.10/tutorial/singers.jpg tutorial.10/tutorial/CreditRoll.class tutorial.10/tutorial/credits.txt		
Tutorial 10	Review Assignments	tutorial.10/review/raintxt2.htm tutorial.10/review/raintxt2.htm tutorial.10/review/logo.gif tutorial.10/review/mrim2.jpg tutorial.10/review/singers2.jpg tutorial.10/review/song.au tutorial.10/review/song.mp3 tutorial.10/review/song.wav tutorial.10/review/welcome.au tutorial.10/review/welcome.mp3 tutorial.10/review/welcome.wav tutorial.10/review/mrim2.avi tutorial.10/review/mrim2.mov tutorial.10/review/CreditRoll.class	rainier3.htm rainier4.htm	
Tutorial 10	Case Problem 1	tutorial.10/case1/lmnhtxt.htm tutorial.10/case1/contact.htm tutorial.10/case1/events.htm tutorial.10/case1/exhibits.htm tutorial.10/case1/hours.htm tutorial.10/case1/support.htm tutorial.10/case1/dino.jpg tutorial.10/case1/dino2.jpg tutorial.10/case1/lincoln.jpg tutorial.10/case1/lmnh1.jpg tutorial.10/case1/lmnh2.jpg tutorial.10/case1/lmnh3.jpg tutorial.10/case1/lmnh4.jpg tutorial.10/case1/sites.jpg tutorial.10/case1/dino.au tutorial.10/case1/dino.wav tutorial.10/case1/dino.avi tutorial.10/case1/dino.mov	lmnh.htm	
Tutorial 10	Case Problem 2	tutorial.10/case2/rftxt.htm tutorial.10/case2/rflogo.gif tutorial.10/case2/sound.gif tutorial.10/case2/tan.jpg tutorial.10/case2/devotion.au tutorial.10/case2/devotion.mp3 tutorial.10/case2/devotion.wav tutorial.10/case2/fireice.au tutorial.10/case2/fireice.mp3 tutorial.10/case2/fireice.mp3 tutorial.10/case2/button.class	rf.htm	
Tutorial 10	Case Problem 3	tutorial.10/case3/fracttxt.htm tutorial.10/case3/flogo.jpg tutorial.10/case3/mandel.jpg tutorial.10/case3/mandel.avi tutorial.10/case3/mandel.mov tutorial.10/case3/Cmplx.class tutorial.10/case3/Controls.class tutorial.10/case3/FracPanel.class tutorial.10/case3/Mandel.class	fract.htm	
Tutorial 10	Case Problem 4	tutorial.10/case4/mbcinfo.txt tutorial.10/case4/schedule.txt tutorial.10/case4/mbc.jpg		mbc1.htm mbc2.htm

HTML File Finder

Tutorial	Location in Tutorial	Name and Location of Data Files	Student Saves File As...	Student Creates New File
		tutorial.10/case4/mbclogo.jpg tutorial.10/case4/concert.rm tutorial.10/case4/folksong.mp3 tutorial.10/case4/CreditRoll.class		
Additional Cases	Case Problem 1	tutorial.add/case1/arctic.txt tutorial.add/case1/flg.txt tutorial.add/case1/frosti.txt tutorial.add/case1/gloves.txt tutorial.add/case1/gmitt.txt tutorial.add/case1/order.txt tutorial.add/case1/pfm.txt tutorial.add/case1/frosti.htm tutorial.add/case1/frosti.css tutorial.add/case1/arcticb.jpg tutorial.add/case1/blueline.jpg tutorial.add/case1/fless.jpg tutorial.add/case1/flogo.jpg tutorial.add/case1/glomitt.jpg tutorial.add/case1/gloves.jpg tutorial.add/case1/polyflce.jpg tutorial.add/case1/sweaters.jpg		gloves.htm gorder.htm gproduct.htm
Additional Cases	Case Problem 2	tutorial.add/case2/comment1.txt tutorial.add/case2/comment2.txt tutorial.add/case2/comment3.txt tutorial.add/case2/comment4.txt tutorial.add/case2/mayer.txt tutorial.add/case2/portraits.txt tutorial.add/case2/specials.txt tutorial.add/case2/weddings.txt tutorial.add/case2/baby.jpg tutorial.add/case2/cactus2.jpg tutorial.add/case2/comment1.jpg tutorial.add/case2/comment2.jpg tutorial.add/case2/comment3.jpg tutorial.add/case2/comment4.jpg tutorial.add/case2/couple.jpg tutorial.add/case2/couple2.jpg tutorial.add/case2/deer2.jpg tutorial.add/case2/family.jpg tutorial.add/case2/family2.jpg tutorial.add/case2/guitar.jpg tutorial.add/case2/guitar2.jpg tutorial.add/case2/mlogo.jpg tutorial.add/case2/slides.gif tutorial.add/case2/wedding.jpg tutorial.add/case2/wedding.avi tutorial.add/case2/wedding.mov		mayer.htm portraits.htm specials.htm weddings.htm
Additional Cases	Case Problem 3	tutorial.add/case3/calendar.txt tutorial.add/case3/chicago.txt tutorial.add/case3/deliver.txt tutorial.add/case3/editor.txt tutorial.add/case3/mbirths.txt tutorial.add/case3/rates.txt tutorial.add/case3/recipe.txt tutorial.add/case3/roles.txt tutorial.add/case3/staff.txt tutorial.add/case3/survey.txt tutorial.add/case3/talk.txt tutorial.add/case3/twintips.txt		articles.htm feature.htm news.htm survey.htm twinlife.htm

HTML File Finder				
Tutorial	Location in Tutorial	Name and Location of Data Files	Student Saves File As...	Student Creates New File
		tutorial.add/case3/deliver.jpg tutorial.add/case3/howard.jpg tutorial.add/case3/kerkman.jpg tutorial.add/case3/kuhlman.jpg tutorial.add/case3/lasker.jpg tutorial.add/case3/lawson.jpg tutorial.add/case3/twinlogo.jpg tutorial.add/case3/twins.jpg tutorial.add/case3/CreditRoll.class		

XML File Finder

Location in Tutorial	Name and Location of Data File	Student Saves File As...	Student Creates New File
Tutorial 1			
Session 1.1			
Session 1.2			Tutorial.01X\Tutorial\Jazz.xml
Session 1.3	Tutorial.01X\Tutorial\Jazz.xml (saved from last session) JW.css	Jazz.xml	
Review Assignment	Tutorial.01X\Review\Rare.txt Tutorial.01X\Review\JW2.css	Rare.xml	
Case Problem 1	Tutorial.01X\Cases\FAQ.txt Tutorial.01X\Cases\FAQ.css	FAQ.xml	
Case Problem 2	Tutorial.01X\Cases\Hamlet.txt Tutorial.01X\Cases\Plays.css	Hamlet.xml	
Case Problem 3	Tutorial.01X\Cases\Staff1.xml	Staff2.xml	
Case Problem 4	Tutorial.01X\Cases\Accounts.txt Tutorial.01X\Cases\Delton.css		Accounts.xml
Tutorial 2			
Session 2.1	Tutorial.02X\Tutorial\FP1text.htm Tutorial.02X\Tutorial\FPInfo.xml	FP1.htm	
Session 2.2	Tutorial.02X\Tutorial\FP1.htm (saved from last session) Tutorial.02X\Tutorial\FPInfo.xml Tutorial.02X\Tutorial\Emp1.xml Multiple jpg files	FP1.htm	
Session 2.3	Tutorial.02X\Tutorial\FP2text.htm Tutorial.02X\Tutorial\FPInfo.xml Tutorial.02X\Tutorial\Emp1.xml Tutorial.02X\Tutorial\FP3text.htm Tutorial.02X\Tutorial\Emp2.xml Multiple jpg files	FP2.htm FP3.htm	
Review Assignment	Tutorial.02X\Review\Invtxt1.htm Tutorial.02X\Review\Invtxt2.htm Tutorial.02X\Review\Invtxt3.htm Tutorial.02X\Review\Refg1.xml Tutorial.02X\Review\Refg2.xml Tutorial.02X\Review\Refg3.xml Multiple jpg files	Inv1.htm Inv2.htm Inv3.htm	
Case Problem 1	Tutorial.02X\Cases\OEInvtxt.htm Tutorial.02X\Cases\OETitles.xml Tutorial.02X\Cases\OE.xml	OEInv.htm	
Case Problem 2	Tutorial.02X\Cases\SListtxt.htm Tutorial.02X\Cases\CHList.xml Tutorial.02X\Cases\bwills.jpg Tutorial.02X\Cases\czims.jpg Tutorial.02X\Cases\emcd.jpg Tutorial.02X\Cases\rshapiro.jpg Tutorial.02X\Cases\taaron.jpg Tutorial.02X\Cases\tdavis.jpg	SList.htm	
Case Problem 3	Tutorial.02X\Cases\AMtxt.htm Tutorial.02X\Cases\AutoOrd.xml	AM.htm	
Case Problem 4	Tutorial.02X\Cases\tour.xml Tutorial.02X\Cases\Castles.jpg Tutorial.02X\Cases\Hebrides.jpg Tutorial.02X\Cases\Highland.jpg Tutorial.02X\Cases\Lake.jpg		Scotland.htm

XML File Finder

Location in Tutorial	Name and Location of Data File	Student Saves File As...	Student Creates New File
Tutorial 3			
Session 3.1	Tutorial.03X\Tutorial\Ordertxt.xml	Order.xml	
Session 3.2	Tutorial.03X\Tutorial\Order.xml (saved from last session)	Order.xml	
Session 3.3	Tutorial.03X\Tutorial\Order.xml (saved from last session) Tutorial.03X\Tutorial\Items.dtd	Order.xml	
Review Assignment	Tutorial.03X\Cases\Pixaltxt.xml Tutorial.03X\Cases\SWListtxt.xml Tutorial.03X\Cases\HWListtxt.xml	Pixal.xml SWList.xml HWList.xml	SW.dtd HW.dtd
Case Problem 1	Tutorial.03X\Cases\EDLtxt.xml	EDL.xml	DL.dtd
Case Problem 2	Tutorial.03X\Cases\newstxt.xml Tutorial.03X\Cases\images.dtd Tutorial.03X\Cases\full_txt.dtd	news.xml	stories.dtd WNS.xml
Case Problem 3	Tutorial.03X\Cases\accounttxt.xml	account.xml	checking.dtd
Case Problem 4	Tutorial.03X\Cases\Members.txt		List.xml
Tutorial 4			
Session 4.1	Tutorial.04X\Tutorial\UHosptxt.xml Tutorial.04X\Tutorial\UHDTDtxt.dtd	UHosp.xml UHDTD.dtd	
Session 4.2	Tutorial.04X\Tutorial\Pattxt.xml UHosp.xml (saved from last session)	Patient.xml UHosp.xml	PSchema1.xsd
Session 4.3	Tutorial.04X\Tutorial\Patient.xml (saved from last session) Tutorial.04X\Tutorial\UHosp.xml Tutorial.04X\Tutorial\Venetian.xsd Tutorial.04X\Tutorial\Flat.xsd	Patient.xml UHosp.xml PSchema2.xsd	
Review Assignment	Tutorial.04X\Cases\CCCtxt.xml	CCC.xml	SSchema.xsd
Case Problem 1	Tutorial.04X\Cases\JWtxt.xml	JW.xml	CD.xsd
Case Problem 2	Tutorial.04X\Cases\Listtxt.xml	List.xml	LSchema.xsd
Case Problem 3	Tutorial.04X\Cases\Partstxt.xml Tutorial.04X\Cases\Grilltxt.xml	Parts.xml Grills.xml	PTSchema.xsd GRSchema.xsd GRStock.xml
Case Problem 4	Tutorial.04X\Cases\Books.txt Tutorial.04X\Cases\Movies.txt Tutorial.04X\Cases\Music.txt		Books.xml Movies.xml Music.xml BSchema.xsd MoSchema.xsd MuSchema.xsd MMart.xml